SEVENTH EDITION

A Short History of Western Civilization

JOHN B. HARRISON
Late Professor Emeritus of History
Michigan State University

RICHARD E. SULLIVAN
Michigan State University

DENNIS SHERMAN
John Jay College of Criminal Justice
City University of New York

McGraw-Hill Publishing Company

New York   St. Louis   San Francisco   Auckland   Bogotá   Caracas   Hamburg
Lisbon   London   Madrid   Mexico   Milan   Montreal   New Delhi
Oklahoma City   Paris   San Juan   São Paulo   Singapore   Sydney   Tokyo   Toronto

to Mary, Vivian, and Pat

The present overwhelms our forgotten selves;
but we are what we were,
with only a frosting of changes
—D.S.

A Short History of Western Civilization

Copyright © 1990, 1985, 1980, 1975, 1971 by McGraw-Hill, Inc. All rights reserved. Copyright © 1966, 1960 by John B. Harrison and Richard E. Sullivan. Printed in the United States of America. Except as permitted under the United States Copyright Act of 1976, no part of this publication may be reproduced or distributed in any form or by any means, or stored in a data base or retrieval system without the prior written permission of the publisher.

2 3 4 5 6 7 8 9 0 **DOH DOH** 8 9 4 3 2 1 0 9

ISBN 0-07-557080-7

This book was set in Palatino by Ruttle Shaw & Wetherill, Inc.
The editors were Christopher J. Rogers and Eleanor Castellano;
the designer was Wanda Siedlecka.
R. R. DONNELLEY & SONS, was printer and binder.

Cover Credit
"TURNER, Joseph Mallord William (1775–1851). *Rain, Steam, and Speed, the Great Western Railway.* National Gallery, London/Bridgeman/Art Resource."

Credits for Part Opening Photos
Part One: Ralph Mandol/DPI; *Part Two:* Alison Frantz; *Part Three:* Anderson/Giraudon; *Part Four:* The British Museum; *Part Five:* Epreuve D'Archives/Rapho-Photo Researchers; *Part Six;* The British Museum; *Part Seven:* The Granger Collection; *Part Eight:* Alinari/Art Resource; *Part Nine:* Historical Pictures Service; *Part Ten:* The Granger Collection; *Part Eleven:* Don McCullin/Magnum; *Part Twelve:* NASA.

Credits for Maps
The maps were executed by Jean Paul Tremblay, Francis & Shaw, Inc., Dyno Lowenstein, and Vantage Art, Inc.

Library of Congress Cataloging-in-Publication Data

Harrison, John Baugham.
   A short history of Western civilization / John B. Harrison, Richard E. Sullivan, Dennis Sherman. — 7th ed.
      p.   cm.
   Includes bibliographies and index.
   ISBN 0-07-557080-7
   1. Civilization, Occidental—History.   I. Sullivan, Richard
Eugene, (date).   II. Sherman, Dennis.   III. Title.
CB245.H32   1990b   89-35193
909'.09821—dc20

CONTENTS

Chart

PREFACE

In this seventh edition of A SHORT HISTORY OF WESTERN CIVILIZATION, we have attempted to achieve the right mix of continuity and change. Those features that made the sixth and previous editions so successful have been retained. We have kept our account brief enough so it offers readers a realistic opportunity to absorb a meaningful overview of the essentials of the history of Western civilization. The scope of the book is not limited to European history; brief treatments of other parts of the world, such as the United States, and non-Western civilizations as they have come to interact with the Western world, are included to put Western civilization into a broader context. The book continues to be organized into sixty chapters, a structure that fits well with most academic calendars. Introductory and retrospective essays at the beginning and the end of each of the twelve units of the book provide a broad summarizing perspective on major historical eras. The interpretative essays featuring points on which historians disagree are designed to encourage readers to develop a healthy skepticism toward accepted generalizations about the past and to learn to ask questions about the meaning of historical investigation. The large number of maps and illustrations highlight and complement the written text. The suggested reading lists offer alternatives for deeper study of topics covered in each chapter. The instructor's manual is a tool available to assist in making full use of this book.

Several important changes have been made in this edition to improve the quality and appeal of the book. There has been an additional infusion of social history and women's history into the text, continuing the changes already made in this direction in the sixth edition. The addition of this material reflects a growing consensus in modern scholarship that such matters need greater attention in order to portray past human experience fully and accurately. Parts of the book have been reorganized, particularly those chapters covering the early modern and modern eras. There have been extensive revisions of the text to include the most recent historical scholarship and, in some cases, new sections have been written. Sixteen pages of color plates have been added, and a large number of illustrations are new to this edition. Most of the maps have been revised and clarified. Five additional "Where Historians Disagree" essays have been added. A new introductory essay on historiography has been written for this edition. The suggested readings have been completely revised and updated.

As in previous editions, our goal is to produce a high-quality, clearly written, useful, and flexible account of Western civilization. We are indebted to numerous teachers and students who have aided us in this effort. We hope this book can serve as the basis for an effective survey of the history of Western civilization, a subject that remains essential for any understanding of who we are and what of significance is happening in the present.

We would like to thank the following reviewers for their many helpful comments and suggestions: Richard L. Bates, Villanova University; Mirian J. Levy, University of Hartford; and David C. Riede, The University of Akron.

RICHARD E. SULLIVAN
DENNIS SHERMAN

History and the Historian

As our readers undertake to expand their knowledge and understanding of the past, we ask them to reflect for a moment on what history is and on how the historian works. These are perplexing questions. At the heart of the problem is the fact that history has a dual meaning. On the one hand, history is everything that has happened in the past: all that an almost infinite number of humans beings did and thought over the millions of years of human existence. On the other hand, history is the reconstruction of these already completed activities and thoughts undertaken by explorers—called historians—who can only be outsiders trying to discover what happened, to explain why something occurred as it did, and to ascertain why such occurrences are in some way meaningful. The gap between what happened in the past and what historians are able to discover about what actually occurred is immense. Our readers can perhaps sense this gap by comparing all the things that must have happened to each of them with what they can accurately reconstruct about all the events of their own lives. As a consequence of the distance between the two meanings of history, the examination of the past goes on continually, and the reconstruction constantly changes as explorers of the past discover more about what happened and as they change their interpretations of why and how humans acted and thought as they did in the past.

There is no law that dictates that the limitless past should be explored, described, and understood. But people continue to find that exercise irresistible. Many have found and still find the past inherently interesting, just as is gazing at stars or watching birds. Others have been and still are convinced that learning about the past has an important social function. It can inform us about who and what we are as human beings. It can shed light on the contemporary situation, either by providing an understanding of how things came to be what they are or by supplying analogies that help us comprehend our situation and formulate solutions to issues that face our society. Societies have especially prized history as an instrument for socializing their members (particularly the young), that is, for teaching them how to behave and to think in ways that are appropriate to their cultural environment. In writing this book, we have assumed that both of these perspectives are equally valid. We firmly believe that gaining knowledge and insight into the past not only is interesting but also is constructively useful to the collective well-being of any society.

In their explorations of the past historians differ in many ways, but most agree that there is a common, basic methodology suited to the task facing them, that is, reconstructing the past. Fundamental to that methodology is the formulation by the historian of a question or a hypothesis about what happened in the past. Obviously, the range of such questions and hypotheses is infinite; as a consequence, historical studies are richly and unpredictably varied. In many ways the vitality of historical studies depends on the imagination and the ingenuity of historians in formulating the problems they wish to study. Once having defined a "subject," the historian starts searching for sources that will provide information about that subject. Of crucial importance are what historians call primary sources, which are surviving pieces of evidence produced by human beings who were directly involved in the activity under investigation or by those in a position to know what happened. Primary sources exist in many forms. Most important are written documents of a variety of kinds in which observers of past events recorded what happened. But other kinds of primary sources can help the historian find out what happened, including buildings, art works, maps, pottery, tools, clothing, and oral traditions. Primary documents do not necessarily speak to the historian in clear and unmistakable terms. Historians must apply critical techniques to them in order to evaluate them and to extract information from them. That criticism can be external, aimed at such things as uncovering forgeries and errors; or it can be internal, aimed at resolving such matters as the motives that moved someone to produce the source or the meaning intended by the creator. In addition to primary sources, historians must also take into account what are called secondary sources. They are the works of other historians and scholars who have examined the same general subject and the same segment of time. Secondary sources must also be critically evaluated.

When historians have completed their search for sources and have extracted from them whatever information they can relative to the question or hypothesis with which they began, they then must present in comprehensible form the results of their research. This is a formidable task. In oversimplified terms it involves a series of choices: what sources to emphasize; how those sources relate to the problem under investigation; what data is not relevant; how to organize information in order to convey a meaningful explanation of what happened; and what literary devices to use in order to permit others to understand what happened in the past. This process can never be totally objective, for historians inevitably decide these issues in terms of their own perspective and their own values about the human condition. As a consequence, many prefer to call the reconstruction of the past an art rather than a science.

Although it is impossible to provide a neat formulation of how history is finally presented, in a rough way historians tend to reflect one of two perspectives in their treatment of the past. Some, representing a humanistic orientation, see the past in terms of unique actions and events that are studied for their intrinsic value and for the insights they provide about the human situation in a particular historical setting. These historians tend to present the past in narrative form, telling a story that unfolds in a chronological order with each succeeding episode somehow related to and conditioned by what went before. Others, reflecting a social science orientation, look for patterns in human thought and behavior over time. They

tend to focus on repetitive commonalities rather than uniqueness, on comparisons rather than chronology, and on the universal relevance of the past rather than the unique, nonrepetitive nature of the past's specific episodes. These historians tend to write history in an analytic style, focusing on explanations, causes, and relationships. In this book, both perspectives will be used.

Given the vastness and the complexity of the past, historians cannot deal with all of history at once. To meet this problem, they have adopted several conventions that permit more effective and meaningful reconstruction. One means is to divide the past into periods, each of which has common features allowing it to be treated as an entity. An example of such a periodization scheme is the one applied to the history of Western civilization. The six-thousand-year span involved in that history is typically divided into four periods: the ancient period; the Middle Ages; the early modern period; and the modern period. As will be illustrated in this book, these larger periods are divided into subperiods. Historians often disagree on periodization schemes, and the boundaries between periods shift considerably. A second way to break up history into manageable segments is to focus attention on topics; sometimes these topics are broad, such as the Reformation, and sometimes they are narrow, such as the consequences of World War I. A third way of segmenting the past is to focus on geographical areas. In this book the area treated is extensive: In geographical terms Western civilization embraces what is today Europe, the Mediterranean basin where Western civilization originated, those areas of the world where offshoots of Western civilization have been established, and areas where there existed non-Western civilizations that were significantly affected by the Western world. Historians often focus on smaller areas: nations, regions or cities. The choice made by historians about how to break up the entire past into manageable units has an important bearing on the way the past is treated.

Historical research and writing are decisively affected by the judgments made by historians as to what aspect of human activity is most important in shaping and explaining the collective destinies of past societies. For example, some argue that political factors are crucial in forming societies, while others insist that economic conditions are decisive. Such formulations have produced several widely recognized categories of history: political history, economic history, social history, intellectual history, religious history, and cultural history. Each of these categories produces its unique version of the past and its unique manner of explaining the historical process. Such categorization also invites some historians to undertake a synthesis that will produce a version of the past embracing all aspects of human activity. The effort to synthesize has played an important part in the writing of this book.

Historians constitute a scholarly community in which knowledge, interpretations, interests, and concepts are shared. As a result, schools of historical thought develop, usually derived from shared assumptions about the fundamental characteristics of human development. An example is one of the best-known schools of thought in the twentieth century, the Marxist school. Proponents of this school argue that modes of economic producton are the determinant force in historical development. Each mode of production serves as a dynamic force creating its own unique political, social, religious, and cultural structures. And each contains within it conflicting class interests that provide the impetus for change and that determine the direction of change. Such schools encourage a collective approach to the past guided by a shared angle of attack and by a common mode of interpretation. They also tend to produce generalized explanations of the past. The constraints implicit in almost any school of historical thought cause most historians to withhold commitment to a particular school. But the existence of such schools often plays a role in shaping the way uncommitted historians approach major historical developments. In this book an effort has been made to represent various interpretations and to emphasize those that seem most useful in explaining a particular situation in the past.

Over the generations there have been numerous changes in what is most challenging both to historians and to their audiences. In recent years three broad developments have been particularly influential. Efforts have been made to integrate some of the results of these developments into this text.

First, there has been a broadening and growing importance of social history. Social historians increasingly emphasize looking at the past "from the bottom up" by studying the everyday experiences and attitudes of "ordinary" people or subordinated groups rather than concentrating on political leaders, elite groups, and great thinkers. To recount the history of these heretofore "silent" people and to assess its significance, social historians have had to ask new questions and to make innovative use of sources often overlooked by traditional historians, such as parish registers, gravestone inscriptions, police reports, manorial records, folk tales, and popular art. Their efforts have greatly enriched our knowledge and understanding of the past in its entirety.

The second development is often termed "the new history" (although, like many elements of social history, its roots go back several decades). The new history has been shaped by the methods and the theoretical constructs formulated by social scientists. For example, historians have applied to the past the methods and the findings of demographers to expand knowledge of changes in population size, age groups, birth rates, age of marriage, fertility rates, family size, and death rates. Other historians have used the methods and findings of modern psychology to expand their understanding of the past. Psychohistorians emphasize emotional factors in explaining individual and group behavior in all kinds of historical situations, including such often-overlooked topics as child rearing, family relations, charismatic leadership, and death. Many historians practicing the new history rely on comparative and quantitative analysis to support their conclusions. Increasingly this approach involves the use of computers and statistical analysis of data pertaining to such things as voting patterns, price fluctuations, and population changes.

A third development has been the growing interests in women's history. Traditionally history has been written from the male perspective and has focused primarily on the thoughts and behavior of men. Women's history attempts to correct this neglect of women in history and the distortions that inevitably result. It focuses on women's experiences and on the roles women played in a large number and variety of historical developments. It also tries to alert us to gender bias in the way historical questions are posed, evidence is evaluated, and history is written.

Perhaps all of these considerations will suggest what is most important: The writing of history involves numerous choices, judgments, and compromises. The history one studies or writes depends on what questions are posed. Historians usually want to know more than only what happened, more than only the facts. They want to know how something of importance happened, why it happened, and why it is significant. They must create some reasoned order out of the chaos of past acts and thoughts. All of these considerations shape how they use historical facts and determine what they make of those facts. It may be true that history defined as all that has happened over the ages is a closed book in which nothing changes. But history defined as reconstructing that past is always in the process of change. Not only are new events happening every day and forgotten events of the past constantly being discovered, but the way we look at and interpret the past also changes as our interests, perspectives, and interpretative modes change. In this book, we have attempted to reflect this dynamic quality of history by making revisions that reflect our changing views and those of our colleagues engaged in exploring the past.

PART ONE

THE ANCIENT NEAR EAST, 4000–300 B.C.

This book will seek to explain the evolution of Western civilization by describing the numerous ingredients that combined over a long period of time to shape its basic features. While the emergence of civilized life on this planet occurred over immense ages, the crucial "roots" from which Western civilization developed began to grow about six thousand years ago in a particular area of the world known as the Near East.

This first section of the book will concentrate on developments occurring in the Near East over a long era stretching from about 4000 B.C. to 300 B.C. After a few introductory remarks concerning the long era of human history that preceded the emergence of civilization in the Near East, we shall focus on the amazing activity that unfolded in two river valley systems in the Near East: the Tigris-Euphrates in Mesopotamia and the Nile in Egypt. For it was in the challenging environment of these river valleys that human communities developed the first complex patterns of institutions, techniques, and ideas that can be called "civilizations." What was achieved in this setting established the foundations upon which Western civilization was to grow. Beyond characterizing the main features of the early civilizations of Mesopotamia and Egypt, we must consider the beginnings of a process as important to the history of the Western world as was the original creation of civilized life—namely, the beginning of the expansion of the river valley civilizations into a large area of northeast Africa and southwest Asia. Not only did this process permit new peoples to raise the level of their existence, but it also created a cultural setting in which they made their own unique contributions to the broadening stream of civilization. Until at least 500 B.C. the peoples of the Near East were on the forefront of the civilized world. This creative population fashioned a priceless heritage that was later exploited by other peoples participating in the shaping of Western civilization.

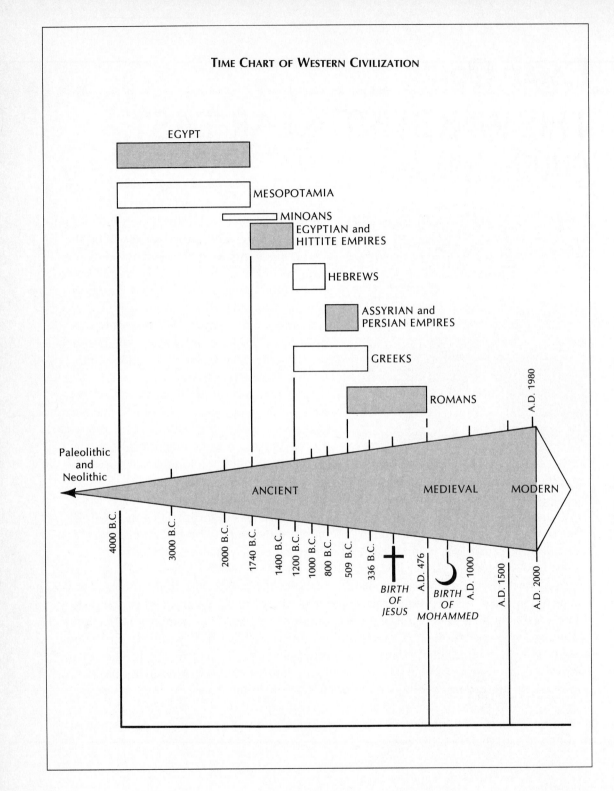

TIME CHART OF WESTERN CIVILIZATION

EGYPT

MESOPOTAMIA

MINOANS

EGYPTIAN and
HITTITE EMPIRES

HEBREWS

ASSYRIAN and
PERSIAN EMPIRES

GREEKS

ROMANS

A.D. 1980

Paleolithic
and
Neolithic

ANCIENT   MEDIEVAL   MODERN

4000 B.C.

3000 B.C.

2000 B.C.

1740 B.C.

1400 B.C.

1200 B.C.

1000 B.C.

800 B.C.

509 B.C.

336 B.C.

BIRTH
OF
JESUS

A.D. 476

BIRTH
OF
MOHAMMED

A.D. 1000

A.D. 1500

A.D. 2000

CHAPTER 1

The River Valley Civilizations: Mesopotamia and Egypt, 4000–1750 B.C.

FIGURE 1.1   A Divine Ruler   The statue of Menkure (an Egyptian pharaoh of the Fourth Dynasty) and his queen conveys the majesty and power that surrounded the rulers of the early river valley societies of the Near East. The ability of such rulers to organize human effort on a large scale was crucial in establishing control over the rich river valleys that provided the material base for the first civilizations. This statue also illustrates the basic characteristics of Egyptian sculpture—rigid posture, stylized clothing, a personal touch revealed in the faces of even the majestic god-kings and their consorts. (Museum of Fine Arts, Boston)

Somewhere just before 3000 B.C. there occurred a decisive turning point in the long history of human beings. The change was marked by the creation of the first higher civilizations based on urban societies. The scene of this accomplishment was a unique one: the special environment existing in the Tigris-Euphrates Valley in Mesopotamia and the Nile Valley in Egypt. The establishment of higher civilization in these areas created the foundations upon which all the subsequent history of Western civilization was built.

1. THE PREHISTORIC BACKGROUND

The emergence of higher civilizations in the Near Eastern river valleys was made possible by complex developments during an immensely long prehistoric period of human preparation—perhaps five hundred times longer than the time span shown on the chart on page 2. Our knowledge of what happened during this prehistoric period is fragmentary, and there is disagreement on how to interpret what is known. In simple terms these vast ages involved three interrelated processes: geological developments, which created the topography and the climate of the earth; biological developments, which produced the human species as well as other creatures and plants; and cultural developments, through which human beings created techniques and practices that allowed them to enhance their capabilities of survival and improvement in a constantly changing physical and biological environment.

On the basis of a meager collection of skeletal remains found scattered over the earth, it appears that the existence of humanlike creatures (hominids) must be extended back at least 3 million years. It was only about forty thousand years ago that the human species (conventionally designated as *homo sapiens*, meaning "thinking man") assumed its present physical form, perhaps first in East Africa or southwest Asia. Over the long period separating primitive hominids from *homo sapiens*, most of it dominated by conditions created by four successive ice ages, something happened biologically to create special creatures endowed with physical traits that provided them with ad-

vantages over other creatures sharing the earth. Especially important were an upright position, stereoscopic vision, a large and complex brain, a voice mechanism that made verbal communication possible, and a unique hand structure that permitted the manipulation of objects.

No less important in preparing for the emergence of higher civilization was the capacity of humans to create objects and techniques that reinforced their biological capabilities and increased their adaptability in their struggle to control the environment in ways beneficial to them. In large part, this ability to create and transmit *culture* was a consequence of the superiority of their brain. The reconstruction of prehistoric cultural development, derived largely from artifacts discovered and interpreted by archaeologists, is as complex and as open to debate as is the biological history of the human species. Despite these difficulties, certain broad lines of development are evident.

Across prehistoric times human cultural activity was most clearly demonstrated in the making of stone tools. For this reason the prehistoric age has been called the Stone Age. Surviving stone tools indicate that during 99 percent of all human prehistory men and women lived as hunters and food gatherers. Although this culture varied in detail from place to place around the globe, it involved certain basic features that permit us to give it a common name—*Paleolithic* (Old Stone Age) culture. Paleolithic peoples lived in small groups dispersed at considerable distance from each other. They were perpetual wanderers, their lives controlled by the movements of animals and the growth patterns of plants upon which survival depended. They sheltered themselves temporarily in caves, holes covered with animal skins, or fragile tents made of skins or branches. At best, their existence was precarious, as is evident from the complete disappearance of some branches of the hominid species, and improvement in the human condition was slow.

But no matter how slowly and painfully, Paleolithic peoples did advance their culture. They developed increasingly complex and effective techniques for making a greater variety of stone tools, eventually complemented by implements made from bone, horn, and wood. These improved tools made them more efficient killers of even the largest and fiercest animals. They accumulated and transmitted a growing store of knowledge about animals and plants that allowed succeeding generations to hunt and gather food more effectively. They learned how to use fire to warm themselves, prepare their food more easily, and scare away predatory animals. Especially important was their ability to shape social structures permitting group activities. The family, perhaps rooted in the demands of child rearing, appears to have been a basic social unit. Several families, perhaps related by kinship ties, joined forces to create a hunting pack that was more effective because of cooperation. Social and economic functions based on gender developed within these groups. The efforts of male hunters were complemented by equally vital activities carried out by female plant gatherers, fire keepers, and child raisers. Interactions within these communities necessitated spoken languages, a prime instrument not only in promoting effective group action but also in passing on knowledge about animals, plants, weather, and toolmaking. Scanty bits of evidence indicate the existence of religious life centered on a belief in the existence, in all things, of spirits susceptible to human manipulation and perhaps in life after death. The cave paintings found at Altamira in Spain and Lascaux in France—as well as crudely shaped human figures, decorated hunting weapons, and jewelry scattered wherever Paleolithic groups passed—suggest an urge and a capacity to express ideas and feelings about the world and to enhance life with created beauty. All of these elements of evolving Paleolithic society leave no doubt that by the time *homo sapiens* had occupied large portions of the globe forty or fifty thousand years ago, the human species had progressed far in establishing mastery over the world and in utilizing its biological and cultural resources to sustain human life with some degree of security.

A culture based on hunting and food gathering had limitations, perhaps too narrow to contain expanding human capabilities. Ultimately, Paleolithic culture gave way to a new pattern of life that changed the human condition in a fundamental way. This great transformation involved the domestication of plants and animals, which allowed human societies to rely on agriculture to provide the material basis for society. This change marked an essential step along the path to higher civilization. The most recent results of archaeological research into human cultural development on a world scale make it almost certain that the change from a hunting and food-gathering to a farming culture first occurred in a relatively limited area of southwest Asia defined by the upper boundary of the Fertile Crescent (as traced on Map 1.1). Not too much later, as time is measured on the scale of human prehistory, agricultural life appeared in most other areas of the world, sometimes borrowed from the original inventors and other times "invented" anew.

The archaeological evidence collected over the past fifty years from many sites in the area where agriculture first appeared suggests that the "revolution" came gradually and was accompanied by much experimentation. The transition period, extending from about 9000 to 6000 B.C. and coinciding in a rough way with the end of the last period of glaciation, has been called the *Mesolithic* (Middle Stone) age. The experimentation occurred in an ecosystem that had a unique combination of features: moderate but regular rainfall; large numbers of wild sheep, goats, cattle, and swine; rich stands of wild cereals, legumes, and plants with oil-bearing seeds; a substantial population sustained by a well-established Paleolithic culture. Perhaps there was a slight change in the climate associated with the retreat of the glaciers that produced conditions favorable to grass-eating animals and cereal plants. And perhaps population pressure prompted people to put their extensive knowledge of plants and animals to new uses. In any case, behavior patterns began to change in Mesolithic times. People stayed longer in one place. Some groups gave increasing attention to the control and selective killing of animal herds, utilizing the harvest of wild grasses to supplement their meat supply. Others concentrated more heavily on the management of wild plants, depending secondarily on hunting. As these practices continued, certain wild animals—sheep, goats, cattle, and pigs—and certain wild plants—especially wheat and barley—were modified genetically to the point where they flourished best under human care. When that happened, human beings were in a position to abandon hunting and food gathering

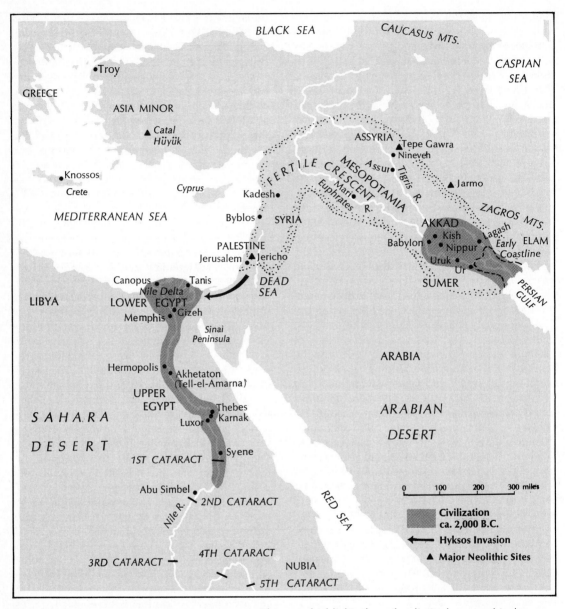

Map 1.1 **EARLY MESOPOTAMIA AND ANCIENT EGYPT** This map highlights the rather limited geographical areas in which higher civilization first appeared. Compared with the vast stretches of territory surrounding them, the areas nourished by the waters of the Tigris-Euphrates and the Nile rivers were small. But what was accomplished there was indeed revolutionary.

in favor of agriculture.

The emergence of agriculture as the basis of life opened what is called the *Neolithic* (New Stone) age. Its revolutionary impact is evident in the remains of several sites excavated in recent years, especially Jericho in Palestine, Halicar and Catal Hüyük in modern Turkey, and Jarmo and Tepe Gawra in modern Iraq (see Map 1.1). People settled permanently in villages, some of which supported populations of several hundred. They built substantial baked-mud houses, featuring not only living quarters but also storage facilities, household shrines, and even burial places. Such public facilities as temples, walls, and wells appeared. Human activity, shared by men and women alike, focused on regular planting and harvesting of wheat, barley, legumes, and fruits, and on the care of domesticated animals, valuable not only for meat but also for milk, cheese, hides, and wool. This new mode of life called for a new kit of stone tools, especially hoes and sickles. Before Neolithic culture progressed far, people were beginning to complement stone tools with copper instruments, heralding a coming age of metals that would make stone tools obsolete. Pottery and basket weaving developed to provide storage for food, and the weaving of fibers emerged to create a new range of clothing.

Besides its new technological features, Neolithic culture had significant new social characteristics. Settled agricultural life demanded greater specialization of labor, which allowed more highly developed skills and better products. Such specialization appears to have given women a greater variety of opportunities to contribute to the village economy; however, the demands of child rearing still limited the extent of that involvement and perhaps increased women's economic dependence on males. Settled life made it possible to accumulate wealth in the form of stored grain and animal herds. This wealth provided the basis of exchange for products that a particular village was unable to provide for itself, thus creating trade, which is clearly evident in the spread of pottery made in a specific area to widely scattered places across the Near East. Increased wealth also made the successful peasant village the target of outsiders, requiring collective action to defend the village. And wealth based on land and animal ownership generated quarrels that posed a threat to internal order in the village. A major consequence of problems related to trade, defense, and adjudication of quarrels was the development of a more complex system of village governance. This system usually took the form of a tribal structure in which several kinship groups or clans acting through family heads selected a village chief who joined the family elders in making and carrying out collective decisions to meet common problems.

Neolithic villagers also had to expand their mental skills to cope with their new situation. The demands of farming called for more complex calculations, extended planning, and disciplined behavior than did hunting and food gathering. Different moral standards were required to fit situations arising from closer contacts with larger numbers of people and from ownership of things. Religion, increasingly centered on the worship of the forces of nature believed to control the fertility of plants and animals, challenged Neolithic villagers with concepts far more complex than those associated with animal spirits. The art created in places such as Catal Hüyük clearly reflects expanding human consciousness. The increasing complexities surrounding religion also led villagers to place greater trust in religious experts— priests—and to dedicate more energy and wealth to winning the favor of the spirits who nourished the crops and animal herds and protected the village. The responsibilities of directing the government of the village and of conducting religious life began to bestow on those involved in these functions a special place of prominence and power in village life, creating the basis for a class system. The evidence strongly suggests that males monopolized these leadership roles as well as family life. Perhaps the emergence of agricultural life created a social system and a set of values that cast women in a position of dependence and inferiority that would be difficult to eradicate. However, it is worth noting that the female figure was a prime symbol used in Neolithic religious cults to represent the regenerative powers of nature. This symbolism suggests a high respect, perhaps even awe, for femininity as a potent force in shaping and controlling human destiny.

2. MESOPOTAMIAN CIVILIZATION: POLITICAL, ECONOMIC, AND SOCIAL LIFE

From a global perspective the development of agriculture had put the peoples of southwestern Asia in the forefront of human activity by about 6000 B.C. Recent studies of the development of some of the area's peasant villages between 6000 and 4000 B.C. suggest some potential for further evolution, but nothing indicates that any of them were capable of developing into complex cities. Urban civilization was created by farmers who learned how to master the more demanding environment existing in the Tigris-Euphrates Valley, a relatively small territory extending about three hundred miles northwest from where the rivers flowed into the Persian Gulf (see Map 1.1).

This flat alluvial plain, called Mesopotamia (a word of Greek origin meaning "between the rivers"), presented both opportunity and challenge to Neolithic peoples on its fringes. As a result of constant silting caused by the annual flooding of the rivers, the soil was immensely rich. Those same floods, brought about by melting snows in the Caucasus Mountains where the Tigris and the Euphrates had their sources, provided a dependable water supply to an area almost devoid of rainfall. However, the potential gifts of Mesopotamia were not easily possessed. The somewhat irregular floods were destructive unless they were controlled, and the rich soil was nonproductive unless the postflood swamps could be drained and cleared of swamp vegetation. And even then the soil was useless unless it could be watered during the arid growing season. Mesopotamia was lacking in many natural resources, especially stone, timber, and minerals. Unless its occupants could organize trading ventures extending over considerable distances, only the most primitive level of culture could be sustained. Finally, Mesopotamia lacked any natural barriers to restrain the raids of peoples living to the east, north, and west.

While agriculture slowly evolved around the fringes of Mesopotamia during the Mesolithic age, that land remained relatively backward. Eventually, perhaps just before 4000 B.C., peasant villages did appear in the river valley. Sometime after

about 3500 B.C. these Neolithic villages began to be overshadowed by larger, more complex, and richer communities. Although the evidence is far from clear, this leap forward appears to have involved more than an inevitable evolution from simple village to complex urban culture. The change was due to a burst of creativity that allowed the formation of larger human communities capable of planning, constructing, and maintaining effective irrigation systems. Systematic irrigation permitted the successful exploitation of the full productive potential of Mesopotamia. Perhaps that achievement was the work of the Sumerians, invaders who settled in south Mesopotamia in a land eventually named Sumer. They succeeded in organizing relatively large and complex communities dependent on an irrigation-based agricultural system. By 3100 B.C. several rich and populous city-states had developed in Sumer, including Ur, Lagash, Uruk, and Umma. Each consisted of two elements: a densely populated urban center defined by walls, impressive temples and palaces, and teeming residential areas occupied by people engaged in pursuits other than farming; and a considerable stretch of irrigated farmland carved out of the chaotic river valley environment by an elaborate system of dikes, canals, and reservoirs and then systematically cultivated by a tightly controlled peasant population. The Sumerian accomplishment soon served as a model for another group of intruders who occupied the area just north of Sumer. These were the Akkadians, a Semitic-speaking people from the Arabian Desert, who developed several thriving city-states in northern Mesopotamia. For at least seven centuries, from about 3100 to 2400 B.C., these independent city-states enjoyed remarkable stability and prosperity.

The key to their success was an effective system of government capable of controlling a large population engaged in a variety of mutually supportive activities. From an early date responsibility for decision making rested in the hands of a single human leader. Perhaps initially that power was held by a high priest (*ensi*), but eventually a secular king (*lugal*) exercising military force came to dominate. In either case authority was grounded primarily in religious belief. The Sumerians believed that each city-state had been originally created by a god or a goddess. The city and its surrounding lands belonged to the divine founder, and its citizens were the founder's slaves. The *ensi* or the *lugal* was the agent through whom the will of the divine owner was carried out. He based his activities in a temple-palace that served as the center of the community. From there flowed divine orders coordinating the numerous activities required to exploit the resources belonging to the patron deity. The efforts of the rulers to control the total population were greatly aided by the development of writing, which allowed the keeping of careful records of what was produced and what was due. Back to the temple-palace came a huge income used to sustain the divine city. Around the temple-palace and supported by this income clustered a wide array of specialists who served to carry out the ruler's orders. They included priests and priestesses, record keepers, engineers, architects, sculptors, traders, artisans, soldiers, and tax collectors. The combined creative efforts of these specialists, whose livelihood derived largely from surplus agricultural productivity made possible by the carefully planned and controlled irrigation system, provided the essential features of civilized urban life existing on a plane far beyond life in Neolithic villages. But none of this would have been possible without an effective political system; higher civilization depended more on the relationships among humans than it did on relationships between humans and the natural environment, as had been the case in Paleolithic and Neolithic cultures.

Although the independent city-state pattern of government dominated Mesopotamia between 3100 and 2400 B.C., political problems emerged that eventually brought changes. The wealth of the city-states led to constant attacks from outsiders, undeterred by any natural barriers shielding Mesopotamia. Equally unsettling were conflicts among the city-states, usually caused by the quest for additional land to support increasing populations and more elaborate urban life. The solution was eventually found in the establishment of *empires* built by conquest and ruled by powerful kings who developed new techniques for keeping peace and order among peoples of diverse backgrounds.

The first attempts at shaping empires were made by strong kings from prominent Sumerian cities who used military force to establish mastery over other cities, but these "empires" were short-lived. Ultimately, the Semites were more successful in uniting Mesopotamia. The first great empire builder was Sargon I (ca. 2370–2315 B.C.) from Akkad. He led his Semitic warriors in campaigns that not only subdued the city-states of Sumer but also extended Akkadian dominance into the Zagros Mountains, Assyria, and Syria. Sargon's empire was sustained by his descendants until about 2200 B.C., but then it collapsed under the combined pressure of internal resistance and external attacks.

For an interval after the collapse of the Akkadian Empire, the Sumerian city-states again enjoyed independence and leadership in Mesopotamia. But soon a new empire-building people, the Amorites, overshadowed them. They were a Semitic-speaking people who entered Mesopotamia from the Arabian Desert about 2000 B.C. Their day of glory came with Hammurabi, ruler of the city-state of Babylon. His reign (ca. 1792–1750 B.C.) was distinguished by a series of conquests that once again created a large empire stretching in a great arc from the Persian Gulf to the Mediterranean Sea. From the great city of Babylon Hammurabi asserted control over a large population and spread the fruits of Mesopotamian civilization to many different peoples. For all its brilliance, the Amorite Empire was relatively short-lived. Shortly after 1700 B.C. outside attackers began to batter its frontiers until eventually the Kassites conquered Mesopotamia; their rule led to a long period of political obscurity.

Hammurabi's career exemplifies the new ideas and practices of government introduced by the empire builders who dominated Mesopotamia between 2400 and 1700 B.C. These contributions, aimed chiefly at using political power to create common bonds among diverse peoples, proved to be among the most important of all Mesopotamian contributions to civilization. One technique used by Hammurabi to unify the peoples over whom he ruled was to impress on them their total dependence on the power of their one ruler. This technique called for a conscious effort to exalt the person of the king as the sole source of earthly power. To heighten his visibility, Hammurabi made his court at Babylon the setting for a vast display of wealth toward which his subjects from "the Four Quarters of the World" could turn for their well-being. He sought to create a common religion in his empire, based on the worship of Marduk, once the patron god of the city of Babylon but now presented as the divine lord of all the other deities and of the earth. Hammurabi proclaimed himself as Marduk's sole agent, alone capable of bringing divine favor to his subjects. But his power was more than appearance. He maintained a well-organized army ready to curb threats to peace in the empire. He established a centralized bureaucracy in Babylon consisting of specialized departments devoted to administration. This central government kept careful watch over governors sent out to administer local units into which the empire was divided and to collect taxes, raise troops, and administer justice.

One of Hammurabi's most significant measures to solidify and unify his empire was his law code. He claimed it was handed down to him from the deities "to destroy the wicked and the evil, so that the strong may not oppress the weak" (see Figure 1.2). Although a modern reader of Hammurabi's law code is taken aback by the brutal punishments imposed on lawbreakers, the code is better characterized by its commonsense, humane approach to basic human problems: protection for women, children, and slaves; fairness in commercial exchange; protection of property; standard procedures for adjudicating disputes; debt relief for victims of flood and drought. It reflected an enlightened concept of justice that drew people of all kinds to accept the rule of a king trying to provide common rules governing the behavior of his subjects.

For its material base Mesopotamian civilization depended largely on a carefully organized and controlled agricultural system. Although there were some technological advances in agriculture, especially the introduction of bronze tools and wheeled ploughs, farming depended chiefly on the traditional crops and animals of Neolithic times. The chief difference was the larger productive capacity of the fertile, irrigated fields of Mesopotamia. The prime agricultural unit was a large farm, usually owned by a member of the aristocracy and tilled by tenants and slaves working un-

FIGURE 1.2 An Ancient Lawgiver This relief, showing Hammurabi receiving a code of laws from a deity, was carved at the top of a stone cylinder upon which were inscribed the provisions of the law written in cuneiform script. Sumerian artists were especially adept in relief carving, an art form that would have an illustrious history. (Giraudon)

der careful supervision of the owner or his agents, whose decisions in turn were guided by directives flowing from the ruler and his agents. Every city supported a large number of skilled artisans who made a variety of fine products consumed in the city or distributed far and wide across the Near East by enterprising merchants in return for the raw materials lacking in Mesopotamia.

The political and economic order in Mesopotamia provided the basis for a more diverse and structured social system than was typical of Neolithic peasant villages. At the summit of society stood an aristocracy made up of priests, landowners, and royal officials who derived their high status from their close association with the ruler and their involvement in the governance of society. This aristocracy benefited most from Mesopotamia's material wealth and created a glittering life for itself. Merchants and artisans enjoyed a prosperous and relatively free life, often closely attached to aristocrats as clients. Each city-state had a large population of urban laborers who performed the menial tasks required to run the city and the households of the powerful. The bulk of the population consisted of farmers, living in villages outside the urban center and devoting themselves to agricultural routines from which they derived meager rewards. Slavery existed but was not a dominant feature of Mesopotamian life. The relationships among various social classes, as well as the rights and responsibilities of each, were carefully defined by law.

At all levels of Mesopotamian society the family was a basic institution. Marriages were arranged by family agreements, and the husband and father exercised almost absolute control over the wife and children. As a consequence, women played a limited role in societal decision making. However, the law did recognize that they had certain rights, especially to the dowries provided them by their fathers at the time of marriage. Surviving records indicate that women often inherited their husbands' property and were engaged in economic ventures of many kinds. Aristocratic women certainly shared in the luxuries that accompanied their husbands' social status. The wives and children of artisans and farmers were actively engaged in the work of the heads of households—and they shared the meager returns for their efforts. As a whole, Mesopotamian society was stable and seldom troubled by social strife and tension.

3. MESOPOTAMIAN CULTURAL LIFE

The emergence of higher civilization in Mesopotamia was marked not only by the advances in government, economy, and social structure just described but also by impressive developments in cultural life—in religion, literature, the arts, and the sciences. By and large, the Sumerians were the prime creators of Mesopotamian culture. The Semites were usually imitators of the Sumerians. The result of this relationship was a common culture based on Sumerian models that ultimately embraced all of Mesopotamia.

A prime force shaping Mesopotamian cultural life was religion. The Mesopotamian religion was *polytheistic,* based on a worship of many deities believed to live in all things and to cause everything to happen. Especially awesome were the spirits that controlled the forces of nature: gods and goddesses of the sky, air, water, sun, moon, storms. One or another of these deities was usually accepted as founder and ruler of each city-state. Particularly appealing to ordinary people who lived close to the soil was the goddess of fertility, called Inanna by the Sumerians and Ishtar by the Semites, whose munificent power renewed nature every spring, usually with the help of a male lover. Sharing the universe with these great gods and goddesses were legions of lesser spirits, each of whom could bring blessings or misfortunes, great or small, to men and women in all stations of life. The Mesopotamians spent considerable intellectual energy trying to define the powers of these deities, their origins, and their relationships to one another and to the human community. The result was a rich and intriguing mythology that had a powerful influence on later religious thinking.

The lot assigned to human beings in the god-dominated universe was not an easy one. They were viewed as slaves of the deities, bound to suffer whatever the angry, vengeful, unpredictable gods and goddesses wished. Especially heavy was the burden of trying to please the deities. To do so required the building of splendid temples where the deities could live, supporting priests and priestesses to attend the divine needs, offering endless prayers and gifts, organizing expensive public festivals, and spending endless efforts to discover the intentions of the gods and goddesses as these might be revealed in the movement of the stars, dreams, and the shapes of the entrails of animals. Not only did the great deities need to be kept pleased, but so did all the lesser spirits to whom honor and tribute were paid at countless shrines in homes, fields, and city streets.

Life was an endless ritual aimed at pleasing a multitude of unpredictable spirits. In return the Mesopotamians expected the material gifts the deities had to offer—the safety and material prosperity of the city-state, the family, and the individual. Most men and women were never sure that the all-powerful gods and goddesses would smile on them. A tone of pessimism and fatalism permeated their view of life. Their religion was lacking in any ethical dimensions that taught that good behavior and good deeds were pleasing to the divine powers. Nor did the Mesopotamians entertain any hope for a happy life after death; the dead passed on to a "land of no return" somewhere underground "where dust is their feed, clay their substance; where they see no light and dwell in darkness." Without a chance to please the deities through good behavior nor a hope for a happy afterlife, perhaps there was little choice but fear of the deities and pessimism about the human lot.

The urge to know and to please the gods and goddesses inspired an impressive literature made possible by the development of a writing system— one of the great inventions in history. The Sumerians were the first to develop writing. In its earliest form their writing consisted of pictures (pictograms) used primarily to record what was due to the deities in terms of cattle and grain. Gradually pictograms evolved into symbols representing sounds that could be combined into words that could express chains of thought of various kinds. For the recording of such thoughts these symbols were pressed onto soft clay tablets with a wedge-shaped stylus and then the tablets were baked; thus the writing is called *cuneiform* (from a Latin word meaning "wedge"). Eventually the Sumerian system of writing was adapted to the Semitic language of the Akkadians, which by Sargon I's time was replacing Sumerian writing in Mesopotamia. However, for centuries learned people continued to study Sumerian texts much as modern scholars learn ancient Greek, Latin, and Hebrew. Thus, much Sumerian literature survived as a model to be followed by other peoples.

While writing in Mesopotamia served a major function in keeping records of a large array of ordinary activities, talented individuals learned to use it for creative purposes. The most impressive literary productions were religious epics, of which the *Creation Epic* and the *Epic of Gilgamesh* are examples. The *Creation Epic* describes how Marduk won supremacy over the spirit world and created earth and human beings, a feat that earned him universal worship in the time of Hammurabi. The *Epic of Gilgamesh* recounts the fruitless struggle of a legendary king of Uruk, Gilgamesh, to find immortality. The Mesopotamians also wrote hymns, chronicles of the deeds of great rulers, and letters. The literary forms, themes, and styles developed by Mesopotamian writers not only enriched their own culture but also asserted an important influence on the literature of later peoples, as is evident in Mesopotamian influences reflected in the Hebrew Old Testament, written a thousand or more years later.

From the beginnings of their civilization, the Mesopotamians showed impressive skills and creativity in the visual arts. The need to provide their deities with suitable dwellings stimulated monumental architecture and produced impressive mud brick temple complexes as the central feature of every city. The crowning feature of the temple complex was the temple tower, called a *ziggurat*, designed as a series of terraces one on top of another, each successive layer smaller than the one below. A sanctuary remote from the world was placed atop the final terrace. Around the ziggurat there usually developed an elaborate complex of lesser shrines, offices, priestly dwellings, storehouses, and workshops, all comprising a sacred precinct where the deities could be served. Hardly less elaborate were the palaces where the kings and their courts lived. The palace at Mari, an important city in the Amorite Empire, covered six acres and contained more than two hundred fifty rooms. Mesopotamian architects knew how to use columns, domes, arches, and vaults, but the lack of stone as a building material limited their ability to exploit these forms fully.

The Mesopotamians were also skilled sculptors. Most three-dimensional statues portray the deities and famous kings. Sculptors took some pains to give a distinctive character to the faces of their subjects but concerned themselves little with a realistic rendering of the human body. Their work, strongly influenced by geometrical forms, is solid, stiff, and motionless (see Color Plate 1).

More realistic and animated scenes were created by sculptors working in low relief to depict historic events or divine exploits (see Figure 1.2). The most exquisite carving was done by seal makers who wrought miniaturized scenes in stone used to press an identifying mark onto documents written in clay. The same deft skill is illustrated in jewelry, metalwork, and decorated pottery.

Chiefly as a result of their efforts to cope with divine forces and with the rivers, the Mesopotamians produced a body of knowledge that can be called science. They devised a system of time reckoning based on cycles of the sun and the moon. They developed a standard system of weights and measures almost universally used by Hammurabi's time. Their numbering system combined a decimal system with units of sixty. They were able to perform the basic functions of arithmetic and geometry. A body of medical knowledge, mixing observations and religious lore, was developed. As a result of the travels of merchants and soldiers, the Mesopotamians amassed a considerable store of geographical information. Inspired by an urge to foretell the future, the Mesopotamians gathered accurate information about the movement of the stars. Although the Mesopotamians were seldom concerned with gathering knowledge about nature for its own sake, the information they did compile about nature in the course of meeting practical problems was stored up for the use of later peoples, particularly the Greeks, as the basis for theoretical science.

4. EGYPT: POLITICAL, ECONOMIC, AND SOCIAL LIFE

Not long after urban civilization took shape in Mesopotamia, a similar leap forward occurred in Egypt. Although bits of archaeological evidence found in Egypt suggest the presence of Mesopotamian influences there at the moment of transition to higher civilization, the basic developments in the Nile Valley were native and the resultant pattern of civilization was unique.

Just as in Mesopotamia, the advent of higher civilization in Egypt hinged on meeting the chal-

lenge posed by a river valley environment. The Nile has its source in the mountains of equatorial Africa (see Map 1.1). From there it flows northward past a series of rapids (cataracts) to trace a narrow, cliff-lined trough seldom more than ten miles wide through bleak deserts almost devoid of rainfall. As it nears the Mediterranean, the river fans out into a series of channels to create the Delta, a triangle of rich land about one hundred twenty miles on each side. The annual floods of the Nile come with predictable regularity to create what the Egyptians called the "black land" of the narrow valley and the Delta, which they contrasted with the dreaded "red land" of the desert. However, the Nile floods had to be controlled and their waters distributed across the "black land" during the rainless growing season before the productive potential of the valley could be realized.

During many centuries prior to the emergence of higher civilization in the Nile Valley, Neolithic agricultural life existed across much of North Africa. However, only somewhere between 5000 and 4500 B.C. did some of these farmers begin to establish their villages on the fringes of the Nile Valley. During the next thousand years these peoples developed the technical and organizational skills that permitted them to move into the valley and to establish irrigation systems capable of controlling the floods and utilizing the immensely rich soil as a basis of village life. By a process that is ill understood, these villages in time were joined together to form small kingdoms.

The era dominated by these small kingdoms, called the Predynastic Age, ended suddenly about 3100 B.C., when Egypt was united under a single ruler, later given the title *pharaoh*. Egyptian tradition ascribed this feat to Menes, who founded the first dynasty of pharaohs (a dynasty was a group of rulers from a single family who followed one another as pharaoh) and opened an era called the Old Kingdom (3100–2200 B.C.). Six dynasties ruled during this long era, the most glorious being the Third and Fourth dynasties. From their capital at Memphis, these pharaohs asserted a beneficial authority that brought peace, prosperity, and the fruits of higher civilization to the entire valley. Egypt benefited especially from freedom from outside attacks, a boon afforded by the formidable natural barriers guarding the Nile Valley: the cataracts, the deserts, the Mediterranean Sea. The massive pyramids built at Gizeh by the powerful pharaohs of the Fourth Dynasty—Menkure, Kephren, and Khufu (Cheops)—mirror the immense wealth of a society unified in exploiting the Nile and the great power of the rulers who directed this collective effort.

The key to this success was the political system that had taken shape by the time of the Third Dynasty. Its central feature was the absolute power of the pharaoh, who was considered to be a god sired by the sun god Ra and destined to eternal life. The pharaoh owned Egypt and its people. Every person was his servant, subject to his unchallengeable orders. Despite their lofty status, most of the pharaohs of the Old Kingdom were active statesmen, well trained for their role and constantly occupied in overseeing the irrigation system, giving justice, directing building programs, and sponsoring trade. They exercised their power through a highly developed administrative system centered at Memphis. Egypt was divided into smaller administrative units, called *nomes*, each controlled by royal officials held closely accountable by the central government for carrying out the pharaoh's orders in the villages of each nome.

During the Sixth Dynasty this highly effective system faltered. Egypt entered a period of anarchy called the First Intermediate Period (2200–2050 B.C.). The pharaohs of this era (Seventh through Tenth dynasties) were shadowy, ineffectual figures. Political power fell into the hands of local rulers whose pursuit of their own interests led to internal wars, lawlessness, injustice, and economic depression.

About 2050 B.C., the princes of Thebes, previously an insignificant city far to the south in the valley, undertook to reunify Egypt. After a fierce struggle, these princes (designated as the Eleventh Dynasty) succeeded and began what is known as the period of the Middle Kingdom (2050–1750 B.C.). Reunited Egypt reached a new peak during the Twelfth Dynasty, especially during the rule of Amenemhet I and Senusret. They consciously restored many of the political institutions and practices characteristic of the Old Kingdom—the divine power of the pharaoh, the centralized bureaucracy, the provincial administration—and labored successfully to revive and even to expand the economic system. Although the main features of the traditional political order were restored, there was a change in the spirit guiding the government of the Middle Kingdom. Less emphasis was placed on the divine power and majesty of the pharaoh and more on the quality of his government. A major concern of the pharaohs was to ensure that *ma'at* prevailed. In Egyptian thought *ma'at* was the principle of right order, justice, and harmony that should prevail throughout the universe, including the human community. During the Middle Kingdom the pharaohs assumed a special responsibility for providing justice, protection, and respect for all of their subjects, including the poor and the powerless who had been badly abused by the powerful during the First Intermediate Period. The concern that *ma'at* should prevail for all society gave the government of the Middle Kingdom a quality not often seen in the history of the ancient Near East.

After about three centuries of orderly government and prosperity, a new period of disturbance brought the Middle Kingdom to an end. A variety of internal problems were aggravated by a threat that Egypt had heretofore not faced: outside invasion. About 1750 B.C. a people called the Hyksos moved into the Delta area from Asia. Once established on Egyptian soil, Hyksos rulers proclaimed themselves pharaohs. Their presence led to divisions within Egypt and to violence and lawlessness. This interlude, called the Second Intermediate Period (1750–1580 B.C.), set the stage for another recovery and a new era of glory in Egypt to be discussed later.

In their fundamental features the economic and social institutions of the Old and Middle kingdoms were strikingly similar to those of Mesopotamia. A carefully controlled agricultural system provided the prime source of wealth in Egypt. The backbone of this system was a numerous peasant population, living in small villages and devoting their lives to the endless round of labor required to maintain the irrigation system and to plant and harvest the crops of wheat, barley, flax, vegetables, and fruit. To these responsibilities was added the burden of extra labor on the immense building programs organized by the pharaohs and their agents and friends. The economy was enriched by the efforts of artisans and merchants who produced or acquired by exchange the luxury goods desired by the powerful and rich in society. Both artisans and traders often worked directly for the pharaohs, the rich officials of his court, the numerous priests, and the powerful provincial nobility.

Egyptian society was dominated by a relatively small aristocracy. At its summit stood the pharaoh and his family, enjoying command over all elements of society and control over the total wealth of the state. The rest of the aristocracy consisted of those to whom the pharaoh chose to extend high status and reward with wealth. Especially influential were the priests who managed the religious system and the officials who assisted the pharaoh in governing Egypt. A mark of aristocratic life was wealth, which its privileged holders spent to create a life of luxury and display.

Despite the efforts of the good pharaohs the lower classes were sometimes exploited and oppressed; their laments constitute a major theme in literature. Yet the surviving evidence, much of it in the form of pictorial representations of the lower classes adorning the tombs of the pharaohs and their nobles, suggests social harmony in Egypt. The scenes depicting peasants and artisans at work and play convey a sense of contentment and even joy. There is very little evidence of the oppression of particular groups in society. Slavery played only a minor role in Egypt during the Old and Middle kingdoms. Women appear to have suffered no special social disability, even though they were subjected to control by fathers and husbands. The consorts of the mighty pharaohs were extended high respect by their divine husbands (see Figure 1.1) and by society in general. Noble women shared most aspects of aristocratic life, especially its material wealth. They owned property and played an important role as priestesses serving the chief deities of Egypt. Lower-class women joined their husbands in working in the fields and played a key role in sustaining the economy. In general, Egyptian society was stable and secure. Most people apparently felt that *ma'at* prevailed to reward a happy, confident society.

5. EGYPTIAN CULTURAL LIFE

The efforts associated with conquering the Nile and exploiting its riches were accompanied by bril-liant and sustained cultural activities. To this day, the early Egyptian cultural achievement impresses the world as one of the major creative bursts in human history.

Egyptian culture was an outgrowth of powerful religious forces that shaped every aspect of Egyptian society. The fifth-century B.C. Greek historian Herodotus concluded that the Egyptians were the most religious of all peoples. From at least some perspectives that seems to be true. Certainly few peoples honored more gods and goddesses; the deities worshiped by the Egyptians numbered in the thousands. These spirits were portrayed in a confusing array of forms—as humans, animals, birds, plants, abstractions, and mixtures of any of these forms. They lived everywhere, roaming freely across the skies and the earth; they were always present wherever and whenever humans were at work or at play. And their influence on human affairs was decisive. While the Egyptians never developed a very precise definition of the nature or the powers of the divine forces, they generally conceived their deities as benevolent toward humans, easy to live with, and not to be feared.

Over the centuries the Egyptians did come to agree that certain deities possessed special powers and deserved universal worship. This mythology accorded special prominence to deities associated with rulers victorious in earthly wars. For example, the falcon god Horus worshiped by Menes, the unifier of Egypt, became a major public deity of the Old Kingdom; likewise, Amon, a minor deity at Thebes, became a powerful national god after the princes of Thebes rose to power as pharaohs during the Middle Kingdom. Two deities ultimately emerged as the most powerful divine forces in Egyptian religion: Ra, the sun god whose worship reflected the power of nature in shaping the good life of the Nile Valley; and Osiris, the god who had the power to grant a happy life after death. But even as gods like Ra and Osiris came to be accepted by all Egyptians, never were the innumerable local deities eliminated as important forces in human affairs.

Another indication of the validity of Herodotus' statement was the energy expended by the Egyptians to please their deities and win their favors. An elaborate set of ritual practices was established early in Egyptian history and changed

FIGURE 1.3 **Judgment Day** This Egyptian funerary papyrus from the tomb of a princess shows some of the steps in the transition to afterlife. In the center, the gods weigh her heart in a balance against the figure of the Goddess of Truth. Any flaw in her life would result in a loss of eternal happiness. (The Metropolitan Museum of Art)

little over the centuries. To the pharaoh belonged prime responsibility for bringing the favor of his fellow gods and goddesses upon his land and his people; no small part of the activities of a typical pharaoh was devoted to religious worship. He was aided by a numerous and powerful priesthood. In the many temples that dotted the land priests and priestesses conducted an elaborate round of rituals to please the deities with food, gifts, song, prayer, and dance. A considerable portion of public income was devoted to these activities. Acts of worship and sacrifice also took place in homes, villages, and city shrines. A rich array of magical practices evolved to attract the attention of the deities and to drive away evil spirits. Much of this religious activity was intended to win the material rewards that the gods and goddesses had to offer—abundant harvests, good health, security, happy times.

Besides earthly benefits, the divine powers held another precious gift for deserving Egyptians—a happy life after death. From early times,

Egyptians believed that every person had a *ka*, a double for his or her body that lived on after death in close association with the divine spirits. The *ka* had to be supplied with what it needed for a happy afterlife. In early Egyptian history a key to caring for the *ka* centered on mummification of the body so that its spirit could continue to live in it. A tomb that would last forever was built to house the mummy and its *ka*. Elaborate arrangements were made to ensure that the spirit would have food, drink, luxuries, company—everything it had enjoyed during life—to make immortal life tolerable. Perhaps only the pharaoh could afford such equipment, but he was willing to build and provision tombs for his wives, his children, his officials, and his friends so that they could continue to be his companions as all enjoyed eternal life.

Although the fate of the *ka* of ordinary people in early Egypt is not clear, the expectation of gaining immortality was gradually democratized and universalized. Perhaps the critical moment in this development came during the First Intermediate

Period as a reaction against the materialism and greed of the ruling class of the Old Kingdom. The broadened concept of immortality found its focus in the worship of Osiris, which by the Middle Kingdom had assumed a central place in religious life and was embodied in a touching myth. Osiris, a god associated with life forces and the Nile, was murdered by his wicked brother, Seth, who dismembered his body and scattered it over the earth. Isis the wife of Osiris, patiently gathered the pieces, whereupon Osiris returned to life. Thereafter, he had the power to raise everyone from death to life. When any Egyptian died, Osiris placed his or her heart on one pan of a balance and a feather on the other. If the heart was heavy with evil, it outweighed the feather and the dead person was judged unfit for a happy hereafter and tossed to a ferocious beast. If it was buoyant with good, its bearer was allowed to live forever in a heavenly place much like the earthly Nile Valley (see Figure 1.3).

A central feature of this concept of immortal life was the idea of moral worth attached to each person. Osiris was concerned with goodness in evaluating people's fitness for eternal life, not with their wealth and social status. In developing a moral dimension to life, the Egyptians introduced a concept unknown in Mesopotamia, but one that would have a rich history. One must be cautious, however, in assessing the impact of moral concerns on Egyptian society. People continued to provide for the material welfare of the dead, although from the Middle Kingdom onward the emphasis was less on the grandeur of the tomb and more on its decoration with a record in pictures and writing that would convince Osiris that its occupant had lived a "good" life; and in time, many busied themselves devising clever formulas to conceal their moral shortcomings.

Out of the immense effort to understand, please, and thank the divine forces there emerged an impressive literature. Egyptian literature in the proper sense was preceded by the development of a system of writing, called *hieroglyphic*, which made its appearance about 3200 B.C. Like cuneiform writing, it began as pictograms out of which evolved symbols representing sounds that could be combined into words. The first use of writing was probably in record keeping and letter writing

connected with the pharaoh's court, but it was not long before more artistic uses were found for writing skills. Much early writing has survived on pyramid walls in the form of hymns, prayers, magical incantations, mythology, and accounts of the deeds of the occupant of the pyramid, all intended to send a message to the divine forces. Besides the pyramid texts other forms of literature survive, set down either on stone or papyrus (a writing material made from the pulp of the papyrus plant pressed into flat sheets). The Egyptians apparently enjoyed collections of maxims and wise sayings, often presented in the form of instructions given by father to son or teacher to pupil. Poetry, often expressing disgust with worldly affairs, was composed. Especially appealing were tales of fancy and romance recounting the adventures of travelers, sailors, and soldiers. On the whole Egyptian literature was confident in mood, more varied and versatile than Mesopotamian literature, but less profound.

The visual arts reflect the character and quality of the Egyptian genius most clearly. In all its forms, Egyptian art mirrors what may be the keystone of Egyptian civilization: the ability of a creative people to work for long ages with set forms and subjects without loss of freshness and vitality. Their artists created for eternity with confidence that the existing order was right and worth sustaining.

Architecture was the queen of all the arts, most of the other forms serving to adorn great buildings. Architects worked with bricks, reeds, and timber, but the most monumental work was in stone, of which there was a plentiful supply in Egypt. The first flowering of architecture came early in the Old Kingdom period and was devoted chiefly to tomb building, which reached its apogee with the construction of the pyramids. The pyramid of Khufu, built about 2600 B.C., still stands as one of the major construction feats of all time. Built on a cliff overlooking the Nile, it measured 755 feet on each side and was 480 feet high. It contained over 2 million blocks of stone, each of which was precut in quarries many miles away and floated down the Nile to the building site, a procedure that required careful planning, skilled engineering, and a huge expenditure of labor. Surrounding the pyramid was a complex of temples and tombs for Khufu's dead family and friends. A roadway led down to the valley where there was another building complex intended to house the priests, officials, and laborers who carried on the many services required to care for the spirit living in the pyramid tomb. Pyramid building continued for many centuries, but later architects never equaled those of the Old Kingdom. Shifting concepts of life after death militated against such massive structures. By the end of the Old Kingdom temples and palaces commanded more attention. The basic temple style, established very early, was the hypostyle hall. Such structures consisted of a high-ceilinged central hall flanked by side halls, each covered with a roof set on columns shorter than those of the central hall. Builders achieved splendid artistic effects by modeling their columns after plants—the palm tree, the lotus plant, the papyrus plant, the reed. Within the temple, numerous chambers were grouped to create a sanctuary where the god or goddess to whom the temple was dedicated could live (see Color Plate 2). Before the temple was an open court surrounded by a columned portico and entered by a massive gate. Scanty surviving evidence indicates that the palaces built for pharaohs and nobles were as splendid as the temples and probably utilized the same basic architectural forms.

Egypt's sculptors matched architects in skill. At a very early date sculptural styles became fixed and changed little over most of Egypt's history. The chief subjects of three-dimensional works were the deities, the pharaohs, their families, and their companions, most such statues being intended to adorn tombs and temples. Human forms were usually massive, stiff, unemotional portrayals following fixed proportions. But the faces were another matter; here the sculptor tried to show feeling and purpose: the power of a god or goddess, the majesty of a pharaoh, the devotion of a royal servant (see Figure 1.1). The artist was not concerned with realistic portrayal of an individual but with projecting a quality embodied in and exemplified by the subject.

Sculptors were also skilled at relief work. Most relief work was carved on the walls of tombs and temples and was intended to record the lives and the deeds of those commemorated (see Figures 2.1 and 2.2). As a consequence, Egyptian reliefs contain a remarkably rich record of everyday life at all levels of society. However, sculptors seldom tried to be realistic. They let the space available determine the size and shape of their figures, and they often used conventional designs to represent objects. Human figures are distorted, the feet and faces usually shown in profile while the main trunk of the body faces the viewer. Many of the reliefs were painted to heighten the effect. Painting, most of which survives in tombs, bears striking similarity to relief work in terms of subject and form.

The Egyptians made advances in technology and science that rivaled the work of the Mesopotamians. They recorded information about the movement of the stars, from which they developed an accurate time-reckoning system based on the annual appearance of the star Sirius and a calendar of twelve thirty-day months plus five days added at the end of each year. They developed a system of numbers that permitted them to perform basic arithmetic functions and to calculate areas and volumes. They accumulated considerable information about the properties of metals and about plant and animal life. In medicine they developed surgical techniques and learned to use a wide range of drugs. Their understanding of anatomy was extensive, undoubtedly a result of observations made in the process of mummifying the dead. However, like the Mesopotamians, the Egyptians had little interest in pursuing knowledge about nature for its own sake. Once they found a practical solution for a problem of engineering, metallurgy, medicine, or discovering the intention of the deities, they sought no further.

SUGGESTED READING

Overview of the Ancient Near East to ca. 330 B.C.

William W. Hallo and W. K. Simpson, *The Ancient Near East: A History* (1971).

Jean Bottéro et al., *The Near East: The Early Civilizations,* trans. R. F. Tannenbaum (1967).

Either of these two books will provide an excellent overview.

Prehistory

Frank E. Poirier, *Understanding Human Evolution* (1987).

Richard E. Leakey, *The Making of Mankind* (1981).

John E. Pfeiffer, *The Emergence of Humankind,* 4th ed. (1985).

Each of these three works provides provocative treatments of the much disputed problem of human origins.

Brian M. Fagan, *People of the Earth: An Introduction to World Prehistory,* 4th ed. (1983). An excellent treatment of prehistoric culture.

Frances Dahlberg, ed., *Woman, the Gatherer* (1981). Informative essays on the role of women in prehistoric society.

Mesopotamia

H. W. F. Saggs, *The Greatness That Was Babylon; A Survey of the Ancient Civilization of the Tigris-Euphrates Valley* (1969). An excellent survey covering all aspects of Mesopotamian history.

H. W. F. Saggs, *Everyday Life in Babylonia and Assyria* (1965). Rich in material on how people lived in ancient Mesopotamia.

Thorkild Jacobsen, *The Treasures of Darkness: A History of Mesopotamian Religion* (1976). An excellent introduction.

Anton Moortgat, *The Art of Ancient Mesopotamia; The Classical Art of the Near East,* trans. Judith Filson (1969).

André Parrot, *Sumer. The Dawn of Art,* trans. Stuart Gilbert and James Emmons (1961).

Either of these beautifully illustrated volumes will provide a good introduction to Mesopotamian art.

Egypt

Cyril Aldred, *The Egyptians,* rev. and enl. ed. (1984).

Barbara Mertz, *Temples, Tombs, and Hieroglyphs: A Popular History of Egypt,* rev. ed. (1978).

Either of these two works will provide an excellent guide to the development of Egyptian civilization.

B. D. Trigger, ed., *Ancient Egypt: A Social History* (1983). Studies by various experts on aspects of Egyptian social history.

Barbara Mertz, *Red Land, Black Land: Daily Life in Ancient Egypt,* rev. ed. (1978).

John Romer, *People of the Nile: Everyday Life in Ancient Egypt* (1982).

These two works are rich in details about how people lived in ancient Egypt.

Erik Hornung, *Conceptions of the Gods in Ancient Egypt: The One and the Many,* trans. John Baines (1982).

A. Rosalie David, *The Ancient Egyptians: Religious Beliefs and Practices* (1982).

Either of these works will help the reader understand the complexities of ancient Egyptian religion.

Kurt Lange and Max Hirmer, *Egypt: Architecture, Sculpture, Painting in Three Thousand Years,* 4th ed., trans. Judith Filson and Barbara Taylor (1968).

W. Stevenson Smith and William Kelly Simpson, *Art and Architecture of Ancient Egypt,* 2nd ed. (1981).

Either of these two works, both well-illustrated, will provide a sense of the basic characteristics of Egyptian art.

CHAPTER 2

The Diffusion of Near Eastern Civilization, 1750–800 B.C.

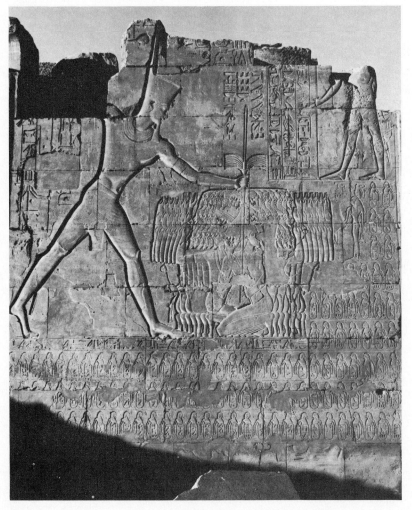

FIGURE 2.1 **Egyptian Imperialism** This scene, from the temple of Karnak, shows the pharaoh Thutmose III (1504—1450 B.C.) grasping Egypt's enemies by the hair prior to striking them to show Egypt's mastery over them. This scene captures the spirit of Egyptian imperialism during the period of the New Kingdom. Such relief carvings occupied a major place in Egyptian artistic activity. (Hirmer Fotoarchiv)

By about 1750 B.C. the Near Eastern world reached a turning point. The higher civilizations produced in the unique environment of the river valleys had matured fully. Well before 1750 B.C. the influence of Mesopotamian and Egyptian civilizations had begun to spread beyond their original settings. During the period 1750–800 B.C. the process of cultural diffusion quickened and became a central theme of Near Eastern history. Not only did new peoples come to share higher civilization, but also many of them made important contributions that enriched the basic patterns of civilized life.

1. DIFFUSION AND THE MOVEMENT OF PEOPLES

Cultural diffusion in this period was a complex process. Ideas, products, and techniques were carried out from the established centers of civilization by traders, soldiers, and diplomats. Imitation of the superior ways of the river valley civilizations by people long settled on their fringes was common. As cultural patterns spread, they were adapted and modified to fit new settings and situations. Especially important as a catalytic force was the movement of peoples into and around the civilized zones to upset the existing order and to create new political entities eager to share the benefits of civilized life.

Two peoples were especially significant in creating conditions that lead to cultural diffusion. One was the Semitic-speaking inhabitants of the Arabian Desert, with whom we are already familiar as intruders into Mesopotamia. After 1800 B.C. these seminomadic desert dwellers continued to pour out of the desert to play a prime role in the history of northern Mesopotamia, Syria, Palestine, and Egypt.

The other people were the Indo-Europeans (sometimes called Aryans). Beginning about 2000 B.C. they fanned outward from their ancient homeland, perhaps north of the Caspian Sea. Their impact was felt over a broad area embracing central Europe, Italy, Greece, the Aegean area, the Near East, Iran, and India. They spoke a language that was new to the Near East and from which later evolved Sanskrit, Latin, Greek, Persian, and most modern European languages. Their general cultural level was more primitive than that of most Near Eastern peoples. However, their superior weapons and military organization allowed them to establish political dominance. Their first settlements in the Near East extended from the upper Tigris-Euphrates valleys westward across much of Asia Minor. Initially they established small principalities led by petty warlords. Eventually, some of these principalities coalesced and expanded by conquering native populations to create larger kingdoms. Among the more prominent were the Kassites, the Hittites, and the Mitanni, all destined to play important roles in the Near East during the period under review. In the process of establishing themselves, these newcomers absorbed and spread major elements of the established civilizations, especially those of Mesopotamia.

2. THE EGYPTIAN AND HITTITE EMPIRES, 1750–1200 B.C.

We have already noted the impact of some of these migrants on Mesopotamia and Egypt. Shortly after 1600 B.C. Indo-European Hittites and Kassites played a major role in dismembering the Amorite Empire founded by Hammurabi. The Kassites were able to establish their political domination over Mesopotamia. They ruled there for nearly four centuries, a period during which Mesopotamia played a secondary role in Near Eastern political life but continued to assert a major cultural influence over many peoples beyond Mesopotamia. To the north of Mesopotamia Indo-European warlords established dominance over an area embracing the upper Tigris-Euphrates valleys and north Syria to create the kingdom of the Mitanni, which flourished from about 1550 to 1350 B.C. Also about 1750 B.C. the Hyksos, predominantly Semitic wanderers from the Palestine area, intruded into Egypt. Although they never succeeded in extending their direct rule beyond the Delta region, they were a factor in causing the chaos in Egypt that characterized the Second Intermediate Period (ca. 1750–1580 B.C.). However, their presence did result in developments that cast Egypt into a new role in Near Eastern history.

The main result of the Hyksos' presence in

Egypt was the emergence of a feeling that foreigners were the cause of Egypt's troubles. That feeling manifested itself in efforts to expel the Hyksos, an enterprise in which many princes aspiring to power became engaged. Eventually, the rulers of Thebes emerged as leaders in this war of liberation. The expulsion of the Hyksos was finally achieved by Ahmose I (1558–1533 B.C.), the founder of the Eighteenth Dynasty. His triumph again placed Egypt under a single ruler and opened a third period of glory in Egyptian history, called the New Kingdom or Empire (1558–1200 B.C.).

During the first century of the Eighteenth Dynasty Egypt was ruled by a succession of able pharaohs. One of the ablest was a woman, Hatshepsut, who is portrayed in a surviving statue with a false beard, suggesting an artist uncomfortable about a woman ruler. These able rulers devoted their energies to restoring internal peace, "cleansing" the land of the taint of foreign rule, and reestablishing order in administration, agriculture, trade, religion, and artistic and intellectual life. In all of these pursuits traditional patterns were highly respected so that the restored system closely resembled that of the Old and Middle kingdoms.

However, a new factor played an increasingly important role: a more aggressive posture toward the outside world. Rooted originally in a haunting fear of a reoccurrence of invasions like that of the Hyksos, this attitude ripened into full-scale imperialism. The first pharaohs of the Eighteenth Dynasty reflected the fear of outside attacks by creating a standing army and by conducting raids against Nubia to the south and into Palestine and Syria, the original homeland of the Hyksos. These raids not only built Egypt's confidence in its strength but also created elements in society with a vested interest in expansionism, especially the military forces and the priesthood. Eventually, during the reign of Thutmose III (1504–1450 B.C.) defensive raiding turned into imperialism (see Figure 2.1). Thutmose led a series of campaigns into Nubia, Libya, and Syria-Palestine that established Egyptian dominance. This expansion brought the Egyptians into contact with other Near Eastern powers, especially the Mitanni, who were rivals for control of Syria-Palestine (see Map 2.1). These confrontations resulted in active diplomatic efforts

that made Egypt's might felt beyond the areas of actual conquest. The Mitanni, the Kassites, and the Assyrians all sought peace with Egypt. For a century Thutmose's successors pursued his policy and made Egypt the dominant power in the Near East.

Successful imperialism brought Egypt a new period of magnificence. Added to the wealth produced by the carefully managed agricultural system was a vast income from tribute exacted from foreign subjects and from greatly expanded trading connections embracing the Sudan, Mesopotamia, Asia Minor, Crete, and the Aegean world. Artistic life blossomed, expressing itself with special brilliance in the magnificent temples built at Luxor and Karnak in honor of Amon-Ra, the chief national god (see Color Plate 2). The influences of Egyptian art styles, literary models, pottery and metal-working techniques, and religious practices were felt throughout the Near East with a force unknown prior to the period of the empire.

But imperialism also brought problems. The burden of controlling conquered peoples required a standing army, the maintenance of garrisons abroad, periodic campaigns to display strength, and complex diplomatic efforts. All of this put a heavy demand on Egypt's resources. A major consequence was an increasing regimentation of Egypt's native populace and a growing reliance on slavery in the service of the state. The concerns of empire distracted the attention of the pharaohs from the welfare of their subjects and created opportunities for oppression by grasping officials, especially the powerful priests of Amon-Ra. New ideas brought to Egypt by foreigners raised questions about the validity of traditional beliefs and practices.

Beginning about 1400 B.C., these problems, complicated by developments outside Egypt, put the New Kingdom to a severe test. The emerging crisis found its focus in the increasing rebelliousness of the dependent princes of Syria-Palestine whose loyalty was a keystone to Egypt's imperial structure. These princes were encouraged to resist Egypt by an aggressive, formidable external foe, the Hittites, whose power base was located in Asia Minor. Of all the "new" people who emerged from the Indo-European invasions, the Hittites enjoyed the greatest success. Their history began in about 1800 B.C., when invading Indo-European warlords imposed their rule on the natives of eastern and central Asia Minor and formed a series of small kingdoms. By about 1600 B.C., several of these kingdoms were united to form a single Hittite kingdom with its capital at Hattusas (modern Boghazköy). The Hittites developed an advanced culture, derived in large part from their borrowing and adaptation of Mesopotamian models. While always reflecting their Mesopotamian origins, Hittite political institutions, religion, literature, art, and technology possessed distinctive features that displayed the creative powers of this "new" people. Their dominance in Asia Minor marked a significant expansion of the area of higher civilization.

Once firmly established in Asia Minor and fortified by their expanding level of material wealth and culture, the Hittites were able to assert a decisive influence in Near Eastern affairs. They forced one of Egypt's chief allies, the Mitanni, into their sphere of influence and eventually destroyed that kingdom. By 1400 B.C. they were actively engaged in encouraging and supporting rebellion among Egypt's client principalities in Syria and Palestine. Hittite power reached its zenith under King Suppiluliumas (1375–1355 B.C.), who threatened to oust Egypt from its Asian holdings (see Map 2.1).

In the face of the mounting threat to its empire, Egypt was distracted by an internal crisis brought on by a religious reform instituted by Amenhotep IV (1379–1362 B.C.) with the help of his queen, Nefertiti. Although his motives have been much debated, it appears that this enigmatic pharaoh acted for both political and religious reasons: to reestablish the pharaoh's absolute supremacy in the face of threats offered by such powerfully entrenched groups as the military establishment, the royal officials, and especially the priests of Amon-Ra and to revitalize a traditional religious system encrusted with contradictory beliefs and overelaborate rituals based on crude materialism. In any case, Amenhotep IV proclaimed a new religion based on the worship of the god Aton, depicted as the source of all life who was represented to humanity in the form of the sun disc giving off rays that sustained all existence (see Figure 2.2). To dramatize his break with the old order, Amen-

FIGURE 2.2 An Egyptian Religious Reformer This scene shows Akhnaton with his wife, Nefertiti, and one of their daughters making an offering to the new deity, Aton, promoted by Akhnaton. The new deity is represented by the sun disc pouring its fruitful rays on the worshipers, who in turn would bestow such benefits on the pharaoh's subjects. The artistic style reflected in this carving is more naturalistic than the traditional Egyptian artistic canon (compare with Figures 1.1, 1.3, and 2.1). (The Metropolitan Museum of Art)

hotep IV changed his name to Akhnaton ("It pleases Aton") and abandoned the old capital at Thebes for a new one named Akhetaton (modern

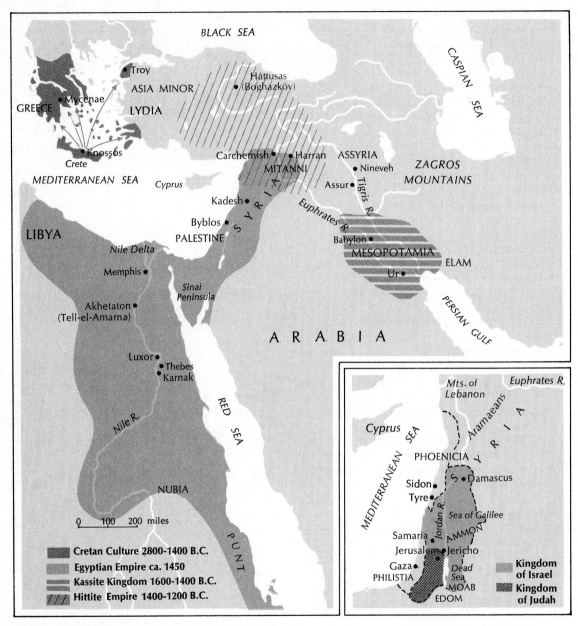

BLACK SEA

Troy
ASIA MINOR
Háttusas (Boghazköy)
GREECE
Mycenae
LYDIA
Knossos
Crete

CASPIAN SEA

Carchemish • Harran
MITANNI
Kadesh
ASSYRIA
Nineveh
Assur •
ZAGROS MOUNTAINS

MEDITERRANEAN SEA
Cyprus

Byblos
PALESTINE
SYRIA
Euphrates R.
Tigris R.
Babylon •
MESOPOTAMIA

LIBYA
Nile Delta
Memphis •

Sinai Peninsula
Ur •
ELAM

Akhetaton (Tell-el-Amarna)

ARABIA

PERSIAN GULF

Luxor
Thebes
Karnak

RED SEA

Nile R.

NUBIA

0   100   200 miles

PUNT

	Cretan Culture 2800-1400 B.C.
	Egyptian Empire ca. 1450
	Kassite Kingdom 1600-1400 B.C.
	Hittite Empire 1400-1200 B.C.

Mts. of Lebanon
Euphrates R.

Cyprus
Aramaeans
MEDITERRANEAN SEA
PHOENICIA
SYRIA
Sidon • Damascus
Tyre
Jordan R.
Sea of Galilee
AMMON
Samaria
Jerusalem • Jericho
Gaza • Dead Sea
PHILISTIA
MOAB
EDOM

| | Kingdom of Israel |
| | Kingdom of Judah |

Map 2.1   THE ANCIENT NEAR EAST, CA. 1450 B.C.   This map illustrates the main centers of political power during the period 1600–1200 B.C. The ambitions of the rulers of the major states led to considerable conflict, especially in Syria and Palestine, where Egyptian and Hittite interests clashed. The map also indicates how extensively the ways of civilized life had spread beyond the original centers of civilization in the river valleys.

Tell el Amarna). The worship of the old deities was forbidden, their temples destroyed, and their priests demoted. New rituals and a new art style, fresh and naturalistic, developed to honor and portray Aton. Some have argued that Akhnaton sought to establish monotheism, that is, a religion based on the worship of a single, universal deity; but close scrutiny of the record does not support this view. Rather, he probably intended to establish Aton as the supreme god to be worshiped and honored by the pharaoh while the Egyptians would worship the god-pharaoh. Many other uncertainties surround what kind of religious system Akhnaton had in mind. Together they raise the intriguing possibility that he intended a religious system that would rid Egyptian society of its restrictive traditionalism, rooted in the old religious order, and equip the Egyptians to take the lead in exploiting the cosmopolitan currents circulating in the Near East in this era of the mixing and mingling of cultures.

However, such questions are moot, for Akhnaton's reforms were stillborn. His proclamation of a new religion raised a storm of protest, led by the priests of Amon-Ra, which for a decade consumed the energy of society. Even before his death Akhnaton's foes had forced him to abandon his reforms. Under his successor, his son-in-law Tutankhamon, the forces of reaction rapidly restored the old order. The restoration of the cult of Amon-Ra is reflected not only in Tutankhamon's name but also in the cult objects found in his tomb, one of the most magnificent reflections of traditional Egyptian art and thought that has survived. Among other things, "King Tut" made a concerted effort to eradicate all signs of Aton worship and all memory of its chief proponent, Akhnaton.

The disturbances associated with Akhnaton's attempted reform and with the efforts to undo it weakened Egypt's capability to defend its empire. Hittite aggression in Syria and Palestine, accompanied by defections of local princes, temporarily ended Egyptian control in that area. Eventually, under the early rulers of the Nineteenth Dynasty, especially Seti and Rameses II, the Egyptians were able to regroup their military forces and to redress the balance in Syria and Palestine after a bitter struggle with the Hittites. The costly and indecisive struggle between these two powers ended about 1270 B.C., when they reached a peace settlement that assigned each a sphere of influence in that embattled area. For an interval both Egyptians and Hittites regained their former vitality as the leading powers of the era.

However, both empires were approaching the end of their greatness; their incessant struggles had sapped their strength. Decisive in determining their end was a new wave of Indo-European invaders, especially formidable because they possessed iron weapons, who spilled over Asia Minor, the Aegean Sea area, and the waterways of the eastern Mediterranean. Their assaults were abetted by new movements of Semitic nomads from the Arabian Desert. The Hittite Empire was completely destroyed about 1200 B.C. Attacks by Nubians, Libyans, and the mysterious "People of the Sea," seafaring marauders probably from Asia Minor, forced the Egyptians back into their old boundaries and for a time established foreigners as pharaohs. These setbacks greatly weakened Egypt internally and reduced its capacity to influence the course of Near Eastern history.

3. THE MINOAN WORLD

The age of diffusion witnessed the development of a vital civilization on the island of Crete, which played an especially important role in history because it provided a link between the ancient Near East and the world to the west—especially Greece. Modern historians have called this civilization Minoan, after Minos, a legendary Cretan king. Minoan civilization owed a great deal to influences from the Near East, but the Cretans put their own unique stamp on their borrowings to give their civilization its own character. A crucial factor in shaping Minoan civilization was the ability of the Cretans to enhance the limited resources of the island by utilizing the seas to reach sources of wealth, ideas, and techniques that stimulated and enriched their society.

By about 6000 B.C. a Neolithic farming culture had been established on Crete. For many centuries thereafter Neolithic farmers shared a simple pattern of culture with other people living in Greece, the Aegean Islands, and Asia Minor. Gradually, over that period the Cretans developed skills in pottery making and metalwork; especially important was the introduction of bronze technology from Asia Minor about 3000 B.C. And the Cretans learned to sail the seas to establish contacts with the advanced civilizations of Egypt and Asia and to gain access to markets and raw materials in the area around the Aegean. By about 2000 B.C. their developing technical skills, increasing wealth, and expanding contacts resulted in the emergence of several full-fledged urban centers, including Knossos, Phaistos, and Mallia. Each was ruled by a king whose magnificent palace was the center of civilized life. Minoan civilization reached its peak between about 1700 and 1450 B.C. During this period Knossos outstripped the other cities of Crete, asserting cultural leadership that provided a common pattern of life on the island and perhaps even establishing a loose political control. Not only did Knossos dominate Crete, but the city's influence was felt over a wide circle of the eastern Mediterranean and the Aegean seas, chiefly through trading ventures. Then between 1500 and 1450 B.C. a disaster struck the Minoan world, destroying many cities, crops, and fleets. Perhaps this catastrophe was a consequence of a devastating volcano on the island of Thera, north of Crete. At about the same time Crete suffered at the hands of invaders from Greece called Mycenaeans. Knossos continued for an interval as a center from which the invaders ruled the island, but shortly after 1400 B.C. it too was destroyed, perhaps as a result of a revolt against the outsiders. Minoan civilization had run its course.

Our knowledge of the major features of Minoan civilization is derived chiefly from archaeological evidence produced by excavations of city sites, especially Knossos. The Minoans did develop their own writing system, called Linear A by modern scholars, but it has not yet been deciphered. About 1450 B.C. that system was replaced by another, called Linear B, which has been deciphered and proved to be based on an early form of the Greek language. It probably represents an adaptation of Minoan writing by the Mycenaean invaders from Greece. The surviving documents in Linear B are chiefly economic records and provide only limited information about Minoan society.

At the height of Minoan civilization Crete was governed by several kings, each controlling a particular city and its surrounding territory. The king of Knossos exercised some form of authority over the other kingdoms, but that overlordship was based on consent rather than force. The fact that Minoan cities were unwalled indicates that the kingdoms lived without serious conflict or great expenditure for arms. The power of Minoan kings rested on strong religious sanctions and on wealth derived from control of the agricultural system and from overseas trade. Royal administration was conducted by a highly developed bureaucracy especially skilled at orderly record keeping. A wealthy and influential nobility made up chiefly of landowners grouped itself around the kings to uphold royal authority.

The Minoan economy was based on a productive agricultural system devoted to the cultivation of grain, olives, grapes, and vegetables and to the raising of livestock, especially sheep. But trade and industry produced the additional wealth necessary to support an advanced urban civilization. Highly skilled artisans laboring in the workshops of the royal palace or in their own shops produced a wide variety of goods that adorned the lives of the rulers, their officials, and the wealthy landowners and merchants. Especially skilled were Minoan potters and metalworkers. Enterprising merchants, sometimes serving the kings and sometimes working on their own, carried Minoan manufactured products over the seas to a wide area around the Mediterranean, including not only the major Near Eastern centers of civilization but also the less developed peoples of the Aegean world. These merchants brought back a variety of raw materials and manufactured goods. The wealth produced by this vigorous economy allowed the Minoan upper class to live in luxurious, well-furnished houses and enjoy fine clothing and abundant jewelry. Upper-class women shared freely in the social life of the palaces and aristocratic households. Every royal city had a considerable population of laborers who performed all kinds of work needed to sustain city life. The rural population clustered in villages where they labored under the supervision of royal officials and powerful landowners. There was little slavery in Minoan society.

The Minoans worshiped a variety of gods and

goddesses, most of them representing the forces of nature. Especially prominent was the goddess of fertility, whose life-giving powers were evoked by all classes of people. A major function of the king was conducting religious services to win the favor of the deities for his entire community, a responsibility that was carried out regularly in each palace. The worship of the gods and goddesses was less elaborate than were the religious practices of Mesopotamia and Egypt. The Minoans built no great temples; they worshiped at simple shrines in private houses, on hills, in groves and caves, and near springs. Priests and priestesses were maintained at the palace to serve the deities, but they played only a limited role in shaping Minoan life and culture. Prominent place in religious ceremonies was given to animal sacrifice, gift giving, dancing, and bull leaping—a dangerous feat in which young men and women vaulted over the horns of a charging bull to do a handstand on its back before dismounting over its rear quarters (see Figure 2.3). The pictorial representations of these rituals suggest a religious life that was joyful and lighthearted, little marked by fear and gloom. There was a belief in afterlife and some attention was given to the care of the dead, but never on the scale that occurred in Egypt.

The genius of the Minoans expressed itself most fully in the visual arts. Their highly developed architectural skills were lavished on palaces and private dwellings rather than on temples and tombs. The immense palace at Knossos reflected a technical mastery of a variety of architectural forms and a fine sense of scale. Many of the multistoried palaces and private dwellings were equipped with a piped water supply, skillfully constructed drainage systems, and indoor toilets. Palaces and houses were decorated with paintings and carvings that focused on nature and human activity. Especially skilled were elaborate frescoes portraying processions of young men and women bearing gifts to the gods and goddesses. Animals, fish, and birds were also favorite subjects of carvers and painters. Minoan decorated pottery reflects a fine sense of form and a love of color. In all its forms Minoan art is mobile, free of stylization, intense, and energetic. It reflects a civilization that was worldly, lacking in fear, eager for change, and pleasure loving. Although strongly

FIGURE 2.3 Minoan Sports This bronze figure dating from the sixteenth century B.C. portrays a favorite Minoan sporting activity—vaulting over a charging bull. Both young men and young women participated in this dangerous game. The artist's ability to convey a feeling of movement on the part of both the leaper and the animal is reflective of much of Minoan art. (The British Museum)

influenced by Mesopotamian and Egyptian models, Minoan civilization contrasts sharply with both; it points not east but west toward a world yet to come—especially to Greece.

4. ERA OF SMALL NATIONS, 1200–800 B.C.: PHOENICIANS AND ARAMEANS

The collapse of the Hittite and Egyptian empires about 1200 B.C., coupled with the decline of Minoan power, left the Near East without a dominant power center for about four centuries. Several small groups seized the opportunity to establish their independence. As these peoples struggled to establish and maintain themselves, they borrowed heavily from the older civilizations. As a result, cultural diffusion continued as a major feature of Near Eastern history.

Two peoples stand out especially as borrowers and disseminators: the Phoenicians and the Arameans. Both were Semitic in origin, the products of the numerous migrations from the Arabian Desert that had been in progress for many centuries before 1200 B.C. These migrants were repeatedly conquered and strongly influenced by Mesopotamians, Egyptians, and Hittites. Consequently, by 1200 B.C. they were already highly civilized peoples; when Egyptian and Hittite power collapsed, they were able to establish political independence. The Phoenicians, located in the narrow coastal area between the Mediterranean Sea and the mountains of Lebanon, developed a number of independent city-states, chief of which were Byblos, Tyre, and Sidon. The Arameans were located east of the Lebanon Mountains between the northern fringes of the Arabian Desert and the Euphrates River. They were organized into a number of small kingdoms centered around Damascus, Kadesh, and Palmyra (see Map 2.1). For about four centuries these city-states and kingdoms were among the chief states in the Near East. Their independence was finally crushed by the Assyrians in the eighth century B.C., as we shall see in the next chapter.

The Phoenicians and the Arameans derived most of their wealth from trade. The Phoenicians took to the seas and established a virtual monopoly on trade in the Mediterranean, chiefly as successors of Minoan traders. Their merchants carried manufactured goods from the entire Near East to the less developed peoples of Greece, Italy, North Africa, Spain, and southern France and brought back the raw materials of these areas. From these traders many peoples to the west got their first taste of higher civilization. The Phoenicians not only traded but also established colonies, notably the North African city of Carthage, destined to become an important center of civilization after 800 B.C. The Arameans were overland traders, exploiting the trade routes that linked Egypt, Mesopotamia, Asia Minor, and points beyond. Both Phoenicians and Arameans reaped a rich reward from their commerce, allowing them to live well and to support a wide range of cultural activities. Neither people was particularly creative in learning and the arts. However, the Phoenicians did perfect an alphabet that later served as a model for the written languages of the Mediterranean basin, and the Aramean language became the chief spoken language of much of the Near East.

5. ERA OF SMALL NATIONS, 1200–800 B.C.: THE HEBREWS

One people emerging into prominence for the first time in this era of small nations had a particularly enduring impact on the history of Western civilization. These were the Hebrews, who left a magnificent literary record of their own version of their history in their Bible, now generally referred to as the Old Testament. This complex document, composed over many centuries by many authors out of a mixture of historical traditions, folklore, legal enactments, moral exhortations, and prophecies, confronts the modern historian with formidable problems. However, the main lines of the story it tells, coupled with supporting evidence from non-Hebrew literary sources and from archaeology, provide a fairly accurate account of the history of the Hebrews during the period with which we are now concerned.

The surviving evidence suggests that the Hebrews were originally nomads, part of the extensive migration of Semite peoples that played a crucial role in the age of diffusion. Early Hebrew history centered on a search for a place to settle. During this age of the patriarchs, as the Old Testament calls it, small tribal groups based on kinship ties left their early places of settlement on the fringes of Mesopotamia and, under the leadership of family heads such as Abraham, Isaac, and Jacob, migrated around the southern fringes of the Fertile Crescent to the area of Palestine. Perhaps this migration began about 1800 B.C., roughly in the time of Hammurabi, and took place over a relatively long period. In the area of Palestine the nomadic Hebrew herders encountered and began to clash with more advanced agricultural societies, especially the Canaanites. This interaction set in motion a slow transition from pastoral to settled agricultural life. An important feature of Hebrew tribal life was a religion rooted in a fierce allegiance among tribal members to a deity who gave special protection to the tribe and interacted with it through its patriarch. Among such deities was Yahweh, the god of Abraham.

Not all of the wandering Hebrews remained in the Palestine area. Some made their way to Egypt, perhaps as part of the Hyksos invasion or as hostages taken during Egyptian expansion into the

Syria-Palestine area during the Eighteenth Dynasty. Assigned lands in the Delta region (the biblical land of Goshen), these foreigners prospered for a time, and some, like Joseph, even found favor at the pharaoh's court, suggesting that the Hebrews accommodated to the higher civilization of the Egyptians. Eventually, however, there arose a pharaoh "who knew not Joseph" and whose mistreatment led to a decisive event in Hebrew history—the Exodus, which probably occurred during the reign of Pharaoh Rameses II (1292–1235 B.C.).

The circumstances surrounding the escape from bondage in Egypt and subsequent period of wandering in the deserts of the Sinai Peninsula pose difficult problems for the historian. However, it seems indisputable that a religious experience occurred that marked a decisive stage in Hebrew history and gave fundamental shape to the religious consciousness of that people. Under the leadership of Moses, the Hebrews of the Exodus came to believe that they as a people had become special partners of Yahweh, who at least some had worshiped during the age of the patriarchs. Master of history and of nature, as he had demonstrated through the events of the Exodus, Yahweh made a *covenant*, or mutual contract, with Moses' people: He selected them as his people and promised to care for them under all circumstances. In return, they pledged to honor him as their only god and to follow his law, set down in the Bible as the Ten Commandments, in the conduct of their collective existence. These fundamental concepts, which thereafter remained central to the Hebrew religion, transformed Moses' "mixed multitude" of tribal groups into "a holy nation," the Israelites, whose unity was rooted in their unique relationship with their god who would brook no rivals.

The people of the convenant now renewed their search for their Promised Land. Their object became Palestine, an area where considerable instability existed in the wake of the collapse of the Egyptian and Hittite empires (see Map 2.1). The Old Testament provides a somewhat simplified account of the Israelite occupation of Palestine, beginning when Joshua led a loose confederation of twelve Hebrew tribes to an initial triumph over the Canaanite city of Jericho about 1200 B.C., fol-

lowed by a succession of victories over the Canaanites that ultimately assured Hebrew control. According to that story, the chief hindrance to success was the unfaithfulness of the Israelites to their convenant with Yahweh, who punished them by allowing their enemies to defeat them. In reality, the Hebrew occupation of Palestine was a complex, drawn-out process involving more than military engagements. To be sure, the Canaanites were formidable foes but not the only ones. Repeatedly the Hebrews had to contend with outsiders equally intent on occupying Palestine, a threat that often necessitated cooperation between Hebrews and Canaanites and to gradual assimilation of the two peoples. The Hebrew effort was impeded by tribal jealousies, especially as the tribal structure became more firmly established and each tribe sought to establish its identity on a territorial basis. These complex situations produced crisis after crisis, sometimes dramatically resolved by charismatic leaders, called "judges," who persuaded the Hebrews to act in unity at least temporarily; such leaders included Gideon, Samson, and Samuel. As the Hebrew occupation proceeded, the newcomers were slowly transformed into farmers, adopting in the process many features of Canaanite culture; this transformation often challenged traditional values and practices and sometimes divided the Hebrews.

After about a hundred and fifty years of struggle and change, the Hebrews were close to dominance. Then they were almost destroyed by the Philistines, warlike newcomers armed with iron weapons who settled along the south Palestine coast after being rebuffed in their attempt to enter Egypt. By about 1050 B.C. the Philistines had made major inroads into Palestine and seemed on the verge of overpowering the Hebrews. The threat of disaster led to a momentous step: an agreement among the Hebrew tribes—forged in large part through the efforts of the most famous of the judges, Samuel—to place themselves under a single king, thereby creating a political "nation."

The unified Hebrew nation lasted for about a century (1020–930 B.C.), embracing the reigns of Saul, David, and Solomon, who collectively brought the Hebrews to the high point of their history in ancient times. These kings were able to organize military resources that expelled the Philistines from Palestine and then subdued not only the Canaanites but also many small principalities on the borders of Palestine, allowing the unified Hebrew kingdom to assume a place as a leading power in an era of small nations. A centralized government was established at Jerusalem, which, especially under Solomon, took on the basic features of a typical Near Eastern absolute monarchy with powers to tax, to impose forced labor, and to spend lavishly on public buildings, support of the arts, and an impressive royal court. The kingdom was greatly enriched by royal economic policies that helped Hebrew traders take advantage of Palestine's strategic location on international trade routes. Solomon was particularly effective in creating an extensive network of diplomatic ties in the Near East that enhanced the prestige of the kingdom and brought its ruling elements into contact with the increasingly cosmopolitan world of the Near East; visible evidence of these contacts was provided not only by Solomon's many foreign wives but also by foreign influences on the arts and on life styles increasingly prevalent among the Hebrews.

Amidst the tribulations and the successes experienced by the Hebrews between 1200 and 930 B.C., their religion—Judaism—continued to develop. The struggles to occupy Canaan and to resist the Philistines brought constant reminders, especially from the aforementioned judges, to remain loyal to the covenant with Yahweh. The success under the early monarchs appeared to vindicate Yahweh's concern for his people and thus keep his worship central in Hebrew life. In fact, the institution of a monarchy, which was believed to be sanctioned in a special way by Yahweh, marked an important step in creating a truly national religion. A prime symbol of this national religion was the establishment by David and Solomon of Jerusalem as the cult center of the Hebrew people, featuring Solomon's splendid temple housing the Ark of the Convenant, a wooden chest containing the commandments Yahweh had given to his people in the time of Moses. The system of law originally set forth in the Ten Commandments was greatly expanded to serve as a common bond among the Hebrews and to relate their new lives as farmers and urban dwellers to basic religious principles rooted in the covenant.

A more complex set of religious practices shaped by an emerging priesthood took on increasing importance in the collective lives of the Hebrews. Despite the repeated outcries in the Old Testament against the dangers of outside religious ideas and practices, the changes in law and worship involved the assimilation of elements from non-Hebrew sources into Judaism. Especially influential was the religion of the Canaanites, based on familiar Near Eastern fertility deities, especially the often-condemned Baal, and on cult practices associated with the agricultural seasons. This process of assimilation sustained constant tension in Hebrew religious life but ultimately resulted in an enriched and flexible common religion attuned to the more advanced level of civilization attained by the Hebrews during the period reaching from the first attempts to occupy their promised land to the culmination of their national history under Solomon.

Even while Solomon reigned in all his glory, deep-seated discontents threatened the unity of the Hebrew kingdom. Among the major causes of this discontent were the autocratic methods of the kings, growing economic and social inequality, rural-urban rivalry, and concerns over foreign religious usages in the rituals of the temple and the royal court. Immediately after Solomon's death these discontents resulted in a division of the kingdom. Dissidents in the northern part of the kingdom refused to recognize his son as king and formed a new kingdom called Israel, with its center at Samaria. The remnant of the previously united kingdom, called Judah, continued under kings descended from the house of David. Each of these nations had a stormy internal history, marked by social and religious conflict. Ultimately, neither was able to survive outside aggression. In 722 B.C. Israel was conquered by the Assyrians and many of its people were carried off into captivity. Judah survived until 586 B.C., when the Chaldeans captured Jerusalem, destroyed the Temple, and took large numbers of Hebrews to Babylon as captives. Although the Persian ruler Cyrus (ca. 560–530 B.C.) allowed those victims of the Babylonian captivity who wished to do so to return to Jerusalem and aided them in restoring the Temple, the political independence of the ancient Israelites had ended. An important consequence of this troubled course of events was the dispersion of many Hebrews across much of the Near East, marking the beginnings of the Diaspora, the scattering of Hebrews into new settings where their religion would undergo new challenges and where they could assert an important influence on the non-Hebrews among whom they lived.

As Hebrew political power eroded and then vanished in the centuries after 900 B.C., Judaism took on new depth. During the period of the divided kingdoms and foreign conquests, religion became the sole force that sustained a sense of commonalty and uniqueness among the Hebrews. Although constantly challenged by the lures offered by non-Hebrew religions, the Hebrew priesthood fashioned a sober, austere cult that cut away much of the magic and superstition surrounding other Near Eastern religions; observance of these practices became a mark of belonging to Yahweh's special community. Much more significant was the reformulation of the traditional concepts of Judaism by a series of powerful religious leaders known as *prophets*. Several of them rank among the world's greatest spiritual leaders: Elijah, Amos, Isaiah, Jeremiah, Ezekiel, the anonymous second Isaiah. Although their careers spanned four centuries and each spoke a unique message appropriate to his own time, these remarkable figures collectively explored with deep spiritual insight many of the essential elements of religious experience. The message of all of them was rooted in a shared conviction, based on their reading of history and their interpretation of their own times, that the Hebrews were guilty of abandoning their covenant with Yahweh. Their mission was to call Yahweh's errant and hardhearted people back to that covenant. In the course of reinterpreting the essence of that covenant, they expanded and clarified certain fundamental concepts that became the essence of Judaism.

First, the prophets proclaimed a true monotheism. They insisted that Yahweh was the only god in the universe and denied that any other deities existed. To give any sign of recognition to any other deity except Yahweh was the greatest of all sacrileges.

Second, the prophets proclaimed a radically new concept of Yahweh's nature. Yahweh was the creator of all things, existing outside of time and nature. Unlike other gods worshiped in the Near East, he was not in nature; he created it and controlled it, making the worship of natural forces idolatry. He was a god of justice, acting according to law instead of whim. He was omnipotent, ruling the entire universe and causing everything in the past, present, and future to happen. He was a god with a plan for the universe and for humanity, a plan that would be worked out in history. He was a god of righteousness, pleased by those who did good, vengeful toward those who did evil. He was a caring god, "merciful and gracious, long-suffering, and abundant in goodness and truth," always watchful over his entire creation.

Third, the prophets projected a new vision of the essence of human nature. As Yahweh's special creatures, human beings were created to become godlike. This end could be achieved only by moral perfection, which involved a choice between good and evil. Human beings were basically moral beings, each endowed with the freedom and the capacity to choose the good. They were not Yahweh's slaves, for whom he cared not and upon whom he might vent his wrath at his whim; rather, each was his child who could earn divine mercy and love and favor by righteousness. Men and women were individuals capable of choosing how they would respond to Yahweh's call, of determining what kind of humans they wished to be. This moral freedom imposed a burden, but it opened avenues of human aspiration and endeavor largely absent in the other religious systems in the ancient Near East.

Fourth, the prophets proclaimed a new basis for defining the conduct of each individual toward others and of a community toward the individuals who were its members. Just as Yahweh treated men and women with righteousness and justice, so also must individuals treat all others according to these same principles. Likewise, the community of Yahweh's followers must conduct its collective actions to promote righteousness and justice. The principles of social righteousness and justice were set forth in a code of law (the Torah) that all were obliged to observe if they were to be counted among those faithful to Yahweh. As that law evolved, it provided detailed regulations for all aspects of individual and communal life. Although some aspects of Hebraic law may seem less than enlightened to today's world, it is firm in its insistence that every individual was worthy of respect and compassionate treatment. Some of the prophets put special stress on the obligation of the rich and the powerful to show mercy, charity, and compassion to the weak and the unfortunate. The ethical dimension of early Judaism was one of its most unique features.

Finally, the prophets reasserted that the Hebrews—the followers of Yahweh—were the people chosen to carry out Yahweh's plan for his creation. No matter what disasters might befall them, they would ultimately emerge victorious over the other peoples of the earth, and through them the one god would eventually be worshiped by all. In the face of the disasters that befell the Hebrews after Solomon, the prophets put special emphasis on Yahweh's eventual intention to send a Messiah to lead the Hebrews to victory. While awaiting their deliverer, the Hebrews must hold fast to their allegiance to Yahweh, maintain their religious ties with one another, and resist the temptation to follow false gods.

As the last centuries of Near Eastern monopoly on higher civilizations unfolded, Yahweh's promise delivered by the prophet Jeremiah seemed unlikely to be realized: "They shall all know me from the least of them to the greatest . . . ; for I will forgive their iniquity and I will remember their sin no more." By about 500 B.C. the Jewish community consisted of a small number of the faithful living around Jerusalem under Persian domination and often at odds with one another. Many of their religious compatriots were scattered around the Near East; they too were under foreign domination and hard-pressed to maintain their ancient faith. The bulk of the population of the Near East remained untouched by the religion shaped by the Hebrews over several centuries; these people preferred their traditional nature deities, their elaborate mythologies, and their complex rituals devoted to winning divine favors. Despite its modest impact on the ancient Near East, Judaism would ultimately have a major impact on history. The Hebrews had written one of the great chapters in the spiritual and moral history of humanity, and the message would not go unnoticed.

SUGGESTED READING

Egyptian and Hittite Empires

P. H. Newby, *Warrior Pharaohs. The Rise and Fall of the Egyptian Empire* (1980). A full treatment of the history of the New Kingdom.

Donald B. Redford, *Akhenaten: The Heretic King* (1984). An excellent study of an enigmatic figure.

T. G. H. James, *Pharaoh's People: Scenes from Life in Imperial Egypt* (1984). Excellent social history of the New Kingdom.

J. G. Macqueen, *The Hittites and Their Contemporaries in Asia Minor*, rev. and enl. ed. (1986).

Johannes Lehmann, *The Hittites. People of a Thousand Gods*, trans. J. Maxwell Brownjohn (1975). Either title will provide an excellent survey of Hittite history.

Ekrem Akurgal, *The Art of the Hittites*, trans. Constance McNab (1962). A well-illustrated study.

Minoans and Phoenicians

R. F. Willetts, *The Civilization of Ancient Crete* (1977).

Arthur Cotterell, *The Minoan World* (1979). Either of these two titles will provide a full introduction to Minoan history and civilization.

Reynold Higgins, *Minoan and Mycenaean Art*, rev. ed. (1981). A sound study that is enriched by excellent illustrations.

Gerhard Herm, *The Phoenicians: The Purple Empire of the Ancient World*, trans. Caroline Hillier (1975).

Raymond Weill, *Phoenicia and Western Asia to the Macedonian Conquest*, trans. Ernest F. Row (1980).

Sabatino Moscati, *The World of the Phoenicians*, trans. Alastair Hamilton (1968). Any of these three titles will help the reader to understand the role of the Phoenicians in the ancient world.

Hebrews

John Bright, *A History of Israel,* 3rd ed. (1981).

Michael Grant, *The History of Ancient Israel* (1984).

J. Maxwell Miller and John H. Hayes, *A History of Ancient Israel and Judah* (1986). Three fine histories of ancient Israel; the Miller and Hayes book provides the fullest treatment.

Bernhard W. Anderson, *Understanding the Old Testament,* 4th ed. (1986). A well-done attempt to weave together history, literary criticism, archaeology, and biblical theology in order to show how Judaism developed.

G. W. Anderson, *The History and Religion of Israel* (1966). A helpful treatment of the evolution of ancient Judaism.

Roland de Vaux, *Ancient Israel: Its Life and Institutions,* 2 vols. (1961). Rich in details about ancient Hebrew society.

CHAPTER 3

The Great Empires: Assyria and Persia, 800–300 B.C.

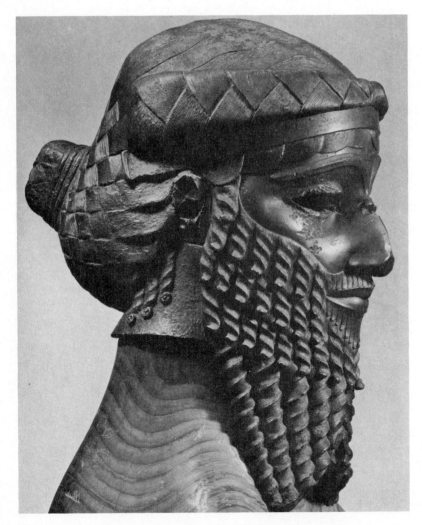

FIGURE 3.1 **A Near Eastern Empire Builder** This portrayal of the Assyrian ruler Sargon II (721–705 B.C.) conveys a sense of power—even arrogant power—that was typical of the rulers of the great Near East empires from ca. 800 to 300 B.C. One can well believe that this man was capable of dominating "the four rims of the world," as Assyrian and Persian empire builders claimed to do. (Hirmer Fotoarchiv)

During the ninth century B.C. significant changes began to occur in the Near East to herald a new era characterized by the formation for the first time of vast empires unifying almost the entire area enjoying the benefits of higher civilization under a single political regime. The ground for this development had been prepared during the previous millennium. The diffusion of the river valley cultures had provided large numbers of diverse peoples with common techniques, religious practices, and literary and art styles. Expanding trade connections had knit distant communities together with common economic interests. Shared cultural, religious, and economic interests invited attempts at political consolidations, and adventuresome leaders appeared to respond to the opportunity.

1. THE ASSYRIAN EMPIRE

The first people to unify almost the entire Near East were the Assyrians. They were a people of Semitic origin who migrated from the Arabian Desert as early as 3000 B.C. and established a homeland on the plateau astride the upper Tigris River, a land that lacked natural barriers and was open to repeated attacks. During the ensuing centuries the Assyrians were powerfully influenced by Mesopotamian civilization; at times, such as under Sargon I and Hammurabi, they were incorporated politically into the empires based in the lower Tigris-Euphrates Valley. The era from 1750 to 1000 B.C. was especially testing for the Assyrians. They were constantly assaulted by Kassites, Hittites, Mitanni, Semitic nomads from the Arabian Desert, and barbarians from the east and north. The hardy farmers of Assyria met this challenge by developing one of the best military forces in the Near East, especially after they adopted the new iron weapons and the horse-drawn war chariots introduced into the Near East shortly before 1000 B.C.

Eventually the fear for the safety of their ancestral homeland, coupled with the absence of any major political powers in the Near East during the era of small nations, provoked the Assyrians to undertake preventive wars against potential enemies. During the ninth century several surrounding nations felt the force of these raids—the Hebrews, the Phoenicians, the Arameans, the Mesopotamians, the mountaineers living to the north and east of Assyria, and the nomads of the northern Arabian Desert. None was able to resist the well-armed Assyrian infantrymen, archers, and charioteers, ably backed by siege equipment and skilled engineers. The effectiveness of the military machine was increased by a deliberate policy of terrorism waged against those defeated by the Assyrians. So awesome did the Assyrians become that many people preferred to "embrace the feet" of the attackers rather than resist (see Figure 3.2).

These raids showed the Assyrians that they could not only defend but also enrich themselves by exacting tribute from their victims. This prospect eventually changed defensive raids into conquest and the establishment of permanent control over Assyria's enemies. The founder of the Assyrian Empire was Tiglath-pileser III (745–727 B.C.), who began the policy of imposing permanent control over conquered peoples. He and a successor, Sargon II (721–705 B.C.), led the Assyrian armies on a series of expeditions that destroyed the chief political powers from Mesopotamia northward and westward to Syria and Palestine. Assyrian governors were imposed on most of the conquered peoples, although a few minor kingdoms, such as Judah, were allowed to exist as tribute-paying clients of Assyria. The central administration of Assyria was enlarged to supervise tribute collection, and effective means of communication were devised to keep the royal court informed of affairs throughout the empire. The army stood ready to crush all signs of resistance; it continued its policy of terrorism, even resorting to the large-scale deportation of conquered peoples, as was the case with a large part of the population of the kingdom of Israel. Once this base of power was established, rulers such as Sennacherib (705–681 B.C.), Esarhaddon (681–669 B.C.), and Ashurbanipal (669–626 B.C.) devoted their energies to dealing with outsiders who insisted on interfering with Assyrian rule. Egypt was forced to accept Assyrian overlordship, and Assyrian influence was extended into Asia Minor, the Zagros Mountains region, Iran, the northern Arabian Desert, and the highland region north of the Assyrian homeland. By 650 B.C. almost the entire civilized Near East stood subject to a single

FIGURE 3.2   Embracing the Feet of an Assyrian King   This carving from an Assyrian royal palace represents Jehu, King of Israel, bowing before his Assyrian conqueror, King Shalmaneser III. It conveys the awe that Assyrian rulers struck in the victims of their conquest. (The Granger Collection)

master, the great king of Assyria, "ruler of the four rims of the world" (see Map 3.1). The arrogant visages of these mighty kings still stare out at us from the remarkable stone busts and reliefs wrought by Assyrian artists to celebrate their deeds (see Figure 3.1); all of them left boastful accounts of their exploits in building the first genuinely ecumenical empire in the Near East.

However, the Assyrian Empire was not as strong as its size and heavy-handed rule suggested. Its brutal treatment of subject peoples aroused their irreconcilable hatred, nowhere better reflected than in the writings of some of the Hebrew prophets. Constant warfare depleted Assyria's human resources and eventually forced its rulers to rely on less efficient levies from conquered subjects. Internal discontent arose, often stemming from dissatisfaction over the distribution of tribute. Worst of all, the Assyrians encountered the plague of all empire builders—enemies beyond the frontiers, aroused by threat of absorption and greed for the riches of the empire. During the reign of Ashurbanipal these problems began to weaken Assyrian power, and troubles mounted rapidly after his death in 626 B.C. The Egyptians

successfully revolted and then stirred up trouble among Assyrian subjects in Syria and Palestine. A Semitic group, the Chaldeans, raised the standard of revolt in southern Mesopotamia, a threat so serious that the Assyrians were forced to commit most of their resources to quelling it. Then the Medes, a people living east of the Zagros Mountains who had learned a great deal by imitating Assyrian military techniques, struck out of the east. In 612 B.C. they and the Chaldeans destroyed the Assyrian capital at Nineveh. Assyrian power collapsed almost immediately, leaving the empire at the mercy of its many foes, who hastened to partition it.

No one in the Near East lamented Assyria's passing. The Hebrew prophet Nahum spoke for all the world: "All who hear the news of you clap their hands at your downfall." However, the Assyrians' bad reputation should not conceal their contributions to history. They broke ground in trying to create a single state out of many different peoples. Their attempt to erect a centralized monarchy was to be imitated by others. The Assyrians wiped out many artificial political boundaries that kept small groups at sword's point. At least briefly

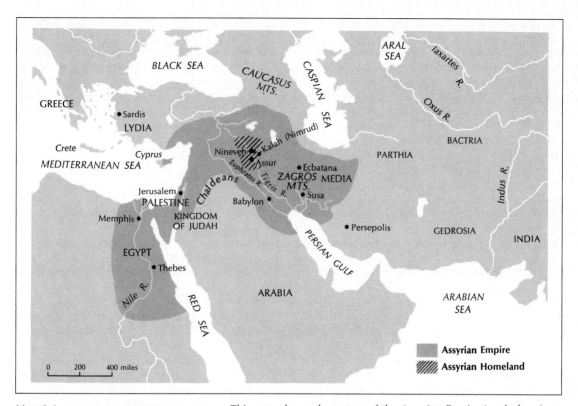

Map 3.1 **THE ASSYRIAN EMPIRE, CA. 662 B.C.** This map shows the extent of the Assyrian Empire just before its collapse. Some idea of its size is illustrated by the fact that it was more than one thousand miles from its capital at Nineveh to Thebes in Egypt—roughly as far as Washington, D.C., is from Omaha, Nebraska. Its size should be compared with that of the earlier empires of the Egyptians and the Hittites (see Map 2.1). A better appreciation of the Assyrian Empire can be gained by making an effort to account for the different peoples we have studied who were included in it.

they imposed a beneficial, albeit burdensome, peace on the Near East, protecting it for nearly three centuries against barbarians who might have destroyed its civilization had they succeeded in seizing control.

Economically, the Assyrian regime had significant effects. The Assyrians themselves added very little to Near Eastern economy, but they encouraged trade and assisted it by breaking down barriers impeding the movement of goods. They encouraged the spread of a common spoken language across their empire, greatly facilitating the exchange of goods and ideas. Through their ef-

forts goods flowed freely over much of the Near East, and technical skills became more widely disseminated.

In cultural activities the Assyrians also made a notable contribution. Their efforts were not creative, but their imitations resulted in the continuation of cultural activity. Their contributions can be seen best in architecture and sculpture. Assyrian kings were avid builders, constructing the great cities of Assur, Kalah (modern Nimrud), and Nineveh as monuments of their power and glory. In these cities earlier Mesopotamian architectural styles were followed closely and thus kept alive.

Temples and palaces were decorated with massive sculptured pieces and with excellent stone reliefs. The vigorous application of traditions from the past gave the Near East a new era of artistic glory. To the tradition they honored, Assyrian artists often gave a unique quality. Especially impressive were the carved friezes done in relief to decorate the walls of royal palaces. This narrative art put together a succession of carved panels to tell in realistic detail the story of a military campaign or a hunting expedition (see Figure 3.2).

In literature the Assyrians devoted a great deal of effort to collecting older works in Sumerian and Akkadian. One of Assyria's kings, Ashurbanipal III, built a huge library at Nineveh as a repository for thousands of copies of cuneiform tablets. Aside from administrative and economic records, most of the writing in Assyrian was a rerendering of earlier literary works, especially the religious epics and creation stories so dear to the Mesopotamians. The Assyrians did show some originality in compiling annals that vividly recounted the events surrounding the innumerable military campaigns of the kings, thereby making a contribution to the art of historical writing.

Assyrian religion was likewise strongly colored by borrowings from Mesopotamia. The great state god of Assyria, Assur, resembled the Amorite Marduk. Assyrian rituals, prayers, and priesthoods are almost indistinguishable from those of the earlier Mesopotamians. Despite the derived character of their religion, there is considerable evidence that the Assyrians were deeply religious. Perhaps even their imperialism was motivated by a genuine desire to assert Assur's dominion over other gods. In many reliefs Assur is shown hovering over the field of battle, ready to take up arms to assure the victory of the king doing battle in Assur's cause. In all these ways the Assyrians kept alive some of the most precious cultural traditions in the Near East.

2. SUCCESSORS OF ASSYRIA, 612–550 B.C.

In the wake of Assyria's sudden collapse several states entered a spirited competition to carve up the empire. Some of these rivals even aspired to replace the Assyrians as masters of the Near East.

One of the competitors was Egypt. After a long period of weakness following the end of the Egyptian Empire about 1200 B.C. (see Chapter 2), foreign rule by the Assyrians again goaded the Egyptians to unify under a single pharaoh, Psammetichus (663–609 B.C.), founder of the Twenty-sixth Dynasty. Egypt again enjoyed a brief period of internal order, prosperity, and international prestige, especially in the Syria-Palestine area. But the Egyptians were incapable of sustaining a role as a great power. The pharaohs had to rely on foreign mercenaries (chiefly Greeks) to provide a military force; these forces were a constant source of internal trouble. A backward-looking spirit dominated thought and expression. A reactionary priesthood used religion as a force to resist change. Old age had gripped Egyptian society. In 525 B.C. the Persians were able to conquer Egypt without much difficulty.

In Asia Minor the small kingdom of Lydia, which first emerged after the fall of the Hittites, benefited from the fall of Assyria. Its rulers, the most famous of which was Croesus (560–546 B.C.), were able to establish control over most of Asia Minor, including several important Greek city-states on the Aegean seacoast. Despite the considerable prosperity of Lydia, it was unable to resist the Persians, who conquered the kingdom in 546 B.C.

Still another participant in the dismemberment of the Assyrian Empire was Media. Based in northern Iran, the Medes had long been restless dependents on Assyria, but they had raised their level of life considerably by borrowing from their oppressors. Eventually they played a major military role in destroying Assyria. After Assyria's fall, they established control of a vast area extending from Iran westward toward Asia Minor. However, the Median kingdom was badly organized. Eventually a vassal prince, Cyrus of Persia, deposed of the Median king and laid claim to the Median realm.

The most spectacular of all Assyria's successors was the kingdom of the Chaldeans, a Semitic people who had established themselves in southern Mesopotamia prior to its conquest by the Assyrians. Their revolt against the Assyrians played a major role in Assyria's downfall. After Assyria's defeat, the Chaldeans established a kingdom based in Mesopotamia. Under the one great Chaldean king, Nebuchadnezzar II (605–562 B.C.), Syria and Palestine were conquered. Among the victims of Chaldean expansion was the tiny kingdom of Judah. Jerusalem and its Temple were destroyed, and many Hebrews were deported to Babylon as captives. Nebuchadnezzar's reign was marked by a conscious effort to cast the Chaldeans in the role of restorers of ancient Mesopotamian civilization; the result was a notable cultural renaissance. The jewel of this revival was his rebuilding of Babylon as his capital. Its massive walls, beautiful temples and palaces, fabulous hanging gardens, impressive sculpture and painting made it one of the most splendid of ancient cities. Even the redoubtable Hebrew prophet Jeremiah, amid his lamentations over the Babylonian captivity of his people, had to admit that "Babylon was a golden cup in the hands of Yahweh." A religious revival in this period restored the worship of ancient Mesopotamian deities, above all Marduk, as a major feature of the civilization of "New Babylonia." However, despite its outward brilliance, the Chaldean Empire lacked military and economic strength. Under Nebuchadnezzar's weak successors, it proved an easy victim of the Persians in 539 B.C.

3. THE PERSIAN EMPIRE, 550–328 B.C.

As is obvious from the review of the competition for the Assyrian Empire, the final victory belonged to the Persians. They were of Indo-European origin, their ancestors having settled shortly after 2000 B.C. in the barren southern part of Iran as simple farmers and herders. For centuries they maintained their political independence. However, during this period civilizing influences penetrated Persia, especially from Assyria, so that the Persians were drawn into the orbit of the higher civilization of the Near East. They did retain significant aspects of their old Indo-European culture, especially in religion and language. In the late seventh century they were forced to accept the overlordship of the Medes, who were closely akin to them in language and culture. About 560

B.C. a Persian prince, Cyrus, overthrew the Median king and proclaimed himself "king of the Medes and the Persians."

With Cyrus' accession to power the Persians began a period of rapid expansion. Cyrus (ca. 560–530 B.C.) was the most successful conqueror. He seized control of Asia Minor by overpowering Lydia. Then he subdued various peoples living to the east, pushing the boundaries of his empire to the frontiers of India, where there existed another highly developed civilization based in the Indus River valley. In 540 B.C. he attacked the Chaldean kingdom and annexed Mesopotamia, Syria, and Palestine. His successor, Cambyses (530–522 B.C.), overran Egypt. Darius I, "the Great" (522–486 B.C.), extended Persian power into Europe by conquering territory in Thrace, but his attempt to subdue the Greeks failed, as we shall see later (see Chapter 5). He also established Persian control over the Indus Valley. When Darius died in 486 B.C., the Persians controlled one of the largest empires ever created (see Map 3.2).

The first Persian rulers were not only successful conquerors but also skilled statesmen whose decisions in the face of the complex problems presented by so large an empire laid the basis for sound government. Cyrus established one basic principle undergirding Persian rule: tolerance toward defeated peoples and respect for their cultural uniqueness. After he overthrew the Median king to launch the Persian rise to power, he drew the Median aristocracy into his regime as participants in his administration and military force. His policy of tolerance was illustrated in an especially dramatic way by his treatment of the Hebrews. Immediately after conquering the Chaldean state, he allowed the Hebrew captives in Babylon to return to Jerusalem, helped them to rebuild the Temple, and encouraged them to reconstitute their religious community. For this generous act the Hebrews hailed Cyrus as Yahweh's "shepherd." Such actions convinced most peoples in the Near East that the Persians did not intend to continue the brutal policies of the Assyrians and made Persian dominance more acceptable.

Darius was the most effective political leader of his dynasty, called the Achaemenids. Borrowing and adapting old ideas and practices in statecraft, he laid the basis for a highly effective po-

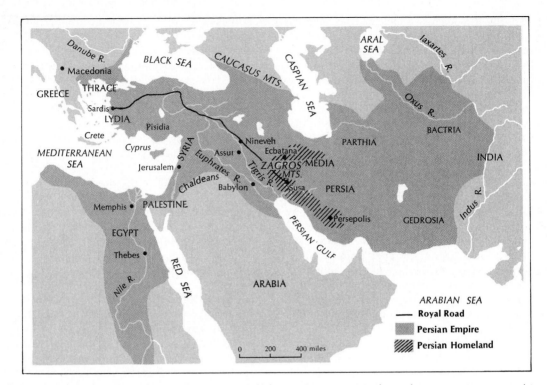

Map 3.2 THE PERSIAN EMPIRE, CA. 500 B.C. At its peak the Persian Empire embraced a vast territory, varied in terrain and climate and occupied by a complex mixture of peoples. In area the Persian Empire was approximately the size of the continental United States. The Persians were able to overcome some of these vast distances by building an excellent road system that fanned out from the capital cities of Susa and Persepolis to key cities across the empire. One of the most famous was the Royal Road, which extended from Susa to Sardis, a distance of about sixteen hundred miles. The Persians developed a system of regular outposts along this road and teams of mounted couriers who, by working in relays, could carry a message from Susa to Sardis in as little as a week.

litical system, often imitated by later empire builders. Like his Near Eastern predecessors, he claimed absolute power with authority to make laws, to judge, and to command obedience and service from his subjects. Court life at his capital cities of Ecbatana, Susa, and Persepolis involved an elaborate etiquette designed to impress everyone that he was indeed "The Great King" (see Figure 3.3). He developed a highly skilled bureaucracy staffed by officials, usually of Median or Persian origin, who represented an elite fanatically devoted to maintaining Persian power.

Darius' most notable innovation lay in the techniques he devised for extending his authority to all parts of his vast empire. He divided the empire into twenty large districts, called *satrapies*, some of which coincided with the boundaries of the kingdoms conquered by the Persians. Over each he appointed a governor, called a *satrap*, usually a Persian and often a member of the royal family, who was given sufficient power to control local affairs. The satraps were removable at the will of the great king and were held strictly accountable for the administration of their districts. Periodically, Darius sent out inspectors to investigate local administration and report to the central government. Contingents of the imperial army under trusted commanders were garrisoned in

FIGURE 3.3 **The "King of Kings" at Work** This relief from the royal palace at Persepolis shows Darius receiving a commander of the royal guard. Behind the king stands his son, Xerxes. (Oriental Institute, University of Chicago)

strategic spots both to support the satraps and to curb their ambitions. An excellent road system and a postal service were developed, permitting rapid communications between the satrapies and the central government. Careful records were maintained by the central government as a means of holding each satrap accountable. By these methods Darius managed to create twenty semi-independent governments, each capable of reacting to situations that were unique to each locality but all guided by common policies shaped by the great king and his high officials seeking to maintain unity amidst diversity.

In the final analysis, Darius' power rested on his armed forces. The Persian army was built around the Immortals, a loyal, disciplined corps of about ten thousand professionals recruited from the Medes and the Persians. When occasion demanded, this elite force was reinforced with contingents mobilized in vast numbers from the subject population of the empire. Although such mass armies could be gathered, armed, and supplied only slowly and although they were hard to control in battle, their sheer numbers made them awe inspiring. The Persians also commanded impressive naval forces, composed largely of hired

Phoenician and Greek ships and crews.

Darius' imperial system endured about one hundred fifty years. The history of the Persian Empire after his death was marked by few events that require our attention. There were numerous wars with outsiders in defense of the empire's immensely long frontiers; the Persians seldom won decisively, but neither did they lose much territory. Rebellions occurred frequently within the empire, but usually they were smashed by the superior power of the great king. The Persians played a major role in the diplomacy of the period, often using their money to build alliances with foreign powers and to manipulate relations among these outsiders; Persian diplomacy was especially significant in the Greek world during the fifth and fourth centuries B.C. Despite its status as a great power, Persian strength gradually eroded during the fourth century. Some of the later kings were deficient in political abilities. Their court became corrupt and torn by intrigue involving royal wives and children, officials, and friends. Ambitious satraps constantly attempted to overthrow the rulers, often putting themselves forward as champions of subject peoples and usually generous in their promises of rewards for those who joined them against the king. A gradual decline in the efficiency and the loyalty of the royal bureaucracy and the armed forces impeded the ability of the kings to control the satraps. By the middle of the fourth century B.C., all that was needed to destroy the Persian Empire was a strong attack from the outside. That attack was soon forthcoming from a powerful Greek/Macedonian army led by Alexander the Great, who was driven in part by an urge to destroy the Persian menace that had haunted the Greek world since the time of Darius the Great. In a brief, brilliant campaign Alexander was able to destroy the Persian power and to take possession of its territory.

The Persians, emerging suddenly from the fringes of the civilized world to master the Near East and confronted constantly with the heavy burdens of holding their huge empire together, devoted most of their talents to administrative, military, and diplomatic affairs. As a consequence, their unique contributions to the cultural development of the Near East were limited. In general, they played a role similar to that of the Assyrians, borrowing from the cultural resources that already existed and synthesizing these borrowings in a way that would create a culture meaningful to a variety of peoples. They continued to utilize already developed languages, especially Aramean, for administrative purposes, although they were able to produce highly sophisticated literary works in their own language. Their kings were lavish in their patronage of art, the results showing chiefly in the royal palaces built at Ecbatana, Susa, and Persepolis. They continued the practice of commissioning artists to render in stone reliefs pictorial records of royal exploits. The kings and their satraps welcomed to their capitals individuals from all over the empire who were schooled in the literary and scientific traditions of the past; as a result, the Persians helped substantially in keeping these traditions alive to serve the cause of learning and expression among later peoples, especially the Greeks, who came to the Persian Empire in large numbers following Alexander's conquests. The tolerant attitude of the Persian masters toward the many different cultural elements embraced in their empire encouraged local cultural activity.

The Persians did make one outstanding contribution to Near Eastern civilization in the form of a new religion, Zoroastrianism. This religion was rooted in beliefs held by the Persians before they became masters of the Near East. Early Persian religion centered around the worship of many deities who represented forces of nature, especially a god of the sky and a god of fire. A complicated ritual, including sacrifices, magic, and prayer, developed as a means of winning the favors of the deities. Priests, called Magi, played a prominent role in directing religious life among the early Persians.

It was into this religious setting that Zoroaster (Zarathustra in Persian) came as a reformer. Although the details of his life are vague and clouded by legend, it appears that he lived about 600 B.C., before the emergence of Persia as master of the Near East. According to tradition, he prepared himself for his ministry by a long period of contemplation in the desert, finally receiving a revelation to guide him to the truth. He then returned to the world to seek converts to his beliefs. At first he enjoyed little success and even suffered persecution, but eventually he began to win adherents, and his religion was implanted in Persian society before the Persians began their rise to dominance.

Zoroaster's exact teachings are as elusive as are the details of his life. His message was eventually set forth in a sacred book called *Zend-Avesta*, but it was compiled over many centuries and contains a confusing array of interpretations and refinements of Zoroaster's original teachings. As a consequence, it is difficult to reconstruct what Zoroaster thought and said. It seems certain that he cast his new message in terms of a protest against existing Persian religion, especially its polytheism and its ritualistic formalism. At its core was a unique concept of the nature of the universe, one based on a principle of dualism. On the one hand, there was the god Ahura Mazda (Lord of Wisdom), the all-powerful, all-pervading lord of creation. This good and benevolent spirit presides over all creation, emanating and personifying such qualities as justice, pure thought, integrity, good intentions, and virtue. But the good Ahura Mazda is opposed by the diabolical Ahriman, an evil force seeking to blot out justice, light, wisdom, and good. The warfare between Ahura Mazda and Ahriman, good and evil, going on since the beginning of the world, provides the dynamic force in the universe. Eventually, in a final day of judgment, Ahura Mazda will prevail; but in the meantime, the conflict will rage, extending into every soul and demanding that each individual elect whether to serve good or evil. On the final day of reckoning, those who have chosen good will be rewarded with eternal happiness, while those who have elected the way of Ahriman will be condemned to eternal misery.

By postulating the struggle between good and evil as fundamental in the cosmic order, Zoroaster made the basic obligation of each human being clear. Only good conduct would win favor in the eyes of Ahura Mazda. The worship of old deities, magic, sacrifices, and priestly ministrations were irrelevant and even constituted a surrender to evil because they diverted attention from doing good. Zoroaster defined a vigorous moral code for his followers, derived in its particulars from the qualities of goodness surrounding Ahura Mazda. Obversely, he set forth a clear concept of sin, rooted in the evil nature of Ahriman. Certainly none of the religions in the world that the Persians were soon to rule, except Judaism, gave such emphasis to ethical issues—and not even Judaism placed the burden of goodness so squarely on each individual. Zoroaster did not associate goodness and righteousness with a particular chosen people or system of law; his message was aimed at all humankind.

Although the record is again confusing, it appears that Zoroaster's religion took firm hold among the Persians and the Medes after the master's death and that it became in some fashion the official religion of the Achaemenid dynasty. However, its acceptance was not universal in the Persian Empire. The general policy of tolerance in the empire permitted other religions to maintain their hold. As time passed, Zoroaster's original message lost its uniqueness. Ritual practices aimed at pleasing Ahura Mazda and warding off Ahriman's evil powers grew increasingly prominent. The role of the Magi again became predominant. Polytheistic concepts crept back into Zoroastriansim. Ahriman was elevated to the status of god, standing equal to Ahura Mazda in the cosmic order. Old Persian deities and hosts of angels and devils reappeared as combatants in the eternal war between good and evil. The concept of the struggle between good and evil tended to associate good with purely spiritual forces and evil with material things. This interpretation of dualism had the effect of belittling the practice of virtue in everyday life and of exalting withdrawal from the world. These developments, tending to make Zoroastrianism like most other Near Eastern religions, blunted its appeal. After the collapse of the Persian Empire, Zoroastrianism declined as a major religious force in the Near East. However, it has survived across twenty-five centuries to the present; its modern adherents, called Parsees, live in Iran and India. Zoroaster's concept of dualism was destined to provide a rich source of spiritual speculation among later religions, especially Christianity.

The sudden end of the Persian Empire at the hands of Greeks and Macedonians must not detract from the importance of the Persians in history. The enlightened and tolerant rule of the Achaemenids built a universal empire in the ancient Near East in which all kinds of people at many levels of civilization were brought together in a viable community. The cosmopolitan environment in that empire permitted local cultures to persist and grow while providing instruments through which all could mix and fertilize each other. In a sense, the resulting amalgam reflected the best the ancient Near East had produced during the thirty-five centuries in which its people stood in the forefront of civilized life.

SUGGESTED READING

Assyrians

H. W. F. Saggs, *The Might That Was Assyria* (1984).

Georges Roux, *Ancient Iraq,* 2nd ed. (1980).

Two well-written treatments of Assyrian history and civilization.

André Parrot, *Arts of Assyria,* trans. Stuart Gilbert and James Emmons (1961). An excellent introduction to all aspects of Assyrian art.

Persians

J. M. Cook, *The Persian Empire* (1983). An effective treatment of Persian history and institutions.

Richard N. Frye, *The History of Ancient Iran* (1983). Surveys Persian history down to the Moslem conquest in the eighth century A.D.

Richard N. Frye, *The Heritage of Persia* (1963). Excellent survey of Persian cultural influence on the larger world.

Mary Boyce, *Zoroastrians: Their Religious Beliefs and Practices* (1984). A brief treatment covering the entire history of Zoroastrianism.

Mary Boyce, *A History of Zoroastrianism,* 2 vols. (1975–1982). A detailed history of early Zoroastrianism.

Roman Ghirshman, *Persia from the Origins to Alexander the Great,* trans. Stuart Gilbert and James Emmons (1964).

Edith Porada, *The Art of Ancient Iran. Pre-Islamic Cultures* (1965).

This and the preceding work provide a full treatment of all aspects of Persian art.

RETROSPECT

When in 330 B.C. Alexander the Great stood in triumph over the body of Darius III, a chapter in world history had ended. The Persians, symbolizing an old order, had given way to a youthful conqueror who represented a vital new order emerging on the western periphery of the Near East. Before shifting our attention to that new setting, a brief epitaph for the ancient Near Eastern world is in order.

For the purposes of this epitaph, let us view the Persians as the last scions of a great family whose origins are rooted in simple Neolithic villages and whose members include all the peoples whose histories have been reviewed in the preceding pages. Over several millennia, especially after 4000 B.C., that family had put together a rich and varied patrimony. They had devised effective systems for extracting sustenance from nature. They had developed impressive techniques for controlling large numbers of people and permitting them to interact with each other. They had learned to enrich lives through a magnificent art and literature. They had interwoven the many

facets of their existence into patterns that gave meaning to their activities and provided them with a sense of direction in a mysterious cosmic order. Their religions provided the integrative, unifying, sense-giving dimension of their civilization. In all these ways the peoples of the ancient Near East had created a priceless storehouse from which future peoples could draw without having to invent higher civilization over again. In one sense, world history is a story of the diffusion of ancient Near Eastern achievements across much of the face of the earth.

Yet, the civilizational pattern of the ancient Near East had limitations. The environment imposed serious constraints, for aside from the river valleys the Near East had limited potential in terms of material resources. Technology imposed another limitation. We must not let the spectacular advances of the last century or two blur a basic fact: Technological advance through most of history has been slow and painful, making difficult all efforts to expand control over nature. The ancient Near East suffered too from the overpowering influence of the river valley peoples. What succeeded so remarkably in early Mesopotamia and early Egypt became the model of civilized life for every people in the Near East. Although they benefited from imitation, those living beyond the valley flood plains became prisoners of modes of life that were creative only in a small geographical setting. Slavish imitation of the river valley pattern of civilization brought people to a certain point— and then stopped them from further advance. Still another limitation on the ancient Near Eastern world was its waste of human resources. It was a world directed by small elites who achieved wonders but who ultimately failed to call forth fresh creative talent. The social structure was too inflexible, too closed, to permit genius to break through from unexpected sources.

However, the greatest constriction on ancient Near Eastern civilization and the ultimate cause of it stagnation lay in the minds of human beings. The world view encased in the great religious systems made it extremely difficult for people to use to full capacity their greatest asset: the power to reason. Instead of freeing them to reflect on the nature and potential of themselves and the things around them, the ancient Near Eastern world view required that people pour their intellectual energies into acts of conformity with the directive forces of the cosmos. Because rationality was smothered, humans failed to discover themselves. They were reaching in this direction, as the Hebrew prophets and Zoroaster testify, but they never broke through the formidable barriers imposed by the assumptions on which their civilization was based. Only someone outside their world still had the freedom to discover what humanity really was. When that discovery was made, the Near Eastern peoples had to surrender the leadership of civilization to others.

Here then is the epitaph of the ancient Near East: It was a world that knew people not well enough.

PART TWO

GRECO-ROMAN CIVILIZATION, 1200 B.C.–A.D. 200

While the civilizations of the Near East were reaching maturity under the political sway of the Assyrians and the Persians, a new civilization was appearing in the lands around the Aegean Sea. It began to emerge about 1200 B.C. and reached its most creative phase in the fifth century B.C. From its Aegean center the new civilization exerted a powerful influence over other peoples. The Greeks themselves propagated their style of life through trading and colonizing ventures that ringed the Mediterranean with their city-states. In the latter part of the fourth century, the Macedonians under the meteoric Alexander the Great joined with the Greeks to burst out of the Aegean basin and overrun the old centers of civilization in the Near East. In the third century B.C. the Romans, just emerging as a world power, became enamored of Hellenic civilization and turned their energies to absorbing and spreading it. The Romans eventually conquered Greece and the Near East but were themselves mastered by the ideas and culture of their victims. The empire that they forged became the setting for a further extension of the Greek pattern of life so that much of western Europe and North Africa fell under Greek influence.

In tracing the complex evolution of Greco-Roman civilization through fourteen or fifteen centuries, one should try to identify in an orderly way the main stages of development and to comprehend the essential ingredients of Greco-Roman civilization. But perhaps most important, one should grasp the extent to which the Greco-Roman world discovered and unleashed a new range of human talents. To many historians, the key to this chapter of human history was the discovery and development of the idea expressed by the Athenian dramatist Sophocles in his *Antigone:* "Many are the wonders of the world, and none so wonderful as Man."

CHAPTER 4

The Origins and Development of the Greek City-State Polity

FIGURE 4.1 The Heart of a Polis The fact that the rocky promontory shown in this photo features the surviving ruins of one of the great artistic achievements in all history should not hide another important consideration: Such physical settings played a prime role all over ancient Greece as focal points that drew people together to form a unique community—the *polis*. That the Athenians chose to invest their wealth and talent in adorning the Acropolis is a reflection of the role that this modest hill played over many centuries as a center of their collective activities. (Hirmer Fotoarchiv)

Greco-Roman civilization originated in a group of small, independent communities located around the Aegean Sea. It is impossible to understand that civilization without grasping the unique nature of these communities. However, none of them sprang full-grown from a void; each was a product of slow growth and long experimentation. This chapter will trace that evolution and show the nature of these communities.

1. THE ENVIRONMENT

Greco-Roman civilization had its origins in the physical environment provided by the Aegean basin. The whole area is blessed with beneficent climate, marked by mild winters and long, dry summers that permit relatively safe travel by sea and allow comfortable life on land without great expenditure on clothing and housing. The topography, especially of Greece proper, is dominated by mountains, valleys, bays, and peninsulas that cut the land into many small pockets of tillable soil and create barriers impeding communication and political unification. The area's resources are not abundant. Tillable soil is limited, poor in quality, subject to erosion, and ill suited to cereal production. Tin, copper, iron, and timber are in short supply. As the Greek historian Herodotus said, "Greece has always poverty as her companion."

But there was an avenue of escape from this restrictive setting: the sea. The Aegean provides excellent harbors and good sailing winds during the summer season. It served as a roadway allowing the Greeks access to a wider world of raw materials and markets and to contacts with other peoples who stimulated and were stimulated by the Greeks.

2. THE MYCENAEAN AND DARK AGES, 2000–800 B.C.: GREEK ORIGINS

The emergence of a unique Greek civilization occurred over a long period of time. Perhaps the first important step was taken when Neolithic culture was introduced to the Aegean area about 6000 B.C. During many ensuing centuries life centered around simple agricultural villages and typical Neolithic institutions. About 2000 B.C. this primitive order was profoundly affected by the intrusion of Indo-Europeans into the area, part of the same movement that disturbed much of the Near East and produced such peoples as the Kassites, the Hittites, and the Persians. The newcomers in Greece imposed their overlordship and their language on the natives, but they adopted from their victims the basic features of agricultural life. For the next four or five centuries, Aegean history centered on the activities of a number of small principalities dominated by aggressive warlords and their armed retainers.

Surviving archaeological evidence indicates that some of these warlords were able to accumulate considerable wealth and that technological skills were advancing rapidly. By about 1500 B.C., the kings of some of the small principalities in southern and central Greece were able to build huge fortress-palaces. The most impressive was located at Mycenae, which has given its name to this phase of early Greek history. The key to the success of these kings appears to have been what they learned from expanding contacts as pirates and traders with the major advanced societies of the Near East and especially with Minoan society in Crete. The rulers of Mycenae and other important cities established well-organized bureaucracies capable of imposing strong economic and political control over the populations living in the areas surrounding their fortress cities. A written form of the Greek language, called Linear B, was perfected to assist kings and their agents in keeping records pertaining to political and economic life.

Mycenaean culture reached its peak about 1300 B.C. As it matured, it moved toward assimilation with the larger pattern of civilization developing across the Near East during the age of cultural diffusion. The art, technology, and religion usages of the Mycenaeans contained features that suggest that the first Greeks were on the way to absorbing the common cultural patterns of the Near East. However, that process was cut short about 1200 B.C. by the decline and then the collapse of Mycenaean culture. The causes are not entirely clear. Perhaps the collapse of Minoan civilization about 1400 B.C. deprived the Mycenaean world of a vital source of inspiration. The disturbances that disrupted the Hittite and Egyptian empires about 1200 B.C. may have severed trade connections so vital to the Mycenaeans. The resulting constraints on the economy of the Mycenaean world caused the warlike kings to turn on each other in search of wealth to sustain their expensive way of life. It was in these troubled times, for instance, that warriors from several Greek kingdoms joined hands to destroy Troy in Asia Minor, a venture immortalized in the poetry of Homer. Whatever the cause, between about 1200 and 1100 B.C. most of the mighty Mycenaean citadels, including Mycenae, were violently destroyed, bringing to an end the first chapter in Greek history.

The collapse of Mycenaean culture led to a period of about four centuries in the Aegean world that modern historians have called a "Dark Age." Information about this period depends largely on archaeological remains, which are scarce and difficult to interpret. Only at the very end of the period does another kind of evidence appear in the form of two literary masterpieces, the *Iliad* and the *Odyssey*, attributed to the poet Homer. Although Homer claims to recount the adventures of heroes living more than four centuries earlier during the Trojan War, he puts these legendary figures in the eighth-century setting he knew. Consequently, his poems provide a picture of the Greek world about 800 B.C.

The scanty evidence leaves no doubt that with the collapse of the Mycenaean world, many aspects of Mycenaean civilization disappeared: the bureaucratic kingdoms, the great palaces, writing, trading, art, technical expertise. Many settled locations disappeared, suggesting a population decline. Life depended on simple farming carried on by the inhabitants of small communities with limited contacts with a larger world. Life around the Aegean had returned to a primitive level.

However, there were developments that established the basis for fresh cultural advance. The Dark Age saw considerable shifting of peoples in the Aegean area. Especially important was the movement of Greeks from the mainland to the Aegean Islands and the coast of Asia Minor, where important contacts with the Near Eastern world were again established. The populating of this entire area with people linked by common cultural traits established the demographic base for future Greek development. The peoples occupying the Aegean basin came to share a common Greek language, although that language had several different dialects. A new writing system, based on the adaptation of the Phoenician alphabet to accommodate the Greek spoken language, was developed to a level that made possible the magnificent Homeric epics. A common pattern of religion, clearly delineated in the Homeric poems, spread among the Greeks. Although the Greek world remained poor, all those living in the Aegean world benefited from technological advances, especially the adoption of iron-age technology and advancing skills in pottery making. Complex processes were working to define a people participating in a common pattern of life; these people would soon call themselves Hellenes, a term that conveyed their sense both of their commonalty and of their uniqueness.

The Dark Age was especially important in shaping political life. The Greek world remained politically fragmented into many petty tribal kingdoms. Over each presided a chieftain who led his people in war, judged their disputes, and represented them before their deities. In marked contrast with the power enjoyed by kings during the Mycenaean Age, the power of these kings was limited by a politically active nobility whose authority was based on patriarchal family ties, loyal personal retainers, and control of the best lands and herds of cattle. The nobles in each kingdom met regularly to share with the king decision making on matters of common interest. Noble power was enhanced by the dominant role aristocrats played in warfare, an activity that contributed in an important way to defining noble values. Peasants and artisans were considered to be free and even participated to a degree in political life through attendance at assemblies, where they shouted their approval or disapproval of decisions made by kings and nobles. By the end of the Dark Age these small political entities—their members united by kinship and personal ties, shared religious life, and active involvement in political decisions—constituted a base from which would emerge the key institution shaping Greek civilization: the city-state, called the *polis* by the Greeks.

3. THE ARCHAIC AGE
800-500 B.C.:
DEVELOPMENT OF THE *POLIS*

Shortly after 800 B.C. the Greek world entered a period of rapid development that historians call the "Archaic Age." During the next three centuries changes occurred in all aspects of life to create the basic elements of Greek civilization. Central to that development was the evolution of the *polis*.

The shaping of the *polis* was a complex process, proceeding at a different pace and in different ways from one place to another. However, among the nearly seven hundred city-states that established an independent identity during the Archaic Age there were certain common patterns of development that provide the key to the basic nature of the *polis* (see Map 4.1 for the location of the major city-states). Central to the emergence of each *polis* were processes that created powerful bonds linking the inhabitants of a relatively small geographical area into a community and that expanded the involvement of the "citizens" of each community in civic life. These communal bonds found their focus in a physical center, an urban center. Already at the beginning of the Archaic Age the rudiments of such urban centers were emerging in the petty kingdoms that had been established during the Dark Age. At such centers were the king's residence and often a hilltop fortress, called an *acropolis*, where those from the surrounding countryside could find protection. There temples were built where members of the community could gather to honor their shared deities. The same center served as a meeting place for the noble clan leaders when they gathered from their rural estates to counsel with the king; some even established residences there. A market, called an *agora*, developed in connection with the fortress. As the Archaic Age progressed, the range of activities affecting group life expanded in each urban center, and increasingly the members of each community developed a sense of belonging to and depending on a special group. At the same time there emerged institutional forms that increasingly gave structure to the shared experiences of those belonging to the community. Involvement and participation in the political, economic, religious, and cultural activities unfolding at each urban center became the central focus in the lives of those belonging to each *polis*.

A major step in shaping the political and social structure of the typical *polis* occurred in all but a few communities during the eighth century B.C. This change involved the replacement of monarchy with a system of government in which authority rested with a council of nobles and the execution of the council's decision was entrusted to elected officials from that same noble class. Aristocratic domination of most city-states persisted until at least 500 B.C. The power of these nobles was based on landed wealth, control over the clan structure that undergirded early Greek society, and dominance of the legal system. Although they were often greedy and always jealous of their authority, the nobles felt a strong attachment to their *polis* and were willing to use their talent and wealth to promote its welfare. Especially crucial was their willingness to take political action to resolve basic problems affecting the entire population. Under their governance the bonds undergirding each *polis* were expanded and strengthened.

Another crucial development in broadening the base of participation in civic life involved the military organization of most city-states. As reflected in the Homeric epics, warfare during the Dark Age had been monopolized by nobles, who alone could afford the horses and equipment needed for cavalry and chariot combat. That system was replaced by a military organization based on the *phalanx*, a massed formation of infantry soldiers, called *hoplites*, armed with shields, breastplates, helmets, swords, and spears. This change brought larger numbers of citizens with modest means into the service of the *polis*, placed a premium on disciplined action in a common cause, and increased the devotion of the new soldiers to the city-state whose safety now depended on them more than on a few noble warriors. Before long these soldiers were demanding a share in making the decisions that determined the activities of the *polis*.

Even more significant in expanding the bonds that attached people to the *polis* were actions taken by aristocratic leaders to cope with major economic and social problems that began to afflict

Map 4.1 **EARLY AND CLASSICAL GREECE** This map identifies the major geographical regions of the Aegean world and locates the most important *poleis*—but by no means all of them. It also reflects the proximity of most Greek city-states to the Aegean Sea. The numerous islands in the Aegean and the inlets and bays penetrating the Greek mainland greatly facilitated seafaring.

much of the Greek world during the Archaic Age. The nature and the impact of the crisis are reflected in a poem entitled *Works and Days*, written about 700 B.C. by Hesiod, a wealthy farmer embittered by the growing poverty and injustice of the times. The causes for the crisis were deep-seated: growing population, competition for lim-

ited land, and the greediness of what Hesiod called "the land-devouring lords" who controlled each *polis*. The chief victims were small landholders who were being forced into debt, economic dependence on noble landlords, and even slavery, thereby losing their status as citizens of their *polis*.

Despite the fact that the aristocracy was part

of the cause of the problem, aristocratic leaders in most city-states played a key role in finding ways of resolving the crisis. A major solution took the form of organizing overseas settlement. In many city-states noble councils and elected magistrates encouraged or even ordered colonizing ventures, usually led by nobles who recruited impoverished followers to take to the seas in search of new homes. A prime target for such ventures was southern Italy and Sicily, an area so completely Hellenized that it became known as Magna Grae-cia (Greater Greece). Other Greek settlements were established on the northern shores of the Aegean, in the Hellespont area, around the Black Sea, in southern France, in Spain, in Egypt, and in modern Libya (then called Cyrenaica). In all of these areas the Greeks imposed control over the native populations and established themselves as farmers, traders, and artisans. The new communities were not colonies in the modern sense. Rather, each was an independent *polis* with its own government, citizens, laws, and civic pride. Although many such new city-states maintained contact with the Aegean city-states from which the settlers had originally migrated, the overseas migrations between about 750 to 500 B.C. marked a massive extension of the *polis* and of what the Greeks called Hellas—the area dominated by Greeks and their culture (see Map 4.2).

Equally important in reducing economic pressures in many city-states was a significant expansion of trade and industry. The colonizing undertakings played a key role in the growth of trade and industry by providing access to raw materials and markets for Greek products. The Greeks proved energetic and enterprising in taking advantage of commercial opportunities, and by 500 B.C. they had become the leading traders in the Mediterranean world, rivaled only by Carthage, originally established as a colony by the Phoenicians. Trade spurred manufacturing in many city-states, and Greek artisans proved skillful in making products in high demand, especially pottery. Even the agricultural system changed as a consequence of expanding trade. Enterprising farmers abandoned the raising of grain in favor of grapes, olives, and livestock, from which were derived products that found profitable markets throughout the Mediterranean area. Increasingly, Greek

city-states imported grain, especially from the Black Sea area. For merchants, artisans, and commercial farmers, the center of economic life shifted to the urban marketplace, creating new ties between citizen and *polis*.

The social structure changed under the impact of economic growth. Some aristocrats became involved in trade and industry and developed interests different from those of their more conservative peers whose status and wealth depended on landownership. This development weakened the class solidarity of the aristocracy and made political changes easier. Many individuals from the lower ranks of society were able to amass considerable wealth through trade and industry and became rivals of the landowning aristocracy for power and prestige. Small farmers, lacking the resources needed to engage in the new forms of agriculture and unwilling to become dependents of great landowners, moved to the urban center to become traders, artisans, or hired laborers. This change dissolved ancient family ties, weakened the control of aristocratic clan leaders over the populace, and thrust upon public authorities new burdens in controlling socially displaced groups.

Changing economic and social structures created pressures for political change. In general, aristocratic regimes in each *polis* tried to relieve mounting tensions by instituting "reforms" that did not require surrender of their monopoly on power. They enacted written codes of law that defined more precisely the rights and responsibilities of all citizens and that limited aristocratic dominance over the administration of justice. They granted relief to debtors and protection to small farmers. They devised policies that sought to gain trading advantages for their city-state. They sponsored projects that improved the public facilities of the *polis*. In these "reforms" the aristocrats were motivated in part by self-interest, but they also were moved by a realization that steps must be taken to retain the allegiance and the services of artisans, soldiers, sailors, shopkeepers, and farmers who increasingly made vital contributions to the welfare of the *polis*.

As important as they were in strengthening the *polis*, these "reforms" were not sufficient in many city-states to maintain stability. The growing attachment of individuals of all social levels to the city-state generated demands for greater political participation than the aristocratic masters were willing to grant. Usually force was required to break the nobles' monopoly on power. In many city-states the assault on aristocratic power was spearheaded by individual leaders called *tyrants* by the Greeks. Often of noble origin and ambitious for personal power, these charismatic figures seized control over the *polis* by force and ruled illegally, sometimes with support from the *hoplites* who dominated the military establishment in many city-states. The typical tyrant made no effort to change existing political structure; rather, each sought to dominate it by filling the council and the magistracies with loyal political followers. Once in power the tyrant launched policies that were popular with the common people, especially those dependent on trade and industry. Measures were taken to depose wealthy, highborn nobles from power, to tax their wealth, and to deprive them of their land, which was redistributed to small farmers. Policies pleasing to nonaristocratic elements in society were pursued, including measures to increase trade and industry, huge expenditures on beautification of the city, and more equitable administration of the law.

The duration of tyranny was relatively brief in most city-states, often lasting only during the lifetime of the first tyrant. Since tyrants had seized power illegally, their regimes depended on their individual talents and their popularity. Eventually, the aristocrats who had been their chief victims took the lead in unseating them and in restoring "legitimate" government. But these aristocrats were unable to reestablish their traditional monopoly based on landownership and kinship ties. In those city-states where aristocratic control continued after the overthrow of tyranny, the ruling element was greatly expanded to include men of wealth but without noble heritage. In some cities that had avoided tyranny, leaders of the old nobility understood the course of affairs well enough to open noble ranks and political power to a wider circle. In many city-states the end of tyranny was accompanied by radical changes in the political system that allowed the total citizen body to take control of civic affairs. With all citizens entitled to participate in government, the last knot that would bind them to the *polis* was tied.

4. ATHENS

The history of Athens during the Archaic Age provides a case study illustrating the evolution of a democratic *polis*. During the Mycenaean Age, Athens was a prominent fortress center exercising control over the surrounding area, called Attica. The general decline occurring over most of the Aegean world during the Dark Age resulted in the emergence in Attica of a number of small agricultural villages led by local tribal leaders. Sometime during the early Archaic Age under circumstances still not well understood, these villages coalesced into a single political entity centering on Athens to constitute an embryo *polis* embracing about a thousand square miles—the largest city-state in ancient Greece except for Sparta. The emerging *polis* was ruled by an hereditary king assisted by a council of clan heads called the *Areopagus* and a popular assembly called the *ecclesia*. For political and military purposes, the citizen body was grouped into four tribes, each composed of brotherhoods (called *phratries*, from whence is derived our word *fraternity*), which in turn were made up of several clans. Citizenship was established by admission to a brotherhood and depended on ties with clans. As a consequence, kinship ties played a crucial role in society.

About 750 B.C. monarchy was abolished and an official, called an *archon*, was elected annually to serve as head of the *polis*. Within a short time other archons were established, including a military leader (*polemarch*) and several judges. These magistrates, nine in number, were elected by the *ecclesia*, but only wealthy men of noble birth were eligible. The real power rested in the Areopagus, composed of aristocratic ex-archons who, upon completion of their terms as elective officials, automatically entered lifetime membership in the Areopagus. Combining their political position with their control over the clan structure, this narrow circle of aristocrats completely dominated Athenian life for two centuries after 750 B.C.

However, during those centuries the Athenians experienced mounting tensions, rooted primarily in the deterioration of the economic and social position of small farmers. Under pressures of a growing population, competition for limited land, and increasing emphasis in agricultural pro-

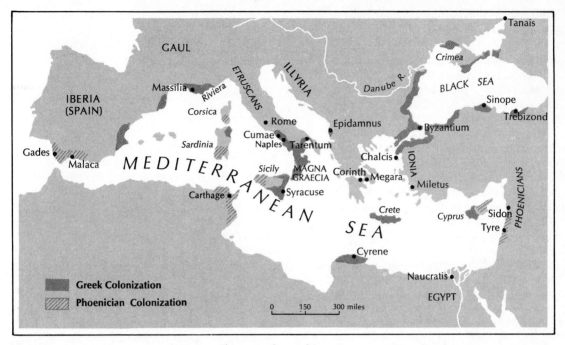

Map 4.2   GREEK COLONIES ABOUT 500 B.C. This map shows the major areas of Greek colonization during the period 800–500 B.C. The location of these settlements make it clear that the Greeks were in a position to dominate much of Mediterranean trade by 500 B.C. Their main rivals were Carthage, originally founded by the Phoenicians, and the Etruscans.

duction on olives and livestock, many of them became debtors obligated to turn over a sizable portion of their crops to their noble creditors as debt payment; some were eventually enslaved because they could not pay what they owed. Athens was slow to seek overseas colonies but ultimately directed its efforts toward the Hellespont and Black Sea areas, suggesting that the city suffered serious food shortage. Toward the end of the seventh century B.C. trade and industry began to expand, creating new economic interests not always satisfied with the policies of the dominant aristocrats whose interests were primarily agricultural.

Ultimately, the ruling aristocracy responded to these pressures by introducing reforms. Perhaps they were prodded in this direction by an aborted attempt in 632 B.C. to establish a tyranny. Also by the seventh century Athens had developed a *hoplite* army that brought a wider circle of citizens into a key role in society. In 621 B.C. a reformer

named Draco drew up the first written code of law, harsh in its details but significant because it curtailed the power of aristocratic judges and family heads to administer justice in their own interests.

Shortly after, there appeared a more significant reformer, Solon, who was elected archon about 594 B.C. Although an aristocrat, Solon was a man of broad vision and strong patriotism whose concern for injustice in Athens is reflected in surviving fragments of his poetry. Central to Solon's program was his effort to aid the poor and oppressed by a "shaking off of burdens." He struck down the ancient debt laws that permitted landlords to extract exorbitant rents from small farmers who fell into debt and slavery. Many who had fallen into bondage were freed. However, while Solon assured personal freedom to those victimized by debt, he did not return their lost land. He apparently realized that Athens could not remain a city-state totally dependent on agriculture. Thus, he took steps to promote new forms of agriculture, notably olive oil production, which would provide products for export. He was especially concerned with encouraging the growth of trade and industry as a means of providing new opportunities for displaced farmers. Particularly important was his encouragement of the immigration of foreign artisans with skills to upgrade the quality of Athenian manufactured goods and with the ability to teach those skills to Athenians.

Keenly aware of aristrocratic abuse of power, Solon introduced political changes designed to curb such abuses; however, these changes were not intended to deprive the aristocrats of dominance in Athens. As a means of limiting the power exercised by aristocratic families through their domination of the brotherhoods, he reorganized the entire citizen population into four classes, each defined in terms of income derived from land. This classification system greatly weakened the grip of the clans over society by allowing one's political role to be defined without reference to family connections. Eligibility for the chief elective offices—from which individuals passed to life membership in the Areopagus—was confined to the two upper wealth groups, but under the new system involvement in the direction of the *polis* was no longer restricted to the highborn. Solon extensively revised Draco's law code to broaden public control over the administration of justice. He also sought to curb abuses in the administration of justice by making the *Heliaea* instead of the Areopagus the final court of appeal. The *Heliaea* was a large panel of citizens drawn by lot from the membership of the *ecclesia* to serve as a court. The new powers bestowed on it by Solon permitted the citizen body to correct judicial inequities perpetrated in the tribal and brotherhood courts, which were totally controlled by noble family heads. While Solon was certainly no democrat, taken together the changes he introduced marked an important step in breaking aristocratic monopoly of power and expanding the role of the citizen body in public affairs.

Solon's reforms failed to resolve the tensions in Athenian society. The aristocrats split into factions competing fiercely for control of the state. The small farmers who had been given freedom by Solon but no land continued to be depressed and uprooted by changing patterns in agriculture. The growing numbers of merchants and artisans clamored for a larger voice in political decisions affecting economic life. The combined force of these discontented elements paved the way for tyranny in Athens.

Athens' first tyrant was an ambitious nobleman, Pisistratus, who after two unsuccessful attempts finally seized control in 546 B.C. with the help of mercenary troops paid out of his own wealth and the contributions of foreign city-states hostile toward Athens. He held power until his death in 527 B.C., and his sons continued his regime until 510 B.C. Pisistratus and his sons made no changes in the constitutional structure of Athens. They sustained their power by controlling the election of archons, which in turn gave them a powerful hold on the Areopagus. They used harsh means, including confiscation of property and exile, to cow the powerful aristocratic families. Like the policy of all Greek tyrants, their major policy was directed toward building a popular following, chiefly among the small farmers and the emerging merchant and artisan groups. They provided jobs by sponsoring public works projects, promoted Athenian commercial and manufacturing interests by an aggressive foreign policy, tried to ensure an equitable administration of justice, and promoted civic religious life (see Figure 4.2). Their policies increased Athens' wealth and expanded the number of citizens whose welfare depended on the well-being of the entire *polis*.

Despite its broad appeal and its role in promoting the advance of Athens as a leading city-state, tyranny marked only a temporary chapter in Athenian history. Under Pisistratus' sons the regime grew more arbitrary and oppressive. Finally, a coalition of aristocratic families with the support of Spartan military forces drove Hippias into exile in Persia in 510 B.C. Although some of the noble victors hoped to reestablish an aristocratic monopoly on power, their dreams were dashed by another noble faction, led by Cleisthenes, which turned to the citizenry for support of reforms aimed at broadening citizen participation in political life as a means of restoring order.

Assuming leadership in 508 B.C., Cleisthenes took the initiative in instituting basic structural

FIGURE 4.2 Greek Civic Religion   An important part of Greek civic life involved public religious ceremonies, the chief of which was the sacrifice of animals. This pottery painting shows Athenians sacrificing to Apollo, whose statue is shown on the right. The priest is placing the animal parts due the god on the bloodstained altar, while the good meat from the sacrificial animal is held on a spit by a youth; it will be cooked and enjoyed by the sacrificers. The scene reflects the familiarity felt by the Greeks toward their deities. (Museum für Vor und Frühgeschichte, Frankfurt)

changes in the political system. He abolished the political functions of the ancient clans, brotherhoods, and tribes, although he left them certain religious and social roles. To replace the kinship-dominated system, he divided Attica into territorial units, called *demes*. All free males living in a *deme* were registered as hereditary citizens, regardless of family connections. The *demes*, perhaps totaling about one hundred fifty, were grouped together to form thirty second-level organizations, called *trittyes*. Three *trittyes* were then combined to create a *tribe*, of which there was a total of ten. In arranging this basic structure, Cleisthenes provided an ingenious twist aimed at overcoming re-

gionalism and reconciling special economic interests. During the sixth century Attica had become divided into three distinct geographical regions, each with special economic interests: the hill or interior country, dominated by poor farmers; the plain, where the land was most fertile and the great noble families were entrenched; and the shore or city, where merchants, artisans, and urban laborers predominated. Cleisthenes created ten *trittyes* in each of these regions. In shaping the ten tribes, he included one *trittys* from each region in each tribe. As a consequence, each tribe contained a cross section of the entire population, requiring that conflicting interests be conciliated before each tribe could determine its position on major issues affecting the entire *polis*. Each *deme* and tribe was a political unit in its own right, with elected officials, courts, shrines, taxes, and military forces. Each offered wide opportunity for direct participation by the citizenry in local affairs.

Cleisthenes then rearranged the main organs of government to fit the new tribal organization. A Council of Five Hundred, composed of fifty citizens selected by lot from each tribe for an annual term, was created as a prime agency in shaping political life of the *polis*. No one could serve on this council more than twice in a lifetime, thus ensuring that many citizens had an opportunity to participate in this all-important body. The Council of Five Hundred was in essence a steering committee for the citizen body, meeting frequently to supervise many aspects of the administration of the city and to prepare an agenda of issues to be presented to the *ecclesia*, which had the ultimate authority in the government. Made up of all male citizens over eighteen years of age voting by tribe, this body met at least once a month to hear debate on issues presented by the Council of Five Hundred and to vote on a course of action. The citizens were further involved in governing the city by their participation in the popular court, the *Heliaea*, which played an increasing role in the administration of justice. Cleisthenes did not change the Areopagus, although it now lacked the authority to guide crucial decisions, and the elected archons remained the executive officers of the *polis*. The magistrates were elected by the *ecclesia* and were still usually from the wealthy, aristocratic segment of the population, but now they had to win the support of the entire citizen body. Perhaps it was Cleisthenes who introduced a powerful instrument for controlling elective officials and overly ambitious aristocrats by establishing the practice of *ostracism*, through which a majority of the *ecclesia* could declare an individual dangerous to the state and order that person into exile for ten years.

Although Cleisthenes' reforms laid the basis for democratic government in Athens, nearly fifty years were required before the citizenry became accustomed to the full exercise of its power. During that time the aristocratic families continued to dominate the *polis*. Not until the time of Pericles,

the chief political figure from 461 to 429 B.C., did Athenian democracy reach full bloom. During that interval changes were made to encourage greater participation. The chief executive offices were increasingly filled by lot, expanding the chances of ordinary citizens to hold high office. The number of magistrates increased steadily, again allowing a larger number of citizens to take part in public life. Especially significant was the establishment shortly after 500 B.C. of a new elective official, called general (*strategos*), from each tribe to constitute a group of ten military leaders who quickly assumed a key role in directing public affairs. In contrast with the archons, who were eligible for only a one-year term, the generals could be elected year after year if they could command sufficient votes in their tribes. Property qualifications for officeholding tended to disappear. The bastion of aristocratic power, the Areopagus, was gradually stripped of its power. A crucial step in the development of democracy came when Pericles introduced public payment for service in the Council of Five Hundred, the *Heliaea*, the elected magistracies, and the army and navy. This step enabled ordinary citizens to serve the *polis* without sacrificing their livelihood. Gradually, the Council of Five Hundred, the *ecclesia*, and the *Heliaea*, all controlled by the citizens, took over direction of public affairs. Increasingly, they were encouraged to do so by leaders such as Pericles, an aristocrat by birth and wealth who felt no fear in entrusting the final political decisions of Athens to the citizens and who sought to convince them that public life was a dignified, responsible, and rewarding activity owed by all who enjoyed the benefit of living in Athens.

In discussing the nature of democracy in Athens or any other *polis*, we must make one important reservation. Participation in political life was confined to males descended from those enrolled as members of a *deme* in the time of Cleisthenes. Women did not qualify for participation in political life in the *polis*. Neither did large numbers of foreigners, called *metics*, or slaves. In the fifth century B.C. the citizen population of Athens was about forty-five thousand; the entire population of Attica was probably about three hundred fifty thousand. Thus, a minority ruled the democratic Athenian *polis*.

5. SPARTA

The history of another important city-state, Sparta, illustrates a different pattern of development of the *polis* in the Greek world.

Sparta emerged as a city-state during the ninth century B.C. as a result of the coalition of several small agricultural villages clustered around the site of the city. After this union the Spartans slowly established control over an area in the southern Peloponnesus known as Laconia, creating a base for future Spartan prominence. Until about 750 B.C. Sparta's development followed a pattern that differed little from most other city-states during the Archaic Age. But then a significant change began to occur that gave Spartan society a unique character. When the Spartans began to feel the economic stresses that gripped most of the Aegean world in the Archaic Age, their solution was to conquer their neighbors and force them to support Spartan society.

Especially crucial was the conquest of Messenia, a fertile agricultural region west of Sparta. The First Messenian War (ca. 720 B.C.) ended in the annexation of Messenia, whose inhabitants were made servile dependents of Sparta forced to labor as tillers of the soil to support their conquerors. In about 640 B.C. the Messenians revolted, with the encouragement of some of Sparta's enemies in the Peloponnesus. After a desperate struggle lasting twenty years, the revolt was suppressed. During the long struggle with Messenia, which tested the military resources of Sparta to the limit, Spartan society was radically restructured so as to ensure military strength sufficient to maintain control over the city-state's subjects. These reforms were attributed to a single lawgiver, Lycurgus, but probably were carried out by several leaders over several decades in the late seventh and sixth centuries B.C.

A fundamental feature of the new order was the division of the population into rigidly defined classes, each with specific responsibilities in the service of the state. Most important were the *Spartans*, a relatively small portion of the total population who were the real citizens. Numbering about ten thousand males considered to be social equals, the Spartans were required to devote their lives to military service in the interest of exerting control over other elements in the population and defending Sparta against outside enemies. The Lycurgan system prescribed a strict regimen for this group. At birth each male child of a Spartan citizen was inspected for physical fitness. If defective, the state ordered death by exposure. If allowed to live, the child remained with his mother until he was seven. Then he joined other males in barracks life, where all were subjected to rigorous military training until they were twenty. At twenty the Spartan became a regular soldier. He was assigned a piece of state land along with laborers to farm it as a source of his livelihood. He could marry after twenty, but he was not permitted to establish his own household until thirty, when he became an "equal" with full rights to participate in the political life of the *polis*. During these long formative years the social life of each Spartan found its focus in a mess group, a small circle of military companions who shared barracks life and contributed payments derived from their state-assigned land allocations to provide common meals. The values and the relationships formed in these mess groups dominated the life of each male Spartan. All Spartans were required to perform military service until they were sixty years of age. Spartan females were likewise rigorously trained to become wives and mothers. Their training emphasized physical fitness and the development of skills in the household arts. As wives, they often played an important role in managing the family economic resources, but there was no place for them in political life.

A second element of the population of Sparta was made of *perioeci*, often living in towns scattered across Spartan territory. This group represented descendants of peoples subjected by the Spartans when they asserted mastery over Laconia. Although they were required to render military service and pay taxes, they were not subjected to the training regimen required of full Spartans. They served the state chiefly as artisans and traders. They enjoyed some degree of control over local town affairs but were not permitted to take part in the governance of the entire *polis*.

Finally, there were the *helots*, state slaves required to spend their lives as agricultural laborers or household servants toiling to support the full

Spartan citizens who had no occupation except soldiering. The helots were allowed to maintain family life and were permitted to keep enough of what they produced to maintain a simple level of life. However, they were treated brutally by the Spartans, apparently to ensure their service as the mainstay of the Spartan economy. The fear of helot revolt remained a constant factor in Spartan life, so much so that the Spartan state declared war on the helots every year, permitting the killing of a suspected helot troublemaker on the spot. Part of the military training of Spartan youths involved seeking out and murdering allegedly dangerous helots.

This rigid social order was held in place by a governmental system that Lycurgus was credited with shaping but that was derived in large part from earlier political institutions. The government was formally headed by two kings, but the actual power of the co-kings was slight unless they were able to distinguish themselves as military leaders. Real power rested with the *gerousia*, a council made up of the two kings and twenty-eight other men over sixty elected to serve for life. This body formulated all legislation, judged the most important cases, and acted as an advisory body in the administration of the state. Its decisions were subject to approval by an assembly made up of all male Spartans over thirty. Theoretically, the assembly could repudiate any proposed policy, but usually its members, trained from childhood to obey orders, were inclined to accept direction from superiors. The execution of laws was entrusted to a board of five *ephors*, elected annually by the assembly, which conducted foreign affairs, supervised military training, policed the helots, controlled state finances, and organized military operations. When supported by the *gerousia*, the *ephors* were able to exercise almost complete control over Spartan political life, despite the fact that the male citizens possessed the power to check them. In essence, Sparta was ruled by an oligarchy of military commanders.

The Spartan political and social system proved effective. Sparta enjoyed an internal stability that was envied by many other Greeks, and the dedication of Spartan citizens to the service of their *polis* was often praised. While the system was not conducive to intellectual and cultural activities, it made Sparta a dominant force in Greek intercity affairs. By 500 B.C. Sparta had forced most of the other city-states in the Peloponnesus to join the Peloponnesian League, whose members followed Spartan leadership in foreign affairs. The combined forces of Sparta and its allies allowed Sparta to play a major role in Greek history after 500 B.C.

6. THE CHARACTER OF THE *POLIS*

To gain a complete understanding of the nature of the Greek *polis*, one would have to study the institutions of several hundred other city-states that had been formed by 500 B.C., each of which believed its institutions to be as typically "Greek" as those of Athens and Sparta. Such a wide-ranging study would certainly highlight variety in the structure of Greek city-states, but it would also reveal certain shared characteristics of the *polis*.

Greek city-states were all small entities within which residents could interact intimately. In each *polis* life focused on an urban center, where were concentrated political, economic, religious, and cultural activities bearing directly on the lives of all. Each made citizenship a distinctive and precious condition of life. In some fashion or other, citizenship involved those who held it—almost exclusively males with the proper family pedigree—directly and actively in civic life. Such involvement was at once a great privilege and a grave responsibility. As Pericles allegedly put it, "We alone regard a man who takes no interest in public affairs, not as harmless, but as a useless character." The giving of one's talent in the service of the *polis* made the citizen a complete human, drawing of the *polis* made the citizen a complete human, drawing each out of clan, calling, and class into participation in a community enterprise. Active involvement nourished patriotism, a fierce pride in and love for the *polis*. Every *polis* was thus a pressure chamber compelling citizens to discover and exercise their talents in the interests of something larger, more enduring, and more splendid than themselves. As such, the *polis* nourished an intensity of life and a level of human achievement seldom witnessed in the human experience and it bred in each citizen a sense of superiority over non-citizens and foreigners that boded trouble for Greek society.

SUGGESTED READING

General Surveys of Greek History

John V. A. Fine, *The Ancient Greeks: A Critical History* (1983).

M. G. L. Hammond, *A History of Greece to 322 B.C.*, 3rd ed. (1986).

Both of these works will provide a full treatment of Greek history down to the time of the Macedonian conquest.

Early Greece to 500 B.C.

John Chadwick, *The Mycenaean World* (1976). An excellent treatment that reflects the best of recent scholarship.

R. J. Hopper, *The Early Greeks* (1976).

Oswyn Murray, *Early Greece* (1980).

Anthony Snodgrass, *Archaic Greece. The Age of Experiment* (1980).

M. I. Finley, *Early Greece: The Bronze and Archaic Ages*, new ed. (1981).

Any of the above four titles will provide an excellent treatment of a period in Greek history that has received significant new interpretations in recent times.

L. H. Jeffery, *Archaic Greece: The City States c. 700–500 B.C.* (1976). Valuable for the attention paid to city-states other than Athens and Sparta.

Chester G. Starr, *Individual and Community. The Rise of the Polis 800–500 B.C.* (1986). A masterful treatment of the forces that produced the *polis*.

A. H. M. Jones, *Athenian Democracy* (1958). This work will provide the reader with a good grasp of how Athenian democracy worked.

W. G. Forrest, *History of Sparta, 950–192 B.C.*, 2nd ed. (1980).

J. T. Hooker, *The Ancient Spartans* (1980).

Two very perceptive treatments of Spartan history.

Economic and Social History

Chester G. Starr, *The Economic and Social Growth of Early Greece, 800–500 B.C.* (1977).

M. M. Austin and P. Vidal-Naquet, *Economic and Social History of Ancient Greece: An Interpretation* (1977).

Either of these two works will provide invaluable information on all aspects of Greek economy. The Austin–Vidal-Naquet work includes original documents illustrating economic development.

John Boardman, *The Greeks Overseas*, rev. ed. (1982). An excellent treatment of a crucial aspect of Greek development.

Sources

Homer, *Iliad and Odyssey* (many translations; among the best are those by Richard Lattimore). Two works that played an essential role in shaping the Greek civic mentality.

Hesiod, *Works and Days*, trans. Richard Lattimore (1959). A picture by a contemporary of the problems that caused stress in the Greek world about 700 B.C.

CHAPTER 5

War, Politics, and the Failure of the Greek City-State Polity

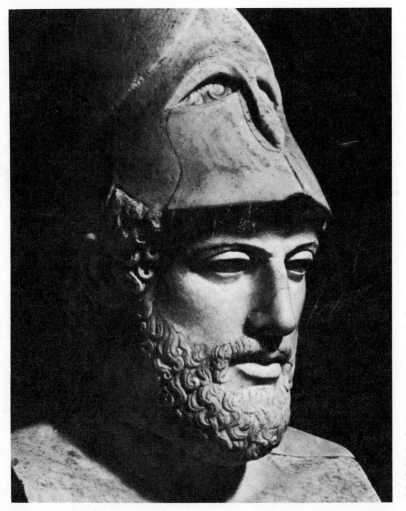

FIGURE 5.1 **Pericles** This statue portrays Pericles under whose leadership the city-state of Athens reached the peak of its power politically, economically and culturally. The key to Pericles' fame rests largely in the faith he had in the Athenian citizen body to decide its own destiny democratically. The artist captures the intelligence, dignity, and political sagacity for which Pericles was honored. (Museo Vaticano/Alinari)

Driven by the energies unleashed in its many city-states, the Greek world enjoyed a Golden Age during the fifth and early fourth centuries B.C. Although each individual *polis* continued to promote the internal well-being of its citizens, another issue grew ever more critical: the problem of relationships among the fiercely patriotic communities, each struggling to strengthen and enrich itself. At the beginning of the fifth century, a threat from the outside demonstrated the need for cooperation, but progressively the city-states surrendered to their parochialism and became embroiled in destructive intercity struggles. In the end they so weakened themselves that they fell easy victims to a powerful external foe.

1. THE PERSIAN WARS, 490–479 B.C.

Prior to 500 B.C. the Greek city-states often warred against one another, but these wars were generally on a limited scale. Nor did any major outsiders threaten the Greeks during the Archaic Age. In fact, there were significant developments promoting cooperation and interdependence among the Greeks. Their common language encouraged a shared culture. Expanding commerce linked the city-states together. Religion was an especially important force promoting pan-Hellenism. It provided a common set of deities, pan-Hellenic festivals—such as the Olympic Games, which drew Greeks together for worship, athletic competitions, and cultural performances honoring their gods and goddesses—and shared shrines, such as the Delphic oracle, where all Greeks came to seek divine guidance. Some progress had even been made in establishing political federations allowing city-states to collaborate without surrendering their autonomy; a prime example was the Peloponnesian League.

The practical need for strong pan-Hellenism was dramatically posed at the beginning of the fifth century by the threat of the Persian Empire. Persian expansion beginning about 550 B.C. had resulted in the conquest of the Lydian kingdom and the subjugation of the Greek city-states of Asia Minor. Although Persian rule was not particularly harsh, the Ionian city-states hated paying tribute and submitting to "tyrants" imposed on them by the Persians. The Persian threat to the entire Greek world increased when Darius invaded Europe in 512 B.C. and established a satrapy in Thrace. Tensions mounted after 499 B.C. as a consequence of a major revolt of the Ionian Greeks. The rebels appealed to their fellow Greeks on the mainland and received support from Athens and Eritrea. Darius eventually crushed the revolt. He apparently decided that Greece must be conquered, moved probably by fear of future Greek intervention in Persian affairs and by ambition to expand his already huge empire. Political scheming among factions within many Greek city-states who saw the Persians as potential allies in the struggles for power and the neutrality proclaimed by several key city-states encouraged Darius to think that the Greek world was ready for conquest.

In 490 B.C. Darius made his move (see Map 5.1 for the Persian campaigns). He sent a fleet and a substantial army across the Aegean, ostensibly to punish Athens and Eritrea for their involvement in the rebellion of the Ionians. After destroying Eritrea, the Persian army landed in eastern Attica, near Marathon. The Greek world had made almost no preparations for the Persian onslaught. Standing alone, the Athenians seemed doomed. But they chose to resist, sending an army to challenge the Persians. Although outnumbered, the Athenian *hoplites*, brilliantly led by Miltiades, defeated the Persians and forced the survivors back to their ships. Miltiades marched his victorious army back to Athens and stood ready to defend the city when the Persian fleet from Marathon appeared there. The Persians elected to return to Asia Minor. Athens celebrated a new breed of heroes whose feats at Marathon rivaled those of the heroes celebrated by Homer.

The Persians were not ready to admit defeat. Although a new attack was delayed ten years by internal troubles, Darius' successor, Xerxes I, was ready by 480 B.C. to mount another assault. In the interval the Greeks made better preparations. In 481 B.C. Sparta took the leadership in organizing a Hellenic League made up of thirty-one city-states willing to pool their military and naval forces under Spartan commanders. Greek armed strength, based on the superb Spartan army, was greatly enhanced by a crucial decision made by Athens. A farsighted leader named Themistocles persuaded the Athenian citizenry to use the income from silver mines recently discovered in Attica to fund a major increase in the Athenian navy, which the Athenians pledged to the support of the Hellenic League. Despite this show of unity, many city-states remained neutral.

Early in 480 B.C. Xerxes began his attack. He chose to trust the Persian cause to a carefully coordinated attack by a huge land army to be supplied by a huge navy. He moved his army across the Hellespont into Europe and advanced slowly around the northern Aegean coast and then southward toward the centers of Greek strength. The Hellenic League made its first stand at Thermopylae, where a narrow pass provided the Greek army a good place to check the huge Persian force and where the narrow sea lanes between the mainland and the island of Euboea could be easily blocked to prevent the Persian fleet from supplying the army. Despite their success in defeating the Persian fleet and the heroic resistance of a Spartan detachment led by King Leonidas, the Greeks were unable to hold at Thermopylae. Having broken through the Greek defenses at Thermopylae, the Persians flooded into central Greece. Athens was captured and burned, although most of its citizens fled to safety.

At this critical point, Themistocles exercised a decisive influence on the course of the war. There was strong pressure in the council of the Hellenic League to withdraw the armies to the Peloponnesus and the fleet to the Gulf of Corinth. Convinced that the fate of the Greeks would be decided at sea, Themistocles combined persuasion with threats of Athens' withdrawal to convince the League to face the Persians in the waters off Attica. In late September 480 B.C., he enticed the Persians into a decisive engagement in the narrow waters between Attica and the island of Salamis. Caught where they could not use their superior naval strength and outmaneuvered by the Greek fleet, the Persians suffered a shattering defeat. Since winter was approaching, Xerxes ordered his fleet back to its bases in Asia Minor and the withdrawal of his army to northern Greece.

In the spring of 479 B.C. Xerxes renewed the campaign by ordering his army southward. The Hellenic League put a major army in the field, anchored by Spartan troops. This force met the Persians at Plataea. Once again the Greek *hoplites* and their phalanx formation proved superior and imposed a major defeat on the larger Persian army. While these events were unfolding, the fleet of the Hellenic League sailed boldly across the Aegean and destroyed the main Persian fleet at Mycale, a victory that triggered a revolt among the Greek city-states of Asia Minor. Xerxes had no choice but to recall his armies from Europe. The jubilant Greeks had saved themselves from what many thought was sure defeat and loss of their independence.

While the Greeks of the Aegean world were throwing back the Persian threat, their fellow Greeks in the West were winning a victory hardly less significant. The struggle here centered on Sicily, where Carthage, a powerful maritime state, was attempting to expand its commercial empire by subduing the Sicilian Greeks. A coalition of Greek city-states, led by Gelon, tyrant of Syracuse, inflicted a decisive defeat on the Carthaginians at the battle of Himera in 480 B.C., ensuring the continued independence of the Greek city-states in Magna Graecia.

2. THE DELIAN LEAGUE AND THE ATHENIAN EMPIRE

Although the Greeks had won a stunning victory in 480–479 B.C., the Persian Empire remained a major power and a real threat. This danger kept alive the spirit of unity among the Greeks. The situation in 479 B.C. demanded that they take the offensive. Leadership for this undertaking passed into new hands. The Spartans, who had led the Hellenic League in the critical days of 480 and 479 B.C., were unwilling to commit their resources to projects remote from the Peloponnesus. Athens now took the lead in summoning a meeting of Greek cities on the island of Delos in 478 B.C. It was quickly agreed to form the Delian League to continue the war against Persia. Policy decisions were to be made by an assembly of League representatives meeting annually; each member city-state would have one vote. Each member pledged to contribute ships and money according to its

Map 5.1 **THE PERSIAN WARS** The map shows the locations of the crucial engagements between the Greeks and the Persians in the campaigns of 490 B.C. and 480–479 B.C. The inset, showing the long route taken by Xerxes in 480 B.C., may suggest the challenge faced by the Persians in their bid to conquer the Greeks, for they had to engage the Greeks in a constricted setting where the Greeks could make the best use of their resources.

abilities. Athens was charged with making the initial assessments and with commanding the League's forces. No city-state would be required to surrender sovereign control over its internal affairs, thus protecting the principle of autonomy.

The League quickly swung into action. An Athenian, Cimon, was placed in command of its joint forces, which enjoyed immediate success. Within fifteen years, all the Greek city-states in Asia Minor had been freed of Persian rule, while the Aegean and the Hellespont area were cleared of Persian naval power. Athens was obviously the most powerful member of the League, but its leaders conducted themselves with marked restraint in relationships with other members. Cimon's policy was conciliatory even toward nonmembers such as Sparta.

This situation was not destined to last, and Athens was largely responsible for the change. As the danger from Persia receded, some members of the Delian League sought to reduce their contributions and even to withdraw. Athens was unwilling to allow the dissolution of the League. Increasingly, Athenian leaders and citizens came to realize that the League's naval force could be turned to commercial ends that would enrich Athens. Beginning about 465 B.C. Athens began to initiate policies aimed at converting the voluntary Delian League into an empire dominated by Athens, a policy that posed a threat to a basic Greek institution: the autonomous *polis.*

The emergence of Athenian imperialism coincided with the final establishment of democracy in Athens. Pericles was the architect of both developments (see Figure 5.1). From his emergence as leader in Athens in 461 B.C. until his death in 429 B.C., Pericles placed the destiny of the city in the hands of his fellow citizens and constantly urged them to support policies that would ensure Athenian dominance in Greece. They responded by supporting with enthusiasm policies that enhanced Athens' dominance, partly because that course enriched the city-state and partly because imperialism fed the Athenians' pride in the greatness of their *polis.* Emboldened by such support, Pericles launched a two-pronged drive to expand Athenian influence. On the Greek mainland he used every device possible to draw more city-states into the Delian League. He supported re-

volts against nondemocratic governments, tried to entice the members of the Peloponnesian League to abandon Sparta, and used Athenian sea power to bottle up such trading powers as Corinth. Meanwhile, Pericles renewed the assault on Persia, carrying the struggle into the eastern Mediterranean. This effort utilized the money and the armed forces extracted from the Delian League with little regard for the wishes of its members.

This aggressive policy enjoyed considerable success, but eventually Pericles realized that Athens was overextending its power. In 454 B.C. an Athenian effort to liberate Egypt resulted in a major naval defeat, which encouraged revolt within the Delian League. The result was some kind of understanding with the Persians that each would respect the other's sphere of influence: Athens' control of the Aegean and the Greek city-states in Asia Minor and Persia's dominance of the eastern Mediterranean coastal area. Athenian aggressive actions on the Greek mainland raised repeated threats of Spartan retaliation so serious that Pericles finally agreed to the Thirty Years' Truce of 445 B.C. in which Athens agreed to halt its aggression against mainland Greek city-states, especially those belonging to the Peloponnesian League, and Sparta promised to recognize Athenian hegemony over the Delian League.

In the years following 445 B.C. the Athenians concentrated on tightening their control over the Delian League. Eventually about three hundred city-states ringing the Aegean were forced to accept Athenian domination. Athens continued to collect funds from these cities, although the Persian danger no longer existed. This "tribute" was used as Athens wished, chiefly to support the system of pay Pericles introduced for the vastly increased number of citizens who performed public service in Athens and to support the artists and writers who made Athens the "school of Hellas." Athens forced many League members to institute democratic governments resembling the Athenian system. The subject cities were compelled to accept the Athenian money system and Athenian weights and measures, thus ensuring that their economies would be subservient to that of Athens. Athenians were settled on lands confiscated from residents of subject city-states, a policy that relieved Athens of excess population and provided a convenient means of shaping internal affairs in dependent members of the Athenian Empire. By any standard Athens treated these formerly independent city-states as dependents and solely for the benefit of Athens.

The subject city-states benefited in some ways. They shared the fruits of increased commerce and the security resulting from enforced peace. Still, their hatred of Athens grew steadily, primarily for political reasons. Athens had usurped their most valuable possession, their right to exist as independent city-states. The mighty, enlightened democratic gem of Greek civilization had, in the eyes of most Greeks, become an oppressor. The proud, triumphant, even arrogant Athenians made no attempt to compensate for depriving their subjects of their independence. They were not permitted to become citizens of Athens, and they were denied any representation in the Athenian government. Some Athenians raised concerns about the destruction of the liberty of any *polis,* but the Athenian citizenry, aware that the economic welfare of Athens and its citizens depended on imperial power and proud of Athens' glory, overrode these voices. Their prideful, self-serving aggressiveness gradually generated an anti-Athenian feeling throughout much of the Greek world. People began to look toward Sparta as the champion of city-state independence. Such sentiments pointed toward a major clash pitting Greek against Greek and testing the viability of the one institution fundamental to Greek civilization: the *polis.*

3. THE PELOPONNESIAN WAR, 431–404 B.C.

Athens' aggressive efforts to expand its interests across the entire Greek world finally plunged the Greeks into the Peloponnesian War. Its outbreak in 431 B.C. resulted from Athenian actions that threatened the commercial interests of Corinth, an important ally of Sparta. Corinth convinced Sparta that Athens was violating the Thirty Years' Truce. The Spartans, increasingly concerned over the expansion of Athenian influence in mainland Greece, were ready to lead the Peloponnesian League and their other allies against the prideful city-state that threatened freedom in Greece. Athens was not unwilling to join the issue. Its large fleet and its huge financial resources derived from commerce and tribute appeared sufficient to offset the superior land forces of the Spartan alliance. Pericles was confident that Athens' enemies were incapable of effective action against the real source of Athenian power—the maritime empire (see Map 5.2 for the alignment of forces in 431 B.C.).

The first years of the war were indecisive. Athens refused to commit itself to a land war; Pericles persuaded the Athenians to withdraw within the city's impregnable walls while the fleet roamed the seas to hold together the empire and bring supplies and wealth to Athens. This strategy left the Spartan armies free to ravage the Attic countryside but unable to strike a telling blow either against Athens or its key imperial strongholds. Within a few years this pattern broke down. The Athenian population grew impatient, watching their beloved land ravaged, especially after a plague struck in 430 and 429 B.C., killing at least one-third of the cooped-up population, including Pericles. The restless populace demanded bolder military action. A militant democratic and imperialistic leader, Cleon, responded by leading Athenian armies outside Attica, especially into central Greece and western Peloponnesus, in an effort to wean away crucial Spartan allies. A resourceful Spartan leader, Brasidas, persuaded Sparta to use its military forces to encourage revolt among the subject cities of the Athenian Empire. Brasidas' activities concentrated on the northern Aegean, especially Chalcidice, posing a threat to Athens' route to vital food supplies around the Black Sea. However, before this new phase of the struggle reached a decisive point, both Cleon and Brasidas were killed in 422 B.C. in a battle for control of the key city of Amphipolis. Their deaths gave powerful peace elements in both camps a chance to end the war. In 421 B.C., Athens and Sparta agreed to a Fifty-Year Truce, which restored the situation to what it had been when the struggle began.

The uneasy peace settlement, which had addressed none of the basic issues, lasted only until 415 B.C. Again the Athenians were responsible for the renewal of hostilities. After the death of Pericles, Athenian political life became increasingly unstable. Afflicted by the burdens of war, the citizens were increasingly swayed by ambitious pol-

Map 5.2 GREECE, 431 B.C. This map identifies the members of the two camps engaged in the Peloponnesian War. Particularly noteworthy is the extent to which Athenian strength was concentrated in a circle of city-states under Athens' control ranging around the Aegean Sea, with Sparta's strength located around the outside of that circle.

iticians willing to promise anything in return for power. Such a figure was the flashy, unscrupulous Alcibiades. Playing upon the imperialistic sentiments so strong in Athens, he persuaded the citizenry to undertake a major expedition against the powerful city of Syracuse in Sicily, an important commercial rival of Athens. This ill-conceived venture, badly led by rival politicians, including Alcibiades who deserted to Sparta to avoid serious criminal charges, ended in a disastrous defeat for Athens in 413 B.C. Worse, the attack on Syracuse provoked Sparta and its allies to renew all-out war against Athens.

After 413 B.C. the fortunes of Athens declined steadily. Internal dissension, pitting prodemo-

cratic forces against a growing faction fearful of the consequences of unbridled democracy, hindered decisive action. The Spartans, brilliantly led by Lysander, mounted a powerful attack on Athenian sea power and a skillful campaign to encourage revolt among the city-states of the Athenian Empire. A decisive step in this campaign was the Spartan success in forming an alliance with Persia, whose wealth and naval power played a crucial role in undermining the Athenian Empire. Athens occasionally won an isolated victory, but the net continued to close around the doomed city-state. Finally in 404 B.C. Athens had to surrender. The victors forced Athens to tear down its walls, to destroy all but twelve ships of its once invincible fleet, and to submit to a government of oligarchs backed by a Spartan army stationed in Athens. Although these Thirty Tyrants, as the Athenians called them, were ousted in 403 B.C. and democratic government was restored, Athens would never recover its former power. And Athens was not the only victim of the Peloponnesian War. Its ravages impoverished many Greek city-states, created bitter rivalries among them, bred internal dissension within each *polis*, caused widespread disillusionment and pessimism, and renewed the threat of Persian domination. Thucydides, the historian of the Peloponnesian War, may have been right when he wrote, "No movement ever stirred Hellas more deeply than this [war]."

4. THE TWILIGHT OF THE WORLD OF CITY-STATES, 404–336 B.C.

The years following the Peloponnesian War marked a troubled time in the Greek world. Two interlocking issues dominated this period: the effort of a succession of leading city-states to establish hegemony over the Greeks and the struggle to sustain internal order and vitality within each *polis*. These issues combined to produce almost constant intercity warfare and bitter civil strife, which gradually sapped Greek strength.

In 404 B.C. Sparta appeared to be the predominant power in the Greek world. For the next thirty years it devoted its energies to asserting its hegemony. The key to Spartan policy was the imposition of oligarchic governments on any city-state that could be bullied into submission, including some of Sparta's old allies. This policy badly undermined Sparta's claim to be the defender of city-state independence. In fact, Sparta did not have the strength to control the Greek world. Its narrowly restricted citizen body was declining in numbers, and its rigid social system prevented Sparta from replenishing its citizens from the ranks of the *perioeci* and helots, who remained a constant threat to internal peace. In the final analysis, Sparta was reluctantly forced to depend on Persian assistance to maintain its hegemony at the cost of allowing the Persians to reestablish dominance over the Ionian Greeks. Growing fear and resentment against Sparta led

to the formation of an alliance led by Thebes. Under the brilliant generalship of Thebes' one great statesman, Epaminandos, this alliance smashed Sparta in a single battle in 371 B.C., a defeat that marked the end of Sparta's long history as a major Greek power.

After 371 B.C. Greek history was marked by a succession of claimants to hegemony. Thebes played an important role for a decade, but even with Persian help it was unable to dominate; its power was smashed in a decisive battle in 362 B.C. by an alliance formed by Athens. In the generation after Thebes' defeat Athens sought to reestablish a dominant position, but its efforts were constantly thwarted by rival city-states. All that resulted was a succession of petty wars that wasted human and material resources and asserted a constant strain on internal life in each *polis*. These internal struggles, usually centered on rivalry between democratic and aristocratic factions for control of political life and on issues involving the distribution of declining wealth in each city-state, were often marked by violence. Increasingly, mercenary forces led by ruthless and adventuresome commanders replaced citizen armies and navies; these professionals much preferred war to peace. Some Greeks were aware of the destructive cost of intercity war. They raised eloquent appeals for some kind of union that would curb it in order to create an environment that would allow city-states to restore internal stability. However, political pan-Hellenism was a lost cause. No Greek *polis* was willing to surrender any of its sovereignty to a superior organization—even in the interests of peace. And great philosophers such as Plato and Aristotle, both of whom lived during the fourth century, vigorously insisted that only the traditional self-defining *polis* was fit for the Greeks.

5. MACEDONIAN CONQUEST OF GREECE

Weakened by the incessant warfare and civic strife, the Greeks became increasingly ripe for conquest. The conqueror turned out to be Macedonia. The Macedonians had played only a minor role in Greek history before the fourth century B.C. Its diverse and unruly population long resisted efforts of Macedonian rulers to unify the kingdom. Although Greek influences had penetrated the area, the people remained backward. However, the situation changed rapidly under the rule of Philip II (359–336 B.C.). A gifted, ambitious ruler, Philip II was able to create a disciplined army and to impose an effective internal organization on his kingdom. Assured of a strong power base, Philip II turned his attention toward the Greek world, driven by an urge to gain access to the Aegean Sea and to bring his backward kingdom into closer contact with the Greek civilization he greatly admired.

The intrusion of Macedonian influence into Greece involved a complex play of political forces. Warring Greek city-states could not resist seeking Philip's support. Philip often intrigued in Greek affairs to create opportunities for his involvement. His skilled diplomacy and his adroit use of military force gave him an increasingly decisive role in Greece. Although many warned of the Macedonian "menace," the Greeks were seldom able to join forces to resist. In fact, some Greeks favored Macedonian dominance as a solution for incessant warfare. Eventually Athens, moved both by fear of Macedonian power and by dreams of using the Macedonian threat as a means of re-creating an Athenian Empire, became the focal point of resistance. Under the leadership of the eloquent Demosthenes, always ready with a speech warning his fellow Athenian citizens of the Macedonian danger and damning those in Athens and elsewhere who advocated peace with Macedonia, Athens was able to form a loosely constituted league dedicated to resistance to Macedonian advances into Greece. Although this alliance occasionally offered assistance to those resisting Macedonian influence, such help was usually too little. Philip finally forced the Athenian alliance to commit itself to battle at Chaeronea in 338 B.C., which ended in a crushing defeat that left all of Greece at Philip's mercy.

Philip treated the vanquished Greeks with mildness, but he did act to end the old order. Soon after his victory he called a meeting of all Greek city-states at which they agreed to form the League of Corinth dedicated to the establishment of a common peace. Members of the League were theoretically entitled to independence, but crucial restrictions were imposed on them. No city-state was to make war on another, to interfere with freedom of the seas, or to change its form of government. Such prohibitions obviously greatly restricted the ancient freedom of the *polis*. The League was to be governed by a council of representatives from each city-state, which would meet regularly and decide League actions to keep peace. Each member was obliged to contribute according to its means to a common military force charged with imposing peace. Macedonia was not a member of the League, but Philip did require that the League sign a treaty of alliance with Macedonia. Philip was also designated as *hegemon* (military commander) of the League, thus putting himself in a position to control its activities. At a meeting of the League council in 337 B.C. Philip proposed that its first undertaking should be joining its forces with Macedonia in a war against Persia, but his assassination in 336 B.C. denied him an opportunity to direct this campaign against an ancient foe of the Greeks. Nevertheless, Philip's statesmanship had achieved a notable end: In the League of Corinth he had provided an instrument under Greek control that would allow the warring city-states to impose peace on themselves without sacrificing completely their sovereignty while enjoying the protection of the potent Macedonian army against outsiders.

SUGGESTED READING

Fifth- and Fourth-Century Greece

Simon Hornblower, *The Greek World, 479–323 B.C.* (1983).

J. K. Davies, *Democracy and Classical Greece* (1978).

Either of these two studies will provide a full treatment of Greek history during the fifth and fourth centuries B.C.

A. R. Burn, *Persia and the Greeks: The Defense of the West, c. 546–478 B.C.*, 2nd ed. (1984). A good account of the clash between the Greeks and the Persians.

P. J. Rhodes, *The Athenian Empire* (1985).

Malcolm F. McGregor, *The Athenians and Their Empire* (1987).

Either of these works will help the reader understand Athenian imperialism.

Andrew Lintott, *Violence, Civil Strife, and Revolution in the Classical City, 750–330 B.C.* (1982).

G. E. M. de Ste. Croix, *The Class Struggle in the Ancient Greek World from the Archaic Age to the Arab Conquest* (1981).

Two provocative treatments of a facet of Greek life that was destructive of the *polis*.

R. J. Hopper, *Trade and Industry in Classical Greece* (1979). A work that will throw light on economic conditions in the period under consideration.

J. R. Ellis, *Philip II and Macedonian Imperialism* (1976).

George Cawkwell, *Philip of Macedon* (1978).

Two excellent studies explaining the Macedonian victory over the Greeks.

Sources

Herodotus, *The Histories*, trans. Aubrey de Selincourt (1955).

Thucydides, *The Peloponnesian War*, trans. Rex Warner (1954).

Most of what we know about the fifth century comes from these two great historians; they are essential reading.

CHAPTER 6

Greek Life and Culture

FIGURE 6.1 **A Greek Goddess** This portrayal of the goddess Athena in mourning suggests the capability of the Greek sculptors to render the human form in an idealized fashion while still injecting feeling into an artistic composition. As the divine protector and patron of the city of Athens, Athena was constantly celebrated in art and literature by the city's artists and writers. She and other deities provided a constant source of inspiration for all forms of cultural creativity. (Acropolis Museum, Athens)

So far our discussion has emphasized the political and economic aspects of the Greek *polis*. However, that institution also had social and cultural dimensions. It provided a milieu where people lived their daily lives. Interactions within its environment stimulated a remarkable achievement in thought and expression. We must now try to summarize that accomplishment, admitting that it would take more than a lifetime of study to fathom the full dimensions of the Greek contribution to thought and expression.

1. DAILY LIFE IN GREECE

The splendid cultural achievements of the Greeks were rooted in the lives of ordinary men and women. Their efforts created the material basis for Greek society; they provided the audiences for creative efforts; and from their ranks came those who produced the literary, artistic, philosophical, and scientific works that constitute the essence of the Greek cultural "miracle."

Most Greeks devoted a significant part of every day to some kind of work related to Greece's diversified economy. In most city-states the bulk of the people earned their living in agriculture. Most farms were small, producing barely enough to sustain a household. There were larger farms managed by aristocratic owners and tilled by tenants and slaves. In the urban center, which was the focal point of each *polis*, large numbers of people worked as traders, artisans, and hired laborers. The scale of operations of retail shops and artisan establishments was small, usually operated by a family household with the help of a slave or two. Only a few enterprises, such as mining and arms making, were large-scale, often utilizing slaves as laborers. As illustrated by the examples of Athens and Sparta, in every city-state a considerable portion of the citizen body lived as employees of the government or as recipients of state-allocated land.

Although most Greeks worked to earn a livelihood, they were not willing to devote all their energies to work; leisure was important. Free time was possible in part because slavery played an important role in the Greek economy. Equally important was the willingness of the Greeks to live

simple lives, made easier by Greece's good climate. Their diet was plain: Bread, olive oil, vegetables and fruit, cheese, fish, and wine were the staple items. Houses were modest in size and sparsely furnished. Most men and women dressed in rough-spun tunics and sandals, although the more affluent favored linen garments and at least some jewelry. However, simplicity of tastes and needs was confined chiefly to private life. The Greeks spent heavily to adorn their city-states with costly temples and public buildings, sculpture, and paintings and to support festivals, games, and dramas at whatever price. They took more joy in expending their wealth on their *polis* than on their private comforts.

The basic unit of Greek society was the family. Kinship bonds always played a prime role in determining citizenship, in defining social status, in controlling property, and in determining associations. The nuclear family—husband, wife, children—living in a single household, perhaps served by a slave or two, stood at the base of the kinship group. But these units always maintained significant ties with a considerable circle of relatives. Marriage contracts were arranged by families, often when the prospective partners were very young. The bride's father provided a dowry, which was returned to the bride if the marriage ended. Actual cohabitation of the contracted couple, an occasion for much celebration, usually began when the girl was fifteen or sixteen; the husband was usually older. Children were important in marriage, but there was constant concern with problems resulting from too many mouths to feed; this concern seems to have resulted in modest-sized families. The Greeks practiced various methods of birth control, and they were not averse to exposing unwanted children to death or to giving them up for adoption. Husbands could divorce their wives easily, but it was much more difficult for a woman to end a marriage.

Greek women had a limited place in society. Despite the facts that powerful and active women were enshrined in Greek legends and celebrated in poetry and drama and that powerful goddesses figured significantly in Greek religion, the lives of most women were severely restricted. Greek literature and philosophical writing, most of it produced by men, is filled with portrayals of women as inferior in intelligence and self-control. That view found expression in legal terms. Although wives and daughters of male citizens were recognized and protected under the law, they were always subject to a male. Women could not own property (except in Sparta) or engage in legal transactions and were excluded from political life. The prime role of respectable women was to direct the household, care for young children, and train their daughters for the same role. Women rarely participated in any aspect of public life, except for religious festivals, and they were usually excluded from the social activities of their husbands. Women of poor households did help their husbands run their farms and shops, thus involving themselves at least to some degree in the affairs of the larger society. But most women were literally out of sight, exerting whatever influence they had within the walls of their home. Some evidence suggests that within the household wives enjoyed the respect and the genuine love of their husbands. A few rare women of beauty, intelligence, and social grace became the sexual companions of important citizens and shared with them their social lives. Prostitution was common in the Greek world.

While the household was the center of life for most Greek women, men appear to have spent as little time there as possible. Shortly after the break of day they were out of the house to occupy themselves with their jobs or with the bustling life of the *polis*. Almost from birth males found their lives enmeshed in a variety of social groups whose activities consumed much of their energy. When they were seven or eight, they went forth daily from their homes to begin their education in reading, writing, and physical education under the guidance of private masters. By the fifth century B.C. in a city such as Athens, that education might continue for years, focusing on skills suitable to political activity, especially rhetoric. The sisters of these young men remained at home to be educated in household arts by their mothers or household slaves. At an early age males were enrolled in a *phratry*, a kinship group that sponsored a variety of religious and social activities. As young men grew older, they gravitated to the *gymnasia*, male gathering places devoted to physical education, athletic competition, and endless talk. It was not unusual for a youth to attract the attention of an adult male who served as a role model in introducing young men to the full range of activities of the *polis*. These relationships, forged in a setting that provided little female influence and that often involved homosexuality, played an important role in shaping male values. No less intriguing to the maturing youth were the marketplace, the theater, and the bordello. Often his adult mentor began to involve him in the endless round of private gatherings, called *symposia*, where males met in private houses to eat, drink, and talk—free even from wives and mothers, who withdrew to special female quarters featured in the typical house. By the time his teenage days were ending, a male entered into the responsibilities of citizenship: military service, participation in the popular assembly, officeholding. For the rest of his life these political activities would command an important part of his time and energies. Perhaps shortly after becoming a full-fledged citizen, the typical Greek male married, but already his life was so involved in the affairs of the *polis* and in the social associations to which he was attached that marriage was incidental to his life. Indeed, involvement in the *polis* was more than a political matter; it defined a broad range of activities that engaged its male members completely. And the Greeks were scornful of any man who did not involve himself in that life.

Even a brief look at the essentials of Greek daily life suggests that Greek citizens enjoyed considerable freedom to do what they wished and that many chose to use that freedom to involve themselves intensely in the varied activities of the *polis*. This environment posed challenges that unleashed powerful creative forces. Thus, daily life in the Greek world and the most sophisticated achievements of Greek culture can never be separated.

2. RELIGION

Religion provided a major link between Greek daily life and cultural achievements. Religious concerns permeated every aspect of daily life, and religious beliefs undergirded all forms of cultural expression. The origins of Greek religion are buried in the earliest stages of Greek history. By the time the first systematic statements describing religious beliefs were made—in the writings of Homer and Hesiod early in the Archaic Age—an elaborate mythology and a complex set of rituals already existed.

Greek religion was polytheistic. Among the vast array of divine forces were certain remote and abstract forces—such as fate, death, justice, love—that provided the basic order governing the universe. But most Greek deities were conceived as having human forms and as conducting themselves much as did earthly humans, except that the gods and goddesses were immortal and more powerful than humans. The most conspicuous and attractive deities were the tumultuous family of major gods and goddesses living on Mount Olympus under the authority of Zeus, whose position resembled that of an earthly father of a noble household. To each of these Olympian deities was ascribed a special role: Zeus was the father of the divine family, controller of the forces of nature; Hera, his wife, was protectress of marriage and the family; Athena was goddess of wisdom; Apollo was the bringer of light and patron of arts; Ares was god of war; Aphrodite was goddess of beauty and love; and so on. One or another of these deities was often protector of a city-state, so that the worship of the Olympian pantheon provided the basis for civic religion. Aside from the Olympian deities, the Greeks believed that the universe was filled with lesser spirits—nymphs, satyrs, demons, spirits of departed heroes and ancestors—who meddled constantly for good and bad in human affairs. A rich body of mythology developed to recount the activities of the deities and to describe their relationships with the human community. Learning that mythology was a fundamental aspect of the life of every Greek.

Most Greeks believed that the deities controlled human affairs and therefore that individuals, families, and city-states had to attune their activities to divine will. There were fear-inspiring aspects of Greek religion, but, on the whole, the Greeks viewed their deities as basically benevolent, approachable, and concerned with human well-being. Although the gods and goddesses could be angry and unpredictable, they were too full of life, too "human," to inflict a burden of terror on human beings. If humans learned the ways of the deities, bent to their will, and refrained from a prideful usurpation of their powers, they could expect divine support in gaining good fortune, long life, honor on earth, and success for their *polis.*

The Greeks devoted considerable energy and talent to pleasing their deities. In general, the gods and goddesses were not much concerned with moral behavior; they expected men and women to approach them in tangible ways. Prayers, sacrifices, and gifts were offered according to carefully defined rituals in shrines maintained in each home and by each clan. More impressive were the splendid civic cults, for which great temples were built and maintained at considerable expense to the city-states. Large numbers of people from all walks of life participated in these civic religious activities (see Figure 4.2). On occasion, the entire Greek world joined in honoring the Olympian pantheon; the Olympic Games, held every four years from 776 B.C. on, represented a pan-Hellenic celebration honoring Zeus. Almost every kind of human activity was acceptable as a way of praising the deities—athletic contests, poetry reading, song, dance, dramatic presentations, and gift offering. As a consequence, religious ceremonies were also cultural and social events. There were no elaborate priesthoods in Greece; fathers conducted rituals in households and clan centers, and public officials served as priests for civic ceremonies. The Greeks spent considerable energy seeking advance information about divine intentions: They interpreted dreams, studied the stars, and read the entrails of animals in search of clues. But most of all, they relied on *oracles,* who were especially gifted people through whom the deities spoke. The most famous oracle was at Delphi, where innumerable Greeks went to implore Apollo to send them messages through special priestesses, who would tell them how to solve problems ranging from personal matters to great political issues.

Complementing the mainstream of Greek religious life embodied in the cult of the Olympian deities was another current, represented by the *mystery* religions, which placed greater emphasis on personal and emotional needs. The Greek mystery religions were rooted in the ancient worship of the regenerative forces of nature and were deeply influenced by ideas and practices from the Near East. The mystery cults centered on a belief in a god or goddess who died and then came back to life as a savior for believers properly initiated. Usually these religions emphasized the power of the resurrected deity to give a happy afterlife. The youthful wine-god Dionysus was the center of such a cult. His worship, based on a belief that he had been torn to pieces by evil gods and then reborn (see page 17 for a comparable concept in Egyptian religion), involved his devotees in a highly emotional initiation ceremony and in ecstatic rites involving wild dancing, drinking, and the eating of raw flesh. Another mystery cult, with its center at Eleusis near Athens, developed around the worship of the fertility goddess Demeter and her daughter Persephone, raised from the dead by her mother's efforts. Over time, the mystery cults became more subdued and respectable, as illustrated by the poorly understood movement called Orphism, which modified Dionysus worship by emphasizing the need for an austere, ethical conduct as a way of pleasing Dionysus and winning escape from the material world into a happy hereafter.

Aside from satisfying deep needs among most Greeks, religion provided a framework for intellectual and artistic growth. It encouraged people to try to understand, explain, and please the deities through literature, art, and philosophy. From it artists and thinkers drew inspiration and a basic store of themes out of which they shaped a variety of masterpieces that still awe and intrigue thoughtful people.

3. LITERATURE

Greek literature represents a magnificent outburst of creativity emerging from a substratum of religious themes. It was born in glory with two epic poems attributed to Homer, the *Iliad* and the *Odyssey*, probably set down in the eighth century B.C. Behind them lay a long tradition of oral poetry sung by bards for aristocratic audiences that loved to hear of the deeds of Mycenaean heroes. Homer, who remains a shadowy figure, drew these oral threads together into unified compositions of great artistry and dramatic power. The *Iliad* recounts the

feats of a circle of heroes during a brief period in the war which the Mycenaean Greeks waged against Troy to avenge the theft of a Greek woman, Helen, by Paris, the prince of Troy. Although filled with an array of striking characters, its central figure is Achilles, whose inflated pride and misdirected anger threaten to destroy the Greeks before he is brought to his senses and takes his place as a great warrior able to turn the tide of battle. The *Odyssey* is an adventure story celebrating the clever talents of one of the heroes at Troy, Odysseus, who needs ten years to overcome a variety of obstacles preventing his return from Troy to his homeland and his patient, long-suffering wife, Penelope. Not a little of the appeal of these epics lies in their gripping plots; but they have other dimensions. They create a heroic picture of men and women—but particularly men—endowed with courage, nobility, and a deep love for life. Homer's heroes served as models for noble character and action for all Greeks and for many people in later ages.

For all its richness, the epic tradition could not contain the Greek literary genius. In about 700 B.C. the poet Hesiod wrote his *Works and Days*, a bitter lament about injustice in the world, and his *Theogony*, a summary of Greek mythology. These works pointed to an outburst of lyric poetry in which new forms were developed to express personal reactions to life. Among the best lyricists were Archilochus of Paros, Alcaeus of Mytilene, and above all the poetess Sappho of Lesbos. A woman of aristocratic origins, Sappho composed lyrics celebrating the beauties of nature and describing her erotic feelings toward young women (later ages coined a word for female homosexuality—lesbianism—from the name of Sappho's native island). The nobility and force of Greek lyric poetry were perhaps best exemplified by Pindar of Thebes (ca. 518–441 B.C.), most of whose works took the form of choral songs in honor of victorious athletes at religious festivals. His poems set forth the classic view of aristocratic (in the Greek sense of "the best") qualities.

The burgeoning poetic talent reflected in epic and lyric poetry reached full fruition in the fifth century, with the development of tragic drama, perhaps the greatest literary achievement of the Greeks. Tragedy originated in the dramatic choruses and hymns developed in connection with the worship of the god Dionysus. By the late sixth century B.C., the dramatic element in these rituals was greatly expanded to allow poets to retell the deeds of the deities and heroes enshrined in Greek mythology and to comment on the meaning of these deeds through choral interludes.

This developing dramatic art suddenly burst forth in full maturity during the fifth century in the work of three of the world's greatest tragedians, all living in Athens amidst the flowering of democracy. The first was Aeschylus (525–456 B.C.). He wrote about ninety plays, only seven of which survive. His tragedies spell out with great power the consequences that follow human transgressions of the dictates of the divine powers. His most impressive surviving work is a cycle of three plays called the *Oresteia*, which traces the tragic fate of the family of Agamemnon resulting from its crime of spilling the blood of its own kin. Aeschylus had a genius for making his suffering characters noble and admirable, capable of bearing their burden of punishment with dignity and even with understanding.

Sophocles (495–405 B.C.), a citizen active in Athenian political life, produced a large number of plays, all but seven now lost. His dramas remained closely bound to the traditional themes provided by religion, but his interest is more human, more intent on searching out the psychological effects of suffering on humans who ran afoul of the gods and goddesses. He portrayed suffering as an uplifting and purifying experience. Many would argue that Sophocles' *King Oedipus* is the greatest tragedy ever written. Essentially it is a drama that reveals the measure of the human spirit by showing the response of a heroic individual. Oedipus' fateful act was unknowingly killing his father and marrying his own mother, vile deeds that violated nature's order and for which he had to atone. In presenting Oedipus' discovery of his crime and his acceptance of his fate, Sophocles evokes a powerful celebration of the greatness of human beings.

Euripides (480–406 B.C.) was a dramatist profoundly touched by the growing disillusionment, skepticism, and pessimism of the later fifth century—the generation of the Peloponnesian War. He utilized tragedy as a vehicle for posing profound questions about human values and problems in a way that arouses the suspicion that human powers are limited. His plays, especially *Medea*, represent a search for some understanding of the full nature of human beings, especially their dark and frightening emotional qualities. Again and again he casts doubt on conventional moral values and accepted religious beliefs. But from his incessant probing emerges a picture of humanity that is fuller and subtler—if not nobler—than the portraits by Aeschylus and Sophocles.

Rivaling tragedy in public appeal was comic drama. Like tragedy, it developed out of religious ceremony, especially the ribald songs associated with the worship of Dionysus. By the fifth century, comedy became independent of religious ceremony and was performed as a distinct art intended to inform and entertain audiences by comic treatment of current politics and social affairs. The master of this form was Aristophanes (ca. 445–385 B.C.), a conservative Athenian whose comedies held up for scorn politicians, democratic institutions, artists, and Athenian social mores. Typical is his play *Lysistrata*, based on the efforts of Athenian women to deny their husbands any pleasures with them until the men gave up warfare.

Prose literature long lingered in the shadow of poetry, but during the fifth century B.C. two historians produced works that demonstrated the Greek genius in that mode of expression. The first was Herodotus (ca. 484–425 B.C.), who wrote a history of the wars between the Greeks and Persians. His work is based on information he gathered through his travels and his search of written records. The result is a dramatic, colorful account of the events relating to the struggle between Greeks and Persians that Herodotus believed decided the fate of the Greek world. The second major Greek historian was Thucydides (ca. 460–400 B.C.), whose masterpiece was a *History of the Peloponnesian War*. With great energy he searched out the details of the military campaigns and the political maneuvers associated with the war in which he was personally involved. Out of this evidence he compiled a brilliant account that not only described the course of the war but also revealed the folly, nobility, chicanery, and bravery of which human beings under stress are capable. His presentation leads one to the conclusion that the Athenians lost because of their own choices; humans emerge as responsible for their own destinies. Not only did Herodotus and Thucydides produce great literary works, but they also pioneered a method of reconstructing the past based on the objective search for and verification of evidence. To this day their histories represent the ideal toward which all historians strive: to find the truth about the past and to let it enrich understanding of the present.

4. ART

The Greek genius in art emerged after a long evolution. The art of the Mycenaean Age, strongly influenced by Minoan models, disappeared during the Dark Age. But near the end of that period appeared the first signs of a uniquely Greek art, best illustrated in finely executed pottery decorated first with geometric patterns and then, by the eighth century B.C., with human forms. During the Archaic Age pottery painters, constantly influenced by motifs and techniques from the Near East, established basic themes and conventions for representing humans and animals in action. Sculptors slowly perfected a unique style of portraying the nude male and the draped female. Drawing heavily on mythology for subject matter, these artists increasingly relied on what they saw in their own world to shape their treatment of mythological figures and themes: naked male athletes, reserved and maternal females, real animals. Out of these observations emerged standards defining proportion, balance, and movement. Also during the Archaic Age, architects developed a basic style for temples and other public buildings: a rectangular ground plan whose elevation featured columns surrounding an inner temple chamber and low-pitched roofs. Increasingly these structures were built with the fine stone available in the Greek world. Although emerging architectural forms and techniques were influenced by Near Eastern models, the Greek concern with proportion and balance provided buildings with unique characteristics. Painters, sculptors, and architects received increasing support from the city-state, whose leaders and citizens were interested in beautifying their *polis* and in elaborating civic religions.

By the beginning of the fifth century, the long apprenticeship was over; a burst of creativity produced a golden age in art. Athens became the focal point of artistic excellence. Unquestionably, the city's crowning glory was the complex of buildings constructed on the Acropolis, the hill dominating the *polis*. Under the sponsorship of Pericles and with funds derived from tribute paid by the subject city-states of the Athenian Empire, three major temples were built there during the fifth century: the Parthenon, the Erectheum, and the temple to Victorius Athena. A splendid stairway and gate, called the Propylaea, gave access to the Acropolis, now the center of Athenian civic religion (see Figure 4.1). The Parthenon, portions of which still stand, embodied the basic features of classical Greek architecture. Built in honor of Athena, it is modest in size (228 by 101 feet). Its two inner chambers, serving as shrines, are surrounded by simple, unadorned columns (in a style called Doric), seventeen on each side and eight on each end, which support the roof and create covered colonnades and entry vestibules. Its majesty stems chiefly from its simplicity, its proportions, its unity, and its balance. The total effect derives not only from the logic of its conception but also from subtle technical devices. For example, the middle of every long horizontal line is slightly higher than the ends to avoid the impression of sagging (see Figure 6.2).

The other Acropolis temples and the Propylaea incorporate the same features as the Parthenon, all adjusted to the size of each structure. The only basic departure was the utilization of slightly more slender and ornate columns (in the Ionic style), which add grace and lightness. Similar temples were built in many other cities throughout Greece. The same basic principles were applied to increasing numbers of public buildings—theaters, gymnasiums, market places, meeting halls—constructed in Athens and other city-states.

The Greek style of architecture, especially temples, provided spaces for decoration by sculptors and painters: the walls and interior space of inner chambers, the entablature built above the columns to provide a rest for the roof, the triangular pediments formed at either end of the structure, and the open spaces before the structure. The best Greek sculptors, represented by Phidias (ca. 500–

FIGURE 6.2 The Parthenon This magnificent example of Greek architecture was the chief structure among a complex of temples adorning the Athenian Acropolis (see Figure 4.1). Begun in the Golden Age of Pericles and dedicated to Athena, its distinctive horizontal lines, its stately Doric columns, and its measured proportions typify the classical Greek architectural style. The pediments above the columns and the triangular space created by the roof were filled with sculpture celebrating Greek deities and portraying themes from Greek mythology. (Marburg)

432 B.C.), Polyclitus (ca. 452–412 B.C.), and Praxiteles (ca. 400–320 B.C.), dedicated their talents chiefly to temple decoration. Phidias designed and executed some of the sculpture adorning the Parthenon. His statues in the round, especially the famed statue of Athena in the inner chamber of the Parthenon, have been lost. Around the walls of that same chamber was a continuous frieze of carved reliefs depicting a procession in honor of Athena; it portrays a teeming scene filled with ordinary people and animals shown in various aspects of everyday life. The external entablature and pediments were covered with powerful representations of divine activities drawn from mythology. Polyclitus devoted his talents chiefly to shaping bronze statues of young men (see Color Plate 3—left). Praxiteles created splendid versions of gods and goddesses in human form (see Figure

6.3 and Color Plate 3—right). All of this sculpture focuses on the portrayal of the idealized human body; the figures are dignified, restrained, beautifully proportioned, filled with the potential for action. The effect of viewing them is to catch a vision of the nobility and the power of human beings extracted from the real world in which human beings lived and acted (see Figure 6.1).

Little has survived of Greek painting, except for pottery painting (see Figure 4.2). There is evidence, however, from literary sources that large-scale paintings decorated temples and public buildings. For example, Polygnotus (mid–fifth century) decorated a colonnade in the Athenian *agora*, the area where political meetings and market activities took place, with painted scenes depicting episodes from the Trojan War. It is highly likely that Greek painting reflected the same traits as sculpture: idealization of the human figure, balance, restraint, and dignity.

5. PHILOSOPHY AND SCIENCE

The Greeks leaped furthest beyond the achievements of earlier cultures in the realms of philosophy and science, areas of inquiry they considered interdependent. Until the sixth century B.C., most Greeks were content to accept the explanations provided by mythology to describe the nature of the universe and the place of human beings in it. Then during the sixth century, just when the *polis* was reaching maturity, some thinkers began to move beyond the mythological world view in search of rational explanations of the cosmos that would take into account what was observable in the natural order.

The prime concern of these early speculative thinkers was to find a simple, unifying principle that would describe and explain rationally what constituted the universe and what made it work in order to replace traditional mythological explanations based on arbitrary, irrational factors. This quest gave rise to several schools of thought. One such school developed a materialistic explanation that argued that such obvious elements as fire or water or air were the basic substances out of which all other things emerged through processes innate in the nature of these basic substances. This materialistic approach continued to be explored until Democritus (ca. 460–370 B.C.) propounded an atomic theory, according to which the universe is composed of identical, indivisible particles floating at random; by mere chance these atoms combined into beings and objects and by the same chance decomposed to end existing things. Another school of philosophers rejected materialism and sought the key to the universe in some nonmaterial force. Perhaps the source of this approach was the sixth-century thinker Pythagoras, whose career combined scientific interest with a strong religious bent. He argued that the basis of cosmic order lay in a numerical relationship among its many parts. Equally influential in shaping this school was Heraclitus (flourished ca. 500 B.C.), who insisted that change was the essence of the material world and therefore no simplistic physical

FIGURE 6.3 Hermes with the Infant Dionysus
Most likely the work of the famed sculptor Praxiteles, this statue is an excellent example of Greek artistic canons; the gods are taken as subject matter and portrayed in an idealized human form that emphasizes physical perfection rather than spiritual qualities. (Hirmer Fotoarchiv)

explanation of the universe could have meaning. This whole school of thinkers ultimately concluded that a nonmaterial, changeless being, endowed with perfect intelligence, supplied the creative force of order in the universe.

Although Greek thinkers always remained interested in finding an explanation of the fundamental nature of the universe, about the middle of the fifth century there emerged an increasing interest in the human condition. A diverse group of thinkers, collectively called the Sophists, led the way into this new realm. The Sophists were primarily teachers interested in preparing their pupils for a role in public life. Out of their concern for what should be taught they articulated ideas that gave philosophical inquiry a new emphasis. The Sophists rejected speculative philosophy on the grounds that objective truth was nonexistent, as demonstrated by the contradictory schemes put forward by prior thinkers. In the words of one of the chief Sophists, Protagoras (485–410 B.C.), a famous teacher in Periclean Athens, men and women were the measure of all things. Human reason should be dedicated to a search for the kind of knowledge that would be useful to humans in their quest for a happy, useful life. Such an approach made it obvious to the Sophists that institutions and standards of behavior were human creations, not the results of an unchangeable natural order. On this basis, the Sophists delivered withering attacks on most things accepted as the truth, arguing that truth is relative and encouraging their disciples to live by any rules that proved workable and beneficial. The Sophists as a group were condemned as skeptics and destroyers of morality. But they made the Greek world increasingly aware of fundamental ethical issues and encouraged humans to trust the power of reason as an instrument for improving the human condition. Out of the ferment they caused emerged the greatest Greek thinkers.

One of these was Socrates (ca. 469–399 B.C.), an Athenian famous in his own time as a provocative teacher. He left no writings; he set forth his ideas orally in the Athenian *agora*, where he engaged all comers in debate about philosophical issues. From what his pupils remembered about his teaching, it appears that Socrates believed that objective truth did exist, contrary to the teachings of the Sophists. Human beings were prevented from discovering that truth by their own ignorance. That ignorance could only be dispelled by rigorous, logical self-examination of beliefs. The Socratic method consisted of asking questions un-

til the error of those who claimed to know something was exposed and then leading the mind through further questioning to the truth by way of precise definition and exact logic. Socrates' goal was to get people to understand themselves and to conduct their lives by the light of their reason. Although his gadfly tactics won him an eager following, he eventually encountered trouble. In 399 B.C., amid the bitterness surrounding the Athenian defeat in the Peloponnesian War, he was accused of corrupting the youth and sentenced to die. Although offered an opportunity to escape, he chose to accept the verdict of his fellow citizens rather than abandon his conviction that knowledge alone led to virtue.

Plato (427–347 B.C.) carried on the work of Socrates, his master. He spent most of his career as a teacher in a school in Athens called the Academy, which he founded. His voluminous works, elegantly written in dialogue form, provide a complete although sometimes confusing record of his thought. Plato was a philosophical idealist; his work brought to full maturity the nonmaterialist philosophical tradition dating back to the sixth century. He argued that the fundamental realities in the universe are ideas, or abstract forms, the chief of which is "the good." The so-called realities that humans perceive with their senses are but imperfect reflections of the perfect universal forms. For example, the justice practiced in Athens was only a shadowy reflection of perfect, transcendental justice; a man or a woman is but a pale image of a higher reality, humanity. Plato argued that the human intellect was capable of comprehending the higher reality of forms. Such truth depends on pure reasoning, which allows the mind to reach a level of comprehension beyond what the senses can reveal.

Much of Plato's writing centers on a search for perfect understanding of universal ideas and an effort to make that wisdom and insight applicable to the problems of human existence. His best-known dialogue, *The Republic*, illustrates his idealism, his method, and his earnest concern for the human condition. This work is devoted to governance. Plato assumes that the purpose of the state is to achieve justice, the ideal state being an earthly embodiment of the perfect idea of justice. He concludes that justice consists in each individual doing that for which he or she is best fitted. The ideal state is one in which every person holds that station and does that job for which he or she is qualified. Such a state, Plato argues, must be ruled by a philosopher-king who will be wise enough to know and recognize the talents of his subjects and put these talents to work. A completely socialistic economy controlled by the wise king must be instituted so that all will be rewarded according to their merits and so that competition and greed can be eliminated from society. In short, the perfect society is a dictatorial state guided by those who are wise by virtue of their rational powers. In his other dialogues Plato conducts a comparable search for an understanding of the nature of love, friendship, courage, the soul—in fact, virtually the whole range of those elements that constitute the ultimate reality, perfect good.

Aristotle (384–322 B.C.) was Plato's most brilliant and productive pupil. As a youth, he came to Athens from northern Greece to study at the Academy. After Plato's death, he spent some time in Macedonia as tutor to young Alexander the Great. He then returned to Athens and founded his own school, the Lyceum. His followers were called the Peripatetics because Aristotle often walked about while lecturing.

During his career, Aristotle produced a massive body of philosophical work ranging across the whole spectrum of human knowledge. Perhaps typical of effective teachers in all ages, he had a passion for systematizing and organizing knowledge, so that his works constitute a kind of encyclopedia of the total learning of the ancient world. Imbedded in his massive scholarship, however, is a basic philosophical position. Aristotle was certainly influenced by Platonic idealism, but his approach is basically different. In his seminal *Metaphysics*, he argues that reality consists of a combination of matter and form (or idea). The form makes the object what it is, but it has no reality except when it exists in matter. Every object has some purpose in a larger universal order, and its perfection consists in serving that purpose. Behind the wilderness of individual objects lies an ultimate "cause," a higher force that animates everything. The philosopher's path is from the study of nature toward the formulation of concepts about the entire universe.

In most of his works, many of which deal with scientific subjects, Aristotle pursued the course laid down in the *Metaphysics*. His *Politics* supplies an illustration of his method. On the basis of a study of the history and organization of more than one hundred fifty Greek city-states, he concluded that the state is a natural grouping of human beings for the purpose of promoting virtue. Men and women are political animals; they cannot fulfill their true nature unless they are members of a state. The state as a "form" manifests itself in many different material shapes: monarchy, oligarchy, tyranny, democracy. Aristotle's analysis of these forms clarified the unique consequences for human beings of each type of state. In his *Ethics* Aristotle asked how men and women should conduct their individual lives and argued that happiness is the proper goal of every human action. Men and women are happy, and therefore good, if they control their passions by the use of reason and if they seek a mean between extremes. Aristotle's principal method of seeking truth was inductive—that is, formulating generalizations on the basis of particular pieces of evidence—and he was the most influential exponent of that method among the Greeks. However, he was also the founder of formal logic, a mode of thinking that employs a deductive method of thinking to extract the truth about specific things from general principles. Aristotelian logic would play a dominant role in philosophical inquiry for centuries to come. As the last great thinker of classical Greece, Aristotle was the most comprehensive.

Aristotle's scientific works mark the culmination of a sustained interest in natural science among the Greeks extending back at least two centuries. That interest resulted in significant work in astronomy, physics, botany, zoology, physiology, and geography. Although Greek scientists borrowed extensively from data about the natural world compiled by Mesopotamians and Egyptians, they made significant additions to scientific knowledge by their own observations of natural phenomena. Illustrative of this approach is the work of Hippocrates (460–377 B.C.), a practicing physician to whom is attributed the famous oath still used today defining the responsibilities of a physician. He insisted that nothing could be known about sickness except through observation

WHERE HISTORIANS DISAGREE

The Irrational in Greek Culture

All historians who try to reconstruct the grand sweep of history quickly become aware of a disturbing consequence of their effort: They find themselves distorting the past by concentrating on what is dominant in any era at the expense of those facets that in their judgment are less important. The conventional treatment of Greek culture provides an example. Modern scholars—including the present authors—have emphatically stressed that the crucial factor in Greek thought and expression was rationalism. But is that the whole story? Have we forgotten something in our eagerness to make the Greeks the model of that desirable human trait, reasonableness?

One of the most perceptive modern classicists, E. R. Dodds, has reminded us not to be too hasty on this matter. In his seminal book entitled *The Greeks and the Irrational* (1951) he developed a strong case for the presence of powerful currents of irrationality in Greek culture. He bases his case on a fundamental postulate established by modern anthropologists and psychologists which argues that in the behavior of all people in all ages there is a powerful element of primitive mentality that finds its expression in religion. He asks: "Why should we attribute to the ancient Greeks an immunity from 'primitive' modes of thought which we do not find in any society open to our direct observation?"

Dodds succeeds in demonstrating persuasively that Greek literary and philosophical leaders were always aware of irrational factors governing human conduct and that they expressed their awareness in religious terms. In other terms, he finds that even the most profound Greek thinkers were never quite satisfied to explain human actions solely in terms of rational behavior. He provides massive evidence to show that many Greeks were constantly fearful of psychic intervention in their lives by divine forces capable of polluting them or driving them to madness. Moreover, he argues that the "enlightened" views of the great cultural heroes of the Greek world were looked upon with suspicion and even hostility by most Greeks, who were never free from a deepseated feeling that forces beyond rational comprehension and control governed human behavior.

Dodd's convincing argument forces us to realize that only a few Greek thinkers affirmed that a human being was a rational creature, and in the long run their belief was overpowered by a more primitive conviction that men and women were essentially irrational. When one adds to this the obvious fact that the great mass of Greeks always accepted a religious interpretation of human nature, the generalization about rationalism as a key to Greek culture becomes exceedingly suspect.

Thus it turns out that the historian who stresses rationalism as a major feature of Greek culture is overlooking a factor of immense importance to the Greeks. This sounds dishonest. Yet in fitting the Greeks into the grand sweep of history, their rationalism is of greater significance than their irrationalism. Their consciousness of the rational powers of human beings marked a fresh insight into the human potential, while their awareness of the irrational aspects of human behavior simply provided a common bond with most other societies in history that have tried to cope with the monumental problems of living. What is important is that some Greeks trusted their rational powers as a means of enriching their lives, for they were the ones that made a difference in the history of civilization.

of sick people and through a search for the natural causes of illness. He repudiated the traditional belief that sickness was due to evil spirits; it was a result of natural causes, and the cure for sickness was a natural process that could be controlled. He collected information about the curative power of drugs and about the effects of diet on health. The collective efforts of Greek scientists allow us to credit the Greeks with the invention of the scientific method, which relies on observation as the source of knowledge about nature. Lacking precision instruments, their observations were often imprecise and their interpretations of data erroneous. Moreover, few were interested in using their knowledge for practical purposes. Scientific knowledge was employed chiefly by philosophers seeking to explain the working of the universe.

6. THE GREEK SPIRIT

Any review of the varied achievements of the Greeks in literature, art, philosophy, and science raises at least two basic questions. Are there any common characteristics undergirding Greek culture in its entirety? Did this splendid outburst of creativity in thought and expression affect the lives of ordinary men and women?

To the first question it seems possible to argue that Greek culture in all its aspects reflects certain basic concepts. Greek thought was intensely *humanistic*; it placed human beings at the center of the universe and celebrated their potential for perfection. Greek cultural leaders were confident that the universe existed to sustain human welfare. They were therefore certain that humans were *in harmony with nature* and had no need to struggle against it, to try to escape it, or shrink from it in fear. Greek culture was *rationalistic*; its creators placed trust in the human ability to understand nature and themselves through human intelli-

gence and to act on the basis of rational decisions to resolve human problems. Rationalism emphasized the need to seek *order* and *symmetry* in all things and to act with *restraint* and *balance*. Greek culture was marked by a *spirit of inquiry* that constantly pushed thinkers and artists toward new knowledge and new ways of expressing themselves. Finally, most Greek intellectual and artistic leaders were *civic-oriented*, ready to offer their talents to the service of the community to which they belonged instead of pursuing individual and introspective ends.

Much more difficult to ascertain is the extent to which the basic values expressed in Greek culture shaped the lives of ordinary Greeks. Like most of the nameless peoples in the past, their thoughts and ideals are lost to us. Probably most Greeks, engaged in the routine of daily life, seldom paused to think about what their pattern of civilization meant, just as most modern men and women seldom dwell on this question. But one thing seems certain: An ordinary Greek would have had trouble escaping contact with the cultural achievements we have described. The best of Greek thought on the human condition was made available to all citizens of each *polis* as an intimate dimension of civic life. Poetry reading accompanied religious ceremonies and athletic competitions. The best drama was played out in public theaters. The best philosophers wrangled in the streets, joined their fellow citizens at *symposia*, and taught in the schools. Architects and sculptors devoted their best efforts to civic art. It seems inconceivable that any citizen could have escaped without being touched by some of the values reflected in Greek culture. We must assume that most Greeks found the values and the ideas engrained in Greek culture as attractive and appealing as did innumerable later generations who found in the Greek way a model for civilized life.

SUGGESTED READING

General Cultural Histories

François Chamoux, *The Civilization of Greece*, trans. W. S. Maguinness (1965). A perceptive overview, well illustrated.

John Boardman et al., eds., *The Oxford History of the Classical World* (1986). Excellent studies of varied aspects of Greek civilization.

Social Life

In addition to the social and economic histories cited in Chapter 4, the following works treat selected aspects of Greek social life.

Maurice Pope, *The Ancient Greeks. How They Lived and Worked* (1976).

Robert Flacelière, *Daily Life in Greece in the Time of Pericles*, trans. Peter Green (1965).

M. T. W. Arnheim, *Aristocracy in Greek Society* (1977).

W. K. Lacey, *The Family in Classical Greece* (1984).

Sarah B. Pomeroy, *Goddesses, Whores, Wives, and Slaves: Women in Classical Antiquity* (1975).

Eva Cantarella, *Pandora's Daughters: The Role and Status of Women in Greek and Roman Antiquity*, trans. Maureen B. Fant (1987).

Yvon Garlan, *Slavery in Ancient Greece*, trans. Janet Lloyd (1988).

K. J. Dover, *Greek Homosexuality* (1978).

Religion

Robert Graves, *The Greek Myths* (1955; illustrated edition, 1981). A full description of the myths undergirding Greek religion.

Walter Burkert, *Greek Religion: Archaic and Classical*, trans. John Raffan (1985). A masterful treatment.

Walter Burkert, *Ancient Mystery Cults* (1987). A well-done guide.

Literature

Jacqueline de Romilly, *A Short History of Greek Literature*, trans. Lillian Doherty (1985).

Peter Levi, *A History of Greek Literature* (1985).

Either of these recent works will provide invaluable guides to the main currents of Greek literary history.

Charles Rowan Beye, *Ancient Greek Literature and Society*, 2nd ed., rev. (1988). A stimulating effort to put Greek literature into its social context.

Art

John Boardman, *Greek Art*, new and rev. ed. (1985). An excellent brief treatment.

John Boardman et al., *The Art and Architecture of Ancient Greece* (1967).

Richard Brilliant, *Arts of the Ancient Greeks* (1973).

Jean Charbonneaux et al., *Classical Greek Art (480–330 B.C.)*, trans. James Emmons (1972).

These three longer treatments, all beautifully illustrated, provide a rich appreciation of the Greek artistic accomplishment.

J. J. Pollitt, *Art and Experience in Classical Greece* (1972). A good treatment of the social and intellectual foundations of Greek art.

Philosophy and Science

Rex Warner, *Greek Philosophers* (1958).

W. K. C. Guthrie, *Greek Philosophers: From Thales to Aristotle* (1960).

Although old, either of these two works will provide a good introduction to the Greek accomplishment in philosophy.

Jean-Pierre Vernant, *The Origins of Greek Thought* (1982). A challenging introduction.

H. D. Rankin, *Sophists, Socratics, and Cynics* (1983). A balanced treatment of the major schools of philosophy in classical Greece.

G. E. R. Lloyd, *Early Greek Science: Thales to Aristotle* (1970). A thorough assessment of the Greek accomplishments in science.

K. D. White, *Greek and Roman Technology* (1984). A well-done assessment of Greek accomplishments in technology.

Sources

Michael Grant, ed., *Greek Literature: An Anthology in Translation* (1973). A rich sampling. Perhaps it will encourage a reader to read Greek writers in their entirety. Good translations of the works of all the authors mentioned in this chapter are easily available.

CHAPTER 7

Greek Imperialism: The Hellenistic World, 336–31 B.C.

FIGURE 7.1 **Alexander the Great** This Roman copy of an original bust of Alexander the Great (perhaps done by the fourth-century sculptor Lycippus) attempts to capture the strength and the idealism of a great hero of the ancient world. (The Granger Collection)

To many Greeks, the coming of the "barbarian" Macedonians spelled doom. But, as is so often the case when contemporaries judge their own age, they were wrong. The Macedonian conquest set the stage for a new chapter in the history of the Greeks. Under Macedonian leadership, they exploded out of their Aegean-centered world to establish their mastery over a wide circle in Asia and Africa. Their genius and their traditions began to mix with Near Eastern civilizations to produce a new culture that historians have called "Hellenistic."

1. ALEXANDER THE GREAT

The military and political genius of Alexander the Great was chiefly responsible for launching the Greeks on this new phase of their history. Endowed with numerous powers—intelligence, ambition, industry, imagination, physical attractiveness, boldness, an iron will—Alexander has never ceased to fascinate students of history (see Figure 7.1). Although Macedonian by birth, he shared the admiration for Greek culture that prevailed at the court of his father, Philip II, and that was deepened by his education under Aristotle's direction.

Only twenty when his father died, Alexander turned his energies immediately to launching the war against Persia that Philip had planned (see Map 7.1). In 334 B.C. he led his Macedonian-Greek army into Asia Minor in order to attack Persia. Although Persia possessed a huge empire, a rich treasury, and a large army and navy, Alexander was victorious from the beginning. Mindful of the role naval power had played in the long struggle between Greeks and Persians, his first campaigns were aimed at depriving the Persians of control of the coastal cities of Asia Minor and Phoenicia, the chief source of Persian naval power. Shortly after entering Asia Minor, Alexander overpowered a major Persian force at a battle on the Granicus River; this victory assured control of the Greek cities along the east coast of the Aegean Sea. From there he moved into Syria and in 333 B.C. won a brilliant victory at Issus. This victory solidified Alexander's control of Asia Minor and opened the way for his conquest of Syria, Palestine, and Egypt. Then he marched on the center of Persian power in Mesopotamia and in the spring of 331 B.C. destroyed the last major military strength of the Persians at the battle of Gaugamela (Arbela). Following this victory, he occupied the major centers of Persian political power, including the capital city of Persepolis, and hunted down the fugitive King Darius III, who was finally murdered in 330 B.C. by his own officials as Alexander closed in on him.

The conquest of the Persian Empire did not satisfy Alexander's ambition. During the next five years he drove on eastward. Battling vast distances, native resistance, and defection among his own troops, he relentlessly destroyed pockets of resistance led by Persian satraps in the regions of Parthia and Bactria. Then he pushed across the Hindu Kush Mountains into the rich land drained by the Indus River, a venture that brought the Greeks into direct contact with Indian civilization. Beyond the Indus Valley his troops refused to go. Alexander therefore turned back westward through southern Persia and into Mesopotamia, where he fell ill and died in June 323 B.C. at the age of thirty-three.

A career so short and so completely occupied with military campaigns left Alexander little time to face the problems of ruling his vast conquests. Probably he had no definite plans when he launched his campaign, but before he died he had made decisions establishing certain broad policies that guided his successors. He moved toward creating a style of rulership that cast him in the role of divine autocrat who enjoyed the special favor of the deities, a kind of rulership foreign both to Greeks and to Macedonians. He at least toyed with the idea of combining the talents of conquered peoples, especially Persians, with those of the conquerors to create a cosmopolitan elite to control his empire. However, his followers found this policy unacceptable. Eventually he had to take steps to ensure that Greeks and Macedonians would rule his empire. This plan required their migration to Asia and Africa, a move that Alexander sought to make attractive by establishing city-states in which the newcomers would have a special place. However, aside from his conquests, Alexander's accomplishments were few. His main influence on the course of history lay chiefly in

Map 7.1 ALEXANDER'S EMPIRE, 336–323 B.C. This map provides a dramatic picture of Alexander's military accomplishment in overpowering the Persian Empire. That the Greeks were able to establish their mastery over this huge territory and impose their pattern of culture on much of it was an amazing achievement. The most intensive Hellenization of Alexander's empire occurred around the eastern end of the Mediterranean from Egypt through Syria and Phoenicia to Asia Minor. But Mesopotamia also felt the powerful force of Greek culture.

his legend: what later generations believed he was trying to do.

2. HELLENISTIC POLITICAL LIFE, 323–31 B.C.

For almost three centuries the consequences of Alexander's conquests dominated the political history of the vast area that fell under his sway. That history was not, however, a simple one. If, as some claimed, Alexander intended to establish a universal empire to be ruled by a philosopher-king

in a way that would bring peace and prosperity to all its people, that was not to be the case. Immediately after his unexpected death, a council of his generals decided to attempt to maintain a united empire under a single ruler. They designated Alexander's incompetent half brother as king, with the understanding that should the child that Alexander's widow, the Bactrian princess Roxanne, was carrying be male, he would share the throne—which is what happened. But this royal pair could provide no effective direction. The generals were soon engaged in a struggle for control. By about 275 B.C. their rivalry had produced a hodgepodge of political entities of various sizes, strengths, and forms of government. By far the most prominent were the major kingdoms established by three of Alexander's companions: Antigonus in Macedonia and the Aegean world; Ptolemy in Egypt; and Seleucus in the vast area stretching from Asia Minor to India (see Map 7.1).

Only the briefest summary of the complex histories of these kingdoms can be undertaken here. Laying claim to the well-established kingdom established by Philip II, the Macedonian kings sustained a fairly effective government during most of the third century B.C. The level of Macedonian economic and cultural life improved, largely due to the continued influx of influences from Greece. Although the Antigonid dynasty always had ambitions to play a major role in the larger Hellenistic world, Macedonian political history centered chiefly on the efforts of the rulers to maintain a hegemony over the Greek city-states and to hold back the barbarians constantly pressing on the northern frontier of Macedonia. These were great burdens, testing the limited human and material resources of Macedonia. Control of the Greek city-states was particularly difficult. Claiming to act in the name of "freedom" for the *polis,* the Greeks constantly intrigued against their masters, often seeking help from outsiders. Macedonian efforts to defuse this resistance by interfering in local city-state political processes and by establishing military garrisons in Greece only sharpened the resistance. And the barbarian assaults never let up. Ultimately, the Macedonian kingdom was incapable of bearing the burden. Shortly before 200 B.C. some of the Greek city-states appealed to Rome for help against what they claimed was Macedonian interference with their freedom. In the ensuing wars, Roman armies conquered both Macedonia and Greece and absorbed them in Rome's expanding empire.

The kingdom established in Egypt by Ptolemy was the most stable Hellenistic state. The Ptolemaic dynasty quickly established an autocratic regime modeled on the ancient Egyptian system of the pharaohs. The key to Ptolemaic power was a bureaucracy and a military force dominated by Greek-Macedonian immigrants. This regime skillfully exploited the native population and the agricultural and commercial resources of Egypt to sustain its power. Internal

stability and wealth permitted the Ptolemies to play an active role in the larger Hellenistic world. They concentrated chiefly on extending their sphere of influence in Syria-Palestine, in Asia Minor, and in the Aegean world. These ambitions involved them in almost constant conflict with other powers in the Hellenistic world, especially the Seleucid kingdom. By the second century B.C. the grip of the Ptolemies on Egypt began to weaken, chiefly because they were forced to rely increasingly on native Egyptians in the army and the bureaucracy and to make concessions limiting their royal income. Growing internal unrest ultimately forced the rulers to seek support from the Romans. Eventually, in 30 B.C., Rome annexed Egypt to its empire.

The Seleucid kingdom had the most troubled history. Its huge size and mixed population provided little basis for unity except what its kings and their Greek-Macedonian followers could impose. Rather quickly the Seleucid rulers lost control over the area east of the Tigris-Euphrates Valley to non-Greeks, who established kingdoms of considerable importance to the future, including Bactria and Parthia. In northern and western Asia Minor local rulers established small but virile kingdoms—Pontus, Bithynia, Cappadocia, Pergamum. Most of the Seleucid political energy was devoted to creating a viable state embracing Mesopotamia, Syria-Palestine, and southeastern Asia Minor. Their authority was based chiefly on military service provided by Greeks and Macedonians established in cities from whence they dominated the native population. Outsiders, especially the Ptolemies, constantly threatened the Seleucids. They also had to contend with native uprisings. For example, a Jewish revolt led by the Maccabees in 167 B.C. was provoked by an effort of the Seleucids to Hellenize the Jews; it resulted in the virtual independence of that long-captive people until they were conquered by the Romans a century later. Ultimately, the Seleucid kingdom was torn to pieces by internal strife and squeezed to death by Parthian pressure from the east and Roman intrusions from the west.

Numerous smaller states shared the political scene with the three major kingdoms. Chief among them were many Greek city-states that remained independent and sought to continue their traditional pattern of governance. A good deal of the political energies of these city-states were devoted to internal affairs, often marked by bitter partisanship and class rivalry. But they also had to concern themselves with the ambitions of other city-states and the threat of the great powers, especially Macedonia. Their fragile independence encouraged many city-states to develop techniques aimed at reducing intercity rivalry and strengthening the religious and cultural ties shared by all Greeks. Especially innovative was the development of effective leagues or federations based on some compromise of total autonomy in the interests of common action emerging from shared political processes. Two particularly important leagues were the Aetolian League embracing several city-states in central Greece and the Achaean League in northern Peloponnesus. Despite their continued existence, the old Greek city-states lost much of their power of self-determination during the Hellenistic Age. Among the smaller states of the era, the most successful were the kingdom of Pergamum in western Asia Minor and the Republic of Rhodes, both of which fared well by capitalizing on commercial activity.

In this world of competing "successor" states that emerged out of Alexander's conquests and Greek-Macedonian domination of the Near East, the conduct of interstate relations took on new intensity and sophistication. As a consequence, the Hellenistic Age marked an important chapter in the history of international relations. Great and small states developed a battery of techniques designed to ensure safety and to gain advantage over others: military force, diplomacy, psychological warfare, internal subversion, economic penetration, arrangements extending privileges to citizens of other states. In a general way, the Hellenistic world moved toward a balance of power aimed at maintaining the status quo. While that balance was constantly in the process of readjustment, it worked fairly well until a major outside power, Rome, moved onto the scene.

The Hellenistic Age witnessed significant developments in terms of political institutions that had an important impact on future history, especially in providing models for the Romans. The very idea of empire itself was important. The Near Eastern world was, of course, familiar with this political concept as a result of the efforts of Amor-

ites, Egyptians, Hittites, Assyrians, and Persians. However, the idea of empire was new to the Greeks, given their enchantment with the microcosmic *polis*. The experiences of the Hellenistic Age put into the Greek vocabulary and mentality the vision of a world state where peoples of many kinds would share a common citizenship and a common destiny. Their concepts of such a political system had an important impact on later political thought.

On a more practical level, the major development in terms of political institutions during the Hellenistic period was the Greek acceptance of the concept of monarchy—an institution that had disappeared from the world of the *polis* as early as the eighth century B.C. During the Hellenistic Age monarchy became the standard form of government among the Greek rulers of the Near East. The system of monarchy practiced by the Greeks was shaped by the traditions of the Near East, but it reflected unique qualities due to Greek influences. In Hellenistic monarchies the king's power was personal. It derived from his feats at arms, his intelligence, his will, and his favor with the deities. By virtue of his personal abilities, he could bestow blessings on his subjects. No constitution or entrenched nobility acted to limit his power. No law other than what he decreed was recognized. Such a concept of royal power clearly reflected the Greek confidence in human ability.

To exercise his vast powers effectively, the king of each Hellenistic kingdom relied on the advice of a circle of "friends" selected because of the king's confidence in their talents and their loyalty. Each ruler developed a well-organized central government featuring a strong army, an elaborate bureaucracy, and an efficient taxation system. Effective military power was the ultimate basis upon which Hellenistic government rested. Greeks and Macedonians filled the chief positions in royal governments and controlled the old structures of local government, which were usually left intact.

The large numbers of Greek and Macedonians who migrated across the Near East to serve Hellenistic kings tended to congregate in cities—some ancient and many newly founded. Into their new abodes the newcomers brought political institutions and practices from their native city-states. As a consequence, assemblies, councils, popular courts, and elected magistrates were established to give the elite outsiders considerable control over their own local affairs. The Greeks and Macedonians in the Near East thus retained their ancient allegiance to the ideal of the small, intimate *polis*, as did their compatriots still living in old Greece. This continued attachment to the ideal of the *polis* detracted from a complete commitment to monarchy. Generally, the Hellenistic kings encouraged and supported the development of such nearly autonomous communities in their kingdoms, chiefly because royal power depended on support from Greeks and Macedonians. However, concerns about retaining their ethnic identity and their elite position in political, social, and cultural life forced all Greeks in the Hellenistic world to turn to the monarchs. As a result, strong, mutually beneficial bonds developed between the monarchs and the Greek-Macedonian city-states of the Near East. The kings could usually count on the support of the local communities and, given their superior resources, were able to impose their will on these communities. Slowly but surely monarchy overshadowed the *polis* as the decisive political force in the Hellenistic world.

3. HELLENISTIC ECONOMIC AND SOCIAL LIFE

Although the Hellenistic era brought prosperity to some areas and to particular groups, on the whole the economic impact of Greek-Macedonian expansion was modest, chiefly because it was not accompanied by changes in the basic structures of production. Agriculture remained the basic source of wealth in the Hellenistic world, but the new masters did not fundamentally change the established system. The conquerors claimed possession of a considerable portion of the agricultural land in their vast empire and imposed on native tenants and increasing numbers of slaves a heavy obligation to till the soil for their benefit. Some Greek owners, including especially the kings seeking revenue, undertook land clearance, new irrigation projects, crop rotation, and the introduction of new crops and equipment; but the resultant increase in production was modest and beneficial to only a few.

An increase in trading activity provided a significant element of prosperity in some areas of the Hellenistic world, especially in a zone embracing the great cities of Egypt, Syria, and Asia Minor. Greek entrepreneurs played a significant role in exploiting the commercial potential of this area and in extending trade connections toward old Greece, Mesopotamia, India, China, and North Africa. Extensive new capital was made available to these entrepreneurs when Alexander confiscated and put into circulation the vast treasury of the Persian kings and the wealth controlled by the Persian aristocracy. Although the Greek and Macedonian newcomers in the Near East spent much of this wealth on luxury goods and the building of new cities, some of it was invested in activities beneficial to commerce: harbors, roads, market facilities, ships, coinage systems, credit and banking operations. Although there was trade in foodstuffs, metals, and timber products, luxury items played a major role in exchange. Hellenistic monarchs, especially the Ptolemies, supported commercial growth to serve political ends and thus created an economic climate favorable to trade.

The Hellenistic economy was marked by significant industrial activity carried on chiefly by native artisans operating small manufacturing establishments. Most manufacturing was devoted to products needed by the populace of each city and thus was highly localized. The surviving evidence suggests that there was no great increase in industrial production and no fundamental change in the organization of manufacturing. Especially noteworthy was the lack of technical progress. Despite some remarkable advances in the level of scientific knowledge, almost no progress was made in applying that knowledge to manufacturing, probably because of the vast supply of cheap native labor and slavery.

Whatever economic expansion there was during the Hellenistic period benefited only a few in society—chiefly the Greek rulers, their political servants, landowners, merchants, artists, and scholars. With the exception of a few natives who adopted Greek ways, most natives were economically exploited. As the Hellenistic era progressed, the gap between the wealthy Greek masters and the poor native farmers, city laborers, and slaves increased. Moreover, economic prosperity was not evenly distributed geographically. Its effects were felt chiefly in the belt extending from Egypt around the eastern end of the Mediterranean into Asia Minor. Increasingly impoverished were the old Greek city-states in the Aegean area, where depopulation and even starvation were not uncommon.

In both the old Greek world and in the vast area conquered by Alexander basic social patterns persisted during the Hellenistic period. In the old Greek city-states family structures and social practices governing daily life remained much as they had been in the fifth century. The chief change involved growing disparities in wealth, hardening class lines, and social tensions breeding conflict and even violence. In "new Hellas" native life was little disturbed by the coming of the Greeks; for most people old masters were merely replaced by new ones. Perhaps the chief new social phenomenon of the period was the implantation into many Near Eastern cities of colonies of Greeks and Macedonians who sought to re-create and perpetuate the social order they brought from their native city-states. But the old social order was difficult to maintain. Wherever Greek migrants settled, they found themselves living among Greeks from many different cities and were constantly confronted by uprooted Greek intellectuals, athletes, soldiers, and merchants seeking their fortunes, a challenge that eroded commitment to local customs based on place of origin. All kinds of opportunities existed to abandon old social ties in order to take advantage of new ways of winning wealth, favor, and high status. Despite their commitment to "Greekness," the contrasts between their way of life and that of the natives eventually modified their patterns of behavior and social values. One aspect of social life so affected involved the status of women. Although still surrounded by legal constraints, many women in the Hellenistic cities of the Near East enjoyed greatly expanded opportunities for education, involvement in cultural and economic life, and even political life—opportunities not available to their ancestors in old Greece.

As the Hellenistic era progressed, the above-noted trends in economic and social life produced a situation that boded ill for the stability of Hellenistic society. Deepening differences in wealth, social¹ strife in the typical Greek *polis*, native re-

sentment against Greek exploitation, and Greek exclusivity generated explosive tensions. The emerging instability represented a serious failure on the part of the Greek masters of the Hellenistic world. In many of the old Greek city-states, intelligent leadership had directed economic and social development toward the improvement of the lot of the deprived, a course that strengthened the entire fabric of society. But the Greek rulers and entrepreneurs of the Hellenistic Age chose to be exploiters, a course that would have a serious cost.

4. HELLENISTIC CULTURE: AN OVERVIEW

The three centuries following Alexander's death marked an important era in cultural history in at least two significant ways. First, that period witnessed the enrichment of the cultural accomplishments of the Greeks. Second, considerable portions of the classical Greek tradition were recast into new forms that became the heritage taken over by non-Greek peoples of later generations. In a sense, much of what survived from ancient Greek culture consists of Hellenistic modifications and adaptations of the Classical Age models.

Hellenistic cultural life was animated by a powerful urge to continue the thought and expression that had developed in Greece during the Classical Age. The Greeks who fought in Alexander's armies and who migrated to populate the cities founded by him and his successors were convinced that they had conquered "barbarians" whose cultural life was not fit for Hellenes. As a consequence, the Greeks felt compelled to take their culture with them into their new world in the Near East and to preserve it in as pure a form as possible. As a result of such feelings, Greek literary, artistic, philosophical, and scientific concepts and forms were implanted across the Near East as the dominant cultural modes.

However, bringing the chief ingredients of Hellenic culture into a new geographical, political, and social setting was not a simple task. In fact, it turned out to be unrealistic, for Hellenic culture began to be transformed almost from the moment of its transplantation. The culturally dominant Greeks found themselves separated from the intimate, tightly knit city-state environment that had originally nourished their culture. They were now widely dispersed in a huge, impersonal world where their destinies were determined by semi-divine monarchs and complicated economic forces. In such a milieu some aspects of their old culture appeared to have little relevance. Moreover, the Greeks soon found that the "barbarian" Egyptians, Syrians, Mesopotamians, Persians, and Indians possessed knowledge, techniques, and ideas that were both new and attractive to the conquerors. These tensions and pressures produced an outburst of activity in literature, art, philosophy, and science, which transformed the old modes of thought and expression in ways that broadened and enriched the classical Greek culture.

During the Hellenistic period cities remained the focal points of cultural life. Many of the old city-states of the Aegean area continued to promote active cultural life; Athens in particular enjoyed prominence in philosophical inquiry. However, the most intense cultural activity of the Hellenistic Age was generated in the new Greek centers in the Near East, especially Alexandria, Antioch, and Pergamum. The population of these cities was cosmopolitan, mixing Greeks from throughout the Hellenistic world with the native peoples. The royal governments that controlled these cities and the affluent Greeks who dominated social and economic life were generous patrons, anxious to attract artists, writers, and thinkers to their cities and eager to provide them with the means to pursue their cultural interests. In Alexandria, for example, the Ptolemaic kings spent huge sums to plan and build a city adorned with the best art and architecture that could be created. They built a large library that contained about seven hundred thousand books (actually handwritten papyrus scrolls) and created a research center, called the Museum, where learned scholars were supported so that they could pursue scientific studies. The best talent flocked to these centers and devoted their skills to satisfying the cultural interests of those who patronized them. The cultural activities generated in these "new" cities addressed a much broader world, a different set of interests, and a new range of problems than had the Greek cultural efforts within the small,

independent *polis* of the Aegean world.

The most active period in Hellenistic cultural life centered in the third and early second centuries B.C. As the second century progressed, complex and subtle changes began to blunt the powerful urge to sustain and elaborate the cultural inheritance from the Greek Classical Age. The ethnocentricity of the dominant population of the great cultural centers began to lose its edge as Greeks and natives merged. Patronage declined as royal governments weakened. Perhaps most important, new concerns began to occupy the attention of people in a way that lessened the importance of the rationalistic, humanistic values of Greek culture and heightened the attractiveness of values embraced in religious systems that had their roots in the ancient traditions of the Near East. But before it could be completely overpowered by the resurgence of religious forces, Hellenistic culture had won the admiration of the conquering Romans and thus lived on under Roman patronage.

5. HELLENISTIC CULTURE: LITERATURE AND ART

The literary output of the Hellenistic Age was massive; the names of a thousand Hellenistic writers have survived. The outpouring was due in part to the patronage of wealthy monarchs, their officials, and private individuals and in part to the increased demand for literature by a growing number of literate people. A simplified version of Greek (*koine* Greek) became the common tongue of government, commerce, and learning. Many natives learned the language; for example, the Hebrew Bible was translated into Greek (the Septuagint) in Alexandria in the third and second centuries B.C. for the use of Jews living there. While the writers of the Hellenistic Age were prolific, they were not especially inventive. Mainly they devoted their energies to imitation of the epic and lyric poems, the tragedies and comedies, and the histories of classical Greece. The poets especially were chiefly concerned with style. They often reworked old subject matter in an attempt to achieve stylistic perfection. There were some authors, however, who produced literature that dealt with current situations and appealed to broader audiences than did the "classics"; such literature included novels and biographies.

The Hellenistic Age also produced a multitude of literary scholars who spent their lives reconstructing earlier Greek literary masterpieces, writing commentaries on their meaning, analyzing their grammar, and discussing their stylistic features. This patient scholarly labor played an important role in establishing and preserving the texts of the Greek classics and in elaborating the rules that governed grammar, rhetoric, and literary form. The scholarly establishment provided endless grist for an education system that was expanding in the Hellenistic Age and becoming increasingly literary and formal. Education played a major role in preparing the Greek ruling elite to discharge its duties and to sustain the cultural brand that was, indeed, its mark of superiority.

The artists of the Hellenistic period were no less active than the literary figures. Again classical Greek models exerted a powerful influence, completely overshadowing the artistic traditions of the Near East. Architecture enjoyed a great boom because of the numerous new cities built by the Greeks and filled with the traditional buildings—temples, gymnasiums, theaters, and centers for public business. Although the basic forms remained classic, there was a tendency to stress size and ornateness in these buildings. Most Hellenistic cities were much better planned than the older Greek cities, with emphasis on a rectangular grid layout, wide streets, adequate water supplies, commercial conveniences, and parks. As a result, they were more impressive than predecessors.

Hellenistic sculpture likewise sought to imitate the masters of the Classical Age; in fact, most sculptors did little more than copy classical models. They remained fascinated with the human figure. Sometimes they were able to capture the full spirit of classical style, as is illustrated by the well-known *Winged Victory of Samothrace*, with its idealized, well-proportioned portrayal of the human form. Hellenistic sculptors showed a greater interest in the nude female than had sculptors of classical Greece; their best work in this respect reflected a pleasing combination of idealization of the body and sensuousness, as is evident in the famous *Aphrodite of Melos* (more commonly known

FIGURE 7.2 An Old Woman of the Hellenistic Age
This portrayal of an old market woman of the third or second century B.C. reflects the concern of Hellenistic artists with portraying the real world about them. The work suggests a world that had its share of suffering and hardship. The contrast with the serene, idealized figures portrayed in the sculpture of the Classical Age in Greece is striking. (The Metropolitan Museum of Art, Rogers Fund, 1909)

as the *Venus de Milo*). Hellenistic sculptors produced impressive relief carvings as a part of temple decoration. Although little evidence has survived, it is clear that the classical tradition in painting was continued during the Hellenistic period. Although classical Greek influences dominated the visual arts, Hellenistic art did develop its unique characteristics. Perhaps the most striking development was the increasing realism reflected in sculpture and painting. In place of the classic quest to create idealized perfection, Hellenistic sculptors came down into the streets for their subjects. Children, old people, common laborers, and barbarians occupied their attention, and they gave vent to emotions, seeking to portray action and violence, passion, sorrow, and suffering (see Figure 7.2).

6. HELLENISTIC CULTURE: SCIENCE AND PHILOSOPHY

The most original cultural contributions of the Hellenistic Age were made in science and philosophy, where investigators and thinkers often moved beyond their Hellenic predecessors. Both fields built upon the achievements of classical Greece, but science and philosophy tended to become separate areas of concern. The moment was especially ripe for scientific advance. Earlier Greek philosophers had postulated challenging theories about the natural world and had argued that nature could best be understood by observing its working. Out of this background there emerged during the Hellenistic Age a strong urge to expand the store of knowledge about the natural world and to interpret its meaning. The expansion of the Greeks put them in touch with a huge body of data compiled over many centuries by learned individuals in the Near East. Hellenistic kings and wealthy Greeks were eager to patronize scientists and to provide facilities to make research possible. The result was active scientific inquiry, centered especially at Alexandria, and an impressive expansion of scientific knowledge, especially in view of the lack of instruments making possible precise observations.

Alexander's conquests and the commercial activities that resulted expanded knowledge of and interest in geography. As a consequence, compilation of geographical knowledge was an important aspect of Hellenistic science. From this new knowledge emerged challenging geographical speculation, illustrated by the work of Eratosthenes (ca. 275–200 B.C.). He calculated the circumference of the earth as 24,662 miles, about 200 miles less than the actual figure. On the basis of his study of tides, he insisted that the Atlantic and Indian oceans were joined and that India could be reached by boat around Africa. He made maps using lines of longitude and latitude and divided the earth into zones still used by geographers. Seleucus (second century B.C.), along with others, studied the tides and came close to relating them to the gravitational force of the moon.

Astronomy likewise attracted attention. The two greatest names were Aristarchus (ca. 310–230 B.C.) and Hipparchus (ca. 185–120 B.C.). Aristarchus insisted that the earth revolved around the sun. Hipparchus denied this premise, working out a geocentric version of the cosmos that involved an intricate array of movements of the sun, moon, and stars around the earth. His system, which took into account what astronomers were then able to observe, won the day and would survive for centuries. He compiled an extensive atlas of the stars and from observation of their movement arrived at an extremely accurate calculation of the solar year. Both these great astronomers tried to calculate the size of the sun and its distance from the earth, but with little success.

Much was also done to advance mathematics. Euclid (323–285 B.C.) compiled a textbook of geometry that remained standard until the twentieth century. Archimedes (287–212 B.C.) calculated the value of pi (the ratio between the circumference and the diameter of a circle). He also devised a system for expressing large numbers, solved the problem of the relative volumes of a cylinder and a sphere, and laid the foundations for calculus. Trigonometry was developed by Hipparchus, and a fundamental work on conic sections was done by Apollonius of Perga (third century B.C.).

Scientific medicine was of great interest to the scholars of this period. Following the lead of Hippocrates, Hellenistic physicians made important progress in anatomy and physiology, chiefly on the basis of careful and systematic observation.

Surgery advanced considerably; so did the use of medicines. Alexandria was especially prominent as a center of medical study, an activity that the Ptolemaic rulers supported even to the extent of supplying the cadavers of prisoners to physicians for dissection.

Hellenistic scientists were also interested in physics, zoology, chemistry, and botany, devoting most of their energies to collecting and classifying data in these areas. Illustrative was the work of Theophrastus (ca. 372–287 B.C.), who compiled descriptive works on botany based on his own observations of plants and their habits. New advances in these fields were limited. However, Archimedes discovered the laws governing floating bodies and developed the theory of the lever.

As Hellenistic science advanced, scientists became increasingly interested in the compilation of encyclopedias intended to summarize knowledge in each scientific field. Euclid's work in geometry has already been noted; other important compilers include Ptolemy (ca. A.D. 85–180) in astronomy and geography, Strabo (ca. 63 B.C.–A.D. 21) in geography, and Galen (A.D. 130–201) in medicine. These encyclopedias served as guides to scientific knowledge at least until the beginning of the great scientific revolution of early modern times.

Hellenistic scientists, like their Hellenic predecessors, had little interest in the practical application of scientific ideas. There were exceptions; Archimedes, for example, developed the windlass, the double pulley, the endless screw for pumping water, and a variety of devices useful in the defense of besieged cities. In fact, virtually the only area where applied technology developed was in the military field. As a consequence, Hellenistic daily life was little affected by the notable advances in science.

Hellenistic philosophy rivaled science in vigor and creativity. The old philosophical interests lived on, as evidenced by the continued activity of Plato's Academy and Aristotle's Lyceum in Athens. However, Hellenistic philosophy was primarily concerned with problems of human conduct and individual destiny, interests that had already attracted the Sophists of the fifth century. This emphasis reflected the stresses felt by Greeks living in a cosmopolitan, impersonal, changing world, which left them seeking reassurance against uncertainty, personal identity, and peace of mind.

The search for individual identity and peace of mind produced several schools of thought that competed loudly and bitterly for public attention. Some attracted popular fancy and aroused ire for their eccentricity and excess. One such group was the Skeptics, who made a principle of doubting everything and who argued that people should live with no concern for truth or values since neither existed. The Cynics were more spectacular; they advocated that society should abandon all its civilized conventions and wealth to return to nature. In search of converts, these disciples of a counterculture took to the streets in filthy rags to deliver diatribes against the establishment and all the amenities of civilized life.

More profound and influential was the teaching of Epicurus (ca. 341–270 B.C.), who taught at Athens. He built his ethical concepts on a materialistic philosophical basis. He argued that the universe consisted of atoms, which by chance formed themselves into beings and things. The deities, if they existed, had nothing to do with this process and therefore need be of no concern to human beings. Death was nothing more than the dissolution of atoms that had come together by accident to bring into being a living creature; thus death need not be feared. Given such a cosmos, human beings should occupy themselves only with happiness and pleasure. Epicurus argued that the path to happiness is not mere physical pleasure but rather those things that bring a peaceful, undisturbed mind. He pleaded with his disciples to withdraw into themselves and avoid excessive wealth, political involvement, superstition, and too great contact with the world. The Epicureans put great confidence in limiting one's association to a narrow circle of intimate friends; "to live in hiding" would shield one from much that could disturb the mind. This philosophy was welcome to many educated people who saw little use struggling in a world where great kings and great wealth determined most things. Although some turned Epicurus' teachings into an excuse for seeking purely physical pleasure, most Epicureans were learned and refined, obedient to public authority, calm, and long-suffering. But they were little given to the active, involved life that was once the ideal for the Greek citizen.

Even more influential in shaping the moral atmosphere of the Hellenistic Age were the Stoics, whose founder, Zeno (336–264 B.C.), taught in Athens while Epicurus was there. Stoicism was based on Zeno's conviction that the material universe of which each human being is an integral part was governed by an unchanging law of nature defined by a Divine Reason. For many Stoics that supreme intelligence was virtually a god who controlled human destiny. Harmony and order would result if the laws of nature were adhered to by all creatures. The course of human beings emerged clearly from such a universal order: They must use their reason to define for themselves a pattern of behavior that would attune them and their actions to the unchanging laws of nature. Such a course would compel all humans to accept the inevitable dictates of the natural order. They must bear all misfortunes with patience since everything that happens has been ordained by an all-knowing providence. All must accept good fortune without pride, since they are not responsible for it. Such submission to the natural order brings tranquility and peace of mind. It ends concern for material things and allows the soul to reach the ideal state—*apatheia* (apathy, absence of feeling). Although in its early stage Stoicism was primarily an individualistic philosophy, it did in time develop a larger dimension that stressed the community of all humans and the need for involvement in public life in order to sustain order and civility, both necessary to peace of mind.

7. HELLENISTIC RELIGION

A major source of ferment in the Hellenistic world was religion. The old civic religions of the Greeks had already been weakened by social stresses within the city-states of the late fifth and fourth centuries and by the assaults of intellectuals. Nonetheless, when the Greeks migrated across the Near East during the Hellenistic period, they sought to transplant and sustain their old beliefs and practices as a part of their "superior" culture. The effort failed. The old deities and the rites in their honor increasingly ceased to answer the basic spiritual needs generated by the changed environ-

FIGURE 7.3 Religious Syncretism This Hellenistic relief illustrates the mixing of religions that was an important aspect of Hellenistic civilization. The seated deity reflects a mixture of Greek and Near Eastern concepts of deity. The priest burning incense in honor of the god is Near Eastern, while the garment of the figure on the right crowning the god is clearly Greek/Macedonian. (Yale University Art Gallery, Duro-Europas Collection)

ment of the Hellenistic world. As a consequence, an important aspect of "Greekness" increasingly suffered eclipse.

To help them in the face of uncertainties and alienation, many Greeks found satisfaction in accepting ideas rooted in the rich religious history of the Near East. These native religious concepts had evolved into well-defined cults, called *mystery religions,* which during the Hellenistic period increasingly won favor among the Greeks at the expense of the old civic religions. Many different mystery religions flourished in the Near East during the Hellenistic period: Isis worship, Mithraism, the Earth Mother cult, Dionysus worship. Whatever their origin, all shared certain fundamental ideas with wide appeal. They centered around the worship of a savior deity, usually identified with the forces of renewal in nature, whose death and resurrection provided eternal life for each individual believer. Those yearning for assurance drew close to that deity by trusting in the deity's saving power, by submitting to a special initiation ceremony, and by participating in emotional rituals, often involving a reenactment of the deity's death and rebirth. Favor with the saving god or goddess depended heavily on the moral conduct of each believer. Since faith in a savior deity, ritual participation, and upright behavior were tests everyone could meet, the mystery religions appealed to men and women of all classes, all levels of wealth, and all ethnic groups. In the cosmopolitan, mobile environment of the Hellenistic world, ideas from various mystery religions constantly mingled. This process, called *syncretism*, pointed toward the emergence of a common faith that not only tended to link Hellenes and native Near Easterners but also created a seedbed out of which would emerge genuinely universal religions (see Figure 7.3).

As the Hellenistic period unfolded, religious attitudes exemplified by the mystery religions increasingly asserted powerful influences over other aspects of thought and expression. Science and philosophy were put to the service of religious thought. Astronomy was transformed into astrology, the "scientist" studying the stars in order to predict the future. The philosopher's effort to learn by rational means the secrets of the cosmic order became an attempt to achieve mystical contact with powerful deities who controlled the universe. This "religionizing" of thought had brought Greek culture and its Hellenistic extension full circle: A culture born out of religion was now being absorbed back into religion. In the process some of the finest achievements of the Greeks were threatened with being twisted out of shape. This transformation was delayed by the emergence of the Romans as champions of Greek culture, but in the long run religious concepts would gain the upper hand, as will be seen in our treatment of the end of Greco-Roman civilization.

The advance of religious values in the Hellenistic world points to a significant dimension of Hellenistic cultural life destined to be an important heritage left to later history. Hellenistic culture was marked by an inner tension. On the one hand, there was a thrust to know the world of people and nature and to understand that world rationally. On the other, there was an equally powerful thrust to retreat from the material world into the spirit world, to abandon thinking in favor of quietude of mind. Although these opposing views sometimes divided the individual mind, in general the first approach was represented by Hellenistic scientists, sculptors, and creative writers, while the second attracted philosophers, literary scholars, and priests. Perhaps the emergence of this polarity in Hellenistic culture was what distinguished it from the Hellenic culture of classical Greece. In any case, the juxtaposition of reason and faith, realism and mysticism, activism and withdrawal at the heart of Hellenistic culture would recur in later chapters of the history of Western civilization as a stimulant to creativity.

SUGGESTED READING

Political History

F. W. Walbank, *The Hellenistic World* (1982).

Michael Grant, *From Alexander to Cleopatra. The Hellenistic World* (1982).

Two challenging syntheses covering all aspects of Hellenistic life.

Robin Lane Fox, *Alexander the Great* (1973). An excellent biography.

Cultural Life

John Ferguson, *The Heritage of Hellenism. The Greek World from 323 B.C. to 31 B.C.* (1973). An excellent overview of the main features of Hellenistic culture.

G. E. R. Lloyd, *Greek Science after Aristotle* (1973). A balanced, readable description of the major accomplishments of Hellenistic science.

A. A. Long, *Hellenistic Philosophy: Stoics, Epicureans, Scep-*

tics (1974). A clear presentation of the teachings of the major Hellenistic schools of philosophy.

Jean Charbonneaux et al. *Hellenistic Art (330–50 B.C.),* trans. Peter Green (1973). A splendidly illustrated treatment of all aspects of Hellenistic art.

John Onions, *Art and Thought in the Hellenistic Age: The Greek World View, 350–50 B.C.* (1979). A challenging effort to interrelate art and thought.

Arnaldo Momigliano, *Alien Wisdom: The Limits of Hellenization* (1975). Discusses how the Greeks dealt with other cultures, especially during the Hellenistic period.

Walter Burkert, *Ancient Mystery Cults* (1987). A good picture of the most powerful religious forces in the Hellenistic world.

Sources

M. M. Austin, *The Hellenistic World from Alexander to the Roman Conquest. A Selection of Ancient Sources in Translation* (1981). A well-selected collection of documents that will help the reader understand many aspects of Hellenistic life as seen and felt by those who lived in that world.

CHAPTER 8

The Rise of Rome to Domination of the Mediterranean World

FIGURE 8.1 A Roman Patrician Honoring His Ancestors This portrayal of a Roman patrician bearing busts of his ancestors conveys the sobriety, seriousness, and respect for family that characterized the aristocratic citizens who acted through the Senate to lead the Roman Republic to ascendancy in the Mediterranean world. (Alinari/Art Resource)

The powerful impulses toward the establishment of a common culture in the Mediterranean basin, loosed first by the Greek city-states and then by the Hellenistic kingdoms, were picked up toward the end of the third century B.C. by a new power emerging from the West: Rome. The rise of the Romans marked the first appearance of a western Mediterranean people in a decisive role in determining the course of history. It is a story that deserves special consideration because the Romans were equipped with unique talents that allowed them not only to sustain the Hellenic and Hellenistic accomplishments but also to advance civilized life to new levels and to spread its fruits to heretofore primitive peoples.

1. THE ORIGINS OF ROME TO 509 B.C.

The emergence of Rome as the dominant force in the Mediterranean owed much to a combination of geographical factors and the human resources of the Italian peninsula. Aside from its strategic location in the Mediterranean basin, Italy had considerable productive farmland, important mineral deposits, and good timber. Its climate was generally mild and conducive to agricultural production.

The Italian population was formed over a long period out of several different ethnic elements whose diverse patterns of culture fragmented the peninsula into a bewildering array of political entities and institutional systems. An ancient native population developed a Neolithic farming culture perhaps as early as 4000 B.C. Beginning about 2000 B.C., Italy, like many other areas of the Mediterranean basin, experienced successive waves of Indo-European invaders. These newcomers fused with the native population, but they did bring superior technical skills and effective military and political structures, which allowed them to dominate the natives. Their language eventually prevailed over much of Italy, creating the base from which classical Latin emerged.

The still backward Italian population was decisively influenced after about 800 B.C. by the settlement in Italy of two outside peoples bringing with them the more advanced civilization of the eastern Mediterranean world. As we have already seen, the Greeks established numerous city-states in southern Italy and Sicily from whence flowed powerful cultural forces affecting the entire Italian population. Even more important were the Etruscans, probably migrants from Asia Minor, who established a series of cities along the western coast of Italy north of the Tiber River. Although each of these cities remained politically independent, they were bound together by strong economic, religious, and cultural ties that allowed them to dominate the natives. Within a short time after their initial settlement, their influence expanded, so that between 650 and 500 B.C. the Etruscans controlled western Italy from the Po Valley to Naples. During this period they transmitted a wide range of technical skills, agricultural and commercial practices, political techniques, religious ideas and usages, and art forms, which provided many Italians with their first taste of urban civilization and helped prepare them for a larger role in history (see Map 8.1).

Among the most precocious pupils of the Etruscans were some villagers living along the Tiber River about fifteen miles above its mouth. These people later created a colorful legend recounting the founding of their city by Romulus and Remus in 753 B.C. Legend aside, the evidence suggests that Rome began as a settling place for herder-farmers from an area just south of the Tiber known as Latium. Tiny villages were built on a cluster of seven hills lying on the south bank of the Tiber. But nothing about the history of these early villages seemed to suggest future greatness.

Shortly after 600 B.C., the several villages were rather suddenly transformed into a single city-state, probably as a consequence of their seizure by Etruscan warlords who imposed political unity on the villages. A single government under a king was established. Although that government may have incorporated institutions and practices from pre-Etruscan times, it was also decisively influenced by Etruscan political practices. The king was advised by a council of elders, called the Senate, composed of about three hundred men of wealth who drew their authority from their headship of families. The freemen, who constituted the bulk of the citizen body, were given a voice in political affairs by membership in two assemblies. The

Map 8.1 **ITALY, 265 B.C.** This map shows the main geographical regions into which Italy was divided and indicates the date at which each was brought under Roman domination. As noted in the text, Roman domination did not mean total loss of independence for the peoples of Italy. Many in central Italy became citizens, as is indicated on the map; most of the rest were allies who retained considerable rights of local control as long as they supported Rome's foreign policy and kept the peace.

most ancient was the Assembly of the *curiae,* so called after a grouping of citizens in thirty units called *curiae;* each unit was made up of a number of clans drawn together for military and religious purposes. At a later date, probably during the sixth century B.C., a military reorganization took place that organized that populace into military units called *centuries.* Assignment to a century was based on wealth. This new arrangement led to the formation of the Assembly of Centuries, made up of all citizens eligible for military service. However, both assemblies were severely limited in their power and did little more than approve the decisions of the king and the Senate. The city-state populace was divided into two distinct classes, *patricians* and *plebeians,* with the former exercising a predominant influence over society. Custom prohibited intermarriage between the two classes. Many plebeians were closely tied to patrician families as *clients,* an institution under which a noble *patron* provided legal protection and material assistance to his client, and the client in return performed various services, including following political directions.

Etruscan techniques in trade and industry were adopted by the fledgling Roman city-state, greatly strengthening its primitive economy. An alphabet was derived from Etruscan models, resulting in the rapid development of written Latin. Etruscan architecture and decoration served as models for the temples and public buildings in the burgeoning city. Primitive Latin religious practices took on more sophisticated patterns reflecting Etruscan usages. Rome was rapidly becoming the center of an advanced culture capable of threatening other communities located in Latium.

Despite their debt to the Etruscans, the Romans chafed under their domination. Shortly before 500 B.C. Etruscan power began to be contested by the dependent subjects everywhere in western Italy, while Greeks and Carthaginians vied with Etruscan forces in the larger setting of the western Mediterranean. The challenge was too much for the Etruscans, whose influence in Italy declined rapidly after 500 B.C. In Rome the patricians took the lead in a revolution that dethroned the Etruscan king and established in his place two *consuls* elected annually from patrician ranks to wield the *imperium,* that is, the highest executive authority of the state. This revolution of 509 B.C. marked the beginning of the Roman Republic, an episode long celebrated by the Romans as the greatest event in their history.

2. ROMAN EXPANSION: THE CONQUEST OF ITALY, 509–265 B.C.

The dominant theme of the first two and one-half centuries of the history of the Roman Republic was Rome's success in establishing dominance over the Italian peninsula (see Map 8.1). Given the fact that in 509 B.C. Rome was only a tiny city-state lost among many other political entities, the Roman victories in themselves represented a remarkable feat. In a larger sense, Roman success created the human and material resources that soon would permit Rome to become a world power.

Rome's expulsion of the Etruscans in 509 B.C. actually weakened the city by depriving it of the powerful support of the Etruscans. For much of the fifth century Rome's survival depended on cooperation with neighboring cities in Latium, which joined Rome to form the Latin League. This League fought a long succession of wars against the Etruscans and the tough mountain peoples trying to gain a foothold in the rich agricultural lands of Latium and Campania. The defensive effort of the League was jeopardized by a Celtic people, the Gauls, who poured into the Po Valley from north of the Alps from whence they raided central Italy; in 390 B.C. they captured and sacked Rome. In the course of their recovery from these attacks, the Romans began to assert pressure on their allies in Latium. Their threat bred fear among the members of the Latin League and caused several of them to rise against Rome in 340 B.C. The "rebels" were subdued within two years, and the League was dissolved, leaving Rome in control of Latium.

From this base, the Romans proceeded to expand their sphere of influence. Between 326 and 290 B.C. they subdued the Samnites, a formidable mountain people living south and east of Rome, who provoked the Romans by challenging them for control of Campania. While engaged in the bitter Samnite Wars, the Romans were attacked from the north by Gauls, Etruscans, and other mountain peoples from north central Italy, but these attacks were thrown back and Roman dominance was gradually established over most of northern Italy lying south of the Po Valley. Hardly had the Samnite Wars ended when Rome was drawn into the affairs of the Greek city-states of southern Italy, chiefly to arbitrate their quarrels. Despite assistance from military adventurers from "old" Greece, the badly divided Italian-Greek city-states could not hold off the Romans. By 265 B.C. Rome had established mastery over all Italy south of the Po Valley and had become a world power— although as yet unproved.

Many forces combined to explain Rome's triumph. The Romans themselves constantly retold the stories of these wars as proof of their superior civic virtues and divine favor. Beneath the legends they created around these struggles there is a core of truth: In these wars the Roman citizens demonstrated bravery, persistence, and self-sacrifice. However, other, more tangible factors played a decisive part in Roman success.

First, the Romans developed a superior military organization. Very early in its history, Rome began to develop a citizen army that required military service of most of the city's population at each soldier's own expense. The effectiveness of this army was greatly enhanced by the development of the *legion* as the basic military formation. The legion was essentially a massed formation of well-armed infantry soldiers, not unlike the Greek phalanx. During the long wars against mountain peoples, the legion formation was modified to create within it small subunits capable of independent action. This modification increased the flexibility of the legion without sacrificing its basic unity and made it a fighting unit that most of Rome's Italian foes were unable to withstand.

A second and even more important factor contributing to Rome's victory in Italy was the innovative policy devised for the treatment of conquered peoples. In its essence this system encouraged conquered people to identify their well-being with Roman success. Rome achieved this end by developing a flexible definition of "belonging" in Rome's spreading network of power. To some conquered peoples, especially those in Latium, Rome extended full rights of citizenship.

The residents of other conquered cities were made what the Romans called "citizens without vote"; these people could not participate in the Roman political process, but they were permitted to trade in Rome and to intermarry with Romans. These cities continued to govern themselves in most matters except foreign affairs, but their half citizens owed to the Roman state the same financial and military obligations as did Roman citizens. Still other communities were made "allies" (*socii*) of Rome, each signing a formal treaty that left it considerable independence in local affairs and imposed on its members the obligation to provide military contingents to serve in Rome's wars. Implicit in these arrangements was the possibility that partial citizenship and ally status would eventually result in full citizenship, especially for those who became Romanized. In many communities that were granted powers of local self-government the Romans gave strong support to continued rule by entrenched aristocracies who found it in their best interests to support Rome. Seeking to provide centers from which conquered territory could be defended, the Romans planted numerous colonies of Roman citizens at various places in Italy. Also, individual Romans were given grants of land upon which they settled at different places in Italy. The presence of Roman colonists and individual settlers became an important factor in the Romanization of Italy. This complex set of arrangements, contrasting so sharply with the way in which other conquerors treated their victims, meant that by 265 B.C. Rome ruled over a loose confederation of Italians, most of whom enjoyed a considerable degree of independence, but all of whom were tied to Rome by virtue of an obligation to serve in its armies, by the hope of achieving full citizenship, and by increasing identification with Roman culture in all its facets. From the Roman point of view this system provided a pool of military resources that ensured Rome's security. But it should be noted that the only way Rome could tap that resource was to engage in war; its Italian subjects paid no tribute. Perhaps this situation served as a major factor promoting imperialism later in Rome's history.

A third element contributing to the conquest of Italy was Rome's ability to adjust its internal political and social structure in a way that promoted allegiance and loyalty among its citizens. When the republic was established in 509 B.C., power fell into the hands of a narrow circle of patricians whose authority rested on birth, wealth, and control of clients. These patricians completely controlled the elective offices, the Senate, and the citizen assemblies. During the next two and a half centuries there ensued what is called the "struggle of the orders." On one side stood the patricians, doggedly determined to maintain their monopoly on power and their exclusive social position. Challenging them were the plebeians, who hardly constituted a homogeneous "class." Some were affluent and ambitious, eager for a share in making political decisions. Most were poor, humble farmers and artisans concerned chiefly with escaping the economic oppression of the patricians and finding more land.

As the struggle of the orders progressed, the patricians grudgingly conceded to the plebeians a larger share in directing the Roman state and took steps to alleviate the most serious economic and social problems facing Rome. Such concessions were often made at moments of crisis created by plebeian leaders; on occasion the plebeians even seceded from the state until their demands were met. Perhaps the ultimate fear of the ruling patricians was that the plebeian soldiers would refuse to serve the state in the wars marking first Rome's struggle for survival and then the conquest of Italy. Whatever the motives and however bitter the struggle, the significant fact was that the dominant patricians did give sufficient ground to prevent civil strife and to avoid alienation of any major segment of the citizen body. As early as 494 B.C., the plebeians gained the right to elect special plebeian officials, called *tribunes*, who were given the power to veto any act of the regularly elected officials that threatened plebeian interests. A new plebeian assembly, called originally the Council of the Plebs and then later the Assembly of Tribes, was instituted to provide a forum where the plebeians could indicate their will to the tribunes. In 450 B.C. plebeian pressure resulted in the famous Twelve Tables, a written codification of ancient legal customs that protected citizens from the arbitrary decisions of patrician judges. A succession of laws gave protection to debtors, permitted marriage between patricians and plebeians, limited

patrician monopoly on the use of public lands, and provided land grants to poor plebeians. One by one the major elective offices were opened to plebeians; particularly important was a law of 367 B.C. that required that one consul be a plebeian, for election to the consulship automatically qualified a Roman citizen for membership in the Senate. Finally, in 287 B.C. the enactments of the Assembly of Tribes were recognized as the ultimate law binding on the entire state, a concession that gave the citizen body final authority.

Viewed from one perspective, the final outcome of the struggle of the orders was the creation of a constitution for the republic that placed the control of the state in the hands of its citizenry— the Roman Senate and the people, as the Romans put it. By 265 B.C. the citizen body theoretically had the final power to decide public policy. They exercised that power through participation in the various assemblies noted above; of these the Assembly of Tribes was the chief instrument for the binding expression of popular will. Aside from the power to make the final laws, the citizens had the power to elect the various magistrates who executed the decisions of the citizens enacted in the assemblies. The Roman executive system was collegiate in form. With minor exceptions, every administrative function was carried out by a board of at least two members of equal rank, each of whom had the power to veto the acts of his colleagues, a system that both constrained rash action by elected officials and led to intricate bargaining in order to achieve any results. The highest executive authority in the state—the *imperium*—was exercised by two consuls charged with the joint management of all civil and military affairs. Next below them were the *praetors*, elected primarily to administer justice but under special circumstances capable of exercising the *imperium.* In time other administrative offices with specialized functions were created to assist in running the increasingly complicated affairs of the expanding republic. Most elective officials were elected for one-year terms. An important exception was the *censor*, chosen every five years to classify the citizens for military service and to judge the moral fitness of citizens for public functions, particularly for membership in the Senate. In times of grave crisis, a *dictator* could be elected for a term of six months with unlimited power to run the state. By law any citizen was eligible for election to these offices, but since there was no pay for service and since electioneering was expensive, few men of humble means aspired to high office and even fewer gained it.

Especially potent in the republican system of government was the Senate, a body of about three hundred men who served for life. Service as consul or praetor automatically qualified a citizen for membership in the Senate, ensuring that it was made up of those with political experience but also that its membership was dominated by the wealthy and the socially prominent. Theoretically, the Senate was an advisory body, counseling the magistrates and the assemblies in making decisions that best served the interests of the state. In fact, its decisions were almost invariably accepted by the assemblies and the magistrates because of the prestige and experience of the senators and because of the influence they asserted on the political process through their numerous clients.

From another perspective the struggle of the orders had resulted in anything but a democratic constitution. During its long course a series of pragmatic compromises had been fashioned that permitted a small circle of wealthy landowners, descendants of a few ancient families, to maintain control of public life in Rome. The members of this circle were convinced that right order in society depended on their collective political wisdom, and thus they acted consciously to control the machinery of government; involvement in the governance of Rome was their career. From the ranks of this circle came most of the elected magistrates, who passed from elected office into the Senate. That body, with its extensive role in decision making, was the bastion of aristocratic control. The power wielders worked as a group to manage the election process and to control the assemblies. Especially effective in achieving these ends was their ability to maintain and to manage their plebeian clients whose support was usually forthcoming in return for public policies that provided economic concessions and protection from oppression under the law. The chief threat to the political power of the patrician families came from enterprising, increasingly wealthy plebeians who sought a share in power. The patricians met this

challenge by absorbing these "new men" into their circle, chiefly by opening public offices and Senate membership to them and by linking them to noble families through marriage. This process tended to shift the basis for political power from kinship to wealth, but it in no way weakened control over political life by a small circle of wealthy families, which the Romans increasingly called the *nobiles*, the ruling nobility (see Figure 8.1). By 265 B.C. most Romans were content to entrust the destiny of the city to these *nobiles*. That trust was based on a deep-seated respect in the Roman citizen body for traditional ways of doing things, on a sense that the leadership of the *nobiles* had been effective in enhancing Rome's power and wealth, and on the assurance that the citizens had the means to curb abuses of power. By 265 B.C. this oligarchic system was so powerfully entrenched and so widely accepted that it seemed to many Romans that the ideal form of government had been fashioned. Perhaps the only issues for the future were whether the ruling *nobiles* could remain united in their collective exercise of power and whether they would remain sensitive and responsive to the needs of the citizen body as a whole.

3. OVERSEAS EXPANSION: THE PUNIC WARS, 264–201 B.C.

By 265 B.C. Rome had completed the unification of Italy and had put in place a system of government that seemed effective. Perhaps without yet knowing it, Rome had become a major power because of these developments. During the next century and a half, Roman history was shaped by an expanding involvement in the complex affairs of the entire Mediterranean world, which resulted in a series of victories that made the Romans the rulers of a large empire (see Map 8.2).

Rome's first encounter with a major Mediterranean power was with Carthage. Originally a Phoenician colony, Carthage had established its independence about 800 B.C. In the succeeding centuries, the Carthaginians had built a thriving commercial empire based on colonies located at strategic places around the western Mediterranean. During much of this period, their main ri-

Map 8.2 **THE ROMAN EMPIRE, 265–44 B.C.** As this map shows, Rome's expansion around the Mediterranean came a bit at a time. By the beginning of the second century B.C. the Romans had established their supremacy in the western Mediterranean, chiefly as a consequence of territory annexed following the Punic Wars. Between about 200 and 125 B.C., the Romans established dominance over Macedonia, Greece, and the west coast of Asia Minor. With that power base it was only a matter of time until further expansion occurred both in the East and in the West. The circumstances surrounding Rome's expansion after 133 B.C. will be discussed in later chapters.

vals for commercial supremacy were the Greek city-states of Sicily and southern Italy. Carthaginian relationships with Rome during this period were generally friendly. Eventually their interests clashed over control of Sicily. In 265 B.C., the Carthaginians, who controlled western Sicily, took steps to protect the Greek city-state of Messana against the aggression of another Greek city-state, Syracuse. After some hesitation, the Romans decided to intervene, perhaps persuaded by fears that Carthaginian control of Messana would result in intervention by a major power in the affairs of

Rome's recently conquered Greek allies in southern Italy. Prospects of booty made the choice easier. Rome's decision meant war with Carthage.

The First Punic War (264–241 B.C.) was a struggle for Sicily. The Romans soon realized that they would need a navy to dislodge the Carthaginians from their seaport strongholds. With great resolve and help from their Greek allies, they soon achieved that end. There then ensued a long series of engagements for control of the waters around Sicily. Although the fledgling Roman navy suffered several defeats, the Romans persevered until

Carthage sued for peace in 241 B.C. By the treaty ending the war, Rome gained Sicily and a sizeable monetary payment to cover war expenses. With the exception of a few Greek city-states given special treatment, Sicily was organized as Rome's first tribute-paying overseas province.

But the issue between the two powers was far from settled. In the years following the peace of 241 B.C., the Carthaginians turned their attention to rebuilding their strength, seriously threatened by the loss of Sicily and the Roman challenge to their sea power. Under the leadership of Hamilcar Barca and his son, Hannibal, Carthage undertook to create an enlarged land empire in Spain as a new base for its power. Hamilcar successfully subdued the native Spanish population, recruited and trained a potent army of Spaniards, and collected a huge war chest derived from Spain's rich mines. The Romans were much too involved in other matters to pay attention to Carthage's recovery: organizing Corsica and Sardinia, treacherously seized from Carthage; extending Roman control into the Po Valley; coping with plebeian agitation for fairer distribution of public land; and curbing piracy in the Adriatic Sea. Only gradually did the Romans turn their attention to the rising power of Carthage in Spain. Their efforts to intervene there soon led to a new war, provoked in 218 B.C. by Hannibal's attack on a Spanish city that Rome claimed as an ally.

The Second Punic War (218–201 B.C.) was certainly Rome's sternest military test, due in large part to the genius of Hannibal. The initial Roman war plan anticipated sending armies to Spain and Africa to destroy the Carthaginian power bases. But Hannibal upset that plan by a boldly conceived plan of his own. His strategy centered on bringing a major military force into Italy in order to deprive Rome of the manpower provided by its Italian allies, whom Hannibal presumed would be glad to rid themselves of the Roman yoke. With characteristic daring he surprised the Romans by leading his army on a thousand-mile march from Spain across southern Gaul and the Alps into northern Italy, where he was welcomed by the Gauls, long enemies of Rome and ready to provide troops to assist Hannibal. On three different occasions between 218 and 216 B.C. the Romans challenged him with large armies, only to be crushed

each time. The last and the most disastrous of these battles, at Cannae, convinced the Romans that they could not match Hannibal in open battle. They adopted a policy of harassing his army, otherwise leaving him free to do as he pleased. Until 203 B.C.—a total of fifteen years—Hannibal maintained an army in Italy, spreading destruction up and down the peninsula; this was a remarkable feat in view of the fact that he received almost no reinforcements or supplies from Carthage or Spain. But he failed to achieve what he counted on to defeat Rome: He never persuaded a decisive number of Rome's Italian allies to desert.

While holding Hannibal at bay in Italy, Rome resolutely undertook the long struggle to crush Carthage. The Romans fought on many fronts and actually won the war outside Italy. Large armies sent to Spain slowly crushed Carthaginian power and cut off Hannibal's reinforcements. Another Roman force was dispatched to Sicily to choke off a rebellion of Greek city-states led by Syracuse in support of Carthage. Roman naval forces patrolled the western Mediterranean and the Adriatic, preventing Hannibal from getting help from Carthage or from its chief ally, the kingdom of Macedon. The Romans encouraged African peoples to attack Carthaginian territories. Rome's counteroffensive culminated in 205 B.C., when a large army under Scipio Africanus was sent to Africa. In him, Rome had found a military talent equal to that of Hannibal. Once in Africa, Scipio attacked Carthage, and Hannibal was recalled from Italy in 203 B.C. to save the city. But even he could no longer stem the tide: He met Scipio in a battle in 202 B.C. at Zama and suffered a complete defeat.

After Zama, the Carthaginians sued for peace. They were forced to surrender Spain to Rome, to destroy their navy, to accept a heavy fine to be paid over the next fifty years, and to agree never again to wage war outside Africa and within Africa only with Rome's permission. Part of Carthage's African territory was turned over to Numidia, a state Rome hoped would balance Carthaginian power in Africa. The use of such client kingdoms as a means of protecting its interests on distant frontiers soon became a regular part of Rome's imperial strategy. This settlement reduced Carthage to a minor power; victorious Rome was dominant in the western Mediterranean.

4. OVERSEAS EXPANSION: THE EASTERN MEDITERRANEAN, 200–133 B.C.

Rome's victory over Carthage was but a prelude to further successful involvement in affairs outside Italy, especially in the turbulent world of the eastern Mediterranean (see Map 8.2). Roman leaders stoutly protested that Rome's engagement there was a "just" cause undertaken to ensure Rome's safety and to protect Roman allies. However, other factors were at work to generate an expansionist, imperialistic policy. The Romans seem to have been plagued by a genuine fear of outsiders, born perhaps from an understandable ignorance about affairs in the East. As we shall see later, aristocratic Roman society was increasingly enchanted by Greek culture, causing many to feel deeply the need to protect it. The Punic Wars had demonstrated clearly that leadership in victorious wars was assurance of fame and power, as illustrated by the career of the immensely popular Scipio Africanus. Equally obvious to all Romans was the fact that successful warfare brought vast riches to Rome in the form of indemnities, tribute, and booty. Developments in the East encouraged many there to turn to "the rising cloud in the West" for help. By 200 B.C., the uneasy balance of power that had existed in the Hellenistic world since the partition of Alexander's empire in the early third century was breaking down. Ptolemaic Egypt grew increasingly weak. Aggressive leaders, such as Philip V of Macedon and Antiochus III of the Seleucid Empire, sought to capitalize on the progressively unstable situation by establishing control not only over Egypt but also over the other independent kingdoms and city-states of the East. To many in the East Rome's intervention seemed the only hope for safety against those threatening the status quo.

Rome's first involvement in the East came during the trying times of the Punic Wars. In an effort to deny the Carthaginians access to the Adriatic Sea, the Romans took steps that challenged the interests of the Illyrians, who controlled the eastern Adriatic coast. Led by an able and ambitious queen, Teuta, the Illyrians resisted and forced Rome to establish a protectorate over the coastal areas. A little later, a new threat arose when Philip V of Macedon formed an alliance with Carthage during the Second Punic War. As a counterbalance, Rome entered into alliances of friendship with Greek cities, especially the Aetolian League. These ventures increased Roman awareness of possible dangers from the East and led to more serious involvement. In 201 B.C. Pergamum, Rhodes, and several Greek city-states appealed to Rome for help against what they argued was Philip V's threat to their freedom. Although the war-weary Roman populace opposed involvement, the ruling oligarchy, led by the pro-Greek Scipio Africanus, declared war on Philip V in 200 B.C. and within three years defeated his forces. He was required to refrain from further involvement in Greek affairs. Amid considerable fanfare and with understandable praise from the Greeks, the Romans reaffirmed the autonomy of each Greek city-state, who henceforth would be Roman allies. The "liberators" of Greece then withdrew without annexing any territory or demanding any tribute.

Peace in the East was brief. In 192 B.C. Antiochus III invaded the Greek peninsula at the urging of the Aetolian League, the members of which were angry at their Roman allies for not rewarding them sufficiently for their assistance in the recent war against Philip V. Rome again sent its armies east, moved in part by the fact that Hannibal was serving as military adviser to the Seleucid army. The Roman legions drove Antiochus out of Greece and in 189 B.C. inflicted a crushing defeat on him at the battle of Magnesia in Asia Minor. He was required to keep out of Asia Minor, his fleet was destroyed, and a staggering indemnity was imposed. Rome turned over large areas of Asia Minor to Pergamum and Rhodes and sanctioned them as Roman-backed peacekeepers. Most of the Greek city-states were restored to independence, although those who had aided Antiochus were fined and forced to surrender some territory to Greek city-states who had remained loyal to Rome. Again the victors annexed no lands.

Despite what the Romans considered to be a policy to ensure peace in the East, the results were otherwise. The reduction of Macedon and the Seleucid state to secondary importance finally destroyed the balance of power in the East and opened the way for rivalry, intrigue, and strife among the petty states of the area. Even the Greeks, whom the Romans had "saved," proved treacherous and unreliable. As the chaos mounted, so did the appeals to Rome for intervention. To the ever-increasing attractiveness of imperialistic ventures was now added growing frustration on the part of the Romans. Slowly they were pushed toward a more drastic solution: direct Roman rule in the East.

Evidence of this new policy came in 171–167 B.C., when Macedonian efforts to court favor among the Greek city-states once again provoked the Romans to declare war on Macedon. Rome easily crushed the Macedonians and their allies. In the ensuing settlements, the Macedonian monarchy was abolished and the kingdom was divided into four weak states upon each of which was imposed a republican form of government. A few years later a minor disturbance in Macedon led the Romans to annex the entire territory as a tribute-paying province under a Roman governor. Persistent intrigue and disturbances among the Greek city-states resulted in increasingly stern Roman reprisals, culminating in 146 B.C. with the savage destruction of Corinth as a example to all Greeks. By that date Rome had forced pro-Roman governments on most Greek city-states. Now they charged the governor of Macedon to supervise the affairs of the Greek city-states, thus ending their freedom. Rome's allies in Asia Minor proved equally unreliable and troublesome. Such harsh measures had to be taken against them that the most important of them, Pergamum and Rhodes, were practically ruined. Finally, in 133 B.C., the last king of Pergamum willed his weakened kingdom to the Romans, who accepted it as a province. Once established in Asia, rich prizes tempted Roman imperialists: Ptolemaic Egypt and the Seleucid Empire, both too weak to offer effective resistance to the Romans.

While concentrating its attention chiefly on the East between 200 and 133 B.C., Rome continued to solidify its power in the West. The occupation of Spain and its organization into two provinces required a long and testing struggle against native resistance. The area of northern Italy between the Alps and the Apennines, called Cisalpine Gaul, was organized into a province. And the Romans finally settled scores with their ancient enemy, Carthage. Although no longer a serious threat, fear of Carthage continued to haunt Rome and prompt actions to humiliate what was now a minor state. The final step occurred in 149 B.C., when Rome declared war on Carthage on the pretext that the Carthaginians had violated the terms of the treaty ending the Second Punic War; Carthage's crime was taking up arms to protect itself against incessant harassment by the kingdom of Numidia, a North African ally of Rome. After a heroic defense Carthage was captured and destroyed in 146 B.C., and its territory was annexed as a Roman province. The destruction of Carthage was a fitting symbol of Rome's position in the Mediterranean world as the second century drew to a close. With provinces on three continents and with unchallenged military forces, the city-state on the Tiber could speak of the Mediterranean as "our sea." The fate of civilization was now in Roman hands.

SUGGESTED READING

Overview of Roman History

Karl Christ, *The Romans: An Introduction to Their History and Civilization*, trans. Christopher Holme (1984). A fine survey.

Early Italy

Jorgen C. Meyer, *Pre-Republican Rome: An Analysis of the Cultural and Chronological Relations, 1000–500 B.C.* (1983). Relying on archaeological evidence, this challenging work throws important light on the origins of Rome.

R. M. Ogilivie, *Early Rome and the Etruscans* (1976).
Michael Grant, *The Etruscans* (1980).
Mauro Cristofani, *The Etruscans: A New Investigation* (1979).
Maja Sprenger, *The Etruscans: Their History, Art, and Architecture* (1983).
Any of the above works will provide a clear picture of Etruscan society and its impact on Rome.

The Republic to 265 B.C.

H. H. Scullard, *History of the Roman World from 753 B.C. to 146 B.C.*, 3rd ed. (1961). A detailed account.

Jaques Heurgon, *The Rise of Rome to 264 B.C.*, trans. James Willis (1973). Traces Rome's development in the total setting of the western Mediterranean world.

Michael Crawford, *The Roman Republic* (1978). A challenging account of political developments with interesting interpretations.

R. Develin, *The Practice of Politics at Rome, 366–167 B.C.* (1985). A detailed study of how the early republican government worked.

E. T. Salmon, *The Making of Roman Italy* (1982). Tells how Rome forged a divided Italy into a single community.

R. M. Errington, *The Dawn of Empire: Rome's Rise to World Power* (1972).

William V. Harris, *War and Imperialism in Republican Roman, 327–70 B.C.* (1979).

These two titles deal in detail with the forces that led to Roman expansion and with its effects on Roman society.

Erich S. Gruen, *The Hellenistic World and the Coming of Rome*, 2 vols. (1984). A detailed study explaining how and why the Hellenistic world came under Roman sway; a landmark study for understanding Roman imperialism.

B. H. Warmington, *Carthage*, 2nd rev. ed. (1969). A fine treatment of the history and civilization of Rome's greatest foe.

Brian Caven, *The Punic Wars* (1980). An excellent treatment of the military history of the Punic Wars.

Biographies

Ernle Bradford, *Hannibal* (1981).

H. H. Scullard, *Scipio Africanus: Soldier and Politician* (1970).

CHAPTER 9

The Failure of the Roman Republic, 133–31 B.C.

FIGURE 9.1 **A Roman Warship** Warships such as the one shown in this relief, created to celebrate Octavian's victory over Antony and Cleopatra at Actium in 31 B.C., played a major role in establishing Roman dominance over the Mediterranean world during the era of the republic. Control over fleets of such ships and the soldiers they carried was also a prime factor in the rise of the military strong men—such as Sulla, Pompey, Julius Caesar, and Octavian—to positions that allowed them to end the republic. (Alinari/Art Resource)

Rome's rise to dominance in the Mediterranean world during the period 265–133 B.C. had understandably generated confidence among the Roman citizenry, especially the ruling oligarchy, that the political and social system of the republic was not only successful but also capable of meeting any situation. Developments after 133 B.C. proved that such confidence was misplaced. Between 133 and 31 B.C. a series of crises tested that system beyond its capabilities and ultimately left the traditional political system in ruins.

1. THE BURDENS OF A WORLD POWER

At the root of the crises that afflicted Rome after 133 B.C. were complex problems that were in large part a result of Rome's expansion from a small city-state to a large empire. Many of them were neglected during the era of expansion, but eventually they surfaced to demand political solutions. They need to be kept in mind if one is to understand the history of the last century of the republic.

First, Rome's conquests created a long frontier to defend and a large, diverse subject population to control. While a military force composed of Roman citizens and Italian allies had conquered this vast empire, the problem of establishing a military system to defend and maintain the empire had not been faced (see Map 8.2 for Rome's expansion during the last century of the republic).

Second, there was the problem of how the conquered subjects would be governed. In contrast with the enlightened policy originally applied to the Italian population, the Romans increasingly viewed conquered non-Italians as subjects to be exploited. Annexed territories were organized into provinces. Control over each province was entrusted to a governor invested with absolute military and civil power; little attention was given to holding these governors accountable. The residents of each province were subject to heavy tribute, the collection of which was entrusted to tax farmers (called *publicans*) who paid the Roman government what it expected from each province and then extorted all they could from the provin-

cials, often in collusion with the governors. This abusive system disrupted order among the provincials and bred discontent, resistance, and hatred.

Third, Rome's Italian allies, whose military service played a key role in Rome's conquests, were increasingly disregarded. Not only did they benefit little from the fruits of conquest, but also the prospect of citizenship implicit in Rome's earlier arrangements grew increasingly remote. As a consequence, the allies became restless and rebellious.

Fourth, Rome's economy underwent significant transformations during the third and second centuries. Rome was greatly enriched by the influx of wealth exacted from conquered peoples. Most of that wealth fell into the hands of a small segment of the population. The beneficiaries not only developed a taste for luxurious living but also sought new opportunities for investment. Although trade and manufacturing investments absorbed some of this wealth, rich aristocrats preferred investment in land and money lending. A basic transformation of the agricultural system provided ample opportunity. The traditional Italian agricultural system, based on the small, independent farm tilled by a freeholder and his family and devoted to cereal crops, was undergoing major changes. Competition from cheaper grain imported as tribute from more productive provinces eroded this system. Many small farms were ruined as a result of the devastation caused by Hannibal's wars in Italy and of the long absence of their owners in military service in far-off places. Often these citizen-soldiers borrowed to save their land, only to find themselves dispossessed for failure to repay their loans. Enterprising Romans with capital began to create large estates (called *latifundia*) by buying or seizing the land of impoverished small farmers and by using political influence to receive allotments of public land. These new agricultural units concentrated on the production of cash crops such as grapes, olives, and livestock. Increasingly the labor supply on the *latifundia* was provided by slaves, most of whom were victims of Rome's wars of conquest, or by former independent farmers forced to accept status as tenant farmer. The real victims of this transformation of agricultural life were Roman citizens and Roman allies whose loyal service as soldiers had won Rome's empire.

These fundamental economic changes caused a fifth set of problems of a social nature. Down to mid–third century B.C. the Roman social order had been relatively simple. Atop the social structure stood a relatively small circle of nobles of both patrician and plebeian origin whose authority was based on family connections, control of political life, and landed wealth. Below them was the rest of the citizen body, chiefly freeholding farmers whose economic and social status made them equals. But changing times slowly made that simple order more complex and brought increasing social tensions. As already noted, the aristocrats became richer; their wealth allowed a style of life that distanced them from the rest of the population. Although these *nobiles* were firmly entrenched at the top of society, they were increasingly challenged by a new group that came to be known as *equites*. The members of this group were wealthy entrepreneurs who grew rich as military suppliers, organizers of large-scale trading ventures, building contractors, bankers, and provincial tax collectors. Their economic interests were intimately linked to public policies with respect to war, provincial administration, public works, and taxes. Consequently, the *equites* were increasingly anxious for a share in political power and for social recognition. The continuing impoverishment of small farmers led to social distinctions within that group. Many were forced to become tenants or hired laborers, with a consequent lowering of their social status. Others in growing numbers left their farms for the cities, especially Rome, to seek livelihood as artisans, shopkeepers, and laborers; their new occupations changed their economic and social needs and concerns. Many citizens who flocked to Rome became members of what the Romans called the proletariat, a rootless and restless population endowed with rights of citizenship but victims of an unstable economic life and an uncertain social status. This volatile "mob," its members ever more dependent on the state or upon rich patrons for their livelihood, offered a tantalizing power base for ambitious political leaders willing to utilize public power to support their interests. At the bottom of the social scale was an expanding slave population; its presence sharp-

ened the concerns of economically and socially depressed freemen whose condition seemed little better than that of slaves. The stresses building up in this increasingly complex social structure had the potential for disrupting the internal order in Roman society.

Finally, Rome's entire citizen body was beginning to feel the unsettling impact of new ideological factors impinging on their lives. Large segments of aristocratic society were deeply affected by concepts and values derived from their adoption of Hellenistic culture and by the style of life their new wealth permitted. Many Romans were intrigued by the emotional, individualistic mystery religions from the East. Incessant military involvement engendered a disturbing tolerance for violence and arrogance. These currents made the Roman populace less willing to abide by traditional values and moral standards associated with the simpler, more rustic world of the early republic.

This array of problems required changes that could only be brought about by innovative political action. By 133 B.C. such decisions were in the hands of the narrow oligarchy, which had established unchallenged control over political life during the long and difficult era of expansion. This dominant group constituted a closed caste that controlled not only access to public office but also the processes by which decisions were made. Most citizens, little understanding the complicated issues of war and diplomacy and duly impressed with the success that came to Rome under the direction of the *nobiles*, willingly allowed the ruling oligarchy to decide Rome's fate. By 133 B.C. the nobles had become so accustomed to unquestioned authority that they assumed it to be their right to direct the state as they saw fit. Their conduct of public affairs between 265 and 133 B.C. suggested little awareness of the problems generated by the expansion they had so successfully managed. While this oligarchic, conservative regime seemed firmly entrenched in 133 B.C., there were ominous signs that the traditional consensus within the ranks of the *nobiles* was in danger of dissolving. Increasingly ambitious members of that group sought wealth, political and military honor, and cultural distinction that would exalt them over their aristocratic peers. Although the ruling oligarchy sought to curb such tendencies, there remained the danger that rivalries among the *nobiles* would become another disruptive force.

Thus, by 133 B.C. a dangerous situation existed. A political order shaped to allow the citizen body of a small city-state to decide its fate had fallen into the hands of a narrow, self-serving ruling caste increasingly divided within its own ranks. That government was faced with massive problems posed by the burdens of ruling a growing empire. Its inability to adjust to the changing situation produced a political upheaval that ultimately destroyed the Roman Republic.

2. ATTEMPTED REFORMS AND FACTIONAL STRUGGLES, 133–79 B.C.

The ordeal of the republic opened with a succession of political struggles that emerged from an effort to institute reforms aimed at resolving some of the most critical problems facing Rome. That effort quickly took the form of a struggle between two factions of the nobility over how the political process should work in reaching decisions about critical issues. On one side was a group known as the *optimates* (the best), representing the established ruling oligarchy, whose members believed that decision making should remain where it had always been—in the hands of the Senate and the elected magistrates drawn from the *nobiles,* a group of approximately two thousand citizens from a narrow circle of powerful families. Opposed was a faction known as the *populares* (the "people") who sought to involve a broader range of the citizen body in political decisions, utilizing for that purpose the ancient political tools of the "people"—the tribunes and the Assembly of Tribes. The *populares* were usually led by men of noble origin, often motivated by a mixture of genuine concern for Rome and ambitions to advance their careers. They sought to achieve these ends by appealing to the plebeian citizens, especially those living in Rome, and the *equites* to use their votes to shape political decisions.

The initial engagement in the struggle for reform and power occurred between 133 and 121 B.C. The champions of the *populares* were the brothers Tiberius and Gaius Gracchus. Aristo-

cratic, well educated, and ambitious, the Gracchi were deeply troubled by the threat posed to Rome's military resources by the declining numbers of citizen farmers and the increasing numbers of urban proletariat, trends that reduced the number of citizens who could afford to perform military service. Elected tribune for 133 B.C., Tiberius proposed a land law aimed at redressing this situation. The law proposed to enforce an older law limiting the amount of public land any citizen could hold. Land recovered by the application of this law would be redistributed to landless citizens. Although the law had some support in the Senate, it threatened the wealth of many *nobiles* who over many generations had gained control of most public lands. In order to pass his proposal, Tiberius resorted to political moves that were not unconstitutional but that ran counter to the way in which decisions were customarily made. He used his power as tribune to put the land law before the Assembly of Tribes; that body approved the measure without senatorial approval and despite the veto of another tribune who was rewarded for his action by being voted out of office. When Tiberius tried to apply his land law, the Senate attempted to thwart him by withholding funding. Tiberius responded by threatening to divert revenues from the provinces for this purpose, a measure that challenged the Senate's traditional control over public finances and foreign affairs. Finally, Tiberius sought reelection as tribune in order to complete his reform. Since such reelection ran contrary to the custom that limited the term of elected offices to one year, the Senate raised the charge that Tiberius was seeking to become a dictator. This inflammatory accusation led to violence and the murder of Tiberius at the hands of those calling themselves *optimates.* After Tiberius' death the application of his land law went forward, suggesting that the substance of the law was not the real issue. Instead, at the heart of the struggle was the threat to the Senate's monopoly on political power posed by Tiberius' political tactics, especially his appeal to the "people" for support.

A decade after Tiberius' death the reform issue was raised again by his brother Gaius. Elected tribune for 122 B.C., Gaius put forward a much more comprehensive program than that of Tiberius. He persuaded the Assembly of Tribes to pass new land laws, to provide cheap grain at public expense for Rome's populace, to establish overseas colonies for the resettlement of impoverished Romans, to extend political privileges to the Italian allies, and to provide to the *equites* greater control over provincial tax collection and over the juries that tried cases involving extortion in provincial administration. These measures, collectively aimed at creating broad *populares* support for Gaius, aroused bitter opposition from the *optimates* and ultimately led to violence they provoked that took the lives of Gaius and three thousand of his followers.

Although the death of Gaius Gracchus left the *populares* leaderless for more than a decade, the Gracchi had formulated a broad reform program that would provide ambitious leaders in the future with a wide range of issues upon which to build popular support. A leader capable of exploiting this situation soon appeared: Marius (ca. 155–86 B.C.). A wealthy man of nonnoble origin with small prospects of a major political role, Marius took advantage of a military crisis to gain power. The occasion was a badly managed war involving Rome with Jugurtha, a claimant to the throne of Numidia, a client kingdom of Rome in North Africa. Growing impatience with the failure of Roman armies to defeat Jugurtha and charges that this clever, unscrupulous king held his own through bribery of Roman officials generated widespread unrest in Rome. Playing upon suspicions of corruption in the Senate and proclaiming his support for *populares* reforms, Marius succeeded in winning the consulship for 107 B.C. He then persuaded the Assembly of Tribes to vote him command of the army in Numidia. In recruiting troops for his campaign, Marius took a bold and fateful step. Disregarding the traditional property qualifications for military service, he enlisted large numbers of propertyless volunteers attracted by hope of rewards from their general. The first step had been taken in the creation of private armies as a political tool.

Marius quickly justified the trust placed in him by defeating Jugurtha in 105 B.C. Then he was annually reelected as consul during the years between 104 and 101 B.C. to conduct campaigns against Germanic tribes threatening northern Italy and southern Gaul. Again Marius was successful,

in no small part because of his skill in professionalizing his volunteer army. While he earned fame as a general, Marius' *populares* allies asserted pressure on the Roman government to provide land allocations for his veterans. However, during his sixth term as consul for 100 B.C. Marius was maneuvered by the Senate into using some of his soldiers to curb the increasingly violent actions of his own political allies. This action ended his leadership of the *populares* cause.

The decade of the nineties was relatively quiet, perhaps because moderate elements in the Senate made efforts to respond to critical problems. However, two issues defied its efforts and provided fuel for the next crisis. One was the festering problem of the Italian allies, long discontented over Rome's failure to recognize their contribution to military conquests and increasingly impoverished by the decline of small-farm agriculture. To relieve their situation, the allies demanded full citizenship. Although Roman leaders from Gaius Gracchus onward often proposed such a step, the Romans repeatedly refused to share the rewards of citizenship with the allies. When one more such proposal was voted down in 91 B.C., the allies joined in a great rebellion, sometimes called the Social War, which threatened Rome's very existence. Sulla (138–78 B.C.), a noble who had established a reputation while serving under Marius in the war against Jugurtha, was chosen to lead the army raised to suppress the uprising. By 89 B.C. Sulla defeated the rebels, whose cause was undermined when the Romans finally granted citizenship. For his success Sulla was elected consul for 88 B.C.

While the Social War was in progress, Rome faced another threat caused by the corruption-ridden, oppressive system of provincial administration. In 89 B.C. Mithridates VI, king of Pontus in Asia Minor, played on this discontent to launch a war of liberation in Asia Minor and Greece. Faced with the threat of loss of its empire in the East, the Senate charged Sulla with leading a campaign against Mithridates. However, a faction of *populares* leaders defied the Senate to vote the command to Marius. Sulla responded by marching his army to Rome, crushing the *populares,* and securing the command by force. His actions left little doubt where real power lay.

Sulla was able to force Mithridates to return to his old kingdom and to reestablish Roman control over the eastern provinces. But he made no decisive settlement in the East; his eyes were on Rome, where developments threatening his career were unfolding. Immediately after his departure for the East, the *populares* under Marius forced their way back into power and imposed a reign of terror on the Senate. They dominated until 83 B.C., when Sulla reappeared in Italy, greatly enriched by booty seized in the East. His battle-tested soldiers routed the *populares,* whose leader had died in 86 B.C. To seal his victory, Sulla ordered the murder of thousands of citizens from all over Italy identified with the *populares* cause and the confiscation of their property, much of which was used to reward his soldiers and his political supporters.

Once in unchallenged control, Sulla had himself appointed as dictator. Intent on restoring control of the republic to the Senate, he enacted legislation that severely limited the power of the tribunes and the Assembly of Tribes to initiate legislation. The size of the Senate was doubled, many of the new seats being granted to *equites* and upper-class Italians. Steps were taken to regularize the election procedures for the magistracies, to improve the administration of justice, and to organize provincial government more efficiently—all sources of political agitation. Confident that he had restored the ancient constitution with the Senate in control, Sulla retired from public life in 79 B.C. In fact, the Senate was in power because a powerful military leader had decreed so. The long, bitter clash between *optimates* and *populares* had resolved few of Rome's basic problems; rather, the struggle created a situation that encouraged bold, ambitious individuals to seek power by exploiting those problems. The republican form of government had suffered a mortal blow.

3. THE ERA OF MILITARY STRONG MEN, 79–31 B.C.

The Senate proved itself unable to bear the burden thrust upon it by Sulla. Its failures created successive opportunities for "strong men" to control Roman political life during the half century following Sulla. Their competition for power and the methods they employed to gain it brought the republic to an end by 31 B.C.

Between 79 and 70 B.C. the Senate was faced with several serious crises: a revolt in Italy led by a disaffected consul seeking to undo Sulla's reforms; a rebellion in Spain organized by a disillusioned Roman governor who enjoyed widespread native support; a slave uprising in Italy led by a professional gladiator named Spartacus; a mounting threat from pirates to the grain supply for Rome; and a new war with Mithridates VI of Pontus. Contrary to the principles undergirding Sulla's settlement, the Senate sought to meet these crises by granting extraordinary powers to ambitious individuals in a fashion that left the Senate little opportunity to control their actions. A protegé of Sulla, Pompey (106–48 B.C.), was given command of forces to deal with the Italian revolt and then with the insurrection in Spain (see Figure 9.2). A rich financier ambitious for a political career, Crassus (ca. 115–53 B.C.), was charged with defeating Mithridates. Both were successful, and although neither was eligible for office, they were rewarded with the consulship for 70 B.C.

During their co-consulship, Pompey and Crassus negated most of Sulla's settlement; their enactments won the applause of the remnants of the *populares* and restored the opportunity for ambitious leaders to exploit popular support as a path to power. But neither Pompey nor Crassus was satisfied. Pompey was the first to move toward greater power. By manipulation he persuaded the Senate and the people to vote him two important military commands: In 67 B.C. he was granted sweeping powers to clear the Mediterranean of pirates, a task he completed in a matter of months. Then in 66 B.C. he was selected to lead an army against Mithridates VI of Pontus, who since 74 B.C. had again challenged Rome's rule in Asia Minor. Pompey quickly defeated Mithradates. He then took it upon himself to reorganize Rome's position in the East. He annexed the combined territories of Bithynia and Pontus into a new province and created another new province in Syria. To protect these provinces, he worked out a series of agreements with small kingdoms beyond Rome's new frontier, making each a client of Rome charged with protecting the frontier in return for Roman support in maintaining each king's power

FIGURE 9.2 Pompey and Julius Caesar These two men, Pompey (left) and Julius Caesar (right), virtually controlled the destiny of the Roman Republic and the Mediterranean world between 79 and 44 B.C. Their busts reflect the talent of Roman sculptors in portraiture. (Pompey, Culver Pictures; Julius Caesar, Alinari/Art Resource)

over his subjects. Pompey also regulated tribute collection in the East so as to greatly increase the return to the Roman government. His efforts represented a major step in solidifying provincial administration; and it won Pompey important support from Romans whose interests were involved in the East.

Pompey's success, reminiscent of Sulla's rise to power, caused constant concern in Rome and drove other ambitious politicians to maneuver to check him. A key figure in this endeavor was Crassus, who found a skilled ally in Julius Caesar (100–44 B.C.), a man of patrician origins but with family connections that linked him with Marius and the *populares* cause (see Figure 9.2). Crassus

and Caesar promoted laws to attract popular support and spent huge sums in an attempt to secure extraordinary military commands such as those held by Pompey. The Senate resisted their maneuvers, supported in its effort by Cicero (106–43 B.C.), a "new" man who clawed his way to the consulship for 63 B.C. by utilizing his skills as an orator and a lawyer. His finest hour as consul came when he earned public acclaim for foiling an alleged conspiracy by Cataline, a frustrated power seeker and sometime agent of Crassus, to overthrow the system. While Cicero shared the ambition for power with most other political leaders of his time, he disdained one-man rule in favor of a "concord of orders" that would link the talents of the old aristocracy and the *equites* into a new ruling force capable of ending senseless political conflict.

Finally, in 62 B.C. Pompey returned from the East. Contrary to expectations, his first act was to disband his army and request that the Senate reward his veterans and legalize the settlement he had made in the East. Under the leadership of intractable conservatives, the Senate chose a course that drove Pompey, Crassus, and Caesar into a political alliance. It not only refused to meet Pompey's requests but also acted to curb a major source of Crassus' wealth by restricting the activities of provincial tax farmers and to discredit Caesar by blocking his election to the consulship. Equally frustrated, the three joined in an informal secret agreement, called the First Triumvirate, designed to ensure that each obtained what he wished. Exploiting his growing popular appeal and with the support of Pompey and Crassus, Caesar won the consulship for 59 B.C. Once in office, he forced through measures that satisfied his fellow triumvirs. His reward was a five-year command to look after Roman interests on its northern frontier in Gaul and Illyria.

During the decade after 59 B.C. Rome's political destiny hinged on the actions of the triumvirs. During the first years of the decade the triumvirate held together uneasily. It was renewed in 56 B.C. with the understanding that Pompey and Crassus would be consuls for 55 B.C. and then be granted governorships of important provinces under terms that would provide them command over armies. Caesar's command in Gaul was also extended for five years. But the arrangement was increasingly shaky. Caesar proved to be a brilliant military leader, conducting a highly publicized series of campaigns that added Gaul as a Roman province and took Roman armies into Germany and Britain. Not only did these victories enhance Caesar's reputation, but they also allowed him to create a loyal, disciplined personal army totally devoted to his cause. Crassus' long search for fame came to an end in 53 B.C. when he was killed in an unsuccessful campaign against a Roman foe in the East, the Parthians. An important link between Caesar and Pompey was broken in 54 B.C. with the death of Pompey's wife, Julia, the daughter of Caesar. Caesar's growing fame fed a familiar fear in Rome—that of a victorious general returning to

impose his will. Pompey increasingly won the favor of the Senate as its protector against such an eventuality and was voted powers that made him virtual dictator. Amid heightening tension fed by fear of Caesar and by the violent actions of his agents seeking to protect his interests, Pompey and the Senate moved to ruin Caesar. As his command in Gaul approached its legal end, Caesar sought to run in absentia for the consulship for 49 B.C. so that he could remain in public office and avoid prosecution for alleged illegal acts committed during his service in Gaul. Early in 49 B.C. the Senate decreed that he must surrender his command in Gaul, and Pompey was empowered to take necessary action to protect the state. Rather than face political ruin, Caesar chose to defy the state. He led his legions across the Rubicon River separating Gaul from Italy and plunged Rome into a civil war.

Caesar quickly demonstrated his military genius in leading his seasoned veterans against the larger forces of Pompey. In a succession of campaigns in Italy, Spain, and finally Greece, he battered Pompey's forces. The defeated Pompey finally fled to Egypt, where he was murdered. Caesar used this crime against a Roman citizen as a pretext to intervene in Egypt, where a struggle for control of the crown was in progress among members of the Ptolemaic family. Caesar supported the claims of Cleopatra against her brother-husband, Ptolemy XIV. Perhaps his decision was prompted by the fact that he had become Cleopatra's lover; but more likely he hoped that by putting the young princess on the throne, he could dominate the last independent Hellenistic kingdom and tap Egypt's fabulous wealth for Rome's benefit. From Egypt Caesar continued his triumphant march through the empire—Asia, Africa, Spain—hunting down Pompey's allies and showing his own power. Finally in 45 B.C., he returned to Rome as undisputed master of the Roman world.

Although Caesar's real power rested on his loyal army, he made an effort to legalize his authority. Despite being elected consul several times, he relied chiefly on the office of dictator as the basis for his actions. He allowed the traditional elective offices to be filled, but with men willing to bend to his will. The Senate was greatly enlarged, the new places being filled with Caesar's supporters. As a consequence, that venerable institution became little more than an advisory council to the dictator. On the basis of his dictatorial power, Caesar assumed control of crucial areas of government previously dominated by the Senate: public finances, provincial administration, command over the military forces. A grateful citizenry heaped a wide range of honors on him, creating around him the aura of superiority over other citizens. In many ways Caesar's position in Rome resembled that of a Hellenistic king; indeed, some of Caesar's contemporaries insisted that it was his intention to establish a monarchy in Rome.

In using these powers, Caesar demonstrated qualities of statesmanship to match his military genius. During his brief rule over Rome, he began shaping a reform program that addressed some of the major problems plaguing Rome: reduction of the citizens dependent on the dole by resettling them in the provinces; debt regulation; curbing violence in Rome; aid to Italian farmers; improvement in provincial administration; extension of citizenship to some provincials; reorganizing local government in Italy. It is not clear, however, whether he planned to reshape the structure of the political system to meet Rome's responsibilities as ruler of the Mediterranean world. Perhaps given more time, Caesar would have faced this issue, but that was not to be. A hard core of conservatives, including such former supporters of Caesar as Cassius and Brutus, formed a conspiracy to end what they saw as a threat to the traditional order. These guardians of "right" order struck their blow for liberty on the Ides of March (March 15), 44 B.C., stabbing Caesar to death while he was attending a Senate meeting just prior to his departure for a major campaign against the Parthians.

Caesar's murder did not lead to the restoration of the old order; rather it produced a new civil war among rivals seeking to replace Caesar. Two candidates emerged as the main contenders. One was Mark Antony (ca. 83–30 B.C.), an experienced politician who had served Caesar as a military commander. The other was eighteen-year-old Octavian, a distant relative whom Caesar had adopted as his son. Faced with efforts by the Senate to eliminate them from power, Antony and Octavian, along with another supporter of Caesar named Lepidus, joined forces in 43 B.C. to form the Second Triumvirate and to force the Senate and people to grant them jointly absolute power in the state. Within a year the triumvirs brutally murdered most of the anti-Caesar senatorial forces, including Cicero, and conducted a military campaign in Greece that destroyed the armies raised by Caesar's assassins, two of whom—Cassius and Brutus—died at the decisive battle of Philippi in 42 B.C.

After 42 B.C. Antony, Octavian, and Lepidus continued to rule Rome under the powers voted them in the legislation that established the Second Triumvirate. Actually, each was making preparations to destroy the others. Antony spent most of these years in the East, seeking to strengthen Roman control there and to mount a war against the Parthians. Although he made some progress in these endeavors, his standing in the Roman world was increasingly tainted by his involvement with Cleopatra, for whom he eventually repudiated his Roman wife—none other than Octavian's sister—and by whom he had two sons. This liaison was cleverly exploited by Octavian to portray Antony as a mad traitor and the pitiful victim of a crafty eastern harlot intent on robbing Rome of its territories to advance her own power and to reward her children.

Octavian proved more adept at building a power base. Under the arrangement agreed upon by the triumvirs, he was charged with the heavy responsibilities of providing land for the veterans from the large army that had defeated the forces of Caesar's assassins, of rooting out powerful remnants of anti-Caesar forces in the West, and of coping with the official government still operating in Rome. He worked patiently to meet these challenges, doing so in a way that gave him a solid hold over Italy and the West. Along the way, he forced Lepidus to retire from the triumvirate. Gradually, Octavian came to be looked upon as the protector of Roman interests against Antony, increasingly portrayed by Octavian's clever propaganda as an enemy of Rome. By 32 B.C. Octavian felt strong enough to refuse to rule jointly with Antony and declared war on Cleopatra. The decisive engagement between the huge armies and navies of the protagonists was fought in 31 B.C. at Actium in Greece (see Figure 9.1). Octavian's forces won an easy victory. The triumphant leader pursued Antony and Cleopatra to Egypt, where Cleopatra made one final effort to entice a Roman to support her cause. When Octavian would have none of her favors, she committed suicide, as Antony had already done. Her kingdom was annexed as a Roman province. Again the Roman world had an undisputed ruler whose sword had raised him to a position comparable to that Caesar had enjoyed in 46 B.C. Rome's future depended on what victorious Octavian would decide to do.

4. ECONOMIC AND SOCIAL TRENDS IN THE LATE REPUBLICAN PERIOD

Octavian's triumph at Actium ended a century of turmoil that from one perspective witnessed a political revolution—the replacement of the oligarchic republican system with a military dictatorship. Accompanying that violent political transformation and in part caused by it were economic and social developments that brought subtle changes in the Mediterranean world.

From an economic perspective, one of the fundamental changes of the late republican period was the emergence of Rome and Italy as the center of wealth in the Mediterranean. In large part that prosperity was due to the immense influx of wealth brutally extracted from the growing numbers of provincial subjects in the form of booty, war indemnities, and tribute. Prospects for even greater wealth remained a prime factor in continued Roman military and political expansion. Rome's predatory policy during the late republican period was economically disruptive, especially in the eastern Mediterranean area. It was not yet fully obvious to Roman decision makers that a basic consequence of this shift of wealth toward Italy was a growing economic dependency of Roman citizens on the total economy of the Mediterranean world. It remained to be seen whether Roman policy would be adjusted in directions that would replace pillage with promotion of provincial economic welfare as a prime source of Roman economic well-being.

Perhaps the realities of shifting economic trends were veiled from most Romans by continued productivity of the Italian economy in the late republican period. Agriculture remained the backbone of that economy. Despite disruptions caused by civil strife, the traditional patterns of agricultural production showed remarkable resiliency. Small farming—constantly fortified by land grants given to dispossessed farmers, landless urban residents, and discharged soldiers—still provided at least a subsistence-level livelihood to large numbers of Roman citizens. The *latifundia* system, devoted to cash crops and dependent on tenant farmers, hired labor, and slavery, continued to expand and to provide large incomes to aristocratic landowners. The expanding urban population of the late republican period stimulated industry and trade. Most industrial production in Italy was devoted to the production of items required for daily life and was organized by artisans running small-scale establishments. The products of these workshops were distributed by shopkeepers who also ran small merchandising operations. However, Rome and Italy became increasingly involved in international trading operations, especially in luxury goods and in grain, requiring capital and organization (see Figure 9.3). Although Roman aristocrats generally disdained trading activities as unworthy of their status, other Romans increasingly became involved in this lucrative activity. Many of them even settled abroad, where they increasingly expanded their participation in trade and their understanding of the interconnection between Rome's continued prosperity and the economic well-being of the entire Mediterranean world.

Outwardly Rome's social structure, rooted in an ancient class system, retained its basic forms during the late republican period. One major change was a large increase in the number of citizens as a result of the extension of citizenship to the Italian allies during the Social War (91–89 B.C.). Although the assimilation of these new citizens was not complete by 31 B.C., they were adapting to the traditional Roman class structure.

Despite the gradual erosion of its monopoly on political power during the last century of the republic, the Roman nobility retained its dominant position in society. The great noble families

FIGURE 9.3   Aspects of Life During the Late Republic   These two scenes reflect important aspects of life in the late republic. On the left laborers unload grain brought by ship from African provinces to feed Rome's growing numbers of unemployed citizens. On the right a Roman aristocrat and his wife are instructed by a Greek slave; to be educated in Greek ways was critical to social respectability in first-century B.C. Rome. (Alinari/Art Resource)

showed remarkable ability to survive political proscription, confiscation of their wealth, and political humiliation at the hands of military dictators. During the last century of the republic the Roman nobility acquired new tastes for luxury and became more sophisticated as a result of expanding contacts with the culture of the Hellenistic world (see Figure 9.3). Many adopted freer life styles. Even aristocratic women, long completely under the domination of male heads of households, began to break the shackles of custom to become property owners, active participants in cultural and social life, and even political forces as key partners in political marriages. Although seldom involved in the mainstream of politics during the late republic, the Italian aristocracy exercised an important role in shaping local affairs throughout Italy. On the whole, the Roman nobility by 31 B.C. remained a formidable force whose support must be sought by anyone who would rule and whose ranks represented considerable talent that could be tapped to reconstruct the Roman political order.

The late republican period was marked by significant changes in the status and role of the *equites*. During a time of political turmoil and Roman expansion, the members of this nonnoble group found countless opportunities to increase their wealth to the point where they rivaled the nobles. Although only occasionally did a member of the equestrian order find his way to the center of political power, as a group the *equites* increasingly played an unofficial role in the conduct of political life. Their engagement in banking, money lending, trade, tax collecting, contracting for public works, and procurement of military supplies made this group an unofficial arm of the government, providing crucial administrative services usually performed by a professional bureaucracy—which was lacking in republican Rome. This involvement gave the *equites* invaluable experience in and insight into foreign affairs, economic life, provincial administration, and military activity. And their expertise whetted their ambitions for a larger share in political life. Any leader who could tap the talent of the *equites* would gain formidable allies in the conduct of political life.

During the last century of the republic the plebeian order grew increasingly diverse in composition and status. Many rural plebeians survived as independent farmers but benefited little from Italy's prosperity. Even more difficult was the fate of former independent farmers forced to become rent-paying tenants or hired laborers in the service

WHERE HISTORIANS DISAGREE

Slavery in the Greco-Roman World

Most experts agree that slavery was an essential element of Greco-Roman society. As a consequence, anyone seeking to understand that society must grapple with slavery. But those who seek to respond to that challenge will soon learn an important lesson about historical investigation: The effort to describe any institution fundamental to a past society generates disagreement.

Central to the disagreement among modern historians about slavery and its role in ancient Greece and Rome is a conceptual issue. Is there such a thing as a "slave society?" That is, is there a society whose essential and unique characteristics are a consequence of the role played in that society by slavery? At this point historians—as well as economists, sociologists, political scientists, and philosophers—do not agree on an answer to this question. As a consequence, the study of slavery in antiquity proceeds from divergent perspectives.

This conceptual disagreement stems in large part from lack of consensus on many matters of fact concerning slavery in antiquity. Historians do not agree on the number of slaves, on the proportion of slaves in relation to other forms of labor, on which facets of economic life were slave-dominated, or on the source of supply of slaves. They argue about when and under what conditions the ancient slave system came into existence and ended. They debate whether slavery flourished because it was economically profitable or because there were social, moral, and psychological factors in Greco-Roman culture as a whole that made slavery necessary. They disagree on the impact of slavery on the mentality and behavior of other segments of the population and on how slaves were treated.

But why should disagreement exist? Why cannot historians working with the same body of information reach a common conclusion?

There are several reasons, which are also instructive about the nature of historical investigation. As already noted, historians often have trouble agreeing on a conceptual approach to important institutions like slavery. The surviving source material providing data about slavery in the ancient world is limited, difficult to interpret, and little concerned with issues in which modern historians are concerned. Perhaps even more significant in generating disagreement among historians is a matter raised by M. I. Finley in his book *Ancient Slavery and Modern Ideology* (1980). He argues persuasively that modern inquiries into Greco-Roman slavery have been decisively shaped by preconceived ideas—ideologies—held by the investigators. For example, the treatment of ancient slavery has been colored by convictions, often rooted in Christian moral values, concerning the moral unacceptability of the institution. Likewise, the study of ancient slavery has been distorted by what one scholar called the "religion of classicism"—the glorification of the universal values of Greco-Roman high culture to the point that whatever made it possible, even slavery, is justifiable. Still again, historians have been distracted from examining the realities of ancient slavery by dogmatic adherence to hypotheses about stages of historical development determined by economic structures, especially the Marxist concept of the slave mode of production as a necessary stage out of which emerged a feudal and then a capitalistic mode of production. In short, historians disagree because they ask different questions and expect different answers in order to support views they believe to be valid.

What then are we to conclude about what Aristotle called "property with a soul"—the slave in the ancient world? Only that there is little agreement on this important matter.

of wealthy owners of *latifundia*. Although citizens, this rural population found it increasingly difficult to participate effectively in the political process unfolding in Rome and, as a consequence, saw its social status deteriorate. The urban plebeians constituted an especially disruptive force, particularly in Rome, by now a city approaching a million residents. Its polyglot mixture of citizens, foreigners, slaves, and freedmen lived in crowded tenements without adequate police and fire protection and with minimal provisions for sanitary conditions. A considerable portion of that population earned an adequate living as artisans, shopkeepers, and laborers. But a large segment of the urban population lacked gainful employment and was dependent on the state or on rich patrons for economic survival. This city "mob" increasingly became the political tool of unscrupulous politicians. Their votes were courted in the assemblies to secure passage of legislation that would advance the personal careers of politicians, and they could be incited to acts of violence to serve political ends. In return, politicians diverted public funds to provide food and entertainment for this helpless, disruptive group. Its control and support increasingly constituted a critical social problem.

Two other components of the social structure need to be noted. First was Rome's expanding slave population, largely victims of Rome's military triumphs around the Mediterranean. Each victory resulted in hordes of war captives dumped into Italy as property of Roman citizens and assigned to labor as household servants, workers in shops and manufacturing establishments, and laborers on *latifundia*. The economic importance of slavery encouraged the development of an active slave trade. Although some slaves, especially educated captives from the Hellenistic world, were treated fairly well and often freed, the great bulk, especially rural slaves, were exploited brutally. Hardly better off were the millions of people living in the provinces who were treated without mercy by Roman armies, governors, tax collectors, and merchants. These voiceless subjects had virtually

no way to protect themselves against their Roman masters. Yet as we have noted, Rome's welfare depended increasingly on their productive skills. By 31 B.C. the hour was fast approaching when the Romans, for their own good, would have to weigh their accustomed ways of treating these subjects.

A final consequence of the long ordeal of the late republic took the form of a transformation of the collective mentality of the Roman citizenry. In various ways there was an erosion of confidence in ancient values and an opening of minds to the need for change. With good reason many groups—the peasantry, the urban proletariat, the *equites*—lost faith in the ability of the republican political order to protect their interests; often powerful individual leaders, no matter how they had come to power, served them better than did rich oligarchs spouting slogans about past glories and patriotic duty. Incessant violence generated a widespread longing for peace and order, even at the cost of some liberty. Particularly appealing to educated nobles and *equites* were the philosophical systems of the Hellenistic world, especially Epicureanism and Stoicism, both of which stressed peace of mind as the object of the good life. Hellenistic mystery religions, promising happiness in the afterlife, appealed to many at all levels of society. Expanding awareness of a world larger and more diverse than Rome not only undermined but even made ridiculous and senseless a narrow dedication to the traditions of a single city-state. Many yearned for a new vision of the good society to provide meaning to their lives in changing times.

While not as dramatic as the political upheaval that occurred between 133 and 31 B.C., these economic and social changes provide further grounds for concluding that a revolution had occurred. And they point up the fact that Roman society required more than the reconstruction of the political order if the Romans were to hold their place as rulers of the civilized world. Such was the challenge that faced Octavian at the moment when the Roman world was his to rule.

SUGGESTED READING

Political Developments

H. H. Scullard, *From the Gracchi to Nero: A History of Rome from 133 B.C. to A.D. 68,* 5th ed. (1982). A detailed history.

Ronald Syme, *The Roman Revolution* (1952).

Richard E. Smith, *The Failure of the Roman Republic* (1955).

Erich S. Gruen, *The Last Generation of the Roman Republic* (1974).

Mary Beard and Michael Crawford, *Rome in the Late Republic: Problems and Interpretations* (1985).

These four works present significant but differing interpretations of the causes of the failure of the Roman republic.

Claude Nicolet, *The World of the Citizen in Republican Rome,* trans. P. S. Falla (1980). A reconstruction of the civic life of the average citizen.

Keith Hopkins, *Death and Renewal* (1983). A study of how power and property were transferred among the members of the Roman elite.

Arthur Keaveney, *Rome and the Unification of Italy* (1987). Describes Rome's treatment of the Italians during the late republic.

A. N. Sherwin-White, *Roman Foreign Policy in the East, 168 B.C. to A.D. 1* (1984). An excellent study.

Economic and Social Developments

Henry C. Boren, *Roman Society: A Social, Economic, and Cultural History* (1977). A brief survey.

P. A. Brunt, *Social Conflicts in the Roman Republic* (1971). A good description of social tensions affecting late republican society.

K. D. White, *Roman Farming* (1970). Clarifies the problems of Roman agriculture during the republican period.

Biographies

A. H. Bernstein, *Tiberius Sempronius Gracchus. Tradition and Apostasy* (1978).

Arthur Keaveney, *Sulla: The Last Republican* (1982).

Peter Greenhalgh, *Pompey: The Roman Alexander* (1980), and *Pompey: The Republican Prince* (1981).

B. A. Marshall, *Crassus: A Political Biography* (1976).

Elizabeth Rawson, *Cicero: A Portrait,* rev. ed. (1983).

Matthias Gelzer, *Caesar: Politician and Statesman* (1968).

Arthur D. Kahn, *The Education of Julius Caesar: A Biography, A Reconstruction* (1986).

Sources

Cicero, *Selected Works,* trans. Michael Grant (1971).

War Commentaries of Caesar, trans. Rex Warner (1960). Contains two of Caesar's political works, *The Gallic Wars* and *The Civil Wars.*

CHAPTER 10
The Roman Empire, 31 B.C.–A.D. 180

FIGURE 10.1 Augustus, First Citizen of Rome This majestic statue of Octavian, or Augustus, as he came to be known soon after he seized power, was intended to idealize and exalt the man who had restored peace to the Roman world after the troubled times of the late republic. (Alinari/Art Resource)

The year 31 B.C. marked a critical point in the history of the Mediterranean world. Its destiny lay in the hands of the Romans, who during the preceding two hundred fifty years had won a series of military victories that subdued all other claimants to power. But even in the midst of victory the Romans suffered a profound internal crisis that ended with the collapse of their traditional political order. They now faced the challenge of restoring order in their own house if their dominance of the Mediterranean world was to continue in a fruitful way. During the first and second centuries A.D. the Romans met that challenge by fashioning their most notable contribution to civilization—a system of government known as the Roman Empire. This system became a powerful force promoting peace and prosperity among millions of people living in a vast territory surrounding what the Romans rightly called "our sea."

1. THE ESTABLISHMENT OF THE IMPERIAL ORDER, 31 B.C.–A.D. 14

The foundation of the Roman Empire was the work of Octavian, one of the truly great figures in all history (see Figure 10.1). His victory at Actium in 31 B.C. made him master of the Roman world by virtue of conquest. The experience of the recent past, especially the case of Julius Caesar, had demonstrated that naked power was not the answer to the ongoing crisis. With an uncanny grasp of the mentality of his times, Octavian sensed the essential issue of the moment. In the minds of the Roman citizenry any form of military dictatorship or monarchy was unacceptable because it flaunted a five-century-old tradition that held that the destiny of Rome could be determined only by the decisions of the Senate and the people acting through a set of institutions that constituted the Roman Republic. Yet the experience of the previous century had taught that the only hope for the management of the vast, problem-ridden Roman world lay in the concentration of power in the hands of a single individual. Octavian's challenge was to reconcile the collective mind-set rooted in tradition with existing reality. His solution, worked out with patience and caution during his forty-five-year rule, was masterful. He retained the outward forms of the republican constitution, but at the same time he obtained by legal means sufficient power to permit him to rule the Roman world.

For some years after 31 B.C. Octavian's legal authority was based on repeated election to the consulship. He realized, however, that a continuous succession of consulships would not serve as a permanent basis for his authority; ancient custom dictated that this highest magistracy be rotated annually among eligible citizens. In 27 B.C. he made a decisive move toward a more permanent solution. He proclaimed before the Senate "the transfer of the state to the free disposal of the Senate and the people." This surrender of all the powers he then held was interpreted as a restoration of the republic, with power again resting in the hands of the Senate, the elected magistrates, and the assemblies. Impressed by this noble gesture, fearful of the recurrence of civil war, and skillfully guided by Octavian, the Senate and the people quickly took legal action to bestow on him a wide array of powers. Included were the power of tribune for life, full consular authority without need to hold that office, *imperium* (full command) over most of the provinces, command of the armies, and the highest priestly office. To these legal powers the grateful citizenry added several honors: first senator; *augustus* ("most revered one"); *imperator* ("victorious general"); and *pater patriae* ("father of the country"). This array of legal powers and tradition-laden honors surrounded Octavian with an aura of authority so great that he began to be called *princeps*, the first citizen of Rome, trusted to do what he wished to rule the Roman world without a hint of illegal abuse of power or of violating tradition. What was essentially crucial in Octavian's position was that he did not have to share the authority legally granted him and that his power need not be renewed regularly. Not unimportant in buttressing his position as *princeps* were his immense personal fortune and his wide circle of political dependents, both created during the period of his rise to power after Julius Caesar's death.

Armed with these great powers, Augustus, as he came to be known by virtue of the title that vaguely suggested a semidivine position, turned his attention to revitalizing the citizen body—basically the population of Italy—on whose shoulders rested the responsibility for ruling the vast empire. Adhering to the ancient and widely held conviction that only a class-structured society could ensure right order, Augustus tried to redefine class divisions and to assign civic responsibilities to each group. Rigid standards of birth, wealth, and conduct were established to define senatorial ranking, resulting in a considerable reduction of those eligible for this rank in society. This elite was assigned a major role in political life. To the Senate, the traditional focus of political life for the *nobiles*, Augustus left important powers in selecting magistrates, judging cases, enacting laws, and governing selected provinces. Members of the senatorial class were expected to fill the traditional elective offices, to serve as provincial governors, and to command armies. He anticipated that the equestrian order (*equites*) would serve the state in a wide array of secondary but critical administrative positions in the army, the tax system, and the judicial system. For the plebeians, Augustus tried to provide order, economic security, and pride of citizenship, in return for which he hoped that that group would exercise its vote in support of his regime and serve as volunteers in the army. While this arrangement was sensitive to traditional class roles, it effectively defined the responsibility of citizenship in terms of service to the state at the direction of the *princeps* rather than in terms of citizen formulation of basic policy.

Beyond restructuring the social order and defining civic roles, Augustus was deeply concerned about the morale of the citizen body. This concern prompted him to take a variety of measures aimed at rebuilding a sense of community and reviving a feeling of pride in Rome, ends he hoped to achieve by playing on tradition. He made a major effort to revive ancient civic religious practices as a central part of public life. He patronized writers, such as Vergil, Horace, and Livy, and artists (see Chapter 11) willing to celebrate Rome's ancient glory and present blessings. Numerous laws were enacted in an effort to curb what Augustus believed to be vices that sapped civic virtue—luxury, sexual irregularities, divorce, childless marriages, gambling, drinking, idleness. Immense sums were spent beautifying Rome and providing better public services in the hope of eliciting pride in what was now "head of the world."

Augustus was particularly concerned with the military system. His solution was shaped by an awareness of the need for a large force to protect Rome's frontiers and by the memory of the disruptive role played by private armies during the last century of the republic. His response was the creation of a professional army directly under the control of the *princeps* consisting of twenty-five legions (about one hundred fifty thousand troops) made up chiefly of Roman citizens serving long terms. Each legion was complemented by an equal-sized auxiliary unit composed of noncitizens recruited in the provinces. Noncitizens serving in both legions and auxiliary units were granted citizenship upon completion of service. A command structure, employing carefully selected members of the senatorial and equestrian orders but always subordinate to the *princeps*, was developed. Steps were taken to provide training, discipline, systematic provisioning, regular pay, and money pensions to the soldiers. The bulk of this force was stationed in frontier provinces facing potential enemies. Only the Praetorian Guard, a select contingent of about nine thousand troops acting as a bodyguard for the *princeps*, was garrisoned in the vicinity of Rome.

During Augustus' reign the army was used both to secure control over existing provinces and to attack external foes. The most important campaigns were waged in an effort to strengthen the empire's European frontier. As a result, the Roman hold on Illyricum was made secure and the new provinces of Raetia, Pannonia, and Moesia were added along the Danube frontier (see Map 10.1). An effort to advance the German frontier from the Rhine to the Elbe ended in a crushing defeat in A.D. 9. Thereafter, Augustus gave up expansion, seeking instead to establish a fixed frontier between Romans and foreigners to be defended by the imperial army.

Well aware of the disarray produced in the provinces by Rome's predatory conduct during the republican period, Augustus made a major effort to improve provincial governance. Rome's several provinces were divided into two groups, those needing the presence of armed forces and those sufficiently secure not to need troops. Au-

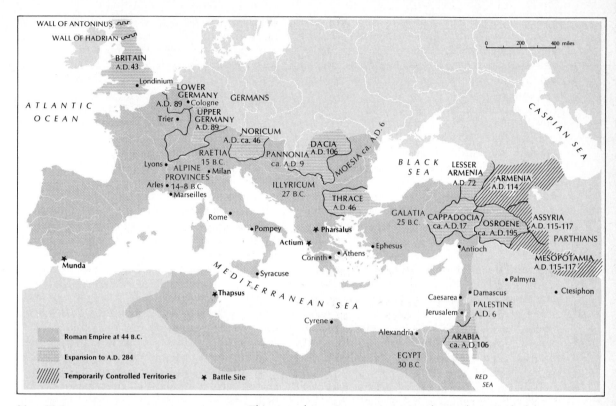

Map 10.1 **THE ROMAN EMPIRE, 44 B.C.–A.D. 284** This map shows Roman expansion during the period of the empire (44 B.C. to A.D. 284). With these additions the empire reached its greatest size. However, by the end of the second century A.D. an uneasy peace existed along the frontiers facing the Germans and the Parthians.

gustus retained control over the first group and directly supervised their administration. He was represented in each by a *legate,* usually a senator, who directed provincial administration in return for fixed pay. The *princeps* was also represented in each imperial province by a *procurator,* usually an equestrian, charged with collecting taxes and accountable to the *princeps.* This arrangement put an end to the rapacious governors and tax farmers who had for so long preyed on the helpless provincials. The provinces not needing armed forces were left under the jurisdiction of the Senate, which annually selected *proconsuls* to act as governors. However, Augustus maintained careful watch over the selection of proconsuls and over their conduct as provincial governors. This new

system almost immediately brought order and equitable treatment to the provincials.

The Augustan system of governance envisaged the sharing of governmental activities between the central government and local authorities. To achieve this end, Augustus encouraged the numerous city-states scattered across the empire to take responsibility for a wide range of matters relating to life in each city-state and its dependent countryside: police regulation, justice, public works, charity, religion. Most city-states had or were encouraged to develop a working system of government based on elected magistrates, a local senate, and assemblies—a system similar to Rome's old republican order. Local aristocracies whose interests were served by cooperating with the Roman government tended to dominate these governments. With Rome's encouragement city-states took on new vigor, and their leaders developed a strong sense of pride that made cities a vital force in promoting order across the vast Roman Empire.

The expanding range of functions associated with the office of *princeps* generated the need for permanent civil servants skilled in administration. Although Augustus and a small circle of confidants managed to handle a huge range of administrative detail, there slowly emerged around the *princeps* a corps of helpers, composed chiefly of freed slaves whose only political attachments were to the *princeps*. This embryonic bureaucracy was destined to play an ever-larger role in directing the imperial regime. In Augustus' time one of its prime accomplishments was the establishment of a sound fiscal system to support the imperial regime, especially its army. The key element of that system was a land tax and a head tax equitably imposed on noncitizens on the basis of regular census taking. Roman citizens contributed to support of the state chiefly through a form of sales tax and an inheritance tax.

Throughout his long reign Augustus was concerned with perpetuating his system. Crucial in this respect was the succession to his position as *princeps*. Fully aware that only the Senate and the people could legally bestow the powers upon which his veiled system of one-man rule depended, he saw the need to establish someone in a position where the Senate and people would have no choice except to grant that person the powers Augustus wielded. He was convinced that he should establish the principle of hereditary succession so that each future *princeps* would enjoy the prestige of descent from Julius Caesar and Augustus. Moreover, he believed that his successor should establish public visibility and gain practical political experience by actual involvement in the governance of the empire under his tutelage. Augustus' problem turned out to be finding someone who could meet these criteria. Augustus had no sons. He arranged three marriages for his only daughter, Julia, in search of an heir, but he outlived two of Julia's husbands as well as two grandsons considered as possible successors. Finally, he chose as his heir an adopted stepson, Tiberius, who was forced to divorce a beloved wife in order to become Julia's third husband and after A.D. 4 was granted ever-greater powers by Augustus with the concurrence of the Senate. When Augustus died in A.D. 14, Tiberius was ready to assume full authority as *princeps*.

This brief summary hardly does justice to Augustus' achievement. He was not a doctrinaire idealist seeking to create a preconceived utopian order. Rather he was a patient, realistic, cautious, pragmatic, hardworking statesman. He kept certain key ideas central to his political program: the need to concentrate power in his own hands; the need to end the use of force in reaching political decisions; the need to honor the ancient political ideals of the Roman citizenry; the need to provide fair treatment to Rome's subjects; the need to set positive goals for all segments of the citizen body. But Augustus was amazingly flexible in devising means to achieve these ends. A long life gave him time to experiment and shift directions. In the end he fashioned a political order that elicited acceptance and active involvement from a crucial element in the Roman world—the Roman citizen body of Italy—and that generated confidence among millions of subjects living beyond Italy that their well-being depended on direction of their affairs by those Roman citizens led by a wise *princeps*.

2. TESTING THE AUGUSTAN ESTABLISHMENT, A.D. 14–96

During the century following Augustus' death, the Augustan system was severely tested but ultimately proved its viability. The testing took place primarily in a relatively narrow political circle involving each *princeps*, his family, his chief political agents, the senatorial class, and sometimes the army. The maneuverings, intrigues, and acts of violence of these elements, set forth in lurid details by the historians Tacitus and Suetonius (see Chapter 11), leave the impression that this era was marked by monumental misrule creating a constant state of crisis. But more constructive developments beyond this circle and outside Rome provide indisputable evidence of the success of the imperial system.

A constant source of tension within the inner circle of power stemmed from the difficulty in finding a ruler who could meet the challenge posed by the office of *princeps* as defined by Augustus. To be effective, a *princeps* needed to combine the administrative ability and the good judgment necessary in running a vast empire with the tact and the sensitivity required to ensure everyone of his respect for the authority the Augustan system entrusted to the Senate and the people. Augustus greatly limited the pool from which such candidates could come by insisting that his successors come from his family. In fact, the first four successors, called the Julio-Claudians, were related to him. But their selection bred intrigue, conspiracy, and violence and produced rulers of limited abilities whose actions provoked incessant opposition and obstructionism from the senatorial order. Augustus' handpicked successor, Tiberius (A.D. 14–37), was an able, experienced leader, but he was also cold, suspicious, distrustful, and easily provoked to brutal retaliation against those he suspected of undermining his power. Gaius (A.D. 37–41), more commonly known by his nickname Caligula, a term meaning "little boots," given to him when he was a boy strutting about military camps in small boots, was an indolent pleasure seeker whose excesses earned him an assassin's knife. Claudius (A.D. 41–54) was a timid, scholarly man who suffered a physical handicap, who was ill at ease in Roman high society, and who was constantly victimized by ill-chosen wives and advisers. Most notorious of all was Nero (A.D. 54–68), a cruel, vain degenerate eventually ousted from office, avoiding assassination by killing himself, but only after he killed his mother and two wives, disposed of numerous senators, persecuted Christians, made a fool of himself posing as an artist, and depleted the treasury to satisfy his expensive whims. It was indeed easy to conclude that none of the Julio-Claudians were worthy of respect and trust as "first citizen."

With Nero's death there occurred a development with ominous implications for the future: control of the choice of *princeps* by the army. In the span of a single year four different men were thrust into office by the army in a climate of violence reminiscent of the late republic. It was with good reason that from this point on the head of the Roman state was increasingly referred to as *imperator* (victorious general) rather than as *princeps* (first citizen). Finally, a general named Vespasian seized the office and put an end to the bloody military competition for control of the political system. Vespasian (A.D. 69–79) devoted his talent to the restoration of the fundamental features of the Augustan system. He sought to resolve the succession issue by instituting a clear hereditary principle that permitted his sons, Titus (A.D. 79–81) and Domitian (A.D. 81–96) to assume power without difficulty. These rulers, called the Flavians, were men of considerable ability who ruled constructively. However, they often acted without deferring to the Senate and thus were constantly charged with being tyrants and were obstructed in their efforts to rule effectively. The mutual disdain between senators and Flavians owed much to the fact that the Flavian family was of nonaristocratic origin. The tension between the Senate and the Flavians highlights an important cause of political turmoil during the first century. Perhaps consciously, Augustus had not precisely defined the powers belonging to the *princeps* and those belonging to the Senate and people. While the Julio-Claudian and Flavian rulers tried to honor the role of the Senate and the people in directing the state, the imprecise line between the two spheres prompted senators to charge repeatedly that rulers were usurping authority and destroying the liberties of citizens. The rulers sometimes reacted by silencing their critics; more often, they simply did what had to be done, disregarding the alleged rights of the Senate and people. Whatever the course chosen, the result was a climate of mistrust so acute that it seemed at times that civil war would again erupt to ruin the Augustan settlement.

In reality, all this strife was little more than an intriguing sideshow detracting from the substantive advances made in achieving the *Pax Romana* envisaged by Augustus. Several of the much-maligned rulers of this era—Tiberius, Claudius, Vespasian, Domitian—were able statesmen who worked patiently and effectively to resolve the problems facing the imperial regime. They maintained Rome's military capability and utilized it to defend the frontiers and to extend Rome's domain: Claudius conquered Britain and annexed

Noricum to strengthen the Danube frontier, and Domitian won territory along the upper Rhine frontier crucial to the containment of the Germanic threat (see Map 10.1). They worked hard to sustain and improve equitable administration of the provinces; especially significant was their willingness to extend citizenship to provincials. They enhanced their concerns for effective administration by promoting the development of a proficient professional bureaucracy. Vast public works were undertaken in Rome, Italy, and the provinces; and trade, industry, and agriculture were given every encouragement. For the most part, the Senate and people demonstrated little interest and less competence in dealing with these crucial matters. Despite their recurrent laments that their liberties were being usurped by rulers unworthy of such honor in terms of ancient standards, by the end of the first century A.D. most people had reached the conclusion that rule by a powerful *princeps*— or *imperator*—was the only ensurance of peace, security, and prosperity. The Augustan system had prevailed.

3. THE EMPIRE AT ITS PEAK: THE "GOOD EMPERORS," A.D. 96–180

With the end of the Flavian dynasty in A.D. 96 much of the conflict that had marked the testing of the Augustan establishment ended. During the next century, the empire enjoyed a golden age, a time of *Pax Romana*—the Roman peace. Seldom has an era produced leaders more highly praised than the five emperors who ruled from A.D. 96 to 180. Nerva (A.D. 96–98) was a respected aristocrat whose conciliatory actions calmed fears of military dictatorship. Trajan (A.D. 98–117), a native of Spain and the first emperor from the provinces, won the admiration of the entire Roman world by his respect for the Roman aristocracy, his brilliant military exploits, and his honest administration. Hadrian (A.D. 117–138) was a cultured humanitarian who spent most of his reign traveling throughout the empire promoting the cause of peace, lawful administration, and material well-being. Antoninus (A.D. 138–161), by the excellence of his character and his humane legislation, earned the title "Pius" ("devoted to duty") from a grateful

Senate. Most illustrious of all was Marcus Aurelius (A.D. 161–180), a noted Stoic philosopher who exemplified a sense of duty, a willingness to work, and a nobility of purpose in the service of the state.

The regime of the "good emperors" was one that produced little history of a conventional kind—battles, intrigues, and so forth. These emperors were sometimes engaged in warfare, chiefly in defense of Rome's sprawling, lightly defended frontiers. Trajan pursued an aggressive policy that resulted in the annexation of a crucial area north of the Danube called Dacia and of extensive territories east of the Euphrates River at the expense of Parthia. Hadrian, however, abandoned expansionism in favor of strong defense of a fixed frontier and diplomacy, a policy that led to the abandonment of much of the territory Trajan had conquered along the eastern frontier. The collective efforts of the "good emperors" by no means solved the problem of protection of the frontier, as was clear from the fact that peace-loving philosopher Marcus Aurelius had to spend most of his reign defending the northern frontier against Germans. Less spectacular were other activities of the "good emperors" related to peace and stability. They effectively removed the disturbances surrounding the succession problem by utilizing an adoptive system whereby each emperor early in his reign adopted as his son a man of ability who was then involved in imperial governance and vested with increasing legal powers to the point where he was able to take over when his "father" died. All these rulers were tactful and respectful toward the senators, who filled most of the high offices and were regularly consulted and who increasingly became staunch supporters of the imperial system. Citizenship was granted to ever-larger numbers of provincials, some of whom were elevated to senatorial rank; this policy facilitated the Romanization of the provincial population. The administrative system was steadily expanded and regularized. The rulers encouraged the development of a unified body of law for the whole empire. They championed humanitarian projects to aid the downtrodden. Every encouragement was given to city-states to determine their own course as long as that freedom did not threaten the imperial peace. The rulers worked tirelessly to establish a sound financial system to support the imperial structure. All these efforts slowly bound the diverse peoples of the empire—numbering perhaps 70 million—into a commonwealth guided from Rome.

In its mature form in the second century A.D. the imperial government was remarkably effective in shaping affairs in the empire. The way that system actually worked to act decisively in people's lives is not easy to describe. One is tempted to oversimplify the imperial government by stressing its structural features without giving sufficient attention to process. The structural aspects of the imperial government can be described in fairly simple terms. At the head of the Roman state stood a single figure, the *princeps* or *imperator,* who was vested with extensive executive, legislative, and judicial powers and with a variety of honors by the vote of the Senate and the people. Theoretically, the emperor exercised these powers by making decisions that were executed through two agencies. First was the bureaucracy, consisting of a central core of specialized departments headed by appointees of the emperor and staffed by paid "civil servants" and of agents dispatched across the empire to carry out imperial orders. Second was the army, a highly professionalized body of about three hundred fifty thousand soldiers commanded by officers appointed by the emperor and capable of enforcing imperial orders if the need arose. The emperor's authority was represented in each of the forty-five provinces into which the empire was divided by a governor (usually called a *legatus*)—with wide powers to keep order, administer justice, and protect Rome's interest—and by a *procurator* charged with collecting taxes. Provincial governors and procurators were supported by staffs of public servants. An elaborate but efficient tax system had been put in place to support this complex apparatus and to allow the imperial government to provide a wide range of public services; the burden of taxation fell most heavily on the provincials. Complementing the imperial government everywhere in the empire were active city-state governments that played a major role in directing local affairs; however, these local regimes were always open to intervention by agents of the emperor's government.

When described in terms of its structure, it is tempting to characterize the imperial government as a highly centralized, bureaucratized machine capable of imposing on a vast population a uniform policy emanating from the decisions of one man. Certainly that potential existed. However, careful study of how the imperial government impacted on the governed in specific situations presents a more subtle and complex picture.

Unquestionably the *princeps* or emperor of the second century A.D. was vested with almost unlimited authority based on legal grants and honors extended to him by agencies that at least the citizen body believed had the right to do so. The universal acceptance of the emperor as the ultimate source of authority was an important factor in giving coherence to political life because it caused everyone to turn to the emperor to get what he or she wanted. Moreover, the traditions associated with the offices upon which the emperor's authority was based dictated that the emperor "do" things; delegation of power was not an acceptable feature of Greco-Roman political thinking. The record shows clearly that second-century emperors were personally swamped with detailed administrative work: conducting military campaigns, arbitrating disputes, responding to petitions for favors, receiving embassies, and seeing to it that public property was properly exploited. Because the Roman record-keeping system was limited, all this detail had to be handled without much knowledge of specific situations. To assist in meeting this burden, emperors relied more often on their household servants than on professional civil servants; members of the imperial household became real power wielders without holding official positions or being constrained by rules defining their conduct of business. The evidence suggests that the emperors often entrusted public business to private contractors who acted according to their own lights once commissioned to perform a service for the state. Perhaps the only area where there was anything like a regularized, empire-wide administrative system was in revenue collecting, and even in this vital activity procedures were haphazard and arbitrary.

Beyond the emperor and his circle, the political process was far from systematic and uniform. It is almost unbelievable to a modern observer to realize how few public officials in the Roman system actually had the *imperium*—the power to make final decisions. Those who did—army commanders, governors, procurators—enjoyed wide latitude in making decisions. The jurisdictions given by their offices were extensive, with the result that they too were swamped with administrative details. Like the emperor, they too relied on their personal servants to assist with these details, and they too depended heavily on private contractors to get things done. All too often, things did not get done; like the famous case involving the Roman official Pontius Pilate, authorities simply "washed their hands" of problems confronting them. The army was especially active in making and carrying out decisions that impinged on the civilian population. Far from being a mechanism through which uniform decisions were imposed upon the population through uniform procedures, the Roman imperial government operated through enclaves of power in which officials vested with the authority of Rome did what they wished in the way they wished.

Probably the lives of most residents of the Roman empire were seldom touched directly by the imperial government—except in the pocketbook. For them the most important political force was the local city-state government whose far-ranging activities were encouraged by the imperial government. Each urban center with its surrounding territory was ruled by a body of local aristocrats (called *decurions*) who formed a local senate. These senates elected local magistrates, collected local taxes, assumed responsibility for keeping order and providing public facilities, held courts, and dealt with imperial officials; in short, they played a major role in governance. Although the imperial government sometimes intervened in their activities, especially in fiscal matters, the city-state regimes were allowed wide latitude to govern those in their jurisdiction as they wished.

In view of these aspects of political reality, it is obviously impossible to think of the Roman imperial regime as one headed by a wise emperor who established general policies on the basis of extensive knowledge of conditions and with the advice of informed councilors and then issued orders that were enacted by a hierarchy of public officials capable of ensuring universal conformance to the emperor's law. Instead, governance depended on the decisions and the actions of a wide array of individuals, some officials and some private parties, acting within a framework of overlapping jurisdictions where pragmatic concerns and individual judgment were more important than rules. To run a vast empire in such a manner would seem to be a formula for chaos. Yet during the second century A.D. the system worked to provide peace and order to millions. One wonders how! The explanation may seem strange to the modern conception of statecraft. Rome was governed by a narrow elite whose shared social status and common culture caused its members to think and to act politically in a common pattern. This elite viewed public life as the highest form of human activity, reflecting an attitude deeply ingrained in the Greco-Roman mentality. Whether they were public officials, senators, local decurions, army officers, or equestrian contractors, their shared social and cultural values prompted each of them to decide on a particular political situation in the same way as did all other power wielders. Thus, without the guidance of clearly formulated policies or rigid rules regulating political behavior, the ruling elite—through myriad decisions shaped by common values—quite unconsciously guided the Roman world in a common direction that especially prized peace and order. Perhaps the tone for this remarkable consensus was set by the "good emperors" whose conduct was shaped by a conviction that power entailed duty in the service of humanity—a political philosophy based on Stoic ideas. Certainly from Augustus onward successive emperors acted to sanction the social status of this elite and to replenish its ranks, especially by extending citizenship to provincials in a position to exercise power. But in the final analysis, it was the political activism of this elite bound together by shared social values and a common culture that ruled the empire in its golden days. The elements which provided the basis for this consensus emerged from the entire fabric of Roman civilization. Consequently, the political dynamism of the imperial system can never be understood fully without a grasp of the intellectual, religious, social, and cultural values shared by its ruling elite. In a real sense the future of the empire depended on the continuation of this consensus among the members of this elite.

4. ECONOMIC AND SOCIAL LIFE IN THE ROMAN EMPIRE

During the first and second centuries A.D. the general level of material life in the Roman world was higher than ever before and not to be equaled again for many centuries—although not all shared that affluence equally. Prosperity was not the consequence of any basic change in the system of production. Rather, it stemmed from the favorable environment created by peace and order, from the integration of formerly isolated areas into the total economy, from the stimulus supplied by the expanding activities of the imperial political system, and from the entrepreneurial activities of nobles and equestrians eager to expand family fortunes.

The basic element in the Roman economy was a diversified agricultural system, which occupied the energies of the great bulk of the population. Everywhere that system included a mixture of small farms cultivated by freeholders or renters and large estates tilled by sharecroppers, hired laborers, and slaves and managed by their noble owners or their stewards. In many areas these farms produced enough to support those who owned them and labored on them as well as a modest surplus to feed the population of local urban centers. However, some areas, such as Egypt and North Africa, produced large agricultural surpluses for export to the empire's great cities, especially Rome. Agricultural expansion was especially notable in Gaul and Spain, stimulated by urban growth and the presence of Roman army camps.

An important key to prosperity during the first two centuries A.D. was an expansion of trade and industry. Most of the commercial activity involved the exchange of agricultural products and simple manufactured goods on a local level. However, there was a significant movement of luxury goods, raw materials, and foodstuffs on a scale embracing the whole empire and even extending beyond to Parthia, India, China, and the Germanic world. The Mediterranean became a busy commercial roadway linking its bordering lands into an interdependent economic community. The famed Roman road system encouraged the movement of goods inland to urban centers and army camps. An array of skilled artisans pursued a variety of small-scale crafts in every major city. Many of these enterprises were financed by nobles whose slaves and freedmen produced goods and shared the returns with their masters. One of the most significant developments of this era was the remarkable expansion of industrial activity in Spain and Gaul as a result of the incorporation of these previously "backward" areas into the mainstream of Mediterranean life. A powerful stimulant to trade and industry during the period was provided by a massive building boom that occurred throughout the empire. Funded from both public and private sources, this outburst filled numerous cities, Rome above all, with forums, basilicas for the conduct of public business, temples, theaters, stadiums, palaces, baths, and private dwellings. Across the countryside were built roads, bridges, aqueducts, villas, and army camps. This vast enterprise required capital, labor, the skilled services of artisans and suppliers, and managerial skills.

Most economic life in the first and second centuries was conducted by private individuals with little interference from the imperial government, which demonstrated limited interest in economic matters except to tap the system through taxation. Yet what we would today call the public sector played an increasing role in the economy. Through its taxation system the Roman government drained off a portion of the wealth of the entire empire. That wealth was redistributed to pay salaries of officials, support the jobless in Rome, beautify the capital city, and maintain the army. As a consequence, most public expenditures tended to be concentrated in Rome and in frontier areas where the army was stationed. Such distribution of public funds tended to stimulate artificially economic activity in these areas while depriving the most productive areas of financial resources needed to sustain and expand economic activity. Moreover, the expanding role of the Roman government in utilizing the wealth of the empire made the economy increasingly sensitive to public policy decisions involving taxation, the size of the army and the bureaucracy, and the frequency of war. This development introduced an element of instability into the basic economic processes.

The basic social order prevailing in the Roman Empire was little changed from the late republican period. The distinction between citizens and noncitizens remained an important social fact, but that division was increasingly blurred by the granting of citizenship to ever-larger numbers of provincials. The citizen population was still divided into various classes recognized by law: nobles, *equites,* plebeians, and slaves. The noncitizen population of the empire was not quite so neatly categorized in legal terms, but in fact over most of the empire there prevailed a social structure similar to that in Rome. The social system provided opportunities for upward mobility, especially through the acquisition of wealth and education and through involvement in public affairs as a consequence of earning the favor of the emperor; especially fortunate in this respect were rich and powerful provincials who were accepted into the Roman nobility when they were granted citizenship.

The Roman social structure and social life were dominated by the nobles. The basis for this group is somewhat elusive to the modern mind. In essence, the nobility was self-defining; its members understood who their peers were on the basis of a variety of factors: family origin, marriage connections, wealth based on land, education, involvement in the highest levels of political life, control over a circle of clients, life style, and values. As best one can tell, the rest of society was willing to accept the superiority of those who met these standards. While small and keenly conscious of its status, the nobility was never totally exclusive. Its ranks were constantly replenished by those who could meet the standards for noble status; most often those who ascended socially were drawn from prominent equestrians and the provincial elite.

Although their wealth was based largely on landownership, Roman nobles were creatures of the city. Rome, of course, was the most attractive center, but many other cities across the entire empire had their noble circles. In this urban setting noble life centered in the family household living in a splendid dwelling, where the *pater familias* (father of the family) ruled as he wished over his wife, children, slaves, and an entourage of clients. He did not "work," as did the lower classes, but "managed" his estates, his investments in trade and industry, his loans, and often some segment of public life entrusted to him through selection

FIGURE 10.2 A Roman Lady This painting portrays a noble Roman lady of the imperial period. It suggests that Roman women were respected for their dignity, sobriety, and strength of character. Women such as this one played an important role in managing the affairs of aristocratic households and sometimes in promoting the political careers of their husbands and sons. (Courtesy of the Detroit Institute of Arts)

for an office. Always uppermost in his mind were increasing the family patrimony and enhancing its prestige. These concerns prompted a keen interest in the education, careers, and marriages of his children, especially sons; success in matters of careers and marriage depended to a considerable degree on his influence among his peers. Roman nobles participated in a constant round of social activities—banquets, festivals, races, gladiatorial contests, cultural events. A worthy noble was expected to provide the major source of funding for many of these activities. Although their legal position was surrounded by constraints that subju-

FIGURE 10.3   Scenes from a Roman Household   These two panels done in relief illustrate some of the activities associated with household life in the Roman world: storing, preparing, and cooking food. The scenes suggest that such households were the setting for a secure and comfortable life. (Alinari)

gated them to their fathers or their husbands, noble women played a prominent role in aristocratic life (see Figure 10.2). Many of them managed the family household, an operation that involved large expenditures and the management of numerous slaves (see Figure 10.3). They owned and managed property and defended their interests in courts. Not only did they take part in many social activities, but they also involved themselves in the sometimes intricate maneuvering involved in gaining and exercising political power. Not a few of them took lovers, just as their husbands did. Some evidence suggests that by the second century the traditional male-oriented mentality of the nobility increasingly viewed wives as equal partners in marriage worthy of respect and considerate treatment. Roman moralists often painted the lives of noble men and women in terms of gluttony, drunkenness, sexual excess, and idleness. However, a close reading of the evidence suggests that noble life was guided by a moral code that placed a high value on sober, ordered, restrained conduct and that sanctioned the use of great wealth to gratify private tastes but also required concern

with and involvement in public affairs in the cause of creating a civilized order. In a general way, the *equites* imitated the noble life style, often successfully in terms of wealth, sumptuous living, and education; however, members of this order were not accepted as being real nobles and thus were excluded from the summit of the social order unless the nobles chose to coopt them into the ranks of the real elite.

Rome and most other cities had a teeming lower-class population: shopkeepers, artisans, minor officials, and idle poor, as well as slaves. In Rome and Italy the bulk of these people were plebeian citizens; in provincial cities they had some status as members of the community. Strong family ties provided a bulwark in the lives of urban dwellers. Most of them devoted their time and energy to ignoble "work" through which they earned a living, an enterprise that often occupied not only heads of lower-class households but also wives and children. Some shopkeepers and artisans fared well, living in comfortable, well-furnished houses and served by slaves. But for most life was marked by poverty, misery, and contemptuous treatment at the hands of their social betters. Large numbers of poor were dependent on the state or noble patrons for the bare essentials; it has been estimated, for instance, that an average of two hundred thousand Roman residents (perhaps a fourth of the city's population) lived off the public grain dole. The Roman imperial government as well as local city-state administrations made serious efforts to provide police and fire protection, an adequate water supply, sanitary facilities, and cheap food. Nevertheless, life in the city was for many marred by poverty, violence, and insecurity.

Still, city life had its compensations, even for the lowliest. Magnificent public buildings and parks provided an impressive setting for one's life. Holidays were numerous—perhaps as many as a hundred a year by the second century A.D. Each was the occasion for splendid religious festivals centering on animal sacrifices that provided free meals, for the triumphs of victorious emperors, and for races, gladiatorial contests, and bloody combats between wild animals and between animals and human beings. Numerous and sumptuous public baths provided attractive gathering places for everyone. Social clubs (called *collegia*), usually made up of individuals sharing a common occupation, provided opportunities for banqueting and help to members in time of need. Taverns abounded as oases where one could escape from the urban desert. For the most part, the urban lower classes seemed content with their lot; there is little evidence of urban discontent.

Those who received the least benefit from the *Pax Romana* were the peasants and the slaves. Isolated from city life, the rural population seldom felt the impact of the forces that gave the Roman world its vitality. Their existence centered around the family, hard work, and simple social activities of the rural village. At best, the material return for their labor was small. Powerful trends were at work in the empire pushing many farmers into dependency on powerful absentee landlords; these dependent agricultural workers (called *coloni*) were increasingly victimized by heavy rents and by an ever-heavier share of the tax burden. To its discredit, the imperial government did little to check the exploitation of the peasantry; in fact, the aristocratic landowners who dominated the political process were quite happy to allow this drift toward peasant exploitation.

Slavery was a prominent feature of Roman imperial society. It has been estimated that in the first century A.D. perhaps one-third of Italy's population of between 7 and 8 million inhabitants were slaves. They worked as household servants, agricultural laborers, workers in urban workshops and merchant stalls, teachers, miners, and rowers; and their reward was minimal. The record is full of instances of brutal treatment by masters whose rights over slaves were complete. There is some evidence that the condition of slaves improved. Many were freed by their masters, in some cases out of gratitude for faithful service. Funerary inscriptions and literary sources suggest amicable associations between masters and slaves. Slaves were allowed to marry and maintain families. Yet in spite of such improvement, no one in the Roman world thought of ending slavery, and that institution continued to debase the lives of the victimized slaves and to poison the minds of their masters.

Even this brief description of the Roman world in the second century A.D. will elicit admiration for its peace, order, prosperity, and unity. That admiration is warranted, but it must always be tempered. The main beneficiaries of the *Pax Romana* were the members of a narrow, proud, self-satisfied, self-serving nobility who were disdainful and unconcerned about those less prominent socially. The empire had its share of poverty, injustice, oppression, and greed. Despite some of its apologists, it was far from a utopia. Some of the flaws in its structure would soon test its strengths.

SUGGESTED READING

Political Developments

Chester G. Starr, *The Roman Empire, 27 B.C.–A.D. 476* (1982).

Colin Wells, *The Roman Empire* (1984).

J.S. Wacher, *The Roman Empire* (1987).

Any of these three works will provide an excellent survey.

Fergus Millar, *The Emperor in the Roman World: 31 B.C.–A.D. 337* (1977). Although massive, this study is vital to understanding how the imperial political system worked.

Fergus Millar, *The Roman Empire and Its Neighbors*, 2nd ed. (1981). Studies the assimilation of the different provincial cultures.

J.B. Campbell, *The Emperor and the Roman Army, 31 B.C.–A.D. 235* (1984). An excellent treatment of an important aspect of the political history of the empire.

Economic and Social History

Peter Garnsey and Richard Saller, *The Roman Empire. Economy, Society and Culture* (1987). An excellent survey.

Géza Alföldy, *The Social History of Rome*, trans. David Braund and Frank Pollock (1985). Rich in details about social conditions.

Ramsay MacMullen, *Roman Social Relations, 50 B.C. to A.D. 284* (1974). Attempts to capture attitudes of major social groups.

Joan Liversidge, *Everyday Life in the Roman Empire* (1976). Excellent treatment of how the Romans lived.

Philippe Ariès and Georges Duby, eds., *A History of Private Life, Vol. I: From Pagan Rome to Byzantium*, ed. Paul Veyne, trans. Arthur Goldhammer (1987). A fully illustrated treatment of aspects of Roman history often neglected.

Judith P. Hallett, *Fathers and Daughters in Roman Society: Women and the Elite Family* (1984).

Jane F. Gardner, *Women in Roman Law and Society* (1986).

These two works, combined with those of Pomeroy and Cantarella cited in Chapter 6, will provide a good picture of the role of women in Roman society.

Keith Hopkins, *Conquerors and Slaves* (1978). A provocative study of social change in the Roman world.

Biographies

A. H. M. Jones, *Augustus* (1970).

Barbara Levick, *Tiberius the Politician* (1976).

Arnaldo Momigliano, *Claudius: The Emperor and His Achievement*, trans. W. G. Hogarth (1961).

Miriam T. Griffin, *Nero: End of a Dynasty* (1984).

Steward Perowne, *Hadrian* (1960).

Anthony Birley, *Marcus Aurelius: A Biography*, rev. ed. (1987).

Sources

Complete Works of Tacitus, ed. Moses Hadas (1942).

Suetonius, *The Twelve Caesars*, trans. Robert Graves (1957).

Two lively treatments of the history of the first century A.D.

CHAPTER 11
Roman Culture

FIGURE 11.1 **The Fruits of Peace** This relief is from a larger composition decorating the Ara Pacis (Altar of Peace) built in Rome during the first century A.D. It glorifies the benefits bestowed by Augustus. The serene goddess of fertility and her happy children are surrounded by symbols of well-being. The work reflects how art was used to promote the greatness of Augustus. (Alinari)

While the Romans were conquering and organizing a vast empire, they also produced writers, thinkers, and artists whose collective efforts made a major contribution to cultural life. Rome's prime role in the history of culture was its assimilation and dissemination of Greek culture. But in the course of adapting the basic elements of Greek culture, the Romans put their distinctive mark on thought and expression, thereby creating a Latin cultural heritage destined to influence the future decisively, especially in western Europe.

1. THE PREPARATION

Prior to the third century B.C. the Romans displayed little interest in cultural pursuits. Although Etruscan cultural models, especially in building techniques and religion, influenced early Roman society, the Romans long remained a simple people occupied chiefly with politics, war, and earning a living. However, their early experiences in these pursuits ingrained in them deep-rooted values that influenced their cultural life throughout their history.

The basic Roman outlook on life formed during the early centuries of Roman history was shaped by four major forces—family life, agriculture, warfare, and religion. The family structure was dominantly patriarchal. The authority of the male heads of households over women and children was total and absolute. Fathers impressed on other members of the tightly knit families a sense of discipline, obedience, and respect for authority and tradition. Farm life made the early Romans a practical, realistic people, content to live simply and frugally. Constant warfare in defense of hearth and city deepened the sense of duty owed to the larger community and strengthened societal discipline.

Religion had the most profound effect on early Roman life and thought. The typical Roman believed that all things in existence were animated by unseen but powerful spirits. The Romans viewed these spirits with high respect, which instilled in them a deep awe for the unseen; the Romans called such awe "piety" and lauded it as a prime virtue. In the early stages of Rome's history the chief objects of this piety were household and agricultural deities: Janus, the protective god of the doorway of each household; Vesta, the goddess of the hearth; the *lares* and *penates*, spirits guarding the productive powers of the family and its lands and flocks. As the city grew, it too developed its divine protectors. Roman civic religion centered especially on a trio of deities, perhaps derived from Etruscan models: Jupiter, the god of lightning and thunder and power; Juno, the goddess of women and family and procreation; and Minerva, the goddess of arts and sciences and wisdom. In time, other deities borrowed chiefly from the Greek pantheon, were added to this trio as major civic deities. Eventually this divine circle protecting the expanding city became the object of an elaborate mythology accounting for the behavior of each of its members. Roman mythology was borrowed in large part from the Greeks. The approach to all the gods and goddesses, whether civic or household, was highly formalized and unemotional. From very early times the Romans developed set patterns for offering sacrifices and prayers to their many deities. They also had well-defined expectations of what the gods and goddesses would return to favor families and the city. Close observance of these customary rituals became a part of responsible citizenship; any deviation threatened to earn the wrath of the deities and misfortunes for men and women. Responsibility for proper worship rested with heads of families and with priests elected to represent the city-state community before the civic gods.

Home, farm, battlefield, and altar combined to define the basic elements of the good life and to establish the values by which a Roman citizen was expected to live. Especially admired were sobriety, industry, discipline, piety, civic responsibility, and honor of the family. Less prized were originality, creativity, and individuality. As time passed, the Roman mentality tended to idealize the values of these early times and to utilize thought and expression as means of recovering the virtues they supposedly induced. This tradition was especially nurtured and prized by the Roman nobles and provided a key ingredient in the shared mentality. Thus, the traits ingrained in Roman society during its early history cast a long shadow over Roman cultural history.

2. THE HELLENISTIC TIDAL WAVE

Beginning in the third century B.C. the simple mentality of the early republic experienced a cultural revolution, brought on largely by Roman expansion. As their armies absorbed first southern Italy and Sicily and then the Hellenistic Near East, Roman aristocrats became aware of Greek culture, especially in its Hellenistic forms. They were so impressed that they were, as the first-century poet Horace put it, taken captive by those they conquered. This experience, which placed a high value on becoming culturally Hellenized, was critical in determining Rome's role in the total stream of cultural history.

One of the major consequences of this fascination with Greek culture was the introduction into Rome of a new education system. Previously, young Romans had been educated at home: males by their fathers, who taught them family customs, the principles of Roman law, civic duties, and religion; females by their mothers, who taught them the household arts. By the second century B.C. that traditional system began to be replaced by the Hellenistic pattern of education. In many aristocratic Roman households Greek slaves were employed to complement basic instruction in reading and writing Latin with instruction in the Greek language and in the Greek "classics" in literature and philosophy. Not only were young men introduced to this new education, but young women were also often involved (see Figure 9.3). Private schools emerged to provide young men with an opportunity to extend their formal education over a longer period of time. They often went to the East, especially to Athens, to finish their education. Grammar (the study of language and literature) and rhetoric (the study of effective expression and argumentation) became the touchstones of the new education. Mastery of these subjects provided the basis for a successful career in public life and for acceptance into the ranks of the *nobiles* and the *equites.*

Their fascination with Greek culture soon spurred the Romans to imitate it. Borrowing heavily from the content and forms provided by Greek models, Latin writers produced epic poems, dramas, histories, and philosophical tracts. As a result, the Latin language was enriched as a vehicle of independent literary expression. Romans were equally captivated by Greek and Hellenistic art. During the wars in the East, numerous art pieces were "liberated" to decorate Roman residences, and Eastern artists were imported to produce copies of Greek statues and paintings. The Greek style of architecture was employed for civic and private buildings so often that Rome resembled a Greek or Hellenistic city.

Even the masses in Rome felt the impact of Greek influences, but they were touched chiefly through religion. The wars of conquest left many people intellectually and emotionally lost. The formal religion of Rome offered little emotional satisfaction. The Eastern religions did. New deities and rituals taken from the Greek civic religions were added to public religion in Rome, but even these additions did not satisfy many. From Eastern slaves they learned about more exciting Hellenistic mystery religions such as the worship of Dionysus or Cybele or Isis. These emotional, personal cults increasingly challenged the traditional religion for the allegiance of the Italian population.

Some Romans fought this cultural revolution. Typical of these cultural conservatives was Cato the Elder, a second-century B.C. statesman who spent his life preaching against the Greek way. He saw the foreign culture as a threat to traditional values. But he was fighting a lost cause. Rome was destined by circumstances and choice to be heir to the magnificent patrimony of the Greeks. Many of Cato's contemporaries saw the perpetuation of Greek culture as a Roman responsibility and acted eagerly to fulfill that mission. For example, no less a person that the powerful Scipio Africanus, along with many of his descendants (including the Gracchi brothers), championed the Hellenization of Roman thought and expression.

During the first century B.C. Roman writers, artists, and thinkers began to put their own stamp on what they had borrowed from the Hellenistic world. This burst of creativity resulted in Rome's "golden age" culturally; the Augustan age marked its high point. After a brief slackening in the first century A.D., there followed a second period of considerable activity during the era of the "good emperors," often called the "silver age" of Roman culture.

3. LITERATURE

Perhaps the most impressive reflection of Rome's cultural genius is its literature. After a long apprenticeship under Greek influence during the third and second centuries B.C., a succession of writers living between about 100 B.C. and A.D. 150 produced a rich and varied body of literature. Almost without exception, these works reflect strong Greek influences in content and form. But their authors demonstrate remarkable talent in adapting Greek modes to the Latin language to produce works marked by stylistic grace and force, depth of personal conviction, a powerful grasp of social and intellectual reality, and a passion for instructing readers.

Outstanding among all Roman writers was Vergil (70–19 B.C.). Born in rural Italy, he grew to manhood during the last years of the civil wars that ruined the republic, and he personally suffered its ravages. Eventually he attracted the attention of Augustus, whose patronage permitted him to devote the last years of his life to writing. Although much of his great talent was poured out in the service of the new Augustan order, it would be erroneous to overemphasize Vergil's role as a propagandist; he wrote in support of the Augustan system out of deep conviction and enthusiasm. His *Georgics* express a strong feeling for nature and for what involvement in pastoral life can mean—especially to those corrupted by the violence and greed surrounding the last days of the republic. Vergil's masterpiece was his *Aeneid*. An epic modeled after Homer and filled with material drawn from Greek legend, this majestic work sought to show that Rome's rise to mastery of the world was divinely ordered. The plot centers on the adventures of a mythical Trojan hero, Aeneas, who after the fall of Troy was ordered by the gods to establish in Italy a new city destined to rule the world. The noble Aeneas is portrayed as an ideal Roman whose virtue is constantly tested by such challenges as the spiteful behavior of the deities, a heartrending love affair with Dido, queen of Carthage, and a horror-filled journey to the underworld. But he persists in fulfilling his mission. Never was the Roman ideal of the dedicated patriot portrayed with more intensity and dignity; and never was the theme of Rome's predestination to greatness more dramatically stated.

Two other poets, Catullus and Horace, illustrate another side of the Roman literary genius. Catullus (ca. 85–54 B.C.) was a product of high society in the late republican period. His life was lived amid a dissolute, pleasure-seeking crowd of young nobles. Among his many adventures was a love affair with a noble lady who was already married and who eventually jilted him. The experience inspired him to pour forth powerful lyric poetry portraying with great intensity the pain caused by lost love. Horace (65–8 B.C.), also a lyric poet, enjoyed the patronage of Augustus and was second in influence only to Vergil. His best work, the *Odes*, represents his personal reactions to hundreds of situations he met in his lifetime. Although he lacked the fire of Catullus, Horace spoke to a wider circle, his poems reflecting the reasoned, thoughtful reactions of an educated, humane Roman to life as a whole—a great spirit looking at the world about him with sanity, intelligence, and wit. He was and remains the ideal of a civilized person.

Lucretius (ca. 95–55 B.C.) demonstrated still another aspect of Roman poetic genius: moral seriousness. A contemporary of Catullus, he was profoundly moved by events of the civil war era. He found his personal salvation in Epicurean philosophy, which he undertook to explain in a long poem called *On the Nature of the Universe*. With almost missionary zeal Lucretius put poetry to the service of instruction. He made a noble plea to educated Romans to seek in philosophy the bases of moral regeneration and personal fulfillment. Seldom has a poet shown greater moral earnestness.

Among the lesser poets were Ovid, Martial, and Juvenal. Ovid (43 B.C.–A.D. 17) entertained Augustan high society with his *Art of Love*, a frivolous but amusing poem on the art of seduction, and his *Metamorphoses*, an entertaining, lively rendering of Greek mythological stories into Latin. Martial (ca. A.D. 38–102) and Juvenal (ca. A.D. 55–140) revealed the shortcomings of Roman society in their brilliant satires.

Cicero (106–43 B.C.) was Rome's most famous prose writer. Although an active lawyer, magistrate, and statesman, he produced a wide variety of writing, of which his speeches form a large part;

he made argumentation an art. Cicero wrote two important essays on political theory, *The Republic* and *The Laws,* defending Roman republic institutions but pleading for the establishment of a first citizen to guide the state. He also wrote several philosophical tracts that attempted to make abstract Greek thought understandable to Roman readers. His numerous *Letters* supply a brilliant picture of Roman politics and society in the first century B.C. This eloquent, learned Roman made Latin prose capable of expressing any idea.

The earliest historical writing in Latin was influenced by Hellenistic models, but the Romans again discovered their own talent. The most influential Roman historian was Livy (59 B.C.–A.D. 17), another of those inspired to creative activity under the Augustan regime. His masterpiece, the immense *History of the Roman Republic,* covers the period 753 B.C. to A.D. 9. Although a large part of the work has been lost, it is clear from what is left that Livy believed Rome had a great historical mission about which he wished to instruct his readers. Livy was not a scientific historian, interested only in the truth; his work was a conglomeration of truth and fiction put together artistically to teach a lesson. Nonetheless, the work presented with great dramatic impact the people and events that made Rome great over seven centuries and highlighted the traditional virtues that would ensure Rome's success for many centuries to come.

Less monumental but equally artistic was the work of Tacitus (ca. A.D. 55–117), who wrote about Roman history during the century after Augustus. His *Histories* and *Annals* covered large portions of the period A.D. 14–96. Although Tacitus was a man of senatorial and republic sentiments, prejudiced against the successors of Augustus, he wrote with brilliance and deep moral sense. Another of his works, *Germania,* gives important information about the Germanic barbarians, who were soon to play a part in Roman life. Suetonius (ca. A.D. 75–150) also treated the rulers from Julius Caesar to Domitian in his *Lives of the Twelve Caesars,* a racy account stressing scandal and excess.

The works of Greek writers swelled the body of excellent histories. One of the greatest was Polybius, who lived in Rome from 167 to 151 B.C. as a hostage. He became an intimate of the pro-Hellenic Scipionic circle and, greatly impressed by the Romans, produced a superb work chronicling Rome's rise to world power. Plutarch (ca. A.D. 46–120) provided a series of biographies of Greek and Roman men in his *Parallel Lives.* Several Romans produced personal memoirs that were of the nature of histories. Probably the best examples were Julius Caesar's *Commentaries on the Gallic Wars* and Marcus Aurelius' *Meditations.*

During the era when Greek ideas and art forms were first sweeping over the Roman world, attempts were made to imitate the magnificent Greek dramatic art. The most outstanding Roman dramatists were Plautus (third century B.C.) and Terence (second), both writers of comedies. But drama failed to take root among the Romans. Moreover, only occasionally did a fiction writer grace the literary scene. These gaps in the scope of Roman literary genres suggest that the creation of highly imaginative literature was foreign to the Romans, who had to be tied to reality—to history, to current moral problems, to personal experience.

4. ART

Originally inspired by Greek forms, motifs, and techniques, the artistic genius of the Romans matured slowly after about 250 B.C., reaching its full maturity during the first two centuries A.D. During that "golden age" the imperial government provided powerful impetus to artistic creativity, perhaps partly for economic and propaganda reasons, but also because a succession of emperors and the members of the ruling class in Rome enjoyed beauty and refinement. This imperial art never lost its Greek imprint, but it reflected innovations that gave Roman art a distinctive character.

Rome's most impressive artistic achievements were in architecture, where important elements were added to what was borrowed. The Romans invented concrete, which provided a cheap, durable, and adaptable building material. This material allowed architects to exploit the arch, the dome, and various forms of vaulting more effectively than had been done before and to create imaginative exteriors by the use of marble and brick facings over concrete. These technical advances permitted larger structures and innovative

FIGURE 11.2 A Roman Aqueduct The Pont du Gard, built across the River Gard to bring water to the Gallo-Roman city of Nîmes, is an impressive monument to Roman engineering skill. The structure rises 160 feet above the river bed and is about 900 feet in length; each of the large arches is about 80 feet across at its base. Roman architects and engineers have seldom been matched in the application of the arch to utilitarian ends. (Art Resource)

variations on the rectangular ground plans and the dominant horizontal elevation lines characteristic of the typical Greek structure.

Unlike the Greeks, the Romans did not excel in temple building; generally, they were content to imitate the Greek style, as is illustrated by the famous Maison Carrée still standing in Nîmes, France. However, they were capable of innovation. The Pantheon, built in Rome in the second century A.D., is one of the greatest round temples ever built. Its domed roof, 142 feet in diameter and supported by niche-filled concrete walls, covers a vast internal space that evokes a sense of awe. A rectangular porch, its gabled roof supported by Greek columns, leads into this inner sanctum, supplying a pleasing mixture of Greek

and Roman architectural ideas.

Much more distinctly Roman were public buildings: forums, baths, ampitheaters, aqueducts, bridges, meeting halls (basilicas), and palaces, built in abundance not only in Rome but also in provincial cities throughout the empire (see Figures 11.2 and 11.3). The Roman Forum, a huge complex of meeting halls, market facilities, and shrines, all laid out on an axial plan, reflects the Roman genius for planning and for adapting architectural forms to a variety of uses. The Colosseum, a massive sports facility begun during Vespasian's reign, accommodated fifty thousand spectators and provided special boxes for the emperors and other dignitaries. It featured an elliptical ground plan above which were elevated four

FIGURE 11.3 Roman Architecture
This photo of an arena and a theater built in Arles in southern France near the end of the first century B.C. illustrates the Roman talent for constructing impressive public buildings to serve as the focus of civic life. Arenas provided the settings for such popular activities as races, gladiatorial combats, and wild animal hunts. The close proximity of a spacious theater suited for drama, dance, song, and poetry reading suggests a wide range of interests among the citizens of a Roman provincial city. (French Government Tourist Office, New York)

levels of arch-covered passageways giving access to the seats looking down on the arena where the bloody combats so beloved by the Romans occurred. The most common Roman building was the basilica, essentially a long hall flanked by side aisles and often featuring a rounded apse at one end. The walls of the main hall extended above the roofs of the side aisles, allowing windows to be cut high in the walls. Arches and columns were skillfully used to permit access from the side aisles into the main hall and to roof the long halls; in the Basilica of Maxentius (early fourth century A.D.) a concrete roof was put over a main aisle eighty feet wide. Roman baths, which consisted of a great central court surrounded by numerous smaller rooms, demonstrated the Roman talent for organizing interior space for utilitarian purposes and for creating internal plumbing and heating

systems. The Romans also built huge imperial palaces (the most famous are those of Nero and Domitian) and rural villas characterized by multistoried layouts featuring different-sized and -shaped rooms and sumptuous internal decor (see Color Plate 4). Not the least accomplishment of Roman architects was the development of living quarters suited to the needs of crowded cities: multistoried concrete structures containing standardized small apartment units suited to the needs of low-income residents.

Roman sculptors were less innovative than were architects. Greek and Hellenistic models were constantly and even slavishly imitated. The best Roman sculpture was devoted to portraiture and to relief work treating historical incidents, both art forms especially useful in serving the purposes of patrons who wished to be remembered either as individuals or as servants of the state. The artists who rendered these statues were remarkably adept at realistic portrayal, but always their work accentuated the dignity of their subjects (see Figures 8.1, 9.2, and 10.1). Roman relief carvings—featured especially on the walls of public buildings, arches and columns celebrating the deeds of emperors, and coffins honoring the dead—were remarkably effective in capturing scenes from everyday life in a way that conveyed a powerful message lauding the feats of those honored, especially in the service of the state (see Figures 9.1, 9.3, 10.3, 11.1, and 12.2). Perhaps the most remarkable example of Roman relief work is the freestanding column erected to celebrate Trajan's military triumph in Dacia. Around the column spirals a continuous scene 700 feet long that depicts in almost photographic detail the activities of about twenty-five hundred figures engaged in a military campaign. The limited survival of Roman painting (see Figure 10.2 and Color Plate 5) and mosaic work (Color Plate 6) suggests that Greek and Hellenistic influences remained strong and that these arts played an important role in decorating interiors, thus being strongly shaped by architectural plans. Painters and their patrons were especially fond of mythological subjects and portrayals of nature.

5. PHILOSOPHY, SCIENCE, AND RELIGION

Philosophical interests in the Roman world followed lines established during the Hellenistic period, focusing chiefly on applying classical Greek philosophical principles to ethical issues facing individuals and society. While many of the most significant philosophers in the Roman world were Greek speakers, educated Romans absorbed their ideas and sought to utilize those ideas to understand and to formulate answers to problems facing the Roman world. The most significant accomplishment of these Roman thinkers lay not in advancing philosophical speculation but in recasting Greek philosophy into a Roman idiom and transmitting that wisdom in the Latin language to later western European society.

Six individuals will serve to illustrate the main currents of philosophical development during the period of Roman domination; most of them were not philosophers in the strict sense but writers, statesmen, or educated citizens seeking personal and social guidance from philosophy. Cicero (106–43 B.C.), famous as a lawyer, statesman, and author, reflected a powerful tendency in philosophical thought to intermingle the viewpoints of various schools into an eclectic response to philosophical issues. But the Hellenistic schools continued to flourish. In his *On the Nature of the Universe*, the poet Lucretius (ca. 95–55 B.C.) used his talent to celebrate the Epicurean ideal of seeking pleasure and peace of mind in a materialistic universe through contemplation and withdrawal from the world. Particularly attractive to many intelligent Romans was the sober philosophy of Stoicism, which was perhaps the most influential philosophical movement of the first two centuries A.D. Three individuals were its noted advocates: Seneca (ca. 4 B.C.–A.D. 65), an essayist who served Nero; Epictetus (ca. 55–135 A.D.), a freedman who, after being exiled from Rome, spent most of his life teaching his ideas to ordinary people; and Emperor Marcus Aurelius (A.D. 121–180), whose famous *Meditations* summarized the Roman version of the Stoic world view. The Roman Stoics did not neglect the emphasis of Hellenistic Stoicism on personal peace of mind, but they gave greater attention to social responsibility and public morality. Especially influential was their expansion of the idea of an all-powerful, unchangeable law of nature governing the universe to provide a justification for a single human community governed by a system of law that conformed to the law of nature. Perhaps the thinker most important for the future was Plotinus (A.D. 204–270), an Egyptian who spent much of his career in Rome teaching a system called Neoplatonism. Derived from Plato's thought, Plotinus' system as set forth in his *Enneads* posited the superiority of the spiritual world over the material, the existence of a supreme being at the summit of spiritual reality, and the possibility of human participation in spiritual reality through a mystical experience that involved the penetration of the supreme spiritual being into the human spirit properly prepared by contemplation. Neoplatonism represented a fundamental aspect of the development of thought during the

Roman period: the merging of philosophy and religion, a trend that perhaps best met the needs of what was increasingly becoming an "age of anxiety" and that would soon provide a fertile field for Christian thinkers.

The Roman period was not marked by significant advances in science. Perhaps the most notable achievement resulted from the effort of scholars, such as Pliny the Elder (ca. A.D. 23–79), Galen (A.D. 131–201), and Ptolemy (ca. A.D. 121–151), to compile great encyclopedias intended to summarize all scientific knowledge contained in Greek and Hellenistic sources. These compilations would long remain the chief guides to understanding nature. The Romans excelled in practical science: the engineering of monumental structures; the construction of roads, bridges, aqueducts; more effective farming techniques. The technical skills developed by engineers, artisans, and farmers formed a precious heritage perhaps as important to the West as was the literary, artistic, and philosophical tradition nurtured and transmitted by Rome.

While the educated upper class of the Roman world absorbed Greek and Hellenistic philosophy and science and adjusted that material to the needs of the Roman world, the basic outlook of the great bulk of society was powerfully influenced by religion. The ancient family and civic religions continued to shape Roman thinking, and attempts were made by rulers such as Augustus to reinvigorate them. Between about 100 B.C. and A.D. 180 religious life everywhere in the empire was greatly enriched by the spread of Hellenistic mystery religions. Particularly appealing were the cults of the Great Mother goddess associated with Cybele, of the Egyptian goddess Isis, and above all of the Persian deity Mithra, which took deep roots in the Roman army. The ideas and practices associated with these religions emphasized personal identification with a deity through highly emotional rituals and life after death earned for good behavior. Such concepts tended to undermine traditional Roman religions that stressed highly formalized rituals performed by collectivities in return for material rewards. The trend already under way during the Hellenistic Age toward religious syncretism—the mingling of beliefs and practices—continued everywhere in the Roman world. The ground was being prepared for the acceptance of a common religion. The advocates of that religion—Christianity—were already spreading their "good news" during the golden age of the Roman Empire.

6. LAW

One of Rome's most enduring cultural monuments was its law, vital not only as a force promoting orderly life throughout Rome's history but also as a legacy handed on to later societies to guide them in establishing effective societal relations. As early as 449 B.C. the principle was set forth in the famous Twelve Tables that citizens had rights that could be claimed and defended in courts. From thence on these rights of citizens, collectively constituting the *ius civile*, were explored, tested, and expanded in the context of changing times. During the republican period the enactments of assemblies enriched the substance of the law. Even more important, the magistrates charged with administering the law, the *praetors*, were allowed to pronounce their interpretation of the law at the beginning of their term; this practice resulted in the constant reinterpretation of the law within a framework that highlighted principles that should govern the *ius civile*. During this same period, the decisions of the judges who actually conducted cases in court constituted an ever-growing body of precedent that had the weight of law. These judges were advised by *jurisconsults*, specialists whose study of the law allowed them to assert a significant role in shaping the precedents that were applied in court as law. Roman expansion presented judicial officials with the problem of settling cases involving noncitizens. The result was the development of a law of nations (*ius gentium*), which represented a mixture of the laws of subject peoples, Roman practices, and the commonsense decisions of judges. With the institution of the Roman Empire the content of the law was further expanded by a vast outpouring of the decrees issued by the emperors attempting to ensure that the huge empire would be ruled uniformly and equitably.

As the body of the law expanded and as the society to which it was applied grew more complex, there was increasing pressure to codify the law into a single, systematic body. This concern had become central to the study of law by the second century A.D., when a series of brilliant *jurisconsults*, working under the patronage of the emperors, focused their attention on defining the principles undergirding sound law and its application. Their efforts were spurred by their realization of the importance of unified law as a tool for governing the empire and by their awareness that the distinction between citizens and noncitizens was disappearing. In addition, their thinking was decisively influenced by Stoic philosophy, which argued that there existed a law of nature (*ius naturale*) governing the universe to which human law must conform. The concept of natural law was a fruitful source of principles according to which all aspects of human law could be arranged and interrelated into a consistent, logical body. The codification of Roman law was not completed until the reign of Emperor Justinian (A.D. 527–565). But as imperial legislators, judges, and students of law moved toward that end, their efforts shaped an immense body of law that became a storehouse to which many people would turn in the future for guidance in the humane, equitable conduct of human affairs.

7. THE ROMANS AS SPREADERS OF CULTURE

When assessing the role of the Romans in cultural history, one must give them due credit for raising the level of culture in large areas previously little affected by higher civilization, especially in the western part of the empire. They were much less exclusive in their attitude toward non-Romans than were the classical Greeks, chiefly because they understood from early in their history the importance of Romanization in establishing and maintaining their domination over their culturally

diverse subjects. The marks of their success as spreaders of culture are still visible. For example, the Italian, French, Portuguese, and Spanish languages are direct descendants of the Latin spread in those areas when the Romans conquered them. A modern traveler in western Europe and North Africa will repeatedly encounter the remains of Roman baths, aqueducts, temples, theaters, and roads—all evidence of the presence of the Romans as a creative force in enriching life in these areas.

The processes through which Romanization was achieved were complex. Roman soldiers, officials, merchants, and colonizers were important agents in carrying Roman culture outward across the empire. The Roman government actively promoted the creation of cities and encouraged those settling in them to imitate Roman ways. Local aristocracies were encouraged to become Romanized as a test for their eligibility for citizenship and for Roman approval of their leadership of local government. In these urban centers, schools were established to teach grammar and rhetoric and to promote the study of literature and philosophy; as a result, a common store of ideas and set of tastes spread to the far corners of the empire. The imperial government promoted extensive building activities, which led to the spread of a common style in architecture, sculpture, and painting. Scholars, religious missionaries, philosophers, artists, and teachers circulated freely throughout the empire to spread a common culture. From the third century B.C. onward, the government and the aristocracy of the city of Rome welcomed artistic and intellectual talent from all over the empire, making the capital of the empire the center of a cosmopolitan culture from which flowed influences affecting life throughout the empire. All of these factors combined to bring large numbers of people under the sway of a common culture that would decisively affect their histories for many centuries to come.

SUGGESTED READING

General Treatments

Pierre Grimal, *The Civilization of Rome,* trans. W. S. Maquinness (1963).

John Boardman et al., eds., *The Oxford History of the Classical World* (1986).

Two insightful surveys of Roman cultural life.

Religion

Margaret Lyttelton and Werner Forman, *The Romans: Their Gods and Their Beliefs* (1984).

John Ferguson, *The Religions of the Roman Empire* (1970).

Ramsay MacMullen, *Paganism in the Roman Empire* (1981).

Any of these three titles will provide rich material on religious life in the Roman world.

Stewart Perowne, *Roman Mythology,* new rev. ed. (1984). A splendidly illustrated description of Roman myths.

Alan Wardman, *Religion and Statecraft among the Romans* (1982). A fine explanation of the role of religion in political life.

Cultural Achievements

Stanley F. Bonner, *Education in Ancient Rome: From the Elder Cato to the Younger Pliny* (1977). A full treatment.

Elizabeth Rawson, *Intellectual Life in the Late Roman Republic* (1985). A landmark study dispelling stereotypes about the lack of Roman intellectual creativity.

Moses Hadas, *A History of Latin Literature* (1952). A clearly written survey.

R. M. Ogilivie, *Roman Literature and Society* (1980). Seeks to relate literature to social conditions.

F. H. Sandbach, *The Stoics* (1975). Describes the basic ideas of the Stoics.

H. F. Jolowicz and Barry Nicholas, *Historical Introduction to the Study of Roman Law,* 3rd ed. (1972). A massive survey.

Richard Brilliant, *Roman Art from the Republic to Constantine* (1974).

Bernard Andreae, *The Art of Rome,* trans. Robert E. Wolf (1978).

Cornelius Vermeule, *Roman Art: Early Republic to Late Empire* (1978).

Three well-written and -illustrated treatments of Roman art.

Sources

Kevin Guinagh and Alfred P. Darjahn, eds., *Latin Literature in Translation,* 2nd ed. (1952). A good sample of Latin literature. Better still would be to read the complete works of the major Latin authors mentioned in this chapter; their works are readily available in good translations.

RETROSPECT

Few epochs in all history witnessed greater achievement than that extending from the time when the Greeks emerged from their Dark Age about 800 B.C. to the generation that saw the Roman imperial order reach its full maturity about A.D. 180—the epoch from Homer to Marcus Aurelius. We might well ask why this epoch was so fruitful. The answer is at once simple and profound: Greco-Roman civilization made humans its central concern. Its motto was spoken by Protagoras: "Man is the measure of all things." Socrates formulated its one commandment: "Know thyself."

We cannot help being impressed at how much the Greco-Roman world discovered about humanity. At grave risk of oversimplification, we might single out a few of these discoveries as being the foundation stones of Greco-Roman civilization. First was human rationality. Second was the ordered universe that provided the setting for human activities. Third was rational humans' capacity for positive good. Fourth was the capability of people to transcend whatever they were at any instant through knowledge and good action. Last was the political nature of human beings, which gave them no alternative except to join others to realize their potential to know, to be good, and to outreach their present condition.

Yet this majestic achievement was somehow flawed, even in the minds of its creators. The Greeks and the Romans were never completely convinced that their own vision of humanity was true. They suspected that in human beings lurked an elusive element of the demonic and that beyond them existed forces they were powerless to control.

Moreover, the kind of society that emerged from the centuries-long effort to create a world fit for reasonable, good, enlightened people had some features that were disturbing. The confidence that political action could achieve perfection had given the state a dangerous dominance over its peoples at the expense of other dimensions of existence. The majestic assumptions about human rationality and capacity for good had given undue power to those who managed to acquire the symbols of rationality and good: an education, offices, wealth, and manners. These aristocrats tended to be oblivious to those who had not been enlightened or blessed with power and prestige: women, slaves, even lower-class citizens. The politicized and intellectualized flavor of classical civilization bred in those who wielded power and participated in the mainstream of cultural life a disdain for other kinds of activity—especially labor—and for other kinds of human behavior—especially that emerging from the emotional side of human nature. The rationalizing of human conduct and of nature bred an intellectual posture that saw things in terms of absolute, fixed forms and found it difficult to accept or to initiate change.

These insights might well have persuaded people living in the second-century Roman Empire of what now seems fairly evident: Classical men and women had learned much about human nature and that knowledge had liberated some of them to enliven and beautify the world, but they had not seen human nature whole. The civilization they constructed had inherent limitations arising from their restricted view of humanity. Perhaps the end product of the classical world is symbolized by a man who revealed his soul at the very end of the period—Emperor Marcus Aurelius. Marcus Aurelius was the embodiment of the best of humanity as conceived in the Classical Age: reasonable, good, serious, politically aware, sensitive to others. As ruler over a marvelous political system, he appeared to have the power to achieve whatever the good of humanity demanded. Yet in his *Meditations* he emerges as the victim of a cruel joke—a man caught up in a mechanical universe running on forever without change, a man who knew and understood but found nothing to do, a man so good that the nature of evil eluded him, a perfect citizen who was destined to the unappetizing business of fending off stupid barbarians. What was there to do but to resign oneself? One suspects that a kind of bloodless, cold, unemotional resignation in the face of what reason and goodness cannot encompass is what classical civilization finally meant. For all its accomplishments, the classical world had still not learned enough about humanity.

But whatever its limitations, classical civilization had changed the course of history. No nation, no people, no civilization of the future could escape its influence—especially not the inhabitants of Europe.

PART THREE
THE FALL OF GRECO-ROMAN CIVILIZATION, A.D. 180–500

During the second century A.D. Greco-Roman civilization had established unchallenged sway over the Mediterranean basin and extended its influence inland from the sea to three continents—Europe, Asia, and Africa. A vast community had been created; within it a bewildering variety of peoples were bound together by powerful forces. The political genius of the Romans, embodied in the imperial system of government, furnished the most potent bond of community. Almost as important were the widely shared cultural concepts that created a common basis of discourse and a common system of values. Derived primarily from the Greeks and finding expression in a remarkable literature, art, philosophy, and learning, this cultural force of unity had been adopted by the Hellenistic world and then spread through the entire Mediterranean world by the Romans. The shared political system and cultural values were powerfully reinforced by common economic ties that linked the many parts of the Mediterranean world in an interdependent material existence. The simultaneous operation of these unifying forces produced one of the most magnificent eras in all human history.

However, no human order, however strong it appears, is perfect, and no community of men and women, however confident they are of their talents, is safe from change and its tensions. As the second century A.D. drew to an end, serious stresses emerged within the basic structures of this splendid Mediterranean community. The long process leading to the formation of that community was reversed, and forces of disintegration became dominant. Within a relatively short time a vast transformation occurred in the Mediterranean basin. Greco-Roman civilization was eaten away by incurable sicknesses within its body and torn apart by the assaults of barbarians from outside. The disintegration of that civilization has always held a fascination for students of the past, prompting them to ask why it is that humanity's greatest achievement—a mature civilization—cannot be made to last. Intriguing as the question might be, the fact is that the end of classical civilization left the vast population of the Mediterranean world with no alternative but to set out again to construct new and viable patterns of life.

CHAPTER 12

The Decline of the Empire and the Rise of Christianity

FIGURE 12.1 The Ascension of Christ This ivory carving from about A.D. 400 portrays Christ's ascension into the hand of God while an angel speaks to the three Marys and soldiers cower in terror. It illustrates how Christian artists adapted classical art styles to Christian purposes; note especially the pagan sarcophagus, which certainly had no part in the scriptural account of this crucial event in Christian history. (Marburg/Art Resource)

An era of transformation of the Roman Empire began with dramatic suddenness during the century following the death of Marcus Aurelius in A.D. 180. In vivid contrast to the *Pax Romana* of the second century, the third century A.D. was characterized by almost incessant civil war that deeply disturbed the internal order of the empire and increased its vulnerability to outside attack. Amid the political crisis, basic economic and social maladjustments surfaced to add to the stress. And intellectual and spiritual confusion sapped the capabilities of society to respond to changing times. In retrospect it is clear that the old Greco-Roman pattern of civilization was dissolving and that a new order was emerging.

1. POLITICAL CRISIS, A.D. 180–284

As the second century came to a close, the peace that had prevailed throughout the Roman Empire under the "good emperors" was shattered. There followed a century of violence that led some contemporaries to believe that the Roman peace was turning to ashes and that the empire might collapse. At the heart of this political crisis were two interrelated problems: the defense of the frontier and the succession question. The resolution of each increasingly rested with the military forces.

Even during the second century the danger to the empire from its outside enemies had been ominous. During the third century that threat reached crisis proportions, especially along the northern and eastern frontiers of the empire (see Map 10.1). The increasing pressure on Roman defenses was due chiefly to developments beyond Roman control. In Parthia, a new dynasty, the Sassanian, seized power in A.D. 224. Its aggressive rulers were dedicated to the restoration not only of Persia's ancient glory but also of its ancient territory—which included most of Rome's Asiatic provinces. Along the long European frontier the Germans became ever more dangerous, chiefly because of developments within the Germanic world that caused massive movements of peoples and the formation of larger groupings of tribes into warrior-led "nations" capable of more effective military actions. During the third century these foes repeatedly intruded into Roman terri-

tory to cause widespread disruption and to focus attention ever-increasingly on the need for stronger military forces.

The ability of the Roman government to respond to the needs of defense was constantly disrupted by internal strife centering on the succession question. The death of Commodus (A.D. 180–192), the son and successor of Marcus Aurelius, was marked by a brutal struggle among segments of the army to decide on a successor to the imperial throne. The victor was Septimus Severus (A.D. 193–211), a man whose career had identified him totally with the army. His dynasty controlled the imperial office until A.D. 235 and succeeded in maintaining internal peace and frontier defenses. But the Severan dynasty followed policies that planted a time bomb. Following the advice of Septimus to favor the troops and forget the rest of the population, the Severi encouraged the soldiery to think that the state should be run to reward the army—a not illogical concept in view of the mounting dangers along the frontiers. Their appetites whetted by the prospect of such favoritism, the soldiers became vitally interested in placing on the imperial throne a leader who would serve their interests.

The intrusion of the army into the determination of succession to the imperial office led to almost constant civil war from the end of the Severan dynasty until A.D. 284. Repeatedly various army units took up arms to elevate their generals to the imperial office in expectation of special favors. Successful leaders of these uprisings—often called "barracks emperors"—barely had time to reward their troops before they were challenged by new rebels and violently removed from office. The incessant civil strife had disastrous consequences. Effective defense of the frontiers was seriously impeded. Civil administration was badly disrupted by the constant change of emperors. An immense new burden was heaped on society to meet the insatiable demands of army units for special rewards. Civil strife disrupted economic life, making it more difficult to provide for the demands of the military and at the same time maintain the level of prosperity that had prevailed during the era of the "good emperors." All of these factors suggested that the disintegration of the empire was at hand.

However, amidst this chaos subtle changes were occurring to transform the essential nature of the imperial government in ways that allowed the empire to survive the third-century crisis. In essence, the political system was becoming militarized and autocratic. The "barracks emperors" were a different breed from earlier rulers. Most were provincials whose entire careers were spent in the army. They had little experience with or sensitivity to the problems of civil administration or the needs of the civilian population. They had little understanding of the fundamental principles undergirding the Augustan principate, which called for sharing power with the aristocracies of Rome and the imperial cities. Their major policy concern was the well-being of the military establishment. The army was enlarged considerably during the third century, often by recruits from outside the empire; and it was reorganized to provide greater mobility—especially in cavalry forces—for containing the outside forces that were able to penetrate the frontier defenses. Increasingly, the chief administrative posts in the imperial government were filled from the army at the expense of the senatorial class. The emperors moved inexorably toward more thorough regimentation of civilian society and economic activity to support the army. They intruded more decisively into the affairs of local city-state governments to limit local self-determination. Rule by a *princeps*, a first citizen on the model of Augustus or Trajan or Hadrian, was being replaced with rule by a *dominus*, an absolute lord over all citizens, increasingly viewed as mere subjects. As the third century unfolded, the fruits of this change began to be evident. For instance, during the reign of Aurelian (A.D. 270–275) Roman armies were able to curb the intrusion of outsiders and to restore Roman control over frontier areas that had become virtually independent. But the path toward military autocracy threatened essential features of the traditional political order.

2. ECONOMIC, SOCIAL, AND CULTURAL STRESSES

During the third century stress and transformation were not confined to the political realm. Economic production decreased, in part due to the ravages caused by civil strife and invasions and in part due to structural limitations inherent in the traditional economic system. Most serious was a decline in agricultural production. There appears to have been a shortage of labor, probably due to a population decline in the entire Mediterranean world resulting from a serious plague. Agricultural technology did not advance to offset soil depletion and erosion. The spread of the *latifundia* was depressive, chiefly because these large estates replaced independent small farmers with dependent *coloni* and because the large-estate owners sought self-sufficiency rather than production for a market. Trade and industry also were depressed. The disturbances accompanying the civil wars impeded the movement of goods. In their search for funds to reward the army the emperors of the third century regularly debased the currency, leading to massive inflation. Increasing regimentation of the economy in the interests of supplying the enlarged army limited opportunities for new commercial and industrial ventures. New capital was scarce because the directive elements in Roman society continued to invest their wealth in land and in nonproductive military expenditures and luxurious living. The aristocratic cast of society continued to preclude any thought of generating economic growth by elevating the standard of living of lower-class members of society.

The whole structure of society was changing in the third century. The ascending military autocrats systematically eliminated the old senatorial aristocracy from their traditional places in imperial administration and military offices. In cities throughout the empire local aristocracies were crushed by the burden heaped on them to provide money and supplies for the armies and deprived of their control over local affairs by the bureaucrats representing the central authority. Artisans and merchants were increasingly forced into compulsory associations (*collegia*) through which their wages and production were controlled in the interests of the state. The peasants were steadily being driven toward hereditary tenancy and dependency on landowners, conditions that made their already depressed condition even worse.

Two elements in Roman society were advantaged by the changing order: great landowners and soldiers. The owners of large estates were able to tighten their control over agricultural production and the labor force. The imperial government, interested chiefly in securing revenue and produce from the land to support the army and the bureaucracy, gave the landowners greater freedom to exploit the peasantry and to pass on to them the burden of taxation. As their control over the *coloni* expanded, the great estateholders moved inexorably toward independence of action and the satisfaction of their self-interest (see Figure 12.2). At the same time, soldiers enjoyed ever-greater status. Men of ability from nonnoble elements of society found the army the chief avenue for social advancement; many rose to key positions in public life—even the emperorship—to challenge the old aristocracy for social dominance. Even the lowest ranks of the army enjoyed favors not open to other citizens. Because the ranks of the army were increasingly filled with recruits from the most primitive areas of the empire or from "barbarian" outsiders, people little acquainted with or committed to traditional Roman ideas and institutions now moved to leadership roles in society.

The shifting patterns of social relationships had two major effects. First, the consensus among the members of *nobiles* that had been so vital to the governance of the empire during the first and second centuries was challenged and began to dissolve. Second, these changes opened the way for the emergence of new talent with entirely different interests and perspectives. Such fundamental transformations were bound to alter the way the Roman world was controlled.

In the face of the crisis of the third century the Roman world seemed paralyzed intellectually. Culturally, the third century was one of the least productive periods of the entire classical era. Writers, artists, thinkers seemed to have lost their ability to address the problems of their time creatively and their faith in the humanistic, rationalistic values of the Greco-Roman tradition. The vaunted powers once attributed to human beings to control their own destinies at last seemed inadequate in the face of the realities of a troubled world.

In fact, the troubled society of the third century increasingly sought and found refuge in another realm—in religion. The era was alive with powerful religious currents that seriously threatened

FIGURE 12.2 Roman Aristocratic Life This scene decorating a third-century A.D. mausoleum reflects important aspects of the daily life of a typical Roman noble—returning from the hunt (top) and settling accounts with his tenants and his financial agent (bottom). (Landesmuseum, Trier)

the classical world view and undermined allegiance to the state in favor of trust in the divine. Although the ancient civic deities of Greece and Rome still had their adherents, the Eastern mystery religions, with their personal deities, emotional rituals, and promises of eternal salvation, won increasing numbers of adherents at all levels of society. There was a vast resurgence of interest in astrology and magic. Even philosophy was permeated by mystical elements. Everyone seemed in search of escape from a meaningless world through mystical contact with the divine. In this quest many Greco-Roman values, including confidence in human reason, seemed irrelevant.

3. THE BEGINNINGS OF CHRISTIANITY

Among the diverse spiritual movements contending for attention during the third century was Christianity. Although still relatively young, this religion was soon to capture universal attention and to play a decisive role in transforming the ancient world.

When it originated early in the first century A.D., Christianity seemed to hold little promise for eventual success. It began as a splinter movement within the world of Judaism, a world charged with tensions born out of repeated frustrations of the Jewish hope to recover lost national independence and the expectations that eventually God's promise of supremacy to his Chosen People would be fulfilled. Since the eighth century B.C. the ancient homeland of the Jews had been ruled by a succession of conquerors—Assyrians, Chaldeans, Persians, the Hellenistic Seleucids, and finally the Romans after 63 B.C. The Romans were willing to concede special privileges allowing the Jews to practice their religion, but they were suspicious of Jewish visions of independence. At first the Romans established a client king in Judea to keep the peace in Rome's name. The autocratic conduct of these kings, typified by the hated Herod (40–4 B.C.), goaded the Jews to constant agitation. Augustus abolished the client kingdom and imposed direct Roman rule exercised by a prefect charged with keeping order and collecting tribute. This system did not pacify the Jews, who eventually revolted in A.D. 66. The Romans reacted savagely, crushing the rebellion in A.D. 70 and destroying the Temple.

The frustration of their national aspiration had by the first century B.C. bred serious division within the Jewish community. Most Jews accepted the idea proclaimed by earlier prophets that a God-sent messiah would deliver them from their oppressors. And they all sought to abide by the Judaic law as it was interpreted by a special group of learned men called *scribes*. But they disagreed on how to act in the immediate historic setting. The Sadducees, chiefly upper-class Jews, clashed with the Pharisees, who enjoyed strong popular backing, over how to deal with the Romans and how to interpret and apply Judaic law as a means of sustaining Judaic identity and purity. Smaller groups opted for more drastic solutions. The Zealots urged taking up arms against the Romans and showed their militancy by acts of terrorism. The Essenes, whose views have become much better known since the discovery of the Dead Sea Scrolls about forty years ago, sought to break through the letter of Judaic law to a new level of spirituality and to realize their ideals by withdrawal from the Jewish community into an ascetic life marked by a sharing of wealth and prayer. Added to these groups were individual prophets, such as John the Baptist, crying out that deliverance was at hand. Of considerable importance were the Jews of the Diaspora—those dispersed by accident or choice across the entire Mediterranean world. They were strongly influenced by Greco-Roman ideas and tended to incorporate these ideas into their religious life; to most Jews of Palestine this attitude raised strong suspicions of compromise, which threatened the purity of historic Judaism.

Into this complex and highly charged scene came Jesus, born into a modest Jewish household in about 4 B.C. at almost the same moment when Augustus was taking steps to bring the Jews under direct Roman rule. When he was about thirty, Jesus began a public ministry among the Jews that lasted about three years. His message was solidly grounded in the Judaic religious tradition but had certain fresh ideas that appealed to many Jews, especially the simple, poor people. He proclaimed himself as the Son of God made man to announce the arrival of God's promised kingdom. He urged his audience to prepare for the new day now dawning by repentance and spiritual renewal based on repudiation of worldly things and on love for God and fellow men and women.

Jesus did not ask his followers to abandon their Jewish heritage but insisted that they must transcend the empty observance of the law and routine performance of the accustomed rituals by opening their hearts to God's grace. As recorded in his Sermon on the Mount, he taught that in his Father's eyes the poor, the weak, the humble, and the peacemakers had a special place; and the rich, the powerful, and the prideful stood to lose their souls. To those who repented and opened their hearts to God he promised worldly cares less than those of a child and eternal salvation. Jesus anticipated that his followers would await the final realization of the Kingdom of God as members of an organized community. He assigned a special leadership role in propagating his word to certain of his followers, whom he called his disciples. He also instituted a ritual life involving a common meal where the faithful would share consecrated bread and wine in his memory.

Jesus' preaching attracted an enthusiastic following, including many women. In his teachings Jesus gave women a place seldom accorded them in contemporary religions. But Jesus also made enemies. His attack on the empty formalism of Jewish religious practice and on the materialism of religious leaders turned "the scribes and the Pharisees" against him. To them, his message was a threat to the whole fabric of historic Judaism. The power establishment in the Jewish community, especially the Sadducees, was disturbed by his appeal to the poor and the oppressed. And many of his early followers lost much of their enthusiasm when he made it clear that his mission was not to create or rule an earthly kingdom. His command to "render unto Caesar what is Caesar's" was proof that he would not take up the sword to liberate the Jews. This was certainly a disappointment to those who had waited so long for a messiah who would recreate a powerful kingdom of the Jews in this world. This combination of hostility from his enemies and defection among his supporters led to his death in about A.D. 29. Members of the Jewish community brought charges of blasphemy against him before the Sanhedrin, the high court of the Jewish community. That body judged him guilty and received approval to crucify him from Pontius Pilate, the Roman prefect, who was afraid that Jesus' preaching would provoke civil strife among the Jews.

Jesus' death triggered a crucial development. A group of his stoutest disciples was convinced that he had arisen from the dead, proving that he was the Christ ("the anointed"), the Messiah, the Savior sacrificed in accordance with divine plan to bring about the salvation of all humanity. This belief set the little band apart from the whole world; in the words of Paul, "We preach Christ crucified, a stumbling block to Jews and folly to the Gentiles . . ." (I Cor. 1:23). A new religion had been born.

4. THE SPREAD OF CHRISTIANITY

In the first years after Jesus' death his followers carried on as a sect of Judaism. They observed the Judaic law while holding to Jesus' precepts, especially his command that they be ready for the return of Christ and for the final establishment of the Kingdom of God. The larger Jewish community continued to regard these strange people with suspicion and hostility. But the flock did grow, in part through the efforts of Jesus' disciples. Christian ideas spread to many cities, particularly in Syria and Asia Minor, where they attracted the attention of Diaspora Jews and of non-Jews (called Gentiles by the Jews) to whom the religious message of Jesus appealed. Before long many were asking to join the new community and were being received. This development posed a grave question for the foundling movement: whether or not new converts were to be held to strict observance of Judaic law and practices. There were those in the primitive Christian community who took a conservative position, but others, typified by Peter, leader of the disciples, increasingly insisted on universalizing Christianity so that it would be acceptable to Jew and Gentile alike.

A major figure in shaping the Christian mission to the Gentiles was Paul of Tarsus. Born into a Jewish family that had earned Roman citizenship, Paul was a representative of the Jews of the Diaspora—an ardent defender of orthodox Judaism but a man who was familiar with the Greco-Roman cultural life of his native city. Early in his adult life he took an active part in resisting the spread of Christianity in the Jewish community, even to the point of persecuting Christians. But then he underwent a dramatic personal conversion to Christianity. Then followed a long missionary career, beginning in about A.D. 46, which took him to Asia Minor, Greece, and eventually Rome. Central to his missionary effort was his determination to win non-Jews to Christianity. His message emphasized what he understood to be the precepts of Jesus that were applicable to all humanity—the redemption of sinners effected by the Son of God through his death, the need for moral regeneration through faith and love of God and humanity, salvation as a reward for belief in Christ and acceptance of God's grace, purity of moral life. He set down these ideas in letters written to instruct those he had converted; these epistles marked a crucial step in establishing the basic formal doctrines of Christianity. By the time of his martyrdom in Rome during the reign of Nero (perhaps in about A.D. 67), the thrust toward making Christianity a religion distinct from Judaism and directed toward a universal audience had become dominant. The separation of the Christian and Jewish communities was hastened by the Jewish revolt of A.D. 66–70, whose savage suppression by the Romans greatly discredited Judaism in the Roman world.

Once launched in the Pauline direction, Christianity steadily spread over most parts of the Roman world. During at least the first century after Jesus' death, a series of dedicated missionary preachers working under all kinds of conditions were the chief agents of expansion. They concentrated their efforts in the major cities of the empire, so that early Christianity developed chiefly as an urban religion. Often these missionary preachers began their activities in the Jewish synagogues of the cities in which they were working. Their efforts usually won a small group of adherents who formed themselves into self-sustaining "churches." The members of these cells then took up the burden of spreading the faith, working in the local communities to increase the flock.

By the end of the third century, vigorous and expanding Christian communities existed everywhere in the empire (see Map 12.1). The heaviest Christian population was in the cities of Egypt, Syria, Palestine, Asia Minor, Greece, and Italy. Christians certainly formed only a small minority of the total population by A.D. 300, but they had become a potent factor in the Roman world, one far exceeding what might have been expected in view of their inauspicious beginning and their early struggles.

The progress of Christianity was not, however, unopposed. From time to time the Roman government persecuted Christians because of their refusal to discharge any civic responsibility—including military service—that involved recognition of the Roman deities. The Christians who suffered were viewed by their fellow believers as martyrs whose heroic example strengthened the resolve of most Christians to remain steadfast. Anti-Chris-

tian feelings were felt in many elements of the Roman populace. Among the masses of people there spread a battery of vile rumors about strange beliefs and immoral, bestial practices, rumors fed by the Christian refusal to participate in public religious rites and by their private, semisecret worship services. Roman intellectuals scorned Christianity, holding up for ridicule its simplistic, illogical concepts. The leaders of the state religion and of the Jewish synagogues constantly charged the Christians with false beliefs and debased practices. Several mystery religions featuring ideas and practices similar to Christianity proved worthy rivals; especially powerful in the third century was Mithraism, which won a wide following in the army.

The Christians made difficulties for themselves as well. From the very beginning there were divisions in their ranks on what constituted right belief and proper usage. The early communities disagreed on the nature of the relationship between Christianity and Judaism. The proper moral posture for a Christian was often a subject for debate, especially because some insisted on a puritanical denial of the world and its pleasures. By the second century and increasingly in the third, Christians disagreed violently on certain fundamental doctrines, especially those relating to the nature of Jesus' relationship to God, thus generating what may be called the first heresies. These conflicts inevitably set Christian against Christian and diverted the faithful from proselytizing.

5. REASONS FOR CHRISTIANITY'S EXPANSION

Yet Christianity did expand—geographically, numerically, and substantively. Its success was due to many factors, not the least of which were favorable conditions in the Roman Empire. Despite sporadic cases of persecution, an atmosphere of religious tolerance generally prevailed. Freedom of movement allowed Christian missionaries to travel where they pleased, as is illustrated by the case of Paul. The general weakening of the traditional civic religions associated with Roman public life caused people to seek individual spiritual sat-

Map 12.1 **THE SPREAD OF CHRISTIANITY TO A.D. 311** This map shows how extensively Christianity had spread across the Roman Empire during the first three centuries A.D. In an important way the journeys of Paul provided a crucial beginning step in this expansion. In general, Christian life was still confined largely to cities by A.D. 311. The heavier concentration of Christians in the East is worth noting; it is perhaps understandable why the newly converted emperor, Constantine, chose to move the capital of the empire from Rome to Constantinople.

isfaction, and the chaos of the third century made the need for personal spiritual security ever more urgent. The existence of a single state uniting diverse peoples into a unified society pointed toward a single, universal religion applicable to all people regardless of origin or status. As noted earlier, powerful forces of religious syncretism had long been at work in the Hellenistic and Roman worlds, preparing for common religious life. In short, the time was ripe for Christianity. But a favorable environment cannot alone explain its expansion. Christianity proved to be a movement rich in inner resources, and it demonstrated an unusual capability to adapt to a changing world.

A fundamental source of Christian strength lay in its appeal as a religion. No matter how far in other directions we push the search for an explanation of its expansion, it is always evident that Christianity won converts primarily because its teachings answered their deepest religious needs. Such ideas as the existence of one almighty, loving, merciful God; his sacrifice of his son to redeem men and women; eternal salvation based on individual worth; damnation for sinners; and universal brotherhood supplied a powerful answer to those seeking to know about God's ways toward men and women. The humanity of Jesus, who had lived on earth not long before, gave intimacy and historical concreteness to Christianity that other religions lacked. Moreover, Christian teachings were dramatically and simply presented in a body of writing, called the New Testament, which took form during the century after the death of Jesus and which came to be accepted as the divinely inspired "good news" brought by Jesus. The Christians linked this holy book with the Jewish Bible, which they called the Old Testament, and gained a powerful weapon for presenting God's ways with respect to the world.

Another reason for Christianity's success was the organization that took shape during the first three centuries of its history. The first Christian communities consisted of a few converts lost in the non-Christian population of the cities of the Roman world. These people met together regularly to pray and sing, to share a common meal commemorating the Last Supper of Christ, and to be instructed. Leaders emerged in these cells; eventually, these leaders were given titles: *episcopus* (bishop), elder, and *diaconus* (deacon). With the passage of time problems emerged that called for firmer organization: larger numbers of Christians, persecutions, increasing wealth available to the community, disagreement over what constituted right beliefs and practice. Authority over all the affairs of the Christian community in each city began to settle on the bishop. Around this office there developed a powerful ideological justification, called the concept of *apostolic succession*. This theory argued that every bishop was a successor to the original apostles and heir to the spiritual authority that Jesus bestowed on those apostles to proclaim the faith and to forgive sinners.

In many large cities the Christian population became so numerous that one place of worship would not suffice to serve them. Additional churches were created with a priest in charge of each. However, the bishop retained final authority over these new establishments, ensuring the organizational solidarity of the Christian community on a citywide basis. This organizational evolution resulted in tightly knot, self-governing local units that reflected a basic entity in the ancient world— the city-state.

While many "churches" were being fashioned

from city to city, the Christians never lost sight of their universal spiritual kinship, rooted in their belief in the one God who had given his son to ensure salvation for all his children. From this kinship resulted efforts to forge bonds of unity that would link the many churches into one Church. Jesus' disciples and the early missionaries such as Paul tried to keep in touch with as many Christian communities as possible by means of extensive travel and letter writing.

By the second century, bishops met together on a regional basis in *councils* to discuss common problems and decide on common solutions that each could apply in his own church. Certain bishops from great cities such as Jerusalem, Antioch, Alexandria, and Rome exerted considerable influence over lesser bishops in the regions surrounding these centers. These influential bishops began to be called "patriarchs" to indicate their preeminence. By the end of the third century there were Christians concerned with vesting ultimate authority over all Christians in the hands of one of these great bishops. A prime candidate was the bishop of Rome, who gained special prestige not only from the fact that Rome was the capital of the world but also from an important doctrine, the *Petrine theory*. According to this doctrine, rooted in a particular scriptural passage (Matt. 16:18–19), Jesus had granted Peter a special place as his vicar on earth; Peter had chosen Rome as the seat of that power; and those who followed him as bishops of Rome after his martyrdom were believed to have succeeded to Peter's authority as head of the total Christian community.

By A.D. 285, Peter's successors as bishops of Rome, increasingly referred to as *popes* (derived from the late Latin word *papa*, meaning "father"), were turning this claim to spiritual supremacy into active leadership in defining doctrine and prescribing discipline for Christian communities over much of the Roman Empire. And many of these communities were seeking the pope's guidance, especially in doctrinal matters. A kind of second Roman Empire was being born, subdivided into well-governed local units and headed by a spiritual "emperor."

Christianity also increased its appeal, especially to the sophisticated upper classes, by developing a systematic, reasoned statement of its

FIGURE 12.3   Honoring the Christian Dead   Following an ancient Roman custom, early Christians sought to perpetuate the memory of the dead by decorating their sarcophagi with scenes from the life of the deceased. This third-century sarcophagus, clearly reflecting pagan art styles, shows the dead man (reading in the center while being prayed for) surrounded by representations of Christian history: the good shepherd, John baptizing Jesus (as a child), Jonah being washed ashore. (Alinari/Art Resource)

fundamental beliefs. This articulation of its doctrine in literary form marked a rather dramatic departure from primitive Christianity. Jesus had preached in Aramaic to an audience that was largely apart from the mainstream of Greco-Roman intellectual and literary life. The early leaders of the new religion were quite open in their rejection of pagan culture and thus established an anti-intellectual bias in the Christian community. For example, Paul could ask: "Has not God made foolish the wisdom of the world?" (I Cor. 1:20). However, this posture did not survive long. As soon as the Christians began their effort to convert Gentiles, they had to employ the Greek and Latin languages and the modes of thought and expression prevailing in the Roman Empire.

By the second century and more pronouncedly in the third, two particular forces spurred the Christians toward intellectualization of their faith: the need to answer the accusations of non-Christian intellectuals that the new religion was irrational, and the problem of resolving differences within the Christian ranks on the meaning of basic doctrines. The "apologists" answering the critics and the theologians defining the exact meaning of the faith borrowed heavily from Greco-Roman philosophy, especially the Platonic tradition. The most influential figures in this movement wedding Christian thought and Greco-Roman culture were two scholars from Alexandria, Clement (ca. 150–216) and Origen (ca. 185–254). Their efforts increasingly persuaded Christians that classical learning had been a preparation for the true revelation and therefore useful in illuminating the meaning of God's word. The absorption of classical learning by Christianity had begun, increasing Christianity's appeal in the Roman world. The Christians were equally adept at adapting Greco-Roman art forms as a means of conveying their message (see Figures 12.1 and 12.3).

The Christians strengthened the appeal of their religion by developing ritual practices that were attractive in a world accustomed to pageantry and spectacles. Originally, Christian worship was simple. The faithful gathered in private houses to share a common meal, called the Eucharist, in commemoration of Jesus, and to pray and sing. As time passed, this ritual life became more complex, marked by the adaptation of Jewish and pagan practices to Christian uses. Special places for worship were built and adorned with art inspired by Christian beliefs. The eucharistic ceremony became more elaborate, constituting what came to be called the Mass. Ceremonies were established for such events as baptism, marriage, and burial. Special holidays—holy days to the Christians—developed to commemorate highlights in Jesus' career and the death of the early martyrs.

The Christian movement also developed a strong social consciousness. Jesus in his teachings and his life repeatedly exemplified the need for charity and kindness in dealing with others. This idea received expression in Christian practice almost from the beginning. Christians poured out their resources to help the sick, the poor, criminals, slaves, orphans, widows, and other unfortunates in society. In spite of their belief that happiness came in the hereafter, the early Christians did not close their eyes to earthly affairs.

The advance of Christianity was an amazing chapter in history. Historians have long debated whether the success of Christianity contributed to the decline of the Roman Empire. There is still no clear answer. In many ways most Christians were good Romans, as Jesus and many early Christian leaders urged them to be. They performed their civic duties as long as they were not required to deny their god. They paid their taxes and obeyed the emperor. They tried their best to help the unfortunate members of Roman society. The books they read on Christian theology contained huge portions of Greco-Roman philosophy. They worshiped in a fashion that bore a strong resemblance to non-Christian worship.

In other important ways, the early Christians were not good Romans. They served a god who would tolerate no rivals, including Roman emperors who claimed divinity. Believing that their god disapproved of the ways of non-Christians, they tended to avoid involvement in worldly affairs and to keep apart from ordinary social life. Their strong sense of sin led them to regard the world, including the Roman Empire, as a perpetual source of evil, hardly worth saving. Their belief in the omnipotence of God and in human frailty caused them to distrust human reason and to put no trust in human ability to build a paradise on earth. They thus found little that appealed to them in the basic premise of Greco-Roman civilization: the conviction that enlightened human activity could create a perfect society on earth. The Christian was a devoted, disciplined member of an organization existing independently of the Roman state. Through its evolving religious ceremonies, the Church kept before the Christians a series of symbols and arguments that made them feel their separateness and their uniqueness. Every Christian convert meant one fewer Roman citizen in the fullest sense of that word.

As the end of the third century A.D. approached, the Roman Empire had reached a critical juncture, resembling in some ways the situation the Roman world had faced at the end of the first century B.C. A long crisis had strained the imperial system and unleashed forces that pointed toward profound transformations of the political, economic, social, religious, and cultural structures of imperial society. The future of the empire depended on what kind of decisions would be made to accommodate the changing situation.

SUGGESTED READING

Decline of the Empire

Peter Brown, *The World of Late Antiquity from Marcus Aurelius to Muhammad* (1971).
Michael Grant, *The Climax of Rome: The Final Achievement of the Ancient World, A.D. 161–337* (1968).
Two provocative treatments of the late Roman Empire.

Joseph Vogt, *The Decline of Rome: The Metamorphosis of Ancient Civilization*, trans. Janet Sondheimer (1969).
Stewart Perowne, *The End of the Ancient World* (1966).
F. W. Walbank, *The Awful Revolution; The Decline of the Roman Empire in the West* (1969).

Michael Grant, *The Fall of the Roman Empire: A Reappraisal* (1976).

A. Ferrill, *The Fall of the Roman Empire: The Military Explanation* (1986).

These five works provide diverse interpretations of Rome's decline.

Rise of Christianity

Jocelyn Godwin, *Mystery Religions in the Ancient World* (1981). A good treatment of religions competing with Christianity.

E. Mary Smallwood, *The Jews under Roman Rule* (1981). A clear picture of the Jewish position in the empire.

Alan F. Segal, *Rebecca's Children: Judaism and Christianity in the Roman World* (1986). A challenging treatment of the interactions between the two religions.

W. H. C. Frend, *The Rise of Christianity* (1984).

Robin Lane Fox, *Pagans and Christians* (1987).

Two masterful, detailed accounts of the rise of Christianity.

R. A. Markus, *Christianity in the Roman World* (1974). An excellent brief account of the rise of Christianity.

Ramsay MacMullen, *Christianizing the Roman Empire, A.D. 100–400* (1984). Examines the reasons for the Christian victory.

Steven Benko, *Pagan Rome and the Early Christians* (1984). Describes how the pagans looked at the Christians.

Marta Sordi, *The Christians and the Roman Empire*, trans. Annabel Bedini (1986). Excellent treatment of relationships between the state and the Christian community down to Constantine.

Wayne A. Meeks, *The First Urban Christians: The Social World of the Apostle Paul* (1983). Excellent social history.

J. G. Davies, *Daily Life in the Early Church* (1952). Provides fascinating glimpses of the simpler aspects of early Christian society.

CHAPTER 13

The Destruction of the Roman Empire, A.D. 284–500

Figure 13.1 Constantine the Great This photo shows the surviving pieces of a huge statue, nearly forty feet in height, that Constantine had placed in a magnificent basilica he built in the Roman Forum. The massive head retains some features of earlier Roman portrait sculpture (see Figure 9.2); however, its creator was more intent in conveying Constantine's lordship than in producing a realistic portrayal of the emperor. (Art Resource)

In A.D. 284 a general named Diocletian seized the imperial throne by force. In itself this act was a repetition of what had happened repeatedly during the preceding half century; however, the accession of Diocletian marked a decisive turning point. He and his most important successor, Constantine (A.D. 306–337), undertook a reform of the empire that prolonged its vitality for another century. Then in the fifth century the empire was unable to resist the onslaught of Germanic invaders, who seized control of the western part of the empire and destroyed the unity of the Mediterranean world.

1. THE REFORMS OF DIOCLETIAN AND CONSTANTINE

Diocletian was by birth of Dalmatian peasant stock. Like so many third-century emperors, he worked his way to prominence in the military service and acquired many of the autocratic ways associated with military life. However, he did have a clear insight into the basic problems facing the Roman world and was aware of the trends unfolding during the third century to threaten imperial society. He acted decisively to carry out political reforms aimed at solving Rome's most serious problems.

Conscious of the chaos resulting from rivalry within the army for control of the succession and of the impossible burden imposed on a single ruler by the mounting problems of the empire, Diocletian sought a new arrangement to ensure orderly succession and a division of administrative responsibility. A system of shared authority was established: He and an associate each assumed the title *augustus* and to each was assigned a subordinate entitled *caesar*. When an augustus died, his caesar would succeed him as augustus and appoint another caesar. In theory the four corulers would share a single *imperium;* in practice each would be responsible for administering one of four newly established territorial units, called *prefectures,* into which the empire was divided. All would follow a common policy.

Diocletian sought to solidify and exalt the authority of the four corulers. The pronouncements of the rulers constituted the final law; no pretense was made of consulting with the Senate and the people. Various practices were adopted to lend a sacred character to the imperial office: Each ruler withdrew from public view as much as possible and adopted an elaborate court ritual designed to associate the ruler with divine powers. Each ruler began to be addressed as *dominus* (lord) rather than *princeps* (first citizen).

A significant expansion and restructuring of the bureaucracy was undertaken to ensure that the autocratic rulers were able to exercise their power. At each imperial court greater numbers of professional civil servants were organized under a chief official, called the *praetorian prefect,* whose powers were extended to embrace all civil affairs in each prefecture. The number of provinces was nearly doubled by dividing old ones, and imperial officials were installed in each to carry out the orders of the central government. An intermediary level of administration was interposed between the provinces and imperial court in each prefecture by the grouping of provinces into thirteen administrative units called *dioceses;* each had its own bureaucratic apparatus responsible to the augustus or caesar or to his praetorian prefect. This elaborate hierarchy gave the central government the means to act directly in local affairs and effectively ended the political role for the once active local city-state governments.

One of Diocletian's major concerns was the army. In part the expansion and the centralization of the bureaucracy was aimed at removing the army from involvement in civil affairs. More important was the need to increase the effectiveness of the army in the face of the external menace. Following initiatives introduced by his immediate predecessors, Diocletian sought to strengthen and regularize the permanent frontier garrisons and to develop a mobile strike force, strong in cavalry, capable of responding quickly to contain crises arising when the frontier forces were unable to cope with outside attackers. This reorganization increased the size of the army considerably—to about six hundred thousand troops—and raised monumental problems of recruitment and support.

The expansion of the bureaucracy and the army placed a massive financial burden on the imperial government. Diocletian tried to meet this challenge by restructuring the taxation system. His motives were many: dependable revenues, more equitable assessments, securing maximum income. A regular census system was instituted, which aimed at identifying units of land and human heads upon which uniform levies could be based. At the same time, the government imposed upon the key productive elements of society a requisition system aimed at extracting crucial produce in kind and services required to sustain the courts, the army, and the bureaucracy. To ensure that money, goods, and services would be available on a regular and permanent basis, Diocletian issued a series of edicts freezing large numbers of people in their occupations. As a further measure to stabilize the economy and control rampant inflation, Diocletian sought to fix prices for a wide range of commodities and services related to the operation of the bureaucracy and the army. He envisaged a regimented economy in which the state had first claim on all products and where all citizens were required to live their lives in the service of the state.

Diocletian's concept of autocracy demanded not only that citizens serve the state with their labor and wealth but also that they focus their minds on its well-being. He was convinced that religious unity was crucial in developing loyalty and devotion to the state. His reign was marked by a major effort to rally the citizenry around a worship of traditional deities, whose agent the semidivine emperor was. This policy brought him into conflict with the increasingly numerous and confident Christian community, which steadfastly refused to honor the pagan deities or to obey the state when it commanded them to do so. Such a position was intolerable to Diocletian, who responded with a series of punitive decrees in A.D. 303 and 304 that were aimed at destroying Christianity. His assault, the most serious ever faced by the Christians, took a heavy toll but failed in its prime objective. It did, however, demonstrate the degree to which religion had come to be viewed as a prime force sustaining autocracy.

When Diocletian decided to abdicate in A.D. 305, it appeared that most of his reforms had been successful in restoring order in the empire. Only one of his reforms was a signal failure—his elaborate plan for regulating the succession. Although

lip service was given temporarily to its provisions, eventually there occurred a renewed outbreak of armed conflicts pitting various contenders and segments of the army against one another. The ultimate victor was Constantine, who between A.D. 306 and 324 won a series of victories that finally left him in sole control of the entire empire. Constantine was a worthy successor of Diocletian (see Figure 13.1). He vigorously pursued the main elements of Diocletian's reform program: strengthening the army; expanding and tightening bureaucratic control over imperial affairs; improving the fiscal machinery; enlarging the emperor's power; and imposing tighter control over the imperial population.

Constantine added important elements to the new order. Most significant was a new religious policy officially proclaimed in A.D. 313, when he and his co-emperor issued the Edict of Milan, granting religious freedom to all in the empire. The edict recognized the right of Christians to follow their faith. Behind the decree was an event of immense psychological impact: the conversion of Constantine himself. In A.D. 311 prior to a decisive battle in his rise to power, he had a vision that promised him victory if he would display the cross as his insignia. He did, and he won. Although Constantine was not baptized until just before his death in A.D. 337, after the Edict of Milan he gave every indication that he favored the Christian cause. He poured out money to build churches, drew clergymen into the councils of state, and extended to them a variety of special privileges. His legislation increasingly reflected Christian teachings. Although he tolerated other religions, he did little to encourage them. Every sign pointed in one direction: The empire was becoming a Christian state.

Contemporary Christians hailed Constantine's conversion as a sign of the fulfillment of God's plan; their enthusiasm laid the basis for designating him as Constantine "the Great." Many have doubted that his motives were totally religious. He certainly stood to gain politically by winning the support of the Christians. Perhaps he sensed that by committing the state to the service of Christian ends, he could create a reliable nucleus of supporters around which to build a unified empire obedient to an emperor who was God's chief servant. On the basis of the record of the preceding three centuries, it was not unrealistic to think that this aggressive religion had the potential to expand its flock to include all Romans. Constantine's behavior was not a cynical manipulation of religion. He was a man of his age, powerfully drawn to religion and especially to Christianity, not the least as a result of the influence exercised over him by his Christian mother, Helen. Whatever his motives, his action in linking the destinies of the Roman Empire and Christianity marked a turning point in history.

Hardly less momentous was his decision to build a new capital at the ancient Greek city of Byzantium, renamed Constantinople. Begun in A.D. 324 and officially dedicated in A.D. 330, this "new" Rome replicated many features of "old" Rome. Constantine's decision to undertake this expensive project was more than an autocratic whim. From the second century onward it was clear that old Rome was not the most advantageous physical center for the empire. With increasing frequency, emperors were chosen whose roots were outside Rome. The whole thrust of political development during the third century minimized the role of Rome's *nobiles* as prime factors in political life. Reflecting the obvious fact that Rome was badly located strategically in terms of frontier defenses, Diocletian's reorganization of the empire into four prefectures resulted in the emergence of new political centers: Nicomedia in Asia Minor, Milan in Italy, Sirmium in the Balkans, and Trier in the Rhineland. Prompted by such considerations, Constantine's choice for his capital was well advised. The site was nearly impregnable against attacks by land or sea. It offered more ready access to the most vulnerable frontiers—the lower Danube and the Euphrates River frontiers. The new city was close to the great centers of wealth in the East, and it was situated where Christian strength was greatest. It also offered its founder freedom from the restrictive traditions of republicanism and paganism, both deeply entrenched in old Rome.

The full impact of the founding of Constantinople was not immediately obvious. Rome remained an important city upon which Constantine continued to shower favors, including a magnificent church built in honor of St. Peter on Vatican Hill. Many could not conceive of Rome as anything except *caput mundi*—head of the world. But to some who especially cherished ancient tradition, it seemed that Constantine had turned the world around, allowing the East to surpass the West, the Greeks to prevail over the Latins. In fact, Constantine had created a bastion that in the not too distant future would serve as the center of a drastically reduced Roman Empire and as a major heir of Greco-Roman civilization (see Chapter 14).

2. AN UNEASY PEACE

Diocletian and Constantine had sought by political action to impose unity on the empire as a cure for its problems, a unity that called on all citizens to commit themselves in body and mind to the service of the state. For a time it appeared that their reforms had saved the empire. By contrast with the third century, the fourth century was one of relative order. Succession to the imperial office was usually peaceful, there was little civil strife, and the frontier defenses seemed secure. The era witnessed vigorous literary and artistic activity, much of it in the service of Christianity but some of it engendered by enthusiasm for traditional Greco-Roman culture. To many contemporaries it seemed again that the Roman political genius had saved the civilized world, as in the time of Augustus.

Yet there were ominous signs of decay in the Roman world that the reforms of Diocletian and Constantine not only failed to resolve but also deepened. Economic production continued to decline, hastened by economic regimentation and by the diversion of an ever-greater proportion of wealth to support the army and the bureaucracy. The burden of taxation, requisition in kind, and compulsory labor for the state fell chiefly on groups especially critical to economic well-being: peasants, artisans, merchants, and local urban aristocrats, all of whom took actions of some kind to avoid the burden at the expense of productivity.

The autocratic imperial government fashioned by Diocletian and Constantine revealed fatal flaws. The exalted emperors became more remote from practical affairs. The costly, ever-growing bureaucracy became intrusive, corrupt, and arbitrary to the point where it was universally detested. Considerable evidence suggests that in terms of effectiveness the army failed to respond to the immense sums spent on it. Increasingly its ranks had to be filled with German recruits, often commanded by their own chiefs, whose loyalty was suspect. The frontier garrisons were undermanned, and their troops often had to devote much of their time to supporting themselves. The actions of the military forces in laying hands on supplies were often arbitrary and brutal, generating deepening hatred between the military and the civilian population. Not a few contemporaries felt and even said that the imperial government had become a monster.

A dangerous manifestation of discontent took the form of withdrawal from public responsibilities. Citizens from all walks of life sought to evade taxation and military service. The senatorial class, once a vital element in imperial governance, turned its attention to accumulating land, creating self-sustaining estates, and living in luxury. Ensconced in their rural strongholds and often openly disdainful of "nonnoble" emperors and their lowly agents and army officers, these powerful figures defied the government's efforts to compel them to bear their share of the public burden. Usually they had their way. In ever-larger numbers peasants accepted a position as dependent tenants under these landlords as a way of escaping taxation, compulsory labor service, and military duty. In city after city across the empire members of local aristocracies fled to the countryside or took service in the imperial bureaucracy or joined the clergy in order to escape the responsibilities thrust on them by the government to deliver the money and the services due from their localities. Such evidence of disaffection pointed toward disunity rather than unity.

Equally disturbing was clear evidence that Constantine's religious policy failed to unify the state and arouse patriotic fervor. Christianity did continue its march to dominance during the fourth century, culminating when Emperor Theodosius (A.D. 379–395) made it the state religion and outlawed all others. The imperial policy of favoring Christianity alienated many Romans, especially aristocrats, who still placed trust in the ancient pagan religions. That resentment surfaced with particular vigor during the reign of Julian (A.D. 361–363), called the "Apostate" by the Christians because he repudiated Christianity and sought to replace it with a restored pagan "church." His effort failed, but it kept alive a fundamental schism in imperial society. Even the Christians were violently divided. During the reign of Constantine a bitter quarrel arose over the question of the Trinity. The Arians made God the Son subordinate to God the Father, denying the absolute divinity of Christ. The outraged Orthodox insisted that the Son was coequal with the Father and that, together with the Holy Spirit, these three "persons" formed a unity. In an attempt to settle this dispute, Constantine summoned churchmen from all over the empire to the ecumenical Council of Nicea in A.D. 325. This assemblage agreed upon the Nicene Creed, which accepted the Orthodox position and articulated a strong trinitarian position that all Christians were obliged to accept. However, the quarrel raged on throughout the century—and so did several other "heresies"—to create disarray among the Christians and to frustrate the efforts of the imperial government to impose unity. Some Christian leaders even challenged the right of the imperial government to interfere in religious affairs, claiming that the Christian community constituted a separate realm exercising an independent jurisdiction when religious issues were at stake. In short, Christianity failed to supply a vitalizing force in the service of the "new" empire; it was a movement with its own ends and strengths, not easily bent to other purposes.

Taken together these trends created divisions within imperial society and undermined the state's ability to muster its material and human resources. Their cumulative impact began to emerge at the end of the fourth century, when the empire had to face a major crisis brought on by a fundamental change in the relationships between the Romans and the Germanic peoples facing each other across the Rhine-Danube frontier.

3. THE GERMANS

In describing the decisive encounter between the Romans and the Germans during the fourth and fifth centuries, historians have traditionally referred to the Germans as "barbarians." The term is appropriate only if used to signify that the Germans differed from the Romans in terms of the basic features of the culture under which they lived. That difference is best reflected in certain fundamental Germanic institutions, each destined to play a part in shaping life in western Europe in future centuries.

The basic Germanic political institution was the *tribe*, headed by a tribal chief who was chosen primarily because of his ability as a war leader. Each tribe was composed of a number of kinship groups, or *clans*. The elders of these clans acting as a council played a decisive role in shaping tribal decisions, but all freemen capable of bearing arms were allowed to have some voice in determining collective action. Tribal government concerned itself with a limited range of affairs: war, religion, and justice. Other matters relating to group life were left largely in the hands of kinship groups; especially crucial was the responsibility of each kinship group to protect its members against injury from others. Each tribe had a body of customary law transmitted orally from one generation to another to regulate such relationships. In its substance Germanic law was primarily concerned with damages against persons. The law prescribed in monetary terms how much compensation could be demanded for various kinds of damage done to a person. That price, called *wergeld*, varied not only according to the nature of the crime but also according to the rank of the person in the kinship group. For example, any damage to a warrior commanded a higher *wergeld* than did the same offense against a woman of childbearing age; in turn, damage done to such a woman called for a higher *wergeld* than did a comparable crime against an aged person. It was the responsibility of those suffering damage or their kin group, not public authority, to initiate judicial processes to collect the *wergeld* defined by law. If the perpetrator of the damage agreed to pay the *wergeld*, then the issue was settled. If not, then the aggrieved kinship group often sought vengeance on the clan of the alleged criminal; the resultant feuds were a common feature of Germanic life. Customary law provided complex procedures for resolving disputes involving damages to persons. One such

procedure, called *compurgation*, involved finding a certain number of individuals—depending on the nature of the crime and the status of the accused—who would swear under oath that the accused was innocent. Another, called *ordeal*, involved putting the accused to a test, such as holding a hot iron or being thrown into water, the results of which could be interpreted as a divine message indicating guilt or innocence.

Early Germanic economy was pastoral, but during the first centuries of the Christian era a simple agricultural economy began to develop. Although kinship groups claimed some rights over land, the basic unit of economic and social life was the household. Generally, Germanic marriages were monogamous, but some rich and powerful men had more than one wife. These households were in large part controlled by males, most of whom were presumed to be equals in early Germanic society. Although dependent on males in many ways, women enjoyed considerable status in Germanic society. Kinship ties were established through both male and female lines of clan groups. Women possessed wealth in their own right, chiefly as a consequence of gifts conveyed to them at the time of marriage. They also played an important part in the economic pursuits that supported family life.

Germanic religion was polytheistic, focusing particularly on the worship of deities embodying the forces of nature dominating the skies and the forests. An orally transmitted mythology existed to explain the nature and the powers of these deities, usually portrayed as remote, terrible forces that must be placated constantly through prayer and offerings. By about A.D. 400 the Germans had just began to develop writing. Yet they did possess a well-developed oral poetic tradition that dealt with the deities and with human heroes. Early Germanic art was devoted especially to jewelry made of precious metals and featuring animal forms and geometric patterns.

Obviously, the encounter between Romans and Germans involved the meeting of two entirely different cultures. It is important to note, however, that the Germans were not locked into a pattern of "backwardness." By the fourth century their society was changing. Small tribal groups were being unified, often by force, into *nations* ruled over by elected kings enjoying considerable powers. Within Germanic society there was also developing a unique institution—the war band (*comitatus*)—composed of warriors united by pledges made under oath to follow a military chief in return for a share of booty. These warriors became a kind of warrior aristocracy, increasingly dominant in society. The emergence of nations and of skilled war bands greatly increased the military capabilities of the Germans. As already noted, Germanic society was moving toward an agricultural economy that encouraged the development of an aristocracy of landowners at the expense of the older, more egalitarian social structure. These changing conditions made Germanic society dynamic, mobile, adaptable, and open to foreign influences.

These two different cultures had faced each other across a fixed frontier for four centuries before their decisive encounter in the fourth century. Although these confrontations had often been hostile, there were more positive aspects. The Germans often demonstrated a desire to share the fruits of Greco-Roman civilization, especially its material wealth. Although the Romans saw the Germans as "barbarians," they respected their physical prowess, their fighting skills, and their alleged moral excellence. They permitted Germans to cross the frontier as long as their movement could be controlled. Large numbers entered the empire as soldiers and farmers and became Romanized; many even rose to high places in Roman society. Roman influences sifted across the frontiers to affect Germanic society. For example, during the fourth century many Goths were converted to Christianity by Ulfilas, himself a Goth educated in Constantinople. Ulfilas provided a Gothic version of the Bible for his converts, a feat that required the creation of a written Gothic language. Such developments suggested that eventually the Germans might be absorbed into the mainstream of Greco-Roman civilization without causing any great disruption of its development. But that possibility depended on the ability of the Romans to control the interactions between themselves and the Germans. From the Roman perspective maintainence of the frontier defense system was the crucial factor.

4. THE GERMANIC MIGRATIONS AND THE FALL OF THE EMPIRE

At the end of the fourth century a dramatic sequence of events occurred within the Germanic world that resulted in a loss of Roman control of relations with the Germans and plunged the Roman Empire into a crisis. About A.D. 370 a horde of nomads, the Huns, suddenly swept out of central Asia across southern Russia. As they moved westward along the northern shores of the Black Sea, they encountered two settled Germanic nations, the Ostrogoths and the Visigoths. The former were quickly overpowered. The terror-stricken Visigoths begged permission to migrate as a nation across the Danube into Roman territory in the Balkans. Their request was granted. They were allowed to keep their own king and were promised land in return for military service. When the imperial government failed to provide for their needs, the Visigoths revolted and inflicted a crushing defeat on a Roman army led by Emperor Valens at the battle of Adrianople in A.D. 378. Rome now had a hostile Germanic nation within its borders. In the meanwhile, the Huns moved farther west where they created a large Hunnic nation north of the Danube and uprooted other Germanic nations (see Map 13.1 for the movements of the Germans).

For a brief time Theodosius, the last ruler of a united empire, was able to confine the Visigoths to the Balkan area by establishing them as Roman allies (*foederati*) to whom were assigned lands in return for military service. But Theodosius' death in A.D. 395 marked the end of the uneasy calm. He bequeathed his office to two sons, one assigned to rule in the West and the other in the East. Neither had much ability, and both allowed the direction of affairs to fall into the hands of ambitious generals whose power depended on Germanic troops. The result was a series of internal power struggles between the eastern and western courts that ended with loss of control over the Germanic hordes pressing on the imperial frontiers.

As the fifth century opened, the Visigoths, led by a capable king named Alaric, were skillfully playing a game of selling their services alternately to the competing emperors. Eventually they

Map 13.1 GERMANIC INVASIONS, FIFTH CENTURY The map shows the movements of the various Germanic nations in the course of their invasions of the Roman Empire in the fifth century. Most of them ended their wandering by establishing a kingdom on Roman soil. Especially important for the future was the kingdom established by the Franks in Gaul.

turned against the West, having been promised by the emperor in Constantinople whatever lands they could conquer. Their repeated attacks on Italy necessitated the recall of troops from the Rhine and Danube frontiers and from Britain, but to no avail. In A.D. 410 they captured and sacked Rome. The frontier defenses in the West broke down, allowing other Germanic nations to pour into the heart of the empire. Their "invasions" led to the

political dismemberment of the empire in the West. In its desperation, the imperial government sought to control the Germans by assigning them areas where they could settle as allies, subject to Roman authority. In fact, wherever the Germans settled and whatever the terms, their kings and warriors soon became the real rulers. As a consequence, during the fifth century a series of independent Germanic kingdoms were founded on

Roman soil in the West to replace the unified imperial regime.

After their sack of Rome in A.D. 410 the Visigoths remained briefly in Italy and then were assigned rich lands in southern Gaul, where they established a kingdom that soon began to extend itself into Spain. Already other Germanic nations who had broken across the Rhine in A.D. 406—Vandals, Sueves, Alains—had made their destructive way across Gaul and into Spain. The Vandals, under the leadership of their one great king, Gaiseric, crossed into Africa in A.D. 429 and carved out a large kingdom that deprived Rome of access to its main grain supply. The Vandals developed sufficient sea power to allow them to pillage Rome in A.D. 455.

The Burgundians created a kingdom in southeastern Gaul in the Rhone Valley, effectively blocking the routes linking Italy to Gaul. Beginning about A.D. 425 Angles, Saxons, and Jutes came by sea to wipe out the badly weakened Roman outposts in Britain and to establish several petty kingdoms; in the process the newcomers drove the native Celtic population into Wales and across the English Channel into Britanny. Without abandoning their original homelands, Franks and Alemanni began the occupation of northern Gaul and the middle Rhine Valley. Late in the fifth century the Franks, led by a ruthless warrior king named Clovis (A.D. 481–511), seized most of Gaul as their base of power; in the process they drove the Gallic Visigoths into Spain and absorbed the Burgundian kingdom as well as much of the territory of the Alemanni. Italy, the last major territory in the West, was taken in A.D. 493 by the Ostrogoths under the leadership of King Theoderic. The confusion caused by the movements of these Germanic peoples was compounded by the presence of a powerful Hunnic kingdom established north of the Danube. Under their feared king, Attila, the Huns harassed the East and then invaded Gaul and Italy in A.D. 451–452, which were successfully defended by a coalition of Roman and Germanic troops. After Attila's death in 453, the Hunnic kingdom quickly broke up, leaving central Europe in a chaotic state.

While the boundaries of these new kingdoms remained fluid, there could be no doubt that by A.D. 500 the Germans had won the West. The fate of the empire in the East during the critical fifth century was quite different. True, German forces repeatedly ravaged imperial territory in the Balkans and sought entry into the eastern provinces. Their assaults were effectively blunted by the money, diplomacy, and military actions of the imperial government in Constantinople, which was not above bribing the Germans into diverting their attacks to the West. As a consequence, the Germans failed to penetrate the East, where the traditional imperial structures survived virtually intact.

The most dramatic result of the Germanic "invasions" was the slow dissolution of the imperial government in the West. Some of the generals serving the incompetent emperors fought valiantly to check the invasions and negotiated desperately to turn Germans against Germans. But the imperial government was simply unable to muster the resources required to contain the Germans militarily. The bulk of the Roman population showed little zeal for defending themselves; perhaps they valued the Roman imperial regime too little to spend much energy in its defense. The imperial regime in the West received little assistance from the richer East in defending the West. Although the Germans were settled under terms that gave the Roman government nominal lordship over them, in fact they took over real power. As the settlement process advanced, the Roman bureaucracy broke down, imperial income dwindled, the imperial armies melted away, and the authority of the successors of Augustus vanished. By A.D. 476 the political realities in the West were officially recognized. A German general, Odoacer, deposed the last Western emperor—ironically named Romulus Augustulus—and turned the insignia of the imperial office over to the emperor in Constantinople. In theory, this act reunited the empire under a single ruler. In reality, the emperor in the East had virtually no control over the West, where the Germans ruled by virtue of conquest. But they dominated without the benefits of the splendid political system created by the Romans. As a result, political chaos threatened.

Beyond the disruption of the imperial political system in the West, the impact of the Germanic migrations must not be overstated. The destruction of life and property was not excessive, and in most cases Germans and Romans settled side by side on peaceful terms. Except in Britain and along a thin stretch of the old empire facing the Rhine, the intruders were not sufficiently numerous to affect the ethnic composition or the language of the old Roman population. Many aspects of Roman civilization survived the shock of the Germanic intrusion to affect in a decisive way the future course of history in the West.

The main result of the Germanic migrations into the western empire was to accelerate and make irreversible certain trends in economic and cultural life that had begun before the Germans arrived. Economic decline continued through and beyond the fifth century. The new German overlords were primarily interested in agriculture; their settlement on the land hastened the trend toward a predominantly agricultural economy. City life suffered badly; most cities in the West shrank to a fraction of their old population and most of them ceased to be commercial, administrative, and cultural centers. Their decline meant the end of the urban aristocracy that had sustained Greco-Roman civilization in the West. While some Roman landlords were displaced by Germanic settlers assigned to their lands, most succeeded in retaining and even enlarging their holdings. Before the end of the fifth century, German and Roman aristocrats were intermingling to create a new ruling force in the West. Political disorder forced increasing numbers of peasants into dependency on great landowners, be they German or Roman. Most large estates became virtually self-sufficient, with the result that the West broke up into thousands of tiny self-contained economic units. Trade was substantially reduced, and manufacturing was increasingly centered in the isolated agricultural estates. All of these developments inevitably eroded the level of economic productivity.

The Germanic migrations also accelerated cultural stagnation in the West. The German rulers and some German aristocrats tried to absorb and sustain Roman intellectual and artistic life, but all they could do was imitate it; all too often their barbarism broke through the thin veneer of their adopted culture. The decline of urban life deprived traditional Roman culture of its basic environment. Educated Romans living in rural settings sought to support education, literature, and art, but their isolation and the growing irrelevance of ancient culture to a changed world made their efforts ineffectual. In fact, cultural leadership was passing into Christian hands whose cultural concerns were markedly different.

5. CHRISTIANITY IN THE LATE EMPIRE

Amidst the events of the fourth and the fifth centuries that disrupted the Roman Empire, Christianity showed great resilience and emerged from the ordeal as a decisive force in society. The fourth century was a particularly glorious period in Christian history during which it became closely identified with imperial society. Massive numbers of converts from all levels of society swelled the ranks of the Christian community to the point where Christians were the dominant religious force in the empire. Christian leaders increasingly advanced to prominent directive positions in society. The Church as a visable organization became a decisive agency in shaping life in imperial society, and its material wealth increased dramatically. The fourth-century Roman government gave powerful support to all of these developments, thereby intertwining the Church and the empire ever more closely. By about A.D. 400 the Roman Empire had truly become a Christian Roman Empire, a fact recognized by Theodosius when he designated Christianity as the state religion.

However, success brought new and serious problems. The avalanche of converts, no longer faced with the terrible possibility that baptism might spell martyrdom, diluted the spiritual fervor of pre-Constantinian Christianity. With the inadequately instructed and spiritually lax converts came an influx of pagan ideas and practices that threatened to obliterate Christian practices of worship and doctrines and that generated heresies that divided Christian from Christian. Discipline within the growing Christian ranks became more difficult. Wealth and power turned the heads of Christian leaders toward worldly pursuits. Especially threatening to the independence of the Christian community was the urge of political leaders to use the Church as a tool to advance political ends. In brief, the success of Christianity in the fourth century threatened to deprive it of its uniqueness, its zeal, its sense of mission, and its independence.

The Christian community of the fourth century proved itself to be highly resourceful in "reforming" itself to meet the challenges posed by changing times. One response was the strengthening of the powers of the clergy, especially the bishops, over individual churches and over the laity. These powers were used to define Christian behavior and modes of worship more precisely and to compel Christians to obey the evolving "law" of the Church, called *canon law.* A major beneficiary of this trend toward a stronger, more hierarchical governance system was the bishop of Rome. The fourth-century emperors showered wealth on the successors of Peter and relied on them to formulate dogma they hoped to impose on the entire empire as a means of combating heresy. The popes responded by expanding their claims to authority and by asserting that authority more vigorously, especially in matters of dogma and discipline.

During the fourth century Christianity found a new source of spiritual vision in monasticism. The monastic movement began in the late third and early fourth centuries in the deserts of Egypt. There a new breed of Christians, calling themselves "athletes of Christ," sought to follow Jesus' command to leave all worldly things behind by fleeing to the desert to seek perfection through prayer and mortification of the flesh. The first desert fathers, exemplified by Anthony, were hermits who sought perfection through individual actions. Soon these hermits began to gather into communities, or monasteries, where spiritual life was governed by rules that defined patterns of behavior and spiritual exercises for achieving perfection. Especially important in establishing modes for communal (*cenobitic*) monastic life were the rules of the Egyptian monk Pachomius and the Greek monk Basil. The spiritual heroics of the early monks electrified the Christian world. By A.D. 400, monasticism had spread over most of the Roman world. While the monastic ethos was excessive in its denial of worldly affairs and in its obsession with the danger of sexuality as a source of sin, it did remind the Christian world of the need to struggle in order to achieve spiritual ex-

cellence. It created a new type of hero to replace the martyrs of old; both men and women alike found its ideal of the Christian life irresistible. And for large numbers of ordinary men and women the holy men forged in the monastic environment became agents through whom divine favors could be gained to relieve the heavy burdens of a troubled, uncaring world.

Although most Christian leaders were quite willing to cooperate fully with the state in the promotion of a Christian empire, some resisted the claims of the state to control religion. They began to articulate concepts that limited the state's control over religion and that argued for religious liberty. Some even contended that Christian ends were more important than were secular ends and therefore must be supreme. On one occasion, for instance, the powerful bishop of Milan, Ambrose (ca. A.D. 340–397), excommunicated the Emperor Theodosius for massacring some of his subjects under circumstances that some thought exceeded the authority of worldly rulers. Ambrose justified his sentence on the grounds that the Church exercised a separate realm of jurisdiction that must take precedence over the power of the state when spiritual issues were at stake. As the concept of the independence of the Church took shape, it spurred discussion of the problem of where ultimate authority in the Christian community lay. More and more Christians agreed that the bishop of Rome, Peter's successor, was the spiritual head of the Christian world.

Perhaps the most significant success of the Christian community was its ability to generate an outburst of cultural activity that resulted in its assumption of cultural leadership in the late empire. That leadership was clearly demonstrated in the arts. Church building provided one of the chief outlets for the talents of architects, sculptors, and painters. They developed new modes of conveying the Christian message by creatively adapting the classical artistic tradition to Christian purposes (see Figures 12.1, 12.3, and 13.2). Some of the most inspired poetry of the age flowed from the pens of Christian writers seeking to express their thoughts and feelings about their faith. Christian writers such as Eusebius of Caesarea (ca. 260–340) recast the writing of history to fit the Judeo-Chris-

FIGURE 13.2   A Sixth-Century Christian Church   This magnificent church was built in Ravenna in honor of S. Apollinare. Its architectural form represents an adaptation of the Roman basilica style (see p. 146) for Christian purposes. The central hall (the nave) served as a gathering place for the faithful. An altar often stood in the semicircular apse at the far end of the nave. Aisles flanked the nave on either side, set off by columns and arches supporting the walls of the nave. These walls rose above the roof over each side aisle. At their upper levels the walls were pierced by windows that lighted the structure's interior. This style of architecture was destined to assert a powerful influence on religious architecture in later western European history. (G. E. Kidder-Smith)

tian version of historical development. Inspired chiefly by the feats of the monks, Christian writers developed a new literary genre, hagiography, devoted to the lives of the saints.

But the jewel of the period was the theological writings of a remarkable group of intellectuals known as the *church fathers*. Among the most prominent were the Greeks Athanasius, Basil, Gregory of Nyssa, and Gregory Nazianus, and the Latins Augustine, Jerome, and Ambrose. Although each was an individual intellectual in his own right, this potent group of thinkers collectively reshaped the basic thrust of intellectual life.

The fruit of their labor was a massive body of literature destined to feed intellectual life for centuries to come. Although their intellectual efforts were rooted in their deep Christian faith, they borrowed boldly and creatively from the content and the methods of the Greco-Roman literary, philosophical, and scientific tradition to build a consistent, logical, articulate statement of the Christian interpretation of the universe. In the process they not only provided reasoned and persuasive doctrinal positions but also literally redefined human values and the purpose of human existence, thereby overpowering the classical

Greco-Roman world view. Yet they did so in a way that made the Greco-Roman intellectual achievement an indispensable tool for understanding what they perceived to be ultimate Christian wisdom.

Of particular importance in establishing Christian intellectual leadership and in shaping the western intellectual tradition was Augustine (A.D. 354–430). Born in North Africa, the son of a pagan father and a Christian mother, Augustine received a good Latin education to prepare him as a teacher of rhetoric. As his education progressed, his searching mind experimented with a variety of pagan philosophical and religious systems, none of which satisfied his yearning for understanding and wisdom. Neither did the mistress he took as a young man nor the child born to that union. Eventually, he converted to Christianity and was chosen bishop of Hippo in Africa.

As a bishop, Augustine's major concern was to be an effective pastor. In that role he worked tirelessly to guide his flock toward sound belief and spiritual perfection and ended his life trying to protect his city from the Vandals. But he also turned out a prodigious body of writing on a variety of theological and moral issues. Much of his writing was prompted by his efforts to combat heresy. In his own time his writings served many as guides to a fuller understanding of the faith; for centuries to come his thought provided the basis for the major positions of the Church on most doctrinal and moral issues. Two of his many works were particularly significant. His *Confessions* recount his own spiritual pilgrimage as an educated Roman through most of the philosophical and religious systems of the ancient world to his final realization that only Christianity could satisfy his spiritual hunger. The work presents not only forceful critiques revealing the failure of Greco-Roman philosophy and religion but also a compelling argument in support of the Christian faith as the only adequate response to life's problems.

Even more influential was his *City of God*, written to answer pagan charges that the Visigothic sack of Rome in A.D. 410 was a punishment imposed on the Romans by their ancient deities who were angry at them for becoming Christians. Augustine sought to demonstrate that this "catastrophe" was only a step in the unfolding of God's plan for the universe. God, he argued, had ordained two cities, that of God and that of the world. The true city of God exists only in the other world; membership will be awarded as God wishes to those who serve the true faith without wavering. On the earth prevails the worldly city, tarnished by sin and due eventually to pass. The Roman Empire was a part of the worldly city. The coming of Christ had established an earthly embodiment of the City of God in the form of the Christian church, into whose body all must now be enfolded. Rome must pass away so that human beings can give their allegiance to the more perfect Christian community. Not despair but joy should greet the passing of Rome, since that event was a preordained step toward a more perfect world planned by God from the beginning. Almost immediately, Augustine's interpretation of the cosmos and of history as the realization in time of the divine plan replaced the various world views offered by classical philosophers.

Other Christian intellectuals helped to assure the victory of a Christian culture. One was Ambrose (ca. A.D. 340–397), bishop of Milan and a key figure in guiding Augustine to his conversion. In his writings Ambrose not only helped to shape the rationale for the independence of the Church but also persuasively articulated the basic principles of Christian morality. He drew heavily on the moral principles developed by classical thinkers, but he skillfully recast their moral values to fit within the framework of Christian doctrine. Another influential figure was Jerome (A.D. 340–419), a man of immense learning and a formidable linguist who was drawn to monastic life despite the great appeal that classical literature had for him. His voluminous letters played a significant role in guiding the spiritual life of an important circle of Roman nobles, including many women. He employed his talents to produce a Latin translation of the Old and the New Testaments. Basing his translation on both Hebrew and Greek versions of Scripture, Jerome's Bible, called the Vulgate, became the standard Latin Bible for centuries. Its existence ensured that Latin would survive as the language of the Church in the West and that its readers would retain an ability to read the literature of classical Latin antiquity. Jerome's extensive commentaries on the Bible also guided later generations in their efforts to interpret the meaning of the Bible.

Firmly in possession of its early traditions and fortified by new sources of organizational, intellectual, and spiritual vitality shaped during the fourth century, the Christian community survived the ordeal of the fifth century amazingly well. In fact, it emerged from the Germanic migrations and the collapse of the imperial government as the most potent force in society. To be sure, the fifth century produced tribulations for the Christian establishment. Churches were destroyed and Christians were killed by the Germans. Particularly disruptive was the fact that almost all of the Germanic invaders were adherents of Arian Christianity, which resulted in clashes with the orthodox Christian population and impeded the assimilation of Romans and Germans. The collapse of the Roman political system in the West deprived the Church of a major protector and a prime source of material support.

But amidst the mounting chaos the Church maintained and even strengthened its position. In many parts of the West, bishops replaced local aristocracies and bureaucrats as keepers of order, administrators of justice, and caretakers of the unfortunate. Pope Leo I (A.D. 440–461), for example, served as virtual governor of the city of Rome and as a forceful diplomat defending the city against attacks of the Vandals and the Huns. Many other bishops played a similar role in cities across the entire West. By A.D. 500 there were clear signs that the Arianism of the Germans was giving way to orthodoxy and that Germans and Romans were finding a common basis in a single faith. A key event in ensuring the victory of orthodoxy was the conversion of the pagan Frankish king Clovis to orthodoxy. Most Germanic kings, whatever their particular religious persuasion, began to lend their support to the Church and to draw on its personnel for assistance in ruling their kingdoms. As the focus of life shifted from the city to a rural setting, the Church began incorporating the neglected peasantry into the mainstream of Christian life. A sign of its concern with rural life was the emergence of a new organizational structure, the rural parish, which provided a local center from which to convert and to guide the spiritual formation of nobles and peasants increasingly bound to a rural environment. As cultural life collapsed in the declining cities, monasteries increasingly provided havens for education and the preservation of culture. By A.D. 500 the Church had become a pillar of order and stability in all aspects of life in the West. It had inherited the leadership role once held by the Roman imperial government, a role that its earliest adherents probably would never have dreamed possible nor perhaps even desirable. That leadership would have a major impact on the future.

SUGGESTED READING

Political, Economic, and Social Developments

The general history of the period covered in this chapter is treated in the works of Brown and Grant cited in Chapter 12. The following works cover more specialized aspects of the period, as indicated by their titles.

Ramsay MacMullen, *The Roman Government's Response to Crisis, A.D. 235–337* (1976).

Diana Bowder, *The Age of Constantine and Julian* (1978).

A. H. M. Jones, *Constantine and the Conversion of Europe* (1948; reprinted, 1978).

Church History

The major developments in church history are treated in the works of Frend and Fox, cited in Chapter 12. The following works treat particular aspects of religious history.

Jaroslav Pelikan, *The Christian Tradition: A History of the Development of Doctrine*, Vol. 1: *The Emergence of the Catholic Tradition (100–600)* (1971). A masterful treatment of the shaping of Christian doctrine.

Derwas J. Chitty, *The Desert a City* (1966). A colorful treatment of the origins of monasticism.

Peter Brown, *Society and the Holy in Late Antiquity* (1982). A brilliant portrayal of spiritual forces that transformed the late Roman world.

John Holland Smith, *The Death of Classical Paganism* (1976). A good account of another side of religious life in the late empire—that of the losers.

The Germans and Their Invasions

Malcolm Todd, *The Northern Barbarians, 100 B.C.–A.D. 300* (1987).

E. A. Thompson, *The Early Germans* (1965).

Either of these works will help the reader understand the nature of early Germanic society.

Hans-Joachim Diesner, *The Great Migrations. The Movements of Peoples across Europe, A.D. 300–700*, trans. C. S. V. Salt (1982). A brief account, beautifully illustrated.

Lucien Musset, *The Germanic Invasions. The Making of Europe, A.D. 400–600*, trans. Edward and Columba James (1975). A more detailed account of the Germanic migrations.

Justine D. Randers-Pehrson, *Barbarians and Romans: The Birth Struggle of Europe, A.D. 400–700* (1983). Especially good on the efforts of the Germans to establish themselves in the empire.

Biographies

Stephen Williams, *Diocletian and the Roman Recovery* (1985).

John Holland Smith, *Constantine the Great* (1971).

Robert Browning, *The Emperor Julian* (1978).

Peter Brown, *Augustine of Hippo: A Biography* (1967).

Philip Rousseau, *Pachomius: The Making of a Community in Fourth-Century Egypt* (1985).

RETROSPECT

During the three centuries prior to about A.D. 500, a complex sequence of events unfolded that brought an end to Greco-Roman civilization. The magnificent political order created by the Romans to bring peace, well-being, and concord to some 70 million people gave way to violence and chaos over large sections of the Roman Empire. Prosperity was replaced by economic stagnation and decline. The enlightened, sophisticated, aesthetically rich culture that once had supplied men and women with a sense of direction, a set of values, and occasion for pleasure lost its vitality and its appeal. Why had Greco-Roman culture not lasted? Why was Rome not eternal, as many believed it would be? Any answer to these questions is apt to convince readers that they have been witness to a great tragedy—almost Greek in character—still to be lamented.

But was the collapse of Greco-Roman civilization a tragedy? It can be argued that by the third and fourth centuries the Roman world had become a prison for the human spirit. Autocratic government, regimented economic life, militarized society, and callous social elitism may have

brought order and security, but the cost was terrible. Traditional values seemed empty forms from which flowed no inspiration capable of mitigating the burdens of civilization.

The emergence of the "barbarian" Germans as a potent force in society may, from one perspective, seem destructive; but from another, their presence infused society with an element of vitality. Here were fresh doers, learners, experimenters. The rapid advance of Christianity may have accentuated modes of thought and patterns of morality that lacked the sophistication of the concepts guiding classical civilization. Again, however, Christianity represented a fresh breeze in the Greco-Roman prison, a new vision of humanity and its destiny that provided a sense of direction and a reason for acting. The "barbarians" and the Christians held the key to the future. Both had potential to advance human destiny.

Moreover, to speak of the fall of Greco-Roman civilization is to utter only a partial truth. When the Roman Empire collapsed, it left behind monuments that would serve as guides to its heirs—a magnificent literature, a great art, model forms of government, a legal system, economic institutions and techniques, moral precepts, philosophical ideals, and scientific knowledge. In a sense, the Greco-Roman accomplishment did not disappear. Little that has happened in a large part of the world—especially the Western world—since A.D. 500 can be understood outside its Greco-Roman background. Many modern societies are children of the classical world, just as were its immediate heirs—the Christian establishment and the recently installed Germanic kingdoms. And no less important: The Roman imperial regime had survived virtually intact in the rich, creative East—that part of the world where higher civilization originated.

So history did not end with the fall of Rome! Nor did the promise of humanity perish with the end of Greco-Roman civilization!

PART FOUR

THE EARLY MIDDLE AGES, 500–1000: STRUGGLE TOWARD A NEW ORDER

The collapse of Greco-Roman civilization left the peoples living around the Mediterranean Sea with a challenge: how to replace the old order with a new civilization pattern. Despite false starts and confusion they met the challenge with remarkable creativity. Between 500 and 1000, called the early Middle Ages by modern historians, three new cultural communities were defined, each based partly on old Roman soil but each extending into "new" territory. One was the Byzantine cultural world with its center in Constantinople, its heartland in Asia Minor and the Balkans south of the Danube, and its frontier in Slavic Europe. The second was the Moslem cultural world with its heartland in the ancient Fertile Crescent, stretching from Mesopotamia to Egypt, and its frontiers eastward to India and westward across North Africa to Spain. The third new civilization was created by the Germanic nations. Gaul and Italy formed its center; its frontiers included England, Germany, Scandinavia, Spain, and the western portions of the Slavic world in central Europe.

In each of these societies there were seminal forces at work generating new institutions and new ideas. The dynamism of this age came from various sources: In all three societies powerful vestiges of Greco-Roman civilization persisted to shape essential features of each new civilization. In two of them—the Moslem and German western European worlds—new peoples, Arabs and Germans, supplied a leavening agent. But perhaps it was religion that furnished the major animating force in this period. Two new universal religions dominated the history of the period. Christianity provided that force in the Byzantine and Germanic western European cultural worlds. Islam, almost immediately establishing itself as a dominant force among the Arab founders of Moslem civilization, played a vital role in shaping the major features of the Moslem world.

Modern historians have often dismissed this age as a "dark age." Before accepting that characterization, we must try to assess the creative aspects of the period.

CHAPTER 14

Heirs to the Roman Empire: The Byzantine and Moslem Empires

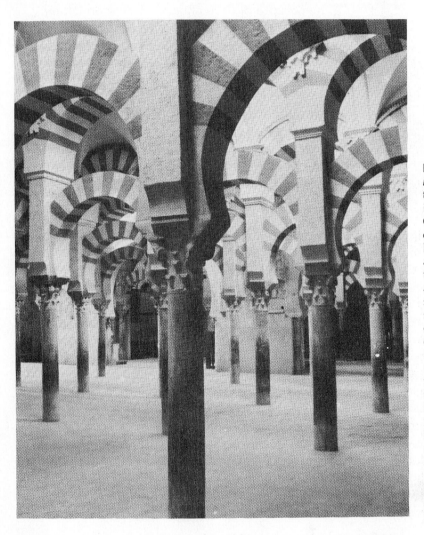

FIGURE 14.1 **Moslem Mosque** This view of the interior of the magnificent mosque—built at Cordoba, Spain, in the eighth century—illustrates key features of Moslem architecture, especially the skillful use of arches and pillars to create spaces for private worship and the employment of geometric decorative designs. Many features of Moslem art represent a creative synthesis of artistic traditions borrowed from earlier cultures embraced in the Moslem world. A comparison of this mosque with a typical Christian basilica (see Figure 13.2) will suggest differences between Moslem and Christian religious practices. (Georg Gerster/Comstock)

Two of the new civilizations emerging from the Greco-Roman world—Byzantine and Moslem—had their centers in the eastern territories of the old Roman Empire. These areas, comprising the most affluent and culturally sophisticated part of the Roman Empire, provided a richer seed bed for development than did the Germanic West. As a consequence, during the early Middle Ages Byzantine and Moslem cultures were more precocious and vigorous than was that of the Germanic West. Since their very success in the early Middle Ages moved them into their own special place in history, apart from development in western Europe, we can only give them limited attention—less than they deserve.

1. BYZANTINE CIVILIZATION: ORIGIN AND HISTORY, 395–1100

Byzantine civilization, so named by modern historians after the ancient Greek city-state of Byzantium where Constantine built his capital, began as a direct continuation of the old Roman Empire. After the division of the empire following the death of Theodosius in 395, a succession of rulers in Constantinople successfully resisted Germanic attacks and maintained the basic features of late imperial society. Their claim to be the heirs to old Rome was validated in 476, when the imperial title in the West was transferred to Constantinople and the Eastern emperors were recognized as legitimate rulers over the entire Roman world, including those parts seized by Germans. But that sequence of events aimed at maintaining the fiction of Rome's survival was marked by developments in the East that by the sixth century pointed toward the shaping of a new society.

The watershed between the old and new Rome can perhaps be placed in the reign of Justinian (527–565), often called the last Roman and the first Byzantine emperor. Justinian's talents and accomplishments have been variously judged across the ages, but few would dispute the fact that he made decisions of immense importance in redirecting the course of history. He was given invaluable assistance by Empress Theodora, one of the most gifted women in history (see Figure 14.2). The daughter of a circus bear trainer, she was an actress and courtesan before Justinian took her as his wife. Intelligent, beautiful, and courageous, she was instrumental in helping her often indecisive husband make policy decisions. She was especially astute in reading the temper of the complex imperial court circle and the factious populace of Constantinople.

Justinian's claim to be called the last Roman stems from the central focus of his policy: a major effort to restore the unity of the old empire. To this end, he set out to reestablish imperial authority over the western provinces held by the Germans. Although his effort was brilliant, his success was partial. The best his armies could do was to recapture North Africa from the Vandals, Italy from the Ostrogoths, and a small strip of southeastern Spain from the Visigoths. Gaul, most of Spain, England, and the upper Danube provinces remained in German hands. More significantly, the price for these limited conquests was great, for Justinian's western policy left the eastern frontiers exposed to the Sassanian Persians, who continued their efforts to recapture the territory held by the ancient Persians. By the end of his reign, it was clear that imperial resources must be concentrated in the East if areas crucial to the survival of the empire were to be held. The Germanic West would have to be abandoned.

Justinian's reign was also significant in shaping a unique governmental system. He saw himself as the direct descendant of the Roman emperors, and he worked actively to perfect the system of absolute monarchy originated by Diocletian and Constantine. An important part of this effort led him to commission a corps of legal experts to organize into a single, consistent code the complex tradition of Roman law, which dated back at least a thousand years. That commission produced the *Corpus juris civilis*, which not only summarized the substance of Roman law as it had been defined in a long series of legislative acts and imperial edicts but also collected legal opinions that defined the principles on which the law rested. While this great monument of legal science was destined to influence considerably the development of law in the future, it served Justinian's age to legitimatize a highly centralized, absolutist government that became a distinctive feature of Byzantine civilization.

FIGURE 14.2 Justinian and Theodora   These mosaic representations of Emperor Justinian and Empress Theodora were created as part of the decoration of the church of San Vitale in Ravenna (built about 574). They reflect a sense of sacred and solemn majesty that increasingly surrounded the Byzantine imperial office. Byzantine artists were highly skilled in creating mosaics to convey a message while adding color to interior spaces. (Justinian, The Granger Collection; Theodora, Scala/Art Resource)

Justinian's reign was also marked by important religious developments. Following the pattern already established by Constantine and his successors, Justinian claimed as part of his imperial authority the right to play a major role as leader of the Christian religious establishment in his empire. Particularly troublesome in his time were several violent disputes over dogmatic issues concerning the relationship between Christ's human and divine nature. The emperor sought repeatedly to settle these quarrels by imperial edicts, often

worked out after extensive discussions with prelates and theologians, which he hoped would curb violence generated by religious passion and restore religious unity. His involvement did implant the idea of a Byzantine church whose organization and doctrines were dependent on the authority of the autocratic, semisacred emperor. But his actions also alienated large numbers of his subjects.

Justinian's reign witnessed the birth of a distinctive Byzantine culture. That culture assimilated the ancient Hellenic component of classical culture with Christian ideology. Into that basic mix it incorporated cultural influences from the Near East, especially from Persia. The great symbol of this new culture was the magnificent church of Santa Sophia built by Justinian in Constantinople.

Byzantine political history from the reign of Justinian until the First Crusade (1095) was dominated by one theme: the constant struggles to fend off attacks from aggressive outsiders, especially from the east and north. These assaults reduced the Byzantine state in size and caused modifications in its internal structure that accentuated its uniqueness among its neighbors (see Map 14.1).

Hardly was Justinian dead when the first blow was struck. In 568 the Lombards, a Germanic nation, invaded Italy and seized a considerable portion of the peninsula, leaving only Venice, a corridor of land from Rome to Ravenna, and southern Italy under Byzantine control. The partition of Italy was significant for two reasons: It left Rome, the seat of the papacy, in Byzantine hands, and it provided a setting in which the Byzantine and German western European worlds would interact.

Little could be done to stop the Lombard assault because the Byzantine Empire was facing a greater menace elsewhere. Late in the sixth century the Sassanids mounted their greatest offensive in the East, seizing Syria, Palestine, and Egypt and advancing through Asia Minor to Constantinople. At the same time the Avars, an Asiatic nomadic people who established a state composed largely of Slavs north of the Danube, moved into the Balkans and toward Constantinople. In the first decades of the seventh century it appeared that the empire would perish in the Persian-Avar pincer. But a savior appeared in the person of Emperor Heraclius (610–641), who regrouped Byzantine resources and flung back the enemies in a war of liberation that permanently weakened both.

The dynasty of Heraclius soon had to face an ever-greater challenge in the form of the rampant Arabs, whose rise to power we shall trace later. Within little more than a half century in the middle of the seventh century, Moslem armies wrested Syria, Palestine, Egypt, and North Africa from Byzantine control. By the early 700s they occupied most of Asia Minor, and in 717 to 718 they placed Constantinople under siege. Again a savior appeared: Emperor Leo III, the Isaurian (717–741), who rescued the capital and eventually succeeded in liberating Asia Minor. However, the eastern provinces were permanently lost, and the Byzantine Empire was reduced to a state comprising Asia Minor and the Balkan peninsula. This was a far cry from the Mediterranean-wide empire that Justinian claimed or even the Eastern Roman Empire that he actually controlled. But it was defensible as a territorial state and would survive nearly intact for seven hundred years.

Despite Leo III's remarkable success in rescuing the Byzantine Empire from what seemed certain destruction, his successors suffered renewed trials that plagued the empire for a century after his death. In part their difficulties stemmed from internal strife brought on by their religious policy (see the next section). But outsiders again contributed to their problems. The Franks seriously undermined the Byzantine position in Italy (see Chapter 16). Even more dangerous was the emergence of a powerful Bulgar state in the Balkans. The Bulgar threat eventually produced another series of strong rulers, the Macedonian dynasty (867–1057), under whose rule Byzantine society reached its high point. The greatest Macedonian emperor, Basil II, the Bulgar Slayer (976–1025), finally destroyed the Bulgar state and extended Byzantine influence deep into the Slavic world of central Europe and Russia. Byzantine power was also increased in the East at the expense of the Moslem world, laying the groundwork for a Christian counterattack against Islam.

By the late eleventh century the Byzantine state began to decline, due in part to internal problems and in part to new assaults from the east by the Seljuk Turks and from the west by Italian cities seeking commercial advantages and Norman princes from southern Italy and Sicily seeking territorial expansion (see Chapter 21). To save the empire from these threats, the emperors appealed to the West for help, and act that was instrumental in launching the crusading movement. But this policy also meant that the fate of the long self-reliant Byzantine Empire was increasingly dependent on outsiders.

2. BYZANTINE CIVILIZATION: INSTITUTIONAL AND CULTURAL PATTERNS

In response to the pressures caused by incessant attacks, the Byzantine world slowly evolved institutional and cultural patterns that not only permitted its survival but also made its civilization unique and distinctive.

A major source of Byzantine strength was its government, based on the absolute authority of the emperor. That authority was defined in terms that combined traditions drawn from the Roman imperial system and from Christian concepts of governance; Constantine served as the model. To the Byzantine populace the emperor was an agent ordained by God to ensure the material and spiritual well-being of God's people. As an intermediary between God and his holy people, the emperor must be obeyed and served loyally. Without the imperial presence at the center of Byzantine life, God's favors would not be forthcoming and chaos would ensue. Although Byzantine court life was often filled with intrigues and violence, and although conspiracies and revolts deprived many emperors of their diadems and their lives, still the divinely sanctioned imperial office provided the prime directive force in Byzantine society.

The Byzantine emperors were served by a large, carefully structured bureaucracy. Each civil servant was assigned a specialized function, a rank, and a salary. Well-educated and loyal, these bureaucrats efficiently kept the fundamental activities of the state in operation. The empire was divided into a number of districts, called *themes*, where officials representing the emperor recruited troops, collected taxes, maintained order, judged cases, and enforced the emperor's edicts. The emperor's power was buttressed by a well-organized army and navy, an efficient system of taxation, and a responsive ecclesiastical establishment. Of crucial importance was the army. During the crises brought on by Persian and then Arab attacks during the seventh and eighth centuries, the government abandoned the long tradition of relying on mercenary soldiers. Instead it developed an army recruited from the free small farmers of Asia Minor and Thrace, who were granted plots of land in return for their military service. The peasant contingents were organized by themes, each under the command of a military governor. For centuries these loyal soldiers, their freedom and land carefully protected by the imperial government, stood against repeated attacks on the Byzantine state.

Agriculture formed the backbone of the Byzantine economy. Large estates, farmed by tenants, existed, but the chief strength of the agricultural system rested with small landowners. The state took a vital interest in keeping agricultural production high so that taxes could be collected from the farmers, whether large or small. The empire also enjoyed tremendous commercial activity; for many centuries Constantinople was the world's chief trading and industrial center. Through it passed a great variety of products coming from and going to places far and wide. The imperial government maintained a sound money system to support this commercial activity. Byzantine traders were supplied with many valuable products by the numerous skilled artisans who practiced their crafts in Constantinople and other imperial cities. All trade and industry were rigidly controlled by the state. Wages, prices, and profits were carefully fixed. Artisans and merchants were compelled to remain in their trades and hand them on to their sons. The imperial government itself monopolized many lucrative businesses.

The Christian religion provided another fundamental force in shaping Byzantine society. While religion touched every aspect of life, perhaps its most important function was to provide a bond linking the populace to the imperial regime, a bond that created a strong and lasting loyalty among the imperial subjects. In terms of beliefs and practices the Christians of the Byzantine Empire were like Christians everywhere. However, with passing time Byzantine Christianity underwent changes that gave rise to a separate religious establishment, now known as the Greek Orthodox church.

Following the pattern established in the fourth-century Roman Empire, the religious establishment in the Byzantine Empire remained closely allied with and subjected to the state. In contrast with the Church in the West, where the collapse of the Roman political order forced religious leaders to act independently, the Greek Orthodox church continued its development in close alliance

Map 14.1 **THE EXPANSION OF ISLAM TO 750** This map shows the amazing success of the Arabs as conquerors during the first century after Muhammad's death in 632; the dates indicate when each major conquest was completed. It indicates clearly that the Persian Sassanian Empire and the Byzantine Empire were the major victims of Arab expansionism. By 750 large numbers of peoples in this empire had accepted Islam as their religion.

with political authorities. The emperor was accepted as the divinely ordained director of both spiritual and secular life; in fact, such a distinction had little meaning in Byzantine society. This system, called *caesaropapism* by modern historians, allowed the emperor to play a decisive role in appointing church officials, defining dogma, settling theological disputes, imposing discipline on both clergy and laity, and using the wealth and the persuasive authority of the religious establishment to serve the state. The episcopal structure of the Byzantine church, headed by the patriarch of Constantinople, served as a powerful force in exercising imperial authority.

Byzantine religious life was given a distinctive quality by a widespread and intense interest in questions of dogma. Diverse opinions on such matters as the Trinity and the relationship between Christ's divine and human nature aroused strong feelings and fierce partisanship that produced serious political crises on many occasions, especially when the emperors tried to resolve such quarrels in the interests of unity. Greek Orthodoxy placed a strong emphasis on ritual practice as a key element of religious life, and over the centuries a rich liturgy featuring elaborate symbolism and unique musical forms evolved as a distinctive feature of Byzantine religion. On occasion both emperors and religious leaders thought this emphasis on ritual life needed to be curbed. The chief such effort led to the bitter iconoclastic struggle that raged from 725 to 843. This quarrel began when Emperor Leo III, backed by part of the clergy, attempted to remove all visual representations (icons) of the deity from churches and rites, insisting that Christians were worshiping the statues instead of God and thus were guilty of idolatry. But these iconoclasts (icon smashers) ultimately failed, and in 843 the use of icons was restored to ritual practices. Byzantine religious life gave a prominent place to mysticism—religious practices by which believers sought direct communion with God through prayer and contemplation. A powerful, active monastic establishment played an important role in encouraging this religious experience.

These unique characteristics of the emerging Byzantine religious establishment, coupled with equally unique developments shaping Christian life elsewhere, led to a growing division in the Christian world. During the fifth and sixth centuries bitter disagreements over dogma and the claims of the patriarch of Constantinople to precedence over the ancient patriarchs of Alexandria, Jerusalem, and Antioch encouraged the Christians of Egypt and Syria to separate themselves from the imperial religious establishment. The Moslem conquest of these areas reduced religious contacts with Christians in the Byzantine Empire and the West. The result was the emergence of separate Eastern churches, such as the Coptic church in Egypt and the Jacobite church in Syria. Differences also began to separate the Byzantine church from the Christians in the West. Dogmatic disagreements (particularly iconoclasm) and different ritual practices played a role in creating the rift. But especially divisive was the ever-deepening quarrel over whether the pope in Rome was superior to or coequal with the patriarch of Constantinople in terms of defining dogma and exercising disciplinary jurisdiction over the entire Christian community. Although the Byzantine emperors constantly turned to the bishops of Rome to sanction

their religious policies, they likewise supported the claims of their patriarch to exercise an authority equal to that of Rome. The slow drift toward separation between Rome and Constantinople finally culminated in 1054, when pope and patriarch excommunicated each other, creating a schism that to the present has proved irreparable.

The growing separation between Rome and Constantinople was promoted by rivalry in the missionary field. From almost the beginning of Byzantine history, Greek missionaries began to penetrate central and eastern Europe, where missionaries from the West were also active. Supported by the diplomatic, military, and material resources of the imperial government and willing to make concessions to local cultures, such as allowing rituals to be performed in native languages, Byzantine missionaries eventually converted most of the Slavs in the Balkan peninsula and Russia and attached them to the Greek Orthodox church. Not only did they give their converts a new religion, but Byzantine missionaries also spread significant aspects of Byzantine political, economic, literary, and artistic life. As a consequence, at a crucial point in the development of Slavic institutions and culture, a large part of the Slavic world was permanently oriented toward Byzantium and set apart from western Europe.

The Byzantine Empire gradually developed its own cultural life, aimed at preserving classical Greek tradition and adapting it to the Christian world view. Within a short time after Justinian's death the use of Latin virtually ceased in the Byzantine world. A vigorous education system flourished in Constantinople. The curriculum was based on a study of classical Greek literature and philosophy. At least in some aristocratic circles women were often provided a literary education in their homes. The system produced many individuals who were conversant with the literary, scientific, and philosophical masterpieces of ancient Greece and the Hellenistic world. This educated group, often associated with the imperial court, the prime patron of cultural life, also collected copies of the classics, commented on them, and wrote in imitation of them. Their efforts ensured the survival of the Greek classics and their widespread dissemination. As early as the ninth century Moslem scholars began to utilize Byzantine sources to gain access to the classical past. The cultural renaissance of fourteenth- and fifteenth-century western Europe depended almost entirely on the Byzantine world to renew knowledge of ancient Greek culture.

The all-pervasive influence of Greek models, however, tended to make Byzantine literature and thought imitative. Probably the most creative figures in Byzantine intellectual circles were the theologians, whose incessant quarrels over dogma produced a huge volume of writing in which philosophical concepts from the classical tradition were applied to Christian teachings. Byzantine historians, influenced by the models of Herodotus, Thucydides, and Polybius, also produced excellent works: Procopius (sixth century) described Justinian's wars and wrote a spicy *Secret History* describing court life; Michael Psellus (1018–1079), a high official in the imperial regime, chronicled the exploits of the Macedonian emperors; and Anna Comnenus (1083–1148), the daughter of Emperor Alexius I, described the career of her father in *Alexiad*. Byzantine poets expressed themselves most originally in hymns, some of which can still be heard in Greek Orthodox liturgy.

Byzantine art is perhaps the best mirror of the spirit of the culture. Architecture was the preeminent art. It represents a skillful fusion of Hellenistic and Near Eastern traditions. The style was formed during the fourth and fifth centuries in Egypt, Syria, and Asia Minor. It was elevated to official status by Justinian's building program in sixth-century Constantinople. The great church of Santa Sophia was based on a floor plan derived from the Greco-Roman rectangular basilica upon which was imposed a great central dome after the Persian manner. The glory of this combination lies in the internal spaciousness it permits. The dome of Santa Sophia is more than one hundred feet across and rises about one hundred eighty feet above the floor of the church. Although it rests on four great arches springing from four massive pillars that form the central square of the nave, the dome indeed seems "to hang by a golden chain from heaven," as a contemporary put it. Justinian, upon viewing the completed church, exclaimed: "I have outdone you, O Solomon."

The architectural style represented by Santa Sophia was widely imitated, and in the course of time a variation gained considerable popularity: A ground plan was based on the Greek cross with its four equal arms; each arm was crowned by a dome, as was the space where the arms cross. The famous church of St. Mark in Venice is an example of this five-domed structure. Byzantine architects also built huge and splendid palaces, most of which have unfortunately disappeared.

Byzantine architecture, for all its technical ingenuity, is incomplete without its decor. The churches and palaces were immense frames for sumptuous decoration. Santa Sophia's interior, for instance, blazed with precious metals, mosaics, paintings, jewels, and fine stone. Byzantine mosaics and frescoes centered primarily on portraying the great episodes of the Christian epic; the best surviving examples are seen in the churches built in Ravenna during the sixth century (see Figures 13.2 and 14.2). Byzantine artists made an immense contribution to the development and enrichment of Christian iconography. They were never basically concerned with portraying the world realistically; rather, they sought to use human, natural, and abstract forms to evoke spiritual understanding. Color, created by glowing combinations of stones, metals, jewels, and paints, played a crucial role in enhancing the impact of every artistic creation (see Color Plate 7).

Byzantine artists were also noted as skillful jewelers, goldsmiths, silversmiths, and manuscript illuminators. In every medium the same features predominated—the fusion of Greco-Roman and Near Eastern motifs and styles, the love of elaborate decoration and color, and the preoccupation with symbolism.

3. MOSLEM CIVILIZATION: ORIGIN AND EXPANSION

A second new civilization emerged in the eastern Mediterranean world during the early Middle Ages to rival Byzantium as an heir of the Greco-Roman world: Moslem civilization, originating among the nomadic inhabitants of the Arabian Desert. Jolted out of their traditional pattern of life by a new religion, called Islam, the Arabs exploded across a vast territory in western Asia and northern Africa and generated a new civilization whose influences still shape the lives of millions of people around the entire globe.

Although peoples from the desolate Arabian Desert had powerfully influenced the course of history in the ancient past (for example, the Akkadians, the Assyrians, and Hebrews), no one living about 600 would have guessed that the desert-dwelling Arabs were soon to have a major impact on the course of history. Although its inhabitants shared a sense of ethnic community rooted in language and common historical experiences, the Arab world was badly divided into numerous competing tribes led by warrior chieftains, called *sheiks*. The desert dwellers, called Bedouins, lived a poverty-stricken life that depended chiefly on the pasturage of animals—particularly camels—around oases. Raids on other tribes were common, so that Bedouin life was dominated by a warrior ethos. Tribal life was bound by rigid custom that governed most social relationships. Especially powerful were kinship ties, which created fierce family loyalties. Bedouin tribal life was deeply influenced by a polytheistic religious system based on the worship of deities representing the forces of nature.

For the most part the Bedouins had been little influenced by the advanced civilizations lying in a great arc around the northern end of the vast desert. However, the Arabs were not completely isolated, a significant factor in the changes that thrust the Arabs into a new historical role during the seventh century. In the long struggle between the Romans (and their Byzantine successors) and the Persians, both parties had tried to win allies among the Bedouin tribes of northern Arabia; as a result, Roman-Byzantine and Persian influences touched the lives of some Arabs in that area. The major religions of these civilizations—Christianity, Judaism, Zoroastrianism—had made modest inroads into the Arab world. Much more significant in bringing outside influences into the world of the Arabs were the overland trade routes that developed along the western side of Arabia. These caravan routes linked the rich cities of Egypt, Syria, and Asia Minor to the Indian Ocean and the Far East. During the sixth century the routes became much more important because Byzantine-Persian rivalry disrupted the trade routes running from the eastern Mediterranean area through Persia to the Far East. Increased trade stimulated the growth and expanded the wealth of the Arabian cities along the caravan routes. Mecca, in particular, became a flourishing cosmopolitan center. Merchants from many places mingled with an ever-growing Arab population attracted to Mecca from the desert by the growing economic opportunities created by trade. Many Bedouin tribes came annually to Mecca to worship at a temple called the *Kaaba*, which contained a black stone that was a cult object for most Arabs. The sharp contrast between the affluent, cosmopolitan life in Mecca and the impoverished, tradition-bound Bedouin desert life began to pose questions about the value of tradition and to generate tensions that pointed toward change.

The forces of change were suddenly unleashed early in the seventh century. The catalyst was a religious prophet, Muhammad, who galvanized the Arab world into unity and jolted it out of its isolation. Muhammad was born in Mecca about 570. Orphaned in his youth, he was brought up by an uncle as a trader. Eventually, he entered the service of a rich widow whom he married, ensuring himself a respectable and leisured career. As a trader, Muhammad came into contact with foreign merchants who came through Mecca. But there is reason to suspect that the decisive aspects of his life were shaped less by these extraneous conditions than by his own introspective, brooding, ascetic spirit, which caused him to spend much of his time in prayer and meditation, often in the solitude of the desert. While the question of his own salvation may have been central to his spiritual searching, there are reasons to believe that he was troubled about the breakdown of communal values and the moral laxity evident in Mecca.

When Muhammad was about forty, he suddenly claimed that God—*Allah* in Arabic—had spoken directly to him and named him his prophet. Throughout the rest of his life these revelations continued, constituting in their entirety a full-bodied new religion. And they gave Muhammad his mission: He dedicated himself to convincing others that Allah had shown him the way to righteousness and truth.

What did Allah reveal to his prophet? The answer to this question lies in the Koran (*Qur'an* in

PLATE 1. *Gudea of Lagash* **(Ruled ca. 2150 B.C.).** This is one of several surviving statues of Gudea, a very active ruler of the Sumerian city of Lagash. Represented in prayer, the ruler's expression reflects the spirit of resignation which characterized the Sumerian world-view. The stylized features and the immobility surrounding the human figure was characteristic of Mesopotamian sculpture. (The Metropolitan Museum of Art, Harris Brisbane Dick Fund, 1959)

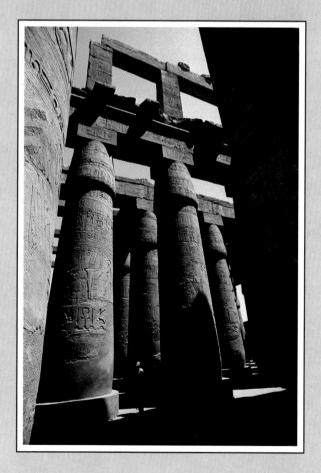

PLATE 2. Egyptian Temple. This photo shows the remains of a massive temple built in honor of Amon-Re at Karnak in the time of Rameses II (1299–1232 B.C.), when the Egyptian empire was at its height. The structure marked the culmination of a long tradition of temple building. The huge columns defined an inner hall which rose above side aisles also defined by columns. The columns contained numerous reliefs and hieroglyphic texts exalting Amon-Re and the feats of the pharaoh. (M. Timothy O'Keefe/Bruce Coleman)

Plate 3 *(left and right).* **Ideal Greek Humans.** These two statues, both Roman copies of Greek originals, reflect the search by Greek artists to represent ideal human beings. The male figure by Polyclitus (fl. ca. 450–420 B.C.) portrays a spearbearer. The female figure by Praxiteles (fl. ca. 350 B.C.) portrays Aphrodite, the goddess of love. These statues reflect the Greek genius for creating a calculated symmetry of the parts of the body without sacrificing the sense that one is observing a living human about to move. *(left,* National Museum, Naples: Scala/Art Resource; *right,* Vatican: Scala/Art Resource)

PLATE 4. A Room in a Roman Villa.
This photo shows a reconstructed room from an aristocrat's villa near Pompey. The decoration of such rooms occupied much of the attention of Roman artists. Paintings dealing with history and nature adorned wall spaces, while elaborate mosaics covered the floors. Examples of such paintings are shown below. (The Metropolitan Museum of Art, Rogers Fund, 1903)

PLATE 5. *Aeneas at the Doctor.* Inspired by Vergil's *Aeneid,* this scene from a villa at Pompeii shows a doctor treating Aeneas; his weeping son stands by while Venus appears with healing herbs. (National Museum, Naples: Scala/Art Resource)

PLATE 6. *The Countryside.* This mosaic formed part of the decoration of a magnificent villa built by Emperor Hadrian near Tivoli. The bucolic countryside was a favorite subject of Roman artists and writers. (Monumenti Musei e Gallerie Pontificie, Vatican)

PLATE 7. *Christ Ruler of the Universe.* This mosaic from the cathedral of Cefalu in Sicily portrays a theme often treated by Byzantine artists. It reflects the skill of Byzantine artists in conveying a spiritual message visually. (Scala/Art Resource)

PLATE 8 *(right).* *Christ Enthroned.* This manuscript illumination from the Irish *Book of Kells* represents one of the major art forms of the early Middle Ages. Churches and monasteries and their patrons highly prized sacred books decorated with such illuminations. (Trinity College Library, Dublin)

PLATE 9. *A Medieval Battle.* As the Latin lettering says, this scene from the Bayeux Tapestry shows the English and the French in battle. This remarkable weaving, nearly 240 feet long, portrays a series of episodes involved in William of Normandy's successful effort to conquer England in 1066. (Scala/Art Resource)

PLATE 10. Stained Glass. One of the most stunning features of a Gothic church was its stained glass windows. Although the effect such windows created is impossible to capture in a photograph, the one shown here from the cathedral at Laon in France shows how an artist could use different colored pieces of glass to tell a story, usually from sacred history. This window treats the childhood of Jesus. (Archives Photographiques, Paris: Jean Feuillie © C.N.M.H.S./S.P.A.D.E.M.)

PLATE 11. A Winter Scene. Very popular in the late Middle Ages were illustrated books of hours used for private devotions. A splendid example was one created for the duke of Berry. It contained a painting for each month of the year. The one above is for February. (Musée Condé/ Chantilly: Giraudon/Art Resource)

PLATE 12. Giovanni Bellini, *Transfiguration of Christ*, Late 1480s. Giovanni Bellini (1430–1516) was one of the leading painters of the Italian Renaissance. In the *Transfiguration of Christ,* the sacred figures, Peter, James, and John crouch below Christ, who stands calmly between Moses and Elijah. In the background is a fifteenth-century town and the hills of northern Italy. The individualism of the figures, the depth and realism of the landscape, the immediacy of the scene, and the religiosity of the subject matter were characteristic of Renaissance art. (Museo di Capodimote, Naples: Scala/Art Resource)

PLATE 13. Raphael, *Portrait of a Man,* ca. 1503. While Renaissance artist's typically painted religious scenes, they also painted secular scenes—often reflecting the tastes and characters of their patrons. Raphael is considered the central painter of the High Renaissance. In portraits such as this, he conveyed the strength and individuality of important secular men without resorting to flattery or conventions. (Borghese Gallery, Rome: Scala/Art Resource)

PLATE 14. Antoine Watteau, *A Pilgrimage to Cythera*, 1717. During the Early Modern period, painting often reflected the tastes of the dominant aristocracy. This was particularly so in eighteenth-century France. This theme is one of classical mythology, but the figures are like eighteenth-century aristocrats gracefully at play in an idyllic garden of nature. The line between life and the roles they are playing blurs in this lush scene. (The Louvre, Paris)

PLATE 15. Peter Paul Rubens, *The Raising of the Cross*, 1609–1610. Baroque paintings are often extraordinarily dynamic and rich. This is particularly so in the large paintings of Rubens. In this altarpiece, the subject matter is religious, but the feeling of the painting is not one of calmness or piety. The heroic, heavily-muscled figures are caught in a moment of dramatic struggle; details are carefully rendered; even the surrounding foliage and the dog are in motion. (Antwerp Cathedral)

PLATE 16. Claude Lorraine, *The Marriage of Isaac and Rebekah (The Mill)*, 1640. This painting, with foreground figures framed by trees under a radiant sky, reveals certain characteristics of the classical style: the geometrically balanced Italian landscape, the figures in classic dress, and the general calm and discipline of the scene. Compared to the dynamic, dramatic nature of Rubens' Baroque style, the classical style is logical and restrained. Claude Lorraine (1600–1682) and Nicolas Poussin (1594–1665) helped make classicism popular in France during the seventeenth century. (Reproduced by courtesy of the Trustees, The National Gallery, London)

PLATE 17. Jan Vermeer, *The Painter's Studio*, ca. 1665. Dutch artists often painted interior scenes, depicting popular and middle-class life. In this painting a woman poses as an allegorical figure of fame. Light spreads smoothly through a window in front of her affecting everything in the studio. A map, something particularly crucial for the commercial Dutch, hangs below a geometrically precise candelabra. (Kunsthistorisches Museum, Vienna)

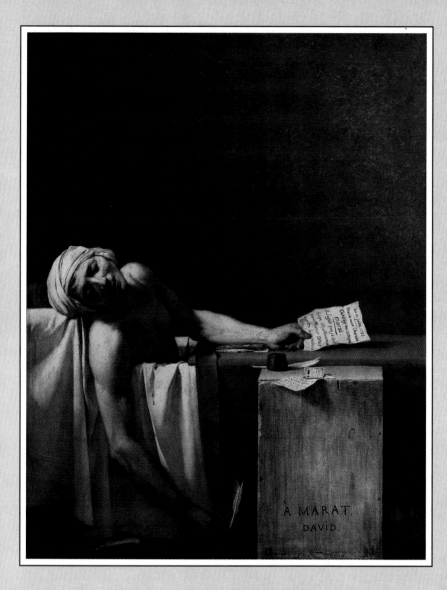

PLATE 18. Jacques Louis David, *The Death of Marat*, 1793. The French artist, David, was an active figure in the French Revolution. Here he shows the death of Marat, one of the chief leaders of the radical second phase of the Revolution. Marat was working in his bathtub when Charlotte Corday assassinated him. The subject matter and the political message is in sharp contrast to earlier eighteenth-century art that reflected aristocratic tastes. (Musées Royaux des Beaux-Arts de Belgique, Brussels)

PLATE 19.   John Constable, *The White Horse,* **1819.** Like many romantic painters, John Constable (1776–1837) was fascinated by nature. Here he depicts a rural scene that is naturalistic (a real scene the viewer might come across) and idyllic. The painting, with its vast living sky and detailed foliage, pulls the viewer into nature. The reality of this image of rural life in nature was already starting to disappear as commercial agriculture, industrialization, and urbanization spread throughout England. (Copyright The Frick Collection)

PLATE 20.   Joseph Mallard William Turner, *The Fighting Temeraire,* **1839.** Turner is considered the greatest of the English romantic painters. In paintings dominated by the light and color, he depicted heroic, tragic struggles mirrored by the overwhelming forces of nature. Here an antiquated battleship sails off into the eternity of the setting sun. The grand ship of the past is replaced by a modern steamship, the smoke from its stack merging into the clouds that frame the sun. (National Gallery, London: Art Resource)

PLATE 21. Eugène Delacroix, *Entrance of the Crusaders into Constantinople*, 1840. Romantic painters such as Delacroix (1793–1863) often glorified the medieval past and the exotic. In this dramatic scene, Byzantine patricians humble themselves before the intruding Crusaders. The scene swirls with passion and color—a romantic vision of the past in sharp contrast to the reality of mid-nineteenth century France. (The Louvre, Paris)

PLATE 22. Gustave Courbet, *The Stone Breakers*, 1849. Realism rejected almost all elements of the Romantic movement. Realistic artists such as Courbet (1819–1877) depicted the mundane, everyday life of workers. Here he portrays stone breakers as a passerby might see them. While there is dignity in their work, Courbet does not glorify them or nature. (Staatlichen Kunstsammlungen, Dresden)

PLATE 23.   Auguste Renoir, *Le Moulin de la Galette a Montmartre*, 1876.   Impressionist painters emphasized the appearance of things as one might see things at a glance. Using new techniques that emphasized applying dabs of colors to the canvas so the eye could mix them, these paintings had great immediacy. Here Renoir (1841–1919), a leading French impressionist most known for his fleshy, optimistic paintings, portrays a festive scene at a Parisian outdoor dance hall. Youthful middle- and working-class figures brim with health and pleasure in this artificial urban environment. (Musée d'Orsay, Paris: Scala/Art Resource)

PLATE 24. Paul Cézanne, *Mont Sainte-Victoire*, 1902–1904. Cézanne (1839–1906) had roots in impressionism, but ultimately rejected it. He tried to display the essence rather than the surface of reality by emphasizing the geometric principles of form and an analytic understanding of color. This landscape is one of a series of paintings of Mont Sainte-Victoire in southern France. Both Cézanne and van Gogh created foundations for twentieth-century painting. (Philadelphia Museum of Art, George W. Elkins Collection)

PLATE 25. Vincent Van Gogh, *The Starry Night*, 1889. Like Cézanne, Van Gogh (1853–1890) had roots in impressionism, but went beyond it. He was able to express his own intense emotions in bold, dynamic paintings. Here he seems to have poured himself into this scene he painted toward the end of his life while at a sanatorium in St.-Remy. The scene swirls with color applied in distinct, broad strokes. It is not a scene of reality one might see, but rather an expression of feelings that mingles with external reality. (Oil on canvas, 29 x 36¼". Collection, The Museum of Modern Art, New York. Acquired through the Lillie P. Bliss Bequest.)

PLATE 26.   James Ensor, *Intrigue*, 1890.
During the late nineteenth century a sense
of dissatisfaction and a criticism of middle-class life grew. This is reflected in ex-
pressive paintings such as those by the
Belgian painter, James Ensor (1860–1949).
Here people are shown as indistinct from
the obnoxious masks they seem to wear.
(Royal Museum of Fine Arts, Antwerp)

**PLATE 27.   Edvard Munch, *The Scream*,
1893.**   Like Ensor, Edvard Munch (1863–
1944) expressed an undermining of middle-class life, but on a deeper, more individual level. In *The Scream*, a nightmare-
like fear is revealed, reflecting an anxiety
and a turning inward toward the unconscious that was growing in late-nineteenth
century intellectual and cultural circles.
Similarities to van Gogh's paintings can be
seen in how paint is used boldly to express emotion. (National Museum, Oslo)

PLATE 28.   Max Ernst, *Europe After the Rain,* 1940–1942.   Max Ernst (born in 1891) became a leader of the surrealists during the 1920s. He painted *Europe After the Rain* while hiding in Paris during World War II. The painting seems to represent the illogical horror and destruction of that era, and it stands as a perhaps prophetic warning to us all. (Wadsworth Atheneum, Hartford, Ella Gallup Sumner and Mary Catlin Sumner Collection)

PLATE 29.   Salvador Dali, *The Temptation of St. Anthony,* 1947.   Surrealism, a relatively popular style of twentieth-century painting, emphasizes the power of dreams and the unconscious. The aim is to depict an unfiltered psychic reality that visually may seem shocking and impossible. One of the most well known surrealists was Salvador Dali (1904–1989). Here the subject is apparently traditional (St. Anthony trying to fend off temptations), but the painting has the feeling and appearance of an improbable nightmare. (Musées Royaux des Beaux-Arts de Belgique, Brussels)

PLATE 30. Piet Mondrian, *Composition*, 1929. The twentieth-century trend away from art that represents external reality toward abstract art was carried to an extreme by the Dutch painter, Piet Mondrian (1872–1944). Here he uses only black, white, and the three primary colors to express his logical, harmonious vision. (National Museum, Belgrade: Scala/Art Resource)

PLATE 31. Fernand Leger, *The Great Constructors*, 1950. This painting by the French artist, Léger (1881–1955), reflects several trends in twentieth century art. Clearly this is an urban scene, showing construction workers and the steel frame of a skyscraper; yet the lines, proportions, and colors scarcely conform to reality. Elements of expressionism—the attempt to convey a feeling about man in this mechanical age—and abstract art—the concern with nonrepresentation lines and colors—abound in this work. (Musée de Biot, France: Josse/Art Resource)

Arabic), the sacred book of Islam, which was compiled shortly after the Prophet's death by his associates as a record of Allah's message delivered through his prophet. The crucial teaching was that there is but one god, Allah; his followers must reject their worship of many gods for monotheism. Muhammad taught that Allah had revealed himself bit by bit down through the ages, the Jewish prophets and Jesus all being accepted as his spokesmen. However, Muhammad was the last and greatest prophet, superseding all others, and his revelation—Allah's final message—was destined to conquer the world. Muhammad insisted that almighty Allah requires complete submission to his will; the religion is thus called *Islam*, which means "submission to God." Every true adherent of Islam, called a *Moslem*, must regulate his or her life so as to abide completely to the will of Allah as revealed to the Prophet. Those who believe in Allah and submit to his law will gain a happy life after death in a sensuous heaven; nonbelievers and the disobedient will be damned to eternal suffering in hell. It is obvious that many of these fundamental teachings were closely akin to beliefs long held by Jews, Christians, Zoroastrians, and pre-Moslem Arabic pagans, a fact that has led to the charge that Muhammad was little more than a borrower of the religious ideas of others. However true this claim may be, it neglects the essential fact: The Prophet brought to the Arab world a religious vision that not only was new to the Arabs but also gave them the historic mission of spreading the true religion revealed in God's final revelation. To the Arab world this message was as radical as early Judaism or primitive Christianity was to their worlds.

To these simple articles of faith Muhammad added a list of duties required of all believers. All must pray five times daily while facing Mecca, give of their wealth to support the poor, fast during the holy month of Ramadan, and, if possible, make a pilgrimage to Mecca once in a lifetime. Muhammad also laid down strict rules regulating diet and marriage, prohibiting drinking and gambling, and demanding honesty, fair play, and respect for others. This code of conduct, strongly reminiscent of that defined for the Jews in the Old Testament, injected a strong ethical vein into the new religion. Each individual was personally responsible to Allah; there was no church, no clergy, no sacraments to assist in gaining Allah's favor.

For several years, the preaching of the new prophet netted only a few converts in Mecca. In fact, Muhammad won many more enemies than followers. By 622 these foes forced him to flee to Yathrib (later renamed Medina, which means "city of the Prophet"), north of Mecca. This flight, called the *Hegira*, marked a turning point in the history of the new religion, which the Moslems recognized by making 622 the first year of their calendar. At Mecca Muhammad—always speaking as Allah's prophet—gave increasing attention to the shaping of a religious-political community dedicated to the advance of Allah's cause by force of arms and to the enforcement of right living on the faithful. Into this community were drawn increasing numbers of Arab converts who subordinated their ancient tribal allegiances to a new, egalitarian companionship based on total submission to Allah and obedience to his prophet. The symbol of the new community was the mosque, the meeting place where the faithful gathered as equals to affirm their faith in Allah and demonstrate their unity in serving his cause. Reflecting the warrior ethos of the Arabic world, this holy community felt justified in living off the booty its warriors seized from nonbelievers, including especially the caravans of the rich Meccans. By 630 Muhammad's following was strong enough to recapture Mecca, a feat that persuaded many Arabs of the validity of Muhammad's message and led them to join his community. During his last years the Prophet used his forces to compel other Arab tribes to accept his leadership, so that when he died in 632 he was the leader of an Arab world virtually united under a religious banner.

Muhammad's success in drawing together the Arab world was impressive enough, but even more astonishing developments were to come. Almost immediately the new "nation" burst out of Arabia and began a series of military conquests that affected most of the civilized world (see Map 14.1). Between 632 and 656, the Arabs destroyed the Persian Empire; wrested the prize provinces of Syria, Palestine, Egypt, and extensive areas of North Africa from the Byzantine Empire; were probing India; and were challenging Byzantine sea power for control of the Mediterranean. After a brief interlude to settle internal problems over Moslem leadership, the advance resumed in the late seventh century. All of North Africa was conquered, and Arab forces pushed into the Indus Valley and the outer reaches of China. An offensive was mounted in Asia Minor that moved closer and closer to Constantinople. Before 700 Moslem naval forces were in virtual control of the Mediterranean. In 711 a Moslem army crossed from Africa into Europe and quickly overran the Visigothic kingdom in Spain. From there the Moslems began to raid Gaul to threaten the Frankish kingdom. But the drive was weakening: In 717 to 718 Arab forces were defeated at Constantinople by Leo III and soon after were driven out of Asia Minor. The Byzantine victory, decisive in checking the Moslem advance into Europe, was complemented in 733 when the Frankish leader Charles Martel defeated a Moslem force at the battle of Tours in Gaul.

The conquest of this vast empire within a century after the Prophet's death represents one of the great military feats in all history. Several factors played a part in this expansion. For one thing, the Arabs' opponents were weak. The Sassanid Empire was exhausted from its long struggle with the Byzantines. Religious disaffection among the Christians in the eastern Byzantine provinces caused the residents to welcome the Arabs as liberators from the religious tyranny and the fiscal exactions of the emperors at Constantinople. The conquerors interfered little with local affairs, making their overlordship easy to accept. They demonstrated great military prowess; their long training as desert warriors paid off. Their enthusiasm for their cause was also a factor. Muhammad had said, "Fight and fear not; the gates of Paradise are under the shade of the swords." Their wars were thus holy wars (*djihad* in Arabic).

4. MOSLEM CIVILIZATION: INSTITUTIONAL AND CULTURAL PATTERNS

The amazing victories of the Arabs presented the conquerors with a wide range of challenges: how to rule a huge empire inhabited by diverse peoples; how to support themselves in a different environment; how to sustain their faith in a world where other religions dominated; how to interact with different cultures. Their responses and the reactions of their subjects to their dominance produced a new, uniquely Moslem pattern of civilization of immense importance to the future history of a large part of the world.

A major problem facing the victorious Arabs was establishing a political system that would permit them to control their numerous subjects. While Muhammad had established the basis for a primitive Arab state, no one could succeed to his special place as Prophet. From his death in 632 down to 661, his close associates picked one from among them to serve as *caliph*—an Arabic term meaning deputy—to interpret and apply the law as revealed in the Koran. This office, bestowing on its holder a vast range of powers sanctioned by religion, became the key element in the Moslem political system. Whoever controlled it and used effectively the authority surrounding it could claim absolute lordship over all Moslems and all who were their subjects. But a major problem in Moslem political life centered on deciding who had a legitimate claim to the caliphate.

As long as Muhammad's personal associates were available, they could legitimately claim the office. But with their passing, a struggle developed for succession. Finally, in 661, a military leader seized control and made the office of caliph hereditary. The dynasty he founded, known as the Omayyads, held power until 750. Its legitimacy was challenged from the beginning by Muhammad's son-in-law, Ali, and his son, Hussein, who claimed authority to interpret the Prophet's word on the basis of their kinship with him. Their claims resulted in their assassinations, but their followers formed a powerful and dedicated religious-political faction, called the Shiites, which for centuries challenged the authority of successive caliphs.

The Omayyads established their center of power at Damascus. Although totally committed to Arab supremacy in the expanding empire, they realized that ruling the lands and peoples conquered by the Arab armies of Allah demanded more complex political institutions than those that characterized Muhammad's first Moslem community. Strongly influenced by Byzantine models, the Omayyads created a centralized court, a bureaucracy, and an efficient tax system. The authority of the Omayyad caliphs was exercised primarily through garrisons of Arab troops established at strategic spots across the vast empire. Bound to the caliph by ethnic and religious ties, the commanders of these garrisons controlled local affairs; often they did so by utilizing already established native political structures. These garrisons were supported by allocations from the caliph's treasury, which was supplied by taxes paid by the conquered non-Moslem population. This system meant that the Moslem world was dominated by an Arab elite whose religious convictions legitimatized for its members their right to possess and exploit what they had won by the sword. For almost a century, this system worked. Arab military supremacy gave conquered subjects little choice. Generally, the isolated, exclusivist Arab garrisons interfered little in local affairs except to collect the tribute that supported them.

But eventually the Omayyad regime was untenable. Arab strength was diluted by its dispersion over the huge empire. More important, as the number of non-Arab converts to Islam increased, resentment against Arab domination grew. Non-Arab Moslems could see no reason why their faith should not make them equal in the sight of Allah to Arab Moslems. That sentiment led to the overthrow of the Omayyads in 750—except in Spain—and the seizure of the caliphate by the Abbasid dynasty, a family of Persian origin claiming distant kinship with Muhammad. Abbasid rule meant the end of Arab domination. The capital was shifted from Damascus to Bagdad, and the political system was reshaped on the model of ancient Persia. The Abbasid caliphs reclaimed the absolute authority to interpret Allah's word for all the faithful, whatever their ethnic origin. Around their court developed a professional bureaucracy made up of educated Moslems. The caliph's authority was extended across the empire through an elaborate system of governorships over which officials representing the caliph administered justice and collected taxes. In this new political environment Arab militancy was greatly diminished.

During the eighth and ninth centuries the Abbasid caliphs enjoyed immense power, exempli-fied by rulers like Harun al-Rashid (786–809), immortalized in the *Arabian Nights*. But by the end of the ninth century Abbasid power began to decline. Rival caliphs, challenging the legitimacy of the Abbasids to interpret Allah's will, were established in Spain, North Africa, Syria, and India and began to compete with each for a dominant position in the Moslem world. Seeking to protect themselves against these rivals, the Abbasids increasingly placed their trust in Seljuk Turkish mercenaries, nomads from Central Asia who by 1055 had made the Abbasids their puppets. By that time, Moslem political unity had vanished forever. Disunity invited attacks from outsiders, especially Byzantine and western European Christians, who had not forgotten earlier Moslem militancy.

Although the benefits were not equally shared, the Moslem world enjoyed significant economic growth. Agriculture remained the basic element of economic life. The early Arab conquerors were little interested in farming except as a source of tribute to support the military elite. As a consequence, the traditional village-farming structure of the Roman-Byzantine and the Persian worlds persisted. Later, under Abbasid rule fiscal policies were introduced that stimulated land clearance, production for urban markets, and the introduction of new crops and techniques, all of which combined to increase agricultural production. Economic growth was most marked in commerce and manufacturing. The emergence of Moslem civilization gave new impetus to urban life. Cities—new and old, large and small—became centers of life for the ruling elite and their dependents. Their needs, ranging from food to luxury items, stimulated trade and industry, which in turn filled cities with merchants and artisans. While much commerce and manufacturing filled local needs, long-distance trade routes stretching from Spain to India developed. Long-distance trade was promoted by the removal of artificial trade barriers, a sound money system, and specialized manufacturing developing in many cities (for example, the steel weapons and textiles of Damascus and the leather goods of Cordoba in Spain). The Moslem political regime allowed merchants and artisans much greater freedom than had been the case in the Byzantine and Persian empires; as a consequence, these groups exercised their entrepreneurial talents to expand wealth. On the whole, the Moslem economy was the most advanced and resourceful in the world during the early Middle Ages.

The Moslem social structure was immensely complex. Arab tradition and the teaching of the Koran emphasized the equality of all male Moslems. In fact, important social distinctions existed, initially between Arabs and non-Arabs and then between Moslems and non-Moslems. As time passed, a social elite emerged defined by office-holding, wealth, education, and living style. This elite congregated in urban centers, where its ranks were constantly replenished by those whose talents as administrators, merchants, artisans, and scholars permitted them to accumulate the wealth and acquire the social graces required for elite status. The bulk of the agricultural population and urban laborers remained outside this elite circle and were considered as inferiors. Non-Moslems, although tolerated, were also treated as inferiors, subject to special taxes and excluded from public life. The stratification of Moslem society was countered to some extent by the force of Moslem law. Already in the Koran there were rigorous prescriptions regulating the behavior of believers. This body of law constantly grew more complex to provide a common standard of conduct binding on all Moslems.

The family was a basic institution in regulating social life. But it was an institution dominated by males. Severe restrictions were placed on women, forcing them into a secluded existence and isolating them from many aspects of social and economic life. Polygamy was legally recognized and widely practiced among the affluent, putting women in a position of competing for a place in the family structure and for control over children. Husbands were able to divorce their wives easily and exercised considerable control over the destinies of children. However, Moslem law did permit women to share in inheritances and sought to protect their interests in their possessions.

The most important forces giving Moslem civilization cohesion and unity were religion and culture. The Islamic religion demonstrated an amazing power to win converts, usually without force, since Arab conquerors seldom insisted that their subjects accept the new religion. They only imposed a special tax on their non-Moslem subjects for the privilege of retaining their old religion and excluded them from government positions. Christians and Jews were extended special privileges because they were, as Moslems put it, "people of the Book" who had received at least a portion of God's revelation. As the years passed, however, devotees of many religions—Christians, Jews, Zoroastrians, and Hindus—were converted in massive numbers, and the vast Moslem Empire became predominantly Islamic. Islam also expanded beyond the boundaries of the empire to win converts in southern Asia and sub-Sahara Africa. Important non-Moslem communities always remained in the empire, including Christian churches in Egypt, Syria, and Armenia and a significant Jewish community in Spain.

Islam itself tended to grow more complex as the centuries passed. This enrichment resulted chiefly from the efforts of a long succession of theologians, philosophers, and lawyers, all of whom reflected on the nature of their religion from different perspectives. The theologians developed a rich body of literature in the form of commentaries (called *sunnas*) on the Koran and on pronouncements attributed to Muhammad but not recorded in the Koran (called *hadiths*). The philosophers incorporated concepts derived from Greek thought into Islam in an effort to illuminate the meaning of the Koran. The lawyers constantly elaborated the body of law that governed Moslem life, seeking to make it consistent, complete, and relevant to the varied conditions of life among the faithful. The collective efforts of theologians, philosophers, and lawyers resulted in an orthodox faith much more complex than the message first proclaimed by the Prophet yet firmly rooted in the basic doctrines set forth in the Koran. The adherents of this orthodox religion, called Sunnite Moslems, constituted the vast majority in the Islamic world. But there were dissenters, the chief of which were the Shiite Moslems, who insisted that the true faith was preserved by Muhammad's blood descendants. They rejected many of the ideas about Islam proclaimed by the Sunnites and often did battle with Sunnites on many issues—a conflict that still divides the Moslem world.

The Islamic world also sustained a long tradition of seeking to deepen spirituality. The quest was carried on primarily by *sufis*, religious mystics who, through contemplation and ascetic practices, sought direct communion with the divine that would deepen their spiritual life as well as that of their followers. Despite these diverse movements, Islam as a common faith provided the prime basis of unity in the Moslem world.

Moslem expansion generated a tremendous cultural revival that brought together into a rich synthesis nearly all the world's great cultural traditions: Greco-Roman, Persian, Mesopotamian, Egyptian, Germanic, Jewish, Indian, and Arabic. Borrowing and synthesis remained a central feature of Moslem culture throughout the Middle Ages. Religion provided the matrix and the inspiration for synthesis. Since Muhammad had forbidden the translation of the Koran into any other language, all Moslems had to learn Arabic; and since the Koran contained the final truth, it was necessary to reconcile the knowledge of older cultures with Moslem religious teachings. The response to these challenges was a brilliant outburst of scholarship that rightly allowed the Moslems to claim to be the cultural heirs of the ages.

Many historians would agree that the greatest Moslem achievements were in philosophy and science. Moslem philosophers devoted their efforts chiefly to reconciling Greek philosophy with the teachings of the Koran. At the same time, they wrestled with the contradictions inherent in the Greek tradition, especially those separating Platonic and Aristotelian thought. Their efforts are closely akin to those of the scholastic philosophers of medieval western Europe (see Chapter 23). In fact, the speculations of the greatest Moslem thinkers Ibn Sina (980–1037) and the Spanish Ibn Rushd (1126–1198), known in the West as Avicenna and Averroës, exercised a direct influence on Western scholasticism.

In science the Moslem achievements were spectacular. Their efforts as collectors put at their disposal a huge body of scientific information from Greek, Indian, Persian, Mesopotamian, and Egyptian sources—more than scientists anywhere in the world had possessed until modern times. To this they added their own contributions, all of which were made widely available to a large circle of people because they were written in Arabic.

In mathematics, the Indian numerical system was adopted and the use of the zero was added to create the Arabic system of numbers almost universally used today. A Moslem, al-Khwarizmi (ca. 780–850), combined Greek and Indian concepts to create algebra. Astronomy advanced tremendously with the joining of Greek views, such as Ptolemy's, to Persian and Mesopotamian. The works of medical writers such as al Razi (865–925) and the philosopher Avicenna represent compilations from numerous sources. Moslem doctors studied diseases, dissected bodies, and experimented with drugs, adding significantly to the existing body of medical knowledge. Geographers and physicists also made significant advances.

Moslem literature demonstrated great vigor and variety. Its poetry, familiar to Western readers chiefly through the works of Omar Khayyám, is marked by brilliant imagery and highly complex technical skill in the use of the Arabic language. Perhaps the most characteristic feature of Moslem literature was the ability of writers to recast subject matter borrowed from various non-Arabic sources into masterpieces attuned to the spirit of Moslem religion and the values of Moslem society. Nothing illustrates this feature better than the *Arabian Nights;* the adventures of Sinbad the Sailor and the feats of Aladdin are stories gleaned from the literary traditions of many non-Moslem peoples, but they are given a unique coloration by the genius of Arabic authors, who retell them in a mode reflecting the spirit and the tastes of their own culture.

Like most of Islam's culture, its art reflects a creative synthesis of many traditions. Architectural talents were devoted chiefly to building mosques and palaces. The mosques, primarily places for individual prayer rather than community worship, are simple structures whose inner space is often divided by rows of graceful columns creating aisles covered by arches. As a rule, the mosques are covered by domes similar to those of Byzantine churches; above them rise graceful towers (minarets) from which the call to prayer is issued. Before each mosque is an open court containing a purification fountain and surrounded by a covered passageway. The greatest mosques, such as those at Damascus and Cordoba, are beautiful structures marked by delicacy and grace (see Figure 14.1). Surviving palaces, such as the Alcazar at Seville and the Alhambra at Granada, reflect the same architectural style but are much more elaborate.

Most Moslem buildings are rather bare on the outside but brilliantly decorated inside, especially with paintings and mosaics in splendid colors. The representation of human and animal forms was discouraged lest the faithful be tempted to compromise their monotheism by worshiping a graven image. Instead, the decorations accentuated floral designs and geometric patterns (arabesques). Exquisite artistry also manifested itself in the crafts; Moslem fabrics, tapestries, carpets, leatherwork, metalwork, weapons, and jewelry were the most prized articles in the medieval world and were key items in international trade.

The vitality of Byzantine and Moslem civilizations far excelled that which emerged in the western part of the old Roman Empire. The Germanic West lagged far behind them until at least the twelfth century. As we shall see, during the medieval centuries no aspect of western European civilization escaped the subtle influences of the Byzantine and the Moslem worlds. That immense debt was often forgotten in the West in later centuries—but not by the heirs of those who created Byzantine and Moslem civilizations.

SUGGESTED READING

Byzantine Civilization

H. W. Haussig, *A History of Byzantine Civilization*, trans. J. M. Hussey (1971).

Robert Browning, *The Byzantine Empire* (1980).

Cyril Mango, *Byzantium, the Empire of New Rome* (1980).

Each of these three works provides a full and balanced general treatment of all aspects of Byzantine civilization.

Romilly Jenkins, *Byzantium. The Imperial Centuries, A.D. 610–1071* (1966). Provides a full political history of the period in Byzantine history covered in this chapter.

J. M. Hussey, *The Orthodox Church in the Byzantine Empire* (1986). An excellent treatment.

Jaroslav Pelikan, *The Christian Tradition: A History of the Development of Doctrine*, Vol. 2: *The Spirit of Eastern Christendom* (1974). A masterful but demanding treatment of the theological issues which challenged Byzantine intellectuals.

D. Talbot Rice, *Byzantine Art*, rev. ed. (1968). A brief treatment, effectively illustrated.

Tamara Talbot Rice, *Everyday Life in Byzantium* (1967). Provides a good feel for how people lived in the Byzantine world.

Moslem Civilization

M. A. Shaban, *Islamic History: A New Interpretation*, 2 vols. (1971–1976).

Hugh Kennedy, *The Prophet and the Age of the Caliphates: The Islamic Near East from the Sixth to the Eleventh Century* (1986).

Either of these two works provides a challenging introduction to early Islamic history and civilization.

Maurice Lombard, *The Golden Age of Islam*, trans. Joan Spencer (1975). Will help the reader to understand economic and social history.

Alfred Guillaume, *Islam*, 2nd ed. rev. (1956). A clear description of the major features of Islamic religion.

Dominique Sourdel, *Medieval Islam*, trans. J. Montgomery Watt (1983). Especially good on the role of religion in shaping Moslem society.

Martin Lings, *Muhammad: His Life Based on the Earliest Sources* (1983). An excellent biography.

W. Montgomery Watt, *The Formative Period in Islamic Thought* (1973). A good introduction to early Moslem intellectual history.

David T. Rice, *Islamic Art*, rev. ed. (1975). A well-illustrated treatment.

CHAPTER 15

Heirs to the Roman Empire: The Germanic West, 500–750

FIGURE 15.1 **Life in a Medieval Monastery** This scene from an illuminated manuscript reflects the essential elements of the daily routine in a Benedictine monastery: the tolling of bells to summon the monks to worship services; studying and copying manuscripts; manual labor. The combination of these activities into a disciplined routine permitted monastic communities to make a major contribution to the shaping of all aspects of medieval civilization, despite the fact that monks sought to escape the world within the confines of their monasteries. (The Pierpont Morgan Library)

The third heir to the Roman Empire, the Germanic society in the West, fared much less well than did the Byzantine and Moslem worlds during the early Middle Ages. Western Europe suffered through an age of instability and disorder. By 750 the first dim outlines of a new order were becoming evident in the form of new institutions and ideas destined to be crucial for the future of Europe.

1. POLITICAL DEVELOPMENTS

A prime factor in the history of the Germanic West between 500 and 750 was political instability stemming from two interrelated factors. First, the West was plagued by the uncertain definition of the territory belonging to each of the various kingdoms established on Roman soil during the fifth century. In 500 the boundaries of those kingdoms—Visigothic, Vandal, Ostrogothic, Burgundian, Frankish, Anglo-Saxon—were still fluid and often a matter of fierce competition. Second, all of these kingdoms lacked well-defined internal political structures capable of maintaining public order.

Between 500 and 750 there was considerable rearrangement of the fragile boundaries of the Germanic kingdoms (see Maps 13.1 and 14.1). Of prime importance was the emergence of the Franks as a major power. During the fifth century, while other Germanic groups were carving out large kingdoms in North Africa, Spain, Italy, and southern Gaul, various groups of Franks slowly penetrated northern Gaul without cutting themselves off from their homeland along the lower Rhine River. Suddenly, under their first great king, Clovis (481–511), the Franks exploded into prominence. A ruthless, able warrior, Clovis unified the Franks and unleashed their military potential. He and his immediate successors wiped out the last remnants of Roman power in northern Gaul, absorbed the Burgundian kingdom, drove the Visigoths out of southern Gaul and claimed their territory, and established dominance over Germanic peoples living immediately east of the Rhine in territories that had not been part of the Roman Empire. The Frankish cause was aided by the conversion of Clovis and his followers to orthodox

Christianity, making their domination more acceptable to the population of Gaul than that of the Arian and pagan rulers they defeated.

The Byzantines and the Moslems also played a role in shaping the political map of the West. As already noted, Justinian's attempt to reconquer the West led to the destruction of the Vandal kingdom in North Africa and the Ostrogothic kingdom in Italy. However, his successors lost northern and central Italy to the last Germanic intruders into the West, the Lombards; the Byzantines retained a band of land extending across central Italy from Ravenna to Rome and southern Italy and Sicily. In 711, Moslem forces overran the Visigothic kingdom and established control over the Iberian peninsula except for small Christian enclaves in extreme northern Spain.

Meanwhile, the political map of the West was being shaped in other areas. In England, where several competing petty kingdoms had been formed by Anglo-Saxon intruders, a variety of forces were at work pointing in the direction of unification. In central Europe large numbers of Slavs moved westward and southward into lands vacated by the Germans and began to develop their own political identity. In the Scandinavian world, new political groupings were taking shape, preparing the people of the North for an important role in western European history in the future.

Thus, by 750 the political map of the West had assumed a more settled shape (see Map 14.1). The heartland of western Europe—northern Italy, Gaul, western Germany, and England—was occupied by kingdoms shaped by three Germanic peoples: the Lombards, the Franks, and the Anglo-Saxons. Facing this German-dominated world on the south were the Byzantines in southern Italy and Sicily and the Moslems controlling Spain, North Africa, and the western Mediterranean Sea. To the east and the north were the Slavs and the Scandinavians.

While the political boundaries of the West took shape, constant experimentation went on as rulers of each Germanic kingdom searched for a workable system of government to replace the Roman imperial regime. That experimentation varied from kingdom to kingdom. As a result, significant regional differences in political institutions emerged in the West during the early Middle

WHERE HISTORIANS DISAGREE

The Division of Times Past

In order to provide a framework into which random data can be arranged, historians divide past time into segments, each treated as a discrete unit that has its unique characteristics. Although necessary, attempts at *periodization* lead to basic disagreement among historians. Nowhere have such disagreements been more apparent than in the attempt to define the division between classical Greco-Roman civilization and what came after in western Europe.

The first widely accepted periodization system relating to the transition from the classical age to a new era was formulated in the early modern period. It was shaped by Renaissance humanists, Protestant religious reformers, and Enlightenment philosophers, whose various interests led them to agree that a major break occurred in the fifth century A.D. This break took the form of a "disaster" marked by the failure of the Roman political system, the triumph of Christianity, and the victory of the barbarian Germans. What followed was a "dark age." This interpretation found particularly persuasive expression in Edward Gibbon's classic, *Decline and Fall of the Roman Empire* (1776), which argued that in the fifth century a new age began with the victory of "religion and barbarism" over the rational, enlightened civilization of classical Greece and Rome.

The periodization scheme defining a decisive break in the fifth century separating the ancient world from a prolonged "dark age" dominated historical thinking well into the twentieth century. Then a new approach was developed, chiefly as a result of the work of the Belgian historian, Henri Pirenne. In his seminal work, *Mohammed and Charlemagne* (1939), he argued that in western Europe the end of the classical world came not in the fifth but in the eighth century when Moslem expansion finally interrupted the economic unity of the Mediterranean basin. In Pirenne's words, "It is . . . strictly correct to say that without Mohammed Charlemagne would have been inconceivable." Thus, it is to the Carolingian era (ca. 750–900) that one must look for the shaping of the essential features of western European civilization, for the "first" Europe. All developments prior to 750 must be annexed to classical history.

Despite heated criticism from many quarters, the Pirenne "thesis" enjoyed wide acceptance among historians for the past half century. However, there are signs that a new periodization scheme is emerging. It is being shaped by advocates of what is sometimes called the "new social history." They are convinced that the determinant forces shaping the historical process are basic social structures that dictate the activities and thoughts of common people, the "silent," neglected actors on the human stage. Their investigations of the medieval world have led them to conclude that somewhere around 1000 there occurred changes in the basic structure of western European society so fundamental that a new age was born. These changes had not to do with politics and war and high culture but with demography, family structures, technology, social groupings, and popular religious mentalities. Compared with these changes, the Carolingian "revival" was a mere episode with little consequences. Before 1000 western Europe was a moribund society, dependent on remnants of the classical world. Only after 1000 did a unique and vibrantly creative civilization emerge in western Europe.

These brief remarks lead to two conclusions. Historians divide time past in terms of what interests them most deeply. And their periodization schemes make a difference in how historical data is organized and interpreted.

Ages, quite in contrast with the unitary political orders characteristic of the Byzantine and Moslem worlds. Out of this experimentation emerged two systems especially important for the future: that of the Franks and that of the Anglo-Saxons. We shall return to the Anglo-Saxons (see Chapter 16); here we shall concentrate on the Frankish political system to illustrate the major features of the new political order in the West.

The Franks—like most other Germans—sought to create a government based on strong monarchy. The basis of royal power was clearly staked out by Clovis. The powers he claimed were derived in part from his position as a victorious German warrior king and in part from authority he assumed as ruler over former Roman subjects. Although ancient Germanic kingship had been elective, Clovis succeeded in establishing the concept that royal power belonged to a single family whose royal blood was believed to be sacred; this principle assured hereditary succession in Clovis' dynasty, called the Merovingians, down to 751. To execute the extensive powers they claimed, Clovis and his successors created a central court of royal officials and established local units of government based on the old Roman administrative system. The kingdom was divided into local territorial units, called *counties*, where *counts* appointed by the king were charged with collecting taxes, rendering justice, maintaining order, and mustering freemen to military duty.

However, the Merovingian dynasty was unable to exercise the power its monarchs claimed in a fashion leading to uniform administration and internal order. As a consequence, royal power steadily declined to the point where the last Merovingians were justifiably dubbed "do-nothing" kings. At the heart of this failure was the inability of the Merovingians to exploit the political concepts and techniques they tried to take over from their Roman predecessors. The kings and their officials remained prisoners of the Germanic concept of king as warrior; as a consequence, rulers repeatedly resorted to force as a means of asserting their authority, often appearing as bloodthirsty tyrants rather than guardians of order and justice. Germanic custom required that warrior chiefs gain approval of their free subjects, or at least the more powerful of them, before taking political action, a

practice that put constraints on royal absolutism. The Merovingian kings had a very limited sense of public service, so that their policies tended to serve dynastic interests and to favor the selfish interests of the warrior followings whose loyal service was the chief guarantee of the survival of the dynasty. Most kings had so little managerial ability that their administrative machinery degenerated into a household officialdom serving only to meet the king's personal needs. Administrative ineptness was compounded by increasing illiteracy among all ranks of the lay population. The Merovingians were unable to sustain an effective system of taxation; increasingly they were forced to depend on their own lands and on booty they could extract by force from their subjects. Following Germanic practice they allowed each of their subjects to be judged by the law under which he or she was born, be it Frankish, Roman, Burgundian, or Visigothic; the result was chaos in the administration of justice. Especially dangerous to royal power was the persistence of the Merovingians in following the Germanic custom of treating the state as private property to be divided among their male heirs. By the early eighth century this practice had split the unified kingdom once ruled by Clovis into three distinct subkingdoms (Neustria, Austrasia, and Burgundy), each ruled by a branch of the Merovingian dynasty and each often at war with the others for control of territory. These dynastic struggles encouraged non-Frankish subject peoples to break away from Frankish control. Disorder was further promoted by feuding among powerful elements in Frankish society, including the royal family itself; following Germanic custom, entire families took up arms to avenge wrongs done to their members by other families, thereby compounding violence and disorder.

Unable to maintain a centralized government capable of exercising the powers they claimed, the Merovingian kings were gradually forced to share power with lay and ecclesiastical landowners. The emergence of the landed nobility as possessors of political power was one of the major developments of the early Middle Ages. The strength of these nobles was rooted in possession of land, family connections, control over dependents, and royal favor. Especially crucial to their advancing power were the favors extended them by the monarchs. In part those favors stemmed from Germanic custom, which demanded that warrior kings generously reward their loyal warrior followers. More significantly, they resulted from the kings' dependence on the nobles for vital political services. Lacking regular income and a professional bureaucracy, rulers were forced to rely on subjects who could and would serve the royal government at their own expense. Only the great noble families could afford such services. In return they exacted from the kings grants of land and rights to govern their possessions as they saw fit. A system of private government thus evolved with great nobles controlling affairs in their localities as they wished. This trend was accentuated by the increasing willingness of the weak in an unstable society to seek the protection of the strong. Through a process known as *commendation* individuals from all levels of society freely pledged under oath to serve others willing to offer protection and material support. Although the specific terms of these arrangements varied considerably, the result was to allow the strong to build up private followings of dependents, often called *vassals*, over whom they exercised control and upon whose services they depended to extend their power. The expanding power of the nobles was a source of incessant strife, for the demarcation between royal authority and noble privilege was imprecise, and the rules governing the relationship of one noble to another were chaotic.

These developments meant that by 750 a unique political order had begun to take shape in the West. It involved several coexisting kingdoms, each ruled by a monarch whose royal office was surrounded by religious and military sanctions that in the eyes of most made the king necessary to right order. In fact, the new monarchy was limited in terms of effectiveness by a narrow concept of public authority and by limited resources, both material and human, at its service. As a consequence, the impact of government on society as a whole was limited, especially when compared with the role played by government in contemporary Byzantine and Moslem societies. Increasingly, monarchs in the West were forced to share rulership with a powerfully established landed nobility whose members took into their own hands the control of many activities previously controlled by the Roman imperial state. It can be argued that the diminution of the power of the state was the most significant feature of the new order emerging in the Germanic West.

2. ECONOMIC AND SOCIAL PATTERNS

During the early Middle Ages economic life in the Germanic West was marked by general stagnation, which resulted in a lower level of wealth than existed in the Byzantine and Moslem worlds. As a result of a succession of plagues, incessant warfare, high infant mortality, and low life expectancy, the West was sparsely populated. Urban life continued to deteriorate, and large areas of land went uncultivated. In many ways this economic recession reflected a continuation of trends that had begun in late Roman times.

Economic life became almost totally agricultural. Possession of land provided not only the key to survival but also the measure of an individual's status in society. Agricultural production was organized in a variety of ways. In some areas, especially around the Mediterranean where Roman survivals were strongest, the *latifundia* system continued. These large estates, increasingly called *villas*, were owned by lay nobles or church officials who reserved part of the land for their own support. That land was tilled by slaves or by tenants. Such tenants were allotted a piece of land sufficient to maintain a household in return for which they performed labor on the soil reserved by the owner of the villa and rendered dues. Their status tended to become hereditary, but such status also assured them permanent use of land sufficient to support the peasant family. In a time of political chaos and population shortage the villa system offered certain advantages. It provided landowners with a permanent labor force, encouraged cooperative effort, and gave security to peasants. Thus it tended to spread across many parts of the West. In other areas, farming was organized around village communities of free landowners; in such communities each family owned and cultivated its own land but also shared common rights in forest and pasture land. Also scattered across the landscape were numerous individual farms cultivated by free peasants. Tilled land was used chiefly for cereal grains and vegetables. Yields were low, so that famine was a constant threat. The products of forests and streams and of animal herds were vital to survival. Agricultural technology was primitive, placing a premium on human labor. However, some advances were made, especially in the development of oxen-drawn ploughs capable of turning over the heavy soils of lands north of the Alps. Although the agricultural system of the Germanic West in the early Middle Ages presents a grim picture, certain developments pointed toward recovery: the disappearance of the voracious Roman taxation system; the formation of agricultural organizations (the villa and the village), which encouraged cooperation between landowners and peasants; the emergence of the family household as a key unit of production; modest technological advances; tentative population growth; and isolated efforts at land clearance.

The shift of the center of economic life to a rural setting was accompanied by the decline of urban-based commerce and industry, again continuing a trend that had begun in late Roman times. Although urban centers survived, cities served chiefly as political and religious centers rather than centers of economic production. Near the Mediterranean in southern Gaul, Italy, Spain, and North Africa, some commercial activity did continue, and contacts with the rich East were maintained. But on the whole the West experienced a diminishing exchange of goods, a declining flow of money, and the virtual disappearance of active merchants and artisans, except as they were supported by owners of large estates to provide for local consumption. What little long-distance trade did survive was increasingly conducted by foreigners, especially Syrians and Jews. One development of the period with great significance for the future was the beginning of trading activity in the North and Baltic seas.

The social structure in the Germanic West changed in response to new conditions. The direction of change was toward a simpler system than had been characteristic of the Roman world. The distinctions between Germans and Romans gradually disappeared. Urban social groups, so

vital in the Roman Empire, vanished. A new aristocracy slowly took shape, composed of resourceful, aggressive, self-made persons capable of acquiring land, seizing political power, gathering dependents around them, and defying public authority. As this new aristocracy (often referred to as the *potentes*, the powerful) took shape, the rest of the population, almost all peasants, tended to be grouped in a single lower class (often called *pauperes*, those without power). While many in this class retained legal status as free persons, increasingly the peasant population became dependents of powerful landowners, bound to the soil of a large estate and subject to various obligations in exchange for possession of a piece of land. Slavery continued to exist, especially as a means of supplying household servants, but there was a tendency to attach slaves to the land in the same fashion as other peasant workers.

Social behavior among the powerful increasingly took on Germanic values and habits at the expense of the more refined standards of conduct of the old Roman world. Increasingly illiterate and generally short-lived, aristocratic males were creatures of violence and passion, their lives centered on fighting, hunting, gaming, and sexual ventures. They loved ostentatious display, particularly in the form of personal adornments made of gold and jewels. Especially important to them were family connections, chiefly because the family circle offered security in an uncertain environment. It was not unusual for aristocrats to collect wives and concubines so as to assure themselves of many children who could be advantageously married to promote family interests. Feuds among competing noble families were a common feature of life. Although male heads of families exercised extensive powers over females, aristocratic women played a significant role in society. Dowries and gifts associated with marriage practices gave them control over considerable property. High respect was paid and special protection was extended to them because of their procreative power, the key to family survival. Their kinship ties provided a basic link in constituting extended families. The social importance of women is illustrated by the prominent role played in public life by several Merovingian queens and by the influence asserted by several gifted leaders of Merovingian monasteries for women. The life of the peasantry was marked by poverty and drudgery. The family was a vital institution to the peasants, chiefly because it was a prime unit in agricultural production.

3. THE CHURCH AND RELIGIOUS LIFE

Of decisive importance in reshaping life in the Germanic West was the Church. Although it emerged from the collapse of the Roman Empire with considerable strength, it was faced with great adversity between 500 and 750. It lost the beneficial support of the Roman government. The emerging political divisions in the West threatened unity, as did the growing isolation of the Church in the West from the Christian communities in the East. The character of religious leadership changed in ways that undermined spiritual concerns. Like all other power wielders in the West, influential ecclesiastical officials, especially bishops, paid increasing attention to gaining land and dependents. Not only did this quest detract them from pastoral duties, but also it made their offices a focus of wealth and power. These offices became the object of competition in which the worldly usually triumphed over the pious. Ecclesiastical offices were prizes that kings used to reward their followers and that self-seeking noble families sought to fill as a means of increasing their wealth and power. Discipline among the lower clergy suffered from the lack of spiritual concern among higher church officials; the result was increasing numbers of unlettered priests, ignorant of basic Christian teaching and morally lax. Powerful nobles often controlled appointments of local priests, especially those serving the increasing numbers of private churches established on local estates by nobles who viewed such churches as private property.

Although the early Middle Ages was a period of intense religious fervor among all people, religious life in general reflected inferior spiritual direction. Pagan and Christian ideas and practices mingled to produce a religious mentality that gave greater emphasis to avoiding evil spirits through magic and the intervention of the saints than to learning basic Christian doctrines and practicing Christian morality. Church writers lamented constantly about sexual promiscuity, marital irregularities, murder, rape, thievery, perjury, illicit forms of worship, and superstition; such complaints were accompanied by pleas for improvement of the clergy and more effective pastoral care.

The disruptive forces in spiritual life producing disunity, worldliness in leadership, debased religious consciousness, and moral laxness were still rampant in 750. However, some forces of renewal had begun to appear, chiefly from within the Church.

A major source of religious vitality was the Church's quest to win new converts. We have already noted that most of the Germanic invaders accepted Christianity as soon as they entered the Roman Empire. In succeeding centuries the Christian frontier continued to advance. During the fifth century missionary forces, spearheaded by St. Patrick, converted Ireland. Missionaries from the Frankish kingdom, itself Christianized late in the fifth century under Clovis, pushed the Christian frontier to the Rhine and beyond during the sixth and seventh centuries. Beginning late in the sixth century the Anglo-Saxons were converted by missionaries from Rome and Ireland. During the late seventh and the eighth centuries, English and Irish missionaries crossed to the Continent to win new converts on the northern and eastern frontiers of the Frankish kingdom. While the Christian frontier was being advanced, the work of converting the rural population of the West went forward. As new converts were won, a network of bishoprics, monasteries, rural churches, and private chapels was developed to ensure pastoral care for new Christians. The missionary establishment was often especially intent on imposing a high level of religious life, thus serving as a model of pastoral care and a source of reforming zeal.

A second positive achievement of the Church was its growing involvement in activities that were not strictly religious. It took on the burden of caring for the weak in society. It maintained the only schools and hospitals. Powerful ecclesiastical leaders played an important role in the councils of kings and royal administration, allowing them to inject Christian ideas of justice and mercy into

FIGURE 15.2   Pope Gregory the Great   Gregory was one of the most influential figures of the formative period of medieval western European society. His varied activities as bishop of Rome put an important imprint on the office of the papacy as the leader of the Christian community in the West. Throughout the Middle Ages his successors looked back to his career as a model of Christian leadership and as a precedent for their actions. (Alinari/Art Resource)

the harsh law codes of the era. Each time the Church intervened in these matters, its prestige as a social agency and its influence over the social order increased.

A third significant development involved the Church's attack on weaknesses within its own body—corruptness and worldliness of the clergy, moral laxness, ignorance of religious precepts, and lack of discipline. Two agencies were especially important in shaping a thrust toward "reform": the papacy and the monastic establishment.

Prior to 500 the papacy had utilized the Petrine theory (see Chapter 12) to establish a strong position as guardians of true doctrine and right practice. That position was reinforced during the troubled fifth century. With the collapse of the Roman imperial government, the bishops of Rome assumed a larger role in governing the city of Rome, as was dramatically illustrated by the role played by Pope Leo I (440–461) in protecting St. Peter's city from the Huns and the Vandals. Leo I was also a fierce defender of the papal right to define orthodox doctrine, especially against the claims of the emperors and the patriarchs of Constantinople. The expanding sense of papal authority was reflected by Pope Gelasius I (492–496) in his "theory of the two swords." He argued that religious and secular power represented two separate realms of authority, each established by God to achieve different aspects of the divine plan and each independent in its own sphere. However, Gelasius maintained, whenever the two powers clashed, the spiritual sword must prevail.

However, many factors limited the ability of the popes to exert their claimed authority. The Arian Ostrogoths who ruled Italy from 493 to 554 were little inclined to respect papal authority. When Justinian reincorporated Rome into the Byzantine Empire, he treated its bishop as one of his religious agents whose authority was no greater than that of the patriarch of Constantinople. The installation of the hostile, aggressive Arian Lombards as rulers of northern Italy after 568 left the popes with no choice but to accept Byzantine protection and to acquiesce to imperial religious policy as defined by the emperor. Finally, papal influence over the Germanic West was disrupted by the control exercised by the newly established Germanic kings over the religious establishment in their realms.

The recovery of the papacy was charted by Pope Gregory I, the Great (590–604) (see Figure 15.2). A well-educated descendant of a noble Roman family, Gregory began his career in public service, ascending to the highest office in the city of Rome, but he soon abandoned the world to become a monk. He was called from monastic life to serve as a papal diplomat in Constantinople, and then he was elected bishop of Rome in 590.

Convinced that the papacy must command material resources to survive in the troubled Italian scene, Gregory spent considerable energy in the management of the patrimony of St. Peter—

that is, the property belonging to the papacy in Italy. He used the large income derived from this property chiefly to expand papal control over Rome, often with little consideration of the officials of the emperor in Constantinople who claimed legal authority to rule the Eternal City. His increasingly powerful position in Rome allowed him to play the Lombards against the Byzantines in a way that not only prevented Lombard conquest of Rome but also undermined Byzantine power in the city. This effort marked an important step in laying the groundwork for a future papal state in Italy.

But Gregory was more than a hard-headed administrator and a wily diplomat. He never forgot the pastoral responsibilities that tradition assigned to the successor of St. Peter. In this capacity he took significant steps toward reshaping the Christian message to fit the unique needs of the Germanic West and toward drawing the western Christian community to Rome for spiritual guidance. He wrote important books on theology and ecclesiastical administration that circulated widely to guide clergymen in explaining the faith and shaping the moral lives of their flocks. His powerful sermons became models for preaching as a means of improving spiritual life. He sought to provide a model of liturgical practice useful in all churches; tradition credited him with a role in developing Gregorian chant as an element of the liturgy. He wrote innumerable letters to kings and clergymen throughout the West, offering them advice on religious matters and reminding them of Rome's authority in the religious sphere. His influence was crucial in converting the Lombards and the Visigoths from Arianism to orthodoxy, thus ending a major cause of religious division in the West. He initiated the missionary effort that played a major role in converting the Anglo-Saxons of England and guided the religious organization of the new converts in a way that subordinated them to Roman authority. In short, Gregory enlarged the role of the papacy in the religious life in the West and began to direct papal efforts toward helping to resolve the particular religious problems of the Germanic West. Although Gregory's immediate successors advanced his program only slowly, the Gregorian model of papal leadership would serve for centuries as a major element in shaping religious life in the West.

A second major force in regenerating religious life in the West came from the monasteries. Monasticism had been imported from the East in the fourth century and had generated an enthusiastic response. But on the whole, early western monasticism failed to sustain its initial vitality, perhaps because it was too imitative of eastern models to address the unique conditions in the West. The West needed its own style of monastic life. Although many spiritual leaders were involved in shaping western monastic practice, two forms were especially influential.

One developed in Ireland, where the severe ascetic practices of the East took deep hold as the standard for monastic life. However, Irish monastic life became thoroughly enmeshed in Irish tribal life and became a decisive force in shaping Christian practice. This situation caused monks to be involved deeply in popular religious life. An example of this engagement was the unique system of penance developed in Irish monastic circles, involving private confession and the use of penitential books that cataloged sins and instructed confessors on the appropriate punishment for each. Irish monasticism placed a strong emphasis on learning as a dimension of piety. As a consequence, monasteries became active centers of education and of the study of sacred literature. Finally, Irish monasteries were incubators of a powerful missionary movement. During the sixth, seventh, and eighth centuries, Irish missionary monks spread over England and the Continent, bringing with them deep piety, skill in uplifting the level of religious life, and great learning.

Another powerful form of monastic life was introduced by Benedict of Nursia (ca. 480–543). Like Gregory I, he was an Italian of noble origin who abandoned the world to follow monastic life. After experimenting with the hermit life, he eventually founded a monastic community at Monte Cassino and formulated a rule to guide the lives of its members. The *Benedictine rule*, combining features from several earlier rules, emphasized that a community of dedicated individuals could serve God and each other better than could the individual hermit isolated from interactions with other humans. However, a "school for the service of God" must be made up of selected individuals willing to make a commitment to perfection. After a rigorous testing period, each new member was required to take vows to renounce all personal wealth, to remain chaste, to obey his superiors, and to remain permanently in the community he entered. The rule entrusted absolute authority over the community to an *abbot* who was responsible before God to direct each monk toward holiness; thus discipline was a key feature of a Benedictine community. A major aspect of the rule was its provision for orderly daily routine for all members of the community, consisting of specified periods of prayer, manual labor, and contemplation and reading (see Figure 15.1). This regimen ensured that the community would be self-sufficient economically and that its members would be engaged in varied activities rather than in endless ascetic practices aimed at suppressing the urges of the body and awareness of the world.

Although Benedict had no intention of devising a rule for all monasteries, his rule—given powerful endorsement by Gregory I in his popular biography of Benedict—was adopted by both male and female communities across western Europe. By 750 monastic houses, especially Benedictine and Irish houses, were asserting a powerful influence in society. Monks and nuns were the new holy people, "athletes of Christ" serving as models of piety and moral excellence for all elements of society. They were able to teach bewildered Christians the basic elements of the faith and the proper way to perform Christian worship. They were the chief preservers and transmitters of learning. They performed numerous acts of charity and goaded the rich and the powerful to emulate them. As a result of their disciplined labors in the service of God, monks carved new estates out of Europe's wilderness and made them the best-managed economic institutions in the West, from which all could learn about farm management and artisanry. They formed a bulwark against both the devil and barbarism, well worthy of emulation.

4. CULTURAL LIFE

Although the chaotic conditions prevailing in the Germanic West from 500 to 750 were hardly con-ducive to cultural activity, certain developments were significant in shaping a new culture. The chief accomplishment was the preservation of significant elements of classical and patristic literature and learning in Latin (the use of Greek virtually disappeared in the West). During the sixth century both secular society and the Church played a role in this enterprise. In Italy, Gaul, and Spain both lay aristocrats and bishops of Roman descent continued to read classical and patristic Latin authors, wrote works imitating them, and supported schools where the young could study rhetoric and grammar. Germanic courts, especially that of the Ostrogoth Theoderic, actively patronized learning and art. A luminary of Theoderic's court, Boethius (ca. 475–525), set out to translate the works of Aristotle and Plato into Latin. His famous *Consolation of Philosophy*, written while he was in prison awaiting execution for alleged treason, was a moving defense of philosophy as a guide to inner peace and happiness. Another of Theoderic's officials, Cassiodorus (ca. 490–583), left the court to found a monastery that became famous for its library of classical and patristic works.

Before the end of the sixth century, secular society ceased to play a role in sustaining cultural life; the burden fell to the Church, especially the monasteries. Irish and Benedictine monasteries established schools to teach new members to read and write, encouraged the copying of the works of classical and patristic authors, and promoted the writing of commentaries on old texts to make them understandable. Especially active in these enterprises were the Benedictine monasteries of England, where Irish and continental influences merged to generate an important outburst of literary and scholarly activity. Monastic intellectual life placed an especially strong emphasis on mastery of Scripture as the prime source of wisdom. The concerns of monks tended to be narrow, governed by a passion to know God, to understand his revealed word, and to pray well. Thus, the monks were selective in their approach to the classical tradition. And they felt no compunction about turning the classical heritage to Christian purposes, sometimes distorting classical thought almost beyond recognition.

A few figures were able to transcend mere

preservation to produce works that revealed creative talent. One was Boethius. Another was a Visigothic bishop, Isidore of Seville (ca. 560–636), whose *Etymologies* consisted of a collection of information about many subjects derived from ancient sources that encouraged the systematic organization of knowledge. Gregory the Great's writings set forth basic theological concepts in simpler terms more suited to the intellectual capabilities of his age than were the sophisticated works of the Latin fathers from whom he borrowed most of his ideas. Especially important in shaping western European intellectual life was Gregory's mode of interpreting Scripture, which sought to discover the hidden meaning behind the literal words of the Bible. A Frankish bishop, Gregory of Tours (ca. 538–594), in his *History of the Franks*, demonstrated skill at compiling historical material. The most outstanding intellectual figure of the age was the English monk Bede (673–735), whose theological, historical, and biographical writings set high standards of learning and style. His *Ecclesiastical History of the English People* is one of the best pieces of history written during the entire Middle Ages. The age was rich in saints' lives, written to celebrate the feats of holy men and women who had surrendered themselves to the service of God.

As a few struggled to preserve education and learning, the lay world sank into illiteracy. Such people were not without culture, as is evidenced by the magnificent epic entitled *Beowulf*, which is a written version in the Anglo-Saxon language of an oral tradition concerning the heroic struggles of warriors against the forces of evil. The illiteracy of the laity created a situation of immense importance for western European cultural history: The languages men and women spoke in their daily lives were different from the language of learning and literature. For centuries learning would remain the monopoly of an elite especially trained to use Latin, the language of the Church. Under such circumstances, it remained a constant challenge to prevent the world of learning from becoming remote from and irrelevant to the realities of life.

The art of the early Middle Ages reflects a mixture of old and new. Greco-Roman forms and themes persisted in architecture, sculpture, and

FIGURE 15.3 Two Thieves Awaiting the Crucifixion This sculpture from the mausoleum of a seventh-century abbot from the Frankish city of Poitiers shows two unhappy thieves bound to crosses while awaiting their end with Christ. While classical art styles persist (e.g., the representation of a building), the portrayal of the human figures indicates that new influences were penetrating artistic expression in the German-dominated world. (Marburg/Art Resource)

painting, but they were constantly modified to serve Christian ends. Many of the churches of the era followed the basilica plan characteristic of Roman structures. However, Byzantine architectural forms, shaped by Justinian's building program, asserted a strong influence on sixth-century Italy, especially in Ravenna (see Figure 13.2), and persisted there to affect building styles in other areas of the West. In sculpture and painting, classical and Byzantine influences merged to create a pictorial art emphasizing symbolical representation of religious motifs (see Figures 12.1 and 15.3). Germanic and Celtic influences asserted their effect on the pictorial arts, especially their decorative style, which used animal and geometric forms to create abstract designs. The vigor of this composite early medieval art is especially evident in designs created to illustrate handwritten manuscripts; prime examples include the Irish Book of Durrow (late seventh century), the English Lindisfarne Gospels (eighth century), and the Irish Book of Kells (early ninth century) (see Color Plate 8). Artistic expression especially emphasized the symbolic representation of religious values at the expense of realistic portrayal of humans and the world of nature.

By 750 the Germanic West had by no means emerged from the time of troubles that followed the collapse of the Roman imperial regime. Habits of violence, ignorance, poverty, and moral laxness had been ingrained into people's lives and would long affect the western European world. However, out of the experiences of the early Middle Ages had emerged innovative institutions and patterns of life: a form of limited monarchy, a new nobility, a stabilized peasantry, an involved Church, the papacy, monasticism, a store of Greco-Roman literature and learning, a new art style. Their potential had not yet been realized, but their existence pointed toward the survival of a vigorous civilization in the West that might in the future equal the level of civilized life already flourishing in the Byzantine and Moslem worlds.

SUGGESTED READING

Political, Economic, and Social History

J. M. Wallace-Hadrill, *The Barbarian West, 400–1000*, 3rd ed. rev. (1967). An excellent general survey.

Henri Pirenne, *Mohammed and Charlemagne*, trans. Bernard Maill (1939). A classic expounding the thesis that only the Islamic invasions of the eighth century brought a break with the classical world.

Edward James, *The Origins of France: From Clovis to the Capetians, 500–1000* (1982).

Katharine Scherman, *The Birth of France: Warriors, Bishops, and Long-Haired Kings* (1987).

Chris Wickham, *Early Medieval Italy: Central Power and Local Society, 400–1000* (1981).

Roger Collins, *Early Medieval Spain: Unity in Diversity, 400–1000* (1983).

These four titles provide excellent treatments of the major continental Germanic kingdoms of the early Middle Ages.

Georges Duby, *The Early Growth of the European Economy. Warriors and Peasants from the Seventh to the Twelfth Century*, trans. Howard B. Clarke (1974).

Renée Doehaerd, *The Early Middle Ages in the West: Economy and Society*, trans. W. G. Deakin (1978).

Two comprehensive treatments of economic and social history.

Richard Hodges, *Dark Age Economies. The Origins of Towns and Trade A.D. 600–1000* (1982). Uses archaeological evidence to revise current opinions about the low level of trade and urban life.

Philippe Ariès and Georges Duby, *A History of Private Life*, Vol. 1: *From Pagan Rome to Byzantium*, ed. Paul Veyne, trans. Arthur Goldhammer (1987). The appropriate chapter in this study is rich in details about social life.

Suzanne Fonay Wemple, *Women in Frankish Society: Marriage and the Cloister, 500 to 900* (1981). A balanced treatment.

Religious and Cultural History

Hubert Jedin and John Dolan, *Handbook of Church History*, Vol. 2: *The Imperial Church to the Early Middle Ages*, trans. Anselm Biggs (1980). A detailed history of all aspects of religious life.

Judith Herrin, *The Formation of Christendom* (1987). Stresses religion as a prime force in shaping the new civilizations of the early Middle Ages.

J. M. Wallace-Hadrill, *The Frankish Church* (1983). A topical approach, rich in interpretations.

Jeffrey Richards, *The Popes and the Papacy in the Early Middle Ages, 476–752* (1979). An excellent treatment.

Pierre Riché, *Education and Culture in the Barbarian West: Sixth through Eighth Century*, trans. John J. Contreni (1976). A work rich in insights into the nature of early medieval culture.

Ludwig Bieler, *Ireland: Harbinger of the Middle Ages* (1963). A brilliant treatment of Ireland's contribution to cultural life.

J. Hubert et al., *Europe of the Invasions*, trans. Stuart Gilbert and James Emmons (1969). An excellent treatment of artistic development during the early Middle Ages.

Sources

Rule of Monasteries, trans. L. J. Boyle (1949). St. Benedict's rule.

Gregory of Tours, *The History of the Franks*, trans. Lewis Thorpe.

Bede, *The History of the English Church and People*, rev. ed., trans. L. Sherley-Price (1968).

Beowulf, trans. D. Wright (1957).

All of these works illustrate various facets of intellectual activity in the early medieval West.

CHAPTER 16

The First Revival of Europe: The Carolingian Age, 750–900

FIGURE 16.1 **Dispensing Justice in the Carolingian Age** This drawing from a ninth-century manuscript shows Emperor Charlemagne and his son, Pepin, king of Italy, presiding over a court of law while a clerk is ready to record their judgment. Concern for justice was an important aspect of the Carolingian effort to provide better government. (Modena Cathedral Archives)

The slow, troubled struggle to create a new basis for society in the Germanic West suddenly quickened in the eighth century. Between about 750 and 900 a narrow but energetic segment of society, spearheaded by kings and clergy, devoted their talents to an effort to "renew" society both on the Continent and in England. Although their ambitions were by no means realized, their limited success had two important results: It made the West visible in the larger world as a coherent culture. And it gave the West an expanded awareness of its unique identity. In a sense, this renewal created the first "Europe."

1. THE RISE OF THE CAROLINGIANS

The central force promoting revival on the Continent was a new Frankish royal dynasty, the Carolingians, so named after its most famous king, Carolus, or Charles. The Carolingians originated as one of the many ambitious noble families whose power and wealth grew steadily under the Merovingians. In the middle of the seventh century, the family utilized its extensive landed possessions and its connections with the Church to gain hereditary control over the office of mayor of the palace in the subkingdom of Austrasia, where the family wealth was concentrated (see Map. 16.1). This key office allowed the family to control the weak Merovingian kings of Austrasia and to utilize royal lands to increase its wealth and its circle of dependents. As their power expanded, the Carolingians sought to extend their influence to the other Merovingian subkingdoms—Neustria and Burgundy. That effort culminated in 687, when Pepin of Herstal, the Carolingian mayor of the palace of Austrasia, defeated the Neustrian mayor and claimed the mayoralty of the entire Frankish realm.

Once established as sole mayor of the palace, Pepin of Herstal and his son and grandson, Charles Martel (714–741) and Pepin the Short (741–751), became the most powerful men in the Frankish state, far overshadowing the "do-nothing" Merovingian kings whom they served. Their efforts were aimed chiefly at checking the forces of disintegration within the kingdom and defending its frontiers. Charles Martel gained undying fame by defeating a Moslem army at the battle of Tours in 733. Their military success was due in part to their ability to take advantage of a significant military innovation that began to spread in the eighth century: the heavily armored mounted warrior. This innovation was perhaps made possible by the invention of the stirrup, which permitted a mounted warrior to keep his mount while striking or receiving blows from sword or spear. The equipping and support of a force of mounted warriors involved costs beyond the means of the impoverished royal government; increasingly it was necessary to rely on men of wealth willing to arm themselves at their own expense. Charles Martel and Pepin rewarded such service by grants of land, called *benefices*, the income from which the recipients used on the condition that they would provide military service at their own expense. Although some of these benefices were derived from royal lands, Charles Martel and Pepin made a regular practice of utilizing Church lands to provide military benefices.

Although condemned by some clergymen as pillagers of the Church, Charles Martel and Pepin courted and won ecclesiastical support vital to their growing power. Their support of missionary activity and of religious reform was particularly welcome among bishops and monks. A key figure in shaping their religious policy was Boniface, an Anglo-Saxon Benedictine monk who came to the Continent in 719 to convert the pagans living beyond the eastern frontier of the kingdom. Until his martyrdom in 755 by pagan Frisians, Boniface not only won many converts but also organized bishoprics and monasteries in newly converted territories and guided the mayors of the palace in shaping a program to reform Frankish religious life. Soon after his arrival in Francia, Boniface sought and received the blessing of the papacy for his varied activities. As a result, papal influence expanded among the Franks and the mayors of the palace gained increasing recognition as supporters of the successors of St. Peter.

Although the Carolingian mayors of the palace clearly exercised control over the Frankish kingdom, they remained legally agents of the powerless Merovingian kings. Finally, Pepin took the logical step to end this incongruous situation by

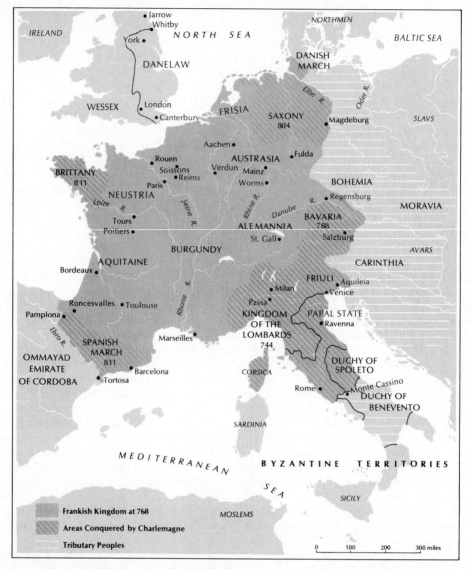

Map 16.1 **THE EMPIRE OF CHARLEMAGNE** One of Charlemagne's great achievements was his military victories, which greatly expanded the Frankish kingdom. This map shows his major conquests. The extent of his holdings indicates that he came close to dominating western Europe, an ambition that would spark the dreams of many later western European rulers. Not long after Charlemagne's death his empire would suffer savage attacks on all its frontiers and would be divided by his heirs.

transferring the crown to his own family. Concerned about the potential hostility that might arise among the Franks by a forced deposition of the ancient dynasty whose sacred blood was held in deep respect, Pepin sought to sanction his action in an unprecedented way. He sent an envoy to Rome to ask Pope Zachary whether the "right ordering of things" did not demand that he who held actual power should wear the crown. On the basis of the pope's affirmative answer, Pepin in 751 deposed the reigning Merovingian and had himself elected king by the Frankish nobles. On the occasion of his coronation, a clergyman (perhaps Boniface) gave him a special anointment never before bestowed on a Frankish king. This sequence of events indicated to many that Pepin's royal office was different from that held by his Merovingian predecessors. Although duly elected by the Franks according to Germanic tradition, papal consent to the dynastic change and anointment by the Church made Pepin an agent of God charged with caring for the material and spiritual needs of the Christian community according to God's will.

Although the bonds between the papacy and the Carolingians had been growing before 751, the papacy was especially anxious to strengthen them at that moment because of significant changes in Italy. Since Justinian's reconquest of Italy, Rome had been under the jurisdiction of the emperor in Constantinople, and the popes had relied—sometimes reluctantly—on imperial protection. During the first half of the eighth century, however, the Moslem assault on Byzantium left the emperors increasingly unable to defend their position in Italy. Moreover, the iconoclastic policy of emperors Leo III and Constantine V was condemned as heretical by Pope Gregory II and his successors. Leo III retaliated by transferring important territories from the ecclesiastical jurisdiction of the pope to that of the patriarch of Constantinople. The decline of Byzantine power in Italy encouraged its longtime rival, the Lombards, to expand their sphere of influence. Beginning early in the eighth century a succession of able Lombard kings undertook military campaigns that increasingly threatened to engulf Rome and to impose a new master on the papacy. Bereft of help from the Byzantine emperors, now both weak and heretical, the popes desperately needed a new protector.

In the face of the mounting Lombard threat, Pope Stephen II (752–757) undertook a journey to Pepin's kingdom in 754, perhaps emboldened by the fact that his predecessor had extended an important favor to the new king. After long negotiations and despite resistance by some Frankish nobles, an agreement was reached. The king agreed to protect the pope from the Lombards. In return, the pope personally reanointed Pepin as king of the Franks and bestowed on him the somewhat ambiguous title of "*patricius* of the Romans," implying Pepin's role as protector of the people of Rome, including the papacy. Pepin undertook campaigns into Italy in 754 and 756 and forced the Lombards to surrender territories in central Italy that they had recently annexed. In a grant known as the Donation of Pepin, he bestowed these lands on the papacy, despite the fact that they legally belonged to the Byzantine emperor. This grant became the basis for the papacy's claim to an independent papal state. During his negotiations with Pepin, Stephen may have persuaded the Frank of the legality of disposing lands that belonged to the emperor by confronting him with a document known as the Donation of Constantine. This document, later proved to be a forgery, claimed to date from the time of Constantine and stated that the first Christian emperor, out of gratitude for being cured of leprosy, had granted Pope Sylvester I (314–335) the rights to the western empire, especially Rome and Italy. Pepin's Donation was therefore only a confirmation of an earlier legal grant made by a universally renowned ruler whose mantle the contemporary emperor in Constantinople had inherited.

2. THE REIGN OF CHARLEMAGNE, 768–814

The foundations established by Pepin of Herstal, Charles Martel, and Pepin the Short were brilliantly exploited by Charlemagne. In the eyes of his contemporaries he possessed many qualities of greatness: imposing physical stature, prowess as a warrior, piety, generosity, intelligence, devotion to family and friends, joy for life. His actions made him a hero not only in his own time but for many future generations of Europeans.

As befitted a Frankish king, Charlemagne was above all else a successful warlord. Few years passed throughout his long reign without a military campaign; the cumulative result was a considerable expansion of his kingdom (see Map 16.1). His most severe test came from the pagan Saxons along the northeastern frontier of his kingdom; only after many campaigns extending over thirty years was he able to conquer and convert them. The northeast frontier was also advanced by the conquest of Frisia. In 774 he crushed the troublesome Lombards, assumed the title of king of the Lombards, and laid claim to all of Italy except the Byzantine territories in the south and the Papal State, over which he continued the protectorship assumed by Pepin. His armies drove down the Danube and annexed territories held by the Avars and Slavs. His attack on Moslem Spain resulted initially in a defeat at Roncesvalles, later immortalized in an epic poem called *The Song of Roland*. But persistent pressure in that direction led to the creation of the Spanish March, south of the Pyrenees. Frankish military might also curbed the separatist aspirations of the people of Aquitaine, Bavaria, and Brittany. Beyond the new frontiers established by conquest, and especially in central Europe, southern Italy, and Denmark, Charlemagne combined force and diplomacy to compel various peoples into a tributary status requiring respect for Frankish territory and Frankish interests.

A tribute to Charlemagne's skill as a military organizer, these victories yielded a rich harvest of booty, which Charlemagne dispersed liberally to sustain the services and the allegiance of the warriors who fought the many battles and to win the favor of nobles and church officials upon whose support royal power depended. But Charlemagne succeeded in surrounding his military ventures with an aura transcending mere material considerations. They were struggles against barbarians, pagans, and infidels, fought to save the Christian world and to win converts for the true religion. For his efforts he won the plaudits of popes, poets, and nobles, who hailed him as "the strong right arm of God."

Charlemagne's military successes were accompanied by a strenuous effort to improve the quality of government within his growing realm by expanding royal power. Charlemagne's concept of kingship was rooted firmly in the Germanic concept of the *bannum*, which entitled a ruler to command his subjects to serve him and to punish those who disobeyed. That Germanic basis of royal authority was elevated and enriched by ideas drawn from Christian concepts of royal authority and responsibility and of the public well-being. The Christian view of the state, rooted in Old Testament precedents and especially in Augustine's *City of God*, which was Charlemagne's favorite book, envisioned the state as a society of Christians linked together by a common faith for the purpose of realizing God's plan for humanity, including the salvation of each individual soul. To achieve that end, society must strive for right order, harmony, and justice, each defined in Christian terms. The key to achieving the good Christian society was the king. Like David, the Christian king was God's agent who, by his anointment to office, was charged with commanding his subjects to do good and with restraining them from evil. He was, in effect, God's minister in the cause of righteousness. This concept of royal power, sometimes called ministerial kingship, provided norms for defining governmental action and political behavior that were much broader than had prevailed in the Frankish state during the Merovingian period.

In applying his expanded concept of royal authority and public responsibility, Charlemagne retained the basic political structures inherited from the Merovingians. What especially marked his reign was his own vigorous action aimed at making those structures work more effectively to realize Christian right order. He was a tireless worker, traveling constantly across his realm, checking incessantly on the performance of his officials, administering justice (see Figure 16.1), and consulting frequently with those upon whom he depended to sustain political order. At the heart of his government was the royal court (called the *palatium*), made up of trusted clergy and lay nobles. Each member of the court was assigned a political function as practical needs demanded: guarding the royal treasury, judging cases, keeping records, conducting diplomatic ventures, commanding armies, providing for the material needs of the royal family. Collectively, the court circle advised the king in shaping policies. The royal court was supported chiefly by the products of extensive royal lands; additional support, never very predictable, came from war booty, tolls on trade, fines, and gifts offered the king in return for favors. The court moved constantly, chiefly to expedite military campaigns and to gain access to the produce from royal estates. Only near the end of his reign did Charlemagne establish a semipermanent residence at Aachen.

To assert his authority on the local level, Charlemagne relied on the traditional system of counties, of which there were about three hundred. In each county the king was represented by a count who administered justice, enforced order, and mustered the freemen of the county to military service. The counts were rewarded by grants of land from which they could derive income as long as they held office. The counts were served by a small group of subofficials, most concerned with administering justice. Bishops and abbots were also assigned important responsibilities in local affairs. Charlemagne tried hard to select capable men for these offices and to supervise their activities. He developed a system of sending out special agents, called *missi,* to investigate what was going on, to instruct local officials on what the king expected, and to report back to the court on local conditions. He issued a constant stream of royal orders (called *capitularies*) to inform local officials of royal intent and to direct their actions on a wide range of matters relating to public order. Almost every year, Charlemagne also called his officials and other great men of the realm to his court to an assembly where he heard their concerns and proclaimed new regulations designed to govern their actions.

The operation of this modest political apparatus, involving only a few thousand officials, depended heavily on the loyalty not only of royal officials but also of all of the king's subjects, especially the great magnates. Charlemagne was constantly concerned with expanding the bonds of loyalty. His own feats as a warrior played an important role in this respect. On several occasions he required all of his free subjects to swear an oath of fidelity, binding them to refrain from activities contrary to public order. He regularly

bestowed gifts, derived chiefly from war booty, on those whose loyalty he especially prized. Most important of all, he greatly expanded the use of commendation and benefices to bind royal officials, nobles, and churchmen to him. Those who were willing to commend themselves under oath to become his vassals were granted benefices, usually in the form of land grants or offices, to be enjoyed as long as the recipients served him faithfully. Unfaithfulness to these oaths was considered a major offense.

As is shown by his capitularies, Charlemagne's prime concern was the curbing of violence and of oppression. From his perspective as a Christian king with a God-given responsibility to sustain the Church in its mission of saving souls, religious life was a prime factor in sustaining concord and justice. As a consequence, a major part of his political program focused on religious reform. Expanding on the program begun by his predecessors, he sought vigorously to revitalize religious life. He encouraged the spread of Christianity by supporting missionary activity, even using force to compel reluctant pagans, such as the Saxons, to receive baptism. He strengthened church organization by reestablishing the authority of bishops and subordinating parish priests to them. He sought to improve the quality of the clergy by imposing higher moral and educational standards on those who assumed ecclesiastical office. Monastic establishments were encouraged to adopt the Benedictine rule as a means of upgrading discipline and spiritual life. Royal authority was used to protect ecclesiastical property and to provide material support for the religious establishment; especially important was the imposition of a tax of 10 percent of income, called the tithe, on all Christians for the support of the Church. Charlemagne made a major effort to establish uniform doctrines and ritual practices as a way of eliminating the diverse practices and bizarre beliefs that passed as Christianity. In formulating and enacting his religious program, Charlemagne relied heavily on guidance from the papacy; especially close was his relationship with Pope Hadrian I (772–795). As a result, a distinct Roman stamp was imposed on religious life in his realm. Charlemagne must be counted as a major architect of the Roman Catholic church and as a major force in enhancing the authority of the papacy in the West.

All of these achievements pointed toward the culminating event of Charlemagne's career: his coronation as emperor. The stage was set for this event when serious disturbances in Rome in 799 led to charges of misconduct against Pope Leo III (795–816), who was forced to flee to Charlemagne's court. In his role as protector of the pope and the Romans, Charlemagne went to Rome in 800 and acted directly to exonerate the pope and restore him to full authority. Then on Christmas Day in the year 800, while the king was attending Mass in St. Peter's Basilica, the pope placed a crown on his head, and the clergy and people in attendance hailed the king of the Franks as "Augustus, crowned by God, the great and peace-bringing Emperor of the Romans." For the first time since 476 a ruler from the West was emperor.

Since that momentous occasion there has been a debate about who instigated the renewal of the imperial office and what it signified. Perhaps responsibility for the event was shared by the pope, Charlemagne, and his advisers as a means of realizing different aspirations. For Leo III the bestowal of the crown certainly enhanced papal prestige. For Charlemagne the new title was a suitable recognition for his accomplishments as conqueror and protector of the Christian world. Some of Charlemagne's ecclesiastical advisers felt that such a title would enhance their ruler's authority to the point where he could play the role of a new David and a new Constantine in promoting Christian unity. Almost everyone in the West shared the opinion that the emperors in the East had failed to serve the Christian cause, especially in view of the fact that a woman, Empress Irene, held the crown at the moment. It is probably also true that the imperial title meant different things to different people. The Byzantine rulers saw it as an outrageous usurpation. The popes, at least in the long run, interpreted the event as a precedent for their right to designate the ruler of the Christian world. For many church leaders the event was a signal to intensify the effort to create the ideal Christian commonwealth.

What Charlemagne thought of his new title is likewise an enigma. He ruled as emperor for fourteen years. Some of his actions suggest that he took the title seriously. He conducted a skillful military and diplomatic campaign that finally compelled the Byzantine emperor to recognize him as emperor. He pursued with renewed vigor his religious reforms, suggesting his responsiveness to the political Augustinianism of those advisers who had encouraged him to become emperor. However, he disdained the trappings of the imperial office, and he insisted on being called king of the Franks. Contrary to all that the imperial title implied about the unity of his realm, he made plans to divide his empire in order to provide a "kingdom" for each of his three sons; such a division was avoided only because a single son, Louis, outlived him. In 813 Charlemagne personally crowned Louis as emperor without papal involvement. These actions suggest that Charlemagne viewed the imperial title as a personal honor that he had earned by his achievements and that he could dispose of as he pleased. Whatever the case, the event of 800, which translated an ancient title rich in political symbolism into a Germanic and Christian context, was of major significance in creating a western European political consciousness.

3. THE CAROLINGIAN CULTURAL RENAISSANCE

Perhaps the most lasting achievement of the Carolingian Age was a cultural renaissance that owed much to the personal interest and effort of the indefatigable Charlemagne. This revival was based on pragmatic motives. Charlemagne was convinced that political and religious renewal could be achieved only through the efforts of better-educated leaders, especially the clergy. Practical though it was, that was a radical idea in a society that had almost lost sight of the connection between learning and public order.

A major factor in generating cultural revival was Charlemagne's ability to utilize the leadership and talent produced by modest cultural revivals that had occurred earlier in several parts of the West—in Italy, Spain, Ireland, and especially England. The setting for the interaction of these leaders was what has been called the palace "school" that the king began to form in the 780s and that took on special vigor in the 790s after Aachen was established as the permanent royal residence. To this somewhat informal circle, often with Charlemagne's personal encouragement, came some of the most learned individuals from all Europe. The palace school served as a highly visible setting where individuals of varying cultural perspectives met to study, write, and reflect on intellectual issues. Because Charlemagne himself was an active and enthusiastic participant, the palace school became a visible symbol of the dedication of his regime to revitalizing cultural life; some even spoke grandly of Aachen as the "new Athens."

More significantly, the palace school became a kind of laboratory, generating ideas and techniques out of which emerged an education system crucial to the Carolingian renaissance. A key figure in shaping this education program was Alcuin (735–804), an English monk reared in the monastic cultural environment that produced Bede and Boniface. Alcuin served at the royal court from 782 to 796 and then became abbot of an important monastery at Tours, where he continued to assert leadership in cultural life until his death in 804. His concepts of education decisively shaped the thinking and the practices not only of his own generation but also of cultural leaders across the entire ninth century and even beyond.

Alcuin, and with him most Carolingian cultural figures, saw education as preparation for understanding the holy literature that contained God's message: the Bible, the writings of the church fathers, the liturgical books, saints' lives. To comprehend the message of salvation contained in the written texts, people must learn Latin. And they must acquire a body of knowledge and intellectual skills that would allow them to grasp the meaning of the holy texts. These educational objectives could best be achieved by organizing education around the old Roman system of the seven liberal arts, which consisted of two basic groupings of "disciplines": the *trivium,* embracing grammar, rhetoric, and dialectic (logic); and the *quadrivium,* comprising arithmetic, geometry, astronomy, and music.

The realization of these educational goals confronted Carolingian leaders with major challenges. They needed to provide textbooks for each of the seven arts, but especially for the *trivium,* which emphasized language study, effective writing, and logical thinking. The material for such textbooks was to be drawn from classical Latin literature, but textbook compilers had to adapt such material to Christian purposes. Once learners had mastered the skills and knowledge embraced in the seven liberal arts, then they needed to apply their minds to the texts containing true wisdom. This objective raised the problem of the quality and the availability of books. A major effort was devoted to establishing authentic versions of Scripture, liturgical books, texts defining ecclesiastical and secular laws, writings of the Church Fathers, and even pagan Latin texts and Germanic legends. The establishment of authentic texts required linguistic skill, broad knowledge, and logical thought. Once scholars had established sound texts, then accurate copies had to be made. This need encouraged the development of workshops, called *scriptoria,* where book copying was systematically pursued; such work was particularly appropriate for Benedictine monks seeking to meet their obligation to serve God by working. Carolingian copyists, concerned with making reading easier, developed a simple but effective system of handwriting called Carolingian *minuscule,* which replaced the almost illegible Merovingian cursive writing with separately formed lowercase letters. The formation of libraries was also encouraged so that good texts would be widely available.

As the tools of education were forged, Charlemagne and his successors employed royal authority to universalize their use. Bishops and abbots were commanded to organize schools and to adopt authentic texts as a basis of teaching. This effort resulted in a significant increase in the number of schools and a heightened concern for the quality of teaching. Many bishops and abbots became active collectors of libraries and organizers of *scriptoria.* Although the palace school had declined in importance by the end of Charlemagne's reign, his successors remained active patrons of culture. However, during the ninth century cultural leadership passed to new centers, especially monastic schools, which effectively sustained the thrust of cultural revival even in the face of political decline.

Although Carolingian reform of education had only a limited impact on the massive illiteracy afflicting all levels of society, it did have significant consequences in shaping an environment more favorable to learning than had existed since late Roman imperial times. The concern with language instruction led to the development of a simplified, flexible version of Latin that became the standard means of literary expression over much of the West. The effort to establish authentic versions of a wide variety of texts created a substantial knowledge base on which a common intellectual life could be erected. That effort also reestablished contacts with the learning and literature of classical Rome and the patristic Church; almost all surviving classical Latin texts date from the Carolingian period. The capacity for clear thinking and effective writing was considerably improved. Taken together, these developments established the base from which a creative, independent western European intellectual and literary life would eventually develop.

A measure of the impact of the Carolingian renaissance can be found in the literary works produced by leading Carolingian writers and scholars. One court luminary and longtime confidant of Charlemagne, Einhard (ca. 770–840), produced an excellent biography of his master; many other writers tried their hands at biography, especially saints' lives. An Italian, Paul the Deacon (ca. 720–799), wrote a *History of the Lombards,* which reflected the capacity of Carolingian writers to produce historical works. Alcuin, Bishop Hincmar of Reims (ca. 806–882), and many others produced lively letters reflecting the major concerns of the age. Theodulf (ca. 750–821), a Spaniard, was but one among many who composed poetry. Several clerics, including Bishop Jonas of Orleans (ca. 780–843), composed books intended to guide princes, which reflect considerable sophistication in political thought. A succession of theologians prepared impressive commentaries on Scripture and compiled significant doctrinal tracts; especially notable as theologians were Hrabanus Maurus (ca. 780–856), abbot of Fulda, and John Scotus Erigena (ca. 810–877), an Irishman who lived in Francia from 850 to 875. Although most Carolingian scholarly work was derived from earlier works, it did reflect an ability to interpret tradition in terms applicable to contemporary issues.

The forces unleashed by the effort to renew Christian life and culture stimulated artistic activity. Carolingian art borrowed from diverse traditions: classical, Byzantine, Germanic, Celtic. The age produced several impressive churches; the most unique was the one built by Charlemagne at Aachen. That octagonal structure, strongly influenced by Byzantine churches in Ravenna, reflects an effort to make architecture a link between religion and the ideology of royalty. The mosaics and frescoes created to decorate churches and the miniature paintings used to illustrate manuscripts reflect skill in narrative art, especially in visually reconstructing episodes from sacred history. Carolingian artists produced fine ivory carvings, metalwork, and jewelry, much of which was employed for liturgical purposes. Underlying most Carolingian art was a powerful urge to deepen religious understanding and promote piety. In this respect, art shared the basic urge that generated and sustained the entire Carolingian renaissance.

4. THE DISINTEGRATION OF THE CAROLINGIAN EMPIRE

Charlemagne left a heavy burden for his successors. His son, Louis the Pious (814–840), continued his father's policies with some success. Although he concerned himself with good government and with defense of the empire, Louis' chief energies were aimed at realizing the universalist ideals embodied in Carolingian political ideology. This inclination led him to a close alliance with powerful churchmen, dedicated to the maintenance of unity, religious reform, and cultural renewal. His reign thus witnessed notable advances in religious reform, including the imposition of the Benedictine rule on the monastic establishment, clarification of the relationship between emperor and papacy, and an expanded role of the clergy in public life. But Louis' course, basically aimed at perfecting ministerial kingship, met resistance from powerful elements in society. The consequent tensions laid bare basic weaknesses in the Carolingian system.

The most disruptive problem in Louis' reign involved the question of succession. As we have already noted, ancient Frankish custom demanded that a ruler divide his realm among his surviving sons. The earlier Carolingians had not had to face that issue. Except for two instances which were quickly resolved, for five generations—from Pepin of Herstal's victory in 687 to Louis' accession in 814—there was only a single son to succeed to the headship of the state. But Louis did have to face the issue. His first instinct, expressed clearly in a document issued in 817, was to preserve the unity of the empire by entrusting it to his oldest son, with the younger heirs receiving minor subkingdoms subordinate to the emperor. But pressure from his younger sons and their supporters and from his second wife, Judith, intent on gaining a share of the realm for her son by Louis, gradually eroded Louis' resolve to maintain the unity of the empire. Eventually Louis agreed to provide a "kingdom" for each of his two younger sons; to the oldest, Lothair, he bequeathed the title of emperor with a vague authority over his younger brothers. Shortly after Louis' death the younger sons declared war on Emperor Lothair and in 843 forced him to sign the Treaty of Verdun. This document legalized the division of the empire into three parts: the kingdom of the West Franks (roughly modern France) to be ruled by Charles the Bald; the kingdom of the East Franks (roughly modern Germany) assigned to Louis the German; and the kingdom of Lotharingia (Lothair's realm), a narrow band lying between the West and East kingdoms and stretching from the North Sea to Italy (see Map 16.2). The Treaty of Verdun provided that the ruler of the Middle Kingdom would hold the imperial title, but his authority over the other kings was vague and ineffectual. Later in the ninth century Middle Kingdom was further divided to create three kingdoms: Italy, Burgundy, and Lotharingia. By this time succession to the imperial office became uncertain and open to competition.

The struggles surrounding the succession issue revealed another threat to imperial authority. Louis found many of his royal vassals ready to desert him and to align themselves with one or another of his sons in return for additional benefices. This situation revealed that Charlemagne's widespread use of vassalage and benefice to create bonds of loyalty to the ruler had its dangers. The granting of land to vassals began to erode the royal property, the basic source of support for government. Unless carefully controlled, the recipients of benefices used the grants of land to expand

Map 16.2 **PARTITION OF THE CAROLINGIAN EMPIRE, 843** This map shows the divisions of the unified Carolingian Empire arranged by the sons of Louis the Pious at the Treaty of Verdun in 843. The kingdom of Louis the German (the Kingdom of the East Franks) and the kingdom of Charles the Bald (Kingdom of the West Franks) became the bases from which Germany and France would evolve. Lothar I's kingdom was later divided into three small kingdoms, the most important of which was the Kingdom of Italy.

their independence without concern for the obligations they owed. Their growing power allowed them to demand new grants in return for service, thus creating a vicious cycle undermining royal authority and expanding the power of the landed nobility. From the end of Louis' reign onward this process accelerated at the expense of royal authority.

Still another problem began to plague the rulers: their inability to defend the Frankish realm against mounting attacks from external foes. From bases in North Africa came assaults by sea from aggressive Moslems, called Saracens, who ravaged the coasts of Italy and southern France. From the east the empire was attacked by new invaders from Asia, the Magyars or Hungarians, skilled at hit-and-run attacks by mounted warriors. Most formidable were the Vikings or Norsemen (Danes,

FIGURE 16.2   The Viking Terror   This representation of Viking ships filled with fierce warriors illustrates why they struck terror in those who witnessed the vessels approaching their undefended shores. One senses that the artist had witnessed such a scene. (Culver Pictures)

Swedes, and Norwegians). Still barbarians and pagans, the Vikings lived along the wild coasts of Scandinavia, surviving chiefly by fishing and piracy. Late in the eighth century, for reasons not entirely clear, they began to expand. Traveling by sea in small groups, they raided an immense area, touching Ireland, England, the Atlantic coast of Europe, the southern shores of the North and Baltic seas, Russia, Iceland, Greenland, and even North America (see Figure 16.2). Wherever they went, they pillaged for booty and struck terror in their victims. Gradually some of them began to settle permanently in the lands they had been raiding, especially in Ireland, northern England, Iceland, a region in northwestern France called Normandy after them, and in the area in Russia around Kiev. Slowly their piracy gave way to trade, and they adopted the religion and culture of western Europeans. But that was too late to spare the Carolingian Empire from the destructive fury of this last wave of Germanic invaders.

The Carolingian armies, organized primarily for attack warfare, were helpless against these highly mobile marauders. The only effective way to deal with them was to organize local defenses under local leaders willing to assume that responsibility and capable of acting on their own. By assuming this burden, nobles greatly expanded their control over local political affairs. From Louis the Pious onward, kings had no choice but to reward these individuals for their military role with additional grants of land and authority, a process that further undermined royal power.

After 843 each of the Carolingian kingdoms witnessed the steady decline of royal authority. The energies of their rulers were absorbed in petty quarrels aimed at snatching territory from one another. They had no choice but to continue seeking the support of the powerful in society by granting new lands and conceding political power. As a consequence, landed nobles tightened their control over local territories, creating increasing numbers of independent principalities and forcing the peasantry into dependence. Invaders continued to pillage western Europe almost at will. The most persistent defenders of royal power were churchmen, but in the long run even ecclesiastical support worked against the interests of the Carolingians. Constantly mindful of the important role Charlemagne had attributed to the Church in creating Christian order, later Carolingian churchmen became bolder and bolder in their claims to supremacy over the state. Frankish bishops repeatedly challenged royal authority and criticized royal conduct. By the middle of the ninth century the pope was openly claiming superior authority over all Christians, including kings and emperors. Pope Nicholas I (858–867) actually tried to assert such claims by interfering in the private lives of Carolingian kings, negotiating to halt civil strife, legislating for the entire Church in the West, taking the lead in spreading Christianity, and doing battle with Byzantine emperors and churchmen over dogma and jurisdiction—all activities that Charlemagne had claimed to control as ministerial king and emperor. And even while expressing lofty sentiments about their role as protectors of Christian order, high church officials joined lay nobles in increasing their landholdings and political powers over local affairs at the expense of the royal government.

By 900 the Carolingian rulers had been reduced to impotence. The dream of Charlemagne to make western Europe a single Christian state where concord and justice prevailed had foundered. However, this failure must not hide the deeper significance of the Carolingian era. The redefinition of the nature of the state and of the role of the Christian ruler, the religious reform, the cultural renaissance, the revival of empire, the expanded role defined for the papacy, and the expansion of personal bonds as an element of public order would all affect the future shape of western European society. Much of later medieval history consisted of working out concepts about civilized life developed in Carolingian times.

5. EARLY MEDIEVAL ENGLAND

While the Carolingians were attempting to renew society on the Continent, active rulers and their followers were pursuing comparable ends in England. The Anglo-Saxon invasions of England in the fifth century had virtually wiped out Roman civilization. Latin culture, including the language, was replaced by Germanic culture and religion. The newcomers established several small kingdoms whose political institutions were almost completely Germanic. From the fifth until the eighth century these kingdoms constantly warred with one another to create a condition almost as chaotic as that prevailing on the Continent between 500 and 750.

The introduction of Christianity into this divided society provided important impetus to the development of a common culture. Late in the sixth century missionaries from Ireland and from Rome came to England and within a century had converted most of the land. For a brief period in the seventh century, Roman and Irish forces clashed over the right to dominate England. The Roman forces won, chiefly because of support offered by Anglo-Saxon kings. This victory ensured uniformity in church organization, ritual, and doctrine and put England in touch with the mainstream of continental religious life. The encounter of Irish monasticism and Roman Benedictine monasticism generated a vigorous cultural revival in England, reaching its zenith in the age of Bede in the early eighth century. As already noted, that revival produced leaders, such as Boniface and Alcuin, who helped shape the Carolingian revival and who strengthened ties between England and the Carolingian world.

Beginning in the eighth century and continuing into the ninth century, England suffered devastating blows from the Vikings. Some of these raiders occupied a large area in northern England known as the Danelaw. The Viking raids also swallowed up several of the old Anglo-Saxon kingdoms. The kingdom of Wessex became the center of resistance and eventually of counterattack against the Vikings. The reign of Alfred the Great (871–899) was the decisive moment. He not only stopped Viking expansion but also laid the groundwork for the reconquest of the Danelaw. Under his leadership the Church and cultural life were revitalized. During the tenth century, Alfred's successors rewon the Danelaw and in the process created a unified kingdom for England.

The unification of England led to a single political system, heavily influenced by ancient Anglo-Saxon institutions. A king, claiming to be supreme judge, army leader, head of the Church, and lawgiver, ruled over the kingdom. Royal authority was supported by household officials who constituted the royal court. The king supported himself and his court chiefly from the income from royal estates. However, he could levy direct taxes on his subjects; for example, several kings collected the Danegeld, a tax levied first in 991 to buy off Viking raiders. The monarch retained the authority to summon all freemen to serve in the army (called the *fyrd*). He could also depend on the military services of his noble retainers, called *thegns*, whose support was won by grants of land. He was advised on matters of public interest by the *Witan*, an assembly of great nobles and churchmen that was held to represent all freemen. However, a strong king could act without this body's approval. This complex of institutions surrounding the king made the central government of England a major factor in public life, much more effective than was that of the late Carolingian monarchs.

A crucial factor in the political order was the system of local government that had developed over a long period. The kingdom was divided into territorial units called *shires*, of which there were about forty in the tenth century. In each shire the king's interests were represented by three officials—the *earl*, the *sheriff*, and the *bishop*. The earl was the most notable in rank and prestige, but the sheriff conducted most of the royal business. A court was held in each shire twice a year, and all free individuals were expected to attend. Royal orders were proclaimed and all civil and criminal cases were adjudicated at this court. The law administered was customary law, dating from far back in Anglo-Saxon history and "remembered" by the influential members of each shire. Each shire was subdivided into *hundreds*, where courts presided over by a royal official met monthly to settle minor cases; the hundreds also provided the basis for recruiting military forces for the *fyrd*. Agricultural villages also had their own courts, usually conducted by landowners. This network of local institutions, providing a means through which royal authority could be applied at the local level, acted as a buffer against the emergence of private political power and political fragmentation so characteristic of the Continent in the tenth century.

Although by the eleventh century the Anglo-Saxon political order began to falter, the pattern of institutions created in the ninth and tenth centuries provided a heritage that would play a major role in shaping a unique English constitutional system in the future.

SUGGESTED READING

The Carolingian World

Most of the works listed in Chapter 15 provide material on Carolingian history. The following titles treat special aspects.

Louis Halphen, *Charlemagne and the Carolingian Empire,* trans. Giselle de Nie (1977). A good survey of political history.

Rosamond McKitterick, *The Frankish Kingdom under the Carolingians, 751–987* (1983). Especially helpful on the later Carolingians.

Jacques Boussard, *The Civilisation of Charlemagne*, trans. Frances Partridge (1968). A balanced treatment of Carolingian society.

Pierre Riché, *Daily Life in the World of Charlemagne*, trans. Jo Ann McNamara (1978). Rich in details on Carolingian life.

Robert Folz, *The Coronation of Charlemagne: 25 December 800*, trans. J. E. Anderson (1974). A balanced treatment of a disputed subject.

Hubert Jedin and John Dolan, eds., *Handbook of Church History*, Vol. 3: *The Church in the Age of Feudalism*, trans. Anselm Biggs (1969). A detailed treatment of religious life.

Rosamond McKitterick, *The Frankish Church and the Carolingian Reforms, 789–895* (1977). A good assessment of Carolingian religious reform.

John Marenbon, *Early Medieval Philosophy (480–1150). An Introduction* (1983). Places the Carolingian intellectual achievement in a larger historical context.

J. Hubert et al., *The Carolingian Renaissance* (1970). A magnificent treatment of Carolingian art.

Russell Chamberlain, *Charlemagne: Emperor of the Western World* (1986). An adequate biography.

The Vikings

Gwyn Jones, *A History of the Vikings*, rev. ed. (1984).

Magnus Magnusson, *Vikings* (1980).

Either of these works will help the reader understand Viking society.

P. H. Sawyer, *Kings and Vikings: Scandinavia and Europe, A.D. 700–1000* (1982). An excellent treatment of the impact of the Vikings.

Anglo-Saxon England

Peter Hunter Blair, *An Introduction to Anglo-Saxon England*, 2nd ed. (1977).

P. H. Sawyer, *From Roman Britain to Norman England* (1978).

Two concise, clearly written surveys of Anglo-Saxon history.

H. R. Loyn, *The Governance of Anglo-Saxon England, 500–1087* (1984). An excellent description of Anglo-Saxon political institutions.

Sources

Two Lives of Charlemagne, trans. Lewis Thorpe (1969). Contains the famous biography by Einhard.

H. R. Loyn and John Percival, eds., *The Reign of Charlemagne: Documents on Carolingian Government and Administration* (1975). Helpful in understanding how Carolingian government worked.

CHAPTER 17

Lordship and Dependency: Feudalism and Manorialism

FIGURE 17.1 The Bastion of Local Lordship: The Medieval Castle Castles such as this one were built over much of western Europe during the eleventh and twelfth centuries as centers from which local potentates and their armed vassals could assert lordship over the surrounding countryside and its inhabitants. This castle, Château Gaillard, built in the late twelfth century on a cliff above the Seine River by King Richard of England to protect his Norman fiefdom from his feudal overlord, the king of France, was virtually impregnable. Outer walls (whose ruins are still visible) and a moat protected the inner fortress and its keep. Living quarters, a great meeting hall, and a chapel were built in the inner courtyard of this structure. (Copyright Stephen T. Johnson)

The inability of the Carolingian dynasty to sustain its effort to renovate society and the devastation caused by the Saracen, Magyar, and Viking assaults produced a new era of instability in western Europe during the late ninth and the tenth centuries. In some respects this period was so chaotic that historians have been tempted to describe it as a "second dark age," resembling the troubled sixth and seventh centuries. However, amidst the difficulties that marked the late Carolingian age, there occurred a basic regrouping of the population of much of the West into institutional patterns that restored stability and set the stage for vigorous growth. For the most part, the new institutional patterns were fashioned from elements that had been present in society since the end of Roman imperial order. Now, just prior to 1000, these usages, some Germanic and some Roman, were brought together to establish new human communities that proved capable of unleashing human talents in a variety of ways. The restructuring of society took a variety of forms across western Europe, thus making any attempt at generalization difficult and misleading. But everywhere certain key patterns emerged to constitute stronger foundations for society.

1. LORDSHIP AND DEPENDENCY

In broad terms a key development of the late-Carolingian period centered on the privatization of political power by powerful landholders. We have seen that a key feature of the Roman imperial order was a strong state in which extensive powers were invested in the hands of officials who exercised those powers in the interests of the public welfare. The Germanic kingdoms that replaced the Roman imperial order attempted to maintain strong central government, but the efforts of their rulers were of limited effectiveness. At the heart of the Carolingian renewal was an attempt to revitalize the state and to reestablish public order. We have traced in the preceding chapter how such rulers as Charlemagne and Louis the Pious sought to achieve this end, with the result that for about at least a century prior to 850 public authority played a prominent role in shaping affairs in the Carolingian Empire.

But the successors to the great Carolingians were unable to sustain their authority. The partition of the Carolingian Empire after 843 resulted in a diminution of royal resources in each of the Carolingian kingdoms. In their attempts to muster support, the late Carolingian kings slowly granted away their royal holdings to powerful nobles and great ecclesiastical officials; technically such grants were made in return for loyalty and service, but the recipients increasingly disregarded their obligations. The inability of the kings to defend their realms against invaders eroded their prestige and necessitated increasing reliance on local power wielders for security. Although kingdoms and kingship survived this ordeal, by the tenth century public authority had become a limited force in the lives of most people in the West.

As royal power and public authority disintegrated, a new force emerged as the dominant feature of political life. *Private lordships* replaced the state as the effective political entities. Individual landholders ruling over principalities of limited area became the only effective political force. The advancing power of landed potentates had been a characteristic of society in the West since late Roman times. By the tenth century the monopoly of power of that group became final. The political map of the West now consisted of hundreds of principalities of varying size in which power was exercised for the private benefit of the lords of these territories.

These lordships were formed in various ways. In some cases, Carolingian public officials, such as counts and dukes, simply arrogated to private use the public authority entrusted to them by the king as well as the lands and the public revenues granted to them by the king as a reward for public service. In other instances, aggressive landowners with the support of armed followers forcefully seized control of a territory and imposed their private rule on its inhabitants. Often the key to the success of such lords was their control of a military strong point, a castle (see Figure 17.1); thus, they are often referred to as *castellans*. In still other cases, enterprising nobles fashioned a lordship out of lands they received as benefices for services rendered to others under the terms of the feudal contract, which will be examined later. But whatever the means, the results were the same:

the fragmentation of kingdoms into a mosaic of private lordships where powerful individuals exercised control over those who lived within their principality. Some of these lords occasionally paid a shadowy allegiance to the impotent kings within whose kingdoms their lordships lay, but in reality each was "king" in his own principality.

As lordship developed, so did *dependency* in various forms. Since late Roman times a variety of forces had been at work encouraging or compelling individuals to place themselves in a position of dependence on other individuals under conditions that regulated their interactions on a private basis beyond the sphere of public authority. By the tenth century almost everyone who did not exercise a lordship lived in a condition of dependency in some form. The conditions of dependency varied infinitely from place to place and from person to person. However, two broad categories existed to determine the condition of most dependents.

First, some lived in a condition of noble dependency. A prime requirement for those who succeeded in creating and then sustaining independent lordships was military force. To provide this force, powerful lords gathered around themselves armed followers willing to provide military service in return for material considerations sufficient to allow them to live a life befitting a warrior. In some cases, lords supported their retainers as a part of their households, but more often military followers were given grants of land from which a living could be derived. As we shall see, the conditions governing the relationships between lords and followers came to be institutionalized in forms that defined a unique way of life for those involved. Although armed retainers were originally drawn from all levels of life, by the tenth century they along with their lords had come to claim a special status for themselves as nobles.

Second, the bulk of the population lived in a condition of servile dependency. In a world where almost everyone from the most powerful to the lowliest depended on agriculture for a livelihood, those who exercised lordship and their armed followers required a peasant labor force to till the soil from which power and wealth were derived. They gained it by asserting their jurisdiction over the peasant population in a way that compelled peasants to perform a range of menial services related to agricultural production and that allowed the exaction of dues from the peasants which supported lordly life. The reduction of the peasantry to dependency had been evolving over many centuries, powerfully abetted by unsettled political conditions that forced peasants to seek security at whatever cost. By the tenth century the dominance of the powerful had become nearly complete, subject to almost no controls by public authority. In the process of establishing domination over their servile dependents, lords had in many cases congregated their peasants into village communities to expedite effective management of their labor and exaction of dues. As was the case with noble dependency, by the tenth century the conditions governing servile dependency had assumed institutional forms that gave stability and permanence to the system.

2. THE COMMUNITY OF THE POWERFUL: THE FEUDAL ORDER

By the tenth century relationships among the powerful were governed by a set of institutions called *feudalism*. This term is surrounded by so many ambiguities that some historians have questioned its usefulness in describing a particular sociopolitical order. However, it can still serve usefully to highlight certain practices through which members of the dominant nobility established order among themselves. Feudalism grew out of the merger, over the course of many centuries, of two practices: personal dependence and shared rights in land tenure. The first was rooted in the Germanic *comitatus* and the Roman clientage system (see pp. 103 and 172) and the second in the Germanic system of gift giving and the late Roman land tenancy system. The confusion and chaos in western Europe following the Germanic migrations encouraged the spread of these ancient institutions between 500 and 750. In search of strong protectors, many were willing to enter a *commendation* agreement, which established a personal bond linking the two individuals—often called *lord* and *vassal*—to each other in a way that was mutually useful. Likewise, those in search of a livelihood or a way to enlarge their holdings were willing to accept the use of another's land in return for some kind of service. Such grants, called *benefices*, remained the property of the grantor and thus could be made without diminishing one's basic holdings. By obtaining the use of land on a conditional basis, the recipient gained real benefit in an unsettled world where use of land was essential.

The Carolingian rulers relied heavily on these usages to expand their control over their subjects, thereby giving these practices status in public law and more precise definition. The Carolingians required the great men of the realm, including public officials, to become their vassals and rewarded them with benefices, now called *fiefs*, in return for services. Such arrangements were especially valuable in providing military service; the fief provided the means by which a vassal could arm himself at his own expense. In many cases, kings also granted their vassals *immunities*, which gave them governing powers over their fiefs and the people living on them. Vassalage and fiefs came to be interconnected to the point where personal dependence almost always involved the grant of a fief. With the breakdown of public authority and royal power after about 850, those seeking to establish private lordships utilized these practices as a means of creating a military following. They gathered around them a circle of followers who agreed to serve as vassals in return for fiefs that gave to each vassal the use of land and a labor force that provided the basis for status, wealth, and security.

Implicit in the arrangements creating the lord-vassal bond was the idea of a mutually binding contract between two free persons. The ritual that had evolved to mark the establishment of such a contract provides a convenient key to the nature of this bond (see Figure 17.2). One man knelt before another, placed his hands between the other's, and declared himself willing to become his "man." By this voluntary act, called *homage* (after the Latin word *homo*, meaning "man"), the first became a vassal and the second a lord. The lord lifted up his new "man" and kissed him, signifying that he accepted him as a vassal. The vassal then swore an oath of *fealty*, binding himself in the sight of God to be faithful to his lord. The lord then gave him some object, such as a clod of

FIGURE 17.2 The Feudal Contract: The Act of Homage This scene pictures the basic act creating the feudal contract—the act of homage by which the kneeling figures became vassals of the seated lord. (Archive of the Crown of Aragon, Barcelona/MAS)

dirt or a ring. This act was called *investiture*, symbolizing the granting of a fief—usually a piece of land but sometimes an office or a money stipend—which the vassal could use to support himself. By the acts of homage, fealty, and investiture, two individuals bound themselves together in a way that gave each rights and imposed on each obligations through which their political and social interactions were controlled. By the tenth century the lord-vassal relationship had become hereditary, ensuring that the bonds created by the contract continued for generations within the same families.

The specific rights and obligations of lords and

vassals came in time to be defined in a special legal system, called feudal law. Although feudal law varied widely across western Europe, certain rights and obligations were fairly standard.

The feudal contract generally established the lord in a position of authority over his vassal. He retained important rights in the fief he had granted to his vassal for the latter's use. The lord was obligated to protect his vassal and to provide him justice—to use his army to defend his vassal against attacks and to maintain a court where the vassal could receive a hearing for any grievances. Put briefly, the lord had the grave responsibility of running a small-scale government to serve the mutual needs of himself and his vassals.

The vassal also had important rights and obligations. He was entitled to the use of the fief and the respect of the lord. In return, he was expected to conduct himself honorably and loyally toward his lord. More specifically, a vassal owed his lord four basic obligations: First was *military service*, which required the vassal to serve at his own expense as an armed knight for a specified length of time each year, usually forty days; such service might involve guard duty at a lord's castle. Second, the vassal had to give *counsel*, usually defined by compulsory attendance at the lord's court. Third, the vassal was obligated to give *aids* in the form of money payments in certain specific situations (for ransoming the lord, the knighting of the lord's eldest son, and the marriage dowry of the lord's eldest daughter). Finally, the vassal had to extend *hospitality* to the lord and his entourage when they visited the fief that the vassal had received. In addition, the vassal was obliged to respect certain usages, called *feudal incidents*, reflecting the lord's rights in the fief. The vassal had to maintain the fief in good condition so as to sustain its value. His heir had to pay the lord an inheritance tax, called a *relief*, when he succeeded to the fief. The lord had the right of guardianship, called *wardship*, over a vassal's minor heir and of approval of the marriage of a vassal's daughter whose husband might someday become heir to the fief. Finally, the vassal was obliged to recognize that if he died without heirs, the fief reverted to the lord (the right of *escheat*).

The enforcement of the terms of the feudal contract was a major problem in a society lacking effective public authority. In fact, lords and vassals had to settle disputes surrounding rights and obligations themselves. The chief instrument was the lord's court, where the custom governing the feudal contract was applied as law. A lord could summon to his court any of his vassals accused of infidelity to be judged by the vassal's "peers"—other vassals—and, if found guilty, punished as custom dictated. To this same court every vassal could bring complaints against his lord or his fellow vassals; again, his peers decided whether he had redress. Despite this machinery, force was always the final recourse, with the result that feudal society was plagued by constant petty wars fought to force fulfillment of obligations and to gain redress for violation of rights. It would be wrong, however, to picture lords and vassals as seeking any opportunity to start a brawl. In a society that knew no other workable system for keeping order, both lords and vassals were often anxious and willing to observe the terms of the contract that served their mutual interests.

A prime result of the feudalization of western Europe's ruling class was to create circles of vassals linked together by their relationships with a common lord. In theory, the feudal order created a sociopolitical hierarchy in which each successive layer of vassals owed allegiance and service to a lord standing one step higher in the hierarchy (see Figure 17.3). At the top stood the king who was supreme lord and theoretical owner of all the land in his realm. At his pleasure he could accept as his direct vassals some of his subjects to whom he might grant large fiefs in return for service commensurate with the size of the fief. The great vassals of the king could then subdivide their holdings into smaller fiefs and grant them to other men willing to become vassals. This process, called *subinfeudation*, could continue until fiefs granted were only large enough to support a single vassal as a warrior.

In practice, the system did not work so neatly. If any lord in the hierarchy granted away too much of his land, he deprived himself of the means to compel his vassals to render him the services they owed and thus was powerless to command their obedience. As we have seen, this depletion of landed resources did happen with the late Carolingian kings; and it also happened to many others

FIGURE 17.3 The Feudal Hierarchy.

amidst the tumult accompanying the establishment of lordships. More threatening to any neat hierarchy was the fact that subinfeudation led to the intersection of lord-vassal circles, creating conflicting loyalties and disparities in the size of landholdings. From the diagram of the theoretical feudal hierarchy, it will be apparent that an enterprising vassal (such as F) could acquire several lords; what is not obvious is where his allegiance lay if he was called upon to serve two lords at once. Moreover, such a vassal might accumulate enough fiefs from a variety of lords to possess more land than any one of them and thus be in a position to defy any of them. Attempts were made eventually to avoid such conflicting loyalties and fragmentation of authority by a system called *liege homage,* whereby a lord required not only his own direct vassals but also their vassals and subvassals to pledge prime allegiance to him. But on the whole, the feudal order led to an almost indescribable maze of contradictory allegiances and accumulations of power that made large-scale communities of lords and vassals nearly impossible. This system served best in the world of limited lordships and small principalities.

Beyond its role in shaping compact circles of lords and vassals within which order could be maintained, the feudal system served another end

vital to political and social stability: It led to the crystallization of a noble class consciously sharing a special ethos and a distinctive style of life. Although the western European nobility had roots reaching back to the Roman and Germanic worlds, the conditions that surrounded lordship and noble dependence provided a sharp focus for noble status. That group consisted of specialists in warfare and governance who felt a responsibility for protecting and ordering society.

The values of the feudal nobility were reflected with special force in two epic poems written to celebrate noble life, the *Song of Roland* and *The Cid* (see page 312). The virtues befitting noble status stemmed chiefly from what was vital to sustaining the bonds of lordship and vassalage: loyalty, bravery, faithfulness, generosity. Above all else stood prowess—the ability to excel in warfare. The life of a noble centered on a career of fighting for his lord, his lands, his family, his dependent peasants—and his God. In early youth, he began to learn his craft as an apprentice in the service of someone who already knew the art, often his father's lord. The culmination of his education was his knighting, an elaborate ceremony surrounded by religious symbolism that climaxed with his investiture with the tools of war; these were used often during his adult life. Of course, he had to sustain himself as a warrior, so the management of the lands received as a fief constituted a part of his vocation. And he had a political function stemming from his position as the vassal of another and probably as lord over still others.

The life of the nobility was generally crude and rough in the tenth century, in part because of the primitive level of economic life. The typical noble residence was a wooden fortress designed for defense rather than comfort. The living quarters were crowded, sparsely furnished, cold, without sanitary facilities, and lacking in privacy. The routine of life featured pursuits typical of male warriors: heavy eating, drinking, gambling, hunting, dancing, wenching, and warfare. Nobles were usually illiterate, "reading" by listening to tales of war sung by bards and to simple preaching of the priests. Marriage was arranged with an eye toward gaining new lands, more vassals, and stronger lords; seldom was it marred by considerations of sentiment. But the family was another matter, for a household rich in strong sons and nubile daughters was a great asset in a world of war, land acquisition, and personal relationships. The crucial importance of keeping landholdings intact and of maintaining ties with a powerful lord began to change the basic structure of the noble family. The earlier system of extended kinship ties and shared inheritance gave way to the patrilineal family in which lineage was traced from father to eldest son and inheritance was restricted to the eldest son. Nobles were religious in a simple way: They trusted God to take care of them if they were brave, faithful, and generous. Their way of expressing their faith was active, impelling them to do something visible to show their piety—build a church, give land to a monastery to assure prayers for their souls, go on a pilgrimage, or fight for God.

The feudal world was a man's world. Women were accorded inferior legal standing. They could not be lords or vassals; their social status reflected that of their fathers and husbands. Their marriage, the crucial event in determining on whom they would be dependent most of their lives, was controlled by males seeking to enhance family status in the feudal world. Unless they betook themselves to a convent, unmarried women were a liability to their families. Noble daughters married young, often to men much older. This situation, coupled with the dangers of warfare, often resulted in widowhood and the burdens of protecting the interests of minor children. Despite their general subservience, women played important roles in sustaining noble society. In a patrilineal family structure, it was the legal wife who bestowed legitimacy on the male heir who would sustain the family and its property. Women took active part in directing household servants who produced most of what was needed to sustain the noble household. On occasion, women managed fiefs when their husbands were absent. Their dowries—over which women maintained control—were often crucially important in expanding their husbands' possessions. Women were frequently called upon to witness legal transactions involving land transfers, suggesting their involvement in sustaining the family fortune and their knowledge of the substance of that fortune.

3. THE COMMUNITY OF THE SERVILE: MANORIALISM

The structures that created a nobility engaged in warfare and governance rested on an agricultural base. The feudal system provided lords and vassals with control over parcels of land of varying sizes that each noble had to exploit in order to sustain himself and his family and to fulfill the complex obligations implicit in noble status. To exploit those lands, the nobility imposed another order of dependency on the peasantry of western Europe. This system, sometimes called the *seigneurial* system, was shaped over a long period out of elements rooted in Germanic and Roman economic and social institutions. By the tenth century the essential features of the system were in place: Each noble had imposed on the peasant inhabitants of the land he controlled an organizational structure that allowed him to command their labor and to take a portion of their produce. As *seigneur*—lord—he controlled a community of humans whose function was essentially economic. Although the way agricultural production was organized varied across western Europe, the *manorial system* prevailed in the most productive areas extending from southern England across northern

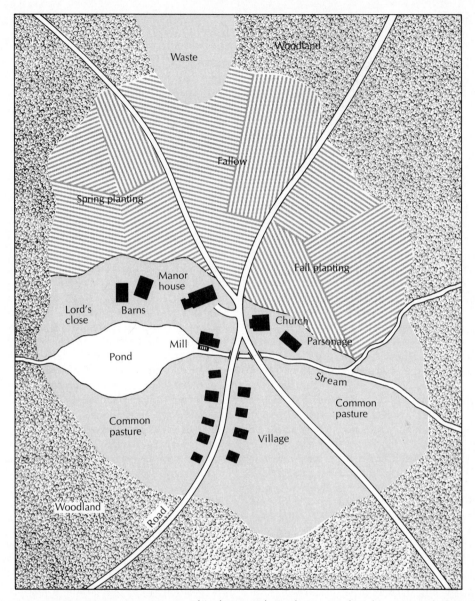

Map 17.1 **A HYPOTHETICAL MEDIEVAL MANOR** This drawing shows how a medieval manor might have been laid out. It will help identify the major components of a medieval manor as described in the text: the seigneur's manor house, the church, the village settlement, the three-field and strip system, the commons, the wood and waste land. All of these components were required to make the manor self-sufficient.

France and western Germany into northern Italy.

The manor was an economic unit organized to produce everything needed by its seigneur and his dependent peasants (see Map. 17.1). It was also a political and social unit providing for the governance of the peasants living there and defining their relationships with their seigneur and with one another. The typical manor's size was determined by the requirements of self-sufficiency. A workable manor required arable land for raising cereal crops, meadowland for animal support, woodland for fuel and building material, and a natural water supply. The seigneur usually reserved one-third to one-half of the arable land as his *demesne* from which he took all of the produce for his own support. The rest was divided into tenancies, called *mansi* or *hides*, each large enough to support a peasant household. Meadows, pastures, and woods were used in common. Under the widely used *open-field system*, the tillable land was divided into large, unfenced plots farmed by the cooperative effort of peasants. Each open field was subdivided into strips. The seigneur reserved a third to a half of these strips in each large field as his demesne; the mansus or tenancy of each peasant was made of strips in each open field.

To protect the fertility of the soil, part of the land was left idle each year. Until about 900 a *two-field system* of rotation was widely used, with half of the manor's tillable land seeded each year while the other half was left idle. Then the more efficient *three-field system* began to spread. The tillable land was divided into three open fields. Every year and in rotation, one field lay fallow, a second was planted in the fall with wheat or rye, and a third was planted in the spring with barley, oats, or legumes (such as beans or peas). Not only did the three-field system put more land under cultivation each year, but also it allowed a greater variety of crops, which improved human diet. Most peasants raised vegetables on small, well-fertilized plots surrounding their huts. In spite of the improved rotation system, yields were small and famines common. Low productivity discouraged the keeping of animals that could lighten work, such as horses and oxen, which were heavy consumers of grain and hay. However, pigs, poultry, and goats, which could live by scavenging in the woods and wastelands, were common.

Since there was little trade in the tenth century, most manufactured goods were made on the manor. Although specialized artisans such as blacksmiths and carpenters plied their trades on some manors, ordinary peasants generally made and repaired equipment, buildings, and furnishings. Women, including noble ladies, made clothing, preserved food, and concocted medicine. Only a few crucial items came to most manors from outside—metals, salt, wine.

The center of the manor was a village containing a manor house, peasant huts, a church and cemetery, granaries, a mill, a bakery, and a brewery. This village was more than a collection of buildings; it was a vital human community with a governing system and a social order. Its governor was the seigneur, who exercised the power to command, judge, and punish his dependent peasants with virtually no interference from authority beyond the manor. If he lived on the manor, the seigneur exercised his lordship in person. If he lived elsewhere, as did many nobles with numerous manors, he entrusted control of the manor to *stewards* and *bailiffs*, usually recruited from the peasantry. Although force provided a means of last recourse, seigneurial control was exercised chiefly through the manorial court. In this court the law, consisting of a body of custom defining every aspect of the relationships among those involved in manorial life, was applied to impose discipline on the peasantry and to allow individuals to gain recourse for damages done to them.

The peasant population of a typical manor included individuals whose legal status ranged from slaves to free individuals. But most were *serfs* or *villeins* who were legally bound to the soil but who held a tenancy from which they could not be dispossessed. Thus, a serf was legally unfree but possessed both a precious right in a piece of land that assured his livelihood and a place in a community that provided protection and a court of law through which rights could be protected. Serf status was passed by inheritance, as was the tenancy to which a serf was attached. Powerful forces were at work both among seigneurs and peasants to merge slaves and free individuals into serfdom.

More important to peasants than their precise legal status were the obligations they owed their seigneur. These obligations, defined by manorial custom, varied greatly over Europe, but every-where certain dues were imposed on peasants. Their chief obligation was labor service. On most manors serfs were required to spend three days a week tilling the demesne of the seigneur. In addition, they might be required to do extra days of work during the planting and the harvesting season (*boon days*) and in maintaining roads and buildings (*corvée*). Often these labor obligations extended to the serfs' wives, who were required to perform such duties as spinning, cleaning, and preparing food in the seigneur's household. Peasants were required to give to the seigneur some share of the produce of their tenancies, thus providing the seigneur with an important supplement to the produce of his own demesne. Peasants had to pay a *tithe* to the Church; often tithes found their way into the seigneur's hands. Fees, called *banalties*, were assessed for the use of the manorial mill, bakery, and brewery—facilities the seigneur alone could afford to build and over which he maintained a monopoly. The seigneur collected a death tax (*heriot*) from each peasant household when the tenancy passed from father to son and a tax (*formariage* or *merchet*) from any peasant whose daughter married outside the manor. There were, of course, fees and fines to be paid by peasants involved in litigation in the manorial court.

It is obvious that the manor provided the seigneur with many opportunities to enrich himself at the expense of the peasantry. Many exploited these opportunities to the fullest. There were limits, however. The seigneur was wholly dependent on the peasants for the one prime ingredient of the manorial economy—labor. Without peasant labor the seigneur's land would go uncultivated and his wealth and his status in the noble world would diminish. There was no other source of labor. The seigneur thus had to act with some restraint toward his laborers if he hoped to get efficient and constant work from them. Peasants were in a position to damage the interests of an overoppressive seigneur by willful neglect of crops, buildings, and animals or by calculated mischief. Killing or maiming or even irritating peasants in the interests of exacting more from them might be more costly than just treatment according to custom. The weight of custom, which tended to fix obligations over long periods, acted as a powerful brake on rapacious seigneurs.

Peasant life in the ninth and tenth centuries was brutally harsh. At best, the manorial system provided a livelihood at subsistence level. Crop failure, sickness, or warfare could erase the thin margin separating subsistence from famine and death. Too many children could overtax the meager supply of food that could be extracted from a tenancy of fixed size. The seigneur or his agents were always at hand seeking any spare wealth. The simple, one-room, scantily furnished huts offered little comfort. Neither did the monotonous diet of bread, soup, beer, cheese, and eggs, with an occasional bit of meat or fish and fruit. Yet there were compensations. The Church was ever-present, offering its solace in the face of life's hardships, including its charity at especially desperate moments, and its hopes of a better life beyond this world. Its ministrations at life's crucial moments—birth, marriage, death—helped to give dignity and significance to human existence, even in the midst of squalor and poverty. Membership in the village community provided the psychological security that stems from living among people long and intimately known. That same community provided an array of simple pleasures, often occasioned by the Church's numerous holy days—beer drinking, gaming, singing, dancing—all capable of easing the burden of a life of bare subsistence.

4. THE CHURCH IN THE WORLD OF LORDSHIP AND DEPENDENCY

The complex processes that surrounded the regrouping of society under a system of lordship and dependency had a profound effect on the Church. The reforming forces unleashed by the Carolingian ministerial kings flagged, and new kinds of problems emerged to make the late ninth and tenth centuries one of the most trying periods in the Church's history.

The Church's major difficulties emerged from its entanglement in the world of lordship and noble dependency, that is, in the feudal order. By the ninth and tenth centuries, the Church held an immense amount of landed property. Its holdings were attached to bishoprics, monasteries, and individual churches and administered by bishops, abbots, and priests. Part of its land came from gifts from the faithful, but much had been acquired in the form of fiefs granted by kings and other powerful laymen, who expected church officials so favored to render services as did any other vassals. In order to protect their holdings in a world where self-help was the key to survival, ecclesiastical officials acted like other lords. They granted church lands as fiefs in return for military and political services and thus became lords in their own rights. Like their lay counterparts, ecclesiastical lords forced the peasants on their lands into a servile condition and gave full attention to asserting their seigneurial authority. They too had to concern themselves with protecting their vassals, holding courts, and collecting dues. Such necessary preoccupations directed their efforts away from their pastoral duties. Lay leaders refused to invest any bishop or abbot with a fief unless he had the qualities of a good vassal, including military prowess and loyalty to the lord rather than to the Church as an institution. In effect, this system meant that secular leaders gained control over elections to ecclesiastical offices, often filling them with loyal kinsmen or proven vassals with little interest in spiritual matters. Secular lords treated church land received as fiefs as if it were private property, diverting the income to uses that had little to do with spiritual needs. This thoroughly secularized officialdom in control of church offices and property neglected discipline, education, charity, and moral guidance. The lower clergy was ignorant and undisciplined. The level of religious life in lay society deteriorated badly; superstition, moral laxity, and corruption of ritual practices abounded. To some contemporary pious souls, especially those who remembered the Carolingian reform effort, religious life had become a scandal worse than had ever been seen. Mammon seemingly had triumphed over God!

With due allowance for the abysmal condition into which the feudalized Church had sunk, it remains necessary to note another dimension of the Church's position in the world of lordship and dependence. Its involvement in that world drew it into contact with the basic institutions and the dynamic elements of society more intimately and directly than ever before. Its feudalized leadership shared the mentality and felt the needs of western Europe's warrior aristocracy and peasantry. Such involvement prepared that leadership to shape a religious order responsive to reality. Even in the midst of a genuine religious crisis evidence of that response began to surface. The Church articulated a social theory positing that right order involved three orders, each with a special social responsibility: those who prayed (*oratores*), those who fought (*bellatores*), and those who labored (*laboratores*). It gave the feudal contract a religious dimension by making the oath of fealty a key element in establishing the relationship binding two men together. Its moral concepts began to shape a code of behavior known as *chivalry* befitting the warrior life (see page 251). Its leaders instituted two practices aimed at curbing violence in feudal society. One, called the Peace of God, sought to restrain acts of war against certain categories of people (the clergy, women, children); the other, called the Truce of God, tried to prohibit warfare during certain periods holy to all Christians (Sundays, major holy days, Lent). A monastic reform beginning in the tenth century, known as Cluniac monasticism (see page 296), encouraged certain practices of piety that appealed strongly to the feudal nobility. The grouping of the peasantry into organized villages provided a setting for the development of a strong parish structure through which the Christian population could be reached. Thus, despite the spiritual disarray caused by the worldliness of the feudalized Church, its immersion in the world of lordship and dependency provided new arenas where it could assert its influence over the development of European society.

The tenth-century world of lordship and dependency, of feudalism and manorialism, does not usually receive a sympathetic evaluation, especially among those who cannot conceive of a civilized order without a strong state. The violence, the oppression, the greed that surrounded the establishment of these political, social, and economic institutions seem the very antithesis of a vital society. However, despite its limitations, the system of lordship and dependency played a fundamental role in preparing a backward society for a new outburst of creativity. Feudalism and manorialism shaped small communities of people capable of concerted, disciplined action. These new groupings created a situation requiring concerted action among peoples of different social status and talents. These collectivities were especially suited to exploit Europe's chief resource, its under- utilized lands and forests. It is not coincidence that western European society began a spectacular pe- riod of growth *after* the system of lordship and dependency had become firmly established.

SUGGESTED READING

Lordship and Dependence

F. L. Ganshof, *Feudalism,* trans. Philip Grierson, 3rd ed. (1964). Stresses the legal aspects of feudalism.

Marc Bloch, *Feudal Society,* trans. L. A. Manyon (1961). A classic, approaching feudalism from a sociological perspective.

Perry Anderson, *Passages from Antiquity to Feudalism* (1978). A Marxist perspective on feudalism and its origins.

Guy Fourquin, *Lordship and Feudalism in the Middle Ages,* trans. Iris and A. L. Lytton Sells (1976). Provides insights into how power was exercised in the feudal world.

Frederic L. Cheyette, ed., *Lordship and Community in Me- dieval Europe: Selected Readings* (1968). Views by ex- perts on how the medieval system of lordship worked.

Timothy Reuter, ed. and trans., *The Medieval Nobility. Studies on the Ruling Classes of France and Germany from the Sixth to the Twelfth Century* (1978). These essays provide conflicting views on the origins and role of the medieval nobility.

Nellie Neilson, *Medieval Agrarian Economy* (1936). A clas- sic description of manorialism.

Georges Duby, *Rural Economy and Country Life in the Me- dieval West,* trans. Cynthia Postan (1968). The best work on manorial economy; provides translations of medieval sources.

Philippe Contamine, *War in the Middle Ages,* trans. Mi- chael James (1984). A good treatment of an important aspect of feudal society.

Sources

David Herlihy, ed., *The History of Feudalism* (1970). A collection of sources illustrating the nature of feudal institutions and practices.

The Song of Roland, trans. Frederick Goldin (1978).

The Poem of the Cid, trans. Lesley Bird Simpson (1957).

Aside from their literary values, these two medieval epic poems reveal a great deal about the mentality of feudal society.

RETROSPECT

In a letter written in 593 or 594, Pope Gregory I called his contemporaries' attention to the strife, suffering, destruction, and injustice seen everywhere. "See what has befallen Rome, once mistress of the world," he mourned. "What is there now, I ask, of delight in this world?"

In a way, Gregory supplied the key to the history of the early Middle Ages. Much of what had characterized Greco-Roman civilization had been lost, and society was poorer. One can easily write—as many have—the history of the early Middle Ages in terms of the destruction of classical civilization; from this perspective the era was indeed a dark age.

However, between A.D. 500 and 1000 much happened to replace what had been lost. Three new civilizations—Byzantine, Moslem, and western European—had been shaped within the confines of the classical world. Each retained precious elements of the old order. Each developed new institutions and ideas to suit its needs and situation. An inventory of what people had fashioned in these difficult centuries gives ample evidence that these "dark" years deserve a decisive place in the continuum of history. By 1000 there were still "things of delight" in the world.

The emergence of three new civilizations was not the only transformation that occurred in the early Middle Ages. In addition to the creative forces at work within each, a new dynamism had developed in the form of interactions among these civilizations. The Greco-Roman world had tended to absorb existing cultures into a unified pattern that stood counterposed to the barbarian world. By 1000 lines of interaction and points of tension existed among civilized societies rather than between the civilized and uncivilized orbits. This distinction was a forceful determinant in the course of future historical development.

The period just reviewed belonged to the East; Byzantium and Islam far surpassed western Europe in every respect. This little appreciated fact demands attention, for the accomplishments of the Byzantine and Moslem worlds in these centuries gave their peoples a proud sense of contribution to the creation of civilized life that other societies later forgot. None benefited more from the achievements of these leaders than the struggling western Europeans, whose future glory would have been different had it not been for what they absorbed from the East during the early centuries of the Middle Ages.

PART FIVE

THE HIGH MIDDLE AGES, 1000–1300: THE REVIVAL OF EUROPE

An eleventh-century chronicler named Ralph Glaber tells us that many Europeans were convinced that, in accordance with ancient prophecy, the world would come to an end at the end of the first millennium of Christian history, that is, in the year 1000. But, wrote Ralph, when that fateful year passed without the appearance of the Antichrist, "it was as if the very world had shaken itself and cast off its old age." Everywhere, he said, people rivaled each other to build better churches and were filled with new ardor for the faith. This bit of medieval legend, whatever its validity in summing up the actual state of mind of western Europeans in the late tenth century, provides a fitting introduction to this section. In actual fact, western European society did enjoy a genuine revival beginning about 1000 and continuing with unabated vigor until about 1300. This era is often referred to as the High Middle Ages. It is the period in which medieval western European society reached its full maturity.

As our account of these effervescent, creative centuries unfolds, it should become increasingly clear that the revival of western European civilization was rooted in certain basic institutions that had been forged during the preceding era: feudalism, manorialism, the Church, the precious treasure of learning stored up by Carolingian scholars. Although primitive in many ways, these institutions and ideas provided basic patterns of organization, social control, thought, and belief that permitted men and women to apply their energies and intelligences constructively. They were suddenly capable of producing new wealth. They found themselves able to construct larger political entities and to form new class relationships. Their spiritual, intellectual, and aesthetic capabilities were expanded so that a wide range of cultural achievements was possible. They found themselves able to turn outward from their beleaguered world to make a major impression on wide areas of the world heretofore little known to them. In short, the High Middle Ages was an era of creative activity that made western European civilization a factor of major significance in the world. The long centuries of painful experimentation that marked the early Middle Ages had clearly ended.

CHAPTER 18

Economic and Social Revival

FIGURE 18.1 Medieval Farming   This miniature used to illustrate an English psalter shows peasants plowing their fields. It indicates that medieval agriculture was a cooperative effort: Peasants combined their labor, their draft animals, and their equipment to till the manor fields. The heavy moldboard plow was a major technological advance of the Middle Ages: It was especially efficient in cutting through and turning over heavy soils. Producing yields sufficient to feed both people and livestock was a major problem. (The British Museum)

Throughout the early Middle Ages a major deterrent to growth was the severely limited and constantly uncertain level of material resources available to western European society. Between 1000 and 1300 that situation was dramatically changed by a major economic expansion accompanied by significant adjustments in the social order. These changes had their source at the base of society; their agents were modest seigneurs, toiling peasants, peddler merchants, and simple artisans. The efforts of these simple people made possible the more spectacular accomplishments of the High Middle Ages in politics, religion, and culture.

1. POPULATION GROWTH

The forces that generated economic growth after 1000 were complex. However, one contributing factor is evident: The population expanded substantially between about 900 and 1350. This demographic change, reversing a trend that had prevailed since late Roman times, resulted in a doubling of the population of western Europe during that period; one generally accepted estimate suggests that the population grew from about 35 million in 900 to about 70 million in 1350. Modern demographers do not yet fully understand the causes of this growth. There is some evidence that during this period Eurasia was relatively free from killer diseases, especially bubonic plague. Perhaps the curbing of the more destructive aspects of warfare and the availability of more and better food contributed. Some have even suggested that the prospects of a better society encouraged people to have more children. Whatever the causes, the simple fact was that for three centuries a constantly expanding population put pressure on the agricultural system for greater productivity and provided a larger work force that could be turned to new enterprises.

There remain a whole series of fascinating and important problems associated with the effects of population growth on the structure of medieval society. For example, it is clear that the population growth was not uniform across western Europe, but the geographic pattern and the regional impact of growth have not yet been clearly established.

Neither is it clear how growth affected different age groups and social classes. What happened to life expectancy, marriage patterns, size of households, and child rearing are still poorly understood. Virtually all one can say is that population increase affected all these matters so vital to the lives of people. As historians become better able to assess the full impact of increasing population, it will be more obvious that population growth was a major dynamic force changing western European society in the High Middle Ages.

2. AGRICULTURAL EXPANSION

The most important aspect of economic growth between 1000 and 1300 was expansion of agricultural productivity. The manorial system, with its reservoir of managerial ability, disciplined labor force, and technical skills, provided the base for growth. At least five major factors were involved in expanding on that base.

First, western Europe's climate improved during this period, especially in northern Europe. Milder winters, more favorable growing seasons, better distribution of rainfall, and fewer violent storms and excessive variations in temperature all seem to have combined to create an improved setting for agricultural pursuits.

Second, as a result of an immense effort devoted to land clearance and peasant resettlement, more land was put under cultivation. Much of this land clearance involved pushing out the boundaries of existing cultivated areas, which in the early Middle Ages stood as isolated, often overpopulated islands of cultivation in vast stretches of forest. In some areas this internal expansion reclaimed lands heretofore useless: Swamps were drained in northern Italy; land was recovered from the North Sea in what is modern Netherlands. But many European cultivators, organized by enterprising landlords, moved great distances to settle on the frontiers of western Europe. The chief areas of colonization were on the German frontier east of the Elbe River, in Spanish lands being wrested from Moslem control, and in southern Italy. It appears that the cultivated acreage in western Europe nearly doubled between 1000 and 1300.

Third, technological advances greatly increased the efficiency of the labor force, especially by supplying new sources of power. The adoption of the horseshoe and the development of new harnesses, especially the shoulder collar, permitted the more efficient horse to replace the ox as a draft animal. Watermills and windmills were greatly improved, and complicated power trains were developed, which allowed the motion from these mills to be applied to such tasks as grinding grain. Traditional agricultural tools—plows, spades, hoes, harrows—were improved by more effective practices of metallurgy. Especially important was the increasing use of the wheeled, moldboard plow, which could cut through and turn over the heavy soils of northern Europe (see Figure 18.1). One suspects that these advances were due to the ingenuity and practical experience of simple peasants searching for ways to make their labor easier and more productive. Whatever the cause, the result was greater productivity and the freeing of human labor for more productive uses.

Fourth, agricultural production was increased in quantity and variety by improved methods of tillage and animal husbandry. Irrigation systems were developed in some parts of western Europe. Agricultural specialization, as in the vineyards of Burgundy and the great sheep-raising granges in England, was made possible by increasing opportunities for exchange, which we shall describe later. Greater attention was given to fertilization. The three-field system of tillage spread, which protected the fertility of the soil, promoted efficient use of labor and equipment, and permitted a greater variety of crops to be grown. Particularly significant was the increased availability of high-protein foods, such as beans, to supplement the mostly carbohydrate diet of earlier times. Better seeds were developed to take advantage of local soil and weather conditions. And improvements in animal breeds produced better animals and more animal products, such as meat and wool.

Finally, production was expanded by what we might call agricultural entrepreneurship. Planning and the adaptation of ancient customs freed labor to clear new lands, to apply new tools and techniques, and to dispose profitably of any excess production. Bold foresight resettled groups of peasants on distant lands. Innovative thinking developed new seeds, bred improved livestock strains, and launched specialized production. Entrepreneurship, exercised in small and undramatic ways, perhaps provides the key to one of the great advances in the history of agriculture.

Modern historians have not been able to quantify very accurately the overall magnitude of the growth of agricultural production between 1000 and 1300. However, in crude terms the consequences are clear. The increased amount of land under cultivation and higher yields permitted everyone to live better and produced a surplus of food, which left more people free to devote their energies to activities other than subsistence agriculture. That critical difference made possible significant changes in all aspects of the society of the High Middle Ages.

3. REVIVAL OF TRADE AND MANUFACTURING

The expansion of agricultural production after 1000 stimulated the revival of trade and manufacturing. Trade had never entirely vanished from the western European scene, but it had declined steadily from late Roman times. By 1000 trade was insignificant in the total economic life of western Europe. Neither had manufacturing totally disappeared, but during the early Middle Ages manufacturing was restricted to the manorial setting where only a limited range of products needed for local self-sufficiency was produced. During the late tenth and early eleventh centuries, a revival began in both commerce and manufacturing; it continued until the mid–fourteenth century. During this era commerce became the catalytic force in European economy, and new forms of manufacturing emerged to provide an expanded range of products for exchange. Among the factors contributing to the commercial and industrial revival were population growth, agricultural expansion, greater political order, outside stimuli, and western European political, military, and religious expansion. But to these must be added the labors and enterprise of men and women whose activities are for the most part unknown to us.

In considerable part, the Europeans' commercial expansion was a story of their ability to break into the flourishing Byzantine and Moslem trading

Map 18.1 **TRADE ROUTES, TWELFTH AND THIRTEENTH CENTURIES** This map shows the major trade routes developed during the twelfth and thirteenth centuries to link western Europeans with the East and to join major trading centers within western Europe. The crucial centers for international trade linking East and West were located in northern Italy, especially Venice, Genoa, and Pisa, and in Flanders, especially Bruges and Antwerp. The internal routes, focusing especially in the towns of Champagne, where great international trading fairs were held annually, spread the products of the East from the Italian and Flemish centers over much of western Europe.

complexes and to gain control of a share of them (see Map 18.1). Western Europe had always remained in touch with the Eastern trade centers, primarily through Byzantine outposts in Venice and southern Italy. In the tenth century trade activity began to quicken. The Venetians took the leading role, steadily enlarging their contacts by sea with Constantinople and bringing an ever-increasing volume of goods to the West. In the eleventh century Pisa's and Genoa's navies loosened Moslem control over the western Mediterranean, and their merchants established trade relations with the Moslems in Spain and North Africa.

The successes of the early crusading movement at the end of the eleventh century (see Chapter 21) allowed the Italian cities to establish and expand important footholds in eastern Mediterranean Moslem cities in the twelfth century. The conquest of Constantinople in 1204 during the Fourth Crusade gave the Venetians virtual control over Byzantine trade. By the thirteenth century the efforts of Italian merchants were reinforced by other traders from coastal cities in France and Spain; collectively they had become the dominant commercial force in Mediterranean trade. The lifeblood of this international trade was luxury items, especially spices and fine cloth.

Meanwhile, another window to the East was opened on the northern fringes of the continent by Viking pirates. Their raiding ventures opened a path through the Baltic Sea and along the rivers of Russia to the Black Sea and Constantinople. Traders from many areas of northern Europe eventually followed the Vikings along this route to carry a variety of goods to and from the lands bordering the North and Baltic seas and Constantinople. The focal point of this northern trading complex came to be Flanders.

No less important than international trade was the growth of trade within Europe. In part, that growth was a result of the efforts of aggressive Italian and Flemish merchants to provide Europe's aristocrats with luxury goods. Their activities created an ever-widening network of routes, especially following the river system of Europe, covering most of Europe. During the twelfth century, the chief meeting places of international traders were the fairs of Champagne in France. Here merchants from all Europe came to display their wares to other merchants, who in turn carried their purchases to local markets and prize customers (see Figure 18.2). By the thirteenth century the fairs were increasingly giving way to permanent markets established in cities.

Complementing the traffic in luxury items was an ever-growing exchange of goods between formerly self-sufficient manors and villages and the growing towns. Local trade in such items as salt, wine, and metals had always existed. From the eleventh century onward, it broadened to provide the growing towns with foodstuffs and raw materials and to carry manufactured products of the towns back to the rural settlements. In volume and number of people involved, the local town-country exchange was undoubtedly the larger component of medieval trade.

The expansion of commercial activity in western Europe promoted the growth of manufacturing. By the twelfth century the towns began to offer opportunities for skilled artisans to make a single product for sale to their fellow townspeople and rural buyers or to merchants who distributed them wherever there was a demand. Artisan manufacturing long remained a vital element of the town economy and put a vast quantity of commonplace goods into trade. Some high-quality items found an international market. By the thirteenth century some areas of Europe, particularly Flanders and northern Italy, had developed more complex manufacturing organizations where merchant entrepreneurs would "put out" raw materials into the households of hired laborers, often rural dwellers. This "putting out" system, or "cottage" industry, was especially applied to wool processing, which became international in scope: Raw wool produced in England was purchased in quantity by a Flemish entrepreneur. He organized the transportation of the wool to Flanders, where it was processed through a series of steps including washing, carding, spinning, weaving, fulling, and dyeing. Each separate operation was performed by specialized laborers, many women, who worked for hire in their own homes. The finished product was distributed by merchants contracted by the entrepreneur. A comparable system for woolen production developed in such northern Italian cities as Florence.

There is no way to tell what the revival of trade and manufacturing meant to the western European economy in quantitative terms. It is probably safe to venture that by the thirteenth century the productivity of western Europe surpassed that of the Greco-Roman world in trade and industry, and probably the contemporary Byzantine and Moslem economies as well. Agriculture was still the most important economic element, but the wealth from exchange and craftsmanship was important also. Moreover, trade and industry increasingly supplied the dynamism that encouraged continued economic growth and diversification.

FIGURE 18.2   A Medieval Fair   In this scene the bishop of Paris is giving his blessing to various merchants who are waiting for the opening of the fair held annually just outside Paris near the monastery of St. Denis. Such fairs provided a major setting for the exchange of goods from far and near. The presence of a figure so important as the bishop of Paris suggests that these fairs were viewed as a vital part of life. (Bibliothèque Nationale, Paris)

4. ECONOMIC CONSEQUENCES OF INCREASED PRODUCTION

The new level of prosperity generated by the increased agricultural, commercial, and industrial productivity in western Europe manifested itself in a hundred ways: better homes, bigger churches, more elaborate dress, greater quantities and varieties of food, more art and literature, more leisure. But aside from the general increase in wealth, greater productivity had more specific results.

First, economic growth revitalized city life. Towns had never disappeared from western Europe. But between the fall of Greco-Roman civilization and about 1000, they became primarily ecclesiastical, administrative, or defense centers, sparsely populated and economically dependent on agriculture. Between 1000 and 1300 ancient towns grew dramatically, and many new towns appeared. By 1300 there were cities of considerable population: Some Italian towns, such as Venice, Milan, Florence, and Genoa, had populations around 100,000; Paris may have had 80,000 people and London had 50,000. The vast majority of medieval cities probably had populations of 10,000 or less, but these modest figures did not detract from their vitality. The growing city population was constantly being fed by migration from rural areas. More significant than numbers was the fact that most urban residents earned their livelihood from trade and manufacturing, thus making the "new" urban centers quite different from the economically nonproductive towns of the early Middle Ages.

In terms of physical growth, many important towns of the era were simply enlargements of older episcopal, monastic, administrative, or military centers. Merchants and then artisans were attracted to these centers for many reasons: security, favor shown them by ruling authorities, access to rivers and roads, availability of buyers. Often they settled haphazardly outside the walls of the old center, their shops, stalls, and households creating a *suburb* (Latin, "under the city"). As commercial activity increased, the walls were extended to enclose the suburbs. Often the suburban marketplace became the center of urban life. During the High Middle Ages new towns were often established at locations favorable to commerce, and their growth resembled that of the old centers. Even some agricultural villages developed into centers of trade and manufacturing.

A second consequence of economic expansion was the growth of a money economy. Money had always circulated in western Europe, but minimally until the eleventh century. Thereafter, its use rapidly expanded to meet the needs of trade. The money economy soon spread to agriculture. The impact of the money economy was revolutionary. A whole new form of wealth emerged to challenge the monopoly held by land. Old economic relationships based on services and payment of obligations in kind were replaced by payments in money. Money could be accumulated in a way that labor services and produce could not. The liquidity of such accumulations encouraged the manipulation of money to create new economic opportunities. The possession of money allowed people to specialize their economic activities and still have the means to obtain the full range of material goods they needed. Money allowed more frequent exchanges. The exploitation of money became a new kind of economic activity.

A third major effect of economic growth was the transformation of agricultural production. The market for surplus food provided by the towns gave manorial seigneurs and peasants money incomes with which they could embellish their lives

with products from the town markets. This new potential for profit changed the emphasis on the manors from self-sufficiency to surplus production. And under this pressure the traditional system of servile dependency began to dissolve.

The dissolution proceeded in two broad directions. In many areas of western Europe, especially in the twelfth century, seigneurs began to break their demesnes into tenancies and rent them to peasants for cash. And they commuted the labor obligations of their serfs and the dues owed them in kind to money payments. Serfs could afford to buy off their obligations because the town market offered them a chance to sell produce and save a little money. But many seigneurs moved in the opposite direction, expanding their demesne and managing its cultivation themselves. A most profitable course was to concentrate on a specialized crop for sale. Seigneurs who did this often displaced peasants from their ancient tenancies and forced them to work for wages. In either case, the old manorial system dissolved over much of western Europe. In its place a variety of forms of agricultural exploitation emerged; all were dominated by the concern for profit, an end that could only be achieved by linking the countryside to the towns, their markets, and their money.

A fourth economic change involved the emergence of a new attitude toward economic activity based on profits. No longer were producers content with self-sufficiency; they worked and planned to gain more worldly goods. They began to devise strategies and techniques that would increase wealth: lending money for profit, speculating in trading ventures, manipulating land for gain, saving money. A protocapitalist economic mentality was taking shape that prized economic growth rather than stability.

Finally, western Europeans had achieved such economic growth by 1300 that they had seized economic leadership in the vast area surrounding the Mediterranean—a leadership that would eventually be extended to the whole world. No longer did Byzantium and Islam stand as advanced economic centers to a backward western Europe. As we shall see later, political factors helped the advance of the Europeans, but it is beyond question that their enterprise played a vital role in establishing their economic leadership.

5. SOCIAL CHANGE: THE BOURGEOISIE

The economic growth of western Europe during the High Middle Ages brought major changes to the simple social order of the world of lordship and dependency. Perhaps the most unexpected and significant change was the emergence of a new social group, the *bourgeoisie*. The shaping of this group represented the efforts of traders and artisans living in towns to define a place for themselves in a world lacking legal or social institutions that fitted their situation. In order to pursue their economic interests effectively, they had to seek various "liberties" or, more accurately, special privileges. Their effort slowly created for them a special collective status, distinguishing them socially from the clergy, noble warriors, and agricultural laborers.

As soon as men and women began to devote full time to commerce and manufacturing, they felt a basic need for personal freedom. Their livelihood depended on freedom to move about in a world that fixed people to fiefs and manors, to dispose of their property at will in a world where property was bound up in an intricate network of obligations, to apply their talent and labor to whatever economic opportunity arose in a world where long-sanctioned customs dictated how people spent their time and efforts. And so the merchants and artisans of the towns struggled for personal freedom and were successful in achieving it. Their methods were various: purchase; force; grants won from kings, feudal lords, and bishops. By 1300 simply living in a town meant personal freedom.

Although personal freedom was vital, it was not sufficient. Townspeople needed liberties that would allow them to determine their collective political destiny, both in terms of defining relationships among themselves and of regulating interactions with those outside their own community. To gain these added liberties, they sometimes banded together into associations to seek special privileges from those who had political authority over them and over the space their city occupied. Their efforts often resulted in a written document, called a *charter*, which defined their status and rights as a corporate body. Initially, such charters had to be fought for or purchased at a high cost, but acquiring a charter soon grew easier as kings, feudal lords, and bishops realized the profits to be gained by having a thriving town on their domains. Charters varied greatly in content. The typical charter recognized the citizen body of the town as a *corporation* that could act legally. Usually charters granted personal freedom to the townspeople and defined what they owed to the granting authority. Finally, charters granted some degree of self-governance. In a few cases, especially in Italy, towns gained complete freedom; such towns were called *communes*. More commonly, the townspeople had only limited privileges of self-government.

In shaping political institutions the townspeople experimented considerably. In most towns there was some degree of popular participation in political life, authority being vested in an elected council. In a typical commune the council usually possessed complete power to legislate, conduct courts, levy taxes, expend money for civic purposes, and negotiate with outside powers. Its only responsibility was to the citizens of the town. Many towns chose a chief administrative official— *mayor, burgomaster, podesta*—who functioned under the supervision of the council. Judicial affairs were entrusted to specially trained judges. Towns with only limited political freedom often had to respect the authority of a royal official or a bishop or a representative of a feudal lord who exercised many powers in judicial and financial matters. Whatever the form of government, the towns quickly created an elaborate new body of law regulating civic affairs.

A grave problem facing the bourgeoisie was the regulation of economic activity among merchants and artisans, a problem for which the rest of society had no solution. The usual answer was the establishment of *guilds* within each town. The merchants of a town usually organized themselves into a single merchant guild; the artisans formed several craft guilds, one for each trade. The merchant guild existed primarily to protect the interests of merchants from outsiders and to restrain the members from taking unfair advantage of one another and their customers. Each guild enacted rules governing prices to be charged, trading practices to be observed, and the conditions under which trade could be conducted. The craft guilds similarly imposed regulations on their members concerning prices, quality of goods, conditions of labor, and quantity of production. They also controlled the conditions for entering a trade. Boys began as *apprentices* to a master, working from two to seven years under his guidance and living in his household. The apprentice then became a *journeyman* who worked for hire until he had saved sufficient money and developed adequate skill to open his own shop and become a *master.* Before he acquired that rank, he had to submit his workmanship to a rigid examination by the guild. Along with their regulative functions, merchant and craft guilds had social functions. Each usually had its own guildhall, where banquets, pageants, and religious affairs were conducted for the entertainment and edification of the members. Each guild also aided its members when sickness or death struck a family.

Like their contemporaries on the farms, city dwellers perfected a variety of technical innovations that aided their economic activities. Market facilities were created to allow the display of goods and to facilitate money-changing operations. Sound coinage systems were established, especially by the Italian towns, whose coins were used in markets all over Europe. Insurance was developed to protect merchants against losses. Bookkeeping systems were devised to keep track of exchange operations and inventories. Merchants created ways to pool their resources for mutual benefits. Partnerships, called *commenda,* were formed to finance specific ventures; under these arrangements one or more merchants provided capital to another merchant to conduct a trading enterprise in return for a specified share of the profit. Eventually permanent companies were formed in which investors made deposits and received regular dividends paid by those who actually conducted the business enterprise.

Particularly significant as a means of providing capital to promote commercial and industrial growth was the development of a credit system and of an institution specializing in credit services: the bank. Bills of exchange became available, allowing merchants to deposit money one place in exchange for a receipt that could be used to pay for goods in another place. Money lending for interest became common. At least in the early stages of commercial growth, the Church strenuously opposed usury, the lending of money for interest, as a sin because it allowed people to profit from the misfortunes of others. Gradually, resistance was modified. The Church conceded that lenders who provided funds for investment in speculative activities were entitled to compensation for the risk, and that borrowers who did not pay their debts promptly should be liable for a penalty. By the thirteenth century large-scale lending operations conducted by banks were a vital part of the economy and a source of great profit.

The urban environment allowed greater social mobility than did the worlds of nobles and peasants. Trade and industry provided diverse opportunities for merchants and artisans to increase their wealth and better their social status. The range of economic activities existing in towns allowed for a more effective use of talent than was possible for nobles and peasants. Urban political and guild life created possibilities for individuals to play a part in shaping political decisions and even to achieve major leadership roles. Women also found a wider range of economic opportunities in the towns than were available to noble and peasant women. Aside from assisting their husbands in trading and manufacturing, women could engage in economic ventures independently. Widows of important merchants often continued their former husbands' trading enterprise. Many women were members of craft guilds, especially in the textile industry. Their rights were specifically protected in guild regulations, and many apparently practiced their craft alongside men, although often at lower wages. Although urban life permitted social mobility, across the period from 1000 to 1300 bourgeoisie society tended to become stratified on the basis of wealth. An oligarchy of rich entrepreneurs, usually merchants, increasingly claimed special status and gained control of city governments and guilds. At the other end of the social spectrum from these patricians was a growing number of poor, exploited laborers who sometimes vented their discontent by rioting.

Perhaps the most tragic victims of medieval urban society were western Europe's Jews. In the early Middle Ages Jews were viewed as a unique social group and were subjected to special legal restrictions. However, they were allowed and even encouraged to engage in commercial activity, ensuring their economic well-being. As more Christians began to engage in trade and manufacturing, measures were taken to exclude Jews from these activities, driving them to rely on money lending as a means of livelihood and causing them to be scorned as usurers as well as adherents of a detested religion. By the thirteenth century Christian bankers were taking over money-lending operations, devising whatever means they could to exclude their Jewish competitors from this lucrative business. Increasingly forced out of the mainstream of urban economic life, Jews were impoverished, forced into menial occupations, compelled to live in ghettos, and often savagely persecuted by urban and ecclesiastical authorities.

The urban environment generated its own cultural needs. Commercial and industrial activities required literacy, computing skills, and rational planning. The activities of the markets and the shops raised a new range of moral problems and special kinds of spiritual longing. The circumstances of city life called for special building needs. The interaction of people from many parts of Europe and the world beyond made city dwellers aware of cultural differences and raised questions about the validity of local customs. As a result of all of these forces, cities became centers of educational, intellectual, and artistic change.

For all its success in defining a unique place for itself in medieval society, the bourgeoisie was still by 1300 not very exalted as a social class. The nobility looked down on merchants and artisans as uncultured and boorish, an attitude that often caused the bourgeoisie to spend their riches aping the habits of the nobles. The Church officially disapproved of many bourgeois activities as violations of Christian morality. The peasants were suspicious of the sharp practices of the townspeople; the "city slicker" is no recent invention of the rural mind. Still, by 1300 the bourgeoisie was solidly established in law and was in fact a dynamic factor in the social order. It is worth noting that neither the Byzantine nor the Moslem world produced a comparable "middle class," although trade, manufacturing, and city life in these societies were older and no less vigorous.

6. SOCIAL CHANGE: THE NOBILITY

In this period of rapid economic change, the nobility remained the dominant social group, its power and influence solidly rooted in feudal bonds and seigneurial control. However, changing economic conditions created new circumstances that affected the status and the life style of the nobility.

Land remained the basis of aristocratic wealth and high social status. However, the manner in which wealth was derived from land changed as the new money economy emerged, and as a consequence, nobles changed their basic modes of exploiting their lands. As noted earlier, nobles became either entrepreneurs managing their own lands or landlords collecting rents. Both courses had risks. Especially tricky was the negotiating of rents that would give them sufficient income to maintain or even improve their social status. In an age of steady inflation many aristocrats made the mistake of agreeing to long-term leases that provided them with fixed returns whose real value declined over time. As a consequence, many noble families saw their wealth and social status reduced; some even lost noble status. Some nobles turned to commercial activities to bolster their wealth, either by extracting money payments from town governments in return for privileges or by investing in commercial ventures. Whether as a commercial farmer, a landlord, or an entrepreneur involved in both agriculture and commerce, a noble of the High Middle Ages had to concern himself much more with economic matters than did his ancestors if he hoped to sustain a key ingredient of noble status: wealth.

A variety of factors were at work during the High Middle Ages to bring about a more complex stratification of the nobility than had existed earlier. The expanding economy led to wide differences in wealth within the noble class, with wealth dependent on the amount of land individuals controlled and how rationally they used its productive potential. The development of strong central governments in many parts of Europe (see Chapters 19 and 20) permitted some nobles to increase their power and prestige by close association with royal governments. Strong government, however, worked to the disadvantage of other nobles, reducing their role in warfare and the exercise of private political jurisdictions. Increasing royal power and differences of wealth also made the personal lord-vassal relationship less important in defining the condition and role of an individual noble. By 1300 the nobility consisted of a variety of groupings whose interrelationships and interactions were defined by an ever more elaborate social code defining status. There was still mobility within the noble class, but on the whole the nobility was becoming an increasingly stratified and closed social order.

In general, nobles of the eleventh, twelfth, and thirteenth centuries enjoyed an increasingly comfortable material life. Their growing wealth coupled with the reduction of violence permitted them to build dwellings that gave more attention to comfort than to physical security. Stone castles, featuring more private chambers, fireplaces vented through chimneys, and improved sanitary facilities, appeared all over Europe. For a price a typical noble could enjoy a much more varied diet, including sugar and exotic spices from the East and fine wine from southern France. A greater variety of clothing was available, especially fine woolens and imported silks. The improved material standards of living subtly refined noble life, which led to a new code of behavior for those of noble status: The code was *chivalry,* especially celebrated in the vernacular literature of the troubadours and the writers of romances (see Chapter 23).

Chivalry as a code defining ideal noble behavior was rooted in the values of the feudal warrior; it stressed loyalty, bravery, generosity, honor, and military prowess. From the eleventh century on, these values acquired new shades of meaning that—at least in ideal terms—converted the crude, brutal warrior of earlier times into the knight skilled in the practice of courtly manners. Under the code of chivalry the ideal noble was still defined as a warrior who required an elaborate training in the arts of warfare before receiving public recognition as a knight. However, chivalry restrained his behavior. He was now expected to treat knights against whom he fought according to rules of honor. He was obligated to help the Church keep the Peace of God, which meant he could not wage war against certain categories of

people (the clergy, women, children), and the Truce of God, which prohibited fighting during certain periods holy to all Christians (Sundays, major holy days, Lent). In fact, the good knight sought some ideal for which to fight, such as crusading to spread the true faith or punishing evildoers who preyed on the weak. Under the chivalric code the warrior instinct tended to be channeled into carefully arranged engagements, called *tournaments,* where the martial arts were practiced under strict rules and amidst a pageantry that featured mannered behavior more than bloodshed and booty taking.

A key ingredient of chivalry was the important role given to women in the social structure. Whereas the old warrior society valued women little except as bearers of children and sources of dowries, the code of chivalry made women objects of devotion, loyalty, and sentimental attachment. A true knight was expected to develop a set of manners that would make his presence pleasing to noble women. In aristocratic circles an elaborate code of courtly love encouraged unmarried knights to demonstrate their prowess by winning the love of a noble lady—usually already married. The pursuit of the love of a lady called for patterns of behavior extending far beyond the ability to wield the tools of war, and it placed a higher value on virtues associated with women: graciousness, the capacity to give love, gentleness.

In order to respond to the new attention extended to them, noble women were expected to develop modes of behavior suited to a more refined world where males and females mixed in a courtly society. Whether the code of chivalry with its emphasis on romantic love between noble men and women improved the status of women remains a disputed question. Certainly women were treated with greater respect and gentleness than in earlier eras, and their participation in courtly social life was greatly expanded. In legal and economic practice, however, their role remained restricted. The prime object of marriage remained improving the economic and political status of the family and rearing children who would sustain the family status; marriages still served male interests and were controlled by males. Some evidence suggests that the new place defined for noble women in the chivalric code required women to be sheltered and protected as sex objects unsuited to participate in the world of work and power.

Taken together, the forces working to transform the conditions of noble life during the eleventh, twelfth, and thirteenth centuries resulted in the definition of the nobility as a leisured class of gentlemen and ladies clearly distinct from the rest of society by birth, wealth, and modes of behavior. The basic elements developed during the High Middle Ages to distinguish this dominant class survived long after the end of the Middle Ages to set the tone for genteel behavior and to define the privileges enjoyed by those claiming aristocracy.

7. SOCIAL CHANGE: THE PEASANTRY

The peasantry was also affected socially by the currents of economic change. During the twelfth and thirteenth centuries, there was large-scale freeing of serfs, especially in France, England, Flanders, Italy, and western Germany. Some peasants purchased their freedom; some gained it in return for colonizing new lands and others by leaving the manors for the city. A more important cause was the willingness of manorial seigneurs to surrender their rights to a serf's produce and services for money payments. In much of the West the serf was thus becoming a legally free tenant farmer, enjoying whatever benefits freedom brought, but also losing the paternalistic protection the manorial lord had often extended.

In a general way, the material life of the peasants improved during these centuries. Their incomes increased as a result of their greater productivity and of the inflationary trends that caused the prices they received for their produce to rise faster than the value of the obligations they owed. As they gained access to local markets, their diet was better, their health and life expectancy improved, and they were able to enjoy a wider range

of products. As might be expected, significant gradations in peasant status emerged as turns of fortune allowed some peasants to acquire the use of more land than others and as some proved more skillful and intelligent than others.

Some evidence suggests that as serfdom declined the peasants gained a greater degree of self-determination than they had had when most of them were locked into the manorial structure, legally bound to the soil as a dependent population. Most peasants continued to live in small villages and had few contacts with the wider world. In some cases they banded together to gain special privileges from their political superiors, which allowed them to control some aspects of village life, much as town dwellers—the bourgeoisie—were doing. They also sometimes directly influenced the affairs of the local church. Free peasants had more opportunity to decide how they would exploit their rented lands and how they would dispose of their crops. They could leave their village to take up farming where conditions were more favorable, or they could seek their fortunes as traders or artisans in the expanding urban centers.

However, we must not push too far in assessing the improved lot of the peasantry. As a class, the peasants remained at the bottom of the social scale. Perhaps they were even further removed from the top because of the increasing complexity, refinement, and class consciousness of the nobility. Peasants became even more the object of scorn by the nobility whose members assumed that their elevated status and expanding economic needs gave them the right to exploit the peasantry economically. For the most part, peasant life remained hard, poor, and limited, and peasant conditions were still largely determined by the dominant aristocracy. As was the case with the nobility and the bourgeoisie, the basic legal and social patterns shaping peasant life became so solidly fixed during the eleventh, twelfth, and thirteenth centuries that they would persist far into the future.

Origins of the Medieval Nobility

During much of this century historians of the Middle Ages have disagreed in explaining the origins of the medieval nobility, the class which dominated political, social, economic, and cultural life.

Early in this century there was general consensus on an interpretation that was given classic expression by the French historian, Marc Bloch, in his seminal work entitled *Feudal Society.* Reflecting a view of aristocracy rooted in the Ancien Régime in France, Bloch defined "nobility" as a social class enjoying specific hereditary privileges defined by law. He argued that such a class did not emerge until the twelfth century. Prior to then there had existed a loosely defined aristocracy, the members of which enjoyed social prominence based on their personal association with royalty and on favors—chiefly land grants and offices—flowing from that connection. This social group was destroyed in the tumult following the collapse of the Carolingian empire. Amidst that chaos, "new," "self-made" men enjoying a monopoly on military power used that power to carve out a legally sanctioned position of privilege transmitted by blood. In brief, the European nobility was derived from the aggressive, ruthless feudal warriors.

Recent investigations have raised questions about this explanation. Many historians, especially those influenced by concepts of social structures formulated by social scientists, argue that noble status embraces more than inheritable legal privileges. They claim that noble status involves factors such as wealth, power over others, life style, and mental perceptions. Any effort to explain the origins of the medieval nobility that focuses on narrow legal concerns without considering these factors is faulted.

Bloch's thesis has been challenged on another ground. He argued that during the tenth and eleventh centuries there was a break in an established order which created an opportunity for "new" men to forge for themselves a unique social status. But recent historians have shown that in many cases there was biological continuity linking Carolingian noble families to noble families of the eleventh and twelfth centuries. It can be demonstrated that some warrior upstarts entered the ranks of nobility during the tenth and eleventh centuries, chiefly by marrying into old noble families. But their social ascent by attaching themselves to existing noble circles does not support the case for a "new" and different nobility in the twelfth century. The issue of origins of the nobility must involve the study of noble status in the early Middle Ages.

Further complicating our understanding of the origins of the medieval nobility is a changing view of the relationship between noble status and the warrior element in society. It was once nearly axiomatic that by the twelfth century every warrior—every knight—was *ipso facto* a noble. Historians are no longer quite so positive. There is much evidence to suggest that many knights held an inferior social status. What seems to have been more important than simply being a warrior was membership in a new kind of family structure in which the material resources of each family were transmitted from father to eldest son rather than being divided among all members of the family, as was the ancient Germanic custom. In other words, noble status in the High Middle Ages originated only with the advent of the patrimonial family structure that permitted the concentration and transmission of wealth in a narrow circle of families.

Their disagreement on the origins of the medieval nobility leaves historians at loss in explaining a key source of dynamism in the medieval world: the processes which allowed some people to establish a position of dominance over society.

SUGGESTED READING

Overview of the Period 1000–1300

Christopher Brooke, *Europe in the Central Middle Ages, 962–1154*, 2nd ed. (1987).

John H. Mundy, *Europe in the High Middle Ages, 1150–1309* (1973).

Taken together, these well-written works provide excellent coverage of the period covered in Part Five.

R. W. Southern, *The Making of the Middle Ages* (1953). A brilliant essay, concentrating on "silent" forces affecting society.

Susan Reynolds, *Kingdoms and Communities in Western Europe, 900–1300* (1984). A challenging effort to identify collectivities that shaped society in the High Middle Ages.

Economic and Social History

R. H. Bautier, *The Economic Development of Medieval Europe*, trans. Heather Karolyi (1971).

N. J. G. Pounds, *An Economic History of Medieval Europe* (1974).

Two excellent general surveys of economic history.

Georges Duby, *Rural Economy and Country Life in the Medieval West*, trans. Cynthia Postan (1968). The best description of agriculture and rural life.

Robert S. Lopez, *The Commercial Revolution of the Middle Ages, 950–1350* (1971). A persuasive defense of an interesting thesis.

Christopher Brooke, *The Structure of Medieval Society* (1971).

Charles T. Wood, *The Age of Chivalry: Manners and Morals, 1000–1450* (1970).

Two studies that seek to describe the general features of the medieval social order.

Philippe Ariès and Georges Duby, ed., *A History of Private Life*, Vol. 2: *Revelations of the Medieval World*, ed. Georges Duby (1987). Rich in details about how people lived during the High Middle Ages.

Frances and Joseph Gies, *Marriage and Family in the Middle Ages* (1987). A good introduction to a complex issue.

David Herlihy, *Medieval Households* (1985). Illuminates the nature of a basic social institution.

Maurice Keen, *Chivalry* (1984). A fine introduction.

Shalamith Shahar, *The Fourth Estate. A History of Women in the Middle Ages*, trans. Chaya Galai (1983).

Margaret Wade Labarge, *A Small Sound of the Trumpet: Women in Medieval Life* (1986).

Eileen Power, *Medieval Women* (1976).

Three of the best of many recent studies of medieval women.

Michel Mollat, *The Poor in the Middle Ages. An Essay in Social History*, trans. Arthur Goldhammer (1986). A pioneering study in a field little explored.

John M. Carter, *Sports and Pastimes of the Middle Ages* (1988). Suggests that people always find ways to have fun.

Urban Life

Henri Pirenne, *Medieval Cities: Their Origins and the Revival of Trade*, trans. Frank D. Halsey (1925).

Fritz Rörig, *The Medieval Town*, trans. D. J. Matthew (1967).

Edith Ennen, *The Medieval Town*, trans. Natalie Fryde (1979).

Howard Saalman, *Medieval Cities* (1968).

Lacking an effective synthesis of a much-studied subject, any of these four titles will provide a helpful introduction.

Joseph and Frances Gies, *Life in a Medieval City* (1969). A good reconstruction of life in a typical medieval city.

CHAPTER 19

Political Revival: The Holy Roman Empire

FIGURE 19.1 The Holy Roman Emperor as "Agent of Christ" This tenth-century ivory plaque shows Emperor Otto I offering a model of the cathedral church of Magdeburg to Christ who is seated in majesty. It reflects the conviction not only that the emperor controlled the Church but also that he was the intercessor between Christ and the faithful Christians on earth. (The Metropolitan Museum of Art, Gift of George Blumenthal, 1941)

While western Europe's lesser men and women were producing new wealth and rearranging their social relationships, its kings were successfully engaged in rebuilding political structures capable of controlling much larger political communities than the principalities that dominated tenth-century western Europe. By 1300 their efforts had produced a level of political order in the West that had not existed since the collapse of the Roman imperial regime. No less important, the major political entities created between 1000 and 1300 marked the origins of states that have persisted until the present. Although state building advanced over all of western Europe, we shall focus attention chiefly on political developments in Germany, Italy, England, and France.

During the High Middle Ages successful kings drew on several traditions to expand their authority: Germanic concepts of warrior kings, the Carolingian ideal of ministerial kingship, Roman law. But central to their success was their exploitation of rights bestowed on them by their position as chief lords in the feudal hierarchy, a status that provided them with extensive rights to command the loyalty, obedience, and services of their vassals. In essence, the states shaped between 1000 and 1300 were *feudal monarchies,* made possible by the exploitation of feudal practices often portrayed as the very antitheses of large states and effective central power.

1. THE FOUNDING OF THE HOLY ROMAN EMPIRE

The earliest and most impressive effort at political reconstruction during the High Middle Ages involved a political entity that later came to be known as the Holy Roman Empire. This state resulted from the combination of kingdoms established by the divisions of the Carolingian Empire. The most important was the kingdom of the East Franks defined by the Treaty of Verdun in 843 (see Map 16.2). To this German core were joined the subkingdoms formed during the ninth century by divisions of the kingdom of Lotharingia; of these, the kingdom of Italy was of special importance as a component of the Holy Roman Empire (see Map 20.1 and Map 16.2). During the late ninth and

early tenth centuries, royal power steadily declined in all of these subkingdoms. In the kingdom of the East Franks—Germany—the dukes who had served the strong Carolingian kings as royal officials usurped royal power to create virtually independent principalities, the chief of which were Saxony, Bavaria, Franconia, Swabia, and Upper and Lower Lotharingia (Lorraine in French) (see Map 20.1). These emerging territorial entities reflected pre-Carolingian tribal groupings. These ethnic ties, combined with the public powers associated with the ducal office, gave each principality an internal solidarity that hindered the complete fragmentation of Germany into petty lordships and the feudalization of relationships among the ruling nobility. An indication of the advance of ducal power came in 911, when the dukes joined hands to depose the last Carolingian king and to elect one of their own, Conrad, duke of Franconia, as king. In the Carolingian kingdoms of Italy and Burgundy-Arles, the process of political fragmentation was also proceeding rapidly; local potentates carved out principalities and imposed their lordship on the local population with little respect for royal power. To complicate the situation, in the late ninth and early tenth centuries this entire area, like most of Europe, was ravaged by the attacks of Saracens, Magyars, and Vikings.

In Germany the drift toward localism was reversed with the election of Henry I, duke of Saxony, as king in 917. His successor, Otto I, the Great (936–973), was the architect of the basic policies restoring monarchical authority. After a long struggle, he compelled the dukes to accept royal overlordship; in the course of this struggle, he managed to dislodge most of the powerful families who controlled the ducal offices, often replacing them with members of his own family. Otto earned fame as an effective warrior king by inflicting a decisive defeat on Magyar invaders at the battle of Lechfeld in 955, ending their destructive raids on Germany. Not content with this notable success, Otto encouraged military expansion, colonization, and missionary activity into the Slavic world, beginning a Germanic "drive to the East" that continued for centuries and found favor among German princes, prelates, and peasants.

Otto's success in these ventures stemmed from

his ability to strengthen the institutional base for royal power. Although he steadfastly insisted on service from the dukes as representatives of public authority, he based his power primarily on a feudal alliance with the clergy. Following a model set by the great Carolingian rulers, he made large grants of royal land to bishops and abbots on a feudal basis, creating ecclesiastical fiefs in every corner of Germany. The church officials who received royal fiefs became royal vassals, obligated to render to the king the military and political services needed to sustain royal authority. To make this policy work, Otto had to be certain of the political capabilities and the loyalty of the men who filled ecclesiastical offices and received as fiefs the lands attached to these offices. He therefore assumed the power to select those who filled clerical offices. As a consequence of this policy, called *lay investiture*, the ecclesiastical establishment became the vital element in royal administration.

Successful in uniting and defending his kingdom, Otto was drawn into Italian affairs. Certainly his urge to imitate the Carolingians was a factor in this fateful step. But political realities played a part. By mid–tenth century many Italians, including the popes, were looking for an outsider capable of doing what their feeble kings could not do: curb internal disorder and protect them from attacks by Magyars and Saracens. Otto was forced to pay heed to Italian affairs because some of his powerful subjects, especially the dukes of Bavaria, were fishing in those troubled waters in search of a power base from which to defy his royal authority. After an initial venture into Italy in 951, which resulted in his assumption of the title of "king of Italy," he returned in 961 to solidify his hold on his new kingdom. In 962 he seized Rome and was crowned emperor by Pope John XII, grateful for being freed from the oppressive clutches of greedy Roman nobles. The office created by Charlemagne was thus renewed; the imperial crown was again worn by the most powerful ruler in the West whose accomplishments had earned him this honor. A vigorous diplomatic campaign ended with recognition of the imperial title by the Byzantine emperor; Byzantine acceptance of Otto's emperorship was fortified by a marriage alliance involving Otto's son, the future Otto

II (973–983), and a remarkable Byzantine princess, Theophano. Otto I forced his authority on the Italian nobility and entrusted the exercise of royal power to powerful church officials who became his vassals. Especially significant was his policy toward the papacy. When John XII refused to accept imperial directions, Otto deposed him, dictated the election of a more pliant successor, and imposed a rule that no pope would be selected in the future without the consent of the emperor. This decision, opening an era of German domination of the papacy, punctuated the fact that the emperor was head of the Christian community, just as Constantine and Charlemagne had been.

2. OTTO'S SUCCESSORS AND THE GATHERING OPPOSITION

From Otto I's death in 973 until 1056, a succession of five emperors continued his policies with considerable success. In Germany the independence of the duchies was curbed, and their leaders were made subservient to imperial authority. The Church was skillfully manipulated to ensure its service to the emperors; in turn, the emperors acted in a variety of ways to promote its interests. To complement the administrative services performed by feudalized church officials, the emperors developed a corps of secular administrators, called *ministeriales*, recruited from the nonfree population under terms that made them totally devoted to royal service. The emperors kept a firm hold on Italy, acting there chiefly through vassal bishops. The empire was expanded on its southwestern border by the absorption of the old Carolingian subkingdom of Burgundy-Arles. Strong pressures continued to be applied in the East, so successfully that by 1056 Poland, Bohemia, and Magyar Hungary all recognized imperial overlordship. The emperors and their ecclesiastical supporters sought to surround the imperial office with a theocratic ideology that stressed the sacred role of the emperor as protector of the Christian order (see Figure 19.1). This effort reached its apogee during the reign of Otto III (983–1002), whose mother, Empress Theophano, joined forces with the leading scholar of the age, Gerbert, now reigning as Pope Sylvester II (999–1003), to promote plans for installing the emperor in Rome in a setting that would exalt not only his sacral role but also his successorship to ancient Roman emperors and perhaps his superiority over contemporary emperors reigning in Constantinople.

But the very success of the German emperors had its cost; it provoked opposition from a variety of sources. The German nobility accepted imperial authority grudgingly; all the while its members strengthened their position by extending their landholdings, consolidating their hold on the peasantry, and building their own alliances with the Church by founding monasteries over which they maintained control. The royal office was particularly vulnerable because it remained elective; despite their efforts, the tenth- and eleventh-century rulers were not able to set aside the ancient Germanic elective principle in favor of hereditary succession. In Italy the nobles resented imperial authority and foreign domination. The emerging Italian commercial cities were eager to establish their liberties at the expense of imperial control. Rulers beyond the imperial frontiers—the French kings in the West and Slavic princes in the East—were suspicious of imperial designs on their independence and their territories.

Finally and most important was the opposition generated by a powerful religious reform movement sweeping over Europe (see Chapter 22). In its ideological aspect this movement challenged the concept that secular rulers—including the emperor—were the divinely ordained leaders of Christian society. In its practical aspect the reform movement was directed against the feudalization of the Church, especially lay control over church offices and property, and against the worldly, immoral clergy produced by these practices. Support for reform came from monks, bishops, and monarchs, including even the saintly emperor Henry III (1039–1056).

Eventually, the reform movement found its leadership in Rome. Since the late ninth century, the papacy had played a modest role in directing Christian life. The papal office was controlled first by local Roman noble families and then after 962 by the Holy Roman emperors. A turning point came when Henry III installed a dedicated German reformer, Leo IX (1049–1054), as pope. Under Leo's leadership, a circle of reformers gathered at Rome, devoting their talents to defining the goals of reform and gathering precedents to justify purifying religious life. Eventually the driving force of this group was a monk named Hildebrand, later to be Pope Gregory VII, who gave the movement a political orientation. He saw the Church as an earthly corporate body that had the responsibility to work out God's will—the salvation of humanity. To achieve that end, the Church must become a visible community with its own head, its own law, its own resources, and its own liberty. All Christians, even the greatest princes, must be directed to the proper execution of their responsibilities in the drama of salvation by the bishop of Rome, the successor of St. Peter as Christ's vicar on earth. Herein lay the radical element of the reform ideology: It denied the role of secular rulers as divinely ordained directors of Christian life. At best, princes were agents of the Church, commissioned by ecclesiastical authorities to assist in directing Christian society and subject to priestly judgment in serving their role.

During Leo's pontificate, the papacy turned its new ideology into a practical reform program that impinged directly on the existing political and ecclesiastical establishments. The concept of papal headship of the Church was widely propagated to remind lesser clergy of their obligation to look to Rome for direction. That claim was even extended to the Byzantine Empire; the result was a bitter quarrel that ended in 1054 when the pope and the patriarch of Constantinople excommunicated each other, creating a schism between the Roman and Greek churches that has persisted to the present. The popes issued a steady flow of legislation against the immorality and corruption afflicting the clergy, especially *simony* (buying and selling of church offices and services) and clerical marriage. Papal agents organized local church councils all over the West to enact reforming legislation. Popes began to build a centralized administrative machinery in Rome to enforce papal rules over all Europe. In 1059 a papal decree provided that henceforth popes would be chosen by the College of Cardinals, a body of ecclesiastical officials centered in Rome who assisted the pope in carrying out church administration. The emperor was deprived of any voice in papal elections except to approve what the cardinals decided. Seeking to strengthen its position, the papacy in 1059 formed an alliance with the Normans, a new political force emerging in southern Italy and Sicily (see Chapter 21); this pact gave the papacy a protector other than the emperor.

This aggressive policy generated resistance in many quarters. Many clergymen, long accustomed to having wives or concubines and to receiving payment for religious services, squirmed at the talk of moral reform. Bishops and abbots resented Rome's growing interference in local religious affairs that tradition had reserved to their jurisdiction. Important lords were uneasy at the prospect of losing the right to appoint church officials and to control the income from ecclesiastical property and offices. Especially vulnerable was the Holy Roman emperor, who not only relied on a subservient, feudalized Church as the chief source of his power but also claimed, by virtue of his exalted office, the God-given right to direct the destiny of Christian society. Such formidable opposition might well have blighted the reform movement had it not been for Gregory VII. A strong, willful man of great political ability and courage, he was not afraid to act to achieve what he believed was right. Once elected pope in 1073, he moved resolutely to sustain the effort to correct religious life. In 1075 he decreed that lay investiture—that is, control by lay authorities over the election and installation of ecclesiastical officials—was illegal. Henceforth, church officials would have to be chosen and installed by the Church itself. And henceforth, property pertaining to ecclesiastical offices would not be subject to lay control. This act, challenging the entire feudal order on a crucial issue, put the papacy on a collision course with most of the kings and lords of western Europe, and especially the Holy Roman emperors, in a contest known as the *investiture struggle.*

3. THE INVESTITURE STRUGGLE

As Gregory moved forward with his reform program, his most formidable foe was the young emperor, Henry IV (1056–1106). He succeeded his father Henry III, under whose rule imperial power had reached its apogee, while still a child. During his minority imperial power was severely chal-

lenged, not only by the papal reformers but also by the German nobility. But when Henry IV assumed full power in 1065, he left no doubt that he intended to follow the policies that had made his predecessors strong. Among other things, he proceeded to appoint men of his choice to episcopal office, despite Gregory VII's prohibition of lay investiture.

The break that was sure to come developed in 1075 in connection with a vacant episcopal see in Milan. Since control of this major city was vital to imperial power in Italy, Henry IV acted decisively to impose his candidate, despite the armed resistance of the city's populace. Late in 1075 Gregory sent Henry a letter ordering him to do penance for violating Church law and threatening him with excommunication and loss of his office. With the backing of most of the German bishops, Henry replied by declaring that "the false monk" Hildebrand was not even pope, since his election had been improper. Whereupon in 1076 Gregory excommunicated the emperor, suspended him from office, and invited the Germans to elect a new king. Many German nobles and bishops leaped at this opportunity to weaken the king. They commanded Henry to appear before a meeting to be held in Germany early in 1077 with the pope in attendance. If Henry could not clear himself of excommunication before this meeting, he would be deposed.

Henry IV faced a crucial issue. The specific question of lay investiture was no longer as critical as the broader implication that the pope could claim to judge the emperor unworthy of his office and bring about his deposition. Henry had to offset this claim to save his regime. His next action was tactically brilliant. He set out to intercept Gregory before the pope could reach Germany to preside over the projected meeting. In January 1077 he found Gregory at Canossa in northern Italy. In the garb of a penitent, the mighty emperor begged the pope's forgiveness. Although Gregory realized that to grant this would free a strengthened Henry to continue the imperial policy, he could not abdicate his responsibility as a priest to forgive repentant sinners. After keeping the emperor waiting in the snow for three days, Gregory absolved him (see Figure 19.2). The pope had won a moral victory by forcing the most powerful ruler in Eu-

FIGURE 19.2   A Humble Emperor: Henry IV   This manuscript miniature from the early twelfth century shows Emperor Henry IV (kneeling) imploring Countess Mathilda of Tuscany and Abbot Hugh of Cluny to intercede in his behalf with Pope Gregory VII just before the fateful meeting of pope and emperor at Canossa. (Biblioteca Apostolica Vaticana, Rome)

rope to admit that he had a superior, but his action deeply disappointed his supporters in Germany and weakened the papal cause against Henry.

Henry moved at once to deal with his most dangerous immediate foes, the German nobility, some of whom persisted in their plans to depose him by electing an antiking. Henry skillfully and speedily beat down their resistance. He then turned to Italy, captured Rome, forced Gregory VII into exile, elevated a supporter to the papal throne, and had himself crowned emperor in 1084. By 1085, the year in which the disillusioned Gregory died, it appeared that Henry IV's cause had been vindicated and the tide of radical reform blunted.

But the victory was a hollow one; the papal challenge had unleashed too many enemies. Henry was unable to hold Rome against the papal allies, led by the Normans, and the papal office was returned to strong and independent hands, especially those of Urban II (1088–1099), who sustained the cause of reform and won ever-increasing support for its ideals. In Germany, the nobles kept up their resistance and slowly undermined royal power. Although Henry defended his power valiantly, by the end of his reign he was a virtual fugitive from the rebellious nobles.

Henry IV's three successors, who ruled until 1152, could not stem the assault on monarchical authority. Imperial power in Italy nearly disappeared, usurped by independent towns, nobles, and the papacy. The imperial crown became a pawn of warring noble factions, with election going to the prince who seemed least likely to exert effective power. Imperial resources were dissipated or usurped, and the administrative machinery broke down. In 1122 Emperor Henry V made peace with the Church over the specific issue of lay investiture by signing the Concordat of Worms, which provided that election to ecclesiastical offices and the formal act of installation into office be made by the Church, while the lands and secular powers associated with the office be invested by the ruler. This compromise gave the emperor an effective veto over elections by allowing him to withhold the property of the office. But it also deprived the monarch of absolute control over its major support, a loyal episcopacy selected by the ruler.

Although the specific problem of lay investiture had been resolved through compromise by the Concordat of Worms, the long struggle to arrive at that settlement had caused a fundamental change in German society (and to a lesser extent in imperial Italy) that undermined the system of royal government shaped by Otto the Great and his successors. During the years of the investiture struggle feudal practices spread rapidly through imperial society. Interminable civil wars drove the weak to seek protection by becoming vassals of the strong and allowed the strong to create independent lordships by surrounding themselves with as many vassals and fiefs as possible. The embattled emperors conceded royal lands as fiefs to princes in a desperate hope of winning support. As the process of feudalization proceeded, a hodgepodge of lordships emerged. There was no hierarchy giving the emperor a theoretical position as the ultimate feudal lord. In fact, the monarchy was left out of the emerging power structure. The real centers of power were powerful noble families who succeeded in surrounding themselves with vassals and fiefs without accepting a position of legal dependency on the emperor. By 1152 the German monarchy had lost touch with the new feudalized society that had emerged during the investiture struggle. A kingdom that had escaped feudalization in the tenth century had now acquired a feudal structure, and the monarchy had limited means of coping with it.

4. THE HOHENSTAUFENS

Despite the destructive impact of the investiture struggle, the Holy Roman Empire survived. At mid–twelfth century a new dynasty, the Hohenstaufens, took up the task of rebuilding the imperial government. The first notable Hohenstaufen was Frederick I, Barbarossa (Red Beard, 1152–1190). He resolutely set about establishing a basis for royal power that would fit the new political realities. In essence, his policy was aimed at turning feudalism to royal advantage in order to build a system of government based not on theocratic principles but on secular principles, principles that Frederick derived largely from the Roman law then enjoying a revival in western Europe.

Frederick's first task was to establish order in Germany by pacifying the powerful noble families. He made broad concessions to a few great nobles in return for their acceptance of vassalage and allowed them to curb their troublesome vassals, the lesser nobles. The chief beneficiary of this policy was the leader of the traditionally anti-Hohenstaufen Welf faction, Henry the Lion, who with royal approval became duke of both Saxony and Bavaria. But Frederick was careful to define his regalian rights clearly and to insist that his great vassals respect them. To enforce these rights, he gave special attention to increasing his royal domain, much of which was concentrated in Swabia (the Hohenstaufen homeland) and in the King-

dom of Burgundy, which became a part of the royal domain in 1156 as a result of Frederick's marriage to its heiress. A corps of nonfeudal civil servants was developed to administer this domain. He continued the old policy of turning the German Church to royal support.

From the beginning of his reign Frederick made it clear that he intended to possess the imperial title and to exercise all the powers that accrued to it. In fact, he was the first to call his realm the "Holy Roman Empire." In Italy this policy brought him into confrontation with three powerful forces: the papacy, the Italian towns, and the Norman kingdom. Initially Frederick's relations with the papacy were cordial, and Frederick was crowned emperor by the pope in 1155. However, he made it clear that he had no intention of admitting papal supremacy or of allowing the papacy to restrict what he considered to be his regalian rights over the Church. In taking this position, he aroused suspicions at the papal court that he intended to challenge the position that the papacy had defined for itself during the investiture struggle.

Even more emphatic was his position with respect to the Italian towns, from which he intended to draw material support for his system of government. By 1158 he laid down a new set of rules to govern the relationship between the emperor and the rich Italian towns. Henceforth, the emperor would reclaim the regalian rights that he argued the towns had usurped. They were to pay regular taxes, accept imperial officials as their rulers, and permit the emperor to coin money and regulate commerce. At one stroke, the freedoms the Italian cities had been fashioning during the previous century were to be severely limited.

Once Frederick had made clear his policy toward the papacy and the towns, the storm broke. For most of his reign he was forced to fight an imposing array of enemies that became known as the Guelf faction (the anti-imperial counterpart in Italy of the Welf faction in Germany). The Guelf struggle against the Hohenstaufen forces (known in Italy as the Ghibellines) was led by Pope Alexander III (1159–1181), a true heir to Gregory VII. Frederick tried to replace Alexander with a pope favorable to imperial interests but with no success. The towns of northern Italy provided the backbone of Guelf strength, especially after they joined hands in 1167 with papal blessing to form the Lombard League. In 1176 at the Battle of Legnano, this league inflicted a defeat on Frederick's army, which greatly impeded his efforts to assert his authority over the towns. The Guelfs could usually count on the support of the Norman kingdom of Sicily in resisting Hohenstaufen power.

In the long run Frederick managed to withstand this powerful coalition, chiefly by compromising some of his ambitions. In 1177 he gave up his attempt to establish a pro-imperial pope and recognized Alexander III. In 1183, at the Peace of Constance, the Italian towns came to terms, recognizing Frederick's overlordship in return for extensive specific rights that assured their actual independence. In 1186 he arranged for his son Henry to marry the heiress of the Norman kingdom of Sicily, detoothing one of his most persistent foes. Frederick's sensible compromises had not gained him full control of Italy nor subdued the papacy, but his authority in Italy was still extensive and his position as emperor intact. His long-standing policy of trying to live with a few great princes in Germany did not prove wholly successful. Eventually, he had to smash the chief Welf prince, Henry the Lion, for unfaithfulness as a vassal. Thereafter, he decided to break up the large principalities and grant the territory to many lesser nobles who would serve as royal vassals. This step relieved the immediate danger, but in the long run, by further promoting feudalization, it proved fatal to royal power.

Frederick Barbarossa's illustrious career ended in 1190 when he was drowned while leading the Third Crusade. He left behind the framework for a strong monarchy, but much needed to be done by his successors to make that system permanent. His son, Henry VI (1190–1197), began as if he would sustain his father's work, fighting a successful war to control the kingdom of Sicily, which he claimed by virtue of his marriage. But then, instead of maintaining effective control over the restless German nobility, he became enmeshed in a series of schemes to extend his power over the Mediterranean to the Holy Land, France, and Spain. As his schemes unfolded, the foes of strong central rule began to join hands. Only a premature death in 1197 saved him from paying the full price

for too great an ambition.

For the next two decades the fate of the Holy Roman Empire was determined by the most powerful of all the medieval popes, Innocent III (1198–1216). In 1198 he assumed guardianship over Henry VI's three-year-old heir, Frederick, and in that role took virtual control over the kingdom of Sicily. He sought to prevent a single Hohenstaufen from ruling Germany and Sicily, a policy that would allow him to safeguard papal power in central Italy. In Germany a faction of the nobles remained loyal to the Hohenstaufens and elected Philip of Swabia as king. Innocent immediately promoted the claims of a Welf candidate, Otto of Brunswick, the son of Henry the Lion; in 1198 Otto was also elected king. This disputed succession led to a civil war that lasted until 1212 and caused great damage in Germany. Both England and France were drawn into this struggle, England in support of the Welfs and France on the side of the Hohenstaufens. Papal diplomacy played the warring factions in Germany against each other and encouraged the northern Italian towns and the nobles of central Italy to throw off imperial control. The work of Frederick Barbarossa seemed completely ruined; the Holy Roman Empire had become a pawn of the papacy.

In 1212, with the aid of the king of France, Innocent engineered the election of his ward to the kingship of Germany and eventually to the Holy Roman emperorship. Frederick II paid for papal support by making sweeping concessions that returned control of the German church to the papacy and fortified papal independence in Italy. But he proved no docile servant of the pope. He took up the battle to build a strong Holy Roman Empire with a political skill, ruthless ambition, and personal qualities that made him one of the most intriguing figures in all medieval history. Highly educated, intelligent, cosmopolitan in tastes and outlooks, his interest in literature, science, and learning so impressed his contemporaries that he was called *stupor mundi*—wonder of the world. His enemies—and they were many—branded him irreligious, immoral, dishonest, cruel, and Antichrist; his admirers saw him as a new man driven by a secular spirit quite distinct from the religious values dominant in his era.

Frederick II took a new approach to the gov-

WHERE HISTORIANS DISAGREE

The Investiture Struggle: A Medieval Revolution?

Many historians view the investiture struggle as a revolutionary event, but they do not agree on why its impact was so important.

One school of thought sees the struggle as a revolt against a deeply imbedded system governing church property and offices. Under Roman law the Church was considered a corporate entity, capable of owning its property. But the Germans brought with them a concept that held that everything connected with a piece of land belonged to the proprietor. As a consequence, proprietors viewed churches built on their land as private property. By extension, they treated the offices and revenues associated with churches as a part of their possession to be disposed of as they saw fit. The investiture struggle was in essence an attempt to liberate church property and offices from private ownership and to vest them in the hands of the corporate Church. The consequent shifting of vast wealth and its accompanying power from secular to clerical hands was of revolutionary importance.

Another view sees the struggle as the cause of a revolution in the political system of the Holy Roman Empire. They argue that between 962–1075 the Holy Roman Empire developed into the strongest, best-organized political unit in western Europe. Its constitution was based on a mutually beneficial union between church and state. Gregory VII's program destroyed that union, thereby undermining the constitutional system of the Holy Roman Empire and allowing the secular nobles to establish independence from the emperor. The result was political chaos in Germany and Italy which kept these areas from developing strong states until the nineteenth century.

Other historians argue that the investiture struggle marked a revolution in sociopolitical ideology. For centuries, western Europeans had accepted the idea that the welfare of Christian society depended on the actions of divinely ordained secular rulers to guide society toward salvation. The royal office combined the functions of both king and priest in order to accomplish divine will. The Gregorian reforms challenged this concept of right order by insisting that priests should direct society toward its ultimate end. The true Christian community was the Church. The clergy, organized under papal control, had the ultimate authority in directing lay society, including kings, toward its God-ordained ends.

Still other scholars see the investiture struggle as a decisive turning point in defining how a Christian should act in the world. During the early Middle Ages the monastic ideal of flight from the world predominated. The investiture struggle dramatized another view: Holy people—exemplified by Gregory VII—should move out of the cloister into the wicked world to attack evil and to persuade sinful kings, nobles, clergymen, and common people to "convert" to the true Christian life. As a result of the investiture struggle the world-denying monk was replaced by the world-involved activist as the ideal Christian.

Whether these issues constitute the "stuff" of revolution is a matter of judgment. However, when a particular episode in history entails control of vast amounts of property, the constitution of a major state, the nature of right order in society, and how people act to change society, then surely major matters are at stake. One test of the argument that the investiture struggle marked a revolution might be to watch for the extent to which these fundamental issues shaped historical development after the investiture struggle.

ernance of the Holy Roman Empire. He had little interest in Germany as the base for imperial power; Italy was the focus of his political concern. After becoming ruler of Germany, he remained there only until 1220. He spent these years surrendering royal power. He was as generous to the great feudal princes as to the papacy: He made their fiefs hereditary, gave them full rights of government over the fiefs, and even turned over to them the strong position the early Hohenstaufens had established in the towns. These concessions ensured that he would receive little help from Germany in his effort to rule the Holy Roman Empire.

As he progressively disengaged himself from Germany, Frederick turned his energies toward creating in his homeland, the Kingdom of Sicily, a centralized, bureaucratic state where royal power would be absolute. Frederick spelled out the program for this regime in a code of law, called the Constitutions of Melfi, issued in 1231. This document, which was strongly influenced by concepts drawn from Roman law and by the model of the Byzantine Empire, gave the king supreme authority as lawgiver and judge, set up a bureaucracy to control local affairs, and virtually abolished all the privileges of feudal lords and towns. Frederick then attempted to impose a comparable regime on Italy. This move aroused the ancient enemies of Hohenstaufen power: the papacy and the Italian communes. Under the leadership of two extremely able and tenacious popes, Gregory IX (1227–1241) and Innocent IV (1243–1254), both uncompromising advocates of papal supremacy, the papacy and the towns battled Frederick for nearly twenty years. The emperor fought skillfully and with great flair, but he lacked the resources to establish control over Italy; papal money and the human resources of the Italian towns were too great. Papal prestige in Europe was too extensive for Frederick to form an effective antipapal alliance; in fact, most European rulers showed little interest in what appeared to be an Italian power struggle. The emperor drew almost no help from his German vassals, who were too busy enjoying the privileges he had extended them. Frederick II died in 1250 far from realizing his ambitions; in fact, his policy had irreparably damaged any realistic base for imperial authority.

Amid bickering and foreign intervention, the German nobles did not agree on a new king until 1273, when they elected Rudolph of Hapsburg, qualified chiefly by his lack of strength. In the interval 1250 to 1273, known as the Interregnum, the last vestiges of effective imperial power were destroyed. Germany had finally broken to pieces politically. Meanwhile a French prince, Charles of Anjou, accepting a papal invitation, assumed the crown of the Kingdom of Sicily in 1266. In the rest of the peninsula each city, each noble, each churchman went an independent way, respecting no higher authority and feeling no attachment to Italy. The Slavic kingdoms that had so long been under strong German influence were also free. One of the cherished dreams of medieval society—a Christian empire in which people who held one faith would enjoy one ruler and one law to guide them in the struggle for salvation—had failed.

SUGGESTED READING

The Holy Roman Empire

K. J. Leyser, *Medieval Germany and Its Neighbors, 900–1250* (1982). The best general history.

Josef Flechenstein, *Early Medieval Germany,* trans. Bernard S. Smith (1978). Especially good on background of the empire of the High Middle Ages.

Horst Fuhrman, *Germany in the High Middle Ages, c. 1050–1200,* trans. Timothy Reuter (1986). Useful on the investiture struggle.

J. K. Hyde, *Society and Politics in Medieval Italy: The Evolution of the Civil Life, 1000–1350* (1973). Effective survey of the complex history of medieval Italy.

R. Folz, *The Concept of Empire in Western Europe from the Fifth to the Fourteenth Century,* trans. Sheila Ann Ogilvie (1969). Treats the concepts undergirding the medieval ideal of universal empire.

Gerd Tellenbach, *Church, State, and Christian Society at the Time of the Investiture Contest,* trans. R. F. Bennett

(1940). A classic on the ideological issues of the investiture struggle.

Uta-Renate Blumenthal, *The Investiture Controversy: Church and Monarchy from the Ninth to the Twelfth Century* (1988). Reflects modern scholarship on a much-disputed problem.

Biography

Peter Munz, *Frederick Barbarossa: A Study in Medieval Politics* (1969).

Thomas C. Van Cleve, *The Emperor Frederick II of Hohenstaufen: Immutator Mundi* (1972).

A. J. Macdonald, *Hildebrand: A Life of Gregory VII* (1932).

CHAPTER 20
Political Revival: England and France

FIGURE 20.1 A Medieval King's Nightmares
These drawings from a manuscript portray a dream of Henry I of England. He dreams that his royal power will not be sufficient to control the major elements of his subjects: the peasants, the nobles, and the clergy. Perhaps because he dreamed what he had to face, Henry I was more successful than most of his contemporaries in winning the support of his diverse subjects. (The President and Fellows of Corpus Christi College, Oxford)

While the German rulers struggled in vain to create an empire embracing Germany and Italy, political consolidation progressed less dramatically but more effectively in England and France. The rulers of each of these kingdoms, chiefly by exploiting their feudal rights as overlords, slowly expanded their power to the point where they exercised extensive sovereignty over all their subjects. Their lordship was made effective by their ability to create institutions of royal government capable of enforcing royal commands. Although royal power in England and France was rooted in political feudalism, the regimes the kings fashioned ultimately superseded feudalism and assumed characteristics associated with modern states.

1. ENGLAND: THE NORMAN CONQUEST

During the eleventh century, the effective system of government that had been established in England earlier (see Chapter 16) showed signs of losing its vitality. The rulers' chief local officials, the earls and sheriffs, steadily secured rights of private government. The kings began to grant royal lands to *thegns* who pledged military service in return but often failed to render it. Many free people were forced to become dependents of the powerful nobles. New Scandinavian inroads undermined royal prestige and encouraged local independence. Canute, a Dane, even took the English crown (1016–1035). He dreamed of drawing England into a vast northern maritime empire based in Scandinavia, but such aims were foiled by his early death and by ineffective successors.

After this interlude of foreign rule, the old Anglo-Saxon royal line was restored with Edward the Confessor (1042–1066) as king. His reign was characterized by a rapid deterioration of royal power to the special advantage of the great earls, of whom Godwin of Wessex was the most powerful. When Edward died without heirs, the Witan elected Godwin's son Harold as king. He was immediately faced with an invasion led by Harald Hardrada, king of Norway, who coveted the English throne. Into this mounting crisis entered William, duke of Normandy. He laid claim to the English crown on the basis of his distant kinship with Edward and his insistence that Edward had promised him the throne. Harald and William chose almost the same moment to invade England to assert their claims, forcing a settlement on the battlefield in 1066. King Harold crushed the invading Scandinavians only to meet disaster a short time later, in October, at the Battle of Hastings, where William's Norman knights overpowered the Anglo-Saxon forces and made it possible for their leader to assume the English crown as William I (1066–1087) (see Color Plate 9).

William made it clear at his coronation that he would observe Anglo-Saxon customs and assume all rights belonging to the Anglo-Saxon kings. To gain the resources he needed to exert these rights and powers, William took a momentous step: He introduced continental feudalism into England. By virtue of his military victory William claimed large tracts of land held by his royal predecessors and by Anglo-Saxon landowners who resisted the Normans. He set aside about one-sixth of it as the royal domain and granted out most of the rest as fiefs to his Norman followers. In return they became his vassals, owing him services, chiefly military, in proportion to the size of their fiefs. Most of his direct vassals (called *tenants-in-chief* or *barons*) subinfeudated their lands and acquired their own vassals. William, however, insisted that all subvassals owed first allegiance to the king, thereby establishing a meaningful feudal hierarchy with the king at the head. Through these steps, he secured not only a valuable royal domain but also the military service of about five thousand knights, enough to ensure his mastery of England. In short, the feudal system allowed him to impose on England a new ruling elite that he as king could control.

As successor to the Anglo-Saxon kings and chief lord of the feudal hierarchy, William had the authority and resources to lay the groundwork for a strong central government. The Anglo-Saxon Witan was replaced by the feudal body called the *Curia Regis* (court of the king), at whose meetings the king's lay and ecclesiastical vassals were expected to judge cases and advise the ruler. To complement the income from his extensive domain, William continued to collect the taxes owed the king from Anglo-Saxon times, the chief one being the Danegeld, originally imposed in 991 to provide tribute payment to the Danes. He also took care to exploit the feudal dues owed him by his vassals. In 1086 William's agents compiled the Domesday Book, a survey of England's wealth fief by fief, which documented what his subjects possessed and how much they owed the king.

William was careful to retain the local units of administration he had inherited, the Anglo-Saxon shires and hundreds, and to see to it that the local officials, especially sheriffs, served royal purposes. Through this system of local government the king kept in direct touch with the English populace in matters of justice, peacekeeping, and taxation. The English system of local government prevented the fragmentation of public authority and its dispersion into private hands.

Overlooking no possible source of power and prestige, William acted to attach the Church to his new establishment. He won the support of the reformers and the blessing of the papacy by promising at the time of the conquest to undertake the reform of the badly corrupted Anglo-Saxon church. Once in control of England, he brought in a Norman, Lanfranc, as archbishop of Canterbury, who vigorously undertook the reform of religious life in England. William generously endowed the Church with property and permitted it liberty to conduct its own courts. However, he never relinquished real control over it, especially in the choice of high ecclesiastical officials.

The Norman conquest was thus a watershed in English history. A disintegrating monarchy was given new political vitality by injecting into its structure certain continental feudal practices that provided the king-lord with the resources to make himself the real master of England. Moreover, the coming of the Normans drew England into the mainstream of western European life by involving its people more directly in the vigorous economic, religious, and cultural forces that were revitalizing society on the Continent. As a consequence, many of the unique aspects of traditional Anglo-Saxon society were slowly effaced during the century following the Norman conquest. Many in England then and later lamented this development, feeling that something precious was lost. But on the whole England benefited greatly from closer contacts with continental Europe.

2. ENGLAND: GROWTH OF THE MONARCHY, 1087–1199

During the century following William I's death, his successors (known as the Norman-Angevin dynasty) were energetic, capable kings who worked hard to expand royal power: the rough, brutal William II (1087–1100); the quiet, prudent, avaricious Henry I (1100–1135); the ambitious, tempestuous Henry II (1154–1189); and the colorful, romantic knight, Richard I, the Lion-Hearted (1189–1199). Only one difficult interlude, brought about by a disputed succession, intervened to cause civil strife between 1135 and 1154. The twelfth-century kings had interests far transcending the governance of England, especially their concerns with their continental possessions, which by the reign of Henry II embraced much of France (see pp. 274–275 and Map 20.1). But we must neglect these aspects of English history in order to concentrate on the efforts of the kings to perfect strong monarchical government (see Figure 20.1).

One of the major achievements of the twelfth-century English kings, especially Henry I and Henry II, was the formation of an effective central administration. They fashioned it by combining and adapting features of the old Anglo-Saxon royal household and of the new Curia Regis in which the king's tenants-in-chief were obliged to serve as part of their feudal obligation to their royal overlord. Development moved along two complementary lines. On the one hand, the kings began to draw men from the Curia Regis who would serve for prolonged periods instead of returning to their private affairs after brief meetings of this body. On the other hand, the kings began to assign specialized functions to various members of this small council of semipermanent servants—the beginning of departments of administration. During the twelfth century, four specialized functional agencies began to take shape: the *Exchequer*, for collecting revenues due to the king from the sheriffs and for judging disputes arising out of financial obligations owed the kings; the *Treasury*, for guarding and dispensing royal money; the *Chancery*, for issuing royal orders and composing royal correspondence; and the *royal law courts*.

The kings continued to sustain and strengthen

Map 20.1 **MEDIEVAL ENGLAND, FRANCE, AND THE HOLY ROMAN EMPIRE** This map shows the major political entities in western Europe about 1300. A major problem for the rulers of these states during the High Middle Ages was the establishment of control over the many principalities into which each was divided.

the traditional Anglo-Saxon system of local government. They resisted the sheriffs' ever-present tendency to usurp royal power for private advantage by using the agencies of the central government to maintain control over the sheriffs and to impose on them a broader range of activities in support of the king. Henry II was especially effective in providing clear definitions of the obligations of the sheriffs.

The kings were careful to guard the financial and military resources needed to support the growing agencies of the royal government and to restrain potential foes. The financial support of the government still depended heavily on the exploitation of the royal domain. Royal agents zealously collected every possible feudal due owed by royal vassals and all fines and fees due to the king for breaking his law or utilizing services performed by his agents. Custom duties were levied on an ever-wider scale, allowing the kings to capitalize on growing trade. The royal government also devised ways of imposing direct taxes on the income and property of its subjects. The revenues from these many sources provided the twelfth-century English kings with a sounder financial base for their power than was enjoyed by any other royal government in Europe. The king's military strength was based on the military service owed by the tenants-in-chief. To complement this feudal army, the kings maintained the ancient royal right to summon the *fyrd*, the army of all freemen in the realm. Toward the end of the twelfth century the kings began to allow those who owed them military service to make money payments, called *scutage* or shield-money, in lieu of personal service; this income was used to hire mercenary troops.

Beyond all doubt, the most important development of the twelfth century was the formation of a royal system of justice. This effort was in large part a response to the confusion surrounding the traditional system of justice. Under the old order courts were conducted by the king, his local representatives in the shires, feudal lords, seigneurs on the manors, the Church, and the towns. In each set of courts different systems of law, different procedures, and different systems of punishment were applied by judges whose legal competence varied greatly. The kings and their legal

advisers sought to diminish this confusion by developing a royal system of justice common to all—a step that had the added attraction of increasing royal income derived from charges for court costs. As the system of royal justice developed, it became one of the positive benefits of strong royal government.

One of the chief measures taken to expand royal justice involved providing greater numbers of royal judges trained to apply a common system of law to cases throughout the realm. Several steps were taken to achieve this end. Henry I began the *circuit court system,* sending itinerant judges at set intervals to shires throughout England to try cases. By the time of Henry II, this system had become a regular practice; and by comparing notes, the itinerant judges were soon able to erect a common set of principles for deciding cases. A *common law* was in the making. Henry II established the first of England's great central courts, sitting permanently at Westminster to handle many cases previously heard by the Curia Regis. Eventually this body began to divide into specialized courts. The decisions of these central courts guided the activities of itinerant judges and contributed to uniformity in the legal system.

As royal judicial activity increased, the kings' agents began to challenge the jurisdiction of the baronial, manorial, ecclesiastical, and town courts. The kings expanded their authority over criminal cases by legislation that defined new crimes against the peace and ordered royal judges to punish violators. Increasing royal control over civil cases, chiefly involving property disputes, was more complicated and met strong opposition, especially from feudal and seigneural lords long accustomed to dealing with property disputes in their own courts. Insisting that no person should lose property unjustly, the kings declared that dissatisfied litigants could purchase *writs* ordering a royal inquiry into their cases. The fertile minds of the royal lawyers soon devised writs that applied to almost every conceivable kind of property dispute. In effect, purchasing a writ amounted to transferring a civil dispute from baronial or manorial courts to royal courts.

To encourage the use of royal courts, important innovations were made to ensure speedier and more efficient judicial processes: regularly scheduled court sessions, clearly fixed court fees, utilization of trained judges, uniform punishments. Most significant in this respect was the introduction of the *jury system.* For a long time English kings and their officials had been summoning groups of their subjects to tell under oath what they knew about some matter of public interest. After 1164 Henry II applied this idea to criminal cases. Sheriffs were ordered to summon in local areas within their shires a *presentment* or *grand jury,* made up of knowledgeable local residents who were required under oath to produce evidence about crimes committed in that area. On the basis of the evidence produced by these jurors, the sheriffs could proceed to bring suspected criminals to trial. By the thirteenth century, comparable groups of men known as *petit* (little) *juries* began to be used to decide on the basis of evidence presented before them the guilt or innocence of those accused of violating the law. The jury system quickly proved superior to traditional practices, which relied on trial by ordeal or by compurgation to ascertain God's will in proving guilt or innocence (see Chapter 13).

As the Norman-Angevin kings shaped a strong monarchical government, they had to concern themselves with their relationships with the Church. In general, the English kings managed the problem in a way that reinforced their authority. William I set the pattern by richly endowing the Church and supporting its reforming efforts while insisting on royal control of ecclesiastical offices and of a portion of the Church's wealth. During the reign of William II, the Church, led by Anselm, archbishop of Canterbury, challenged the monarchy's right to appoint church officials. This struggle was resolved by the Compromise of Bec in 1107, which allowed the Church to elect its own officials but gave the king the privilege of investing these officials with their lands. A more serious struggle arose in 1164 when Henry II issued the Constitutions of Clarendon, which ordered that clergymen accused of crimes be tried in royal instead of ecclesiastical courts. A one-time loyal servant of Henry II, Thomas à Becket, then archbishop of Canterbury, resisted with great vigor this attack on what he considered the Church's liberty. For his efforts he was murdered under circumstances that made it seem that the much-

FIGURE 20.2   Murder in the Cathedral: The Making of a Martyr   This manuscript illustration shows agents of King Henry II murdering Archbishop Thomas à Becket in the cathedral at Canterbury. (The Walters Art Gallery, Baltimore)

provoked king was responsible. Thomas' martyrdom forced the king to concede considerable freedom to the Church in judicial matters (see Figure 20.2). On the whole, however, the English kings exercised a powerful control over the Church, and the Church gave its support to the strengthening of monarchy. Unlike the Holy Roman Empire, England was spared the disruptive impact of the investiture struggle.

3. ENGLAND: LIMITING ROYAL POWER, 1199–1307

During the twelfth century the rapid, aggressive expansion of royal authority generated surprisingly little resistance. During the thirteenth century, however, the kings met more formidable opposition. Nobles, clergy, and the rising bourgeoisie joined hands to compel the kings to recognize a principle inherent in the feudal order: that lordship—even royal lordship—was limited by the "law" of the feudal contract.

The conflict broke into the open during the reign of John (1199–1216). Politically able, although devious and rash, John brought part of his trouble on himself by making inordinate fiscal demands on his subjects. He also had the misfortune of having as his adversaries two of the most formidable personalities in medieval history, King Philip Augustus of France and Pope Innocent III. Philip captured a considerable part of the French territories under English control in a war that required John to impose a heavy burden of service and taxation on his subjects in a losing cause. John also became embroiled in a clash with Innocent III over the appointment of the archbishop of Canterbury. Again he lost and was forced to acknowledge that he was a vassal of the pope, holding England as a fief.

These rebuffs, coupled with a series of tyrannical acts by John, resulted in a great meeting of powerful nobles and clergy called in 1214 to organize a rebellion. It was led by Stephen Langton, the archbishop of Canterbury whom John had once tried to keep from office. John extricated himself from this grave danger by signing the Magna Carta in 1215. Endlessly celebrated by later generations as a charter of liberty, the Magna Carta basically affirmed the traditional privileges of nobles, clergy, and townspeople. The king promised to limit the extension of royal authority in certain areas, chiefly taxation, the administration of justice, and landholding. The charter was therefore conservative, seeking to curb unlimited expansion of royal power. Its framers had no thought of destroying effective royal government or of making all people equal. They insisted on the principle that certain of the king's subjects had rights, defined by law, custom, and contract, which the king must respect.

John's concession in no way resolved the clash between the king and the privileged over the extent and limits of royal power. It continued throughout the long reign of his weak, extravagant, foolish son, Henry III (1216–1272). Henry III caused problems for himself by spurning the advice of his own barons in favor of foreign advisers, making outlandish concessions to the papacy, and pursuing costly but futile foreign military adventures. The exasperated nobles resisted him in a variety of ways: forcing him to reissue the Magna Carta, using their influence to compel him to dismiss his foreign advisers, and forming a council of nobles to reform and supervise the operation of royal government. When these efforts failed, they resorted to a major uprising in 1264–1265 led by Simon de Montfort. The rebels won the upper hand temporarily and de Montfort summoned the nobles, the clergy, and representatives from the towns and shires to a *Parliament* that sought to establish control over the monarchy. This effort was thwarted by the inability of the rebels to agree and by the actions of Henry's son, Edward, who mustered royal arms and crushed the rebels.

The astute, capable Edward I (1272–1307) saw that few of the nobles who had opposed John and Henry III wished to end strong monarchy or destroy its institutions. In fact, during the troubled times of John and Henry III these institutions had continued to develop in complexity and effectiveness. The expansion of royal power was not the issue; the protest was against the misuse of royal authority and the abuse of ancient rights. More significantly, Edward recognized that a *community of the realm* had begun to emerge, consisting of great barons, lesser nobles, clergy, and townspeople, all of whom felt a common interest in the political affairs of England as a nation. This feeling led them to act together in confronting the royal government and to transcend on occasion the narrow confines of feudal contracts, ecclesiastical privileges, and town charters. This communal effort provided the basis for an emerging English national spirit and for new political institutions through which the community of the realm could find expression.

Edward I's reign represented an attempt to

strengthen the central government by taking these views into account. He first took steps to remove complaints that the nobles, clergy, and townspeople had raised about the administrative and judicial systems. Second, a series of fundamental laws was enacted, defining more clearly the rights and powers of the crown and how these should be exercised. In general, this legislation further limited the power of feudal lords and the Church while expanding that of the king and his courts, but Edward's political skill usually disarmed protests before they became dangerous.

Edward's chief means of avoiding opposition was the regular use of Parliament. Advisory bodies, such as the Witan and the Curia Regis, had long played a part in English political life but within a narrow framework of feudal practices. Simon de Montfort's Parliament of 1265 was a new kind of structure, joining representatives of the shires and towns to the feudal barons and clergy to create a body claiming to direct the affairs of the realm. Edward I clearly sanctioned this precedent in his Model Parliament of 1295. He commanded that each county and town select two representatives to Parliament to take counsel with the barons and ecclesiastical lords. The Parliament was soon accepted as a body with power to represent the interests of England's free population and as a place where these interests could voice their concerns about the state of the realm. Edward called Parliament primarily to serve his own purposes—especially to get extra money or to gain approval of some piece of legislation. Meetings of Parliament also served important judicial functions, so that the institution came to be viewed as the highest court in the land. Finally, Parliament provided an institutional setting where complaints against the royal government could be voiced and suggestions for change proposed; from these pleas emerged the right of Parliament to initiate legislation binding on the king and the entire realm. For at least another century Parliament's organization was vague and its powers not clearly defined. Its importance lay in Edward's recognition that the king had to listen to the demands of his subjects and his willingness to promote an institution that gave them a voice in government in a way that strengthened the emerging political community under an effective royal government.

4. FRANCE: FOUNDATIONS OF ROYAL POWER, 843–1180

The emergence of effective monarchy proceeded more slowly in France than in England and under different circumstances. Medieval France originated as the kingdom of the West Franks, a subdivision of the Carolingian Empire created by the Treaty of Verdun in 843 (see p. 221 and Map 16.2). Except for brief intervals, the Carolingian family held the crown of this kingdom until 987. During that period royal power steadily declined. The kingdom was fragmented into numerous small principalities controlled by feudal lords. These powerful figures recognized the weak kings as their feudal overlords but seldom rendered any services as vassals. The great fiefs that they had been granted became hereditary possessions virtually immune from royal control.

In 987 the French nobles and clergy finally ended the Carolingian dynasty by electing as their king one of the chief feudal lords in the kingdom, Hugh Capet, count of Paris. Hugh's descendants, called the Capetians, held the throne without interruption until 1328. The first four Capetians, who ruled from 987 to 1108, exercised almost no power outside their own royal domain, a modest but strategically well-located territory around Paris known as the Ile de France (the area shown on Map 20.1 as the royal domain in 987). Even there royal authority and resources were constantly threatened by unruly vassals. Throughout the rest of the kingdom powerful royal vassals did as they pleased in their principalities, many of which were larger and richer than the royal domain. The first Capetians did manage to establish an hereditary claim to the throne and to retain the support of the Church. And with the help of churchmen, they did maintain the important fiction inherited from the Carolingian world that the royal office was surrounded by a sacral quality and that its occupant was supreme feudal suzerain.

Between 987 and 1108 the history of France must be told in terms of the history of each of its many principalities (see Map 20.1). Most of them had been Carolingian administrative districts granted to dukes, counts, and viscounts in return for public service. These royal vassals made their fiefs hereditary and used their public authority to establish private lordships. Most of them subinfeudated their fiefs to surround themselves with supportive vassals owing feudal obligations. In many cases these secondary vassals carved out for themselves territorial enclaves, called castellanies, over which they exercised a private jurisdiction at the expense of their lords.

During the eleventh century the long process of political fragmentation slowed markedly, but not as a result of royal action. The change stemmed from the successful efforts of dukes, counts, viscounts, and castellans to establish effective lordship over their vassals. These lords, many of them royal vassals, brought order to their principalities primarily by a rigorous assertion of their rights as feudal lords. They shaped institutions that permitted them to amass sufficient military strength and fiscal resources to compel the obedience of their noble and servile dependents, to assume control over the administration of justice, and to command the support of the local ecclesiastical establishment. This local consolidation was most notable in the great royal fiefs of northern France, especially in Normandy, Flanders, Anjou, Maine, Champagne, Burgundy, and Blois. The effectiveness of such lords was exemplified by William, duke of Normandy, who was able to muster resources that permitted him to conquer England. In southern France, where feudal usages had developed more slowly, the great royal fiefs such as Aquitaine, Gascony, and Toulouse remained more fragmented; numerous petty princes paid little heed to the counts and dukes who claimed lordship over them. The kings of France played almost no role in this process of local consolidation. They were fully occupied with ruling their limited royal domain. Only rarely and seldom in any decisive way did they assert their rights over their powerful vassals whose power was increasing as a result of their expanding control over their fiefs. But neither did the kings surrender their rights.

As the twelfth century opened the position of the Capetians began to improve. Beginning with Louis VI (1108–1137), the king undertook to do what many of his vassals had already done—establish effective control over the royal domain. Louis patiently set about forcing his vassals in the royal domain to end their lawlessness, and he created an administrative machinery that allowed him to collect the dues owed the king as their overlord. His control over the royal domain provided him with sufficient resources to expand his role in the affairs of his vassals outside the Ile de France. With increasing frequency he acted as judge in disputes involving his vassals, protected weaker ones against stronger, influenced the succession to fiefs held from the king, and added small territories to his royal domain by asserting his rights under feudal law. Illustrative of his expanding strength was the decision of the dying duke of Aquitaine to entrust his daughter and heiress, Eleanor, to the protection of his overlord, the king of France. Louis VI promptly arranged for the marriage of his ward to his own son, thereby setting the stage for the annexation of Aquitaine to the royal domain.

The modest progress made by Louis VI in expanding royal influence led to a crisis in Capetian history under the reign of his successor, Louis VII (1137–1180). Thanks to the work of his father's administrators, especially the able and devoted Suger, abbot of the royal monastery of St. Denis, Louis VII maintained a firm hold on the royal domain. But beyond the royal domain, the king fared badly. He proved incapable of controlling Aquitaine, where local lords continued to act in defiance of the king's authority. Louis VII's participation as a leader in the Second Crusade not only won him no glory but also cost him a wife and her dowry. The attractive Eleanor accompanied him on that venture and was rumored to have dallied with some of the more attractive knights in the crusading army, including her uncle. This scandal was too much for the pious Louis. Moreover, Eleanor had produced no son to assure the survival of the Capetian dynasty. Perhaps Eleanor, a patroness of troubadour poets and a devotee of the ideals of courtly love, had also had enough; she is alleged to have said that she discovered she had married a monk instead of a king. In any case, Louis arranged to have the marriage dissolved; one price for this act was the surrender of his wife's dowry, the duchy of Aquitaine.

The hapless king's major difficulty, however, did not stem from his political and marital ineptitude. During his reign an unusual sequence of events unfolded to create what historians call the

Angevin "empire," which consisted of several major royal fiefs in France joined together in the hands of a single vassal of the French king. The original architects of this unusual conglomeration were the counts of Anjou, who were important royal vassals. Through an intricate process involving acquisition of fiefs, conquest, and marriage alliances, the lords of Anjou managed to establish control over a substantial territory, including Normandy, Anjou, Brittany, Maine, and the Touraine (see Map 20.1). In 1151 that territory was inherited by a certain Henry, who the next year married the recently divorced Eleanor and acquired Aquitaine as her dowry. For all of these territories, Henry was vassal of Louis VII. Then in 1154, the already well-endowed Angevin became Henry II, king of England. Obviously, his "empire" provided him with resources far exceeding those of his lord, the king of France. In fact, the very survival of the French monarchy was in question, its future put to the test by a development that could only occur in the feudal world.

5. FRANCE: THE CONSOLIDATION OF ROYAL POWER, 1180–1328

The response of the Capetians to the challenge posed by the Angevin "empire" led to the rapid expansion of royal power. The decisive turn of events came during the reign of Philip II Augustus (1180–1223), who over a long period bent every effort to destroy Angevin power in his realm. During the first two decades of his reign, he maneuvered skillfully to thwart the efforts of his vassals, Henry II and Richard I, to solidify their hold on their continental territories. With the accession of John came the opportunity to move decisively. As we have already seen, John was beset by serious challenges in England that weakened his position. His tyrannical conduct alienated many of his vassals in France, causing them to turn to his overlord for justice and protection. When John refused to appear before Philip to be judged in a case that involved John's taking as a wife a princess already betrothed to one of his vassals, Philip pronounced him an unfaithful vassal and in accordance with feudal law confiscated his fiefs. By force of arms the French king annexed Normandy, Anjou,

Maine, the Touraine, and parts of northern Aquitaine to the royal domain. Philip's control of these key territories was assured by a victory in 1214 at the Battle of Bouvines, where he crushed the forces of John and his Welf allies from the Holy Roman Empire. As master of a greatly enlarged royal domain, made up of principalities well organized by their former feudal overlords, Philip finally had the resources needed to assure his supremacy over any of his vassals.

Philip II's successors continued to follow his policy of extending the royal domain (see Map 20.1), a task made easier by the resources available from his victory over the Angevins. The kings employed a variety of means to claim territory: marriage alliances that permitted the Capetian family to inherit fiefs; confiscation of fiefs held by vassals judged unfaithful; purchase; escheat of fiefs held by vassals who died without heirs. A major addition to the royal domain, the county of Toulouse, resulted from the leadership by Philip II and Louis VIII (1223–1226) of a Church-sponsored crusade against the heretical Albigensians in southern France (see p. 301). The English sought to thwart the expansion of the royal domain and reclaim the fiefs lost to Philip II, but finally in 1259 they agreed to a treaty giving up their claims in France except for a small territory in Gascony. By 1328 a large part of France had been consolidated under direct royal rule; a kingdom of France had become a reality.

The later Capetians, especially Philip II, Louis IX (1226–1270), and Philip IV (1285–1314), worked vigorously to develop political institutions that would allow them to govern their expanding holdings effectively. They constantly enlarged the definition of their royal authority, combining concepts drawn from feudalism, Roman law, and Christian political ideology. To exercise these enlarged powers, they adapted and expanded primitive institutions inherited from the early Capetians: the Curia Regis, a court of the king's vassals; the royal household (*hôtel*), made up of officials who cared for the personal needs of the royal family; and the *provosts*, agents who managed the royal estates.

One major accomplishment of these kings was the development of a central administration located at Paris and capable of guarding the royal interests throughout the expanding domain. The Curia Regis and the royal household were gradually merged to constitute a single judicial and administrative body, which was charged with an ever-greater range of responsibilities. Originally the jurisdiction claimed by the central government was derived chiefly from the king's power as feudal lord, but by mid–thirteenth century kings were issuing ordinances to extend royal jurisdiction. The original small body of vassals and household officials serving the central government was greatly expanded by the addition of full-time, salaried administrators, many of them lawyers. During the reigns of Louis IX and Philip IV, the Curia Regis began to divide into specialized departments: the *conseil,* a small group of royal advisers; the *parlement de Paris,* concerned with administering royal justice; the *chambre des comptes,* which handled financial matters; a *chancery,* charged with producing royal orders and keeping records. Lawyers associated with the central government began efforts to establish a unified body of law, a formidable task as a result of the diverse customs that had emerged in the feudal principalities. By the reign of Philip IV the central administration of the kingdom had become a fully professionalized body of officials completely devoted to enhancing royal power and capable of asserting a collective force that guaranteed obedience to the royal will.

As the royal domain grew, the kings were faced with the monumental task of devising a system of local government. Unlike the situation in England, where kings were served by the ancient system of shires and sheriffs, local government in France had long been monopolized by feudal and manorial lords. Philip II attacked this problem by creating special officials known as *baillis* (bailiffs), whose numbers and powers were increased by his successors. Usually selected from nonnoble personnel of the royal court, these salaried officials were assigned to specific territories within the royal domain to hold courts, collect taxes, and keep order in the name of the king. Louis IX established special officers called *enquêteurs* (investigators) to check on the conduct of the bailiffs and to report misdeeds to the central government. Although the local nobility continued to perform many political functions, the bailiffs, acting in the name of the kings, steadily assumed political functions once monopolized by feudal and seigneurial lords.

The broadening range of royal activities, especially the waging of war and supporting the expanding royal administration, placed a heavy financial burden on the kings. A significant part of royal income continued to be derived from royal lands, but other sources of revenue had to be found. Aside from feudal dues, fines, and fees for royal services, the royal government had few sources of regular income. As a result, the kings often had to resort to arbitrary exactions from any source possible: towns, the Church, Jews, foreign bankers and merchants, nobles who fell out of royal favor. Especially during the reign of Philip IV, the measures used to satisfy the ravenous royal appetite for money produced complaints of royal tyranny and aroused resistance in many circles.

In the early fourteenth century, the Capetians instituted another practice that strengthened their authority. Expanding on the feudal practice of seeking counsel by calling their vassals to the Curia Regis, they began to summon representatives of the three major social groupings (*estates*)— the nobles, the clergy, and the townsmen—to advise them and approve their policies. Philip IV convoked three of these *Estates General.* In each case the assembled representatives meekly did what the king wished. But their approval added tremendous weight to royal power by making it appear that the entire nation approved of royal action. The Estates General was much more a tool of the French monarchs than was the English Parliament, chiefly because the major power groups in France, especially the nobles, failed to develop a sense of shared interest in and concern for the affairs of the entire realm.

Throughout most of the long period during which the Capetians were consolidating their hold on France, they drew invaluable aid from the Church. The kings bestowed wealth on the Church, supported reform, took its side in the investiture struggle, and respected its liberties. In return, the Church supported the royal claims to greater power and lent its wealth and talent to royal service. This fruitful relationship did not end until the reign of Philip IV, who became embroiled in a bitter struggle with Pope Boniface VIII (1294–1303) over the extent of the king's power to tax

FIGURE 20.3 A Queen at Work This manuscript illustration shows Queen Blanche of Castile, wife of King Louis VIII (1223–1226), keeping close watch over the education of her son, King Louis IX (1226–1270). Even while she was asserting her role as a mother, she was acting as regent for a kingdom that Louis IX inherited when he was an infant. Her son became a great king and a saint. (Bibliothèque Nationale, Paris ms. fr. 5716)

church property and judge the clergy. As we shall see (Chapter 25), Philip IV won a stunning victory over the mighty head of Christendom, so long successful in thwarting the Holy Roman emperors. The explanation is clear: By the early fourteenth century the king of France possessed a power base that the pope could not dissolve by simple command.

The victory of Philip IV over Boniface VIII points to a final achievement of the Capetians: their ability to endow their royal office with an image that showed kingship at its best. The prestige of the Capetians is best exemplified by Louis IX, eventually recognized as a saint by the Church. In no small part because of his actual accomplishments, Louis was hailed in his own time as a lover

of justice, true Christian, gallant knight, crusader, peacemaker, promoter of morality, ideal son, husband, and father—in short, the perfect prince (see Figures 20.3 and 21.1). Most of the Capetians shared at least some of the aura of superiority so generously heaped on Louis IX, proving them as skillful in fashioning an image as in shaping effective political institutions. That image did much to enhance their real power.

Thus between 1000 and 1300 political leaders in England and France had found a solution to a problem that had persisted since the dissolution of the Roman Empire—how to create a stable political order capable of binding men and women into a large-scale community that promoted common goals. These leaders achieved that end by exploiting rights and obligations implicit in the feudal system. However, in fashioning strong monarchies, they had learned to respect the rights of privileged groups—vassals, clergy, townspeo- ple—as partners in the tasks of government. Their accomplishment laid the basis for a notable institution that would play a decisive role in the future of western Europe—the nation-state.

SUGGESTED READING

England

Christopher Brooke, *From Alfred to Henry III, 871–1272* (1961). A brief, well-written survey.

Frank Barlow, *The Feudal Kingdom of England, 1042–1216,* 3rd ed. (1972).

M. T. Clanchy, *England and Its Rulers, 1066–1272: Foreign Lordship and National Identity* (1983). Fuller accounts stressing the evolution of political institutions.

Doris M. Stenton, *English Society in the Early Middle Ages (1066–1307),* 4th ed. (1965). Particularly strong in relating economic, social, and cultural factors to political history.

R. Allen Brown, *The Normans and the Norman Conquest,* 2nd ed. (1985). Excellent treatment of Norman expansionism and its impact.

W. L. Warren, *The Governance of Norman and Angevin England, 1050–1272* (1987). A fine synthesis.

G. O. Sayles, *Medieval Foundations of England,* 2nd ed., rev. (1964). A provocative interpretation of constitutional development.

France

Elizabeth M. Hallam, *Capetian France, 987–1328* (1980). A balanced survey.

Jean Dunbabin, *France in the Making 843–1180* (1985). Especially good in its treatment of France's principalities.

John W. Baldwin, *The Government of Philip Augustus: Foundations of French Royal Power in the Middle Ages* (1986). A massive work, but useful in understanding the building of royal power.

Biographies

David C. Douglas, *William the Conqueror: The Norman Impact Upon England* (1964).

W. L. Warren, *Henry II* (1973).

Amy Kelly, *Eleanor of Aquitaine and the Four Kings* (1950).

Frank Barlow, *Thomas Becket* (1986).

John Gillingham, *Richard the Lionheart* (1978).

W. L. Warren, *King John,* rev. ed. (1978).

John Chancellor, *The Life and Times of Edward I* (1981).

Margaret W. Labarge, *Saint Louis: Louix IX, Most Christian King of France* (1968).

CHAPTER 21
The Medieval Expansion of Europe

FIGURE 21.1 **Departure on a Crusade** This scene depicts King Louis IX of France leaving Paris on the Seventh Crusade. It captures some of the solemnity surrounding the crusading movement. With their eyes seemingly on their distant goal in the Holy Land, Louis and his knights depart without a look backward at the group of monks blessing them. (The British Museum)

The increasing material wealth and the more effective political organization of western Europe set the stage for a decisive change in the relationship between the West and the world beyond. Between 500 and 1000 western Europeans had been almost constantly on the defensive. After 1000 that situation was reversed. During the next three centuries they employed a variety of means to expand their sphere of influence over a wide area. These efforts marked the beginning of an outward thrust by western Europeans that would continue for centuries.

1. RELIGIOUS EXPANSION

Since its beginnings Christianity had been an expansionist religion. The missionary urge remained vigorous during the High Middle Ages. As a result, the Christian world was substantially enlarged.

A major area of expansion was in Scandinavia. While the first efforts to convert the Scandinavians began in the ninth century, the crucial era in the Christianization of Denmark, Norway, Sweden, and Iceland came in the late tenth and eleventh centuries. In most cases the conversion of the kings was the decisive event. The new Christian kings received assistance in their effort to convert their people from missionaries from the south, especially from England and Germany.

Meanwhile, Christianity was carried eastward into the Slavic world. In this area the major impetus for expansion was provided by the rulers of the Holy Roman Empire and their ambitious lay and ecclesiastical vassals. Beginning in the late tenth century, the Bohemians, Poles, and Hungarians were gathered into the Roman Catholic fold. Somewhat later and again with German support, the religious frontier was advanced along the Baltic to convert the Wends, the Prussians, the Finns, the Livonians, and the Lithuanians. During this same period missionary forces from the Byzantine Empire were spreading Christianity among the eastern Slavs, especially the Russians.

During the thirteenth century missionaries from the West made efforts to win converts among the Moslems of North Africa and the Near East, and some even ventured as far afield as the Mongol Empire and China. Although these ventures produced no significant results, they opened vast new prospects for the future.

Wherever the missionary effort succeeded—Scandinavia, central Europe, Iceland, the Baltic area—the newly established Church introduced its new converts to many aspects of western European culture. As a consequence, the lives of people in these areas were decisively changed; they were "westernized" in terms of their institutions and their way of thinking.

2. COLONIZATION AND COMMERCIAL EXPANSION

The western Europeans who thrust outward with the cross were often accompanied—and sometimes led—by others driven beyond Europe's boundaries primarily by economic interests. As we have already seen, one of the great accomplishments of western Europeans during the era from 1000 to 1300 was the opening and colonization of an extensive agricultural frontier on the eastern fringes of Europe—in today's terms, a territory comprising northern Poland, most of East Germany, large areas of Czechoslovakia, and Austria. This Germanic "drive to the East" had the support of the Holy Roman emperors and of the Church, but mainly it was carried out by landowners and peasants seeking new lands to exploit. Their occupation of this frontier zone was accompanied by the implantation of western European institutions.

Likewise, between 1000 and 1300 merchants reached beyond Europe to establish the western European presence in a much larger world (see Map 18.1). Italian merchants wrested control of the Mediterranean seaways from the Byzantines and the Moslems and established trading posts in Constantinople and several Moslem seaports in Syria, Egypt, and North Africa. Northern Europeans, spearheaded by the Vikings, established settlements at Novgorod, Smolensk, and Kiev; from these emerged the Kievan principality that constituted the first effective state in Russia. Scandinavian raiders also settled Iceland and drew it into the European world. After the armies of the Fourth Crusade conquered Constantinople in

1204, western European merchants established bridgeheads around the Black Sea, which opened access to the cities of Central Asia and China. Italian traders roamed across the Asian world, reaping rich profits and reporting the potential of that vast area in travel accounts such as that composed in the late 1200s by the Venetian Marco Polo. A few bold Europeans were finding their way toward the waterways leading to India and the Indies. Simultaneously, Western seafarers were pushing southward along Africa's west coast, drawn chiefly by the fame of the gold mines of Senegal.

3. MILITARY EXPANSION IN SPAIN AND SOUTHERN ITALY

The most spectacular form of expansion during the High Middle Ages was military conquest. Europeans were impelled by a variety of motives: land hunger, quest for markets, adventure, religious zeal. Military expansionism manifested itself around the whole rim of the European heartland, but the thrust was aimed primarily at Byzantium and Islam.

One of the most important areas of expansion was the Iberian peninsula. When the Moors (as Moslems are called in Spanish history) conquered the Iberian peninsula in the eighth century, they failed to subdue small pockets of Christians in the extreme northwestern part of the peninsula. In the late eighth and early ninth centuries the Carolingians created the Spanish March from territory won from the Moors in northeastern Spain. Prior to 1000 several petty states developed in these Christian enclaves—Leon, Castile, Navarre, Aragon, and Barcelona. In these states in the early eleventh century a drive to rewin Spain was generated—a thrust that turned into a war of liberation called the *Reconquista.* The disintegration in the early eleventh century of the once powerful caliphate of Cordoba and the emergence of numerous warring Moslem principalities made the task of the Christians easier. Given this opportunity, the militant Christians turned their energies to a common assault on the Moors, usually with the strong encouragement of the Church. Large numbers of Christian knights from outside Spain,

especially from France, joined the fray. A powerful religious spirit animated these warriors, as is illustrated by two great vernacular literary works written to celebrate the feats of Christian warriors against the Moorish infidels, the *Song of Roland* and *The Cid.* The first phase of the Reconquista culminated in 1085 with the capture of the key city of Toledo. With the aid of Berber reinforcements from northwest Africa, the Moors were able to halt the Christian advance temporarily and by the mid–twelfth century even threatened to reclaim territory lost to the Christians. Shortly thereafter the Christian offensive was renewed, culminating in 1212 at the battle of Las Navas de Tolosa, where the Christian forces won a decisive victory over the combined forces of the Spanish Moors and their Berber allies. By 1300 the Christians had occupied all of the peninsula except a small region in the south called Granada (see Map 21.1).

Three major Iberian kingdoms—Castile (to which Leon was joined), Aragon, and Portugal—grew out of the territory rewon from the Moslems during the Reconquista. Each developed its own system of government, although all had certain basic similarities. Monarchy was the basic institution, and the kings steadily gained prestige as a result of their leadership of the Reconquista and Church support of their cause. Newly conquered lands gave them a chance to settle people as farmers or town dwellers under conditions that allowed the king to retain his authority. These factors initially retarded the coming of the feudal system, but eventually, feudal practices not unlike those of the French did develop. Hereditary fiefs were granted to nobles in return for services, and some vassals gained a large degree of immunity from royal control. The kings also granted extensive privileges to Spanish towns, many of which continued to be populated by Moslem and Jewish communities. The Spanish monarchs sought to develop centralized administrations, well-organized financial systems, and effective courts. Several thirteenth-century kings of Aragon and Castile legislated extensively to define royal powers and appointed local officials, comparable to the French bailiffs, to represent them. Nobles and townspeople resisted the expansion of royal power and in the long run compelled kings to accept limitations on their authority. In each king-

Map 21.1 **CHRISTIAN EXPANSION IN IBERIA**
This map shows the progress made by Spanish Christian warriors in reconquering the Iberian peninsula from the Moors during the Middle Ages. Three major kingdoms emerged from the Christian victories—Aragon, Castile (to which Leon was joined), and Portugal.

dom there developed a *Cortes*, a representative body composed of nobles, ecclesiastical leaders, and townspeople with considerable power to limit royal decisions on a variety of matters, including taxation.

As the Spanish kingdoms ruled by feudal monarchs developed, society in each took on many features common to the rest of Christian western Europe. But Spanish society retained its unique features, which were by-products of the merging of Christian and Moslem institutions and ideas during the long period of the Reconquista. As a result, Spain played a special role in the medieval West as the channel through which many Moslem influences flowed into the mainstream of western European society.

Another area of European military expansion was southern Italy and Sicily. Norman warriors from northwest France were the aggressors here. They first came to southern Italy as adventurers who, in return for land, were willing to sell their military services to local rulers competing for

power. Especially anxious for their services were Byzantine officials, seeking desperately to retain control over the area in the name of the emperor in Constantinople. Soon, however, these resourceful warriors, constantly reinforced by new migrants from Normandy, succeeded in establishing dominance over their supposed masters. By mid-eleventh century the papacy legally recognized a Norman principality in southern Italy; in return, the Normans agreed to support the papacy in its struggle with the Holy Roman emperors. These same aggressive warriors then proceeded to snatch Sicily from the Moslems. In 1130 these aggressive feats were formally recognized when the papacy sanctioned the creation of the Kingdom of Sicily, embracing southern Italy and Sicily, with a prince of Norman descent, Roger II, recognized as king. A strong monarchy was soon shaped. It incorporated a mixture of northern European feudal, Byzantine, and Moslem practices. The Kingdom of Sicily passed into Hohenstaufen hands at the end of the twelfth century and reached its apogee under Frederick II (see Chapter 19). Thereafter, the kingdom began to decline, chiefly because it became a pawn of outside powers. But it remained in western European hands, a prize of expansion.

4. MILITARY EXPANSION: THE CRUSADES

The most dramatic expansionist effort of the western Europeans involved a succession of military campaigns directed toward the eastern Mediterranean world over the course of nearly two centuries. These campaigns, called the Crusades, were viewed by contemporaries as religious wars against Islam for control of the holy places where Christianity originated. However, as they progressed, their objectives became more complex.

In part, the crusading movement began because developments in the Near East offered western Europeans opportunities and inducements. As early as the ninth century, the vast Abbasid caliphate began to break up into independent caliphates bitterly contending with one another for territory and for the right to represent the true version of Islam. The rivalry was especially keen in Syria and Palestine. The aggressive Shiite Fatimid caliphate based in Egypt sought to absorb this area at the expense of the Sunnite Abbasids. The Byzantine Empire also had ambitions in this area, which it still claimed as part of the old Roman Empire. In its efforts to protect its claims and to bolster its declining strength, the Abbasid dynasty brought a vigorous new force into the picture: the Seljuk Turks. They were a people of Asiatic origin who had entered the Eastern Moslem world in the tenth century, became converts to Islam, and used their military prowess to expand their influence. By the mid–eleventh century, the Seljuks established their dominance over Bagdad and made the Abbasid caliphs their puppets. They then turned their energies westward in an effort to enlarge their sphere of influence. This thrust brought them into conflict with the Fatimids and the Byzantine Empire and made the eastern Mediterranean world a confusing battleground. The Turkish menace became especially critical in 1070 and 1071, when the Turks seized Jerusalem from the Fatimids and inflicted a crushing defeat on the Byzantines at the battle of Manzikert (see below). In the midst of this confusion, local Moslem leaders established several small principalities in Syria and Palestine; they were willing to make any arrangements that would thwart the efforts of the major rivals to establish control over this crucial territory.

The Byzantine Empire was also undergoing a crisis in the eleventh century. Under the Macedonian dynasty (867–1057) it had enjoyed its most glorious days. But after the death of the greatest emperor of this dynasty, Basil II (976–1025), ineffectual rulers allowed the defense system to deteriorate by failing to protect the free peasantry that constituted its backbone from increasing exploitation by the aristocracy. The Normans wrested southern Italy from imperial control and posed a growing threat to imperial control in the Balkans. The Italian city-states, especially Venice, challenged Byzantine sea power. More seriously, in 1071 at the battle of Manzikert Byzantine forces suffered a crushing blow from the Seljuk Turks, who in succeeding years conquered most of Asia Minor. This deepening crisis finally produced an effective ruler, Alexius Comnenus (1081–1118). His most pressing problem was to recover Asia Minor. But Alexius needed military help. He began to appeal to the pope and the princes of western Europe, arguing for help against the aggressive infidels who threatened Christendom. The plight of the Byzantine Empire presented westerners with fresh opportunities and inducements to become involved in the East.

Despite the volatile and inviting situation in the East, there would have been no crusading movement without the confluence of a variety of factors in the West. Increasing material wealth provided the means for more ambitious military undertakings, and the greater political order curbed local warfare and freed the war-loving aristocracy for foreign ventures. Changing patterns of landholding, which confined inheritance to eldest sons, created a large pool of young warriors seeking new opportunities to make a fortune. The military potency of feudal society was being demonstrated by victories on the German, Spanish, and Italian frontiers. The Italian cities were eager to advance their commercial interests in the eastern Mediterranean. The long-standing religious animosity toward Islam was sharpened by the wars in Spain and Italy. The wave of religious reform sweeping over western Europe emphasized the idea that Christians must serve God by working collectively through outward, active demonstrations of their piety. One way in which that activist vision expressed itself was through an increasing interest in pilgrimages. Thousands of people joined organized voyages to holy places all over Europe and increasingly to the Holy Land, where they were sometimes victimized by warring Moslem factions. The religious revival had an especially important impact on the chivalric ideal. Increasingly, it emphasized the responsibility of the true warrior to devote his prowess to holy war that would promote the cause of the Church and scourge its enemies, especially the hated infidels.

It was the papacy that translated the opportunities emerging in the East and the forces of militancy surging through western European society into a specific form of military action. The key figure was Pope Urban II (1088–1099), who conceived and initially proclaimed the idea of organizing an armed pilgrimage of Christian warriors who would achieve a variety of ends for the good of the true faith. This army would respond to an appeal that Alexius Comnenus made to the pope in 1095 for aid in defending the Byzantine Empire against the Moslem Seljuk Turks. In return for this help Urban hoped to gain Byzantine recognition of papal supremacy over the whole Christian world, thus ending the schism that had occurred in 1054, when the pope and the patriarch excommunicated each other. Finally, this force, aided by the Byzantines, would crush the infidels and capture the holy places in the East as a supreme act of piety in the service of God.

In 1095, after discussing his idea with important ecclesiastical and lay leaders, Urban made public his plan for a crusade in a stirring speech delivered at Clermont in France before a large audience gathered for a church council. He called on Christian knights to put aside their petty quarrels and join forces under papal leadership in an attack on the Moslems that would save Christianity in the East and liberate the Holy Land. Urban proclaimed measures to protect the property and the families of those who were willing to take up the cross and promised that each would be rewarded in heaven for fighting this holy war.

The pope's speech at Clermont was greeted with shouts that it was God's will to do what Urban asked. That enthusiasm was soon transmitted over much of Europe by preachers of the crusading ideal. A number of feudal potentates (but no kings) began gathering separate armies in various areas. Before these armies of knights could be organized, an undisciplined horde of peasants and artisans, stirred by the appeals of enthusiastic preachers, began what has been called the Peasants' Crusade. After savagely attacking Jewish communities in several German cities, this ragtag mob moved eastward down the Danube Valley and across Hungary and Bulgaria, causing havoc as it advanced. When it finally reached Constantinople, Emperor Alexius Comnenus quickly dispatched it to Asia Minor, where it was immediately annihilated by the Turks.

By the summer of 1096 four major armies of knights began to move toward the East by different routes (see Map 21.2). Their first goal was Constantinople, where they expected to unite their forces for the attack on the Turks and the march to Jerusalem. As the armies one by one reached Constantinople during the fall and winter, protracted negotiations were necessary. The leaders of the armies from the West had no common plan of action. Although Urban II had designated a distinguished bishop to direct the crusading effort, the doughty nobles leading the various armies were unwilling to accept direction. Alexius Comnenus had expected mercenary contingents that he could simply take into his pay and order to do what he wished; the armies now converging on his capital were anything but soldiers for hire. Thus, Alexius had to negotiate an agreement with each leader. Eventually, by means that increased the distrust of the proud crusaders for the "Greeks," Alexius persuaded each of the crusading leaders to swear a personal oath of allegiance to him and to promise to release to Byzantine control conquered territories that had previously belonged to the empire. In return, he promised to provide supplies and military support.

In the spring of 1097 the crusaders began their march across Asia Minor. One decisive battle at Dorylaeum brushed aside the modest resistance

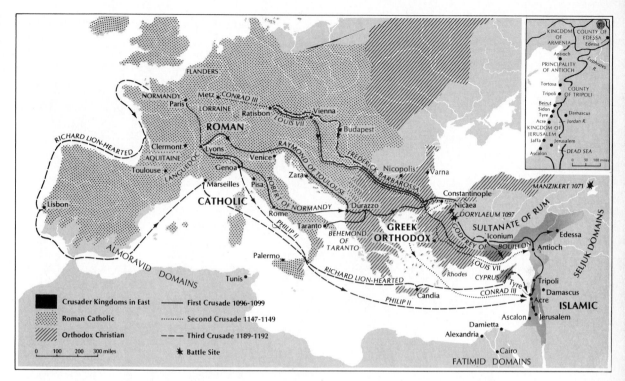

Map 21.2 **THE EARLY CRUSADES** This map shows the major land and sea routes taken by various crusading armies during the First, Second, and Third crusades. The leaders of the major armies are also indicated. The distances involved in these military ventures suggest the challenges faced by the crusaders. The First Crusade established the Latin Kingdom of Jerusalem, far removed from where the armies started their trek. Most successive crusades were prompted by the need to defend that kingdom from the Moslem forces that surrounded it.

of the Turks, who were badly divided at the moment, and allowed the crusaders to pass on toward the Holy Land, paying little attention to Alexius' interest in liberating Asia Minor. Once in Syria, the armies began to split up, chiefly because their leaders were anxious to ensure their private fortunes. One group left the main body to establish control over Edessa and its surrounding territory. After the key city of Antioch had been captured in June 1098, a Norman prince, Bohemond, refused to leave it, claiming it as his by right of conquest. Not until July 1099 was Jerusalem captured by the remaining crusaders, who vented their fury by slaughtering hundreds of its inhabitants (see Figure 21.2). This great victory, a re-

markable feat considering how far the crusading armies had come and the severe tribulations they had faced for three years, made the First Crusade a success.

The crusaders disregarded both their pledge to Alexius to serve as his vassals and a papal plan to create a state subordinate to Rome. Instead, in 1100 they elected Baldwin of Flanders, a leading crusader who had established himself as count of Edessa, as king of the Latin Kingdom of Jerusalem. Baldwin retained a sizable territory around Jerusalem as the royal domain and granted out the territories of Edessa, Antioch, and Tripoli as fiefs to major crusading leaders, each of whom became his vassal. The princes acquired vassals of

FIGURE 21.2 The Capture of the Holy City, 1099 This manuscript illustration shows the crusaders making their final assault on Jerusalem in 1099 to mark the successful end of the First Crusade. Their victory ended with the slaughter of those shown defending the city. (Snark International/Art Resource)

their own, creating a typical western European feudal order. The king ruled this kingdom with the advice of his vassals, who met regularly at Jerusalem. A Latin patriarch of Jerusalem was installed, subordinating the Christian establishment to Roman authority. The native population was disturbed very little by the newcomers.

Once the Latin Kingdom of Jerusalem had been established, the defense of "Overseas" (*Outremer*, as western Europeans called their distant outpost) became a major problem. Almost immediately after the capture of Jerusalem, most of the knights from the West returned home, having fulfilled the vow they had taken to liberate the holy places. Those who stayed were few in the face of the

Moslem forces whose lands they had occupied. These few took steps to protect themselves. With the aid of Italian navies they seized the chief Mediterranean seaports in Syria and Palestine; this success allowed the Latins to control the sea routes facing the Latin Kingdom, which was of decisive importance in holding their positions. They built a series of impregnable castles at strategic locations in the Holy Land. Before 1130 they established the two great crusading orders, the Knights Templar and the Knights Hospitaler; both were modeled on monastic organizations, but their members vowed to serve God by defending Christians living in and coming to the Holy Land. Later, a third such group, the Teutonic Knights, was established. Despite these measures the Christian position was always weak. That weakness repeatedly persuaded western Europeans over the next two centuries to go crusading as a way of serving God. Almost every year some western European knights at least temporarily lent their efforts to defending the Latin Kingdom. On occasion, especially at moments of crisis in the ongoing struggle, efforts were made in the West to organize more substantial forces to defend the holy places, thus permitting historians to speak of successive "crusades."

The Second Crusade (1147–1149) was prompted by the loss of Edessa in 1144 to the Turks. Papal appeals for action attracted two kings as its leaders: Conrad III, Holy Roman emperor, and Louis VII, king of France. Despite such prestigious leadership, the crusading armies were virtually destroyed by the Turks in Asia Minor. When the two rulers did arrive in the Holy Land with remnants of their forces, their misdirected military efforts aided little in the defense of the Latin Kingdom.

During the years following the Second Crusade, more effective leadership began to emerge in the Moslem world surrounding the Christian holdings. The most brilliant of these new leaders was Saladin, who joined the Moslem forces of Egypt and Syria into a powerful threat to the Latin Kingdom of Jerusalem. By 1187 he captured almost all the Christian holdings except Tyre, a few isolated castles, and the northern counties. When the news of this disaster reached the West, the pope called for a new crusade and received the promises of Henry II of England, Philip II of France, and Frederick Barbarossa of Germany to lead armies against Saladin. Frederick left first but was drowned en route. Henry II also died before he could begin his march; however, his successor, Richard the Lion-Hearted, stepped into his place. He and Philip, almost always at odds, made their way to the East by 1191. Philip was anxious to snatch away Richard's French possessions; therefore, he stayed on the scene only a minimum time. The colorful English king remained for over a year. After several inconclusive engagements with Saladin, Richard finally agreed to a truce that left Jerusalem in Moslem hands and allowed Christians to visit it. Aside from the return of a few

coastal cities to Latin control, the Third Crusade did little to improve the Christian position.

The Fourth Crusade, which in the eyes of many made a travesty of the crusading movement, was initially prompted by Pope Innocent III. However, the pope soon lost control over the forces that were raised. To ensure transportation to the East, the crusading leaders turned to the Venetians, who invested far more in ships to transport the crusaders than the disappointingly small crusading force was able to collect. To resolve this problem, the Venetians and the crusading leaders agreed to support a claimant to the Byzantine throne in return for trade concessions for Venice and money and troops for the crusaders to attack Egypt. But having ensconced the Byzantine ally in the imperial office, they found him unwilling or unable to deliver on his promises. The crusaders and the Venetians therefore decided to take Constantinople for themselves.

Their attack was successful; the city fell into Western hands in 1204 and was savagely pillaged. The crusaders immediately proclaimed a Latin Empire of Constantinople and elected a Flemish noble as emperor and a Venetian cleric as patriarch of the Greek Orthodox church, thus reuniting the Church for the moment. Somewhat reluctantly Innocent III gave his sanction to the whole arrangement. The crusading nobles immediately began to carve out rich fiefs for themselves. The Venetians, who assumed control over the chief port cities of the empire, were the real beneficiaries of the whole undertaking. The Latin Empire of Constantinople survived until 1261. Its history was mainly a story of the defense of the westerners against Greek forces whose leaders kept alive a legitimate Byzantine government in Asia Minor and fought valiantly to oust the usurpers.

After the Fourth Crusade, the crusading movement lost much of its appeal to Europeans. Innocent III organized a fifth crusade, but he died before it got underway in 1217. Its armies attacked Egypt and captured Damietta, a major Mediterranean port. The crusaders could have traded it for Jerusalem, but greed led them deeper into Egypt, where they were trapped by a Nile flood and destroyed by the Moslems.

Frederick II led the next crusade, chiefly because he wanted to secure possession of the Holy

Land, to which he had a legal right by virtue of his marriage to the heiress of the Latin Kingdom of Jerusalem. Frederick's crusade was fraught with difficulties from the very beginning. Because he refused to accept papal direction, he was in the bad graces of the papacy when he departed for the Holy Land. Once in the East, he chose to gain his ends by diplomacy rather than by the sword. In 1229 he signed a treaty with the Moslems that restored Jerusalem to the Latins and provided for a cessation of war between Christians and Moslems. This was a great victory, but the way it had been gained outraged many in the Christian West. When Frederick occupied Jerusalem, he was under a sentence of excommunication, and the city was immediately placed under papal interdict.

After this, the turmoil among the Christians in the Latin Kingdom of Jerusalem increased, making it more vulnerable; and in 1244 the Moslems again captured the Holy City. This loss prompted Louis IX of France to organize what amounted to the last major crusade (see Figure 21.1). He spent four years in the Holy Land, but his presence did little to strengthen the Christian position. In fact, his Egyptian campaign increased the danger by providing the opportunity for a strong, aggressive ruling dynasty, the Mamelukes, to establish itself in Egypt.

The increasing pressure on the Latin Kingdom of Jerusalem was relieved temporarily in the mid–thirteenth century when Christians and Moslems allied against the Mongol threat. Early in the century a great leader, Genghis Khan, had transformed the Mongol nomads of Central Asia into a potent military force that swept over Eurasia and fashioned a huge empire stretching from China to central Europe. The Mongol threat began to lessen after 1260, and the old hostilities between Moslems and Christians were renewed. In 1291 the Mamelukes took the last Christian strongholds in the Holy Land. After nearly two centuries, the Latins had finally been ousted from Syria and Palestine.

So ended the most overt and dramatic manifestation of medieval western European expansionism. However, the loss of Outremer should not detract from how significant that expansionism in all its various forms had been in changing the position of western Europe with respect to the rest of the world. Nor should it tempt us to minimize the importance of the crusading movement. Historians are not unanimous in their assessments of the consequences of the crusading movement, but they agree that at least in some respects the effects were enduring. The Crusades generated an interaction between East and West, which "educated" Europeans to new ideas, products, and styles of life. The ventures certainly extended and solidified western European commercial power. They decisively affected the histories of both the Byzantine Empire and the Moslem world, weakening the former and provoking the latter to a new aggressiveness that was to have a significant impact on Europe during the late Middle Ages and well into early modern times. Perhaps the most significant legacy of the crusading movement was the negative image of western Europeans it generated among people in the East: the greedy, faithless, crude warrior; the crafty, grasping merchant; the ambitious, worldly church official—all of whom would do anything to acquire land, wealth, and power. Such images poisoned East-West relationships for centuries.

SUGGESTED READING

Expansion in Spain, Southern Italy, and Sicily

Anwar G. Chejne, *Muslim Spain. Its History and Culture* (1974). A fine introduction to Muslim Spain.

Thomas F. Glick, *Islamic and Christian Spain in the Early Middle Ages* (1979). Treats the interaction of Islamic and Christian societies.

Angus MacKay, *Spain in the Middle Ages: From Frontier to Empire, 1000–1500* (1977). Traces the rise of the Christian kingdoms.

C. H. Haskins, *The Normans in European History* (1915). A classic.

Richard F. Cassady, *The Norman Achievements* (1986). A sound recent assessment of the role of the Normans in Europe.

The Crusades

Jonathan Riley-Smith, *What Were the Crusades?* (1977). A stimulating analysis of the nature of the crusading movement.

Carl Erdmann, *The Origin of the Idea of Crusade,* trans. Marshall W. Baldwin and Walter Goffart (1977). A fundamental work stressing ideological factors.

Jonathan Riley-Smith, *The First Crusade and the Idea of Crusading* (1986). A provocative study, challenging Erdmann's ideas.

Jonathan Riley-Smith, *The Crusades. A Short History* (1987).

Hans E. Mayer, *The Crusades*, trans. John Gillingham (1972).

Two fine short histories; perhaps the Riley-Smith work is better.

Erick Christiansen, *The Northern Crusades: The Baltic and the Catholic Frontier, 1100–1525* (1980). A full treatment of an overlooked aspect of medieval crusading.

Joshua Prawer, *The Crusaders' Kingdom: European Colonization in the Middle Ages* (1972). Portrays what happened to the Europeans in the Near Eastern environment.

Norman Daniel, *The Arabs and Medieval Europe,* 2nd ed. (1979). Treats European attitudes toward Islam.

Benjamin Z. Kedar, *Crusade and Mission: European Approaches Toward the Muslims* (1984). Examines the interactions between crusading and missionary concepts.

Michael Angold, *The Byzantine Empire, 1025–1204; A Political History* (1984). Will help the reader understand the Byzantine role in the Crusades.

Malcolm Cameron Lyons and D. E. P. Jackson, *Saladin: The Politics of the Holy War* (1982). A perceptive study of a great Moslem leader.

The works of Shaban and Kennedy cited in Chapter 14 are useful in portraying conditions in the Moslem world during the crusades.

Sources

James A. Brundage, ed., *The Crusades: A Documentary Survey* (1972).

Louise and Jonathan Riley-Smith, eds. and trans., *The Crusades: Idea and Reality, 1095–1274* (1981).

Two collections of materials throwing light on how contemporaries experienced the crusading movement.

CHAPTER 22

The Revival and Triumph of the Church

FIGURE 22.1 The Last Judgment This magnificent scene carved above the main portal of the west façade of the Gothic cathedral at Chartres illustrates a fundamental idea of medieval Christian teaching: the Last Judgment—when Christ will make a final determination of the eternal lot of all people. Christ is surrounded by symbols of his glory and by life-size representations of individuals who played a role in the unfolding of the Christian drama. The scene conveys a powerful message to the faithful who might stray into sin: The time is at hand to enter the church and partake of grace-giving sacraments so that one will be ready to receive Christ's approval at the final hour. (Scala/Art Resource)

Between 1000 and 1300 powerful religious movements surged through western European society to bring about changes that some refer to as a "reformation." The reform movement of the High Middle Ages was complex, involving diverse approaches to the structuring of Christian society and to the attainment of Christian perfection. It tested to the limits a variety of traditional assumptions about religion and society. It called forth a major intellectual effort seeking to discover in the rich Christian tradition guides that would help shape a fuller religious life. Its impact was felt at all levels of society. In its totality the reform movement represented the major force binding all Europeans into a unified civilization. Thus, in a real sense, the medieval reformation constitutes the central "event" in the history of the High Middle Ages.

1. ORIGINS OF THE REFORM MOVEMENT

As we have seen (see Chapter 17), religious life in western Europe reached a low ebb in the tenth century, chiefly as a result of the feudalization of the Church's property and its leadership. Even in the midst of that difficult time the signs of religious renewal began to appear. Its first manifestations came in the monastic world, which for centuries had served as a focal point for those intent on the quest for spiritual perfection. Especially important was the monastery of Cluny, founded in Burgundy in 910 by a pious lay prince (see p. 296). The new monastery was dedicated to strict observance of the Benedictine rule, to freeing the community from lay control, and to elevating the intensity with which God was worshiped. A succession of dedicated abbots worked diligently to spread the Cluniac model, so that by the early eleventh century Cluniac establishments existed all over Europe as centers of spiritual guidance. Monastic reform was not confined to the Cluniac movement. During the tenth century monastic reforms were initiated in Lotharingia, Italy, and England, each stressing various patterns of renewal: denial of the corrupt material world in favor of poverty; a search for moral perfection; a quest for a better understanding of the Christian heritage.

Many bishops sought ways to improve the moral condition of the lower clergy under their jurisdiction and to intensify the teaching of their flocks. Pious rulers, and especially their queens, began to patronize reform activities. Some feudal potentates gave generous support to reformed monastic houses, especially Cluniac establishments, attracted chiefly by the willingness of the monks to pray for their souls after death. Even the peasantry felt the pull of reform, chiefly by outcries against abuses and corruption.

At its beginnings in the late tenth and early eleventh centuries, the quest for spiritual renewal was diffuse, disorganized, lacking in specific direction, and even contradictory. Although elements of spontaneity continued to surround the reforming effort until well into the thirteenth century, from the early eleventh century onward certain major trends dominated the medieval "reformation." One of them, spearheaded by the Roman popes with the support of some secular rulers and the intellectual establishment, sought to establish the "liberty" of the Church, to perfect its organization, and to impose on the faithful a uniform discipline and doctrine. A second, focused chiefly in the monastic world but also drawing strength from intellectuals, constantly probed for deeper spirituality, for moral improvement, and for more meaningful ways of worshiping God. A third involved a vibrant upsurge of popular piety, seeking ways by which the poor and the meek might share the promises of Jesus. Although these major components of the reform movement constantly intersected and reinforced each other, an examination of each of them separately will provide the most effective means of comprehending the magnitude of religious ferment during the High Middle Ages.

2. PAPAL REFORM: ORGANIZATION AND UNIFORMITY

The medieval reformation was well under way before the papacy began to play a significant role in its progress. An ancient tradition, reinforced during the Carolingian Age, attributed to the bishops of Rome headship over the Christian community by virtue of Jesus' commission to Peter, the first bishop of Rome. But during the tenth and early eleventh centuries the papacy had become bogged down in corruption and was dominated first by Roman nobles and then the Holy Roman emperors. As a consequence, it earned little respect from the Christian community of western Europe. In fact, that community was fragmented into many churches, most of which were led by a feudalized clergy dominated by secular lords and concerned chiefly with issues of power and wealth.

The situation began to change in the middle of the eleventh century when a circle of radical reformers, led by Hildebrand, later Pope Gregory VII (1073–1085), established control over the papacy. These reformers were men of deep moral convictions and well schooled in the traditions of the Church. They were convinced that the moral degeneration afflicting the contemporary religious world could only be cured by the reassertion of the authority of the Church. As we have seen (see Chapter 19), the Gregorian reformers envisaged the Church as a visible earthly community charged with guiding the members of that community to salvation. They believed with a passion that the community needed its own head, its own laws, its own resources, and its own liberty. On the basis of the ancient Petrine theory, they claimed for the bishop of Rome the divinely sanctioned authority to head the Christian community as God's earthly vicar. Borrowing from patristic thought and the pronouncements of earlier popes, they argued that God entrusted to his vicar two kinds of divinely ordained power, spiritual and temporal. The pope held the spiritual sword but granted the temporal sword to lay princes to be used to repress evil forces that impeded the faithful from gaining God's favors on earth and from earning eternal salvation. He retained full authority to direct the use of the temporal sword by any prince and to withdraw it if spiritual needs so dictated.

As pope, Gregory VII acted to convert this ideology into a reform program that addressed what he perceived to be the evils of his day. He launched an effort to free the Church from lay control by prohibiting lay investiture of clergymen with their offices and lands, thereby opening a prolonged political struggle with the princes of western Europe, especially the Holy Roman emperors. He initiated a legislative program aimed at using papal authority to eliminate moral abuses among the clergy, especially the selling of church offices and services (simony) and clerical marriage. To ensure that these efforts at reform were observed, he charted a program aimed at centralizing ecclesiastical authority in papal hands. Even before his pontificate, the papal reformers had instituted the College of Cardinals as the body empowered to elect the pope, thereby putting the papal office beyond lay control. Gregory took important steps to make that body the nucleus of a papal administrative machine. Papal *decretals* (legislative enactments) were issued with increasing frequency, laying down regulations for church governance and clerical conduct. Papal legates were sent across Europe to enforce this legislation. The papacy encouraged regional church councils to enact measures aimed at correcting abuses wherever they existed in the Christian world. Provisions were made to expedite the appeal of difficult cases to Rome for settlement. Special attention was given to regularizing and increasing papal income so as to ensure independence of action.

Gregory VII did not live to see his program succeed, but it remained a blueprint for his successors. The consolidation of papal power met resistance from many quarters, particularly from bishops and princes, who rightly sensed that their ancient freedoms were threatened. But Gregory's successors pursued his policy of centralization with skill and persistence. Their efforts were abetted by the willingness of the popes to retreat from Gregory's radical position on the supremacy of ecclesiastical over secular power. This compromise led to extensive mutual support between Church and state in establishing a more effective ecclesiastical organization; many kings found such an organization useful in supporting their own efforts to curb stubborn nobles and towns. By the thirteenth century such popes as Innocent III (1198–1216), Honorius III (1216–1227), Gregory IX (1227–1241), and Innocent IV (1243–1254) presided over an immense organization capable of directing religious life all over western Europe in minute detail.

These thirteenth-century papal monarchs controlled an elaborate Church bureaucracy located in Rome and called collectively the papal *curia*. This body was divided into specialized departments dealing with finances, correspondence and records, judicial cases, doctrine, and the discipline of sinners. It was staffed by trained clerical specialists who made careers of papal administration. The College of Cardinals, made up of churchmen especially selected by the pope, sat with the pope in special meetings (called *consistories*) to formulate major policies; its members often served as heads of the specialized departments that handled routine administrative matters. From the curia flowed a steady stream of legislation touching on every conceivable aspect of religious life. The papal court system handled an ever-increasing volume of cases appealed to Rome from throughout Europe. The Roman curia extended its authority beyond Rome through a system of papal agents, called *legates*, sent from Rome to supervise the enactment of papal orders. Some legates resided for extended periods in specific areas, while others were commissioned to deal with a specific problem. The legatine system, coupled with the curia's extensive correspondence and judicial appeals to Rome, kept the popes well informed about local affairs throughout Europe. A huge and constantly increasing income—derived from papal property, gifts, fees for judicial services, payments for dispensations from papal regulations, and assessments levied on the lower clergy and the laity— sustained this huge organization.

Papal authority was extended downward through the age-old hierarchy of archbishops, bishops, and priests. By 1300 the exact functions of each level were carefully defined, and papal control over the election and supervision of archbishops and bishops was extensive. Each archbishop was entrusted with the supervision of several bishops in his *province*, and each bishop was empowered to direct the activities of the priests and the laity residing in his *diocese*. These officials headed a small-scale model of the papal curia, called a *cathedral chapter*, staffed by *canons* who had a voice in episcopal elections, advised their superior, and carried out provincial and diocesan administration. The administration included conducting judicial proceedings, collecting and dispensing revenues, managing episcopal property, and supervising parish priests who were charged with ministering the sacraments and preaching to the Christian populace. One of the major accomplishments of the era was the establishment of a firm structure of local parishes across western Europe. For the most part, these territorial units, often coinciding with manors and agricultural villages or with specific quarters in urban centers, were freed from lay control over the appointment of priests and parish income and placed under episcopal direction. They provided a key element through which Christian teaching and practices could be extended to all people.

Although by 1300 some were beginning to think otherwise, the inspiration behind this effort at centralization was not merely a quest for power. Papal leaders and many of their episcopal subordinates genuinely believed that only through effective organization could the Christian flock be guided toward right behavior and right belief. As a consequence, a major aspect of the papal reform movement was an attempt to define and standardize church law and doctrine vital to the proper care of souls.

By the eleventh century the Church possessed an immense body of law derived from many sources: scriptural precedents, the writings of the early Church Fathers, the acts of a long succession of church councils, and the pronouncements of many popes and bishops (some of which were forged) on issues dealing with religious practices and discipline. Many of the provisions of this body of law were confused and contradictory, and some no longer applied to contemporary realities. Moreover, the issues posed by the reform movement demanded new legal solutions. These problems produced a new breed of specialists: trained lawyers working to create a consistent, organized body of law that would sustain the effort to create an independent religious community with its own rules. A decisive figure in the effort to create a "code" of law for the Church was Gratian. In 1140 he published his *Decretum*, which represented an effort to apply the rules of logic to the vast body of past precedents in a way that would remove contradictions and produce a consistent set of laws. Gratian's work immediately became the guide for Church administration and discipline. Among many other things, his code defined the powers of each rank of the clergy, the jurisdiction of ecclesiastical courts, crimes against the Church and their punishments, the proper use of Church income and property, and the manner of conducting religious ceremonies. Throughout the work ran one predominant idea—the supremacy of the papacy in the governance of the Church. Subsequent codifications that incorporated new legislation and extensive commentaries aimed at relating canon law to the real world greatly enriched the Church's law. By 1300 a powerful instrument for directing Christian society had been forged.

A comparable movement occurred in the field of doctrine. By 1000 the Church had accumulated a rich body of teachings defining right belief, but this material was disorganized and often contradictory. To cope with this problem, another kind of specialist, the trained theologian, emerged. Perhaps the decisive figure in developing systematic theology was a French schoolmaster, Peter Abelard (1079–1142). Calling attention to the conflicting teachings of Scripture, the Church Fathers, and tradition on certain doctrine questions, he urged that scholars apply human reason to resolve these differences. Most theologians adopted his approach, which came to be called Scholasticism. During the thirteenth century, a series of great theologians, the chief of whom was Thomas Aquinas, worked to systematize the Church's teachings and eliminated most of the earlier confusion. In the process, they tried to weave all human knowledge into a unified body consistent with revealed truth, giving the Church a single truth to teach to all.

Although the essence of Christian doctrine was stated in succinct form in the Nicene Creed, originally promulgated in 325, at the heart of the theological system of the twelfth and thirteenth centuries stood the doctrine of grace and the sacramental system. According to the theologians, God had created human beings in order that they might enjoy eternal salvation, human life being but a test of worthiness. Since humans were corrupted by original sin—the stain imposed on all by the disobedience of Adam and Eve—men and women needed God's grace to save them. That grace was bestowed through the sacraments instituted by Christ as an essential part of his mission of redemption (see Figure 22.2).

By the twelfth century the number of sacraments was set at seven; each drew its efficacy by virtue of the fact that it was administered by the Church, without whose services no Christian could expect to be saved. *Baptism,* usually administered at infancy, removed the stain of Original Sin and initiated its recipients into the Christian community; without it no Christian could be saved. *Confirmation,* usually received during the difficult years of adolescence, infused into Christians the Holy Ghost, strengthening their faith and fortifying them against the devil at a particularly critical moment. *Extreme unction,* administered to those in danger of death, strengthened them at the moment they must face the judgment of the Almighty and removed from their souls the stain of minor (or venial) sins. *Marriage* sanctified the wedded state and family life. *Holy orders,* or ordination, conferred on select Christians the priestly powers that permitted them to act as valid successors of Christ and the apostles in teaching the faith and administering the grace-giving sacraments, especially the Eucharist and penance. The *Eucharist* was the sacrament by which Christ himself was present to the faithful. Its exact nature was not defined until the Fourth Lateran Council in 1215, held under the direction of Innocent III, pronounced the doctrine of *transubstantiation:* When a priest consecrated bread and wine at Mass, their substance changed miraculously into the body and blood of Christ, although their external accidents (color, shape, taste, etc.) remained the same. Partaking of this sacrament—receiving Communion—infused the grace of Christ's substance into the soul. No punishment was more terrible than excommunication—being cut off from receiving the Eucharist. The last sacrament was *penance,* whereby Christians who confessed their sins to a priest and resolved not to repeat them received God's forgiveness, provided that they made some sacrifice or did some good work assigned by the priest. Since the stain of sin barred one from heaven, Christians constantly needed to resort to the confessional to ensure that their souls, freed from Original Sin by baptism, were constantly repurified by the removal of all stains caused by the sins they committed in the course of their lives. The Fourth Lateran Council decreed that the faithful must confess at least once a year.

FIGURE 22.2 The Sacraments These scenes from a fourteenth-century manuscript illustrate three of the seven sacraments—baptism, the Eucharist, and marriage. According to the Church's teaching, only through participation in the sacraments could a Christian gain salvation. (Bibliothèque Nationale, Paris, ms. n. s. fr. 4509)

Embroidered on the sacramental system was a rich array of Church-sanctioned practices and beliefs to facilitate the winning of God's favors. By the thirteenth century Christian life was surrounded by an array of prayers and ritual ceremonies that invoked God's help in every conceivable situation. Sacred objects, especially relics, available to almost every Christian possessed powers to draw God and the devout faithful together. An army of saints filled heaven to plead the cause of humanity with God and to assist in frustrating the hordes of devils that schemed under Satan's command to corrupt men and women. These adjuncts to the sacramental system were enlarged and enriched during the High Middle Ages, a process that added a powerful emotional dimension to the rather awesome concepts of the sacramental system.

The major fruits of papal reform—the centralized administrative system, the wide-ranging body of canon law, and the theological system making the Church essential to the salvation of all—permitted Church leaders to extend their influence far beyond the religious sphere. Nothing illustrates this influence better than the role played by Innocent III in European affairs. We need only recall how he manipulated affairs to make his ward, Frederick II, Holy Roman emperor. He took an active role in the complex political interactions involving the numerous Italian city-states. After a long quarrel he compelled Philip II of France to take back a wife he had repudiated. He forced or persuaded John of England and several other rulers to accept the status of vassal of the pope. Innocent was active in promoting the crusading movement. He was instrumental in organizing a crusade against the heretical Albigensians of southern France, thereby helping the French kings to expand their royal domain. Innocent's story was replicated in the careers of most thirteenth-century popes and, on a smaller scale, in those of countless bishops. In short, papal monarchs and their episcopal agents used religious weapons to gain political ends and political and economic pressures to advance ecclesiastical interests. They often summed up their authority by speaking of their God-given right to exercise "the fullness of power" over all Christians. By that they meant that they had the right to make the final decisions affecting any aspect of Christian society. While they conceded that lay leaders had the authority to direct worldly affairs, they claimed the ultimate authority to judge how well these authorities used their power to achieve Christian ends.

3. MONASTIC REFORM: SPIRITUAL SEEKING

While the quest for greater order in the organization of the Church and its law and theology was advanced by popes, bishops, canon lawyers, and theologians, others sought for deeper spiritual understanding. Although those promoting reform on the papal model were always concerned with spirituality, it was in the monastic world that the urge to deepen spiritual life was felt most strongly. Those interested in expanding spiritual horizons faced a religious mentality of limited dimension in the year 1000. Most believed in a God perceived as a stern judge whose wrath might fall on helpless, sin-tainted humans at any time and in any form (see Figure 22.1). Human life was surrounded by constant danger from the devil and his demons, present everywhere and armed with almost irresistible powers to entice men and women ever deeper into sin, for which God's anger would only be greater. The best humans could hope for was to do something that would be pleasing to God or that would persuade the legions of angels and saints who served the judgmental deity to intercede in their behalf. As a consequence, religious life was highly externalized. Men and women sought to propitiate God by offerings of their material goods, acts of charity, prayers, and veneration of relics of the saints. They searched for acts of penitence to win forgiveness for their sins—fasting, abstinence from fleshly pleasures, pilgrimages. Nothing brought greater comfort

than miracles whereby God or his agents overturned the natural order to cure sickness, turn sure defeat in war into victory, save the harvests, or confound the devil at the crucial moment when he was about to trap someone into sin.

The dominant monastic force during the tenth and eleventh centuries was the Cluniac movement. The Cluniacs reinforced the ancient ideal that God could be served best by a retreat to a cloistered stronghold. The movement sought to restore the primitive purity of the Benedictine rule as a means of ensuring that an elite would serve God well. The founder of Cluny, a pious French noble, freed it from lay control, and its first abbots sought successfully to extend its influence by founding dependent houses that took directions from the abbot of the mother house. In a spiritual sense, the Cluniac movement emphasized an elaborate daily round of prayer and celebration of sacred rites as the main duty of the monks. The Cluniac liturgy was a splendid model of externalized religion that the contemporary world found so attractive. Many feudal aristocrats established close ties with Cluniac communities, chiefly to gain assurance that the monastic congregations they supported would include them in their prayers for the dead. As sponsors of the Peace and the Truce of God, the Cluniac order made a notable contribution to curbing feudal warfare and promoting the concept of holy warfare as an act pleasing to God. And as promoters of the cult of saints and pilgrimages, the Cluniac monks provided an important outlet for the widespread urge for penitential actions pleasing to God.

By the end of the eleventh century the Cluniac movement began to lose its appeal. In part, this decreased interest was a consequence of the excessive wealth and the spiritual complacency of the Cluniac order. More important, spiritual seekers increasingly found the externalized forms of piety promoted by Cluny unduly limited and not attuned to changing concepts of the nature of God, of human capabilities, and of the needs of Christian society, especially as highlighted by the Gregorian reform. These views tempered God's harsh judgmental qualities with a new emphasis on his love for humanity (see Figure 22.3). They invited a search for the human capacity to absorb God's love internally and to progress toward perfection through human powers. They encouraged activities born of human love that promoted the welfare of earthly society.

The expanding confidence in the human capacity for personal perfection led to a revival of hermit life based on the model provided by the desert fathers of the fourth and fifth centuries. Many of the hermits of the eleventh and twelfth centuries pursued their search for perfection individually. However, the hermit ideal did produce the Carthusian order, established in France in the late eleventh century. Selecting the most unattractive sites for monastic houses and imposing a severe regimen of poverty, fasting, and prayer, the Carthusian order encouraged its members to strive for a spiritual condition that would open the human heart to divine love. The order impressed upon an admiring world a model of denial of self and of the world as a means of preparing to meet God.

The monastic movement that during the twelfth century played the most important role in shaping a new spiritual vision and in projecting it into the world was the Cistercian order. Founded in 1098 by a Benedictine who felt that the ancient rule was not being properly observed by the then-dominant Cluniacs, the Cistercian movement stressed the need for separation from the world and for an austere life of prayer and labor. Cistercian houses were usually established on remote, uncultivated sites; like other agricultural colonizers of the era, the Cistercian monks employed their labor and technical ingenuity to create thriving agricultural establishments. Cistercian houses, both male and female, soon sprang up all over Europe, held together by a unique provision in the Cistercian rule stating that policy and regulations for all houses would be decided by regular meetings of their heads.

Especially influential in shaping the Cistercian spiritual message was Bernard of Clairvaux, who viewed monastic life as a preparation for action in the cause of God. That preparation was aimed at the inner spiritual development of each individual monk rather than the elaborate, communally organized round of external religious acts that characterized Cluniac practice and that dominated the religious mentality of most contemporary Christians. Monks needed to practice physical depri-

FIGURE 22.3 A Loving, Caring God This sculpture from Chartres Cathedral shows God creating Adam. This Creator is not the awful judge of the last day (see Figure 22.1). Rather, this scene reflects the new understanding of God that had such a powerful effect on the spirituality of the twelfth and thirteenth centuries. (Archives Photographiques, Paris)

vation, work, and prayer as a part of their spiritual training. Equally important was contemplation and devotion. Bernard's prescription for individual spiritual development focused attention on a loving God reaching out to unleash the potential of the human soul to participate in divinity. The human spirit could best reach back toward that God by contemplating the human, suffering Jesus and by seeking to share the feelings of Mary, Mother of God, of Jesus' disciples, and of those he taught as all of them lived in the presence of God made human for the salvation of other humans. Bernard was fully confident that the love and understanding flowing from such an approach to God would prepare human beings to go forth to fight sin and spiritual poverty without fear of corruption. In his own life he exemplified this new kind of spiritual activism. During his long career in the Cistercian order (1113–1153), he was involved in nearly every important event in Europe as a spiritual activist. He was the chief instigator of the Second Crusade, proclaiming that involvement was a manifestation of love for God and of service in the divine cause. He served the papacy doggedly in rooting out corruption in the clergy (he even censured papal conduct on occasion). He was a relentless foe of unorthodox and heretical thinking. He hounded Europe's kings constantly to improve their lives and their governments. He had no peer as a popular preacher and as a promoter of the use in the entire Church of the devotional practices that were at the heart of Cistercian spirituality. He and other Cistercians served as industrious soldiers of Christ whose chief armament was their sense of godliness derived from their inner spiritual life. Their target was the souls of men and women who possessed but did not properly use the power to make themselves better Christians.

Other developments in the monastic world of the twelfth century contributed to the deepening of religious life and the expansion of monastic influence on society. The number of monastic houses for women—nunneries—increased dramatically, usually governed by a version of the Benedictine or the Cistercian rule. These centers enlarged the visibility of women as models of piety and offered many of them opportunities for education and service. An order called the Augusti-

nian Canons was organized as a means of improving the moral quality of the clerics who served in cathedral chapters. Its rule bound the canons to poverty, prayer, and moral excellence while permitting them to continue their responsibilities as pastors and episcopal administrators. Perhaps the most unusual application of the monastic model was the establishment of the crusading orders— the Templars, the Hospitalers, and the Teutonic Knights. Following a model defined by Bernard of Clairvaux, those who entered these orders took a monastic vow stressing obedience, poverty, and service to God as warriors defending the Christians in the Holy Land. Their service earned these orders not only high respect but also immense wealth, which led to their involvement in landholding, commerce, and money lending.

The expansion of monastic involvement in the world and the monastic search for new spiritual horizons reached a culmination in the early thirteenth century with the establishment of the *mendicant* (begging) orders, the Dominicans and the Franciscans. These orders were a response to several problems that increasingly challenged the Church's traditional pastoral activities: the growth of urban life, with its unique institutions and tensions; the emergence of more sophisticated law and theology; the growing criticisms of the wealth and power of the ecclesiastical establishment; and doctrinal heresy. The mendicant movement sought to prepare pastors who could go forth into the world to address these problems without being burdened by material concerns or by the stigma of wealth—widely believed to be a barrier to spiritual perfection. To achieve this end, the mendicant orders insisted on absolute poverty after the model of Jesus and his disciples; neither the individual monk nor the corporate order was to possess wealth. Material support was to be derived from charity extended by those being served; begging for such charity was a key element of the vocation of the mendicants. Although the mendicants were mindful of the necessity of developing inner spiritual life, the range of problems they sought to address as pastors called for the development of intellectual skills. As a consequence, their preparation for active monastic life stressed education devoted to mastering the intricacies of canon law and theology and to developing skills needed for effective expression of the Church's teachings.

The Dominican order drew its name from its founder, a Spanish canon named Dominic (1170–1221). He was inspired to found a new order as a result of a tour through southern France, where the Albigensian heresy was rampant despite the efforts of the local bishops and Cistercian monks to curb it. Dominic became convinced that orthodoxy would prevail only if preachers learned in theology and free from all suspicion of wealth mingled intimately with the heretics to teach them the true faith. In 1215 Pope Innocent III authorized him to organize a new order dedicated to the destruction of heresy by preaching. The rule provided that Dominic's followers would commit themselves to complete poverty and to preaching; their collective activities would be directed by a master general and his subordinate priors who commanded the provinces into which the order was divided. The rule placed heavy stress on the education of each monk in theology and law. The Black Friars, or Friars Preachers, as the order came to be called, quickly established themselves as a major force across Europe, active in preaching and in controlling the formulation and teaching of theology in the universities. Their involvement in university education allowed them to play a major role in shaping the religious leadership of the entire Church during the thirteenth century.

The inspiration for the Franciscan order was supplied by one of the most appealing figures in all religious history, Francis of Assisi (1182–1226) (see Figure 22.4). The son of a wealthy Italian merchant, Francis, while still a young man who had previously enjoyed the pleasures of life, underwent a fundamental spiritual conversion that convinced him that he must imitate Christ in a most literal sense. As he put it, he married "Lady Poverty" and turned his energy to preaching and performing charitable works. He was especially charismatic as a preacher, exuding joy and a sympathy for all God's creatures, especially unfortunate, suffering human beings. To his followers, he was "God's own troubadour," filled with happiness and love. Almost immediately both men and women began to follow him. They surrendered their wealth, worked or begged for a livelihood, and preached a simple message of love for

FIGURE 22.4   Francis of Assisi: "God's Own Troubadour"   St. Francis of Assisi, portrayed here in a painting done by Cimabue ca. 1280, was perhaps the most powerful spiritual force in the thirteenth century. His ideas on poverty and love deeply affected many of those searching for religious values in his age. (Alinari/Art Resource)

God and humanity. In 1210 Francis asked Innocent III for permission to organize a formal religious order that would practice absolute poverty and dedicate its efforts to preaching and good works. Innocent hesitated, feeling that Francis' demands on his followers were too severe and perhaps concerned that the simple message of love and repentance would breed a crop of dissenters with little regard for the machinery that the organized Church supplied for saving souls. Finally, however, he consented. Between then and 1226, when Francis died, the order grew rapidly, spreading to nearly every part of western Europe and even beyond. As the order expanded, its governing rule was modified to provide a more structured organization and a discipline more formal than the founder's simple command that his followers imitate Jesus. The rule of absolute poverty was modified to allow the order to acquire wealth and to place greater emphasis on formal education as preparation for a preaching career. To many devoted Franciscans these compromises represented a denial of the Franciscan ideal; as a result of these concerns, the order was plagued by bitter internal conflicts. The Friars Minor, or Grey Friars, also met strong opposition from local clergy, who resented their exaltation of poverty and their effective skills as preachers and confessors. Despite these obstacles, the Franciscans asserted a powerful influence on religious life at all levels of society. Together, the Franciscans and the Dominicans became pillars of strength for the thirteenth-century Church in terms of propagating its teachings, containing voices of dissent, and expanding spiritual consciousness.

4. POPULAR REFORM: ENTHUSIASM, DISSENT, HERESY

The highly visible efforts of reformers to impose order on religious life and to expand spiritual visions were accompanied by considerable religious ferment among people of modest social status. Reform of this kind manifested itself in the activities of diverse peoples: simple priests, maverick monks, peasants, merchants, artisans, women, even children. What motivated their efforts at religious renewal are difficult to discern. Perhaps they were stimulated by a deeper understanding of the Christian message brought to them by the priests and monks produced by the papal and monastic reform movements. Perhaps they were introduced to new religious ideas by the slowly expanding number of literate laypersons, especially in towns, who were able to explore sacred literature and articulate their own interpretation of its meaning. The social and economic changes affecting society at all levels created new pressures that provoked a rethinking of traditional religious values. In reviewing the evidence, one suspects that many simple, uneducated, illiterate people were able to extract from their limited knowledge of God's ways and of Jesus' message fresh religious insights that made their lives more meaningful. Whatever the source, there can be no question that the period 1000 to 1300 witnessed significant religious stirrings throughout the population.

One manifestation of popular religious ferment was the enthusiastic response of simple people to externalized cult practices aimed at seeking God's favor and doing penance for sins. Such people eagerly participated in the cult of relics and the veneration of saints. Simple people participated in pilgrimages to holy places, whether the holy place be a shrine located a few miles away or the scene of Jesus' earthly life in distant Palestine. The infamous Peasants' Crusade reflects the fervor aroused in the popular mind by the crusading movement; even more bizarre was the Children's Crusade of 1212 during which several thousand children were organized for an expedition to the Holy Land and proceeded as far as Marseilles in southern France before less pious merchants sold them into slavery.

Another fairly frequent manifestation of popular religious enthusiasm was the response given to charismatic preachers, who some credit with laying the groundwork for a Christian evangelical movement. Building their message around Jesus' poverty, humility, and love, these preachers often established bands of followers who shared their wealth, engaged in works of charity, cared for the sick, and worshiped in unique ways that emphasized emotion and intimate companionship. Some of these leaders spiced their exhortations to live like Jesus and his apostles with passionate attacks on the moral flabbiness of the clergy and the wealth of the contemporary Church, thus making anticlericalism a regular part of popular religious reform. On occasions, this anticlericalism led to overt action against the established clergy. For instance, in 1145 an Italian monk, Arnold of Brescia, so aroused the populace of Rome against the wealth and secular power of the papacy that the pope was forced to flee and only succeeded in recapturing control of the city by calling upon Frederick Barbarossa to use force to capture and execute Arnold.

On occasion such popular reform efforts extended beyond what the Church and secular authorities would tolerate as dissent and became heresy. Such was the fate of the Waldensian movement. This group was inspired by Peter Waldo, a rich merchant from Lyons in France. In 1173 he gave away his wealth and took up a life of poverty in imitation of Christ—much as Francis of Assisi would do later. Soon after he began his preaching, Peter went in person to Rome to seek papal permission to establish a monastic order based on poverty. The pope denied him permission to continue his work. Disregarding this prohibition, the group continued, gradually becoming more radical. Practicing poverty and a strict moral life reflecting many Cistercian ideas about sobriety, temperance, and simplicity, Waldensian leaders went among the common people, especially in urban centers, preaching and praying in the vernacular language. They condemned the clergy, arguing that all Christians could serve a priestly function, and denied the need of the sacraments in gaining salvation. They developed their own ministers and their own ritual practices. Eventually they were accused of heresy, and the Church undertook to suppress the movement. Some Waldensian groups, especially in France, returned to orthodoxy, but in northern Italy the movement withstood persecution and has survived to the present.

Far more radical were the Cathari (from a Latin word meaning the "pure"), also called Albigensians (from Albi, the southern French city where the movement was especially strong). Their fundamental belief was rooted in a radical dualism, a concept that originated in the Near East as early as the fourth century, probably from the mixing of Christian and Zoroastrian ideas. The movement spread slowly westward, finally reaching northern Italy and southern France in the tenth century. By 1200 its influence was felt throughout Europe, with its major center of strength in southern France, a land that was politically fragmented and culturally unique

The Cathari believed that two powers, good and evil, coexist and constantly compete in the universe. Only things spiritual, including the human soul, were good. Everything material was evil, including the flesh within which the soul is entrapped and the earth itself. This position caused the Cathari to deny the humanity of Jesus and the validity of what he had instituted in this world as instruments of salvation, including the earthly Church, the ordained priesthood, and the

sacraments, all of which partook in some way in the evil material world. True Cathari—the "perfect," as they called themselves—sought to liberate their souls by escaping the material world. They refused to marry, holding that human procreation was the greatest of all evils. They ate no meat, milk, or eggs, all the products of sexual union. They owned no property and refused to shed blood. Allowances were made in the Cathari communities for those incapable of the rigorous life imposed on the "perfect." Second-grade Cathari, called "believers," were permitted to indulge in things material more freely, although "believers" hoped someday to join the ranks of the "perfect" who alone would be saved. The Cathari developed their own clergy, their own religious services, and their own rules of conduct. Their fervor and discipline produced communities that were remarkably resourceful in asserting political and economic dominance over the areas where they lived. But above all else, the Cathari impressed those around them with their austerity and moral earnestness.

Needless to say, the unique beliefs and the material success of the Cathari aroused the ire of those outside their exclusive communities and brought charges of heresy against them. As a consequence, the Church moved to suppress the movement. Local bishops attempted to convert them by persuasion; that failing, they then hailed them before Church courts to try and punish them under the provisions of canon law that provided death sentences for heresy. As we have noted, first the Cistercians and then the Dominicans tried to persuade the Cathari to return to orthodoxy. However, these measures failed, in part because of the dedication of the Cathari and in part because the movement had support from many local nobles. Pope Innocent III finally took a more drastic step: He organized a force of French knights, most vassals of kings Philip II and Philip III of France, to mount a "crusade" against the heretics. This ferocious Albigensian Crusade (1209–1229) destroyed the main centers of Cathari power and exterminated many members of the movement. To hunt down those that remained, the papacy utilized a special court, the Inquisition, and empowered it to employ special legal techniques, including secret witnesses and torture, to identify suspected heretics and to bring them to trial that resulted either in their return to orthodoxy or their death. These drastic measures provided a final solution for Catharism.

5. THE CONSEQUENCES OF THE MEDIEVAL REFORMATION

During the thirteenth century there were increasing signs that the reform movement was losing its vitality. Most of the forces that generated reforming ideas and practices during the eleventh, twelfth, and early thirteenth centuries had been successfully encapsulated into the formal structures of the Church as official parts of its organization, its doctrine, its law, its ritual, its moral code, and its spirituality. In a sense, what we identified as papal reform had absorbed and legitimized most other kinds of reform. There remains but one question: What were the consequences of all the energy spent trying to elevate the level of religious life? Historians have differed widely in their answers to this question, chiefly because they cannot agree on a standard by which the quality of religious life can be judged. But perhaps most would accept certain outcomes of the medieval reformation.

First, the medieval reformation certainly strengthened the organization of the Church. In contrast to its position in 1000, the Church by 1300 had the power and the resources to impose on its vast membership one body of belief, one code of conduct, and one set of religious practices. Seldom in history has an institution been in a position to direct society so decisively. But that position was not gained by accident; it required sustained creative effort.

Second, the reformation redefined the relationship between church and state. Whereas in 1000 the Church was dominated by secular powers whose authority was surrounded by a sacral aura, by 1300 the Church had defined for itself an area of liberty into which no other authority could intrude. Acting within this sphere, the Church was able to play a vital role in influencing societal development according to religious norms. The existence of separate realms for church and state would powerfully affect Europe's future.

Third, the challenges posed by the effort to renew religious life unleashed intellectual and artistic talents in ways that stretched the mental capabilities and the artistic sensibilities of western Europeans far beyond the boundaries of the mentality existing in the year 1000. In short, religious renewal sparked a multifaceted cultural renaissance that might not otherwise have happened except for the troublesome issues raised by the intense search for God and for more effective ways of serving his will.

Fourth, the medieval reformation broadened the range of spiritual possibilities far beyond what had been available to Christians in the early Middle Ages. The probing for the meaning of religious life that occurred between 1000 and 1300 in the monastic world and among simple people produced spiritual concepts that greatly enriched Christian life. Perhaps the most notable discovery was the spiritual frontier that existed within the individual Christian.

Finally, it can be argued that the medieval reformation caused as many religious problems as it solved. As its most notable monument, the medieval reformation created a powerful, rich, highly structured institution, deeply involved in the affairs of the world. In its theology and its law, that Church had defined a highly formal system of religion that claimed to hold the keys to salvation. It remained to be seen whether society would continue to accept that monolithic system in its entirety. Would kings and princes allow the Church to direct many aspects of worldly society according to its own rules? Would men and women find the answers to their spiritual needs in the strictly defined system of belief and worship prescribed by the Church? Was there any flexibility within this highly centralized, legalistic, formal religious structure to allow adjustment to changing times and ideas? In short, did the far-reaching consequences of one powerful religious reformation create conditions that would soon demand another?

SUGGESTED READING

General Surveys of Church History

Bernard Hamilton, *Religion in the Medieval West* (1986). A valuable guide to the basic tenets and practices of the Christian faith.

Jeffrey Burton Russell, *A History of Medieval Christianity: Prophecy and Order* (1968). A good brief treatment.

Hubert Jedin and John Dolan, eds., *Handbook of Church History*, Vol. 4: *From the High Middle Ages to the Eve of the Reformation*, trans. Anselm Biggs (1970). A detailed history of religious life.

R. W. Southern, *Western Society and the Church in the Middle Ages* (1970). Stresses relationships between the Church and the world.

Reform: Papal, Monastic, Popular

Walter Ullmann, *A Short History of the Papacy in the Middle Ages* (1972). A compact, provocative summary of papal history.

Charles M. Radding, *The Origins of Medieval Jurisprudence. Pavia and Bologna, 850–1150* (1987). Treats the origins of medieval canon law.

Jaroslav Pelikan, *The Christian Tradition. A History of the Development of Doctrine*, Vol. 3: *The Growth of Medieval Theology (600–1300)* (1978). A challenging treatment of the search for a uniform body of doctrine.

Bernard Hamilton, *The Medieval Inquisition* (1981). A clear study.

Christopher Brooke, *The Monastic World, 1000–1300* (1974).

C. H. Lawrence, *Medieval Monasticism: Forms of Religious Life in Western Europe in the Middle Ages* (1984). Two good descriptions of various forms of medieval monasticism.

R. I. Moore, *The Origins of European Dissent* (1977). Traces the development of dissent, with a stress on social factors.

Walter L. Wakefield, *Heresy, Crusade and Inquisition in Southern France, 1100–1250* (1979). Excellent on the Cathari.

Rosalind and Christopher Brooke, *Popular Religion in the Middle Ages: Western Europe, 1000–1300* (1984). A fine introduction.

Biographies

Helene Tillmann, *Pope Innocent III*, trans. Walter Sax (1980).

Watkin Williams, *Saint Bernard of Clairvaux* (1953).

Adolf Holl, *The Last Christian*, trans. Peter Heinegg (1980). Treats Francis of Assisi.

Etienne Gilson, *Héloise and Abelard*, trans. L. K. Shook (1951).

Pierre Mandonnet, *St. Dominic and His Work*, trans. Mary Benedicta Larkin (1945).

CHAPTER 23

Intellectual and Artistic Achievements

FIGURE 23.1   Gothic Sculpture
These Gothic figures from the south portal of the cathedral at Chartres, France, illustrate the warmth and realism of Gothic sculpture. (Jean Roubier)

The crowning achievement of western Europeans during the High Middle Ages was their original and creative work in thought, literature, and art. The foundations for this cultural outburst had been painfully shaped during a long apprenticeship culminating in the Carolingian revival; the immediate stimulus was provided by the powerful political, economic, and social changes occurring after 1000. The achievements played an important role in giving western European civilization its unique character and in establishing western European preeminence in a world setting.

The cultural achievement of the High Middle Ages can best be understood by a topical approach concentrating on certain areas of cultural activity that dominated thought and expression. However, it is important to note that the cultural development occurring during the period from 1000 to 1300 had a chronological dimension. In broad terms, cultural change occurred in two phases. The first, extending from about 1000 to 1170, was marked by vigorous exploration and experimentation that immensely expanded the cultural horizons and skills of thinkers, writers, and artists. As one American scholar put it, that era witnessed a "renaissance." As the twelfth century neared its end, the cultural climate began to change. The buoyant, questing spirit gave way to a concern for organizing and summarizing the diverse accomplishments of the earlier period. This age of synthesis, extending across the thirteenth century, produced the most mature expressions of medieval culture, but its accomplishments lacked the freshness and spontaneity characteristic of the earlier "renaissance."

1. THE WORLD OF LEARNING: EDUCATION

The cultural life of the High Middle Ages was divided into two distinctive spheres. In one, Latin was the vehicle of expression. In the West, Latin was the language in which the prime sources of the Christian faith were enshrined: Scripture, the writings of the Church Fathers, the liturgy, the canon law. And it was the language employed to explain the meaning of the faith. Those who used that language, chiefly members of the clergy, became the "learned" in society, a group accorded high respect because its members had access to the written sources that opened the way to salvation. In the other cultural sphere, the languages of the people, the vernacular tongues, prevailed, first as spoken vehicles of communication and then as written languages devoted chiefly to expressing the interests, tastes, and values of the nobility. Although these two cultural spheres intersected and interacted, each made its own unique contributions to the cultural life of the High Middle Ages.

In the world of the "learned" education was of crucial importance. During the early Middle Ages Latin increasingly became a foreign language that had to be learned by those seeking access to religious truth. This crucial need required schools designed primarily to sustain Latin learning. What was taught in those schools and how it was taught became a prime factor in shaping the mentality of the learned world.

As we have already noted (see Chapters 15 and 16), prior to 1000 educational activity was largely confined to monastic schools, although by 1000 a few modest cathedral schools still survived from Carolingian times, and in Italy some municipal schools continued. A curriculum based on the study of the seven liberal arts had been fixed, and basic textbooks defining the content of these disciplines had been established, chiefly during the Carolingian period. The monastic schools touched a narrow segment of the population and cultivated a limited range of intellectual interests.

During the eleventh and twelfth centuries the educational system underwent a significant expansion and a fundamental change in character. Part of the stimulus came from intellectual ferment within the monastic world (see Chapter 22). More decisive, however, was a shift in the social value of education. Education became the avenue by which increasing numbers prepared themselves for career opportunities opened up by the demand in the Church, royal governments, and towns for literate people capable of handling the complexities of administration and commercial exchange. Cathedral and municipal schools were better prepared to meet this challenge than monastic schools and enjoyed a remarkable growth in number and size. Especially in the cathedral schools there was a marked intensification and expansion of the study of the seven liberal arts, particularly the *trivium*—grammar, rhetoric, and dialectic (logic). In the municipal schools in Italy, the study of law took on new vigor. Many of the most prominent cathedral schools of the early twelfth century, such as those at Paris, Chartres, Laon, and Reims, owed their fame to individual masters who specialized in one of the liberal arts and was thus able to enrich its content and its methodology. In fact, being a master became a career in itself, marking the appearance of the professional intellectual as a key force in the world of learning. The content of grammar, rhetoric, and dialectic derived chiefly from classical Latin models, so that the cathedral schools became centers of more intensive and critical study of the classics. The other four liberal arts (the *quadrivium*)—arithmetic, geometry, astronomy, music—were less important in training literate, articulate people to serve new social roles. Still, their content was constantly expanded, chiefly as a result of the renaissance of classical studies.

Toward the end of the twelfth century the monastic, cathedral, and municipal schools no longer met the needs of the world of learning. Because they were often dependent on a single master teaching a specialized discipline, they lacked continuity and curricular breadth. Also, their masters had opened up intellectual vistas and generated specialized scholarly interests that abbots, bishops, and town councils had little practical interest in fostering. Moreover, during the last half of the twelfth century western Europe was flooded with a huge body of new knowledge coming from the Greek and Moslem worlds. Primarily philosophical and scientific in content, this new knowledge challenged existing religious beliefs and demanded levels of learning well beyond that needed to prepare people for careers. The response was a new institution, the university, consisting of a community of teachers and learners engaged in a collective effort to expand, organize, and transmit knowledge and intellectual skills.

The earliest universities, those at Bologna and Paris, came into existence about 1200; not long after others emerged in various urban centers across Europe. Following a pattern already used by urban dwellers and by merchants and crafts-

men seeking to establish a place for themselves in society, the founders of universities organized themselves into self-governing corporations, or guilds (the general Latin term for "guild" was *universitas*). At Bologna the students, for the most part law students, formed a *universitas* because they felt they needed protection from the townspeople and their masters. At Paris the teachers of the arts in the city's episcopal school broke away from the bishop's control and founded a self-governing body, the faculty of the arts, to control the educational process. A crucial step in establishing a university was gaining legal recognition from a public authority—king, bishop, town council—allowing the corporation to exercise certain privileges. The privileges claimed were wide-ranging, but one was vital: the right to grant a degree certifying that a learner had completed a specified program of training defined by a faculty. Once a guild of teachers and students had established its legal status, it developed its own internal structure and operating rules. This process was often lengthy and beset by fierce struggles within the *universitas*.

The core curriculum of the typical university was based on training in the seven liberal arts conducted by a faculty of masters of arts, each a specialist in one of the arts. Completion of the arts program, usually requiring four years, resulted in a bachelor of arts degree, which qualified its literate recipients for a variety of careers. Those wishing to teach the arts either in a university or some other kind of school pursued their studies in one of the arts for another year or two and earned a master's degree. Those who aspired to a teaching career beyond instructing students in the liberal arts or who hoped to serve in high places as authorities on technical disciplines could pursue a doctorate in theology, law, or medicine. This degree required additional years of study, research, and public professing. At Paris, for example, the theology doctorate took at least thirteen years of study. Although the ultimate objective of university study was earning a degree, many students spent time at universities without earning degrees; just being at a university earned them preferment in advancing their careers and some degree of social respectability.

The basic teaching method at universities focused on acquainting students with authoritative texts in the various disciplines. Usually these texts were works by ancient authors; but as the High Middle Ages progressed, the works of "modern" authorities were added (such as Peter Lombard and Gratian). Since books had to be handwritten, they were scarce and expensive. In the face of this problem, the master read the text (thus the origin of the lecture method, derived from the Latin word for reading, *lectio*), and the students took notes. As the master read the text, he commented on the issues it raised, often citing the opinions of other authorities on each issue and employing logical argumentation to reconcile differences. The purpose of this enterprise was to convey fundamental truths and to train students in the art of defending them through argumentation (*disputatio*)—an art that required acquiring a body of knowledge, developing a capacity for logical thinking, and perfecting skills in oral argumentation. Proof of worthiness for a degree was established by a student's performance in a public examination. Such a test required the student to expound on a text, develop and defend a thesis with respect to it, and respond to challenges to the thesis posed by the examining masters. This method produced minds that held a high respect for established authorities, were adept at textual analysis, were skilled in reconciling contradictory positions by logic, and were inclined to settle differences by argumentation.

The early universities were communities of people rather than physical entities. Most classes were held in rented halls. Students took lodgings in private homes. In time, however, universities did take on a physical presence. Patrons began to endow establishments, called *colleges,* for housing and feeding students. The first such institution was the Sorbonne at Paris, named after its patron, Robert de Sorbon, a rich courtier. Chapels, manuscript-copying services, and libraries were built to serve those engaged in learning. Thus, a university quarter began to emerge in some medieval cities, usually a welcome adornment to urban life.

University students were almost exclusively male and came from a mixed social background; predominantly they were the offspring of people of modest means—petty nobles, merchants, artisans, even affluent peasants—who saw education as a means of economic and social advancement. They ranged in age from fourteen or fifteen to thirty or thirty-five. Since universities were few, students gathered at each from afar, thus constituting a population of strangers in most university towns. Many were supported by their parents or by patrons—usually inadequately, if we can believe the constant pleas for funds voiced in surviving student letters. These letters, however, seldom talk of student expenditures in taverns and on other frivolous pursuits that are recorded in other surviving documents. Students engaged in endless clashes with townspeople, who viewed them as foreigners, idlers, and wastrels but also as targets for exploitation. Since students were legally considered members of the clergy and of a privileged corporation, it was difficult for town governments to exercise legal control over them. Town-gown rivalry, often surrounded by bitter recriminations and even violence, became a regular part of urban life in every university center.

2. THE WORLD OF LEARNING: THE MEDIEVAL "SCIENCES"

The evolution of the medieval educational system promoted the structuring of intellectual activity into what medieval scholars would have called "sciences," by which they meant bodies of interrelated knowledge capable of describing and explaining meaningful segments of the universe. In a sense, each of the seven liberal arts constituted a science in the medieval scheme of things, and medieval scholars and teachers greatly enriched each of them, but especially grammar and dialectic. However, the chief monuments of medieval intellectual activity came in more exalted "sciences": theology (which embraced what we would call philosophy), or the study of God; law, or the study of human society; and nature, or the study of the material order. Aside from the challenging intellectual issues innate in each of these areas, various pressing problems in a changing society forced learned men to explore each and to struggle to bring order to what was known.

The queen of medieval "sciences" was theology. Although it had always engaged Christian thinkers, theology made a quantum leap forward during the High Middle Ages. That advance was due in part to the urgent need felt within the Church to unify and systematize its basic teachings as an aspect of its effort to reform Christian society. But also stimulating theological activity were the expanded competence in thinking techniques and the critical issues raised by new knowledge.

During the early Middle Ages theological inquiry sought primarily to understand and to explain the meaning of certain authoritative texts that contained the divine truth—above all else, Scripture. The approach was primarily literary, seeking by careful reading and meditation to discover the levels of meaning contained in the word of God. In the eleventh century, a subtle change in approach to texts began to occur, providing the key to the emergence of the "science" of theology. Prompted by their growing awareness of the contradictions in Scripture and in the way past authorities had interpreted the revealed truth, scholars began to explore the extent to which human reason could be useful in grasping religious truth. In this pursuit they turned to the methodology of dialectic or logic, using the rules of formal thinking to test and to demonstrate the validity of religious propositions.

Some of the early proponents of this new approach were naïve and were viewed with suspicion because of their unorthodox conclusions. A key figure in turning the tide was Anselm (1033–1109), abbot of the monastery of Bec in Normandy and later archbishop of Canterbury. A man of learning and of unquestioned orthodoxy, Anselm proclaimed as his central intellectual tenet that faith should seek understanding, by which he meant that one steeped in revealed truth should strive to understand that faith in human terms. To demonstrate his point, he undertook to develop a logical proof of the existence of God, one that could stand on its own without dependence on revelation. His famous proof, which has intrigued many generations of thinkers, legitimized human reason as a valid tool in the search to understand what revelation meant.

The study of dialectic and its application to various problems became a passion in the schools of the early twelfth century. A leader was Abelard (1079–1142), a key figure in creating the science of

theology. Son of a minor Breton noble family, Abelard studied with several leading masters in various cathedral schools in France and then became a successful master himself. His promising career was disrupted by a love affair with one of his pupils, Heloise, which led to secret marriage, a child, the emasculation of Abelard by Heloise's outraged kinsfolk, and the separation of the lovers. These "calamities," as Abelard put it, condemned the victim to a life of wandering from monastery to monastery and school to school— perhaps always haunted by his memory of true love but also driven by an urge to know and to understand more fully. Abelard's career was filled with controversy, stemming partly from his prideful, combative personality and partly from the force of his ideas, which posed a revolutionary challenge to traditional theological inquiry.

Superbly skilled as a logician, Abelard made a major contribution to systematizing the use of dialectic as a tool of theological inquiry. In a bold book entitled *Sic et Non (Yes and No)*, he set down a series of cases in which authorities disagreed on fundamental doctrinal questions. His approach implied that only the use of reason could resolve these contradictions. Abelard also developed new insights into how human beings came to know. He maintained that the truth consists of concepts formed in the mind from the study of created things, such concepts being the nearest approximation to the perfect knowledge that is God. A philosopher's task is to organize in a logical fashion all that is known so as to create a mental image of God's universe. Abelard's dialectical approach to theology aroused strong opposition, led by the formidable Bernard of Clairvaux. But the resistance was to no avail, and the new theology became predominant. It was given special impetus by Peter Lombard (1100–1160), who used the dialectical methodology as the basis for his *Sentences*. In it Peter employed logic to resolve contradictory positions contained in Scripture and the writings of the Church Fathers on a large number of topics relating to basic Christian doctrine. The result was a unified body of theology, systematically organized. The *Sentences* quickly became the basic text for teaching theology, and its dialectical methodology became standard.

The value of the dialectical approach became

even more evident during the late twelfth and thirteenth centuries, when scholars in the West came into possession of a vast body of new knowledge derived from Greek philosophy and scientific knowledge along with the Moslem commentaries on that material. During the early Middle Ages western Europeans had lost contact with almost all of Greek philosophy and science. However, from as early as the ninth century Moslem scholars became deeply interested in this material, had translated most of material into Arabic, and had commented on it extensively (see page 197). Beginning in about 1150 this huge body of knowledge again became available in the West, primarily as a result of the labors of scholars working chiefly in Spain and Sicily to translate Arabic texts into Latin. The new material included most of Aristotle's writings, and he quickly became the leading authority on logical methods and on philosophical and scientific learning—the Philosopher, as Western thinkers soon called him. The new learning posed a serious challenge: Not only did it provide scholars with heretofore unfamiliar knowledge about a wide range of matters, especially about the natural world, but it also confronted them with logically demonstrated systems of truth that directly contradicted many basic Christian teachings.

The major concerns of thirteenth-century theologians, collectively called the Scholastics, centered on mastering the new knowledge, organizing it into a rational system, and reconciling it with Christian doctrine in a way that met the tests of logic. Their assault on these problems was motivated not only by the intellectual challenges innate in these issues but also by their urge to serve the Church in its quest for doctrinal clarity and uniformity. These concerns, explored most intensely in the universities, evoked a variety of responses, often accompanied by bitter intellectual warfare that belies the notion that the Middle Ages was a time of uniformity and conformity in the realm of ideas.

One especially controversial approach to these fundamental issues was formulated by a group of scholars called the Averroists, after a famous Moslem thinker who had commented extensively on Aristotle's works. The adherents of this school wholeheartedly accepted Aristotelian rationalism,

arguing that reason was capable of defining an order of truth that had its own validity irrespective of the tenets of the faith. At the opposite pole was a school of thought that found Aristotelianism to be of little value in leading to the truth. This school reasserted the Platonic-Augustinian tradition that had long prevailed as the prime approach to theological wisdom. The most notable figure in this group was Bonaventura (1221–1274), a Franciscan teacher in Paris who later became head of the Franciscan order. Bonaventura argued that reason could not discover the ultimate truth, which must come to the intellect intuitively through an illumination from divine sources beyond the power of human reason. Although Bonaventura did not deny the value of a rational consideration of natural phenomena, he held that no fundamental truth would result; in fact, he was convinced that rationalism would ultimately end in doctrinal error.

But the most representative response to the major issues posed by the new knowledge was formulated by a succession of scholars who tried to reconcile revelation and reason. By far the most influential advocate of this approach was Thomas Aquinas (1225–1274), an Italian Dominican whose active career was divided between teaching at the university in Paris and serving at the papal court. During his career as teacher and scholar he produced a huge body of theological writing. His chief works, the *Summa contra Gentiles* and the unfinished *Summa Theologiae,* represent medieval theological and philosophical thought at its most advanced level. In all of his works Thomas begins with the assumption that God created the universe in such a way that all its parts fit together and have a single purpose. Every human being has the duty to know God and his works, and each has the ability to achieve that end as a result of human reason. There are two paths to this single, unified order of truth: revelation and reason. The task of the mind is to seek the truth by applying itself to those things that are the proper subjects for reason while accepting on faith those things that can be learned only by revelation. Thomas accepted on faith such doctrines as the Creation, the Trinity, and the Incarnation but applied reason to such problems as the existence of God, immortality, the operation of the natural world, the nature of government, and ethics. He was certain that reason directed to the proper ends and guided by sound methodology would provide the intelligence with an order of truth that fitted into the order of truth contained in revelation. If there is a conflict between revelation and reason, it results from faulty reasoning.

Following the rules of logic formulated by Aristotle and relying heavily on him for knowledge of subjects proper to human reason, Thomas measured the whole realm of human knowledge item after item with a view toward reconciling that knowledge with the revealed truth. His method consisted of a rigorously applied series of steps: formulating a proposition stating some aspect of the truth, setting forth all possible contrary positions, demonstrating the logical fallacies in these contrary positions, and finally showing the logical validity of the true position. Each single truth in Thomas' system is part of an interlocking structure of thought that relates all things to a perfect truth. The final result of his work—his *summae,* or summations—is a synthesis of all knowledge into one vast structure glorifying God and demonstrating the perfection of his creation in terms comprehensible to the human mind. The Thomistic synthesis perhaps best represents the overall spirit of medieval thought: the quest to integrate existing knowledge into a single structure; new knowledge was seldom a concern of theologians or philosophers.

Another "science" that developed during the High Middle Ages involved the systematic study of law. Although several universities had faculties of law, the major center of legal studies was at the University of Bologna. By the eleventh century strong pressures were felt in society, especially in the Church and the royal courts, to develop unified, consistent bodies of law as an instrument promoting order in society. However, legal systems existing at that time were surrounded with confusion and contradictions. Like the theologians, students of law began to employ dialectic as a tool to resolve this problem. We have already noted the work of Gratian, who in his *Decretum* (1140) created a model compendium of canon law, based on the collection and rational reconciliation of a wide range of precedents. Gratian's work became the basic text used in teaching canon law.

A long succession of twelfth- and thirteenth-century canon lawyers continued the work of compilation and commentary; by the thirteenth century their labors had produced a highly sophisticated, consistent body of law essential to the governance of the Church.

The development of canon law was greatly stimulated by a revived interest in the study of Roman law. Except for a few places where written law had remained in use during the early Middle Ages, such as southern France and northern Italy, Roman law had long been neglected in the West. But then in the eleventh century its study was taken up with great vigor, mainly because the chief embodiment of Roman law, the Code of Justinian, provided an ideal model of law organized on a rational basis. Civil lawyers spent their energies writing commentaries (called *glosses*) on the code to try to elucidate its meaning and relate its principles to existing society. Aside from producing an immense body of legal literature, their work decisively influenced the kind of law administered in the rising monarchies and shaped the concepts defining royal power. The legal concepts set forth by the students of Roman law prompted efforts to codify the confused bodies of customary law existing over much of western Europe. An example was the important treatise on English common law compiled by Henry Bracton in the thirteenth century.

Although a precise "science" of society did not emerge in the High Middle Ages, theologians and lawyers had much to say about the nature of human society and of the political order. Discussions on these matters were spurred by a variety of influences: explorations by religious reformers of the ancient Christian concepts of the nature of the state and society; the conflict between church and state; the need to justify the claims of the new monarchies; the revival of Roman law; the recovery of classical Greek and Roman works on political theory (especially Aristotle). Gradually the serious study of political theory led to a new view of the nature of society and the political order. Traditional political thought, derived chiefly from Augustine, viewed the state as an instrument for suppressing the sinful nature of human beings; by filling this negative role, rulers prepared the ground for the spiritual perfection of human beings through the efforts of ecclesiastical leaders. Increasingly during the twelfth and thirteenth centuries the state came to be defined as an integral part of the natural order asserting a unique and necessary positive force for the full realization of human potential.

Thomas Aquinas played an important role in articulating this new view of the state. Strongly influenced by Aristotle, he argued that the state is a part of the natural order, existing to permit human beings to live in an ordered community where each could realize his or her innate potential for good. The proper form of government was a result of rational reflection on human needs. In Thomas' view, the ideal state was one in which various classes performed specific functions under the guidance of a just ruler in the interests of providing for the needs of all. Such a system ensured justice, which was the ultimate objective of government. Upon the ruler of the good state fell the heavy responsibility of discovering and applying the principles of natural law required to regulate human society in accord with the divine order. In discovering a positive role for the state as an instrument shaped by rational human actions for promoting human welfare, the political theorists of the High Middle Ages established the foundations for future study of the state and its functioning in a context which took into account existing realities.

In the "science" of the natural world the achievements of medieval thinkers seem pale by the standards of later ages. The most advanced area of scientific study was medicine, which constituted a separate field of study in some universities, especially at Salerno in Sicily. The study of medicine focused primarily on mastering medical knowledge derived from the Hellenistic and the Moslem worlds. However, the High Middle Ages did witness one development of major significance for the study of the natural world. During the early Middle Ages thinkers had adhered to a view of nature rooted in Neoplatonism. This view considered the natural world an inferior order of reality, representing an illusory reflection of nonmaterial perfect forms. As this Neoplatonic concept was translated into a Christian idiom, nature came to be viewed as part of the universe corrupted by the Fall. Given powerful impetus by a monastic ideal that spurned material things, early medieval thought was biased against serious concern with nature. That changed during the High Middle Ages. The Scholastic effort to unite all knowledge into a single truth and the vastly increased knowledge of nature resulting from the rediscovery of Greek and Moslem scientific works generated an effort to study the natural world as a prime manifestation of God's created cosmos. That study led to the conclusion that the material world was good by virtue of being part of God's creation, that there was order in nature because it was part of God's perfect order, and that the natural world was intelligible to human reason. In short, nature had to be understood if theological and philosophical knowledge was to be complete. This fundamental shift in attitude constituted a prime achievement of the medieval search for truth. The discovery—perhaps rediscovery is a better term—of nature provided the starting point for great advances in knowledge *about* nature.

Even in the High Middle Ages the first tentative steps were taken to learn more about the natural world than was contained in the ancient authorities, especially Aristotle and Scripture. An important group of scholars, most of them Franciscans, centered at Oxford in the thirteenth century pointed the way. Robert Grosseteste (1168–1253) and his pupil Roger Bacon (ca. 1214–1294) were its most distinguished members. These men insisted that the truth about the natural world could be gained only through observation and experimentation. Bacon argued that most Scholastics put too much trust in ancient authorities, and he engaged in experimentation, especially in optics. The efforts of Bacon and his fellow scholars were helped by an increasing body of knowledge and technical expertise being accumulated by artisans, medical practitioners, mechanics, and farmers engaged in the routine affairs of life. The ground was being prepared for a later explosion of scientific knowledge.

3. BEYOND THE LEARNED WORLD: VERNACULAR LITERATURE

Complementing the writings of theologians, lawyers, and scientists was another rich and varied body of literature created during the High Middle Ages. It aimed primarily at instructing and entertaining a broader audience than the learned world.

Much of this second kind of literature was written in Latin to serve the increasing numbers of Latin readers and speakers produced by the schools. This literature was strongly influenced in style and language by classical Latin authors whose works provided the models upon which the study of grammar and rhetoric was based. However, Latin authors in the High Middle Ages demonstrated considerable skill in using those models in innovative ways. The Latin vocabulary was constantly enriched by the infusion of new words and meanings, and classical literary forms were modified to permit Latin authors to treat matters that concerned them in creative ways. Perhaps the best Latin writing of the High Middle Ages took the form of lyric poetry on religious themes, often composed to serve the religious liturgy, especially as hymns. Much of this poetry used a new verse technique based on rhyme and accent rather than on long and short vowels, the classical technique. The new style lent itself to nonreligious poetry, exemplified by the many student songs, collectively called Goliardic poetry, celebrating drinking, sensual love, gambling, and other worldly themes. Between 1000 and 1300 there was also a great outpouring of prose literature devoted to history, biography, saints' lives, devotional literature, letters, and political polemics.

But it is vernacular literature, written in the tongues that Europeans spoke in their daily lives, that represents the most creative literary accomplishment of the High Middle Ages. By 1000 the language map of western Europe had become a tower of Babel. That map had emerged slowly during the early Middle Ages out of three basic root languages: classical Latin, which evolved into Romance tongues, such as French, Provençal, Italian, Spanish, and Catalan; Old German, out of which came German, English, and the Scandinavian tongues; and Celtic, which evolved into Irish and Welsh. Each of these basic vernacular languages was further divided into local dialects, and many of them were enriched by extensive borrowings from each other. How these various tongues came to be instruments of written expression is

badly understood, but the fact that writers did develop the capability of using these languages to create unique literary works marked a major landmark in western European cultural development.

Most vernacular literature was written for an aristocratic audience and reflects the values of that class. One of the earliest forms was the epic, a song setting down in writing the deeds of great warriors that had been preserved in oral tradition. The great Anglo-Saxon epic *Beowulf*, composed about 800, recounts the deeds of a warrior living in a pre-Christian Germanic society. So also do the Scandinavian sagas, the *Poetic Edda* and the *Prose Edda* of Snorri Sturlson, not put in written form until the twelfth and thirteenth centuries but reflecting a much earlier pagan society dominated by violence. The chief Germanic epic, the *Nibelungenlied*, composed about 1200, reflects a tradition dating back to the time of the Germanic invasions. The chief *chanson de geste* ("song of deeds") produced in French was the *Song of Roland*, written about 1100 to retell the story of Charlemagne's expedition of 778 against the Moors in Spain, which ended in the defeat of the Frankish forces at Roncesvalles. However, the unknown author adorned his account of this historical event and its hero, Roland, with the ideals and customs characteristic of eleventh-century feudal society; particular emphasis is given to Roland's prowess as a warrior, his loyalty to his lord, and his willingness to give his life to defend his faith. The same themes dominate the Spanish epic, *The Cid*, which glorifies the deeds of a famous knight involved in the Reconquista of Spain from the infidel Moors.

The epic genre was rivaled by a new vernacular literary form, the lyric, which during the twelfth century enjoyed a tremendous vogue in the courtly circles of the chivalric nobility. This poetry developed first in Provence, in southern France, and soon spread over most of Europe. Its creators, called *troubadours*, were chiefly young men whose lack of great fiefs and firm family ties rooted in proper marriages placed them on the fringes of noble society. Through their poetry they sought to expound their sensual love for a noble lady, usually already married, in a fashion that would earn them honor in her eyes and thus status in the society to which she belonged. The troubadours (called *trouvères* in northern France and *min-nesängers* in Germany) formulated a new set of values for noble society. Their poetry argued that the emotions associated with love—longing, suffering, anticipation of a lover's favor—had the power to ennoble just as much as did prowess in battle or loyalty to a male feudal lord. The search for self-understanding and the emotional probing associated with the quest for love refined the inner spirit and evoked patterns of behavior that combined to create the gentleman as the epitome of noble existence. The lyric writers thus played a crucial role in transforming values and behavior patterns upon which the concept of male excellence was based. They also were instrumental in attributing to women a vital role in shaping nobility, a role based on their sexuality and their power to give pleasure. The impetus for this new morality derived primarily from qualities innate in human nature and had little to do with moral values rooted in religion, an interpretation that raised grave suspicions in the minds of church leaders about troubadour poetry.

Toward the end of the twelfth century, the epic and the lyric traditions merged to produce a third type of vernacular literature, the *romance*. Romances were stories combining the love theme with adventure, written chiefly to entertain court society; the immensely popular romances enjoyed the special patronage of high-placed noble women, such as Eleanor of Aquitaine. The adventure element in these stories was drawn from sources with vague roots in history, especially materials relating to King Arthur and his court. The authors of the romances used this "historical" material with complete freedom. The treatment of love in these stories reflected continued probing of themes contained in troubadour poetry. The most gifted romance writers fashioned works with enduring appeal. Among them was Chrétien de Troyes, a late-twelfth-century French author who skillfully exploited the Arthurian material to create an intriguing picture of the ideal knight struggling to achieve chivalric excellence through pursuit of love and adventure and of the noble lady serving as a prime agent in shaping the consummate knight. Another writer, the thirteenth-century German Gottfried von Strasbourg, in *Tristan and Isolde*, masterfully reveals the meaning of love in

the lives of two who were its prisoners. *Parzival*, written by his countryman Wolfram von Eschenbach, is an appealing picture of a man pursuing an unobtainable ideal, symbolized by the Holy Grail. The mature concepts of chivalry found their fullest expression in the romances. The themes and actions treated in them had a powerful impact on the behavior of the nobility for centuries and continued to intrigue writers and audiences down to the present, influencing poetry, operas, and even modern musicals.

While the epics, lyrics, and romances were being written, sung, and read by nobles, other forms of literature evolved to appeal to the tastes and interests of nonnobles. Especially notable were dramas and *fabliaux*. Medieval drama began as part of church liturgy; dramatized parts of services eventually moved outside the church into the marketplace. By the thirteenth century the guilds had taken over the responsibility for producing these dramas on religious festivals. Each guild would take responsibility for presenting one scene from a connected series of scenes that constituted the entire play. Several types of dramatic production developed: mystery plays, enacting scenes from the Bible; miracle plays, treating the highlights of saints' lives; morality plays, personifying human virtues and vices. The presentation of these serious, sacred dramas was punctuated by earthy language and comical portrayals of the key characters. The *fabliaux* were short tales recited in public squares to entertain the crowds. Whatever the subject—it could be almost anything—the *fabliaux* were always close to city life, representing everyday events in the lives of ordinary people. They were filled with vulgar humor and satire aimed especially at priests, betrayed husbands, and scheming women effective in getting what they wanted from young men. The most famous collection of *fabliaux* was the *Romance of Reynard the Fox*, made up of stories in which animals symbolize people and human characteristics.

Of the many writers during the High Middle Ages one genius, Dante Alighieri (1265–1321), towers above all others. He was to literature what Thomas Aquinas was to theology. Dante was a product of the vibrant urban life of Florence. In his youth he fell in love with a girl named Beatrice, who later married someone else and died young.

Beatrice became for Dante the ideal woman as defined by the code of courtly love. Dante was a learned man who wrote on a variety of subjects. He was also active in Florentine political life, ultimately suffering expulsion from the city because of his identification with a faction that lost control of the city government. While suffering in what he called "an undeserving exile," he wrote in his native Tuscan dialect his masterpiece, *The Divine Comedy.* Outwardly, it tells of Dante's journey through hell, purgatory, and heaven. Tired, discouraged, and confused at the outset, the pilgrim slowly begins to comprehend the harmony, order, and purpose in the universe; his spirit is progressively uplifted and his soul cured of its discontents. Guided through hell and purgatory by the Latin poet Vergil and through heaven by his beloved Beatrice, he is permitted to see all things from the depths of hell to God himself. Within this framework Dante weaves with dazzling poetic skills a rich tapestry reflecting medieval thought. He is a philosopher, presenting with consummate skill the medieval idea that all things in the universe are ordered by God in a cohesive, intelligible scheme. He is a mystic, yearning to the depths of his soul to catch a glimpse of God so that his longing may be satisfied. He is a love poet; Beatrice, his guide in heaven, is a symbol of human love, a purifying and uplifting emotion. He is a scientist, incorporating into his poem many medieval ideas about the structure of the physical universe. He is an admirer of Greek and Roman writers and thinkers, although he has to condemn them to hell as non-Christians. He is a keen political observer, full of fierce partisanship. On his long journey from the gates of hell to its very pit, where Lucifer chews up three great traitors, Brutus, Cassius, and Judas, Dante discusses with Vergil nearly every kind of sin, showing a deep understanding of human nature and its weaknesses. The ascent from hell through purgatory to the seat of God in heaven offers him equal chance to discourse on every aspect of virtue. Few artists have grasped human life and human aspirations more fully or written of them with greater artistry.

4. THE VISUAL ARTS

During the High Middle Ages the visual arts provided the cultural media common to all, rich and poor, literate and illiterate, learned and ignorant. This era marked a decisive epoch in art history. Two major styles, Romanesque and Gothic, were perfected between 1000 and 1300. Both styles were preeminently religious in inspiration, created primarily to provide suitable places of worship, and the Church was the prime agency promoting artistic endeavor.

The Romanesque and Gothic styles were the fruits of a long artistic evolution. The starting point of medieval church architecture was the Roman basilica, the rectangular meeting hall. The early Christians placed their altars in the semicircular *apse* at the rear and conducted the mass there. The *nave* provided space for the faithful participating in the sacred rites. Side aisles often flanked the nave. The upper walls of the nave rose above the side aisles and were pierced with windows allowing light into the nave. A lateral

Romanesque Barrel and Groin Vaults

Gothic Ribbed Vault

aisle, called the *transept,* sometimes crossed the nave just in front of the apse, so that the early church took the form of a cross. Over the centuries, this basic ground plan of church architecture and the art that decorated it were considerably modified by influences from the Byzantine, Germanic, and Celtic worlds and by new creative forces emerging from daily life. During the High Middle Ages artists finally succeeded in blending these many tributaries into distinctive new styles.

Romanesque architecture first appeared in the late Carolingian period and flourished through most of the twelfth century. Its main features are admirably illustrated by several churches still standing: Notre Dame la Grande in Poitiers, the cathedral of Saint-Sernin in Toulouse, the cathedral church of Worms, the Abbey Church of Maria Laach in Germany, and the church of Sant' Ambrogio in Milan. The Romanesque style was characterized both by technical innovations and by a new spirit. The monastic world, especially the Cluniac reformers, played a dominant role in developing and spreading this style. The Cluniac emphasis on elaborate rituals and their concern for providing the proper setting for the veneration of relics and for gatherings of pilgrims dictated churches large enough to house a number of chapels and accommodate great crowds. Architects also wanted to find a replacement for the traditional wooden roofs, which were so often destroyed by fire. The solution was a capacious church built entirely of stone.

So that liturgical needs were met, the basic ground plan of the traditional basilican structure was modified. The nave was extended beyond the transept to create a *choir,* a space where the main altar was located and where the clergy and monks could gather for worship. The side aisles were also extended around the choir, creating a passageway or ambulatory that encircled the nave and the choir. A series of chapels were constructed off the side aisles and the choir ambulatory, providing spaces for many simultaneous religious services and special shrines for relics. To replace the wooden roof, architects developed techniques that allowed them to throw a barrel vault made of stone over the full length of the nave and choir and the side aisles. These heavy roofs were supported by massive stone walls. Where openings were needed through these walls—such as passages between the nave and the side aisles—round arches set on heavy pillars were used to support the structure above the opening. Groin vaults, again supported by arches and pillars, were evolved to cover the square or rectangular area where the axis of the nave and the choir was crossed by the transept. However, the barrel vault system of creating a stone roof was satisfactory only for relatively small structures. As the Romanesque style evolved, architects developed a method of building stone roofs over larger naves and choirs. They begin to break up the long barrel vault with rib arches crossing the nave and choir and resting on pillars on opposite sides of the nave and the choir. This technique created a series of bays or "squares" marked off by pillars at each of the four corners. Each bay could then be covered with cross vaults. The space between the rib and the cross vaults could be filled in with relatively light stone pieces, reducing the roof weight and concentrating its downward thrust on the pillars at the corners of each bay (see illustration, p. 314). Despite these innovations, the stone vaulting covering the structure remained massive and exerted tremendous downward and outward thrust. For this reason Romanesque churches required heavy walls and massive internal columns; the few windows had to be kept small. Thus the typical Romanesque structure had an atmosphere of muted darkness and mystery that was not dispelled by the decorative paintings on piers, arches, and walls and the candles that supplied artificial light. Yet this atmosphere was also due to the religious mentality of an age that viewed the church as God's citadel standing against a world filled with evil forces, a sacred fortress where men and women could commune with the God who protected them from the howling demons and the frightening forces of nature that raged outside this holy refuge (see Figure 23.2).

By the mid–twelfth century the European world was changing rapidly, and the new environment produced a new architectural style, the Gothic. It appeared first in Ile de France, the domain of the Capetians; the earliest full-scale Gothic church was the Abbey Church of St. Denis near Paris, built in 1137–1144 by Abbot Suger, the adviser to kings Louis VI and Louis VII. From here the Gothic style spread over much of Europe.

The Gothic style evolved out of a desire for height and light in churches, a desire derived largely from new intellectual and spiritual concepts that fostered a more rational view of God and saw his chief attributes in terms of reason, light, and proportion. The Gothic church was an attempt to leave behind the mystery-shrouded, awesome world of the Romanesque and move into the light and purity of paradise—the paradise Dante pictured in poetry. Among the Gothic structures that achieve this effect magnificently are the cathedrals at Paris (Notre Dame), Chartres, Reims, Amiens, Strasbourg, and Bourges in France; at Lincoln, York, and Salisbury in England; and at Cologne in Germany.

Technically, this transformation was made possible by the pointed arch, which carried thrust downward, and the ribbed vault, used to concentrate the thrust at a few points. Architects were able to combine them to fashion tremendously tall skeletons of stone whose weight flowed to earth through a series of slender pillars. The outward thrust, greatly reduced by the pointed arches and concentrated by the rib vaults, could be offset by thickened columns at the outside of the building or by flying buttresses, pillars set away from the main structure and joined to it by bracing arches high above the ground (see illustration, p. 315). Thin walls, supporting nothing but their own weight, could be filled in between pillars. More important, light could be let into the structure by great arched windows cut through the thin walls. These windows, often interlaced with delicate decorative stonework, pierced the lofty clerestory and the side aisles, and majestic round windows were placed high above ground level at the ends of the nave, the choir, and the transept. The windows were often filled with many-hued stained-glass figures or scenes that suffused the interior with a breathtaking display of colored light (see Figure 23.3 and Color Plate 10).

Nearly every other visual art was put to work to decorate medieval churches. The exterior of a Romanesque church was generally plain except for the west façade, where the great arches built to provide doorways leading to a nave and side aisles provided a setting for sculpture. As illustrated by churches at Arles and Vézelay, these spaces were filled with massive, highly symbolic sculpture done in high relief; they portrayed human figures, animals, and abstract decorative patterns. A favorite subject was the Last Judgment, in which a stern Christ was portrayed relegating men and women to heaven or hell (see Figures 22.1 and 23.2). Within a Romanesque church there was more sculpture, chiefly decorative carving adorning the massive piers. The wall spaces were decorated with frescoes portraying scriptural scenes, particularly those that stressed the suffering of Christ and his judgment on humanity. Romanesque sculpture and painting is somber, with human beings small, powerless, and dependent, surrounded with symbols of the terrors that beset spiritual life; it grips the emotions rather than the mind.

Gothic architecture brought about changes in the other arts. The exteriors of Gothic churches

FIGURE 23.2 Romanesque Art These photos of the church of Sainte Madelaine at Vézelay in France illustrate some of the main features of Romanesque art. The nave (top right) features round ribbed arches, heavy columns, and thick walls pierced by small windows. Above the main portal (upper left) is a sculptured complex showing Christ instructing his disciples; comparable scenes over entrances were usual in Romanesque churches. The many capitals atop the pillars (lower left) of the nave and the porch leading to the main entrance provided space for carved scenes illustrating biblical themes. Romanesque sculpture was less concerned with realism than with reminding viewers of a religious truth and with moving their emotions. (Nave, Marburg; portal, Scala/Art Resource; sculpture, Marburg/Art Resource)

provided innumerable places for decorative sculpture, giving stone carvers an opportunity to experiment with a fantastic array of decorative motifs. Statues, sometimes executed in the round as well as in relief, became more realistic and humanistic, expressing more the human qualities than the mystical powers of Jesus, the Virgin, the apostles, and the saints (see Figures 22.3, 23.1, and 23.3).

The interior of Gothic churches offered less space for painting and sculpture than did Romanesque churches; decoration was concentrated chiefly on columns and arches. Not images but light fills the Gothic church. The painted walls of the Romanesque church were replaced with stained-glass windows. Their creators drew their themes chiefly from scriptural sources, but in their renditions they reflected in amazing detail the daily activities of medieval people. The stained glass at Chartres and in the beautiful Sainte-Chapelle built by Louis IX in Paris enthrall the viewer.

A variety of minor arts were employed to adorn these structures and to serve in carrying out religious services. Skilled metalwork was used for door handles and hinges, candleholders, chalices and pitchers, reliquaries, and railings to divide the space within the church. Woodwork provided pulpits and highly adorned seats for the celebrants of sacred services. Intricate needlework was employed to create splendid vestments for the clergy and tapestries to cover wall spaces. Skilled copyists and miniature painters fashioned beautiful liturgical books: bibles, missals, psalters, hymnals. Ivory carvings were used to fashion covers for these books. In all these forms, artists demonstrated highly developed skills and imagination to create works that fitted the grand style dictated by architecture and that reinforced the atmosphere of sanctity proper to holy places. Attendance at religious services constantly exposed the entire population to a dazzling display of the visual arts.

Another art associated with religious activity, music, also developed significantly during the High Middle Ages. Church music consisted primarily of melodies with verses taken from Scripture (especially the psalms) or composed for liturgical events (such great hymns as *Dies Irae* and *Stabat Mater* came from the Middle Ages). *Gregorian chant* (its alleged inventor was Pope Gregory I) or *plain song* developed as early as the sixth century. At first, the singing was in unison, but over the centuries variations worked on plain song developed into contrapuntal music. By the thirteenth century, complex and moving contrapuntal compositions, rendered by many voices and various instruments, filled the churches with sounds almost as heavenly as the light that poured through the stained-glass windows.

The great cathedrals commanded the best artistic talent and the bulk of the wealth that medieval society had to devote to art. However, there were other lines of artistic pursuit. Living quarters for bishops and the cathedral clergy and for monastic communities were constructed in both the Romanesque and Gothic styles. Many feudal castles, massive rather than elegant or comfortable, were built in the Romanesque style. In the towns, especially from the thirteenth century onward, beautiful town halls and guildhalls were constructed, putting Gothic principles to new uses. These buildings were decorated with paintings and carvings and furnished with skillfully wrought furniture and utensils for daily living. These structures were impressive signs that the Church never completely absorbed artistic energies.

5. THE UNDERLYING SPIRIT OF MEDIEVAL CULTURE

Certainly it is not easy to find a common denominator for Thomas Aquinas, Dante, the architects and sculptors who built the churches at Poitiers, Amiens, and Chartres, the troubadours, the romance writers, and the authors of *fabliaux*. However, the more one experiences medieval culture, the more one senses an underlying, unifying spirit.

Medieval thought, literature, and art are permeated by a quest for truth and light beyond the world of human existence. This reaching out of the mind and the imagination sprang from the almost universal belief that God controlled the universe and that it was the duty of mortals to know and worship him. The artist and the writer stood in awe of God and humbly used their talents to serve him. Medieval culture viewed as a whole,

FIGURE 23.3   The Gothic Style   The splendid church of Notre Dame at Amiens in France exemplifies the Gothic style. Its lofty nave (top left) is vaulted with pointed arches whose ribs carry weight down to the columns flanking the nave. Note the high arches that lead to aisles on either side of the nave. Above these arches is the clerestory, pierced by huge windows lighting the nave; the expanse can be seen in the apse at the far end of the building. The aerial view of the structure (bottom left) shows the flying buttresses used to offset the outward thrust of the roof on its supporting stone skeleton. Also evident is the transept crossing the nave. The façades of the main structure and the transept were decorated with numerous sculptures. Greeting those who entered the south transept was the "Golden Virgin" (top right), a wonderful example of the warmth and realism of Gothic sculpture. (Aerial view, Hunting Aerofilms; nave and sculpture, Archives Photographiques, Paris)

therefore, has an atmosphere of otherworldliness and of surrender to a power beyond human understanding.

Yet intertwined with this aspiration toward and submission to the divine is a warm, sympathetic feeling for humankind. Medieval people believed that a human being was God's finest creation. Artists and writers were never disdainful of human powers and potentialities. They took joy in presenting humanity as it was and wrestled constantly with the problem of understanding human nature more fully.

The medieval genius shines most brillitantly in attempts to synthesize these two outlooks. Thinkers, writers, and artists seldom felt that otherworldliness and secularism, spirituality and humanism were contradictory terms. They respected their own powers enough to believe that they could reach out toward God—by building higher cathedrals or by putting together greater *summae* of knowledge or by flights of poetic fancy. Yet they were filled with a faith great enough to believe that their human quest would lead them to a power infinitely greater than themselves and that ultimate illumination would allow them to realize their full potential as God's creatures.

SUGGESTED READING

General Surveys

John W. Baldwin, *The Scholastic Culture of the Middle Ages, 1000–1300* (1971). A perceptive brief survey.

C. H. Haskins, *The Renaissance of the Twelfth Century* (1927). A classic treatment.

Philippe Wolff, *The Cultural Awakening*, trans. Anne Carter (1968). A good assessment of the revival of cultural life.

Robert L. Benson and Giles Constable, eds., *Renaissance and Renewal in the Twelfth Century* (1982). An informative collection of essays on various phases of medieval cultural revival.

The Learned World

Alan B. Cobban, *The Medieval Universities: Their Development and Organization* (1975). A good description of medieval universities.

Michael Haren, *Medieval Thought: The Western Intellectual Tradition from Antiquity to the Thirteenth Century* (1985). Especially good in showing continuity between the ancient and medieval worlds.

John Marenbon, *Later Medieval Philosophy (1150–1350): An Introduction* (1987). A clear treatment; should be used along with Marenbon's volume on an earlier period, cited in Chapter 14.

Etienne Gilson, *History of Christian Philosophy in the Middle Ages* (1955). A classic treatment providing a positive assessment of medieval thought.

Richard E. McKeon, ed., *Selections from Medieval Philosophers*, 2 vols. (1929–1930). Selections from medieval philosophers.

Harold J. Berman, *Law and Revolution: The Formation of the Western Legal Tradition* (1983). A seminal study rich in insight.

A. C. Crombie, *Medieval and Early Modern Science*, 2nd ed., 2 vols. (1959). A good survey.

Walter Ullmann, *A History of Political Thought: The Middle Ages* (1965). A provocative survey.

Ewart Lewis, ed., *Medieval Political Ideas*, 2 vols. (1954). A collection of medieval writings on political theory.

Literature and Art

W. T. Jackson, *The Literature of the Middle Ages* (1960). A useful survey. More valuable is reading medieval literary works; the works mentioned in this chapter are easily available in excellent translations.

Georges Duby, *History of Medieval Art, 980–1440* (1986). A topical approach with splendid illustrations.

Henri Focillon, *The Art of the West in the Middle Ages*, 2nd ed., 2 vols., trans. Donald King (1969). A masterful detailed treatment.

Georges Duby, *The Age of the Cathedrals: Art and Society, 980–1240*, trans. Eleanor Levieux and Barbara Thompson (1981). A challenging attempt to interrelate art and social developments.

Jean Gimpel, *The Cathedral Builders*, trans. Teresa Waugh (1984). Describes the techniques of medieval builders.

Henry Adams, *Mont-St.-Michel and Chartres* (1913). A classic work contrasting the spirit of Romanesque and Gothic art.

Erwin Panofsky, *Gothic Architecture and Scholasticism* (1951). A stimulating effort to interrelate the intellectual and artistic worlds.

RETROSPECT

The era from 1000 to 1300 was of decisive importance in shaping the essential features of western European civilization. It was a time of remarkable expansion changing every aspect of the primitive society that had been so painfully and tenuously pieced together in the first five centuries after the collapse of the Roman order. After 1000 there occurred at every level of society and in every phase of life sustained, creative activity that increased wealth, secured order, shaped a more complex social order, expanded mental horizons, deepened understanding of the human condition, and enlarged the capabilities for expression. Many of the creations of the High Middle Ages remained essential features of western European society almost until the present. Included were the youthful national states, towns, the centralized Church, the universities, the basic social classes (nobility, bourgeoisie, peasantry), the vernacular languages, Romanesque and Gothic art, legal systems, and commercial and agricultural technologies. Any attempt to understand later European history must take these medieval creations into account.

But the era had another, equally important dimension. While gathering strength internally, western European society began to impinge on the world beyond its boundaries. During the High Middle Ages the first decisive steps were taken toward the establishment of European preeminence in the world. Anyone who would understand the contemporary world situation would be well served by attempting to identify the forces that by 1300 had given western Europeans the capabilities to influence the destinies of non-Europeans.

In reflecting on developments during the High Middle Ages, one is struck by the fact that as western European society matured, its institutional and ideological fabric was interlaced with dichotomies and contradictions. Examples leap immediately to mind: strong monarchy opposed to the privileged Church, nobility, towns; universal empire in competition with national states; Church versus state; urban society contrasted with rural society; universal Latin culture opposed to localized vernacular cultures; faith pitted against reason; the spirit against the flesh; guild protectionism versus capitalistic enterprise. One is almost forced to conclude that as a consequence of its historical development during the High Middle Ages, western European civilization became, in a unique way, an order compounded of contradictory thrusts. It was like a Gothic cathedral in which height competed with thrust, light with dark.

Can we say perhaps that this juxtaposition of opposites that emerged in the period between 1000 and 1300 constitutes the essence of postmedieval western European civilization? Dare we suggest that these medieval contradictions have supplied the Western world with its dynamism? Might we suspect that the history of the West after 1300 may be a story of the resolution of these contradictions? These issues are worth watching.

PART SIX

THE LATE MIDDLE AGES, 1300–1500

Historians have used various and contradictory phrases to label the late Middle Ages, that is, the period from 1300 to 1500: "the age of the Renaissance," "an age of transition," "the dawn of a new era," "the autumn of the Middle Ages," "the waning of the Middle Ages," "the age of adversity." All of these labels suggest that change was the keynote of the era; but they also suggest that historians do not agree on the direction of that change. Some emphasize new forces emerging; others stress the dissolution of old ways.

We shall take our clue for our treatment from those who lived during the period. Reading the literature and viewing the art of the era, one is struck by the bitterness, frustration, morbidity, and doubt gripping people's minds. They seemed to have sensed that something was amiss, and they reacted by losing confidence and hope. Their state of mind suggests that they saw their age as a time of decline and disintegration. Following that lead, our treatment will seek to show that the equilibrium established in the thirteenth century began to break down, resulting in widespread tensions and the deterioration of old patterns of civilization. But in taking that approach, we need to be mindful that those tensions also generated powerful new forces, capable of transforming society; we shall return to them in later discussions. However, men and women living during the period from 1300 to 1500 could not sense their promise as well as we can, gifted as we are with hindsight. To those people their times were disturbing, marked by the passing of the known and the familiar.

CHAPTER 24
Political, Economic, and Social Tensions

FIGURE 24.1 **Medieval Siege Warfare** This scene portrays the siege of an English castle in southern France by French forces during the Hundred Years' War. It illustrates very accurately the main weapons used in warfare. Engagements of this type drained large amounts of resources from both the English and the French royal governments. Providing the needs of the armies in these encounters often resulted in the pillaging of the countryside, which disrupted agricultural production and commercial exchange and caused untold misery to many. (The British Museum)

Politically, the fourteenth and fifteenth centuries were filled with disorder and strife. All of the major political entities that had been shaped during the High Middle Ages suffered dislocation in some form. Their inadequacies bred civil strife, class struggles, internal wars, and internal misgovernment throughout western Europe. In part, these political troubles rose from structural limitations and weaknesses in the institutions of these states. In part, they were a consequence of a new range of problems that the existing regimes had not previously faced. The most serious of these new problems were economic and social difficulties arising from the limitations and inadequacies of the traditional agricultural, commercial, and industrial systems.

1. THE DECLINE OF THE HOLY ROMAN EMPIRE

We have previously traced the efforts of a succession of rulers between 950 and 1250 to join Germany, Italy, and the western fringes of the Slavic world into a Holy Roman Empire and the powerful opposition, led by the papacy, these efforts generated (see Chapter 19). The death of the last great medieval emperor, Frederick II, in 1250 marked a decisive turning point: Not only did the empire as an institution disintegrate in the late Middle Ages; so did the political ideal that had given it a rationale—that a Christian commonwealth uniting the faithful under a single Christian prince could be created and sustained.

Frederick II's death opened a long period of decline in the authority of the emperor in Germany. After a strife-torn period without a ruler (called the Interregnum, 1250–1273), the German nobility elected a succession of rulers from three different families—the houses of Hapsburg, Luxembourg, and Bavaria—only to repudiate each family in turn when its ruling representative threatened to become too powerful. While demonstrating their unwillingness to accept a ruler with any effective power, the nobles, clergy, and townspeople successfully extended their independence from the central government. The resistance to effective monarchy was given legal definition by Emperor Charles IV (1347–1378), who in 1356 issued a decree called the Golden Bull. It provided that the German ruler would be chosen by seven princes designated as *electors:* the archbishops of Cologne, Trier, and Mainz, and the princes of Saxony, Brandenburg, the Palatinate, and Bohemia. Each elector was granted almost complete independence within his own territory.

After 1356 the Holy Roman Empire progressed rapidly toward decentralization. Other princes and cities demanded and gained the same kind of independence enjoyed by the electors, making the empire little more than a confederation of hundreds of independent political entities. The emperor could call together the princes, church leaders, and representatives of the towns in meetings called *diets,* but he lacked any means of enforcing decisions; he had no national army, no tax system, and no court system. Within their small principalities, many princes created stable, well-organized political systems—Germany was not a lawless, ungoverned land by any means. But Germany did lack unity, a condition that would cost it dearly in the future.

In Italy, the trend toward decentralization after 1250 was even more pronounced. The elected emperor was in theory the ruler of Italy, and from time to time some Italians did seek to have him exert his authority. After the early fourteenth century, the emperors seldom even tried to exercise any influence over their Italian realms, and a welter of independent states emerged. Among them, a few stand forth as most important.

In southern Italy the old Norman-Hohenstaufen state was divided after 1282 into the Kingdom of Naples, ruled by a French prince, and the Kingdom of Sicily, ruled by a member of the royal family of Aragon. Their rivalry and misrule brought steady decline to this once rich area. Finally, in 1435 the two kingdoms were united under Aragonese rule. However, by that time the area was so disturbed that it was destined to remain poor for centuries. The Papal States dominated central Italy. Papal overlordship was bitterly resisted by the local nobles, and it was badly compromised by the absence of the papacy from Rome during much of the fourteenth century (see Chapter 25). However, during the fifteenth century a succession of able, ruthless popes restored their authority, making the Papal States a major force in Italian political life.

Northern Italy was divided into many small city-states, most of which were constantly agitated by political conflicts. By the beginning of the thirteenth century concessions forced from their political overlord, the Holy Roman emperor, assured their political independence. After the death of Frederick II, they battled one another for land, trading advantages, power, and security. Some of the more powerful of the city-states, especially Milan, Venice, and Florence, were able to impose their rule on other small cities to create territorial entities that tended to dominate political life in northern Italy.

Internally, the political system of most of the city-states tended to move from an order with considerable citizen participation toward a system dominated by a single individual (the *signore*, "lord") or by an oligarchy of the rich. The pressure of intercity warfare and of class strife within each city-state encouraged the trend. Milan was taken over by a despot early in the fourteenth century when the Visconti family established its power. Visconti domination, which made Milan rich and greatly expanded its territory, lasted until 1447, when the Sforza family replaced them. Florence resisted despotism longer; in fact, through most of the period Florence retained the façade of a republican form of government that allowed its citizens considerable power to decide public issues. Under this system the city was constantly agitated by political strife. Gradually there emerged a behind-the-scenes power that used patronage, bribery, and personal influence to control rivalry and shape political decisions. After about 1430 that role was played by members of a rich banking family, the Medici. Although they held no exalted titles, the Medici in effect ran Florence as if they were despots. Venice always remained subject to an oligarchy of rich merchants whose methods did not differ greatly from those of the despots. The turbulent, strife-filled times in Italy promoted a new style of politics, later described brilliantly in Machiavelli's *The Prince*. The new order tended to place heavy emphasis on the absolute sovereignty of the state, its right to create its own moral sanctions, its superiority over its subjects. Many historians see these developments as prototypes for the absolute sovereignty claimed by modern states.

Despite the vitality of the Italian Renaissance states, the fragmentation of the peninsula doomed Italy to weakness in the face of larger, better-organized states, such as Spain and France and even the larger German principalities. In 1494 Charles VIII of France was called into Italy by the Sforza ruler of Milan in order to gain advantage for his city; the French invasion opened a long era when the many states of Italy became pawns in European power politics.

2. THE FAILURE OF FEUDAL MONARCHY IN FRANCE, ENGLAND, AND SPAIN

After 1300 England, France, and the Iberian kingdoms encountered troubles nearly as serious as those of the Holy Roman Empire. As the fourteenth century progressed, the well-organized feudal monarchies developed during the twelfth and thirteenth centuries (see Chapter 20) began to show signs of instability and inadequacy. The heightening of tension in each kingdom led to civil wars that pitted the crown against the nobles and noble factions against each other. Under constant stress, the essential features of feudal monarchy and the concepts that animated the political order of the High Middle Ages broke down.

The histories of France and England from 1300 to 1500 were linked together by the Hundred Years' War (1337–1453). This struggle was an extension of a conflict that began in the twelfth century over possessions on the continent held by English kings as fiefs from the French kings. The first phase of the struggle, highlighted by Philip II's victory over John, was settled by the Treaty of Paris (1259), which recognized the French king's control over the northern part of the old Angevin Empire but left the English king holding as a fief important territories in Aquitaine (see Map 24.1). However, the rivalry continued, especially as a result of pressures exerted on English holdings by the strong French kings, Louis IX and Philip IV. English and French interests also clashed in the county of Flanders, where the English sought to resist French domination to protect their interests in the Flemish woolen industry, which depended on English raw wool. French support of the efforts of the Scots to win their independence also troubled the English, especially after the Scots virtually assured that end with their victory at the battle of Bannockburn in 1314.

These festering issues came to a head during the reign of Edward III of England (1327–1377). In 1328 the last member of the direct Capetian line died. Although Edward III had the best hereditary claim to the French throne, the Estates General selected as king Philip of Valois, representing a collateral line of the Capetian family. Philip VI acted aggressively to assert his authority in Flanders, provoking a revolt there. The pro-English Flemish rebels urged Edward to claim the French throne so that he could become their king. In the meantime, Philip began to harass the English territory in Aquitaine and to press his claim to lordship over his vassal, the king of England. When Edward resisted Philip's demands, the French king confiscated Aquitaine in 1337 on the grounds that Edward had refused to honor his obligations as a vassal. Edward III then asserted his claim to the French throne, provoking a major war.

The first phase of the Hundred Years' War, lasting until 1360, was nearly fatal to France. Having established control of the English Channel, the English put armies in France, which in two great battles at Crécy (1346) and Poitiers (1356) cut to pieces the flower of the French nobility. At Poitiers, King John of France was captured and taken to England. An internal crisis ensued in France, marked by an effort of the Estates General to take control of the government, by a peasant rebellion, called the *Jacquerie*, in 1358, and by the ravaging of a large part of France by bands of unpaid soldiers. Eventually John bought his release by agreeing to the Treaty of Brétigny (1360) in which he agreed to pay a huge ransom and to give Edward III full title to Guienne as well as a small territory in northern France, including the key port of Calais. Edward renounced his claim to the French throne.

The Treaty of Brétigny did not end the ancient rivalries. The next phase of the war, extending from 1364 to 1415, saw sporadic but indecisive fighting. Effective military action was impeded by serious internal problems in both of the rival kingdoms. France enjoyed a brief recovery under Charles V (1364–1380), who rebuilt French military strength and increased royal income to the point where he seriously threatened England's hold on Guienne (see Figure 24.1). However, these gains were undone during the reign of his pitiful successor, Charles VI (1380–1422). A minor when he became king, Charles VI was victimized by greedy relatives acting as regents. The most powerful was an uncle, Philip, duke of Burgundy, who was determined to control the weak monarch in order to enlarge his already substantial principality. Philip was thwarted, however, when Charles, on reaching his majority, fell under the spell of his brother, Louis, duke of Orléans. Moreover, Charles began to suffer spells of insanity, each of which required a reinstitution of the regency. Burgundians and Armagnacs (partisans of the duke of Orléans) competed bitterly for control of the regency and the kingdom. Powerful nobles joined the struggle in an effort to serve private interests. This selfish, violent rivalry plunged France into civil chaos from which much of the population suffered badly.

England was hardly less troubled during these years. Edward III ruled until 1377 amid deepening trouble. To wage the increasingly costly war against France, he needed money, and the easiest way to get it was to call Parliament. Frequent meetings resulted in the rapid development of parliamentary organization: The *House of Lords*, comprising the great feudal barons and high church officials, separated from the *House of Commons*, made up of townspeople and of the lesser gentry representing the counties. Aside from its extensive control over taxation, Parliament began to gain a voice in spending money, controlling royal officials, and initiating legislation through petitions presented to the king. The advancing power of Parliament became particularly notable in the reign of Richard II (1377–1399). His reign was troubled by economic and social problems that led to a Peasants' Revolt in 1381 and by deep dissatisfaction among the nobles with the king's autocratic ways. Eventually, Parliament deposed Richard II and chose in his place Henry IV (1399–1413), whose sole right to rule was based on Parliament's approval. Obviously, that institution had assumed a crucial role in political life. However, Parliament proved neither capable of directing the kingdom nor willing to trust the king to do so. It became a forum for factional agitation aimed at dominating the king in order to gain greater privileges.

Henry V (1413–1422) hastened both England and France on their troubled ways by reopening the Hundred Years' War. In 1415 he invaded France and crushed a French army at Agincourt. With the support of the Burgundian faction, he established control over most of France north of the Loire River. In 1420 he forced the humiliating Treaty of Troyes on Charles VI. By its terms, Henry married Charles' daughter; Henry or his heir by that marriage would rule France after Charles' death; in the meantime Henry would serve as regent. The legitimate heir to the throne, the dauphin Charles, was disinherited. France seemed on the verge of destruction.

But the English were not to enjoy their triumph long. After both Henry V and Charles VI died in 1422, leaving the infant Henry VI as king of both nations, the French made a spectacular recovery. The rallying point was the dauphin Charles, who controlled considerable territory south of the Loire and had the support of many royal officials, military captains, and nobles. Timid by nature, Charles did not capitalize on these resources until he was moved to action by a strange turn of events. In 1429 a simple peasant girl, Joan of Arc, came to him claiming God had revealed to her that Charles must free France of the English and assume the crown that rightly belonged to him. Her message bestirred the dispirited Charles and pumped new confidence into the French soldiers loyal to him. Dressed like a man, Joan herself was with the army that in 1429 defeated an English army besieging the key city of Orléans; this was the first French victory for many years. On the strength of it, Joan persuaded Charles to be crowned king, a venture that turned into a triumph.

From 1429 to 1453, the French won victory after victory, until the English held only Calais. But Joan did not live to see these triumphs. In 1430 she was captured by the Burgundians and turned over to the English. She was tried by the Church for heresy and burned at the stake in Rouen in 1431. Despite her tragic end, Joan's dream of a reborn France soon came to pass. Under Charles VII, royal power made a remarkable recovery in France. Well served by excellent ministers, Charles was able to build a well-trained army paid for by the king, thus ending his dependence on a feudal army and on troublemaking mercenaries. In 1439 the Estates General granted the king power to impose a direct tax, called the *taille*, on his subjects. Although many powerful nobles in France continued to act in their own interest, political life more and more focused on the royal government with its increasing ability to establish order and curb the irresponsible behavior of the princes. The old feudal basis for royal power was rapidly eroding. In its place was a growing consciousness of the king as the head of a nation of subjects held together by common interests that the state should serve. When Charles VII died in 1461, his son, Louis XI (1461–1483), inherited a solid base from which to rule. His accession marked the beginning of a new era.

England was in a less happy state during much of the fifteenth century, chiefly because of a deepening factionalism among a few privileged families seeking control of the government as a means of enhancing their power. Surrounding themselves with private armies, these factions pushed England toward civil war. The struggle began to take shape during the reign of Henry VI (1422–1461). Because he became king in infancy, there was a

Map 24.1 THE HUNDRED YEARS' WAR In the Hundred Years' War the English fought to regain their once extensive possessions in France (see Map 20.1), and the French sought to add these territories to the royal domain. The map shows the ebb and flow of that prolonged struggle. When the war began in 1337, England held only a modest territory in southwest France. At the height of their fortunes in the first half of the fifteenth century, they controlled most of northern France. But not for long. When the war ended in 1453, the French had driven them off the Continent except for the city of Calais.

NORTH SEA

E N G L A N D

★ BOSWORTH FIELD

London •

SLUYS 1340 ★
Bruges • • Antwerp
Calais • COUNTY OF DUCHY OF
Cassel • BRABANT
AGINCOURT 1415 ★ FLANDERS
Arras • COUNTY
• OF NAMUR
CRÉCY HAINAUT
1346

ENGLISH CHANNEL

Rouen •
Compiègne • Reims •
NORMANDY Seine R. Paris • CHAMPAGNE
Brétigny • ALSACE
DUCHY OF
BRITTANY Rennes • LORRAINE
MAINE Troyes • Domremy •
Orléans •
Angers • Dijon •
ANJOU Loire R. DUCHY OF
Chinon • Bourges • BURGUNDY COUNTY
POITOU (Supporting OF
English Claim) BURGUNDY
POITIERS 1356 ★

BAY OF BISCAY

AUVERGNE

Kingdom of France in 1339
English Areas in 1339 Bordeaux •
English Controlled Areas in 1429 Dordogne R.
Burgundian Areas in 1441 Garonne R. AQUITAINE
★ Battle Site A Q U I T A I N E

GUIENNE Avignon • PROVENCE
ARMAGNAC • Aix
Bayonne • GASCONY

NAVARRE

MEDITERRANEAN SEA

0   50   100 miles

ARAGON

Meuse R.
Marne R.
Moselle R.
Rhine R.
Saône R.
Rhône R.
Durance R.

long regency. Moreover, his family, the Lancastrians, elevated to the throne by parliamentary act in 1399, did not have as strong a hereditary claim to the throne as did another family, the Yorkists. Followings of nobles formed around the Lancastrians and the Yorkists, leading to a bitter civil war, the War of the Roses, so called because the opposing forces adopted the white and the red rose as their symbols. While this struggle for the crown raged, the regular processes of orderly government were disrupted. Tyranny, intrigue, murder, confiscation of property, and pursuit of private ends were the order of the day. Finally, in 1485, Henry Tudor, a Lancastrian, defeated his Yorkist rival, King Richard III, in a pitched battle at Bosworth Field and assumed the throne as Henry VII.

Although Henry's claim to the crown was extremely tenuous, the nation, weary of civil disorder, was willing to follow anyone who promised to restore peace and security. The desire for order was strong among the lesser nobles, the *gentry* made up chiefly of rural landowners, the prosperous peasant yeomen, and the well-to-do bourgeoisie. Taken together these elements constituted a substantial force willing to support effective royal government. The old noble factions were badly discredited as a result of their brutal, self-seeking conduct during the War of the Roses. As a result, the new king had considerable freedom to act as he pleased. Henry used the opportunity to end the feudal state and create a strong central government that united the English people into a nation.

The three major Iberian kingdoms—Aragon, Castile, and Portugal—also had their difficulties during the late Middle Ages. By 1300 the holy war against the Moslems had ceased to be the significant factor in Spanish affairs, for the Moslems had been confined to the narrow territory of Granada (see Map 21.1). The Christian kingdoms then turned on one another, competing bitterly for territory. At the same time almost constant civil strife raged within each kingdom, replicating the struggles in England and France. Castile was plagued by a long series of disputed successions that undermined royal authority. Aragon's internal order was compromised by the aggressive overseas policy pursued by its kings, especially in Italy, a policy seldom favored by the nobility, and by conflict between the landed and the commercial interests. These senseless quarrels finally began to abate in 1469 when the heiress of Castile, Isabella, married Ferdinand, the heir of Aragon. In 1479, when this couple had succeeded to both thrones, they quickly took steps to end the strife, unify their lands into a single state, and to impose stronger royal control over their subjects.

Portuguese kings did not meet such violent resistance as did the other Iberian kings, and their heroic struggle to prevent Castile from absorbing Portugal won them broad internal support. They also promoted commercial ventures throughout the fifteenth century, backing Portuguese merchants who expanded southward along the African coast and found lucrative markets.

3. EASTERN EUROPE AND THE MEDITERRANEAN WORLD

While the western European states were undergoing internal crises and engaging each other in rivalries that sapped their strength, highly significant political changes were unfolding along Europe's eastern and southeastern frontiers. These developments drastically altered the relationships that had been established between the West and these eastern areas in the High Middle Ages (these changes can be followed on Map 24.2).

The Byzantine Empire never fully recovered from the attacks of the Seljuk Turks in the late eleventh century and the capture of Constantinople by western Europeans in 1204 during the Fourth Crusade. After the Europeans were finally ousted in 1261 and Greek emperors again assumed

Map 24.2 CENTRAL EUROPE AND WESTERN ASIA, ca. 1500 This map shows the major political entities in central Europe and western Asia about 1500. Especially threatening to Poland, Lithuania, and Hungary—and to western Europe in general—were two rapidly expanding powers: the Ottoman Empire and the Grand Principality of Moscow (the future Russia).

ARCTIC OCEAN

Ob R.

FINLAND

L. Onega

L. Ladoga

KINGDOM OF SWEDEN

Stockholm

Novgorod

Moscow

Ural R.

BALTIC SEA

TEUTONIC ORDER

Riga

Königsberg • Vilna

Smolensk

Volga R.

Danzig

DUCHY OF
PRUSSIA

GRAND DUCHY
OF
LITHUANIA

KHANATE OF THE GOLDEN HORDE (TARTARS)

ARAL
SEA

Oder R.

Vistula R. • Warsaw

KINGDOM
OF POLAND

Kiev

Dnieper R.

HOLY
ROMAN
EMPIRE

UKRAINE

Don R.

Astrakhan

Vienna

Pruth R.

Dniester R.

Budapest

MOLDAVIA

SEA OF
AZOV

CASPIAN SEA

KINGDOM OF HUNGARY

Belgrade

WALLACHIA

Danube R.

BLACK SEA

BOSNIA

SERBIA

BULGARIA

Varna

ADRIATIC SEA

Kossovo

Sofia

Nicopolis

Constantinople

Trebizond

MACEDONIA

Thessalonica

AEGEAN SEA

RHODES

MAMELUKES

MEDITERRANEAN
SEA

CRETE

CYPRUS

	Ottoman Possessions ca. 1355
	Byzantine Possessions ca. 1355
	Ottoman Possessions ca. 1481
	Grand Principality of Moscow ca. 1300–1505
▬▬▬	Boundary of Holy Roman Empire
·······	Western Boundary of Mongol Expansion, 13th Century

Note: Crete, to Venice, 1204–1669;
    Cyprus, Crusader Kingdom to 1489, then to Venice until 1571;
    Rhodes to Knights Hospitallers, 1309–1523

power, a fatal illness afflicted the empire. Civil strife slowly sapped the strength of its government. The Italian city-states, led by Venice, deprived the empire of much of its trade, and bit by bit its territory was pared away, especially by the Ottoman Turks. The emperors of the fourteenth and fifteenth centuries appealed desperately to the West for help but received little. Finally, in 1453 Constantinople was captured by the Ottomans, who made the city their capital under the name Istanbul. The fall of Constantinople ended forever the power that had so long shielded Europe.

The Ottoman victory in 1453 marked the reappearance of a Moslem threat to the West, a danger that western Europeans had not faced for centuries. The Ottoman Turks were originally Asiatic nomads who were uprooted and pushed westward by the Mongols. They settled in Asia Minor in the thirteenth century, accepted Islam, and adopted many of the ways of Moslem society. Under their first great ruler, Osman (or Othman, whence the term *Ottoman*) (1290–1326), the new state began to expand in Asia Minor and then into the Balkans, largely at the expense of the Byzantine Empire. Early in the fifteenth century, Ottoman power was nearly destroyed by Tamerlane, a Mongol warrior who sought to reconstruct the empire of Genghis Khan (see Chapter 21). Tamerlane's empire collapsed soon after his death in 1405, allowing the Ottomans to recover their power and continue their expansion. They completed the conquest of the Byzantine Empire by 1453. Early in the sixteenth century, they conquered Syria, Palestine, and Egypt. As the Middle Ages ended, their vast empire loomed as a major threat to the West.

As the Ottoman Turks extended their territorial sway, they fashioned political institutions that gave their empire strength and stability. The Ottomans constituted an elite claiming supremacy over their subjects, many of them Christians, by right of conquest. They retained a strong sense of community based on their ethnic identity and their religion. The Ottoman state was headed by the *sultan,* whose extensive power over all aspects of life was based on his claim to be the successor of Muhammad, empowered to interpret the Moslem law that all followers of Allah were required to obey. A well-organized bureaucracy developed,

modeled on both Byzantine and Abbasid models. Local units of government were developed across the empire to carry out the sultan's policies, collect taxes, and administer justice. In practice, the Ottoman regime allowed local communities broad authority to regulate their own affairs as long as they did not disrupt internal peace or challenge the sultan's supreme power. Aside from taxes, the Ottomans extracted human resources from their subject population to sustain their regime. Young boys, often of Christian or Jewish origins, were claimed as slaves, converted to Islam, and rigorously trained for specialized duties in the civil service or the army. The military corps created from these slaves, called the Janissaries, developed into a highly professional, dedicated force that played a key role in Ottoman expansion and in maintaining Ottoman domination over the large empire. Young girls were also enslaved to serve in Ottoman harems, including that of the sultan.

Central and eastern Europe began to assume a modern shape in the wake of the decline of the Holy Roman and Byzantine empires. The south coast of the Baltic Sea was dominated by Germans, an expansion spearheaded by the crusading order of the Teutonic Knights who brought traders, missionaries, and agricultural colonists in their wake. Their presence filled the Slavs of central Europe with an abiding distrust and fear of the Germans. The Germanic threat resulted in a union of the ruling houses of Poland and Lithuania under the Lithuanian prince Jagiello, who married a Polish princess and governed both states as King Ladislas II (1386–1434). The house of Jagiello exerted strong military pressure on the Baltic Germans and the Russian states to the east during much of the fifteenth century, but it never succeeded in creating an effective government for its huge kingdom. To the south, Hungary continued to develop, but its energies were increasingly absorbed in defending itself against the Ottoman Turks and holding back ambitious German nobles bent on taking the Hungarian throne. Until the Ottomans seized control of the Balkans at the end of the fourteenth century, a flourishing Serbian kingdom dominated that area; after its destruction, the Hungarians stood as western Europe's outpost against the Turks. Farther east a vigorous Russian state was emerging. We shall return to the story of its development later (see Chapter 34). Suffice it to say here that by 1500 Russia was beginning to play an important role in determining the fate of eastern Europe.

4. ECONOMIC AND SOCIAL TENSIONS

The political difficulties of the late Middle Ages were brought on partly by basic economic and social problems troubling most of Europe. By 1300 the long period of economic growth that western Europe had enjoyed since about 1000 (see Chapter 18) was ending; for the next century and a half its economy suffered contraction and depression, and social disequilibrium grew. Although the nature and impact of economic and social dislocation varied from region to region, certain broad patterns affected western Europe generally.

The economic growth of the period from 1000 to 1300 had been powerfully stimulated by sustained population growth. The depression that afflicted western Europe after 1300 was in important ways a by-product of a dramatic population decline. Modern demographers have produced considerable evidence to suggest that by 1300 much of western Europe had reached the point where the population level was straining the food supply. Also, the early decades of the fourteenth century were marked by a succession of famines, due in part to unfavorable climatic conditions and in part to increasing dependence on poorer agricultural lands. Perhaps the combination of a population pushing the limits of productive capacity and an increasingly unfavorable pattern of weather might have been sufficient to cause a population downturn. To these conditions, however, was added a demographic catastrophe.

That disaster took the form of a devastating pestilence: the Black Death, an epidemic of bubonic plague that first spread over Europe with deadly effect between 1347 and 1350 and then returned periodically during most of the fourteenth century and far beyond into the seventeenth century. The scourge was brought to Europe from the East by rats infested with fleas whose bites transmitted the bacilli to the human bloodstream. Once the disease was loosed in

FIGURE 24.2   The Plague   This painting captures the terror inflicted on the population of a city by the Black Death. Even while shrouding the dead for burial, people were suddenly struck down, as is the man shown falling to the ground. Neither the prayers of the clergy nor the pleas of the saints, represented in this scene by St. Sebastian, could help. (The Walters Art Gallery, Baltimore)

western Europe, it caused an immense loss of life. The best estimates suggest that a third of Europe's population was wiped out between 1347 and 1350. Periodic recurrence of the plague continued the downward spiral of the population, so that by the early fifteenth century western Europe had barely half as many people as it had had in 1300. Such a drastic demographic change had massive effects on the level of production, the demand for goods, the labor supply, prices, social relationships, and mass psychology (see Figure 24.2).

While population decline was a prime force in curbing economic growth in the late Middle Ages, it was only one factor. The economy also suffered from structural limitations rooted in the traditional system of production and from disruptive forces outside the economic system. Especially damaging to economic life during the fourteenth and fifteenth centuries was the reduction of commercial exchange. The population decline drastically reduced demand and limited the productive processes that supplied goods for exchange. Vast disturbances in eastern and central Asia ended opportunities to penetrate new areas of commercial opportunity. The rise of the Ottoman Empire seriously disturbed the favored position that Italian merchants had long enjoyed in the eastern Mediterranean. The independent cities that had been the source of commercial growth earlier became increasingly restrictive, chiefly in an effort to protect local merchants and to monopolize regional trade. Sustained cooperation among commercial cities for mutual benefit proved nearly impossible. The most successful effort of this kind was the Hanseatic League, which linked about seventy cities in northern Germany, Scandinavia, and the Low Countries. But ultimately the League declined, chiefly because its members refused to sacrifice local interests.

Industrial production experienced a comparable constriction. Labor shortages increased labor costs to the point where many kinds of industrial production were unprofitable. To redress this situation, some manufacturers—particularly in the wool industry—began to move their operations into rural areas where labor was cheaper. And they joined landowners to pressure governments to pass legislation, such as the English Statute of Laborers (1351), attempting to freeze wages. The guild system, which had once promoted industrial production, grew increasingly restrictive. Seeking to protect their monopoly over the production of goods in each city, the guilds passed rules limiting the volume of production, setting prices, excluding the products of outsiders, barring technical changes, and limiting entrance into each craft. Although some industrial operations, such as wool production, continued to flourish, the general effect of such measures was to depress industrial production.

Agricultural production was likewise depressed and dislocated. Widespread and persistent warfare ravaged many lands. Colonizing opportunities had nearly disappeared. Famine and plague decimated the rural labor force and sharply reduced the urban demand for food products, especially cereal grains. Large areas of marginal land were taken out of production, dislocating many agricultural workers. Many landowners were sorely pressed to make ends meet. Their solution usually involved abandoning the traditional manorial system. Some rented their domains to enterprising peasants eager to gain access to more land. Others enclosed their manors in order to concentrate on specialized crops and livestock raising; these operations increasingly depended on hired labor. Both solutions resulted in the dislocation of serfs traditionally attached to the land.

Economic dislocation and contraction led to widespread social tension and disturbance in the late Middle Ages. As we noted earlier, even before 1300 Europe's aristocracy was becoming stratified, chiefly on the basis of wealth. That stratification continued and became even more pronounced during the late Middle Ages. These were tenuous times for the highest nobility, not only because changing economic conditions strained their fortunes but also because the unsettled political situation demanded their involvement in violent factionalism and civil war if they were to retain their position of prestige and power. Some did not survive the murderous conflicts. However, the powerful aristocratic families that did survive held their fortunes and increased their privileges, so that their social position became more distinct than ever. Increasingly, these powerful nobles owed their status to their close connections with the monarchs. The high aristocracy pursued an ever more splendid and exclusive life style; it was based on an exaggerated practice of behavior patterns dictated by the code of chivalry.

Although many lesser nobles were also sorely tested by the agricultural depression, they solidified their position as a country gentry asserting a powerful influence over local life. Their key to success was the careful management of production on their landholdings and the exploitation of the local labor supply. They often strengthened their local position by allying themselves with great nobles and by seeking favors from royal governments. While duly impressed by the life style of the great nobles, the lesser nobles were not able and did not try to imitate it. They began to develop a simpler life style attuned to the activities of the small country estate and the local town. By 1500 this gentry had become a powerful force interested primarily in order and stability and support for their economic interests; they became a source of support for the increasingly strong kings. Thus, by 1500 a powerfully entrenched aristocracy continued to dominate society. However, its inner structure as a class was being altered, and its power base was shifting from the relationships defined by feudal connections to those defined by birth, by wealth, and by royal favor.

The peasant world underwent significant changes during the late Middle Ages. The developments in agricultural production noted above gave added impetus to the decline of serfdom, so that by 1500 servile dependence—a key component of the agricultural system before 1300—had virtually disappeared in western Europe. While this development improved the legal status of most peasants, it deprived many of the economic security that had characterized serf status in earlier times. Population decline and the dismantling of manors seriously disrupted community groupings that had been a vital part of peasant life. Economically, peasants were thrown more and more on their own as renters or hired laborers, often with disastrous results in a period of economic instability. Hard-pressed landlords preyed on peasant misfortunes to force on them added financial obligations, higher rents, and lower wages. Royal taxes fell heavily on the peasants, and the wars they thus paid for often ravaged their farms. With reduced opportunities in the troubled cities and a vanishing frontier, many peasants were trapped in a position of poverty and oppression. They expressed their discontent by frequent and violent rebellions, most of which were brutally crushed by kings, nobles, and clergy (see Figure 24.3). Despite the generally grim picture surrounding peasant life in the late Middle Ages, there were peasants who succeeded in increasing their landholdings either by purchase or by renting and who found ways of expanding their productivity and wealth in a volatile age. This element of the peas-

FIGURE 24.3 Peasant Violence Pressed by a variety of miseries, peasants often resorted to violence in the late Middle Ages, as illustrated in this drawing showing peasants attacking a knight with axes and daggers. (Bibliothèque Nationale, Paris, ms. fr. 87)

ant class would eventually make important contributions to the agricultural recovery of western Europe (see Color Plate 11).

Equally disadvantaged and discontented were certain elements of the urban population. The depression in manufacturing and exchange reduced many small-scale artisans and shopkeepers to the status of laborers for hire or to the ranks of the unemployed. They were also increasingly deprived of a significant voice in urban government, such as they had enjoyed during the twelfth and thirteenth centuries. Dominated by rich entrepreneurs, city governments and the guilds sought to regulate more stringently the economic activities and the wages of urban laborers. This element of the bourgeoisie demonstrated their discontent by frequent rioting and rebellion, usually with little more success than the peasants had.

The social group making the greatest advance in the fourteenth and fifteenth centuries was an elite segment of the bourgeoisie engaged in capitalistic ventures. Their success is exemplified by the Medici and the Bardi in Italy, the Fuggers in southern Germany, Jacques Coeur of France, and some of the entrepreneurs associated with the Hanseatic League. Members of this group amassed huge fortunes in such fields as banking, money lending, and the wool industry. Seeking to use that wealth to create more, these entrepreneurs increasingly determined the course of economic development. They seized political control of most city governments and found favor with kings. Culturally they were able to patronize the learning and art of the Renaissance movement advancing in much of Europe and to set standards of fashion. In a sense, this group now represented the bourgeoisie; others who had formerly been counted in this class—simple artisans and small shopkeepers—were becoming a group apart, a laboring class. The new bourgeoisie was destined to play a major role in the future of the West.

By approximately 1450 the worst of the economic and social stresses of the late Middle Ages was over, and there were signs of recovery everywhere. Aside from the return of political order accompanying the restoration of royal authority, the population had begun to grow again. The agricultural system became increasingly stable, chiefly on the basis of a rental system that bound landlord and peasant together on a money basis and a more rational management of land and labor in relation to the realities of the market. Innovative techniques were being devised for accumulating capital and organizing large-scale manufacturing production and commercial enterprises. New technological advances were being made and were being applied more widely—water mills in the textile industry, better mining techniques, printing, improved shipbuilding, the compass, the astrolabe, gunpowder. New frontiers were opening by way of the seas that washed Europe's western shores. All these forces pointed toward new growth in western Europe. It was obvious, however, that this growth would be achieved in ways different from those that prevailed in medieval Europe.

SUGGESTED READING

Overview of the Period 1300–1500

Robert Fossier, ed., *The Cambridge Illustrated History of the Middle Ages*, Vol. 3: *1250–1520*, trans. Sarah Hanbury Tenison (1986).
Daniel Waley, *Later Medieval Europe: From Saint Louis to Luther*, 2nd ed. (1985).
George Holmes, *Europe: Hierarchy and Revolt, 1320–1450* (1975).
Any of these three works will provide an excellent overview of the major developments during the period.

Western Europe

Bernard Guenée, *States and Rulers in Later Medieval Europe*, trans. Juliet Vale (1985). A comparative study of political developments.
F. R. H. DuBoulay, *Germany in the Later Middle Ages* (1983). A clear treatment of Germany's complex history.
Brian Pullan, *A History of Early Renaissance Italy. From the Mid–Thirteenth to the Mid–Fifteenth Century* (1973). Helpful in showing general political and economic trends in Italy.
George Holmes, *The Later Middle Ages, 1272–1485* (1962).
Trevor Rowley, *The High Middle Ages, 1200–1550* (1986).
Either of these works will provide a clear picture of developments in late medieval England.
John Gillingham, *The War of the Roses: Peace and Conflict in Fifteenth-Century England* (1981). Stresses the political and military aspect of England's internal strife.
P. S. Lewis, *Later Medieval France: The Polity* (1968). One of the few works in English on late medieval France.
Christopher Allmond, *The Hundred Years' War. England and France at War c. 1300–c.1450* (1988). A well-done treatment stressing the effects of the war.

Eastern Europe

Donald M. Nicol, *The Last Centuries of Byzantium, 1261–1453* (1972). A clearly presented account.

Halil Inalick, *The Ottoman Empire: The Classical Age, 1300–1600*, trans. Norman Itzkowitz and Colin Imber (1973). The best treatment of a subject not always given an objective evaluation.

David Morgan, *The Mongols* (1986).

G. Vernadsky, *The Origins of Russia* (1959). A brilliant treatment.

Economic and Social History

C. M. Cipolla, *Before the Industrial Revolution: European Society and Economy, 1000–1700* (1976). Effectively places late medieval economic and social history in a larger context.

Harry A. Miskimin, *The Economy of Early Renaissance Europe, 1300–1460* (1969). A detailed study; more general treatments can be found in the works of Bautier and Pounds, cited in Chapter 18.

Specialized aspects of late medieval economic and social history are treated in the following works.

Johannes Schildhauer, *The Hansa: History and Culture*, trans. Katherine Vanovitch (1985).

Robert S. Gottfried, *The Black Death: Natural and Human Disaster in Medieval Europe* (1983).

Graham Twigg, *The Black Death: A Biological Reappraisal* (1984).

Michel Mollat and Philippe Wolff, *The Popular Revolutions of the Late Middle Ages*, trans. A. L. Lytton-Sells (1973).

CHAPTER 25

The Decline of the Church

FIGURE 25.1 Pope Boniface VIII This fresco from the Church of St. John Lateran in Rome shows Pope Boniface VIII proclaiming the great jubilee held in Rome in 1300. The artist, perhaps Giotto, catches something of the autocratic spirit of the proud pontiff whose efforts to assert papal authority led to deep trouble for the Church. (Alinari/Art Resource)

The tensions that beset western European political, social, and economic institutions in the fourteenth and fifteenth centuries afflicted the Church even more severely. After 1300 this powerful institution, which had earlier decisively influenced all aspects of human activity, encountered increasing difficulties in asserting its traditional leadership role. Its teachings, its system of government, and its leaders were subjected to merciless criticism and open defiance. And the Church failed to discover effective ways to respond to these mounting criticisms.

1. A CRISIS IN CHURCH GOVERNANCE

One of the major results of the reform movement of the High Middle Ages had been the creation of a highly centralized, hierarchical system of church governance capable of imposing a uniform pattern of belief and discipline on the Christian community of western Europe. During the late Middle Ages that structure faltered in a variety of ways.

The most dramatic challenge to that system focused on its very center: the papacy. The authority of the papal office, brought to its apogee by the talented popes of the thirteenth century, was vigorously contested during the pontificate of Boniface VIII (1294–1303). This vain, ambitious "prince of the new Pharisees" (see Figure 25.1), as Dante called him, met stern resistance from the kings of England and France. His failure to respond effectively to that test dramatized the vulnerability of the papacy and led to increasing attacks on the papal office.

Boniface's first setback came when he attempted to stop Edward I of England and Philip IV of France from imposing new taxes on the Church in their realms to help finance their wars with each other. In a pronouncement intended to be binding on all Christians (called a papal bull) entitled *Clericis laicos*, Boniface forcefully maintained that only with papal consent could taxes be laid upon the Church. Edward and Philip responded by cutting off revenues from their kingdoms to Rome, forcing Boniface to retreat from his position.

Before long Boniface and Philip again clashed, this time over the question of whether the king or the Church had jurisdiction in legal cases involving the clergy. Against the strong-minded pope stated his case unequivocally. In a bull entitled *Unam sanctam* he not only stated the Church's right to judge its clergy but also insisted that the French king and all other Christians must subject themselves to the pope to be saved. Philip countered with a masterful propaganda campaign, highlighted by blatant distortion of the papal position, which successfully discredited the pope in the eyes of the French public. He capped that campaign by sending his agents to Italy to capture Boniface. They were successful, and the pope escaped what might have been an even more painful defeat by dying. St. Peter's vicar had suffered a humiliating defeat.

Philip IV capitalized on his victory by using his influence over the College of Cardinals to ensure the election of a French bishop as pope. Aware that he would be unwelcome in the turbulent Papal States, the new pope in 1309 took up residence at Avignon, a city located on the east bank of the Rhone River, just outside French territory. Until 1377 this city remained the residence of the papacy. During these years of what the Italian writer Petrarch called the "Babylonian Captivity"—referring to the episode in Jewish history when God's chosen people were held captive in Babylon by the sinful Chaldeans, now equated with the French monarchy—the popes were accused, unfairly, of being pawns of the French kings. The English, who were locked in the Hundred Years' War with the French, used the situation to reduce papal control over English ecclesiastical affairs. The German emperors and princes were equally defiant. Many Christians were troubled by the fact that the pope's claim to power was based on succession to St. Peter as bishop of Rome, not Avignon. These critics were not impressed by the plea of the papacy that Rome was not safe; neither had it been for Peter nor for many earlier popes. The Babylonian Captivity caused scholars and writers to raise major questions regarding church government and to arrive at answers that challenged papal supremacy.

The Avignon papacy was extremely active in pursuing policies intended to strengthen papal control over the entire ecclesiastical organization of the Church. Several of the Avignon popes were highly skilled administrators whose efforts brought the long-standing trend toward centralization of Church organization to a culmination. Their most pressing concerns were financial. Cut off from the traditional revenues derived from their control of the Papal States in Italy, these popes worked hard to exploit old sources of revenue from across all Europe and to develop new forms of income. They vastly expanded their control over appointments to major ecclesiastical offices, "reserving" for themselves the right to fill these offices with those willing to pay the price. Payment usually took the form of conceding to the papacy all or part of the income associated with the office for a specific period of time. The popes earned a lucrative income by granting dispensations from the regulations of canon law for a broad spectrum of matters ranging from the dissolution of marriages to the relaxation of obligations associated with holding religious offices. Another expanding source of income was the sale of indulgences, a practice that allowed sinners to do penance by making payments in money. They steadily increased the number of cases that had to be adjudicated in papal courts and derived a huge income from this activity. They enlarged the papal bureaucracy beyond anything previously known. In terms of revenues, subordinates, and business transactions, the Avignon popes were actually more powerful than even their illustrious thirteenth-century predecessors.

However, this emphasis on organizational affairs did their prestige more harm than good. Abuses of the worst kind began to plague the papal government. The growing horde of papal bureaucrats engaged in every type of corruption, such as selling offices and accepting bribes to assure the desired outcome of judicial cases tried in papal courts. Many buyers of Church offices were interested only in income and never went near the office; absenteeism thus became a major problem. It was common for one individual to purchase several offices; this pluralism again contributed to neglect of the responsibilities associated with religious office. Bishops and abbots in all parts of Europe resented growing papal interference in local Church affairs and tried to escape papal control, often by turning to their kings, who gladly protected them—for a price. Papal taxation aroused bitterness and resistance everywhere. Edward III of England reflected the dislike of the money-grabbing popes when he said: "The successor of the Apostles was ordered to lead the Lord's sheep to the pasture, not to fleece them." Perhaps the king's criticism was less than candid. One reason why the popes were able to increase papal income was that they shared their take with the royal governments of western Europe, which were not too disturbed by additional burdens on their subjects as long as they profited. The officials of the papal curia spent much of this wealth on luxurious living; a symbol of their luxury was the splendid papal palace built in Avignon. The ecclesiastical life style of the city, which Petrarch called "the sewer of the world," aroused the bitter anger of many in Europe whose lot was poverty and suffering in the wake of the Black Death and widespread economic depression. The Avignon popes seemed powerless to curb these excesses, and thus suffered the blame.

The Babylonian Captivity finally ended in 1377 with the return of the pope to Rome. However, this move led to the election by a part of the College of Cardinals of a second pope, who continued to live at Avignon. Thus began the Great Schism, forty years in which the Church was headed by two popes directing two administrations, two tax systems, two sets of Church courts. Everyone was at a loss to know who was the right pope. Corruption and fiscal exactions increased. Rival popes played politics furiously, each seeking to gain enough allies to oust the other. Many Europeans—and especially princes—thought in terms of obeying the pope who offered the most advantageous concessions in terms of controlling Church wealth within each kingdom or principality. Few took seriously the claim of either pope to be spiritual leader of Europe; popes who competed with one another and encouraged the division of Christendom seemed little better than greedy politicians.

As a result of the schism, many leaders—bishops, canon lawyers, theologians, and even princes—began to search for ways of ending what seemed a scandalous situation. Their search eventually focused on an institution that had played a major role in the early history of the Church: a general council. The chief advocates of the conciliar theory argued that an ecumenical assembly of bishops possessed an authority superior even to that of the pope and thus provided a legitimate means of healing the schism and reforming the clergy. Despite the threat of conciliarism to the concept of papal supremacy, its advocates carried the day. Between 1409 and 1449 four councils were held, each a stormy affair marked by interminable negotiations. The Council of Pisa (1409) addressed the issue of the schism but ended with the installation of a third pope to further complicate that problem. The Council of Constance (1414–1418) finally succeeded in restoring a single pope.

In the subsequent two councils, the popes devoted singular attention to controlling proceedings and thus disarming this dangerous threat to papal authority. Their task was not too difficult, since the council membership was often divided by quarrels among ecclesiastical leaders representing different nations. A major tactic used by the popes to curb the claims of the conciliarists to exercise final authority over the Church was to make concessions to monarchs in return for their support of papal power. For example, the pope accepted the Pragmatic Sanction of Bourges, issued in 1438 by Charles VII of France with the backing of the French clergy; this agreement gave the French monarch extensive rights over ecclesiastical income and the clergy. Comparable agreements worked out with other rulers seriously limited papal power and hastened a trend toward the creation of "national" churches.

Probably the greatest failure of the councils was their inability to institute meaningful reform. Despite numerous attempts to enact legislation aimed at curing many of the Church's ills, the members of the councils were never able to agree on a practical reform program. When the last council disbanded in 1449, most people had lost confidence in this means of revitalizing the Church. The greatest influence of the conciliar movement was indirect: It opened the Church's traditional organization to question and caused many to conclude that the pope's claim to the "fullness of power" was not divinely ordained.

The popes of the last half of the fifteenth century concentrated on strengthening their control over the Papal States in Italy and competing in the many power struggles raging in Italy in this period. On the whole, they were successful. But the methods they employed led many to view the pope as nothing more than a secular prince, scheming, bribing, and brawling to get what he desired for himself, his family, and his friends and enjoying a luxurious existence. A few led scandalous lives and several became patrons of Renaissance artists and writers who were openly advocating ideas and values that challenged Christianity. The popes ceased to enjoy the respect and veneration of most Christians. No one would deny that the popes were powerful in terms of wealth and political resources. What they had lost was the moral authority that had been their chief source of influence in the thirteenth century, and without that authority, the papacy was in no position to exercise effective authority over the faithful.

The disarray in church governance resulting from the problems besetting the papacy and the decay of papal prestige was compounded by a steady deterioration of the effectiveness of the entire body of the clergy in the performance of their pastoral and administrative responsibilities.

Especially pronounced was the decline of monasticism. Between 1300 and 1500 not a single new order of any importance was established in western Europe, and many of the older monastic institutions became increasingly corrupt and ineffectual in providing spiritual leadership. Monasteries were no longer a refuge for the spiritually dedicated or a stage from which the zealous could launch their efforts to purify religious life.

The Franciscans and the Dominicans were the most powerful and active orders during the late Middle Ages. Except for a few purists, most mendicants forgot their ideals of poverty and pastoral service and turned to the pursuit of wealth and power. Most of the other orders fell into the same pattern. Monks and nuns were lax in observing monastic rules governing discipline and defining moral norms. Little attention was paid to the quality of recruits entering monasteries; many were aristocratic ladies who could not find husbands, younger sons without land, and commoners who sought to escape the hardships of life. Absentee abbots thought only of garnering the income from monastic property. Of course, not all monks were

FIGURE 25.2 Misconduct of Monks Some of the most savage criticism of the late medieval church was aimed at the monastic establishments. These scenes reflect some of the causes of that criticism. Left, a monk and his mistress are held in stocks for passersby to jeer at. Right, a monk drinks excessively. (The British Library)

morally lax or without religious fervor. However, the culprits, as usual, caught the public eye and the innocent shared their bad reputation. One needs to read only a little of the literature of the fourteenth and fifteenth centuries, such as some of the stories in Boccaccio's *Decameron* or Chaucer's *Canterbury Tales,* to realize that monasticism was held in low repute. Monastic life had come to signify laziness, greed, immorality, and hypocrisy (see Figure 25.2).

The secular clergy, charged with the Church's everyday ministry to the Christian populace, was equally plagued by corruption and moral laxness. The tone was set by the powerful officials of the papal curia, especially the cardinals, whose vast entourages, immense wealth, and talent for political machinations indeed made them "princes of the Church." Many bishops purchased their offices, paying prices that left them little choice but to wring money out of their subjects, and heavy papal taxes tempted them and the lesser clergy to undertake shady financial practices. Some held several offices at once, making it impossible for them to perform the duties of any. Absenteeism was common; many bishops and priests preferred life at Avignon or at a royal court to life in their episcopal sees or parishes. Absentee clergy often turned their religious duties over to poorly trained, poorly paid clerks who were incapable of guiding religious activities. Services, instruction, confessions, preaching, and counseling were slighted, leaving people with religious problems lost and unhappy.

Given these conditions, it was not difficult for many people in the fourteenth and fifteenth centuries to judge the Church as an institution harshly. In their minds it was too rich, too power-hungry, too bloated with self-serving officials. It had become an institution chiefly concerned with sustaining its power and wealth at the expense of a vast Christian community that was already troubled by a variety of economic, social, and political dislocations.

2. CHALLENGES TO TRADITIONAL RELIGION

Especially damaging to the Church's traditional leadership role was its inability to accommodate or control the frequent and extremely heterodox religious movements welling up in the tension-filled society of western Europe during the late Middle Ages. Chiefly as a result of the intense effort to impose uniformity on religion during the High Middle Ages, after 1300 Roman Catholic belief and religious practices fell into a rather unbending, formal pattern that became ever more mechanical; most ecclesiastical leaders were content to equate piety with going through the motions of attending services, receiving the sacraments, and obeying the clergy.

Dissatisfaction with this situation was demonstrated in many ways. One of the most important was an increase in the number of mystics, that is, persons who believed they could experience and know God directly through intuitive powers. Mysticism was present throughout the Middle Ages; St. Bernard and St. Francis of Assisi were mystics. But the fourteenth and fifteenth centuries produced an especially large number of people who sought ways to catch their personal vision of God. Many of the most influential were simple men and women who never wore clerical garb, like Joan of Arc. None was more prominent than Catherine of Siena (1347–1380). On the basis of visions of Christ she claimed to have experienced, as well as through her efforts to help the poor, the sick, the criminals, and the downtrodden, she earned a reputation as a saint. Although she, as well as many like her, was never seriously at odds with the Church, Catherine practiced a kind of Christianity unfamiliar to contemporary officials of the cult.

The activities of the mystics led to the development of communal movements that operated almost independently of the Church. A prime example was the Brethren of the Common Life (and its female counterpart, the Sisters of the Common Life), founded by a lay preacher named Gerard Groote (1340–1384), who was one of the many spiritual heirs of the great German mystic Meister Eckhart (1260–1327). This loosely knit movement was a product of a new kind of piety, called the *devotio moderna*, which stressed prayer, love, and direct communion with God. Devotees of the new piety joined together as brothers and sisters in communities where they shared their worldly goods, joined in common worship, confessed their sins to each other, devoted themselves to works of charity, sought to educate members of the community, and even produced their own devotional literature. One of the best examples of their literature, still read today as a spiritual guide, is Thomas à Kempis' *Imitation of Christ*. The many communities of brethren seldom strayed into heresy, but their piety, their puritanical life, and their mysticism set them apart. Not surprisingly, the brethren were often attacked for spreading dangerous ideas; perhaps there was some substance to this charge in view of the fact that such important later reformers as Erasmus and Martin Luther were educated in their schools. Akin to the brethren were the Beguines, associations of laywomen who led a common life, committed themselves to chastity and good works, and supported themselves by working or begging. Similar communities of men, called Beghards, were also established. More radical were the Brethren of the Free Spirit, who among other things denied the existence of sin on the basis of their belief that God existed in all things, an idea that resulted in their condemnation.

The fourteenth and fifteenth centuries produced a hardier crowd of radicals—usually condemned as heretics—who voiced ideas that provoked many to violent actions against the Church. Some were intellectual figures, such as Marsiglio of Padua, whose devastating book, *The Defender of the Peace*, appeared in 1324. Its thesis was that the Church was obligated to fulfill certain spiritual duties but was not entitled to any secular powers. Marsiglio advocated that it be deprived of its wealth and made a branch of government, subservient to the ruler. He argued that the Church as a community of all Christians should be ruled by a council representing all elements in Christian society, not by a clerical hierarchy headed by the pope. He denied that the papal office had divine sanction; the pope was simply an ecclesiastical administrator whose powers were defined by the Christian community and who could be limited any way that community wished.

Somewhat later, John Wycliffe (1320–1384) delivered even heavier attacks on the Church. This Oxford scholar and teacher entered the ranks of rebellion late in life, apparently moved by a growing tide of anticlericalism and antipapalism emerging in an England troubled by the Hundred Years' War and internal stresses. In his first attacks on the Church he argued that the Church had abused its right to hold property and that all church property should be confiscated by the state. Later he advocated the destruction of the whole clerical hierarchy on the ground that salvation depended not on the clergy but on the power of God; every person was his or her own priest. Here, of course, he was striking at a key idea on which the medieval Church based its institutional position: the idea that salvation depended on the ministry of a clergy set apart from and above the laity by the sacrament of ordination. Wycliffe also attacked many of the religious practices of the Church—elaborate rituals, prayers to saints, veneration of relics, pilgrimages, and the like. He even questioned the validity of the sacraments as necessary to salvation. He argued that Scripture alone must be the authority for Christian doctrine and translated the Bible into English so that all could read it.

Although Wycliffe was soon condemned as a heretic and forced to leave Oxford, his teachings attracted many followers, known as the Lollards, and for many years Lollard preachers and writers agitated for their master's ideas in England. In time, however, they came to challenge all authority, and the English kings of the fifteenth century joined the clergy in destroying the movement.

Wycliffe's ideas had their most significant effect not in England but in Bohemia (modern Czechoslovakia). The leading disciple there was John Huss (ca. 1373–1415), a priest who taught at the University of Prague. When his preaching of Wycliffe's precepts raised a protest from the clergy and ruling faction, most of whom were German and were passionately hated by the native population, Huss became a national hero of the Bohemians. Like Wycliffe, he too was excommunicated. Eventually, Huss sought and received permission to appear before the Council of Constance to defend his teaching. The Holy Roman emperor promised him safe conduct for his appearance. Once in Constance, however, Huss was imprisoned, tried, and executed as a heretic in 1415. A rebellion broke out immediately in Bohemia and raged until 1436. Crusade after crusade was preached by the papacy against the Hussites; several German armies, led by an emperor who was anxious to reclaim Bohemia, were soundly thrashed by the aroused Bohemians. Eventually peace was restored when certain religious concessions were granted to the Hussites. However, a faction of the followers of Huss and Wycliffe, called Taborites, was not satisfied by these concessions and became practically a church apart in the last years of the Middle Ages.

Manifestations of religious ferment and frustration took many other forms during the four-teenth and fifteenth centuries. Any number of fiery preachers proclaimed the end of the world and the coming of God's wrathful final judgment. Wildly emotional cults, such as the Flagellants, who whipped one another to atone for the world's sins, preyed on people's religious sensibilities, especially in times of great crisis such as the Black Death. Brutal massacres of the Jews in the name of Christian righteousness marred the histories of many cities. A fear of witches flourished on an unprecedented scale, accompanied by numerous trials of those suspected of witchcraft. Increasingly people sought assurances of salvation by purchasing indulgences, which they believed would ensure that the punishment due for sins would be removed. Never were relics more appealing and more brazenly manipulated, as illustrated by Chaucer's pardoner with his bag full of "pigs' bones." Literature, art, and sermons were preoccupied with death in particularly horrible forms. All of these unusual forms of religious expression reflected a psychology of fear and uncertainty, sometimes reaching the proportions of mass hysteria.

Clearly, religious ferment in Europe was powerful and widespread. Neither the gentle mystics nor the fiery-tongued rebels, neither the adherents of the occult nor the victims of hysteria were at home in the Roman Catholic church. People were striking out in all directions, questioning ritual, organization, and dogma. But the institution that claimed to care for the souls of the disturbed and the dissatisfied either ignored the quest for religious satisfaction or ruthlessly crushed the discontent. The Church was failing its central mission: to meet the basic religious needs of its vast flock. More importantly, it seemed unable to discover ways of restoring its power to cure souls.

3. THE FAILURE OF INTELLECTUAL LEADERSHIP

The Church suffered another serious blow as a consequence of fundamental shifts in the intellectual development of the late Middle Ages. This transformation was not dramatic, but it undermined the Church's control over a supportive intellectual establishment and generated new criticism of the world view upon which the Church's authority was founded. Outwardly, the life of learning continued down familiar paths. The universities remained the focal points of scholarship and teaching in the liberal arts, theology, law, medicine, and science and provided the major attraction to most intellectuals. The Scholastic method, although increasingly pedantic and trivial in its approach and its accomplishments, reigned supreme. But the emphasis in intellectual endeavor underwent a subtle change. The majestic Scholastic synthesis of the thirteenth century, exemplified by the works of Thomas Aquinas, failed to hold its sway over theological and philosophical deliberations. It left so many questions unanswered that many thinkers not only despaired of the dream of reconciling revelation and reason into one consistent, complete order of truth but also began to attack the basic proposition that faith and reason were compatible. Synthesis gave way to analysis. As we have seen, even while the Thomistic synthesis was being hammered out, some people refused to accept it; the resistance intensified after 1300.

Shortly after Thomas Aquinas' death in 1274, the attack on his position quickened and took forms that raised fundamental philosophical questions. The Franciscan scholar John Duns Scotus (ca. 1266–1308) argued with great force that God's freedom and power were so exalted that all attempts to describe his attributes rationally imposed untenable limits on divine power. In effect, Duns Scotus was saying that theology was not a proper matter for rational speculation. This trend of thought was expanded by William of Ockham (ca. 1300–1349), an English Franciscan who taught at Oxford and served in the court of Emperor Louis IV of Bavaria until the Black Death claimed his life. A powerful logician, Ockham assailed the basic rational supports of Thomistic theology. In his mind knowledge of such things as the existence of God and the immortality of the soul came only by intuition and mystical experience. Theology and philosophy thus became separate "sciences," incapable of reconciliation. In defining the realm of reason, Ockham argued that only by sense perception of individual objects could humans know; in this respect he was a philosophical *nominalist,* repudiating the long tradition that

ideas constituted the ultimate reality (philosophical *realism*). Duns Scotus and William of Ockham gained powerful disciples who followed up the assault on Thomism. The crescendo of attacks shattered the thirteenth-century confidence in one all-embracing truth and with it a powerful prop of the Church.

The disarray among the Scholastics encouraged thinkers to take new intellectual paths. Since reason was distinct from faith, political theorists like Marsiglio of Padua constructed new concepts of the governance of church and state that were especially destructive to theologically based justifications of the Church's power over the social order. The attack on rational theology nourished mysticism and opened the way for the radical theological concepts of Wycliffe and Huss. Many intellectuals, disillusioned by the barren exercises of late medieval Scholasticism, found intellectual sustenance in classical literature and philosophy, drawing from these sources a secular, humanistic world view and value system. Most important for the future was the growing interest in science. Following Ockham's argument that rational inquiry must confine itself to tangible objects, scholars, especially at the universities of Paris and Oxford, produced a considerable body of scientific knowledge and provided significant corrections to Greco-Arabic scientific generalizations. Their efforts laid the groundwork for the revolutionary scientific discoveries of Copernicus, Galileo, and others in the sixteenth and seventeenth centuries. As intellectual life became more pluralistic and more oriented to worldly, secular concerns, the potential for criticism of the Church increased, and the Church's ability to control intellectual activity for its benefit decreased.

4. THE THREAT OF NEW FORCES

While the Church decayed from within and was unable to cope effectively with religious and intellectual movements diverging from traditional patterns, it had to contend with powerful forces outside the sphere of religion that challenged its leadership and depleted its following. Many of these forces portended a new era in western European history; they will receive fuller treatment later. Here, it is important that they be noted as threats to the Church's dominance.

The aggressive national states beginning to take shape in the fifteenth century represented one such force. Although still Catholic, ambitious rulers sought to limit and dominate the religious establishment in their realms. In England kings and Parliament joined in enacting laws to prevent the papacy from taxing church property and controlling ecclesiastical appointments. In France, the royal government worked steadily, often with the help of the French clergy, to establish a "Gallic" church, independent of the papacy and subservient to the crown. In Spain late in the fifteenth century the monarchs even undertook to reform the Church independently of the papacy. These cases were all clear indications that as 1500 approached, "national" churches were becoming a reality at the expense of the universal Church.

Equally threatening to the Church's position was the capitalistic ethos emerging in economic life, especially among urban patricians but also among members of the rural gentry and affluent peasants. Challenging the Church's ancient distrust of wealth and materialism, this new ethos viewed wealth and its acquisition as a positive force in society. Its adherents would have liked to see the Church's wealth put to new uses. Most of them paid little heed to religious arguments condemning the charging of interest, price manipu-

lation, and profit seeking. Implicit in the capitalist ethos was a mentality oriented toward competition, worldliness, individualism, pragmatism, and a work ethic—all values that did not fit easily into the Church's concept of how the drama of salvation should be played.

Finally, a new breed of thinkers, writers, and artists, sometimes collectively called *humanists,* was emerging to criticize many teachings and practices supported by the Church. The new humanism, developing first and most vigorously in Italy and then spreading to other parts of western Europe, found its intellectual sustenance and its aesthetic values in classical rather than medieval models. It posed a major challenge to the world view long promoted by the Church in the name of Christian truth.

The irresolvable internal difficulties and challenging outside forces that combined to undermine the authority of the Church in the late Middle Ages provided the surest indication that an epoch was ending. Admittedly the stresses and strains affecting political, economic, and social institutions all pointed toward the transformation of basic structures characteristic of medieval western European civilization. However, for centuries the religious establishment—the Church—had been the main force giving that civilization its unique features. The faltering of the Church truly heralded the end of an epoch in western European history.

SUGGESTED READING

Decline of the Church

Francis Oakley, *The Western Church in the Later Middle Ages* (1979).

Steven Ozment, *The Age of Reform (1250–1530). An Intellectual and Religious History of Late Medieval and Reformation Europe* (1980). Two excellent treatments of all aspects of religious history.

Yves Renouard, *The Avignon Papacy, 1305–1403,* trans. Denis Bethell (1970). A concise survey; good on the impact of this chapter in papal history.

Walter Ullmann, *The Origins of the Great Schism: A Study in Fourteenth Century Ecclesiastical History* (1948). A careful analysis of the factors that produced the Great Schism.

Daniel MacCarron, *The Great Schism: Antipopes Who Split the Church* (1982). Biographical sketches of the popes involved in the schism.

Brian Tierney, *Foundations of the Conciliar Theory; The Contributions of the Medieval Canonists from Gratian to the Great Schism* (1955). Stresses the legal basis for conciliar ideas.

Antony Black, *Council and Commune: The Conciliar Movement and the Fifteenth-Century Heritage* (1979). Discusses the political ideas of the conciliarists in the context of history and theology.

New Religious Movements

Rufus M. Jones, *The Flowering of Mysticism; The Friends of God in the Fourteenth Century* (1939).

James M. Clark, *The Great German Mystics: Eckhart, Tauler, and Suso* (1949).

Anne Bancroft, *The Luminous Vision: Six Medieval Mystics and Their Teachings* (1982).

Any of these three titles will help the reader to understand the nature and influence of late medieval mysticism.

Albert Hyma, *The Christian Renaissance: A History of the "Devotio Moderna,"* 2nd ed. (1965). A full treatment of a movement that deeply affected late medieval religious life.

Richard Kieckhefer, *Unquiet Souls: Fourteenth-Century Saints and Their Religious Milieu* (1984). Rich in insights into the nature and causes of religious "unquiet" in the fourteenth century.

Norman Cohn, *The Pursuit of the Millennium: Revolutionary Millenarians and Mystical Anarchists of the Middle Ages,* rev. ed. (1970). A brilliant description of aberrant religious movements in the later Middle Ages.

Malcolm Lambert, *Medieval Heresy: Popular Movements from Bogomil to Huss* (1977). An excellent synthesis.

Cultural History

Georges Duby, *Foundations of a New Humanism, 1280–1440,* trans. Peter Price (1966). A remarkable synthesis linking many aspects of late medieval cultural history.

Gordon Leff, *The Dissolution of the Medieval Outlook: An Essay on Intellectual and Spiritual Change in the Fourteenth Century* (1976). A perceptive but challenging interpretation of late medieval intellectual development.

RETROSPECT

By 1500 there were many signs that western European society was again on the threshold of a remarkable era of expansion, comparable in many ways to the great leap forward that occurred between 1000 and 1300. Yet it is understandable that most people living in 1500 were dimly, if at all, aware of the promise before them. Like men and women in most ages, they were better instructed by the immediate past and the present than by the unrealized future. Our treatment of the late Middle Ages has made it clear that both past and present were troubled, filled with tensions rooted in limitations inherent in the basic structure of medieval western European civilization. Given the magnitude of those troubles, it is not surprising that people's thoughts were filled with pessimism and anguish and that their reactions to life were marked by excess and violence.

In retrospect, the causes of the adversities of the late Middle Ages seem clear. The major institutions, thought patterns, and value systems shaped prior to 1300 as essential features of civilization had unstable features that began to emerge after 1300. The medieval ideal of a Christian commonwealth was flawed by fundamental disagreement about the leadership of that commonwealth and by deep-seated localism. Feudal monarchies were beset by conflicts between royal authority and private privilege. The universal Church, with its central leadership and uniform doctrine, law, and liturgy, could not contain the ferment that was seeking new ways of understanding and living Christian life. Localistic, monopolistic, self-sufficient economic structures contended with international, profit-seeking, individualistic enterprises. Faith and reason, Latin and vernacular cultures, religious and secular values vied for people's minds. The precarious balance among such conflicting elements, which had been shaped during the High Middle Ages, began to fall apart in the late Middle Ages. Thus the turmoil of that age.

Some aspects of the history of the late Middle Ages remind one of the events of the third and fourth centuries that resulted in the collapse of classical Greco-Roman civilization. But the situation was fundamentally different; a catastrophic collapse of an established civilization was not at hand. It was not the exhaustion of a total civilization that caused the troubles of the fourteenth and fifteenth centuries. Rather, those troubles stemmed from the clash of contradictory elements folded into the medieval synthesis. Once the collective decision was made to opt for one way or the other between the alternatives posited by the medieval synthesis, new energies were released. By 1500, choices began to be made in favor of strong central government, national states, rationalism, religious diversity, a pluralistic culture, and a capitalistic economy as the essential components of European life. All these were medieval in origin, just as were their opposites. Postmedieval Europe was thus shaped by choices made from the rich, varied institutional and ideological creations of medieval people. "Modern" Europe originated in the Middle Ages. Its history is unexplainable and unintelligible without a knowledge of medieval history.

PART SEVEN

The Beginning of Early Modern Times: Fifteenth and Sixteenth Centuries

In the previous section, we observed the various tensions and weakening institutions that marked the decline of the medieval world during the fourteenth and fifteenth centuries; now we shall see how the institutions we have come to call early modern grew out of the decaying medieval system.

The earliest changes occurred in the urban societies of northern Italy. There, during the fourteenth and fifteenth centuries, the culture of the Renaissance was born. Strongly rooted in classical Greek and Roman civilizations, this self-conscious culture developed thought, values, and institutions that would characterize early modern times. During the later fifteenth and the sixteenth centuries, the Renaissance spread north of the Alps, where scholars, writers, and artists adapted it to their own needs and concerns.

In place of the declining feudal monarchies and empires, powerful monarchs created the national or territorial state, which became the dominant political institution of the early modern era. The first of these national states to emerge were Spain, France, and England. From then until now, the history of the Western world has revolved around them and the other national states that were patterned after them.

The overseas expansion of Europe reflected the political vitality of the age. National states supported voyages of discovery and the establishment of empires around the globe. This expansion took advantage of and stimulated new economic development. Europe's medieval economy, characterized by subsistence agriculture, monopolistic guilds, and localism, slowly gave way to capitalistic practices and institutions. The old landed aristocracy that had dominated the medieval economy now found itself challenged and threatened by new intruders into its class and by a new middle class of aggressive merchants and entrepreneurs.

The decline of the Western Christian Church in the last two centuries of the Middle Ages culminated in the Reformation. During the first half of the sixteenth century, the Western Church itself split, and much of northern Europe became Protestant. This split, in turn, hastened reform within the Roman Catholic church. In this deeply religious age, however, such a momentous disintegration of religious unity created turmoil and violence. For almost a hundred years religious and political conflict became intertwined in the bloody Wars of Religion.

Since these five great movements—the Renaissance, the rise of national states, the expansion of Europe, the rise of commercial capitalism, and the Reformation (Protestant and Roman Catholic) occurred primarily during the fifteenth and sixteenth centuries, it may be useful to conceive of the fifteenth as a century of transition and the sixteenth as the first century of the early modern era.

CHAPTER 26
The Renaissance: Italy

FIGURE 26.1 **Leonardo da Vinci, "The Virgin of the Rocks," ca. 1485** With Leonardo da Vinci (1452–1519), Renaissance painting, with its emphasis on humanism, reached its peak. In this painting, the Virgin is a beautiful woman, and the Christ child is a playful, cuddly little boy. The rock formation is authentic, and the plants are identifiable specimens. (Archives Photographiques, Paris)

While most of European society during the fourteenth century was still medieval, Italian society was already changing, developing some of the characteristics that would become common during the early modern period. Most important, Italian society produced a new culture with roots in both medieval Christian civilization and classical Greek and Roman civilizations. This culture, called the Renaissance, would continue to grow in Italy during the fifteenth century and then spread throughout Europe. The Renaissance became a basis upon which thought, literature, and art during the early modern period rested.

1. ITALIAN ORIGINS

Although historians have debated the causes for the rise of the Renaissance in Italy, they usually point to a few factors that distinguish Italy, and particularly northern Italy where the Renaissance was centered, from the rest of Europe.

Above all, northern Italy was unusually urbanized—there were more and larger cities than in most other areas of Europe. The first and most important Renaissance city was Florence, but other cities such as Venice, Pisa, and Milan became centers of the Italian Renaissance. By the fourteenth century these cities had gained economic prosperity from long-distance trade, commerce, industry, and banking.

These cities marshalled their economic strength to expand and gain power over surrounding lands once controlled by the landed aristocracy. They also took advantage of the exhausting struggles between the Holy Roman emperor and the papacy, two powers that might have been strong enough to hinder the growing political independence of the cities. Political life within the cities became dynamic, often chaotic, but most of the time controlled by the new commercial elite.

The society of these large, commercial cities became more fluid as position began to be determined more by wealth than by blood. Medieval aristocratic strictures were weakened. The elite of the cities, continually infused with new members of the wealthy bourgeoisie and outside talent attracted to the vibrant cities, participated in commercial and industrial exploits—activities usually rejected as inappropriate to the aristocracy elsewhere in Europe. This elite included a large number of relatively young people, more aggressive and individualistic than traditional groups elsewhere.

This urban elite needed to be literate and well educated in practical matters. Schools arose to serve them and taught a curriculum appropriate for their practical interests. The elite also had great wealth to spend, and they turned to culture in general and art in particular. They may have wanted art as an investment, as a means for promoting their own political and social ambitions, or as a matter of civic pride. In any case they became patrons of the arts. Now art was being produced not only for clerical and traditional aristocratic patrons but also for rich, middle-class, and urbanized aristocratic patrons who had different outlooks.

As the demand for art grew, so did the prestige of the artist. In medieval society artists were little more than low-paid artisans. In Renaissance society they became well-paid professionals and part of a respected intellectual elite that included writers and philosophers.

Finally, the physical and human environment of the Italian cities included advantages not present elsewhere in Europe. The remains and traditions of Greco-Roman civilization were still evident in Italy and its cities. Moreover, these cities, thanks to their proximity to the East and their commercial and political ties to Byzantine lands, often came into contact with the sophisticated Byzantine culture.

Thus the thriving Italian urban society—with its commercial wealth, its political independence, its social fluidity, its schools, its artists, its intellectual elite, and its cultural environment—was the fertile ground in which the Renaissance first grew.

2. GENERAL NATURE

The term *renaissance* means "rebirth." One of the central characteristics of the Renaissance was the self-conscious revival of classical civilization and the sense of creating something different from medieval civilization. Renaissance scholars rejoiced in discovering, mastering, and making available the cultural products of Greece and Rome. At the same time they criticized medieval Scholasticism and medieval culture in general. They envisioned themselves as being part of a new civilization based on a revival of classical civilization intertwined with the purest elements of Christian civilization.

The emphasis on reviving classical civilization reflected greater concern with secular life. The medieval focus on theology—concern with the spiritual world and formal religious doctrines—changed toward a focus on human beings, their nature and their actions. Medieval Christian theologians distrusted the flesh as an enemy of the spirit and human wisdom as unable to perceive divine truth by rational processes unless guided by Christian inspiration. Renaissance scholars and artists glorified the human form as beautiful and the human intellect as capable of discovering all truth worth knowing. They viewed human beings as three-dimensional, part of an immediate, concrete, recognizable physical environment.

However, care must be taken in characterizing Renaissance culture as secular. The Renaissance was not antireligious; there was no fundamental questioning of Christian beliefs in this still-religious age. Much of the secularism of the Renaissance was in a Christian and even a pious context. Part of the concern with reviving secular classical civilization stemmed from a desire to better understand early Christianity and Christian principles. Moreover, the secularism of the Italian Renaissance was not a sharp, sudden break with the immediate past. Secular interests had never completely died out, even at the peak of the Church's prestige in the Middle Ages. The twelfth century had already witnessed a revival of interest in classical civilization. It would be better to say that during the Italian Renaissance there was a significant intensification of the secular spirit in thought, literature, and art, all still within a fundamentally Christian environment.

Individualism was another important facet of the Renaissance spirit. In this respect, the difference between the medieval and the Renaissance spirit was primarily one of degree. Christianity did much to elevate the dignity of the individual soul and the individual personality. But the medieval clergy feared pride as a sin. They taught that the individual ego must be carefully held in check. Medieval monasticism attempted to suppress the individual ego and submerge it in the group. In practice, then, medieval Christianity tended to be collectivist. Church artists and writers usually did not sign their names to their work, which was supposed to contribute only to the greater glory of God. Renaissance individualism was prideful, even lusty. People of accomplishment were self-consciously confident, even boastful. They wanted the glory that their work would bring them. People such as Boccaccio (1313–1375), Alberti (1404–1472), Machiavelli (1469–1527), and Cellini (1500–1571) were proud of their identity and uniqueness.

Many of these great scholars and artists displayed another element of the Renaissance ideal—versatility. The educated person of the Middle Ages was usually a specialist—a theologian or church artist or administrator. But the most renowned Renaissance schoolteachers taught many subjects in addition to the traditional formal ones—dancing, fencing, poetry, and vernacular languages to mention a few. Many of the Renaissance schools broadened the old theology-oriented seven liberal arts and made much greater use of pagan classical literature and philosophy in the curriculum. One of the most popular books in Europe in the sixteenth century was Castiglione's *Book of the Courtier*. The ideal courtier, said Castiglione, is not only a gentleman and a scholar but also a man of action—a soldier and an athlete. Probably the best illustration of versatility in any age is Leonardo da Vinci (1452–1519). This revered Renaissance figure, one of the most celebrated painters of all time, was also an able sculptor, architect, mathematician, philosopher, inventor, botanist, anatomist, geologist, and engineer.

Finally, the Renaissance was urban and socially limited. While many products of the Renaissance were public and even unavoidable in Italian cities, only an elite participated in or directly supported the Renaissance. It scarcely touched most people in the cities and was unheard of in the countryside. Moreover, the Renaissance was of different significance for women than men, even among the elite. On the one hand, women often participated with men in the new urban schools and played a growing role within the household. Indeed, marriage patterns often resulted in widowed women retaining the family's wealth while not remarrying, giving them considerable economic freedom. On the other hand, women during the Renaissance were losing some of the status and public position they held during the Middle Ages. More than before, they were relegated to domestic life, where they played a supportive, decorous, and sexually inferior role to their husbands. This changing status was particularly evident within the rising middle class, but even noble women lost power and the independence they had enjoyed when medieval courtly manners and love held sway. Women were generally excluded from active, public participation in the culture and society of the Renaissance.

3. HUMANISM

During the fourteenth century, Italy witnessed the rise of humanism. Historians have debated the exact meaning of Italian humanism. Narrowly defined, it means classical scholarship—the study of original Latin or Greek manuscripts. Broadly defined, it means the recovery of classical manuscripts, educational reform to include greater emphasis on classical scholarship, rejection of medieval Scholasticism and professionalism, and optimistic emphasis on human beings—on their capabilities as powerful, rational Christian and secular beings on this earth. Understood in this broad sense, humanism encompasses in its literature, its educational reforms, and its philosophy the main characteristics of the Italian Renaissance.

Literature

The characteristics of Renaissance humanism are richly illustrated by the Italian literature of the fourteenth century. The best of that literature was produced by the Tuscan Triumvirate—so called because it consisted of three men who lived in Florence in the old Etruscan province of Tuscany. The first was Dante Alighieri (1265–1321). In an earlier section (see Chapter 23) we discussed Dante as the greatest of the late medieval writers.

His masterpiece, the *Divine Comedy*, is so full of medieval Christian lore and theology that it has been called a *Summa Theologiae* in poetry. Nevertheless, there is so much of the humanistic spirit in the *Divine Comedy* and in Dante's other writings that he belongs also to the Renaissance. In the "Inferno" of the *Divine Comedy*, Dante paints vivid, sensuous word pictures that seem to characterize this world rather than the next. The blazing fires and sulfurous fumes of hell, the cries of lament and curses of the damned come alive in our imagination. Furthermore, the author venerates such pagan classical writers as Vergil and Cicero to a much greater degree than had the medievalists (although a number of medieval writers had tried to make Vergil a Christian).

Dante's other major writings are even more humanistic. His love lyrics, written in his native Tuscan vernacular and addressed to Beatrice, are among the most beautiful in any language. In fact, Dante's writings greatly enriched the Florentine dialect and raised it eventually to the status of the national language of Italy.

Dante was also versatile; he was a man of public affairs as well as of letters. An active participant in the turbulent politics of Renaissance Italy, he was exiled from his native Florence when his faction lost. Dante even went so far as to fill hell in the *Divine Comedy* with his political enemies.

Petrarch (1304–1374), the second of the Tuscan Triumvirate, is often considered the father of Italian humanism. In his writing and his life he rejected medieval Scholasticism and culture as inferior to classical culture. He argued for the recovery of classical manuscripts, the mastering of Latin, and educational reform. He is best known for his superbly crafted letters to great figures of the past, such as Cicero, Vergil, Livy, and St. Augustine, and for his love sonnets in the Tuscan vernacular to Laura, a married woman whom he saw at mass and loved from afar.

Boccaccio (1313–1375) did for Italian prose what Dante and Petrarch did for Italian poetry. In his *Decameron*, a collection of one hundred tales or novelettes, Boccaccio exhibits little Christian restraint. He relates bawdy romances with skill and grace, condoning and even glorifying the seamy side of human nature.

Classical Manuscripts

The passionate quest for Latin and Greek literary manuscripts sometimes conflicted with the creation of original Italian literature by siphoning off the interest and energy of the writers. This conflict is illustrated by Petrarch, who rather early in life ceased writing what he called his "worthless" lyrics in order to discover lost classical manuscripts and to copy their style. He did succeed in bringing to light many priceless classical literary gems, but his epic *Africa* (relating the exploits of Scipio Africanus), written in Latin after the style of Vergil's *Aeneid*, lacks spontaneity and is all but forgotten.

Petrarch interested Boccaccio in the recovery of Greek and Latin manuscripts, and the search soon spread. Popes, princes, rich merchants, and bankers subsidized the humanists. In the fifteenth century, Italy was busy with professional humanists hunting, copying, translating, and editing ancient manuscripts.

Educational Reform

Working with classical manuscripts was related to a broader educational reform encompassed in the humanist movement. Humanists such as Petrarch argued that medieval schooling was too narrow, that the goal of education should be to produce more rounded, eloquent, virtuous individuals who were able to pursue the good life. Classical literature became a larger part of an educational curriculum that increasingly stressed practical learning. Educational reformers such as Pietro Paolo Vergerio (1349–1420) and Vittorino da Feltre (1378–1446) modified the Scholastic tradition and infused the curriculum with physical exercises, music, philosophy, Latin, and Greek as well as classical literature.

Philosophy

The study of classical masterpieces led to a variety of philosophical inquiries. This phase of humanism had many facets, including a new stress on the rational capabilities of humans, the development of a critical attitude, and a change in the concept of politics.

In 1396 Manuel Chrysoloras, a Byzantine scholar from Constantinople, was invited to Florence. He and other Greek scholars stimulated the study of Greek manuscripts during the fifteenth century. This study led to a revival of interest in Platonism and the establishment of the Platonic Academy in Florence under Marsilio Ficino (1433–1499) and Pico della Mirandola (1463–1494). They believed that, properly understood, Platonic philosophy and Christianity were compatible. They argued that human beings had great freedom and abilities, above all an ability to use will and reason to strive for the good life.

Another element of the humanistic view of life was the development of an analytic attitude. When Lorenzo Valla (1407–1457) proved by linguistics that the Donation of Constantine was a forgery, the scholarly and secular-minded pope raised no objections, although this was one of the documents upon which the papacy had based its claims to temporal power in the West. In fact, Pope Nicholas V made Valla his secretary. By making this discovery, Valla established himself as the father of modern critical historical scholarship.

The Florentine Niccolò Machiavelli (1469–1527), in his celebrated *The Prince*, suggested that Christian morals have little to do with the actual practice of politics. To acquire and maintain political power, the prince (or ruler or governing officials) must be willing to use both amoral and ruthless means. Since politicians, like all human beings, are self-seeking animals, the prince should assume that all rival princes and even his own lieutenants are conspiring for his power. Therefore, the prince should be willing to set his own chief subjects against each other and maneuver them into impotence. A wise prince deceives and treacherously attacks his foreign rivals at the most favorable moment before they can do the same. While Machiavelli was trying to remedy the deplorable reality of a divided Italy overrun and pillaged by more powerful foreign enemies, he also reflected the reality of secular attitudes and politics in fifteenth- and sixteenth-century Italy. His was a political theory that separated politics from ethics, stressing how people behaved rather than how they ought to behave. Few books have had more influence on, or been more descriptive of, modern political thought and practice.

4. FINE ARTS

Several characteristics of the Italian Renaissance are vividly illustrated in the Italian fine arts of the fourteenth, fifteenth, and sixteenth centuries.

Painting

Medieval painting in Europe had been closely allied with the Church. Painters deliberately penalized human flesh in order that the spirit might shine forth unimpeded. The figures, nearly always saints, were stiff, haggard, flat, and elongated. The physical world too was blanked out with solid gold backgrounds. The styles were stereotyped.

In the early fourteenth century Giotto, a contemporary of Dante, began to break this medieval mold of artistic custom by humanizing his figures and painting functional landscape backgrounds. Although his magnificent frescoes in the church of St. Francis at Assisi depicting the life of St. Francis were still rather flat, with diffused lighting, this did not make them less decorative—an artistic principle known to ancient Egyptian artists. True, Giotto's subject matter was almost entirely religious, but his treatment of it was such that the humanistic spirit made definite advances at the expense of the medieval. In the early fifteenth century Masaccio greatly developed the trend begun by Giotto a century earlier. He increased the illusion of depth by introducing atmospheric perspective and by further developing linear perspective. He also introduced the principle of the known light source, which thereafter replaced diffused light in painting. His nude human forms were further rounded and humanized (see Figure 26.2). His landscape backgrounds were realistic and detailed. With Masaccio and later painters such as Bellini (see Color Plate 12) and Botticelli (see Figure 26.3), the transition from medieval to Renaissance painting was completed and the stage set for such towering geniuses of the

FIGURE 26.2 Masaccio, "Expulsion of Adam and Eve" Masaccio, early in the fifteenth century, developed still further the trend toward humanism and naturalism begun a century earlier by Giotto. His "Expulsion of Adam and Eve from the Garden of Eden" depicts a religious subject in a human, realistic, and detailed manner. The nude figures are rounded and individualized. (Alinari/Scala Art Resource)

FIGURE 26.3 Botticelli, "Adoration of the Magi," ca. 1477 The theme of this painting is religious, with the Christ child in the center. However, the human figures are depicted with individualism, and the models (Lorenzo de Medici kneeling next to the Christ child; the artist, Botticelli standing proudly to the far left) are secular and contemporary. (Uffizi/Art Resource)

Italian High Renaissance as Leonardo da Vinci, Michelangelo, Raphael, and Titian.

It would be difficult to find a more representative figure of the Italian Renaissance than Leonardo da Vinci (1452–1519). All the colorful facets of the Renaissance spirit are richly illustrated by the career and work of this versatile genius. Leonardo was an illegitimate child, as were a number of the famous figures of the Renaissance. He was born near Florence and began his career there, but some of his most productive years were spent in the employ of the duke of Milan. He finally followed King Francis I to France, where he died. Like most Renaissance artists, Leonardo dealt primarily with religious subject matter; but, also like the others, his treatment of it was more secular and human. In his *Virgin of the Rocks* (see Figure 26.1), for instance, Leonardo creates with exquisite grace and beauty the Virgin Mary and the Christ child. The Virgin, however, is the loveliest of women, and the Christ child is a plump and playful baby boy. The characters are human, not divine. The background is a strange rock formation, naturalistic enough to reveal a keen interest in this material earth and yet arrestingly abnormal. The plant forms in the background are actually identifiable. Leonardo's *Last Supper* depicts the reactions of the twelve disciples to Christ's words, "One of you shall betray Me." This celebrated fresco, exhibiting the artist's complete mastery of technique and draftsmanship, is essentially a study in human psychology—a subject in which Leonardo showed a special interest. The famous *Mona Lisa* is not religious in subject matter; it is the portrait of a real woman. The mysterious half smile—the mouth smiles but the eyes do not—so captivates the viewer that one is likely to overlook other features of the picture, including the hands, which are said to be the most sensitive ever painted.

Michelangelo (1475–1564) is second only to Leonardo da Vinci as a versatile Italian High Renaissance genius. Since Michelangelo was primarily a sculptor, his painting is sometimes called "painted sculpture." Although a Florentine, much of his life was spent in Rome, where he labored in the service of the popes. His greatest painting was the ceiling fresco in the Vatican Sistine Chapel. The hundreds of individual figures, representing nine scenes from the book of Genesis, marvelously blend together into one harmonious whole. Later Michelangelo painted the *Last Judgment* as an altarpiece for the same chapel. The Christ in this picture is more like a pagan giant than the Jesus of medieval Christianity.

Some critics believe Raphael (1483–1520) to be the greatest painter of all time; others say that he merely synthesized the original work of others. The output during his brief life was enormous. His favorite subjects were religious, but his Madonnas were feminine, gracious women and his Christ child pudgy and mischievous. His best-known paintings, the *Sistine Madonna* and the *Madonna of the Chair*, both in oil, well illustrate this secular treatment of a sacred theme. Many of his vivid portraits are of lay princes and tycoons (see Color Plate 13). His monumental fresco *The School of Athens* reveals the veneration felt for the glory of Greece during the Renaissance.

The fourth of the great painters of the Italian High Renaissance was Titian (1477–1576). A citizen of Venice, the most powerful commercial city of the fifteenth and early sixteenth centuries, Titian reflected the humanistic spirit of the Renaissance to an even greater degree than his three renowned contemporaries. Although a considerable portion of his painting was of religious subjects, his focus was nearly always the pomp and pageantry of the Church rather than its teachings. But a large part of his subject matter was more secular. The wealth and brilliance of Venice, overflowing with cargoes of luxurious fabrics, tapestries, and gems from the East, provided a challenging array of sensuous and colorful material for the artist to depict. And in the use of color, particularly vivid yellows, reds, and blues, Titian had no peer. He painted the hair of his women a reddish-gold hue that has come to be called titian. His portraits of some of the great lay personages of the sixteenth century, such as Francis I of France, Emperor Charles V, and Philip II of Spain, are masterful character studies. With Titian, the break with medieval painting begun by Giotto and Masaccio and widened by Leonardo, Michelangelo, Raphael, and many other great Italian painters was completed.

Sculpture

In sculpture, the artist without peer in any age is Michelangelo. It is true that he had Roman copies of the sculpture of Hellenic Greek masters such as Praxiteles and Scopas to guide and inspire him. But the gifted Florentine was no mere copier. The Greek masterpieces, for all their beauty and grace, were idealized types—half human, half divine. Michelangelo and his lesser-known immediate predecessors and contemporaries added a typically Renaissance characteristic to sculpture: individuality. The statues of the Italian Renaissance are not only human beings but also human individuals. Even Michelangelo's *Pietà*, which represents the mother of Jesus holding the dead body of her son as she looks down piteously, is a study in human emotions. The helplessness and hopelessness of the huge, all-engulfing mother displays the human resignation at the finality of death—not the Christian hope of resurrection and eternal life. His *Moses* portrays the fierce and rugged strength of man, not God. Moses' beard, as crude as icicles beneath a water tank in the month of January, displays the sculptor's ability to distort deliberately for effect. The three-dimensional medium of marble enabled Michelangelo to exploit to the full his favorite subject, the masculine nude. Numerous statues of David are used to convey not only the virile muscular power but also the agile grace of the male animal. His *Dying Slave* (see Figure 26.4) is a sublime portrayal of both the human form and the human spirit struggling to free themselves from bondage. Some critics think that the great sculptor's finest genius is displayed in the companion statues of two members of the Medici family—Lorenzo, the contemplative type, and Giuliano, the man of action. In these two pieces the master craftsman and artist exhibits every technique of sculpture. The work of Michelangelo is probably our best example of the Renaissance glorification of the human being.

The subject of Renaissance sculpture cannot be dismissed without brief mention of the work of Benvenuto Cellini. His work in gold and silver was of an exquisite delicacy that has never been equaled. His most famous larger work is the bronze statue of Perseus holding up the Gorgon's head. In this amazing conglomeration of unrealities, Cellini showed complete disregard of all accepted traditions and standards, yet with happy results. Such bold and original pioneering was typical of the self-confident, secular nature of the Renaissance mind.

Architecture

Renaissance architecture, like Renaissance sculpture, drew heavily from Greek and Roman sources (see Figure 26.5). From Greece by way of Rome came columns (now merely decorative) and horizontal lines; from Rome came the dome, the arches, and the massiveness that characterized Renaissance buildings. All of these features (except massiveness) represented a revolt against the Gothic architecture of the later Middle Ages, although the Gothic style had never gained much of a foothold in Italy.

FIGURE 26.4   Michelangelo, "The Dying Slave"
The genius of Michelangelo, master sculptor of the Renaissance, is exemplified in this work, "The Dying Slave," now in the Louvre, which glorifies both the human form and the human spirit. (Courtesy Michigan State University)

The two greatest monuments of Italian Renaissance architecture are the dome of the cathedral in Florence and St. Peter's Basilica in Rome. The Florentine cathedral is essentially Tuscan Gothic. Its ornate rectangular façade and bell tower reflect Byzantine and Islamic influences. But its most distinguishing feature is its gigantic octagonal dome, designed and constructed by Brunelleschi in the

FIGURE 26.5   Circle of Piero Della Francesca: An Ideal Town   This mid-fifteenth-century townscape painting expresses ideals of Italian Renaissance architecture: geometry, logic, individuality with order, lightness, and spaciousness. (Anderson/Art Reference Bureau)

early fifteenth century. This symbol of the grandeur of ancient Rome served as a model for such later great domes as St. Peter's in Rome, St. Paul's in London, and the Capitol building in Washington, D.C.

But the most grandiose achievement of Renaissance architecture is St. Peter's. This magnificent structure was to the Renaissance era what the Pyramids, the Parthenon, the Colosseum, and the Gothic cathedrals were to their respective epochs. It was built by the popes during the sixteenth and early seventeenth centuries at a cost that shook all western Europe religiously and politically. Its numerous architects drew primarily on classical Greek and Roman sources for their inspiration. Even seventeenth-century baroque features eventually entered into its design. Raphael served for a time as chief architect, and Michelangelo designed the dome. One has to step inside St. Peter's to appreciate the breathtaking grandeur of this awesome structure. Its lofty proportions and gigantic pillars, its brilliant paintings and sculptures, its gold, marble, and mosaic decorations all glorify the material things of this world as well as the spiritual aspects of this world and the next.

Music

Music was another field of art in which many original contributions were made during the Renaissance period, particularly the sixteenth century.

Although most of these developments occurred in northern Europe, especially the Netherlands, Italy was a scene of some importance. Instrumental music became popular, and great improvements were made in the instruments. The harpsichord and the violin family of instruments came into existence. Musical techniques such as major and minor modes, counterpoint (the blending of two contrasting melodies), and polyphony (the interweaving of several melodic lines) rapidly developed. The most illustrious musician of the sixteenth century was Palestrina, chief musician to the pope and probably the greatest master of polyphonic music of all time. Although most of the music of the Renaissance still centered about the Church, it was now more sensuous and versatile. Moreover, new secular forms appeared. The madrigal, popular throughout Europe in the late sixteenth century, was a musical rendition of stanzas of secular lyrical poetry. Renaissance musicians laid the foundations for modern classical music in all its major forms—concerto, symphony, sonata, oratorio, and opera.

5. DECLINE

During the sixteenth century, the Italian Renaissance lost some of its vigor and originality. Certainly this loss did not occur overnight. For decades, and even into the seventeenth century, Italy was recognized as a center of the fine arts and cultural sophistication. Italian art, heavily patronized by the Church, retained much of its momentum. However, the center of Renaissance activity was shifting from Italy to northern Europe, paralleling the shift of commerce from the Mediterranean to the Atlantic. When Venice, Florence, and Milan were the most prosperous commercial and banking centers in Europe, they were the most vigorous seats of Renaissance culture. With the shifting of the trade routes to the West, their cultural vigor declined.

Other sixteenth-century developments probably played roles in the decline of the Italian Renaissance. The invasions of Italy by the French, Spanish, and German armies and the general military and political instability of the sixteenth century seem to have contributed to the decline. The flowering of culture and relative political stability in other parts of Europe may have made Italy a less important or attractive cultural center. In any case, cultural momentum shifted northward as the Renaissance spread outside of Italy.

SUGGESTED READING

General

G. A. Brucker, *Renaissance Florence*, rev. ed. (1983). A useful book on Renaissance Florence.

J. Burckhardt, *The Civilization of the Renaissance in Italy* (1867, 1983). A classic that has influenced all subsequent studies of the subject.

J. R. Hale, *Renaissance Europe: The Individual and Society, 1480–1520* (1978). Strong on individualism.

L. Martines, *Power and Imagination: City-States in Renaissance Italy* (1980). A highly respected recent study.

J. H. Plumb, *The Italian Renaissance* (1965). A good, well-written survey.

Humanism

F. Chabod, *Machiavelli and the Renaissance* (1960). A solid analysis by a leading authority.

Paul O. Kristeller, *Renaissance Thought: The Classic, Scholastic, and Humanistic Strains* (1961). A highly respected study of Renaissance thought.

W. H. Woodward, *Vittorino da Feltre and Other Humanist Educators* (1964). A good study of Italian humanist education.

The Fine Arts

James Beck, *Italian Painting of the Renaissance* (1981). A good recent study.

Bernard Berenson, *The Italian Painters of the Renaissance* (1968). A classic.

Sources

B. Castiglione, *The Book of the Courtier* (1976). Contemporary textbook for gentlemanly behavior.

B. Cellini, *Autobiography* (1956). The artist's own account of an adventuresome life.

N. Machiavelli, *The Prince* (1961). A classic of political theory.

P. Taylor, *The Notebooks of Leonardo Da Vinci: A New Selection*. Well illustrated.

CHAPTER 27

The Renaissance: The North

FIGURE 27.1 Dürer, "The Four Horsemen of the Apocalypse," ca. 1497–1498 In this woodcut the great German artist Albrecht Dürer exhibits a skill in his engraving and woodcutting that matched the painting genius of his Italian contemporaries, Leonardo and Michelangelo. His painting of this apocalyptical scene reveals the piety, the mysticism, and the concern with death that were important elements of the northern Renaissance. (The Art Museum, Princeton University)

The northern Renaissance occurred later than the Italian Renaissance and was in large measure imported from Italy. Although northern scholars such as Chaucer visited Italy as early as the fourteenth century, it wasn't until the late fifteenth century, when journeys by scholars, students, and merchants to Italy were commonplace, that the Renaissance flowered in the North. The northern Renaissance also had its own roots and characteristics. It was located more in the courts and universities than in large commercial cities. Northern humanism was more intertwined with Christian pietism than in Italy. In a broad sense, the northern Renaissance sought to humanize Christianity, to reconcile the sacred and the secular.

1. NORTHERN HUMANISM

The trend toward humanism as a basic attitude toward life began in earnest in northern Europe in the late fifteenth century. One of the central figures of northern humanism was Johann Reuchlin (1455–1522), a German scholar. After a sojourn in Italy during which he became imbued with the ideas of the Italian humanists, Reuchlin undertook to introduce the new classical learning into Germany. Specifically, he sought to broaden and enrich the university curriculum by establishing the study of the "un-Christian" Hebrew and Greek languages and literature. The Church and university interests vested in the medieval order of things attempted to thwart him, invoking the Inquisition to try him on grounds of heresy. Reuchlin fought back courageously and enlisted a large and enthusiastic following. Eventually the pope condemned him to silence. However, the victory really lay with Reuchlin and his humanist supporters. During the first few decades of the sixteenth century the new humanistic curriculum became established in all the major universities of Germany.

Meanwhile, in England a group of Oxford professors was accomplishing with less opposition what Reuchlin had fought for in Germany. John Colet (1467–1519) was the most prominent member of this group. He, too, visited Renaissance Italy. In true northern humanistic fashion he gave a critical and rational slant to his preaching and teaching of the Scriptures at Oxford. Probably the greatest of Colet's contributions to the new learning was the founding of St. Paul's grammar school in London, with a largely classical curriculum. To guarantee its humanistic orientation, he chose as trustees a guild of London merchants. St. Paul's soon became a model for many other such schools throughout England.

The most famous of the early-sixteenth-century English humanists was Sir Thomas More (1478–1535), Lord Chancellor of the Realm. More's *Utopia*, like Plato's *Republic*, blueprinted an earthly, not a heavenly, paradise. In picturing his ideal commonwealth, More indicted the social, religious, and political events of his own time. Utopia was a society in which private property and profits were unknown. Much attention was given to public health and education. The economy was planned and cooperative. War was outlawed except in self-defense. Religious freedom was granted to all but atheists. Although More eventually was to accept death by beheading rather than to recognize Henry VIII as head of the English church in place of the pope, his ideal society was ethical and secular. Humans through their own wisdom would create their own perfect world here on earth.

Towering above all the other northern humanists was Desiderius Erasmus (1466–1536). Erasmus was born in Rotterdam in the Netherlands, the illegitimate son of a priest. Reared as an orphan, he was educated in a school run by the Brethren of the Common Life, a pietistic order of laymen that taught the Greek and Latin classics and emphasized simple inner piety rather than ritual and formal creed. (Martin Luther, the great contemporary and adversary of Erasmus, also attended a school of the Brethren of the Common Life.) At the age of twenty-one Erasmus entered an Augustinian monastery (again like Luther) and was eventually ordained. Instead of serving as a priest, however, he studied his beloved classics—a pursuit he was to continue at the Sorbonne and for the rest of his life.

Erasmus' vast erudition combined with his great personal charm made him a much sought-after man. His first book was *Adages*, a collection of wise sayings of the Greeks and Romans with his own comments. It was an immediate success, and other books soon followed. His greatest work was the *Praise of Folly*, in which he ridiculed with subtle humor and delightful satire the ignorance, superstition, credulity, and current practices of his day, particularly those connected with the Church. The folly that he praised was a very human lightheartedness, a sense of humor. Wherever Erasmus went—France, England, Italy, Switzerland, Germany, the Netherlands—he was received with admiration and awe. No other individual so advanced the cause of northern humanism by popularizing the study of the Greek and Latin classics.

In addition to popularizing the new humanistic learning north of the Alps, Erasmus is significant in history for at least two other reasons—his influence on religious and social reform, and his efforts to humanize and intellectualize Christianity. He was at his best when laughing to scorn the abuses and superstitious practices of the Roman Catholic church. The taking of money from the poor and ignorant masses by wealthy and corrupt clergy, veneration of relics, and unquestioning belief in the miraculous were in the eyes of Erasmus beneath the contempt of enlightened men and women. But he was clever enough to sheathe his barbs with humor, thus making them more subtle and effective. Erasmus, however, was no Protestant. When Martin Luther first began his attacks on the Roman Catholic church, Erasmus thought that he was merely seeking to correct glaring abuses and hailed him as a fellow spirit. But when Erasmus discovered that the German reformer was primarily interested in doctrinal reform and that the Protestants were as dogmatic as the Roman Catholics, Erasmus would have nothing more to do with him. Nevertheless, Erasmus' incessant attacks on the abuses in organized Christianity undoubtedly encouraged both Protestant and Roman Catholic reformers.

Erasmus made great efforts to humanize Christianity. Although he never did specifically say so, the implication running through his writings is that Jesus was also a human being—a person to emulate. Erasmus would bypass formal creed, dogma, ritual, organization, and seek the "historical" Christ. Erasmus attempted to steer Christi-anity into a practice of following the example of a humanized Christ, stressing love, piety, civic virtue, and the best of classical values.

2. LITERATURE

During the late fifteenth and early sixteenth centuries Renaissance literature in the North was closely connected to the spirit of northern humanism with its stress on combining classical scholarship and Christian concerns. Scholars and educators such as Ulrich von Hutten (1488–1523) in Germany, Jacques Lefèvre d'Etaples (1454–1536) in France, Francisco Jiménez de Cisneros (1436–1517) in Spain, and William Grocyn (ca.1446–1519) in England helped establish traditions of literary humanism in their countries. During the middle of the sixteenth century Renaissance literature in the North became more distinctly secular. The most important literary developments in the decades from the mid–sixteenth to the early seventeenth centuries were in England, France, and Spain.

The reign of Elizabeth I (1558–1603) was a period of great energy and optimism in England, and this was reflected in its literary outpourings. England became "a nest of singing birds" such as the world had never seen nor heard. Edmund Spenser's *Faerie Queen* (1590) glorified the versatile individual of the Italian humanists, particularly the ideal set forth by Castiglione in his *Book of the Courtier*. Christopher Marlowe (1564–1593) in his brief life wrote human-centered plays of such caliber that some critics think he would have achieved the stature of Shakespeare had he lived. His *Tamburlaine the Great* and *Edward II* treat the worldly drama of royal ambition. The central figure in *The Jew of Malta*, a forerunner of Shylock, is a product of the revived commercial capitalism. *Doctor Faustus* dramatizes the theme, later immortalized by Goethe, of the intellectual who in true Renaissance fashion sold his soul to the devil in return for earthly knowledge and pleasure.

Mightiest of all the writers of the English Renaissance was, of course, William Shakespeare (1564–1616). So little is known of Shakespeare's life that some still wonder whether he actually wrote all the poems and plays we attribute to him.

Although his lyrical poetry was beautiful, his most important work was in drama. Here he was heavily indebted to his contemporary, Christopher Marlowe, as well as to the ancient Greek and Roman dramatists. Marlowe developed the blank verse form, which Shakespeare perfected. In plays such as *Hamlet, Macbeth, Othello, King Lear, The Merchant of Venice, As You Like It, Henry IV, Romeo and Juliet*, and *Julius Caesar*, Shakespeare displayed a mastery of every known technique of the dramatic art.

More important for the student of history, he exemplified and dramatized the secular spirit of the Renaissance. The individual is Shakespeare's subject matter. Rugged, distinctive human personalities are the heroes and villains of his plays. No human emotion, aspiration, or psychological conflict escapes his eye. On the whole, Shakespeare, unlike the Greek dramatists, makes each person the master of his or her own fate. Admiration for Greece and Rome, a keen interest in newfound lands, the first stirrings of modern natural science, the commercial revolution and social problems arising from the emergence of the capitalistic middle class, the rise of national monarchy and a national patriotic spirit—all enter into the fabric of the plays.

The two chief figures in French Renaissance literature were François Rabelais (1494–1553) and Michel de Montaigne (1533–1592). Rabelais was a renegade priest, a bored physician, and a loving student of the classics. Although he stumbled quite by accident and late in life upon his gift for writing, he turned out to be one of the great creative geniuses in the history of literature. His masterpieces are *Pantagruel* and *Gargantua*. They are fantasies about two completely unrestrained giants who wallow and revel unashamedly in sensual pleasures. These works are an open assault on Christian moral standards and restraints. The wit is coarse and lewd and sympathetic toward the frailties of human nature. Rabelais' rich imagery, his marvelous gift of expression, and his graceful artistry combine to make him one of the founders of modern French prose.

Montaigne was a prodigy born of a wealthy family. Like Rabelais, he was an ardent lover of the classics. The result of his life of study and reflection was his *Essays*. Montaigne was a skeptic.

To arrive at reliable truth, he believed, one must rid oneself of all religious prejudice. He was a moral and spiritual relativist, rejecting all absolutes. Unlike his successors of the eighteenth-century Enlightenment, he distrusted the authority of human reason. Unable to replace the authority of Christian dogma with any other firm conviction, Montaigne was nearly always negative in his conclusions. But he immensely enjoyed this game of intellectual hide-and-seek. In fact, Montaigne believed that the chief purpose of life is pleasure—not the "eat, drink, and be merry" pleasure of Rabelais, but urbane, sophisticated, restrained, intellectual pleasure. The influence of Montaigne has been enormous—obviously on essayists from Bacon to Emerson and later, but also on the development of modern rationalism in general.

Standing out above all others in Spanish Renaissance literature are Miguel de Cervantes (1547–1616) and Lope de Vega (1562–1635). Cervantes was a contemporary of Shakespeare, the two dying within a few days of each other in 1616. Cervantes' early life, like Shakespeare's, is obscure. In time he became a soldier of fortune, fought heroically and was wounded in the great naval battle of Lepanto with the Turks, suffered a five-year imprisonment in Algeria, and finally served as a quartermaster for Spain's Invincible Armada. In poverty-stricken later life he settled down to write his famous novel *Don Quixote*. This masterpiece of Spanish literature relates with urbane grace and humor the adventures of a confused knight, who filled his noble head too full of the lore of chivalry, and of his groom, Sancho Panza. Sancho, a squat plebeian on a donkey, and Don Quixote, an emaciated knight on a tall, lean horse, go about Spain from one delightfully charming adventure to another. Cervantes' most immediate purpose was to satirize what was left of medieval chivalry. At a deeper level he probes the balance between the idealism of Don Quixote and the realism of Sancho Panza, revealing that there is some of each in all of us. Finally, since all types and classes of people throughout Spain are lucidly portrayed, *Don Quixote* is a valuable historical source for descriptions of life in sixteenth-century Spain.

Lope de Vega wrote a fabulous number of works in practically every known genre. His plays

FIGURE 27.2   The Gutenberg Bible
An illuminated page from the Gutenberg Bible, after a facsimile. This forty-two-line Bible, printed by Johannes Gutenberg in about 1456, is the earliest known book printed by movable type in the Western world. The craftsmanship exhibited by this illustration is remarkable. Gutenberg's invention launched a revolution in communications. (Rare Book Division, New York Public Library, Astor, Lennox and Tilden Foundations)

alone exceed in number those of any other writer, whether we accept the writer's own claim to at least eighteen hundred or recognize only the five-hundred-odd plays that can be accounted for to-day. The secular person, pictured in every conceivable dramatic situation, is the hero of the great Spanish playwright.

Thus the writers of the northern Renaissance had much in common. Their chief interests were contemporary human beings and the exciting, rapidly expanding material world around them. Their chief inspiration was the classical literature of Greece and Rome. They were on the whole nationalistic and wrote in the new national vernaculars.

3. PRINTING WITH MOVABLE TYPE

The spread of humanism and literature in general was stimulated by the invention of printing on paper with movable type. In ancient and medieval times manuscripts were written and copied in longhand on parchment or papyrus, a slow and costly process that greatly retarded the dissemination of knowledge. In the fourteenth century printing from carved wooden blocks came to western Europe from China by way of the Moslem world and Spain. This process too was tedious, costly, and limited. Also from China came paper, made of various fibers, silk, cotton, or flax. Paper was a great improvement over parchment or pa-

FIGURE 27.3 Matthias Grunewald, "The Crucifixion," ca. 1510–1515 This northern Renaissance painting from the "Isenheim Altarpiece" by the German artist Grunewald combines a deeply pious subject matter reminiscent of late Gothic traditions with Renaissance perspective and individualism. (Musée Unterlinden, Colmar)

pyrus for purposes of mass production. [Even the art of printing by movable type itself was a Chinese (Korean) invention, although this is not believed to have influenced its invention in the Western world.]

Johannes Gutenberg set up the first practical printing press using movable type in Europe at Mainz in western Germany. The Gutenberg forty-two-line Bible printed in about 1456 is the earliest known book to be printed by the new process (see Figure 27.2). The invention was an immediate success and spread quickly to all the other countries of western Europe. It is estimated that by the end of the fifteenth century more than twenty-five thousand separate editions and nearly 10 million individual books had been printed. Printing was now much cheaper, much quicker, and much more accurate. Its effects spread beyond greater access to religious and secular literature. The printing press encouraged a growth of literacy and made the spread of political and commercial documents easier.

4. ART, ARCHITECTURE, AND MUSIC

Northern Renaissance art was influenced by Italian art and shared many of its characteristics, but it had stronger roots in the Christian, pietistic culture of the late Middle Ages. Generally the subject matter of paintings was less secular than that of Italian Renaissance paintings. Northern artists tried to bring the concrete details of Christian life into immediate focus and with great emotional impact (see Figure 27.3).

The most noteworthy fifteenth- and sixteenth-century painters in the North were the Flemings (Belgians) and the Germans. The Van Eyck brothers, Hubert and Jan, lived in Ghent in the Flemish Netherlands in the fifteenth century. Like Masaccio, their Italian contemporary, they brought to near completion the transition from medieval to Renaissance painting (see Figure 27.4). Their greatest joint work is *Adoration of the Mystic Lamb*. Not the least of their contributions to painting was

FIGURE 27.4 Jan Van Eyck, "The Virgin and Chancellor Rolin"
The Van Eyck brothers, Hubert and Jan, of Ghent in the Netherlands, were fifteenth-century contemporaries of Masaccio. This painting illustrates the clear, naturalistic perspective, the precision of line and detail, and the religious theme that were characteristic of northern Renaissance painting. (Scala/Art Resource)

the development of oil as a medium. It was from them that Leonardo da Vinci learned to work in this medium, which he perfected in such masterworks as the *Mona Lisa* and the *Virgin of the Rocks*.

In sixteenth-century Germany, Albert Dürer of Nuremberg and Hans Holbein the Younger of Augsburg were the leading painters. Dürer was primarily a master craftsman of delicate and graceful line. Probably for this reason, his woodcuts and engravings are better than his paintings, and in these media he is without peer in any age (see Figure 27.1). Holbein was a skillful sketcher and woodcutter, but he made his greatest contributions in the field of portrait painting. He painted several portraits of Erasmus and illustrated Erasmus' *Praise of Folly* with pen-and-ink drawings. Many of his most productive years were spent in England in the employ of Henry VIII. Among his greatest portraits are those of Henry VIII (see Figure 28.1), Edward VI, Mary Tudor, and Sir Thomas More.

Renaissance architecture was less prominent in the North. The largest Renaissance structure outside Italy is the vast Escorial near Madrid, which Philip II of Spain built as a royal palace and mausoleum. Its rugged massiveness, rectangular shape, and horizontal lines typify the Renaissance style. Some of the best examples of northern Renaissance architecture are the Renaissance wing of the Louvre in Paris, which is the world's largest and probably greatest art gallery, and some of the largest chateaux along France's Loire River. This architecture was essentially derivative; the French Renaissance chateaux were really fortresses being played with.

The music capital of the Western world during the Renaissance period was the Netherlands. It was from the Flemings that the Italian Renaissance musicians, including Palestrina, derived much of their knowledge and inspiration (see p. 360).

5. SIGNIFICANCE OF THE RENAISSANCE IN HISTORY

In retrospect, then, it is apparent that the Renaissance was part of a transition from the Middle Ages to the early modern period. In some measure it was a rebirth of the classical civilizations of Greece and Rome, but it was not merely that. There was much in the Renaissance that was fresh and original, and there was a self-consciousness among Renaissance scholars, writers, and artists that they were part of something new. In some ways the Renaissance represented a new emphasis on secularism and a rejection of the scholastic Christian culture of the Middle Ages, particularly in Italy. Yet in other ways it remained fundamentally a Christian civilization and an era that, in our terms, was quite religious. Indeed, the depth of religious sentiment during the Renaissance, particularly in the North, is revealed by the Reformation.

The intellectual and cultural themes established during the Renaissance would continue to grow throughout the early modern period. As we shall see, their effects would be felt in the politics, the commerce, and the society of Europeans during the sixteenth, seventeenth, and eighteenth centuries.

SUGGESTED READING

General

J. Huizinga, *The Waning of the Middle Ages* (1954). A superb interpretation important for an understanding of the early northern Renaissance. (See also items at the end of Chapter 26.)

Northern Humanism

E. H. Harbison, *The Christian Scholar in the Age of the Reformation* (1956). By a leading scholar in the field.

J. Huizinga, *Erasmus and the Age of the Reformation* (1957). Probably the best single volume on Erasmus.

R. Marius, *Thomas More: A Biography* (1984). A recent study.

M. M. Philips, *Erasmus and the Northern Renaissance* (1965). A good general study.

England, France, and Germany

Fritz Caspari, *Humanism and the Social Order in Tudor England* (1968). Focuses on connections between humanism and sixteenth-century English society.

L. Febvre, *Life in Renaissance France* (1977). A highly respected account.

Werner L. Gundersheimer, ed., *French Humanism 1470–1600* (1969). A solid collection of essays.

J. H. Overfield, *Humanism and Scholasticism in Late Medieval Germany* (1984). Focuses on universities.

Lewis Spitz, *The Religious Renaissance of the German Humanists* (1963). Broad and well written.

Art and Printing

Elizabeth Eisenstein, *The Printing Press as an Agent of Change* (1978). A superb, exhaustive interpretive study.

W. Stechow, *Northern Renaissance Art: 1400–1600* (1966). A useful survey.

CHAPTER 28
The Rise of National States

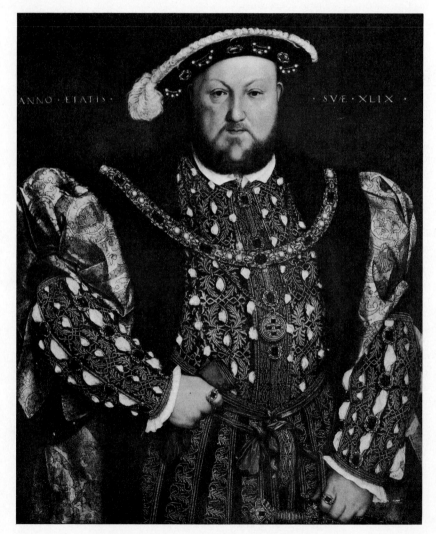

FIGURE 28.1 Hans Holbein the Younger, "Portrait of Henry VIII," 1540 Henry VIII and his father, Henry VII, were two of the most forceful of the new monarchs that arose in Europe between 1450 and 1550. These monarchs increased the power of the central government as well as their own personal power. (Alinari/Art Resource)

I n the fifteenth and sixteenth centuries, monarchs in western Europe succeeded in creating powerful national states. These monarchs, often referred to by historians as the "new monarchs," aggressively built their dynastic power in three main ways. First, they undermined their competitors, above all the feudal barons. Monarchs turned to members of the lesser nobility and the middle class for backing. Second, they developed new methods of financial and administrative support. National taxes gave monarchs new, independent sources of income, and expanding governmental bureaucracies staffed by officials who owed allegiance to the monarchs extended royal authority throughout the land. Third, they brought the Church more under their command. In some cases they gained the right to appoint church officers within their lands; in other cases they actually established new official churches.

The new monarchs used other methods as well and took advantage of developments occurring at that time. Applying principles of dynastic succession, they married to expand and unify their lands. They increased their income by promoting and tapping into reviving commerce, which brought with it a moneyed economy and a prosperous middle class. With their greater financial resources, new monarchs established standing professional armies that could use the new military tactics and technology that were lessening the importance of the independent mounted armored knight. They suppressed internal violence and made law enforcement more the responsibility of their own agents. To legalize their growing power, the monarchs utilized the principles of Roman law, which considered kings to be sovereigns in whose hands the welfare of all the people was placed.

The most important of these new monarchs arose in Spain, France, and England. Although other factors retarded unification in Italy and Germany until the nineteenth century, Spain, France, and England were already well on their way to becoming powerful national states in the late fifteenth century.

---

[1]Isabella ruled Castile from 1474 to 1504, and Ferdinand ruled Aragon from 1479 to 1516.

1. SPAIN

Spain became the most powerful and influential of the new states at the opening of the early modern era. The energy and enthusiasm that Spain displayed at this time may be attributed in part, at least, to her long and finally successful struggle against the Moors. By the middle of the thirteenth century the Moors had been driven out of the entire Iberian peninsula except for the southernmost province of Granada. Furthermore, the numerous medieval feudal holdings in what is now Spain had been consolidated into four large kingdoms—Castile, Aragon, Granada, and Navarre (south of the Pyrenees). The marriage of Ferdinand of Aragon and Isabella of Castile in 1469 united to some extent the two largest kingdoms. During their reign (1474–1516)[1] Granada and Navarre were conquered and ties between their lands were strengthened. Thus, within a forty-seven-year span from 1469 to 1516 the Spanish national state was created.

Ferdinand and Isabella strove for political and religious unity. In order to suppress further the jealous nobility, they allied themselves with *hidalgos*—members of the lesser nobility—and the middle class, leaning heavily on them for financial and administrative assistance. In return, the joint sovereigns did everything in their power to advance their fortunes. Vigorous enforcement of law and order, stabilization of the currency, building of roads and bridges, tariff protection of home industries—all served to advance the economic prosperity of Spain in general and the middle class in particular. This commercial expansion was greatly enhanced in 1492 with the discovery of the New World in the name of Spain. The ensuing profits and loot further strengthened the hands of the Spanish sovereigns by freeing them from dependence on the Cortes (the representative bodies dominated by the nobility) for funds.

In religious affairs, also, Ferdinand and Isabella gained power over the Church and unified their country. They acquired the right to appoint bishops, reformed the Church, and gained access to some of its wealth. By the end of their reign, the Church in Spain was in effect at the command of the Spanish state. Against the two non-Christian groups in their realm, the Jews and the Moslems, the "Catholic Sovereigns" waged a campaign of conversion or expulsion. The Jews had long been the object of hatred and persecution in Christian Europe. In part this hatred derived from religious differences, but there was also an economic factor. Church laws against usury had given the Jews a monopoly on money lending, a precarious but often profitable activity. The envy and hatred of the Christians led to periodic outbreaks of violence. In the late fourteenth century, an outbreak of unusual severity forced many Spanish Jews to seek safety in outward conversion. But these Marranos, as the pseudoconverts were called, were the object of increasing suspicion. Finally, Ferdinand and Isabella, despite some reluctance, introduced the Inquisition into Spain. At the mercy of this court, the Marranos were terrorized by imprisonment, torture, and loss of life and property. In 1492 the remaining Jews were ordered to leave the country. The exiles thus banished (estimated to be in the neighborhood of one hundred fifty thousand) took much of their wealth and all their economic energy and skills with them.[2]

Shortly afterward the Moslems suffered a similar fate. Upon surrendering their last stronghold in Granada, in 1492, they had been promised religious freedom in return for submission to the political authority of the Spanish crown. However, again the "Catholic Sovereigns" yielded to the increasing pressure of religious intolerance, and in 1502 the Moslems were ordered to accept Christianity or leave Spain. Although thousands did leave, even more thousands remained and went through the farce of outward conversion. But these "converts," called Moriscos, only delayed their fate. In the two succeeding reigns they too were persecuted and expelled.

Spain, then, was unified religiously under the crown, but at an economic and intellectual cost. Nevertheless, territorially consolidated and politically unified by Ferdinand and Isabella, enriched by the wealth of the New World, and inspired by the crusading zeal of a purified and triumphant religion, Spain was to be the most powerful and influential of the new national states during the first century of the early modern era (see Figure 28.2 and Map 28.1).

2. FRANCE

The reign of Louis XI (1461–1483), known as the "Spider King," may be said to mark the beginning of France as a modern national state. Louis came to the throne of France eight years after the end of the Hundred Years' War with England. His predecessor, Charles VII, had used the war emergency to obtain powers over taxation (*taille*) and a standing army for the crown. During the last phase of the war a great upsurge of French national spirit, aided by the exploits of Joan of Arc, made possible, at long last, the expulsion of the English invaders. Louis XI put these inherited advantages to clever use. First of all, he set out to crush the power of the feudal nobility who had taken advantage of the royal distress during the Hundred Years' War to assert their virtual independence of the crown. By craft and by direct military force he broke up the league that the insubordinate nobility formed against him and reduced the individual nobles to submission. In order to achieve this goal, Louis utilized the rising middle class. In return for its support he placed many members of this class in his councils and in key administrative posts, enabling some to enter the nobility. He also did what he could to foster commerce and industry. Roads, harbors, and waterways were improved. Shipbuilding, commerce, and industry were encouraged by royal subsidies and protective regulation.

Louis XI virtually completed the territorial consolidation of the French national state. He brought province after province under direct royal control, until by the end of his reign France had acquired all of its modern territory except the northwesternmost peninsula of Brittany (which was acquired by Louis' son) and a few territories along the fluid northeastern frontier. This expansive movement brought Louis XI into conflict with Charles the Bold of Burgundy. Charles the Bold (perhaps "the Rash" would have been a more accurate title) had inherited rich and strategically

---

[2]The Jews had earlier been expelled from England, France, and the German states.

FIGURE 28.2 Ferdinand and Isabella A coin of Ferdinand and Isabella, sovereigns of Spain. Spain was the most powerful of the new national monarchies and her coins enjoyed wide circulation in Europe and predominance in the Spanish and English empires in North and South America during the sixteenth, seventeenth, and eighteenth centuries. The Spanish piece-of-eight was commonly called the "dollar," and in 1787 the dollar was adopted by the United States as its standard unit of value. (American Numismatic Society)

located territories that included the Netherlands, the duchy of Burgundy, and the free county of Burgundy. These he hoped to consolidate into a great national state—the old Middle Kingdom of Charlemagne's grandson Lothair—between France and Germany. Had he succeeded in doing so, the course of history might have been changed significantly. However, Charles the Bold and his successor, Mary of Burgundy, were no match for the "Spider King" of France. Charles was killed battling the Swiss, and Mary was unable to prevent Louis XI from seizing the duchy of Burgundy, Picardy, and part of Flanders. (The abortive Burgundian "Middle Kingdom" has been a battleground between France and Germany throughout much of the modern period.) Thus consolidated and enlarged, France was to play a dominant role in European affairs in the centuries that followed.

Louis XI's schemes, however, did not include the betterment of the condition of the lower classes. Having paid for his ambitious programs with heavy taxes but having received little in return, the lower classes remained disaffected and discontented.

3. ENGLAND

Early modern times, so far as English history is concerned, may be said to have begun with the reign of Henry VII (1485–1509), the first of the Tudor dynasty. The political unity of the English national state had been brought about as early as 1066 by William the Conqueror (aided to a considerable degree by geography). However, the feudal system, with its decentralization of administration and society, the Hundred Years' War with France (1337–1453), and the Wars of the Roses (1455–1484) between the rival houses of Lancaster and York, had by the last quarter of the fifteenth century brought England to a state of turmoil bordering on anarchy. Henry Tudor acquired the English throne by victory on the battlefield over the Yorkish King Richard III, who was slain. Himself a member of the Lancastrian family, Henry ended the bloody dynastic feud by marrying Elizabeth of York.

The most pressing task confronting the strong-willed new monarch was the suppression of the turbulent nobility. The great feudal barons had

Habsburg Dominions
Ottoman Empire
Boundary of the Holy Roman Empire

NORWAY
Bergen
Oslo
Stockholm

SCOTLAND
Edinburgh

NORTH SEA

SWEDEN

DENMARK
Copenhagen

BALTIC SEA

IRELAND
Dublin

ENGLAND
York

London
Canterbury

ATLANTIC OCEAN

Danzig

Hamburg
BRANDENBURG
Berlin

Vistula R.
War

DUTCH NETH. Munster
Antwerp
BELG. Brussels Cologne
NETH.
Wittenberg
SILESIA
Breslau
SAXONY
Schmalkalden
BOHEMIA
Prague
MORAVIA
Crac

LUX.
Trier
Worms

St. Malo
Rouen
Metz
PALATINATE
Ratisbon
Strasbourg
Augsburg
Vienna
AUSTRIA
Paris

Orléans
BAVARIA
Munich

Bu

Bourges

FR. COMTE Basel
SWISS CONFEDERATION
TYROL

Angoulême
FRANCE

Bordeaux
Geneva
SAVOY
Trent
Venice
Milan
Parma
VENETIAN REPUBLIC

Mohacs

DAUPHINE
Avignon
Marseilles
Genoa
Florence
DALMATIA

BOSNIA

Santiago
Bayonne
PYRENEES

Oporto
Valladolid Burgos
NAVARRE

PORTUGAL
SPAIN (Castile)
ARAGON
CATALONIA
Barcelona

Corsica (to Genoa)
Elba (to Florence)
Rome
PAPAL STATES

MONTENEGRO

Lisbon
Escorial
Madrid
Toledo

Valencia
Balearic I.

Sardinia (to Aragon)

NAPLES (Aragon)
Naples

Seville
Cadiz
Granada
GRANADA

MEDITERRANEAN SEA

Palermo

Ic
(\

Sicily (to Aragon)

Melilla (Spain)
Algiers
Tunis

Malta (Knights of St. Joh

SULTANATE OF FEZ
SULTANATE OF ALGIERS
SULTANATE OF TUNIS

B A R B A R Y   S T A T E S

0   100   200   300 miles

taken advantage of the decades of civil war and of the long rule of a weak king prior to the war to defy royal authority. They retained their own private armies and overawed the local courts. At once and with great vigor Henry VII proceeded to enforce the laws against livery and maintenance,[3] thereby destroying the illegal feudal armies. Since the regular local courts were too weak to proceed against the nobility, Henry set up his own Court of Star Chamber, which, backed by the royal army, was able to overawe the most powerful barons and bring them to justice and to submission to the crown.

In these undertakings Henry VII had the support of the lesser gentry and the middle and lower classes, all of whom yearned for peace and order. The middle class, particularly, desired stability for the sake of its growing business activities, and it was with this class that the Tudors allied themselves. Henry selected many of his counselors and administrators from the ranks of the bourgeoisie. He made favorable commercial treaties with the Netherlands, Denmark, and even with Venice, the jealous queen of the rich eastern Mediterranean trade. Navigation acts were passed to protect English shippers. Henry's frugality and careful collection and handling of revenues not only were good business but also freed the king of dependence upon Parliament for funds.

Henry VII died in 1509, but he passed along to

---

[3]So called from the practice of the peasantry's wearing the lord's badge or livery, signifying membership in his private army, in return for the lord's promise to maintain (support) them in courts of justice.

Map 28.1 EUROPE, 1526 This map indicates how widespread the Hapsburg dominions were under Charles V. In addition, Charles V exercised some indirect control over most of the territory within the Holy Roman Empire as its selected emperor. As the Spanish monarch, his lands included Spanish holdings in the New World. The map also shows France nearly surrounded by its Hapsburg rivals and the Isamic Ottoman Empire as a threat to Christian Europe.

his glamorous son, Henry VIII, a united and orderly national state and a well-filled treasury. And under his granddaughter, Elizabeth, England rose to a position of first-rate importance in European affairs.

4. ITALY, GERMANY, AND THE HOLY ROMAN EMPIRE

Italian- and German-speaking people have played a vital role in modern European history, particularly in making important contributions to the arts and sciences. However, they did not achieve political unity at the opening of the early modern period, and that disunity created political problems that persisted into the nineteenth and twentieth centuries.

At the opening of the early modern period the Italian peninsula was divided into five major independent states: the Kingdom of Naples, the Papal States, Florence (Tuscany), Venice, and Milan. The Kingdom of Naples, the poorest of the Italian states, occupied the southern third of the peninsula and at times the large island of Sicily (see Map 28.2). During the fifteenth and sixteenth centuries it was a bone of contention over which France and Spain repeatedly fought. The Papal States occupied the central portion of the peninsula. These states were ruled by the pope not only as a supreme pontiff but also as political head. Florence and Venice, republics in name, were dominated by rich banking and commercial families. Milan, another thriving center of commerce, was ruled by an autocratic duke.

The main reason for Italian disunity in the early modern era was the long tradition of independence among the city-states. There the spirit of local rather than national pride and loyalty prevailed. Instead of forging common bonds, the major Italian city-states such as Florence, Venice, and Milan competed with each other for control over the smaller ones, such as Ferrara, Modena, and Mantua. Possibilities of unification under the papacy or the Holy Roman emperor were undermined by a long history of struggles between these two powers. For awhile, the Treaty of Lodi (1454–1455), which allied Florence, Milan, and Naples, and alliances between Venice and the Papal States

created a balance of power and some stability on the Italian peninsula. But this stability broke down in 1494. In the following decades Italy was repeatedly invaded by France and the Holy Roman Empire. The political division of the Italians in an age of powerful national states continued to be a standing invitation to aggression against them.

During the fifteenth century German-speaking peoples remained split up into more than three hundred virtually independent units. The only political bond between them was the impotent government of the Holy Roman Empire. This ramshackle institution—a survival of the organization set up by Charlemagne in 800 and revived by Otto the Great in 962—purported to be a restoration of the old Roman Empire, but it never was. In the Middle Ages, when the Spanish, French, and English sovereigns were consolidating their territories and their authority, the German emperors were frittering away their time and energy trying to bring Italy under their control. While they were away from Germany on these quixotic ventures, the local feudal barons conspired against them, consolidated their own power, and built up hereditary states of their own within the empire. Meanwhile, territory after territory slipped from under the emperor's control, until by the opening of the early modern period, the Holy Roman Empire included for all practical purposes only the German-speaking states (plus Czech-speaking Bohemia).

Eventually seven of the emperor's most prominent subjects gained the right to elect him. This elective feature not only diminished the prestige of the emperor but also forced candidates to bribe the electors and bargain and promise away any chance of strengthening the imperial office. Since the emperor had no sure income, he had no military force with which to enforce his will. Even to defend the empire, he was forced to call upon his subject princes to furnish troops. The lawmaking and taxing powers lay in the hands of the Diet, which was composed of three houses: the house of electors, the house of lesser princes, and the house of representatives of the free imperial cities. The Diet had no regular time or place of meeting and was seldom able to reach agreement on any important question. In the late fifteenth century an imperial court was set up to settle disputes between member states. However, lacking any

Map 28.2 ITALY, 1454 Italy as unable to overcome her political divisions, with the large but weak Kingdom of Naples controlled by outside powers, the center controlled by popes opposed to national unification, and the rich urbanized North divided among cometing states.

means of enforcing its decisions, this instrument too proved ineffective.

The one factor that gave any semblance of vitality to the Holy Roman Empire was the Hapsburg family. A Hapsburg was first elected emperor in 1273. After 1438, with only one brief exception, no one but a Hapsburg was elected until the empire finally died at the hands of Napoleon in 1806. By marriage and diplomacy, the Hapsburgs expanded their original Austrian lands until they possessed at the opening of the early modern period one of the largest and richest dynastic estates in Europe. Although, therefore, the Holy Roman emperor as emperor was virtually powerless, as head of the house of Hapsburg he was one of the most influential of monarchs. Nevertheless, all efforts of the Hapsburgs to strengthen the central government of the empire foundered on the rocks of German particularism—the local interests of the jealous princes.

During most of the first half of the sixteenth century the house of Hapsburg was headed by Emperor Charles V (see Figure 28.3). Charles V inherited from his parents and four grandparents a vast array of territories and claims. From his grandfather Maximilian he inherited the Hapsburg provinces generally spoken of as Austria, to which were added in Charles' lifetime Hungary, Bohemia, Moravia, and Silesia. As a Hapsburg, he also inherited a good claim to the imperial crown of the Holy Roman Empire. From his grandmother Mary he inherited the Burgundian lands: the free county of Burgundy (Franche Comté), the Netherlands, Luxembourg, Flanders, Artois, and claims to the duchy of Burgundy and Picardy, which had been seized by Louis XI. From his grandfather Ferdinand he received Aragon, the Kingdom of Naples, and numerous islands in the Mediterranean. From his grandmother Isabella he received Castile and a claim to the entire Western Hemisphere based on the papal Line of Demarcation (1493) and the Treaty of Tordesillas (1494). And from Ferdinand and Isabella jointly, he inherited Granada and Spanish Navarre.

The very size of Charles V's far-flung holdings spelled perpetual trouble. (See Map 28.1.) The language problem alone was appalling. To this were added differences in local customs, tastes, and eventually religion. Moreover, Charles V was sure

FIGURE 28.3 This 16th century engraving by Sichem shows Emperor Charles V with symbols of the Holy Roman Empire, sword and crossed Globe. (The Bettmann Archive)

to become involved in all the major international conflicts of Europe. Born and reared in the Netherlands, Charles was accepted in Spain only after a serious opposition and open revolt. His efforts to strengthen the government of the Holy Roman Empire and to raise money and troops there were frustrated by the local German princes. Finally, the Lutheran revolt further split the empire and shattered completely the personal power of Charles in Germany.

5. INTERNATIONAL RIVALRIES, 1516–1559

The rise of national states failed to bring peace to Europe. The national monarchs, supported by the bourgeoisie, had justified their own aggrandizement on the grounds that it was necessary to end the interminable feudal wars, and they had in fact established a large measure of internal law and order. However, the little feudal wars were followed by big national and dynastic wars. Although these monarchs established modern diplomatic institutions (earlier developed by Italians in the fifteenth century), such as permanent ambassadors, they also utilized larger armies and new military technology in their wars.

Throughout the sixteenth century international strife revolved around the house of Hapsburg. Charles V found himself almost continually at war with Francis I of France. Each feared the other's power. Francis I had continued the process initiated by his predecessors of increasing the power of the French monarchy, above all by securing new revenues through the sale of governmental offices, by swelling the state bureaucracy, and by gaining the right to appoint France's bishops and abbots. Francis vigorously contested Charles' election as Holy Roman Emperor. They fought over conflicting territorial claims in Italy, the Burgundian lands, and along the French-Spanish border. Charles won nearly all the battles, but he was never able to make his victories permanent.

The relations between Charles of Hapsburg and England were limited to a personal family quarrel. When Henry VIII sought an annulment of his marriage to Catherine of Aragon, the aunt of Charles V, Charles used his influence with the pope to block the proceedings, thus touching off a chain of events that ended with Henry taking over the Church in England and separating it from the Roman Catholic church. It was under Charles' son, Philip II, that conflict between Spain and England was brought to a climax.

Among Charles V's more concrete achievements were his marriage to Isabella of Portugal, which brought about a brief union of Spain and Portugal under Philip II, and his repulse of the Ottoman Turks. The Ottoman Turks had migrated to Asia Minor from Central Asia in the thirteenth century, converted to Islam, and by the beginning of the sixteenth century had built an empire that extended from Egypt to the Danube. Under Suleiman the Magnificent (1520–1566), their ablest ruler, they crushed the Hungarians at Mohacs (1526), swept across Hungary, and in 1529 laid seige to Vienna, the capital city of Hapsburg Austria. At the same time they conquered all of North Africa as far west as Morocco, and their fleets dominated the Mediterranean. It was feared that all Western Christendom might fall to the Moslems. At this point, Charles V rallied the forces of the empire and the Hapsburg provinces and drove the Turks back into Hungary. His captains also administered some defeats to the Moslem Barbary pirates in the western Mediterranean.

In 1555 Charles V began to divide his holdings between his son, Philip II, and his brother, Ferdinand. To Philip he gave the Burgundian provinces and Spain, with its appanages in Italy, the Mediterranean, and the New World. To Ferdinand he gave the Austrian provinces and successfully promoted Ferdinand's candidacy to the crown of the Holy Roman Empire. Henceforth there were two branches of the Hapsburg dynasty—Austrian and Spanish—both of which would long continue to play important roles in European and world history.

In 1559 the Treaty of Cateau-Cambrésis ended the dynastic wars between the Hapsburgs and the French Valois kings. Spain gained dominance in Italy, the center of power in Europe shifted to Spain, and a new era of revolts and wars entwining religion and politics unfolded.

6. THE POLITICAL MAP OF EUROPE IN 1559

At the beginning of the early modern period, then, powerful monarchs established national states in Spain, France, and England. These national states rose to dominate Europe. Germany and Italy were divided into many small states. The German states and Slavic Czech-speaking Bohemia were in the Holy Roman Empire. The Netherlands, owned by the Hapsburgs, was a part of the empire. Switzerland, nominally in the empire, was in reality an independent confederation of semiautonomous cantons. Elsewhere in Europe, Scotland was still independent, and England's control over Ireland was only tenuous. Denmark owned Norway and was in temporary union with Sweden. Poland, including Lithuania, occupied a large stretch of territory east of Germany, but its anemic government made Poland impotent at home and abroad. Russia, under Ivan III, had just freed itself from Mongol overlordship and as yet counted for little in European or world affairs. The Balkan peninsula and most of Hungary were part of the Otto-man Empire.

Spain, France, and England represented the political wave that most of Europe would eventually follow. But their new internal strength brought not a more peaceful international order but war on a larger, more violent scale.

SUGGESTED READING

General—The Fifteenth and Sixteenth Centuries

Margaret Aston, *The Fifteenth Century: The Prospect of Europe* (1968). A general survey with emphasis on social history.

De Lamar Jensen, *Renaissance Europe: Age of Recovery and Reconciliation* (1981). A good recent treatment.

Eugene F. Rice, Jr., *The Foundations of Early Modern Europe, 1460–1559* (1970). The best general survey of the period, with an excellent bibliography.

The New National Monarchies

J. H. Elliott, *Imperial Spain, 1469–1716* (1964). An excellent account of Spanish history during this period.

G. R. Elton, *The Tudor Revolution in Government* (1959). An important analysis of English political history during the fifteenth and sixteenth centuries.

J. Lockyer, *Henry VII* (1972). A recent biography with accompanying documents.

R. J. Knect, *Francis I* (1982). An authoritative study.

J. J. Scarisbrick, *Henry VIII* (1968). A fine biography.

J. H. Shennan, *The Origins of the Modern European State* (1974). An excellent brief analysis.

A. J. Slavin, ed., *The "New Monarchies" and Representative Assemblies: Medieval Constitutionalism or Modern Absolutism?* (1964). A sampling and comparison of scholarship on the political history of the period, particularly the rise of the "new monarchs."

The Hapsburgs

K. Brandi, *The Emperor Charles V: The Growth and Destiny of a Man and of a World Empire* (1939). A classic biography.

H. B. Koenigsberger, *The Hapsburgs and Europe: 1516–1660* (1971). A solid account of Hapsburg rule.

CHAPTER 29

European Expansion, Commercial Capitalism, and Social Change

FIGURE 29.1   **Columbus Discovers the New World**   This illustration is from a letter of Columbus to the treasurer of the king of Spain, published in Basel a year after his first voyage. Here the Spaniards are offering the Indians gifts as they approach the West Indian island. The Indians are portrayed as naked and perhaps even childlike, emphasizing the European perception of them as lesser, uncivilized beings. Pictures such as this excited the wonder and greed of many Europeans during the Age of Discovery. (NYPL Picture Collection)

The rise of national states was closely associated with the expansion of Europe and new economic development. Monarchs who created national states supported voyages of discovery and the overseas conquests that resulted. They took advantage of the wealth that poured in to finance their growing governments and their wars. They also allied themselves with the rising middle class against the feudal aristocracy. The strength of this middle class lay in its commercial wealth and its use of capitalistic methods to gain that wealth. Together, this European expansion and economic development represented a new level of power and wealth that would make Europe dominant over large parts of the globe.

1. THE AGE OF DISCOVERY

In the late fifteenth and early sixteenth centuries European mariners made a series of daring voyages in which they discovered not only the New World but also new and much better routes to the East (see Map 29.1). These voyages were made possible by a number of recent developments. Important improvements in the technology of shipping and navigation were being made. New armaments and military tactics gave Europeans advantages over those resisting them. Commercial and organizational skills increased the chances of success for these risky voyages. The governments of the national states along the Atlantic coast promoted these voyages and provided needed financial support. Their principal motive was a desire to bypass the Venetians, the Moslems, and the land barriers that separated them from the riches of the East. But there was also a powerful outward impetus in the spirit of inquiry and adventure kindled by the Renaissance interest in the secular world, and in the Christian missionary zeal that had always been a spur to expansion.

The first to begin these voyages in the fifteenth century were the Portuguese. During the first half of the fifteenth century, Prince Henry the Navigator (1394–1460) established a school of navigation and base of operations on the southwestern tip of Portugal from which he sent expeditions down the west coast of Africa. In addition to curiosity, his motives were mercenary and religious:

He wanted to capture the gold trade in western Africa and hoped to find the legendary Christian kingdom of Prester John. A broader goal of this Portuguese effort was to find a new route around Africa to India. Pushing steadily down the coast of West Africa, the Portuguese developed a lucrative trade in gold, ivory, sugar, and slaves. In 1488 Portuguese explorers rounded the Cape of Good Hope. In 1498 Vasco da Gama, in what was probably the greatest voyage in the history of navigation, reached India, the object of the quest. Vasco da Gama was out of sight of land ninety-three days—three times as long as Columbus on his voyage to the New World. That the Portuguese knew what they were up to is proved by the fact that Vasco da Gama's return cargo sold for sixty times the cost of the expedition. These glad tidings sent a host of Portuguese adventurers hurrying to the East Indies, where they carved out a huge commercial and political empire. One of these adventurers, Cabral, swinging too far westward, touched the eastern bulge of South America, thus laying the basis for Portugal's claim to Brazil. With their discovery of this all-water route to the East, the Portuguese broke the Arab and Venetian monopoly over the spice trade. From that point on, the center of commercial activity shifted westward toward the Atlantic seaboard.

Meanwhile, Spain was sending its mariners westward, for by the late fifteenth century most educated people in western Europe assumed that the earth was round, although they greatly underestimated its size. Many navigators therefore believed that the East Indies could be reached by sailing west. The first European to attempt it was Christopher Columbus. (Nothing had come of the tenth-century voyages to Greenland and northern America of the roving Norsemen, Eric the Red and Leif Ericson.) Columbus was born in Genoa but moved to Portugal. When, however, Portugal failed to support his proposed westward voyage, he turned to Queen Isabella of Castile, who gave him the necessary backing. His three ships touched a West Indian island on October 12, 1492. Thinking that the West Indies were islands off the east coast of Asia, Columbus made three further voyages in the hope of bypassing these barriers and sailing on to his real goal, the East Indies. Instead, he was turned back by the South and

Map 29.1 **EXPLORATION AND CONQUEST, FIFTEENTH AND SIXTEENTH CENTURIES** This map shows the routes taken by some of the early explorers. It indicates some of the distinctions between the Portuguese and Spanish empires—the Portuguese concentrated in Africa and the East and focused primarily on sea power and trading posts; the Spanish concentrated in the New World and focused primarily on conquest and colonization. Early English and French efforts were more limited and farther north.

Central American mainlands and died disappointed, not having realized the magnitude of his discovery.

But others soon realized it, and in the first half of the sixteenth century, Spanish expeditions to the New World multiplied. In 1493 the pope drew a line of demarcation dividing the non-Christian world between Spain and Portugal. This line was somewhat altered in favor of Portugal the following year by the Treaty of Tordesillas. Since all of North and South America except the eastern part of Brazil and most of Greenland fell to Spain, the Spanish sailors continued to move westward. Ponce de Leon, de Soto, and Coronado explored the southern part of what is now the United States. Balboa crossed the Isthmus of Panama and looked out upon the Pacific Ocean. In 1519 Magellan set out around the world by way of the Straits of Magellan. Although he himself was killed in the Philippines, one of his ships in 1522 completed the circuit. Also in 1519 Cortez began the conquest of the Aztec Empire in Mexico. In 1531–1532 Pizarro conquered the Inca Indians in Peru.

The other two national states, England and France, were relatively inactive in discovery and exploration during the fifteenth and early sixteenth centuries. The English crown did, however, sponsor voyages to northern North America by the Italian mariner John Cabot in 1497–1498. These voyages became the basis for England's claims to North America, where England later built a great empire. The French government sponsored Jacques Cartier, who in 1535 sailed up the St. Lawrence to what is now Montreal and claimed Canada for France. Nonetheless, it was not until the seventeenth century that Spain and Portugal were replaced as the world's leading imperial powers.

2. THE FOUNDING OF THE SPANISH NEW WORLD EMPIRE

Although much of the Western Hemisphere at the beginning of the sixteenth century was sparsely inhabited by native or "Indian" tribes, the Spaniards encountered two highly organized societies: those of the Aztecs in Mexico and the Incas in Peru.

The first inhabitants of the Western Hemisphere are generally believed to have immigrated from Asia across the Bering Strait, perhaps as long as forty thousand years ago. They organized into hundreds of tribes throughout the North, Central, and South America.

The first of these tribes to build a highly organized society were the Mayas. They are believed to have come into what is now Guatemala and the Yucatán peninsula of southeast Mexico from the northwest about 1000 B.C. Their civilization reached its height between A.D. 400 and 600. It was a city-state civilization resembling that of ancient Greece approximately a thousand years earlier. Their writing, most of which has been lost, was a combination of pictures and ideographs.

Their best art was brightly colored pottery, gems, gold and silverware, and sculpture. Probably their most remarkable creations were a system of mathematics based on the decimal (actually vigesimal) system and a calendar based on astronomy, both of which were in advance of those used in contemporary Europe. Their massively walled stone cities were connected by elaborately paved roads. These cities, however, were continually at war with one another, and in the twelfth century the less culturally developed but better-organized Toltecs conquered the Mayan city-states much as Philip of Macedon conquered the Greeks.

In the fourteenth century the warlike Aztecs came down from the north and founded a city on an island in Lake Tezcoco—the present Mexico City. From this base they conquered and organized a military empire or confederacy comprising most of what is now southern Mexico. The Aztecs were the Romans of the New World, and like the Romans they acquired most of their culture from the earlier civilization (Mayas). Theirs was the gift of military and political organization. They developed an elaborate, though stern, system of justice. Their religion was important and highly organized. Several thousand priests, both regular and secular, tended the impressive temple and supervised education and morals. The numerous gods, taken mostly from the Mayas, were headed by the terrible war god, who demanded human sacrifice, usually prisoners of war. And yet the rank-and-file Aztecs were gentle lovers of poetry and art. Flourishing commerce, agriculture, and mining added to the wealth obtained by conquest.

An even more colorful civilization was that of the Incas on the Andean Plateau of South America. In the eleventh century the Inca Indians began to extend their sway over their neighbors until their empire covered an area fifteen hundred miles long and three hundred miles wide—including present-day Ecuador, Peru, and parts of Bolivia and Chile. An elaborate system of roads and communications tied this vast and lofty empire together. Incan society was a combination of benevolent despotism and socialism. The all-powerful Inca ruler was treated as a god. However, he had a body of advisers and administrators, chosen from the upper classes. All land and all production were owned and directed by the state. The regi-

FIGURE 29.2 The Aztec Perception of the Spanish Although there are many Spanish records of their arrival and explorations in the New World, this Aztec manucript (ca. 1519–1522) is one of the few surviving Indian versions of the coming of the Europeans. This illustration shows Cortez arriving in Mexico. Note the depiction of some of the crucial elements of Cortez's conquest: the sword, the horse, the flag, and the cross. (Biblioteca Apostolica Vaticana, Rome)

mented lower classes did all the work under close supervision and shared from the common stores. A high degree of specialization was practiced. Agriculture was well advanced, and huge terracing and irrigation projects had been developed to overcome the difficulties of the Andean terrain. Religious worship, particularly of the sun god, was an important feature of national life. Outstanding were Incan pottery, architecture, textiles, and gold and silver ornamental objects.

The native American civilizations were no match for the marauding Europeans. Spanish military men, particularly those of the lesser nobility (*hidalgos*), were part of a centuries-old tradition of crusading for Church, crown, and profit. Cortez, with a band of some six hundred soldiers and eighteen horses, overcame the Aztecs by a combination of treachery, tactics, weapons, and determination. He took advantage of divisions and hostilities between the Aztecs and the subject tribes as well as the Aztec belief that the Spaniards were ancient gods whose return had long been expected. Once inside the capital city, the Spaniards were too strong to be expelled. They slaughtered and looted the poorly armed Aztecs without mercy (see Figure 29.2).

Even more spectacular was the conquest of the Incas. Like Cortez, Pizarro used disunity within the Incan Empire as well as trickery and brutality to defeat the Incas. At one point, Pizarro enticed the Incan emperor into a conference. At a given signal Pizarro's small but well-armed band of Spanish soldiers fell upon the splendidly dressed but primitively armed Incan troops and slew them by the thousands. Pizarro promised to free the Incan chieftain in return for a ransom of gold objects sufficient to fill a room seventeen by twenty-two feet to a height of nine feet, plus a larger amount of silver. This ransom was collected and paid, but Pizarro, who never really intended to free the emperor, had him put to death anyway.

Spanish administrators soon replaced these conquerors, and throughout the sixteenth century Spaniards flocked to the New World. By 1607, when the first permanent English colony was founded in North America, a quarter of a million Spaniards had settled in the vast Spanish Empire stretching from what is now Arizona to Cape Horn. A number of distinguished missions and cathedrals had been erected, and several thriving universities had been founded. The native civilizations had been almost wholly destroyed and replaced by the Christian civilization of Spain.

3. CAPITALISM AND THE COMMERCIAL REVOLUTION

The discovery of the New World and of all-water routes to the Far East fueled an expansion of European commerce that was already underway. A crucial aspect of this expansion was the development of capitalistic methods. The use of capitalistic methods and the scale of commercial growth was so great that the term *commercial revolution* is used to describe it.

The term *capitalism*, stripped to its barest essentials, means a system whereby private individuals put money to work to make more money. Individuals, competing in a market to maximize their profits, determine what to produce, how to produce it, and what price to charge. It involves, among other things, private property, the profit motive, a substantial amount of free enterprise,

the hiring of labor for wages, and the lending of money for interest.

Elements of capitalism had been in existence for centuries, but to a lesser degree and in much more limited form than during the sixteenth century. During most of the Middle Ages agriculture operated at only a subsistence level and was carried out under feudal restrictions. Commerce was a trickle of luxuries for the rich and necessities such as iron, implements, and salt. Guilds hampered commercial and industrial enterprises. The Church supported the concept of the "fair price" rather than competitive pricing and frowned on the lending of money for interest (usury).

During the eleventh century, commercial activities began to revive, and by the thirteenth century a pronounced recovery was underway. The Crusades contributed significantly to this revival. The huge movement of men and supplies from western Europe to the Holy Land enriched the merchants and shippers of Venice and other Italian cities. Some of them set up permanent trading posts in the Near East and introduced the luxuries of the materially more advanced Moslem and Byzantine worlds to western Europe. The Fourth Crusade, which the Venetians diverted to the looting of Constantinople, was particularly fruitful. The Venetians seized not only a great hoard of gold and silver in the stricken Eastern imperial capital but also a large part of the territory of the Byzantine Empire itself. This wealth flowed into the stream of western European commerce.

Foremost among the centers of this newly revived commerce and capitalism were the city-states of northern Italy, such as Venice, Genoa, Florence, and Milan. Venice was the queen of the Mediterranean in the thirteenth, fourteenth, and fifteenth centuries. After crushing the sea power of her chief rival, Genoa, in the fourteenth century, Venice enjoyed a virtual monopoly over the lucrative trade with the East. At the peak of its prosperity, Venice's merchant marine numbered some thirty thousand sailors. Milan was the starting point of the overland traffic across the Alps to northern Europe. In the late fourteenth century Milan gained control of the port city of Genoa. Florence manufactured large quantities of fine woolen textiles on a capitalistic basis, and in the fourteenth and fifteenth centuries it was the banking capital of the Western world. The Medici family alone possessed at one time some two hundred branch banks scattered throughout western and central Europe.

In northern Europe, the Hanseatic League, composed of some eighty German Baltic and North Sea cities, enjoyed a brisk trade in such commodities as fish, furs, grain, and timber. In southern Germany and the Rhine Valley, numerous trading centers such as Augsburg, Nuremberg, and Cologne sprang up along the overland route between Italy and northern Europe. Finally, the Netherlands, Paris, and London shared in this early period of revived commercialism.

As the main trade routes shifted from the Mediterranean to the Atlantic during the fifteenth and sixteenth centuries, new commercial centers to the west began to flourish. Contrary to what one might have expected, Spain, surfeited with gold and silver from Mexico and Peru, never developed a thriving commercial capitalism. And although Lisbon became the first great terminus of goods pouring in from the East, the Portuguese, like the Spanish, were so preoccupied with their vast overseas empire that they neglected the marketing opportunities in Europe itself.

These lucrative opportunities were first seized by the Dutch. Enterprising Dutch merchants purchased the goods in Lisbon, shipped them to the Netherlands, and sold them at a nice profit throughout northern and western Europe (see Figure 29.3). In the sixteenth century Antwerp, with its excellent harbor and location, was the leading commercial center in Europe. In the seventeenth century, following the sack of Antwerp in 1585 by Spanish troops, Amsterdam and London led the commercial world. The Dutch even took advantage of their newly won independence from Spain and of Portugal's temporary conquest by Spain in 1580 to seize the best part of Portugal's Eastern Empire, the area of present-day Indonesia.

Another phase of the commercial revolution was the advent of more bounteous supplies of commodities. Spices, coffee, tea, sugar, dyes, tropical fruits, fine textiles, tapestries, and precious stones, long known but in scarce supply and too expensive for all but the very rich, now came into Europe in ever-increasing volume. From the New World came potatoes, corn, tobacco, and

FIGURE 29.3 Jan Gossaert, 'Portrait of a Merchant,'' ca. 1530 This portrayal of a banker by the Flemish painter Gossaert reflects the spirit of commercial capitalism. This serious, self-assured banker works with pen in hand and business letters in the background. His clothes and rings reveal controlled wealth. (National Gallery of Art, Washington, D.C.; Alisa Mellon Bruce Fund)

chocolate (all of which were previously unknown to Europe), new dyes and medicines, gold and silver.

A different kind of new product—black slaves—also helped to swell the rising stream of commerce. This modern traffic in human beings was first begun in the later fifteenth century by the men of Portugal's Prince Henry the Navigator. It was later taken over by the Spaniards to supply labor for their empire in the New World. Native Indian populations were decimated by disease and the harsh conditions imposed by the Spaniards. Those that survived proved to be poor·slave laborers. The Spaniards turned to tropical Africa to supply slaves for their mines and plantations. Thousands of blacks were bought from local chieftains and crowded into the holds of ships. Many of them died during the crossings, but the survivors were sold like cattle for a high price in the New World markets. So heavy was this immensely profitable traffic that the racial and social complex of the New World society was drastically altered.

New types of business organizations were developed to accommodate the expanding volume of commerce. *Chartered companies* were organized to bypass the medieval guilds, which were unable or unwilling to meet the new demands. The most efficient type of chartered company proved to be the joint stock company. The members of a joint stock company pooled their resources, hired or elected their management, and shared in the profits in proportion to the amount of stock owned. In this way permanence was achieved, since the stock of any individual member could be bought or sold while the company remained intact.

Two of the earliest joint stock companies were the British East India Company, founded in 1600, and the Dutch East India Company, founded two years later. The British company was given not only a trading monopoly over British India but political control of the area as well. The Dutch company was given a monopoly over all Dutch trade east of the Cape of Good Hope. Annual profits of 300 percent were not uncommon for these giant companies. The annual profits of the Dutch East India Company never fell below 12 percent over a period of two hundred years.

Banking expanded in proportion to commerce. In the sixteenth century the Fugger family of Augsburg occupied the place in the financial world that the Medicis of Florence had held in the fifteenth. Jacob (the Rich) Fugger loaned Charles V the money with which he bribed his way to the emperorship of the Holy Roman Empire. In the seventeenth century the Bank of Amsterdam and the Bank of England were founded on a seminational basis. Both of these banks were really private joint stock companies, but in return for certain monopolies, such as the handling of government funds and the issuance of currency, they were obliged to accept a degree of government regulation. Banks of this size were able to mobilize sums of money and credit sufficient not only to launch and control large-scale commercial ventures but to influence government as well.

The commercialization of agriculture was of especially great significance. In some areas, particularly England, it sped up the process of combining smaller plots of land oriented toward subsistence farming into larger plots of land specializing in certain crops or herding for export. The commons—land available for the use of poor tenants—was taken away by large commercial landlords. Increasingly, small farmers were turned into wage laborers, either on the lands of commercial farmers or in the cities. The ranks of the landless poor swelled, while the productive commercial farmers gained wealth.

Industrial activity expanded in this period, particularly mining, shipbuilding, printing, armaments, and textiles, but guilds and governmental restrictions hindered the spread of capitalistic methods in these industries. The greatest expansion of capitalistic practices came with the growth of the domestic, or "putting out" system. Merchants or entrepreneurs would purchase the raw materials and distribute them to artisans, who would do the piecework in their cottages. Then the entrepreneur would collect the finished products, pay the cottagers for their work, and market the goods at a profit. While this system had certain advantages, it limited the volume of production. Until the coming of the machine and the factory system in the late eighteenth and early nineteenth centuries, therefore, large-scale capitalism was to remain commercial rather than industrial.

Part of this commercial revolution was fueled by the extraordinary rise in prices during the sixteenth century. This price inflation was probably related to the dramatic influx of gold and silver from the New World into Europe. However, historians now point to other causes for the price inflation that were perhaps more important, including the increase of population, the growing sense of confidence, and the increased purchasing of goods by governments; all combined to push demand for goods beyond available supplies. Traders, merchants, and commercial farmers were in a particularly good position to benefit from the rising prices for commodities, which encouraged them to invest in commercial activities.

4. MERCANTILISM

Governments attempted to exercise some control over economic developments. From the beginning of the Age of Discovery in the late fifteenth century until the end of the eighteenth century, all the governments of western Europe except the Dutch Netherlands pursued a policy that has come to be called *mercantilism*. Mercantilism was, in essence, economic nationalism. While the monarchs of the new national states were consolidating their political power, they were also attempting to unify and centralize their national economies. Efforts were made to standardize national currencies and weights and measurements. Internal commerce was encouraged by improving communications and reducing or removing internal tariff barriers. These efforts, however, were only partially successful. More attention was paid to the aggrandizement of each nation's economy at the expense of its neighbors. The basic assumption of mercantilist theory was that gold and silver are the true measure of national prosperity and power. Gold and silver, the mercantilists believed, in addition to being convenient mediums of exchange, could purchase anything—consumer goods, armies, navies, and administrative personnel. Spain's good luck in Mexico and Peru and its sixteenth-century brilliance and influence undoubtedly strengthened this view.

Spain alone was fortunate enough to come upon the gold and silver directly. All the other states had to devise more roundabout means of acquiring the precious metals. The favorite device was to seek a favorable balance of trade. The importation of expensive manufactured goods was discouraged by high tariffs, whereas the exportation of manufactures was encouraged, if need be, by subsidies. The reverse was true of inexpensive raw materials. The national aim was to buy low and sell high. Colonies were sought as sources of raw materials and markets for manufactured goods. But the colonies were not to be permitted to compete with the manufacturers and shippers of the mother country. Navies were advocated for the protection of the colonies. Sometimes the mercantilists closely regulated a nation's manufactures with a view to maintaining a reputation abroad for high quality. This phase of mercantilism reached its highest development in France in the seventeenth century under Louis XIV's economic minister, Colbert. It was not until the latter part of the eighteenth century that the British economist Adam Smith and the French Physiocrats began to undermine faith in the validity of mercantilist principles and to prepare the way for an era of *laissez faire*, or free trade.

5. POLITICAL AND SOCIAL CONSEQUENCES

One immediate political consequence of the rise of commercial capitalism in western Europe was the strengthening of royal absolutism. The monarchs made use of the merchants and bankers in order to increase their own power at the expense of the rival nobility. More money was now available for the royal treasury and the royal army. The middle classes, of course, shared the benefits of their alliance with the royal monarchs. Many members of the bourgeoisie were appointed to key positions in the royal administrations. With their increased wealth came increased social and political influence. The strongholds of their influence were the towns and cities whose growth paralleled the expansion of commerce. Western European society was becoming more urban—yet another change from the medieval pattern.

As the power of the national monarchs and the middle class grew, the position of the old nobility weakened. Their wealth and power were based on land, and now money was of growing importance. The inflation of prices further hurt the old nobility in relation to the moneyed bourgeoisie. Not overnight, but slowly and with occasional setbacks over the decades and centuries, the old nobility of western Europe was being displaced in political and social influence.

Yet in some ways the nobility was not being replaced but was rather being infused with new, though suspect, blood. The successful, wealthy middle class generally dreamed of joining the privileged nobility rather than replacing it as a social class. They did just that by purchasing aristocratic titles, acquiring large estates, and marrying into the nobility. Moreover, various opportunities were grasped by bolder but less established members of the nobility. Many nobles of minor importance in Spain were able to become wealthy and powerful in Spanish lands overseas. In England and the Netherlands many members of the aristocracy openly engaged in business operations, thereby adjusting successfully to changing economic conditions.

The ascendance of the middle class and changes within the nobility did not bring an immediate improvement in the condition of the lower classes. Indeed, the *nouveaux riches* often proved to be harsher taskmasters than the older aristocracy, who had stronger ties to medieval traditions of social responsibility. The urban wage earners were especially hard-hit by the inflation. Sixteenth-century cities, while increasing in size and number, witnessed an even greater growth of poverty, begging, vagrancy, and crime. In France and England some peasants who had converted their feudal dues to money payments profited, but most of the peasants in western Europe and all of those in central and eastern Europe suffered from the inflation. Landlords and those wealthier peasants who adapted well to the commercialization of agriculture profited, but they usually left in their wake large numbers of peasants worse off than before. Distressed landlords were likely to pass their hardships along to the peasantry. The number of landless poor grew. Peasant revolts became common throughout Europe in the sixteenth century. However, the rise of the middle class and the weakening of feudal class lines produced a more fluid social structure and made possible future political change. Money is more easily acquired by the commoner than is blue blood or title.

Finally, commercial capitalism probably diminished women's economic status. Most women still worked in traditional occupations—remaining in the countryside, assisting in their husbands' trades, or engaging in typical women's jobs such as domestic service, midwifery, and nursing. In the newer commercial, industrial, or professional occupations stimulated by commercial capitalism, women usually were either excluded or relegated to the lower-status and lower-paid jobs such as carding and spinning wool. As work became increasingly defined as labor for paid wages, the domestic tasks performed by women lost their status as work. Ultimately some women would gain options for greater independence from spreading commercial capitalism, but they had much to overcome.

6. EUROPEAN DOMINATION OF THE GLOBE

Thus we see Europe's agricultural, collectivist, "fair price" economy was being transformed into a much more dynamic, urban, competitive, profit-motivated economy. The rise of commerce and capitalism not only changed the nature of European society but also provided much of the explosive force that enabled tiny Europe to dominate most of the rest of the world.

During Europe's Age of Discovery much of the Western Hemisphere, southern Asia, and the coastal areas of Africa were quickly brought under European domination. This amazing expansion continued until by the end of the nineteenth century practically the entire world was dominated by Europe and European civilization. Spanish, Portuguese, English, French, and Dutch colonists, followed later by the nationals of all the other European countries, flocked to the New World, taking their Western Christian culture with them. The brilliant Aztec and Incan civilizations of Mexico and Peru were destroyed. The tribes of American Indians were exterminated, absorbed, or confined to reservations. The Moslem, Hindu, Buddhist, and Confucian civilizations of Asia and Africa were not so quickly or extensively destroyed, but they were clearly affected. The details of European expansion (and eventual contraction) constitute a considerable portion of the history of Western civilization since the sixteenth century.

SUGGESTED READING

The Age of Discovery

C. M. Cipolla, *Guns, Sails, and Empires: Technological Innovation and the Early Phases of European Expansion, 1400–1700* (1965). Stresses connections between technology and successful expansion.

D. P. Mannix and M. Cowley, *Black Cargoes: A History of the Atlantic Slave Trade* (1968). An excellent detailed account.

J. H. Parry, *The Age of Reconnaissance* (1963). A good survey of the causes and consequences of the early voyages.

Overseas Empires

Charles R. Boxer, *The Portuguese Seaborne Empire* (1970). An excellent study of the Portuguese Empire.

Charles Gibson, *Spain in America* (1966). A good study of the Spanish Empire in the New World.

B. Keen and M. Wasserman, *A Short History of Latin America* (1984). A useful recent text.

Commercial Capitalism and Social Change

F. Braudel, *Civilization and Capitalism, 15th–18th Century,* trans. S. Reynolds, Vol. 2: *The Wheels of Commerce* (1982). Highly acclaimed and sophisticated.

R. Bridenthal, C. Koonz, and S. Stuard, eds., *Becoming Visible: Women in European History, Second Edition* (1987). Contains good material on this period.

C. M. Cipolla, *Before the Industrial Revolution: European Society and Economy* (1980). Particularly good on demographic and economic change.

Ralph Davis, *The Rise of the Atlantic Economies* (1973). Contains a good survey of sixteenth-century economic history.

Richard Ehrenberg, *Capital and Finance in the Age of the Renaissance* (1963). A good study of sixteenth-century capitalism and the Fugger bank.

CHAPTER 30

The Reformation

FIGURE 30.1 **Cranach the Younger, "Protestant Reformers," 1543** This painting shows some of the crucial figures of the Protestant Reformation. In the center stands Elector John Frederick of Saxony, whose family protected Luther and other Protestant reformers. Luther is to the far left, his associate Philip Melanchthon is to the far right, and between Melanchthon and Frederick is Huldreich Zwingli, a leading reformer in Zurich. (Toledo Museum of Art, Toledo, Ohio; gift of Edward Drummond Libbey)

Sixteenth-century Europeans were intensely interested in religion. Although Renaissance culture, political developments, and commercial expansion were of great concern, the church was still at the very center of their lives. The Reformation probably touched more people than any other development of the sixteenth century.

The Protestant Reformation, initiated in the second decade of the sixteenth century by Martin Luther, swept through much of northern Europe. Reform within the Roman Catholic church, often called the Catholic Reformation, followed and included both internal reforms initiated independently of the Protestant Reformation and reforms undertaken to counter Protestantism. In the end, the Reformation split western Europe into hostile religious camps, destroying the medieval unity of the Western Christian Church.

1. BACKGROUND

In the late Middle Ages, discontent with the Church grew. Large numbers of people felt spiritually dissatisfied with what the Church offered. Greatly concerned with their own salvation and with leading a more pious life, people looked outside the formal institutions of the Church for guidance and examples. The growth of lay religious organizations such as the Brethren of the Common Life, the popularity of traveling preachers, the continuing search for mystical experiences, and the graphic pious art all testified to widespread and deep spiritual needs that were not being met through the Church. The Church seemed to have departed too far from the spirit and practices of the apostles and early fathers.

People voiced other complaints about the Church, particularly about many abuses that arose during the fourteenth and fifteenth centuries when the Church was torn by the Babylonian Captivity, the Great Schism, and the struggles between popes and councils (see pp. 339–342). The lack of education and the worldliness of the clergy, the sale of Church offices and services (simony), the favoring of relatives for lucrative Church offices (nepotism), and the holding by one man of more offices than he could adequately serve (plu-

ralism)—all were subjects of loud and growing complaint. Many of the higher clergy, even the popes, became preoccupied with their own secular concerns and Renaissance culture. Those who recognized a need to remedy these problems were unable to do enough until it was too late. Eventually the Church hierarchy took steps to remedy abuses, but not until much of Western Christendom had already left the Roman Catholic fold.

In addition to these spiritual dissatisfactions and complaints about abuses within the Church, other developments made certain areas of Europe fertile for the growth of reform movements. In Germany the Holy Roman Empire lacked the political unity that had helped national monarchs in Spain, England, and France gain control over their national clergy and access to the accumulated wealth of the Church. Local governments grew jealous of the immunities from civil laws and taxation enjoyed by the clergy. People resented the drain of wealth to the clergy and the institutions of the Church outside their territories, especially to Italy. These localities supported lay preachers, who gave numerous popular sermons throughout the year. In some of these same areas, particularly in university towns, Christian humanism took hold. Thanks to the printing press, criticisms of the Church by Erasmus, Ulrich von Hutten, and other humanists became widespread.

For the most part, this growing dissatisfaction with the Church was not revolutionary and did not yet challenge the fundamental doctrines of the Church. There was no widespread sense that the Church was about to be torn apart or that the only alternative was to make a complete break from the Church. On the other hand, the depth of the problems facing the Church is indicated by the radical reform movements occurring prior to the sixteenth century. As early as the fourteenth century reformers such as John Wycliffe in England and John Huss in Bohemia had voiced their protests against the Church. These protests turned into threatening movements of heretical dissent and social revolt, and authorities put them down only with great difficulty. When movements of dissent and revolt against the Church arose in the sixteenth century, they proved to be too powerful and well supported to be suppressed.

FIGURE 30.2   Cranach the Elder, "Martin Luther,"
1521 Martin Luther often referred to himself as "a peasant, the son of a peasant." His father, though of peasant stock, was an ambitious miner who moved into the ranks of the bourgeoisie. A complex character, Luther had the brilliant mind and personal force of one of the great leaders and movers of history. (Culver Pictures)

2. LUTHERANISM

The Protestant Reformation was composed of four major distinct but related movements—Lutheranism, Calvinism, Anglicanism, and Anabaptism. From these four main stems have sprung the hundreds of Protestant denominations that exist today. The Lutheran revolt was first in point of time.

Martin Luther (1483–1546) was the son of an ambitious miner of central Germany (see Figure 30.2). At a boarding school run by the pietistic

Brethren of the Common Life he, like his contemporary Erasmus, was introduced to a type of Christianity that emphasized simple piety rather than dogma and ritual. Later at Erfurt University he received a traditional liberal arts education. He was an excellent student. However, upon the completion of his undergraduate course and just as he was ready to begin study of the law, he suddenly renounced the world and entered an Augustinian monastery. This decision was no passing whim. As a child, Luther had been much concerned over the fate of his soul, and throughout his university days, his religious yearning had increased.

But the young friar found no satisfaction in the monastic life of the sixteenth-century Church. He scourged himself, donned beggar's garb, and went out among his former fellow students with sunken cheeks and gleaming, feverish eyes. It was not until, on the advice of a perceptive supervisor of his monastic order, he began to read the writings of St. Augustine and St. Paul that Brother Martin found the answer to his lifelong quest. On reading in Paul's Letter to the Romans (1:17) "the just shall live by faith," he concluded that here was the true means of salvation—not good works, sacraments, and rituals, but simple faith in Christ. Over a period of years he developed a theology based on the fundamental concept that righteousness is a gift of grace from God attained by faith in Christ's righteousness—justification by faith alone.

In the meantime Luther had become a member of the faculty of the newly founded University of Wittenberg in Saxony. For several years he taught philosophy and theology, quite unaware that his belief in salvation by faith alone was in fundamental conflict with the dogma of his church. Students flocked from afar to listen to him.

One day a friar named John Tetzel came into the vicinity of Wittenberg selling indulgences. According to the doctrine of indulgences, which had grown up in the late Middle Ages, Christ and the saints, by their good works while on earth, had accumulated in heaven a treasury of excess merit that the pope could apply to the credit of penitent sinners, thereby shortening for them or their loved ones their stay in purgatory. By the opening of the sixteenth century the dispensing of this vague, extrasacramental means of grace had become hardly more than a money-making venture. Huge sums, taken from all over Europe, were brought to Rome for the construction of St. Peter's or for other costly papal projects.

On October 31, 1517, Martin Luther posted on the church door in Wittenberg his Ninety-Five Theses, or propositions, concerning the doctrine of indulgences, which he proposed to be debated publicly. It did not occur to him that this event would mark the beginning of an upheaval to subside only after nearly half of Western Christendom had broken away from the Roman Catholic church. He was astonished and at first dismayed to find himself suddenly the national hero of all the various disgruntled elements throughout Germany. When, however, two years later in a public debate at Leipzig Luther finally realized that his position was hopelessly at odds with that of the Church, he lost no time in making the break clean. He published a series of pamphlets in which he violently denounced the pope and his organization and called on the German princes to seize the property of the Church and make themselves the heads of the Christian Church in Germany.

A papal bull of excommunication (which Luther publicly burned) soon followed. A few months later Emperor Charles V called the troublesome monk to appear before the Diet of the Holy Roman Empire at Worms (1521). There Luther boldly refused to recant and was outlawed by the highest civil authority in Germany. Although Luther remained under this death sentence with a price on his head for the rest of his life, he was protected by his prince, the elector of Saxony, and by German public opinion.

By this time all Germany was in religious and social turmoil. Nearly everyone with a grievance of any kind was looking to Luther for leadership. Religious zealots, such as the Anabaptists, began preaching individualistic and more radical doctrines in his name, and he found it necessary to repudiate them. Taking a somewhat more conservative stand, he decided that only those features of the Roman Catholic church that were opposed to the Scriptures ought to be rejected. In the early stages of the conflict Erasmus and many other humanists thought they saw in Luther a kindred spirit, but this alliance was short-lived. Erasmus soon found Luther to be as dogmatic and uncompromising in matters of doctrine as the Roman Catholic theologians, if not more so.

Luther also found it necessary to break with a group of rebellious peasants in south Germany. The condition of the peasants was bad and growing worse. The landed aristocracy, themselves losing ground to the rising middle classes, were depriving their peasants of long-established manorial rights such as free use of meadows and woodlands. In 1524 widespread disturbances broke out in southwestern Germany. The next year the peasants published a list of demands, including an end to serfdom, elimination of certain taxes, confiscation of Church property, and reform of the clergy. When these were refused, the peasants rebelled in the name of Luther, whom they believed to be against all oppressive authority. Luther was sympathetic with some of their demands, particularly the confiscation of Church property and reform of the clergy, but otherwise he proved to be socially and politically too conservative. He rejected their attack on authority as too broad and pleaded with them to refrain from violence. When the rebellious peasants did not follow Luther's advice and continued their violent uprisings in Luther's name, he repudiated them and called on the civil authorities to suppress the revolt by force. The armed authorities did so with a vengeance.

Luther's new religion, as he eventually formulated it, made the Scriptures the sole authoritative source of Christian dogma. That all might have access to the Bible, he translated it into German.[1] He conceived of the Church as the whole body of believers in Christ, not the Roman Catholic church or any other specific organization. He abolished the hierarchy of pope, cardinals, and bishops, and he reduced the importance of the clergy in general, proclaiming the priesthood of all believers. The ritual of worship was made much simpler. Of the seven sacraments of the Roman Catholic church, Luther kept only the two he found mentioned as sacraments in the Bible: baptism and the Eucharist. He rejected the Roman

---

[1]Luther's translation was in such excellent German that it had great influence on the standardization of the modern literary German language.

Catholic doctrine known as transubstantiation.[2] Luther interpreted the scriptural passages that refer to the Holy Eucharist, or Lord's Supper, to mean that during the administration of the sacrament Christ's body somehow enters into the bread and the wine, but the bread and wine remain—consubstantiation. He denied the Roman Catholic belief that a sacrifice is involved. He abolished monasteries and the celibacy of the clergy. Luther himself married a former nun. In general, he sharply distinguished religious matters from political and social matters, leaving the believer spiritually free and the secular rulers in charge of political and social matters.

The Emperor Charles V was greatly distressed by this religious revolution, which further divided his scattered and chaotic empire. Many German princes saw in Lutheranism a chance to increase their own political and financial independence from Charles V and the Italian papacy. Although determined to suppress the Protestants, Charles V was too busy with his wars against the French and the Turks to make much headway. Years of indecisive fighting between the Roman Catholics under Charles V and the Protestants ended in 1555 with the compromise Peace of Augsburg. Each of the more than three hundred German princes was left free to choose between Lutheranism and Roman Catholicism; his subjects were to abide by his choice. Luther himself died in 1546, just before the fighting began. By this time, Lutheranism had triumphed in the northern half of Germany and soon had spread, under the leadership of Scandinavian monarchs, to Denmark, Norway, Sweden, and most of the Baltic provinces (now Latvia, Estonia, and Finland), which were then under Swedish control. In addition, Lutheranism heavily influenced all later Protestant movements, the most important of which was Calvinism.

3. CALVINISM

John Calvin shares with Luther the position of first importance in the founding of Protestant Christianity. Born in France in 1509, John Calvin was twenty-six years younger than Luther. He was the son of a lawyer who was secretary to the bishop of Noyon in Picardy. Young Calvin had a radiant personality that made for warm friendships. Long association with aristocratic friends probably accounts for his elegant manners. His father sent him first to the University of Paris for a thorough grounding in the humanities and theology and then to the best law schools in France. Upon finishing his legal training, he entered a humanistic literary career. Suddenly, at the age of twenty-four, after reading Luther's writings and having an intensely personal religious experience, Calvin converted to Protestant Christianity.

The zealous young reformer soon aroused the ire of Roman Catholic authorities in France and of the French government and was forced to flee for his life. Calvin then spent the next two years in hiding writing the first edition of *The Institutes of the Christian Religion*. Published in Basel, Switzerland, when Calvin was only twenty-six, this theological treatise was to become the most influential writing in the history of Protestantism. Its precise and forceful logic reveals the fine legal training and powerful intellect of the author. Its lucid and facile style influenced the formulation of modern literary French. It immediately made Calvin an important name in literary and theological circles.

Probably Calvin's most significant contribution to Christian theology is his sublime concept of the majesty of God. To the author of the *Institutes*, the Divine Creator is so majestic and awe inspiring, and human beings so insignificant by comparison, that salvation by election, or *predestination*, as it is more often called, seems to follow logically. According to Calvin, God in the beginning planned the whole universe to the end of time. For unfathomable reasons of his own, God selected those human beings who would be saved and those who would be damned. He planted in the minds of the elect a saving faith in Christ and an insatiable desire to live the Christian life and to bring about the Kingdom of God on earth. In no other way could one acquire this faith and this desire. Calvin based this doctrine on the Scriptures (particularly the writings of St. Paul), which he considered to be the sole authoritative source for Christian the-

[2]*The New Catholic Dictionary* defines transubstantiation as "the marvellous and singular changing of the entire substance of the bread into the entire substance of the Body of Christ and of the entire substance of the wine into His Blood."

ology. St. Augustine, the most influential of the early Church Fathers, and Luther also believed in salvation by election, but neither they nor anyone else had ever spelled out the doctrine so precisely.

Shortly after the publication of the *Institutes*, Calvin went to Geneva. That city, like most of the rest of Switzerland, was in the throes of religious and political revolt brought on partly by the influence of Luther and the native Swiss reformer, Ulrich Zwingli (1484–1531). At first accepted by Protestant leaders, then rejected, Calvin finally returned in 1540 to try to make Geneva a model city of God on earth. Calvin, by sheer force of personality and intellect, soon rose to a position of great power in the city. He brought the town council, which was remarkably democratic and representative for the sixteenth century, under the dominance of a consistory composed of Protestant pastors and laity. Under Calvin's leadership the town council and the consistory set up a strict system of blue laws. Churchgoing was compulsory. Dancing, cardplaying, theatergoing, drinking, gambling, and swearing—all were forbidden. Enforcement was vigorous and penalties severe, even for the sixteenth century. The most famous penalty was the burning of Michael Servetus, an eccentric amateur scientist and theologian whom the Roman Catholic church had already condemned to death for heresy.[3] Servetus escaped his Catholic persecutors and came to Geneva. When Servetus arrived, he was seized, tried, convicted, and burned at the stake.

Calvinist ritual was even simpler than that of the Lutherans. The worship service consisted of preaching, praying, and psalm singing. Like Luther, Calvin retained only two of the seven sacraments—baptism and the Holy Eucharist, or Lord's Supper. But to Calvin, Christ was present only in spirit in the bread and wine and only for the elect. Calvin patterned his system of church government after that of the very earliest church as described in the Bible (Acts of the Apostles). The local churches were governed by laymen called *elders* who were elected by the congregations. A measure of unity in faith and practices was maintained by means of a hierarchy of representative assemblies.

During the second half of the sixteenth century it was Calvinism rather than Lutheranism that became the most dynamic force in Protestantism. Protestant Christians came from many countries to sit at the feet of Calvin and to study at the University of Geneva, which he founded. John Knox, who came from Scotland to study under Calvin, called the Genevan theocracy "the most perfect school of life that was ever on earth since the days of the apostles." Calvinists combined vigorous evangelical appeals with a systematic theology and a well-organized church. The Calvinist ethic of "the calling" to one's station on earth, no matter what it was, dignified striving and hard work.

Calvinism became dominant in most of Switzerland (Swiss Reformed), the Dutch Netherlands (Dutch Reformed), Scotland (Presbyterian), and the German Palatinate. It also had a strong minority following in England (the Puritans) and a smaller but vigorous following in France (the Huguenots), Bohemia, Hungary, and Poland. The Calvinists played an important part in the founding of the United States, particularly the Puritans in New England, the Dutch Reformed in New York, and the Scotch-Irish Presbyterians along the frontiers of all the original states. Such well-known denominations in present-day America as the Congregationalists, the Presbyterians, and the Baptists are Calvinist in origin.

4. ANGLICANISM

Foundations for the Reformation in England had been developing for many years before it was actually initiated by the actions of King Henry VIII (1509–1547). Lollardy, a movement of religious and social dissent stretching back over a hundred years, persisted as an underground movement into the sixteenth century. Humanism and anticlerical sentiments were gaining in strength. In 1525, William Tyndale (1494–1536), influenced by Luther, started printing an English translation of the Bible. However, the occasion of the beginning of the Reformation in England was the desire of

---

[3]The most serious of Servetus' heretical views were his denial of the Trinity, which cast doubt on the divinity of Christ, and his rejection of childhood baptism.

Henry VIII for a new wife and a male heir. Catherine of Aragon, to whom he had been married for eighteen years, had given him only a daughter, Mary. When it became apparent that Catherine would have no more children, Henry decided to ask the pope to annul the marriage. The pope, however, was in no position to grant the annulment. Catherine was the aunt of the Emperor Charles V, whose troops were at that very moment in control of the city of Rome. When Henry finally realized the pope was not going to accommodate him, he took matters into his own hands. At his bidding a subservient Parliament passed the Act of Supremacy (1534), making the king of England, not the pope, head of the Church in England. Later the monasteries, strongholds of papal influence, were dissolved and their holdings confiscated by the crown. Meanwhile, Thomas Cranmer, whom Henry made archbishop of Canterbury, had arranged the annulment, and Henry had married Anne Boleyn. (He was to marry six times in all.) Henry was, of course, excommunicated by the pope.

But Henry VIII was no Protestant. In the days before the annulment controversy the pope had given him the title "Defender of the Faith" for his anti-Lutheran writings. Now he had Parliament pass the Six Articles reaffirming the Catholic position on all controversial doctrinal points except that of papal supremacy. Protestants, on the one hand, and Roman Catholics who refused to acknowledge the headship of Henry VIII in place of the pope were persecuted with equal severity.

It was during the reign of Henry VIII's young son, Edward VI (1547–1553), that the Anglican church first became Protestant. Archbishop Cranmer drew up a *Book of Common Prayer* and Forty-two Articles of Faith that were definitely Calvinist in flavor. Edward VI was succeeded by his elder sister, Mary (1553–1558), who was the daughter of Catherine of Aragon and a devout Roman Catholic. Mary's ambition was to restore her kingdom to the Roman Catholic fold. Her first step was to marry her cousin, Philip II of Spain, the most powerful champion of resurgent Roman Catholicism in all Europe. Next she asked and received papal forgiveness for her wayward people. Finally, "Bloody Mary" burned at the stake some three hundred Protestants, including Archbishop

Cranmer. But Mary's marriage to a man soon to be king of Spain, England's most dangerous rival, and her persecutions were extremely unpopular in England; in the long run her policies hurt rather than helped the Roman Catholic cause there.

Elizabeth I (1558–1603), the Protestant daughter of Anne Boleyn, followed Mary on the English throne. This high-spirited, cynical, and politically minded queen found theology tiresome. Her chief interest was to find a satisfactory compromise that would unify her people. During the course of her long reign the Anglican church became definitely, but conservatively, Protestant. Cranmer's *Book of Common Prayer* was readopted with slight alterations. The Forty-two Articles were changed to the Thirty-nine. Some of the more controversial doctrinal points that seemed to prevent the various Protestant sects from uniting were reworded. Although celibacy of the clergy was abandoned, the episcopal system (government of the church by bishops) was retained. A rather elaborate ritual was adopted. Two of the sacraments, baptism and the Eucharist, were retained.

Although the great majority of the English people appeared to have accepted Elizabeth's compromise settlement, two groups remained dissatisfied. An extreme Calvinist element sought to "purify" the Anglican church of all remaining traces of Roman Catholicism. These Puritans were to increase in strength until under Oliver Cromwell's leadership in the next century they gained temporary control of the country. The Roman Catholic minority, on the other hand, lost steadily in numbers. The support that some Roman Catholics gave to Philip II's attempt to conquer England and to the effort of Mary, Queen of Scots (a Roman Catholic), to overthrow Elizabeth (see Chapter 31) tainted all of them with the suspicion of treason and played into Elizabeth's hands. By the end of her reign, England was one of the Protestant countries of Europe.

5. THE ANABAPTISTS

Some reformers believed that Luther, Calvin, and the Anglican leaders had not gone far enough. They would break more sharply with all the existing institutions of the early sixteenth century—

political, economic, and social as well as religious. Hence the term *radical* is often applied to them. Since these "radicals" were highly individualistic in their approach to religion, it is difficult to generalize about the many sects with their widely differing views and points of emphasis.

Generally, these sects tended to emphasize the evilness of the world, the mystical communion with God, the Second Coming of Christ, and the righteousness of the poor in their struggle against the rich. In some cases, religious reform became a means of social reform—a revolt of the poor against the rich.

These sects commonly rejected the doctrine of infant baptism. The true Christian, they believed, was one who was "born again" and baptized as an adult according to Scripture. Those who had been baptized as infants must be rebaptized. Anabaptism means *re*baptism. The Anabaptists believed that the true church of Christ on earth is a gathered church composed only of born-again Christians. The Anabaptists attempted to live lives of uncompromising holiness as dictated by the Bible or by the Holy Spirit speaking directly to each individual. These sects refused to recognize or participate in civil government, take oaths of allegiance, recognize titles, or serve in armed forces. Some practiced a shared economy. Most of them were poor. They were feared and persecuted by Roman Catholics, Lutherans, Calvinists, Anglicans, and secular leaders alike.

A few of the early Anabaptist leaders were violent activists, such as Thomas Müntzer, who inflamed the peasant rebels of southwest Germany, and John of Leyden, who set up a violent dictatorship in Münster in northwest Germany. This bizarre "heavenly Jerusalem" held out for more than a year against besieging Lutheran and Roman Catholic armies. The leaders were then tortured to death and their bodies hung in iron baskets from a church tower as a warning to radical dissenters. But the great majority of the Anabaptist leaders were pious and gentle—in fact, pacifists. Conrad Grebel, the first prominent Anabaptist leader, was a humanist from an upper-class family of Zurich, Switzerland. Probably the most successful and influential of all the Anabaptist leaders was the convert Menno Simons, a gentle former Roman Catholic priest from the Dutch

Netherlands. His followers, the Mennonites, spread throughout much of western Europe and later the United States. Also in the Anabaptist tradition was the Society of Friends, commonly known as Quakers. Founded by George Fox in England in the mid–seventeenth century, this pietistic and pacifistic sect has spread to many parts of the world.

6. CATHOLIC REFORM

The rise of Protestantism touched off an aggressive Catholic reform movement during the 1530s and 1540s, but even before this movement some efforts to revitalize Roman Catholicism had already taken place. In Spain, around the turn of the sixteenth century, Cardinal Ximenes had forestalled a possible protest movement by enforcing strict discipline on the clergy and waging bitter warfare against heresy. During the first few decades of the sixteenth century several religious orders such as the Theatines, the Capuchins, the Barnabites, and the Ursulines were founded and dedicated themselves to clerical reform and education within the Catholic church. Even before the revolt of Luther and Calvin, Catholic leaders from several countries pushed for the calling of a general council to authoritatively enact badly needed reforms. However, the secular interests of the Renaissance popes and the popes' fears that an assertive reform council might again challenge the absolute authority of the papacy prevented a coordinated European-wide reform. The last council to meet before the Reformation, the Fifth Lateran Council (1513–1517), bowed to the pope's control and enacted no major reforms.

After the 1520s and 1530s, with area after area becoming Protestant, countermeasures of a rather drastic nature became imperative. There were two schools of thought concerning the proper course of action. One, led by the liberal Cardinal Contarini of Venice, advocated compromise and conciliation. Contarini eventually went so far as to meet with Melanchthon, a close friend of Luther and an important figure in the Lutheran revolt, in earnest quest of an acceptable compromise. They were unsuccessful; the two religions appeared to be incompatible. The other school of thought was led by the conservative Cardinal Caraffa of Naples. Caraffa believed that many corrupt practices in the Church needed to be reformed but that no compromise whatever should be made in the dogma. He believed that the Protestants were heretics and could reunite with the Roman Catholic church only by recanting and submitting to the pope. This is the school of thought that triumphed, and Caraffa became Pope Paul IV. The upshot of this line of thinking was the calling of a Church council at Trent, an imperial city in northern Italy.

The Council of Trent

The Council of Trent, which was in session off and on for eighteen years from 1545 to 1563, was probably the most important council in the history of the Roman Catholic church. The popes skillfully controlled its membership and voting procedure. The ultimate decisions of the council were in two categories: dogmatic and reformatory. In matters of faith or dogma, all the traditional doctrines of the Church were reaffirmed and redefined, especially controversial ones such as the sacraments, transubstantiation, auricular confession, celibacy of the clergy, monasticism, purgatory, invocation of the saints, veneration of relics, and indulgences. The dogmatic canons and decrees of the council concluded: "Anathema to [accursed be] all heretics! Anathema! Anathema! Anathema!" The council also took stern measures to stop corrupt practices. Simony, nepotism, pluralism, and immorality and ignorance among the clergy were condemned. Schools for the education of the clergy were advocated. Bishops were admonished to exercise closer supervision and discipline over the lower clergy. To implement its canons and decrees, the council endorsed the Inquisition, which had recently been set up in Rome to combat heresy, and inaugurated the Index of Forbidden Books to prevent the reading of heretical literature except by authorized persons. Both instruments were placed under papal control and supervision.

Thus the Roman Catholic church at last spoke out, selected its weapons, and girded itself for more effective battle against the Protestants. At its service was the militant new Society of Jesus.

FIGURE 30.3   Ignatius Loyola (1491–1556)   Ignatius Loyola, by founding the Society of Jesus (the Jesuits), played a key role in the Catholic Reformation. Although not as scholarly as Luther or Calvin, he was a superb organizer and leader. (Culver Pictures)

The Society of Jesus

The founder of the Society of Jesus, Ignatius Loyola (1491–1556), was a member of the Spanish lesser nobility, and until early middle life he was an obscure soldier (see Figure 30.3). In a battle with the French his leg was crushed by a cannonball. During the months of agony and convalescence Loyola read lives of the Christian saints and underwent a deep spiritual conversion. He determined to devote his tremendous energies and latent talents to the service of the Roman Catholic church—to become a soldier of Christ, the Virgin Mary, and the pope. He set off for the University of Paris to begin his education. Loyola was, how-

WHERE HISTORIANS DISAGREE

The Meaning of the Reformation

Most historians agree that the Reformation was of major significance, but when they address the more difficult questions of its exact causes and nature, agreement ends.

Before the twentieth century, historians often confused their own religious preferences with historical analysis, becoming more interested in assigning blame or praise. Protestant scholars focused on the corruption of the Roman Catholic church, the heroic piety of Protestant figures, and the positive force of the Protestant Reformation in the modern world. Catholic scholars contended just the opposite, arguing that there was no crying need for doctrinal reform, that Protestant leaders were self-centered and ignorant theologians, and that the Protestant Reformation was to blame for the flood of secularization in the West.

Most twentieth-century historians look at the Reformation in more complex terms. Many favor sophisticated religious and cultural interpretations of the Reformation. These historians argue that the Reformation grew out of deep and widespread spiritual longing and dissatisfaction with the practices of the Catholic church. They emphasize that whatever other qualities Protestant leaders may have had, they were deeply religious people whose reforming doctrines and practices appealed to the spiritual and cultural needs of many. These historians also stress the spiritual concerns revealed in Catholic reform. To these historians, the sixteenth century was an age of religious reform.

Other historians think of the Protestant Reformation in primarily political terms. They stress that the time was ripe for the Reformation not only because of religious tensions but also because secular authorities favored it. They emphasize that vast numbers of people became Protestant or remained Catholic (or reconverted) because their political leaders de-manded it. They view the various religious movements of the sixteenth century as associated with nationalism. They believe it to be significant that the Protestant Reformation began in Germany, where there was no strong central government and where Luther strongly and openly appealed to German nationalism against Rome. By contrast, the strong rulers of France and Spain were able to extract such concessions from the pope as to create what amounted to a Gallican church and Spanish Catholic church, while successfully withstanding the Protestant challenge. The various Calvinistic churches were generally set up along national lines, such as the Swiss, Dutch, German, and Scottish Reformed churches. And of course the Anglican church was a national church.

Still other historians interpret the Reformation from an economic perspective. They point out the hunger for the rich lands held by the Roman church, the resentment over the tax exemption of these lands and over the draining away of money to Rome, and the opposition of the commercial class to the Church's ban on usury. Related to these points is the "Weber thesis." Max Weber and other scholars have argued that the hard work and asceticism which Calvinism stressed fit well with the emerging spirit of capitalism, which emphasized hard work, savings, and reinvestment. Thus Calvinism appealed particularly to commercial centers in Holland, England, Switzerland, and New England. From this perspective, then, Protestantism helped solve various economic problems of the era.

The long history and depth of these controversies over the meaning of the Reformation reveal how difficult evaluation of major religious change can be for the historian.

ever, not a scholar nor theologian but a man of action. He soon began to attract a band of followers, with whom he organized the Society of Jesus.

The Jesuit order, as the Society of Jesus was commonly known, was founded along military lines. Absolute and unquestioning obedience was the first requirement. Loyola admonished his followers, ". . . if she [the Church] shall have defined anything to be black which to our eyes appears to be white, we ought in like manner to pronounce it to be black." Applicants for membership were carefully selected and trained. For the spiritual guidance and inspiration of the members of the Society, Loyola wrote the *Spiritual Exercises*. The *Exercises* guide the member through a solid month of concentrated meditation, a week each on the horrors of sin, the life of Christ to Palm Sunday, his suffering and crucifixion, and his resurrection and ascension. This remarkable work has proved to be a powerful tool for training and rededication. Jesuits served as priests, teachers, medics, diplomats, or in almost any other capacity suitable to their talents and training—but always with the interests of the Catholic church in mind. After years of service a few of the most outstanding were admitted to the highest circle of officers who, under a general elected for life and residing in Rome, governed the order.

Loyola's high standards, far from deterring applicants, served as a challenge and an attraction. The Society of Jesus grew rapidly. As priests, the Jesuits were nearly always the best trained, the most popular, and the most influential. As teachers, they were usually more highly educated, devoted, and attractive than their competitors. They have always been keenly aware of the power of education, especially for the very young. "Give me the child, and I care not who has the man." The Jesuits soon gained control of education in most Roman Catholic countries.

These dedicated soldiers of Christ also made the best missionaries. In North and South America the dauntless Jesuits went among the Indians and converted most of them to Roman Catholic Christianity. In the Far East, Francis Xavier, second only to Loyola himself in Jesuit history, converted tens of thousands.

Not the least important of Jesuit activities was that of gaining the confidence of kings, princes, and other political personages, and thereby influencing state policy. This militantly zealous order was a powerful stimulant to the wavering cause of Roman Catholicism. In Italy, Spain, Portugal, and Ireland, where Protestantism had only a weak foothold, the Jesuits helped stamp it out altogether. In France and Belgium they helped to turn the tide against the Protestants. In southern Germany, Poland, and the Austrian Hapsburg lands, all of which seemed to be on the verge of going Protestant, the Jesuits reversed the trend and helped make those lands strongholds of Roman Catholicism.

7. WOMEN AND THE REFORMATION

As with the Renaissance, scholars question whether the Reformation benefited women socially or in any aspect of public life. Although Luther may have encouraged greater sharing within the household—the ideal of the companionate marriage—and acceptance of sexuality within the marriage, it is difficult to argue that his reforming ideas greatly improved the condition of women. In his eyes, women were expected to be satisfied as pious wives, mothers, and household managers, remaining clearly under the authority of their husbands. Despite some advocacy of mutual cooperation within the marriage, Calvin also rejected female independence and placed the husband at the head of the household.

The Protestant abolition of monasteries included women's religious orders, thereby eliminating one of the few occupational outlets available to sixteenth-century women. Protestantism offered no comparable alternatives for the thousands of women who left the often socially prestigious Catholic convents. Only well into the seventeenth century and in certain Protestant sects such as the Quakers did women start to play a public role as preachers.

Catholic reform resulted in few if any significant changes for women. Only the growth of pious Catholic women's organizations, such as the Ursulines, who were devoted to teaching girls, gave women some opportunity to play a more active role within the Church.

If the direct effect of the Reformation on women is uncertain, it is clear that women during that era suffered from an explosion of witch-hunts and prosecutions for infanticide. Beliefs in witchcraft dated back for centuries, but it was not until the sixteenth century that large numbers of women were actually prosecuted and put to death on charges of witchcraft. Protestants and Catholics alike charged women, usually older, lower-class women living in rural villages, with the heretical crime of making a pact with the devil and causing harm to their enemies. Tens of thousands of women were tried for witchcraft and perhaps a third of them were put to death.

Concurrent with these witchcraft hunts of the Reformation era came a flood of prosecutions for infanticide. While authorities prosecuted far fewer women for infanticide than witchcraft, those prosecuted were more likely to be found guilty and executed. Usually the objects of these prosecutions were poor unmarried younger women living in cities.

How much the Reformation itself had to do with this wave of lethal prosecutions of women is unknown. Perhaps more important were the growing efforts by the state to regulate behavior, the environment of fear during this period, and the general suspicion of women out of the norm in this male-dominated society. In any case, during the sixteenth and seventeenth centuries both Catholic and Protestant authorities, whether religious or secular, found sufficient theological and civil justifications to carry out these prosecutions that cost so many women their lives.

8. SUMMARY

Protestantism grew out of a widespread desire for greater spiritual satisfaction and correction of abuses within the Western Christian Church. Political and economic factors soon came into play to broaden the appeal and strength of the Protestant Reformation. Towns, princes, and kings saw the advantages of acquiring control over religious institutions and the tremendous wealth controlled by these institutions. This wealth and control served to strengthen their own political power. Since religious affiliation was viewed as integral to political and social order, conversion of political leaders eventually meant conversion of most of their people.

Initially Lutheranism was the dominant Protestant denomination, but in the second half of the century Calvinism became the most dynamic. By the end of the third quarter of the sixteenth century, Protestantism had triumphed in the northern half of the Germanies, in Scandinavia, in most of the Baltic provinces, in most of Switzerland, in the Dutch Netherlands, Scotland, and England. In addition, it had gained a strong minority following in France, Poland, Bohemia, and Hungary.

No matter how much the various Protestant denominations disagreed among themselves, they shared beliefs that put them at odds with the Roman Catholic church. They believed in justification by faith alone. They believed that the Roman Catholic church had departed so far from the spirit and practices of the apostles and early Fathers that it could no longer be considered God's appointed custodian of the Christian religion. Scripture alone, not the decisions and traditions of the Roman Catholic church, was their sole authoritative source for Christian dogma. They emphasized the direct relationship between human beings and God. They thought of the church as a priesthood of all believers. They rejected papal supremacy, the divine sanction of the Roman church, the celibacy and indelible character of the priesthood, monasticism, and such other characteristic Roman Catholic doctrines as purgatory, transubstantiation, invocation of saints, and veneration of relics.

The Roman Catholic church was not impotent in the face of these challenges. It had already initiated some internal reform efforts of its own prior to the outbreak of Protestantism, and those reform efforts grew throughout the sixteenth century. It also initiated a broad-based counter-Reformation to strengthen its hold in areas that remained Roman Catholic and to try to regain areas lost to Protestants. Despite some successes, however, it was never able to reconquer or reconvert the territories in which Protestants had gained a clear majority. The Reformation definitively split Western Christendom into hostile religious camps, and this religious hostility would spill over into decades of bloody wars and revolts.

SUGGESTED READING

General

G. R. Elton, *Reformation Europe 1517–1559* (1966). Particularly good for its treatment of the political context.

H. J. Grimm, *The Reformation Era* (1973). Sound and readable.

De Lamar Jensen, *Reformation Europe, Age of Reform and Revolution* (1981). A very good work.

R. L. de Molen, *Leaders of the Reformation* (1984). Portraits of key figures.

L. W. Spitz, *The Protestant Reformation* (1985). A solid, recent survey.

Lutheranism

J. Atkinson, *Martin Luther and the Birth of Protestantism* (1968). Good introduction.

E. Erikson, *Young Man Luther: A Study in Psychoanalysis and History* (1962). A highly important and influential interpretation.

H. G. Haile, *Luther: An Experiment in Biography* (1980). A modern treatment.

Calvinism

J. T. McNeil, *The History and Character of Calvinism* (1967). By a leading authority.

W. E. Monter, *Calvin's Geneva* (1967). Fine study of the Reformation in Geneva.

F. Wendel, *Calvin: The Origins and Development of His Thought* (1963). A good introduction to Calvin and Calvinism.

Anglicanism

A. G. Dickens, *The English Reformation* (1974). Best survey.

The Anabaptists

G. H. Williams, *The Radical Reformers* (1962). Excellent survey.

J. J. Scarisbrick, *The Reformation and the English People* (1985). A short survey.

Catholic Reform

A. G. Dickens, *The Counter Reformation* (1969). A brief well-written introduction.

René Fülop-Miller, *Jesuits: A History of the Society of Jesus* (1963). A thorough study with a psychological perspective.

H. Jedin, *A History of the Council of Trent*, 3 vols. (1957–1961). The standard, definitive work on the subject.

Women and the Reformation

M. J. Boxer and J. H. Quataert, eds., *Connecting Spheres: Women in the Western World, 1500 to the Present* (1987). Includes useful material on the period.

R. Bridenthal, C. Koonz, and S. Stuard, eds., *Becoming Visible: Women in European History, Second Edition* (1987). Includes a good chapter on this period.

CHAPTER 31
Politics and the Wars of Religion

FIGURE 31.1. François Dubois, "St. Bartholomew's Day Massacre" This painting of the St. Bartholomew's Day Massacre in 1572, by François Dubois, a contemporary Protestant painter, shows soldiers indiscriminately killing Huguenots in Paris. (Musée Cantonal des Beaux-Arts, Lausanne)

The Peace of Augsburg in 1555 brought an end to war between Catholics and Lutherans in Germany, and the Treaty of Cateau-Cambrésis in 1559 ended the Hapsburg-Valois wars. But these halts to long conflicts did not bring an end to the bloodshed. On the contrary, the period between 1560 and 1648 witnessed an outbreak of revolts, massacres, civil wars, and international wars that was unprecedented. While people in several areas suffered, the most intense and extended fighting occurred within the boundaries of the Holy Roman Empire. By the end of the Thirty Years' War in 1648, probably a third of the German population had died from the war.

Certainly religious differences were involved in these conflicts and accounted for the ferocity of the struggles (see Map 31.1). But politics and greed were also intertwined, with leaders vying for political gain and mercenaries thirsty for loot. Both crossed religious lines to make war for their own purposes.

1. THE CRUSADE OF CATHOLIC SPAIN

Emperor Charles V had bequeathed the greater part of his vast empire to his son Philip II (1556–1598) (see Figure 31.2). In addition to Spain, Philip's inheritance included the Netherlands, Franche-Comté, Milan, the Kingdom of Naples, Sardinia, and the Spanish Empire overseas. In 1580 Philip conquered Portugal in the name of his Portuguese mother and became master (at least in name) of Portugal's huge Eastern empire.

Philip II, unlike his father, was a native Spaniard. He utilized the gold and silver flowing in a steady stream from the New World and the lucrative commerce of the East Indies and of the busy Netherlands in the interests of Spain. Ignoring the Cortes and the local rights of Aragon and tending personally to the myriad details of government, the meticulous and stubborn Philip brought Spain under his sway to an extent that Ferdinand and Isabella and Charles V had never been able to do. With the best army in Europe and the will to use it, there is little wonder that the king of Spain was the most feared man in Western Christendom.

The Roman Catholic church was of great im-

FIGURE 31.2. Philip II Philip II of Spain was the most feared monarch in the Western world during the second half of the sixteenth century. A meticulous and stubborn ruler, he struggled to extend his own power and the dominance of the Roman Catholic church over Protestantism. (Alinari/Scala/Art Resource)

portance to Philip II. He conceived it to be his chief mission in life to use the great wealth and power of Spain to restore the dominion of the Roman church over all of Western Christendom. In the Netherlands, in England, and in France, Philip II threw the might of Spain on the side of the Roman Catholics in their counteroffensive against the Protestants.

Revolt in the Netherlands

Philip II, unlike his father, Charles V, was considered by the Netherlanders to be an unsympathetic foreigner who taxed their prosperous commerce and industry for the benefit of Spain. The abso-

Map 31.1 **RELIGIOUS MAP OF EUROPE, CA. 1560** This map indicates the religious divisions in Europe during the Reformation. In the turmoil between 1560 and 1648, most of those areas that had already turned Lutheran or had established Calvinist churches would remain Protestant. Those areas in which Protestant groups were in the minority would be subject to pressures and change.

lutist monarch and his Spanish administrators also overrode the traditional political privileges of the nobles and the cities in the Netherlands. Nonetheless, religion was the foremost cause of dissension. By mid–sixteenth century, nearly half the

people in the Netherlands had become Protestant. Most were Calvinists, but a considerable number were Anabaptists. Philip II, who would tolerate no heresy in his empire, took stern measures to stamp out Protestantism. The Inquisition was used to enforce the laws against heresy. In 1566, bands of outraged Protestants began to deface Roman Catholic churches. Philip thereupon dispatched Spanish troops under the duke of Alva to reduce the Netherlands to submission. A six-year reign of terror followed, in which thousands were put to death.

Far from being cowed, however, the Netherlanders resisted fiercely. They found a brilliant leader in William of Orange, or William the Silent, as he came to be known. They took to the sea, playing havoc with Spanish commerce and communications. When, in 1580, Philip conquered and annexed Portugal, the hardy Dutch "Sea Beggars" seized the richest parts of the Portuguese Empire in the East Indies. The Spanish infantry quickly overran the ten southern (Belgian) provinces, but against the seven northern (Dutch) provinces, made up largely of islands and peninsulas and skillfully defended by the Dutch fleet, Spain's armies could make little headway. Most of the Protestants soon fled north from the Spanish-occupied southern provinces. Likewise, most of the Roman Catholics fled south from the Protestant-dominated north. In 1579 the ten Roman Catholic southern provinces (now Belgium), fearful of the growing power of the Protestant northern provinces (which also spoke a different language), submitted to the Spanish yoke. The seven northern provinces, however, banded together in the Union of Utrecht and continued the struggle for independence. When in 1584 William the Silent was assassinated by a hireling of Philip II, other able leaders arose to take his place. Finally in 1609, eleven years after Philip's own death, Spain agreed to a twelve-year truce, and in 1648 Spain recognized the complete independence of the Dutch Netherlands, as the seven northern provinces are commonly called. In the seventeenth century the little Dutch republic led the world in commerce, in banking, and in painting and was second to none in science and philosophy.

Thus Philip II's crusade in the Netherlands was only partly successful. He saved the southern provinces for Spain for another century, and for the Roman Catholic church, but the Dutch provinces, the richest in his empire, were lost both to Spain and to the Church.

Struggles with England

Most grandiose of all Philip II's crusading efforts was his attempt to restore wayward England to the Roman Catholic fold. His first move was to marry England's Roman Catholic queen, Mary Tudor. They wed in 1554, two years before his own rule over the Spanish Empire. However, Mary's marriage to the king of a feared and hated rival power and her persecution of English Protestants only increased her own unpopularity and that of the Roman Catholic cause in England. Moreover, the marriage failed to produce an heir. When Mary died in 1558, Philip sought to continue his influence in England by trying to marry her successor, Elizabeth. But Elizabeth, a Protestant and a high-spirited English patriot, refused.

Elizabeth proved to be one of England's ablest monarchs (see Figure 31.3). In style and policy, she was a *politique*—a ruler who avoided strong religious stands and emphasized moderation, pragmatism, tolerance, or avoidance in religious matters. For her, like other *politiques* such as William of Orange, religious concerns were subordinated to the need for political unity. She guided the Anglican church to a moderate Protestant position.

Spain's military successes led Elizabeth to support Spain's opponents. In the 1570s and 1580s she signed an alliance with France and aided the Dutch Protestant rebels. She also encouraged English sea dogs to plunder Spain's treasure ships sailing from its New World colonies—indeed, to plunder the colonies themselves. When in 1587 Spanish plots against Elizabeth clearly implicated Mary, Queen of Scots (a Catholic), Elizabeth was forced to execute her. It was then clear that England would not peacefully rejoin the Catholic fold.

Philip II tried to conquer England by direct military action. In 1588 his "Invincible" Armada sailed forth—130 ships, many of them great galleons. Aboard was a formidable Spanish army. The Armada was to go first to the Netherlands and pick up additional soldiers. In the English Channel it met the somewhat larger English fleet, composed mostly of smaller but swifter and more heavily armed ships. The Spaniards fought well

FIGURE 31.3.   Marcus Gheeraert, "Queen Elizabeth I"   Marcus Gheeraert's portrait of Queen Elizabeth I shows this monarch at the height of her power (a picture of her victory over the Spanish Armada in the background, the crown to her right, her right hand on the globe) and wealth (her jewel-laden attire). (Cooper-Bridgeman Library)

until finally their formation was broken by English fire ships sent into their midst. Once scattered, the Spanish ships were no match for the English fleet. Storms played a major role in the loss of Spanish ships. Only about half the ships ever reached Spain. It was at this point that England began to wrest control of the seas from Spain. Not only had Philip II failed to exterminate Protestantism in England, but the Roman Catholic cause there was now tainted with treason, and Protestantism was stronger than ever.

Confronting the Ottoman Turks

In the sixteenth century, the Ottoman Empire under Suleiman had grown in power to its greatest extent. Victories over Christian troops in Hungary had threatened central Europe. Ottoman fleets dominated large parts of the Mediterranean. The Hapsburgs had traditionally led in the struggle against the Ottomans and Islam in general, and Philip II took up the challenge with vigor. Under the urging of the pope, Venice, Genoa, and Spain amassed a fleet of more than two hundred vessels under the command of Philip's illegitimate half brother, Don Juan. In 1571 this fleet caught and annihilated the somewhat larger Turkish fleet off Lepanto on the coast of Greece. This was one of the few clear-cut successes of Philip's career. Lepanto greatly diminished the Turkish menace to Christendom by sea and marked the beginning of a long, slow period of decline for the Ottoman Empire.

2. THE RELIGIOUS WARS IN FRANCE

In France and Germany during the late sixteenth and first half of the seventeenth centuries, struggles between Protestants and Catholics combined with conflicts between different political factions to break out into bitter wars, usually called the Wars of Religion.

In France Calvinism had made slow but steady progress during the reigns of Francis I (1515–1547) and Henry II (1547–1559) in spite of vigorous persecution by those Roman Catholic monarchs. By 1559 the Huguenots, as the French Calvinists were called, numbered possibly a twelfth of the total population. However, since their ranks included many of the prosperous bourgeoisie and some of the greatest noble families of France, their influence was far greater than their numbers would indicate. Enmity between the Huguenots and the Roman Catholics, which had smoldered under the strong rule of Francis I and of Henry II, broke into open and consuming flame under Henry II's three ineffective sons, who ruled in succession from 1559 to 1589. All three were dominated by their powerful and ambitious mother, Catherine de Médicis. This situation invited political as well as religious faction and intrigue, and in the civil wars that followed politics and religion were intertwined.

The leadership of the Roman Catholic faction was assumed by the powerful Guise family; that of the Protestants by the influential Bourbon family, who were related to the royal line. The first eight years of fighting were ended in 1570 by an uneasy truce. However, Catherine de Médicis became fearful of the growing influence of the Huguenots. She turned for support to the Catholic

Guises, and under their influence she agreed to a plan to massacre the Huguenots. At a given signal at midnight, August 24, 1572 (St. Bartholomew's Day), the Roman Catholics in Paris fell to slaughtering the Protestants. The massacre soon spread to the provinces and went on for a number of weeks. Thousands of Huguenots were slain.

The ablest of the Huguenot leaders, young Henry (Bourbon) of Navarre, escaped and rallied the remaining Protestant forces for the war that was now renewed in earnest. The wealth and energy of the numerous bourgeois and noble members of the Huguenot faction, plus the brilliance of their dashing young leader, offset the superior numbers of the Roman Catholics. Eventually Henry III, the third son of Catherine de Médicis to rule France, organized a moderate Roman Catholic faction to stand between the uncompromising Guise faction and the Protestants. The struggle now became a three-cornered "War of the Three Henrys" (Henry, duke of Guise, Henry of Navarre, and Henry III, king of France). Philip II of Spain threw his support to Henry, duke of Guise. Henry III, now regarding Henry, duke of Guise, as the greater menace to his own royal authority, had him assassinated in 1588. The next year an agent of the Guises assassinated Henry III. This left Protestant Henry of Navarre, by right of succession, King Henry IV of France. However, it was only when he abjured Protestantism four years later and went through the formality of becoming a Roman Catholic that the great majority of his subjects, who were Roman Catholics, allowed him to enter Paris and be legally crowned. "Paris is worth a Mass," he is alleged to have remarked. Five years later (1598) he issued his famous Edict of Nantes (see p. 420), which, by granting tolerance to the Protestant minority, ended religious strife in France for nearly a century.[1] By these acts, Henry revealed himself as a *politique*, favoring national unity over religious concerns. He enjoyed some of the same success and popularity as other *politiques*, such as Elizabeth I in England and William of Orange in the Netherlands.

---

[1]The Huguenots rose up in a brief rebellion (1627–1629) against Cardinal Richelieu when he removed their military and political privileges (see p. 421).

FIGURE 31.4. **The Thirty Years' War**   This print shows Magdeburg, where in 1631 one of the battles of the Thirty Years' War was fought. The last and the bloodiest of the religious wars that accompanied the Reformation, the Thirty Years' War devastated much of Germany and exhausted its participants. (NYPL Picture Collection)

3. THE THIRTY YEARS' WAR IN GERMANY

The Peace of Augsburg (1555), which had brought to a close the first armed conflict in Germany between the Roman Catholics and the Lutherans, proved to be only an uneasy truce. Since the signing of the treaty, which recognized only Roman Catholics and Lutherans, the Calvinists had made strong headway in several states of the Holy Roman Empire and demanded equal recognition. Furthermore, lands of the Roman Catholic church were constantly being secularized in Protestant areas in violation of the treaty. On the other hand, the Roman Catholics, being more aggressive as a result of the clarification of their position by the Council of Trent and the activities of the militant Jesuits, talked of exterminating Protestantism in the Holy Roman Empire and recovering all their lost lands and souls. The Protestants in alarm formed a defensive league. The Roman Catholics countered by forming a league of their own.

The increasing tension finally erupted into the Thirty Years' War (1618–1648) (see Figure 31.4). In this war the religious issue was complicated and often confused by political and dynastic issues. The individual princes of the empire were struggling to maintain or even increase their independence from the emperor. The Hapsburg dynasty, both Austrian and Spanish, threatened to become so powerful that the apprehensive Bourbons of France entered the war against them. The upshot was that eventually the Roman Catholics, the Holy Roman emperor, and the Hapsburg dynasty (the emperor was an Austrian Hapsburg) formed one faction against which were arrayed the Protestants, most of the individual princes of the empire, and the Bourbons.

The long-brewing Thirty Years' War began in 1618 when a group of Bohemian nobles, mostly Calvinists and fearful of losing both their religious and their political rights, declared their Hapsburg ruler deposed and chose the Calvinist elector of the Palatinate as their king. The Hapsburg Holy

Ottoman Empire

Austrian Hapsburgs

Spanish Monarchy

Swedish Dominions

Brandenburg-Prussia

— Boundary of the Holy Roman Empire

0   100   200   300 miles

SHETLAND I.

NORWAY

• Bergen

SWEDEN

• Stockholm

ORKNEY I.

KINGDOM OF
DENMARK AND NORWAY

SCOTLAND

• Edinburgh

NORTH SEA

DENMARK

• Copenhagen

BALTIC SEA

BRANDENBURG-PRUSS

SCHLESWIG

SWEDISH
POMERANIA

• Danzi

IRELAND

• Dublin

ENGLAND
(COMMONWEALTH
1649–1660
UNITED KINGDOM
1707)

HOLSTEIN

• Hamburg

POMERELIA

Vistul

HANOVER

Bremen •

BRANDENBURG

GREAT
POLAND

ATLANTIC OCEAN

London •

UNITED
PROVINCES

Amsterdam •
Ryswick •

• Berlin

ENGLISH CHANNEL

SPANISH
NETH.

• Brussels

• Leipzig

SAXONY

L
PO

SILESIA

C

Paris •   • Verdun

MINOR
GERMAN STATES

BOHEMIA

MORAVIA

FRANCE

Toul •

LORRAINE

ALSACE

FRANCHE
COMTÉ

• Augsburg

BAVARIA

AUSTRIA

• Vienna

Kingdom of Hungary

• Bu

HUNGAR

SWISS
CANTONS

SAVOY

PIEDMONT

REP. OF VENICE

• Milan

• Venice

SLAVONIA

• Parma

PORTUGAL
(TO SPAIN
1580–1640)

PYRENEES

CATALONIA

Marseilles •

TUSCANY

• Zara

BOSNIA

ADRIATIC SEA

MONTENEGR

S

• Madrid

CASTILE

ARAGON

CORSICA
(Genoa)

PAPAL
STATES

Rome •

• Bari

Lisbon •

SPAIN

BALEARIC I.

MINORCA

SARDINIA

IONIAN
(Venice

MAJORCA

KINGDOM OF NAPLES

Naples •

GIBRALTAR

Tangier
(Portugal)

• • Ceuta (Spain)

• Algiers

MEDITERRANEAN

• Palermo

SICILY

• Oran (Spain)

Tunis •

SEA

FEZ AND MOROCCO

BARBARY   STATES

ALGERIA

TUNISIA

MALTA (Spain)

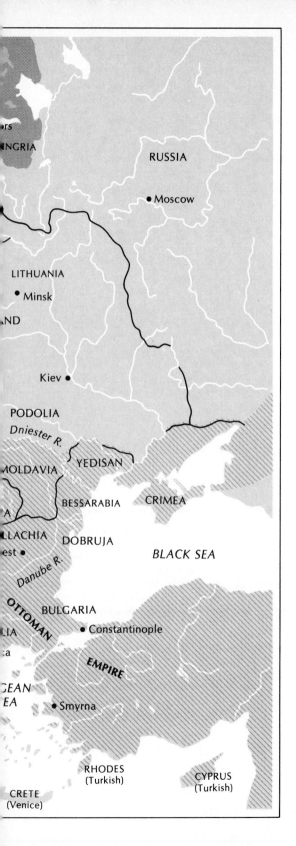

Roman emperor, aided by the Roman Catholic League and by Hapsburg and Roman Catholic Spain, took the field and easily crushed both Bohemia and the Palatinate. Hundreds of Calvinist Bohemian nobles were executed and their property confiscated. Protestantism was outlawed in Bohemia. The Calvinist Palatinate was annexed to Roman Catholic Bavaria. This quick and crushing victory by Roman Catholic and imperial forces frightened not only the Protestant princes of northern Germany, but also the Protestant neighboring states.

In 1625 Lutheran King Christian IV of Denmark, who held numerous bishoprics in Germany that had been illegally secularized, entered the war against the Roman Catholic and imperial forces. Christian IV was aided by English subsidies and numerous German Protestant princes. At this critical juncture a brilliant soldier of fortune, Albrecht von Wallenstein, offered his services to the emperor. This military genius raised a volunteer army of fifty thousand adventurers of various nationalities. Wallenstein's army, together with the regular imperial and Roman Catholic forces, defeated Christian IV and drove him out of Germany. The Danish king was deprived of nearly all his German holdings. Upon the conclusion of this phase of the war in 1629, the victorious emperor issued the Edict of Restitution, restoring to the Roman Catholic church all the lands illegally secularized since the Peace of Augsburg—more than a hundred tracts, large and small.

The whole Protestant world was now genuinely alarmed at the resurgent power of the Roman Catholics. The German princes were faced with the loss of their powers to the Holy Roman emperor. The French Bourbons were concerned

Map 31.2 EUROPE, 1648 This map of Europe after the Treaty of Westphalia in 1648 shows that what would eventually become unified into Germany during the nineteenth century was still greatly divided within a Holy Roman Empire that was weaker than ever. With the rapid decline of Spain, most political conflict in the century after 1648 would be between France, England, Austria-Hungary, and Brandenburg-Prussia.

about the rapidly growing strength of the Hapsburgs. At this juncture another Protestant champion stepped forward—Gustavus Adolphus of
Sweden. This Lutheran "Lion of the North" was
a military leader of great ability. Furthermore, he
was well backed by French gold. Gustavus Adolphus led his army victoriously through the Germanies, gaining allies among the Protestant
princes as he went. The Hapsburg emperor hastily
recalled the ambitious Wallenstein, whom he had
dismissed upon the conclusion of the Danish
phase of the war. Two of the ablest military commanders of early modern times now faced each
other. In the battle of Lützen (1632) Wallenstein
was defeated, but Gustavus Adolphus had been
killed and the victory was far from decisive. For-
tunately for the Protestants, Wallenstein was dismissed and two years later was assassinated. Since
Sweden had failed to turn the tide of the war, the
Bourbon king of France in 1635 threw the full
weight of his military might directly into the fray.
For thirteen more years the war dragged on until
all participants were exhausted. The Treaty of
Westphalia in 1648 finally brought the struggle to
a close (see Map. 31.2).

In general, thanks largely to the intervention
of France, the Roman Catholics, the Holy Roman
emperor, and the Hapsburgs suffered a setback.
Not only were the Roman Catholics thwarted in
their efforts to exterminate Protestantism in Germany, but the Calvinists now gained equal status
with the Lutherans and Roman Catholics in the
Holy Roman Empire. The Edict of Restitution was
nullified. The Holy Roman Empire practically fell
apart. According to the terms of the Treaty of
Westphalia, each of the more than three hundred
individual princes could now make his own treaties. Three of the most important princes, the rulers of Brandenburg, Bavaria, and Saxony, made
sizable additions to their territories. Sweden
gained strategic territories along the German Baltic
and North Sea coasts. France gained the important
bishoprics and fortress cities of Metz, Toul, and
Verdun, and the province of Alsace except for the
free city of Strasbourg. These former imperial territories gave both Sweden and France a vote in
the Diet of the Holy Roman Empire and a say in
German affairs. The complete independence of
Switzerland and the Dutch Netherlands was officially recognized. The Austrian Hapsburgs retained their hereditary possessions but lost prestige as emperors of a disintegrating Holy Roman
Empire. Also, their relative position declined as
that of France rose. The Spanish Hapsburgs fared
worse. After eleven more years of fighting with
France they yielded a strip of the Spanish Netherlands and another strip along the Spanish border to France. Spain's days of greatness were finished.

The immediate effect of the Thirty Years' War
on Germany was disastrous. For three decades
hostile German and foreign armies had tramped
back and forth across Germany, killing, raping,
and looting the defenseless inhabitants. In the
wake of Wallenstein's army of fifty thousand, for
instance, swarmed one hundred fifty thousand
camp followers bent on plunder. To the usual horrors of war was added religious fanaticism. Some
30 to 40 percent of Germany's inhabitants lost their
lives from this war. Many years would be required
for Germany to recover from these wounds.

The Thirty Years' War was the last and the
bloodiest of the religious wars that accompanied
the Reformation. Although there would still be
much religious strife and controversy, the religious map of Europe henceforth would change
very little. After 1648 political rather than religious
affairs would occupy center stage in the Western
world.

SUGGESTED READING

General

T. Aston, ed., *Crisis in Europe 1560–1660: Essays from Past and Present* (1965). An important interpretation of the whole period as one of general crisis.

R. Dunn, *The Age of Religious Wars, 1559–1689* (1979). A good, brief survey.

T. Rabb, *The Struggle for Stability in Early Modern Europe* (1975). Analyzes the "crisis" interpretation.

The Crusade of Catholic Spain

W. T. MacCaffrey, *Queen Elizabeth and the Making of Policy, 1572–1588* (1982). A good recent analysis.

G. Mattingly, *The Armada* (1959). Brilliantly shows the impact of the Armada's failure on all of Europe.

Geoffrey Parker, *Spain and the Netherlands, 1559–1659* (1979). A clear introduction.

P. Pierson, *Philip II of Spain* (1975). A well-written biography.

Religious Wars in France

J. H. M. Salmon, *The French Wars of Religion: How Important Were Religious Factors?* (1967). A collection of provoking interpretations.

J. H. M. Salmon, *Society in Crisis: France in the Sixteenth Century* (1975). Focuses on French institutions.

The Thirty Years' War

Georges Pagès, *The Thirty Years' War: 1618–1648* (1971). A clear history of the conflict.

T. K. Rabb, ed., *The Thirty Years' War* (1981). A collection of differing interpretations of the war and its significance.

Retrospect

During the fourteenth and fifteenth centuries, various tensions and a weakening of social institutions marked the transformation of the medieval world. During the fifteenth and sixteenth centuries, the institutions and developments that would characterize early modern times grew out of the changing medieval system. The five most important developments of the fifteenth and sixteenth centuries were the Renaissance, the rise of national states, the expansion of Europe, the rise of a capitalistic economy, and the Reformation.

The first challenge to the medieval system came in the cities of northern Italy during the fourteenth and fifteenth centuries. There the ideas, values, and culture of the Renaissance arose. Scholars, writers, and artists began looking back to classical Greece and Rome for models instead of accepting medieval scholastic authority. Cultural leaders focused more on individual human beings living in a concrete, material, Christian world rather than on medieval theology.

Western Europeans of the social and cultural elite were becoming more self-centered, proud, versatile, and materialist. These Renaissance qualities produced new, vibrant literature and art, making northern Italy the cultural center of the West.

During the fifteenth and sixteenth centuries the Renaissance spread from Italy to northern Europe, particularly to the courts of princes and kings and to university towns. There the Renaissance took on a more piously religious character as northern humanists tried to reconcile Christian and classical cultures.

In place of the declining feudal monarchies and empires arose the national or territorial state, which became the dominant political institution of the early modern era. The rise of the national states ended the independence of numerous feudal lords by bringing them under the authority of national monarchs. Talented monarchs such as Ferdinand and Isabella in Spain, Louis XI in France, and Henry VII in England increased their own power and established foundations for the continued growth of national monarchical power. Those areas that did not unify into national states, such as in Germany and Italy, suffered from political weakness.

National monarchs encouraged Europeans to expand into the non-Western world. Voyages of discovery soon led to commercial trade, spreading Christianity, and political control. During the fifteenth and early sixteenth centuries, Portugal and Spain led in this expansion of Europe. England, France, and the Netherlands soon followed. By the end of the sixteenth century, large parts of the rest of the world, particularly in the Western Hemisphere, southern Asia, and coastal Africa, had come under European economic and political domination.

The expansion of Europe was also stimulated by new economic developments. Europe's medieval economy, characterized by subsistence agriculture, monopolistic guilds, and localism, slowly gave way to capitalistic practices and institutions. Increasing population and rising prices spurred commerce and created social turmoil, with poorer peasants suffering the most. The old landed aristocracy was now threatened by newcomers into the class and by a new middle class of aggressive entrepreneurs, merchants, bankers, and lawyers. It is true that the bourgeoisie sought most of all to enter the ranks of the nobility, and did so whenever possible, and that the nobility held the upper hand politically and socially for two or three more

centuries. But by 1600 class lines had become more fluid.

The fifteenth and sixteenth centuries were marked by a deepening concern for religious matters. During the 1500s the Western Christian Church, which had monopolized religious life and strongly influenced the intellectual, political, and economic life of Europe during the Middle Ages, was split asunder by the Reformation. Great religious leaders such as Martin Luther and John Calvin broke from the Roman church and laid the foundations for the various Protestant churches. Much of northern Europe became Protestant. This advance of Protestantism stimulated reform efforts already underway within the Roman Catholic church. Catholic doctrine was forcefully affirmed at the Council of Trent, and new religious orders such as the Jesuits reinvigorated the Church.

The religious struggles of the Reformation combined with political forces to give rise to the Wars of Religion. From the middle of the sixteenth to the middle of the seventeenth centuries, much of Europe was struck by war and political turmoil that was connected to religious issues. The most devastating of these wars was the Thirty Years' War, which broke out in Germany in 1618 and was not concluded until 1648 with the Peace of Westphalia. By this time, the developments initiated during the fifteenth and sixteenth centuries were achieving a new maturity. Europe was already entering into the Age of Royal Absolutism.

PART EIGHT

THE AGE OF ROYAL ABSOLUTISM, SEVENTEENTH AND EIGHTEENTH CENTURIES

As we have seen, the fifteenth and sixteenth centuries were a period of change and upheaval. The Renaissance, the Reformation and the Wars of Religion, the rise of the new monarchs, the commercial revolution, and the expansion of Europe marked the period as substantially different from the preceding Middle Ages and as the beginnings of early modern times. The seventeenth and eighteenth centuries constituted a period when the society, culture, and institutions of early modern Europe matured. The mid-seventeenth century to the last decades of the eighteenth century was a period of relative stability. Historians have often referred to this period of European history as *"l'ancien régime,"* the Old Regime before the French Revolution of 1789.

The dominating development of this period was the growing power of central governments, particularly in the form of royal absolutism. The government of France under Louis XIV epitomized this royal absolutism. An important contrasting trend to royal absolutism was constitutionalism, where the king lost the struggle for greater power. The most striking examples of constitutionalism were in England and the Netherlands.

In most other ways the society and culture of the seventeenth and eighteenth centuries evolved only slowly, reflecting the growing power of central governments and their reigning monarchs. Aristocrats remained socially dominant but with some exceptions, such as in England and the Netherlands, were domesticated by royal monarchs or integrated into the service of the crown's central government. Life for most people still took place in the countryside and in traditional villages, which were only starting to evolve as the tentacles of central governments and economic change reached them. Here it was only in the second half of the eighteenth century that the agricultural revolution and the spread of cottage industry quickened economic and social change. Most religious affiliations remained as determined during the course of the Reformation and Wars of Religion, with established churches usually working hand in hand with monarchs and aristocrats. The most important cultural trends—the baroque and the classical styles—reflected royal grandeur and aristocratic tastes.

Intellectually, however, two developments occurred that would eventually undermine this traditional order of early modern Europe and provide a foundation for the modern society of the nineteenth and twentieth centuries: the Scientific Revolution and the Enlightenment. Yet even these intellectual developments took place only among a small elite and within the political and social context of the seventeenth and eighteenth centuries.

This period, then, is best organized around its most dominating and striking development—the rise and maturation of royal absolutism. The first two chapters examine royal absolutism and the challenges to royal absolutism in western Europe. The third chapter traces the rise of royal absolutism in eastern Europe. The next chapter turns to the competition among states for power, colonies, and empire—in many ways another element of the growing power of central governments. Focus then broadens to economic, social, cultural, religious, and intellectual developments of the period, most of which in some ways reflect the rise of and struggle with royal absolutism in the seventeenth and eighteenth centuries.

CHAPTER 32

The Dominance of France:
The Age of Louis XIV

FIGURE 32.1. Pierre Patel the Elder, "Versailles," 1668 This painting shows Louis XIV's palace and grounds at Versailles in 1668. The scale and order of Versailles reflected the grandeur of the French monarchy at its height. Other European monarchs modeled their palaces after Versailles in an attempt to increase their own prestige. (Lauros-Giraudon/Art Resource)

France was the dominant nation in Europe throughout most of the seventeenth and eighteenth centuries. Under Louis XIV royal absolutism not only reached its peak in France but also served as a model that other monarchs sought to emulate. The well-lighted stage across which the "Sun King" strode was set for him by three able predecessors—Henry IV, Richelieu, and Mazarin.

1. THE RISE OF FRANCE UNDER HENRY IV, RICHELIEU, AND MAZARIN

When Henry IV became king of France in 1589, his country was torn from several decades of bitter religious war. Respect for law and order had broken down. The feudal nobility had in many cases reasserted its own authority. The finances of the central government were in chaos. Roads and bridges were in disrepair. French prestige abroad was at a low ebb; even the city of Paris was garrisoned by the Spanish troops of Philip II.

Henry of Navarre, the first of the Bourbon dynasty to rule France, set out to change all this. The new king, in his prime at the age of thirty-six, was debonair and witty, courageous, generous, and optimistic. His slogan, "A chicken in the pot of every peasant for Sunday dinner," was more than an idle phrase; it is little wonder that *Henri Quatre* became the most popular monarch in French history. The romantic Henry had in the duke of Sully an able, methodical administrator to serve and steady him. The most urgent task was to restore the authority of the central government. This Henry set out to do by vigorously suppressing brigandage and enforcing the law. The lesser nobility was brought to heel directly and quickly. The powerful nobility was dealt with more gingerly, but by the end of Henry's reign real headway had been made toward reducing the nobles to obedience to the central government.

Henry and Sully launched a comprehensive program of economic reconstruction. Agriculture and commerce benefited from the increased security of life and property, from the repair of roads, bridges, and harbors, and from the freeing of internal and external commerce of many obstructions and tariff barriers. Marshes were drained for farming. Better breeding methods were introduced. The peasants' livestock and implements were protected against seizure for debt or taxes. New industries producing glass, porcelain, lace, tapestries, and fine leather and textiles were subsidized and protected by the state. Silk culture, which brought vast wealth to France, was introduced. The building of France's overseas empire began in 1608 when Champlain founded Quebec, the first French colony in the New World.

When Henry IV came to the throne, only about a fourth of the heavy taxes, from which the clergy and the nobility were largely exempted, ever reached the national treasury. The rest went into the pockets of corrupt officials and tax farmers, that is, the collectors who bid a fixed sum for the privilege of collecting the taxes and were permitted to keep anything over and above the contracted amount. Sully was unable to change this vicious system, but by means of careful bookkeeping, efficient administration of expenditures, and elimination of corruption, he was able to show a surplus for the first time in many years.

Another major achievement of Henry's reign was the granting of religious toleration to the Huguenot minority. A *politique*, Henry abjured Protestantism in order to gain acceptance as king of an overwhelmingly Roman Catholic nation. The Edict of Nantes, which Henry IV issued in 1598, granted the Huguenots not only complete freedom of conscience and limited public worship but also civil and political equality. Moreover, they were given military control of some two hundred fortified cities and towns as a guarantee against future oppression.

Having laid the foundations for royal supremacy, economic health, and religious toleration, Henry IV in the last years of his reign devoted an increasing amount of attention to foreign affairs. His goal was to make France first secure and then supreme in Europe by weakening the power of the Spanish and Austrian Hapsburgs. In 1610 he readied his armies for a campaign, but just as he was preparing to join them he was assassinated by a fanatic.

After fourteen years of retrogression under Henry IV's Italian wife, Marie de Médicis, and their young and inept son Louis XIII (1610–1643), Cardinal Richelieu gained active control over the

FIGURE 32.2. Champaigne, "Cardinal Richelieu"
The imperious and ruthless Richelieu played a major role in making the royal power supreme in France and France the supreme power in Europe. Here he poses in church robes befitting his office as a cardinal. (Scala/Art Resource)

government of France (see Figure 32.2). Although technically a mere servant of the fickle Louis XIII, the masterful cardinal made himself so indispensable that for eighteen years (1624–1642) he held firm control over French affairs. Handsome, arrogant, and calculating, Richelieu was a true Machiavellian. His twofold policy, from which he never veered, was similar to that of Henry IV—to make the royal power supreme in France and France supreme in Europe.

Believing the high nobility and the Huguenots to be the chief threats to royal absolutism, Riche-

lieu crushed them both. With the royal army at his disposal, he boldly destroyed the castles of the nobles who remained defiant, disbanded their private armies, and hanged a number of the most recalcitrant. The special military and political privileges that the Huguenots enjoyed under the Edict of Nantes were considered by Richelieu to be intolerable, giving them the status of a state within a state. After a bloody two-year struggle, he stripped the Huguenots of these privileges, although he left their religious and civil liberties intact.

In order to bypass local political influence, which in some provinces was still strong, the dynamic minister divided France into some thirty administrative districts called *généralités*, each of which was placed under the control of an *intendant*,[1] who was an agent of the crown. So absolute was the power of the *intendants* over local affairs, even of the most minute nature, that they came to be called the "thirty tyrants of France." They were chosen from the ranks of the bourgeoisie and were shifted around frequently lest they become too sympathetic with the people over whom they ruled. The royal will was thus extended to every part of France.

Although Richelieu was a cardinal in the Roman Catholic church, he did not hesitate to plunge France into the Thirty Years' War in Germany on the side of the Protestants. His purpose, of course, was to weaken the Hapsburgs, chief rivals of the French Bourbons for European supremacy. When Richelieu died in 1642, he had gone far toward bringing to fruition Henry IV's policies of royal supremacy in France and French supremacy in Europe. Richelieu, however, did not share Henry IV's concern for the common people. Their lot became harder under the imperious and ruthless cardinal, at whose death they rejoiced.

Richelieu was succeeded by his protégé, Cardinal Mazarin. Louis XIII's death in 1643, one year after that of his great minister, left the throne to Louis XIV (1643–1715), a child of five. Mazarin played the same role in the early reign of Louis XIV that Richelieu had played during most of the

---

[1]The *intendants* existed before Richelieu's time, but he greatly increased their power and functions.

reign of Louis XIII. From the death of Richelieu in 1642 until his own death in 1661, Mazarin vigorously pursued the policies of his predecessor. The Thirty Years' War was brought to a successful conclusion. All who challenged the crown's absolute authority were crushed.

The most noteworthy events during his administration were a series of uprisings between 1648 and 1652, known as the *Fronde*. The Fronde was a revolt of the disgruntled nobility and townspeople against the ever-increasing authority of the central government. At times it looked as if the rebels might succeed, but the rebellious factions could not unify. In the end only Mazarin and the monarchy represented order in the face of apparent chaos, and the rebels were defeated. The failure of the Fronde marked the last overt resistance to royal absolutism in France until the French Revolution in 1789. When Cardinal Mazarin died in 1661, he passed along to young Louis XIV a royal power that was at last absolute and a national state that was easily the first power of Europe.

2. LOUIS XIV AND HIS GOVERNMENT

Louis XIV was twenty-three years old when, in 1661, he stepped forth as the principal actor on the world's gaudiest stage. Young Louis was well fitted for the part. He had a sound body and a regal bearing. His lack of intellectual brilliance and of deep learning were more than offset by a large store of common sense, a sharp memory, a sense of responsibility, and a capacity for hard, tedious work. From his Spanish mother, from Mazarin, and from his tutors he had gained the conviction that he was God's appointed deputy for France. In Bishop Bossuet he had the most famous of all theorists and exponents of royal absolutism. Bossuet in numerous writings argued that absolute monarchy is the normal, the most efficient, and the divinely ordained form of government. He contended that, furthermore, the royal monarch, the image of God and directly inspired by God, is above human reproach and accountable to God alone. These ideas as acted out by Louis gained and held the ascendancy throughout the continent

of Europe during the late seventeenth and most of the eighteenth centuries.

Absolute though he might consider himself [the words *"L état, c'est moi"* ("I am the state") are often attributed to him], Louis could not possibly perform all the functions of government personally. Actually, the great bulk of the decisions and details of government were handled by a series of councils and bureaus and were administered locally by the *intendants*. Distrusting nobles, Louis appointed members of the middle class to the important offices of his government. The functions of the chief councils, such as those of state, finances, dispatches, and the privy council, appear on paper to have been overlapping and ill defined. As supervised by the industrious Louis XIV, however, the administrative machinery worked smoothly and efficiently. In fact, it was the envy of his fellow monarchs and probably constituted his most constructive achievement. There was no semblance of popular participation in government. The role of the people was to serve and obey; in return, they enjoyed reflected glory and received such benefits as the monarch might be willing and able to bestow on them. The Estates General was not called once during the seventy-two years of Louis XIV's reign or the fifty-nine-year rule of his successor.

3. THE KING AND HIS COURT: VERSAILLES

In line with Louis XIV's concept of divine right absolutism, he believed that he should have a palace worthy of God's chief deputy on earth. Hating tumultuous Paris, congested and crowded with vulgar tradespeople, he selected Versailles, eleven miles southwest of the city, to be the new seat of government. There as many as thirty-five thousand workmen toiled for thirty years, turning the marshes and sandy wastes into the world's most splendid court. The cost was so staggering that Louis destroyed the records. The greatest artists in the land were employed in the creation of the palace and the grounds. The most costly marbles, glass, tapestries, paintings, and inlaid woods were used in profusion in the ornate baroque style

FIGURE 32.3.   Charles Lebrun, "Chancellor Seguier"   Chancellor Seguier, a patron of the seventeenth-century French artist Lebrun, is shown here as an ambitious courtier to Louis XIV. In formal robes, this member of France's new nobility *(noblesse de robe)* is attended by pages as if he were a monarch. (The Louvre, Paris)

of the period. Hundreds of acres of gardens, parks, walks, canals, and artificial lakes were laid out with mathematical precision. Playing fountains and marble statues formalized the landscape.

Around his court Louis XIV gathered the great nobles of France (see Figure 32.3). Henry IV, Richelieu, and Mazarin had broken their power; Louis XIV turned them into court butterflies. The inevitable jostling for the king's attention, which was the one source of preferment, and the conflicting claims of so much titled rank necessitated

the drawing up of an elaborate code of etiquette. The king was dressed and undressed, bathed, and fed by the highest noblemen in the land—all in strict ritual. The household personnel consisted of ten thousand soldiers in brilliant uniforms and four thousand civilians. Nor was the pageant of Versailles mere glitter alone. Louis XIV subsidized or gathered around himself the leading French artists and literary figures.

But there was a reverse side to the coin. Versailles was a showplace, not a comfortable home for the king. It was cold, drafty, and inconvenient. The balls, parades, hunts, and social ritual were not sufficient to absorb the energy of the vivacious and ambitious nobility of France. The court seethed with gossip, scandal, and intrigue. Nor did the hard-toiling, heavily taxed French masses, who were supposed to enjoy the reflected glory of the monarch, always appreciate such extravagant glamour. Indeed, there were increasing expressions of discontent.

4. COLBERT AND THE FRENCH ECONOMY

Louis XIV was fortunate to have at his command during the first half of his reign a prodigious financial manager. Jean Baptiste Colbert (1619–1683) was an inordinately ambitious social climber who realized that, because of his bourgeois origin, his only means of advancement was through indispensable service to the king. An engine of efficiency, he toiled endlessly, supervising the countless details of the French economy.

Colbert's first and probably his most difficult task was to balance the national budget, which had become badly unbalanced under Richelieu and Mazarin. The careful accounting of receipts and expenditures that Sully had inaugurated three-quarters of a century earlier was resumed. Some of the debts that the government had contracted at exorbitant rates of interest were canceled; on others the rates were reduced. Dishonest tax collectors were dismissed and punished.

With Colbert, mercantilism reached its peak. French industries were protected by prohibitive tariffs, while exports and new industries were subsidized. Raw materials, however, were strictly husbanded. Imperial and commercial activities in India and North America were vigorously promoted. To protect this growing empire and the commerce that it generated, a large navy was built. But Colbert did not stop with these traditional mercantilist practices. In order to gain a world-wide reputation for the uniformly high quality of French products, all manufacturing was subjected to the most minute regulation and supervision. So many threads of such and such quality and color must go into every inch of this textile

and that lace. A veritable army of inspectors enforced the regulations. This extreme policy of mercantilism, the economic adjunct to royal absolutism, has come to be called Colbertism. It achieved its immediate end so far as quality and reputation were concerned, but it stifled initiative and retarded future industrial development. That Colbert was able to balance the budget and achieve general economic prosperity in the face of Louis XIV's lavish expenditures, including the building of Versailles, was a remarkable feat. It is well, however, that Colbert died in 1683, for Louis' wars of aggression eventually wrecked most of the great minister's work. Much of Europe copied Colbert's policies and techniques during the latter part of the seventeenth and most of the eighteenth centuries.

5. ABSOLUTISM AND RELIGION

It was virtually inevitable that Louis XIV's concepts of divine right monarchy would have religious repercussions. First, they ran counter to the claims of the pope. All his life Louis considered himself to be devoutly loyal to the Roman Catholic faith, as were the majority of his subjects. But when it came to matters of church administration Louis was not willing to have his royal authority limited, even by Rome. Numerous conflicts between king and pope led to the calling of a great council of the French clergy in 1682. This council, under the domination of Bishop Bossuet, faithful servant of Louis XIV and famed exponent of the theory of royal absolutism, drew up a statement of Gallican Liberties, special privileges or freedoms of the French church from Roman domination. The Gallican Liberties brought the French church to a position close to that of the English church under Henry VIII. They might even have led to eventual separation from Rome had not Louis XIV in later life fallen increasingly under the influence of the Jesuits and the pious Madame de Maintenon, who were able to rekindle his loyalty to the pope.

Louis' absolutism also ran afoul of the Jansenists, so called because they were followers of a Belgian bishop, Cornelis Jansen. This group represented a Puritan movement within the Roman Catholic church. The Jansenists had no intention of breaking away from the Church, to which they considered themselves entirely loyal. It was their wish to return to the teachings and practices of the Church in the days of St. Augustine. They emphasized predestination, inner piety, and the ascetic life. A number of intellectuals and people of means were attracted to their ranks, including the dramatist Racine and the mathematician and philosopher Blaise Pascal. At Port Royal near Versailles a group of prominent Jansenists practiced a communal life and established an excellent school that attracted much favorable attention. Eventually the Jesuits persuaded the pope to declare Jansenism heretical and aroused Louis XIV against the Jansenists. He outlawed the sect and destroyed its buildings.

The chief religious victims of Louis XIV's absolutism were the Huguenots. Although the Huguenots numbered not more than a tenth of the total population in France, many of them were industrious, prosperous, and educated members of the middle class. The Huguenots were subjected to a variety of persecutions. Regular army troops were quartered in Huguenot homes and instructed to cause havoc. Whole Huguenot communities would abjure their faith at the approach of the troops. Finally, in 1685 the Edict of Nantes was revoked and the Protestant religion outlawed. Although Huguenots were forbidden to emigrate, many—probably a quarter million—succeeded in doing so, taking much of their wealth and all their economic knowledge and skills with them. Not only were these industrious citizens lost to France, but they strengthened some of France's rivals and enemies, such as England, the Dutch Netherlands, and Brandenburg, which welcomed them. Forbidden to enter the underpopulated French colonies, many Huguenots helped to people the English colonies in America.

6. LOUIS XIV'S WARS OF AGGRESSION

The Sun King was not content to rule the world's most powerful nation. Louis' immediate and expressed goal was to extend his rule to France's natural frontiers. Since the French boundaries were already delimited by mountains and sea on every side but the northeast, it was in that direction that Louis looked for expansion. He claimed that only the Rhine River would provide France with an adequate natural strategic boundary on that side. An advance to the Rhine would involve France in war with most of Europe. Between the French frontier and the Rhine lay the Spanish Netherlands, much of the Dutch Netherlands, imperial territory belonging to the Austrian Hapsburgs, and many German states. England, too, would be threatened, and the balance of power upset. But Louis felt himself equal to the task of defeating these powers.

Louis' war minister, Louvois, organized France's huge military establishment on a scientific and businesslike basis, replete with supply depots and hospitals. He introduced strict discipline, uniforms, and marching drill. Vauban was one of the great designers of fortifications and of siege operations. It was a common saying that a city defended by Vauban was safe and that a city besieged by Vauban was doomed. Condé was an able and dashing military leader, and Turenne a masterly planner of campaigns and battles.

During the last four decades of his seventy-two-year reign Louis XIV fought four wars of aggression. In 1667 he unceremoniously sent French armies in to conquer the Spanish (Belgian) Netherlands. Spanish power had declined rapidly since the sixteenth century, and Louis' armies captured one fortress city after another. The Dutch, however, took alarm and formed an alliance with England and Sweden to check the French menace. This array of powerful nations along with Spain caused Louis to accept a peace that granted him only a slice of the Spanish Netherlands.

The frustrated Grand Monarch determined to punish the upstart prosperous Dutch. He sent huge French armies into the Netherlands. The cause of the Dutch seemed hopeless, and in desperation they opened their dikes. Large portions of their land were flooded, but the French were held at bay. Meanwhile, the power of France frightened Spain, the Holy Roman emperor, Brandenburg, and several small German states into joining the Dutch in alliance. Louis XIV won many victories over the allies, but when the English Parliament forced Charles II to break his agreement with the French king and join the alliance against him, Louis XIV decided to make peace. Again hapless Spain was the loser, giving up to France the long-coveted Franche-Comté (free county of Burgundy) and another strip of the Spanish Netherlands.

At the end of the Dutch War (1678) Louis XIV stood at the peak of his power (see Map 32.1). He had defeated all the greatest military powers on the western European continent and had gained valuable territories. But the tide was about to turn. Turenne was killed near the end of the Dutch War, and the aged Condé retired at the end of the war. No comparable generals were found to replace them. Colbert's hard-won surplus and balanced budget were now things of the past, and France's economy was suffering. All Europe had become alarmed by the French aggression.

No sooner had the Dutch War ended than Louis began trumping up claims to various territories in Alsace and Lorraine and sending in his armed forces to occupy them. The result was another defensive alliance against Louis composed of the Dutch Netherlands, Spain, Sweden, the Holy Roman emperor, and a number of small German states. The heart of the alliance was William of Orange, stadholder of Holland, and when the redoubtable Dutchman became King William III of England after the Glorious Revolution of 1688, England, too, was brought into alliance against Louis. The alliance was called the League of Augsburg. After nine years of fruitless struggle, Louis accepted a peace giving him only the city of Strasbourg.

But the Sun King was not about to give up. He persuaded the last monarch of the Hapsburg line in Spain just before he died in 1700 to choose one of Louis' grandsons as king. The prospect of Spain and the Spanish Empire joined to the already inordinately powerful French monarchy frightened the other powers of western Europe into once more forming an alliance against France. The ensuing War of the Spanish Succession lasted eleven years (1702–1713). The allies administered to the French and Spanish armies a series of severe defeats. In 1713 Louis XIV, beaten and exhausted, was forced to accept the Treaty of Utrecht. The settlement was complicated, but France had been somewhat humbled. It was beginning to lose ground overseas to Great Britain and in Europe had been halted short of the Rhine. But France was still the most powerful single nation in Europe.

Louis XIV lived only two years after the signing of the Treaty of Utrecht. He had long outlived his popularity. As the body of the grandest of all the absolute monarchs was drawn through the streets of Paris, some of his abused people cursed in the taverns as the coffin passed.

7. THE DECLINE OF FRENCH ABSOLUTISM

The French monarchy never again achieved the power it wielded under Louis XIV. Certainly France remained a first-rank power, with a large army, a centralized bureaucracy, and a growing economy. But between 1715 and 1789 the monarchy slowly declined.

Louis XIV was succeeded in 1715 by his five-year-old great-grandson, Louis XV. Louis XV was never interested in the day-to-day affairs of government like Louis XIV. Most historians consider him a mediocre king, concerned with his own pleasures and willing to leave governmental administration to his ministers, most of whom were of questionable quality. Until 1720 the duke of Orléans ruled as regent. He diminished the prestige of the monarchy by backing the financial schemes of John Law, which resulted in a scandal known as the Mississippi Bubble. The duke of Orléans also opened the door to the crown's greatest competitor—the aristocracy—by strengthening the *parlements*—courts dominated by aristocrats that declared laws or acts of the monarch valid or invalid.

From 1726 to 1743 Cardinal Fleury served as chief minister. The most effective of Louis XV's ministers, Fleury brought relative stability to political affairs and a needed period of peace. But neither he, nor the less effective advisers of Louis XV that followed, nor the monarchy of the indecisive Louis XVI that succeeded in 1774 were able to solve fundamental problems weakening the monarchy.

Map 32.1 **THE GROWTH OF FRANCE UNDER LOUIS XIV** These maps indicate the extensiveness of the wars waged by Louis XIV during his reign and the areas in which he made the most significant gains—along the eastern border of France.

Expensive wars and unreformed taxation policies left the treasury depleted after Louis XIV's death. The clergy and nobility retained most of their immunities from taxation despite efforts of several ministers to break those privileges. The debt grew, and the monarchy was weakened by its inability to reform its finances to lessen the burden of that debt.

Underlying these political and financial problems was a resurgence of the aristocracy. In the decades between 1715 and 1789 the monarchy was faced by an increasingly assertive aristocracy, anxious to recapture some of its old political power. Ambitious aristocrats thwarted the kings' efforts to reform taxes. They set themselves up as centers of aristocratic opposition to the monarchy, above all through their control of the *parlements* (law courts).

Thus by the middle decades of the eighteenth century, the French monarchy had clearly declined from its heights under Louis XIV. When problems came to a head in the 1780s, the king was unable to handle them and the monarchy was toppled by a great revolution.

SUGGESTED READING

General

P. Anderson, *Lineages of the Absolutist State* (1974). A good Marxist analysis.

G. N. Clark, *The Seventeenth Century* (1961). Good brief survey, emphasizing cultural aspects.

R. N. Hatton, *Europe in the Age of Louis XIV* (1979). A well-illustrated survey.

Rise of France Under Henry IV, Richelieu, and Mazarin

L. A. Moote, *The Revolt of the Judges: The Parlement of Paris and the Fronde 1643–1652* (1971). A detailed analysis of the Fronde.

V. L. Tapié, *France in the Age of Louis XIII and Richelieu* (1974). A good survey.

Louis XIV and His Court

W. F. Church, ed., *Louis XIV in Historical Thought* (1978). Conflicting interpretations of Louis XIV.

P. Goubert, *Louis XIV and Twenty Million Frenchmen* (1970). A respected study of French society and politics.

H. Rowen, *The King's State: Proprietary Dynasticism in Early Modern France* (1980). Analyzes the theory of Louis XIV's rule.

A. Trout, *Jean-Baptiste Colbert* (1978). Analyzes his economic policies.

J. B. Wolf, *Louis XIV* (1968). An excellent biography.

The Decline of French Absolutism

A. Cobban, *A History of Modern France, Vol. 1* (1966). A clear, well-written interpretation.

Sources

L. R. Saint-Simon, *The Memoirs of the Duc de Saint-Simon*. A disgruntled courtier's detailed eyewitness account of Versaille under Louis XIV.

Marie de Sévigné, *Letters from Madame la Marquise de Sévigné*, ed. and trans. Violet Hammersley (1956). Well-written eyewitness account of life at Versailles.

CHAPTER 33

The Challenge to Absolutism: England and the Dutch Netherlands

FIGURE 33.1. The English Cabinet This scene shows Robert Walpole, who served as prime minister of England from 1721 to 1742, presiding over a session of the cabinet. Walpole and the other cabinet members shown here all were members of Parliament and belonged to the majority party in that body. In sessions such as this they decided upon the major policies to be followed by the government; their control of Parliament allowed them to enact their decisions. Thus, the cabinet became the effective executive power in Great Britain, a position that it still holds today. The emergence of the cabinet system was one of the major outcomes of the bitter political struggle in seventeenth-century England. (The Bettmann Archive)

While royal absolutism was being perfected in France and elsewhere on the Continent, England and the Dutch Netherlands moved toward a form of government that placed limitations on the authority of the executive and on the power of the state. This constitutional system gave to a representative body the authority to define the law. It also sought to create a balance between the power of the state and the rights and liberties of citizens of the state. The constitutional changes made in England and the Dutch Netherlands during the seventeenth century strongly influenced later struggles against absolutism in many parts of the world.

1. EARLY STUART ABSOLUTISM

The absolutism shaped by the Tudors (see Chapter 28) was subjected to serious challenges during the seventeenth century. "Good Queen Bess" died in 1603 without a direct heir. She was succeeded by a distant cousin, James Stuart (1603–1625), king of Scotland. He was an avowed absolutist, but he was woefully ignorant of the delicate working of the Tudor political system and not suited by temperament for the hard work nor gifted with the political adroitness needed to keep that system working. His political ineptitude led to a progressive breakdown of the Tudor system and to a polarization of political forces.

But not all of the troubles of James I's reign were the making of a king known in his own days as "the wisest fool in Christendom." New problems were facing England that threatened the general satisfaction that most people had felt toward Tudor governance. Major economic changes were in process, creating new opportunities in agriculture, manufacturing, trade, and the professions. Enterprising groups seeking to take advantage of these opportunities were eager to assert greater control over royal policy in order to promote their economic interests. These same changes were adversely affecting other groups, especially rural tenants and laborers, thereby fostering popular discontent. A major realignment of power was taking shape in Europe, marked by the ascendancy of France. This development encouraged the English rulers to seek closer ties with their traditional enemy, Spain, a course that many still basking in the glories of the victory over the Armada viewed as unpatriotic.

The very structure of the Tudor political system lacked key elements conducive to effective absolutism. Too much depended on the personal qualities of the monarch and a narrow circle of royal advisers. There was not a well-developed bureaucracy nor a well-organized military force. The central government had limited control over local government, dominated by a local gentry, the members of which were jealous of their offices and protective of their local interests. The traditional system of common law served to limit arbitrary acts by the royal government. Most serious of all were the limited financial resources of the crown. It could not manage on the traditional sources of revenue—income from royal lands, customs duties, and feudal dues. Additional income could only be derived from taxes, which Parliament had long since established the right to approve. If absolutism was to continue, significant political reforms aimed at increasing the power of the monarch were required. Such changes posed a threat to powerfully entrenched interests in England.

Another increasingly acute source of tension involved religious issues. Many were not satisfied with the Anglican settlement carried out during Elizabeth's reign (see Chapter 31). The major dissenters were the Puritans, who wanted reforms that would make the established religion more "Protestant": simpler ritual, more emphasis on Scripture, less episcopal control over local churches. There also remained many Roman Catholics who hoped to undo the Reformation; their presence was a cause of constant concern for all Protestants.

During James I's reign these issues found their focus in Parliament, especially in the House of Commons, a body theoretically representing the entire English populace but actually dominated by the country gentry, merchants, and lawyers. The king was forced to summon Parliament because of the constant and increasing need for money. Although Parliament usually provided some financial aid, its members constantly raised issues that challenged royal policy. They criticized James I's royal advisers for corruption, favoritism, and incompetence. They questioned his unwavering support of Anglicanism and his lenient policy toward the Catholics. They condemned the alliance he made with Spain early in his reign and his failure to support the Protestant forces when the Thirty Years' War began in 1618. James responded by repeatedly dismissing Parliament. He then tried to utilize other means of raising money, but these efforts were challenged in the courts as contrary to custom and thus illegal. The king answered by dismissing judges, leading to more parliamentary criticism. Throughout this long series of clashes, Parliament proved itself to be an undisciplined, intemperate body. But its confrontations with the king heightened the fear that the royal government was bent on extending its prerogatives to the point where the constitution and the law would be subverted, opening the way to tyranny.

Under James' successor, Charles I (1625–1649), the conflict deepened into civil war. Charles was no less stubborn than James in his insistence on royal absolutism and in his refusal to bend before the claims of Parliament and the courts. The king's major problem continued to be a need for funds, a need made more desperate by a blundering foreign policy that resulted in costly military ventures in France and Spain that produced no victories. Charles was forced to request taxes from Parliament, which responded by challenging royal policy on a variety of issues. Increasingly, the leaders of Parliament began to make specific their definition of what they meant by royal violation of the constitution and the law. Their views found expression in the Petition of Rights submitted to the king in 1628. This bold document demanded that the king desist from various illegal acts: imposing martial law in peacetime, levying taxes without Parliament's approval, imprisoning citizens without trial, and quartering soldiers with private citizens. Desperate for money, Charles accepted the Petition of Rights, thereby admitting that he had acted illegally. But when Parliament in its next session in 1629 insisted that the king respect the petition's provisions on taxation, Charles dismissed Parliament, over the bitter protests of its leaders.

For the next eleven years Charles ruled without Parliament. To do so he was forced to rely on a variety of means of raising funds that pushed royal authority to the limits of legality. Ultimately, it was Charles' religious policy that forced him once again to confront his enemies on their ground—in Parliament. With Charles' support, his chief religious adviser, William Laud, archbishop of Canterbury, initiated a vigorous "reform" aimed at giving greater emphasis in the Church of England to elaborate rituals, episcopal authority over local churches, and the doctrine of free will. To the Puritans Laud's reforms were detestable, the very opposite of the most fundamental precepts of Protestantism. Many of them fled to the New World in search of a setting where they would have the freedom to institute real Protestantism. Laud's policies also alarmed many Anglicans, who sensed that England was on a course that would lead it back to Roman Catholicism. But it was the absolute refusal of the Scotch Presbyterians to accept the "beauty of holiness," as Charles called Laud's reforms, that precipitated a crisis. In 1639 they revolted, posing a military crisis that forced Charles to summon Parliament into session in 1640 in order to raise money to resist the Scotch threat to the kingdom.

The first Parliament of 1640, called the Short Parliament, was dismissed after three weeks because it again challenged royal authority. But the Scots continued to press and Charles was forced to capitulate. He summoned the Long Parliament, so called because it was to sit for twenty years. With an amazing show of unity Parliament proceeded to legislate the end of Stuart absolutism. It forced Charles to sacrifice his chief ministers, including Laud. It abolished the hated extraordinary courts, including the Star Chamber and the Court of High Commission, which had long been tools used by the crown to avoid the common law. An act was passed requiring a meeting of Parliament every three years and curbing the power of the king to dismiss Parliament. Severe limitations were placed on the king's power to tax without parliamentary approval. To all of this Charles acceded, chiefly because he needed money to fight the Scots.

Up to this point Parliament had succeeded brilliantly in legislating what amounted to a bloodless revolution that established limited monarchy. But the parliamentary forces then began to falter over the question of how to use Parliament's power. In general, its leadership was forced in directions that caused alarm in many quarters and drove many back toward support of the king. Charles helped to cause this split by giving every sign that he would resist being a limited monarch. Suspicion of his motives caused parliamentary leaders to remove from his hands control of the administration and the army and to impose taxes that seemed as burdensome as those imposed by Charles earlier. Religious opinion in Parliament moved in the direction of ending Anglicanism "root and branch" in favor of some form of Presbyterianism. This mounting extremism caused many influential leaders to believe that Parliament was setting a course that would upset the established order. The division in the parliamentary ranks emboldened Charles to try to restore his control; he went so far in early 1642 as to attempt to arrest the leaders of Parliament. This action was a call to arms, pitting against each other elements of a ruling class that had lost its community of interest, an interest that had long focused on the monarch.

2. ENGLISH CIVIL WAR, COMMONWEALTH, AND PROTECTORATE (1642–1660)

The opening of armed strife divided England along lines that defy easy definition. The opposing forces did not represent clear-cut economic interests or social classes. A considerable following, soon known as the Cavaliers, rallied around Charles, who represented himself as the champion of the established order against the political and religious radicals in Parliament. The backbone of the Cavalier forces came from the great noble families and their clientele among the country gentry living in the more economically backward areas of northern and western England. Although the opposition, called the Roundheads, had its noble supporters, it drew its main strength from lawyers, the gentry of the south and the east, and the commercial interests; many from these elements were Puritans. This core was soon reinforced by radical elements from the poor and oppressed, especially those living in London. In the intricate matter of choosing sides, there figured complex personal factors—family ties, friendships, personal loyalties—much after the fashion of the American Civil War.

The first phase of the civil war lasted through 1646. While neither side was prepared militarily, for a time the Cavaliers seemed to have the upper hand. But the Roundheads had forces working in their favor: support of the navy, domination of the richest part of England, control over the regular administrative system and Parliament, power to vote taxation. In 1643 the Roundhead cause was bolstered by an alliance with the Scots. But ultimately the outcome of the struggle was determined by the success of the Roundheads in creating an effective army. The chief architect of the victorious army was a simple farmer with strong Puritan convictions, Oliver Cromwell. He organized a cavalry regiment of disciplined, deeply religious recruits who proved more than a match for the Cavalier forces they faced. His system was soon applied to the entire Roundhead force to create the New Model Army, made up of selected troops paid and equipped in a businesslike fashion. It quickly proved itself superior to the Cavalier army, so that by 1646 the Cavalier army was crushed and Charles was forced to surrender.

However, with victory in their grasp, the Roundheads were unable to work out an acceptable settlement. After the defeat of the Cavaliers the Roundheads were led by moderates who wished to establish a limited monarchy and a Presbyterian religious order. Charles remained unwilling to accept such a settlement and raised fears of a renewal of the civil war by fleeing his captors and allying himself with the Scots. More ominous was the increasing prominence of Roundhead leaders who demanded a more radical religious reform favoring the independence of local churches and freedom of conscience. These religious Independents were joined by the Levellers, political radicals who advocated the end of monarchy, democratic elections, and the redistribution of wealth. The strength of these religious and political radicals became centered in the New Model Army, where discontent was fed by the fact that pay was considerably in arrears. Fearful that the radicals would seize complete control, the moderate Roundheads ordered the army demobilized. And they turned back to the king, who suddenly expressed considerable enthusiasm for parliamentary control over the monarchy and for Presbyterianism. The Independents, led by Cromwell, would not be denied. They destroyed the hope of Charles and his Scotch army in a single battle in 1648 and, along with it, the cause of the Cavaliers and the moderate Roundheads. Backed by the New Model Army, Cromwell acted decisively to ensure the position of the Independents. He purged the Long Parliament of all members not dedicated to his cause and gave to the so-called Rump Parliament chief authority in the land. It immediately legislated out of existence the Anglican church, the House of Lords, and the monarchy. And at Cromwell's urging it decreed the execution of the king in 1649 on the grounds that he was "a tyrant, traitor, and murderer."

For eleven years after Charles I's death Cromwell's forces sought to rule England without a king. Always in a minority and dependent on the army, their desperate experimentation failed to establish a stable order. England steadily retreated from revolution.

The first experiment sought to create a republican form of government called the Commonwealth. A one-house Parliament was made the supreme authority, with a state council of forty-one members charged with conducting the daily affairs of government. The political and religious extremists in the army were curbed, and considerable toleration was extended to all Protestants. Severe measures were taken to subdue the rebellious Irish and the Scots. An aggressive foreign policy, aimed at promoting English commercial and colonial interests, was undertaken. Navigation acts were passed to ensure that trade within England's emerging empire would be monopolized by England. War was waged on the Dutch, England's chief commercial rival. None of these policies, however, helped to popularize the Commonwealth. The Cromwellians could not shed their image as regicides and Puritan extremists (see Figure 33.2). Resistance to the Commonwealth grew steadily.

Cromwell ultimately blamed the failure of the

FIGURE 33.2. A Satire on Cromwell The deep religious fervor of the Puritans and the taint of regicide that lingered throughout the Commonwealth and the Protectorate are satirized here as Oliver Cromwell is shown at prayer while Charles I is being executed. (NYPL Picture Collection)

Commonwealth on what he considered the self-seeking leaders of the Rump Parliament. Finally, in 1653, he dissolved the Rump by force and tried to replace it with a handpicked body (called the Barebones Parliament, in honor of Praise-God Barebones, the first name on its roll). This body failed to distinguish itself in any way, and it too was dissolved. Finally, the very instrument that had stood against tyranny—Parliament—was gone. The tide of revolution had peaked with Cromwell and his army in control.

In pursuit of what he called a "healing and settling" course for England, Cromwell tried one more experiment, called the Protectorate. A written constitution was drawn up entrusting power to a lord protector (Cromwell), who was advised by a Council of State and guided by a one-house Parliament elected by property holders. From the beginning the lord protector and Parliament clashed on most issues, largely because the elected Parliament represented political and religious positions that ran contrary to the convictions of those who alone could sustain Cromwell in power, the "godly" men of the New Model Army. Despite the constant turmoil the Protectorate achieved some successes. The specter of radical political change was dispelled by the suppression of the Levellers. The central administration was honestly administered. Traditional patterns of local government were restored. A variety of Protestant groups enjoyed considerable independence and freedom of religious choice. Cromwell pursued a firm foreign policy that pacified Ireland and Scotland, extended English overseas colonies, and promoted commercial interests. But never could Cromwell escape the fact that the army, not civilian consent, kept him in power.

As the Protectorate floundered, opinion began to run in favor of the restoration of monarchy. In 1657 Parliament asked Cromwell to become king, an honor he declined, but he did agree to remain lord protector for life. Thus, when he died in 1658, the wheel had come nearly full circle: A man who had led his soldiers to the abolition of monarchy was himself king without title.

At Cromwell's death, his son, Richard, became lord protector. This weak figure was soon swept aside by forces favoring the restoration of monarchy. By 1660 elements in the New Model Army joined with people of property and commerce to end the Protectorate. The Long Parliament voted to dissolve itself. A new Parliament was elected and soon invited Charles Stuart, the son of Charles I, to return from exile and assume the crown in 1660.

3. THE ENGLISH RESTORATION (1660–1688)

The Restoration of the Stuarts by no means resolved the basic problems that had divided England since 1603, particularly those involving the relationship between king and Parliament and the religious establishment. Between 1660 and 1688 these problems continued to disturb society. However, the struggles of the Restoration era were more moderate than had been the case in the preceding two decades.

The reign of Charles II (1660–1685) began in a climate of forgiving compromise. The king and Parliament joined in repealing all the acts of the Commonwealth and the Protectorate. Only a few Cromwellians were punished for their part in killing Charles I. Confiscated property was returned to property owners. The king was assured of a sizable income on a regular basis, but he was deprived of many ancient feudal rights that had allowed his predecessors to exact taxes without approval of Parliament. Not only was control of taxation reserved to Parliament, but the Triennial Act was passed to ensure that it would meet every three years whether or not the king so wished. However, this settlement did not get to the basic political issue: where ultimate authority rested.

Even less satisfactory was the religious settlement embodied in a series of parliamentary acts passed in 1661 and 1662 and known as the Clarendon Code after Charles II's chief adviser, the earl of Clarendon. These acts not only reestablished the Anglican church but also threatened to destroy the Independents and Presbyterians. The Act of Uniformity required all clergy to abide by the Book of Common Prayer. The Corporation Act ruled that all members of city governments worship in the Anglican church. The Conventicle Act made religious meetings other than Anglican illegal, and the Five Mile Act forbade all preachers who were not Anglican to come within five miles of any city. In brief, the Clarendon Code promised to nonconformists (that is, non-Anglicans) little better than criminal status.

These troublesome issues soon began to surface, to divide opinion and generate conflict. They were intensified by a series of disasters that befell England during the early years of Charles' reign.

He involved England in a war with the Dutch that led to a humiliating defeat. In 1665 a plague struck England, to be followed the next year by a fire that destroyed most of London. Many god-fearing English felt that these misfortunes were divine retribution for the immorality of the royal court, where the model of profligacy was set by the king himself.

Parliament again became the center of dissatisfaction. It reacted to public wrath by forcing Clarendon out of office in 1667 and by becoming stingier in approving taxes needed to fund an unsuccessful war and Charles' personal extravagances. Charles paid little heed to the growing opposition, choosing instead to pursue two policies he personally favored: an alliance with France and religious tolerance in England that would permit Roman Catholics to worship freely. In 1670 he signed a treaty with Louis XIV agreeing, in return for a subsidy, to join France in a war on the Dutch and to promote the Catholic cause in England. In 1672 Charles issued a Declaration of Indulgence, which set aside laws restricting the practice of Roman Catholicism. An outraged Parliament forced the king to withdraw the Declaration of Indulgence and passed the Test Act (1673), which excluded Catholics from all public offices. And when Charles joined France in another unsuccessful war against the Dutch in 1672–1674, Parliament forced him to seek peace by refusing financial support.

Although the tensions continued, especially those involving religious issues, Charles showed considerable ingenuity in neutralizing Parliament during the last years of his reign. An improving economy resulted in growing tax returns, minimizing Parliament's power to control the crown by controlling taxation. Louis XIV's subsidies helped ease the financial burden on the king. More significantly, Charles skillfully built a political following—an embryonic "party"—devoted to strong monarchy and Anglicanism. Its members, scornfully dubbed "Tories" (a term used to designate Irish bandits) by the opposition, could often control Parliament in support of the king. An opposing "party," committed to parliamentary supremacy and religious tolerance for all Protestants, was also formed; its members were called "Whigs" (after a term used to designate Scottish

horse thieves and murderers). Charles' successes led many to feel that absolutism was returning to England. But one obstacle kept Charles from totally controlling English political life: a rising fear that the king was determined to restore Catholicism.

James II (1685–1688) inherited a strong position from his brother, based in large part on the Tory majority in Parliament, a sound financial position, and general satisfaction with legitimate succession. But he soon dissipated this strength by his open avowal of Catholicism and attempts to improve the position of Catholics in England, which neither Tories nor Whigs would tolerate. When in 1688 a son was born to James and his Catholic wife and baptized in the Catholic faith, ensuring that the Stuart dynasty would be perpetuated by a Catholic successor, Tory and Whig leaders invited James' Protestant daughter, Mary, and her husband, William of Orange, the stadholder of several provinces in the Dutch Netherlands, to assume England's throne. When William invaded England in late 1688, the great majority of the people rallied to his side; James II fled to France. For a second time, the unhappy Stuarts had been forced off England's throne, but this time the revolution was bloodless.

4. ENGLAND'S GLORIOUS REVOLUTION AND ITS CONSEQUENCES

The flight of James II, unlike the execution of Charles I, did not lead to radical political experimentation. Instead, what the English call a Glorious Revolution was carried through in the form of several fundamental legal enactments that pacified England and established the basis for its future political system.

Immediately after the triumph of William and Mary, Parliament declared the throne vacant by reason of James' abdication. It then voted to grant the crown to William and Mary. A Bill of Rights was passed in 1689. This fundamental charter asserted Parliament's authority to depose a king and choose a new one. It assured to the members of Parliament the right of free speech, immunity from prosecution for statements made in debate, and freedom from royal intervention in elections. It forbade a variety of acts that had long been the basis for royal absolutism: taxing without consent of Parliament, dispensing with laws, maintaining a standing army in peacetime, requiring excessive bail, depriving citizens of the right to trial in the regular courts, interfering with jurors, and denying people the right to petition the king. The Bill of Rights implied that government was based on a contract between ruler and ruled, a concept of government increasingly attractive among "enlightened" leaders in western Europe. This theory of government was set forth with special force by John Locke in his *Two Treatises on Civil Government*, published in 1690. Locke argued that a government was the product of a contract entered into by rational people in order to establish an authority capable of protecting rights that belonged to all humans by the laws of nature: the right of life, liberty, and property. Any government that violated these natural rights broke the contract that brought it into existence; in this event its subjects had a right to correct or even overthrow it. For settlement of the long-standing religious issue a Toleration Act was passed, allowing religious freedom to Puritans and Independents but not to non-Protestants. Finally, the Act of Settlement was passed in 1701 to ensure that none but Protestants could inherit the throne.

The initial settlement marking the Glorious Revolution certainly addressed in a positive way fundamental issues that had troubled England for nearly a century. However, there remained problems still to be resolved. The accession of William and Mary resulted in a basic reorientation of England's foreign policy, which called on the nation to commit its resources to a long, burdensome series of wars in many parts of the globe to prevent France from establishing world dominance. We have already seen (Chapter 32) the decisive role that England played in foiling Louis XIV's ambitions. Closer to home Ireland was brought under English control. Early in his reign William led an army into this unhappy land, where discontent had long festered and which now became a center of Stuart intrigue—funded by the French—aimed at recovering the English throne. Having established control by force, William instituted a policy of suppression, reducing Ireland to colonial status, a policy that provided splendid opportunity for English landlords to uproot Irish Catholic landowners and take possession of their property. Scotland enjoyed an easier fate in the face of increasing English power. Early in his reign William began negotiations with the Scots that finally bore fruit after his death. In 1707 Parliament passed the Act of Union, which joined the two kingdoms into a single nation henceforth known as the United Kingdom of Great Britain. The settlement gave the Scots a liberal number of seats in Parliament and guaranteed their Presbyterian religious establishment.

The burdens of global war placed stresses on the political system and led to important changes. As we have already seen, Parliament was actively engaged in defining the settlement after the Glorious Revolution. Its role in political life intensified thereafter, chiefly because its approval was needed for taxes. Annual government expenditures increased threefold between the reign of Charles II and the reign of William and Mary. To meet these expenditures, the monarchs had to call Parliament nearly every year. Frequent sessions of Parliament required that the royal government pay special attention to the election process in search of sufficient votes from qualified voters—chiefly property owners—to secure a majority in Parliament willing to support royal policy. Because Parliament was increasingly important, party strife between Whigs and Tories became a decisive feature of political life. Party leaders played an ever-larger role in counseling the rulers and overseeing public affairs. This ever-increasing identification of Parliament with the management of the nation's affairs probably did more than the noble principles of the Bill of Rights to make secure parliamentary control of public life.

The progress toward parliamentary supremacy following the Glorious Revolution left unresolved one major constitutional issue—that of the exact nature of the executive power responsible for the conduct of the routine affairs of state. For centuries, English kings had relied on powerful ministers to assist them in conducting government affairs and in shaping policy. Until 1688, these ministers had usually been chosen by the king and were responsible to him. After the supremacy of

Parliament was established in 1688–1689, this system began to change with the emergence of the *cabinet system*. Royal ministers were increasingly chosen on the basis of their ability to influence Parliament, especially the House of Commons. Since Commons tended to divide into parties that controlled large blocs of votes, it proved wisest for the rulers to seek out party leaders from that body for appointment as ministers responsible for exercising executive functions.

With the accession of Anne (1702–1714), this trend developed rapidly. Neither she nor the first Hanoverians, George I (1714–1727) and George II (1727–1760), were especially qualified for or interested in the rigorous tasks of administration. As a consequence, the direction of the government and the formulation of policy fell into the hands of royal ministers able to secure from Parliament approval to carry on the affairs of state in the name of the monarch. This *cabinet* of ministers slowly learned to accept mutual responsibility for the total operation of the government, which required that they all be members of the same party and that they use their collective influence in Parliament to ensure approval of their program. If they failed to command a majority in that body, then they had to surrender their positions as ministers in favor of a new cabinet that did have a parliamentary majority. One member of the cabinet, the *prime minister*, came to be recognized as the leader and spokesperson of the whole group; a major qualification for this designation was leadership of the majority party in Commons.

Although Queen Anne relied heavily on John Churchill, duke of Marlborough, to conduct her government, the first real prime minister and architect of the cabinet system was Robert Walpole (see Figure 33.1). A longtime member of Commons, he became George I's chief minister in 1721, primarily because of his leadership of the dominant Whig party in Commons. From then until 1742 he virtually ran England by surrounding himself with fellow ministers who could control votes in Parliament. Not until he lost control of Commons over a foreign policy issue was he forced to relinquish his position as prime minister. However, the king had little choice but to appoint another prime minister and cabinet that could command a majority in Parliament. Henceforth to the

present the executive functions of government in Great Britain would be carried out in the name of the monarch by a circle of party leaders who could command a majority in the House of Commons but who were likewise required to render account to that body for their conduct of public affairs.

The Glorious Revolution and the settlement that followed it marked a turning point in Great Britain's history. Two great decisions had been reached. First, royal absolutism had been repudiated in favor of a limited monarchy in which ultimate authority was entrusted to an elected Parliament. Second, religious uniformity had given way to religious toleration for all Protestants. The resolution of these issues restored Great Britain's internal stability and provided a basis for its rapid advance to the status of world power. However, the "revolution" had its limitations: Even as it unfolded, steps were taken to limit eligibility for Parliament to men of wealth, chiefly landowners. Until the nineteenth century these "gentlemen" dominated Great Britain in a fashion that served their collective interests.

5. THE DUTCH NETHERLANDS

Absolutism was also successfully challenged during the seventeenth century by the Dutch. Their success led to the creation of a new nation in which prevailed a political and social environment that allowed the Dutch to forge for themselves a leadership role in European commerce, banking, and intellectual and artistic life. That new nation emerged from the Dutch refusal to accept the absolutist system that Philip II of Spain attempted to force on them (see Chapter 31). Although Philip II was able to impose Spanish rule over the ten southern provinces of the Netherlands (now Belgium; see Map 33.1), the seven northern provinces resisted and by 1609 had established effective independence as the United Provinces of the Netherlands; independence was officially recognized by the Treaty of Westphalia (1648).

The new state adopted a republican form of government. Each province, ruled by an elected executive (called the stadholder) and a provincial representative assembly, retained extensive control over local affairs. Although most of the stad-

Map 33.1 THE UNITED PROVINCES, 1609
This map illustrates how small a territory the Dutch Republic occupied in its golden age—no larger than a corner of England. Yet through the cities of this small area flowed much of the commerce of the seventeenth and eighteenth centuries. With that commerce came a flow of money that made such cities as Amsterdam the financial centers of the world.

holders came from the landed aristocracy, especially from the House of Orange, a powerful family that had played a crucial role in the struggle for independence, the provincial governments were dominated by commercial and financial leaders who resisted the establishment of strong central government. The only truly national political institution was the States General, made up of delegates from each province who acted only on instructions from the provincial governments. It enjoyed limited powers and asserted very little direction over national affairs. The citizens of the Dutch Netherlands enjoyed considerable freedom to pursue their personal and collective interests. Particularly noteworthy was religious freedom. The Reformed church, strongly Calvinist in doctrine and practice, was established by law, but other religious groups, including Roman Catholics and Jews, were tolerated, a fact that attracted religious refugees from other European nations.

The Dutch Netherlands, a nation of only about one million, made its chief mark on the seventeenth-century world in commerce and finance. That success was based on the seafaring skills of its people and the entrepreneurship of its vigorous bourgeoisie. Those talents, developed over many centuries, allowed the Dutch to become world leaders in commerce. Experienced Dutch sailors plundered Spanish commerce and overseas colonies to reap a rich reward. When Spain temporarily annexed Portugal in 1580, the Dutch seized most of Portugal's lucrative holdings in the East Indies. The Dutch East India Company, set up in 1602 to develop trade with the East Indies, returned huge profits to its stockholders during the entire seventeenth century. The Dutch established a flourishing colony in North America. Dutch traders also took advantage of their favorable geographical position at the mouth of the Rhine and its tributaries and of their excellent harbors along the northern European trade routes to gain a near-monopoly of the carrying trade of Europe. A large

FIGURE 33.3.   Rembrandt, "Syndics of the Cloth Guild"   In the Dutch Netherlands of the seventeenth century, commerce was king. Under the leadership of such men as shown here, the tiny Dutch Nether-lands attained a first-rank position in the world of science, philosophy, and trade. Rembrandt, one of the greatest portrait painters of all time, was probably also the greatest of the baroque painters. (Fotocommissie Rijks-museum Amsterdam)

proportion of Europe's ships were built in Dutch shipyards.

The extensive trading activities of the Dutch led to a huge flow of wealth into the hands of Dutch merchants. This capital allowed them to become Europe's leading money lenders, serving princes, merchants, and landowners willing to pay for the use of Dutch capital. The financial activities of the Dutch were institutionalized in the Bank of Amsterdam, set up in 1609. It became a model for national banks later established else-where in western Europe. Its location in Amster-dam reflected the fact that that city had become

the world's chief commercial and financial center.

The wealth and the freedom of Dutch society generated a vigorous cultural outburst. Some of the chief intellectuals in Europe found refuge in the United Provinces, including the philosophers René Descartes from France, John Locke from En-gland, and Baruch Spinoza, a Jewish refugee from Portugal. Among the notable Dutch intellectuals was Hugo Grotius, whose *On the Law of War and Peace* was the first great treatise on international law and has remained a classic on the subject ever since. Freedom of the press enabled the United Provinces to become the leading European center of book publishing. This was the golden age of Dutch painters. While baroque painters in other countries were glorifying royalty and nobility, Jan Vermeer, Franz Hals, and above all, Rembrandt van Rijn were celebrating the spirit of Dutch society by dignifying—sometimes glamorizing—the middle and lower classes (see Figure 33.3). Dutch scientists played an important role in advancing the Scientific Revolution, including the invention of the telescope and the microscope. All of these activities gave the Dutch an important role in western European literary, intellectual, and artistic life.

As the seventeenth century drew to a close, the Dutch preeminence in commerce and banking began to decline, especially in the face of England's sea power and France's land might. But that decline could not efface the notable contributions of the Dutch to seventeenth-century western European civilization, a contribution due at least in part to the freedom enjoyed by Dutch citizens to assert their talents as they chose.

SUGGESTED READING

General Treatments

J. P. Kenyon, *Stuart England* (1978).
Barry Coward, *The Stuart Age. A History of England 1603–1714* (1980).
Either of these works will provide a fine overview of Stuart England.
Derek Hirst, *Authority and Conflict: England, 1603–1658* (1986).
J. R. Jones, *Country and Court, England, 1658–1714* (1978).
These two volumes, parts of a new general history of England, give a balanced treatment of the period.
Christopher Hill, *A Century of Revolution, 1603–1714*, 2nd ed. (1982). A provocative study from a Marxist perspective.
C. G. A. Clay, *Economic Expansion and Social Change, England, 1500–1700*, 2 vols. (1984). An excellent synthesis, rich in details.

From Civil War to the Glorious Revolution

Robert Ashton, *Reformation and Revolution, 1558–1660* (1985). Helps to establish the background for England's revolutionary age.
Lawrence Stone, *The Causes of the English Revolution, 1529–1642* (1972). Analyzes various interpretations of the causes of the English revolution.
G. E. Aylmer, *Rebellion or Revolution? England, 1640–1660* (1986). A balanced treatment of the civil war and the era of Cromwell.
C. V. Wedgwood, *The King's Peace, 1637–1641* (1955); *The King's War, 1641–1647* (1959); and *A Coffin for King Charles* (1964). Brilliant treatments of the crucial years of the English civil war.
Christopher Hill, *The World Turned Upside Down: Radical Ideas During the English Revolution* (1972). An important work on radicalism.

Patrick Morrah, *Restoration England* (1979). A good social history.
John Miller, *The Glorious Revolution* (1983). A brief, thoughtful description and assessment of the Glorious Revolution.
P. Laslett, *The World We Have Lost*, 2nd ed. (1971). A brilliant evocation of the English society of about 1700.

The Dutch Netherlands

Pieter Geyl, *The Netherlands in the Seventeenth Century*, rev. ed., 2 vols. (1961–1964). An excellent detailed treatment.
Charles Wilson, *The Dutch Republic and the Civilisation of the Seventeenth Century* (1968).
K. H. D. Haley, *The Dutch in the Seventeenth Century* (1972).
Two brief treatments that will help the reader to understand Dutch society in its most glorious age.
C. R. Boxer, *The Dutch Seaborne Empire, 1600–1800* (1965). A good description of the source of much of Dutch wealth.
Simon Schama, *The Embarrassment of Riches. An Interpretation of Dutch Culture in the Golden Age* (1987). A brilliant portrayal of social life.

Biographies

Pauline Gregg, *King Charles I* (1981).
Antonia Fraser, *Cromwell. The Lord Protector* (1973).
Antonia Fraser, *Royal Charles: Charles II and the Restoration* (1979).
S. Baxter, *William III and the Defense of European Liberty, 1650–1702* (1966).

CHAPTER 34

Eastern Europe and the Rise of Prussia and Russia

FIGURE 34.1. Frederick II Before His Troops   During the seventeenth and eighteenth centuries, the rulers of Brandenburg-Prussia used their armies to build up the state, making it one of the major powers of eastern and central Europe. Here, Frederick II of Prussia is shown in a characteristic military pose, exemplifying the strong alliance of the monarchy and army. (The Mansell Collection)

At the beginning of the seventeenth century eastern Europe exhibited certain characteristics that set it in sharp contrast to western Europe. Economically, the states east of the Elbe River were less commercially developed than those in western Europe. Estate agriculture (large landed estates owned by lords and worked by their serfs) remained the rule. Socially, the landed aristocracy dominated these areas to a greater extent than in western Europe. Indeed, this aristocracy had generally succeeded in reversing medieval trends toward greater freedom for the peasantry and the growth of towns. During the fifteenth, sixteenth, and seventeenth centuries serfdom was reimposed with greater severity than ever, and the landed aristocracy won in its struggle with competing urban centers. Politically, many areas lacked the strong central government found in the western European states. In political struggles the nobility had sometimes gained the upper hand over monarchs. Nowhere was this pattern more marked than in Poland, where there was a corresponding decline in the strength of the state to the point that Poland was literally divided and annexed by outside powers during the eighteenth century. Yet the seventeenth and eighteenth centuries would witness some important changes in eastern Europe, particularly in political affairs.

The most significant political developments in central and eastern Europe during the seventeenth and eighteenth centuries were the rise of Prussia and Russia. At the opening of the seventeenth century, the two chief powers in central and eastern Europe were the Ottoman and Hapsburg empires. Although the Moslem Ottoman Turks had been restrained by Hapsburg military power in the sixteenth century on both land and sea, they were about to renew their effort to conquer Christian Europe. The Austrian Hapsburgs, in addition to disputing the control of southeastern Europe with the Turks, dominated the Holy Roman Empire, which included all the German states. In northeastern Europe, Sweden, Prussia, Poland, and Russia competed for hegemony. Among all these powers, Prussia and Russia had hitherto been the least conspicuous in world affairs. During the seventeenth and eighteenth centuries, Prussia and Russia would become major powers and assume active roles in international politics.

1. THE EARLY HOHENZOLLERNS

The history of Prussia is in large measure the history of the Hohenzollern family. This aggressive and prolific dynasty was first heard of in the tenth century. At that time the Hohenzollerns were obscure counts ruling over the castle of Zollern and a tiny bit of surrounding territory in southwest Germany just north of the Swiss border. In the twelfth century they became burgraves of Nuremberg, an important commercial city in Bavaria. Early in the fifteenth century the Holy Roman emperor, looking for an able ruler for the mark of Brandenburg, a military province near the exposed northeastern border of the empire, chose the head of the house of Hohenzollern. Although its ruler was one of the seven electors of the Holy Roman emperor, Brandenburg was a bleak and thinly populated little province. Yet around this nucleus the Hohenzollerns built the important state of Prussia and, later, the German Empire (see Map 34.1).

From the time the Hohenzollerns became margraves of Brandenburg (1415) until they were finally overthrown at the end of World War I in 1918, they followed a threefold policy: militarism and territorial aggrandizement, paternal despotism, and centralized bureaucracy. The first to take major steps toward making Brandenburg an important power was Frederick William (1640–1688), the Great Elector. One of the ablest of all the Hohenzollerns, he acquired several new territories at the end of the Thirty Years' War. He centralized and administered the governments of his scattered territories with energy and skill. He won in his struggles with the Estates, the representative assemblies of the realm, gaining the crucial power to collect taxes and eliminating the Estates as a functioning institution. He established and strengthened his standing army. He managed an important compromise with the landed aristocracy, allowing them complete control over their serfs but committing them to his government as members of his bureaucracy and his military officer corps. He protected the native industries, improved communications, and aided agriculture. In a most intolerant age he followed a policy of religious toleration. When Louis XIV revoked the Edict of Nantes in 1685, Frederick William wel-

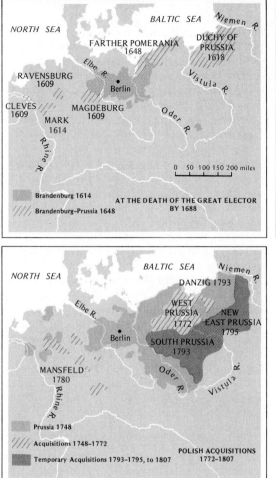

Map 34.1 **THE GROWTH OF PRUSSIA, 1614–1807**
These maps show the growth of Brandenburg-Prussia during the seventeenth and eighteenth centuries. The maps reveal the lack of connections between many of Brandenburg-Prussia's lands; one of Prussia's long-term goals in the eighteenth and nineteenth centuries was to connect those territories it already controlled as well as to expand its holdings.

comed thousands of industrious Huguenots to Brandenburg. At the death of the Great Elector in 1688, Brandenburg was on the road to becoming a great power.

The next Hohenzollern, Frederick I (1688–1713), acquired the title of king for the dynasty. The Hapsburg Holy Roman emperor in 1701 granted Frederick the title in return for aid against Louis XIV in the War of the Spanish Succession. Frederick I chose Prussia rather than Brandenburg for the name of his kingdom, since Prussia was outside the Holy Roman Empire and a free sov-

ereign state. Hence Brandenburg became Prussia.

From 1713 to 1740 Prussia was ruled by a vigorous militaristic autocrat, Frederick William I (since he was the first Frederick William to be king). Unquestioned absolutism, machinelike centralized bureaucratic administration, and, above all, militarism were his obsessions. He built the Prussian army into the most efficient and one of the largest fighting forces in Europe. And yet Frederick William was so efficient and miserly that he was also able to pass along to his talented son, Frederick II, a well-filled treasury.

2. COMPETITION WITH THE AUSTRIAN HAPSBURGS AND THE EMERGENCE OF PRUSSIA AS A GREAT POWER

In the same year that Frederick II became king of Prussia (1740), the beautiful and gracious young Maria Theresa became archduchess of the Austrian Hapsburg dominions. These dominions included, in addition to the Austrian lands, the Kingdom of Hungary and the triune crown of Bohemia, Moravia, and Silesia. After the Thirty Years' War, the Austrian Hapsburgs initiated a long policy of centralizing their power in those lands they directly controlled (rather than the Holy Roman Empire) and expanding to the east. This policy was effectively carried out during the second half of the seventeenth century and the eighteenth century. The monarchy improved its administration, established a powerful standing army, gained at least a fragile allegiance of the nobility, and acquired territories at the expense of the Ottoman Empire and Poland. Maria Theresa's father, Emperor Charles VI, had spent much time in his last years attempting to safeguard his daughter's accession to the Hapsburg throne. He succeeded in obtaining the signatures of virtually every European sovereign, including the king of Prussia, for a document called the Pragmatic Sanction, which guaranteed the integrity of Maria Theresa's crown and territories. Two months after Charles VI died, however, Frederick II, without a declaration of war, marched his troops into and seized Silesia, one of the richest of the Hapsburg provinces. This Machiavellian act of the young Prussian king plunged most of the major European states into a series of wars for the mastery of central Europe.

The War of the Austrian Succession lasted for eight years (1740–1748). Maria Theresa successfully repelled the Bavarians, Saxons, French, and Spaniards, but she was unable to dislodge Frederick II from Silesia. Frederick, on his part, cynically deserted his allies as soon as he had achieved his own purposes. The Treaty of Aix-la-Chapelle in 1748 brought the hostilities to an end. Frederick retained Silesia, and Maria Theresa's husband, Francis of Lorraine, was recognized as Holy Roman emperor. The only real gainer from the war was Frederick II. Silesia, a fertile province inhabited by more than a million German-speaking people, nearly doubled the population and resources of Prussia.

The Hapsburgs, however, had no intention of being thus despoiled of one of their fairest provinces by the upstart Hohenzollerns. Proud rulers over territories many times the size and population of Prussia and for centuries emperors of the Holy Roman Empire, they viewed the Hohenzollerns with condescension. Maria Theresa's able diplomat, Count Kaunitz, was soon at work lining up allies. Saxony, Sweden, Russia, and even France were won over. Spain, now ruled by the Bourbons, later followed France into the alliance. This time, however, Great Britain took the side of Prussia. Great Britain did this in order to oppose its archenemy France, with whom it was already at war in India and North America, and to safeguard Hanover. This double shifting of alliances came to be called the Diplomatic Revolution.

Frederick was not one to wait for his enemies to strike first. As soon as he became aware of their designs, he opened hostilities by overrunning Saxony. Thus began the Seven Years' War (1756–1763). Frederick, with his slender resources, soon found himself at bay; the four greatest military powers on the continent of Europe were closing in on him from all directions. After tenaciously holding his enemies off for six years, defeat appeared to be near. Then in 1762 the Russian Tsarina Elizabeth, one of his bitterest enemies, died and was succeeded by the ineffective Peter III, who was an ardent admirer of Frederick II and who put Russia's forces at the disposal of Prussia. Although Peter III was soon murdered by a group of his own officers and court nobility and Russia withdrew from the war, the remaining allies had no further stomach for the fight. The Peace of Hubertusburg in 1763 left things as they were at the beginning of the war, Prussia retaining the controversial Silesia. In the same year the Treaty of Paris brought to a close the colonial struggle between Great Britain and France in India and North America, leaving Great Britain master of both.

Having so narrowly escaped destruction, Frederick the Great spent the remaining twenty-three years of his life reconstructing his war-ravaged territories. He encouraged agriculture, subsidized and protected industry, and invited immigrants into his well-governed territories. At no time, though, did he neglect his war machine. In 1772 he joined Austria and Russia in the first partition of Poland. Frederick took West Prussia, thus joining East Prussia with the main body of the Prussian state. When Frederick II died in 1786, Prussia had been raised to the status of a great power, sharing equally with Austria the leadership of central Europe. During his reign Prussia's size and population had more than doubled, and its military exploits pointed to a spectacular future.

3. RUSSIA BEFORE PETER THE GREAT

While Prussia was becoming a great power in central Europe, Russia was rising to prominence to the east. The first shaping of some of the Slavic tribes of eastern Europe into what eventually became the Russian national state was begun by Viking invaders in the ninth century. These intrepid seafarers moved out from their Scandinavian homes in all directions—across the Atlantic, into the Mediterranean, and up the rivers of what are now England, France, Germany, and Russia (the word *Russia* is apparently derived from the Swedish word for rower). Their most important commercial and political center in eastern Europe was Kiev, which became Russia's first capital. Eventually the Norse invaders adopted the Slavic culture of their subjects.

In the tenth century Christianity was brought to Russia by missionaries from Constantinople. Through the influence of the Greek Orthodox church, whose headquarters were in Constantinople, Russia became a somewhat Byzantine civilization, differing from the Greco-Roman and Roman Catholic culture common to the countries of central and western Europe.

A second crucial influence on Russian civilization was the Mongol conquest of the thirteenth century. Around the turn of the thirteenth century the Mongol conqueror Genghis Khan (1162–1227) had established a vast empire in eastern Asia. Shortly after his death the Golden Horde, as the

Mongol warriors were called, swept westward into Christian Europe. The thirteenth-century Europeans were no match for the Mongols. Russia was easily overrun, and in 1241 a combined German and Polish army was defeated at Liegnitz in the heart of central Europe. All Christian Europe appeared to be at the mercy of the invaders. At that moment, however, the great khan died in eastern Asia, and the Mongol commander withdrew his forces to Russia and hastened back to seize his share of the spoils. The Golden Horde never resumed its triumphal surge westward, but for two and a half centuries it inundated Russia and there was considerable mixing of cultures.

During the Mongol occupation the grand dukes of Muscovy managed to ingratiate themselves with their Mongol masters and build up their own influence and power. The first of the grand dukes of Muscovy under whom Russia took on the shape of a modern national state was Ivan III (1462–1505). In 1480 Ivan III defeated the rapidly declining Mongols and limited their power in Russia to the southeastern area. Ivan greatly extended his sway both to the north and to the west by military conquest. After his marriage to Sophia Palaeologus, heiress to the now-defunct Byzantine (Eastern Roman) Empire, Ivan declared himself successor to the Eastern Roman Caesars—hence the title Tsar. When he died, the foundations of a Russian national state had been laid (see Map 34.2).

Ivan IV (1533–1584), "the Terrible," added both to the authority of the Russian tsars and to the territories over which they ruled. He destroyed the remaining power of the Mongols in southeastern Russia and annexed most of their territory. The Ottoman Turks, however, seized the strategic Mongol territory north of the Black Sea. Although Ivan IV established trade relations with England by way of the White Sea and the Arctic Ocean, his efforts to gain a foothold on the Baltic were frustrated by Sweden and Poland. It was during Ivan IV's reign that Russia's conquest of Siberia was begun. Half a century later the Russian flag was planted on the shores of the Pacific.

The twenty-nine years following the death of Ivan IV are known as the Time of Troubles (1584–1613). Weak rulers and disputed successions resulted in such anarchy that the Poles were able to

Map 34.2   THE GROWTH OF RUSSIA IN THE WEST   These maps show the steady expansion of Russia to the west and south, acquiring access on the Baltic Sea and Black Sea under Peter the Great and extending its territories further in the course of the eighteenth century.

capture Moscow and hold it briefly. To end the political chaos, a group of leading nobles in 1613 chose Michael Romanov as tsar.

The early decades of the Romanov dynasty, which was to rule Russia until the Revolution of 1917, were not easy. There were great popular discontent and numerous uprisings between the late 1640s and the early 1670s as the lower classes rebelled against the nobles and the central government, who were making serfdom even more onerous and life for townspeople more difficult. The discontent reached a climax with the revolts led by Stenka Razin in the late 1660s and early 1670s. Razin was finally caught and executed, soon ending that series of threats. During this

same period problems within the Russian Orthodox church broke out as many, known as the Old Believers, rejected liturgical changes initiated by the patriarch of Moscow. The effect of this controversy was to drive the Church into greater dependence on the secular government. Nevertheless by the final decades of the seventeenth century the Romanov tsars had managed to overcome these problems, improve the central administration, and extend their authority. They gradually established commercial and cultural contacts with the West. Increasing numbers of traders, artisans, and adventurers from central and western Europe, particularly Germany, came to Russia to seek their fortunes. Thus the stage was set for Russia to become more fully involved in European affairs. This involvement became especially important during the reign of Peter the Great.

4. RUSSIA UNDER PETER THE GREAT, 1689–1725

Peter I (1689–1725) was an unusually large, vigorous, and ambitious individual (see Figure 34.2). At the age of seventeen he seized the reins of government from his elder sister. For the next thirty-six years he devoted his boundless energy to the twofold policy of strengthening his own authority and his military forces and of gaining access to the west on the Baltic and Black seas.

Peter concluded that one of the best ways to increase his own political and military power was to copy Western practices. He traveled in western Europe and learned much about Western customs and techniques, which he proceeded to introduce into Russia. After crushing a revolt of his body-guard with a ruthlessness that cowed all potential troublemakers, he adopted the bureaucratic system of western European monarchs in both central and local government to make his authority more absolute. Western technicians were brought to Russia in large numbers and new industries were subsidized and protected by mercantilist policies. Western, particularly French, social customs were introduced to the upper and middle classes of Russian society. Women were brought out of seclusion, and the long beards and flowing Oriental robes of the men were banned. These reforms hardly touched the peasant masses, who were increasingly tied down in a system of serfdom bordering on slavery—a process that had been going on in Russia throughout the sixteenth and seventeenth centuries. When the patriarch of the Russian Orthodox church opposed the tsar's authority and some of his Westernizing policies, Peter abolished the patriarchate. He placed at the head of the church a Holy Synod composed of a committee of bishops and presided over by a lay procurator-general, all appointed by the tsar. Henceforth, the Orthodox church was a powerful instrument of the Russian government. But Peter the Great's chief concern was always his military

FIGURE 34.2. Peter the Great Peter the Great was a physical giant. This portrait gives us a hint of the vigor and forcefulness that he put to use in Westernizing and modernizing Russia, making the nation a military power to be reckoned with. (Culver Pictures)

establishment. He built a navy and patterned his conscript army after that of Prussia. By the end of his reign, Russia had one of the major fighting forces of Europe.

When Peter became tsar, Russia had no warmwater access to the West. Sweden held the coveted shores of the Baltic Sea, and the Ottoman Turks occupied the territory north of the Black Sea. Peter's efforts to dislodge the Ottoman Turks were not very successful, but after an extended, costly war with Sweden, in which Peter lost early battles to his adversary Charles XII, Peter's efforts were rewarded. By the Treaty of Nystad in 1721, Russia received the Swedish Baltic provinces of Livonia, Estonia, Ingria, and Karelia. On the Neva River near the Baltic, Peter built a new modern capital, St. Petersburg, facing the West. At his death in 1725, Russia was a great and growing power ready to play a major role in European affairs.

5. RUSSIA UNDER CATHERINE THE GREAT, 1762–1796

Peter the Great was followed by a succession of weak or mediocre rulers. After an interval of thirty-seven years, Catherine the Great (1762–1796) ascended the Russian throne. Catherine was an obscure princess from one of the little German states. She had been married for political reasons to young Peter III, grandson of Peter the Great, while he was still heir to the Russian crown. After he became tsar, Peter III quickly alienated all classes of his subjects. Less than a year after her husband became tsar, Catherine conspired with a group of aristocratic army officers, who murdered Peter and declared Catherine tsarina of Russia.

The Machiavellian tsarina prided herself on being an enlightened despot, as was fashionable in the late eighteenth century, but few of those enlightened ideas were translated into political or social deeds. Some apparent reforming efforts ended when Russian serfs rose in one of the greatest insurrections in history. In 1773, under the able leadership of a Don Cossack, Pugachev, hundreds of thousands of serfs marched against their masters. The rebellion was put down with difficulty. The cruel repression left Russian serfs almost as slaves to the privileged nobility.

The chief significance of Catherine the Great in political history lies in her aggressive foreign policy (see Figure 34.3). Peter the Great had reached the Baltic by despoiling the Swedes. Catherine reached the Black Sea, the Balkan peninsula, and the heart of Europe by defeating the Turks and destroying Poland. In two major wars between 1768 and 1792 Catherine defeated the Turks and seized all of their territory north of the Black Sea as far west as the Balkan peninsula. Russia also gained a vague protectorate over the Christians in the Ottoman Empire, which provided a standing opportunity to meddle in the internal affairs of the Turks. But Catherine fell short of her

real goal, Constantinople. By 1772 Russia, Prussia, and Austria had already seized strips of Poland. In 1793 Russia and Prussia enlarged their holdings, and in 1795 the three powers divided among themselves the remainder of the once huge Poland. Catherine's share, which was about two-thirds of the total, brought Russia's western boundary deep into central Europe. The second and third partitions of Poland and concern over the French Revolution, which began in 1789, absorbed Catherine's energies during the last years of her life. When she finally died in 1796, Russia was a nation ominous in size and power and a major factor in European and world affairs.

6. THE DISAPPEARANCE OF POLAND AND THE DECLINE OF SWEDEN AND THE OTTOMAN EMPIRE

Poland, at the opening of the eighteenth century, was the third largest country in Europe, exceeded in size only by Russia and Sweden. In the sixteenth and seventeenth centuries it had appeared that Poland would become a major power. Taking advantage of Russia's Time of Troubles (1584–1613), the Poles had captured Moscow. In the latter part of the century they had saved Vienna from the Turks.

Actually, however, the Polish nation was far from strong. Sprawling over a large area between Russia and the German states, it enjoyed no natural boundaries either to the east or the west. The eastern half of its territory was inhabited by Russian-speaking people. The northern provinces were peopled largely by Latvians, Lithuanians, and Germans. There were also many Germans in the west. Religious cleavages followed the language lines.

Moreover, there was no strong middle class to vitalize Poland's economy. In the late Middle Ages a sizable overland commerce between the Black and Baltic seas had flowed across Poland. But with the shifting of commercial routes and centers to the west in the early sixteenth century, Poland's commerce had withered. Furthermore, the Polish nobility, jealous of its own power and fearful of

L'ENJAMBÉE IMPERIALE.

Constantinople

Russie

FIGURE 34.3. **Catherine the Great** Catherine the Great's territorial ambitions are satirized in this cartoon, which shows her leaping toward her coveted goal, Constantinople, as the pope and other European leaders look on in dismay. (NYPL Picture Collection)

an alliance between the bourgeoisie and the king, deliberately penalized commerce with severe restrictions. The great mass of the people were serfs, tilling the soil of the powerful nobility.

In the face of so many divisive forces, only a strong central government could have made Poland a stable national state. But here lay Poland's greatest weakness. The kingship was elective, and the great nobles who held the elective power saw to it that no strong king ever came to the throne.

During the eighteenth century the kings were all foreigners or puppets of foreign powers. The legislative Diet was completely monopolized by the nobility. So that each noble's rights were safeguarded, unanimity was required for the passage of every measure. Thus any noble could veto any proposed law (*liberum veto*). In addition, any noble could disband ("explode") the Diet and cancel all its acts. This system guaranteed virtual political anarchy. National spirit was weak. The all-pow-

Map 34.3 EASTERN EUROPE, SIXTEENTH–EIGHTEENTH CENTURIES Between the sixteenth and eighteenth centuries, political power in central and eastern Europe shifted fundamentally. The first map shows the Holy Roman Empire, Poland, and the Ottoman Empire in the sixteenth and early seventeenth centuries. The second map shows that by the eighteenth century, these powers had all but been replaced by Prussia, the Russian Empire, and the Austrian Empire.

erful nobles were far more concerned for their own private interests than for the well-being of the nation.

It would have been surprising had such a power vacuum as eighteenth-century Poland not invited the aggression of its ambitious neighbors. In 1772 Catherine the Great and Frederick the Great bargained to take slices of Polish territory. The somewhat less greedy Maria Theresa of Austria, fearful of being outdistanced by Russia and Prussia, joined them. This aggression at long last stirred the Poles to action. Sweeping reforms were passed, improving the condition of the peasants and the bourgeoisie and giving the king and the Diet power to act effectively. But it was too late. Russia and Prussia were determined to prevent the emergence of a vigorous Polish nation. In 1793 they marched in and seized additional slices of territory. The Poles, under the leadership of Thaddeus Kosciusko, now flew to arms, although the arms were often only agricultural implements. They were no match for the professional armies of Russia, Prussia, and Austria, who in 1795 divided the remainder of Poland among themselves.

Poland was not the only victim in eastern Europe of the powerful Russian, Prussian, and Austrian armies. Sweden and the Ottoman Empire declined, both relatively and actually. Sweden had become the dominant military power in northern and eastern Europe under Gustavus Adolphus in the early seventeenth century. At the opening of the eighteenth century Sweden was second only to Russia in size among the nations of Europe, holding large areas east and south of the Baltic in addition to the homeland. However, its population and resources were too small to hold for long such far-flung territories, which were coveted by ambitious and growing Prussia and Russia. Charles XII made a spectacular effort to hold them, but in the end he lost all his trans-Baltic territories except Finland, and he dissipated Sweden's strength in so doing. Sweden has never been a major power since.

The Ottoman Turks, after reaching the gates of Vienna early in the sixteenth century and again late in the seventeenth century, weakened rapidly. The Treaty of Karlowitz in 1699 limited their power in Europe to the Balkan peninsula and a strip of territory north of the Black Sea. Their two serious defeats at the hands of Catherine the Great marked the beginning of the breakup of the Ottoman Empire.

By the end of the eighteenth century, the three dominant powers in central and eastern Europe were the relatively static Austrian Hapsburg Empire and the two rapidly rising states—Prussia and Russia (see Map 34.3). Each of these states had developed strong central governments with standing armies, large bureaucracies, and organized systems of taxation under the monarch's control.

SUGGESTED READING

General

D. McKay and H. Scott, *The Rise of the Great Powers, 1648–1815* (1983). A good recent survey.

I. Woloch, *Eighteenth-Century Europe: Tradition and Progress 1715–1789* (1982). A recent, thorough introduction.

Rise of Prussia

F. L. Carsten, *The Origins of Prussia* (1954). A solid, brief account of the reign of the great elector, Frederick William.

G. Craig, *The Politics of the Prussian Army, 1640–1945* (1964). A highly respected analysis of the influences of the Prussian Army.

H. Holborn, *A History of Modern Germany 1648–1840* (1966). Best on the subject.

H. C. Johnson, *Frederick the Great and His Officials* (1975). Focuses on Prussian administration.

The Austrian Hapsburgs

R. J. Evans, *The Making of the Hapsburg Empire, 1550–1770* (1979). A solid, recent account.

Rise of Russia

P. Dukes, *The Making of Russian Absolutism: 1613–1801* (1982). A solid survey.

I. de Madariaga, *Russia in the Age of Catherine the Great* (1981). Highly regarded recent study.

B. H. Sumner, *Peter the Great and the Emergence of Russia* (1962). A brief introduction.

A. Yanov, *Origins of Autocracy: Ivan the Terrible in Russian History* (1981). Excellent recent analysis.

Disappearance of Poland and Decline of Sweden and Ottoman Empire

P. Coles, *The Ottoman Impact on Europe, 1350–1699* (1968). A well-written study.

O. Halecki, *A History of Poland* (1961). Sound coverage of the partitions.

R. N. Hatton, *Charles XII of Sweden* (1968). An excellent, thorough biography.

CHAPTER 35

Overseas Colonization and Competition for Empire

FIGURE 35.1. **The Taking of Quebec, 1759** This eighteenth-century engraving shows British forces capturing Quebec from the French in 1759. This victory was a major turning point in the eighteenth-century competition for world empire. (Library of Congress)

During the age of royal absolutism, the European nations intensified their competition for overseas possessions and commerce. They were spurred on in large part by the riches that flowed to Europe from these possessions but also by a conviction that overseas possessions enhanced the power of nations. Whereas Spain and Portugal had led the way beyond the Atlantic frontier during the sixteenth century, England, France, and the Netherlands threw themselves vigorously into colonizing and commercial expansion in various quarters of the globe during the seventeenth and eighteenth centuries. The newcomers indeed outstripped their older rivals and established themselves as the leading European colonial powers. As large as the world beyond western Europe was, the competition for it led to struggles among the leading European powers; the outcome of these struggles decisively affected the power relationships among the competing nations. And while the Europeans colonized, traded, and competed around the globe, European civilization spread with them, impacting with varying results on the native populations encountered by the Europeans. The seventeenth and eighteenth centuries marked a decisive turning point in the establishment of western European domination over much of the world. No less significantly, European expansion laid the basis for a global economy.

1. THE NEW WORLD: THE ENGLISH, THE FRENCH, AND THE DUTCH

One of the areas attracting the English, French, and Dutch was the New World, where all three nations established thriving colonies during the seventeenth century and eventually became embroiled in bitter rivalry for dominance. The northern European nations had their appetites whetted by the fabulous profits reaped from the New World by the Spanish and the Portuguese during the sixteenth century. These two powers retained their vast empires in Central and South America during the seventeenth and eighteenth centuries and continued to earn a rich reward from their enterprises. During the seventeenth century the hauls of gold and silver declined, and the Spanish

and Portuguese turned their energies toward creating large plantations worked by oppressed natives and imported African slaves to produce products marketable in western Europe. Their presence in South and Central America forced the attention of the English, French, and Dutch toward North America and the Caribbean area.

The English were the most successful colonizers in North America. Although some settlers were prompted by political and religious reasons, most were lured by the prospects of available land. Colonizing ventures were organized by joint stock companies chartered by the government to plant settlements in the New World or by individual leaders granted huge tracts of land for the purpose of colonization. Between 1607, when the first colony was planted at Jamestown, Virginia (see Figure 35.2), and 1733, when a colony was founded in Georgia, England established control of the Atlantic seaboard from Maine to the Spanish colony in Florida. In the thirteen colonies a stable order soon emerged that showed considerable potential for agricultural and commercial growth. This growth was promoted by a steady flow of emigrants, not only from England but also from other northern European nations. By the beginning of the eighteenth century the English settlers were beginning to push westward out of the coastal colonies in search of new lands to occupy. English explorers and traders penetrated into the Hudson Bay area in Canada and claimed for England a huge territory, where soon a profitable trade in fur developed. Flourishing English colonies were established in the West Indies, the chief ones being Barbados, Jamaica, and Bermuda. In this area the English concentrated on developing highly profitable sugar plantations, utilizing African slaves as a labor supply.

France also undertook to colonize in the New World, although not as successfully as England. Its first American colony was established by Samuel de Champlain at Quebec on the St. Lawrence River in 1608. Champlain later explored and claimed for France the entire St. Lawrence Valley from the Atlantic to the Great Lakes. Toward the end of the seventeenth century during the reign of Louis XIV the French extended their holdings in North America by claiming a huge territory called Louisiana, stretching down the Mississippi

FIGURE 35.2.   The New World Frontier   This representation of the first settlement at Jamestown, Virginia, suggests something of the drastic changes that affected those who left European society—symbolized by the great ship standing at anchor—to face the wilds of the New World. (Culver Pictures)

Basin from the Great Lakes to the Gulf of Mexico. The French also established prosperous colonies in the West Indies, especially on Martinique and Guadeloupe, where sugar production was the major economic activity.

Except for the West Indies, settlers were slow to come to France's vast, rich lands in the New World, in part because of governmental policy. France closed its empire to non-Catholics, thus excluding an element so important in populating England's colonies—the religiously dissatisfied. By adopting a policy of land allocation that favored the aristocracy, the French government made it difficult for commoners to obtain land overseas. The opportunities for profits offered by the fur trade discouraged agricultural settlement. When England seized France's American empire in 1763, perhaps no more than eighty thousand settlers lived in New France, compared with the 1.5 million inhabitants of the English colonies. But that sparse population left its marks, especially in the form of Roman Catholicism, the French language, and the imitation of French social practices by

settlers in the St. Lawrence Valley and southern Louisiana—marks that persist to the present to give a distinctive character to society in these areas.

The Dutch also became involved in the colonizing of North America. In 1621 the Dutch West India Company was chartered to undertake colonizing and commerce in the New World. In 1624 a Dutch colony was planted on Manhattan Island, a location made especially attractive because of its potential as a center from which trade could be controlled. Soon other Dutch communities were established in the valleys of the Hudson, Connecticut, and Delaware rivers. However, the Dutch did not push their colonizing effort very seriously. Their interest was chiefly in trading activities, leading them to concentrate their energies on the more profitable East Indies. Their American colonies became a bone of contention in the Anglo-Dutch struggles that preceded the Glorious Revolution in England. In 1664 the English seized New Netherland, ending Dutch colonization in North America.

2. EUROPEAN PENETRATION OF THE FAR EAST AND AFRICA

During the sixteenth century, Portugal had established supremacy in the Far East. In the seventeenth century, however, the Dutch, English, and French aggressively entered into the area (see Map 35.1). The Dutch were the first. In 1602 all the competing Dutch companies interested in Far Eastern trade were joined into a single Dutch East India Company, to which the Dutch government gave almost complete freedom of action. The company soon drove the Portuguese out of the Spice Islands, which became the center of the Dutch trading empire. In 1641 Malacca on the Malay peninsula was seized, giving the Dutch control of the seas around the East Indies. Ceylon and the Celebes were also captured. The English tried to seize a share of this rich area, but they were driven out by the Dutch as early as 1623. To safeguard the sea route to the Indies, the Dutch established a colony at the Cape of Good Hope in South Africa. Its growth was slow, but the Dutch influence was eventually strong enough to influence the history of South Africa to the present. To watch its interests in the Indies, the Dutch East India Company established a governor-general in Java, who in turn set up several other fortified governmental centers in the island empire.

For years after, the Dutch continued to profit from their holdings in the Indies. They demonstrated remarkable skill in utilizing the native agricultural economy to produce commodities such as spices that were in great demand in western Europe. Consequently, their presence disturbed very little the existing patterns of life in the area. The Dutch also made attempts to penetrate China and Japan but enjoyed only limited success, chiefly because neither the Chinese nor the Japanese welcomed them. Both were too strong to permit entrance by force.

The English, although shut out of the East Indies by the Dutch, made rapid progress toward replacing the Portuguese in India. The English East India Company was chartered in 1600 and given a monopoly of English trade in the East. This company concentrated chiefly on India, slowly forcing the Portuguese to let English traders into that rich land. The company founded its own "factories" (trading posts) at key locations—Surat, Madras, Bombay, and Calcutta (see Figure 35.3). For a long time the East India Company was content to exploit the trading opportunities available in these cities; the merchants interfered little with Indian affairs and had little influence on Indian society.

Rather belatedly, the French entered the competition in the Far East. Colbert organized a French East India Company (1664), which soon established a French outpost at Pondicherry in India. From this center the French company built up a prosperous trade that returned large profits.

During the seventeenth and eighteenth centuries, western Europeans made significant crossroads into sub-Saharan Africa. Again the Portuguese had been the early leaders, but they were eventually joined by others. It was the establishment of the plantation system in the New World that sparked a new interest of Europeans in Africa. The plantations needed labor; African slaves could provide that commodity. Portuguese, Dutch, English, French, and North American traders and adventurers, acting with the support of their governments, established a series of trading posts along the West African coast stretching from modern Senegal to Angola chiefly for the purpose of purchasing slaves to be transported to the New World.

3. THE IMPACT OF EUROPEAN EXPANSION: THE NATIVE AMERICANS

The increasing presence of European colonists and traders around the world during the seventeenth and eighteenth centuries had a significant impact on the native populations of the areas to which Europeans went. In many ways these encounters between Europeans and natives set a pattern that was destined to impose a bitter heritage on the modern world.

Of all the non-Europeans who felt the impact of the white man, the native Americans—the American Indians—were perhaps most immediately and drastically affected. Their patterns of life, ranging from the highly sophisticated civilizations of the Incas in Peru and the Aztecs and Mayas in

Mexico and Central America to the simple pastoral and hunting cultures of the North American Indians, were irreparably disrupted by the onslaught of the intruders.

We have already described the destructive impact of the Spanish and Portuguese *conquistadors* on the Aztecs, Mayas, and Incas. During the seventeenth and eighteenth centuries, the dislocation continued. Spanish and Portuguese colonial policies cast the Indians into the role of laborers on the expanding plantation system and in the reviving mining enterprises from which the Europeans drew huge profits. To add to the disruption of native social and economic life, the new masters imported large numbers of black slaves from Africa. Although the foreign Europeans were few in number, they dominated political, economic, and

social life with little respect for the established practices of native life.

Despite their indifference to established native American culture, the Europeans in Latin America were never numerous enough to exterminate the native Americans or their cultures. Inexorably, their blood and their culture intermingled with those of the native Americans. As a result, significant elements of native American culture survived, especially in family structure, agricultural techniques, art motifs, and even religion. Although the ancient Indian civilizations of Central and South America were forever disrupted, enough Indian culture survived to give Latin American society a special hybrid character that has survived to this day.

The Indians of North America suffered a dif-

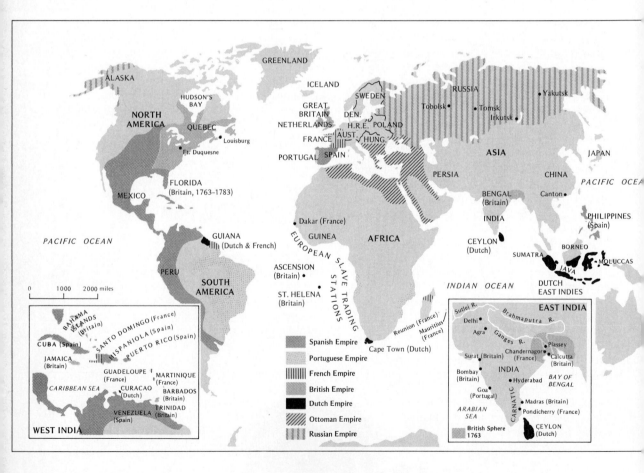

ferent, and perhaps a crueler, fate. In general, the interactions between French settlers and the Indians were not particularly disruptive to Indian society, chiefly because the French were few in number, usually more concerned with trade than land occupation, and interested in the Indians as potential converts to Christianity. The English settlers pursued a more ruthless course. From the beginning they were chiefly interested in occupying and exploiting the land, an intent that demanded the displacement of the natives. Although English-Indian relationships were occasionally marked by friendliness and mutual assistance, the burgeoning seaboard population began to assert inexorable pressure on the Indians. As a consequence, the Indians began to disappear from "new" America; their demise was often accompanied by conniving and brutality on the part of the settlers, who began to perceive themselves as *the* "Americans." In the effort to protect their land, the Indians fought back savagely. Their resistance nourished a feeling among the colonists that the native Americans were inferior savages whose extermination would best serve everyone's interest. The British government struggled from afar to establish an Indian policy aimed at respecting Indian rights to their lands and dealing with them honorably in resolving conflicts. But the westward-bound, land-hungry newcomers paid little heed and proceeded with the grim business of displacing or exterminating the Indians in the vast Indian stronghold lying between the Appalachians and the Mississippi. The resultant dislocations completely undermined the foundations of native American culture and condemned the Indians to a long-standing inferior status in America.

Map 35.1 OVERSEAS POSSESSIONS, 1763 This map shows the extent to which the major European powers had established control over the world by the middle of the eighteenth century. It especially points up the success of England in the quest for overseas possessions. The rich trade flowing to and from Europe to the overseas possessions had become a vital factor in the economies of these nations. Increasing its overseas possessions and trade was of vital importance to every Euorpean state.

4. THE IMPACT OF EUROPEAN EXPANSION: THE FAR EAST

In contrast with the impact of Europeans on the New World, their impact was minimal on the peoples of the Far East. Few Europeans went to that part of the world as colonists. Those few who did isolated themselves in trading depots located in seaboard cities in India and the East Indies, where their contacts with the natives were slight. The limited impact of the Europeans on the world of the Far East resulted also from the fact that the newcomers encountered ancient cultures and solidly established societies.

When the Europeans first began the penetration of India, that ancient land was politically unified for one of the rare moments in its history. Unity had been imposed by Moslem foreigners, the Moguls, a branch of the Mongol horde of Tamerlane. Mogul rule brought prosperity to India's upper classes and a brilliant chapter in India's already rich cultural history. As the seventeenth century progressed, Mogul power began to decline. Political power increasingly fell into the hands of native local princes, a development that proceeded rapidly during the eighteenth century. Because this situation aided the English and the French in establishing their commercial interests in India, the intruders encouraged political localism. Thus, their presence had a significant impact on the political structure of India.

However, Indian society retained its cohesion and its unique identity despite the presence of the foreigners, be they Moslem Asiatics or Christian Europeans. Its primary social institutions—the family, the village, and the caste system—remained intact, fundamentally untouched by the outsiders. Undergirding these ancient social institutions were powerful religious beliefs and practices, embodied above all in Hinduism, which emphasized the acceptance of the existing order as a part of the divine order. Hindu Brahmins, or priests, played a crucial role in sustaining the traditional order. Indian social institutions, religion, and culture combined to incline Indians to accept their situation in the present world because each individual's lot represented a necessary step in the progression toward ultimate fulfillment in another

FIGURE 35.3. **A Refuge in a Foreign World.** This drawing shows a European factory, or trading settlement, built in seventeenth-century India. Within the confines of such structures were warehouse, places of residence, market facilities, and even a church. The structure illustrates how the Europeans isolated themselves from the native population in the Far East. (The Bettmann Archive)

world. Progress, competition for wealth, and the search for new things did not hold the same attraction for Indians as they did for Europeans. Indians were not impressed by European civilization. They were convinced that they had reflected as deeply on human problems as the foreigners and had arrived at superior answers. Indians could point to a remarkable art and literature as proof of the vitality of their way of life. Little the Europeans could offer to India seemed able to improve on Indian institutions and values. The outsiders found that a few hundred soldiers and a few cannon could not shake the Indians'

confidence in their village and family life, their caste system, their religion, and their culture. Moreover, the continued existence of the basic pattern of Indian civilization in no way impeded the Europeans from reaping huge profits from their commercial enterprise in India. Only slowly and almost imperceptibly did the European way of life make any significant impression on India. And as time passed, Europeans developed a deep respect for some aspects of Indian civilization.

The Dutch presence in the East Indian world likewise had little effect on native society. In fact, the Dutch found it in their interests to sustain the existing order because it lent itself easily to commercial arrangements favorable to the outsiders.

The other major cultural centers in the Far East—China and Japan—were also little affected by the intrusion of Europeans during the period from 1500 to 1800. Again, this was a consequence of the vitality of native civilizations. In China the Manchu dynasty established a strong political regime during the seventeenth century that brought internal peace, prosperity, and a revitalization of Chinese social, religious, and cultural life along traditional patterns. Chinese civilization came to be greatly admired in Europe in the eighteenth century. However, the Manchus carefully controlled the activities of Western traders—called "Ocean Devils" by the Chinese—with the consequence that European influences were barely felt in China. Japan also enjoyed internal stability under the rule of the Tokugawa shoguns, who in the early seventeenth century established firm control over Japan's ancient feudal system and encouraged close adherence to ancient social, cultural, and religious customs and values. The new rulers soon adopted a policy of excluding all Europeans from access to Japan, a policy of isolationism that continued until the nineteenth century and that ensured that European influences would be minimized.

5. THE IMPACT OF EUROPEAN EXPANSION: SUB-SAHARAN AFRICA

European expansion into sub-Saharan Africa during the seventeenth and eighteenth centuries had a decisive effect on the societies existing in that vast territory. The centuries prior to 1500 had witnessed the formation of several prosperous states across a wide belt of territory south of the Sahara from the Atlantic to the Indian oceans and then far southward along that inviting sea. These states—Ghana, Mali, Songhay, the kingdoms of Hausaland, and the Swahili city-states on the east coast of Africa—were strongly influenced by Moslem religion, culture, and technology from North Africa. However, in all of them the imprint of much older native African cultures was also strongly felt, producing an amazingly cosmopolitan culture, especially in the cities that dominated these states. The remarkable affluence of these states depended on a vigorous trans-Saharan and Indian Ocean trade that carried gold, ivory, slaves, and many other products northward to the Moslem world and Europe and eastward to India. In fact, many of these states were brought into existence by enterprising native chieftains who organized extensive realms so as to control more effectively the trading ventures that brought such great riches. Because their existence depended so heavily on trade and because the techniques their rulers borrowed to assert their power had little impact on the great bulk of the native population, these African states tended to be unstable. Nonetheless, their creation and their active intercourse with outside cultures marked an important stage in the development of sub-Saharan Africa and its involvement with the larger world. Farther to the south, beyond the sphere of Moslem influence, the native population continued its agricultural existence according to ancient customs, as yet little touched by developments to the north.

These developments in pre-1500 sub-Saharan Africa created a situation that made Africa particularly susceptible to the onslaught of the western Europeans, chiefly because the destiny of so many African states was tied directly to trade with the outside world. Coming by sea to the coastal areas of sub-Saharan Africa, the Europeans almost instantly caused a redirection of trade routes from the traditional trans-Saharan routes toward the coastal regions that gave access to western Europe and the expanding European empires in the New World and the Far East. The newcomers made little effort to settle in sub-Saharan Africa, partly because the Africans resisted their settlement but more importantly because they could get what they wanted by doing little more than establishing a few trading posts in the coastal cities of Africa. What they wanted were the valuable raw materials of Africa, especially gold, and then before long the Africans themselves—as slaves to perform the arduous labor of creating a rich agricultural establishment in the New World. Throughout the seventeenth and eighteenth centuries massive numbers of black Africans—perhaps as many as 9 or 10 million—were uprooted from their native soil, often as a result of the efforts of their black compatriots, sold into the hands of English, French, Dutch, Portuguese, Spanish, and American slave traders, and distributed under inhuman conditions far and wide to toil as chattels in the service of white landowners intent on exploiting the vast agricultural potential of the New World.

As the Europeans opened slave stations along the coasts of sub-Saharan Africa, significant new political alignments occurred in Africa. African kingdoms along or with access to the Gold Coast flourished as a result of their domination of trade flowing from inland into the hands of European traders. Among the most prominent of these kingdoms were Oyo, Benin, Asante, Kongo, and Ngola. Often the ruling elements of these kingdoms became prime agents in supplying slaves to the Europeans, leading them to intervene among inland tribes to find slaves to sell. Native chiefs living inland likewise became caught up in the slave trade. Armed with deadly weapons from Europe, the native tribes began to wage war on one another as a means of procuring slaves. The Europeans asserted subtle influences on the coastal states in order to enhance their own trading interests, thus promoting a slow deterioration of the capability of the Africans to control their own destiny. As the demand for slaves increased and the prices commanded by the African slave suppliers rose, European traders moved farther and farther south along the west coast of Africa to turn the attention of more and more native Africans toward serving European trading interests, especially slavery, with the same disruptive consequences. European influences, especially Portuguese, on the east coast of Africa were equally disruptive of the brilliant Swahili civilization flourishing there. Only deep in the central part of Africa did the native population remain relatively free of the impact of European intrusion.

On the whole, the development of sub-Saharan Africa was seriously impeded by the encounter of its peoples with the western Europeans during the seventeenth and eighteenth centuries. Africa's human resources were depleted, her natural resources plundered, and her political and social structures disoriented. The Europeans gave little in return, especially when compared with what the Moslems of North Africa had contributed to the enrichment of sub-Saharan Africa prior to

1500. Despite the traumatic consequences of European expansion in this era, the Africans retained many elements of their native tradition, which would later reassert itself as a significant aspect of the liberation of Africa from European domination. And those who were uprooted from Africa in this period took much with them to add important elements to the civilization that was forming in the New World, where they were laboring as slaves.

6. THE STRUGGLE FOR OVERSEAS EMPIRE

In spite of the vast lands to occupy in the New World and rich trading opportunities to exploit in the highly civilized East and in sub-Saharan Africa, the aggressive European nations could not keep out of one another's way in their overseas expansion. As a consequence, the rivalry of European nations became global. The outcome of these struggles began to determine the destinies of peoples only remotely involved in the competition of the European states.

The competition for empire was rooted in two interrelated factors: the essential importance of overseas trade to the expanding economies of the major European nations and the policy of mercantilism practiced by most European powers.

The growing importance of overseas commerce to national economies was abundantly clear. New products from abroad—among others, spices, sugar, tobacco, cotton, silk, tea—were in high demand. So also were some manufactured goods from the Far East, especially cotton textiles and chinaware. Colonists needed the products of European manufacturers. The opportunities to transport these goods stimulated shipbuilding. The need to distribute products from abroad created new opportunities for merchants. The funding of overseas trading and colonizing ventures stimulated the development of banking and credit. The profits garnered from overseas trading activities not only improved the standard of living of those who earned the profits but also became a prime source of capital for investment in agriculture, manufacturing, and commerce. Even governments relied on the gains from overseas trade to provide taxes and loans. In short, Europe's economy had become the focal point for a global system. Control of that economy was vital to the well-being of European nations, even to the point of fighting others for a share of the lucrative overseas trade.

The realities of seventeenth- and eighteenth-century economic life found expression in the widely accepted economic policy of mercantilism, which accentuated the importance of competition for overseas trade and colonies. Mercantilist policy was based on the conviction that the economic well-being of a nation depended on directing the total national economy in a way that would produce a favorable balance of bullion coming into the economy. Among other things, this policy saw colonies as a source of cheap food and raw materials and an outlet for manufactured goods that would return a profit to the mother country. Such a view made the accession and the careful management of the colonies crucial to each nation that aspired to be powerful. Especially important was the need to monopolize trade with a nation's colonies, which placed a premium on developing naval power. Likewise, mercantilism dictated that every effort be made to restrict the colonizing ventures of rival nations and to deprive them of their colonial possessions whenever possible. Thus, every conflict among the major European nations in the seventeenth and eighteenth centuries was extended to their colonies, and every major peace settlement included a redistribution of overseas possessions (see Chapters 32 and 34 for the European aspects of these wars).

The competition for the fruits of overseas empires began in the sixteenth century with the English and Dutch assaults on Spanish and Portuguese trading activities and overseas holdings. By the middle of the seventeenth century competition began to intensify and to become more general. More than any other country, England allied governmental economic policy with private commercial interests, with a view toward promoting national well-being. This approach cast England into a particularly aggressive role in the competition for empire and trade. As early as 1651 England passed its first Navigation Act, providing that all goods coming to and from England and its overseas possessions must be carried in English ships.

This policy posed a challenge to Dutch commercial power, which was especially successful in providing shipping services to other nations. It also encouraged the growth of the English merchant fleet and the navy, badly neglected during the early Stuart period. On three different occasions between 1651 and 1688, England engaged the Dutch in warfare. As a result, Dutch commercial ascendancy began to be undermined while England's commercial power grew; the Dutch also lost their North American colonies.

Toward the end of the seventeenth century the English and the Dutch began to see that France was the chief threat to both. The result was an Anglo-Dutch alliance made by William of Orange when he became king of England in 1689. By that time the Netherlands was no longer the major sea power in Europe. The Dutch were increasingly content to keep their already established holdings in the East Indies, to continue their declining but still profitable carrying trade, and to reap a great profit as the chief bankers and money lenders of Europe.

From 1689 until 1763 England and France fought each other regularly in Europe, and each engagement had its repercussions abroad (see Map 35.1). Several times during the War of the League of Augsburg (1688–1697), the English and the French forces engaged in North America, where the war was called King William's War. Neither in Europe nor in America was the action decisive, and no changes were made in the holdings of either combatant. England had more success during the War of the Spanish Succession (1702–1713). In North America, where the struggle was called Queen Anne's War, England captured Acadia (Nova Scotia) and received recognition of its claims to Newfoundland and Hudson Bay. From France's ally, Spain, England received Gibraltar and Minorca, assuring entrance into the Mediterranean. Spain also granted to England the right to supply Spain's colonies with slaves (the *asiento*) and the privilege of sending one ship a year to the Spanish colonies in America. These concessions ended Spain's long effort to close its empire to outsiders and gave England the advantage over other nations in exploiting trading opportunities provided by the Spanish overseas holdings.

From 1713 to 1740 England and France remained at peace. During this calm neither nation was idle in overseas matters. France, realizing the weakness of its position, was especially active in North America. France tried to protect its holdings from English sea power by building a strong fort at Louisburg at the mouth of the St. Lawrence. France also began constructing and garrisoning a series of forts in its territories west of the Appalachians designed to keep the English colonists pinned to the Atlantic seaboard. England concentrated its efforts on widening the commercial breach it had made in Spain's empire in 1713. A new European war in 1740, the War of the Austrian Succession, led to a sharp conflict between England and France in America (King George's War) and in India. At the end of the war in 1748 each power restored its spoils to the other, England giving up Louisburg and France restoring Madras.

An eight-year truce ensued in Europe, each side preparing desperately for the struggle that everyone knew would soon reopen. In North America, France went back to the policy of building a barrier against the westward expansion of the English colonies. The inevitable clash came in 1755, when the British unsuccessfully tried to stop the French from occupying Fort Duquesne, at the present site of Pittsburgh. The issue was clearly joined; one power must destroy the other in America.

In India a no less dramatic struggle was shaping. France had entered the scene later than England but had made steady progress up to 1740. Between 1740 and 1756 the French and British manipulated the internal chaos in India resulting from the decline of Mogul authority to wring for themselves concessions from India's various princes or political factions. Competition became so vicious that soon an undeclared war was on in India. Thus, at the opening of the Seven Years' War (French and Indian War in America) in 1756, France and England were pitted against each other on three continents. In that war England, led by William Pitt, threw its chief efforts into the naval and colonial war and won a smashing victory. In North America the French held their own until 1757. After that the superior British forces, supported by the navy, overpowered the French outposts one by one. The decisive blow came in 1759, when the British captured Quebec, opening all Canada to the British (see Figure 35.1). British naval units captured the chief French holdings in the West Indies. In India, Robert Clive, a resourceful agent of the East India Company, gave the British a decisive victory at the battle of Plassey in 1757. Clive added large territories to England's sphere of influence by conquering several native Indian states.

The Seven Years' War ended in 1763 with the Treaty of Paris. France surrendered Canada and all Louisiana east of the Mississippi (except New Orleans) to England. Spain, which had been an ally of France, ceded Florida to England. By a special treaty France compensated Spain for this loss by giving Spain the rest of Louisiana (west of the Mississippi). All French possessions in the West Indies except Guadeloupe and Martinique also fell to England. France's empire in India likewise went to Britain. The French were permitted to enjoy trading privileges in India and to keep Pondicherry, but Britain controlled the chief centers of trade, ending any hope of a French recovery of power there. The Treaty of Paris closed an era in European expansion. Although the Dutch and the Spanish still had extensive holdings abroad, Great Britain had fought its way to supremacy in colonial and commercial affairs. The English could now turn to the exploitation of that empire.

Since Columbus' voyage the Europeans had wrought an important change around the world. Energetic colonizers had planted European civilization on the soil of the New World. Enterprising merchants had begun to tap the wealth of a considerable part of the Far East and of sub-Saharan Africa, creating for the first time a global economy in which the level of prosperity in European nations was directly related to their access to the labor and products of peoples all over the earth. European patterns of civilization had begun to alter the lives of peoples who had developed their own cultures long before the Europeans came. For good or bad, the Europeanization of the world had begun. And European history never again ceased to have a world-wide scope.

SUGGESTED READING

European Expansion

J. H. Parry, *Trade and Dominion: The European Oversea Empires in the Eighteenth Century* (1971).

Holden Furber, *Rival Empires of Trade in the Orient, 1600–1800* (1976).

Either of these studies will provide an excellent account of the building of commercial empires.

The Impact of European Expansion

Bernard Bailyn, *The Peopling of British North America: An Introduction* (1986).

W. J. Eccles, *France in America* (1972).

These two works will help the reader understand the occupation of North America by Europeans.

Wilcomb E. Washburn, *The Indian in America* (1975). A good survey.

Karen Ordahl Kupperman, *Settling with the Indians: The Meeting of English and Indian Cultures in America, 1580–1640* (1980).

James Axtell, *The Invasion Within: The Contest of Cultures in Colonial North America* (1985).

Two excellent studies of the impact of European civilization on native American life.

James Lockhart and Stuart B. Schwartz, *Early Latin America: A History of Colonial Spanish America and Brazil* (1983). A good survey.

Stanley Wolpert, *A New History of India,* 2nd ed. (1982). The appropriate parts of this work will provide a good introduction to Indian society at the time of the European intrusion.

Roland Oliver and Anthony Atmore, *The African Middle Ages, 1400–1800* (1981). A clear treatment of a complex subject.

James A. Rawley, *The Transatlantic Slave Trade. A History* (1981). A balanced account.

Imperial Rivalry

W. L. Dorn, *Competition for Empire, 1740–1763,* rev. ed. (1963). A classic work.

CHAPTER 36

Society, Faith, and Culture in the Seventeenth and Eighteenth Centuries

FIGURE 36.1. Gainsborough, "Miss Catherine Tatton" Although the middle class was growing during the early modern era, the culture of the period was still dominated by the aristocracy. This portrait of an aristocratic lady by Thomas Gainsborough (1727–1788) reflects the luxury and tastes of the eighteenth-century aristocracy, which commissioned many such paintins. (Scala/Art Resource)

For most people the structure of society, the way of life, and the relevant social institutions changed only slowly throughout most of the seventeenth and early eighteenth centuries. More rapid change occurred thereafter, but it was usually concentrated in certain areas and classes. Despite the continued rise of the bourgeoisie and considerable political change, the aristocracy remained socially dominant and governments headed by kings generally continued to centralize their power. Religious faith remained of great importance to most people, but after the middle of the seventeenth century new religious movements such as pietism were no longer the revolutionary force they had been during the previous century. The literature and arts of the period reflected the spirit of royal absolutism and the values of the aristocracy, with their exaltation of kings, princes, and nobility and also their concern for order and form. The classical style prevailed in literature and music and shared dominance with the baroque in painting and architecture.

1. SOCIETY

Population Growth and Social Structure

One of the greatest sources for change in Western society has been population growth. As we have seen (see pp. 388–390), European population grew substantially during the sixteenth century, putting pressures on economic life, adding to social turmoil, and creating changes in the quality of life for different classes of people. This population growth leveled out during the first two decades of the seventeenth century. On the whole, Europe's population was able only to maintain itself or grow slightly during the seventeenth century. In some areas population declined markedly. The typical enemies of population growth were poverty, disease, famine, and war. Most people lived close to the subsistence level. Any disturbance—a poor harvest, a natural catastrophe, a war—quickly used up their meager reserves of food and opened the door to hunger, declining health, disease, and famine. The Thirty Years' War was particularly devastating, leading to a decline in German population of some 40 percent during the

first half of the seventeenth century. The relatively late age of marriage—in the late twenties for men, the mid-twenties for women—also helped keep down the number of births in a society in which life expectancy was short and only about half of the babies born would reach maturity.

During the eighteenth century, particularly after the 1730s, European population grew sharply—from approximately 110 million in 1700 to 190 million in 1800. Although the causes are unclear, it seems that an increasing birth rate and declining death rate were achieved by earlier marriages, better and more regular nutrition, fewer plagues, and less devastating wars. Agricultural and commercial prosperity, along with continuing improvements in transportation facilities, diminished the periodic famines in many areas. Historians credit in particular the introduction of the potato from the New World and its widespread cultivation in eighteenth-century Europe with crucially increasing supplies of nutritious food. Certainly medical practices were not one of the causes for population growth. With the exception of developing small pox inoculation, which was little used outside of England until the nineteenth century, eighteenth-century doctors, hospitals, and medicines probably caused more deaths than they prevented.

Seventeenth- and eighteenth-century people viewed their society as divided—into different occupational groups and classes—and hierarchically ordered—the different groups and classes ranked from high to low status by birth, office, wealth, or education. Mobility between these ranked orders of society was viewed as the exception. People considered the social order to be relatively rigid and correct. In fact, however, mobility and change occurred. Wealth, education, and new opportunities for governmental service opened avenues for middle-class merchants, bankers, and professionals to move into the ranks of the aristocracy. Nevertheless, social mobility was never the option for many, as it would become during the nineteenth and twentieth centuries.

Rural Life

Seventeenth- and eighteenth-century Europeans lived predominantly in rural settings. In western

FIGURE 36.2. Louis Le Nain, "The Cart," 1641 In contrast to most seventeenth-century artists, Le Nain shows the life of the French peasantry. This farmyard scene (notice the mixture of ages), so typical of the countryside, contrasts sharply with life for the aristocracy. (The Louvre, Paris)

Europe approximately 80 percent still lived in the countryside; in the less urbanized eastern Europe the percentage was even higher. In rural areas life was centered on the traditional village (see Figure 36.2). There life was communally oriented: villagers knew each other, strangers stood out, and almost all effective authority was local. Community pressures limited what we today would consider the rights of dissent or privacy.

This pattern of life was slowly being altered. The traditional village was experiencing intrusion from the outside, change in its age-old pattern of life, and loss of people to the growing cities. The political isolation of the village was being broken by the increased presence of officials from the growing central governments, by the growing absence of the local nobility (who were attracted to the courts and capital cities), and by the decline of communal political institutions. Above all, economic life was being changed by the agricultural revolution and by the spread of cottage industry—both facilitated by improving means of transportation.

The Agricultural Revolution At the beginning of the seventeenth century, crops and animals

were raised in western Europe much as they had been since the Middle Ages. Most fields were open and divided into various strips of land. Crops were rotated and land allowed to lie fallow (unplanted) one out of every two or three years to keep the soil fertile. Large strips of land were set aside as "commons"—open areas where villagers grazed their animals and gathered food and hay. Decisions about crops, animals, and land use were usually determined by tradition and the practices of the community.

During the seventeenth and eighteenth centuries, changes in agricultural production initiated in Holland spread to England and then to other areas of western Europe. These changes were so important that they have been called an agricultural revolution. New crops such as potatoes, turnips, and clover were introduced. New methods of rotating crops, such as from grains to tubers (potatoes and turnips) to hay (grasses for animal fodder), were developed. Fertilization of the soil was increased by using manure from larger animal herds. These changes enabled farmers to eliminate fallow land. In addition, Dutch innovators developed methods of draining wetlands so that new crops and methods could be introduced easily.

They also experimented with breeding to create new strains of productive cattle.

In the early eighteenth century, the new crops and methods spread to England. Charles "Turnip" Townsend experimented with crop rotation and the use of turnips and clover. His contemporary and compatriot, Jethro Tull, advocated the use of a seed drill, which made planting more efficient and productive. Another Englishman, Robert Bakewell, improved the existing types of sheep and cattle by selective breeding.

These changes were sometimes connected to the enclosure of open fields and commons, particularly in England. The consolidation and enclosure of scattered strips and farms allowed larger landowners the freedom to apply new agricultural methods. Enclosures had been used in Great Britain since the sixteenth century, but the profits that could be made in commercial agriculture employing new crops and methods stimulated numerous landlords to seek enclosures during the eighteenth century. After 1750 Parliament authorized a wave of enclosures that transformed the British countryside. While these enclosures hastened the agricultural revolution, they left large numbers of rural poor unable to survive as small farmers. Many of them were forced into the ranks of rural or urban workers.

Cottage Industry During the seventeenth and eighteenth centuries, "cottage industry," or the "putting-out system," expanded greatly in rural areas. According to this system, a merchant-capitalist provided raw materials (usually for textile production such as wool or linen) and sometimes equipment (such as a handloom or spinning wheel) to peasants. Peasants, working in their cottages, turned these raw materials into finished products—spinning and weaving wool into cloth (see Figure 36.3). The merchant periodically returned, paid for the peasants' labor by the piece, and distributed the finished products to distant markets. The pay was low, lower than that offered in cities, but it was enough to help large numbers of peasants and rural workers to survive. The growth of cottage industry during the eighteenth century, particularly in Great Britain and parts of France and Germany, helps explain how so many people could remain in rural areas.

Urban Life

Cities grew during the seventeenth and eighteenth centuries, but unevenly. Until the middle of the eighteenth century, most of the growth was in the capital and port cities, particularly in northern and western Europe. These cities swelled with the growth of central governments and commerce. After the 1750s new cities arose and small cities grew, reflecting the general population growth and new concentrations of agricultural and industrial activity—particularly in Great Britain.

This urban growth meant greater prosperity for some, but the urban masses were not the beneficiaries. Most continued to live precariously at little more than a subsistence level. Any improvement in the standard of living was enjoyed almost exclusively by the middle and aristocratic classes, particularly those taking advantage of opportunities in commerce and industry and in the expanding governmental bureaucracies. A growing class of urban professionals attended institutions of higher education. In an expanding number of colleges they joined young aristocrats sent by families who felt that more education and culture was appropriate to members of the aristocracy. The middle classes continued to use their wealth to enter the aristocracy through the purchase of titles and offices, the acquisition of large estates, and judicious marriages.

The Family

The family, so central to social life and the socialization of future generations, is usually one of our most conservative institutions, evolving only gradually over time. This pattern of subtle, slow change held true for most of the seventeenth and eighteenth centuries.

The family functioned as both a social and an economic unit. In this household economy (or family economy), everyone who could worked for the good of the household. Husband, wife, children, servants, and apprentices were part of this unit of production and consumption. Even those who earned wages elsewhere usually sent part of their earnings back to the family. Children were often sent away to other households when they could earn more outside their own family.

Child rearing and attitudes toward children

FIGURE 36.3. Cottage Industry   Most cottage industry was in textiles. Here the various members of a rural household in Ireland work together, beating and combing flax into linen, which will be spun and woven. (The Mansell Collection)

were strikingly different from those of today. Children were generally not at the center of family life nor of primary concern. Infanticide was not unknown, abandonment was a common practice, and what we would consider neglect was more often the rule than the exception. Much of this behavior may be explained by the high rate of infant mortality, the generally precarious state of the household economy, and simple poverty. Parents usually had to view their children not only as family members, but as assets or liabilities in the survival of the family. With life so precarious for their children, great emotional involvement with them was risky.

It was once thought that most people lived in extended families—more than one married couple and their children in the same household; how-

ever, most historians now agree that as a rule people lived in a nuclear family household consisting of one couple and their children. Nevertheless, the typical family household during the sixteenth, seventeenth, and most of the eighteenth centuries was a much more populated, public place than the household of a modern nineteenth- and twentieth-century nuclear family. At various times a variety of relatives lived in or moved through the household, as did domestics and laborers. The household was far more open to members of the community and pressures from the community at large. The father, older children, other relatives, and community adults in general participated with the mother in raising and socializing young children.

Marriages continued to be entered into for primarily economic and social reasons. The land, the wealth, the skills, and the position one held were the most important considerations in contemplating marriage; sentiment, particularly being in love, played a secondary role. Children were the expected product of a successful marriage. Typically, a married woman gave birth to more than five children, though odds were that many of those would fail to reach adulthood or even get beyond the first few years of childhood.

Significant change came during the second half of the eighteenth century. Sentiment was becoming more important as a motivation for marriage; economic and social considerations, while still important, were not quite as dominant as before. Premarital sex and sex outside of marriage were on the increase, as evidenced by the growing number of births registered within a few months of marriage and by rising rates of illegitimacy. People were marrying at an earlier age and moving around more. Child rearing and homemaking were being turned into a woman's profession in middle-class households. Along with the rising likelihood that most babies born would survive came a changing perception of children as more special, precious, and loved—not miniature adults to be used, as they were more often perceived in the sixteenth and seventeenth centuries. Indeed, what was happening during the second half of the eighteenth century was a slow transformation to the modern family, which would come into bloom with the spread of industry and the dominance of the middle class during the nineteenth century.

Women

Women, while continuing to play a subordinate role to men, were central to the economic well-being of the family among the lower classes. Their work started when they were children, helping with the lighter tasks of farming or cottage industry. In her early teens, a girl often left home to work as a servant, trying to gain the skills and money for her future marriage and the establishment of a new household. As a married woman, her tasks as a child bearer and child rearer were important but secondary to her other economic and social functions. In addition to the standard household chores, women were expected to work

as much as possible. Women participated in the collecting and threshing of grain, took primary responsibility for gardening, raised the poultry, supervised and processed dairy production, and shared in the manufacture of household items and products for commerce (particularly spinning) as the putting-out system spread. When women worked in wage-earning occupations, it was generally at less pay and in lower-status positions than men. The line between acceptable "women's work" and "men's work" widened as the emphasis on women's domestic responsibilities grew. Outside a household, women were particularly vulnerable. They lacked many legal rights and were denied most alternatives for independent employment.

Middle- and upper-class women had fewer opportunities for participation in economic life. Respectable careers open to unmarried middle-class women were limited to those of governess or lady-in-waiting. Once married, the middle-class woman was at the center of the family, but for any real economic independence she had to wait for the death of her husband. More than lower-class women, middle-class women were increasingly seen as responsible for upholding standards and supervising the help within the home. Aristocratic women were similarly limited in the economic roles they played, but they could turn to influential social and cultural roles (see Chapter 38).

2. FAITH: THE GROWTH OF PIETISM

After the end of the Wars of Religion in the mid–seventeenth century, a relative status quo existed between Catholicism and Protestantism. While hostility still existed between believers of different Christians faiths, it no longer broke out into the violence and revolution characteristic of the Reformation era. Religious life remained centered in the local parish. In his church, the priest or pastor conducted services and supervised various charitable and educational activities. Although most people retained allegiance to established Catholic or Protestant churches, some new religious movements did arise during the seventeenth and eighteenth centuries. The most important were a number of pietistic sects, which stressed the importance of active faith in leading a religious life.

In Germany Philipp Spener (1635–1705) and Count Zinzendorf (1700–1760) became leaders of pietist movements of considerable dimensions. Spener, a Lutheran pastor, recoiled from the formal officiousness that his church had fallen into after the heated religious strife of the sixteenth and early seventeenth centuries. He minimized dogma and external forms in favor of inner piety and holy living. His largely Lutheran following included some of the leading intellects of Germany. Count Zinzendorf, a well-to-do Saxon noble man, undertook to restore the Bohemian Brethren, the persecuted and scattered followers of the early-fifteenth-century reformer John Huss. He called his group the Moravian Brethren. The Moravians, too, shunned intricate dogma and formal ritual. They set up model communities based on brotherly love, frugal living, hard work, and inner piety.

In Lutheran Sweden, Emanuel Swedenborg (1688–1772), a distinguished scientist, inventor, and public servant, founded a movement somewhat like the Moravian Brethren, based on his visions, which he took to be direct revelations of God. Swedenborg wrote several learned theological works stressing inner and outward piety and individual communion with God.

England, however, was the seat of the most widespread and influential pietistic movements of the seventeenth and eighteenth centuries. The first was the Society of Friends, or the Quakers, as they were generally called, founded by George Fox (1624–1691). Fox, a man of great energy and stubborn independence, detested formalism in religion as well as in society and government. He believed that true Christianity is an individual matter—a matter of plain, pious living and of private communion with God under the guidance of divine "inner light." Opposed to war, to rank, and to intolerance, the Quakers refused military service, the use of titles, and the taking of oaths. In these respects the Quakers were different from most of the other pietists. They were considered dangerous to the established order and were severely persecuted.

A more moderate and popular pietist move-

ment was Methodism. The prime mover in Methodism was John Wesley (1703–1791). John Wesley and his brother, Charles, became converted to a more fervent, evangelical type of Christianity. When the Anglican churches closed their doors to John Wesley, he preached emotional sermons to huge throngs in the streets and fields. George Whitefield, the most eloquent of all the early Methodists, electrified tens of thousands in England and America and converted many to pietistic Christianity. The real founder of Methodism in the American colonies was Francis Asbury (1745–1816), who duplicated in many respects the work of John Wesley in England. In both England and America the Methodists grew rapidly in numbers, mostly among the middle and lower classes.

The various pietist groups were definitely not political revolutionaries. They were intensely interested in social reform—in education, health and sanitation, temperance, penal reform, and abolition of the slave trade. But they hoped to achieve these reforms by private charity rather than political action. They tended to accommodate themselves to political status quo in the belief that spiritual and social conditions could be improved within that framework of government.

3. CULTURE

The cultural styles of the seventeenth and eighteenth centuries reflected the dominance of royal and aristocratic tastes—particularly in the baroque, classical, and rococo styles. The main exceptions came in the Dutch Netherlands and eighteenth-century England, where paintings and literature often reflected the tastes of the ascending middle class.

Literature

The reign of Louis XIV (1643–1715) was the golden age of French literature. The elegance, the sense of order, and the formalism of the court of the Grand Monarch were all reflected in the literature of the period, sometimes called the Augustan or the classical period of French literature. It was in the field of the drama that the French writers attained their greatest success. Corneille wrote elegant tragedies in the style of and often on the same subjects as the ancient Greek tragedies. The struggles of human beings against themselves and against the universe furnish the dramatic conflicts. Corneille's craftsmanship and style are handsomely polished, though often exalted and exaggerated.

Even more exquisitely polished were the perfectly rhymed and metered couplets of Racine's tragedies: *Andromaque* relates the tragic story of Hector's wife after the death of her husband at the hands of Achilles and the ensuing fall of Troy. *Phèdre* is about the wife of the legendary Greek king Theseus who falls in love with her stepson. This story had also been the subject of plays by Euripides, Sophocles, and Seneca.

One of the greatest of all the French dramatists was Molière. In his charming and profound comedies—such as *Tartuffe, Le Misanthrope,* and *Les Femmes Savantes (The Learned Ladies)*—Molière devastatingly portrays and satirizes the false, the stupid, and the pompous: egotists, pedants, social climbers, false priests, quack physicians. The tragic conflicts and the personality types of Corneille, Racine, and Molière are universal and eternal.

Other major French writers of the age of Louis XIV were Blaise Pascal, the scientist and mathematician who also wrote the marvelously styled *Provincial Letters* against the Jesuits and the deeply reflective *Pensées (Thoughts);* Madame de Sévigné, who wrote almost two thousand letters to her daughter, each a work of art; and duke de Saint-Simon, who spent the latter part of his life writing forty volumes of *Mémoires.* Madame de Sévigné and the duke of Saint-Simon, both of whom were eyewitnesses of the court of Louis XIV, constitute two of the most important sources we have for the history and the life of that period.

The common denominator among all these writers is their emphasis on and mastery of elegant and graceful form. In this emphasis they reflect the spirit of royal absolutism at its height. However, the form is valued not merely for its own sake but as an artistic clothing for subtle and critical thought. French literature in the late seventeenth century overshadowed that of all other countries of Europe, much as did French military and political influence. The lucid and graceful French language became the fashionable language of most of the royal courts and courtiers on the European continent.

French literature in the eighteenth century continued for the most part in the classical vein. Voltaire wrote dramas and poems carefully tailored to the dictates of classical formalism. His prose works exalted logic and the ideals of Greece and Rome. Only Rousseau among the major eighteenth-century French writers departed from the classical spirit to anticipate the romanticism of a later era.

Next to France, England produced the most important literature in the seventeenth and early eighteenth centuries, and like the French, the English authors generally wrote in the classical vein. The giant of English letters in the mid–seventeenth century was John Milton (1608–1674). This learned Puritan was steeped in the literature of ancient Greece and Rome. His exquisite lyrics *L'Allegro* and *Il Penseroso* and incomparable elegy *Lycidas* are thickly strewn with references to classical mythology. The conscientious Milton contributed much of his great talent and energy to public affairs. During the Puritan Revolution he went blind while working as pamphleteer for the Puritan cause and as secretary for Oliver Cromwell. The chief literary product of this period of his life is *Areopagitica,* probably the noblest defense of freedom of the press ever penned. Milton's masterpiece is *Paradise Lost,* written in his blindness and after the restoration of the Stuart kings had ruined his public career. *Paradise Lost* is a poem of epic proportions based on the Genesis account of the rebellion of Satan against God and the temptation and fall of human beings. This majestic theme is treated in stately blank verse of formal elegance. Even in this deeply religious work, Holy Writ is interwoven with classical pagan myth.

The two greatest poets to succeed Milton were John Dryden in the late seventeenth century and Alexander Pope in the early eighteenth century. Both were satirists, both displayed a massive knowledge of Greek and Roman lore, and both wrote chiefly in the formal rhymed couplets typical of the classical period. In the precision of their form, as in the sharpness of their satire, their appeal was to reason rather than to emotion.

The eighteenth century in English literature was an age of great prose. Following the upheavals of the seventeenth century, the Puritan and Glorious revolutions, it was a time of political and religious bitterness and bickering. In pungent and incisive prose Jonathan Swift, in his *Gulliver's Travels* and political essays, and Richard Sheridan, in his numerous dramas, pilloried the fops, pedants, bigots, and frauds of the day, much as Molière had done a century earlier across the channel. It was in the eighteenth century that the English novel was born. More than other literary forms, it was aimed at and reflected the tastes of England's rising middle class. Samuel Richardson, in *Clarissa Harlowe,* and Henry Fielding, in *Tom Jones,* used this medium to analyze human personality, emotions, and psychology, just as Corneille and Racine had used the poetic drama in France for the same purpose.

In the eighteenth century several writers—Robert Burns in Great Britain, Rousseau in France, Schiller and Goethe in Germany—anticipated romanticism (see Chapter 45). But the prevailing spirit in eighteenth- as in seventeenth-century literature was classical. Precision, formalism, and ofttimes elegance marked the style. Ancient Greece and Rome furnished the models. The appeal was generally to reason. The royal monarchs and their courts had little to fear from this literature. They could derive comfort from its formal order and laugh with the rest of the world at its satire, which was aimed at humankind in general rather than at ruling regimes.

Painting and Architecture

If the literature of the seventeenth and eighteenth centuries did not offend the absolutist kings and their aristocratic courtiers, the visual arts of the period usually glorified them (see Color Plate 14). The dominant style of painting and architecture during the seventeenth century was the baroque, which used elaborate swirling forms and colors to achieve dramatic, emotional effects. The baroque style was originally associated with the Roman Catholic Reformation and reflected the resurgence of a revitalized Roman Catholic church led by the militant Jesuits. Later its massive and ornamental elegance reflected the wealth and power of the absolutist monarchs and their courts, then at the peak of their affluence.

The most popular of the baroque painters of the early seventeenth century was the Fleming Peter Paul Rubens (1577–1640). After studying the work of the Italian High Renaissance masters, Rubens returned to Antwerp and painted more than two thousand pictures, many of them huge canvases. He operated what amounted to a painting factory, employing dozens of artists who painted in the details designed and sketched by the master. Rubens, a devout Roman Catholic, first painted religious subjects (see Color Plate 15). His later subjects were pagan mythology, court life, and especialiy voluptuous nude women—all painted in the most brilliant and sensuous colors (see Figure 36.4).

Spain boasted two of the greatest seventeenth-century painters: El Greco and Velásquez. El Greco, whose real name was Domenikos Theotokopoulos, was a native of the Greek island of Crete (hence "The Greek"). After studying the Italian Renaissance masters, he settled down in Toledo and developed a style of his own. By deliberate distortion and exaggeration he achieved sensational effect. *View of Toledo, St. Jerome in His Study,* and *Christ at Gethsemane* illustrate his genius. El Greco's favorite subject was the reinvigorated Church of the Roman Catholic Reformation. Considered to be a madman by his contemporaries, he is now regarded as the forerunner of several schools of nineteenth- and twentieth-century painting. Velásquez was a painter of great versatility. Although much of his earlier work was of a religious nature, he also painted genre subjects (depicting the life of the common people) and, later, portraits. He is considered one of the greatest of portrait painters. As official court painter, he exalted and glorified the Spanish royalty and ruling classes at a time when they had really passed their peak in world affairs.

During the second half of the seventeenth and then the eighteenth century, classicism, with its greater emphasis on control and restraint, gained favor. Good examples of classicism are in the works of the French artists Nicolas Poussin and Claude Lorrain (see Color Plate 16). Poussin spent most of his life in Italy studying the Renaissance masters. Although his biblical and mythological

FIGURE 36.4. Peter Paul Rubens, "Henry IV Receiving the Portrait of Marie de Médicis," 1621–1625 Rubens was commissioned by Marie de Médicis, widow of King Henry IV of France, to paint this allegorical scene showing Henri IV considering a proposed marriage to Marie de Médicis. The swirling lines, dramatic perspective, rich color, and opulence are typically baroque. (The Louvre, Paris)

scenes are more vibrant and pulsating than the Italian Renaissance paintings that inspired them, they are much more serene, subtle, and controlled than the works of Rubens and El Greco.

In eighteenth-century Great Britain, Reynolds, Gainsborough, Romney, and Lawrence vied with each other for commissions to paint the portraits of royalty and aristocracy. The results were plumes, jewels, buckles, silks, brocades, and laces in dripping profusion (see Figure 36.1).

In the Dutch Netherlands painting did not reflect royal and aristocratic tastes. Here in the busy ports and marketplaces commerce was king, and the great Dutch painters of the seventeenth century, notably Frans Hals, Jan Vermeer, and Rembrandt van Rijn, portrayed the bourgeoisie and the common people (see Color Plate 17). Rembrandt is universally recognized as one of the greatest artistic geniuses of all time. As a portrayer of character he has never been surpassed. His mastery of light and shade (*chiaroscuro*) made it seem as if the very souls of his subjects were illumined. *Syndics of the Cloth Guild, Night Watch*, and *Anatomy Lesson of Dr. Tulp* (see p. 439) are among his most powerful portrait studies. These three paintings also vividly depict the commercial prosperity, the festive urban life, and the growing interest in natural science, respectively, in seventeenth-century Dutch Netherlands.

Baroque architecture, like baroque painting, was an elaboration and ornamentation of the Renaissance and a product of the Roman Catholic

FIGURE 36.5. The Baroque Style This photo is of the interior of the basilica St. Andrea della Valle, which was built in the latter part of the seventeenth century. It well illustrates the elaborate, gaudy splendor of the baroque style, the hallmark of the age of royal absolutism and affluence. In this case the royal monarch was the pope, ruler of a Church reinvigorated by the Roman Catholic Reformation. (Alinari/Scala/ Art Resource)

Reformation (see Figure 36.5). In the late sixteenth, the seventeenth, and the eighteenth centuries Jesuit churches sprang up all over the Roman Catholic world. The most important and one of the best examples of the baroque style is the Jesuit parent church, Il Gesù, in Rome. Also, like the painting, baroque architecture was later used to represent the gaudy splendor of the seventeenth- and eighteenth-century absolute monarchs and their courts.

Towering over all other monuments of baroque architecture, much as St. Peter's towered over all

other Renaissance structures, was the Versailles Palace of Louis XIV (see Figure 32.1). The exterior of Versailles is designed in long, horizontal, classic lines. The interior is lavishly decorated with richly colored marbles, mosaics, inlaid woods, gilt, silver, silk, velvet, and brocade. The salons and halls are lighted with ceiling-to-floor windows and mirrors and crystal chandeliers holding thousands of candles. The palace faces hundreds of acres of groves, walks, pools, terraces, fountains, statues, flower beds, and clipped shrubs—all laid out in formal geometric patterns. So dazzling was this symbol of royal absolutism that many European monarchs attempted to copy it. The most successful attempt was Maria Theresa's Schönbrunn Palace in Vienna.

In England Sir Christopher Wren was the greatest architect of the baroque period. The great fire that destroyed most of the heart of London in 1666 provided Wren with an opportunity to build numerous baroque structures. His masterpiece is St. Paul's Cathedral, with its lofty dome and columns.

In the eighteenth century, architecture tended to become less massive, relying heavily on multiple curves and lacy shell-like ornamentation. This style is usually referred to as rococo. One of the best examples of the rococo style is Frederick the Great's Sans Souci Palace at Potsdam. The rococo style, like the baroque, represented an age of royal and aristocratic affluence.

Music

The classical spirit pervaded the music of the seventeenth and eighteenth centuries as it did the literature and the visual arts; and like the literature and the visual arts, the music was an outgrowth of Renaissance developments.[1] The piano and the violin family of instruments, whose forebears appeared in the sixteenth century, developed rapidly in the seventeenth. In the late seventeenth and early eighteenth centuries, three Italian families, the Amati, the Guarneri, and the Stradivari, fashioned the finest violins ever made. The seventeenth century was also marked by the rise of the opera. Alessandro Scarlatti in Italy, Lully in France, and Purcell in England popularized this grandiose combination of music and drama. The eighteenth was the great century of classical music—the age of Bach, Handel, Haydn, and Mozart.

Johann Sebastian Bach (1685–1750) was a member of a German family long distinguished in music. Noted in his own lifetime chiefly as an organist, he composed a vast array of great music for

FIGURE 36.6. Mozart Mozart, shown here as a boy, gained fame as an infant prodigy. Mozart died when he was thirty-five, but this prolific genius composed over six hundred works. (Mozart Museum, Salzburg)

organ, harpsichord, and clavichord (forerunner of the piano), orchestra, and chorus, much of which has been lost. Most of Bach's compositions were religiously inspired, and he holds the same position in Protestant music that the sixteenth-century Palestrina does in music of the Roman Catholic church. Bach was not widely appreciated in his own day. It was not until Felix Mendelssohn in the nineteenth century "discovered" him that he became widely known.

George Frederick Handel (1685–1759) was born in central Germany in the same year as Bach and not many miles distant. He studied Italian opera in Germany and Italy and wrote forty-six operas himself. He became court musician of the elector of Hanover. Later he made his home in England, as did the elector, who became King George I of

---

[1] Some music historians designate the music of the seventeenth and early eighteenth centuries, including that of Bach and Handel, as baroque, which was a forerunner of the classical.

England. Handel wrote an enormous quantity of music, both instrumental and vocal. All of it is marked by dignity, formal elegance, and melodious harmony—fitting for and appreciated in an age of royal splendor. His best-known work is the majestic oratorio *The Messiah,* heard every Christmas season.

Franz Joseph Haydn (1732–1809), unlike Handel, was primarily interested in instrumental music; he was the chief originator of the symphony. During his long career in Vienna, which he helped to make the music capital of the world, he wrote more than a hundred symphonies in addition to scores of compositions of other forms of music, particularly chamber music. It was in his hands that orchestral music really came into its own. All his work is in the formal, classical style. He became a friend and an important source of inspi-

ration for the younger Mozart.

Wolfgang Amadeus Mozart (1756–1791) is regarded by many students as the greatest musical genius of all time. Born in Salzburg, he spent most of his adult life in Vienna. Mozart began composing at the age of five (possibly four), and gave public concerts on the harpsichord at the age of six (see Figure 36.6). At twelve he wrote an opera. Before his untimely death at the age of thirty-five, he wrote more than six hundred compositions in all the known musical forms. Symphonies, chamber music, and piano sonatas and concertos were his favorite forms. His best-known operas are *The Marriage of Figaro, Don Giovanni,* and *The Magic Flute.* In the masterful hands of Mozart the classical style reached the peak of its perfection. Never was music so clear, melodic, elegant, and graceful.

SUGGESTED READING

General

F. Braudel, *The Structures of Everyday Life: The Limits of the Possible* (1982). A massive, highly respected social history.

H. Kamen, *European Society, 1500–1700* (1985). A solid survey.

G. Rudé, *Europe in the Eighteenth Century* (1972). Emphasizes social history.

Society

P. Ariés, *Centuries of Childhood: A Social History of Family Life* (1962). A path-breaking work.

J. Blum, *The End of the Old Order in Rural Europe* (1978). Excellent comparative study.

M. W. Flinn, *The European Demographic System, 1500–1820* (1981). A recent survey.

P. Laslett, *The World We Have Lost* (1965). A classic study of English society during the period.

E. Shorter, *The Making of the Modern Family* (1975). Interpretive, controversial, and well written.

L. Stone, *The Family, Sex and Marriage in England, 1500–1800* (1977). A sophisticated interpretation.

L. Tilly and J. Scott, *Women, Work and Family* (1978). A highly respected work.

J. de Vries, *European Urbanization, 1500–1800* (1984). Broad recent survey.

Faith

A. Armstrong, *The Church of England, the Methodists, and Society 1700–1850* (1973). A broad survey.

G. R. Cragg, *The Church and the Age of Reason* (1961). A solid survey.

Culture

A. Adam, *Grandeur and Illusion: French Literature and Society 1600–1715* (1972). A thorough survey of French literature and its relation to seventeenth-century society.

P. Burke, *Popular Culture in Early Modern Europe* (1978). Focuses on ordinary people.

C. Palisca, *Baroque Music* (1968). Excellent survey.

C. Rosen, *The Classical Style: Haydn, Mozart, Beethoven* (1972). Excellent study.

V. L. Tapié, *The Age of Grandeur: Baroque Art and Architecture* (1960). A solid survey of art history.

I. Watt, *The Rise of the Novel: Studies of Defoe, Richardson, and Fielding* (1957). A good introduction.

CHAPTER 37

The Scientific Revolution

FIGURE 37.1. Isaac Newton Isaac Newton (1642–1727) became the leading figure of the Scientific Revolution, employing the new methods of science and drawing together discoveries in astronomy and physics to create a systematic explanation of the physical laws of the universe. This portrait suggests his youthful vigor and keenness. He was still in his twenties when he developed some of his greatest theories. (The Bettmann Archive)

Until the seventeenth century even the most learned scholars of Europe agreed with the standard medieval understanding of the physical nature of the earth and the universe. This medieval understanding was based on the views of the fourth-century B.C. Greek, Aristotle, as modified by Ptolemy and medieval Christian scholars. According to this Christian medieval understanding the earth was stationary and at the center of the universe. Around it moved the planets, the sun, the stars, and the heavens in an ascending series of spheres. This universe was finite and and focused on the earthly center of God's concern. "Scientific" investigation generally took the form of making deductions from accepted, authoritative medieval assumptions about the physical universe. The questions asked were usually the more philosophical or theological ones of ultimate causes for an event—guesses on why something occurred.

During the seventeenth century a relatively small number of scholars undermined this medieval understanding of nature and replaced it with a modern scientific view. According to this new scientific view, the earth was a moving body and no longer at the center of the universe. Rather it, along with the planets, moved around the sun in an infinite universe of other similar bodies. Scientific investigations generally took the form of observing, measuring, experimenting, and coming to reasoned conclusions through the use of sophisticated mathematics. Medieval assumptions about the physical universe were viewed with a skeptical eye. The questions asked were usually the more concrete, pragmatic ones of how an event occurred rather than the ultimate reasons for why such an event occurred. The new scientific synthesis was one of a mechanistic universe of forces acting according to mathematically expressible laws and open to human reason and investigation.

Until the eighteenth century the impact of this modern scientific view, known as the Scientific Revolution, was limited. Nevertheless, it was an intellectual revolution of great significance, for with it Western civilization was making a turn from its medieval assumptions and embarking in a direction unique among the cultures of the world. Science would grow to become one of the main factors distinguishing the West and accounting for its power and dynamism.

1. CAUSES AND SPREAD

There were several causes for the development and spread of the Scientific Revolution, some of which extend back to the late Middle Ages and Renaissance. Medieval universities had been growing for some time and included the study of philosophy and other subjects that would be central to the Scientific Revolution, including astronomy, physics, and mathematics. Certainly the emphasis and the greatest prestige was accorded to theology and nonscientific study in these medieval universities, but nevertheless there were places on the faculty for many of the central figures of the Scientific Revolution, such as Galileo and Newton.

The Renaissance involved a search for classical writings. The discovery of Greek authorities who contradicted Aristotle and the growth of Neoplatonism as an alternative to Aristotelian thought in Renaissance Italy encouraged scholars to question medieval scientific assumptions. The Renaissance stimulated interest in analyzing and describing physical reality, a key concern of the Scientific Revolution. The Renaissance was also an age of commercial and geographic expansion in the West, which created a demand for new instruments and precise measurements, particularly for navigation in the open seas. This demand encouraged scientific research, especially in astronomy and mathematics. In turn, the better instruments developed during the Renaissance helped scholars make accurate measurements, something crucial for the new science. During this same period, the printing press was invented, which facilitated the dissemination of the new science, even if initially to only a select few.

The Reformation played a mixed role in the Scientific Revolution. Generally, both Catholics and Protestants criticized the scientific discoveries that so threatened the medieval-Christian view of the universe. During the sixteenth century there was perhaps more room within the Catholic church for scientific research than among Protestants, but by the middle of the seventeenth century this was clearly not the case. By then the Counter-Reformation Catholic church had turned into an enemy of much of the new science, while Protestants began to accept it. This was particularly so in England, where the Puritans encouraged the new science and where science took hold most firmly.

During the seventeenth century, governments gave support to science, in part hoping that scientific inquiry would yield discoveries that would increase the power and prosperity of the state. With governmental support scientific academies were established and played a significant role in the advancement of science. The earliest and most important of these were the Royal Society in England, chartered in 1662 by Charles II, and the Académie des Sciences in France, founded by Colbert four years later. These organizations and others patterned after them furnished laboratories, granted subsidies, brought scientists together to exchange ideas, published their findings, and encouraged scientific achievement generally. They also helped make scientists a more socially acceptable group and contributed to the creation of a new set of values supportive of the new science.

Finally, religious and psychological factors played an important, if difficult to evaluate, role in the development and spread of the Scientific Revolution. Many of the new scientists had strong, though not always traditional, religious motives for their work, particularly a desire to gain insight into the perfection of God's universe.

2. ASTRONOMY AND PHYSICS: FROM COPERNICUS TO NEWTON

The first branches of modern natural science to attract systematic attention were astronomy and physics. Discoveries in these fields would dramatically alter the perception of nature and the earth's place in the universe.

Nicolaus Copernicus

The first steps were taken in the sixteenth century by Nicolaus Copernicus (1473–1543), a Polish cler-

gyman interested in astronomy, astrology, mathematics, and church law. Like so many other northern European scholars in the fifteenth century, he crossed the Alps to study in an Italian university. There he was influenced by the rediscovery of Greek scholarship, particularly Platonic and Pythagorean thought, that differed from the accepted, mathematically complex Aristotelian-Ptolemaic tradition. This rediscovered Greek thought emphasized the importance of a hidden, simpler, mathematically harmonious reality underlying appearances. With a religious, mystical passion, Copernicus sought a simpler mathematical formulation for how the universe operated. This search convinced him that the earth was not the center of the universe but, rather, that the sun was the center. Moreover, the earth was not stationary but moved in perfect divine circles around the sun, as did other bodies in the universe. This change from an earth-centered (geocentric) to a sun-centered (heiiocentric) universe has come to be known as the Copernican revolution (see Figures 37.2 and 37.3).

Copernicus worked on his heliocentric model of the universal for almost twenty-five years, but fearing the ridicule of the laity and the ire of the clergy, he did not have it published until 1543, the year of his death. Few knew of his views and even fewer accepted them. Nevertheless, their significance and their threat to the Christian conception of the universe would be recognized and condemned by Catholic and Protestant authorities. They denounced the Copernican system as illogical, unbiblical, and unsettling to the Christian faith. Nevertheless, his views would stimulate other scholars investigating the physical nature of the universe.

Tycho Brahe

After Copernicus, the most important astronomer of the sixteenth century was a Danish aristocrat, Tycho Brahe (1546–1601). He persuaded the king of Denmark to support him, and he built the most advanced astronomy laboratory in Europe. There he gathered unusually accurate, detailed information about the planets and stars (even though the telescope had not yet been invented). Partic-

FIGURE 37.2.   The Medieval View of the Universe
This woodcut (1559) shows the traditional Ptolemaic conception of the universe. At the center is the earth, surrounded by ascending spheres of air, fire, the sun, the planets, the stars ("firmament"), the crystalline ring, and the "primum mobile." (The British Museum)

FIGURE 37.3.   The Copernican conception of the universe (woodcut, 1576).   At the center is the sun, surrounded by the circling planets (one of which is the earth), all bounded by an infinity of stars and the heavens. One of the central developments of the Scientific Revolution was the replacement of the Ptolemaic geocentric by the Copernican heliocentric conception of the universe. (The British Museum)

ularly important were his discoveries of a new star in 1572 and a comet in 1577, both of which undermined the Aristotelian assumptions about a sky of fixed, unalterable stars moving in crystalline spheres. He did not share Copernicus' belief in a heliocentric universe nor did he grasp the sophisticated mathematics of the day. He believed that the earth remained the stationary center of the universe, as argued by Aristotle and Ptolemy, but he concluded that the other planets revolved around the sun, which itself moved around the earth and moon. However, the astronomical observations he gathered would be used by other scholars who became convinced that the earth moved around the sun.

Johann Kepler

Tycho Brahe's assistant, Johann Kepler (1571–1630) built upon Brahe's observations while returning to the Copernican heliocentric theory. A German Lutheran from an aristocratic family, Kepler believed there was an underlying mathematical harmony of mystical significance to the physical universe. He sought such a mathematical harmony that would fit with Brahe's observations. His most important findings were the three laws of planetary motion, proposed between 1609 and 1619: first, that the planets moved in ellipses around the sun; second, that their velocity varied according to the distance from the sun; and third, that there was a physical relationship between the moving planets that could be expressed mathematically. He thus further undermined the Aristotelian universe accepted by medieval thought and provided support for the Copernican revolution. Moreover, he extended the Copernican revolution in ways that would be fully realized by Galileo and Newton.

Galileo Galilei

The Italian astronomer, physicist, and mathematician Galileo Galilei (1564–1642) believed, like Copernicus and Kepler, that there was a hidden harmony to nature. He felt that this harmony could be discovered through experimentation and mathematics. He investigated motion through controlled experiments and demonstrated that motion could be described mathematically. He showed that bodies once set in motion will tend to stay in motion and described mathematically the speed of falling bodies. He thus undermined Aristotelian physics and established rules for experimental physics.

Galileo then moved to astronomy, using a telescope he built in 1609. The telescope revealed to Galileo that the moon had a rough surface not unlike the earth's, that Jupiter had moons, and that the sun had spots. He confirmed the Copernican hypothesis and provided support for the view that other heavenly bodies were like the earth and imperfect. By implication, this finding meant that the natural universe was ordered and uniform, without the hierarchical distinctions of the accepted medieval view.

Galileo aggressively published and defended his views against detractors, most notably in *Dialogue on the Two Chief Systems of the World*, published in Italian in 1632. This text brought him into conflict with conservative forces in the Catholic church, which condemned his theories at an Inquisition in 1633, forcing him to recant.

Isaac Newton

The uphill trail blazed by Copernicus, Brahe, Kepler, and Galileo was continued on to a lofty peak by Isaac Newton (1642–1727). As a student at Cambridge University, he distinguished himself enough in mathematics to be chosen to stay on as professor after his graduation. Starting in his early twenties, Newton came forth with some of the most important discoveries in the history of science—or indeed of the human intellect. He developed calculus and investigated the nature of light. He formulated and described mathematically three laws of motion: inertia, acceleration, and action/reaction. He is probably best known for the laws of universal attraction, or gravitation. The concept matured and was refined in Newton's mind over a period of years. As it finally appeared in 1687 in his *Principia (The Mathematical Principles of Natural Knowledge)*, the law is stated with marvelous simplicity and precision: "Every particle of matter in the universe attracts every other particle with a force varying inversely as the square of the distance between them and directly proportional to the product of their masses." This law, so simply expressed, applied equally to the movement of a planet and a berry falling from a bush. The secret of the physical universe appeared to have been solved—a universe of perfect stability and precision.

What Newton had done was to synthesize the new findings in astronomy and physics into a systematic explanation of physical laws that were true for earth as well as for the heavens. This Newtonian universe was uniform, mathematically describable, held together by explainable forces, atomic in nature. The universe was essentially matter in motion.

Newton, like most other figures of the Scientific Revolution, was profoundly religious; he believed in God and a God-centered universe, as well as alchemy. By the later years of the seventeenth century and the beginning of the eighteenth century, the new science was becoming more acceptable than it had been for Newton's predecessors, as is illustrated by his career. He became a member of Parliament and served for many years as director of the Royal Mint. He was knighted by Queen Anne. His acceptance, as contrasted with the ridicule and persecution suffered by Copernicus and Galileo, indicates the progress that had been made by the scientific attitude between the sixteenth and the eighteenth centuries.

3. SCIENTIFIC METHODOLOGY

The scientists who made discoveries in astronomy and physics succeeded in undermining the medieval view of the universe as stable, fixed, and finite, with the earth at its center. They replaced it with a view of the universe as moving and infinite, with the earth merely one of millions of bodies, all subject to the laws of nature. In the process they were also developing and using new methods for discovery, for ascertaining how things worked, and for determining the truth. Indeed, at the heart of the Scientific Revolution was the new methodology of science. According to this new methodology, earlier methods for ascertaining the truth, which primarily involved referring to traditional authorities such as Aristotle, Ptolemy, and the Church and making deductions from their propositions, were unacceptable. The new methodology emphasized systematic skepticism, experimentation, and reasoning based on observed facts and mathematical laws. The two most important philosophers of this new scientific methodology were Francis Bacon and René Descartes.

Francis Bacon

Francis Bacon (1561–1626) was a politician and once was lord chancellor of England under James I. He had a passionate interest in the new science. He rejected reliance on ancient authorities and advocated that scientists should engage in the collection of data without holding preconceived notions. From that information, scientific conclusions could be reached through inductive reasoning—drawing general conclusions on the basis of many particular concrete observations. He thus became a proponent of the empirical method, which was already being used by some of the new scientists. In addition, he argued that true, scientific knowledge would be useful knowledge, as opposed to medieval Scholasticism, which Bacon attacked as too abstract. He had faith that scientific discoveries would be applied to commerce and industry and generally improve the human condition by giving human beings greater power over their environment. He thus became an outstanding propagandist for the new science as well as a

FIGURE 37.4. Title Page of Bacon's *Novum Organum* This title page from Francis Bacon's *Novum Organum (New Instrument)*, published in 1620, shows a ship of discovery sailing out into the unknown. Below is the quotation, "Many shall venture forth and science shall be increased." (The Bettmann Archive)

proponent of the empirical method (see Figure 37.4). He did not, however, have a good understanding of mathematics and the role it could play in the new science. Descartes did.

René Descartes

René Descartes (1596–1650) was born in France and received training in Scholastic philosophy and mathematics. He spent his most productive years as a mathematician, physicist, and metaphysical philosopher in Holland. In 1619 Descartes perceived connections between geometry and algebra that led him to discover analytic geometry, an important tool for scientists. He expressed his philosophy and scientific methodology in his *Discourse on Method* (1637), a landmark in the rise of the scientific spirit. It was an eloquent defense of the value of abstract reasoning. He would question all authority no matter how venerable—be it Aristotle or the Bible. He tried to remove systematically all assumptions about knowledge to the point where he was left with one experiential fact—that he was thinking. "I think, therefore I am," he believed to be a safe starting point. From this starting point he followed a rigorous process of deductive reasoning to come to a variety of conclusions, including the existence of God and the reality of the physical world. He argued that the universe could be divided into two kinds of reality: mind, or subjective thinking and experiencing; and body, or objective physical substance. According to this philosophy, known as "Cartesian dualism," the objective physical universe could be understood in terms of extension and motion. "Give me extension and motion," said Descartes, "and I will create the universe." Only the mind was exempt from mechanical laws.

Descartes, like Bacon, rejected Scholastic philosophy as not useful (although there were similarities in his deductive method and the reasoning used in Scholastic thought). He emphasized the power of the rigorous, reasoning individual mind to discover truths about nature and turn them to human needs. Unlike Bacon, he emphasized mathematical reasoning, not empirical investigation. By challenging all established authority, by accepting as truth only what could be known by reason, and by assuming a purely mechanical, physical universe, Descartes was in dispute with medieval thought and established an influential philosophy and methodology for the new science.

4. OTHER DISCIPLINES

The individuals who made the great discoveries of the Scientific Revolution all used, to varying degrees, the new scientific methodologies promoted by Bacon and Descartes during the first half of the seventeenth century. Clearly astronomy and

FIGURE 37.5. Modern Anatomy   This illustration from an anatomy book published in 1639 by William Harvey shows the circulation of blood. Harvey's empirical, descriptive approach was typical of the new science. (Art Resource)

physics led the way, but important discoveries were made in other sciences as well.

In the sixteenth century Vesalius, a Fleming living in Italy, wrote the first comprehensive textbook on the structure of the human body to be based on careful observation. Because he dissected many human bodies in order to make his observations, he ran into serious opposition from clerical authorities. In disgust he gave up his scientific studies and became the personal physician of Emperor Charles V. In the seventeenth century William Harvey, an Englishman who also studied in Italy, discovered the major principles of the circulatory system, thus making it possible for surgeons to operate on the human body with somewhat less fatal consequences than had previously been the case (see Figure 37.5). Vesalius and Harvey are regarded as the founders of the science of anatomy.

In the seventeenth century, an Irish nobleman, Robert Boyle, laid the foundations for modern chemistry by attacking many assumptions inherited from the ancients and by beginning the systematic search for the basic physical elements. He relied on the experimental method and argued that all matter was composed of atoms. He discovered a law of gases that still bears his name.

The language in which science is expressed is mathematics. In the early seventeenth century a Scotsman, Sir John Napier, invented logarithms, by which the process of multiplying and dividing huge numbers is greatly simplified. Shortly afterward the system was applied to the slide rule. About the same time, René Descartes adopted the symbols now used in algebra and devised analytic geometry, a method of combining and interchanging algebra and geometry. In the latter part of the seventeenth century Newton and the German Wilhelm Leibnitz, working independently, invented calculus, upon which many of the most intricate processes of advanced science and engineering are dependent.

During the seventeenth century some of the basic scientific instruments were invented. Both the telescope and the microscope were products of the Dutch Netherlands. However, it was Galileo who first used the telescope in systematic astronomical observations. Leeuwenhoek, a Dutchman, was the chief pioneer in the use of the microscope. He discovered bacteria two hundred years before Pasteur learned how to combat them; he also observed the cellular structure of plant and animal tissue, the structure of the blood, and its circulation through the capillary system. Another Dutchman, Huygens, invented the pendulum clock, making possible for the first time in history the precise measurement of small intervals of time.

The methods and discoveries of the Scientific Revolution spread to disciplines outside of what are usually considered the sciences. A good example is political theory, with the seminal thought of Thomas Hobbes (1588–1679) and John Locke (1632–1704).

Hobbes gained contact with the new sciences from several quarters. As a young man he served as a secretary to Francis Bacon. While traveling on the continent, he came into contact with René Descartes and Galileo. He studied the writings of William Harvey. Hobbes acquired an expertise in both geometry and optics. Toward the middle of his life Hobbes became involved in the political events of his times and turned his attention to political theory. Dismayed by the civil strife raging during the civil war in England, Hobbes developed a political theory justifying absolutism in the name of law and order. In his *Leviathan* (1651), Hobbes started from a very few principles about human nature and rigorously deduced explanations for the founding and proper functioning of the state. He argued that human beings are most concerned with the preservation of their own lives, the avoidance of pain and the pursuit of pleasure, and the striving for power to protect themselves and get what they want. In the hypothetical state of nature, people are in a continual competitive struggle with each other. Self-interest and reason eventually lead people to exit the state of nature by way of a social contract between themselves. This social contract creates and grants massive powers to a sovereign, who uses those powers as necessary to keep the peace. Hobbes, like other seventeenth-century scientists, assumed a mechanistic, materialistic universe. His reasoning was much like Descartes'—rigorous, mathematical, and deductive. In the end, Hobbes concluded that absolutism was in accordance with natural law, though his method of reasoning pleased neither kings nor aristocrats.

John Locke was also heavily influenced by the new seventeenth-century science. He acquired a medical education at college, read the works of leading scientific thinkers such as Francis Bacon and Isaac Newton, and was a friend of Robert Boyle. Like Hobbes, Locke was involved in some of the political events of his times. Locke also started with human beings in a state of nature, made some basic assumptions about the human condition, and traced the exit from the state of nature by way of a social contract. Yet Locke came to some significantly different conclusions. Assuming that human beings were not quite so self-centered and that things were not so bad in the state of nature, Locke argued that the sovereign had far fewer powers than Hobbes had claimed and that individuals retained the right to revolt under certain circumstances. Applying reasoning similar to that of seventeenth-century scientists, Locke concluded that British constitutionalism was in accordance with natural law.

Thus both Hobbes and Locke extended the Scientific Revolution to new fields. While their conclusions differed, they set a new standard for political theory, becoming two of the most influential political theorists of modern times.

By the end of the seventeenth century, the Aristotelian-medieval world view had been broken and replaced by the Copernican-Newtonian world view. The methodology of modern science was established. Scientists had created the foundations for the modern sciences of astronomy, physics, mathematics, chemistry, and anatomy, and study in other disciplines was underway. Although the new scientists' work had gained considerable acceptance, their ideas were still known to only a few. During the Enlightenment of the eighteenth century, the ideas of the Scientific Revolution spread widely and were applied in new ways.

SUGGESTED READING

General

J. Ben-David, *The Scientist's Role in Society* (1971). A sophisticated social interpretation.

A. R. Hall, *The Scientific Revolution 1500–1800: The Formation of the Modern Scientific Attitude* (1966). A good analysis.

M. Jacob, *The Cultural Meaning of the Scientific Revolution* (1987). A strong interpretation.

A. G. R. Smith, *Science and Society in the Sixteenth and Seventeenth Centuries* (1972).

Astronomy and Physics

Ludovico Geymonat, *Galileo Galilei* (1965). A solid biography.

T. S. Kuhn, *The Copernican Revolution* (1957). An excellent analysis.

F. Manuel, *A Portrait of Isaac Newton* (1968). Uses a psychoanalytic perspective.

R. S. Westfall, *Never at Rest: A Biography of Isaac Newton* (1981). An excellent new biography.

Scientific Methodology

T. S. Kuhn, *The Structure of Scientific Revolutions* (1962). An important, influential interpretation of the Scientific Revolution.

Other Disciplines

P. Laslett, *Locke's Two Treatises of Government* (1970). Includes an introductory analysis with the texts.

C. B. MacPherson, *The Political Theory of Possessive Individualism: Hobbes to Locke* (1962). A controversial, Marxist interpretation.

Sources

M. B. Hall, ed., *Nature and Nature's Laws: Documents of the Scientific Revolution* (1970). A good collection.

CHAPTER 38
The Enlightenment

FIGURE 38.1. "Madame Geoffrin's Salon," 1755   Meetings in aristocratic Parisian salons such as this were typical of the Enlightenment. Here thinkers, artists, musicians, writers, and aristocrats exchanged views and helped spread the philosophy of the Enlightenment. (Giraudon/Art Resource)

As a period of intellectual history, the eighteenth century is usually referred to as the Enlightenment, or the Age of Reason. The Enlightenment was initiated toward the end of the seventeenth century by a number of intellectuals who attempted to popularize the ideas of the Scientific Revolution. During the eighteenth century this popularization continued, and new attempts were made to apply the methods of natural sciences to human behavior and social institutions. Western thinkers were speculating on the broader meaning of science—its ethical, political, social, and economic implications. They subjected almost everything to the critical standard of reason. In doing so, Enlightenment thinkers rejected the assumptions of their medieval and Renaissance predecessors who looked to the Christian or classical past for guidance. Enlightenment thinkers argued for reform and change. They felt that people were ready to shrug off the shackles of tradition and custom and participate in the progress of civilization; to these optimistic intellectuals, people were ready to become enlightened.

The Enlightenment was limited in some respects. During the eighteenth century the Enlightenment was centered in western Europe. Moreover, Enlightenment thought spread primarily to only the elite of the urban aristocracy and middle classes. Nevertheless, the ideas and attitudes developed during the Enlightenment would come to dominate most parts of Western civilization over the next two centuries.

1. ENLIGHTENMENT CONCEPTS

Although Enlightenment thinkers differed widely among themselves, they shared a belief in certain broad concepts that together make up the philosophy of the Enlightenment. The three most important concepts were reason, nature, and change and progress.

Enlightenment thinkers argued that all assumptions should be subjected to critical and empirical reasoning. Traditional institutions or customs should not be accepted because they have been long-lasting but rather should be examined critically and held up to the standard of reason. True knowledge is gained empirically. All we know and all we can ever know is what we perceive through our senses and interpret with our reason. There are no such things as innate ideas or revealed truth.

Enlightenment thinkers believed that nature is ordered, functions reasonably, and constitutes a standard for judgment. Nature is governed by a few simple and unchangeable laws. Those who think they can change one of these laws—who think they can, by praying, for instance, bring down the rain on parched crops and perchance a neighbor's unroofed house—are dupes of their own egotism. Nature does not act capriciously. Proper empirical analysis will show that nature functions in line with the laws of reason. Nature is good and beautiful in its simplicity. Human beings have corrupted it with their complex political, social, and religious restrictions. A move to nature is a move toward wholesome vigor and freedom.

Most Enlightenment thinkers felt that change and progress work hand in hand as human beings work to perfect themselves and their society. Change should not be viewed with distrust as a deterioration from a previously superior, more perfect state of things. Change, when dictated by reason and when in line with nature, liberates individuals and should be pursued. Such change contributes to individual and social progress on earth. Human beings are naturally rational and good, but the proponents of mystic religions have distorted human thinking and prevented proper progress by preaching false doctrines of original sin and divine moral laws. Rid people's minds of these religious hindrances and they can and will build for themselves a more perfect society.

The concepts of reason, nature, and change and progress worked together in the minds of Enlightenment thinkers and generally formed a structure for their more specific ideas. Enlightenment thinkers used reason and nature to criticize institutions and customs of the past, which still dominated their eighteenth-century society. Reason and nature further guided these thinkers as they determined what changes should take place. They felt that as individuals and societies made appropriate changes, human life would become more informed by reason and more compatible with nature. They believed human beings were on the verge of enlightenment—of great progress—if people would simply open their eyes and become mature, reasoning adults. This progress would take the form of people leading increasingly happier, freer, more moral lives.

2. THE *PHILOSOPHES*

Enlightenment ideas were put forth by a variety of intellectuals who in France came to be known as the *philosophes*. *Philosophes* is French for philosophers, and in a sense these thinkers were rightly considered philosophers, for the questions they dealt with were philosophical: How do we discover truth? How should life be lived? What is the nature of God? But on the whole the term has a meaning different from the usual meaning of "philosopher." The *philosophes* were intellectuals, often not formally trained or associated with a university. They were usually more literary than scientific. They generally extended, applied, popularized, or propagandized ideas of others rather than originating those ideas themselves. The *philosophes* were more likely to write plays, satires, histories, novels, encyclopedia entries, and short pamphlets or simply participate in verbal exchanges at select gatherings than to write formal philosophical books.

It was the *philosophes* who developed the philosophy of the Enlightenment and spread it to much of the educated elite in western Europe (and the American colonies). Although the sources for their philosophy can be traced to the Scientific Revolution in general, the *philosophes* were most influenced by their understanding of Newton, Locke, and English institutions.

The *philosophes* saw Isaac Newton as the great synthesizer of the Scientific Revolution who rightly described the universe as ordered, mechanical, material, and only originally set into motion by God, who since then has remained relatively inactive. Newton's synthesis showed to the *philosophes* that reason and nature were compatible: Nature functioned logically and discernably, and what was natural was also reasonable. Newton exemplified the value of reasoning based on concrete experience. The *philosophes* felt that his empirical methodology was the correct path to discovering truth.

John Locke (1632–1704) agreed with Newton but went further. This English thinker would not exempt even the mind from the mechanical laws of the material universe. In his *Essay Concerning Human Understanding* (1690), Locke pictured the human brain at birth as a blank sheet of paper on which nothing would ever be written except by sense perception and reason. What human beings become depends on their experiences—on the information received through the senses. Schools and social institutions could therefore play a great role in molding the individual from childhood to adulthood. Human beings were thus by nature far more malleable than had been assumed. This empirical psychology of Locke rejected the notion that human beings were born with innate ideas or that revelation was a reliable source of truth. Locke also enunciated liberal and reformist political ideas in his *Second Treatise of Civil Government* (1690), which influenced the *philosophes*. On the whole Locke's empiricism, psychology, and politics were appealing to the *philosophes*.

England, not coincidentally the country of Newton and Locke, became an admired model for many of the *philosophes*. They tended to idealize it, but England did seem to allow greater individual freedom, tolerate religious differences, and evidence greater political reform than other countries, especially France. England seemed to have gone furthest in freeing itself from traditional institutions and accepting the new science of the seventeenth century. Moreover, England's approach seemed to work, for England was experiencing relative political stability and prosperity. The *philosophes* wanted to see in their own countries much of what England already seemed to have.

Many *philosophes* reflected the influence of Newton, Locke, and English institutions, but perhaps the most representative in his views was Voltaire (1694–1778) (see Figure 38.2). Of all the leading figures of the Enlightenment, he was the most influential. Voltaire, the son of a Paris lawyer, became the idol of the French intelligentsia while still in his early twenties. His versatile mind was sparkling; his wit was mordant. An outspoken critic, he soon ran afoul of both church and state authorities. First he was imprisoned in the Bastille; later he was exiled to England. There he

FIGURE 38.2   Frederick the Great with Voltaire
Voltaire, seated, talks with Frederick the Great.
This picture reveals the image of the great Enlightenment thinker at work with books, papers, and pen and with the international stature sufficient to gain the ear of enlightened despots such as Frederick. Yet Frederick's enlightenment may have been more form than substance. Bibliothèque Nationale, Paris)

encountered the ideas of Newton and Locke and came to admire English parliamentary government and tolerance. In *Letters on the English* (1733), *Elements of the Philosophy of Newton* (1738), and other writings, he popularized the ideas of Newton and Locke, extolled the virtues of English society, and indirectly criticized French society. Slipping back into France, he was hidden for a time and protected by a wealthy woman who became his mistress. Voltaire's facile mind and pen were never idle. He wrote poetry, drama, history, essays, letters, and scientific treatises—ninety volumes in all. The special targets of his cynical wit were the Catholic church and Christian institutions. Few people in history have dominated their age intellectually as did Voltaire.

The work that best summarizes the philosophy of the Enlightenment is the *Encyclopedia*. The *En-cyclopedia* was a collaborative effort by many of the *philosophes* under the editorship of Denis Diderot (1713–1774) and Jean le Rond D'Alembert (1717–1783). This gigantic work undertook to explore the whole world of knowledge from the perspective of the *philosophes*. Its articles on subjects ranging from music to machinery expressed the critical, rationalistic, and empiricist views of the *philosophes* (see Figure 38.3). The practicality of science and knowledge in general was emphasized. One of the work's main messages was that almost anything could be discovered or understood or clarified through reason. An underlying current was criticism of the irrational and of whatever stood in the way of the Enlightenment, whether it was religious intolerance or traditional social institutions. The first volume appeared in 1751. Its threat to the status quo was recognized by governmental and Church authorities, who censored it, halted its publication, and harassed its editors. Thanks in great part to the persistence of Diderot, who fought the authorities and dealt with a difficult group of contributing authors, the project was completed with the publication of the final volume in 1772. The *Encyclopedia* sold well and played an important role in the penetration of Enlightenment ideas outside the major cities and courts.

By this time the Enlightenment was evolving to a different stage. The *philosophes* were becoming more quarrelsome among themselves. This argumentation reflected a greater acceptance of the fundamental philosophy of the Enlightenment, for the debates tended to center on how far Enlightenment concepts could be extended. Some *philosophes*, such as Baron d'Holbach (1723–1789), verged on atheism in attacks on organized religion. Others, such as Marie-Jean de Condorcet (1743–1794), were so optimistic that they almost made a religion out of progress itself. Enlightenment thinkers were also tending to specialize. Some laid the foundations for the development of the social sciences during the nineteenth century. For example, Cesare Beccaria (1738–1794) contributed works on modern criminology and penology, and Adam Smith (1723–1790) wrote what would turn into the fundamental text of classical economics. Finally, some Enlightenment thinkers took more challenging positions, often contradicting some of the ideas of the Enlightenment itself and providing a transition to the succeeding intellectual traditions. The most important example of these thinkers is Jean-Jacques Rousseau (1712–1778).

One of the most original thinkers and writers of all time, Rousseau crusaded for a return to nature—beautiful, pure, simple nature. The message struck home in a society weary of arbitrary and often corrupt governmental bureaucracy and an oppressively artificial and elaborate code of social etiquette. Rousseau was lionized. Great ladies, including the queen of France, began playing milkmaid. In his novel *La Nouvelle Heloise*, Rousseau extolled the beauties of free love and uninhibited emotion. In *Emile* he expounded the "natural" way of rearing and educating children. He would let children do what they like and teach them "practical" knowledge. Rousseau shared much with other *philosophes*, even contributing to the *Encyclopedia*, but after the 1750s he broke from them for personal as well as intellectual reasons. In *Origin of Inequality Among Men* (1753), Rousseau argued that civilization was not necessarily a progressive boon to humanity, that human beings had lost much since their exit from the state of nature. In *The Social Contract*, Rousseau became one of the few *philosophes* to make a fundamental contribution to political theory. Rousseau generally placed greater faith in emotion, feeling, and intuition than in reason. In this he was a forerunner of the romantic spirit and expounded its principles long before that movement reached its peak.

The *philosophes* had a self-conscious sense of a spirit of enlightenment. They felt that they were leading a mission of liberation, that by striking the match of reason the darkness of the past would be dispelled and humanity would quickly and easily liberate itself. By becoming thus enlightened, humanity could move from childhood to adulthood. They attacked war and the military values of the traditional aristocracy. They rejected artificial social distinctions. They lauded most forms of freedom, including freedom of the press, of speech, and of religious belief. They supported the application of science to economic activity, a view appealing to the middle class and liberal aristocracy. They believed that their eighteenth-century civilization was ready for enlightenment and the great progress that would result. Yet the optimism of most of the *philosophes* was not wild-eyed; indeed, there was an underlying current of pessimism in the works of thinkers such as Diderot, de Sade, Rousseau, and even Voltaire.

In characterizing the *philosophes*, historians have disagreed. Some view the *philosophes* as shallow, self-concerned dilettantes who had few deep or original ideas and who were afraid of real reform. Most historians, however, argue that the *philosophes* were thoughtful, sincere thinkers who performed an important service by laying the intellectual foundations for modern society.

FIGURE 38.3. **The Encyclopedia** This engraving from one of the many technical articles in the *Encyclopedia* shows workers preparing type for printing, with detail of materials used in the process. It reveals the optimistic faith in the ease and practicality of learning typical of Enlightenment thought. (French Embassy Press and Information Division)

3. WOMEN AND THE SOCIAL CONTEXT

There were several centers of Enlightenment thought in the cities and courts of Europe, particularly western Europe, but the heart of the Enlightenment was in Paris. Several regular gatherings were held in the salons of wealthy Parisian patrons, usually women of the aristocracy or upper middle class such as Madame du Deffaud or Madame Geoffrin. There the *philosophes* met with each other and members of the international upper middle class and aristocratic elite. They debated the ideas of the Enlightenment in an environment lush with art, music, and wealth. These gatherings facilitated the spread of Enlightenment ideas among social and intellectual elites and added much to the social respectability of intellectuals.

As patrons and as intellectual contributors to these gatherings, women played an important role in the Enlightenment. Women such as Madame Geoffrin provided essential financial support to several *philosophes*, particularly for the *Encyclopedia*. Other women corresponded by letter with leading intellectual, political, and social figures throughout Europe, using letter writing as an art just as conversation was an art in the salons. The salons were open to women with the right intellectual or social qualifications. The *philosophes* tended to support improving the education and position of women. The Enlightenment emphasis on individualism theoretically and in the long run led toward accepting the idea of political and social equality between men and women. Nevertheless, it cannot be said that the *philosophes* advocated equal rights for women in a modern sense nor that they challenged fundamental assumptions about the subordinate public roles appropriate for women. One of the few people to argue for real change in the condition of women in the eighteenth century was Mary Wollstonecraft (1759–1797). In 1792 she published *Vindication of the Rights of Women*, but generally her plea for equal rights for all human beings fell on deaf ears.

Meetings in Paris salons were paralleled by smaller meetings in other French and foreign cities as well as by less organized meetings in coffeehouses and homes of the liberal aristocracy. Enlightenment ideas were read and discussed in local academies, Freemason lodges, societies, libraries, and clubs.

4. ENLIGHTENMENT AND RELIGION

The Enlightenment was profoundly secular in character, but religion played an important role. Very few Enlightenment thinkers were either atheists or traditional Christians. Most were skeptics, influenced by the arguments of Pierre Bayle (1647–1706). Many believed in some form of deism. They believed that this wonderful mechanism called the universe could not have come into being by accident. Some infinite Divine Being must have created it and set it in motion. However, the finite mind of human beings cannot comprehend the infinite. Therefore, God is unknowable. Furthermore, God, having set his perfect mechanical laws in motion, will never tamper with them nor interfere in human affairs. God is impersonal.

It is readily apparent that the beliefs of the *philosophes* were diametrically opposed to the doctrines of the Christian churches—Roman Catholic, Protestant, and Orthodox alike. Christian theologians argued that God remained active in the universe, that God's ways are revealed through religious literature and institutions, and that faith constitutes a valid alternative to reason. Enlightenment thinkers and Christian leaders were soon engaged in debate, both spending much time and effort attacking each other. In countries such as France and Italy, where clerics were strongly entrenched in government, they censored the writings of the *philosophes* and sought to interrupt their work. In the long run, however, the ideas of the Enlightenment spread, and the Church probably lost more than it gained by so ardently attacking the *philosophes* and their ideas.

5. POLITICAL AND ECONOMIC ASPECTS OF THE ENLIGHTENMENT

Enlightenment thinkers devoted much thought to matters of government. If human beings are by nature rational and good, then surely, if given the opportunity, they can devise for themselves efficient and benevolent political institutions. Corrupt tyrannies were no longer tolerable. Of the numerous "enlightened" thinkers in the field of political science, three stand out above the others in influence: Locke, Montesquieu, and Rousseau.

Locke's most eloquent plea was for the natural rights of human beings, which are life, liberty, and property. He theorizes, in his *Two Treatises of Civil Government*, that to safeguard these rights individuals voluntarily contracted to surrender a certain amount of their sovereignty to government. The powers of the government, however, whether it be monarchical or popular, are strictly limited. No government may violate the individual's right to life, liberty, and property. If it does, the people who set it up can and should overthrow it. These ideas were fundamental in the thinking of the makers of both the French and the American revolutions. Jefferson wrote many of Locke's ideas into the Declaration of Independence, frequently using his exact words. They likewise appear in the United States Constitution and in numerous French declarations of liberty.

Baron de Montesquieu (1689–1755) was less a theorizer than a discerning student of history and shrewd analyst of political systems. His masterpiece is *The Spirit of the Laws*. Although a great admirer of the English government after the Glorious Revolution, Montesquieu came to the conclusion that different types of government are best suited to various conditions. For instance, absolute monarchy is best for countries of vast area, limited monarchy for countries of moderate size like France, and republics for small states like Venice or ancient Athens. Not only did he approve of Locke's doctrine of limited sovereignty, but he specified how it can best be secured—by a separation of powers and a system of checks and balances. The powers and functions of government should be equally divided among king, lords, and commons, each one being checked by the other two. This theory was probably Montesquieu's greatest practical contribution to the science of government. The principle was incorporated into the United States Constitution—kings, lords, and commons becoming executive, judicial, and legislative branches of government.

The real father of the theory of modern democracy was not Locke nor Montesquieu, both of whom distrusted rule by the masses, but Rousseau. This morbid, erratic genius based the conclusions in his *Social Contract* and in his *Second Discourse* upon pure imagination. People in the state of noble savagery were free, equal, and happy. It was only when some began marking off plots of ground saying "this is mine" that inequality began. In order to restore their lost freedom and happiness, people entered into a compact, each with all the others, surrendering their individual liberty to the whole. Since sovereignty is indivisible, the general will is all-powerful. Although Rousseau never made it clear just how the general will would actually operate in practice, he apparently assumed that the individual would be free by virtue of being part of the general will. Rousseau had great influence on the leaders of the second and more radical phase of the French Revolution.

Some of the eighteenth-century planners of the better life through reason turned their thoughts to economics. Since the late fifteenth century, mercantilism had been the dominant economic theory and practice in western Europe. This system of regulated nationalistic economy reached its peak in the seventeenth century. Only the Dutch Netherlands held out for free trade. But if, according to the fundamental assumptions of the Enlightenment, the universe is run by a few simple mechanical laws, why should there not be a similar natural order in the field of economics? A group of French Physiocrats, led by Quesnay, personal physician to Louis XV, began to teach that economics has its own set of natural laws, that the most basic of these laws is that of supply and demand, and that these laws operate best when commerce is freed from government regulation. This doctrine came to be known as *laissez faire* (or free trade and enterprise).

The chief developer of the theory of laissez faire was Adam Smith, a Scottish professor of philosophy who associated with the Physiocrats while sojourning in France. His *Wealth of Nations*, published in 1776, has remained the bible of laissez-faire economics ever since. The ideas of the French Physiocrats and Adam Smith strongly influenced the leaders of the American and French revolutions.

6. ENLIGHTENED DESPOTISM

While critical and combative, the *philosophes* were not political or social revolutionaries. They hoped for rather painless change from above rather than a revolutionary transfer of power to the still unenlightened masses. Many followed Voltaire in believing that enlightened despotism was the form of government that offered the greatest chances for enactment of enlightened reforms. By the middle of the eighteenth century several monarchs found these views attractive, styled themselves as enlightened monarchs, and attempted to enact reforms that at least appeared to fit with Enlightenment thought. These monarchs have been distinguished from their predecessors and termed "enlightened despots." To what extent this is a valid characterization of their rule remains to be seen.

The most sensational of the enlightened despots was Frederick the Great of Prussia (1740–1786). Frederick had from boyhood loved music, poetry, and philosophy. At the end of the Seven Years' War (1756–1763), the second of his two wars of aggression, he settled down as a model enlightened despot and attempted to apply the laws of reason to statecraft. Frederick was an avid reader of the French philosophers. He even invited Voltaire to visit him at Potsdam, but Prussia was not big enough to hold two such egos at once. The two quarreled and, after several years, parted.

Frederick made much of religious toleration. However, he continued to penalize the Jews and never ceased to ridicule Christians of all denominations. He was a strong advocate of public education, although he spent very little on it in comparison with what he spent on his army. The centralized Prussian bureaucracy became the most efficient government in Europe. True to the prevailing thought of the Enlightenment, however, he had no faith in popular self-government. Nor did he make a move to free the serfs or to end the feudal system in Prussia. Probably the most lasting of Frederick's contributions to Prussia were his codification of the law and improvements in the administration of justice. In the field of economics, Frederick was a mercantilist, although he did share the Physiocrats' appreciation of the importance of agriculture.

The most sincere of all the enlightened despots was Joseph II of Austria (1780–1790). Unfortunately, he lacked the practical sagacity of Frederick the Great. His well-meaning but ill-conceived efforts to centralize the administration of the far-flung Hapsburg territories, to replace the numerous languages of his subjects with German, to secularize the strongly entrenched Roman Catholic church, and to free the serfs in a society still based on feudalism, all backfired.

Other monarchs, such as those of Sweden, Sardinia, Spain, and Portugal, attempted or enacted reforms that could be seen as enlightened. Even in Russia, Catherine the Great made apparent efforts at enlightened reforms, but ultimately she did not put most of those reforms into practice.

Significantly, France alone of the great powers on the Continent failed to produce an even faintly enlightened despot. Upon attaining the French throne in 1774, the well-meaning Louis XVI appointed the Physiocrat Turgot as minister of finances. Turgot, a friend of Voltaire, initiated a program of sweeping reforms that might have forestalled the French Revolution. However, within two years' time the powerfully entrenched vested interests persuaded the weak-willed king to dismiss him.

Whether there was a phenomenon of enlightened despotism occurring during the eighteenth century remains a debated question among historians. If there was, it was usually a matter more of form than content. Several eighteenth-century monarchs acted in certain enlightened ways, believed themselves to be enlightened, admired some of the *philosophes,* and were admired in return. Several supported culture, favored a less religious and more rational justification for their rule, and consulted with *philosophes*. Yet most of their "enlightenment" was superficial. Many of the reforms they made were simply an update in the long process of making the central government more effective and powerful. Few tried to enact fundamental social, political, or economic reforms dictated by Enlightenment thought, and even those who tried, such as Joseph II, generally failed to effect those reforms.

7. CONCLUSION

Enlightenment thinkers applied and popularized a secular, rational, reformist way of thinking that undermined the intellectual foundations of traditional society. These thinkers, probably unknowingly, laid the intellectual foundations for the revolutions that swept Europe and America from the last quarter of the eighteenth century to the mid–nineteenth century. Moreover, their way of thinking and the ideas that arose from it would form the intellectual core of the liberal middle-class ideology that was ascendant during the nineteenth century and is still strong in the twentieth century.

SUGGESTED READING

General

C. Becker, *The Heavenly City of the Eighteenth-Century Philosophers* (1932). An influential, thought-provoking volume by a leading historian.

E. Cassirer, *The Philosophy of the Enlightenment* (1951). An important synthesis, but difficult.

P. Gay, *The Enlightenment: An Interpretation. Vol. I: The Rise of Modern Paganism. Vol. II: The Science of Freedom* (1969). Detailed treatment of a leading authority.

P. Hazard, *The European Mind, 1680–1715* (1963). Excellent on the early Enlightenment.

L. Krieger, *Kings and Philosophers, 1689–1789* (1970). A broad survey making connections between thought and politics.

H. Payne, *The Philosophes and the People* (1976). Focuses on the gap between the *philosophes* and the people.

The *Philosophes*

T. Bestermann, *Voltaire* (1969). A solid biography.

A. M. Wilson, *Diderot* (1972). An excellent biography.

Enlightened Despotism

J. Gagliardo, *Enlightened Despotism* (1967). A good introduction.

E. Wangermann, *The Austrian Achievement, 1700–1800* (1973). A good study of enlightened monarchs.

Sources

L. G. Crocker, ed., *The Age of Enlightenment* (1969). A good anthology.

P. Gay, ed., *The Enlightenment: A Comprehensive Anthology* (1973). A good selection of documents

RETROSPECT

The seventeenth and eighteenth centuries were the apogee of royal absolutism as a form of government in the Western world. The clearest example of royal absolutism arose in France, where under Henry IV, Richelieu, Mazarin, and Louis XIV, the Bourbon monarchy achieved a degree of control that was virtually complete and a position of dominance in Europe that has seldom been equaled. European history during the years 1661–1715 has been called the age of Louis XIV. Louis and his court were the envy of all other monarchs, who sought to emulate them. France possessed a military strength so great that the major states of western and central Europe working in combination held France in check only with difficulty.

The most noteworthy exceptions to royal absolutism in western Europe were found in England and the Dutch Netherlands, where constitutionalism prevailed. In England royal absolutism had reached its peak during the sixteenth century under the vigorous and politically crafty Tudor rulers. The Stuart kings, who came to the throne in 1603 when Elizabeth I died childless, were full of fine absolutist theories but were unable to carry them out smoothly. They soon found themselves in a running fight, mostly over money matters and power, with Parliament, a stronghold of the landed and commercial interests. In a showdown—the Puritan Revolution—the parliamentary forces, under the able leadership of Oliver Cromwell, triumphed. Before the century had ended, one Stuart king had been executed, another invited to the throne on terms, and a third driven out of the country. During the course of the seventeenth and eighteenth centuries England's parliamentary and cabinet system gradually took shape. Constitutionalism had prevailed over royal absolutism. The landed and commercial interests now in control of the English government, however, were no less aggressive in foreign and colonial affairs than had been the royal monarchs.

The Dutch Netherlands, while somewhat unique, also developed a political system emphasizing constitutionalism rather than royal absolutism. Lacking the military resources and potential of their larger neighbors, France and England, the Dutch nevertheless achieved a phenomenal commercial and financial dominance in the Western world. Their economic exploits were accompanied by a preeminence in the fields of painting and philosophy. The Dutch lived under a republican form of government and enjoyed a degree of individual freedom that could not be matched in Europe.

Royal absolutism dominated political forms in central and eastern Europe during the seventeenth and eighteenth centuries. There the most important political developments were the rise of two military despotisms—Prussia and Russia. The Hohenzollerns of Prussia, consistently pursuing the policies of royal absolutism, militarism, and territorial aggrandizement, more than doubled their territory and population and challenged Austria for the leadership of the German-speaking world. Russia, under two strong absolutist monarchs, Peter the Great and Catherine the Great, decisively defeated Sweden and the Ottoman Turks and gained valuable territory facing the West. Poland, failing to develop a strong central government, disappeared from the map, carved up by Russia, Prussia, and Austria.

While Prussia, Russia, and Austria were struggling for the mastery of central and eastern Europe, the French, the English, and the Dutch were competing for dominance in North America and Asia. In this contest the English emerged victorious in North America and India, and the Dutch in the East Indies. The English found it relatively easy to drive the Indians out of eastern North America and colonize the continent with Europeans. In Asia the English and the Dutch defeated the natives but were unable to Europeanize these people who had such firmly established societies, cultures, and religions.

The economy and society—rural, based on agriculture, and with a vast mass of peasantry dominated by the privileged aristocracy—changed only slowly for most of the period. Gradually the central governments, the growing cities, and the middle classes altered life within the traditional village. The pace of social change quickened in the mid–eighteenth century as population grew, agriculture was revolutionized, and cottage industry spread. Religious affiliations changed little; established Catholic and Protestant churches remained committed to the hierarchical social order and the dominant political systems of their states. Even the numerous pietist and quietist religious sects that arose during this period passively accepted, for the most part, the political authority of the established and usually absolutist governments.

The baroque and classical styles, which prevailed in literature and the arts in western Europe throughout most of the seventeenth and eighteenth centuries, generally harmonized with and often exalted the absolutist monarchs and their courts. These styles stressed a combination of grandeur, richness, and order that appealed to monarchs and the privileged orders, who so often were the patrons of the arts.

The seventeenth and eighteenth centuries spawned two developments that would eventually undermine the intellectual foundations of the traditional Christian Western society: the Scientific Revolution and the Enlightenment. The Scientific Revolution challenged the traditional, theological, earth-centered conception of the universe and offered a new perception of the universe as infinite, moving, and lawful, with the earth merely one of many bodies. Truth would no longer be based on custom, faith, or authority but, rather, on rigorous reasoning founded on observed facts and mathematical laws. In the process of this Scientific Revolution, the foundations for the modern natural sciences were established. The Enlightenment popularized and extended the Scientific Revolution. The main Enlightenment thinkers—the *philosophes*—used reason to criticize traditional customs and institutions. They optimistically believed that people could easily become enlightened and thereby progress to a new level of maturity. Their ideas would play an important role in the revolutions of the late eighteenth and the nineteenth centuries and would form a basis for the liberal ideology that would rise to dominance during the nineteenth and twentieth centuries.

Yet even these intellectual developments properly belong to the seventeenth and eighteenth centuries. They stressed order and power, which were so important to the period. They reflected the dynamic between royal absolutism and constitutionalism—particularly in the Enlightenment admiration for English political institutions and enlightened despotism. They remained limited to a small elite, just as the glamour, affluence, and power of the period remained limited almost entirely to the royalty, the aristocracy, and the small upper middle class. The lower classes, whose labor and blood made so much regal and military splendor possible, received few benefits and were unaware of the fundamental intellectual developments that were occurring. From the late eighteenth century on, much would change.

PART NINE

THE AGE OF REVOLUTIONS, 1776–1850

The period between the last quarter of the eighteenth century and the middle of the nineteenth century was an era of revolution in the Western world, both in Europe and in America. The most dramatic and striking of the revolutions occurring during this period were political, starting with the American and French revolutions in the late eighteenth century and ending with the Revolutions of 1848 that swept the European continent. The more subtle but even more historically significant revolution of this period was economic: the Industrial Revolution. Starting in Great Britain toward the end of the eighteenth century, the Industrial Revolution spread to continental Europe and the United States during the first half of the nineteenth century and would eventually extend to most of the rest of the world.

Both the political and economic revolutions reflected stirrings of change already underway within the still fundamentally traditional society of the eighteenth century. The Enlightenment was propagating liberal ideas that had politically revolutionary implications. The growth of commerce and industry, particularly in certain parts of western Europe, was altering the old economy. The bourgeoisie was increasing in strength and numbers and was exerting pressure on the aristocracy. The peasantry, too, and even the urban workers were becoming restive.

When the privileged classes steadfastly refused to yield and traditional institutions proved unable to cope with demands for political change, a series of revolutionary upheavals ensued. The first occurred in America, where in 1776 the British colonies revolted and declared their independence as the United States. The American Revolution was followed by the French Revolution of 1789, which was of considerably greater significance, for it represented an almost complete overthrow of traditional institutions in a powerful country in the heart of Europe. During the succeeding two decades, elements of the French Revolution were spread throughout Europe by imitation and by the revolutionary and Napoleonic armies. After 1815 conservatives, representing the traditional forces of order, reasserted control and struggled with the revolutionary forces unleashed by the French Revolution. But the era of revolutions was not over. Uprisings, usually inspired by some of the same liberal goals as the French Revolution of 1789, occurred in several areas during the 1820s and 1830s. A culmination of many of these struggles came in 1848 when revolutions toppled governments almost everywhere.

The Industrial Revolution was only seemingly less of an upheaval than these political revolutions. As economic activity shifted from the farm to the factory, cities grew, classes changed, and ultimately society itself was transformed. By 1850 a new industrial society was firmly entrenched in Great Britain and was clearly establishing itself elsewhere.

Together the political and economic revolutions occurring between 1776 and 1850 transformed Western civilization. Indeed, so massive were the changes stemming from these revolutions that historians usually mark this period as the beginning of modern times.

CHAPTER 39

The American Revolution

FIGURE 39.1. The Constitutional Convention This painting, by Junius Brutus Stearns, represents the Constitutional Convention in session in Philadelphia in 1787 with George Washington presiding. At times the proceedings of the Convention were less sedate and reflective than this scene portrays; nonetheless, it catches the sense of high purpose that the delegates believed they were serving in seeking to strengthen the new nation. (The Granger Collection)

The forces of change that were building up during the seventeenth and eighteenth centuries found early expression in a somewhat unexpected place—in the British colonies in North America. The American colonists waged a successful rebellion against Great Britain and established the new nation of the United States of America. The forces that produced the American Revolution and gave shape to the new nation reflected in important ways the ferment working everywhere in western Europe to threaten traditional society. Placed in a global setting, the American Revolution was a major event in shaping the modern world.

1. AMERICAN COLONIAL SOCIETY

The American Revolution was a complex movement, but behind it lay one fundamental fact: During the century and a half prior to 1776, American society had become different from British society in particular and European society in general. Its uniqueness was due chiefly to the fact that European immigrants and their offspring had to adapt traditional patterns of life in order to survive in a new environment. As a consequence, the colonists came to think of themselves as a separate people. This realization, coupled with Great Britain's efforts to bend colonial society to British purposes, led the colonials to act in the name of independence and nationhood.

By 1776 an obvious sign of the vitality of colonial society was its large population, which had reached about 2.5 million. During the eighteenth century population had grown faster in America than in Europe. The growth was in large part due to emigration from Europe and Africa (by 1776 blacks constituted 20 percent of the population). Americans were also reproducing more rapidly than Europeans, largely because of longer life expectancy and earlier marriage in a land where it was easier to establish a new household than it was in traditional European society.

The rapidly growing population had created a bustling, diverse economy in the American wilderness. Its backbone was agriculture, ranging from the small, independently owned family farms of New England and the Middle Atlantic colonies to the great plantations worked by slaves in the southern colonies. The American soil and climate permitted a variety of crops: grain, tobacco, cotton, rice, indigo, vegetables, fruits, livestock. After the first hard years the colonists were more than able to feed themselves; some of their crops, especially tobacco, found markets in Europe. And off to the west lay vast areas of rich, unexploited land to attract the growing population.

The colonists had not neglected commerce and industry. Colonial merchants, especially in New England and the Middle Atlantic colonies, did a thriving business within America, and some of them traded with Great Britain, the West Indies, and continental Europe. The bulk of the international trade involved colonial raw materials, which were exchanged for manufactured goods and slaves. By 1776 the colonists were producing considerable amounts of manufactured goods, sometimes in defiance of British mercantilist regulations. The colonists were by no means self-sufficient, but neither were they totally dependent on Great Britain and Europe. American entrepreneurs were increasingly intent on protecting their commercial and manufacturing interests and on minimizing external constraints.

By 1776 American society was becoming stratified into a class structure that bore an outward resemblance to the society of Great Britain. An aristocracy of wealth made up of merchants, plantation owners, and successful professionals dominated many aspects of life and grew increasingly conscious of its status. A large, enterprising group of independent farmers, shopkeepers, artisans, and modestly successful professionals ranked below the aristocrats. Still lower were numerous tenant farmers and laborers—a group that was increasing in size and economic hardship. Finally, there were black slaves, whose position as property gave them no status in society and whose lot was harsh in every respect. However, social stratification in America was not as rigidly defined nor as inflexible as was the class structure in Europe. The chief forces that sanctioned aristocratic status in Europe—birth, royal favor, tradition, unique life style—simply did not exist in America. Few European aristocrats migrated to America; the family trees of most American aristocrats had shallow roots. In America aristocratic status rested chiefly on wealth amassed in America through farming or commercial activity. It was possible for a capable, enterprising, and lucky individual of low status to advance to aristocratic status by amassing a fortune. The frontier also offered escape for those who resented aristocratic control. Colonial conditions thus loosened the bonds of aristocratic society and provided a measure of freedom for people of lesser status and means—except black slaves.

Early American society was dominated by males whose authority as heads of the basic social unit, the family, allowed them to dominate women and children. Marriages were usually arranged by families. Under the terms of English law, which prevailed everywhere in the colonies, a married woman was legally subject to her husband and barred from participation in almost all aspects of public life. In addition to the legal constraints on women, the social code stressed the virtue of submission by women to male authority. In the typical household on farms and in the cities, women were expected to carry out an array of tasks generally viewed as "women's work": preparing food, making clothing, tending animals, raising a garden, raising children. Particularly harsh was the treatment of slave women. Although slaves were permitted to maintain family units, traffic in slaves often disrupted these households. Slave women were frequently sexually abused by their masters. In the upper classes, women of wealthy families enjoyed considerable comfort and leisure but little independence. The cities offered some economic opportunity for single women and widows to lead a more independent life as nurses, teachers, or shopkeepers. But on the whole colonial women had almost no opportunity to assert their talents beyond the confines of the household.

Religious life in colonial America took unique forms. Generally, the founders of each colony attempted to define a single religious establishment for that colony, usually based on a European model. One such establishment was the Puritan order that emerged in New England. Based on the principles of local control of each congregation by those who believed themselves to be saved, simple ceremonies involving Scripture reading and preaching and austere moral codes, the Puritan congregations exercised a powerful influence on the manners and morals of New England society. However, the Puritans were never able to exclude from their society those who would not conform and eventually were forced to tolerate dissenters. Elsewhere an effort was made to implant Anglicanism as practiced in Great Britain. A variety of factors combined to make the Anglican church in America different from that in Great Britain. No Anglican bishoprics developed in America, and there was a shortage of educated clergymen trained to sustain the elaborate Anglican services. As a consequence, a hierarchically directed Anglican system based on uniform doctrines and rituals failed to develop. Local Anglican churches fell under the direction of local lay leaders, who tended to define religious practice as they saw fit. The Anglican establishment moved in the direction of a congregational system that allowed considerable room for local differences and thus toleration. To some extent the same fate befell the other highly structured religions established in colonial America, especially Lutheranism and Roman Catholicism. Each found it difficult to maintain uniformity and conformity to traditional practices. The common tendency was toward the acceptance of religious diversity and toleration.

Prior to 1776 the colonists distinguished themselves only modestly in cultural activities. They did establish lower schools and colleges in an attempt to prepare people for careers. Newspapers and book publishers appeared in many areas. The rudiments of a distinct architectural style emerged. But in the main American cultural life depended on western Europe. Perhaps the most notable cultural development was the ability of some colonists to keep abreast of Europe's chief intellectual and cultural movements, especially those associated with the Enlightenment and science.

Especially significant in setting the stage for the rebellion in America were the differences that emerged between the political system of Great Britain and that of its colonial subjects. In theory one system applied to both. The colonials recognized the British monarch as the head of state, but the colonials had no active role in the government presided over by the British ruler. Every colony developed its own local government. Each had a governor, usually appointed by the monarch, who represented the authority of the crown and who provided a channel through which the concerns of the colonists were conveyed to the British government. Each colony (except Pennsylvania) had a two-house legislature. The lower house was elected by property owners, and the upper house was appointed by the king or the colonial governor. The property qualifications were such that a much larger proportion of male colonials were eligible to vote than was the case in Britain; as a consequence, colonial legislatures reflected a broader spectrum of society than did the British Parliament. The powers of colonial legislatures were never clearly defined, but in general they had extensive authority to control local affairs and to levy taxes. The governors had nearly absolute power of veto over legislatures, but they were not usually in a position to exercise these powers because they depended on legislatures for their salaries and operating funds. The colonists developed a system of courts patterned after the British court system, and they enjoyed the legal rights of British subjects as incorporated in English common law. Although the Americans recognized that the British government had authority over them, the system of local government that developed in the colonies encouraged them to feel that they had a right to decide their own political destiny. One hundred fifty years of experience in self-government created a breach wider than the Atlantic between Great Britain and its American colonies.

Although by 1776 there were wide differences between American and British societies, these differences did not preordain an American effort to establish independence. Most colonists still felt that they were British and still were attached to a European tradition. What eventually aroused American resistance to British rule was a conviction that the British were denying them the right to sustain the tradition they shared. That perception drew much of its substance from the fact that American society had become different, causing the Americans to view tradition in a different way.

2. THE AMERICAN REVOLUTION: FROM SALUTARY NEGLECT TO WAR

The numerous forces working to create a unique society in America were little understood in Great Britain. In conformity with mercantilist thought, America was viewed as a source of scarce raw products and a market for manufactured goods. This view was legislated by the Navigation Acts of the mid–seventeenth century, which implied that Britain would act politically and economically to shape the colonial economy to serve its own interests. It was assumed that the colonists would benefit by conforming to British direction. However, until mid–eighteenth century Britain was lax in enforcing its mercantilist policies. During this interval American economic development took its own direction and shaped its own interests. And political evolution accustomed the Americans to asserting considerable control over their destiny.

With the end of the Seven Years' War in 1763, British policy began to change in the direction of tightening control over its colonial empire. The vast lands won from the French needed some kind of administration that would ensure their sensible utilization and deal with the Indian population whose frustrations were expressed with frightening emphasis by a general Indian uprising in 1763, led by the Ottawa chief, Pontiac. Great Britain was faced with a huge debt, incurred in part to save Americans from the French and the Indians; it was time for the colonials to share that burden. Britain's rapidly growing population and the increasing importance of manufacturing to its economy produced a need for imported foodstuffs and for larger markets for manufactured goods. All of these considerations prompted a series of acts, such as the Grenville (1764–1765) and the Townshend (1767), designed to increase revenues and tighten administration in America.

The colonists were hardly in a mood to bend before British interests after so long enjoying the "salutary neglect" of earlier years. They felt they had made sufficient contributions to the British victories in the wars of the first half of the eighteenth century to relieve them of further responsibility. They resented what they felt was treatment as inferiors by the British forces sent to drive the French and Indians out of land that belonged to the Americans. The American population was growing even faster than that of Great Britain, creating powerful pressures to expand the American economy and to move westward into the territories won from the French. The growing demand for manufactured goods created an unfavorable balance of trade, which increasingly made many Americans debtors to England. To correct this situation, the Americans needed to increase native manufacturing and expand markets in Europe, both of which ran counter to British mercantilist policy. A depression following the Seven Years' War sharpened the growing tension.

The Americans reacted to Britain's changing policy with fiery speeches, boycotts of British goods, protest meetings (such as the Stamp Act Congress of 1765), and occasional riots. They complained that they were being taxed without representation in Parliament and that their own legislatures, long the chief source of governing regulations, were being disregarded. Although British reaction to American resistance was inconsistent, its government pressed on in its effort to tighten its hold on America. It increased its military presence in America and ordered royal officials to seize American property in ways that paid little heed to British law. Between 1768 and 1774 sterner measures, such as the Tea Act, the "Intolerable Acts," and the Quebec Act, were imposed to bring the colonials under tighter control. Resistance in America spread, reflected by the meeting of the First Continental Congress in 1774. And it was fed by growing radicalism, which focused on British violation of fundamental rights as justification for independence and self-government.

In Great Britain a few leaders realized the danger, and some even sympathized with the principles upon which the protests of the colonists were based. But these forces could not muster enough parliamentary support for conciliatory actions aimed at reassuring that considerable segment of the colonial population still not ready to break with Britain or for a fundamental change of policy that would take into account the realities surrounding relationships with colonists whose interests no longer coincided with those of the mother country. The British leaders agreed on only one thing: that it was an act of rebellion and a perversion of the British constitution to claim that British subjects had a right to disobey laws passed by Parliament, as indeed Americans were doing with increasing frequency. This attitude prompted an increase in British armed forces in America, an action that appeared to reinforce King George III's words: "Blows must decide whether they are to be subject to the Country or Independent."

Indeed, it came to blows. Armed hostilities opened in April 1775 when American militiamen challenged British forces in skirmishes at Lexington and Concord. In May 1775 the Second Continental Congress assembled. Led by men ready to break with Great Britain, the Congress took steps to organize the war and to appoint George Washington as commander of the American armies. The hour had come to settle long-debated issues on the field of battle.

When the war began, Britain seemed to enjoy overwhelming superiority. In fact, the British government took the rebellion lightly; one royal official characterized the rebels as a "rude rabble without a plan." But such a view proved erroneous. It did not take into account Britain's ineffective military leadership, the distance to the battle scene, and the determination of the rebels. For almost a year after the encounters at Lexington and Concord, the main British forces were pinned down in Boston by an American militia drawn chiefly from New England. The Second Continental Congress proceeded with plans for raising money, supplying a military force, and winning allies. A variety of actions were taken to transfer power from British officials into the hands of American authorities. Most significant of all, once the shooting started, opinion in America moved rapidly toward acceptance of the idea of independence.

Popular sentiment in favor of independence crystallized in 1776, when several colonies instructed their delegations to the Second Continental Congress to break with Britain. On July 4, 1776, Congress issued the Declaration of Independence, crafted chiefly by Thomas Jefferson. Its magnificent preamble, leaning heavily on the political philosophy of John Locke and European disciples of the Enlightenment, justified rebellion on the grounds of "self-evident" truths, especially natural rights and government by contract. The British government had violated these "inalienable" rights and thus had no claim to the allegiance of its subjects, who were entitled to form a new contract to ensure their rights. For many, the Declaration of Independence elevated the struggle above mere revolt; it became a struggle for an "enlightened" polity. The principles enunciated in the Declaration would inspire later generations to act in the name of rights so fundamental that they were beyond the authority of any government.

However, the Americans were far from united. Many—perhaps 20 percent—opposed independence and the war. Some of these loyalists—contemptuously dubbed "Tories"—fled to Canada and Great Britain; those who remained were a source of concern to American leaders and a target of British efforts to promote dissension. Many Americans were essentially neutral; only under duress did these neutrals contribute to the war effort. Some black slaves saw the war as an opportunity to shed their shackles and enjoy the liberty of which the patriots spoke so much. Loyalists and British tried to exploit this hope; the fear of slave revolts dampened enthusiasm for the war in the southern colonies. Even among the patriots there was perpetual disagreement on how to conduct the struggle for independence. The fact that the Americans could sustain their cause in the face of these divisions was remarkable. In part, success was due to the leadership provided by men like George Washington, John Adams, Thomas Jefferson, and Benjamin Franklin, all of whom demonstrated considerable talents for leading armies, organizing resources, rallying popular support, and negotiating with foreign powers.

The war itself unfolded indecisively during 1776 and 1777 (see Map 39.1). While there were victories and defeats on both sides, the British seemed to be gaining the upper hand, especially when they undertook a major campaign in the Hudson Valley aimed at isolating New England from the other colonies. However, that campaign ended in October 1777 with the surrender of a major British force at Saratoga. This victory not only raised flagging American spirits but also was decisive in persuading a hesitant France to commit itself to the American cause. In 1778 a formal alliance was concluded, and France began to supply needed money, ships, and troops. Subsequently, other European powers showed increasing friendliness toward America; Spain and the Dutch eventually declared war on Britain, and several other nations threatened to do likewise. Britain now had a world conflict on its hands; the pressure on America was considerably relieved.

After 1777 military activity spread over a large area. The British concentrated their main force in New York City, where it could be reinforced by sea. In a series of hotly contested engagements in New York, New Jersey, and eastern Pennsylvania the Americans managed to contain British forces and avoid a decisive defeat in the crucial Middle Atlantic area. The British undertook a major offensive in the South in 1780 and 1781. The campaign ended in a stunning defeat at Yorktown, Virginia, in October 1781. This was the last major battle of the war. By 1781 Britain was anxious to end a costly war that threatened its position around the world. Prolonged negotiations, involving not only Britain and America but also France and Spain, finally ended with the Treaty of Paris in 1783. In its essential provisions, Britain recognized American independence and ceded to the Americans all territories east of the Mississippi from Canada to Spanish Florida. The new nation had won a magnificent victory.

3. THE AMERICAN REVOLUTION AND THE DEMOCRATIZATION OF SOCIETY

The American Revolution was more than a successful war of independence carried out by determined colonial subjects against a somewhat inept mother country. Between 1775 and 1783 a variety of steps were taken within American society that resulted in a new political and social order unique in the contemporary world. The changes accompanying the Revolution did not uproot the old order entirely, but they did modify it in ways that reflected many of the ideas of the Enlightenment. The thrust toward restructuring society and government found its chief inspiration in the concept of republicanism. Rooted in a tradition that

Map 39.1 REVOLUTIONARY WAR CAMPAIGNS This map portrays at least in broad outline the central strategy involved in the revolutionary war. With their main strength concentrated in New York City, where they could be reinforced by sea, the British tried to cripple the Americans first by attempting to seize control of the Hudson Valley and then by an extended campaign to win the South. The Americans countered both of these moves successfully while still containing the main British forces in New York, New Jersey, and eastern Pennsylvania.

reached back to ancient Greece and Rome, republicanism visualized the ideal society as one composed of equals living in small communities under a government of limited power controlled by its constituents. In such a society, the natural virtue of people would constrain anyone from infringing on the rights of others and would allow all to pursue their individual interests. It was the success the Americans achieved in moving toward the republican ideal that caught the attention of a world standing on the brink of other, more drastic revolutions.

The first important efforts at reordering society on republican principles were made within the several states (as the colonies were called after July 4, 1776). New governments, based on British principles of government, colonial political experience, and theoretical concepts derived from Enlightenment thought, were formed in all the states. The framers of these governments tried to create a political order that would protect the people's liberties without becoming tyrannical. Nearly every state drew up a written constitution carefully defining the structure and functions of government. Elaborate bills of rights, stressing traditional British liberties, were included in the constitutions. Since sovereignty rested with the people, all official positions were filled by elections and the right to vote was extended. Two-house legislatures were established in most states, the lower houses being controlled by property-holding voters and the upper houses being selected by the lower chambers. Systems of representation were devised to ensure that each elected representative spoke for roughly the same number of voters. Legislatures were given wide-ranging powers that assured their control over public affairs. Especially significant were the powers granted to legislatures to control and check executive officials, who were universally suspected of being the chief instigators of tyranny. Independent judiciaries were almost universally adopted. The concept of separation of powers was thereby incorporated into the new state governments, signifying a strong conviction that the powers of government must be limited by constitutional safeguards. Taken as a whole, the state constitutions framed between 1776 and 1780 inaugurated a degree of popular control over government unknown in the contemporary world, although none of them was completely democratic.

The Revolution brought about changes in other areas of life as significant as those altering the political structure. Several states took steps to disestablish state-supported churches, to institute religious toleration, and in general to separate political and religious life. Many states passed new land laws that tended to make it easier to gain ownership of property. Especially significant was the abolition of primogeniture, which required that the eldest son receive all his father's land. Slavery was abolished in some northern states, in part at least because this institution seemed out of place in a society dedicated to the principles of the Declaration of Independence. Efforts were made to expand educational opportunities and to take more adequate care of society's unfortunates. In the name of republicanism people spurned the old social customs that called for deference to aristocrats and replaced them with behavior patterns that reflected greater egalitarianism. Even the lot of women improved somewhat. In writing to her husband, John, in 1776 Abigail Adams chided him to "remember the ladies" in his schemes to increase liberty in America. Women came to be credited with playing a major role in building the virtues on which a republican society must rest. And expanding opportunities for occupations outside the household began to emerge for women. All these liberalizing movements pointed toward an increasingly greater freedom in the future.

Quite accidentally, the Revolution had an important leveling effect in terms of the distribution of wealth. An inflation, caused by the efforts of the Americans to pay for the war with paper money, wiped out fortunes, aided debtors, and allowed new fortunes to be built. Many established merchants suffered heavy losses from the disturbance of foreign trade, but new opportunities in trade and industry emerged once America was free from the British commercial system. Small farmers flourished during the war, bolstered by easy money and high prices. Under these varied pressures, the prerevolutionary social order did not survive intact. Again, a greater degree of social equality and personal freedom emerged to characterize life in the new nation.

4. LAUNCHING THE NEW NATION

Once independence had been declared, American leaders were faced with creating a central government. In responding to that challenge, they were guided by the above-noted principles working to democratize society. Movement toward a national political system had to contend with republican distrust of large-scale government and with the existence of thirteen separate states long accustomed to independent action. But the realities of a war for survival, the dangers inherent in a world of large and ambitious nations, and the sense of a shared experience in creating a new society in the American wilderness gave irresistible force to a national government.

The first attempt at forming a national government was carried out by the Second Continental Congress. Dominated by men who had a deep distrust for strong government over which the populace had no control, the Congress shaped the Articles of Confederation, finally approved by all of the states in 1781. The articles established a loose union of thirteen nearly independent states headed by a central government that could not compel the states to do anything but could only encourage them to cooperate. The inadequacies of the confederation and the self-serving actions of state governments rather quickly generated sentiment in favor of a stronger central government. As a result, in May 1787 a convention was summoned to consider revising the Articles of Confederation.

The convention immediately decided to scrap the Articles and to write a new constitution (see Figure 39.1). Once this task was undertaken, the delegates found themselves in broad agreement on many crucial issues. They agreed that a republican form of government based on a written constitution enumerating the powers of the central government was necessary, that there must be popular control over the central government, that there must be separation of powers with built-in checks among the various branches of government, that the states must enjoy certain jurisdiction, and that the central government must have authority to deal independently with matters affecting national interests. Working from these premises, the delegates forged a constitution out-

FIGURE 39.2. Congressional Debate This cartoon shows a "discussion" in the House of Representatives in 1798 between a Vermont Republican (with the tongs) and a Connecticut Federalist (with the cane). It reflects the intensity of party strife just prior to the key election of 1800. (New York Public Library Picture Collection)

lining the basic framework for a new government. A two-house legislature, an elected president, and a national judiciary were established. Each branch was assigned specific functions, and an elaborate system of internal checks was devised to constrain each branch from exercising too much power. The powers of the national government were specifically enumerated, while other powers were reserved to the states. However, specific provisions were made allowing the central government to coerce the states in those matters over which it had jurisdiction. This principle of federalism was a unique feature of the new government. A major roadblock centering on the fears of smaller states

was overcome by a compromise providing equal representation of each state in one branch of the legislature, the Senate, and representation in proportion to population in the other, the House of Representatives. To ensure a degree of flexibility, provisions were made for amending the constitution.

By 1789 a sufficient number of states had approved the new Constitution to allow the new government to begin operation with George Washington as president and with elected representatives who were committed to the Constitution (Federalists) in control of Congress. During the next decade the new government proved its worth. Congress enacted legislation that filled in vital details: a bill of rights, a federal court system, and administrative departments to assist the president in discharging his responsibilities. Taxes were levied and collected, public credit was established, and new states were added to the nation as a part of the process of utilizing the vast territory ceded by Britain in 1783. As president, Washington conducted himself in a way that gave the office dignity and allayed deep-seated fears of executive tyranny. Under the guidance of his cabinet, especially Alexander Hamilton as secretary of the treasury and Thomas Jefferson as secretary of state, policies were formulated that helped to restore prosperity and to steer the fledgling nation along a path of neutrality in the stormy international scene agitated by the French Revolution.

Despite the successes of the new government under Washington and his successor, John Adams, there was mounting discontent with the Federalists who dominated it (see Figure 39.2). This party made it increasingly clear, especially through the policies promoted by Alexander Hamilton, that it intended to make the central government as strong as possible and to bind the wealthy to the cause of strong central government by favoring their economic interests. This direction aroused opposition not only from those who felt their economic interests threatened but also from those philosophically suspicious of strong government, those committed to human equality, and those confident of the political wisdom of the common people—ideas powerfully reinforced by the French Revolution. This opposition began to rally around Thomas Jefferson to form a new party, called the Republicans (not to be confused with the present Republican party, founded in 1854). The emergence of political parties added an element to the new political system that the makers of the Constitution had not foreseen. In a close and bitter election in 1800, Jefferson and the Republicans won the presidency in what has been called "the Revolution of 1800." Perhaps it would be more accurate to say that this election completed the revolution begun twenty-five years earlier. It provided final proof of the workability of the new government by demonstrating that the voters controlled the state and that they did not have to rebel to force a government to be responsive to the wishes of a majority.

Between 1775 and 1800 the Americans had put on an impressive display for a changing world. By force of arms they had rid themselves of a political regime they perceived to be tyrannical. To replace it, they had fashioned, by a rational process, thirteen state governments and a national government capable of effective governance but restricted from abusing the rights of people. These governments proved sensitive to popular control and made the exercise of popular sovereignty a fact. Liberal, enlightened people everywhere saw their ideals become a reality in America. Here was inspiration and guidance for those elsewhere who aspired to change society. Many believed, as the German poet, Goethe put it, "America, thou hast it better/Than has our Continent, the old one." The age of revolutions had been launched in practice as well as in theory.

SUGGESTED READING

Colonial Society

Daniel J. Boorstin, *The Americans: The Colonial Experience* (1958). A challenging portrait.

James A. Henretta and Gregory H. Nobles, *Evolution and Revolution. American Society, 1600–1820* (1987). A stimulating treatment of many aspects of colonial society.

Edwin J. Perkins, *The Economy of Colonial America*, 2nd ed. (1988). A brief but effective description of colonial economy.

Gary B. Nash, *Red, White, and Black: The Peoples of Early America*, 2nd ed. (1982). An interesting study of race relations in colonial America.

C. Duncan Rice, *The Rise and Fall of Black Slavery* (1975). A fine study with an historiographical analysis.

Patricia U. Bonomi, *Under the Cope of Heaven: Religion, Society, and Politics in Colonial America* (1986). A broad survey stressing the vitality of colonial religious life.

Mary Beth Norton, *Liberty's Daughters: The Revolutionary*

Experience of American Women, 1750–1800 (1980). A fine study.

The Revolutionary Era

John C. Miller, *Origins of the American Revolution* (1959). A provocative exploration of the forces that produced the Revolution.

Marc Egnal, *A Mighty Empire. The Origins of the American Revolution* (1988). A challenging treatment stressing the role played by upper-class factions in the struggle against Great Britain.

Bernard Bailyn, *The Ideological Origins of the American Revolution* (1967). A brilliant study.

Edmund S. Morgan, *The Birth of the Republic, 1763–1789*, rev. ed. (1977). A brief account of major events.

Robert Middlekauff, *The Glorious Cause: The American Revolution, 1763–1789* (1982). A full narrative account.

Don Higginbotham, *The War of American Independence; Military Attitudes, Policies, and Practices, 1763–1789* (1971). A fine military history.

Merrill Jensen, *The American Revolution Within America* (1974). Stresses the impact of the Revolution on American society.

The New Nation

John C. Miller, *Toward a More Perfect Union: The American Republic, 1783–1815* (1970). A good narrative account.

Richard B. Morris, *The Forging of the Union, 1781–1789* (1987). A superb analysis of the path toward the Constitution.

Gordon S. Wood, *The Creation of the American Republic, 1776–1787* (1969). Especially good on the growth of republican thought.

Richard B. Bernstein with Kym S. Rice, *Are We to Be a Nation? The Making of the Constitution* (1987). An exciting account of the Constitutional Convention.

John C. Miller, *The Federalist Era, 1789–1802* (1960). An excellent study of the first years under the new Constitution.

CHAPTER 40

The French Revolution, 1789–1799

FIGURE 40.1. David, "The Tennis Court Oath," June 20, 1789 This painting by the sympathetic artist Jacques Louis David glorifies a crucial step in the French Revolution when the leaders of the newly formed National Assembly swear to draw up a constitution for France. In the center representatives of the three Estates—clergy, nobility, and commoners—join in a cooperative gesture. (French Embassy Press and Information Division)

In 1789 the French monarchy was brought to its knees by one of the greatest and most far-reaching upheavals in the history of Western civilization—the French Revolution. During the following ten years revolutionaries eliminated the centuries-old French monarchy, overturned the social system of France's old regime, and transformed France's religious institutions. Underlying these changes was the spirit of the Revolution, best summarized by its slogan: *Liberté, Égalité, Fraternité* ("Liberty, Equality, Fraternity").

The Revolution was so fundamental, so dynamic, and so threatening that it could not be contained within France. The news alone of what was happening in France spread fear among those hoping to maintain the status quo and stirred the hopes of those longing for change. Then by force of arms the French carried the ideas and institutions of the Revolution beyond France's borders. For France, and for much of Western civilization, the Revolution was a watershed that would mark the beginning of the modern world.

1. THE LAST DAYS OF THE OLD REGIME IN FRANCE

France at the succession of Louis XVI, though somewhat weakened by the defeats and failures of Louis XV, was still the richest and most influential nation in continental Europe. During the course of the eighteenth century, France's commerce and prosperity had steadily increased. Half of all the specie in Europe was to be found in France. The French enjoyed a relatively high standard of living. It is not, therefore, to desperation born of poverty that one must look as an explanation for the French Revolution but, rather, to frustration caused by existing institutions—social, religious, political, economic—that had failed to adjust to changing conditions.

French society on the eve of the French Revolution was divided into three distinct orders, or *estates*. The first estate was the clergy, numbering approximately one hundred thousand out of a total population of some 24 million. The Catholic church in France owned over 10 percent of the land—the best land—and from its lands and tithes and fees enjoyed an income probably half as large

as that of the government itself. It controlled all educational institutions and censored the press. It monopolized public worship and continued to harass all other religious groups at a time when the spirit of religious tolerance was rising throughout most of the Western world. The clergy itself was sharply divided. The upper clergy—the bishops and the abbots—were rich and powerful. They were drawn exclusively from the ranks of the aristocracy and were generally looked upon by most of the lower clergy and the common people as parasites. The lower clergy—the priests and the monks—came from the lower classes. The income of the priests was modest. They shared the lives of the people they served and were generally popular, but they had almost no influence on Church policy.

The second estate was the nobility, numbering approximately four hundred thousand. The nobility owned over 20 percent of the land of France but was exempt from all direct taxation. The richest of them lived at Versailles as absentee landlords, where they hunted, intrigued, made love, and read the books of the *philosophes* of the Enlightenment. They were reputed to possess the best manners and the worst morals of any class in Europe. The most haughty of the nobility—the most jealous of their rights—were the newcomers, the *noblesse de la robe* (nobility of the gown). They were former rich bourgeois who had purchased judgeships in one of the high law courts. They led the newly reassertive eighteenth-century French aristocracy that had, since the death of Louis XIV in 1715, recouped some of their power and influence at the expense of the king and the bourgeoisie. By the second half of the eighteenth century, almost all high governmental posts were held by the nobility. This nobility was emboldened to challenge the authority of the monarchy when it sought reform and to assert ancient rights and privileges that had fallen out of use against those below them.

The third estate was composed of commoners—the bourgeoisie, the proletariat, and the peasantry—and comprised about 96 percent of the total population. Of all the social and economic groups in France in 1789, the bourgeoisie were probably the most frustrated. They were business and professional people—the bankers, merchants, shopkeepers, and lawyers—who had grown into a middle class between the nobility and the peasantry. By the late eighteenth century France's upper bourgeoisie had gone as far as their wits and energy could take them. Some had become richer by far than most of the nobility—only to find the highest levels of government and society closed to them. Others, less wealthy but well educated and ambitious, resented the second-class status assigned to them by the nobility.

The urban populace was a mixture of groups—wage earners, servants of the rich, artisans, and the unemployed. There was enough distress among them to create tensions—tensions that would increase with the maladjustments caused by the Revolution. During the course of the eighteenth century, the price of bread had risen three times as fast as wages. Paris was the only city in France with an urban populace large enough to make its influence strongly felt. There, they included about three hundred thousand citizens (about half the total population of the city)—enough to play a significant role in a revolution.

At least 90 percent of the French people in 1789 were peasants, tillers of the soil. Although they were probably better off than most peasants elsewhere in Europe (they owned at least 30 percent of the land, and serfdom had virtually disappeared), they were on the whole discontented. Most peasant-owned land was subject to feudal dues. Probably a majority of the peasants owned no land at all but were sharecroppers who gave up 50 percent of their produce to the lord in addition to the feudal dues (the fees paid by the peasant for use of the lord's mill, oven, wine press, and breeding stock, death taxes, inheritance taxes, sale-of-property taxes). Not only were peasants forbidden to hunt; they could not even protect their crops from the lord's hunting parties—nor, for that matter, from the game itself. Although French peasants no longer had to donate their labor to the lord, they were still required to furnish so many days' labor for roads and public works. On them fell nearly all the direct taxes levied by the national government. Altogether, peasants gave up much of their income in taxes to their landlords, to the church, and to the state.

The life of the peasantry too had evolved only slowly since the Middle Ages. Peasants generally lived in little rural villages, the houses close together. The house usually consisted of one room, with a dirt floor, thatched roof, and neither chimney nor glass windows. The livestock were frequently under the same roof. The peasants' daily diet was made up almost entirely of dark bread and wine; meat was reserved for special occasions. Entertainment centered around the Church. On Sundays and holy days, of which there were many, their attire and attitudes were festive and gay. Ambitious young French peasants, unlike the peasants in most other parts of Europe, did have opportunities for advancement. Many engaged in cottage industry. A peasant could buy some land, become a priest or the lord's steward, a blacksmith or innkeeper, or seek a new life in the city. Only relatively few, of course, would succeed.

The government of France was arbitrary. Usually the king's decree was, in effect, law. The Estates General, the French counterpart of the British Parliament, had not met for nearly two centuries. Justice was capricious and corrupt. There were 237 different codes of law to confuse the litigants. There were no juries as in Great Britain. The king could arrest and imprison at will (although Louis XV and Louis XVI seldom did). The judges of the thirteen superior courts, called *parlements*, purchased or inherited their titles and were all members of the nobility. It was therefore impossible for commoners to obtain justice in a case against the nobility. The arbitrariness and inherent injustice of this system, which had long been taken for granted, clashed with the widely circulated ideas of the Enlightenment.

2. THE BREAKDOWN OF THE OLD REGIME

The breakdown of the Old Regime in France began in the field of finance. Louis XVI had inherited a large and constantly growing national debt. It was not excessive for a nation as rich as France; Great Britain and the Netherlands had higher per capita debts. But when combined with the exemption of the nobility and the clergy and much of the bourgeoisie from direct taxation and the extravagant cost of maintaining the military establishment and servicing the national debt (most of which had been incurred by past wars), it spelled eventual bankruptcy. Furthermore, France lacked an adequate banking system and was still burdened with the corrupt system of tax collection (called tax farming) that allowed much revenue to be diverted from the treasury into the pockets of private collectors.

Upon assuming the throne, Louis XVI appointed the Physiocrat Turgot, a friend of Voltaire, as minister of finance. Turgot initiated a series of sweeping reforms designed to clean up the mess. However, those with vested interests in the old system brought about his dismissal at the end of two years, and his reform measures were rescinded. A succession of ministers then tried all kinds of palliatives, such as borrowing, pump-priming expenditures, and better bookkeeping, but to no avail. By 1786 the debt was 3 billion livres,[1] and the annual deficit had reached 125 million. Bankers refused to lend the government more money. In a desperate effort to save his regime, Louis called an Assembly of Notables in 1787 and attempted to persuade the nobles and the clergy to consent to be taxed. But the privileged orders refused and demanded, instead, a meeting of the Estates General, thinking that they could control it and thereby assert their own interests. Pressured by a virtual revolt of his own nobility, the king gave in.

3. THE TRIUMPH OF THE THIRD ESTATE

During the early months of 1789 elections were held for members of the Estates General. All France was agog with excitement. Hundreds of pamphlets appeared, and there was widespread public debate. By tradition, each of the three es-

tates, the clergy, the nobility, and the commoners, elected their own representatives. All males who had reached the age of twenty-five and paid taxes were permitted to vote. Since the third estate, which included the bourgeoisie, the peasantry, and the urban populace, comprised more than nine-tenths of the total population, it was given as many seats as the other two combined. However, by tradition the three estates sat separately and each group had one vote.

By April 1789 the delegates began to arrive at Versailles. Goodwill prevailed. Violent revolution was far from anyone's mind. The delegates came armed only with *cahiers*, the lists of grievances that had been called for by the king. Of the six hundred representatives of the third estate, not one was a peasant. Except for a handful of liberal clergy and nobles who were elected to the third estate, they were all bourgeois. Nearly all the members of the third estate, as well as many members of the two privileged estates, were acquainted with the philosophy of the Enlightenment. They held inflated hopes of quickly solving long lists of problems that had been growing for years.

The first formal session was held on May 5. Immediately a sharp debate began over the method of voting. The two privileged estates demanded that, according to custom, the three estates meet separately and vote by order—that is, each estate cast one vote. This procedure would mean that all attacks on privilege and inequality would be defeated by a vote of two to one. The third estate demanded that the three estates meet jointly and that voting be by head. Thus all measures for fundamental reform would pass, for not only did the third estate have as many members as the other two combined, but a number of liberal clergy and noble men sympathized with the cause of reform. Both sides realized that the outcome of this issue would be decisive.

On June 17, after six weeks of fruitless haggling, the third estate, bolstered by the support of a few priests from the first estate, declared itself to be the National Assembly of France and invited the other two estates to join it in the enactment of legislation. Three days later, on June 20, when the members of the third estate arrived at their meeting hall, they found it locked. Adjourning to a

---

[1] The livre was technically worth about twenty cents, but its purchasing power in the eighteenth century was much greater than that of the late-twentieth-century American dollar.

nearby building used as an indoor tennis court, they took the "Tennis Court Oath," vowing never to disband until France had a constitution. It was the third estate's first act of defiance. On June 23 the king met with the three estates in a royal session at which he offered many liberal reforms but commanded the estates once and for all to meet separately and vote by order. The king, his ministers, and members of the first two estates filed out, but the representatives of the third estate defiantly remained seated. When the royal master of ceremonies returned to remind them of the king's orders, Mirabeau, a liberal noble man elected by the third estate, jumped to his feet and shouted, "Go and tell those who sent you that we are here by the will of the people and will not leave this place except at the point of the bayonet!" When the startled courtier repeated these words to his master, Louis XVI, with characteristic weakness, replied, "They mean to stay. Well damn it, let them stay." A few days later he reversed himself and ordered the three estates to meet jointly and vote by head. The third estate had thus won the first round.

The monarchy might have still been able to reassert control had not the new National Assembly received unexpected support from two sources: the Parisian populace and the French peasantry. Both had been suffering from unusually poor economic conditions initiated by poor harvests. Revolutionary events raised expectations in these hard times, making both groups unusually volatile. The first important disturbances came in Paris. In early July alarming news began to arrive that the king was calling the professional troops of the frontier garrison to Versailles. It appeared that he was at last preparing to use force. At this critical juncture, the Parisians countered the threat of force with force. On July 14 a riotous crowd searching for arms marched on and destroyed the Bastille, a gloomy old fortress prison in the working-class quarter that symbolized the arbitrary tyranny of the old regime (see Figure 40.2). (July 14 has long been celebrated as the French national holiday.) This show of force stayed the king's hand.

At the same time the forces of order were faced with uprisings in the countryside. During July and August peasants revolted against their lords throughout France, burning tax rolls, attacking manors, reoccupying enclosed lands, and generally rejecting the burdens of feudalism. These revolts were further inflamed by what has come to be known as the Great Fear—unfounded rumors that brigand bands, perhaps raised by nobles, were creating havoc everywhere. A panic swept the countryside. Many nobles fled from France (the émigrés). For all practical purposes, feudalism came to an end. The legal end of feudalism came on August 4 during a night session of the National Assembly when, in an effort to make the best of a bad situation, one noble man after another stood up and renounced his feudal rights and privileges.

These defeats suffered by the forces of order enabled the third estate in the National Assembly to take further actions. The most important of these actions occurred on August 26, when the National Assembly proclaimed the Declaration of Rights of Man and the Citizen. This document, which followed the English Bill of Rights by an even hundred years and preceded the American Bill of Rights by two years, was replete with the phrases of the philosophers of the Enlightenment. "Men are born and remain free and equal in rights." The natural rights were declared to be "liberty, property, security, and resistance to oppression." Liberty of opinion "even in religion," freedom of the press, and freedom from arbitrary arrest were all proclaimed.

The forces of privilege and reaction, however, still had to be brought to terms. The king not only refused to sign the August decrees but began once more to assemble troops around Versailles and Paris. In answer to this new threat of force, a huge mob of Parisian women on October 5 and 6 marched eleven miles out to Versailles, surrounded the palace, and with the help of the bourgeois National Guard, forced the king to accompany them to the city, where he became a virtual prisoner of the populace. As the carriage bearing the royal family rolled toward Paris, the surrounding crowd shouted jubilantly, "We have the baker, the baker's wife, and the little cook boy! Now we shall have bread!" A few days later the National Assembly moved its sessions to Paris, where it came increasingly under the influence of the radical populace of the great city. The third estate had triumphed.

FIGURE 40.2.   The Storming of the Bastille   The storming of the Bastille represented the first act of crowd violence of the French Revolution. Actually, the crowd of Parisians was merely looking for arms to defend itself against rumored attack by the forces of the king. However, the Bastille was believed to have held hundreds of political prisoners and was a symbol of all that was oppressive under the Old Regime. Its fall symbolized a direct blow for freedom and stayed the hand of the king, who was contemplating suppressing the defiant third estate. (Culver Pictures)

4. MAKING FRANCE A CONSTITUTIONAL MONARCHY

The National Assembly could now at last settle down to the task of transforming French institutions. During the next two years the Assembly passed a series of sweeping reforms that may be conveniently classified as follows.

Judicial

The *parlements,* and the manorial and ecclesiastical courts with their arbitrary procedures and overlapping jurisdictions, were swept away. An orderly system of lower and higher courts was established. The administration of justice was decentralized and democratized. Judges were to be elected for six-year terms. Torture was abolished. In criminal cases juries were to be used for the first time in French history.

Economic

In accordance with the doctrine of laissez faire, guilds, labor unions, and trading associations were abolished. All occupations were declared open to all classes. Feudal obligations, including labor on the public roads, had already come to an end on the night of August 4. Internal tolls and customs were abolished.

Financial

The complex and unequal taxes, direct and indirect, were swept away. They were replaced by a tax on land and a tax on the profits of trade and industry. Both were uniform and no one was exempt. Tax farming was at long last abolished. Expenditures were henceforth to be authorized only by the national legislature. To meet the pressing financial needs of the government, the National Assembly issued paper money called *assignats* to the value of 400 million livres. To back up this paper money, the property of the Roman Catholic church, valued at approximately that amount, was confiscated.

Religious

The seizure of its property was the first step toward the nationalization of the Church. Monasticism was abolished. The clergy was to be elected by the people (including non-Roman Catholics) and their salaries paid by the state. The bishops were reduced in number, wealth, and power. They were no longer to be invested by the pope. These measures were incorporated in the Civil Constitution of the Clergy, to which all members of the clergy were required to take an oath of allegiance in order to perform their functions and draw their salaries. The pope, whose control over the organization and the clergy of the French church would have been broken, declared the Civil Constitution of the Clergy to be founded upon heretical principles and ordered the clergy to refuse to take the oath of allegiance. A majority of the clergy, including nearly all the bishops, followed the pope's command. The defection of the "nonjuring clergy" and of thousands of their devoted parishioners was the first serious split in the ranks of the revolutionists.

Political

Under the new constitution, which was completed in 1791, judicial, legislative, and executive powers of the central government were separated. Law-making was given to the single-chamber Legislative Assembly of 745 members elected for two-year terms. Voting, however, was limited to males at least twenty-five years of age who paid taxes equivalent to three days' wages. It is estimated that some 4 million adult males ("active" citizens) could meet these qualifications and that some 2 million remained "passive" citizens. Actually to sit in the Legislative Assembly required the payment of taxes amounting to fifty-four livres. Only some seventy thousand Frenchmen could meet this qualification, and the weight of power fell to the bourgeoisie. The king was granted a suspensive veto over all but financial and constitutional measures, but three successive legislatures could pass a bill over the king's veto. The conduct of foreign relations was left in the hands of the king, but he could not declare war or make treaties without the consent of the Legislative Assembly. The king's expenditures were limited to a sum voted by the legislative body. France was greatly decentralized. For purposes of local government and administration, the country was divided into eighty-three departments, each of which was administered by a small elected assembly. The execution of the national laws was placed almost entirely in the hands of the local authorities.

In October 1791 the National Assembly, having completed its work, gave way to the Legislative Assembly, which had recently been elected under the new constitution. Within a brief span of two years and with very little bloodshed, France had been made over. The monarchy had been limited and made subject to a written constitution. The Roman Catholic church had been subordinated to the state. Feudalism had come to an end. Individual rights and liberties and legal equality had been defined and established.

5. FOREIGN WAR AND THE FAILURE OF THE MODERATE REGIME

The new government so optimistically launched lasted less than a year. The chief gainers in the French Revolution thus far had been the bourgeoisie and the peasants. The bourgeoisie had gained political control over the country and

WHERE HISTORIANS DISAGREE

The Origins of the French Revolution

No subject has provoked more historical research and debate than the French Revolution. The literature has become so extensive that several books have been written on the historiography itself.

Of all the aspects of the French Revolution, the most central and debated has been its origins. Why did it happen?

The most dominant interpretation of the twentieth century has viewed the Revolution as a struggle between rising and falling social classes. According to this view, which has a Marxist core, the Revolution was really a series of social revolutions. Most important was the revolution of the rising bourgeoisie, increasingly wealthy and numerous thanks to the growth of capitalism, commerce, and industry, but prevented from matching its economic dominance with social and political power. The bourgeoisie revolted against the assertive aristocracy, economically declining because of its ties to feudalism and agriculture but jealously fighting to retain its old social and political dominance. Adding to this fundamental struggle was the revolt of the urban proletariat at crucial points during the Revolution and the revolt of the peasants during the key months of summer 1789. Together, these revolts were too much for the monarchy, which along with the other institutions of the old feudal order were swept away and replaced by middle-class institutions. In each case, the social classes involved pursued their own interests. The base of this social revolution, which led to such sweeping political change, was the long-term shift from agriculture to industry and from feudalism to capitalism. Thus political change followed and was subordinate to socioeconomic change.

During the last twenty-five years, this dominant interpretation has come under increasing attack. Many historians now argue that the social conflict between the bourgeoisie and aristocracy has been exaggerated. They point out that the social backgrounds of those supporting or opposing the Revolution show no clear pattern, that the aristocracy lost less than assumed during the revolution, and that the rising industrial and commercial bourgeoisie were not the key supporters of the Revolution. New research seems to show that there was more mobility between the bourgeoisie and the aristocracy than previously known, that the aristocracy was more progressive and open to Enlightenment ideas than assumed, and that the aristocracy was not so firmly tied to the old economic order as argued. Apparently it was not the commercial and industrial middle class who were most important in pushing for revolution but, rather, lawyers and administrators—especially those who were young and most frustrated with the lack of social, economic, and political positions to match their talents and expectations.

Some of these revisionist historians place new stress on the political breakdown of the monarchy that began during the decades before 1789. According to this view, political conflict was shifting from the confined sphere of the central government, as had been the rule under royal absolutism, to the public sphere, as would be the rule under modern constitutional forms of government. As early as the 1750s and 1760s, the French monarchy was becoming unable to contain political debate. By the 1780s, the monarch's political authority was being undermined. Thus, political causes should not be subordinated to socioeconomic causes for the Revolution; political developments had a crucial force of their own.

A full explanation for the origins of the French Revolution must link social and political forces, which combined to bring down the monarchy and establish a new system. Exactly how those links are forged will remain of acute interest and debate among historians.

greater social mobility. Most adult male peasants, who constituted the bulk of the French male population, could now vote, and all of the peasantry was at least free from feudal obligations. To the many peasant landowners who owned their land before the Revolution were now added others who had seized the lands of émigré nobles or had purchased confiscated Church lands. Most of the bourgeoisie and the landowning peasants were satisfied and wished to see the Revolution stop where it was, lest they lose their sacred property and their political dominance.

However, other groups were quite dissatisfied. The royal family, the aristocracy, most of the clergy, and the army officers yearned for the restoration of their privileges. And many of Paris' urban populace, both men and women, wanted to see the Revolution continued in a more radical way. They had gained little except theoretical rights and legal equality. Owning no property, they could not vote. Yet they had supplied much of the physical force that had saved the third estate and made the moderate reforms possible.

Leadership for these disgruntled groups was found among radical members of the bourgeoisie, who came to favor overthrow of the monarchy and extension of the Revolution. These radicals, although a definite minority, were well organized and ably led. They came together in numerous clubs, which were formed to debate and plan political matters. The most important was the Jacobin Club. Although the Jacobins were and remained predominantly intellectual bourgeoisie and were moderate at first, they gradually became the most radical group in France. Three Jacobin leaders came to tower over all others. Jean Paul Marat, Swiss by birth, was an inordinately ambitious and frustrated physician and scientist turned popular journalist (see Color Plate 18). His was the gift of rabble-rousing journalism. He incessantly demanded the beheading of all those leaders who opposed the further extension of the Revolution. Georges Jacques Danton, a former lawyer in the king's council, was a thundering orator of great energy and ability. Maximilien de Robespierre was also a lawyer. This determined idealist was influenced by Rousseau and bent upon the creation of a virtuous republic.

Events soon played into the hands of the radicals. The kings of Austria and Prussia, fearful of the spread of revolutionary ideas to their own lands and urged on by the French émigrés, began to make threatening moves and to issue meddlesome warnings to the French revolutionaries. In France the reactionaries believed that a successful war would enhance the prestige and power of the throne and that a defeat would result in the restoration of the Old Regime. Most of the radicals believed that war would expose the inefficiency and disloyalty of the king and bring about his downfall. When, therefore, in April 1792 Louis XVI appeared before the Legislative Assembly to request a declaration of war against Austria and Prussia, only seven negative votes were cast. Thus lightly was begun a series of wars that was to last twenty-three years and embroil most of the Western world.

The French armies, almost leaderless since nearly all the high-ranking officers were members of the nobility and had either fled or been deposed, were badly defeated. As the Austrian and Prussian armies advanced toward Paris, there was panic in the city. The king, who had already forfeited his credibility when he attempted to flee the country in June 1791, was now rightly suspected of being in treasonable communication with the enemy. A huge Parisian crowd of men and women advanced on the king's palace. The royal family fled for its life to the Legislative Assembly. The interior of the palace was wrecked, and several hundred of the Swiss guards were slain. The Legislative Assembly suspended and imprisoned Louis XVI and called elections for a national convention to draw up a new constitution to take the place of the one that had just failed.

6. THE TRIUMPH OF THE RADICALS AND THE REIGN OF TERROR

The elections to the constitutional convention took place in an atmosphere of panic and violence. During the interim between the overthrow of the limited monarchy and the meeting of the convention, Danton assumed emergency leadership of the nation. Feverishly he superintended the gathering of recruits and rushed them to the front. As the recruits were preparing to leave Paris, rumors spread that their wives and children would be murdered by the reactionary clergy and nobles.

FIGURE 40.3. Execution of Louis XVI In January 1793, Louis XVI was executed by guillotine in a public square before troops and a large crowd of citizens. Here the scene is portrayed as a triumph of the Revolution. (The Bettmann Archive)

Violent elements began murdering members of the nonjuring clergy and reactionary nobles who were being held in the prisons of Paris. During the first three weeks of September 1792 more than a thousand such victims were massacred. In the elections of the National Convention, held amid this hysteria, the radicals won a sweeping victory. Most of the conservative elements fearfully stayed away from the polls.

In the National Convention a long-simmering struggle between different Jacobin factions came to a head. The Girondins, so called because many of their leaders came from the vicinity of Bordeaux in the department of the Gironde, had once been the dominant and most radical faction of the Legislative Assembly—the Left.[2] In the National Con-

vention the Girondins found themselves on the Right. The new Left was made up of the Jacobin followers of Marat, Danton, and Robespierre, mostly from the city of Paris. They came to be called the Mountain, since they occupied the highest seats in the convention hall. This radical convention, elected for the purpose of drawing up a new constitution, was to rule France for the next three years (1792–1795).

The first act of the National Convention was to declare France a republic. The next move was to dispose of the king. After a close trial he was found guilty of treasonable communication with the enemy and sent to the guillotine—an instrument adopted by the revolutionists for the more mechanical and humane beheading of the condemned (see Figure 40.3). The execution of Louis XVI, accompanied by proclamations of world revolution by the evangelical Jacobins, sent a shudder of horror through the royal courts of Europe. Furthermore, the hastily recruited French revolution-

---

[2] The present political connotation of the terms *right* and *left* derives from this period. In the revolutionary assemblies the conservatives sat quite by chance on the speaker's right, the liberals and radicals on his left.

ary armies, which had checked the Austrians and Prussians at Valmy in September 1792, had taken the offensive and overrun the Austrian Netherlands.

Austria and Prussia were now joined by Great Britain, the Dutch Netherlands, Spain, Portugal, Sardinia, and Naples in a great coalition bent upon the destruction of the French Revolution and the restoration of the Old Regime. The French armies were unable to stand up to such an array of armed might. But the defeats and invasions were not the worst disasters to confront the revolutionary government. The peasants of the Vendée region in western France, who had been stirred up by the nonjuring clergy, rebelled against the radical government. The rebellion spread until some sixty of the eighty-three departments were involved. Major provincial cities such as Bordeaux, Lyons, and Marseilles were in revolt. Toulon, the chief French naval base on the Mediterranean, invited in the British fleet. Inside the convention itself many of the moderate Girondins were sympathetic to the rebels.

Faced with what seemed to be inevitable disaster to their radical cause and indeed to the Revolution itself, the leaders of the Mountain decided on drastic action. For support they turned to the Paris Commune, as the city government was called, which was controlled by radicals, and the *sans-culottes*—the common laborers, small shopkeepers, and artisans who wore trousers rather than the aristocratic knee breeches (or *culottes*). The men and women of this urban populace had already played an important role in the Revolution by opposing the old forces of order and supporting leaders of the third estate at crucial times, such as in the storming of the Bastille. By 1793 they wanted to carry the Revolution further, and for the next two years their wishes and actions would have considerable weight in France. Economically, they favored price controls to keep the cost of bread down and other governmental intervention in the economy to narrow the gap between rich and poor; they envisioned a society of small shopkeepers, artisans, and small farmers as ideal. Politically, they were antimonarchical and strongly republican, indeed favoring as much direct democracy as possible. While leaders of the Mountain did not fully agree with the *sans-culottes*, they were willing to work with them. On June 2,

1793, the National Convention, now dominated by the Mountain and surrounded by a threatening Paris crowd urged on by *sans-culottes* leaders, voted the expulsion and arrest of twenty-nine Girondin leaders. Having thus silenced all opposition within the convention, the leaders of the Mountain and their followers inaugurated a "reign of terror" against their political enemies. Their goals were to unite France and to save and extend the Revolution.

The National Convention delegated unlimited powers to a Committee of Public Safety, composed of twelve men working in secret. The most influential member of this all-powerful committee was Robespierre. At its call was the Committee of General Security, a national police force. A Revolutionary Tribunal was set up to try, condemn, and execute suspects without the usual legal procedure and as quickly as possible. Members of the National Convention were sent out in pairs to carry the Terror to every nook and cranny of France. Although tens of thousands of persons, possibly half a million, were imprisoned during the Reign of Terror, only some twenty-five thousand are believed to have been executed. The drastic policy was remarkably successful. The disaffected elements were quickly silenced, and the rebellions quelled. The defense of the republic was entrusted to Lazare Carnot. A *levée en masse* was ordered. All men, women, and children were called to the colors. The able-bodied young men were rapidly trained and rushed to the front. Everyone else contributed to the war effort on the home front. This common activity for defense of country produced a high state of morale—the first mass national patriotism in history. Able new officers were found. The armies of the coalition were defeated on every front and hurled back beyond the frontiers.

While Robespierre and his associates were saving the Revolution, they were also busy extending it to more radical ground. Robespierre was determined to make France a utopian republic where virtue and fraternity would reign supreme. During the emergency of 1793 a maximum price was placed upon the necessities of life for the protection of the consumer, particularly the *sans-culottes*. Efforts were made to control inflation by forcing people to accept the badly inflated *assignats* at their face value. New measures made it easier for peasants to acquire land. The metric system was adopted; the Louvre Palace was turned into an art gallery; the national library and national archives were founded; a law (never implemented) provided for a comprehensive national system of public education. Women adopted the flowing robes and hair styles of ancient Greece. Silk knee breeches, the symbol of aristocracy, gave way to trousers. Titles of all kinds were discarded and "Citizen" and "Citizeness" substituted. Even the calendar was revolutionized. The months were made equal and named after the seasons. Weeks were made ten days long, with one day of rest (thereby eliminating Sunday, a day of traditional Christian importance). The Year I was dated from September 22, 1792, the date of the declaration of the republic.

Meanwhile, discontent with Robespierre and his policies was increasing. The defeat of the invading armies of the coalition and the suppression of the internal rebellion appeared to most people to remove the justification for the Terror, yet the Terror was intensified. Robespierre felt that the republic of virtue for which he yearned had eluded him. When Danton counseled moderation, Robespierre sent even him and his most prominent followers to the guillotine. No one, not even the members of the National Convention, felt safe any longer. Finally, in July 1794, the Convention found the courage and the leadership to overthrow Robespierre and send him to his own guillotine.

7. REACTION AND THE RISE OF NAPOLEON

Since Robespierre was overthrown on July 27, which was 9 Thermidor by the revolutionary calendar, the reaction that followed is known as the Thermidorian Reaction. The propertied bourgeoisie, who quickly gained control of things, had been frightened and angered by the restrictive measures of Robespierre's regime. All such measures still in force were repealed. The Terror was brought to an end, and the chief terrorists executed. Armed bands of bourgeois hirelings went around for some time beating or killing Jacobins. Many individuals, weary of discipline and restraints, reveled in an outburst of licentious living. In 1795 the National Convention finally got around to the task for which it had been elected three years earlier: the drawing up of a new constitution. The resulting constitution reflected conservative reaction. Only property owners could vote for members of the legislative bodies. Executive functions were placed in the hands of five directors, who were chosen for five-year terms by the two legislative bodies. In October 1795 the National Convention turned over its powers to the Directory, the name that was given to the new government.

The most significant development of the period of the Directory, 1795–1799, was the rise to power of Napoleon Bonaparte. The directors, though men of reasonable competence, were unable to restore peace and political and social tranquillity. Though peace had already been made with Spain and Prussia, war with Great Britain, Austria, and Sardinia dragged on. Government finances were chaotic, and brigandage was rife. More and more people longed for a strong man who could bring peace abroad and order at home. Napoleon proved to be the man, and the story of his rise to power will be toid in the next chapter. When in November 1799 Napoleon overthrew the Directory and made himself dictator, the French Revolution had run full cycie from absolute Bourbon monarchy to absolute Napoleonic dictatorship.

SUGGESTED READING

General

C. Brinton, *The Anatomy of Revolution* (1956). Seeks to discover a common pattern in revolutions by comparing the English, American, French, and Russian revolutions. Fascinating.

F. Furet, *Interpreting the French Revolution* (1981). An influential new interpretation.

N. Hampson, *A Social History of the French Revolution* (1963). A well-written, detailed account.

R. R. Palmer, *The Age of the Democratic Revolution,* 2 vols. (1959, 1964). Places the French Revolution in a broader transatlantic context.

S. Schama. *Citizens: A Chronicle of the French Revolution.* (1989). A vivid, revisionary account.

The Old Regime and the First Phase of the Revolution

William Doyle, *Origins of the French Revolution* (1980). Surveys recent interpretations.

G. Lefèbvre, *The Coming of the French Revolution* (1947). By one of France's leading authorities, it covers the first phase of the Revolution.

Alexis de Tocqueville, *The Old Regime and the French Revolution* (1955). A classic analysis with useful insights.

M. Vovelle, *The Fall of the French Monarchy, 1787–1792* (1984). A new synthesis.

Second Phase

M. Lyons, *France Under the Directory* (1975). A good brief treatment.

R. R. Palmer, *Twelve Who Ruled: The Committee of Public Safety During the Terror* (1941). Best book on the Reign of Terror.

A. Soboul, *The Parisian Sans-Culottes and the French Revolution 1793–1794* (1964). The most highly respected analysis of the *sans-culottes.*

Sources

J. H. Steward, *A Documentary Survey of the French Revolution* (1951). Excellent, broad collection of documents.

CHAPTER 41

The Era of Napoleon, 1799–1815

FIGURE 41.1. David, "Napoleon's Coronation" This painting by David was intended to glorify Napoleon at the height of his powers. Having just crowned himself emperor with a laurel wreath (alluding back to Roman emperors) in an 1804 ceremony presided over by Pope Pius VII (on his right), Napoleon prepares to crown Josephine as empress. (Alinari/Art Resource)

No individual in modern times has enjoyed a more meteoric career than Napoleon Bonaparte, the modern counterpart of Alexander the Great and Julius Caesar. He was essentially a product of the Enlightenment and the French Revolution. He rose to power in France quickly, both undoing and securing changes initiated during the French Revolution. As he extended his rule throughout Europe by military conquest, he spread revolutionary forces of change to other lands.

1. NAPOLEON'S RISE TO POWER

Napoleon was born on the French island of Corsica in 1769. At the age of nine he was sent to a military school in France. An unusually self-reliant individual, he studied history, geography, and mathematics. At sixteen he received his commission as second lieutenant of artillery. During several years of boring garrison duty he stuffed his photographic mind with history, the classics, and the philosophy of the Enlightenment.

The French Revolution provided unprecedented opportunities for soldiers of talent to rise in the officer corps. Most of the prerevolutionary army officers were nobles and had fled the country or been deposed. Moreover, the expanded size of the army created new demand for skilled officers. Napoleon took advantage of his opportunities. In 1793 he gained attention in the recapture of Toulon. In 1795 Napoleon was again called upon, this time by the National Convention, which was threatened by a Parisian crowd. Using artillery—his famous "whiff of grapeshot"—Napoleon quickly dispersed the crowd and became the hero of the Convention. He used his new prominence to secure command of the French army still fighting in northern Italy. Napoleon's dynamism and skill quickly galvanized the lethargic French forces, who defeated the Austrians and Sardinians and forced them to sue for peace. He personally negotiated a favorable peace with Austria and sent back glowing reports of his exploits.

Napoleon then turned toward France's most formidable opponent, the British. The British navy was too powerful for France to dare an invasion of the British mainland. Napoleon concluded that an expedition to Egypt would be a telling blow to British commerce with its colonies and to the British Empire in general. Moreover, it might prove to be an unexpected thrust and thus an easy victory, something to contribute to Napoleon's image as a daring heroic conqueror. Militarily, the expedition was a failure; Admiral Nelson (1758–1805) decisively defeated the French fleet at the Battle of the Nile on August 1, 1798. Yet Napoleon avoided personal disaster by slipping back to France with a few chosen followers and cleverly managing the reports that arrived from Egypt.

Meanwhile, matters were turning worse for France's government, the Directory. The expedition to Egypt prompted Great Britian, Austria, and Russia to join in a second coalition against France. By 1799 French armies had suffered defeats and France was threatened with invasion. Internally, support for the Directory was weakening as the economic situation worsened and as political factions vied for power. One of the conservative factions, led by Abbé Siéyès (who was already one of the directors), concluded that the Revolution had gone too far. The members of this faction wanted to return to a more authoritarian form of government, which respected the changes initiated during the first, moderate phase of the Revolution in 1789. This situation provided Napoleon with another opportunity. Siéyès and others conspired with Napoleon to overthrow the Directory in a coup d'état. This coup occurred on 18 Brumaire (November 9, 1799). Napoleon was only thirty.

2. THE CONSULATE—PEACE AND REFORM, 1799–1804

Having seized power by conspiracy and force, Napoleon had a constitution drawn up to conceal what amounted to a military dictatorship under the cloak of parliamentary forms. He gave himself the title of First Consul with the power to appoint key civilian and military personnel, declare war and make treaties, and initiate all legislation through a hand-picked Council of State. Two other consuls without any significant powers served as camouflage. Two legislative bodies were selected from a iist of candidates elected by all adult French males. But since they could not propose new laws, their power was very limited. Thus the voters were led to believe that they were participating in the government, whereas in reality their voice was but faintly heard. Local government was again brought under the strict control of the centrai government by placing each of France's eighty-three departments under the control of a powerful agent of the central government called a *prefect*.

Napoleon lost no time in making a treaty (1800) with the United States, bringing to an end a two-year undeclared naval war that had grown out of French seizures of American vessels and the pro-British and anti-French policies of John Adams' administration. Slipping over the Alps with a French army, Napoleon crushed the Austrian army in northern Italy in the battle of Marengo, knocking Austria out of the Second Coalition. Tsar Paul of Russia was cajoled with flattery and promises into making peace. Even Great Britain was persuaded to sign the Peace of Amiens in 1802. Shortly thereafter Napoleon cut his losses in North America and sold Louisiana to the United States.

Napoleon next proceeded to gain social support for his rule and create new permanent institutions. He approved the end of feudal privileges and the transfers of property, thereby winning favor with the peasantry. By affirming property rights as inviolabie and formal equality before the law for adult males, he gained support from the middle class. He also welcomed back all but the most reactionary émigrés, most of whom had been part of France's old aristocracy. He deterred opposing groups by creating a secret police force under Joseph Fouché and suppressing political organizations. For those who displayed loyalty and achieved the most, he created the prestigious Legion of Honor.

Some of these measures were institutionalized in Napoleon's most important reform, the creation of the Civil Code of 1804 (the Napoleonic Code), which would later be copied by many other nations. The Civil Code, along with other codes for criminal and commercial law, reduced to order the dozens of different legal codes in existence. Generally they affirmed the reforms sought in the beginning stages of the French Revolution while rejecting the more radical measures enacted after

1792. But for women, the code was a clear defeat. Rather than granting them legal or political equality, it gave authority over the family to men and left married women legally and economically dependent on their husbands.

Napoleon was keenly aware of the political and social importance of religion. "Always treat the pope," he counseled his diplomats, "as if he had 200,000 men." He himself was a deist and a cynical moral relativist, believing that God was "always on the side with the most cannon." One of his first steps was to make peace with the pope and end the ten-year struggle between the French revolutionary governments and the Roman Catholic church. After arduous negotiations, the First Consul and the pope signed the Concordat of 1801, which was to govern the relations between the French state and the Catholic church until the beginning of the twentieth century. The Catholic religion was declared to be the religion of the majority of the French people, but freedom for other religions was also to be protected. The state was to appoint the bishops, but only the pope could invest them in their offices. The bishops were to appoint and discipline the lower clergy, thus restoring the traditional episcopal principle of the church. The salaries of the clergy were to be paid by the state, and the clergy were to take an oath of allegiance to the state. The pope accepted the permanent loss of church property seized by the National Assembly. While the Catholic clergy was never pleased with the Concordat (indeed, Pope Pius VII eventually renounced it), it ended the religious cleavage that had harassed France since the early days of the revolution.

Napoleon initiated several other institutional reforms. He established the Bank of France to handle government funds and issue paper money. He brought order and efficiency to government finances. He created a long-lasting system of secondary schools tied to the University of France. He established several professional and technical schools.

The first five years of Napoleon's rule were spectacularly successful. Law and order at home and peace abroad had been attained. Financial stability, equal and efficient justice, religious tranquillity, and the foundations of an effective educational system had all been achieved. Public morale was high. However, Napoleon was not satisfied with his accomplishments. He yearned for more glory. In 1804 he crowned himself emperor of the French and sought further fields to conquer.

3. THE EMPIRE—WAR AND CONQUEST

Great Britain, France's inveterate foe, had become increasingly alarmed at Napoleon's growing strength. Napoleon had not only continued to build up his military forces but had also taken advantage of the Peace of Amiens to further his commercial and imperial schemes at Great Britain's expense. Before the end of 1803 the British government declared war and the next year joined with Austria and Russia to form a third coalition against France. This was what Napoleon expected and wanted. He soon appeared at the English Channel at the head of a force sufficient to conquer the British Isles, if only the twenty-four-mile water barrier could be crossed. In the Channel, however, lay the world's mightiest fleet, commanded by the greatest of all Britain's admirals, Lord Nelson. Meanwhile, he was watching the movements of the Austrians and Russians and readying his own army. When the time was ripe, he suddenly marched his army eastward, surrounded an exposed Austrian army at Ulm in southwest Germany, and forced it to surrender. But the day after Ulm, Nelson sighted the combined French and Spanish fleets off Cape Trafalgar on the southwest point of Spain and annihilated them (October 21, 1805). Although Nelson was killed early in the battle, his victory saved Great Britain from the menace of a Napoleonic invasion and limited the scope of the French emperor's conquests to the continent of Europe.

On land, however, Napoleon seemed invincible. Moving his army eastward from Ulm, he met and crushed the oncoming combined forces of Austria and Russia at Austerlitz. Austria immediately sued for peace, and the demoralized Russians retreated toward their home country. At this juncture Prussia declared war on Napoleon. The time was inopportune, and the Prussian army was no match for Napoleon. At Jena and Auerstädt

Napoleon overwhelmed and virtually destroyed the Prussian forces (1806). Two weeks later the French were in Berlin. Hearing that the Russian troops were re-forming in Poland, Napoleon moved eastward to meet them. After being held to a draw by the Russians in a blinding snowstorm at Eylau, he defeated them decisively a few months later in the great battle of Friedland (1807). Tsar Alexander I now sued for peace. Although the Treaties of Tilsit (July 1807) were technically between equals, they actually left Napoleon master of the European continent and Alexander I only a junior partner. Russia was given a free hand to deal with Turkey in eastern Europe but was not permitted to take Constantinople, the prize the Russians most desired. In return for a dominant hand in eastern Europe, Alexander promised to join Napoleon against Great Britain and to force Sweden to do so. Tilsit recognized the changes that Napoleon had already made in central and western Europe and left him free to make any others he wished.

Between 1806 and 1808 Napoleon remade the map of Europe. The puppet Duchy of Warsaw was created out of part of Prussia's (and later, part of Austria's) Polish territory. Prussia's territory west of the Elbe was made a part of the kingdom of Westphalia, over which Napoleon's youngest brother, Jerome, was made king. Prussia was thus virtually halved in size. The Holy Roman Empire was at long last abolished, and its hundreds of little principalities greatly consolidated. A strip of German territory along the North Sea was annexed outright to France. The rest of German territory west of the Elbe was brought into the Confederation of the Rhine, with Napoleon as protector. Napoleon's younger brother, Louis, was made king of Holland; but when Louis began to favor the interests of his Dutch subjects over those of the French Empire, Napoleon deposed him and annexed his territory to France. The Italian peninsula was brought under French dominance. The coastal areas along the northeastern Adriatic Sea were detached from Austria and annexed to France. In 1808 Napoleon overthrew the weak Spanish royal house and made his elder brother, Joseph, king of Spain. Shortly before, the Portuguese royal family had fled to Brazil at the approach of a French army. Denmark (including

Map 41.1 **EUROPE, 1810** This map shows the Napoleonic empire at its height. Generally, French revolutionary and Napoleonic institutions spread most in those areas closest to France and under its direct control. Napoleon's empire was weakened when he tried to extend his control to Europe's geographic extremes—Spain and Russia.

Norway) became Napoleon's most faithful ally.

Thus, by 1808, most of Europe was under French control or French influence (see Map 41.1). No other conqueror has so dominated Europe. In all those territories under direct French control, Napoleon's "enlightened" institutions and administrative efficiency were introduced. The rest of Europe, impressed with the effectiveness of the French revolutionary ideas and institutions, adopted many of them voluntarily.

4. DECLINE AND FALL OF THE EMPIRE

A number of factors contributed to the decline and fall of the Napoleonic empire. One of the most obvious was British sea power. Because of it, Great Britain alone of the European powers was able to withstand the Napoleonic military onslaught. After Trafalgar had dashed Napoleon's hopes of invading the British Isles, he sought the destruction of "perfidious Albion" by economic pressure. In order to wreck the economy of the "nation of shopkeepers," he attempted to blockade the entire continent of Europe against British shipping. All British goods were confiscated. French privateers were set upon British merchant ships. These measures, known as "the Continental System," did cause Great Britain distress. However, with control of the sea, Great Britain was able to apply a more effective counterblockade against the Napoleon-dominated Continent. The Continental System created ever-increasing resentment in France's satellite states against Napoleon's rule.

Another factor that undermined the Napoleonic empire was the rise of a national spirit among the subject peoples. The mass spirit of intense patriotism or nationalism, which had its origin in France during the *levée en masse* of 1793, spread to the rest of Europe in the wake of Napoleon's conquering armies. The first people to rebel openly against the French yoke were the proud Spaniards. Hardly had Napoleon's brother Joseph been placed on the Spanish throne when his unwilling subjects rose up and chased him out of Madrid. The superior French armies, even when led by Napoleon himself, were ineffective against the hit-and-run guerrilla tactics invented by the Spaniards. The British government, observing Napoleon's predicament in Spain, sent an army under Arthur Wellesley, the future duke of Wellington, to exploit the situation. Spain became a running abscess that drained away much of Napoleon's military strength. Meanwhile, Prussia, after the humiliation of Jena, had begun a rejuvenation under the leadership of Baron von Stein. Partly in secret and partly in the open, the Prussians modernized their army and their civil institutions and prepared for the day of liberation. In 1809 Austria declared war on Napoleon in a premature effort to free itself from subservience to the French emperor. Although Austria was once more defeated, the heroic valor with which the Austrian armies fought served notice of the rising spirit of national pride and resistance. Napoleon could no longer enjoy the advantage of fighting with soldiers fired with the heady wine of nationalism against lethargic professional armies.

The beginning of the end was a disastrous campaign against Russia in 1812. With their own interests pulling them apart, the alliance between Alexander I and Napoleon became strained. Napoleon, against the advice of his closest associates, decided to invade Russia. Amassing an army of six hundred thousand, the mightiest army ever assembled up to that time, he plunged into the vastness of Russia. Many of his troops, however, were unwilling conscripts from the puppet states. The Russian army retreated into the interior of the huge country, following a scorched-earth policy and drawing Napoleon ever-farther from his base of supplies. Finally, after the bloody battle of Borodino about seventy-five miles from Moscow, Napoleon's hosts entered the city. But Alexander I refused to make peace. A fire destroyed much of Moscow, leaving the invaders without shelter in the face of approaching winter. Napoleon began his retreat too late. The Russian winter caught his forces burdened down with loot. Tens of thousands froze or starved. Russian Cossacks, riding out of the blizzards, cut down or captured other thousands. Of the six hundred thousand men who marched into Russia, no more than one hundred thousand returned.

Napoleon dashed back to France to raise fresh conscripts, but the flower of French manhood was gone. One nation after another rose up to join the

WHERE HISTORIANS DISAGREE

Who Was Napoleon?

Few individuals in history have inspired such passionate debate as Napoleon. In part, this controversy is a result of his meteoric rise to the heights of power and his string of military conquests. And in part, it is a consequence of the charismatic quality of his leadership. He combined personal dynamism and charm, which created faith in masses of followers and enabled him to dominate many of those with whom he came into contact. The debate is also related to difficulties separating the myth of Napoleon from the reality of Napoleon. Finally, all sides of the debate can find some support in the varied, contradictory legacy of Napoleon's intentions and deeds. Therefore it is not surprising that historians have bitterly disagreed over how to characterize Napoleon.

Many historians argue that Napoleon was fundamentally a dictator. They point to the methods he used to acquire power—the fame associated with military prowess, the coup d'état, and the plebiscite that seemed to affirm democratically his power without offering a real choice—as methods typical of modern dictators. They also point to his actions after acquiring power—crowning himself emperor, eliminating freedom of speech and press, removing the substance from representative institutions, initiating a systematic crackdown on political opponents, and creating a secret police—as characteristic of military dictatorships.

Other historians, see him as a preserver of the Revolution. They stress his familiarity with Enlightenment ideas and his early support of the French Revolution. They point out that Napoleon did affirm the end of feudalism, the overthrow of the old aristocracy, the establishment of equality before the law for men, and the rights of property. They also argue that his most important service may have been in spreading the ideas and institutions of the Revolution beyond France's borders—in particular, the rejection of aristocratic privilege and the spread of the Napoleonic Code. In short, Napoleon affirmed the fundamental reforms of the early French Revolution, institutionalized them, and then helped spread them elsewhere in Europe.

Still other historians argue that Napoleon is best viewed as the last in a line of eighteenth-century enlightened despots. They point out that like other enlightened despots, such as Frederick the Great of Prussia and Joseph II of Austria, Napoleon was most interested in maximizing the political and military power of the state. Like them, he saw that to do so required centralizing and rationalizing the government, improving finances, codifying laws, and supporting the armed forces. He shared their tendency to make religious concerns secondary to political unity and to gain support through the creation of educational institutions. Thus from an eighteenth-century perspective, Napoleon is recognizable as an enlightened despot.

Many historians argue that individual leaders themselves, even as extraordinary as Napoleon, do not decisively affect history's mainstream. More important are the forces, circumstances, and people that surround them. Other historians maintain that individuals, above all rare charismatic leaders such as Napoleon, can have significant historical consequences.

Which of these interpretations best fits the historical record depends greatly on the perspective of the viewer and on what aspects of Napoleon's personality and rule are emphasized. At the same time, how much can be attributed to the actions of any historical figure must be kept in mind in deciding exactly who was Napoleon.

Russians in a war of liberation. At Leipzig in central Germany, in October 1813, Napoleon was at last decisively defeated. The next year the allies entered Paris and exiled Napoleon to the island of Elba, off the coast of Italy. When the allies began to squabble over the peace settlement, Napoleon escaped back to France and raised another army, but he was finally defeated in June 1815 by the duke of Wellington and the Prussians under Marshal Blücher at Waterloo in Belgium. This time he was imprisoned on the island of St. Helena in the South Atlantic, where six years later he died.

5. OVERSEAS EFFECTS: LATIN AMERICA

One vast area outside Europe upon which the impact of the revolution of Napoleon was strong and immediate was Latin America. During the eighteenth century, discontent with colonial rule had been steadily mounting in the Spanish and Portuguese colonial empires in North and South America. As in the thirteen English colonies in North America, resentment was directed primarily against economic and political restrictions. As the native-born "Creoles" had come to outnumber the Spanish- and Portuguese-born settlers, the ties of loyalty to the mother countries had become more and more tenuous. The liberal writings of the French and British philosophers of the Enlightenment were smuggled into Latin America and made their converts, particularly among young intellectuals. These liberal Latin Americans could not help being impressed by the successful revolt of the English colonies to the north and the setting up of a liberal New World republic. The French Revolution had an even more profound influence on them. When, therefore, Napoleon overthrew Ferdinand VII of Spain and placed his own brother, Joseph Bonaparte, on the Spanish throne, the sentiments of loyalty on the part of the colonies for the mother country, which were already weak, became confused.

By 1810 the colonies were in open revolt. As with the English colonists three decades earlier, the cause of the Latin American revolutionists seemed hopeless. In addition to the regular Spanish troops, they had to struggle against most of the wealthy Spanish settlers and the local Roman Catholic hierarchy. Eventually two brilliant young leaders, Simón Bolívar and José San Martín, emerged to overcome the seemingly impossible obstacles and to lead the South American revolutionists to success. By 1822 the independence of Spanish South America was won. In the same year the issue was decided in Spain's Central American colonies and in Mexico, which then included the southwest quarter of what is now the United States. In all the former Spanish colonies, republics were established, although a long period of troubled apprenticeship preceded the establishment of effective popular governments. Real stability has continued to be a problem for Central and South American nations.

In the huge Portuguese colony of Brazil, the independence movement was delayed by the flight of the Portuguese royal family to Brazil in 1807. However, the return of the king to Portugal six years after Napoleon's fall and the efforts of the Portuguese government to reimpose the colonial status on Brazil quickly fanned the embers of revolt into flame. In 1822 the Portuguese king's son, Pedro, whom he had left behind as regent, yielded to native pressure and declared himself king of independent Brazil. In all of free Latin America the Napoleonic Code was adopted as the basis of civil law, and the impact of the Enlightenment on political institutions was clearly visible.

6. SIGNIFICANCE OF THE FRENCH REVOLUTION AND NAPOLEON

The French Revolution and its Napoleonic sequel had a profound effect on the course of history. Like Pandora when she lifted the lid of that fateful box, they let loose forces and ideas that have influenced and shaken the world ever since, especially the revolutionary ideals of *Liberty, Equality, Fraternity*. Originally conceived in the eighteenth century by the philosophers of the Enlightenment, they were born materially in the American and French revolutions and spread by Napoleon.

In the era of the French Revolution, the ideal of *liberty* meant freedom from arbitrary authority—political, religious, economic, or social. It meant freedom of speech, press, conscience, assembly, person, and profession, and the sacredness of property. During the moderate first phase of the French Revolution, a great deal of progress toward these goals was made; in the tumultuous and bloody second phase, a good deal was lost. Under Napoleon's rule there was no political liberty. However, he claimed that the efficiency, prosperity, and honor of his regime more than made up for the lack of popular government, for which, he believed, the world was not yet ready.

Equality meant essentially equality under the law and equality of opportunity for gain and advancement. Generally, it did not apply to women, even though women played important roles during the Revolution and had hoped for gains that never came. It was only during the brief dominance of Robespierre that even partial social equality of all male citizens became a goal. Napoleon's law codes were a great boon to the more moderate kind of equality among men. The codes left women devoid of political rights and legally dependent on men.

Fraternity manifested itself in the mass movements (sometimes violent) for reform, in the comradeship in the conscripted armies, and above all in the new popular and dynamic spirit of nationalism. These forces, released by the American and French revolutions, spread first to the rest of Europe, then to Latin America, and eventually to the rest of the world. Much of the history of the world since the era of the French Revolution has revolved around these forces.

In another sense, the French Revolution and the Napoleonic era constituted a decisive political watershed marking the beginnings of modern times. The French Revolution opened the road to constitutional government and democratic institutions. Although there would be numerous reversals, constitutional governments and democratic institutions would generally flourish over the course of the succeeding two centuries and come to characterize politically modern times. The administrative bureaucracy and legal codes established during the Napoleonic era would be imitated and also come to characterize modern political systems.

Finally, the French Revolution and the Napoleonic era provided two images that would invite study and imitation throughout the nineteenth and twentieth centuries. The first image was that of the successful popular revolution. While the French Revolution was not the first revolution, it was the one that occurred in the heart of Western civilization and toppled not only the government but the major institutions of traditional society. This revolution would inspire revolutionaries and warn those representing the status quo for decades to come. The second image was that of Napoleon as a nationalistic, charismatic leader who could suddenly grasp power and exert his will with great effect. During the nineteenth and twentieth centuries, this powerful image would inspire individuals who envisioned themselves as potential Napoleons and people who yearned for easy, decisive solutions to deeply felt problems.

SUGGESTED READING

General

P. Geyl, *Napoleon, For and Against* (1949). Good study of changing interpretations of Napoleon.

J. C. Herold, *The Age of Napoleon* (1983). Entertaining, well-written survey.

R. Jones, *Napoleon. Man and Myth* (1977). A fine recent treatment.

G. Lefèbvre, *Napoleon*, 2 vols. (1969). Scholarly treatment by a leading authority.

F. Markham, *Napoleon* (1966). An excellent biography.

France

L. Bergeron, *France Under Napoleon* (1981). A good recent analysis.

R. B. Holtman, *The Napoleonic Revolution* (1967). Good on domestic policy and propaganda.

The Empire

D. Chandler, *The Campaigns of Napoleon* (1966). Focuses on military history.

O. Connelly, *Napoleon's Satellite Kingdoms* (1965). A good study of Napoleonic rule in Europe.

F. Markham, *Napoleon and the Awakening of Europe* (1965). A good study of Napoleon's influence outside of France.

W. S. Robertson, *The Rise of the Spanish-American Republics* (1965). Good brief account.

CHAPTER 42

Restoration and Reaction, 1815–1830

FIGURE 42.1. Cruikshank, "The Peterloo Massacre," 1819 This painting by George Cruikshank depicts the troops of the conservative British government breaking up a rally for liberal political reform, including demands for universal suffrage and religious freedoms. During the restoration, many European governments attempted to repress liberal movements. (The Mansell Collection)

The overthrow of Napoleon in 1815 brought to an end, in Europe at least, the heroic and tumultuous epoch that had begun in 1789 with the meeting of the Estates General. The intervening twenty-six years had been filled with great expectation, experimentation, turmoil, and war. Now there was disillusionment and weariness. The European royalty and aristocracy, at long last triumphant over revolutionary France, were determined to put an end not only to the Mirabeaus, Robespierres, and Napoleons but also to the ideas of the Enlightenment.

The returning holders of power—the monarchs, the aristocrats, the established Christian churches, and the elite of the governmental and military bureaucracies—generally subscribed to a conservatism that was dominant between 1815 and 1830 and that would remain a powerful force throughout the nineteenth century. Conservatives tended to believe that a hierarchical Christian society authoritatively guided by traditional monarchs, aristocrats, and clergy was time tested and best. Edmund Burke (1729–1797), Great Britain's most influential conservative thinker, and conservatives in general rejected the abstract rationalism of the Enlightenment and the reforms of the French Revolution. Any rapid change was suspect, and the attempt by the middle class to grasp political power was a presumptuous act by individuals who simply did not know how to rule. For conservatives the experience of the French Revolution was a lesson in what to avoid.

In order to achieve their conservative goals, to redraw territorial boundaries and to establish lasting stability in Europe, the leaders of the victorious powers gathered at the Austrian capital of Vienna in the autumn of 1814. To this conference also flocked representatives of every state in Europe, hundreds of dispossessed princes, agents of every conceivable interest, and adventurers.

1. THE CONGRESS OF VIENNA (1814–1815)

The Congress of Vienna was dominated by the four major victors over Napoleon (see Figure 42.2). Great Britain was represented by her able foreign minister, Lord Castlereagh. Prussia's mediocre

king, Frederick William III, headed his own delegation, as did Russia's tsar, the idealistic young Alexander I. Austria's emperor, Francis I, played host to the assembled great. However, the real leader of the Austrian delegation—and, indeed, the dominant figure of the whole congress—was the Austrian chancellor, Prince Klemens von Metternich. As guiding principles on which to base their decisions, the conferees decided on "legitimacy" and "stability." By *legitimacy* they meant that in the redistribution of various territories, attention would be paid not to the desires or interests of the people concerned but to the claims of the victorious—the former and the future sovereigns. By *stability* they meant establishing and maintaining a balance of power within Europe, with particular focus on restraining France. Many of the decisions formalized at Vienna had already been made by the four major powers shortly before and after Napoleon's overthrow in April 1814 (see Map 42.1).

Thanks in no small measure to the presence of the clever and able Talleyrand, France, the cause of all the turmoil, got off lightly. Prussia would have severely punished and weakened France, but her three major colleagues were fearful of upsetting the balance of power. Already saddled with the restored Bourbons, France was merely reduced to almost the same boundaries it had had before the wars of the revolutionary era. The Congress of Vienna had originally imposed no indemnity on France. But because of Napoleon's return from Elba in the midst of the congress and his hundred-day fling that ended at Waterloo, the four great powers compelled France to cede the Saar Basin to Prussia, to pay an indemnity of 700 million francs, and to return the art treasures stolen by Napoleon from the various galleries of Europe. Allied forces were to occupy France until the indemnity was paid. To contain France within its frontiers and to discourage future French aggression, Prussia was given a sizable block of territory along the Rhine, the Austrian Netherlands (Belgium) was annexed to the Dutch Netherlands, and Piedmont was enlarged by the annexation of the city-state of Genoa.

The main powers, taking advantage of political changes that had occurred over the previous twenty-six years and trading among themselves,

FIGURE 42.2. **Jean B. Isabey, "Congress of Vienna"** The principle figures of the Congress of Vienna are portrayed by Jean Baptiste Isabey. From left to right: Metternich is standing before a chair, Castlereagh is sitting with crossed legs, and Talleyrand is sitting with his right arm on the table. (Culver Pictures)

received new territories. Great Britain gained several strategic islands and colonies, increasing her sea power and overseas dominance. Prussia added some areas in central Europe that made it more homogeneously German and Western. However, the Rhineland territory was not contiguous to the Prussian homeland—a situation that invited further aggression. Russia's acquisition of Polish territory made the great majority of the Polish-speaking people subjects of Russia and brought Russia farther into the heart of central Europe. Austria, in exchange for the Belgian Netherlands, took the two rich Italian provinces of Lombardy and Venetia. Its preeminence in Italy, together with the presidency over the German Confederation, made Austria the dominant power in central Europe. The Holy Roman Empire, which Napoleon had destroyed, was not restored, but in its place was erected the weak German Confedera-

tion under the permanent presidency of Austria. Napoleon's consolidation of the more than three hundred German states into thirty-nine was allowed to stand, bringing the German people that much more political unity.

The Congress of Vienna has been both admired and criticized by observers ever since 1815. Critics point out that the peoples and territories of Europe were moved about by the great powers at Vienna like pawns on a chessboard, in complete disregard for the wishes of the people or for the spirit of nationalism that was now an increasingly virile force. Instead of trying to deal constructively with the budding forces of liberalism and nationalism, the great powers tried to ignore or repress them. Admirers point out that the Vienna settlement was not vindictive toward France and did establish a reasonable balance of power, both of which contributed to a century of freedom from European-wide war. While one may not agree with the conservative goals of the conferees, a settlement was achieved at Vienna and at least temporarily maintained in succeeding years.

2. THE CONCERT OF EUROPE

Metternich and his colleagues, pleased with their work, set up machinery for perpetuating it. Conveniently at hand was the Holy Alliance, conceived by Alexander to establish and safeguard the principles of the Christian religion. Russia (Orthodox), Austria (Roman Catholic), and Prussia (Protestant), the three bastions of conservatism, were to form the nucleus of the alliance. All Christian states of Europe were invited to join, and only Great Britain and the Papal States did not. Metternich considered the Holy Alliance a "sonorous nothing" but saw in it an opportunity for influencing the tsar. Intended by Alexander I as a bulwark of Christianity, the Holy Alliance became a symbol of reaction and repression.

Much more earthly an agency for perpetuating the Vienna settlements was the Quadruple Alliance. This was a military alliance of Austria, Russia, Prussia, and Great Britain created in November 1815 for the purpose of guaranteeing for twenty years the territorial boundaries established by the Vienna settlement. Metternich was determined to make of the alliance an international military police force that would suppress any liberal or national movements. It was arranged that the four member powers should hold periodic congresses to carry out the purposes of the alliance.

The first congress was held at Aix-la-Chapelle in northwest Germany in 1818. The purpose was to arrange the withdrawal of occupation forces from French soil. Since France had demonstrated good behavior under the restored Bourbon king, Louis XVIII, it was not only freed of occupying forces but was admitted to the Quadruple Alliance. Congresses at Troppau in 1820 and at Laibach in 1821, both on Austrian soil, concerned themselves with an insurrection that had broken out in Naples against the tyrannical Bourbon king, Ferdinand I. An Austrian army was authorized to put down the insurrection and reestablish the

hated Ferdinand I on his throne. The Neapolitan liberal volunteers, no match for the Austrian regulars, were soon defeated and their leaders executed, imprisoned, or exiled. What turned out to be the last of the congresses met in 1822 at Verona to deal with a liberal revolt in Spain against the reactionary Ferdinand VII. With the sanction of the Congress of Verona a French army crossed the Pyrenees and easily put down the rebellion.

The first of the alliance powers to repudiate the Metternich system was Great Britain. At the Troppau congress, the British clearly indicated their opposition to interfering in the internal affairs of other states. When the Verona congress decided, over British protest, on intervention in Spain, Britain's representative withdrew from the congress.

The Metternich system soon received further blows, some from unexpected quarters. At the Congress of Verona, the like-minded Austrians, Russians, and Prussians had been alarmed not only by the rebellion in the Spanish homeland but also by the revolt of Spain's New World colonies. When the corrupt government of Ferdinand VII proved incapable of putting down the revolt, Alexander I, with Metternich's blessing, proposed to send a Russian fleet to help coerce the colonies. Great Britain, enjoying a lucrative trade with the rebellious colonies, did not wish to see them restored to Spanish dominion and commercial monopoly. The British minister, Canning, who had succeeded Castlereagh in 1822, proposed to the government of the United States that Great Britain and the United States issue a joint statement against interference by the "Holy Alliance" in the affairs of the Western Hemisphere. However, Secretary of State John Quincy Adams foresaw that the time might come when the United States would wish to invoke such a policy alone, perhaps even against Great Britain. In 1823, President Monroe announced what has come to be called the Monroe Doctrine: The United States would regard any interference on the part of European powers in the affairs of the Western Hemisphere as an "unfriendly act." The United States was at the time, of course, a new and relatively weak nation, but Canning's immediate support of the American policy killed any further thought of "Holy Alliance" intervention in the New World,

German Confederation Boundary

Kingdom of Prussia

Austrian Empire

Kingdom of Sardinia

...lian States
...EDMONT
...PAL STATES
...NGDOM OF TWO SICILIES
...PARMA
...MODENA
...LUCCA
...TUSCANY
...SAN MARINO

...rman States
...USSIA
...HANOVER
...OLDENBURG
...MECKLENBURG-SCHWERIN
...NASSAU
...HESSE-CASSEL
...HESSE
...SAXONY
...BADEN
...WURTTEMBERG
...BAVARIA AND PALATINATE

Map 42.1 EUROPE, 1815 As this map indicates, the settlement at the Congress of Vienna left France with its lands little changed from 1789, but now France was bordered by strengthened states: the Kingdom of the Netherlands, Prussia, and the Kingdom of Sardinia. The victorious powers gained territories, but a balance of power was maintained.

for Great Britain had unchallenged dominance of the seas. The Monroe Doctrine marked the beginning of active participation by the United States in affairs beyond its own immediate shores.

The next blow to Metternich's concert of Europe came when the Greeks turned against their Moslem Turkish overlords in the revolt of 1821–1829. The valiant efforts of the Greeks were not sufficient to resist the power of the Ottoman Empire. By 1827 they were on the point of being hopelessly crushed. However, the sympathies of the great powers were being aroused for the courageous Greeks. Russia, Great Britain, and France in particular displayed a growing concern over the events in Greece. Russia's Orthodox Christian religion was the same as that of the Greeks. Furthermore, the Russians had long desired Constantinople, which controlled Russia's natural strategic and commercial outlet to the Mediterranean. Great Britain was concerned over the possibility of Russia's dominance in the Near East. In addition, the ruling classes in Great Britain and France were steeped in the classical culture of ancient Greece. Lord Byron, the most popular literary figure in Europe, lost his life fighting as a volunteer for Greece. In 1827 these three powers, over Metternich's protest, intervened in the Greek revolt and defeated the Turks on land and sea. The Treaty of Adrianople in 1829 granted independence to most of the Greeks on the home peninsula and local autonomy to the Serbs and Rumanians. The successful revolt of the Greeks was a victory for the resurging revolutionary principles of liberalism and nationalism. The intervention of Russia, Great Britain, and France further weakened the already battered concert of Europe.

3. THE BOURBON RESTORATION IN FRANCE

When the victorious armies of the coalition powers entered France and deposed Napoleon in the spring of 1814, they brought "in their baggage" the members of the Bourbon royal family who had fled the Revolution. In their wake trooped the émigré nobility. A younger brother of the guillotined Louis XVI was placed on the throne as Louis XVIII. (The son of Louis XVI, who had died in prison in 1795, without having ruled, was considered to be Louis XVII.) The "restored" Bourbon king was now fifty-nine and too fat and gouty to walk unassisted. He had traveled much and unwillingly during the long, lean years of his exile. When Napoleon returned from Elba in 1815, Louis XVIII had to flee once more. After Waterloo he returned to his throne, which he considered "the most comfortable of armchairs," determined to do nothing that might force him to leave it again.

Upon assuming the throne, Louis XVIII issued a charter, or constitution, that retained Napoleon's administrative and legal system and civil and religious liberty. Lawmaking was placed in the hands of a two-chamber legislature. The upper house was made an aristocratic stronghold, and the lower house was elected by a highly restricted electorate. Only those who paid direct annual taxes of three hundred francs could vote; this limited the suffrage to about one hundred thousand out of a total population of nearly 30 million. The lower house could be prorogued, or dissolved, by the king. Since the king also appointed and controlled his own ministers and the host of civilian and military officials, carried on foreign relations, controlled the military forces, and enforced the laws, his power was only somewhat limited by the charter.

Louis XVIII set out to use his powers with moderation so that tranquillity might be restored. There were no wholesale punishments of revolutionary leaders. The peasant and bourgeois purchasers of church and noble lands were not dispossessed. However, most of the returned émigrés—largely from the highest ranks of the clergy and the nobility—were of a different spirit. They came back from their unhappy exile angry and vengeful, demanding their old privileges and indemnification for their lands. Their leader was the king's younger brother, the Comte d'Artois— a typical Bourbon who had "never learned anything and never forgotten anything." The reactionaries controlled both houses of the national legislature, since even in the lower elected house, suffrage restrictions heavily favored the aristocracy and the *nouveaux riches* bourgeoisie. Louis XVIII found it increasingly difficult to hold these fire-eating reactionaries in check. Shortly before he died in 1824, he warned his incorrigible brother of the danger to the Bourbon dynasty if he did not adopt a more moderate attitude.

Unfortunately, Charles X, as the Comte d'Artois now styled himself, was a stranger to moderation. He quickly aroused animosity against his regime to an explosive pitch. The Napoleonic generals who had brought so much glory to France were immediately retired from duty. An indemnity was voted the émigrés for their confiscated lands, the money to be raised by reducing the interest on government bonds from 5 percent to 3 percent. This angered the upper bourgeoisie, who were the chief bondholders. The peasants were alarmed by a proposed establishment of primogeniture, which seemed to endanger the principle of equality and the security of land titles. The Jesuits were brought back to France, and favors were bestowed on the Catholic church. Opposition mounted rapidly. By 1827 Charles X had lost his majority in both houses of the national legislature. Totally blind to the political realities of the day, he twice dissolved the lower chamber and attempted to force the election of a friendly majority by censoring the press and using official pressure on the electorate. The hostile majorities only increased in number. Finally in July 1830 the king in a set of ordinances dissolved the newly elected chamber, called for new elections, restricted the suffrage so drastically that only about twenty-five thousand very rich citizens could vote, and abolished completely the freedom of the press. These measures set off an uprising in Paris. The Parisian proletariat erected barricades in the streets that the disaffected rank and file of the army were "unable" to break. After three days of desultory fighting, the insurgents had the upper hand, and the last Bourbon king of France was on his way to exile in England.

4. RESTORATION AND REPRESSION IN THE GERMANIES

In central and eastern Europe, particularly in the Germanies, Italy, and Russia, the conservatives and the Metternich system were more secure. The Germanies in 1815 consisted of thirty-seven little states and two large ones—Prussia and Austria. In all of them the influence of Metternich was strong. The German Confederation was an improvement over the old Holy Roman Empire, which Napoleon had destroyed, only in the sense that Napoleon's consolidation of the more than three hundred states down to thirty-nine was allowed to stand. The Diet was only a gathering and debating place for the representatives of the rulers of the thirty-nine states. The confederation had no treasury and no army at its command. There was not even a flag to symbolize its German national character. Reactionary Austria enjoyed a permanent presidency over it.

The German nationalism and liberalism that existed in 1815 centered primarily in the little states, some of whose rulers defied Metternich by granting liberal constitutions. The national and liberal activities here were largely the work of university students and professors, who shortly after 1815 began to form *Burschenschaften*, or brotherhoods, for the purpose of promoting German nationalism, liberalism, and the Christian religion. In 1817 in commemoration of the three hundredth anniversary of Luther's publication of his Ninety-five Theses, the *Burschenschaften* staged a giant festival at Wartburg, where Luther had hidden and had begun his translation of the Bible. Although the festivities were primarily religious in character, enough enthusiasm for German nationalism and liberalism was displayed to fill Metternich with anxiety. The murder two years later of a reactionary propagandist by a fanatical student gave Metternich his opportunity to strike. Calling together the princes of the leading German states at Carlsbad, he joined them in drawing up a set of harsh decrees designed to crush the embryonic national and liberal movements. The *Burschenschaften* were outlawed. Strict censorship was established. Classrooms and libraries were supervised. Liberal students and professors were terrorized by spies and police. The Carlsbad Decrees succeeded in suppressing for a number of years this first outcropping of the revolutionary spirit in Germany since the overthrow of Napoleon.

In Prussia the militaristic, paternalistic, despotic Hohenzollerns reigned. Behind them stood the equally reactionary landed aristocracy, the *Junkers*. The Junkers served as officers in the Prussian army and filled the key posts in the civil service and administration. These military lords hated not only liberalism in any form but also German nationalism. They did not wish to see virile, martial Prussia contaminated by association with the lesser German states that were now infected with the French disease of liberalism. It was only in the economic field that German unity received any encouragement from Prussia. Because its territory was separated into two noncontiguous segments, Prussia in 1819 began making commercial treaties with its smaller German neighbors, providing for the free flow of trade among them. By 1834 nearly all the states of the German Confederation except Austria had joined the Prussian-sponsored *Zollverein* (customs union). Though it was not so intended, the *Zollverein* proved to be a forerunner of German political unity under Prussian leadership.

As was to be expected, conservatism reached its height in Austria. The spirit of the French Revolution and Napoleon, with the one exception of nationalism, had hardly touched the Hapsburg state and its feudal society. In addition to the natural conservatism of the Hapsburgs and their chief minister, Austria had a language problem that caused its rulers to fear liberalism and nationalism like the plague. Austria proper is German-speaking, but during the sixteenth, seventeenth, and eighteenth centuries the Hapsburgs had annexed territories inhabited by Hungarian (Magyar), Czech, Slovak, Ruthenian, Polish, Rumanian, Serb, Croat, and Slovene language groups. In 1815 two Italian-speaking provinces were added. Before 1789 these various language groups remained relatively quiet under their feudal lords, the Hapsburg dynasty, and the Roman Catholic church. In the wake of the French Revolution, they began to stir with national consciousness.

Metternich saw clearly that if this new force was not suppressed, the Hapsburg state would fall apart. Furthermore, nationalism unchecked would cause Austria to lose its dominance over Germany and Italy. The various German and Italian states would be drawn together into powerful national states from which Austria would be excluded, for most of the people in the Hapsburg state were neither German- nor Italian-speaking. When these facts are considered, it is not surprising that Austria in 1815 was the most reactionary state in Europe save Russia. In the Hapsburg provinces Metternich's police and spies were everywhere. Permission to enter or to leave the country was made very difficult, lest dangerous ideas be brought in from the West. Classrooms, libraries, bookstores, and organizations of all kinds were considered suspicious and closely supervised. Even music (in the country of Mozart and Beethoven) was censored for fear that musical notes would be used as a cryptic code for conveying revolutionary ideas. On the surface, these policies appeared for some time to succeed. Nevertheless, Metternich was aware that the Hapsburg state stood on shaky ground.

5. RESTORATION AND REPRESSION IN ITALY

Austria dominated Italy even more completely than Germany. Lombardy and Venetia were annexed outright. Modena, Parma, and Tuscany were ruled by Austrian princes. The Papal States and Naples were under Austria's protection and guidance in both domestic and foreign affairs. In all these states the deposed aristocracy and clericals trooped back, full of hatred for French institutions and for the Italian liberals who had cooperated with Napoleon (see Figure 42.3). Nearly all the Italian intelligentsia were soon in prison or in exile. In the Papal States the Inquisition and the Index were restored, and such Napoleonic innovations as street lighting were done away with. Of all the Italian states, only Piedmont in the extreme northwest was free of Austrian control, but even here the restored heads of the house of Savoy were so reactionary as to cause Metternich only joy.

6. CONSERVATISM IN GREAT BRITAIN

Although Great Britain had been for years a home of representative government, its government in 1815 was far from democratic. The suffrage was

FIGURE 42.3.   Repression in Italy   This illustration shows Italians being shot as suspected revolutionaries; it epitomizes the spirit of reaction and repression as the great powers of Europe tried to restore the old order and stifle the new currents of liberalism and nationalism. (Historical Pictures Service, Chicago)

so severely restricted by property qualifications that only about 5 percent of the adult males could vote. Furthermore, the industrial cities of the north, which had emerged since the last distribution of seats in Parliament, were not represented at all. Both houses of Parliament were therefore monopolized by the landed aristocracy. It must be remembered, however, that the cleavage between the middle class and the aristocracy was not so sharp in Great Britain as on the Continent. The law of primogeniture in Great Britain granted the eldest son the entire landed estate and permitted him alone to assume the title. The younger sons sought careers in the church, in the military, or in business. This process brought

about much intermingling between the upper and the middle classes. The long-sustained prosperity of British commerce had produced a merchant class wealthy enough to purchase respectability, lands, and sometimes titles. The aristocracy frequently invested in commercial enterprises and later in industry. These facts help to explain why the great political and social struggles in nineteenth-century Britain, though sometimes bitter, lacked the violence of those on the Continent.

A period of economic depression and unrest in Great Britain followed the ending of the Napoleonic wars in 1815. For twenty-two years, with only one brief interruption, Britain had been engaged in a desperate struggle with France, a struggle that was economic as well as military. Meanwhile, British industrial expansion had gone on apace. The war's end found British warehouses piled high with unsold goods. Thousands of returning veterans found no jobs. Strikes and riots, which had begun during Napoleon's blockade, increased. The conservative Tory party, which had seen the country through the war, was strongly entrenched in power. Both the Tories and the slightly more liberal Whigs were still badly frightened by the specter of French revolutionary Jacobinism. The government therefore took strong measures against the restless workers. The writs of habeas corpus were suspended. The climax came in 1819 when troops fired on a crowd that had assembled outside Manchester to listen to reform speeches. A number were killed and hundreds injured in this "Peterloo Massacre."

Within a few years, however, as the postwar crisis of depression and unrest eased, the Tory government yielded slightly to the pressure for reform. We have already seen how Foreign Secretary Canning by 1822 had deserted Metternich's reactionary concert of Europe and aided independence movements in Latin America and Greece. During the 1820s the navigation laws were somewhat relaxed and the tariff slightly lowered. The Combination Laws were partially repealed, permitting laborers to organize unions, though not to strike. The civil disabilities against nonconforming Protestants and Roman Catholics were removed, permitting them to participate in political life on an equal basis with Anglicans. These measures, however, welcome as they were, did not get at the fundamental issue: a broadening of popular participation in the government. The pressure for suffrage reform would continue to mount, particularly from the industrial bourgeoisie, which was rapidly gaining in wealth.

7. REACTION AND REPRESSION IN RUSSIA

Even Russia had not escaped the influence of the French Revolution and Napoleon. Russia had joined in the second, third, fourth, and fifth coalitions against France, had been invaded and ravaged as far as Moscow in 1812, and had played a major role in the wars of liberation against Napoleon in 1813–1814. Meanwhile, the young tsar, Alexander I, and many of his aristocratic young army officers had picked up romantic and liberal ideas from the West. But Russia was not yet ripe for Western liberalism. It was a vast agricultural nation with a feudal social structure and a very small urban bourgeoisie that could serve as a liberal base. The Orthodox Christian church, dominated by an upper clergy drawn from the aristocracy, was a handy governmental agency for controlling the masses. The unstable Alexander I soon fell under the influence of Metternich and of his own reactionary boyar magnates and repented of his liberalism.

There was no trace of romanticism whatever in Nicholas I, Alexander's younger brother, who succeeded him in 1825. Nicholas was a handsome, austere autocrat whose military career wedded him to the concepts of discipline and authority. A quixotic revolt by a group of young liberal officers on the occasion of his ascension to the throne and a full-scale revolt by his Polish subjects in 1831 further embittered him against liberalism in any form. Both revolts were crushed with an iron hand. For thirty years (1825–1855) Nicholas I ws to stand as the perfect symbol of absolute reaction and the armed guardian of the Metternich system. When at the end of the nineteenth century Russia did begin to yield to liberal and revolutionary forces, it was with disorder and violence.

8. CONSERVATISM AND THE CHALLENGE OF LIBERALISM

Between 1815 and 1830 the forces of conservatism were dominant. They acted both in reaction to the events of the French Revolution and the era of Napoleon and in accordance with their own ideology—a set of beliefs and policies in support of a traditional Christian, ranked, aristocratic society wedded to old institutions and suspicious of change. In the international field this conservatism was epitomized by Metternich's policies, the Holy Alliance, and the concert of Europe. In domestic politics, this conservatism was characterized by the restoration of power to the traditional monarchs and aristocrats, the renewed influence of

Christianity, and the suppression of liberal and nationalistic movements. Yet conservatives were faced with formidable opponents even during the early years after the fall of Napoleon. The struggle between conservatism and liberalism, which would last into the twentieth century, had just begun.

SUGGESTED READING

General

F. Artz, *Reaction and Revolution, 1814–1832* (1968). The standard survey of the period.

E. J. Hobsbawm, *The Age of Revolution, Europe 1789 to 1848* (1970). A good Marxist survey covering this period.

J. Weiss, *Conservatism in Europe, 1770–1945* (1977). A good analysis of conservatism in its broad context.

The Congress of Vienna

C. Brinton, *The Lives of Talleyrand* (1963). Sympathetic biography of one of the leading participants.

H. Kissinger, *A World Restored* (1964). An interesting, sympathetic interpretation.

H. Nicolson, *The Congress of Vienna: A Study in Allied Unity 1812–22* (1970). Excellent volume on the subject.

The Bourbon Restoration in France

A. Jardin and A. J. Tudesq, *Restoration and Reaction* (1984). Covers France well.

P. Mansel, *Louis XVIII* (1981). A good recent biography.

Reaction in Central Europe

T. Hamerow, *Restoration, Revolution, and Reaction: Economics and Politics in Germany, 1815–1871* (1958). A respected, difficult analysis encompassing the period.

A. J. P. Taylor, *The Hapsburg Monarchy, 1809–1918* (1965). Lively and scholarly.

Conservatism in Great Britain

N. Gash, *Aristocracy and People. Britain, 1815–1867* (1979). Balanced coverage.

Reaction and Repression in Russia

A. Palmer, *Alexander I: Tsar of War and Peace* (1974). A thorough biography.

A. Ulam, *Russia's Failed Revolutionaries* (1981). Contains a good analysis of the Decembrists.

CHAPTER 43
Liberalism and Revolution, 1830–1850

FIGURE 43.1 **The Reform Bill of 1832** This engraving from the April 15, 1832, issue of *Bell's Weekly Messenger* depicts the successful struggle to enact the liberal Reform Bill of 1832 in Great Britain. At the top, under the banner of reform, Whig leaders unite with the king to pass the bill. At the bottom, the British lion uses reform to defeat the fleeing Tories and the dragon representing the rotten-borough system. (The Mansell Collection)

During the Restoration years following the defeat of Napoleon, liberalism was suppressed by the conservatives who came back into power. Between 1830 and 1850 liberals gained a series of victories, often by way of revolutions or threatened revolutions, marking this period as a heyday for liberalism (see Map 43.1). By the early 1830s Greece, Belgium, and most of Spain's New World colonies had gained their freedom. The restored French Bourbons had been overthrown in a liberal revolt. In Great Britain the Reform Bill of 1832 marked a new liberal era. A new constitution in 1834 brought liberal institutions to Spain. Liberal revolts and movements had at least raised their heads in Poland, Italy, and parts of Germany. By 1850 liberal institutions had spread and revolutions, almost all of which included strong liberal elements, had occurred in nearly every country of continental Europe.

1. GENERAL NATURE OF NINETEENTH-CENTURY LIBERALISM

Liberalism is a difficult term to define. It has various shades and from time to time changes its complexion. During the nineteenth century, liberalism had developed into an ideology—a loose set of beliefs about the world and how it should be.

The roots of liberalism stretch back through the French Revolution and the Enlightenment to the seventeenth-century political thoughts of John Locke and others. At the base of liberalism was a belief in individualism. Liberals optimistically believed that individuals, unaided and free from outside forces or institutions, should pursue their own interests. Individuals deserved equality before the law and the right to embark on careers open to talent. Government should be constitutional and based on popular sovereignty. The people should be represented by an elected legislature, to whom government ministers were responsible. Government should be limited in its powers, with such individual freedoms as freedom of the press, of speech, and of assembly guaranteed. The role of the government should be that of a passive police officer, enforcing laws

and contracts. Government should interfere in economic life as little as possible, leaving that realm to private enterprise. Liberals were also anticlerical; that is, they opposed interference in government by organized religion. During the first half of the nineteenth century, liberals were usually nationalists, since nationalism at that time was primarily concerned with freeing peoples from alien rule and uniting them under one flag, and nationalism seemed consistent with popular sovereignty, constitutional government, and people's rights. Liberals, particularly during the first half of the nineteenth century, were not democrats; liberals wanted to limit the right to vote to those holding wealth and the educated. Only later in the nineteenth century did liberals begin to favor universal male suffrage.

Liberals typically came from the middle class—the commercial and industrial bourgeoisie, the professionals, and the intellectuals. Their chief opponents were the vested interests of traditional society—the aristocracy, the clergy, and the military—seeking to retain their favored positions. The peasantry was still generally conservative, strongly influenced by the clergy and sometimes by the aristocracy, and not very active in politics. Liberals were sometimes contemptuous of the propertyless masses below, forming alliances with them against conservatives only so far as necessary. Middle-class liberals' contempt for those below them was often a mask for fear; their contempt of the aristocrats above them was tinged with envy.

Liberals stood in contrast to conservatives. Liberals were optimistic about the individual; conservatives were pessimistic. Liberals had great faith in reason; conservatives argued that reason was too abstract. Liberals favored many of the ideas and reforms of the Enlightenment and French Revolution; conservatives attacked them. Liberals valued the individual over the society; conservatives felt the individual was secondary. For liberals the state was an agent of the people; for conservatives the state was a growing organism not to be tampered with.

After 1850 the nature of liberalism would change. The outcomes of the revolutions occurring between 1848 and 1850 were a blow to liberals. As commerce and industry spread, the bourgeoisie

Map 43.1 **EUROPEAN REVOLTS, 1820–1831 AND 1848–1849** The first map indicates the location and dates of revolts, both major and minor, taking place between 1820 and 1831. The second map indicates the location of revolutions between 1848 and 1849. While the specifics of each outburst differed, most involved demands for liberal reform. Together, these maps reveal the geographical breadth of revolutionary activity during this period.

acquired wealth and power, and soon the vested interests of this class made it more hostile to rapid political and social changes. Its place in movements for political and social change was taken by the industrial working class, which was slowly becoming politically active. Groups deriving from the working classes, lower middle classes, and intelligentsia began to advocate greatly increased government intervention in economic affairs on behalf of the masses as well as the participation of the masses in political life. More progressive advocates of liberalism joined these groups in arguing for greater democratization of political life and government intervention in economic and social affairs. This, however, takes us beyond the primary concerns of this chapter. Liberalism flowered between 1830 and 1850, and this story needs to be told.

Sites of Revolts 1848-1849
Boundary of German Confederation

0   200 MILES

2. POLITICAL AND SOCIAL REFORM IN GREAT BRITAIN

During the 1820s Great Britain had already taken some moderate steps on the road to liberal reform (see pp. 541–542), but these steps did not go to the heart of the matter—broadening the franchise. Pressures mounted on the conservative Tories to effect electoral reform, but they were unwilling or unable to do it. Finally in 1830 the aristocratic but more liberal Whigs, long out of power, drove the Tory government from office.

The new prime minister, Earl Grey, immediately introduced and forced through Parliament the Reform Bill of 1832. This bill redistributed the seats of the House of Commons, taking away many from the "rotten boroughs" (once-important towns that had dwindled in population or had even disappeared) and giving them to the industrial cities of the north. The suffrage was extended to all those who owned or rented property with an annual value of ten pounds. It is estimated that the number of eligible voters was thereby increased from approximately four hundred and fifty thousand to eight hundred thousand out of a total population of some 16 million. Although on the surface the Reform Bill of 1832 appears innocuous, it represents a great turning point in British history. The long era of dominance of the conservative landed aristocracy was ending and that of more liberal property owners, including the commercial and industrial bourgeoisie, had begun. The supremacy of the House of Commons over the House of Lords, which had opposed the Reform Bill, was established. A new period of political and social reform had opened.

Both political parties recognized the new era. The Whig party, supported by the industrial bourgeoisie but containing a right wing of liberal aristocrats and left wing of intellectual radicals, changed its name to the Liberal party. For the next half century the Liberals were often in power, under the leadership of such personalities as Lord Grey, Lord John Russell, Viscount Palmerston, and eventually William E. Gladstone. The Tory party was still predominantly the party of the landed aristocracy, but it contained some bourgeois elements, and its more liberal wing, led first by Sir Robert Peel and later by Benjamin Disraeli, was now in ascendancy. The somewhat discredited "Tory" designation was changed to "Conservative."

Both parties, conscious of the rising importance of public opinion, supported a series of reforms. In 1833 slavery was abolished in the British Empire with compensation for slave owners. The Municipal Corporations Act applied the principles of the Reform Bill of 1832 to local government. The old penal code was reformed, reducing the number of capital offenses to three and generally softening the punishment of criminals. The penny post increased the circulation of mail and literature. Parliament granted small but gradually increasing subsidies to the schools, most of which were run by the Anglican church. Between 1833 and 1847 Parliament passed a series of laws that prohibited the employment in textile mills of children under nine and limited the hours of older children and of women to ten hours a day. The employment of women and children in underground mines was prohibited. In 1846 the Corn Laws (the import tariff on grain), long opposed by liberals and the object of a major reform movement, were repealed, reducing the price of bread.

These reforms were not the work of the masses but of wealthy middle-class and aristocratic liberals along with a few intellectual radicals. The only reform movement initiated by the laboring classes in this period was the Chartist movement (see Figure 43.2). The hard-pressed urban workers, bitterly aware that they had been bypassed by the Reform Bill of 1832 and that they were not sharing in the unprecedented national prosperity, were dissatisfied with the reforms of the bourgeois liberals. In 1838 working-class leaders drew up a People's Charter, which demanded (1) universal male suffrage, (2) the secret ballot, (3) removal of property qualifications for members of Parliament, (4) pay for members of Parliament, (5) annual elections, and (6) equal electoral districts. The charter was twice presented to Parliament and twice summarily rejected. In 1848, the Chartists planned a huge petition and demonstration in London. The frightened government prepared to use force. However, only a few mild disorders followed the third rejection, and the movement came to an end. Nevertheless, the Chartist movement had its influence. The most immediate result of the movement was to make both political parties aware of the growing influence of the working classes and of the advisability of winning their favor. In the following decades, all the demands in the charter were enacted into law.

3. LIBERAL REVOLUTIONS IN BELGIUM AND FRANCE

The year 1830 was a bad one for conservatives in Belgium and France. The union forced upon Belgium and the Netherlands at Vienna had never been a happy one, and Belgian discontent with Dutch rule had been mounting for fifteen years. In addition to differences in language, the Belgians were Roman Catholic, whereas the Dutch were predominantly Calvinist. The Belgian economy was based on industry, the Dutch on commerce. Belgium, more populous than the Netherlands, was not given its fair share of representation in the government. When the halfhearted efforts of the Dutch failed to suppress the revolt, Austria and Russia threatened to intervene in the interests of legitimacy and tranquillity. They were deterred by British and French support of Belgian independence, which was therefore achieved. Belgium soon adopted a liberal constitution and would remain a liberal nation throughout the nineteenth century.

The July Revolution in France was an even more serious blow to conservatism. Liberals and the people of Paris had toppled the reactionary

Figure 43.2. **Chartist Print**   This print shows Chartists in a powerful but peaceful procession in London. (The Mansell Collection)

regime of Charles X, the last of the Bourbons. There was strong sentiment to form a republic, but a coalition of liberal legislators and leaders of the wealthy bourgeoisie wanted only a constitutional monarchy. They set themselves up as a provisional government and named a new king: Louis Philippe (1830–1848), head of the house of Orléans and a cousin of the departed Bourbon.

Louis Philippe, recognizing that a new era had come to France, catered to the rich. He assumed the role of the Citizen King, casting aside the trappings of royalty and donning those of the Parisian upper middle class. His eighteen-year reign came to be called the bourgeois monarchy (see Figure 43.3). His twofold policy, from which he never veered, was order and prosperity at home and peace abroad. One of his first acts was to lower the taxpaying requirements for voting from three hundred francs to two hundred francs per year. This act raised the electorate from approximately

one hundred thousand to two hundred fifty thousand in a nation of some 32 million people and placed political control in the hands of the wealthy. Louis Philippe's chief minister during the 1840s was the historian François Guizot. He was a thoroughgoing liberal. He believed in government by the property-owning classes, particularly the bourgeoisie. He therefore opposed any further extension of the suffrage, even to members of the intelligentsia like himself.

Beneath the surface, problems simmered. The national prosperity was not shared by the working class, who suffered the usual hardships, insecurity, and maladjustments that accompanied the advent of industrialization. Slums mushroomed in Paris and the industrial cities of the northeast. Workers clamored for the right to vote and the right to organize unions but got neither. Poor harvests, financial crises, and growing unemployment in 1846 and 1847 heightened the frustration.

4. THE REVOLUTION OF 1848 IN FRANCE

The mounting discontent came to a climax in February 1848 when the government prohibited the holding of a reform banquet. Street brawling broke out in Paris. Louis Philippe attempted to quiet people by dismissing Guizot, but the appeasement failed. A shot fired during a brawl between a mob and the troops guarding the residence of Guizot unnerved the troops, who fired a murderous volley into the mob and set off a full-scale insurrection. Barricades flew up all over Paris, and when the disaffected national guardsmen began going over to the rebels, Louis Philippe followed Guizot into exile in Great Britain.

The working classes of Paris had triumphed, but only for a fleeting moment. A group of bourgeois liberals led by Alphonse de Lamartine hastily set up a provisional government that was republican in sentiment but in which the only prominent radical member was the socialist Louis Blanc. The provisional government immediately called for the election by universal male suffrage of an assembly to draw up a new constitution. Under the pressure of the Paris populace, the provisional government admitted the workingmen to the national guard, thereby arming them, and set up emergency-relief national workshops. The workshops, however, were a parody of those outlined by Louis Blanc, who cried that they were deliberately planned so as to ensure their failure. Workers of all kinds were assigned to hastily arranged projects, and when more workers enrolled than could be used, the surplus workers were paid almost as much to remain idle. Tens of thousands rushed to Paris to join the workshops. The resulting demoralization of labor and the cost to the taxpayers thoroughly frightened all property owners, the peasants as well as the bourgeoisie. The elections held in April 1848 resulted in an overwhelming victory for the conservative republicans and limited monarchists, in part thanks to the conservatism of the landowning peasants, who constituted the great majority of the French population. The socialists were crushed. Even in Paris, their only real stronghold, they won a mere handful of seats.

One of the first acts of the newly elected constitutional assembly was to abolish the national workshops. The workers were told either to join the army or to go look for work in the provinces. The desperate Paris working class resorted to arms and the barricades: "Better to die from bullets than from starvation!" For four days all-out war raged in the streets of Paris between the working class, armed with national guard rifles, and the regular army of the conservative constitutional assembly, using artillery in addition to small arms. When the last barricade had been destroyed, some fifteen hundred, mostly workingmen, had been killed. Several hundred were sent overseas to French colonial prisons. Louis Blanc fled to Great Britain. The bloody "June Days" widened the cleavage between radical urban Paris and conservative rural France—a cleavage that has long complicated France's public life.

The inexperienced constitutional assembly hurriedly drew up a constitution establishing the Second French Republic. (The First French Republic had been declared by the revolutionists in 1792 and had been overthrown by Napoleon in 1804.) Legislative power was given to a single-chamber legislature elected by universal male suffrage. All executive and administrative powers were placed in the hands of a president, also elected by universal male suffrage. The first presidential election, in December 1848, resulted in a sweeping victory for Louis Napoleon Bonaparte, nephew of Napoleon Bonaparte, as president. It took this ambitious and clever politician only three years to destroy the weak constitution and to take power in a coup d'état.

The Revolution of 1848 in France involved the first violent reaction of the urban working class against bourgeois liberalism. The working class was too small as yet to make any headway outside Paris. The revolution shattered against the solid mass of landowning peasantry allied with the propertied bourgeoisie. Its bloody suppression left a heritage of bitterness that would cloud the future of France.

5. THE REVOLUTION OF 1848 IN CENTRAL EUROPE

The February explosion in Paris set central Europe aflame with revolt (see Figure 43.4). However, the Revolution of 1848 in central Europe was a rising

FIGURE 43.3.   Daumier, "The Chamber of Deputies" This print by the French artist Honoré Daumier presents a satirical view of the French Chamber of Deputies during Louis Philippe's July Monarchy. This governmental body, though clearly more liberal than its predecessor under Charles X, was dominated by the relatively wealthy, satisfied upper classes. (The Art Institute of Chicago)

of the intelligentsia and the middle classes with a little support from the working class. Furthermore, in 1848 the cause of liberalism in central Europe was entwined with that of nationalism. The two forces frequently conflicted with each other, nationalism proving to be the more virile of the two.

The most crucial center of revolution was Vienna. This beautiful metropolis was the seat of the Hapsburg government, which not only ruled over the various language groups of the Austrian Empire but also dominated both the German Confederation and Italy. When early in March 1848 news of the events in Paris arrived in Vienna, the long-repressed student liberals began rioting in the streets and clamoring for an end to the Metternich

system. As the uprising gained in momentum, Metternich was forced to flee for his life. The Hapsburg emperor, Ferdinand I, hastily abolished the repressive laws, ended serfdom, and promised constitutional representative government. However, he too was soon forced to flee his own capital. Meanwhile, the Magyars in Hungary, under the leadership of the eloquent Louis Kossuth, set up a liberal autonomous Hungary. The Czechs did the same in Bohemia and called for a Pan-Slavic congress to meet at Prague. In Austria's Italian provinces of Lombardy and Venetia the rebellious populace drove the Austrian garrisons into defensive fortresses and declared their independence. By June 1848 it appeared that the Hapsburg Empire would become liberalized, fall apart along

FIGURE 43.4. Revolution in Germany In central Europe in 1848, liberal sentiment emerged in the form of public demonstrations by the intelligentsia—particularly the university students. Here, in June of 1848, German students convene at Wartburg, the castle that had once served as a refuge for Martin Luther. (Copyright Staatsbibliothek, Berlin)

national (language group) lines, or both.

In Berlin, the capital of Prussia, the news from Paris and Vienna set liberals demonstrating in the streets. The vacillating Hohenzollern king, Frederick William IV, promised a liberal constitution and support for German national unity. As in Paris, an unauthorized volley into the mob set off bloody street fighting, which the king ended by making further concessions to the liberals. Hohenzollern Prussia, like Hapsburg Austria, appeared for the moment to be on the road to liberal government.

Meanwhile, in the rest of the German states a group of self-appointed liberals called for a pop-ularly elected assembly to meet at Frankfurt to construct a liberal German nation. The two questions confronting the Frankfurt Assembly were whether the German-speaking portions of the multilingual Hapsburg Empire should be included in the projected German nation and who should head the new nation. Tied in with the Austrian question was that of religion. With Austria (and Bohemia, which was alleged to be predominantly German), the Roman Catholics would predominate, and without Austria and Bohemia, the Protestants. For eleven precious months these knotty problems were debated. Eventually Austria virtually excluded itself by refusing to consider coming into the new German nation without its non-German provinces. By a narrow margin it was decided to offer the emperorship to the king of Prussia. But now it was too late. The situation in Vienna and Berlin had drastically changed.

In Austria the inexperience and weakness of the liberals and the rivalries and conflicts among the various language groups played into the hands of the Hapsburgs. Skillfully playing off one group against another, the Austrian rulers beat down the liberal and national revolts one after the other. In Hungary they had the help of the reactionary Nicholas I of Russia, whose army crushed the rebels.

In Prussia, too, the liberals were weak and inexperienced. The unstable Frederick William IV, after his first uncertainty, gradually fell under the influence of his militaristic and reactionary Junker advisers. Further stiffened by the news from Vienna that the Hapsburgs had regained their autocratic position, he spurned the German crown offered him by the Frankfurt Assembly and replaced the constitution drawn up by Prussian liberals with one that was a travesty of liberalism.

The Hohenzollerns' rejection of the crown of a united liberal Germany blasted the hopes of the Frankfurt Assembly. When a few of the most determined attempted to continue their efforts, they were dispersed by Prussian troops.

6. REVOLUTION IN ITALY

On the Italian peninsula 1848 was a year of revolution. These revolts reflected an already long history of liberal and nationalistic movements in Italy. Soon after 1815 Italian nationalists began to form secret societies, called *Carbonari* (charcoal burners), which met at night around charcoal fires to plot freedom from Austrian and local tyranny and to plan for national unification. In 1821 revolts erupted in Naples, Sicily, and Piedmont, but all were short-lived. In the early 1830s a romantic young intellectual, Giuseppe Mazzini (1805–1872), organized the Young Italy society, which was dedicated to the task of achieving a free, united Italian nation. Although the first uprisings inspired by the Carbonari and Young Italy were crushed by Austrian arms, the Italian national movement, once aroused, could not so easily be suppressed.

In 1848 revolutions occurred in Sicily, Naples, Piedmont, and Tuscany. By 1849 republics had been established in Rome and Venice, and other Italian states had adopted liberal constitutions. Yet the time for the permanent overthrow of Austrian rule and the unification of Italy had not yet arrived. Austrian arms (and in Rome, French arms) prevailed. It would be another ten years before liberalism and nationalism, under the leadership of Piedmont, would gain a more lasting victory in Italy.

7. AN ASSESSMENT

The struggles between liberals and conservatives, which had resulted in several liberal victories since 1830, came to a climax with the revolutions of 1848. Economic turmoil, demands for liberal reform, nationalistic sentiments, and ineptitude by frightened governments combined to spell a series of stunning victories for revolutionaries in almost every major country in Europe. The major exceptions were England, which had compromised in response to demands for liberal reform, and Russia, which remained the bastion of reaction. Once in power, revolutionaries initiated major reforms, most of which fit well with the recognized canons of liberalism.

Nevertheless, the revolutionaries' victories were short-lived. By 1850 the conservative forces of order had regained control. Louis Napoleon, soon to be Napoleon III, sat as president in France. The Prussian king regained control over his lands and ended hopes for a liberal unified German nation. In Austria and Hungary the Hapsburgs were again in power, just as they were in their Italian lands. Liberalism and nationalism were not yet strong enough to form new, lasting governments in these areas.

Several factors account for the defeat of liberal and nationalist forces, though the situation differed in each case. First, the alliance between middle-class liberals, radicals, socialists, artisans, and workers was one of convenience. Once revolutionary forces were in power, the interests of the various groups were too divergent for the alliance to hold. This division was most clearly evident in France, where the frightened middle class and conservative peasantry broke with the Parisian working classes, as revealed by the outcome of the elections and the bloody June Days. Second, liberalism and nationalism were forces that worked together when out of power; once in power they often were at cross-purposes. This lack of harmony between liberalism and nationalism was particularly so in central Europe where the aspirations of German, Polish, Magyar, Croatian, Serbian, and other nationalities conflicted with efforts to form new governments with liberal institutions. Third, the strength of conservatism and the forces of order should not be underestimated. With industrialization only beginning in central Europe, the main source of liberal strength, the industrial middle class, and an important source of revolutionary urban discontent, the working class, were weak. Revolutionary liberal leaders were inexperienced, particularly in central Europe and Italy. Once the shock of initial defeat was over, experienced conservatives marshalled their resources, and forces of order overcame the now divided revolutionary forces.

The reestablished governments had learned lessons from 1848 and maintained themselves with new vigor. In a few cases liberal reforms initiated between 1848 and 1850 were retained, and in other cases those reforms in modified forms would be passed in succeeding years. But the great period of revolutionary liberalism ended in 1850.

SUGGESTED READING

General

W. L. Langer, *Political Upheaval, 1832–1852* (1969). Excellent survey of the period.

Liberalism

G. de Ruggiero, *History of European Liberalism* (1959). A classic study.

J. S. Schapiro, *Liberalism: Its Meaning and History* (1958). Good brief summary; includes readings.

Reform in Great Britain

D. Beales, *From Castlereagh to Gladstone, 1815–1885* (1969). A useful study of political history.

M. Brock, *The Great Reform Act* (1974). Solid, scholarly, respected.

D. Thompson, *The Chartists: Popular Politics in the Industrial Revolution* (1984). A thorough, recent study.

The Bourgeois Monarchy in France

D. Pinkney, *The French Revolution of 1830* (1972). Excellent study of the topic.

J. B. Wolf, *France, 1814–1919: The Rise of a Liberal Democratic Society.* (1963). Excellent survey.

Central Europe and Italy

I. Deak, *The Lawful Revolution: Louis Kossuth and the Hungarians, 1848–9* (1979). Excellent study of the individual and the revolution.

T. Hamerow, *Restoration, Revolution, Reaction 1815–1871* (1966). Highly respected analysis of Germany.

Gaetano Salvemini, *Mazzini* (1957). Excellent introduction to Mazzini's ideas.

The Revolutions of 1848

G. Duveau, *1848: The Making of a Revolution* (1967). Excellent study of the 1848 revolutions in France.

L. B. Namier, *1848: The Revolution of the Intellectuals* (1964). An eminent historian shows how nationalism wrecked the liberal movement.

P. Robertson, *The Revolutions of 1848: A Social History* (1960). Scholarly and lucid.

P. Stearns, *1848: The Revolutionary Tide in Europe* (1974). A good summary.

CHAPTER 44

The Industrial Revolution

FIGURE 44.1.   François Bonhomme, "Workshop with Mechanical Sieves," 1859   This realistic painting of a factory interior in France shows the mixture of raw material (zinc ore), machines, and division of labor that epitomized the Industrial Revolution. Men, women, and children work together in this dismal environment; but the men have the more skilled jobs (a foreman sits in the rear to the left), while the women and children are assigned to the less skilled jobs (sorting and splitting chunks of ore). (Conservatoire National des Arts et Métiers)

The term *Industrial Revolution* refers to the vast economic and social changes initiated in Great Britain during the last few decades of the eighteenth century and spreading to the Continent and other parts of the world during the nineteenth and twentieth centuries. It involved a shift from production by individuals alone or in small groups using hand tools powered by muscles, wind, and water to production by organized groups of people in factories using machinery powered by steam. These changes in the methods of production resulted in sustained economic growth. In the process of industrializing, nations experienced rapid population growth and a general shift from a rural society based on agriculture to an urban society based on manufacturing. Along with the French Revolution, the Industrial Revolution set in motion changes that would transform almost all aspects of life in the West during the nineteenth and twentieth centuries.

1. THE COURSE OF THE INDUSTRIAL REVOLUTION

The Industrial Revolution began in Great Britain for several reasons. Demand for the production of goods in Great Britain was growing rapidly during the eighteenth century, thanks to relatively widespread domestic prosperity, a growing population, and abundant markets within Britain's large colonial empire. Great Britain was well positioned to meet this growing demand for goods. It had an abundance of conveniently located raw materials, such as coal and iron. Investment capital amassed from merchants and landowners was available to enterprising entrepreneurs through family connections, partnership arrangements, and banks. Thanks to their leading role in the eighteenth-century agricultural revolution, Britain's farmers could more efficiently produce food for urban populations (see pp. 466–467). A large, mobile force of skilled and unskilled workers provided industrial entrepreneurs with a cheap supply of labor. Hindrances to commerce and industry so common in other countries were not present to the same degree in Great Britain. British transportation facilities were good, there were fewer governmental restrictions on commerce, and wealthy citizens did not disdain involvement in commerce and industry. Britain's government had been stable since 1689 and was strongly influenced by capitalistic landowners, merchants, and bankers.

British inventors and entrepreneurs responded to these conditions by developing new machines, sources of power, transportation facilities, and factories. These new developments increased production and trade tremendously and made Great Britain an early leader in the Industrial Revolution. By the middle of the nineteenth century, Great Britain was the first industrialized society. It was urbanized, covered with railway lines and canals, and dotted with factories. It produced far greater quantities of textiles, metals, and machines than any other country.

During the eighteenth century, nations on the Continent lacked this combination of circumstances so conducive to British industrialization. In addition, between 1789 and 1815 the Continent suffered from the economic, social, and political turmoil of the French revolutionary and Napoleonic periods. After 1815, and particularly after 1830, the Industrial Revolution spread, first to Belgium, shortly thereafter to France, parts of Germany, and the United States, and later to other areas of Europe. At first Continental entrepreneurs copied British inventions and imported skilled British laborers and technicians. Governments recognized the British lead and became more directly involved in promoting industrialization by supporting the construction of railways, subsidizing certain industries, and erecting protective tariffs for domestic industries. By the end of the nineteenth century, countries that once lagged far behind Great Britain were competing successfully for industrial markets.

2. TECHNOLOGY AND TRANSPORTATION

Probably the most dramatic change the Industrial Revolution brought about was the continual creation of new technology and transportation facilities (see Figure 44.2). A virtual explosion of inventions increased productivity and mechanized productions, above all in textiles, mining, and metallurgy. The steam engine provided a vast new

FIGURE 44.2. Railroad, Ship, and Factories This nineteenth-century print shows the outward signs of the Industrial Revolution: railroads, steamships on canals, and smoke-belching factories. (The Bettmann Archive)

source of reliable power. New roads, canals, and especially railroads provided regular, inexpensive means of transportation for people and materials.

The cotton textile industry was the first to become mechanized. In 1733 John Kay invented the flying shuttle, which doubled the speed at which cloth could be woven. In 1764 James Hargreaves hitched eight spindles to his wife's spinning wheel instead of one. The result was the far more efficient spinning jenny (named after his daughter Jenny). The number of spindles was soon multiplied. Five years later, Richard Arkwright patented the water frame, a system of rollers driven by water power, which spun a much finer and firmer thread than the jenny. In 1779 Samuel Crompton, combining the principles of the spinning jenny and the water frame, produced the hybrid spinning mule—a great improvement over both. In 1785 Edmund Cartwright invented the power loom.

The mechanization of both spinning and weaving greatly increased demand for cotton. In 1793 a young American, Eli Whitney, invented the cotton gin, which helped meet this demand. Removing the seeds from cotton fiber by hand was a tedious process; one person could separate only five or six pounds a day. Cotton was therefore grown only in small patches. Whitney's gin not only made possible an adequate supply of cotton for Britain's mills but also brought into existence the huge cotton plantations worked by black slaves in the American South.

Meanwhile, better sources of power were being developed. In 1769 James Watt significantly improved on earlier, inefficient steam engines and invented the first steam engine that could be used to drive machinery. The power that could be generated by the steam engine was almost unlimited.

Constant improvements were made in the mining of coal and the production of iron, crucial for heavy industrialization. As large quantities of relatively inexpensive coal and iron became available, still better machines were produced and a sufficient supply of fuel was available to drive them.

An integral part of the Industrial Revolution was the improvement of transportation and communications. Without both, sufficient quantities of raw materials to feed the hungry machines and adequate markets to absorb the finished products would not have been available. Moreover, the massive population shifts accompanying industrialization would have been much more difficult.

The last decades of the eighteenth century and the first decades of the nineteenth were a time of road and canal building in Great Britain, France, and the United States. Around the turn of the century Thomas Telford and John McAdam in Great Britain pioneered in the construction of well-drained and surfaced roads. In Great Britain canals were particularly useful for transporting coal. In the United States completion of the Erie Canal in

1825 opened up the Great Lakes region to lucrative world communications and ensured the primacy of New York City as the chief port and metropolis of the United States.

A more dramatic revolution in transportation came with the application of the steam engine to locomotion. In 1807 Robert Fulton demonstrated the practicability of the steamship by steaming his *Clermont* the one hundred fifty miles up the Hudson from New York to Albany in thirty-two hours. In 1825 George Stephenson in Great Britain convincingly demonstrated the usefulness of the locomotive by hauling a train of thirty-four cars twenty-five miles at twelve miles an hour. By the middle of the nineteenth century, railway lines covered Great Britain and were spreading rapidly on the Continent and in North America. The railroad transported people and material, opened up areas to commerce and urban growth, constituted a major source of demand for industrial products such as coal and iron, and symbolized the spread of the new industrialized society.

3. THE FACTORY SYSTEM

Many of the components of the Industrial Revolution were brought together by the development of the factory system. Industrial capitalists invested considerable funds in machines, buildings, and raw materials. They trained workers to do specific jobs in conjunction with artificially powered machines, which increasingly determined the pace and nature of the work. Industrial capitalists organized the process of producing goods into a series of steps and specialized tasks. Their new factories pumped out unprecedented quantities of manufactured goods.

Before the factory system was instituted, goods were produced either by craft guilds or under the domestic, or "putting out," system. (See Chapter 36.) Under this system workers did as much or as little work as they wished without supervision. The operations were necessarily small in scale, much time was lost distributing the raw materials from cottage to cottage and collecting the finished products, and uniformity of quality was virtually impossible to attain.

The spread of the factory system spelled the end of the domestic system of manufacturing. The rise of the factory system resulted in a tremendous growth of productivity in manufacturing and a seemingly fantastic increase of manufactured goods. Artisans, although not immediately displaced, found it increasingly difficult to compete with factories that were producing similar products much more rapidly and inexpensively. As the factory system took hold, hastily and cheaply built living quarters for workers and their families were crowded around factories. This factory system was the origin of the modern mill town and industrial city. It also contributed to the dramatic urbanization of industrial societies in the nineteenth century and fundamental changes among social classes in these societies.

4. SOCIAL CHANGES

Population Growth and Urbanization

A large variety of far-reaching social changes are related to the Industrial Revolution. The broadest changes were demographic. Population increased dramatically. In Great Britain population grew from about 9 million in 1780 to almost 21 million in 1850. European population as a whole rose from about 188 million in 1800 to 266 million in 1850. The exact causes for this explosion of population are difficult to pinpoint, but it was probably a result of a declining death rate (thanks to a decline in epidemics and an increase of food supplies) and a rise in the birth rate (caused by an earlier departure from home, earlier marriage, and earlier child bearing in an increasingly mobile population).

A more direct result of industrialization was the shift of population from rural to urban areas and the growth in size and number of cities. In England and Wales in 1800 about 17 percent of the population lived in cities of over twenty thousand inhabitants. By 1850 the figure grew to about 35 percent. This pattern was being repeated in other areas of Europe as they industrialized. The consequences were all too apparent. Already overcrowded, devoid of mass transportation facilities, equipped at best with vastly inadequate sanitation facilities, the cities became more densely packed and unhealthy each year. At the same time, these cities exhibited a vibrancy and image of opportunities that continued to attract people. Often the alternatives available in the countryside were even less appealing hovels and rural slums.

Social Classes

Even before the Industrial Revolution, the French Revolution had already altered many people's perceptions of the social order. Industrialization added economic and social foundations to this new understanding of society. People viewed themselves less as part of a rigid, ranked, ordered society and more as part of a flexible society of a few classes with mobility between classes both possible and proper. Class membership was not a formal designation but a description of the amount of money, the type of work, the style of life, and the beliefs held by people. Nevertheless, this does not mean that society had in reality become egalitarian. As in centuries before, there remained sharp differences between different classes of people.

The two classes most firmly tied to traditional rural society, the aristocracy and the peasantry, were doomed by the Industrial Revolution. Over the nineteenth century they would decline in number, wealth, position, and influence. Yet the extent and speed of this decline should not be overestimated. It was not until the second half of the nineteenth century that urban dwellers outnumbered rural populations in even the most industrialized nations; in some countries, such as France, the small farm was more the rule than the exception. Moreover, the aristocracy remained influential even in industrializing nations, commanding considerable wealth and prestige. Aristocrats still dominated many localities, staffed upper levels of government, and controlled certain professions such as the diplomatic and military officer corps.

The middle classes as a whole and the industrial bourgeoisie in particular grew in numbers and profited from the Industrial Revolution. Those who benefited most were the large factory owners, bankers, and merchants, who amassed great fortunes and rose toward the top of society. The smaller factory owners, professionals, shopkeep-ers, and "white-collar" workers who made up the various ranks of the middle class also benefited. They gained their wealth by mental rather than physical labor and by the investment or manipulation of capital. This middle class tended to favor liberal reforms and believe in certain values such as hard work, thrift, careers open to talent, and prudence. Over time they outdistanced their two main competitors: the aristocracy, which remained dependent on the traditional society and rural economy, and the artisans, who were increasingly unable to compete with factory production. Though still a minority (even in the largest cities such as Paris they constituted no more than 25 percent of the population), the middle classes gained in prestige, political power, and cultural influence thanks to their growing wealth and numbers. During the second half of the nineteenth century they would gain dominance over much of Western society.

The urban working classes changed, grew, and suffered during the Industrial Revolution. Many of these workers were domestics, and this class grew still larger as the middle classes gained the wealth to hire them. Artisans remained a large class throughout the nineteenth century. On the whole they commanded better pay than the less skilled factory workers, and wealthier purchasers demanded their products. However, new factories increasingly displaced the artisans, and they often reacted radically, sometimes violently, to the changes brought by industrialization. They tended to join radical political organizations, lead in union-organizing activities and strikes, and be the most active elements of violent and revolutionary protests. After mid-century, this class would decline in size.

The industrial proletariat was the newest class. Demand from new factories swelled the ranks of the factory workers. Large numbers of surplus agricultural workers and displaced artisans were absorbed into factory work along with part of the overall increase in population. It was this industrial proletariat that most visibly grew with industrialization and stood in most striking contrast to the industrial bourgeoisie.

Factory workers were ruthlessly exploited by factory owners, particularly during the early stages of the Industrial Revolution. Wages for a

FIGURE 44.3. Child Labor This woodcut, dated 1853, portrays the supervisor of an English cotton factory whipping a young boy. Incidents similar to this were not uncommon during the first phase of the Industrial Revolution. Such conditions spurred speculation on ways to control industrial capitalism. (New York Public Library)

work week of six or seven days at twelve to sixteen hours per day were kept to a subsistence level. Unmarried women and orphaned children were more cheaply and easily exploited than men and were thus employed in the new factories. Contracts were made with orphanages for the employment of the children. Young children were marched off before daybreak to work all day in the factories. If they fell behind the pace set by the machines, they were beaten (see Figure 44.3). Sometimes they were chained to their machines.

After the first few decades of the Industrial Revolution, a pattern of hiring whole families to work in the new factories emerged. Although this system meant that the amount of wages necessary for subsistence was kept to a minimum, it at least allowed the working-class family to stay together. By the middle of the nineteenth century the practice of hiring families and children was declining, but life for the industrial working class remained oppressive. The factories and mines were dark, dirty, and dangerous. The dwellings of the workers were likely to be hovels clustered around smoky, noisy mills or mine entrances. The workers were frequently compelled to spend their wages at company stores, paying monopoly prices arbitrarily set by the owners. Work lost its dignity. The factory workers were disciplined to the clock and the machine. The dull, monotonous, robotlike repetition of a single operation on a machine brought the workers none of the satisfaction and pride of skilled craftsmanship.

Many historians and social scientists argue that statistics show that the early factory workers received higher wages and enjoyed a better standard of living than they had ever had as agricultural or urban workers. Clearly, industrial workers were reaping material benefits from the Industrial Revolution after 1850, but in the years before 1850 workers may have lost more than they gained. Certainly the life of the agricultural laborer or artisan should not be romanticized: The conditions of work and life among the agricultural and urban poor had always been hard. But industrial work involved vast changes that were extraordinarily painful. The longer hours, the greater insecurity, the limits on freedom, and the more frequent unemployment of the uprooted slum-dwelling factory worker of the early nineteenth century do not appear in statistics of wages and prices (see Figure 44.4). The overall picture of the industrial proletariat during the first half of the nineteenth century is dismal and can be justly characterized as a new kind of slavery—slavery to the machine and the machine owner.

One of the industrial proletariat's first reactions was violence. Throughout the winter of 1811 to 1812, when the pressure of the Napoleonic war and the blockade against British commerce was added to the maladjustments of the Industrial Revolution, a wave of personal violence and machine smashing swept throughout Great Britain (the Luddite riots). Parliament, composed entirely of members of the property-holding classes, quickly made industrial sabotage a capital offense and suppressed violence with a heavy hand. Several dozens of offenders were hanged. Sporadic outbreaks of violence, however, continued for several years. This story was repeated in other countries as the Industrial Revolution spread. In the United States in the middle decades of the nineteenth century, violence broke out among the Irish immigrants working in the anthracite coal mines of eastern Pennsylvania. The exploited miners formed secret terror societies called Molly Maguires. For a number of years they intimidated, even murdered, unpopular bosses and uncooperative nonmembers. They were eventually ferreted out by civil authorities and ruthlessly suppressed.

More peaceful efforts of the industrial proletariat to bring group pressure to bear on their employers by organizing unions also at first met with defeat. In 1799 and 1800 the British Parliament passed the Combination Acts, which outlawed all labor combinations organized for the purpose of securing better wages, hours, or working conditions. In 1824 trade unions were legalized in Great Britain, but their activities were still severely restricted. In other countries strikes and union activities were outlawed. In some cases, as in the United States, the owners themselves organized for the purpose of breaking up labor unions. Private detectives and police were set upon labor leaders, who were beaten, fired, and blacklisted. It was not until the second half of the

FIGURE 44.4. Doré, "A London Slum" This woodcut by Gustave Doré portrays the squalor of an overcrowded London slum in the early nineteenth century. (Prints Division, New York Pubic Library, Astor, Lenox, and Tilden Foundations)

nineteenth century that labor unions were able to make consistent headway in major struggles with employers.

Nevertheless, factory workers and other elements of the working classes managed to assert themselves in various ways even during the first half of the nineteenth century. Many local working-class organizations were established and survived. A few larger organizations, such as the Grand National Union in Britain, had at least temporary life. Strikes, whether legal or illegal, were numerous and widespread if not always well organized. There were even significant working-class political movements in this early period, the most important of which was Chartism in Great Britain. Chartism, organized by the London Working Men's Association, arose in the 1830s and 1840s. Chartists agitated for various political and economic reforms and at times seemed to be a powerful, organized, even revolutionary threat in England. Although the movement had broken up by mid-century without having achieved its goals, it did reveal some of the potential political strength of an organized working class.

Social Institutions

Industrialization had a strong impact on social institutions during the nineteenth century. Some of the most subtle but significant and long-lasting changes took place in the family, particularly the middle-class family.

During the nineteenth century, what many historians and sociologists call the "modern family" predominated in the West, particularly in western Europe and the United States, and above all within the middle classes. Compared with the family of early modern times, this modern family was more tied together by emotional bonds, more child-centered, and more private. Within the middle-class modern family, which increasingly served as an accepted standard for all families, there was a growing division of roles and labor between the sexes. Ideally the middle-class man was authoritative, competent, and controlled. His wife was supposed to be deferential, emotional, and even frail—almost on a pedestal as a showpiece of success and propriety. Men increasingly specialized in the competitive world of work outside the home, while women specialized in domestic management. Proper middle-class women were excluded from almost all paid occupations, with the exception of such jobs as governess or elementary-school teacher, directly connected to the domestic role. Home was idealized as a "haven in a heartless world" of ruthless industrial capitalism to which the husband returned after work. The wife was to provide the emotional support for the husband, who supplied the money to support the household. The wife was to make sure the house was clean, the meals were served. In addition to being in charge of any domestic servants (a requirement for any middle-class home), she was supposed to be the all-caring mother. Her children were at the center of the family, and their childhood was more extended than ever before.

Outside the middle class, patterns differed. In aristocratic families, the wider social and political connections remained important and still played a major role in the selection of marriage partners. In peasants' and artisans' families, the household economy was still a reality. In industrial working-class families, women were more likely wage laborers, though for less pay and in lower-status positions than men.

Many other social changes exacerbated by industrialization, such as poor housing, lack of public transportation, horrible sanitation, child labor, and periodic unemployment, did not go unnoticed. Demands for social reforms grew. The wealthier classes were most comfortable supporting charitable institutions and self-help organizations, which proliferated during the nineteenth century. But pressure increased for governmental intervention. Public health organizations, sanitary codes, and housing regulations spread after the 1830s and 1840s. Governments took on greater responsibility for primary and secondary education. By mid-century, governments in industrializing areas had passed several laws to restrict child labor and control a few of the worst social conditions accompanying industrialization. But many of these laws were not effectively enforced until the second half of the century. Moreover, it was not until after 1850 that governmental programs such as urban planning, public sanitation (sewers and piped water), and urban transportation (horse-drawn and electric streetcars) had a real impact.

5. NEW ECONOMIC AND SOCIAL THOUGHT

The Industrial Revolution and the social changes related to it, like the French Revolution, were accompanied by new theories and doctrines. The increasingly dominant set of ideas, values, and beliefs—or ideology—was liberalism. Most middle-class liberals applauded both the Industrial and French revolutions while rejecting some of their "excesses" (see Chapter 43). Economic liberalism was more directly related to the economic and social changes accompanying industrialization. Socialism was another newer and more critical line of thought. Like economic liberalism, socialism directly related to industrialization, but not from the perspective of the middle class. Over the course of the nineteenth century, socialist ideology would grow and become the main alternative to economic liberalism.

Economic Liberalism

The growing middle classes, who were prospering from the Industrial Revolution, found intellectual support and justification for their interests in the doctrine of economic liberalism. This doctrine has been best stated by the Scottish philosopher Adam Smith in his classic *Wealth of Nations* (1776). The essence of Smith's theory is that economics, like the physical world, has its own natural laws. The most basic of the economic laws is that of supply and demand. When left to operate alone, these laws will keep the economy in balance and, in the long run, work to the benefit of all. If the sanctity of property and contracts is respected, competition and free enterprise will provide incentive and keep prices down. Government regulations and collective bargaining only impede the workings of the natural laws of economics and destroy incentive. Government should therefore follow a policy of laissez faire, limiting its activities in the economic field to enforcement of order and of contracts, public education and health, national defense, and in rare instances the encouragement of necessary industries that private enterprise does not find profitable. Here was a theory ready-made for the industrial capitalists, who already held all the trump cards.

A strong boost was given to laissez-faire thinking by a young Anglican clergyman, Thomas Malthus, who in 1789 published his *Essay on Population*. Malthus argued that since population increases by a geometric ratio whereas the food supply increases only by an arithmetic ratio, it is a basic natural law that population will outstrip the food supply. This alleged law has two important implications. One is that nothing can be done to improve the lot of the masses. If their condition is temporarily bettered, they will immediately produce children in such numbers that the food supply will be outstripped and starvation will threaten all. Only poverty and privation hold them in check. The second implication is that the rich are not to blame for the misery of the poor; the poor are themselves responsible because of their incontinence. These ideas were so soothing to so many of the book-buying upper classes that Malthus quickly attained fame and wealth.

David Ricardo supplied further support for policies of economic liberalism. Having made a fortune in stock market speculation while still a young man, Ricardo purchased a seat in Parliament and spent the rest of his life thinking and writing on economics. In *The Principles of Political Economy and Taxation* (1817), he propounded the law of rent and the iron law of wages. Rent is determined by the difference in productivity of land. Take off all restrictions and subsidies, and the poorest land goes out of cultivation, reducing the rent on the more productive lands proportionately. He argued for this idea so forcefully that it played an important part in the repeal of England's Corn Laws, which had maintained the price of grain at an artificially high level. Lower grain prices meant lower bread prices, which enabled industrial capitalists to pay lower subsistence wages to their workers. More important in economic thinking was Ricardo's iron law of wages, according to which the natural wage is the subsistence level and the market wage tends to conform to it. Raise the market wage and the workers will multiply so rapidly that soon the law of supply and demand will bring the market wage down below the subsistence level. Then the workers will die off from malnutrition and disease and slow down their reproduction rate. Eventually, they will become so scarce as to be able to bid the market wage up above the natural wage. Always, though, the pull is toward the subsistence level. This theory again was music to the ears of the industrial capitalists.

These economic liberals, being some of the earliest thinkers to analyze the economics of industrial capitalism, are often called the classical economists. Their ideas were popularized in Great Britain and spread to the Continent. There they were modified and expounded by men such as Jean Baptiste Say and Frédéric Bastiat.

A related stream of economic liberalism was initiated by the British Utilitarian philosopher Jeremy Bentham as early as 1789, in his *Principles of Morals and Legislation.* Bentham was an eighteenth-century materialistic rationalist who lived on until 1832, bridging the eighteenth and nineteenth centuries with his life and thought. The Utilitarians believed that the useful is the good and that the chief purpose of government and society is to achieve "the greatest good to the greatest number." But since every individual is the best judge of his or her own best interests, the surest way to achieve general happiness is allow individuals to follow their own enlightened self-interest. Individualism, then, is the best safeguard of the general welfare. At the same time Bentham himself and several of his followers saw the necessity for the state to act for the common welfare. Utilitarians became active during the middle decades of the nineteenth century in promoting legislation and creating governmental bureaucracies to handle some of the economic abuses and social problems connected with the Industrial Revolution.

Over the nineteenth century, economic liberalism evolved as industrial capitalists proved unwilling to adhere to laissez faire when it did not suit their interests, as the economic and social inequities of industrialism became too abhorrent to humanitarian sensibilities, and as perceptive criticisms of economic liberalism became persuasive. The most influential thinker to lead in this evolution of economic liberalism was John Stuart Mill (1806–1873). Mill, a child prodigy, was brought up to be a good Benthamite. However, he was too sensitive and humanitarian to remain in the hard materialist camp of the Utilitarians. Moreover, living a generation after Smith, Malthus, Ricardo, and Bentham, he was able to see

some of the social effects of the Industrial Revolution. Although Mill in no way rejected private property and free enterprise, he believed that in the industrial age restrictions must be instituted by the state for the protection of the poor. Although production is bound by the laws of supply and demand, the distribution of goods is not. Public utilities such as railroads and gas and waterworks are natural monopolies and should be owned by the state. The state should provide free compulsory education for all and regulate child labor. He favored income and inheritance taxes as economic equalizers. Mill's chief work on economics, *Principles of Political Economy,* was published in 1848. Mill was also the first influential philosopher in modern times to advocate equal rights for women. His *Subjection of Women,* which appeared in 1869, came to be considered the classic statement on the subject of women's rights. In his later years he considered himself a moderate socialist. More than other nineteenth-century liberals, many of his views fit those of twentieth-century liberalism.

Utopian Socialism

During the first phase of the Industrial Revolution the economies of the industrialized countries belonged to the bourgeoisie in thought as well as in deed. The theories of the economic liberals enjoyed ascendancy. The hard-pressed proletariat, though increasingly disconcerted, did not formulate new economic theories. However, as early as the opening of the nineteenth century, a number of intellectuals from the upper classes began to question the fundamentals of the existing system, such as private property and private enterprise for profit. They stressed the need for economic planning and wanted to base society on cooperation and community rather than competitive individualism. The ideas of these intellectuals were speculative and had limited impact, particularly when compared with those of Marx and other hard-headed socialists of the later nineteenth century. A number of these early, speculative intellectuals came to be called Utopian Socialists.

One of the first Utopian Socialists was the French nobleman Henri de Saint-Simon (1760–1825). He and his followers believed that society should be reorganized on a "Christian" basis, that all should work, and that the inheritance of private property should be abolished. His ideal society would be run according to the formula "from each according to his capacity, to each according to his deserts." Saint-Simon would reward the superior artists, scientists, engineers, and business people according to their merits. But he laid down no plan of action for achieving his ideal society.

Charles Fourier (1772–1837), a Frenchman of middle-class origin, advocated doing away with economic competition, the source of so much evil. In his utopian society, agriculture and industry would be carried on by voluntary cooperatives whose members would pool their resources and live in communal apartment houses. Distribution of goods and profits would be based on a mathematical formula: workers, five-twelfths; capitalists, four-twelfths; management, three-twelfths. Although Fourier's elaborate plans included many impractical ideas, some of his ideas found their way into practice.

A step forward in socialist thinking was taken by Louis Blanc (1811–1882), another middle-class Frenchman. Louis Blanc would abolish the evils of selfish competitive capitalism by setting up a system of social workshops. The government would lend money to voluntary workers' cooperatives, which would establish and run the workshops. Distribution of the proceeds would be according to the formula, "from each according to his ability, to each according to his need," the formula later adopted by Karl Marx.

A different kind of Utopian was Robert Owen (1771–1858). Born in Wales, Owen quickly made an industrial fortune in Manchester and bought large cotton mills in New Lanark, Scotland. He set out early in the nineteenth century to make New Lanark a model socialist utopia. Wages were raised, hours shortened, working conditions improved, child labor abolished, educational and recreational facilities provided, sickness and old-age insurance established. Owen spent the rest of his life and fortune drawing plans for and setting up model socialistic communities. Several were established in America, notably New Harmony, Indiana. All were short-lived; nor was Owen's benevolent example followed by other industrialists.

The Utopian Socialists were all strongly influenced by the materialistic rationalism of the eighteenth-century Enlightenment. They recognized some of the deeper significance of the Industrial Revolution and the alternatives it presented. They attacked the unbridled pursuit of profits in an unregulated economy. They attempted to show how a well-organized community or state could eliminate the misery of industrial capitalism and create a society of happy people. They opposed existing organized religion, although Saint-Simon believed that his ideal society should be dominated by a new social Christianity—a brand of Christianity that had never yet been tried. Most of the Utopian Socialists had little influence on their own times. They did, however, start a trend of economic and social thought that was to become influential. During the second half of the nineteenth century a more virile type of socialism would arise. For the most part, this later socialism would be organized, revolutionary, and bear the stamp of Karl Marx. •

Marxian Socialism

During the second half of the nineteenth century a stronger type of socialism was formed—a type whose foundations were established in the social and intellectual atmosphere of the 1840s. For the most part, this socialism would be organized, revolutionary, and bear the stamp of its founder, Karl Marx (1818–1883).

Marx was born into a German middle-class family. His father was a Jewish lawyer who had converted to Christianity. A brilliant student, Karl Marx attained his doctorate in philosophy and history, but he was denied an academic position because of his radical views. After embarking on a career in journalism, he was exiled from Germany and later from France because of his radical ideas. He spent the last thirty-four years of his life in London working on his ideas and trying to build organizations to put them into action. Marx collaborated with his friend Friedrich Engels, son of a wealthy German manufacturer, in writing the *Communist Manifesto* (1848). This work, along with the later *Das Kapital* (the first volume of which appeared in 1867), contains the fundamentals of Marxism. Marx built his ideology on a basis of

German philosophy (Hegelian idealism), French social thought (what he referred to as the Utopian Socialists), and British economics (particularly the economic liberalism of David Ricardo). The most salient points of Marx's ideology are summarized next.

Economic Interpretation of History Although people and history are complex, material economic considerations are most important. Economic interests and motivations underlie the most critical actions of human beings, just as the dominant characteristic of an historical epoch is its prevailing system of economic production. Societies are formed around the means of production, around the principal ways that human beings make a living. The political system, the religious system, and the cultural system that develop must conform to the necessities of the economic system and the social system, which form around the economic realities of life.

Class Struggle Societies are broadly divided into the haves and the have-nots. The haves are the owners of the means of economic production; the have-nots are the exploited laborers for these haves. The haves and have-nots are opposing classes with opposing interests. Above all, the haves are interested in maintaining a fundamental status quo, while the have-nots have much to gain from fundamental change. Thus, "the history of all hitherto existing society is the history of class struggles": in ancient times freeman versus slave; in medieval times landlord versus serf; in modern times capitalist versus proletariat. The bourgeoisie (the capitalists), having overcome the aristocracy (the feudal landlords) in a revolutionary struggle (such as the French Revolution), will in time be displaced by the proletariat (the industrial working class) in a new revolutionary struggle.

Surplus Value In the capitalistic industrial economy, the law of surplus value prevails. According to this law, the workers, who are paid only subsistence wages, create, by their work, value in excess of their wages. This excess, surplus value, is the illegitimate source of profit for the capitalist.

Inevitable Destruction of Capitalism Capitalists are locked into a competitive struggle with each other. This struggle forces them to continually introduce new, costly machines while keeping wages to a minimum. Larger factories must be built, fewer and fewer capitalists succeed in the competitive struggle, and greater and greater quantities of goods are produced in a system running out of control. Correspondingly, the capitalist system is characterized by alternating periods of prosperity and depression. Under capitalism, then, the law of surplus value plus the increasingly more frequent and deep periods of depression will finally produce such misery that the working class will revolt, seize the means of production from the capitalists, destroy the capitalist system, and ultimately establish a classless socialist society.

Internationalism Workers in all countries have more in common with each other than they have with capitalists of their own country. Therefore workers should unite across national boundaries in their struggle against the common enemy—the capitalist bourgeoisie.

When the *Communist Manifesto* first appeared in 1848, it had little impact on the already developing revolutionary events of that year. It reflected, however, the intellectual and social turmoil being produced by the Industrial Revolution. In the following decades, Marxian Socialism would grow to become a major theoretical and ideological force in the West (see Chapter 50).

6. THE ARRIVAL OF INDUSTRIAL SOCIETY

The industrialization of Western societies during the nineteenth century was of tremendous significance. Indeed, industrialization has become a measure of whether a society is considered "modern" or "traditional." Industrialization carried in its wake fundamental changes in literally all aspects of life, from the concrete reality of an individual's everyday life to the arrangement of classes in society. Conflict wrought by these changes was inevitable and widespread, whether in an intellectual realm, at the work site, or at the barricades. Generally, it was the industrial bourgeoisie that emerged victorious in these struggles, establishing its control over the economy and the government in the industrialized countries. It is the story of these struggles, combined with the political changes stemming from the French Revolution, that constitutes much of the meat of nineteenth-century history.

SUGGESTED READING

Economic Aspects

T. S. Ashton, *The Industrial Revolution, 1760–1830* (1968). An "optimistic" historian who plays down the horrors of the Industrial Revolution.

P. Deane, *The First Industrial Revolution* (1975). Balanced brief analysis.

D. S. Landes, *The Unbound Prometheus: Technological Change and Industrial Development in Western Europe from 1750 to the Present* (1969). Thorough, insightful description and analysis of the developing technology of the Industrial Revolution.

S. Pollard, *Peaceful Conquest: The Industrialization of Europe* (1981). Up-to-date general survey.

Social Changes

R. Bridenthal and C. Koonz, eds. *Becoming Visible: Women in European History* (1976). Contains chapters on the significance of the Industrial Revolution for women.

C. Morazé, *The Triumph of the Middle Classes* (1968). A sympathetic survey.

P. N. Stearns, *European Society in Upheaval* (1967). A general survey of social classes and social history during the nineteenth century.

P. Taylor, ed., *The Industrial Revolution: Triumph or Disaster?* (1970). Samples a variety of views on the benefits and burdens of industrialization.

E. P. Thompson, *The Making of the English Working Class* (1963). Challenging interpretation stressing the culture and activities of the working class.

L. Tilly and J. Scott, *Women, Work and Family* (1978). A highly respected work.

E. A. Wrigley, *Population and History* (1969). Introduction to demographic changes during the Industrial Revolution.

Economic and Social Thought

R. Heilbroner, *The Worldly Philosophers* (1972). A well-written history of economists and their ideas.

A. S. Lindemann, *A History of European Socialism* (1984). A good modern treatment.

D. McLellan, *Karl Marx: His Life and Thought* (1977). An excellent biography and introduction.

F. Manuel, *The Prophets of Paris* (1962). A study of the French Utopian Socialists.

CHAPTER 45

Romanticism in Philosophy, Literature, and the Arts

FIGURE 45.1. Schinkel, "Medieval Town on a River," 1815 This painting by the German romantic artist Karl Friedrich Schinkel contains many of the key elements of romanticism: glorification of nature, religious mysticism, adoration of the medieval, and concern with the emotional. With these characteristics, romanticism stood in contrast to many of the industrial, secular, and rationalistic trends of the period. (Neue Pinakothek, Munich)

Schools of thought and art do not fall neatly into chronological patterns. Nevertheless, one is frequently able to observe a prevailing style that characterizes the culture of a given era. Thus, although romanticism began in the eighteenth century, the prevailing style until the last years of that century was still classical. Similarly, although classicism continued on through the nineteenth century and into the present day, romanticism was the dominant spirit in the last years of the eighteenth century and the first half of the nineteenth century.

1. THE NATURE OF ROMANTICISM

The romantic spirit had many facets, but essentially it was a reaction against the rationalism and formalism of the classic spirit. Whereas classicism extolled reason and perfection of form, romanticism appealed to the emotions, to feeling, and to freedom and spontaneity of expression. Whereas the classicist was interested in the natural order and the laws of human beings and the universe, the romanticist loved to sing of woods and lakes and lovers' lanes and to dream of faraway or imaginary times and places.

Romanticism was associated with and was in part a product of the French Revolution and Napoleon. Many classicists had been interested in peacefully reforming society in accordance with the natural law. They did not anticipate the violent upheaval that came, although many of the radical revolutionary leaders and Napoleon believed themselves to be in the tradition of classical Greece and Rome. It was the romanticists, breaking sharply with past forms and traditions and with bold abandon trying the new, who reflected the revolutionary spirit. This does not mean that all romanticists were political radicals or even liberals. Some, like Shelley and Heine, were. Others, like Edmund Burke and Sir Walter Scott, were conservatives representing a reaction against the excesses of the revolution.

Nationalism was another facet of romanticism. Whether liberal or conservative, the romanticist was likely to be an ardent nationalist. The romantic poet Lord Byron lost his life fighting for Greek national independence against the Turks. The dreamer and orator Mazzini was called the soul of Italian nationalism. He spent most of his adult life in exile because of his labors for a free and united Italy. Herder, as early as the eighteenth century, had pleaded eloquently for a German national culture. The fraternity and the freedom so common to the national movements before 1850, no less than pride in real or imagined national achievements, gave outlet to the emotions of the romanticist.

Romanticism also represented a reaction against the rationalistic deism of the eighteenth century and a return to mystic religion. In literature and art, romantics stressed the emotion of Christianity and the presence of God in nature. Romantic theologians such as Friedrich Schleiermacher (1768–1834) emphasized that the important part of religion was emotional—the feeling of dependence on an infinite God—not religious dogma or institutions. The revival of religion as part of the romanticism of the early nineteenth century brought about a renewed interest in the Middle Ages. The classicists had drawn their inspiration from pagan Greece and Rome. Now in the early nineteenth century the Knights of the Round Table and Siegfried and Brünhild came back in style once more. No more perfect example of the romantic spirit can be cited than the novels and verse of Sir Walter Scott, whose subject matter was primarily medieval. Gothic architecture enjoyed a revival. The "Dark Ages" were transformed into the "Age of Faith."

Finally, the interest in the Middle Ages and in nationalism reflected another aspect of romanticism: its passionate concern with history. History, written by people such as Thomas B. Macauley (1800–1859) in Great Britain and Jules Michelet (1798–1874) in France, was literary, exciting, and dramatic—a story of heroic individuals, national struggles, and great accomplishments. It became a subject of great interest among scholars as well as the reading public.

2. THE PHILOSOPHY OF IDEALISM

Any discussion of romantic thought should begin with Rousseau (1712–1778), even though this French genius lived during the heyday of rationalistic classicism and before romanticism came into full flower. Rousseau, like most of his fellow philosophers of the Enlightenment such as Voltaire, Diderot, Montesquieu, was a deist, believing in the mechanical universe of natural laws. However, he differed sharply with them over the place of reason. Far from believing that a person can know only what is perceived through the five senses and interpreted by reason, Rousseau stressed feeling, instinct, and emotions. He also anticipated the romantic movement in his inordinate love of nature. He would stretch himself out on the ground, dig his fingers and toes into the dirt, kiss the earth, and weep for joy. This emotional genius was a true romanticist in his revolt against the rules of formal society. Free love, undisciplined childhood and education, the noble savage—all were features of Rousseau's revolt. His influence on later generations was enormous.

It seems a far cry from the rough genius of Rousseau to the exquisitely ordered thought of Immanuel Kant (1724–1804), but the German philosopher was admittedly indebted to Rousseau. Kant, who was partly of Scottish ancestry, was a native of Königsberg in East Prussia. A frail and insignificant-looking man who never traveled more than fifty miles from the place of his birth, he slowly developed into one of the most powerful and influential thinkers of modern times. He was often in difficulty with the Prussian government because of his liberal and unorthodox views. Kant started out as a scientist and always respected the methods of natural science. He was also steeped in the philosophy of the Enlightenment. However, he was not satisfied with the conclusions of the eighteenth-century materialistic rationalists. Eventually he thought on beyond them. Kant came to believe that there are in reality not one but two worlds—the physical realm and the spiritual realm, or the realm of ultimate reality. The first he called the realm of phenomena; the second the realm of noumena. In the physical realm of phenomena the approach to truth of Descartes, Locke, and Voltaire—sense perception and reason—suffices. But in the spiritual realm of noumena, these methods fail. Ultimate spiritual truth may be attained only by faith, conviction, and feeling. Truths in the realm of the noumena, such as the existence of God or the immortality of the soul or

the existence of good and evil, cannot be proved by reason. And yet we are justified in believing them because they reinforce our moral sense of right and wrong. His principal work, *Critique of Pure Reason,* was a metaphysical answer of the highest intellectual order to the philosophers of the Enlightenment. These ideas came to be called the philosophy of idealism. Kant and his early nineteenth-century followers represented a sharp reversal in the philosophical trend toward rationalism and materialism, which in a sense began in the thirteenth century with the efforts of Albertus Magnus and Thomas Aquinas to rationalize Christian doctrines.

The most influential of Kant's disciples was Georg Wilhelm Hegel (1770–1831). Hegel's chief interest was the philosophy of history. Like his master, he rejected the mechanistic amoral universe of the Enlightenment. He believed, rather, that a benevolent but impersonal God created and runs the universe, making human society better by a process of purposeful evolution. This evolution is achieved by a dialectical system of thesis, antithesis, and synthesis. Any given system or civilization (thesis) is challenged by its opposite (antithesis). From the struggle emerges a new system containing the best elements of both (synthesis). This synthesis then becomes a new thesis, which when it has served its purpose is challenged by a new antithesis, and so on. Hegel believed that every historical epoch is dominated by a *zeitgeist* (spirit of the time). The zeitgeist of the nineteenth century was German civilization, whose greatest contribution was freedom through disciplined order. Hegel exalted the state. Only in and through the state can the individual find meaning and be free. Hegel's influence on romanticism and on the early nineteenth century in general was substantial.

3. ROMANTIC LITERATURE

The spirit of romanticism can be made to come alive in no better way than by a study of the British romantic poets. A number of British writers began to break with classicism during the course of the eighteenth century. The best-known and probably the most representative of these writers was Robert Burns (1759–1796). Born in a humble clay cottage, the Scottish poet lived an undisciplined life as if he had been reared in accordance with Rousseau's *Emile*. Burns idealized nature and the rustic rural life with which he was intimately acquainted. In spontaneous verse written in his native Scottish dialect, he wrote an ode to a field mouse, "Wee, sleekit, cow'rin', tim'rous beastie," which he had turned up with his plow. In *The Cotter's Saturday Night* we are given a charming and sympathetic picture of village life among the poor of Scotland. "Auld Lang Syne" is sung with nostalgia every New Year's Eve by millions throughout the English-speaking world. *John Anderson My Jo*, a touching tribute to love in old age, could never have been written by Racine or Alexander Pope.

The romantic spirit, early reflected in the poetry of Robert Burns, reached maturity with William Wordsworth (1770–1850) and Samuel Taylor Coleridge (1772–1834). The two were warm friends. Both were closely associated with the beautiful lake country of northwest England, Wordsworth by birth and Coleridge by adoption. They took a trip to Germany together, where they fell under the influence of Kant. Both, as young men, were ardent social reformers. The two collaborated on *Lyrical Ballads*, which appeared in 1798. *Lyrical Ballads* contains some of the best work of these gifted poets, such as Wordsworth's *Tintern Abbey* (see Figure 45.2) and Coleridge's *Ancient Mariner*. Both men were masters of versification and poetic expression. They were also lovers and students of nature, and both of them, particularly Wordsworth, sensed a brooding, mystical presence of the divine. Wordsworth's *Intimations of Immortality* is sublime in its spiritual depth and insight. In their ardent love of nature, their introspective concern for the individual, their preoccupation with the spiritual rather than the material, and their greater attention to substance than to form, Wordsworth and Coleridge broke distinctly with the spirit of classicism.

Once the vogue of romanticism was dignified and popularized in Great Britain by Wordsworth and Coleridge, a host of romantic writers appeared. A younger trio of poetic geniuses of the highest order, Byron, Shelley, and Keats (all of whom lived briefly and died between the years 1788 and 1824), are well known and loved. All

FIGURE 45.2.   J. M. W. Turner, "Tintern Abbey"
Tintern Abbey, a twelfth-century Gothic ruin in Wales, was the object of both literary and artistic romanticism. Here Turner, the leading English romantic artist, evokes the power of nature, religion, and the medieval past. (The British Museum)

three gave spontaneous and unrestrained vent to their emotions. Byron and Shelley combined an exquisite esthetic sense with irrepressible revolutionary zeal, defying the forms and customs of society. Keats was a gentler soul, who after a life-long quest for the beautiful died at the age of twenty-five.

Meanwhile, Sir Walter Scott in novel and verse was devoting his longer life (1771–1832) to glorifying the Middle Ages and his native Scotland. Scott, unlike Byron and Shelley but like Wordsworth and Coleridge in their mature and mellow later years, was conservative in his attitude toward public affairs.

On the other side of the Atlantic, Longfellow,

Cooper, and Irving were founding an American national literature. In their subject matter, their style, and their attitudes, they reflected the European romantic spirit. Many other American writers in the early nineteenth century wrote in the romantic vein. Ralph Waldo Emerson (1803–1882) was considered a religious radical and skeptic in his day. He gave up his Puritan pastorate (by then Unitarian) at Boston's Old North Church because of his heterodoxy. However, in his essays and poems it was the romantic philosophy of Kantian idealism, not the rationalism of the Enlightenment, that he introduced into America. Edgar Allan Poe (1809–1849), short-story writer, literary critic, and romantic poet of a high order, was in a sense an American Shelley, though less ethereal and more morbid. Henry David Thoreau (1817–1862) took Rousseau's back-to-nature idea more seriously than did its author. Rousseau, for all his passion for nature, would never have withdrawn from society for two years to live by Walden Pond in introspective solitude. Emerson, Poe, and Thoreau were all individualists to the point of being mild social revolutionaries. Thoreau preached civil disobedience and allowed himself to be put in jail rather than pay taxes for what he considered to be unworthy causes. The sensitive Poe, enduring oblivion and poverty, turned to drink and an early grave. Emerson weathered a storm of hostility from organized religion and society for his nonconformist views.

Romanticism came to German literature in the latter half of the eighteenth century, partly under the influence of the early British romanticists and partly as a result of the conscious effort of the Germans, led by Herder, to free themselves from bondage to French classical culture. Foremost among all German writers is Johann Wolfgang von Goethe (1749–1832). Like Shakespeare, Leonardo da Vinci, and Beethoven, Goethe is a genius of such proportions that he cannot be confined to any single cultural school or movement. However, insofar as it is possible to classify him, he belongs more nearly to the romantic tradition than to any other, both in time and in spirit. His prodigious energies were devoted essentially to a lifelong (eighty-three years) search for the secrets of happiness and wisdom. His encyclopedic mind delved fruitfully into literature, philosophy, sci-

ence, and public affairs. His novels, lyrics, essays, scientific and philosophical treatises, and dramas fill one hundred thirty-two volumes. No writer except Shakespeare has had so many of his lyrics set to music. Goethe's masterpiece is *Faust*, a philosophical drama written in exquisite verse (see Figure 45.3). It is about a medieval scholar who, dissatisfied with the fruits of knowledge, sells his soul to the devil in return for earthly pleasure and wisdom. Goethe explores the depths of human experience and aspiration. *Faust* was sixty years in the making. In his medieval interests, his fresh emotional spontaneity, his love of nature and of individual personality, and his courageous, robust, pioneering spirit, Goethe was a romanticist.

Goethe's friend and protégé, Friedrich Schiller (1759–1805), was more popular in his own day than the master himself. Schiller drew heavily on the Middle Ages and on nationalism (when national aspirations were associated with freedom) for his dramas, histories, and lyrics. *William Tell*, a drama based upon the Swiss struggle for freedom from Hapsburg tyranny, is probably Schiller's best-known work. Neither Goethe nor Schiller can be considered a German nationalist in the narrow sense; both were universal in their interests and their appeal.

Heinrich Heine (1797–1856) was considered to be Goethe's successor as a writer of German lyrics, though not of Goethe's stature. Most of Heine's voluminous writing was in the field of romantic lyrical poetry. One of his most representative works was an ode to the Silesian weavers who rose up against the hardships caused by the Industrial Revolution, which was just coming to Germany, and were shot down by Prussian troops. Because of the hostility of the various German governments in the age of Metternich to his radical political ideas, Heine exiled himself from Germany. The last twenty-five years of his life were spent in Paris. Many of his later lyrics show a touch of the light gaiety of the French.

Literary romanticism flowered later in France than England or Germany. Francois René Chateaubriand (1768–1848), a disillusioned noble man who began writing during the reign of Napoleon I, was one of the first French writers of influence to react against the rationalism of the Enlightenment. His *Genius of Christianity* is a return to mystic

FIGURE 45.3. Delacroix, Scene from *"Faust"*
This lithograph by Delacroix depicting the devil on the left and the scholar Faust on the right is an illustration for Goethe's masterpiece, *Faust*. (Prints Division, New York Public Library, Astor, Lenox, and Tilden Foundations)

religion. He also dreamed and wrote of glorified Indians in far-away tropical America. At almost the same time, Madame de Staël (1766–1817) analyzed and helped popularize romanticism. Alexander Dumas the elder (1802–1870) has continued to delight young and old alike with his romantic and melodramatic *Three Musketeers and Count of Monte Cristo*, painting the haunting afterglow of medieval chivalry. George Sand (1804–1876), an unconventional woman and gifted author, wrote numerous popular novels filled with romantic

passion and idealism. Victor Hugo (1802–1885) in his long and tumultuous life wrote a vast quantity of exquisite lyrics, dramas, essays, and fiction in the romantic tradition. His *Hunchback of Notre Dame* is medieval in setting. In *Les Misérables* he immortalizes and idealizes the masses of underprivileged humanity, preaching redemption and purification not by planned social reform but through suffering. Jules Michelet crossed historical and literary lines in his seventeen-volume *History of France*. He tells the thrilling story of France's long and glorious achievements, usually with skillful historical craftsmanship and always with matchless grace.

The first great figure in Russian literature was the romantic poet Alexander Pushkin (1799–1837). The chief inspiration for his great lyrics, dramas, histories, novels, essays, and tales came from French and British writers, particularly Byron. Because of his revolutionary radicalism (of the French variety), he was for a while exiled by the Russian government to southern Russia. Later he became a Russian nationalist and took many of his themes from Russian history. His tragic drama *Boris Godunov* (patterned after Shakespeare) is considered to be his masterpiece.

4. THE ROMANTIC SPIRIT IN THE ARTS

Words fail to convey the messages and the meanings expressed in the visual and musical arts. This is particularly true of art, whose appeal is primarily to the emotions.

The leading painters glorified nature, religion, and nationalism (see Figure 45.1). John Constable (1776–1837) in Great Britain, Camille Corot (1796–1875) in France, and George Inness the elder (1825–1894) in the United States painted landscapes fit to have illustrated the moods of Wordsworth or Thoreau (see Color Plate 19 and Figure 45.4). Their idealizations of nature and the rural life would have delighted Rousseau and Burns. J. M. W. Turner (1775–1851) in England caught the romantic mood in his eerie, misty impressions of seascapes and mythological subjects (see Color Plate 20). Jean François Millet (1814–1875) idealized both the French rural life (*The Sower* and *The*

FIGURE 45.4. Millet, "The Angelus" The spirit of romanticism that dominated art during the first half of the nineteenth century was marked by a religious revival and by an admiration for the simple, rural life, which Millet effectively captures in painting. (Giraudon)

Gleaners) and mystic religion *(The Angelus)* (see Figure 45.4). His compatriot, Eugène Delacroix (1798–1863) depicted on canvas Byron's *Prisoner of Chillon.* On great murals in the Louvre, the library of the Chamber of Deputies, and the Hôtel de Ville he portrayed glorious scenes from history (see Color Plate 21).

The romantic movement was less pronounced in the field of architecture. Its chief manifestation was a revived interest in the Gothic style. The French, after several centuries of apathy if not scorn for anything associated with medievalism, suddenly showed a renewed interest in their magnificent Gothic monuments. The Houses of Parliament, constructed in London in the early nineteenth century when England was rapidly becoming industrialized, were built in the Gothic style.

The romantic spirit was caught and expressed by a host of great musicians. They went beyond the controlled classical music, trying to translate emotions into sound. First and foremost was Beethoven (1770–1827), who was not only one of the greatest of classic composers but also the first of the romanticists. His earlier work was in the spirit of his idol, Mozart. In maturity his originality overflowed the bounds of classic forms, becoming freer, more individualistic, and emotional. Beethoven lived through the upheavals of the French Revolution and Napoleon, and his keen interest in these dramatic events is reflected in his music. His Symphony No. 3 (*Eroica*) was dedicated to Napoleon, whom Beethoven at first regarded as the embodiment of the democratic ideals of the French Revolution. His Fifth and Seventh symphonies were inspired by the German nationalistic upsurge, which helped to overthrow Napoleon. Karl Maria von Weber (1786–1826), Franz Schubert (1797–1828), Felix Mendelssohn (1809–1847), and Robert Schumann (1810–1856) carried on in the spirit of the great Beethoven.

These gifted and youthful Germans expressed in their melodic music the same spontaneous and emotional spirit that their contemporaries Byron, Shelley, and Keats were expressing in English verse. A German by adoption was the colorful Hungarian-born Franz Liszt (1811–1886). Liszt is believed to be the greatest concert pianist of his time. His glamorous personality and sensational, emotional compositions greatly popularized romantic music. Although Liszt was an international figure, his Hungarian folk music was characteristic of the growing national sentiment of the time. He befriended the youthful Richard Wagner, who later married one of Liszt's illegitimate daughters.

The romantic spirit is nowhere better illustrated than in the work of the Polish-French pianist-composer, Frédéric Chopin (1810–1849). Chopin could express his sweet sorrows in lilting nocturnes, his sunny gaiety in bright waltzes and mazurkas, his national patriotism in stirring polonaises, or his deeper, dramatic moods in more formal ballades and concertos—all with equal skill and all in the romantic tradition. Meanwhile, other notable Frenchmen were writing romantic symphonies and operas. Gounod's *Faust* is an operatic version of Goethe's great theme. The haunting melodies of Bizet's (1838–1875) *Carmen* are widely known and sung. The greatest Italian romantic composer was Giuseppe Verdi (1813–1901). His operas *Aida, La Traviata, Il Trovatore,* and *Rigoletto* are still sung every season in opera houses all over the world. Verdi was Italy's national cultural hero during the long, uphill fight for freedom and unity.

Richard Wagner (1813–1883) brought to a dramatic climax the romantic era in music. Wagner's tempestuous life, like his music, illustrates and marks the transition from the romantic, moderately liberal and nationalistic early nineteenth century to the more violent and restless spirit of the late nineteenth and early twentieth centuries. In his youth Wagner was a radical and was exiled from Saxony in 1849 for his revolutionary activities. Later he became an extreme German nationalist—even a German "master racist" of the type that has brought so much violence to the twentieth-century world. His operas, though containing some of the world's greatest music, are also grandiloquent and often stridently nationalistic. *Tannhäuser, The Meistersingers, Siegfried, Götterdämmerung, Lohengrin,* and *Das Rheingold* are an important part of the opera repertory today.

Romanticism in the arts, as in literature and philosophy, reflected a new recognition that human beings are complex, emotional, and only sometimes rational creatures. In a civilization that was becoming more scientific, materialistic, industrial, and urban, romanticism was a counterweight for the human experience. Although new cultural trends such as realism would appear during the middle of the nineteenth century (see Color Plate 22), romanticism would remain a strong current in Western civilization well into the twentieth century.

SUGGESTED READING

General

K. Clark, *The Romantic Rebellion* (1973). Clearly written, useful.

M. LeBris, *Romantics and Romanticism* (1981). A well-illustrated recent survey of romanticism in its political context.

S. Prawer, ed., *The Romantic Period in Germany* (1970). A good collection of essays.

H. B. Schenk, *The Mind of the European Romantics* (1966). A solid survey.

J. L. Talmon, *Romanticism and Revolt: Europe, 1815–1848* (1967). Survey of romanticism in its broad historical context.

The Philosophy of Idealism

E. Cassirer, *Kant's Life and Thought* (1981). Excellent, though difficult.

R. Stromberg, *European Intellectual History Since 1789* (1975). Surveys the topic well.

C. Taylor, *Hegel* (1975). Excellent introduction.

Romantic Literature

M. H. Abrams, *Natural Supernaturalism: Tradition and Revolution in Romantic Literature* (1971). A good survey of romantic literature.

J. S. Allen, *Popular French Romanticism* (1981). Relates literary romanticism and popular culture.

Romanticism in the Arts

A. Hauser, *Social History of Art* (1958). Relates artistic trends to social developments.

H. W. Janson, *History of Art* (1977). The standard survey with a section on romanticism.

RETROSPECT

The era between 1776 and 1850 was a period of great—some historians think the greatest—political, economic, and social upheavals. Politically and socially, it was a time of high expectation and excitement. In a matter of weeks—and sometimes days—the kind of fundamental changes that usually require decades took place. Time-honored institutions, privileges, and customs toppled. Wealth, power, and rights were redistributed. Economically, changes came only somewhat slower but were even more fundamental. Goods and services were produced in different ways and in different places. Where people lived, how they made a living, and how they related to each other were changing in irreversible, revolutionary ways.

The New World was the stage for the first of these revolutions. The American Revolution was primarily a matter of the thirteen English colonies winning their independence from the mother country. As a result of the Revolution, loyalist lands were redistributed, and the royal governors and their aristocratic councils gave way to the more democratic legislatures. The Declaration of Independence and the new Constitution were filled with the ideas of the Enlightenment.

The changes brought about by the French Revolution were more dramatic and significant for Western civilization. French society on the eve of the Revolution was still essentially feudal, with its privileged clergy and nobility. Government was in the hands of a monarch. The Church was intolerant and oppressive. Within a few months of the outbreak of the Revolution in 1789, a series of sweeping reforms had occurred—the end of feudalism, the Declaration of the Rights of Man, and the drawing up of a liberal but moderate constitution.

But the nobility and the clergy were not willing to see their privileges so easily lost. Nor were the radical Jacobins convinced that the Revolution had gone far enough. They wished to see the principles of "Liberty, Equality, Fraternity" extended beyond France's borders. When Austria and Prussia intervened in behalf of the French royalty and nobility, the radicals deposed and beheaded Louis XVI. All the great powers of Europe except Russia formed a coalition for the purpose of ending this threat to the established order. The revolutionary radicals, now in control, inaugurated a Reign of Terror for the purpose of uniting and mobilizing the nation. It was remarkably successful; the internal enemies of the Revolution were terrorized into silence or support, and the foreign enemies were defeated and driven back beyond the frontiers. But no one seemed able to consummate the Revolution and restore peace. The radical Jacobins were overthrown by the bourgeois moderates, and the Terror ended; but the moderates, too, proved unable to bring peace at home and abroad.

In 1799 a coup d'état brought Napoleon Bonaparte to power. Over the next few years he instituted stabilizing reforms that affirmed some of the changes wrought by the French Revolution and destroyed others. His fifteen-year rule was marked by almost continual warfare.

At the Congress of Vienna in 1814–1815, the major powers structured a peace settlement in accordance with the principles of conservatism. In many ways the ensuing decades between 1815 and 1850 were a struggle between these forces of conservatism and the newer forces of liberalism. Despite various revolutionary rumblings, the forces of conservatism generally remained in control until 1830. After 1830 reform and revolution in the name of liberalism started to wrestle control from the conservatives, culminating in the great liberal and nationalistic revolutions of 1848. Yet this great defeat for the conservative forces of order was short-lived. By 1850 most were back in power again and the great period of liberal revolution was over.

Meanwhile another kind of revolution had been taking place in western Europe—the Industrial Revolution. By the end of the eighteenth century new factories, using new sources of power, new machines, and new methods of production, were sprouting up in Great Britain in great numbers. Great Britain's economy was experiencing unprecedented, sustained growth. The Industrial Revolution had begun. After 1815 it spread to western Europe and the United States. Great social changes followed in the wake of industrialization. Cities grew, the class structure changed, new social institutions developed, and even the function of the family and the role of women evolved. The first beneficiaries of the Industrial Revolution were the industrial bourgeoisie—the factory owners. Whether the industrial proletariat benefited is questionable. While their wages may have risen, they lost skills and security and became the virtual slaves of factory owners. These radical changes in production and distribution and the ensuing stresses prompted new economic and social thought—economic liberalism, Utopian Socialism, and Marxism.

Both an affirmation of and a reaction to the revolutionary spirit that engulfed the Western world between 1776 and 1850 was reflected in the romanticism that characterized the philosophy, literature, and arts of the period. For liberals romanticism affirmed the optimism, the individualism, and the heroism epitomized by the French Revolution, Napoleon, and the revolutions of the first half of the nineteenth century. For conservatives romanticism rejected the rationalism of the Enlightenment and affirmed the glories of the prerevolutionary and preindustrial world where the mysteries of nature and religion dominated. Although romanticism would remain an influential and popular cultural style after mid-century, the ensuing period would be more accurately reflected by realism.

Part Ten

NATIONALISM AND INDUSTRIALIZATION, 1850–1914

Nationalism had been growing as a force since the beginning of the Age of Revolutions and had played a particularly important role in the Revolutions of 1848. Between 1850 and 1914 nationalism became a much more pervasive force in the West. During the 1850s and 1860s nationalistic unification movements led to the creation of two new nation-states in Europe: Italy and Germany. At that same time the forces favoring national unification defeated forces struggling for separation in the United States. In France, Great Britain, and elsewhere, the nation-state was greatly strengthened as more citizens acquired the right to vote and as central governments acquired more power and took on greater responsibilities. Nationalism supported and was used by both liberals and conservatives striving to promote their own interests and struggling in a competitive international arena. By the later decades of the nineteenth century nationalism had taken a more militant tone and had even spilled over into a new imperialism. National pride and prestige helped drive Western nations into a race for new colonies and imperial influence in the non-Western world.

Industrialization, like nationalism, had been a growing force during the Age of Revolutions. But in 1850 only England and a few areas in western Europe were industrialized. Between 1850 and 1914 several nations in western Europe, along with the United States, became mature industrial powers, and eastern Europe had begun to industrialize. During this period industrialization interacted with nationalism. Nationalistic pride demanded that a nation have a modern industrial economy (also important for a strong military), and the creation of a modern industrial economy seemed to require national unification. Moreover, nationalism and industrialization joined hands to justify, and even seemed to require, the great imperial expansion of the West between the 1880s and 1914.

The forces of nationalism and industrialization were reflected in the social, intellectual, and cultural developments of the period. A mature industrial society was an urban society, and during this period the urban working classes were growing in numbers and self-consciousness. They were forming their own labor organizations, acquiring their own ideologies, gaining the right to vote, and becoming more educated—all often despite the distrust and hostility of the dominant bourgeoisie. This industrial society also depended on and admired science. The spread of the natural and social sciences along with the growing power of nationalism challenged Christianity, which was wedded to traditional society. Thought, literature, and art were influenced by nationalism, industrialization, and science. Indeed, certain cultural developments of the Age of Nationalism and Industrialization foreshadowed the disillusioning period of war and upheaval following the outbreak of World War I in 1914.

CHAPTER 46

Nationalism and the Nation-State, 1850–1871

FIGURE 46.1. Garibaldi Landing in Sicily The period between 1850 and 1870 was marked by a strong growth of nationalism and the successful unification of Italy and Germany. Here the lifelong nationalist Garibaldi is heroically portrayed landing in Sicily in 1860 as part of the struggle for Italian unification. (Historical Pictures Service, Chicago)

By 1850 many of the liberal and nationalistic aspirations of revolutionaries were dashed as conservative, authoritarian rulers came to power. However, nationalism as a dynamic force remained powerful and would continue to increase in strength during the nineteenth and twentieth centuries. Between 1850 and 1871 almost all political leaders, whether liberal or conservative, recognized the strength of nationalism. Nationalism's political impact was manifested most dramatically in Louis Napoleon's rise to power in France and in the successful struggles for national unification in Italy and Germany. More broadly, nationalism played a crucial role in the growing authority of the nation-state. Increasingly, central governments had to justify and bolster their authority by reference to a nation of citizens rather than dynastic links to the past. The period from 1850 to 1871, then, marks the beginning of a time when nationalism grew from earlier roots to become a dominant force in Western political life, and when the nation-state took on new authority and new functions.

1. THE NATURE OF NATIONALISM

Nationalism may be defined as feelings of common cultural identity and loyalty to one's country. What are the essential factors that contribute to these feelings? What makes a person a German or a Pole, even when there is no German or Polish national state?

The most important factor is language. Language brings people together in understanding and separates them from those they cannot understand. Probably second in importance is a historical tradition of unity. The Belgians with their two languages and the Swiss with their three languages and two religions illustrate the importance of this factor. Religion can be a powerful factor, too, though not so important as language. The German Empire with its common language came and held together in spite of a serious religious cleavage, and the Austrian Empire fell apart along language lines in spite of a common religion and a long tradition of unity under the Hapsburgs.

Territorial compactness and natural boundaries frequently contribute to nationalism.

Until the French Revolution, national loyalty was chiefly centered on the ruling monarch or dynasty and was limited for the most part to the educated upper classes who participated in the government of the nation. The French Revolution gave birth to a new and more virile kind of nationalism. The establishment of equal rights and popular representative government, together with the abolition of old provincial boundary lines, brought the masses of people into direct partnership with the national government. Universal conscription into the revolutionary armies gave the people a sense of fraternity in a righteous cause—a crusade. Nationalism acquired attributes of a religion. Such mass dynamism helped make the revolutionary and Napoleonic armies irresistible.

Nationalism soon spread to the other peoples of Europe. In the decades following the Napoleonic era industrialization and policies toward industrialization were becoming connected with nationalism. The Revolutions of 1848 clearly demonstrated the revolutionary potential of nationalism. By mid-century nationalism had grown from its deeper roots to become entwined with the central political, economic, and social forces of modern times.

2. THE SECOND EMPIRE OF NAPOLEON III

In France, Louis Napoleon Bonaparte blended support from below, reform, and authoritarian nationalism in his Second Empire, which was established in 1852 and lasted until 1870. Louis Napoleon was originally elected president of France's Second Republic in 1848. He benefited from his illustrious name, his appeal to property owners longing for order, and his well-publicized promises to link democracy from below with reforming leadership from above. When the National Assembly refused to change the constitution so that he could run for a second term, he organized a coup d'état and seized power on December 2, 1851. Resistance was limited, though thousands were arrested and deported. He quickly granted

FIGURE 46.2. Rebuilding Paris Under Napoleon III Under Napoleon III, numerous slums and old winding streets were torn down to make room for new, wide boulevards. The boulevards made it easier for authorities to maintain order and more difficult for revolutionaries to raise barricades. (The Mansell Collection)

universal male suffrage, and during the following year he held two plebiscites in which over 90 percent of the voters supported him and made him hereditary emperor—Napoleon III.

Under the new constitution, most power resided in the emperor. Although there was an elected legislative body, it could not initiate legislation or exert control over Napoleon III's ministers. The emperor controlled elections by manipulating the electoral machinery, exerting official pressure, and supporting official candidates. He kept the press under scrutiny. Thus politically the Second Empire was clearly authoritarian, at least during the 1850s.

It was also during the 1850s that Napoleon III enjoyed his greatest successes. Economically, France prospered, in part thanks to Napoleon III's policies. He encouraged industrialization and economic growth by promoting railroad construction, public works, and financial institutions. Two giant investment banking corporations, the Crédit Mobilier and the Crédit Foncier, mobilized huge amounts of capital for industry, railroads, and real estate. The Bank of France expanded until each of the country's eighty-six departments had at least one branch. George Haussmann, the prefect of Paris, had large parts of Paris torn down and rebuilt (see Figure 46.2). With a new sewer system, new parks, and new large boulevards, Paris took on an envied image that would last well into the twentieth century.

Napoleon III also encouraged educational and social reforms, thereby increasing his popularity among a variety of groups. Hospitals, nurseries, and homes for the aged were built. Government subsidies kept the price of bread low. A system of voluntary social insurance for workers was instituted. Cooperatives were encouraged, and labor unions with limited rights to strike were partially legalized for the first time.

The peak of France's revived national prestige was reached during the Crimean War (1854-1856). Like his uncle, the second Napoleon was not satisfied with spectacular domestic achievements. His opportunity for glory in foreign affairs came when Tsar Nicholas I of Russia attempted to dismember the Ottoman Empire, "the sick man of Europe," and to achieve Russia's historic goal: Constantinople and access to the world through the Turkish Straits. France did not relish the prospect of an ambitious new rival in the Mediterranean. (Great Britain, with its vast holdings and interests in the Near and Far East, was even more sensitive to this threat than was France.) A second source of Franco-Russian conflict arose when the tsar, as the great champion of Orthodox Christianity, attempted to gain a protectorate over all Christians in the Ottoman Empire and over the Christian holy places in the Turkish province of Palestine. Since the Crusades France had been the leading champion of Catholic interests in the Near East, including the Christian shrines in the Holy Land. And Napoleon III's strongest ally in France was the Catholic church.

In 1853 the Russian army and navy suddenly attacked the Turks. Early the next year Great Britain and France sent their naval and military forces into the Black Sea and laid siege to Russia's naval base, Sebastopol, on the Crimean Peninsula. Sardinia came into the war to gain the friendship of France and Great Britain. Austria maintained a hostile and Prussia a friendly neutrality toward Russia. The war was fought with gross inefficiency on both sides. The only real hero was the British nurse Florence Nightingale, whose efforts helped to inspire the creation of the International Red Cross a few years later (1864).

Nicholas I died in 1855, humiliated by the knowledge that his creaking military machine was going to fail. The Peace of Paris in 1856 prohibited Russia's naval forces on the Black Sea and maintained the integrity of the Ottoman Empire. The autonomy of Serbia and the Rumanian provinces of Moldavia and Wallachia under the suzerainty of Turkey was guaranteed by the great powers. The Catholics were left in control of their shrines in the Holy Land. Great Britain at long last agreed to neutral rights on the high seas.

The chief loser of the Crimean War was Russia, whose massive military no longer looked so formidable. But more broadly a loss was suffered by the already crumbling "concert of Europe," which no longer could wield significant influence on behalf of a conservative international status quo. An immediate beneficiary of the Crimean War was Napoleon III. He played host to the peace conference and, of course, made it into a colorful spectacle. French nationalism and international prestige rose to new heights.

By 1859 Napoleon III had obtained not only the loyalty of the great majority of his own people but also some hegemony in the affairs of the European continent. France was prosperous and powerful. Then things began to go wrong. The dynamic force of nationalism, which he understood and used so well in France, he greatly underestimated abroad. In his efforts to control the Italian and German national movements he failed dismally—in the latter case fatally.

The first serious blunder came in 1859, when he made war on Austria in behalf of Italian freedom. The defeat of Austria set off a frenzy of Italian nationalism that threatened to dispossess all the rulers of the local states of Italy, including the pope. This situation alarmed and angered the French Roman Catholics, who blamed Napoleon. But when the French emperor deserted the Italian nationalists in the midst of the campaign, with the agreed-upon job only half done, he further alienated the French liberals, who were already unsympathetic to him.

Napoleon's efforts to create an overseas empire brought France little immediate profits and much trouble. The most ambitious and disastrous was his attempted conquest and control of Mexico. In 1862 he joined with Great Britain and Spain and seized several Mexican ports, ostensibly to collect debts owed by the revolutionary Juárez government. As soon as the British and the Spaniards saw that Napoleon had more ambitious plans in mind, they withdrew. The French armies then marched on to Mexico City, drove the Juárez government into the hinterland, and set up a Hapsburg prince, Maximilian, as puppet emperor for France. The government of the United States protested vigorously in the name of the Monroe Doctrine, but embroiled in its own Civil War, it could do no more. As soon as the Civil War ended early in 1865, the American government dispatched victorious Union troops to the Mexican border. Napoleon III, now hard-pressed at home, agreed to withdraw his troops. No sooner had the last French soldiers left Mexico City in 1867 than the Juárez forces captured and shot the well-meaning puppet emperor Maximilian. The Mexican fiasco added to the growing unpopularity of Napoleon III with the French people.

On the Continent, Napoleon III was attempting to slow the rapid growth of Prussia and to offset it by annexing territories on the left bank of the Rhine. His failures in this area of foreign policy would eventually prove fatal to his regime.

Meanwhile, the booming prosperity subsided after 1860. The Cobden Treaty, which lowered tariffs between Great Britain and France, flooded France with cheap British manufactured goods with which the less advanced French industries could not compete. The French textile industry also suffered heavily as a result of the American Civil War, which cut off its cotton supply. Both the industrial bourgeoisie and proletariat were hard hit. Overexpansion and speculation began to take their toll.

The emperor attempted to allay the mounting discontent of liberals and workers. Beginning in 1859 he made one concession after another until by 1870 the Second Empire was, at least on paper, a limited constitutional monarchy with a liberal parliamentary government. But 1870 was too late. The showdown with Bismarck's rapidly forming German nation was at hand. The sick and discouraged Napoleon III blundered into a war with Germany for which his armies were woefully unprepared (see pp. 591–592). He was defeated and captured, and his government was overthrown.

3. CAVOUR AND THE MAKING OF ITALIAN UNITY

For centuries Italy had been politically divided into various city-states, kingdoms, and provinces. After 1815 nationalistic sentiments and movements stirred throughout Italy. By 1848 three different plans for uniting Italy into a sovereign state had been developed; each had its own following. One plan was to make Italy a liberal democratic republic. This was the plan of Giuseppe Mazzini, an inspiring speaker and writer but not a very practical organizer or man of action. His movement was called Young Italy. The second plan was to form an Italian confederacy under the leadership of the pope. The third plan was to make Italy a limited monarchy under the leadership of the house of Savoy, the ruling dynasty in Piedmont-Sardinia. During the Revolution of 1848, the first two plans were discredited. Mazzini's chaotic Roman Republic, which he set up after the rebellious populace had driven out the pope, outraged the Roman Catholic world and was overthrown by a French army of Louis Napoleon. After this experience the pope bitterly opposed the unification of Italy, fearing that it would mean the loss of his political control over the Papal States.

At the same time, the heroic role played by Piedmont-Sardinia in battling the Austrians against hopeless odds won for the house of Savoy the devotion and confidence of Italian nationalists. However, the powerful Austrians were still in Lombardy and Venezia, the unsympathetic pope still ruled the Papal States, and the rest of the Italian states were weak and divided. Despite the new prestige of Sardinia, therefore, the task of uniting Italy required the work of a great political leader. He soon appeared: Camillo Benso, Count di Cavour (1810–1861).

Cavour was born into a well-to-do noble family of Piedmont. By the 1840s he was a successful businessman and had become enamored with moderate liberal ideas. Shortly before the Revolution of 1848, he founded a newspaper called *Il Risorgimento (The Resurgence)*, which never ceased to preach Italian unity. In 1850 Cavour was made minister of commerce and agriculture, and two years later prime minister of Sardinia.

Cavour's goals were limited: to modernize economically Piedmont, to make Piedmont the center of the national unification movement, and to form a new Italian state as a constitutional monarchy rather than a democratic republic. To these ends, he worked to lower tariffs, build railroads, and balance Piedmont's budget. He supported the nationalistic Italian National Society, which worked toward national unification under Piedmont. Finally, he used diplomacy and Piedmont's relatively small army to gain international support and overcome the primary obstacle to unification—Austria.

Cavour sent Piedmont's army into the Crimean War in the hopes of winning French sympathy. The plan worked, and at the Paris Peace Conference in 1856, he was given an opportunity to state impressively to the world Italy's case against Austria. In 1858, Cavour and Napoleon met at Plombières, a French spa, and there Cavour persuaded him to fight Austria. Sardinia would provoke Austria into a declaration of war; France would help Sardinia drive the Austrians out of Lombardy and Venetia, which would then be annexed to the kingdom of Sardinia. In payment Sardinia would cede the two little French-speaking provinces of Savoy and Nice to France.

When everything was in readiness in April 1859, Cavour easily provoked unsuspecting Austria into a declaration of war. To Austria's surprise, French armies poured across the Alps to fight alongside the Sardinians. In the two bloody battles of Magenta and Solferino, the Austrians were defeated and driven out of Lombardy. But to the dismay of Cavour, Napoleon suddenly made a separate peace with Austria (the Agreement of Villafranca) on condition that Sardinia receive Lombardy but not Venetia. Napoleon appears to have been motivated by the surprising bloodiness of the battles, the threatening attitude of Prussia, and the anger of the French Roman Catholics, who feared that the wild outburst of nationalism all over Italy following the victories over Austria threatened the independence of the Papal States. News of Magenta and Solferino set all Italy aflame with nationalistic fervor. Early in 1860, under Cavour's supporters, Tuscany, Modena, Parma, and Romagna (the northernmost of the Papal States) joined Piedmont, bringing together all of northern Italy except Venezia.

At this juncture, the rawboned Giuseppe Garibaldi, the most colorful of all the makers of the Italian nation, performed a daring exploit. With a thousand civilian warriors dressed in red shirts and slouch hats, he sailed aboard two little Piedmontese ships for southern Italy. His goal was the conquest of the Kingdom of Naples, the largest and most populous of the Italian states, with a regular army of 124,000 men and a sizable navy. Cavour officially condemned the seemingly foolhardy expedition of the thousand but secretly aided it. Garibaldi's exploits read like a fairy story. He conquered the large island of Sicily, crossed the Strait of Messina, and entered triumphantly into Naples. The opposing troops had little heart for their cause and deserted to Garibaldi by the thousands after his first victories. Moving northward in the direction of Rome, Garibaldi defeated the last Neapolitan forces.

Not wanting to lose control of the situation and fearful that the daring but undiplomatic Garibaldi would march on Rome and bring down French armies, Cavour sent troops southward and seized all the pope's remaining territory except Rome and the territory immediately surrounding it. When Victor Emmanuel at the head of his army approached the forces of Garibaldi, the gallant warrior and patriot submitted to his king and retired to the rocky island of Caprera (see Figure 46.3). The Kingdom of Italy was formally declared in March 1861, with Victor Emmanuel II as king and the liberal Sardinian Constitution of 1848 as the national charter. The red, white, and green Sardinian flag now flew over all of Italy from the Alps to Sicily except Venetia and Rome (see Map 46.1). Those two provinces were not joined to the Italian state until 1866 and 1870, respectively, when, as we shall soon see, first Austria and then France was defeated by Prussia.

Cavour did not live to enjoy the fruits of his labors. Less than three months after the birth of his beloved Italian nation, he was dead. Paunchy, with ill-fitting glasses and a myopic stare, he was anything but impressive in appearance. Neither was he an orator. "I cannot make a speech," he once truthfully said, "but I can make Italy."

Map 46.1 **THE UNIFICATION OF ITALY** This map shows the various stages of Italian unification after 1859. Most of Italy was unified under the leadership of Piedmont by 1860. The new Italian nation took advantage of international affairs to gain other territories after 1860.

FIGURE 46.3. **Victor Emmanuel and Garibaldi** This English engraving portrays King Victor Emmanuel and the heroic Garibaldi shaking hands in 1860, culminating the unification of Italy. (Culver Pictures)

4. GERMAN UNIFICATION

During the decade of the 1850s both liberalism and nationalism began to make rapid headway in the German states. The area was industrialized rapidly. In Prussia the rise of a middle class, imbued with liberalism and German nationalism, challenged for the first time the dominance of the Junker aristocracy, who abhorred liberalism and whose national loyalty was limited to Prussia. The conversion of the Hohenzollerns and the Prussian Junkers to German nationalism was facilitated by the "Humiliation of Olmütz" in 1850. Shortly after the vacillating Frederick William IV had spurned the German national crown offered him by the Frankfurt Assembly in the spring of 1849, he attempted to reorganize the German Confederation under Prussian leadership. The Hapsburg government of Austria, now completely recovered from

its embarrassments of 1848–1849, mobilized its superior army and ordered him to cease. At the town of Olmütz in Austrian territory, the king of Prussia abjectly yielded. After this, the Hohenzollerns and more and more of the proud Junkers sought an opportunity to avenge the national insult to Prussia and replace Austria as leader of the Germanies (see Map 46.2).

In 1858 the unstable mind of Frederick William IV gave way, and his younger brother, who three years later became King William I, assumed leadership of the Prussian government as regent. Unlike his romantic and idealistic brother, William I was a militarist. His first move was to rejuvenate and greatly strengthen the Prussian military machine. The liberals, now strong in the Prussian Landtag, began to take alarm. Might not this all-powerful military machine be used to suppress liberalism? The liberals hoped that by holding up

Map 46.2 **THE UNIFICATION OF GERMANY** During the 1860s Prussia won its struggle with Austria for leadership in Germany. Through wars and diplomatic maneuvering, Bismarck welded numerous German states into a single nation by 1871.

the military budget they might bargain for a stronger role for the legislature in the Prussian government. After several years of haggling the liberals in 1862 finally defeated the military budget. Liberalism and nationalism had collided head-on. William I, unskilled in and unsympa-

thetic with parliamentary government, threatened to resign. As a last resort, he called to the chancellorship Otto Eduard Leopold von Bismarck (see Figure 46.4).

Bismarck would remain chancellor for the next twenty-eight years. He stamped his iron will and

FIGURE 46.4. Bismarck Otto von Bismarck had little faith in democratic processes for achieving purposes of state. Rather, he trusted "blood and iron." The German Empire bore in large measure the stamp of his personality and ideals. (The Granger Collection)

his domineering personality not only on Prussia and Germany but also to a considerable degree on the rest of Europe. Upon assuming the chancellorship of Prussia in 1862, Bismarck, with the backing of the king and army, defied the liberal opposition in the Landtag, violated the constitution, and collected illegally the funds necessary for the military program. "Not by speeches and majority resolutions," said Bismarck, "are the great questions of the time decided—that was the mistake of 1848 and 1849—but by blood and iron." He came to be known as the "Iron Chancellor." Prussian liberalism was crushed. Bismarck believed that military victories won on foreign soil would turn the Prussian liberals into fervent German nationalists. This prediction soon came true.

Bismarck lost little time in putting his new mil-itary machine to work. An opportunity soon presented itself in the form of a dispute with Denmark over the long-standing and complex Schleswig-Holstein question. Schleswig and Holstein were two little provinces lying between Prussia and Denmark. Their population was partly German speaking and partly Danish speaking. Since 1815 they had been ruled by the king of Denmark, though they had not been incorporated into Denmark. In 1863 the Danish king suddenly annexed Schleswig outright. Bismarck, seeing an opportunity to test the Prussian army, to annex some territory, and also to embroil Austria, declared war on Denmark (1864). Since Holstein was a member of the German Confederation, Austria also entered the war against Denmark lest the leadership of the confederation pass to Prussia. Denmark sued for peace and Bismarck made the peace settlement as complicated as possible. Schleswig and Holstein were to be ruled jointly by Prussia and Austria.

Bismarck soon used this unworkable arrangement to stir up trouble with Austria. His first task was to obtain the support or the neutrality of the other three continental powers, Italy, Russia, and France. Prussia had been the first great power to recognize the new Kingdom of Italy. Now, promising Venetia, Bismarck drew the new nation into an alliance against Austria. It was always a cardinal principle of Bismarck to maintain friendly relations with Russia (at Prussia's back door). When Russia's Polish subjects revolted once more in 1863, Prussia alone of the great powers supported Russia. Bismarck neutralized Napoleon III by personal persuasion and deception. By the spring of 1866, with everything in readiness, Bismarck created by threats and maneuvers a state of alarm in Austria, finally manipulating Austria into a declaration of war.

In the Austro-Prussian War most of the little German states supported Austria. Their military forces, however, were quickly crushed beneath the Prussian steamroller. Prussia's armies overwhelmed Austria, a nation twice the size and population of Prussia and long the dominant power in central Europe. Bismarck saw that Austria was now harmless to Prussia and would make a valuable ally or at least friend in Prussia's future wars. Restraining his king and his generals, he

FIGURE 46.5. Victorious German Troops in Paris Victorious German troops march down the Champs-Elysées (with the Arc de Triomphe in the background) at the end of the Franco-Prussian War. (Historical Pictures Service, Chicago)

made the terms of the Treaty of Prague extremely lenient. Austria was to pay no indemnity and to accept the rearrangement of Germany by Prussia. Austria was also forced to cede Venetia to Italy as Italy's reward for fighting on the side of Prussia.

Following the victory over Austria, Bismarck reorganized Germany. Hanover, Nassau, Frankfurt, and Hesse-Cassel were annexed to Prussia outright, bridging the gap between Prussia's Rhine province and the main body. The remaining twenty-one states north of the Main River were bound to Prussia in a North German Confederation. The confederation was completely dominated by Prussia, which alone constituted four-fifths of its area and population. Prussia's king and prime minister were made president and chancellor of the confederation, for which Bismarck drafted the constitution.

Its government was fundamentally autocratic, despite some democratic and liberal forms. The chief administrative officer was the chancellor (Bismarck), who was responsible only to the king of Prussia as president, by whom he was appointed. The legislative body was composed of the Bundesrat, whose members were really ambassadors of the twenty-two state governments, and the Reichstag, whose members were elected by universal male suffrage. All new laws required the approval of both bodies. The Reichstag had no control over the chancellor and his cabinet, as in Great Britain, and little control over the budget and the army and navy. If the Reichstag failed to vote a new budget, the old one automatically continued in force. This document later became the constitution of the German Empire.

Meanwhile, the former liberals in the Prussian Landtag, caught up in the nationalistic fervor following the victory over Austria, repented of their sins of having opposed Bismarck and voted him exoneration for having violated the constitution. The four predominantly Roman Catholic states south of the Main River (Bavaria, Würtemberg, Baden, and part of Hesse-Darmstadt) were left out of the North German Confederation at the insistence of Napoleon III and because Bismarck preferred to have them come in later by their own choice. Bismarck recognized that the reluctant German states could be brought into the fold if German nationalism could be rallied against a foreign threat. France, itself stirred by nationalistic ambitions, provided that threat.

Bismarck's opportunity to confront France came in 1870 when the Spanish crown was offered to a Hohenzollern prince. Bismarck persuaded the reluctant prince to accept the Spanish offer, and the French immediately took alarm at the prospect of being surrounding by Hohenzollerns. Heavy French pressure was exerted on Prussia, to which both the prince and King William I yielded. However, the French ministers were still not satisfied and demanded more. After a meeting at Ems between the French ambassador and the Prussian king, the chancellor saw an opportunity to provoke the French into war. Cleverly editing the Ems dispatch so as to make it appear that the French ambassador and the Prussian king had insulted each other, he published it to the world. The French government, walking into Bismarck's trap, declared war.

The prevailing world military opinion was that this time Prussia had overreached herself and that Bismarck's work would be undone. But as in the case of the Austro-Prussian War, the military might of Prussia was grossly underestimated. The four predominantly Catholic south German states, far from joining Catholic France as Napoleon III had hoped, threw in their lot with Protestant, German-speaking Prussia as Bismarck had anticipated.

The issue of the war was decided in a matter of weeks. Moltke's superior hosts moved into France. The French were overwhelmed. One French army was surrounded at the fortress city of Metz, where it surrendered three months later. Another French army under Marshal MacMahon and Emperor Napoleon III was surrounded at Sedan and surrendered on September 2. Napoleon III himself was one of the captives. When this news reached Paris two days later, the liberals overthrew the government of the Second Empire and declared the Third French Republic. Within a matter of weeks, Paris was surrounded by the Germans. For four months the great city held out; starvation forced it to surrender on January 28, 1871 (see Figure 46.5).

Bismarck forced stricken and helpless France to sign a treaty designed to cripple the nation beyond recovery. The Treaty of Frankfurt required France to pay an indemnity of 5 billion francs in gold. German troops would remain on French soil until this amount was paid in full (which Bismarck mistakenly hoped and expected would take a long time). The province of Alsace and the greater part of Lorraine were ceded to Germany. Since these provinces contained much of France's vital iron reserves, the seizure of Alsace and Lorraine long poisoned Franco-German relations.

On January 18, 1871, while the big German ~~French~~ took guns were still battering Paris, the heads of the twenty-five German states at war with France met on Bismarck's call at Versailles (behind the German lines) and in the Hall of Mirrors proclaimed Wilhelm I emperor of the German Empire. The constitution that Bismarck had drafted for the North German Confederation became the constitution of the German Empire. Bismarck, of course, became its chancellor, and he lived to rule over his creation for the next nineteen years. The German Empire had now replaced France as the dominant power on the European continent and became a new rival of Great Britain for world hegemony.

In Germany, as in Italy, nationalism had succeeded. In the decades after 1871 the two new nation-states would join the competition in international affairs. And nationalism was strengthening the political institutions of other nation-states, furthering a trend that had already become apparent in France during the 1850s and 1860s. Nationalism would also contribute to the new imperialism of the late nineteenth century, which in turn would further increase the power of the na-

tion-state and eventually help spread nationalism to the non-Western world.

SUGGESTED READING

General

W. E. Mosse, *Liberal Europe, 1848–1875* (1974). A useful comparative history.

N. Rich, *The Age of Nationalism and Reform* (1976). A solid survey.

The Nature of Nationalism

B. Shafer, *Faces of Nationalism* (1972). A good summary.

A. Smith, *Theories of Nationalism* (1983). A comparative approach.

The Second Empire of Napoleon III

A. Plessis, *The Rise and Fall of the Second Empire* (1985). A recent account.

N. Rich, *Why the Crimean War? A Cautionary Tale* (1985). A concise political and diplomatic interpretation.

T. Zeldin, *France, 1848–1945,* 4 vols. (1973–1980). Sophisticated, insightful, and thorough.

Cavour and the Making of Italian Unity

D. Beales, *The Risorgimento and the Unification of Italy* (1982). Brief survey with accompanying documents.

R. Grew, *A Sterner Plan for Italian Unity* (1963). Excellent analysis of the movement for Italian unification.

D. M. Smith, *Cavour* (1985). A highly respected work.

D. M. Smith, *Italy: A Modern History* (1969). Scholarly survey covering the period.

German Unification

T. S. Hamerow, *The Social Foundations of German Unification, 1858–1871* (1972). Relates economic, social, and political factors behind German unification.

H. Holborn, *A History of Modern Germany,* 3 vols. (1959–1969). Detailed, scholarly survey.

M. Howard, *The Franco-Prussian War* (1969). Excellent analysis.

O. Pflanze, *Bismarck and the Development of Germany* (1963). An excellent political analysis covering Germany during this period.

CHAPTER 47

Politics in the Age of Progress, 1871–1914

FIGURE 47.1. Bismarck and the Socialists The satirical illustration from the September 28, 1878, edition of the British magazine *Punch* shows the German chancellor Bismarck in military dress vainly struggling to keep down the Socialist "Jack in the Box." Although Bismarck banned the Social Democratic party in 1878, it would not die. In the years just prior to World War I it became Germany's largest single party. Other socialist parties grew throughout Europe during the same period. (*Punch*, September 28, 1878)

From the end of the Franco-Prussian War in 1871 until the outbreak of World War I in 1914, the West was free from major wars. Despite some changes and shaky beginnings, European nations survived the period with their governments intact. When the considerable economic expansion, cultural production, and imperial success are added to this political picture, the years between 1871 and 1914 could be viewed as a time of great progress for Europe.

Nevertheless, some disturbing trends were evident. The freedom from war was accompanied by a growing militarism in several nations and a new precarious complexity in international affairs. Moreover, governmental survival did not mean political peace; political unrest and even some revolutionary activity threatened many European nations. Imperial success was purchased at a price of heightened international rivalries. These disturbing trends would bear bitter fruit with the outbreak of World War I in 1914.

The strongest political forces of the period were the spread of democratic institutions and nationalism. Both forces had been underway since 1850. However, the spread of democratic institutions occurred quite unevenly. And nationalism, while it differed according to the conditions in each country, took on more conservative, aggressive, militaristic, and even racist overtones. The political developments between 1871 and 1914 can be well exposed by stressing the themes of democracy and nationalism and dividing our examination of European nations roughly between western and eastern Europe.

1. WESTERN EUROPE: THE SPREAD AND REFORM OF DEMOCRATIC INSTITUTIONS

Most western European countries had formed a national identity and initiated democratic reforms before the eastern European countries. Between 1871 and 1914 democratic institutions continued to spread in western Europe and, in general, encountered fewer problems than in eastern Europe.

Great Britain

During the second half of the nineteenth century Great Britain was in a strong position. The country had avoided the revolutionary turmoil that struck the European continent between 1848 and 1850, largely due to the government's ability to reform and adapt just enough to contain pressures for radical change. Liberalism seemed to be working well. The British economy was the most modern in the world, and the British people were relatively wealthy (although the condition of the working class was still unenviable). Yet Great Britain was not immune from the forces of nationalism that were growing everywhere in the West. In the decades following 1850 British nationalism grew, and liberal and conservative British politicians increasingly used it to gain support, increase the responsibilities of the national government, and justify foreign policy.

For most of the 1850s and 1860s liberals controlled the government. Lord Palmerston, a liberal Whig, was prime minister and leader of the Whigs for much of the period between 1855 and 1865. While modest domestic reforms to modernize government and increase allegiance of the people to the government were instituted under his ministry, he relied on nationalistic sentiment for support. He willingly paraded British naval might whenever possible and sympathetically supported movements for national liberation abroad. But he did not bend to those who demanded greater inclusion in the political system by increasing suffrage.

By 1865 William E. Gladstone had risen to leadership within the Whig party and was transforming it into the more modern Liberal party. In 1866 he and the Liberal prime minister, Lord Russell, introduced a suffrage reform bill. Although the bill was defeated and the Liberal ministry was forced to resign, the narrowness of the defeat plus the popular demand for suffrage reform convinced the rising young leader of the Conservatives, Benjamin Disraeli (1804–1881), that reform was inevitable. The shrewd Disraeli decided to seize credit for the inevitable by introducing his own reform bill. The result was the Reform Bill of 1867, which, as amended by the Liberals, doubled the electorate and gave the vote to males in the lower middle class and upper working class for the first time.

Gladstone's Reform Bill of 1884 enfranchised most of the rural males. After 1884 virtually every male householder or renter in Great Britain could vote. Restricted woman's suffrage would come in 1918 and full suffrage in 1928.

Several liberal reforms were enacted during the 1850s, 1860s, and 1870s, making government responsible for primary schools, requiring competitive examinations for civil service, and removing some religious restrictions on non-Anglicans. Yet until the end of the nineteenth century, both the Conservative and Liberal parties were still controlled by the aristocracy and the wealthy bourgeoisie. Although both parties were fairly benevolent toward the working classes, the large and discontented industrial proletariat wanted its fair share in the government. Between 1881 and 1906 its leaders turned to a program of moderate socialism, and with the aid of a number of intellectual radicals, notably George Bernard Shaw, H. G. Wells, and Sidney and Beatrice Webb, the Labour party was formed.

In 1906 the rejuvenated Liberal party came to power under the actual, if not official, leadership of the fiery young Welshman David Lloyd George, who also had the backing of the Labour party. Between 1906 and 1911 Lloyd George put through Parliament a revolutionary program of accident, sickness, old-age, and unemployment insurance. To meet this and other increased costs to the government, he forced through the reluctant House of Lords his famous budget of 1909, which shifted the "heaviest burden [of taxation] to the broadest backs." A steeply graduated income tax and high taxes on unearned income, inheritances, idle parks of the landed aristocracy, and mining royalties struck heavily at the rich. The Parliamentary Reform Act of 1911 stripped the House of Lords of most of its former power and made the popularly elected House of Commons supreme. In 1914 the long-festering Irish question was resolved by granting self-government to Ireland, although the outbreak of World War I in that year delayed its implementation. And conflict between Protestants and Catholics in northern Ireland promised to persist. However, by 1914 Great Britain was on the road to greater social, economic, and political democracy.

Between 1871 and 1914 Britain increased its imperial holdings (see Chapter 49) and joined other nations in a dangerous international rivalry that combined nationalism and militarism. In the face of Germany's swift rise to power and prestige, the British took renewed pride in their dominant navy and in their empire, which contained one-fourth of all the earth's territory and people. Many well-to-do Britishers thought themselves to be so superior to the other peoples in Europe that they became the most unpopular of all travelers on the Continent. To some observers, it appeared that Great Britain was as big a bully on the seas and overseas as Germany was on the continent of Europe.

France

With the end of the Second Empire of Napoleon III during the Franco-German War of 1870–1871, the Third French Republic was proclaimed. However, the first elections, held in February 1871 after the surrender of Paris, resulted in a sweeping victory for the monarchists. This somewhat surprising result may be explained by the fact that the republican leaders wanted to continue the hopeless war with Germany. The city of Paris, made up largely of the liberal bourgeoisie and the radical proletariat, was unwilling to submit to the domination of conservative rural France. It declared its independence from the rest of France and set up its own city government, or commune. The Paris Commune gained a reputation as an experiment in Marxian socialism. In reality the Commune was dominated by a mix of different socialistic and republican groups and was more radically democratic than anything else. Two months (April–May 1871) of fighting, culminating in a week of all-out warfare in the streets of Paris, were required for the rest of the French nation (with the regular army) to subdue the Paris Commune (see Figure 47.2). Some twenty thousand Parisians were executed after they had surrendered, and seventy-five hundred were deported. The fall of the Paris Commune ended a threat to the integrity of France, heartened conservatives, and created martyrs for socialism.

The royalists, though in the majority, were split into a Bourbon faction and an Orléanist fac-

FIGURE 47.2. **Executions During the Paris Commune**   Bloodshed and bitter reprisals were common on both sides during the Paris Commune. Here, in 1871, Communards (including women) execute hostages in response to a previous execution of Communard leaders. (BBC Hulton/The Bettmann Archive)

tion, neither of which was willing to yield to the other. Meanwhile, as this stalemate dragged on for several years, the liberals grew in strength. Finally, in 1875, the frustrated and frightened monarchists consented (by a single vote) to the adoption of a republican constitution. The constitution provided for a Chamber of Deputies elected by universal male suffrage, a Senate elected by a complicated indirect method, and a rather powerless president to be elected by the two legislative bodies. Most of the executive functions of the republic were to be carried on by a cabinet of ministers dependent on the Chamber of Deputies. It was not until four years later, however, that the liberal republicans under the leadership of the eloquent Léon Gambetta gained actual control of the republic.

But the Third French Republic, so furtively born, was still not safe. Powerful groups were hostile to it. The chief of these were the various factions of monarchists (Bourbons, Orléanists, and Bonapartists), the professional military, the Roman Catholic hierarchy, and large numbers of

peasant proprietors. In the late 1880s these factions rallied around a handsome man on horseback, General Boulanger, who became so popular that he might have overthrown the republic had he been bolder and more skillful or had the republican leaders been less courageous. As it turned out, when he was summoned to answer charges of treason against the republic, he fled the country and eventually committed suicide.

In the 1890s the antirepublican forces rallied again around a group of army officers who had falsely accused a Jewish army captain, Alfred Dreyfus, and sent him to prison on Devil's Island. This time the enemies of the republic were aided by a rising militant nationalism and anti-Semitism. It required twelve years for the republicans, inspired by the novelist Émile Zola, to get Dreyfus acquitted and the army officers who had imprisoned him punished. The Dreyfus case strengthened the republic and discredited its enemies.

Democratic government did not work as smoothly in France as in Great Britain. The tradition of extreme individualism, the animosity between clericalist and anticlericalist, the sharp cleavage between radical urban Paris and conservative rural France, lingering provincial loyalty, and a historic suspicion of strong government and high taxes—all contributed to the formation of a multiplicity of political parties. Thus the cabinet was forced to rely on the support of a precarious combination of parties (a *bloc*) in order to carry on the executive functions of government. In France the Chamber of Deputies could overthrow a cabinet without having to risk an immediate national election, as was the case in Great Britain. As a result, there was a rapid turnover of French ministries. During the forty-three years from 1871 to 1914, no fewer than fifty-one ministries attempted to govern France. Nevertheless, the French government was not as unstable as it might appear. The same groups of ministers often rotated in and out of office, sometimes simply exchanging one ministry for another. Moreover, the actual details of administration were carried on with relatively little interruption by a stable civil service, firmly built in the tradition of Richelieu and Napoleon I.

As the twentieth century opened, democratic government in France appeared to be firmly established and increasingly responsive to the will of the masses. Trade unions had been legalized, a modern system of public education that bolstered support for the republic was well established, and (in 1905) all formal ties between the state and the Catholic church were broken. Factory laws were giving the workers increased protection. Between 1905 and 1910, a limited program of unemployment, old-age, accident, and sickness insurance was inaugurated. This program of social legislation, however, was only a modest beginning; and the French masses, becoming more politically conscious and active, expressed their discontent in strikes and more votes for the Socialists.

France, like Great Britain, was subject to the growing nationalism of the period that was related to international rivalries, imperial expansion, and military buildup. The already strong French pride had only been intensified by France's defeat at the hands of Germany in 1870–1871. The statue dedicated to the city of Strasbourg in the Place de la Concorde in Paris was draped in perpetual mourning as a constant reminder of the day of revenge. France greatly speeded up its overseas

empire building and increased the size of its armed forces until they were larger in proportion to the population than those of the German Empire. France sought and found military allies. When a general strike in 1910 threatened the nation's military security and war preparations, Aristide Briand, himself a radical and former Socialist, did not hesitate to use the armed forces to break it up.

Italy

Italy entered the 1870s in a much weaker position than France or Great Britain. Italy had only just become a nation-state, and even that status was weakened by strong regional differences—particularly between the more economically developed north and the poorer south. Italy's new government was liberal, but the right to vote was limited to the middle and upper classes, who constituted a small minority of the nation's population.

Between the 1870s and World War I Italian governments weathered various political crises that sometimes reached revolutionary proportions. The nation was painfully modernizing and entering into the international arena. Italian governments became involved in the shifting international alliances of the period and the nationalistic race for colonial possessions. Toward the end of the period there were signs that Italy would follow the democratic pattern set in other Western nations. Economic and social reforms to benefit the working classes were enacted under the government of Giovanni Giolitti, and in 1911 universal male suffrage was enacted.

Smaller Countries of Northern Europe

The people of the smaller countries of northern Europe also witnessed the triumph of democratic government during this period. Belgium adopted universal male suffrage in 1893. Here the weighted vote was established, men of wealth and education getting two or three additional votes. The Dutch Netherlands extended the suffrage in 1887 and again in 1896; in 1917 all adult men and women were given the right to vote. Norway adopted universal male suffrage in 1898, Sweden in 1909, and Denmark in 1914. In 1913 Norway became the first European country to grant the vote to women. In these five nations, the traditional respect for government and the relatively high degree of literacy made democracy a vigorous reality.

2. EASTERN EUROPE: CONSERVATISM, MILITARISM, AND NATIONALISM

The democratic trends characteristic of western Europe were also occurring in eastern Europe, but they were longer in arriving, less firmly established, and not as complete as in western Europe. Moreover, nationalism, which was a general phenomenon, took on more strident, aggressive tones in eastern Europe where national identity was less comfortably fixed. Most of eastern Europe remained in the control of conservative groups. The governments were autocratic in nature and more dependent on the military for support.

The German Empire Under Bismarck and Kaiser Wilhelm II

The center of these trends in eastern Europe was the German Empire. Its creation by the blood-and-iron method, its autocratic constitution (despite the establishment of universal male suffrage), and its strong-handed leadership, first by the Iron Chancellor and then by Kaiser Wilhelm II, guaranteed that the German Empire would be an enlarged Prussia. The German Empire possessed a powerful army, a large, energetic, and disciplined population, a rapidly growing industrial machine, a fervent and restless national spirit. Bismarck ruled over his creation as chancellor for almost twenty years.

His first concern after the defeat of France and the declaration of the empire in 1870–1871 was to complete the consolidation and nationalization of the German states and people. The law codes, the currencies, and the military forces of the twenty-five lesser states were brought into conformity with those of Prussia. Banking and railroads were placed under control of the national government. The empire's spawning industry was protected against British competition by a high tariff. The

French in Alsace-Lorraine, the Danes in Schleswig, and the more than 3 million Poles in the eastern districts were pressured to give up their language and traditions.

Two other groups in Germany excited Bismarck's suspicion and wrath: the Roman Catholics and the Socialists. Any German who had a foreign loyalty was intolerable to Bismarck. From 1872 to 1878, Bismarck waged a political power struggle with the Roman Catholics that came to be called the *Kulturkampf* (battle for civilization). The Jesuits were expelled, civil marriage was made compulsory, and all education, including that of Roman Catholic priests, was brought under state control and largely secularized. When the Roman Catholic clergy and most of the laity, which constituted approximately one-third of the total German population, resisted and rallied to the pope, hundreds of priests and six bishops were arrested. But it was all to no avail. The Roman Catholic Center party in the Reichstag became stronger, and by 1878 Bismarck wanted its support for what he considered to be a struggle of greater importance—that against the Socialists. In 1878 upon the accession of a more conciliatory pope, Leo XIII, Bismarck "went to Canossa" and had the most severe of the anti-Catholic legislation repealed.

In the same year he began a twelve-year crusade against the internationally minded Socialists. He outlawed their publications, their organizations, and their meetings, and set the German police force upon them. But he only drove them underground. Throughout the decade of the 1880s, Bismarck sought to undercut the Socialists' appeal to the working class by setting up a comprehensive system of social insurance. Accident, sickness, and old-age insurance was provided for the industrial proletariat, the funds being raised by compulsory contributions from the workers, the employers, and the state. Although Bismarck's motives were not benevolent or humanitarian, his measures gave impetus to a trend toward state responsibility for social security. Nevertheless, the Socialists were not appeased, and Bismarck continued to fight them as long as he remained chancellor.

Bismarck's foreign policy after 1871 was one of security and retrenchment. He knew that France would be unforgiving and revengeful, forever seeking an opportunity to regain Alsace and Lorraine. Of France alone he had little fear, but France in league with other powers, particularly Russia and Great Britain, would be formidable. Therefore, his consistent policy was to maintain a close military alliance with Austria-Hungary and cordial relations with Russia and Great Britain. In 1873 Bismarck formed the Three Emperor's League among Germany, Austria-Hungary, and Russia. When the interests of Austria-Hungary and Russia proved to be incompatible, this league was replaced in 1879–1882 by the Triple Alliance among Germany, Austria-Hungary, and Italy. A separate "reinsurance treaty" of friendship and neutrality was made with Russia. Of course, Bismarck did not depend wholly on diplomacy. Throughout this period, the German military machine was made even more powerful.

In 1888 Wilhelm II (1888–1918) became kaiser. Wilhelm II was twenty-nine years of age when he ascended the throne. He had been brought up in the army, which was his first love. Egotistical and bombastic by nature, he was a dabbler in theology, history, and the arts and gave advice and instructions freely to the leading figures in those fields. He was also an eloquent and willing speaker and had his generous and humanitarian moments.

The young kaiser's personality and policies soon clashed with those of Bismarck. In 1890, just two years after he became emperor, Wilhelm II accepted Bismarck's reluctant resignation as chancellor. The immediate cause of the break was a disagreement over the control of the ministry and the repeal of the anti-Socialist laws, which Bismarck wished to be continued. The real reason, however, was that there was simply not room enough in Germany for two such prima donnas.

Bismarck's foreign policy was quickly reversed. The reinsurance treaty with Russia was immediately allowed to lapse, as the kaiser assumed a keen interest in extending German hegemony over the Balkans and the Ottoman Empire, areas the Russians considered to be vital to their own interests and ambitions. In 1894 Russia formed an alliance with France, the very thing that Bismarck had work so hard to prevent. Wilhelm II also soon alienated Great Britain. His extension of German influence in the Near East, particularly his Berlin-to-Bagdad railroad project (see pp. 622–623),

threatened an area in which Great Britain had many vital interests and through which ran its "lifeline" to India and the Far East. In China, too, German interests began to rival those of the British.

It was the kaiser's naval policy, however, that alarmed the British the most. Wilhelm was an ardent and lifelong navalist. "The waves beat powerfully at our national gates," he cried, "and call us as a great nation to maintain our place in the world. . . ." Germany's "place in the sun" was a favorite phrase of the Hohenzollern emperor. The Reichstag voted an enormous naval building program that was steadily increased until in 1908 it called for twenty-eight new battleships of the biggest and latest design. The purpose of this program was to give Germany a battle fleet so great that "a war against the mightiest naval power would endanger the supremacy of that power."

Great Britain, whose food supply as well as her empire depended on naval supremacy, took utmost alarm. Failing in efforts to reach an understanding with the kaiser's government, Britain launched a huge and costly naval building program of its own. In 1904 Britain joined France, and in 1907 Russia, in the Triple Entente, which was in reality a defensive military alliance. The interests and policies of Great Britain, France, and Russia had long been so discordant that nothing less than maximum alarm could have brought them together. Thus in seventeen years Wilhelm had undone Bismarck's work and brought about the "encirclement" of the fatherland by three of the world's greatest powers.

Germany's economic exploits under Bismarck and Wilhelm II were no less phenomenal than those in the military realm. In 1871 Great Britain was the world's leading nation in manufacturing and commerce; the Industrial Revolution was still in its early stages in Germany. By 1914 Germany was a close second to Great Britain in industry and commerce; in many areas, such as the production of steel and machinery, Germany had far outstripped Britain. In the up-and-coming chemical and electrical industries and in scientific agriculture and forestry, Germany was far in advance of all other nations. Germany was also first in the application of science to industry and in industrial and scientific research. By 1914 the German merchant marine had captured the lion's share of the lucrative transatlantic passenger traffic.

At a time when other industrial nations, particularly the United States, were beginning to restrict the giant monopolistic trusts, the German imperial government was encouraging and subsidizing its cartels in order that they might compete more effectively with foreign companies. More and more of the world's market was captured by German business. "Made in Germany" became a familiar mark from the Andean plateau to the Congo jungles. Germany's population, keeping pace with its economy, increased from 41 million in 1871 to 65 million in 1914. Meanwhile, heavy emigration (which had reached a peak in the 1880s of some two hundred fifty thousand a year, most of it to the United States) dwindled to a mere trickle. In 1914 the number of German emigrants was less than the number of workers coming into Germany from neighboring countries. Only the United States was keeping pace with Germany in overall economic advancement.

The industrialization of Germany, although accompanied by the growth of a large and prosperous bourgeoisie, did not produce a tide of liberalism as it had in the other Western industrialized nations. The middle classes allied themselves with the conservative government. Only the Social Democratic party (working class) and the small and weak Progressive party (intellectuals, professionals, and small-business people) advocated liberal or radical reforms. But even the Social Democratic party, by 1914 the largest party in the empire, was inundated by the flood of nationalism that welled up during the international crises that preceded World War I.

Russia

Until the 1850s, Russia had remained relatively untouched by the Industrial Revolution and liberalism. Russia's government was autocratic under the tsar, its society was still feudalistic with serfs bound to the land and their lords, and its large army enjoyed an aura of near invincibility. Russia had earned the reputation of being the most conservative and unreforming of the European powers. After the Crimean War of 1853–1856,

FIGURE 47.3. Red Sunday In January 1905 the tsar's guards shot down hundreds of peaceful demonstrators in front of the royal palace in St. Petersburg. This event, known as "Red Sunday," left a bitter memory with Russia's liberals and radicals. (The Granger Collection)

it was clear that things would have to change soon.

Russia's army was humiliated in the war. Its leaders quickly realized that Russia was being left behind by the other powers, that the country lacked the economic and social foundations for a modern war—the railroads, the armaments industry, and the social support. The new tsar, Alexander II (1855–1881), announced a series of reforms. The most important was the freeing of the serfs in 1861. While the measure put an end to that form of human bondage and did transfer land to the freed peasantry, it did not make the peasants fully independent and self-sufficient. In general they received only the poorest land, they remained burdened by payments owed to the state, and they were tied by collective ownership to their village commune (the *mir*). Other reforms made the local judicial system more independent, created elected local political institutions, encouraged primary and secondary education, relaxed censorship, and modernized the military. At the same time, the government initiated a program of railway construction, which stimulated related industries. In Russia's cities a still small middle and working class began to grow.

A strong wave of dissatisfaction arose during the later years of Alexander II's rule. The former serfs had been cruelly disappointed by the fruits of emancipation. Another revolt of Russia's Polish subjects in 1863 made Alexander II more reactionary. His failure to follow through with more sweeping reforms after the emancipation of the serfs disappointed liberals, populists, and others, who were mostly intellectual young aristocrats. In despair over the possibility of reforming the huge Russian Empire by orderly methods, these young intellectuals became radical. They set out to undermine Russia's society, government, and church in order to build a new and modern Russia from the ruins. When their efforts were spurned by the masses whom they were seeking to uplift, a more violent wing of the revolutionaries turned to terror and assassination to achieve their ends. Numerous bureaucrats and police officials were slain by terrorists, and Tsar Alexander II himself was killed by a bomb.

The new tsar, Alexander III (1881–1894), was a harsh, reactionary autocrat. Blaming his father's death on softness, he set out to exterminate all liberalism in Russia. The ruthless Plehve was made head of the secret police, and its agents were soon everywhere. Thousands of suspects were arrested. Some were shot or exiled to Siberia. Alexander initiated a sweeping reactionary program of Russianization. The censored press, the closely supervised schools, the secret police, and above all, the clergy of the Orthodox church became potent agencies for Russianization. Non-Orthodox religions were persecuted. Language minority groups—the Poles, the Baltic peoples, the Finns, and even the Ukrainians—were forced to use the Russian language. The Jews suffered the harshest persecution. They were subject to such abuse, including bloody pogroms, that more than a quarter million of them fled, mostly to the United States.

Alexander III was succeeded by Nicholas II (1894–1917), also reactionary but less effective. Although Nicholas attempted to continue the policies of his father, he was unable to make them

work. During the 1890s, Russia experienced a new surge of industrialization, stimulated by the aggressive policies of Sergei Witte, the finance minister, and the infusion of foreign capital into Russia. A larger industrial bourgeoisie and proletariat emerged and with them movements for liberal and radical reform. Of the various liberal and radical parties that emerged, the one of greatest significance for the future was the Social Democratic party. This was a Marxist party whose leadership was made up almost entirely of intellectual radicals. Their chief concern was for the industrial proletariat. In 1903 the Social Democrats split into a moderate, gradualist wing called the Mensheviks (minority) and a violent revolutionary wing called the Bolsheviks (majority). The Bolsheviks were led by the brilliant and dynamic Vladimir Lenin, who was living in exile in Switzerland.

Taking advantage of the embarrassment of the tsar's government because of Russia's defeat by Japan in 1904–1905 (see p. 621), the various liberal and radical groups clamored for reform. In July 1904 the hated Plehve was assassinated. In January 1905 hundreds of peaceful demonstrators were shot down in front of the royal palace in St. Petersburg by the tsar's guard. This bloody event, known as "Red Sunday," fanned the flames of discontent (see Figure 47.3). In October 1905 a general strike completely paralyzed the country for ten days. Nicholas II, yielding at last, issued a manifesto that promised civil liberties and a popularly elected Duma. However, before the Duma could be elected, the return of the Russian troops from the Far East and a huge loan from Russia's ally, France, strengthened the hand of the tsar. During the next two years he and his advisers succeeded in reducing the Duma to an undemocratically elected body that had little real control over the government. Nevertheless, a break had been made in Russia's autocratic system. Russia's rural society had broken from its feudal bonds, its economy was industrializing, and its political system included parliamentary institutions that promised to gain authority in the future.

National Movements in Southeast Europe

While nationalism between 1871 and 1914 was crushing minority language groups in the German

Map 47.1 LANGUAGE GROUPS, AUSTRIA-HUNGARY This map indicates the difficulties facing the Austro-Hungarian Empire in an age of growing nationalism. Satisfaction of demands for independence by the various ethnic or language groups would spell dismemberment of the empire.

and the Russian empires, it was pulling the Austrian and Ottoman empires apart along language lines. After Austria's defeat by Prussia in 1866, the dominant German minority in Austria felt obliged to take into partnership the aggressive and restless Magyars of Hungary. The *Ausgleich* (compromise) of 1867 set up the Dual Monarchy of Austria-Hungary. Each country had its own separate parliament. But the two were united under a common ruler, the head of the house of Hapsburg; common ministries of war, finance, and foreign affairs; and joint delegations from the two parliaments whose

duty was to coordinate policies wherever possible. This arrangement was essentially an alliance between the Germans of Austria and the Magyars of Hungary against the Slavic, Rumanian, and Italian language groups, which constituted a majority of the total population of the Dual Monarchy. In effect, the Germans said to the Magyars: "You take care of your subject language groups [mostly Slavs] and we will take care of ours" (see Map 47.1).

Austria followed a relatively moderate policy in dealing with its subject language groups. Cultural autonomy was granted, and the suffrage was gradually extended until in 1907 all adult males were given the vote. However, the subject peoples were more interested in nationalism than in democracy. The various language groups developed images of a glorious cultural and political past. The prosperous Czechs of Bohemia were especially adamant. The problem was confounded by the fact that many of the language groups had kinspeople outside the Dual Monarchy whom they wished to join and who deliberately stirred up their disloyalty. Such groups were the Italians, the Poles, the Ruthenians (Ukrainians), the Serbs, and the Rumanians. Parliamentary sessions in Austria frequently degenerated into shouting, inkstand-throwing melees among the various language groups. Moreover anti-Semitism was growing in Austria, a development not unrelated to these problems among different ethnic groups.

Hungary made no pretense of conciliation. The Magyar aristocracy ruled over the Slovak, Rumanian, Serb, and Croat minorities with an iron hand. The aristocracy also refused to permit its own Magyar masses to participate in the government. The nationalist discontent in Hungary was even greater than it was in Austria; the Yugo (southern) Slavs (Croats and Serbs) were particularly troublesome. This explosive nationalism threatened to blow the Austro-Hungarian monarchy apart and, because of the network of entangling alliances, to draw the other major powers into a world conflict.

The Balkan portion of the Ottoman Empire between 1871 and 1914 was a hornets' nest of nationalism (see Map 47.1). The hatred of the Christian Balkan language groups for their Moslem Turkish masters was equaled only by their distrust for each other. The once potent Ottoman Empire crumbled throughout the course of the nineteenth century, and one Balkan language group after another, now aflame with national pride and ambition, emerged as an independent nation. Meanwhile, all the great powers of Europe became involved in the strategic and troubled area of the Near East. Russia, Austria-Hungary, Great Britain, France, Germany, and Italy had important imperial, economic, and military interests in the Balkans. In addition, Russia and Austria-Hungary had serious nationalistic interests there. Russia considered itself the big brother and protector of the Slavic-speaking Serbs and Bulgarians. Austria-Hungary's large Rumanian and Yugoslav populations desired union with their free kinspeople in Rumania and Serbia. Between 1829 and 1913 first the Greeks, then the Serbs, Rumanians, and Bulgarians, and finally the Albanians gained their independence from the Ottoman Empire. In each case a major crisis occurred among the great powers. These Balkan crises became progressively more severe, until finally one crisis got out of control and exploded into World War I.

SUGGESTED READING

General

A. J. Mayer, *The Persistence of the Old Regime in Europe to the Great War* (1981). A controversial, recent interpretation.

N. Stone, *Europe Transformed, 1878–1919* (1984). Fine new survey.

A. J. P. Taylor, *The Struggle for Mastery in Europe, 1848–1918* (1971). A good, interpretive study of international politics.

Great Britain

M. Bentley, *Politics Without Democracy, 1815–1914* (1984). Fine political coverage.

D. Read, *England, 1868–1914. The Age of Urban Democracy* (1979). Related politics and socioeconomic developments.

France

D. Johnson, *France and the Dreyfus Affair* (1967). Excellent study.

J. M. Moyem and M. Rebérioux, *The Third Republic from Its Origins to the Great War, 1871–1914* (1984). A thorough synthesis.

R. L. Williams, *The French Revolution of 1870–1871* (1969). Excellent analysis of the Paris Commune.

Italy

J. A. Thayer, *Italy and the Great War: Politics and Culture, 1870–1915* (1964). A solid analysis of Italian political history.

D. M. Smith, *Italy: A Modern History* (1969). A good survey.

Germany

G. Craig, *Germany, 1866–1945* (1980). Particularly good on German political history during this period.

P. Pulzer, *The Rise of Political Anti-Semitism in Germany and Austria* (1964). A well-written analysis.

C. Schorsky, *German Social Democracy, 1905–1917* (1955). Excellent analysis of the Social Democrats.

H. U. Wehler, *The German Empire, 1871–1918* (1985). A recent interpretive study.

Russia

W. Blackwell, *The Industrialization of Russia* (1982). Good on this important topic.

A. B. Ulam, *Russia's Failed Revolutionaries* (1981). Good study of Russia's revolutionary groups prior to 1917.

H. Rogger, *Russia in the Age of Modernization and Revolution, 1881–1917* (1983). Excellent synthesis.

Southeast Europe

B. Jelavich, *History of the Balkans* (1983). A useful recent survey.

L. S. Stavrianos, *The Balkans, 1815–1914* (1963). Relates domestic and international developments.

CHAPTER 48

Democracy, Expansion, Civil War, and Reform in the United States, 1800–1920

FIGURE 48.1. **Manifest Destiny** This painting, "Manifest Destiny," by John Gast, reveals the idealized myth of westward expansion. Moving from the Atlantic coast cities of the East across the plains and mountains toward the Pacific, the goddess of Destiny carries a schoolbook in one hand and a telegraph wire in the other. Below her come white male hunters and settlers, pushing Indians and buffalo farther west in retreat. In her wake follows the railroad. (Library of Congress)

By the end of the eighteenth century the United States was experiencing many of the same trends and developments as other nations of Western civilization. As we saw in Chapter 39, the United States was influenced by Enlightenment ideas, experienced a revolution, and established liberal political institutions—a pattern familiar to France and some other European nations. With the exception of the black slaves, almost all citizens of the new nation were from European stock. Most people worked the land, but there were some growing cities and early industrial establishments—again a pattern not too different from many areas in Europe.

There were some important differences between the United States and other nations of Western civilization in 1800. It had only recently emerged from colonial status and remained separated from Europe by the Atlantic Ocean. Politically and socially, the United States did not carry a strong legacy of monarchical rule or aristocratic distinctions. There was a surplus of land, thanks to the willingness of American citizens to take from the Indians, and a supply of cheap, noncompetitive labor, thanks to slavery.

During the nineteenth century the United States again shared in trends sweeping through Western civilization while remaining strikingly distinct in some important ways. In this chapter we will emphasize the pattern of shared trends and distinctions as we trace major elements of United States history in rough chronological order. By the end of the second decade of the twentieth century, the United States will have reached a point where its development can be better viewed as integrated with that of other Western nations.

1. DEMOCRACY AND GEOGRAPHIC EXPANSION, 1800–1861

Democracy in the young American republic received a boost with the election of Thomas Jefferson as president in 1800. Jefferson represented the ideals of a nation of small farmers and the realities of a political democracy with a party system. The coming to power of this liberal theorist—the author of the Declaration of Independence—was a shock to the more elitist Federalists, who flourished under presidents Washington and Adams. The conservative Founding Fathers had felt that the capable elite should rule and that political parties, or "factions," would undermine the new political system. Although the rich and well-born raised a cry of anguish at the triumph of Jefferson, he was a moderate individual who in fact did little that was radical as president. Although he was supported in the election by the yeoman farmers, he was an elegant Virginian and a scholarly philosopher rather than a man of the masses.

The War of 1812 with Great Britain resulted in an upsurge of American nationalism, which helped mold America's evolving political institutions. A new crop of nationally minded statesmen appeared, the ablest of whom were Henry Clay, John C. Calhoun, and Daniel Webster. The war itself ended indecisively, yet the United States emerged with a stronger national economy and a greater sense of being a nation with its own character and institutions rather than a former British colony.

The War of 1812 also produced a hero, Andrew Jackson. His rise to the presidency signaled a new stage in the development of America's democratic institutions. Not only did it represent the rise of a common man to the presidency—he defeated formidable, established, sophisticated political giants—it also marked the rise of western frontier states to national political importance and the early development of modern, mass-based political parties. During the Jacksonian era, which extended some two decades after his election in 1828, democracy advanced as new states without property qualifications for voting were rapidly admitted to the Union and as the older states eliminated property qualifications from their voting requirements. Artisans and small farmers used the egalitarian rhetoric of the Jacksonian era to assert their own interests and power. Yet much of the so-called Jacksonian "revolution" was more superficial than substantial. American Indians and blacks fared worse during the Jacksonian era than before, and like Jefferson, Jackson as president did little that was radical.

Meanwhile, the United States was expanding (see Map 48.1). Between 1800 and 1861 the United States was the most rapidly growing nation in the world, both in area and in population. The pur-

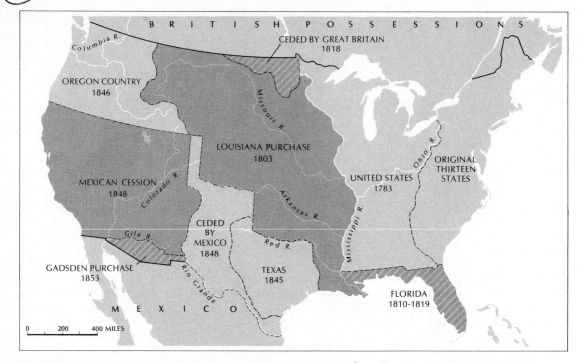

Map 48.1 **TERRITORIAL EXPANSION OF THE UNITED STATES, 1783–1853** Through a variety of means, including wars, purchases, treaties, and expropriation, the United States more than trebled its territory between 1800 and 1861. This territorial expansion kept land in surplus despite an unprecedented rate of population growth.

chase of the Louisiana Territory by Thomas Jefferson from Napoleon in 1803 for some $16 million doubled the original area of the United States. In 1819 Florida was purchased from Spain for $5 million. Texas, which was even bigger than now, was annexed in 1845. The next year the Oregon Country was annexed after the settlement of a long-standing dispute with Great Britain. The annexation of Texas resulted in a war with Mexico (1846–1848). After a quick and easy victory, the United States took a huge block of Mexican territory, comprising the present states of California, Arizona, New Mexico, Nevada, Utah, and parts of Colorado and Wyoming. This territory was enlarged to the south in 1853 by the Gadsden Purchase from Mexico ($10 million). These additions within a period of fifty years more then trebled the original territory of the young American nation. Yet the

cost was higher than the money paid for some of the territory. Indians had to be slaughtered and dispossessed. Wars of conquest had to be fought (Mexico), and other wars had to be risked (Great Britain). Westward expansion was not simply a sanitary, heroic struggle to a destined end.

The growth in population was keeping pace with the increase in area. Between 1800 and 1861 the population of the United States increased from approximately 5 million to 32 million. Adding to the high rate of natural increase was an ever-increasing tide of immigration from Europe. After 1840 the largest immigrant groups were the Irish, most of whom settled in the cities of the Northeast, and the Germans, most of whom pushed on to the fertile lands of the Middle West.

Between 1800 and 1861, then, American political institutions had evolved along democratic and nationalistic lines. Voting rights had been extended to essentially all adult, white males. Political power had been wrestled from the elite circles of the old colonial well-to-do. A modern political party system had been developed. Americans pridefully thought of themselves and their institutions as distinct within Western civilization. The United States had expanded westward to the Pacific Ocean. The western frontier itself was one of the greatest of nationalizing influences. To it came people from all the seaboard states and from abroad who looked to the national government for protection, for roads and canals, and for land titles. It was in this period that American culture began to free itself from strictly European influence. The American Indian was idealized by Henry Wadsworth Longfellow and James Fenimore Cooper. Washington Irving's pen made the legends of American colonial days enchanting. Gilbert Stuart and Charles Willson Peale made idealized portraits of American heroes. American schools and universities were teaching a particular American version of civilization and world affairs.

2. SLAVERY, CIVIL WAR, AND RECONSTRUCTION, 1861–1877

The central event for American history during the nineteenth century was the Civil War, which broke out in 1861 and lasted until 1865. The nature of the Civil War has been debated endlessly, but certain features stand out. The North was increasingly a growing, urban, industrial society based on free labor (see Figure 48.2). The South remained agricultural, dependent on large plantation crops such as cotton and based on slave labor (see Figure 48.3). The North was enjoying increasing influence over national policies and generally favored federal over state power. The South saw its influence over national policies slipping and increasingly favored states' rights over federal power. The North seemed to represent a modernizing, democratic, nationalistic society; the South a traditional, unegalitarian, regional society. In great part, the Civil War was a clash between these increasingly different societies with different interests. But the issue that provided much of the emotional energy to this clash and that prior to

1861 tied together the issues dividing North and South was black slavery.

The first boatload of blacks was brought to Virginia in 1619, one year before the Pilgrims landed at Plymouth Rock. Because of the tremendous amount of labor required to clear the American wilderness, the African slave trade flourished throughout the colonial period. By the time of the American Revolution, black slaves constituted approximately one-fifth of the total population of the thirteen colonies. Slavery was recognized and protected by the national constitution. Because of the climate and the diversified economy, however, slavery was proving to be unprofitable in the Northern states, and between 1777 and 1804 all the states north of Maryland passed emancipation laws. South of the Mason and Dixon line (the boundary between Maryland and Pennsylvania), where agriculture reigned supreme, slavery continued to be profitable and prevalent. But by 1789 many Americans, in the South as well as in the North, disliked the institution. After the Revolution scores of antislavery societies were founded. It appeared possible that slavery in America was on its way to an early and peaceful end.

Some unforeseen developments, however, changed the attitude of the South toward emancipation, and a sharp line was drawn between the North and South over the slavery issue. The first of these developments was Whitney's invention of the cotton gin in 1793. This machine made the raising of cotton so profitable that soon large cotton plantations worked by black slaves grew up throughout the South. The American South became the chief supplier of Britain's textile mills. By the mid–nineteenth century, the black slaves outnumbered the whites in South Carolina and Mississippi, and in the rest of the Deep South slaves were about equal in number to the whites. The Southern economy had become so wedded to cotton and to black slavery that the Southern antislavery movement had faltered, and the defense of slavery had gained momentum. Even more important than economic considerations in the development of proslavery sentiment in the South was the social problem. Black slaves were seen not only as the basis of wealth but also as the basis of power and status by Southern slaveholders. White slaveholders accepted as given the inferi-

ority of blacks. The Southern whites did not believe that they could absorb into their society or even live alongside so many free blacks under any circumstances.

The critical issue became the extension of slavery to the western territories. The population of the Northern states, with their growing industry, was rapidly outstripping that of the South. As the northwestern territories clamored for statehood without slavery, the Southerners took alarm. Already they were hopelessly outnumbered in the House of Representatives, whose membership is based on population. Their only security in the national government lay in the Senate, where each state has two members. The Southerners did everything in their power to slow down the settlement of the West and insisted that the admission of every free state must be accompanied by the admission of a slave state in order that equality in the Senate be maintained. But time and tide were on the side of the North. Geography, population, the growth of industrialization, and the march of liberalism in the Western world were irresistible.

In 1854 the Republican party was founded as a strictly Northern party committed to the restriction and, seemingly, ultimate extinction of slavery. In 1860, with Abraham Lincoln as its candidate, it won a sweeping victory over the Democrats, now split between North and South over the question of slavery. Rather than accept an inferior position in the nation and face the prospect of eventually having their power and status destroyed by some 4 million black slaves forcibly freed in their midst, eleven Southern states (about half the territory of the Union and a third of its population) seceded and set up an independent government.

The North had an overwhelming preponderance in population, wealth, industry, transportation, and naval power. But the South enjoyed brilliant military leadership and the further advantage of fighting on its own soil for what it believed to be the survival of white civilization. The war lasted four bloody years. For three of the four years it looked as if the Union could not be restored. But after numerous discordant elements in the North were brought together, Great Britain and France tactfully neutralized, and the winning commanders and strategy found, the Southern armies were finally crushed.

Slavery was abolished and the authority of the national government restored, never to be seriously threatened again. However, the war left a legacy of sectional bitterness. The conciliatory Lincoln was assassinated just five days after the war ended. The radical Republican congressional leaders, who now gained control of the government, treated the defeated and devastated South as a conquered province. They sought to achieve basic reforms and to ensure political and civil rights for the freed slaves. The effort ended by 1877 when the last federal troops were finally withdrawn from the South. Over the course of the next twenty years many of the gains made by blacks were lost. By this time a different dynamic was taking hold of American life and changing it in unprecedented ways: industrialization.

3. INDUSTRIALIZATION AND URBANIZATION, 1865–1901

INDUSTRIAL REVOLUTION

Although the earliest factories were already present in the United States by the end of the eighteenth century, the growth of industrialization during the nineteenth century was at first quite slow. The French and British blockades during the Napoleonic wars and the War of 1812 with Britain cut the United States off from British manufacturers and caused much American commercial capital to be diverted to manufacturing. By the middle decades of the nineteenth century, industrialization was spreading, particularly in the Northeast. However, it was not until the years immediately

---

FIGURE 48.2.   A Northern Factory   (Top) This lithograph of the Stillman, Allen & Co. Novelty Iron Works of New York City shows the more industrial, urban nature of the North in the middle decades just prior to the Civil War. (Museum of the City of New York)

FIGURE 48.3.   A Southern Plantation   (Bottom) This picture, Charles Giroux's "Cotton Plantation," shows the contrasting rural society with a large population of black slaves typical of the South. Courtesy, Museum of Fine Arts, Boston, M. and M. Karolik Collection)

FIGURE 48.4. Cornelius Vanderbilt This cartoon attacks Cornelius Vanderbilt, who in the 1860s gained control over several railroads and amassed a great fortune. He is portrayed exercising monopolistic corporate power over the nation's railroads. (Culver Pictures)

following the Civil War that the United States joined other Western nations as a leading industrial power.

In most ways industrialization in the United States proceeded much as it did in other Western countries. New machines and sources of power were applied to the manufacturing process. Large factories sprang up in the East and Midwest, turning raw materials into finished products in great quantities. Working-class and urban populations connected with industrialization grew, fed both by migration from rural areas and massive immigration from Europe. The United States proved subject to the same problems that plagued other industrializing nations: poor working conditions, low pay, child labor, urban slums, inadequate sanitation, and few social services.

However, there were a few elements that seemed to characterize the United States' growing industrialization between 1865 and 1901. Above all, the degree to which business became concentrated in the hands of a few individuals and corporations was striking. Industrial capitalists such as Andrew Carnegie (steel), John D. Rockefeller (oil), Cornelius Vanderbilt (railroads), and J. P. Morgan (finance) amassed unbelievable fortunes and power (see Figure 48.4). The corporations they founded, such as U.S. Steel and Standard Oil, soon gained monopolistic control over vast resources.

More than in most other nations, in America governmental policies during this period favored business in general and these huge industrial firms in particular. Not surprisingly, then, in the United States the unionization of labor was relatively slow to emerge. In part this result was due to the continued abundance of cheap land and the influx of cheap mobile labor from Europe. But unionization was also deterred by the determined resistance of industrial capitalists backed by private and public police power, and by governmental policies and officials unsympathetic to unionization. Despite some earlier beginnings in various trades (such as the Knights of Labor), it was not until 1886 that Samuel Gompers, an immigrant from Great Britain, organized the American Federation of Labor—the first successful national labor organization in America.

By the end of the nineteenth century the United States not only was a major industrial power but also had outstripped the world in industrial production. The government and the economy of the country were still dominated by big-business interests that controlled the dominant "Old Guard" wing of the Republican party. Although the United States enjoyed enormous overall economic development, wealth was very unequally distributed, causing widespread discontent. Western and southern farmers had been clamoring for public regulation of the railroads, on which they were dependent. Small business, labor, and consumers demanded protection against the monopolistic practices and prices of the great trusts and corporations, which were protected by a prohibitively high tariff. The United States government remained behind almost all other industrial nations in its willingness to deal with social abuses stemming from industrialization. Millions deplored the city slums, the corrupt spoils system in the civil service, and the squandering of natural resources by private interests. The forces of reform were growing and would break out in the two decades following the turn of the century.

4. REFORM AND PROGRESSIVISM, 1901–1920

The great reforms of the progressive era are usually dated from 1901, when Theodore Roosevelt assumed the presidency. Roosevelt firmly believed in the capitalistic system, but he was convinced that the time had come when the superiority of the government over private business must be asserted. After assuming the presidency in 1901 upon the assassination of McKinley, "T.R.," as he was popularly known, immediately launched a vigorous program of reform. The Interstate Commerce Act of 1887 and the Sherman Antitrust Act of 1890, which had lain dormant, were activated. Organized labor was given a little support in its unequal fight with organized capital. Pure food and drug acts were designed to restrict the corporations and safeguard the public health. More than 200 million acres of forest and mineral lands

and water power sites were withheld from private exploitation. He strengthened the merit system in the federal civil service. Many of his reform efforts were blocked by Congress and the federal courts, which were still controlled by the Republican Old Guard.

In 1912 the Democrats, under the leadership of Woodrow Wilson (1856–1924), gained their first clear-cut victory since the Civil War. Wilson proved to be more liberal than Roosevelt. With the Democrats in control of both houses of Congress, Wilson's administration sharply lowered the tariff, passed the Clayton Antitrust Act (more specific than the Sherman Act), gave further encouragement to organized labor, and set up the Federal Reserve Banking System, which removed control of the nation's financial policies from the hands of private interests on Wall Street and placed them in the hands of the federal government.

The passage of the long-struggled-for women's suffrage in 1920 was the last reform of the progressive era. The return to power of the conservative Republicans under Warren Harding in 1920 brought to a close the progressive period. However, in those two decades American institutions and policies had adjusted to at least some of the social and economic realities of a modern democratic industrial society. At the same time the United States had joined other imperial powers with its acquisition of territories in Latin America, the Pacific, and Asia. Finally, the United States had become embroiled in World War I. From this point on, the United States would be too integrally connected to world-wide economic and political affairs to act in isolation.

SUGGESTED READING

General

R. Current et al., *American History: A Survey* (1987). A balanced, solid text.

Democracy and Geographic Expansion, 1800–1861

R. Billington, *Westward Expansion: A History of the American Frontier* (1974). An excellent survey.

J. Ellis, *After the Revolution: Profiles of Early American Culture* (1979). A useful survey of culture.

J. R. Howe, *From the Revolution Through the Age of Jackson: Innocence and Empire in the Young Republic* (1973). Good study of political development.

E. Spicer, *A Short History of the Indians of the United States* (1969). Useful introduction to the topic.

Slavery, Civil War, and Reconstruction, 1861–1877

M. Dillon, *The Abolitionists: The Growth of a Dissenting Minority* (1974). Concise summary.

E. D. Genovese, *Roll, Jordan, Roll: The World Slaves Made* (1974). A scholarly study of slave society.

J. H. Franklin, *Reconstruction After the Civil War* (1961). A classic study.

P. J. Parish, *The American Civil War* (1975). Includes chapters on the preceding and succeeding periods.

Industrialization and Urbanization, 1865–1901

D. J. Boorstin, *The Americans: The National Experience* (1965). Useful sections on the impact of modernization.

T. C. Cochran and W. Miller, *The Age of Enterprise* (1968). A broad, scholarly study covering the period.

E. C. Kirkland, *Industry Comes of Age: Business, Labor, and Public Policy 1860–1897* (1967). A good survey of industrialization.

Reform and Progressivism, 1901–1920

J. M. Cooper, Jr., *The Warrior and the Priest: Woodrow Wilson and Theodore Roosevelt* (1983). A comparative biography.

R. Hofstadter, *The Age of Reform: From Bryan to FDR* (1955). A classic.

A. Link and R. McCormick, *Progressivism* (1983). A succinct modern review.

S. M. Rothman, *Woman's Proper Place* (1978). Focuses on women's changing roles.

R. H. Wiebe, *The Search for Order, 1877–1920* (1968). Contains good material on reform and progressivism.

CHAPTER 49

Imperialism

FIGURE 49.1. Imperial Glory This picture of colonial troops parading in London in celebration of Queen Victoria's Diamond Jubilee in 1897 reveals some of the forces behind late-nineteenth-century imperialism: nationalistic pride, military power, social cohesion, and romantic sentiments. (Culver Pictures)

We have already seen that from the fifteenth to the eighteenth centuries the national monarchies of the West "discovered" and conquered most of the Western Hemisphere, the west coast of Africa, and southern Asia. Then from 1763 until 1871 there came a lull in expansion; Europe was busy with revolution, industrialization, and nation building. Imperial powers such as Spain, Portugal, and France lost many of their overseas holdings during this period, leaving Great Britain as the only Western nation with an extensive empire. Even some of Britain's holdings in North America had been lost during the American Revolution, and imperialism seemed incompatible with liberalism in the mid–nineteenth century. In the period from 1871 to 1914, however, a new burst of European expansion, the "new imperialism," brought practically all the remaining portions of the earth's surface under Western influence or domination.

1. CAUSES FOR THE NEW IMPERIALISM

One of the chief impulses behind the new imperialism was economic. The rapid expansion of industry in Europe and the United States created a demand for greater markets, new sources of raw materials, and investment outlets for surplus capital. Many people in Western nations pushed for imperial expansion, optimistically assuming that the new markets, the new sources of raw materials, and the new investment outlets could be found. These advocates of imperialism were primarily those most directly in a position to profit from it—certain financiers, merchants, shippers, settlers, and colonial officials as well as industrialists with specific economic interests in non-Western lands.

Probably a greater impulse to the new imperialism was nationalism. It flattered the national ego to see its colors spread over the map. It also provided military and naval bases and personnel for the hungry military machines that were an integral part of late-nineteenth-century nationalism. In Europe the conservative parties based on the landed aristocracy were even more imperialistic than the liberal parties based on industrial

and commercial interests. Most of the imperial governors, generals, and admirals came from the conservative aristocracy. National egotism also gave the citizens of the great Western powers a sense of mission; they were bringing the blessings of their civilization to backward peoples. Rudyard Kipling expressed the belief of many Westerners when he sang in rhyme of the "white man's burden" to hold in tutelage and to civilize the "lesser breeds" of the earth.

Another motivating factor in the new imperialism was the evangelizing zeal of the Christian religion. Christianity had long taken to heart the command, "Go ye into all the world and preach the gospel to every creature." At the very time that Christianty was wavering under attack in its homeland in the West, it was carrying on foreign missionary activity of unprecedented scope and intensity. More often than not, where the missionaries went, so went Western explorers, traders, troops, and officials.

In addition, political and diplomatic developments became intertwined after the 1880s to make colonial claims increasingly valuable assets. These claims could be used by Western nations to forge alliances or bargain with competitors in the growing international disputes of the period.

Finally, the processes involved in imperial expansion and the circumstances of the West help explain the new imperialism. Science and technology gave industrialized nations such a military advantage that they could easily conquer and control the nonindustrialized lands. Almost any penetration into such areas as Africa, southern Asia, or the Pacific quickly led to greater involvement and eventual control. Once missionaries or traders established their presence in a new area, home governments were called on to provide support, enforce contracts, or protect private interests. To provide that support and protection, they had to create new facilities in the new lands, thus increasing the Western presence. The governments soon requested the cooperation of the native political leaders, and when it was not forthcoming, they used force. Thus, initial contacts by Western explorers, missionaries, or traders blossomed into full imperial control by Western nations.

WHERE HISTORIANS DISAGREE

The New Imperialism

Scholars have debated the causes of the new imperialism almost since its appearance in the final decades of the nineteenth century. For years, there were two major competing interpretations for the causes of imperialism: The first focused on economic motivations, the second on nationalism.

The earliest explanations for the new imperialism were economic. In 1902 J. H. Hobson argued that imperialism was caused by industrial capitalism in general and influential financial capitalists in particular.

In 1916 Lenin, argued that capitalist competition produced monopolies that were being forced to look overseas for new areas to exploit. Many historians have favored related broad economic interpretations of imperialism. Their basic argument is that industrialization demanded ever-widening markets. As industrialization spread to several Western countries during the second half of the nineteenth century and as European markets were being limited by increasing tariffs, competition for markets intensified. At the same time the need for raw materials expanded, as did the search for new, profitable investment opportunities. These economic motives were translated into the new imperialism.

Opponents of economic interpretations for the new imperialism point out that the biggest markets, the largest sources of raw materials, and the most investment outlets for capital remained within Western civilization even during this period. Moreover, the imperializing Western nations did not necessarily profit economically from imperialism. Much of the territory seized between 1880 and 1914 had little economic value; some, in fact, was an economic liability. Many of these historians argue that the chief cause of the new imperialism was nationalism. They point out that the outbreak of the new imperialism occurred shortly after the unification of Italy and Germany and during a period in which nationalism was on the rise throughout Europe. This nationalism turned into a new competitive struggle for international prestige among Western nations that spilled over into non-Western areas after 1880. Imperial conquest became a measure of status, proof that a nation had become first rate. To be left behind in the imperial race was to be marked as a second-class nation. Thus economic motives were secondary; on the whole, imperialism was a nationalistic phenomenon.

Recently, several historians have pointed out that there is little evidence that European statesmen felt pressured to acquire colonies by wealthy capitalists or public patriotism during the crucial period of the 1880s and 1890s. Rather, the key to the new imperialism lay in political and diplomatic developments. In some cases, political problems within a territory only indirectly controlled by a European power pressured that power to annex the territory. This situation occurred in Egypt during the 1880s, when Great Britain took control and then expanded its interests to neighboring Sudan. In other cases, the new style of politics and diplomacy within Europe turned colonies into political assets that had to be acquired. Here Bismarck set a pattern of making claims to colonial territories and using those claims as bargaining chips against other powers. His tactics forced other nations to make their own claims, which led to the virtual partition of Africa.

Many historians take the middle road, arguing that the best way to explain the new imperialism is to include economic, nationalistic, and political-diplomatic factors. But here judgment is crucial, for historians must determine what elements of each argument are most valid and what weight should be given to them.

2. THE EXPLOITATION AND AWAKENING OF CHINA

One of the most important scenes of European imperialism during the nineteenth century was China. This huge and populous country was the seat of the oldest continuous civilization in the world. For some five thousand years China had been a vast melting pot, absorbing invading peoples and cultures and welding them into a tough but resilient civilization. The military conquerors were always themselves swallowed up or conquered by Chinese culture.

Over time, the Chinese chose to isolate themselves from the outside world. A great wall (never completed) originally constructed to defend China's northern border later symbolized its effort to retain the old and keep out the new. Although they admitted some European traders and Christian missionaries in the sixteenth and seventeenth centuries, they closed their doors rather tightly thereafter. By the nineteenth century their medieval society, under the corrupt and declining Manchu dynasty, constituted a power vacuum that tempted exploitation by the West.

The first Europeans to force themselves upon the Chinese were the British. Going to war in 1839, when Chinese officials interfered with their sale of opium in China, the British, with their modern weapons, easily defeated the Chinese. By the terms of the Treaty of Nanking (1842), the Chinese ceded Hong Kong to the British, opened many of their ports to foreign trade free of restricting tariffs, and granted the foreigners extraterritorial rights. This was the first of a series of unequal treaties and the signal for all the great Western powers to rush into China and seize what they could. In the ensuing scramble it was the rivalry among the great powers themselves rather than

Map 49.1 **IMPERIALISM IN ASIA, 1840–1914** As this map indicates, almost all the Western powers participated in the imperial expansion into Asia. Once Japan westernized, it too joined the imperial race.

ARCTIC OCEAN

ALASKA
*(Purchased by U.S.A.
from Russia, 1867)*

BERING SEA

ALEUTIAN I. (U.S.A., 1867)

KAMCHATKA

SEA OF
OKHOTSK

Lena R.

Yakutsk

S I B E R I A

SAKHALIN

KURILE I.
(Japan, 1875)

AMUR PROVINCE
1858

KARAFUTO
(Japan, 1905)

Ob R.

Yenisei R.

N   E M P I R E

Khabarovsk

MARITIME
PROVINCE
(Russia, 1868)

Tobolsk

Tomsk

L. Baikal

Chita

Amur R.

MANCHURIA

Vladivostok
1860

JAPANESE EMPIRE

Omsk

TRANS-SIBERIAN RAILROAD

Irkutsk

Harbin

SEA OF
JAPAN

Urga

Mukden

KOREA
(1905, 1910)

Tokyo

L. Balkhash

OUTER MONGOLIA
(Autonomous, 1912 Russian Sphere)

INNER MONGOLIA

JEHOL

Port Arthur
(Japan, 1905)

1854

Peking

Tientsin

Kiao-chow
(Germany, 1898)

PACIFIC OCEAN

Tashkent 1860-65

SINKIANG

Shanghai
(Britain, 1842)

HARA 1876

Kashgar

Huang Ho

Nanking

Ningpo
1842

EAST
CHINA
SEA

1895

KASHMIR
1846

T I B E T

C H I N A

Hankow

MARIANA I.
(Germany, 1899)

RYUKYU I.

Indus R.

PUNJAB

HIMALAYAS

Lhasa

Chungking

Yangtse R.

Foochow

GUAM
(U.S.A., 1898)

Delhi

NEPAL

BHUTAN

Brahmaputra R.

YUNNAN

KWANGSI
(French Sphere)

Amoy

Canton
(Britain, 1842)

FORMOSA *(Japan, 1895)*

PESCADORES *(Japan, 1895)*

Ganges R.

Hong Kong *(Britain, 1842)*

Macao *(Portugal, 1557)*

INDIA

Calcutta

BURMA
(Britain, 1852, 1885)

Hanoi

HAINAN

Kwang-chow
(Lease to France, 1898)

CAROLINE I.
(Germany, 1899)

B R I T I S H   I N D I A

1852

ANNAM

Manila

PHILIPPINE I.
(U.S.A., 1898, 1899)

YAP

gal

Rangoon

1826

SIAM

FRENCH
INDOCHINA
1884, 1907

SOUTH
CHINA SEA

nbay

Hyderabad

Yanaon
(France)

Bangkok

Mekong R.

PALAU I.

Goa
(Portugal)

BAY OF BENGAL

Saigon

Madras

Pondicherry
(France)

ANDAMAN I.
(Britain)

BRITISH
NORTH BORNEO
1888

NEW GUINEA

KAISER WILHELMS
(Germany, 188

Karikal *(France)*

CEYLON

SARAWAK
1888

MALAY STATES
(Britain, 18 0, 1824)

BORNEO

CELEBES

Singapore
(Britain, 1819)

SUMATRA

D U T C H   E A S T   I N D I E S

NDIAN OCEAN

Batavia

JAVA

TIMOR

(Portugal, 1859)

Darwin

AUSTRALIA

Chinese resistance that saved China from complete loss of independence.

The British got the lion's share. In addition to Hong Kong and concessions in the Canton area of the southeast, they gained a virtual trading monopoly in the Yangtze Valley, which was the richest and most populous part of China. In the north they gained footholds in the capital city of Peking and its port city of Tientsin, in the Shantung Peninsula, and in Manchuria. They gained dominion over Tibet. In the 1880s they seized control of Burma, which owed a tenuous allegiance to China. The French took large areas in Southeast China and Hainan Island as their sphere. In the 1880s they completed the detachment of Indochina from Chinese sovereignty. The Russians took Manchuria as their sphere, annexed a large strip of China's northeast coast, including the port of Vladivostok, and became active in Korea. The Germans carved out for themselves much of the strategically located Shantung Peninsula and built a powerful naval base at Kiaochow. In 1894 the rejuvenated and modernized Japanese went to war with China. They easily defeated China and not only took away Formosa and Korea but also forced China to pay a huge indemnity. Even the United States got into the act. The United States had launched an imperialist program in the Far East in 1898 by seizing the Philippine Islands and Guam from Spain. Now, fearful for its growing trade with China, the United States attempted to gain a sphere of influence in Fukien Province and demanded an Open Door policy in China with equal trading opportunities for all.

Meanwhile, Chinese nationalism was being aroused by the Western and Japanese aggressions against the "Celestial Empire." In 1899–1900 a serious uprising against the foreign exploiters, known as the Boxer Rebellion, took place. Thousands of Chinese Christians and a number of foreigners were slain. This liberation movement was put down by British, French, German, Russian, Italian, Japanese, and American troops. The nationalist leaders were severely punished, and China was forced to pay the foreign governments a large indemnity.

A more far-reaching revolutionary movement, aimed not only at freeing China from foreign exploitation but also at modernizing and democratizing its society and government, was being organized by Dr. Sun Yat-sen (1866–1925). Sun Yat-sen, the son of a poor Chinese farmer, studied in a British mission school in Hawaii, became a Christian, and later graduated from the British medical school at Hong Kong. Eloquent and dynamic, he organized his followers into the Kuomintang party, which was committed to a three-point program: (1) national independence, (2) democratic government, (3) social justice. In 1911 the reformers launched a revolution against the Manchu dynasty, declared a republic, and elected Sun Yat-sen as a provisional president. The revolution swept most of China. The Manchu officials in Peking, their power having evaporated, declared China a republic and abdicated in favor of General Yuan, organizer of the New Army of North China. Early in 1912 the idealistic Sun Yat-sen, in behalf of national unity, and fearful of rising anarchy and warlords within and the possibility of Japanese and Russian intervention from without, yielded to General Yuan. Yuan, however, soon proved to be more interested in power than in liberal reform. When the Kuomintang party won the elections of 1913, he suppressed the party and had its most promising young leader assassinated. Sun Yat-sen disassociated himself from Yuan's dictatorship and resumed his liberal activities in South China. When World War I opened a new era in 1914, China was torn with revolution and division.

3. THE EMERGENCE OF JAPAN

Japan's reaction to Western intrusion was quite different from that of China. The Japanese people inhabit four large islands and some three thousand small ones stretching along the eastern coast of Asia for a distance of about two thousand miles. Like China, Japan had admitted the sixteenth- and seventeenth-century European traders and Christian missionaries but had evicted them and closed its doors after observing what was happening everywhere in Asia where Europeans were admitted. At mid–nineteenth century the Japanese were living in isolation. Their stage of technical knowledge and their feudal society ruled over by

FIGURE 49.2. Japanese Silk Factory, 1905 By the early twentieth century Japan had successfully adopted Western industrial methods. In this 1905 photograph of a silk-weaving factory, supervising men are in formal Western attire and women work on the machines. (California Museum of Photography, University of California, Riverside)

military chieftains were quite similar to those of Europe five hundred years earlier.

In 1853, eleven years after the Treaty of Nanking opened up China, an American fleet commanded by Commodore Matthew C. Perry steamed into Tokyo Bay and so overawed the Japanese that they opened their ports to shipwrecked American sailors and to American trade. The alert Japanese were much impressed by the technological superiority of the Americans. In 1868, just fifteen years later, a group of forward-looking young Japanese overthrew the existing government and began reorganizing the Japanese government and society along modern Western lines. Taking what they considered to be the best from the various Western nations, they patterned their business methods after those of the United States,

their legal system after the French, and their navy after the British. But it was Bismarck's Germany that impressed the Japanese the most. They built a military machine and an authoritarian government and education system on the model of the German Empire.

In an incredibly short time Japan became a modern, industrialized, military, and, on the surface at least, a westernized power (see Figure 49.2). In 1894 Japan attacked China, defeated it with ease, and forced it to pay a large indemnity and to give up Korea (which Japan annexed in 1910) and the island of Formosa. In 1902 Great Britain became the first Western power to treat an Oriental nation as an equal by entering into a military alliance with Japan. Thus strengthened and reassured, Japan attacked Russia in 1904 and, to everyone's surprise, defeated Russia on land and at sea. As a reward, Japan took the southern half of Sakhalin Island and Russia's railroad and port concessions in southern Manchuria, thereby becoming the dominant power in that large and valuable section of China. By 1914 Japan was a first-rate westernized power—industrialized, militaristic, and imperialistic.

4. COMPETITION FOR THE STRATEGIC NEAR AND MIDDLE EAST

The term *Near East* usually refers to the area at the eastern end of the Mediterranean: Egypt, the old Ottoman Empire, and the Balkan peninsula. In the period 1871–1914, the term *Middle East* usually meant the area of the Persian Gulf, the territory northwest of India, and sometimes Tibet. (By the middle of the twentieth century the term *Middle East* was generally used to designate the whole area from and including Egypt and Turkey to the western borders of India.) Before the development of its oil resources after World War I, this area (with the exception of the Balkan peninsula) was relatively poor. It was inhabited chiefly by Moslems who were hostile to Europeans. The main importance of the area, therefore, was strategic. It is the land bridge between the world's two largest land masses—the continents of Eurasia and Africa. The opening in 1869 of the Suez Canal, which shortened the sailing distance between western Europe and the Far East by five thousand miles, doubled the strategic value of the Near and Middle East. Indeed, Suez quickly became probably the most vital single commercial and military focus point in the world.

The Suez Canal was built by a French company between 1859 and 1869. However, in 1875 Great Britain, taking advantage of the Egyptian government's financial distress, purchased the khedive's controlling portion of the canal stock. Seven years later, to quell an anti-European insurrection, the British occupied Egypt with their military forces. The French acquiesced in the establishment of Britain's control over Egypt and the Suez Canal in return for British support of French dominance in Morocco.

Serious competition for the British in the Near East soon came from an unexpected source. Wilhelm II, upon becoming kaiser of the German Empire in 1888, immediately began to show a keen interest in the Ottoman Empire. Sultan Abdul Hamid II (1876–1909) was such a cruel slaughterer of his Christian subjects that he was called in the Western world "Abdul the Damned." Nevertheless, Wilhelm II in 1889 paid Abdul Hamid a visit in Constantinople and declared himself to be the friend and benefactor not only of the Turks but also of all the Moslems. Friendship was followed by economic concessions and German investments in the Ottoman Empire. A second visit by the kaiser in 1898 led to a concession to Germany to build a railroad from the Bosporus to the Persian Gulf. This, with its European connection, was the famous Berlin-to-Bagdad railroad. The British took alarm. The Bagdad Railroad, with a fortified terminus on the Persian Gulf, would undercut Britain's longer water route to the East and threaten India, Britain's richest colonial prize. A projected branch running down through Syria and Palestine to Hedjaz would menace the Suez Canal itself.

Russia was equally concerned. Since the days of Ivan III in the fifteenth century, one of Russia's major ambitions has been to gain a warm water outlet to the world through the Turkish Straits at Constantinople. Russia had long looked to Constantinople as the seat and legitimate capital of its Orthodox religion and Byzantine culture. The decay of the Ottoman Empire in the nineteenth century encouraged Russia to try for Constantinople, and only the intervention of Great Britain and France in the Crimean War (1854–1856) prevented Russia from attaining its goal. In 1877–1878 Russia defeated Turkey and threatened to dominate the whole Balkan peninsula. This time Great Britain and Austria-Hungary forced Russia to submit to a general settlement by the European powers. At the Congress of Berlin, 1878, Russian ambitions in the Near East were once more thwarted. Bismarck's support of Austria-Hungary and Great Britain at the Congress of Berlin marked the beginning of German-Russian estrangement. Russia's defeat by Japan in 1904–1905 caused Russia to intensify its pressure toward the Middle and Near East. Russia's southward expansion so menaced India that Great Britain extended the northwest Indian frontier to the Khyber Pass and crossed over the Himalayas to checkmate Russian influence in Tibet, Afghanistan, and Persia.

The new German threat in the Near and Middle East, however, caused the British and the Russians to settle their long-standing differences. In 1907 they neutralized Tibet and Afghanistan and divided Persia into three spheres of influence—a Russian sphere in the north, a British sphere in the south, and an "independent" sphere in the center. Great Britain, Russia, and France, now diplomatic allies, prevented the sale of Bagdad Railroad bonds in their respective countries in an effort to embarrass the financing of the costly undertaking. Germany went right ahead, however, with the extension of its influence in the Balkans and the Ottoman Empire. In 1913 Germany dispatched a military mission to Constantinople to reorganize and instruct the Turkish army. The Ottoman Empire's friendship and eventual alliance with Germany was undoubtedly motivated by a greater fear of Russia. By 1914 the area of the Near and Middle East was a giant powder keg with fuses leading to St. Petersburg, Berlin, and London.

5. THE SCRAMBLE FOR AFRICA

At the opening of the nineteenth century, Africa was not the seat of ancient and highly developed civilizations, as was Asia. The brilliant civilizations of Egypt, Carthage, and Rome had long since disappeared. The Moslem religion still existed throughout North Africa, but the once vigorous Moslem civilization had declined. The Portuguese, Spanish, British, and French had trading posts along the gold, ivory, and slave coasts on the west. The Dutch and Portuguese had posts and settlements around the southern cape. But most of the huge continent still lay dark and mysterious.

By 1880 the African scene had still not changed very much. During the middle decades of the nineteenth century, the interior was explored for the first time, notably by David Livingstone, a Scottish missionary, and Henry Morton Stanley, a British journalist. The French had conquered Al-

geria and made it a part of France and had pushed up the Senegal River in the west. The British had taken the Cape Colony from the Dutch by the Treaty of Vienna in 1815, and the Dutch settlers had moved northward into the interior.

After 1880, however, the tempo of European activity changed drastically. The explorers' tales of strange wild animals and primitive peoples, of jungles, ivory, and gold, excited the imagination of western European adventurers and evangelical Christians. European politics, industrialism, and nationalism supplied much of the impetus. There took place such a mad scramble for Africa among the powers of western Europe that by 1914 the only independent areas left were Ethiopia in the east and Liberia in the west. Ethiopia, with French aid, had repulsed an invading Italian army, and Liberia had been sponsored by the United States as a hoped-for receptacle for liberated black slaves. The rest of the huge continent had been seized by France, Great Britain, Germany, Portugal, Belgium, Italy, and Spain (listed in the approximate order of size of territory held). (See Map 49.2.) The treatment of the natives was very similar to that accorded the New World Indians in the sixteenth and seventeenth centuries.

The seizure of so much territory did not occur, of course, without serious international incidents and crises. One such incident occurred at Fashoda in the Sudan in 1898. A French expedition under Major Marchand, bent on establishing an all-French axis across Africa from west to east, arrived at Fashoda and hoisted the French flag. The British, however, claimed the Sudan as an appendage of Egypt. Furthermore, they were interested in a Cape-to-Cairo railroad running through all British territory, even though they were already blocked by German East Africa. Lord Kitchener therefore hurried down from the north with a superior British force and compelled the French to withdraw.

In South Africa the British fought a major war with the Dutch settlers (1899–1902). When British settlers began to move into Cape Colony after the Congress of Vienna had ceded it to Great Britain in 1815, the Calvinist Dutch Boers (farmers) who had settled there in the seventeenth century trekked northward far into the interior. Eventually the British recognized the independence of the two Boer states, Transvaal and Orange Free State.

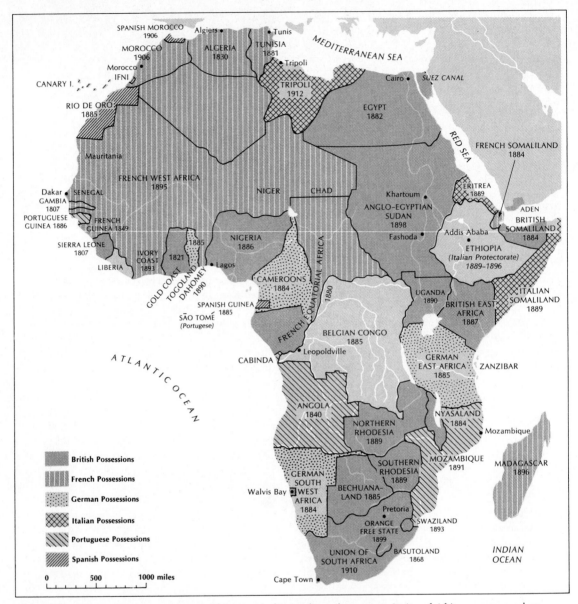

SPANISH MOROCCO
1906

Algiers • Tunis

MEDITERRANEAN SEA

MOROCCO
1906

ALGERIA
1830

TUNISIA
1881

Tripoli

Morocco
IFNI

CANARY I.

TRIPOLI
1912

Cairo •

SUEZ CANAL

RIO DE ORO
1885

EGYPT
1882

Mauritania

FRENCH SOMALILAND
1884

FRENCH WEST AFRICA
1895

NIGER   CHAD

Khartoum •

ANGLO-EGYPTIAN
SUDAN
1898

RED SEA

ERITREA
1889

ADEN

Dakar •

SENEGAL

GAMBIA
1807

PORTUGUESE
GUINEA 1886

FRENCH
GUINEA 1849

BRITISH
SOMALILAND
1884

Fashoda •

Addis Ababa •

SIERRA LEONE
1807

IVORY
COAST
1893

1885

NIGERIA
1886

ETHIOPIA
(Italian Protectorate)
1889-1896

LIBERIA

GOLD COAST
TOGOLAND
DAHOMEY
1890

Lagos •

CAMEROONS
1884

UGANDA
1890

ITALIAN
SOMALILAND
1889

SPANISH GUINEA
1885

BRITISH EAST
AFRICA
1887

SÃO TOMÉ
(Portugese)

FRENCH EQUATORIAL AFRICA

1880

BELGIAN CONGO
1885

ATLANTIC OCEAN

CABINDA

Leopoldville •

GERMAN
EAST AFRICA
1885

ZANZIBAR

ANGOLA
1840

NORTHERN
RHODESIA
1889

NYASALAND
1884

Mozambique •

MOZAMBIQUE
1891

MADAGASCAR
1896

British Possessions

French Possessions

German Possessions

Italian Possessions

Portuguese Possessions

Spanish Possessions

GERMAN
SOUTH
WEST
AFRICA
1884

Walvis Bay

BECHUANA-
LAND 1885

SOUTHERN
RHODESIA
1889

Pretoria •

SWAZILAND
1893

ORANGE
FREE STATE
1899

BASUTOLAND
1868

INDIAN
OCEAN

UNION OF
SOUTH AFRICA
1910

Cape Town •

0   500   1000 miles

Map 49.2   IMPERIALISM IN AFRICA, 1914   This map indicates how the vast majority of Africa was carved up by European nations in the two decades of the 1880s and 1890s.

FIGURE 49.3. British in India
This photo of Indian servants catering to a British gentleman indicates the gulf between the British ruling class and the Indians they governed. It also reveals the appeal to Britishers of foreign service. (BBC Hulton/ The Bettmann Archive)

When, however, the richest gold mines in the world were discovered in the Transvaal in the 1880s, British immigrants (Uitlanders) flooded in. The unwelcome Uitlanders were badly treated by the Dutch Boers. The British empire builder Cecil Rhodes, with the support of powerful interests back home, was determined to brush aside the two little Boer republics. When the able Boer president, Paul Kruger, saw the British intent, he opened hostilities. What the world expected to be an easy victory for the British took three years of all-out military effort involving severe casualties and enormous costs. Britain's treatment of the defeated Boers, however, was lenient. They were taken into partnership in the Union of South Africa, and their war hero, General Botha, was elected the Union's first prime minister. During the course of the struggle, a telegram of congratulation from the German kaiser to President

Kruger and the British seizure of a German ship attempting to violate the British blockade caused great tension between Great Britain and Germany. Only the superiority of the British navy, as the kaiser admitted, prevented him from going to war.

The British navy also proved decisive in two crises over Morocco. In 1905 France, with the approval of Great Britain, Italy, and Spain, began the conquest of Morocco. France claimed that it was necessary because of continual raids by wild Moroccan tribes on French Algeria. The German kaiser, seeing an opportunity to assert his own power and possibly to break up the Triple Entente, which France, Great Britain, and Russia were then forming, appeared at the Moroccan port of Tangier on a German warship and indicated his support of Moroccan independence. Great tension followed. At an international conference at Algeciras, France, supported by her own ally, Great Britain,

FIGURE 49.4. Imperialism Satirized   This cartoon, which appeared in 1899, satirizes the attitudes of smug righteousness and superiority with which the Americans, the British, and the European nations extended their dominance over the rest of the world. The United States was dominant in the Western Hemisphere; the European imperialist powers in the Eastern Hemisphere. (New York Public Library Picture Collection)

and by Germany's ally, Italy, won a limited control over Morocco. Disorder continued, however, and in 1911 France sent a conquering army into Morocco, at which point Germany dispatched a cruiser to the Moroccan port of Agadir. Again tension mounted. In the face of Germany's threat to France, Britain's chancellor of the exchequer, Lloyd George, talked loudly of war. Again Germany backed down. Between Germany and Morocco stood the British navy. These two efforts of the kaiser to drive a wedge between the Entente powers had the effect of driving them closer together. Moreover, his own ally, Italy, had proved uncertain. These two crises growing out of imperialism hastened the coming of World War I.

6. THE BRITISH EMPIRE

Of all the European overseas empires, the British was by far the most successful. Indeed, it was the dazzling size and wealth of the British Empire that helped to excite the other European powers to greater imperialistic activity. By 1914 the British Empire included one-fourth of all the land and people of the earth.

Great Britain's commerce with its empire was enormous. In 1914 Britain's foreign investments, most of which were in the empire, totaled $20 billion—one-fourth of the total wealth of the homeland. (By comparison, France had $9 billion invested abroad; Germany, $6 billion. The United States was a debtor nation.) The empire, furthermore, provided lucrative and often glamorous careers for thousands of British governors, army and navy officers, diplomats, and civil servants of every description.

In the latter part of the nineteenth century, Great Britain adopted the policy of granting self-government to the English-speaking portions of its empire. Canada, which had gained self-government in 1849, was granted dominion status in 1867. With dominion status, the only remaining effective bond was allegiance to the British crown. The British governor-general was only a figurehead like the king at home. Australia was made a self-governing dominion in 1901, New Zealand in 1907, and the Union of South Africa in 1910. The policy was successful. All the dominions rallied to the mother country in both world wars.

Great Britain's richest imperial prize was India (see Figure 49.3). India's more than 300 million inhabitants accounted for at least three-fourths of the total population of the whole empire. India was nearly twenty times as large as Great Britain and more than seven times as populous. It was the mother country's best customer and supplied many minerals and raw materials. Until 1858 India was governed by the British East India Company, a private stock company. However, the great Sepoy Mutiny of 1857, the first large-scale uprising of the Indians against British rule, caused the British government to take over the government of India from the company. Between 1858 and 1914 Great Britain spent millions of dollars in India on railroads, industries, education, and public health. The enormous growth of India's population, which more than doubled during the period, is testimony to some improvement in the conditions of life under British rule. But the British took out of India more than they brought in, and they showed no inclination to grant self-government. Indian dissatisfaction with British rule mounted steadily. In the late nineteenth century, nationalism, which had provided so much aggressive energy for Europe, was coming to Asia—to India as well as to Japan and China. In 1885 the All Indian Congress party was formed for the purpose of achieving Indian independence. By 1914 it was becoming obvious that India would not remain a placid and profitable colony much longer.

7. THE LEGACY OF IMPERIALISM

The Western world's technology, its dynamic capitalism, and above all its aggressive nationalism had enabled it between 1880 and 1914 to subject most of the rest of the world to its domination (see Figure 49.4). In the process of dominating the non-Western world, Western nations not only exploited the natural and human resources of conquered lands but also profoundly undermined the cultures, societies, and political organizations of native peoples. Few in the West were able or willing to recognize how destructive this policy could be. By 1914 most people in the Western world had come to view imperialism as a normal and permanent state. In the course of the twentieth century, however, some of the very forces that accounted for the new imperialism would lead to its demise. The non-Western world was irreversibly changed by Western imperialism, but it would not remain under the thumb of Western nations for long.

SUGGESTED READING

General and Causes

D. K. Fieldhouse, *The Colonial Experience: A Comparative Study from the Eighteenth Century* (1982). A good introduction.

D. Headrick, *Tools of Empire* (1981). Examines what made imperial expansion relatively easy.

D. Mannoni, *Prospero and Caliban: The Psychology of Colonization* (1964). An excellent analysis from a psychological perspective.

T. Smith, *The Patterns of Imperialism* (1981). A good recent survey.

H. Wright, ed., *The "New Imperialism"* (1975). An anthology of different views.

The Exploitation and Awakening of China

J. K. Fairbank, *The United States and China* (1979). A scholarly, lucid history of China by a leading expert.

I. Hsu, *The Rise of Modern China* (1975). A useful survey.

The Emergence of Japan

J. W. Hall, *Japan, From Prehistory to Modern Times* (1970). A useful survey.

M. Hane, *Japan: A Historical Survey* (1972). Good on the nineteenth and twentieth centuries.

Competition for the Near and Middle East

S. N. Fisher, *The Middle East: A History,* 2nd ed. (1969). Reliable text.

The Scramble for Africa

J. Gallegher, R. Robinson, and A. Danny, *Africa and the Victorians: The Climax of Imperialism* (1961). A good, controversial analysis.

E. J. Murphy, *History of African Civilization* (1972). Solid on the nineteenth and twentieth centuries.

The British Empire

W. Baumgart, *Imperialism: The Idea and Reality of British and French Colonial Expansion* (1982). Up-to-date study.

B. Porter, *The Lion's Share, A Short History of British Imperialism, 1850–1970* (1975). A solid survey.

CHAPTER 50

Industrial Society, Social Classes, and Women

FIGURE 50.1. The Urban Classes
This French cartoon of 1845 shows a typical Parisian apartment house in which the various social classes lived in close proximity but different conditions. The bourgeoisie live on the first (American second) and second floors in wealth and prudent comfort. The lower classes, and aspiring artists, live on the bottom and upper floors in increasing poverty—thanks to their imprudence. (Bibliothèque Nationale, Paris)

Between 1850 and 1914 new areas in the West were industrializing, new industries were being developed, new methods of production were being used, and new business structures were emerging. The quantity and quality of industrial production underwent such a great change that historians have come to call these industrial developments the "second Industrial Revolution." During the same period social developments initiated during the earlier period of industrialization were maturing and evolving. Some, such as the rise of working-class organizations and ideologies, were directly connected to the industrial process. Others were more broadly based—the growth and movement of populations, the evolution of classes, and the developing experiences of women in an increasingly urbanized society. In short, mature, modern industrial economies and societies were becoming firmly established throughout the West.

1. THE SECOND INDUSTRIAL REVOLUTION

The first Industrial Revolution was initiated in Great Britain during the last decades of the eighteenth century. It spread to certain limited areas of western Europe and the United States during the first half of the nineteenth century. This early industrialization was based primarily on steam, iron, and textiles. During the 1850s and 1860s industrial production continued to expand, but mostly in the same areas and along the same lines as in earlier decades. In 1871, Great Britain was still the industrial leader, producing more industrial goods than the rest of the world combined. Besides Great Britain, only Belgium and parts of France, Germany, northern Italy, and the United States were industrially well developed.

The second Industrial Revolution was initiated in the last third of the nineteenth century. It was more widespread than the first Industrial Revolution and was based more on electricity, oil, steel, and chemicals. Great Britain, failing to invest sufficiently in new processes, falling behind in marketing techniques, and relying too heavily on old plants, lost its industrial leadership. Between 1871 and 1914, the United States and Germany sur-

passed Great Britain. By 1914 the Industrial Revolution had penetrated central and eastern Europe, Japan, Canada, Australia, and New Zealand; even India had a small textile industry. However, it was still in western Europe and the United States that most of the world's industry was to be found, and the greater part of Asia, Africa, and Latin America was still not industrialized. Moreover, it was in western Europe that both the prosperity and the uncertainties of economic life—exemplified by the industrial boom of 1850–1873 and the depression between 1873 and 1896—were experienced most.

New Products and Processes

Steel has been the mainstay of industry and transportation since the latter part of the nineteenth century. Until the mid–nineteenth century, steel was hard to make and very expensive. The discovery of the Bessemer process (1856) and the Thomas-Gilchrist process (1878) of removing impurities from molten iron greatly speeded up and cheapened the production of steel. In 1871 the total annual steel production in the entire world was approximately 1 million tons, of which about half was produced by Great Britain, a fourth by Germany, and an eighth by the United States. By 1914 the world's annual production had increased more than fiftyfold; the United States was producing approximately half the total, Germany a fourth, and Great Britain an eighth. Out of this steel were made tools and machines that constantly increased in numbers and efficiency. By 1914 in the industrialized countries, these increasingly automatic machines fabricated most metal, textile, leather, and wood products (see Figure 50.2).

The power to drive the steel machines was increasing in like proportion. In 1914 probably nine-tenths of the world's industrial power was still provided by the steam engine. Other and more efficient power generators, however, were rapidly coming to the fore. Between 1831 and 1882 the dynamo for generating electricity was developed by a number of inventors, the most important of whom were Michael Faraday (British), the Siemens brothers (German), and Thomas A. Edison (American). Sir Charles Parsons (British) pat-

FIGURE 50.2. Krupp Works   Germany industrialized rapidly during the last quarter of the nineteenth century. This photo shows the armaments factory at the Krupp works in Essen, Germany. (Culver Pictures)

ented the steam turbine in 1884. The turbine proved to be so efficient that it was soon used to drive the largest ships and eventually to generate most of the world's electric power. In 1888 the electric motor was invented by Nikola Tesla, a naturalized American born in Croatia. The first practical internal-combustion engine was invented by Gottlieb Daimler (German) in 1886. One year later he put it to work in the first automobile. In 1892 the diesel engine, efficiently burning cheap crude oil, was invested by Rudolf Diesel (German). The invention of these two engines gave impetus to the oil industry.

In the last decades of the nineteenth century, pure science was playing an increasingly vital role in industry, and both science and industry were being applied to agriculture. Physics contributed most heavily to the rapidly growing electrical industry. Chemistry made possible such important industries as synthetic dyes, wood pulp, paper, plastics, synthetic fibers, photography, and motion pictures. The electrical and chemical industries were most highly developed in Germany. The mechanization of agriculture made its first big advances in the great grain-growing areas of the United States, Canada, and Australia, although western Europe was also steadily increasing its agricultural yields through the use of farm machinery and scientific farming techniques.

Transport and Communications

Between 1850 and 1914 a large part of humanity became mobile. Whereas before 1850 relatively few people had ever seen more of the world than could be seen on journeys by foot or on horseback, by 1914 millions of people were traveling considerable distances, often by rapid conveyance. Even in places such as China, Turkey, and Brazil, trains chugged along, hauling people for distances and at speeds unknown before.

This was the greatest era of railroad building in history. There had been a rather lively building of railroads before 1850 in western Europe and the United States. However, between 1850 and 1914 the world's railway system was fundamentally completed. There has been relatively little railroad building since.

At the same time, the steamship was making comparable progress, although it had stiff competition from the sailing ship until near the end of the nineteenth century. Steel hulls of great size, turbine engines, and screw propellers were too much for the beautiful sails. The opening of the Suez Canal in 1869 and the Panama Canal in 1914, together with the increase in the size and speed of ships, brought the world and its peoples, commodities, and markets much closer together.

During the last three decades of the nineteenth century, the humble bicycle became a common and important means of locomotion, especially in Europe. But the bicycle was not fast enough for the industrial age. When Gottlieb Daimler attached his little combustion engine to a wagon in 1887, the automobile was born. It quickly captured the imagination of daring pioneers. Daimler sold his patent to a French company, and until the end of the century the French led the field in automobile development and production. Leadership passed to America with the founding of the Ford Motor Company in 1903. Henry Ford, who started out as a bicycle mechanic, applied the assembly-line method of mass production to the new automobile industry. The rapid spread of the automobile created vast new industrial empires in oil, rubber, and concrete.

After the turn of the century the airplane was invented. The first successful heavier-than-air flying machine was flown by Wilbur and Orville Wright in 1903 over the sand dunes at Kitty Hawk, North Carolina. Aviation was still in its infancy in 1914, but already its tremendous future was obvious.

Communications were developing faster yet. In 1844 Samuel F. B. Morse sent a message by wire forty miles from Baltimore to Washington. The telegraph, transmitting messages instantaneously from one end of any length of wire to the other, caught on rapidly. In 1866 a telegraph cable was laid across the Atlantic, enabling news to travel from New York to London as quickly as from New York to Brooklyn. Ten years later Alexander Graham Bell, an American born in Scotland, invented the telephone, and in 1895 Guglielmo Marconi, an Italian, sent the first message by wireless telegraphy. Together with the revolution in transportation, these developments in communications accelerated the Industrial Revolution by greatly facilitating the large-scale mobilization of capital, raw materials, labor, and markets.

The Growth of Corporations and Monopolies

At the same time that industry was growing, individual companies were growing larger and combining to form monopolistic mergers or trusts. Such undertakings as railroads, shipping lines, and iron and steel mills were too large for all but a very few individuals to finance. As a rule, therefore, enterprises of this scope were carried on by joint stock companies. Entrepreneur capitalists would raise the necessary capital outlay by organizing a corporation and selling stock in it to other capitalists. All the industrialized countries encouraged the investment of capital in corporations by passing laws that limited the liability of stockholders to the amount of money invested (hence the "Ltd." usually seen after the name of a British corporation or combine). By 1914 most of the world's industry was controlled by large corporations and trusts. Although their stockholders were numbered by the thousands, they were really controlled by a relatively few banks and wealthy individuals. And between the owners of these corporations and the millions of workers, there lay a great gulf. The actual operation of the larger industries would be carried on by hired managers, who hired and fired and supervised the workers.

The giant corporations were ruthless in dealing with each other. In this era of unrestrained competition, the big and strong frequently destroyed the small and weak. The premium was on size and strength. The results were combines, mergers, and monopolistic trusts. The spectacular success of Rockefeller's Standard Oil Trust in the 1880s soon made it the model for many others, particularly in the United States, Germany, Japan, and to a lesser extent, Great Britain. The German monopolistic combinations such as the giant I. G. Farben Industries (chemicals and dyes) were called *cartels*. They received government encouragement and support, particularly in their operations abroad. In Japan three-quarters of the nation's industry was controlled by five giant family corporations.

2. THE RISE OF WORKING-CLASS ORGANIZATIONS AND IDEOLOGIES

Labor Unions and Cooperatives

Wherever industrialization occurred, distressed laborers almost immediately attempted to protect themselves by banding together. However, until the 1870s inexperience, poverty, hostile governments, and unfavorable public opinion effectively hindered their efforts. Anti–labor union laws were not fully repealed in Great Britain until 1875 and in France until 1884. In Germany Bismarck persecuted labor unions until his dismissal in 1890. Until the 1880s, the union movement in Europe was limited chiefly to skilled workers, organized by crafts, who were moderate in their aims and methods.

In the 1880s unionization spread rapidly to unskilled workers, cut across craft lines, and adopted socialistic programs (often Marxist) and more radical methods. In Great Britain the labor unions formed the national Trades Union Congress in 1868, and later they became identified with the

Labour party, which was founded between 1881 and 1906. In Germany the individual unions in 1890 formed a national organization that was frankly Marxist. In France in 1895 the various unions banded together in the giant CGT (Confédération Générale du Travail—General Confederation of Labor) with a radical program. By 1914 the working class in the industrialized countries was sufficiently large and organized (though only a minority was as yet unionized) to make itself a power to be reckoned with, both in the factories and mines and at the polls.

Meanwhile, a much bigger portion of the working class was participating in the milder cooperatives of various types. In 1910 in Great Britain membership in cooperative retail stores, fraternal insurance (friendly) societies, and credit associations is estimated to have been some 14 million, the great bulk of whom were wage earners. These organizations also provided much-needed social fellowship for workers. In the 1880s Denmark became the home of the agricultural cooperative movement. By 1914 nearly all of Denmark's agricultural commodities were cooperatively produced and marketed, and the movement had spread to most of northern Europe, to Italy, and to the United States.

Socialism

During the second half of the nineteenth century socialism became a major ideological force within the working class and came to influence the society and politics of the West in important ways. The most prominent source of socialism was Karl Marx, who, along with Friedrich Engels, had already produced the *Communist Manifesto* in 1848. (See Chapter 44.) Marx argued that modern industrial society in the capitalist West was being split increasingly into two opposing classes: the capitalists (factory owners) and the workers. According to Marx, capitalism was doomed to be overthrown by a revolution of the working class and replaced by a socialist system.

Marx continued to write during the 1850s, 1860s, and 1870s, publishing his most important book, *Das Kapital*, in 1867. He played a key role in translating his ideas into actions by helping union organizers to form the International Working

Men's Association (the First International) in 1864. The association was an amalgam of non-Marxian socialists (such as followers of Louis-Auguste Blanqui and Pierre Joseph Proudhon), anarchists (such as Mikhail Bakunin), and Marxists, and it was divided at the start. Soon, however, Marx and his followers gained control. Although this organization proved to be fragile, falling apart in the 1870s after the Paris Commune, it helped spread Marx's socialism—particularly in Germany. The Second International was formed in 1889 and lasted until 1914. An international federation of socialist parties, it worked to spread socialism, maintain doctrinal purity, and develop socialist strategies.

After Marx's death in 1883, his followers split into various groups and often disagreed over the "correct" meaning of Marxism. The most important modification of Marxism was a moderate revisionism, led by the German socialist Eduard Bernstein (1850–1932). Bernstein argued that Marx had made some errors and that a revolution would not be necessary. He advocated cooperation with the capitalistic classes to obtain all the immediate benefits possible for labor and a gradual approach to socialism.

In Germany, where socialism had its greatest success before 1914, the Social Democratic party formally rejected Bernstein's moderate revisionism but in practice often tended to follow it after the 1890s. By 1914 the party was able to poll some 4.5 million votes and had become the largest party in Germany. The French Socialists were more radical than the Germans. In 1905 the orthodox and the revisionist wings of the French Socialists joined to form the United Socialist party under the leadership of the scholar-orator, Jean Jaurès. By 1914 they numbered 1.5 million voters and had 110 seats in the Chamber of Deputies. Contrary to the expectations of Marx, socialism in Great Britain was weak and mild. Among the earliest British Socialists were George Bernard Shaw, H. G. Wells, and Sidney and Beatrice Webb. These intellectual radicals formed the Fabian Society, which was committed to moderation and gradualism. The Labour party, founded between 1881 and 1906, was also mild and grew slowly before 1914. Neither the Fabian Society nor the Labour party could be called Marxist, although both were influenced by Marx. In the United States, the socialist movement was relatively weak and (in retrospect) mild. The first prominent American Socialist, Eugene V. Debs, did manage to poll nearly a million votes for president in 1912 and again in 1920.

Anarchism

Anarchism was an extremely radical movement that has often been confused with Marxism. While both were anticapitalist and gained most of their support from the working classes, anarchists stressed much more the elimination of the state and any authority that impinges on human freedom. Anarchists optimistically believed that human beings, once freed from the corrupting institutions that oppressed them, would naturally cooperate with one another. Anarchism's two most influential leaders were the Russian activist Mikhail Bakunin (1814–1876) and the exiled Russian theoretician Prince Pëter Kropotkin (1842–1921). Anarchism became particularly influential in France, Spain, and Italy and among artists and intellectuals as well as members of the working classes. A relatively small wing of the anarchist movement turned to violent means to gain their ends. Among its victims were Tsar Alexander II of Russia in 1881, President Carnot of France in 1894, King Humbert of Italy in 1900, and President McKinley of the United States in 1901. This image of violence has tainted the general perception of anarchism ever since.

3. THE GROWTH AND MOVEMENT OF POPULATION

Since the eighteenth century, European population had been growing at a rapid pace. This growth continued as industrialization spread throughout Europe in the nineteenth century. Between 1850 and 1914 Europe's population expanded from 266 million to 450 million. However, there were important changes underlying this growth of population during the second half of the nineteenth century, particularly after 1870.

In many areas, particularly western Europe, increasing birth rates were no longer a prime generator of population growth; in fact, birth rates were declining. A trend starting in the middle class and spreading to the working classes of marrying later and intentionally having fewer children was limiting the size of families. Because parents could rely more on infants surviving into adulthood, there was less need to have so many children. Moreover, parents who wanted to ensure their own and their children's rising economic well-being and social position elected to have smaller families, which were less expensive and required less division of assets. Despite the declining birth rate, population grew, fueled by an even greater decline in the death rate. This decrease was caused by a combination of improved public sanitation, economic growth, and medical advances.

This European population was not only growing but also moving in vast numbers in two main ways: from Europe to overseas areas, particularly the United States, and from the countryside to the city.

The overseas migration of Europeans between 1850 and 1914 was phenomenal. Ever since the first settlements in the New World, there had been a sizable trickle of Europeans to the Americas. This trickle had become a flowing stream in the mid–nineteenth century. Great numbers of British, Irish, and then German immigrants landed in the United States during the 1840s, 1850s, and 1860s. After 1870 the stream of Europeans migrating overseas swelled into a rushing torrent as peoples from southern and eastern Europe joined the flow. In the brief span of forty-three years between 1871 and 1914, more than 30 million Europeans left their homelands and migrated to the New World or to the British dominion territories. The great bulk of them came to the United States.

Several factors help explain this massive movement of Europeans overseas. Perhaps the greatest impetus was the growth of population. The growing numbers led to increasing competition for land in rural areas and for living space and jobs in urban areas. As different areas of Europe underwent the economic and social transformations connected with industrialization, people were uprooted from traditional ways of life. When these upheavals were accompanied by political turmoil, many found additional reasons to migrate. As

these developments pushed Europeans from their homelands, opportunities in the New World, both real and imagined, pulled them across the Atlantic (see Figure 50.3). Land and economic opportunity seemed abundant in such places as the United States, Canada, Argentina, and Brazil. Improvements in transportation—railroads and steamships—made travel to these faraway places easier. This combination of push from Europe and pull from the New World induced millions of relatively poor, young, and often unmarried Europeans to migrate overseas. Although it is difficult to know how most of them experienced this change, clearly not all were satisfied. Approximately one-third of those migrating from Europe overseas eventually returned.

Europeans were moving from the countryside to the city at an even faster pace than they were moving overseas. In 1850, despite a long process of urbanization, in no country did those in cities outnumber rural inhabitants. This picture changed rapidly during the second half of the nineteenth century. By the turn of the century more than half the population in western Europe lived in urban areas. Agriculture had become an occupation for the minority in Great Britain, Belgium, the Netherlands, Germany, and France.

The movement to the city was brought about by the opportunities in industry and commerce, the growing attractiveness of urban life, and the application of mechanization and science to agriculture, which now required far fewer workers to produce greater yields. The social problems of the cities were being recognized and attacked. A public health movement to improve water supplies and public sanitation by introducing piped water and sewer systems was initiated in England during the 1840s. Urban areas in other countries followed England's lead in the succeeding decades. Urban life was altered by the introduction of mechanized, regular, and reliable means of public transportation, particularly electric streetcars in the 1890s. This development widened opportunities for better housing, since people no longer had to live so close to work. Central areas, which had housed people of all social classes together, were becoming dominated by public buildings, retail outlets, businesses, and theaters. Around the central areas new residential districts and suburbs

FIGURE 50.3.   "Welcome to the Land of Freedom"   In this romanticized painting a variety of emotions is displayed on the faces of immigrants as they pass the Statue of Liberty in New York Harbor on their way to a new life. Between 1871 and 1914, more than 30 million Europeans immigrated overseas, most of them to the United States. (The Granger Collection)

formed, often separated into working-class and middle-class sections. Some limited private and public programs were initiated to facilitate the construction of cheap housing.

Cities were thus becoming more attractive. Urban planning spread throughout Europe in the second half of the nineteenth century. The general pattern was initiated in Paris during the 1850s and 1860s, where the government tore down old, overcrowded, and almost inaccessible areas of the city and built large boulevards and parks and provided for more open spaces. Other cities such as Vienna and Cologne followed the example of Paris. Together the spread of sanitation facilities, public transportation, urban planning, and new

housing in Europe's cities was making life in urban areas relatively safe and appealing compared with life in the countryside.

4. SOCIAL CLASSES

The class divisions of industrial society continued to develop along the lines already established during the first half of the nineteenth century. The aristocracy continued to shrink in size and significance, yet it still retained some vestiges of wealth, prestige, and position. In part, it was supported by the increasingly conservative elite of the upper middle class. These families, who had gained great wealth from industry, commerce, and banking, mingled with the old aristocracy and copied much of its exclusive and expensive life style. Numerous servants, at least one country house surrounded by an estate, membership in exclusive clubs, extensive travel, major contributions to good causes, and support of culture were almost requirements for full membership in this elite, which constituted less than 5 percent of the population.

The bulk of the middle class, ranging from small factory owners, shopowners, schoolteachers, and professionals to clerks and minor officials, continued to benefit from industrial expansion and urbanization. During the second half of the nineteenth century, however, there were some important changes in the outlook and composition of this class. Before 1848, the middle class was often revolutionary and certainly at the forefront of progressive political change. After 1848, the middle class ceased to be revolutionary and more often fought to retain the status quo rather than promote progressive reform. For the most part, the middle class was gaining what it wanted and was achieving dominance in Western society. In composition, the middle class was not only growing (to some 20 percent of the population) but also adding new groups to its numbers. The two most important of these new groups were the professionals and the white-collar employees. The professionals included people such as engineers, chemists, accountants, and architects as well as public and private managers. These people utilized their education and expertise to fill specialized needs created by industrialization. In wealth, attitudes, and style of life they resembled the traditional middle-class entrepreneurs, merchants, and bankers they served. The white-collar employees were placed toward the bottom of the middle classes. They included the growing numbers of clerks, secretaries, bureaucrats, and salesmen who usually worked for large firms and earned little more than members of the skilled working class. But they self-consciously considered themselves apart from the working classes below them, ascribed to middle-class attitudes, and tried their best to follow a middle-class style of life—at least in appearances.

Generally members of the middle class copied as much of the envied life style of the wealthier upper middle class as they could. With care, most could afford one domestic, good food, a well-furnished apartment or house, schooling and perhaps music lessons for the children, attendance at cultural events, fashionable clothes, and travel.

In values and beliefs, middle-class people thought that they represented what was correct and best in Western society. They believed that prudence, control, rationality, and hard work were the keys to success. They respected traditional Christian morality, sexual purity, and marital fidelity, while they denounced drinking, crime, excesses, and even poverty as vices. They felt they should be able to live up to these standards, at least in appearances if not always in practice. Money remained an important consideration for marriage, but the union was supposed to be centered on sentiment. While this was the period of Victorian sexual propriety for the middle class, it now appears that there was increasing acceptance and expectation of sexual enjoyment within the marriage. Children were at the center of the family and fewer in number; they remained at home through the adolescent years and were more extensively educated.

The working classes—the wage laborers with little if any capital—were headed by an elite of workers whose skills as artisans, machinists, foremen, or specialists were in great demand. Often they struggled to distinguish themselves from the bulk of the working classes below them by adopting a stern, moralistic attitude, copying the appearance of the middle class, and striving to ensure that their children would maintain or surpass their own position in the social hierarchy. The bulk of the working classes were factory laborers, construction workers, transport workers, unskilled or semiskilled day workers, and domestics.

Clearly, the working classes were benefiting from industrialization during the second half of the nineteenth century. Real wages were on the rise, perhaps doubling in Great Britain between 1850 and 1914. The working classes engaged in the proliferating leisure-time activities, which included public drinking and socializing in cafes and pubs, watching organized sports such as soccer, boxing, and racing, and attending music halls, vaudeville theaters, and amusement parks. Nevertheless, the working class was still located toward the bottom of the social and economic scale, continually experiencing or being threatened by poverty, unemployment, poor housing, and insecurity. They may have been participating in an expanding industrial society, but that expansion did not benefit all equally. The gap between rich and poor remained wide; the upper 20 percent of the population usually received more national income than the combined total of the remaining 80 percent.

This society of the late nineteenth century and early twentieth centuries had acquired some permanence that reflected its mature industrial base. It was a society that was more affluent than ever but was still divided into classes of greatly differing status and wealth. Tensions ran through this society, as did great movements of people and ideas. Nevertheless, when the generations after World War I looked back to this society, it seemed enviable despite its faults.

5. WOMEN'S ROLES AND EXPERIENCES

It is difficult to summarize the situation of women between 1850 and 1914. Women's roles and experiences differed sharply according to class lines, and even within classes many of the relevant developments were contradictory. What generally unified women's experiences during this period, as before, was their legal inequality to men, their lack of political rights, their economic dependence and inferiority, and their social restrictions. In an age in which liberal values—stressing individualism, political rights, and equality before the law—were becoming firmly established, women were still relegated to a secondary position or actually excluded from most aspects of public life.

For middle-class women, the contradictions were greatest. The sexual division of labor, separating the woman's sphere from the man's sphere, was rigidified by the growing cult of domesticity. Accordingly, women were glorified as caring mothers, supportive wives, and religious beings. Their place was in the home, where they were in charge of the domestic scene. The wife was supposed to defer and cater to her husband and take

FIGURE 50.4. Emmeline Pankhurst Women led numerous demonstrations in their struggle to gain the vote, particularly in Great Britain. Here a policeman is arresting a leading suffragette, Emmeline Pankhurst. (Culver Pictures)

personal responsibility for nursing and rearing the children. The children's education and the religious well-being of the family was her realm. As domestic manager, she was supposed to have expertise as a consumer, and in turn she was the object of consumer advertising. She was also assumed to be interested in charity and willing to donate time for worthy causes. The middle-class wife was not expected to engage in paid occupations outside the home. The more successfully middle class the family was, the less likely it was that the wife engaged in paid work. Nevertheless, toward the end of the nineteenth century some professions such as schoolteaching, social work, and nursing were expanding and opening to even married middle-class women. Still, most of these occupations were associated with women's domestic roles, were relatively low paying, and were considered most appropriate for unmarried women.

Within the working class, middle-class views about the separate spheres of women and men and the particular domestic nature of women hovered and had some important effects, but the actual experience of women differed. In general working-class women were much more likely to work for wages than middle-class women. A common pattern was for young women to take jobs as domestics before they were married—often moving to cities for this purpose. In addition to the more traditional jobs for women in textiles, food processing, and retail outlets, some of the newer occupations in nursing and secretarial work were opening to women. When jobs were unavailable, prostitution (generally legal and regulated) remained at least a temporary alternative for some. After marriage, women were effectively excluded from several of the options they had when single. One of the main ways for working-class women to earn money was in "sweated industries," where they worked in small factories or at home, usually in textiles or decorating, and were paid by the piece. In all these occupations, women continued to be discriminated against; they received lower pay than men for the same work and were excluded from many jobs open to working-class men. Often middle-class notions of domesticity were used to justify the lower pay and status of women's work, employers arguing that women's primary role was not in paid labor. Women were the first to be affected by new legislation controlling the hours and conditions under which workers could be employed, although these laws were often poorly enforced.

During this period some organized efforts to challenge the role and status assigned to women arose. The strongest feminist movements arose in Great Britain and the United States, particularly movements to extend voting rights to women. In Great Britain organizations such as the National Union of Women's Suffrage Societies, led by Millicent Fawcett (1847–1929), and the more radical Women's Social and Political Union, led by Emmeline Pankhurst (1858–1928), petitioned, lobbied, and marched for the franchise (see Figure 50.4). Some women used more violent means to bring attention to their cause. But the government resisted and success was achieved only at the end of World War I.

In other countries, women's organizations argued for the right to vote and for changes in women's social and economic position, but these organizations were often splintered and rarely achieved their goals. Many continental feminist leaders such as Louise Michel in France, Clara Zetkin in Germany, and Anna Kuliscioff in Italy associated themselves with socialist or radical movements. Only in Norway did women gain the right to vote in national elections before World War I. However, the issues of feminism were now being raised publicly as never before and would become more powerful during the twentieth century.

SUGGESTED READING

General

E. J. Hobsbawm, *The Age of Capital* (1975). Examines middle-class life during the second half of the nineteenth century.

N. Stone, *Europe Transformed, 1878–1919* (1984). A broad survey.

E. R. Tannenbaum, *1900: The Generation Before the Great War* (1976). Good essays on social history.

The Second Industrial Revolution

A. S. Milward and S. B. Saul, *The Development of the Economies of Continental Europe, 1850–1914* (1977). A good treatment of the second Industrial Revolution.
D. S. Landes, *The Unbound Prometheus: Technological Change and Industrial Development in Western Europe from 1750 to the Present* (1969). Excellent survey emphasizing technological change.
S. Pollard, *Peaceful Conquest: The Industrialization of Europe* (1981). An up-to-date survey.

The Rise of Working-Class Organizations and Ideologies

L. R. Berlanstein, *The Working People of Paris, 1871–1914* (1985). A comprehensive study.
J. Joll, *The Anarchists* (1964). A good examination of anarchism and anarchists.
G. Lichtheim, *Marxism* (1971). Highly respected treatment.
W. Sewell, Jr., *Work and Revolution in France* (1980). Good treatment of French socialism.
E. Wilson, *To the Finland Station* (1953). Classic study of socialist leaders.

The Growth and Movement of Population

A. Briggs, *Victorian Cities* (1970). A good examination of Britain's industrial cities.

C. M. Cipolla, *The Economic History of World Population* (1962). A standard introduction.
J. Merriman, ed., *French Cities in the Nineteenth Century: Class, Power, and Urbanization* (1982). A good selection of recent essays.

Social Classes

J. Donzelot, *The Policing of Families* (1979). An important interpretation stressing governmental interference with family life.
P. Gay, *The Bourgeois Experience: Victoria to Freud,* 2 vols. (1984–1986). Excellent study of sexuality and the middle class.
P. N. Stearns, *European Society in Upheaval* (1967). Solid, if traditional, social history covering the period.

Women

M. Boxer and J. Quataert, eds., *Connecting Spheres: Women in the Western World, 1500 to Present* (1987). Fine chapters covering the period.
P. Branca, *Women in Europe Since 1750* (1978). A useful study.
R. Bridenthal and C. Koonz, *Becoming Visible: Women in European History* (1977). Contains good chapters covering the period.
M. Vicinus, *Suffer and Be Still: Women in the Victorian Age* (1972). Good essays on Victorian women.

CHAPTER 51

Science and the Challenge to Christianity

FIGURE 51.1. Eakins, "The Gross Clinic," 1875 This realistic painting by Thomas Eakins of an operation in progress conveys the sense of power of modern science and the optimism with which science was viewed in the nineteenth century. The lack of religious refernces in this medical scene indicates some of the potential challenge of secular science to Christianity. (Jefferson Medical College, Thomas Jefferson University, Philadelphia)

By the middle of the nineteenth century, science had gained much prestige. It was increasingly connected with the inventions and technology of industrialization, which provided wealth and power. It seemed to go hand in hand with the rationalism and prevailing bourgeois liberalism of the period. Over the course of the nineteenth century, people assumed that scientists had, or soon would have, a firm understanding of the physical world. They were optimistic that scientific methods would provide a similar understanding of human society. Although this sense of certainty and optimism would be somewhat undermined in the decades surrounding the turn of the century, the period between 1850 and 1914 must be considered one of great progress in the sciences.

At the same time Christianity faced serious and fundamental challenges. It was attacked from several quarters, but at the base of the many challenges were the successes and increasing prestige of science. Christian leaders often had difficulty adjusting their theology and institutions to the scientific, liberal, and secular assumptions of the period.

1. THE PHYSICAL, BIOLOGICAL, AND MEDICAL SCIENCES

The greatest advances in the field of the physical sciences in the nineteenth and early twentieth centuries centered on discovering the nature of matter, energy, and electricity. John Dalton (1766–1844), a gifted British scientist and teacher, started a fruitful line of inquiry by reviving the theory that all matter is composed of atoms. Dalton eventually concluded that what distinguishes the various chemical elements is the weight of the atoms of which each element is composed. Building on Dalton's theories, the Russian chemist Dmitri Mendeléev (1834–1907) in 1870 worked out a periodic chart showing the atomic weight of all the known elements and indicating by gaps in the chart that others remained to be discovered. Both Dalton and Mendeléev thought that the atom was an indivisible solid. But in the 1890s the British physicist Joseph Thomson (1856–1940) and the

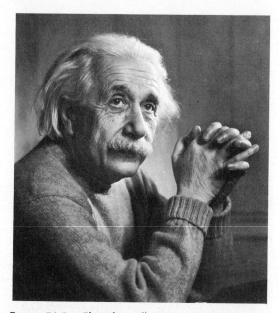

Figure 51.2. Einstein Albert Einstein (1879–1955) became one of the most recognized figures of the twentieth century. His theory of relativity, first proposed in 1905, undermined the concept of a stable material universe that Newton had so beautifully formalized early in the eighteenth century. (Karsh, Ottawa/Woodfin Camp & Associates)

Dutch physicist Hendrik Lorentz (1853–1928) independently discovered that atoms are composed of small particles, which Lorentz named electrons. Shortly thereafter another British physicist, Sir Ernest Rutherford (1871–1937), further developed Thomson's theories. Rutherford conceived of each atom as a miniature solar system, the nucleus being the sun, and the electrons the planets. Furthermore—and this was most startling—Thomson and Rutherford suggested that the protons and electrons might not be matter at all but merely positive and negative charges of electricity.

Meanwhile in the 1890s the German physicist Wilhelm von Roentgen (1845–1923) discovered X-rays, and the French physicist Pierre Curie (1859–1906) and his Polish wife Marie Curie (1867–1935) discovered radium and added to what was known about radioactivity.

During this same period, Albert Einstein (1879–

1955), a German physicist who later fled to America, was assailing time-honored concepts not only about the stability of matter but also about time, space, and motion (see Figure 51.2). Einstein derived a formula equating mass and energy: $E = mc^2$ (E = energy in ergs; m = mass in grams; c = speed of light in centimeters per second). According to this formula, the atomic energy in a lump of coal is some three billion times as great as the energy obtained by burning the coal—a truth that was proved several decades later with the development of the atomic bomb. In 1905 Einstein proposed his theory of relativity, which made time, space, and motion relative to each other and to the observer, not the absolutes they had always been conceived to be.

These stunning discoveries in physics and chemistry were triumphs, reflecting new sophistication in scientific theory and experimentation. But by the turn of the century a sense of uncertainty was creeping into elite scientific circles—a sense that the more we learn, the less solid and reliable the material world seems. This sense of uncertainty, particularly in physics, would spread in the early decades of the twentieth century.

The intellectual world was even more interested in and influenced by developments in the biological sciences. Evolution, like the atomic theory, had been suggested by the ancient Greeks and from time to time afterward. With the revival of scientific interests and attitudes in the seventeenth and eighteenth centuries, the thoughts of a number of scientists turned to the problem of the origin of the present world and its phenomena. By the mid–nineteenth century, the concept of a slow and gradual development of the earth's crust and its inhabitants was not at all uncommon among intellectuals. The time was ripe for a first-rate scientist to supply the evidence. That man was Charles Darwin (1809–1882).

Darwin was of a distinguished British family. His study of medicine at Edinburgh and theology at Cambridge failed to challenge him. The world of plants and, to a somewhat lesser extent, animals was his first love—or rather, his consuming passion. In spite of frail health, he turned his powers of observation and reflection to the amassing of biological knowledge. Gradually he developed his concept of evolution. Of great influence on his thinking was Malthus' *Essay on Population* (1798), which described the struggle of human beings for food and survival, and Sir Charles Lyell's *Principles of Geology* (1830–1833), which was the first truly scientific treatise on geology. Lyell demonstrated by the study of fossils the likelihood of a gradual evolution of the earth's crust and of plant and animal forms over eons of time. Darwin published *On the Origin of Species by Natural Selection* in 1859. In this historic work he described with an impressive array of factual data, convincing reasoning, and lucid prose, the long, slow evolution of present plant and animal species from simpler forms through a process of natural selection. In the struggle for survival in nature's jungle, the fittest survived. Those specimens that possessed the more useful characteristics—for instance, the horse with the longer legs—survived to produce more offspring and to transmit their superior qualities, both inherited and acquired, to future generations. Twelve years later (1871) in his *Descent of Man,* he undertook to show how humans evolved from more primitive species by the same process. Although Darwin's work leaves many fundamental questions unanswered, his main thesis quickly gained general acceptance in the scientific world.

Few books in history have had so much influence as *On the Origin of Species*. The industrial bourgeoisie seized upon Darwin's theory as an explanation and a justification of its own success. Rulers and dominant groups everywhere derived comfort from it. Philosophers, notably Herbert Spencer, undertook to broaden the principle of evolution to make it the key to all truth. Meanwhile, Darwin's brilliant work not only popularized but also significantly contributed to the advancement of the biological sciences.

Medical science lagged far behind the physical and biological sciences at the opening of the nineteenth century. The seventeenth- and eighteenth-century scientists had made great progress in discovering the secrets of the stars, of the elements, and of plants and animals, but where the ailments of the human body were concerned, they were still holding to theories of Galen, a Greek physician of the second century A.D. George Washington was bled to death in 1799 by a physician who was following the standard practice of the time.

Much groundwork had been laid, however, for medical progress. In the sixteenth century Vesalius made great advances in the study of human anatomy. In the seventeenth century Harvey discovered the circulatory system, and Leeuwenhoek and Malpighi were using the newly invented microscope to explore the structure of human tissue and to discover the existence of microbes. By the late eighteenth century the British physician Edward Jenner was successfully inoculating against smallpox, though he did not understand the secret of its success. During the 1840s anesthesia was discovered and used successfully. But the whole field of germ diseases and infections was still a mystery.

The secrets of bacteria, their nature and their control, were first explored by the French chemist Louis Pasteur (1822–1895). During the 1860s Pasteur, after intensive and imaginative research, discovered that fermentation is caused by airborne bacteria that could be destroyed by boiling (or by pasteurization). Later he discovered that many diseases of humans and animals are also caused by bacteria and that some of them can be prevented by vaccination. His spectacular services to French agriculture and to humankind made him the most honored man in France. Robert Koch (1843–1910), a country doctor in eastern Germany, hearing of Pasteur's first discoveries, picked up the trail and discovered the germs causing anthrax (a deadly disease of cattle), tuberculosis, sleeping sickness, and many other diseases. He became a professor at the University of Berlin and was awarded the Nobel Prize.

Also building on Pasteur's foundations was the renowned British surgeon Joseph Lister (1827–1912), who applied the new knowledge of bacteria to the use of antiseptics and disinfectants in surgery. His amazing success in controlling infection opened a new era in surgery, and Lister was raised to the peerage by the British government. The honors bestowed on Pasteur, Koch, and Lister, in contrast with the persecutions suffered by many of the sixteenth- and seventeenth-century scientists, are striking evidence of the triumph of science and the scientific spirit in the nineteenth century.

2. THE RISE OF SOCIAL SCIENCE

The spectacular successes of the natural sciences in the nineteenth century encouraged scholars to apply the techniques and principles of natural science to the study of the human mind and society. The result was the birth of modern psychology and sociology, both of which soon became popular.

Until the middle of the nineteenth century the mechanistic and associational approach to psychology stemming from the theories of John Locke (1632–1704) still prevailed. In the second half of the nineteenth century a number of psychologists began to systematically apply an empirical approach to the study of human behavior. One of the first to bring psychology into the laboratory was Wilhelm Wundt (1832–1920). In his famous laboratory at Leipzig he and his enthusiastic students tested human reactions and tried all sorts of carefully controlled and measured experiments on cats and dogs, assuming that the findings would also be applicable to human beings.

The Russian scientist Ivan Pavlov (1849–1936), pursuing Wundt's line of attack, excited the intellectual world with the discovery of the conditioned reflex. Pavlov showed meat to a hungry dog and the dog's mouth watered. Then Pavlov rang a bell while showing the meat. Eventually the dog's mouth watered when only the bell was rung. The implication was that many of our human responses are purely mechanical reflexes produced by stimuli of which we are often unaware.

Sigmund Freud (1856–1939) created the greatest stir of all in the rapidly growing field of psychology. Freud was a Viennese neurologist who became the father of psychoanalysis. Freud concluded that much of human behavior is irrational, unconscious, and instinctual. He argued that conflict is a basic condition of life, particularly conflict between our innate biological drives (such as sex or aggression) and our social selves. These conflicts are worked out on a mostly unconscious level and in stages during childhood. These conflicts invariably cause frustration. Freud believed that much neurosis and psychosis stemmed from the suppressed and frustrated drives of early life—frustrations that then festered in the subconscious. He concluded that the correct therapy for such neuroses was to make the sufferer conscious of the facts and circumstances of the original frustration. He stressed the interpretation of dreams as a key tool for revealing the unconscious. Freud and his followers developed psychoanalysis into an influential theory of human behavior, an insightful method of psychological investigation, and a useful therapy for certain problems.

During the second half of the nineteenth century sociology acquired status as a social science. This new discipline was founded and named by Auguste Comte (1798–1857), an eccentric Frenchman of great energy and imagination. The history of humankind, said Comte, can be divided into three epochs. The first was religious, when mystical or supernatural explanations were assigned to all phenomena. The second was metaphysical, when general laws and abstract principles were taken as explanatory principles. The third, which humankind was on the point of entering, was the specific or positive, when the truth would be discovered by the scientific gathering of factual data. Comte had utter scorn for the first and little respect for the second epochs. He believed that humans and society are as susceptible to scientific investigation as minerals, plants, and the lower animals. His religion was the worship of humanity, and he had great faith in its future. These ideas were called *positivism*. Comte's followers, eager and numerous, placed great faith in statistics. They amassed vast arrays of statistical data on every conceivable social problem.

Second only to Comte in importance in the founding and promotion of sociology was the Englishman Herbert Spencer (1820–1903). Spencer shared Comte's scorn for mystical religion and denied that morals should be based on religion. He also shared Comte's faith in the progress of humanity. In his ten-volume *System of Synthetic Philosophy*, Spencer undertook to synthesize all human and social phenomena into one grand evolutionary system.

People's interest in themselves and in human society, together with the scientific spirit of the times, guaranteed for the social sciences great popularity. Anthropologists and archaeologists dug feverishly into the physical and cultural past of the human race. Political scientists and economists tended to forsake theory for the statistical

and "practical." Strenuous efforts were made to make history a social science. Leopold von Ranke (1795–1886) strove to make history coldly scientific and morally neutral. History, he insisted, should be based on an exhaustive accumulation and analysis of documentary evidence. Ranke's historical attitude and methodology were imported from Germany into the United States. They became the standard in both countries.

Between 1850 and 1914 natural scientists appeared to be solving the last mysteries of the material universe. Medical scientists appeared to be banishing pain and disease from the earth. Social scientists were amassing voluminous knowledge about the human mind and social relationships. Science had become one of the mainstays for the widely popular belief in progress.

3. CHALLENGES TO CHRISTIANITY

The rapid growth of science was just one of several challenges faced by organized religion in the West. Christianity seemed to be threatened by most of the major forces of modernization.

Industrialization was in many ways inimical to Christian faith and practices. Industrialization contributed to the mass migration of people from farm to city and from country to country, tearing them loose from old social patterns and institutions, of which the church had long been one of the most important. Members of the flocks became separated from their pastors. Once in the active and exciting industrial cities, many of the newcomers seemed no longer to need the church for their social life and entertainment.

The liberal and radical political movements of the late nineteenth century were for the most part anticlerical. The established churches in Europe, particularly the Catholic church, had long been allied with the conservative aristocracy and royalty. Liberals, when they came to power, often attacked the powers, the privileges, and the property of the established church. France is a good example. After the revolutionary era had ended with the overthrow of Napoleon, the Catholic church made a comeback. It allied itself with the Bourbon regime and with Napoleon III's Second

Empire, and it opposed liberal movements, including the setting up of the Third French Republic. The liberal leaders of the Third Republic soon adopted anticlerical policies. During the 1880s the Ferry Laws loosened the hold of the Church on education by setting up a rival and favored system of public secular schools, in which the teaching of religion was banned. In 1901 the Associations Law virtually destroyed the Church's schools by outlawing the Catholic teaching orders or associations. In 1905 church and state were completely separated. In all the industrialized countries in this period, public secular education made great strides, usually under the sponsorship of liberal parties.

Another factor inimical to organized religion during the second half of the nineteenth century was the growth of nationalism, which afflicted all the great industrialized powers. International Catholicism and international Judaism were seen as competitors for nationalistic allegiance. Between 1872 and 1878 Bismarck waged *Kulturkampf* (battle for civilization) against the Catholic church in Germany (see p. 599). Bismarck regarded as intolerable the allegiance of millions of German citizens to a non-German pope and the formation of a Catholic political party in Germany. The anti-Semitism that arose in many countries at this time may be attributed in part to the resentment against the international character of Judaism and also to racism, which was often connected to strong nationalism. The Dreyfus case in France is an example (see p. 597). Bloody pogroms in Russia drove tens of thousands of Russian and Polish Jews to America. Many Jews themselves, after centuries of dispersion, became nationalistic and started a movement (Zionism) to set up a Jewish national state in Palestine.

In most of these challenges to Christianity, science—whether through use or abuse—was used to bolster or lend some credibility to the attack. During the twentieth century Christianity would learn to coexist with science, but in the nineteenth century the two were at odds with each other.

With the exception of the evolutionary hypothesis, the challenge to Christianity by natural science was more indirect than direct. The discovery of more and more of the secrets of the material world allowed people to attribute to natural causes many phenomena that previously had been attributed to divine intervention. Disease germs, for instance, now appeared to be doing things that had long been ascribed to God.

The greatest conflicts between natural science and the Christian religion to emerge in the nineteenth century grew out of Darwin's evolutionary hypothesis. The publication of *On the Origin of Species* in 1859 created an immediate religious storm. The proposal of a long, gradual, and seemingly mechanistic evolution of all present species from simpler forms appeared to contradict the account of divine creation given in the first chapter of Genesis. The whole process of evolution as suggested by Darwin appeared to leave God entirely out of the affairs of the universe. Any doubt concerning Darwin's place for human beings in his evolutionary hypothesis was removed twelve years later, when he published *The Descent of Man.* Human beings, like all other living things, evolved from more primitive species. According to Darwin's hypothesis, in the view of many readers, a human being seemed to be just another animal, albeit the highest.

Clerics raged against Darwin and his hypothesis. Efforts were made, sometimes successfully, to suppress the reading of Darwin's books and the teaching of the evolutionary hypothesis in the schools. Darwin was not lacking in champions able and willing to assail the forces of religion. Thomas Huxley (1825–1895), a biologist, surgeon in the British navy, and president of the Royal Society, popularized Darwin's work in dozens of vigorous and lucid books and pamphlets and heaped withering scorn upon the clergy. He called himself "Darwin's bull-dog." Herbert Spencer was carried away with Darwin's thesis and built a whole system of philosophy around the idea of evolution. Spencer considered evolution the key to all truth and all progress. Ernst Haeckel (1834–1919), a prolific German scientist and popularizer, made great claims for evolution and for science. He proclaimed that scientists would very soon be solving all the remaining mysteries of life and even creating life. The conflict between the evolutionists and the Christian clergy that raged in western Europe in the last four decades of the nineteenth century did not reach its climax in the United States until the 1920s.

The assault of social science upon Christianity was much more direct and severe than that of natural science. Anthropologists dug into the human race's distant past to unearth the primitive origins of its culture, of which religion is always an important part. Nearly all of them concluded that religion is based on primitive superstition. In 1890 Sir James Frazer (1854–1941) published *The Golden Bough,* a vast and fascinating history of early myths, superstitions, and cults from which he believed that modern religions, including Christianity, were derived.

Psychologists often viewed religion as a fantasy or illusion created by human beings. God served as a powerful parental figure to turn to when difficult problems drove human beings into a more childlike psychological state—someone who could be relied on to deal with a threatening world. Religion also provided psychological ecstasy as well as ways to enforce constraint and control.

But it was the sociologists who were the most persistently and pointedly hostile to religion. Supernatural religion had no place whatever in Comte's positivism, humanity itself being the object of worship. Through volume after volume of Herbert Spencer's sociological writings ran a vein of hostility to mystic religion in general and to Christianity in particular. Mechanical evolution became, for Spencer, the key to all social progress. Even morals evolved. Religious faith, said Spencer, retarded social progress and obscured human vision of the evolutionary social process.

Finally, the scientific spirit brought forth a number of biblical scholars who subjected the Bible to searching scrutiny and analysis—some for the purpose of establishing its exact meaning, and others for the purpose of detecting error or fraud. This type of scholarship is called "higher criticism."

The first prominent nineteenth-century "higher critic" of the Bible was David Strauss (1808–1874), a Lutheran theologian at the University of Tübingen in Germany. After long years of laborious work, Strauss brought out a *Life of Jesus* in two volumes that stripped Christ of his divinity and undertook to explain in natural terms the miracles and prophecies recorded in the New Testament. Strauss asserted that the New Testament was a very unreliable document, that the authorship of the four Gospels could not be proved, and that the four accounts of the life of Jesus were contradictory.

Much more popular and influential was the charming one-volume *La Vie de Jésus* by Ernest Renan (1823–1892), a French scholar and a Catholic. Renan pictured Christ in solely human and natural terms. Renan attributed Christ's belief in his own divinity to hallucinations. But it was these psychological aberrations that gave him his power and drive and much of his appeal. The work of Strauss, Renan, and the numerous other "higher critics" appeared to many to bring religion within the compass of onrushing science.

4. THE CHRISTIAN RESPONSE

The first reaction of Christianity to the new challenges was angry rejection of the new ideas and forces. In 1864 Pope Pius IX (1846–1878) issued a *Syllabus of Errors,* errors that Roman Catholics were to avoid. These errors, eighty in all, included separation of church and state, civil marriage, secular education, freedom of speech and press, religious toleration, liberty of conscience, liberalism, and materialism. In 1870 Pius IX called a Vatican council (the first general council since that at Trent in the sixteenth century), which pronounced the doctrine of papal infallibility. According to this doctrine, the pope, when speaking *ex cathedra* (that is, officially *from the chair* of St. Peter) on a matter of faith or morals, is not subject to error. This was the most authoritarian position that the Church and the pope had ever taken, and it came at a time when the intellectual, political, and religious trends seemed to be in the opposite direction. In the late nineteenth and early twentieth centuries, the Catholic hierarchy excommunicated numerous members and several priests who had compromised the official doctrines of the Church.

Many Protestants also rejected the new ideas and forces, particularly fundamentalist sects that interpreted the Bible literally. More established churches, such as the Anglicans in Great Britain and Lutherans in Germany, resisted but had to contend with undisciplined dissent within their

FIGURE 51.3. Pope Leo XIII Leo XIII (1878–1903) was the first pope to face up to issues raised by science and modernization. While clinging to the traditional doctrine of the Church, he accepted new scientific discoveries and supported some liberal reform movements. (UPI/Bettmann Newsphotos)

ranks and secular authorities that supported the new developments.

The second reaction of Christianity to the nineteenth-century challenges and assaults was to surrender to them. Many Christians, Catholics and Protestants alike, lost their faith and left their church. But many more who lost the traditional faith remained in their church and attempted to change its doctrines. They granted the claims of science and the "higher criticism," and they sympathized with the materialism, liberalism, and nationalism of the day. They continued to go to church, to sing the hymns, to say the prayers, and to recite the creeds, but they did not believe what they sang, said, and recited. They would reject the supernatural and deny the divinity of Christ. They would make the Bible a book of good literature and high ethical ideals; Christ, a great social

reformer; and the church, an instrument for the promotion of good will, wholesome fellowship, racial tolerance, temperance, charity, patriotism, and so on. These Christians came to be called *modernists.* The Catholic church declared officially against modernism in 1907, and by 1914 it appeared to have either suppressed the modernists in its ranks or driven them under cover. In the various Protestant churches in Europe modernism competed with fundamentalism, both extreme and moderate, and by 1914 modernism had tended to gain the upper hand. In the United States modernism in the Protestant churches did not reach its peak until the 1920s and 1930s.

The third reaction of Christianity was moderate compromise: an acceptance of proved scientific facts and reasonable deductions therefrom together with attempts to harmonize the findings of science with the fundamentals of the Christian faith. This attitude involved interpreting certain passages in the Bible figuratively, particularly the first chapter of Genesis, and admitting to a few errors in various versions of the Bible. This harmonizing Christian reaction led to an increased awareness of the responsibility of the Christian churches to participate actively in the social and political problems of the day.

The Catholics were the first to reach this middle position. Leo XIII (see Figure 51.3), pope from 1878–1903, promoted the theology of Thomas Aquinas, which stressed the compatibility of faith and reason. He welcomed new scientific beliefs on condition that they be proved. He and his successors gradually took the position that natural science was not the province of the Church; that evolution could be taught in the Church's schools as a hypothesis; that the first chapter of Genesis should be taken figuratively; and that within these premises belief in evolution was a private and individual matter.

Leo XIII also faced up to some of the economic and social challenges of industrialization. In 1891, in the most famous of all his encyclicals, *Rerum Novarum* ("of new things"), he denounced materialism and Marxian socialism and proclaimed the sanctity of private property. He did, however, declare limits to the use of private property. Labor must not be treated as a commodity; workers must be paid a fair living wage and protected against too long hours, injury, and disease. Leo XIII advocated a wider distribution of property, labor unions for collective bargaining, and farming co-operatives. Roman Catholic labor unions were soon organized to challenge the socialist-dominated unions.

Christianity, so beset on its home grounds by challenges, assaults, and internal divisions during the late nineteenth century, was never more zealous in sending out missionaries to propagate the faith abroad. Roman Catholic, Protestant, and Eastern Orthodox missionaries vied with one another in Asia and Africa. By 1914 more than 40 million people outside Western Christendom professed the Christian faith. But since the Christian missionaries in Asia and Africa were often associated with Western imperialism and exploitation, they frequently aroused resentment. In 1914 Christianity in the West was still on the defensive.

SUGGESTED READING

General

O. Chadwick, *The Secularization of the European Mind in the Nineteenth Century* (1975). A useful, well-written study.

C. C. Gillispie, *The Edge of Objectivity* (1960). Good survey of modern science.

The Physical, Biological, and Medical Sciences

M. Ruse, *The Darwinian Revolution* (1979). An excellent introduction.

E. Mayr, *The Growth of Biological Thought* (1982). A good recent survey.

The Rise of Social Science

R. Aron, *Main Currents in Sociological Thought*, 2 vols. (1965, 1967). An excellent survey of the founders of modern sociology.

P. Gay, *Freud: A Life for Our Time* (1988). A well-regarded study.

Challenges to Christianity

J. L. Altholz, *The Churches in the Nineteenth Century* (1967). A solid survey.

H. Daniel-Rops, *A Fight for God* (1966). A good history of the Catholic church during the period.

J. McManners, *Church and State in France, 1870–1914* (1972). Solid and scholarly.

A. Vidler, *The Church in an Age of Revolution* (1961). A solid study of church and state during the period.

CHAPTER 52

Thought and Culture in an Age of Nationalism and Industrialization

FIGURE 52.1. **Picasso, "Les Demoiselles d'Avignon," 1906–1907** Between 1850 and 1914 artistic styles evolved rapidly, moving from realism to the beginnings of modernism. Pablo Picasso (1881–1973) was one of the most influential artists during the latter part of this period and throughout the twentieth century. This painting reflects the sense of revolt, the rapidly changing values, and the tendency to turn inward that characterized many cultural products of the late nineteenth and early twentieth centuries. (Oil on canvas, 8' × 7'8". Collection, The Museum of Modern Art, New York. Acquired through the Lillie P. Bliss Bequest)

The nationalism of the increasingly powerful Western nation-states, the challenges to established religious and moral values, and the tensions of industrial society are reflected in the thought and art of the period between 1850 and 1914. There was no sudden or drastic break with the spirit of idealism and romanticism that prevailed in the thought and art of the Age of Revolutions, 1776–1850. Both idealism and romanticism continued throughout the nineteenth century and beyond. Nevertheless, after mid-century, realism tended to replace the romanticism of the early nineteenth century. As the bourgeoisie played a more dominant role in the culture of the period, artists, writers, and intellectuals became more of an *avant garde*—increasingly critical of bourgeois values and tastes. By the end of the nineteenth century and the beginning of the twentieth, these artists, writers, and intellectuals were injecting a theme of pessimism and painful introspection into Western culture.

The nationalism that was such an important component of political and social developments during the period was reflected in a growing body of thought. Nationalism was also one of the elements behind the spread of state-sponsored educational reforms, which led toward expanded literacy and the growth of popular journalism.

In literature a stream of realism and naturalism, characterized by an almost scientific examination of life, seemed to focus on individual and social failings. Art tended to slip away from the grasp of the ordinary viewer as photography displaced traditional representational art and impressionists applied a new understanding of the physical world and optics to their paintings. Post-impressionists veered into even more disturbing styles as art, like the new scientific disciplines, became more specialized.

1. POPULAR EDUCATION AND JOURNALISM

During this era of nationalism and spreading industrialization, and particularly after 1871, there were great advances in popular education. In 1871 northern Germany and Scandinavia were the only places in the world where practically everyone could read and write. In the United States most of the states had free public elementary schools, but a fifth of the total population was still illiterate. In Great Britain a third of the people were still illiterate, in France and Belgium a half, in Spain and Italy three-fourths, in Russia and the Balkans nine-tenths. Between 1868 and 1881 national systems of free and compulsory public education were established in nearly all the nations of western and central Europe and the United States. For the most part, the systems were as yet limited to elementary schools. Nevertheless, by 1914 illiteracy had practically ceased to exist in Scandinavia, Germany, Great Britain, and the Netherlands. The illiteracy rate was less than 10 percent in the United States, Canada, France, and Belgium. In Italy it had been reduced to 50 percent, in Spain, Russia, and the Balkans to a little more than 50 percent. Literacy, of course, is only the first step toward education.

The rise in literacy was reflected in a growth of popular journalism. In 1850 newspapers were relatively few, small, expensive, and written for a limited educated clientele. The London *Times*, probably the world's most influential newspaper, had a daily circulation of less than fifty thousand. During the second half of the nineteenth century, nationalism and industrialization were accompanied by a new kind of newspaper, one that was cheap, sensational, and popular in its appeal. One of the pioneer popular journalists was Joseph Pulitzer (1847–1911), a Hungarian immigrant to the United States. Pulitzer founded the St. Louis *Post Dispatch*. He bought and built up the New York *World* until it became the country's biggest newspaper. With screaming headlines, flag-waving patriotism, easy catchy style, sensational news, popular causes and features, and, above all, comics, he made a fortune and became influential in politics. In the 1890s William Randolph Hearst built a great newspaper empire patterned after Pulitzer's. In Great Britain Alfred Harmsworth founded the halfpenny popular *Daily Mail*, made a fortune, and then bought the London *Times*. Before the end of the century five newspapers—two in London, two in Paris, and one in Berlin—had a daily circulation of more than a million each. *Le Petit Journal* in Paris had a circulation of more than two and a quarter million. This type of newspaper not only catered to the masses but also became a powerful molder of public opinion. Hearst boasted, with a modicum of truth, that he manufactured the Spanish-American War. Since the popular newspapers made their money chiefly from advertising rather than from sales, they came increasingly to reflect the viewpoints of their chief advertisers, the great corporations. The big newspapers were themselves of course, big business. Although they catered to the masses, they generally did not represent the interests of the masses.

2. CURRENTS OF THOUGHT: NATIONALISM AND DISENCHANTMENT

During the nineteenth century a strong current of thought reflected and supported the growing nationalism of that era. German thinkers in particular contributed to the intellectual foundations of nationalism. In the first half of the century, Georg Wilhelm Hegel (1770–1831) was most influential. Among other things, he argued that individual freedom depends on ordered discipline under a strong state and that the zeitgeist (spirit of the time) of the nineteenth century was the spirit of German civilization.

Even more directly supportive of nationalism were the ideas of people such as Heinrich von Treitschke, probably the most influential German historian of the decades surrounding the turn of the century, who proclaimed that Germany's victory over France demonstrated the superiority of military autocracy over liberalism. Only strong states ought to exist. Dissident minorities, individualism, and parliamentary inefficiency must not be tolerated.

German thinkers were not the only ones to reflect the nationalism of the period in their ideas. The French historian Hippolyte Taine blamed France's defeat in 1870–1871 on the corrupting influence of liberalism born in the French Revolution and bred during the nineteenth century. He would take France back to the days of the Old Regime. In Great Britain, Thomas Carlyle in thunderous prose exalted heroes and hero worship, specifically the Prussian variety. Rudyard Kipling put his poetic gifts to use to sing of the glorious British Empire and the "white man's burden" of ruling and civilizing "backward" peoples.

The most extreme set of ideas underlying nationalism during the second half of the nineteenth century was racism. People of every nation began to think and talk of themselves as a distinct and superior breed. Language was more than ever confused with race. Thus one spoke of the various "races" in the Austro-Hungarian Empire. By far the most popular and serious of all the racial cults was the Aryan myth. The term *Aryan*, which was originally a linguistic term referring to the ancient Persians (Iranians) and later to all peoples speaking Indo-European languages, was now applied to the Germanic- or Teutonic-speaking peoples or to the Nordic (tall blond) type of northern European. After Germany's spectacular military triumphs and economic developments under Bismarck, the term *Aryan* came to be applied more specifically to Germans and to the energetic, aggressive, military qualities they were supposed to possess. Oddly, the two chief formulators of the Aryan myth were a Frenchman, Comte de Gobineau, and the renegade Englishman Houston Stewart Chamberlain, who left his homeland and became a German citizen. Their ideas, however, were taken much more seriously in Germany than in France or Great Britain. They argued that race was the key determinant of history. Chamberlain's racist ideas veered off into anti-Semitism, as did the ideas of other racist writers such as Richard Wagner. Wagner wrote violent propaganda tracts and composed grandiose operas stridently extolling the virtues of the early Nordic (German) supermen—Siegfried and the Nibelungs.

Although many philosophers of Social Darwinism and liberalism remained optimistic about the evolution of human beings and human society ever onward and upward, a new, strong strain of disenchantment surfaced in late-nineteenth-century philosophy. A forerunner of these pessimistic philosophers who were to have so much influence on the twentieth century was Arthur Schopenhauer (1788–1860). In *The World as Will and Idea*, published in 1819, forty years before *On the Origin of Species*, this German thinker set forth the idea that one force governs and motivates the whole world of animate life, and that force is will—the will to survive. The world, therefore, is a cruel and heartless place full of struggling and competing creatures, a place where the strong and fierce devour the weak and gentle. The only possible happiness to be found in it is by ascetic denial and withdrawal. They suffer least who participate least in the hard, competitive world.

This line of thinking (at least a variation of it) was carried to its ultimate by an admirer of Schopenhauer, Friedrich Nietzsche (1844–1900). Nietzsche was a disillusioned German theological student turned philosopher. He was a pain- and nerve-racked genius. Two of his most influential works are *Thus Spake Zarathustra* and *Beyond Good and Evil*. Like Schopenhauer, he believed that the greatest force in the animate world is will. However, this will is not only to survive but also, in the strong at least, to achieve power. "The will to power" was Nietzsche's key phrase. If a superior society is to emerge, it will have to come about through the efforts of strong and gifted individuals who will rise to power because of their superior strength, will, and intelligence. Anything that contributes to power is good, be it strength of will, boldness, cunning, or intelligence. Whatever leads to weakness is bad, be it gentleness, modesty, generosity, or compassion. The two greatest enemies of the good society are democracy and Christianity. Democracy is the rule of mediocre masses, cattle. But it was against Christianity that Nietzsche hurled his sharpest invective; he believed Christianity to be the greatest curse of Western civilization: a religion that extols the vices of slavery, such as meekness, compassion, sacrifice, and charity, to compensate for actual weakness. He went on to attack many other accepted foundations of nineteenth-century civilization, including liberalism, rationalism, and science. Although not a nationalist or racist himself, his ideas would later be used by others to support militant nationalism and even racism.

Less caustic and far more popular was the French philosopher Henri Bergson (1859–1941). Like Nietzsche he attacked bourgeois liberalism and extolled the instincts and the subjective will. His sense of the world as an evolving, vital, spontaneous place fit well with other trends in thought

and the arts during the early decades of the twentieth century.

Also popular was the philosophy of pragmatism. The chief expounder of this school of thought, which has been so potent and widespread in the twentieth century, was William James (1842–1910), a professor of psychology and philosophy at Harvard University. Pragmatism reflected the uncertainties aroused by atomic physicists around the turn of the century. James rejected all absolutes of logic and religion. Truth is relative, depending on the individual and the circumstances. A thing is true if it works and is useful. We cannot know ultimate religious or moral truths, for instance, but if a particular religious faith gives an individual confidence and peace of mind, then it is practical and therefore true for that person. Thus spiritual, moral, and human values become as relative in the minds of William James and the pragmatists as the physical world in the mind of Albert Einstein.

3. REALISTIC LITERATURE

Much of the literature of the second half of the nineteenth century, like the philosophy, reflected the materialism, the cynicism, and the pessimism of the age. However, there was a strong carryover of romanticism beyond 1850 and into the twentieth century. The romantic Victorian poets Victor Hugo, Robert Browning, and Alfred Tennyson lived on until 1885, 1889, and 1892, respectively. Although Browning was a rugged and analytical realist when probing the depths of human psychology and emotions, he tended at times to be an idealist and an optimist, believing that "God's in his heaven, all's right with the world." And although in 1850 the young Tennyson in his *In Memoriam* revealed a religious skepticism bold for the time, in 1889 he hoped to see his "Pilot face to face" when he had "crossed the bar." Nevertheless, the prevailing and most significant trend in literature was realism. It was expressed most generally in the novel and drama rather than poetry. Realism tended to depict the seamy, sordid side of human nature and society. It villainized the *nouveau riche* industrial bourgeoisie and its religious and moral hypocrisy without idealizing the uprooted and distressed working class.

France took the lead in realistic literature. Balzac, who died in 1850, had foreshadowed realism. In his scores of novels and tales he subjected the dominant middle class to increasingly exact and severe scrutiny. The first French novelist to catch the full flavor of realism was Gustave Flaubert (1821–1880). His *Madame Bovary* related the illicit sex life of the wife of a small-town French physician in such full and unblushing detail that it scandalized a public not yet accustomed to such unrestrained "realism." *Madame Bovary* became a model to other novelists.

Émile Zola (1840–1902), though interested like Flaubert in individual personality, was more concerned with social problems, particularly those created by industrialization. Zola was a bold and radical republican who played a major role in finally securing justice for Dreyfus. In twenty penetrating but sometimes tedious novels he depicted and analyzed the problems of a changing society. His sympathy was with the industrial working class, but he suffered no illusions as to the natural goodness of people, including the distressed lower classes.

Charles Dickens (1812–1870) in Great Britain combined romanticism and realism. In his sentimentality, his moralizing, his optimism, and his spontaneous gush of words, he was a romantic. In his zeal for social reform, his pillorying of bourgeois arrogance and corrupt bourgeois institutions, and his graphic and often sordid detailing of the life of the urban working class, he was the first of the British realists. In *David Copperfield*, *Oliver Twist*, and *The Pickwick Papers*, three of the best-known of his numerous and lengthy novels, a galaxy of characters of the middle and lower walks of life in industrial Britain parade realistically before us.

Mary Ann Evans (1819–1880), writing under the pen name George Eliot, wrote popular novels depicting the realities of British social life. In *Middlemarch: A Study of Provincial Life*, she sensitively related psychological conflicts to the determining social realities that surround her characters.

Thomas Hardy (1840–1928), unlike Dickens, had a pessimistic view of the universe. His vivid characters—ordinary English countryside folk—struggle Darwin-like against fate, environment, and their own frail natures without any help from God or Hardy. *The Return of the Native*, *The Mayor of Casterbridge*, and *Tess of the D'Urbervilles* are some of the best examples in any language of the realistic novel.

Probably the most typical of all the British realists was George Bernard Shaw (1856–1950). Of Irish birth, Shaw early crossed over to London, where he long remained the gadfly of bourgeois society. In scores of urbane and sophisticated novels, essays, and plays, he charmingly but caustically taunted Christianity, capitalism, and democracy. Shaw was a cynic, a Socialist, and a stark materialist. He was the epitome of late-nineteenth-century and early-twentieth-century realism.

In the United States, the era of the realistic novel began with the works of Theodore Dreiser (1871–1945). Dreiser's novels depicted in hard, rough detail the life and the philosophy of the disenchanted and uprooted proletariat living in a materialistic, industrial world of changing values. His first novel, *Sister Carrie*, which appeared in 1900, was an American industrial version of *Madame Bovary* told with raw unrestraint. To escape poverty, Carrie became the mistress of a succession of men. The progressive degeneration of the characters constitutes the theme of the novel. Editors were so shocked at the frank and open presentation of lurid details that Dreiser had great difficulty getting the book published. The success of *Sister Carrie* was immediate, and other novels in a like vein followed.

One of the most influential of the realists was the Norwegian playwright Henrik Ibsen (1828–1906). A frustrated artist embittered by youthful poverty, Ibsen ridiculed bourgeois society in his popular dramas. In what is probably his best-known play, *A Doll's House*, one of his heroines rebels against the "doll's house" that her stodgy, hypocritical, middle-class husband created for her. In *An Enemy of the People*, Ibsen reveals the fickleness of the masses and their unfitness for democratic government. *Ghosts* deals with the social and personal problems of syphilis.

In Russia, Ivan Sergeyevich Turgenev (1818–1883) and Fyodor Dostoyevski (1821–1881) combined realism with romanticism in much the same manner as did Dickens in Great Britain. In his masterpiece, *Fathers and Sons*, Turgenev grapples

FIGURE 52.2. Claude Monet, "La Grenouillère," 1869 Monet was a leading French impressionist. His bold use of color, his emphasis on the play of light, and his focus on the appearance of things were typical of impressionistic painters. (The Metropolitan Museum of Art, Bequest of Mrs. H. O. Havemeyer, 1929. The Havemeyer Collection)

powerfully with the problems of the older conservative Russian generation versus the modern, sophisticated, and radical younger generation. Dostoyevski's two greatest novels are *Crime and Punishment* and *The Brothers Karamazov.* In them he delves psychologically and mystically into the problems of evil and purification through suffering. He was deeply religious, but not in any formal or orthodox sense. Leo Tolstoy (1828–1910) was more completely dedicated to realism and devoted his life and writing almost exclusively to social reform. His masterpiece is *War and Peace.* In this gigantic novel, scores of personalities along with more impersonal social forces so interlace with and influence each other that not even the strongest individual—not even Napoleon—can work his will alone. In his later years Tolstoy sought to combine Christianity with socialism, giving up his great inherited wealth to set a good example. Anton Chekhov (1860–1904) wrote polished but realistic and pessimistic plays about Russian life. Maxim Gorky (1868–1936), up from the proletarian ranks, analyzed the social problems of the Russian masses in his dramas and novels.

Realistic literature, with all its varieties, had many things in common. It reflected almost invariably the social dislocation brought about by the Industrial Revolution, particularly in its more advanced second phase. It reflected the materialism of an age of science and technology. It displayed over and over again the influence of Darwin and, later, of Freud. It was increasingly concerned with the disillusionment and cynicism brought about by changing religious and moral values.

4. IMPRESSIONIST AND MODERN PAINTING AND SCULPTURE

France, the birthplace of realistic literature, was also the chief seat of the impressionistic and modern painting and sculpture that predominated during the second half of the nineteenth century. Impressionism was a mild and sophisticated revolt against the artistic standards that had prevailed since the late fifteenth century. It reflected the intellectual challenge to traditional values and institutions that arose after mid-century. It took its chief inspiration from the seventeenth-century

FIGURE 52.3. Rodin, "Heroic Head" Auguste Rodin, "Heroic Head" (Pierre De Weissart), 1889, bronze. Rodin's powerful figures represent both a new departure in sculpture and a bridge from the nineteenth century to the twentieth. He brought the impressionistic spirit to his work, and he was a forerunner of much of the abstract and symbolist sculpture of the twentieth century. (Norweb Collection, The Cleveland Museum of Art)

Spanish painters Velázquez and El Greco, from Japanese art, which was rediscovered after 1853, and from new scientific knowledge concerning the nature of color and light. Impressionistic painting was informal, unposed, and random-angled. It sought to convey by studied casualness the impression of a view one gets at a glance. The chief founder of the impressionistic style of painting was the Frenchman Édouard Manet (1832–1883). Among his more illustrious disciples were

Claude Monet (1840–1926), Auguste Renoir (1841–1919), and Camille Pissarro (1830–1903) (see Color Plate 23 and Figure 52.2). These artists painted sunlit parks and landscapes, shimmering lakes and rivers, and subtle, sophisticated portraits. They omitted much detail, painting in only suggestive shapes, forms, and colors as first impressions, and leaving the rest to the imagination. Their work was sensuous, decorative, and mildly iconoclastic.

The breach that the impressionists made with long-established traditions was greatly widened near the end of the nineteenth century and early in the twentieth by more radical modern painters. The new trend was led by Paul Cézanne (1839–1906), a lifelong friend of Émile Zola (see Color Plate 24). Cézanne distorted freely in order to achieve a more powerful effect and applied thick paint to attain the appearance of solidity and roundness. Going far beyond Cézanne, the gifted but eccentric Frenchman Paul Gauguin (1848–1903) and Dutchman Vincent van Gogh (1853–1890) broke openly with artistic standards of the past. Gauguin was interested in painting not the literal document of his subject but only what the subject meant to him. He painted patterns formed in his mind by objects rather than the objects themselves, using violent reds, yellows, and greens. He finally became primitive, deserting Western civilization for the South Sea Islands. Gauguin's friend, van Gogh, would squeeze out paint directly from the tube on to the canvas to achieve striking effects (see Color Plate 25). Like Gauguin, van Gogh was an expressionist, freely distorting the images of nature to make them express his own feelings. Cézanne, Gauguin, and van Gogh were the forerunners of many iconoclastic schools, such as cubism and futurism, that marked twentieth-century painting.

Two of the most influential of the revolutionary modern painters were the Frenchman Henri Matisse (1869–1954) and the Spanish-born (French by adoption) Pablo Picasso (1881–1973), both of whom received their chief inspiration from Cézanne. In some of their work they carried distortion to great extremes. Matisse became enamored with primitive culture. Picasso's figures during one phase of his long career became geometric (hence cubism) and disjointed (see Figure 52.1).

He occasionally gave up color entirely for black and white.

It is characteristic of an age of intellectual revolt and changing values that the artists turn inward (see Color Plates 26 and 27). During the late nineteenth and early twentieth centuries, painting became highly individualistic. The artists tended to paint such objects as fruit, still life, and mandolins. Furthermore, they turned to figures on the periphery of a disintegrating society, such as prostitutes, solitary drinkers, blind beggars, and circus performers. The figures were separate from one another. This disjointedness and the symbols of science, machinery, and speed, which were so prominent in this painting, represented an age of intellectual revolt against traditional values, of materialistic science and technology, and of social tension. Unfortunately, much of this painting was so technical and highly specialized that it could be appreciated only by relatively few at a time when the many were seeking enlightenment.

The rapid growth of cities and of wealth during the second Industrial Revolution was responsible for the production of a large quantity of sculpture to decorate the new public buildings, squares, and parks. Most of it was patterned after the styles of the past, either classical or baroque, more often the latter. Probably the two sculptors of the period who most truly reflected the spirit of their own time and of future trends were Constantin Meunier (1831–1905) in Belgium and Auguste Rodin (1840–1917) in France. Meunier was the first great sculptor to recognize the importance of the industrial proletariat. Among his rugged and realistic statues are "The Hammersmith," "The Puddler," "The Mine Girl," and "The Old Mine Horse." Rodin introduced impressionism into sculpture (see Figure 52.3). His most famous statue, "The Thinker," illustrates not only impressionistic art but also the influence of the classical, Renaissance, baroque, and romantic styles. Rodin was the forerunner of much of the modern, abstract, and symbolist sculpture of the twentieth century.

5. FUNCTIONAL ARCHITECTURE

The architecture of the period 1850–1914, like the sculpture, combined the old with the new. The

Figure 52.4. Sullivan's Carson-Pirie-Scott Department Store The Carson-Pirie-Scott Department Store in Chicago was designed by the American architect Louis Henry Sullivan (1856–1924), who was the first to determine that function is the sole purpose of the style of a building. Sullivan designed the world's first steel-supported skyscraper. (Hedrich Blessing)

prevailing style in the numerous and increasingly large public buildings continued to be classical or baroque. Gothic architecture, which enjoyed a revival in the early part of the nineteenth century, was now limited primarily to university buildings and to churches. Even Byzantine, Moorish, and Oriental models appeared here and there throughout the West as the world was brought closer together by rapid communications.

The first great architect to develop a style appropriate to an age of steel, science, and speed was the American Louis Henry Sullivan (1856–

1924). Sullivan argued that "Form follows function." That is to say, the style of buildings should be determined by their intended use and by the materials used in their construction (see Figure 52.4). The architectural devices of the past had lost their utility, were purely decorative. And in fast-moving, crowded, and growing New York and Chicago, what sense did horizontal Greek or Moorish lines make? Sullivan designed the steel-supported skyscraper.

But Sullivan and his followers were not satisfied with the principle "Form follows function." They decided that function is the prime purpose of architecture. The application of this principle came to be known as "functional architecture." Structural steel, reinforced concrete, and glass brick made it possible for the functional architects to achieve unbroken horizontal lines impossible for the Greeks and towering heights combined with gracefulness and light that the medieval Gothic builders could not have contemplated. Furthermore, the spirit of intellectual revolt against the standards and values of the past gave the architects a freedom to experiment never before enjoyed. Finally, unprecedented wealth and technological advances provided them with the means to execute their ideas. Some of the massive utilitarian structures of this and later periods are creditable monuments to an age of materialism.

6. MUSIC OLD AND NEW

Of all the arts, music showed the least responsiveness to the economic and social trends between 1850 and 1914. Some of the greatest romantic composers lived well on into the second half of the nineteenth century. Wagner lived until 1883, Verdi until 1901. Their ranks were joined in the late nineteenth century by such great romanticists

as Camille Saint-Saëns (1835–1921) in France and Peter Tchaikovsky (1840–1893) in Russia. Nor was there any lessening in the spirit of nationalism in music, which was such an important ingredient of romanticism. Wagner's nationalism became more militant after 1870. Tchaikovsky combined Russian nationalism with his romanticism. More strictly nationalist in their themes and folk tunes were the Russian Nikolai Rimsky-Korsakov (1844–1908); the Czech Antonín Dvořák (1841–1904); the Norwegian Edvard Grieg (1843–1907); and the Finn Jean Sibelius (1865–1957).

Not only romanticism but also classicism was carried over into the late nineteenth century by the great German composer Johannes Brahms (1833–1897). Spending the last thirty-five years of his life in the Hapsburg capital of Vienna, Brahms became an ardent Hungarian nationalist without giving up loyalty to his native Germany. Probably more than any other musician, Brahms resembles Beethoven in style. Like Beethoven, he combined the classical spirit with the romantic.

The most important innovator in music of the period was the French composer Claude Debussy (1862–1918). Debussy was the father of impressionistic music. Experimenting with subtle and sophisticated dissonances, he was to music what Manet and Renoir were to painting. Meanwhile, in Germany Richard Strauss (1864–1949) was startling and scandalizing his pre–World War I audiences with his complex and sometimes harshly dissonant "realistic" tone poems. He is often said to have ushered in the "modern" period in music. In Russia, Igor Stravinsky (1882–1971) was beginning his long career of composing music that was still more iconoclastic and abstract. He is called the father of the expressionist school. Stravinsky, with his more violent and impetuous dissonances, bears somewhat the same relationship to Debussy as does Picasso to Monet in painting.

SUGGESTED READING

General

F. L. Baumer, *Modern European Thought* (1977). Good general introduction.

H. S. Hughes, *Consciousness and Society* (1956). A superb study of intellectual history during the period.

S. Kern, *The Culture of Time and Space, 1880–1918* (1983). An important, interpretive work.

G. Masur, *Prophets of Yesterday* (1961). A good examination of key intellectual figures.

C. E. Schorske, *Fin-de-Siècle Vienna: Politics and Culture* (1980). An excellent study of one of Europe's cultural centers.

R. Shattuck, *The Banquet Years* (1968). A well-written account of the social and cultural life of late-nineteenth-century Paris.

Popular Education and Journalism

C. M. Cipolla, *Literacy and Development in the West* (1969). Covers the rise in literacy during the period.

R. Williams, *The Long Revolution* (1961). A good study of literacy and popular literature in England.

Currents of Thought

W. Kaufmann, *Nietzsche: Philosopher, Psychologist, Antichrist* (1974). Highly respected analysis of Nietzsche and his thought.

K. Löwith, *From Hegel to Nietzsche: The Revolution in Nineteenth-Century Thought* (1964). A good analysis.

G. L. Mosse, *Toward the Final Solution: A History of European Racism* (1978). A useful introduction.

L. Poliakov, *The Aryan Myth: A History of Racist and Nationalist Ideas in Europe* (1971). An excellent introduction.

Realistic Literature

R. Pascal, *From Naturalism to Expressionism: German Literature and Society, 1880–1918* (1973). A good survey.

Art, Architecture, and Music

P. Collaer, *A History of Modern Music* (1961). Well-written survey.

G. H. Hamilton, *Painting and Sculpture in Europe, 1880–1940* (1967). A useful survey.

A. Hauser, *Social History of Art*, Vols. III and IV (1958). Connects art to social developments of the period.

H. R. Hitchcock, *Architecture: 19th and 20th Centuries* (1958). A good survey.

J. Rewald, *The History of Impressionism* (1961). A useful introduction.

RETROSPECT

Between 1850 and 1914 developments in Western civilization were dominated by the spread of nationalism and industrialization. Both had their roots in the preceding Age of Revolutions, but until the middle of the nineteenth century they were relatively limited in scope and intensity. During the second half of the century nationalism spread to new areas, achieved new successes, and took on a more pragmatic and aggressive quality. At the same time, industrialization matured in Western societies and spread eastward to Russia and westward to the United States.

Between 1850 and 1871 nationalism was used to strengthen the political institutions of the nation-state. The Second Empire of Napoleon III provides an outstanding example of nationalistic state building during this period. Domestically, Napo-

leon III involved the government in a series of new economic and social programs; in foreign affairs he intervened in areas stretching from Russia to Mexico. However, the fruits of nationalism were even more significant in Italy and Germany. First Italy, under the guidance of Piedmont and its prime minister Cavour, unified most of the diverse states of the Italian peninsula into a single nation in 1860. Then Prussia, under the leadership of Bismarck, used war and diplomacy to unify Germany into a powerful new nation in 1871.

Between 1871 and 1914 Europe was characterized politically by the spread of democratic institutions and the growth of a more militant nationalism. While the spread of democracy occurred in some form throughout Europe, it was more complete and more closely associated with liberalism in western Europe. In eastern Europe the spread of democracy was much less complete and, in some cases, more a matter of form than substance. There, governments such as those under Kaiser Wilhelm II in Germany, the tsars in Russia, and the emperor in Austria-Hungary tended to be conservative and authoritarian.

Meanwhile, in the United States many of the main developments occurring during the nineteenth century roughly paralleled European developments. Democratic institutions, along with a growing sense of nationalism, were spreading as the country expanded. At the same time that the Industrial Revolution was spreading from Great Britain to other areas of Europe, the United States was industrializing its economy—particularly after the Civil War in 1865. And like other Western governments, the American government attempted to adjust to the pressures of a mature industrial society by instituting political reforms toward the end of the nineteenth and the beginning of the twentieth centuries.

After 1880 nationalism and industrialization combined to thrust the leading nation-states of the West into a new imperial race. Within two decades the Western powers carved vast areas of Africa, Asia, and the Pacific into colonies and territories of imperial interest. As a result of this imperial expansion, non-Western societies were undermined and irreversibly changed, and Western powers became locked into added rivalries that would bear fruits of war in 1914.

Meanwhile the second Industrial Revolution was taking place in the West. Steel, chemicals, and electricity were replacing iron, textiles, and steam as the basis of new industrial development. Countries such as Germany and the United States successfully challenged the long leadership of Great Britain in industrial production. Industrial societies became much more urbanized and were dominated by the middle class, but the working classes were now rising to the fore with their own organizations and ideologies. Most significant was the rise of Marxian socialism, a powerful ideology that won many adherents and that was thrust into public life by socialist unions and socialist political parties.

Thought and culture between 1850 and 1914 reflected the influence of nationalism and industrialism. Both stressed secular beliefs and a certain pragmatic scientific approach. Both contributed to the growing problems facing Christianity during the period. The spread and the prestige of the natural and social sciences was particularly strong and was reflected in some of the literary and artistic trends of the period. Toward the end of the nineteenth century and the beginning of the twentieth century, however, a new strain of disillusionment, uncertainty, and even pessimism was appearing in philosophy, literature, art, and even science. This disturbing cultural trend foreshadowed the devastating turmoil of the decades following the outbreak of World War I in 1914.

PART ELEVEN

THE ERA OF THE TWO WORLD WARS, 1914–1945

Despite some growing social tensions, some expressions of uncertainty and doubt in intellectual circles, and some concern over deepening international rivalries and entanglements, in 1914 there was cause for the general sense of optimism that prevailed in Western civilization. Looking back over the previous century, one could see a long period of relative peace, political reform, economic growth, social adjustment, and cultural accomplishment. Western civilization seemed to have advanced greatly during the nineteenth century, and the twentieth century looked promising. Even the outbreak of war in August 1914 did not shatter this optimistic vision, for most anticipated a cleansing, short, painless, and victorious outcome. By the war's conclusion in 1918 reality had overwhelmed the early optimism. World War I initiated a new era of destruction, upheaval, and revolutionary change in the West.

But developments in the 1920s and 1930s were frightening to the liberal democratic powers who had won World War I at such a great cost. Revolutions in Russia had not only brought down the tsarist government but also had brought to power the Bolsheviks. The Bolsheviks, first under Lenin and then Stalin, transformed Russia into the Communist Soviet Union, which by the 1930s was a totalitarian nation pursuing policies in fundamental opposition to the principles of the liberal capitalistic West. Fascism arose in Europe, first in Italy under Mussolini and later in Nazi Germany under Hitler. Fascism directly and violently identified liberalism and democracy as enemies. Meanwhile, hopes for the spread of liberal democracy in southern Europe, eastern Europe, and Japan were dashed as these areas turned to authoritarian forms of government.

The democratic West reacted to these threats with disunity, confusion, and immobility. Nations such as Great Britain, France, and the United States had their own problems, heightened by the Great Depression of the 1930s. In the end Germany in Europe and Japan in the East were not to be restrained from their expansive goals. World War II broke out in 1939 and proved to be far more destructive than War I. At the war's conclusion in 1945, the aggressor states had been clearly defeated. Whether, and how, Western civilization would recover from this era of destruction remained to be seen.

CHAPTER 53
World War I, 1914–1918

FIGURE 53.1. Trench Warfare This photo of French troops on the western front in World War I illustrates the type of war it was: fought in deep trenches covered with barbed wire by foot soldiers wearing masks against poison gas. Despite the assumptions to the contrary by offense-minded generals, the advantage was with the defense. (Roger-Viollet)

The first blow that rocked the twentieth-century world was World War I. To most people, busy with their daily tasks, it seemed to be a sudden and unforeseen disaster. To statesmen and informed students of world affairs, it was the snapping of long-developing tensions.

1. ORIGINS OF THE WAR

World War I began as a showdown between two hostile alliances of European powers: the Triple Alliance, composed of Germany, Austria-Hungary, and Italy; and the Triple Entente, composed of Great Britain, France, and Russia. This system of alliances was begun by Bismarck shortly after the defeat of France and the creation of the German Empire in 1870–1871. In 1873, as a safeguard against a revengeful France, or indeed against any hostile combination against Germany, Bismarck formed the Three Emperors' League, composed of Germany, Austria-Hungary, and Russia. When the interests and ambitions of Austria-Hungary and Russia proved to be incompatible, Bismarck replaced Russia with Italy (1882) to form the Triple Alliance. However, as long as he remained at the head of the German government, he carefully nurtured cordial relations with Russia and also with Great Britain. This policy left France isolated.

Bismarck's diplomatic work was quickly undone by Kaiser Wilhelm II, who ascended the German imperial throne in 1888 and forced Bismarck's resignation two years later. Wilhelm II immediately dropped the friendship pact with Russia and began to antagonize Great Britain by his grandiose schemes in the Near and Far East and by his huge naval building program. France was now able to form an alliance with Russia (1894) and an entente (understanding) with Great Britain (1904). In 1907 the Triple Entente was formed after Great Britain and Russia had settled their long-standing differences in Asia. Growing fear of Germany helped reconcile the sharply divergent interests that had long existed among these three powers.

Suspicion and fear between the two power combinations mounted steadily. A ruinous armaments race ensued; the powers of the Triple Entente strove desperately to overcome Germany's long lead in land forces, while Germany sought to erase Great Britain's naval advantage. Rivalries and conflicts among the various members of the two alliances cropped up all over the world, threatening to embroil all the other members. In 1905–1906 and again in 1911 two such clashes occurred in Morocco between France and Germany. In both these crises, as we have seen (see pp. 625–626), Germany was forced to back down by the threat of the superior British navy. Two occurred in the Balkan peninsula between Russia and Austria-Hungary. In 1908 Austria-Hungary suddenly annexed two provinces, Bosnia and Herzegovina, which were inhabited by Serbs and Croats. Serbia had planned to annex these territories, peopled by its own linguistic king. Serbia appealed to its big Slavic brother, Russia. Russia threatened Austria-Hungary, whereupon Germany rattled its mighty sword and forced Russia to back down.

A second Balkan crisis occurred in 1912–1913. The various Balkan states defeated Turkey and then fought among themselves over the spoils. Victorious Serbia threatened to expand. Austria-Hungary not only thwarted Serbia's expansion to the Adriatic Sea but also threatened to annihilate Serbia. Again Serbia appealed to Russia and again Germany forced Russia to back down. Each of these crises brought the world close to war, increased international tension, and speeded up preparations for a final showdown.

It was in the Balkans that the fatal explosion finally occurred. Here the interests of Russia and Austria-Hungary clashed head-on. The Serbs, Bulgarians, Rumanians, and Greeks were religious (Orthodox) and cultural (Byzantine) kin of the Russians. The Serbs and Bulgarians were also linguistic (Slavic) kin of the Russians. Moreover, the Balkan peninsula was of great economic and strategic importance to Russia.

Austria-Hungary's interests in the Balkans were, perhaps, even more vital than those of Russia. The Dual Monarchy's chief interest in the area grew out of the polyglot nature of its empire. It was composed of numerous language groups, some of which, particularly the Serbs, Croats, Slovenes, and Rumanians, had linguistic kin in the Balkans. As the Ottoman Empire in the Balkan peninsula disintegrated in the nineteenth and early twentieth centuries, the various Balkan language groups emerged as independent nations.

Map 53.1 WORLD WAR I This map indicates the surrounded position of the Central Powers and the areas of greatest fighting (and greatest destruction) during World War I.

These free peoples constituted a strong attraction for the members of their language groups in Austria-Hungary, who wished to break loose and join them. This was particularly true of Serbia, which attracted the Hapsburg's Yugoslav subjects (the Serbs, Croats, and Slovenes). But if the Yugoslavs should join Serbia, Austria-Hungary's other language minorities—Italians, Czechs, Slovaks,

Poles, Rumanians, and Ruthenians—would also demand their freedom from Austrian and Hungarian rule and the Dual Monarchy would fall apart. Austria-Hungary therefore felt it must control the Balkan peninsula in self-defense. It was also the only direction in which it could expand, particularly after its exclusion from Germany in 1866.

Overlying the clashing interests of Russia and Austria-Hungary in the Balkans were those of Germany and Great Britain. Germany felt it must maintain the integrity of the Dual Monarchy, which was its only effective and reliable ally. Then, too, Germany's own ambitions in the Balkans and the Near and Middle East were great. One of Kaiser Wilhelm II's chief imperial projects was the Berlin-to-Bagdad railroad (see p. 622), which would make German power dominant in the Ottoman Empire if not the whole Near and Middle East. This scheme gravely menaced Great Britain's own imperial lifeline running through the Suez as well as its immediate interests in the Near and Middle East. Germany's project threatened to blight permanently Russia's hopes of gaining an outlet through the Turkish Straits and to cut Russia off strategically from its allies. France and Italy had their own interests in the Balkans and in the Near and Middle East, although their primary concern was their commitments to their respective allies.

When, therefore, a third crisis occurred in the Balkans in the summer of 1914, all the great powers of Europe were automatically involved. The two Moroccan crises, the two Balkan crises, and the feverish armaments race had brought the tension in Europe to the breaking point. All that was needed was an incident.

2. THE FATAL EXPLOSION

The incident was the shooting at Sarajevo (in Bosnia) of the Austrian Archduke Francis Ferdinand by a Serb on June 28, 1914. The assassination was a deliberate plot involving numerous Serbian army officers. Francis Ferdinand, heir to the Austro-Hungarian throne, was singled out because the Serbs feared that his liberal policy toward the Yugoslavs in Austria-Hungary would allay their dis-

content, thereby lessening their desire to break away and join Serbia. After the assassination, the government of Austria-Hungary decided to crush Serbia and establish its own dominance in the Balkans once and for all. This tactic would require the backing of Germany, for clearly Russia would not stand aside and allow its Serbian kin and allies to be so treated or its own national interests to be thus violated. At a fateful conference in Berlin eight days after the shooting, the German government gave Austria-Hungary a "blank check." The Germans urged Austria-Hungary to act quickly while world opinion was still outraged by the assassination and promised support in any emergency.

Armed with Germany's blank check, Austria-Hungary presented Serbia with an impossible ultimatum. When Serbia failed to yield to all of its terms, Austria-Hungary declared war and invaded Serbia. Russia mobilized its forces against Austria-Hungary and Germany. Germany sent harsh ultimatums to Russia and to France. When Russia failed to reply and France gave an unsatisfactory reply, Germany declared war on Russia on August 1 and on France two days later. The next day, August 4, when German troops violated Belgian neutrality on their way to attack France, Great Britain declared war on Germany. Thus, by August 4, 1914, all the great powers of Europe except Italy were at war (see Map 53.1). Italy claimed that it was not obligated to aid its allies, Germany and Austria-Hungary, since they were the aggressors. The following year, after receiving promises from France and Great Britain that it would reap the spoils of victory, Italy entered the war on the side of the Entente powers. To the side of Germany and Austria-Hungary came Turkey and Bulgaria; these were referred to as the Central Powers. To the side of the Entente powers, who came to be called the Allies, eventually came much of the rest of the world—some thirty-two nations in all. This was truly a world war.

3. GERMANY'S NEAR TRIUMPH

In a long drawn-out war, the advantage would appear to lie with the Allies in view of their superior manpower and resources and their control of the seas. However, Germany had no intention of fighting a long war, and few world observers saw much possibility of the Allies preventing the superior German army from winning a quick and crushing victory on the mainland of Europe. The German high command had long anticipated the military situation that confronted it in August 1914 and had developed a plan of operation known as the Schlieffen plan. This plan called for a holding action against the slow-moving Russians while the main German forces thrust through neutral Belgium to quickly knock out France, which possessed the only army in the world that gave the Germans any real concern. Then the Germans would concentrate on and destroy Russia with relative ease. Great Britain, her allies gone, would sue for peace.

The Schlieffen plan nearly succeeded. Stubborn Belgian resistance held up the Germans long enough for the French to redeploy their forces to the north and for the British to throw their small army across the Channel. Nevertheless, the seemingly irresistible German juggernaut crunched ahead; four weeks after the beginning of hostilities, it was outside Paris ahead of schedule. At this juncture, the desperate French and British armies turned on the Germans and in the bloody seven-day Battle of the Marne not only defeated them but drove them back a few miles. Both sides extended their lines from the Swiss border to the North Sea and entrenched. The First Battle of the Marne was one of the decisive battles in history, for it forced on the Germans a long war of attrition that made possible their ultimate defeat.

An important factor in the German defeat at the Marne was the detachment at the critical moment of one hundred thousand of their best troops for use against the Russians, who had invaded Germany with unexpected speed. Generals von Hindenburg and Ludendorff, with several divisions, were hastily transferred from the western to the eastern front. Under their command the reinforced German armies trapped the Russians at Tannenberg and administered a crushing defeat that sent them reeling back into Russia. Meanwhile, the British navy swept the Germans from the surface of the seas and set up a blockade of Germany. However, the Germans quickly discovered Britain's Achilles' heel with a new weapon:

the submarine.

In 1915 the Germans staged a holding operation in the west while they delivered a series of hammer blows on the Russians, driving deep into Russia and inflicting immense casualties. A major Anglo-French effort to come to the aid of the hard-pressed Russians by breaking through Turkish defenses at the Dardanelles was beaten back with heavy losses. In 1916 Germany returned to the assault in the west. In the nine-month Battle of Verdun, the French held the Germans back, but at an enormous cost in men and supplies. The four-month Battle of the Somme between the British and the Germans was even bloodier. Like Verdun, it ended in a stalemate. In the Battle of Jutland, the biggest naval battle in history up to that time, the British fleet thwarted the effort of the German fleet to break the blockade but suffered serious losses.

4. THE HOME FRONT

Most people expected the war to last a matter of weeks. But as the months dragged on and the toll of lives and material spent on the war rose, it became apparent that whole societies would have to be mobilized to support the war effort. World War I would be a total war that blurred distinctions between combatants and civilians, between the battle lines and the home front.

The most pressing need was to organize the economy to produce the materials consumed by modern warfare—most obviously the high quantities of bullets, shells, guns, and armaments of all types (see Figure 53.2). But a vast array of other materials were also necessary—everything from food and uniforms to trucks and railway cars. Over the long haul, war needs demanded both an advanced industrial capability and efficient organization of that industrial capability to produce what was needed and get it where it could be used. To varying degrees, the governments of the major powers, particularly Germany, Great Britain, and France, took control of their economies. Production, consumption, wages, and prices were determined by governmental agencies rather than the free marketplace.

FIGURE 53.2.
Women War Workers During World War I, the British created large armaments plants under the Ministry of Munitions. Under the wartime pressure, women replaced men in numerous occupations usually reserved for men. (Imperial War Museum, Great Britain)

The mobilization of resources included human resources. Not only were men drafted into the armed services, but women and men at the home front were often required to work in accord with priorities determined by the government. Labor unions were brought into partnerships with the government. Women's roles changed as they assumed jobs previously reserved for men. Class distinctions blurred as more and more members of society were included in the war effort.

Politically, governments became intolerant of dissent. Constitutional or democratic processes were often ignored in the name of authority and efficiency. Propaganda was used to create support for the government and hatred for the enemy.

Those nations less able to organize and maintain this vast effort—such as the Austro-Hungarian and Russian empires—faltered first. They lacked the strong industrial base and organizational strength of Germany, France, and Great Britain. But over time, even the strongest nations weakened under the strain. By 1917 the threat of mutiny by troops was accompanied by political

and social protests against the war. It had become clear that the war was to be won or lost on the home front as much as on the battle lines.

5. THE ENTRY OF THE UNITED STATES AND THE VICTORY OF THE ALLIES

By 1917 Germany and its allies, though beginning to show signs of strain, appeared to be close to victory. French morale dropped at the front and behind the lines; numerous units of the battered army mutinied. The Germans launched an unlimited submarine campaign against British shipping. The combined German and Austro-Hungarian forces administered a crushing defeat to Italy. In November 1917 Russia, suffering unbearable hardships at the front and behind the lines, succumbed to the Communist revolution and soon thereafter withdrew from the war. Although the harsh terms forced on helpless Russia by the Germans in the Treaty of Brest-Litovsk[1] showed the remaining Allies what they could expect from a victorious Germany and strengthened their will to fight to the finish, the Germans were now able for the first time in the war to concentrate their full strength on the weary French and British. The prospects for the Allies seemed dim. It was at this critical juncture that the United States entered the war.

When the war had begun in 1914, President Woodrow Wilson had admonished the American people to remain neutral in thought as well as in deed. However, from the beginning, the great majority of public opinion in the United States was that Germany and its allies were the aggressors. During the course of the war, the United States increasingly became economically tied to the Allied cause. The sinking of American ships by German submarines, however, provided the immediate impetus for the entry of the United States into the war. When the Germans first began large-scale sinkings of merchant and passenger ships in 1915, President Wilson had protested so vigorously that the Germans finally agreed to desist. Great Britain and France, it is true, had seized some American ships attempting to evade the blockade of Germany, but no lives had been lost and damages had been paid. Early in 1917 the German high command decided to launch an unlimited submarine campaign against enemy and neutral shipping alike. At about the same time, British intelligence turned over to the United States the Zimmermann note, in which Germany offered United States territory to Mexico as a reward for attacking the United States.

German leaders fully expected that these policies would bring the United States into the war, but they believed that Great Britain and France would be crushed before any appreciable American weight could be brought to bear in Europe. The American government immediately broke off diplomatic relations with Germany. After several American ships had been sunk, Congress, on April 6, at the request of President Wilson, declared war on the German imperial government.

Although a full year elapsed before American troops were able to play an important role at the front, the boost in Allied morale was immediate, and the Americans lost no time supplying financial, material, and naval aid. The total contribution of the United States to Allied victory was relatively small compared with that of France and Great Britain, but America's role, coming as it did when both sides were approaching exhaustion, was probably decisive. At the beginning of 1918 the race was between Germany and the United States. Germany transferred troops from the Russian front to overwhelm Great Britain and France before large numbers of American troops could arrive, while the United States strove to raise, train, and transport to France sufficient forces to stem the German tide. Again the advantage appeared to lie with Germany.

In March 1918 Field Marshall Ludendorff, now in command of the German armies, launched the first of a series of massive blows on the western front designed to end the war. The British and French were driven back with heavy losses. In desperation, they at long last agreed to a unified command under France's General Ferdinand Foch. The Americans, under General John J. Pershing, also accepted his command. By the middle of June, Ludendorff had launched four great drives, and the Allied lines had been battered so thin that when the climactic fifth drive began along the Marne River in mid-July 1918, Ludendorff wired the kaiser: "If the attack succeeds, the war will be over and we will have won it." When Foch heard the opening German barrage, he wired his government: "If the present German attack succeeds, the war is over and we have lost it." The Germans were stopped by a narrow margin. Foch, now receiving a swelling stream of fresh American troops and armaments, immediately ordered a counterattack. In the Allied counterattack, the tank, developed by the British, proved to be the breakthrough weapon. German strength and morale waned rapidly; the war was lost.

The first of the Central Powers to go out of the war was Bulgaria, which at the end of September 1918 surrendered to French, British, and Serbian forces operating from the Greek port of Salonika. A month later Turkey surrendered to British im-

---

[1] Russia was forced to give up territory containing one-third of its European population, three-fourths of its iron, and nine-tenths of its coal deposits, plus a heavy indemnity.

FIGURE 53.3. The Big Four
The "Big Four" as they posed for newsreels at Versailles in 1919. Left to right, David Lloyd George, Vittorio Orlando, Georges Clemenceau, Woodrow Wilson. The biggest controversy that developed at the peace conference was between Clemenceau, who demanded a harsh treaty with Germany, and Wilson, who insisted upon a "just" treaty. (UPI/Bettmann Newsphotos)

perial forces in the Near East. Austria-Hungary, its various language groups in revolt, surrendered on November 3 to Italian, British, and French forces driving in from Italy. The following day a full-fledged mutiny that had been brewing for several days broke out in the German navy and quickly spread throughout Germany. Popular uprisings brought down the kaiser's government. On November 11 the German commanders, their armies hopelessly beaten and in full retreat from France and Belgium, accepted Foch's armistice terms, which amounted to outright surrender. However, the German commanders manipulated events so that most of Germany's population was unaware of the extent of Germany's military collapse (no foreign soldiers were yet on German soil), and a new civilian government of republicans and socialists had to accept responsibility for the surrender. This tactic set the stage for future charges that Germany had not really been beaten but had been "stabbed in the back" by the political forces that would rule Germany during the 1920s.

6. THE PEACE SETTLEMENT

The Allied statesmen who gathered in Paris in January 1919 to try to make a lasting peace were confronted with a formidable task. Hate and disillusionment poisoned the atmosphere. Although all thirty-two of the victorious Allies were represented at the Paris Peace Conference, the great decisions were really made by the leaders of France, Great Britain, and the United States (see Figure 53.3). The French delegation was headed by Premier Georges Clemenceau, the aged "Tiger of France." As host to the conference and the head of the nation that had done the most to defeat Germany and that had suffered greatly, he expected to dominate the decisions. Leading the British delegation was the eloquent and fiery "Little Welsh Attorney," Prime Minister David Lloyd George. As spokesman for the British Empire, which comprised one-fourth of all the land and people in the world, he also expected to dominate the conference. At the head of the American del-

NORTH CAPE

ARCTIC OCEAN

• Murmansk

Reykjavik •   ICELAND
                (Denmark)

Narvik •

Archang

Areas Lost by Germany
Areas Lost by Russia
Areas Lost by Ottoman Empire
Austria-Hungary 1914

NORWAY

SWEDEN

FINLAND

L.

0   100   200   300 miles

FAEROE I.
(Denmark)

Helsinki •   • Leningrad
             Reval •
     Oslo •   ESTONIA
   • Stockholm   Riga •
                        LATVIA
             ORKNEY I.
             SCAPA FLOW   LITHUANIA
                        Memel •
DENMARK   Kaunas •
ULSTER   Edinburgh •   Copenhagen •   EAST   Vilna •   WHITE
IRISH   PRUSSIA   RUSSIAN
FREE STATE GREAT BRITAIN   Hamburg •   Danzig •   S.S.R.
   Dublin •   Liverpool •   POLISH
                                       CORRIDOR   POLAND
                 NETHERLANDS
ATLANTIC   Amsterdam •   Bremen •   Warsaw •   Brest-
                          Berlin •   Litovsk •
OCEAN   London • Rhine R. GERMANY   • Kiev
                  Brussels • WEIMAR REPUBLIC
                  BELGIUM RUHR Weimar •
                  LUX. Cologne •   Prague •   GALICIA
            Paris •   SAAR Frankfurt • CZECHOSLOVAKIA
         Versailles • Metz • Stuttgart •   BUKO-
                   ALSACE- Strasbourg • Vienna • Budapest • VINA
                   LORRAINE   Munich • AUSTRIA   BESSARABIA
         FRANCE   SWITZERLAND   HUNGARY TRANSYLVANIA
                   Geneva • Locarno   Trieste •   RUMANIA
    Bordeaux •   Fiume • Belgrade • Bucharest
                                    Zara   YUGOSLAVIA   Danube R. DOBR
      Bilbao •   Marseilles •   Trent • (Italy)   SERBIA
PORTUGAL   Florence •   SERBIA   Sofia •
Lisbon   Madrid •   Barcelona •   ITALY   BULGARIA
        SPAIN   Rome •   ADRIATIC
                                          SEA   ALBANIA
         Seville • CORSICA   Naples •   AEGEAN
Cadiz • Gibraltar (Britain) (France)   SEA   Smyr
Tangier • SPANISH   BALEARIC I. SARDINIA   Athens •
         MOROCCO   (Spain)   SICILY   GREECE   DODECA
              Algiers •   (Ital)
MOROCCO   ALGERIA   TUNISIA   MALTA (Britain)   CRETE
(France)   (France)   (France)   MEDITERRANEAN SE

Map 53.2 EUROPE, 1923 As a result of World War I the Austro-Hungarian and Ottoman empires were dismembered and both Germany and Russia suffered important losses of territory. However, the newly established states of eastern Europe were vulnerable and cut off from their strongest potential support: France and Great Britain.

egation was the idealistic President Woodrow Wilson.

A fundamental and bitter clash immediately developed between Clemenceau, who wanted a hard peace that would mutilate Germany and make it harmless in the future, and Wilson, who wanted a "just" peace free of vindictiveness of any kind. In the end Wilson received support from Lloyd George. Great Britain needed the trade of a recovered Germany and did not wish to see France become too dominant on the Continent. The Treaty of Versailles with Germany reflected Wilson's ideas in fundamental principles, though not in every detail.

Six months of hard work and bitter wrangling were required to draw up the treaty (see Map 53.2). Its most important terms were, in brief, as follows: Germany and its allies were forced to accept full responsibility for the war. Germany was compelled to give up all its overseas colonies and concessions. Alsace and Lorraine were returned to France. The Polish-speaking areas of eastern Germany were ceded to the resurrected Polish state. With one exception, wherever doubt existed as to the wishes of the people in the affected areas, plebiscites were held to determine their desires. The exception was the "Polish corridor," which was cut along the Vistula River to give Poland an outlet to the sea. Germany's army was cut down to one hundred thousand officers and men, who were to be long-term volunteers to prevent a rapid turnover of trained personnel. Germany's navy was reduced from the world's second greatest to six small battleships, six cruisers, and a larger number of auxiliary vessels. Germany was permitted no submarines, no military aviation, no poison gas (which it had introduced during the war), and no offensive weapons such as tanks and heavy artillery. Germany's Rhineland was to be permanently demilitarized, and its munitions industries were made subject to Allied inspection. Germany's general staff was to be dismantled and its top war leaders tried for violations of the rules and customs of war, and if found guilty, punished. (The kaiser fled to the Netherlands just before Germany collapsed, and the Netherlands refused to give him up.) Finally, Germany was held liable for an indemnity that in 1921 was set by an Allied reparations commission at approximately $33 billion. Wilson and Lloyd George believed these terms to be just. Clemenceau considered them to be suicidally lenient.

The treaties with Germany's allies were actually more severe than the Treaty of Versailles because the principle followed in territorial rearrangements was freedom or union of all national language groups, and Germany was more homogeneous linguistically than were its allies. The polyglot Austro-Hungarian Empire was split up along language lines. The Czechs and Slovaks were formed into the new state of Czechoslovakia, which unfortunately also included sizable German and other minorities. The Poles were joined to Poland, the Rumanians to Rumania, the Italians to Italy, and the Serbs, Croats, and Slovenes to Serbia, which now became Yugoslavia. Thus the Dual Monarchy was cut down from a nation of 50 million, second in area only to Russia among the nations of Europe, to an Austria of 6.5 million German-speaking Austrians and a Hungary of 8 million Magyars. Turkey was shorn of its far-flung non-Turkish territories. The new national boundaries, in spite of the painstaking care with which they were drawn, left many pockets of discontent to breed future conflicts.

Wilson placed his chief hopes for peace in an association of nations that would settle peaceably the tensions and conflicts that were certain to arise in the future. He insisted that its framework be incorporated in the treaty with Germany. The first twenty-six articles of the Treaty of Versailles therefore constitute the convenant of the League of Nations.

The League of Nations had no military forces at its command. Its only teeth, so to speak, were Article X and Article XVI. Article X stated that every member undertook to guarantee the territorial integrity of every other member. In other words, if one member was attacked, all the other members were morally obligated to come to its aid. However, there was no way to compel them to do so. Article XVI stated that if a nation went to war in violation of a decision of the League, all the members of the League were to boycott the aggressor. This weapon (economic sanctions) could have been a potent deterrent if faithfully applied.

In the last analysis, however, the success of the League of Nations depended primarily upon the support of the Big Three victorious democracies—the United States, Great Britain, and France. The refusal of the United States to join the League (see pp. 701–702) was a body blow. Great Britain and France immediately lost faith in it and began to pursue their traditional nationalistic aims. Moreover, a defensive alliance between France, Great Britain, and the United States, desperately wanted by France and agreed to at the conference, was not ratified by the governments of Great Britain or the United States. France felt betrayed and left alone to face a resentful Germany.

7. THE EFFECTS OF WORLD WAR I AND THE PEACE SETTLEMENT

World War I profoundly affected the West. Much of Europe was shattered by this war of unprecedented scope and destructiveness. Over 10 million people had been killed, some 3 million of them civilians. Even more died of diseases or hardships traceable to the war. Over 20 million had been wounded. The cream of a generation of Europe's future leaders had been lost, a reality that helps account for the poor quality of leadership during the 1920s and 1930s. The financial and material losses were incalculable. A tenth of the richest part of France had been laid waste. The most developed part of Russia was devastated. European nations were saddled with heavy debts. The German, Austro-Hungarian, Ottoman, and Russian empires had collapsed. The British and French empires were seriously weakened. The economic system of capitalism, based on a relative lack of governmental control over economic and social affairs, was undermined during the war as central governments mobilized and managed their na-

WHERE HISTORIANS DISAGREE

Causes for World War I

World War I shattered the world of 1914 and nearly destroyed a whole civilization. It is natural, then, that many historians and others should spend a great deal of time and thought trying to assess the causes and assign responsibility for such a disaster.

Initially, people had great difficulty distinguishing causes from responsibility. Most nations were allies or supporters of the victors, and they held Germany responsible for the war. To them, that was little different than concluding that Germany caused the war. This view was formalized in Article 231 of the Treaty of Versailles.

During the 1920s a reaction against this harsh judgment set in. Several historians offered "revised" analyses of responsibility for World War I. Harry Elmer Barnes concluded that primary blame did not rest with Germany but rather with Russia, France, and Serbia. Sidney Bradshaw Fay argued that World War I was a war that no one really wanted, and that if blame must be assigned, it should go to Russia, France, and England as much as anyone.

Responses to these "revisionist" judgments soon appeared. Since then the scholarly and ideological struggle has continued, some historians pointing to Germany, others to the Allies, and still others to Austria-Hungary.

In recent decades scholars have tended to avoid assigning responsibility or blame for the war and instead to focus on what were the crucial causes for the war.

Many historians point to the system of alliances developing in the decades prior to 1914. These alliances divided nations into hostile, distrustful camps. In this system of alliances the acts of one nation became tied to the acts of another. Increasingly, each nation lost its ability to be flexible. Thus, when a relatively local problem between Serbia and Austria-Hungary got out of control, other nations were sucked into a conflict they did not want by the terms of the alliances they had formed and feared to violate.

Other historians focus on nationalism as the real underlying cause for the war. They argue that it was nationalism that caused nations to view everything in terms of rivalry. It was nationalism that spurred the imperial struggle, the buildup of arms, the willingness to fight, the refusal to compromise, and the underestimation of war costs.

More recently, some historians have emphasized the social tensions of European nations as the more profound underlying cause for the war. They point to growing social unrest in almost all European nations and the revolutionary threat in some. These social tensions made governments and people unusually willing to go to war as a means for letting off social pressure and bringing internal unity in the face of an external threat. The near collapse of all opposition to war once war was declared (even among committed socialists) seems to support this view.

Finally, there are those, particularly Marxist scholars, who argue that World War I stemmed from economic rivalries. They emphasize that as industrial and financial capitalism developed, so did the international interests of influential economic groups. Economic rivalry led to imperial rivalry and eventually to military rivalry. It was these economic factors that set the stage for the particular events leading to the outbreak of World War I.

Ultimately, there are always individuals who make the decisions leading to war. The deeper question is what forces created the situation where such decisions occur and result in a major war such as World War I.

tions' economies as never before. Propaganda was unleashed on a massive scale and would thereafter become an important fixture of twentieth-century life.

The peace settlement negotiated in Paris left no one satisfied and many deeply resentful. Russia, which had suffered great losses, was not even invited to the conference. Germany, which would have to play an important role in postwar Europe, was not allowed to participate in the talks—rather, its representatives were presented with a treaty and offered little choice but to sign a humiliating and weakening settlement. The United States gov-

ernment refused to sign the treaty. France's thirst for revenge was not satisfied and France soon felt isolated. The settlement left newly established nations in eastern Europe in a weak position. Certainly, the task facing the negotiators was difficult and perhaps overwhelming. The passions and destruction unleashed by the war may have been so great that no settlement would have been satisfactory. However, the Treaty of Versailles left a legacy of disappointment and resentment to be built upon during the two decades separating World Wars I and II.

SUGGESTED READING

Origins of World War I

F. Fischer, *Germany's Aims in the First World War* (1967). Controversial account stressing Germany's responsibility for the war.

L. Lafore, *The Long Fuse* (1971). A good analysis of the causes of the war.

J. Joll, *The Origins of the First World War* (1984). Excellent analysis.

The War

C. Falls, *The Great War* (1961). A brief narrative stressing military affairs.

A. Solzhenitsyn, *August 1914*. Inspired, detailed account of the Tannenberg campaign that virtually knocked Russia out of the war.

B. Tuchman, *The Guns of August* (1963). Well-written account of the immediate background and opening campaigns of World War I.

A. J. P. Taylor, *The First World War* (1963). A well-written account.

The Home Front

F. L. Carsten, *War Against War* (1982). A good study of radical movements in Great Britain and Germany.

G. D. Feldman, *Army, Industry, and Labor in Germany, 1914–1918*. Excellent analysis of the social effects of the war in Germany.

J. Williams, *The Home Fronts: Britain, France, and Germany, 1914–1918* (1972). A comparative study of the domestic impact of the war.

The Peace Settlement

A. Link, *Wilson, the Diplomatist: A Look at His Major Foreign Policies* (1965). By a foremost authority on Wilson.

H. Nicolson, *Peacemaking 1919* (1965). Good examination of the Versailles process and settlement.

The Effects of World War I

R. Albrecht-Carrie, ed., *The Meaning of the First World War* (1965). Stress on international affairs.

P. Fussell, *The Great War and Modern Memory* (1975). Stresses the psychological significance of the war.

J. Roth, ed., *World War I* (1967). Excellent collection of essays analyzing the significance of the war.

Historical Fiction

E. Hemingway, *A Farewell to Arms*. Famous novel based on the author's experiences on the Italian front.

E. M. Remarque, *All Quiet on the Western Front*. Has brought home to millions the horrors of trench warfare in World War I.

CHAPTER 54

Revolution and Communism in Russia

FIGURE 54.1. Serov, "Lenin Proclaiming Soviet Power" This painting shows Lenin, with Stalin and other Bolshevik leaders, proclaiming to the revolutionary forces the Bolsheviks' assumption of power in 1917. The style of the painting, social realism, is typical of Soviet art during the 1920s and 1930s. (Sovfoto)

World War I not only was militarily devastating for Russia but also was something that the centuries-old tsarist government could not survive. In March of 1917 the government of Nicholas II was swept from power by a revolution. This was the beginning of an extended period of revolutionary events in Russia that eventually resulted in the rise to power of the Bolsheviks, who in turn attempted to establish their vision of a Communist society in Russia. By the 1930s Russia was ruled by a totalitarian government that was effecting a massive economic, social, and cultural transformation of the nation and that was seen as a threat by most nations of the West.

1. THE RUSSIAN REVOLUTION OF 1917

Without the strain of World War I, revolution might not have occurred as it did and when it did in 1917, but that a revolution occurred in Russia should not be surprising. The violent Russian upheaval of 1917 was the result of maladjustments and discontent that had long been developing. Russia, except for a handful of intelligentsia, had been virtually bypassed by the great liberalizing movements, such as the Enlightenment and the French Revolution, that had influenced western Europe. The Industrial Revolution, which brought in its wake liberalism and radicalism, reached Russia only in the 1890s. While western and parts of central Europe and the United States were becoming politically, economically, and socially modernized, Russia remained a land of peasantry, feudal aristocracy, and tsarist autocracy. Many of the frustrated Russian intelligentsia in the latter half of the nineteenth century turned to revolutionary doctrines and even terrorism in an effort to effect rapid change. Others, including elements from the small but growing middle class, hoped for more moderate liberal reforms. But the tsarist government, particularly under Nicholas II (1894–1917), was generally reactionary and unbending.

The growing pressures for change exploded in the revolution of 1905. With little support and faced with dissension and revolt on all sides, Nicholas II was forced to grant some liberal reforms and promised to give the elected Duma some real powers. But as soon as the crisis passed, Nicholas II returned to old policies and rejected the substance of the liberal reforms.

The outbreak of the war in 1914 brought some temporary national unity as most factions rallied to the support of the nation. Soon, however, the strains of war proved too much for the inept Russian government. Russia suffered staggering losses at the hands of the German armies. Behind the lines the suffering of the civilian population, much of which could be attributed to the corrupt bureaucracy of the tsar, was acute. Members of the Duma and others increasingly demanded liberal reform, but the tsar and his ministers refused to share power. The disintegration of Russia's military forces was reflected in a disintegration of Russia's government. The tsar increasingly fell under the influence of his unbending wife, Alexandra. She in turn fell under the influence of Grigori Efimovich Rasputin (1871?–1916), an uneducated Siberian monk who claimed powers to heal the tsar's hemophilic son. Even the tsar's aristocratic supporters, a group of whom murdered Rasputin late in 1916, were demanding fundamental change.

In early March 1917, the dam broke. Demands for bread in Petrograd quickly turned into riots and strikes. The tsar's troops were unable to restore order, often refusing to fire on the rioters or actually joining them. On March 12 the Duma organized a Provisional Government and three days later Nicholas II resigned. The new Provisional Government was dominated by liberals and moderate socialists. The leading figures of this government were Pavel Milyukov and Prince Georgi Lvov, both relatively moderate liberals. The Provisional Government enacted into law civil liberties, religious freedom, equality before the law, union rights, and other typical liberal reforms. Its more moderate faction promised to turn Russia into a Western-style political democracy and enact fundamental social reforms; others demanded more radical change. However, in addition to its inexperience, its differing factions, and the pressures for change, the Provisional Government labored under two burdens. First, it had to share power with the newly organized soviets—political organizations of workers, soldiers, and radical intellectuals—particularly the powerful Petrograd Soviet. Second, it chose to continue the war that was draining Russia. Some of the crucial connections between these two burdens are indicated by the Petrograd Soviet's issuance of Order Number 1, which declared that military officers would be democratically elected by soldiers and military decisions would be democratically made. Order Number I contributed to the continuing disintegration of the Russian forces.

In May the liberal leaders of the Provisional Government resigned and the socialist Alexander Kerensky (1881–1970) became the leading figure in the government. By this time, however, the Bolshevik wing of the Marxist Social Democratic party was starting to play an important role in Russian affairs.

2. THE RISE OF THE BOLSHEVIKS

Marxism became influential among some intellectuals toward the end of the nineteenth century. In 1898 Russian Marxists formed the Social Democratic party, whose principal leaders were Gregory Plekhanov (1857–1918) and his disciple Vladimir Ilich Ulyanov (Lenin) (1870–1924). Repression by the tsar's government forced the Social Democrats into exile. At a London conference in 1903 the radical Bolshevik wing under Lenin split from the more moderate Mensheviks.

Until 1917, Lenin's Bolsheviks remained only a minor party. Its leaders were hunted down by the state police and shot, imprisoned, or exiled. For some seventeen years Lenin remained in exile in Switzerland, keeping his party alive and plotting for the eventual overthrow of the tsar's government. During that time Lenin developed theoretical and tactical principles for the successes the Bolsheviks would enjoy in 1917. Three of these principles were crucial. The first was that the party should not be open and democratic but rather should be an elite, highly trained, and constantly purged group of dedicated Marxist revolutionaries. The second was that the socialist revolution need not be a revolution of only the industrial working class; in Russia it could also be a dual revolution of workers and peasants—all part of an even broader socialist revolution that would

sweep other countries of Europe. The third was a continuing opposition to World War I.

Lenin and the Bolshevik's chance came in the months after the fall of the tsar's government in March 1917. In April 1917 the German government transported Lenin from his place of exile in Switzerland to the Russian border in an effort to increase the chaos and remove Russia from the war. Lenin refused to cooperate with the Provisional Government and instead unleashed a barrage of appealing slogans such as "peace to the army, land to the peasants, ownership of the factories to the workers." Meanwhile, the Socialist Kerensky came to power, but he was unable to extract Russia from the war. Bolshevik influence was growing, particularly among the Petrograd workers and soldiers. In July the Bolsheviks decided the time was ripe to seize power, but the effort failed. The Bolsheviks were not yet a dominant force, and the Kerensky government arrested many Bolsheviks and forced others, including Lenin, to flee to exile in Finland. The Kerensky government was further weakened by the failure of a new Russian offensive in the war and threatened coup d'état of General Kornilov. This threat led Kerensky to release the Bolsheviks and rely on the soviets to defend the capital in September. By October the Bolsheviks under the leadership of Lenin and the brilliant Leon Trotsky (1877–1940) gained control over the Petrograd and Moscow soviets. Lenin again judged the time was ripe for revolution, and this time he was right. On November 6 Trotsky conducted a well-organized revolution, seizing the crucial centers of power and arranging for the transfer of power to the soviets and Lenin. On November 7 the Bolshevik majority elected Lenin the head of the new government.

3. THE BOLSHEVIKS IN POWER, 1917–1927

The Bolsheviks immediately moved to fulfill their promises and consolidate their power. In place of the old tsarist hierarchy, a pyramid of people's councils, or soviets, was set up. These councils were elected by universal suffrage but were actually dominated by a relatively few Communist party members. When national elections failed to turn a Bolshevik majority to a Constituent Assembly, Lenin had the Red Army disperse it. Capitalism was abolished. A barter system of exchange replaced money—the value of the ruble having been destroyed by inflation and devaluation. All industry and commerce were placed under the management of committees of workers responsible to party commissars. The land was nationalized and its management turned over to local peasant committees. They in turn distributed it to individual peasants to be worked by their own labor. All crop surpluses were turned over to the state. Church lands were expropriated by the state.

In order to free the new regime for the enormous task of refashioning Russian society, Lenin immediately opened peace negotiations with the Germans. The Germans, realizing Russia's helplessness (Russian troops were deserting in droves), demanded the harshest of terms. Lenin attempted to stall them off, but when the Germans threatened to march on Petrograd and Moscow, he was forced to sign the Treaty of Brest-Litovsk (March 1918). Russia lost Finland, Estonia, Latvia, Lithuania, the Ukraine, Bessarabia, its Polish provinces, and some of its Trans-Caucasian territory. These lands contained one-third of Russia's European population, three-fourths of its iron, and nine-tenths of its coal. In addition, Russia was compelled to pay a heavy indemnity.

But these hard terms were not the end, nor the worst, of Lenin's woes. Two years of bitter civil war followed the peace with Germany. The aristocracy, including most of the higher army officers, launched a counterrevolution against the Bolshevik regime. These "white" forces were aided by various other disaffected groups and by French, British, Polish, Japanese, Czech, and American troops. It was with the greatest of difficulty that the "red" armies, hastily organized by Trotsky, finally defeated the "whites." In doing so, the Bolsheviks regained the Ukraine. However, a large additional strip of territory was lost to Poland, thanks largely to French armed intervention on the side of the Poles.

Russia's war-torn economy was a shambles. The civil war compounded the destruction already suffered from World War I. Indeed, part of the reason for the Bolshevik victory in the civil war

was their policy of "war communism," which succeeded in mobilizing Russia's economy and society for the war effort but also further disrupted normal economic activities. Lack of experience and some unpopular policies added to the economic difficulties. Often workers did not know how to run factories and trains. The distribution of goods was in inexperienced hands. When peasants saw that their surpluses would be seized by the government, they often resisted or refused to raise more than they needed for themselves. By 1921 some 30 million Russians were threatened with starvation, and in spite of considerable foreign relief, particularly from the United States, many did starve.

Lenin, a realist, saw the necessity for retreat. In 1921 he launched the NEP (New Economic Policy), which was a temporary compromise with capitalism. In order to provide incentive, industries employing fewer than twenty workers were permitted to operate under private ownership. These little industrial capitalists were called *nepmen*. Enterprising peasants, called *kulaks*, were permitted to own and rent land and hire laborers. Money and credit were restored. This small-scale capitalistic activity was closely supervised and regulated by the state. However, the NEP provided enough incentive to pull the Russian economy out of chaos. In 1923, just as the new policy was beginning to function, Lenin suffered a paralytic stroke and died the following year.

Lenin's death precipitated a power struggle among his chief associates (see Figure 54.2). Most assumed that his successor would be Leon Trotsky. He had been the chief organizer of the Red Army and had planned its victory over the Whites. A brilliant and eloquent Communist theorist, he was an apostle of world revolution. Trotsky, however, underestimated Joseph Stalin, executive secretary of the Communist party. This unobtrusive and taciturn man was an unscrupulous behind-the-scenes operator. Stalin was the son of poverty-stricken ex-serfs. Expelled from an Orthodox seminary because of his Marxist views and activities, he became a professional revolutionist and terrorist. (*Stalin* is a pseudonym meaning "man of steel.") He was repeatedly arrested and imprisoned and repeatedly escaped. World War I found him in exile in Siberia. Taking advantage of the

Figure 54.2.   Trotsky and Stalin   This rare photograph, taken in 1923 at a party meeting, shows the feud between Stalin (seated, at right) and Trotsky (standing, at left) that ended with Trotsky's murder in Mexico in 1940. As the brilliant, eloquent Trotsky speaks, the taciturn Stalin, son of ex-serfs, eyes him coldly. (UPI/ Bettmann Newsphotos)

amnesty granted to all political prisoners by the Kerensky regime in 1917, Stalin hastened to Petrograd, where he became a devoted associate of Lenin. He played a prominent role in the civil war against the Whites and became executive secretary of the Communist party. In this key position he made himself master of the all-important party machinery.

In this struggle for leadership, Trotsky took the position that all efforts must be made to bring the socialist revolution to other parts of Europe, and that without support from other more advanced socialist nations, socialism in Russia would fail. Trotsky also favored ending the NEP and immediately launching a policy of massive industrialization. Stalin took a more moderate stand, arguing that socialism in one country (Russia) was possible and therefore all efforts should be pointed toward securing what had already been gained in Russia. Trotsky was the more compelling speaker and accomplished theorist, but he also conveyed an element of arrogance. Stalin was more adept at political in-fighting. By conspiring with prominent groups of Bolsheviks and playing one faction against another, Stalin isolated Trotsky and had him expelled from the party and exiled from Russia. By the end of 1927 Stalin had maneuvered himself into a position of dominance over the Communist party and dictatorship over the Soviet Union.

4. THE FIVE-YEAR PLANS AND THE PURGES

In 1928 Stalin launched the first of a series of five-year plans (see Figure 54.3). They were units of planned economy with certain specific goals or objectives to be achieved every five years. They marked the end of the NEP, which had served its purpose of pulling the Communist economy through its first major crises. The objectives of the First Five-Year Plan were (1) the elimination of the last remnants of capitalism, (2) the industrialization of the Soviet Union, (3) the collectivization and mechanization of agriculture, and (4) national defense. However, underlying these objectives were even more fundamental goals: to transform the economy and society of the Soviet Union into a Communist economy and society, and to train and socialize Soviet citizens to be adaptive participants in this Communist system. Rarely has such an ambitious program been undertaken.

Achievement of the first goal meant the liquidation of the *nepmen* and the *kulaks*. When tens of thousands of the independent peasant-proprietor *kulaks* resisted, Stalin eliminated them. The consolidation of their farms into mechanized collectives and the organization of giant state farms went on apace. The state farms were huge outlays up to three hundred thousand acres in size run by party managers and hired laborers. Every effort was made to mechanize them. Vast tracts of land in southeast Russia and Siberia were brought under cultivation for the first time. The collective farms were of various types. In the most common type, independent farmers surrendered their lands and horses but retained their houses, gardens, cattle, pigs, and chickens for their own private use. The collective farm was run by elected managers who were instructed and supervised by party officials. Elimination of the tiny individual tracts, each one of which had been surrounded by ditches or hedgerows, made mechanization possible. A certain amount of the harvest was set aside for taxes, insurance, improvements, and feed. A large part had to be sold to the state at a fixed price. The rest was distributed to the peasant members in proportion to the amount of their original contribution to the collective in land and horses and to the amount and quality of their work. The mechanization of Russia's agriculture required the construction of huge quantities of tractors and farm machinery.

Since the Industrial Revolution was still in its infancy in Russia in 1928, industrialization meant building almost from the ground up and concentrating on producer rather than consumer goods. Western engineers and technicians were lured to Russia with high salaries. Capital was obtained by exporting scarce supplies of wheat, often at ruinously low prices. At the cost of much privation, enormous strides were made. Steel mills, power plants, foundries, mines, refineries, and railroads were built all over the Soviet Union. At Dnepropetrovsk on the Dnieper River, the world's largest dam and hydroelectric power plant were constructed. At the end of 1932 it was announced that all the goals of the First Five-Year Plan had been reached several months ahead of time.

During the 1930s the second and third five-year plans were launched. Generally the stress remained on the collectivization and mechanization of agriculture and on heavy industrialization. However, there was a new emphasis on the production of consumer goods to enable the masses to enjoy a slowly rising standard of living.

The results of the five-year plans are difficult to evaluate accurately. What might have happened if the policy choices had been different is unknown. The results in agriculture were most questionable. There was tremendous resistance to collectivization as well as mismanagement and drought. At times famine became a reality, as did a state of near civil war in the countryside. At one point Stalin admitted that problems with collectivization had claimed some 10 million human victims and brought about the destruction of half of

FIGURE 54.3. **Stalin, "The Five-Year Plan in Four Years"** In this 1930s Soviet propaganda poster, "The Five-Year Plan in Four Years," Stalin is portrayed leading industrial development against the reactionary forces of capitalism and religion. (The Fotomas Index, London)

the nation's draft and farm animals. Yet by 1939 over 90 percent of Soviet agriculture was collectivized and much of it was mechanized.

The results of the five-year plans in industry and defense were more gratifying and, in many ways, phenomenal. In 1928, at the beginning of the First Five-Year Plan, the Soviet Union was far behind other nations in industrial production. During the First Five-Year Plan industrial production doubled, a record equaled again in the Second Five-Year Plan. During this period the Soviet Union managed to achieve an unprecedented rate of growth in industrial output, but at great human cost. By 1941, when the Germans invaded the Soviet Union, it had become the fourth greatest industrial power in the world. In a number of categories it had surpassed both Great Britain and Germany and was second only to the United States. The Soviet Union could never have withstood the German assault had this not been true.

The 1930s were also the time of the Great Purges. In 1934 Sergei Kirov (1888–1934), a high Soviet official, was assassinated. It is unclear whether Stalin's enemies were responsible or whether Stalin himself ordered the assassination only to use it as an excuse to eliminate potential rivals. However, a long period of party purges,

arrests, trials, imprisonments, and executions soon followed. Eventually almost all the original Bolshevik leaders were removed from power and from the party, as were most of the Red Army's top officer corps. By the end of the Great Purges in 1939, hundreds of thousands—perhaps millions—of people had been affected. The government, the Communist party, and the military were now staffed by new, generally younger figures all beholden to Stalin.

Stalin's motives for the Great Purges are a matter of debate. Some argue that the purges were a manifestation of his paranoia; others argue that they were a logical step in the process of moving the Soviet Union from a revolution in 1917 to a totalitarian Communist state in the 1930s. In any case they did consolidate Stalin's power and eliminate all potential pockets of resistance to him.

5. TOTALITARIAN CONTROL

Between 1917 and 1939 the government effected totalitarian rule in the Soviet Union. The government was dominated by the Communist party and the party head served as virtual dictator. Not only did the party enjoy a monopoly over political affairs and the armed forces, but it also controlled to an unprecedented degree the economic, social, religious, and cultural life of the nation.

The Soviet Political System

On coming to power, the Bolsheviks divided the Russian Empire into eleven socialist republics— Russia proper and ten other language or dialect areas. In 1939–1940 five more were added from territories seized by Russia at the outbreak of World War II. The Soviet Union was in theory a union of autonomous republics. (U.S.S.R. stands for Union of Soviet Socialist Republics.) Actually, however, Russia itself constituted at least four-fifths of the total area and population and dominated the Union.

The Soviet system of government as originally set up consisted of a pyramid of elected councils— village, district, county, and provincial—culminating in the Union Congress of Soviets, which met once very two years and chose executive and administrative boards. Voting was by show of hands in mass meetings. The urban vote was given more than double the weight of the rural vote, since bolshevism's chief concern was the industrial proletariat. In 1936 Stalin promulgated a new constitution, which appeared to be more democratic. Voting was to be by secret ballot, the differential between the urban and the rural vote was abolished, and the members of the various soviets in the pyramid were to be elected directly by the local districts. The member republics in the Union were allegedly granted complete autonomy.

Only the Communist party was permitted to engage in organized political activity. It named the official candidates, made all political policies and platforms, and conducted all election promotion and propaganda. Opposition to the party's official candidates and program was considered to be disloyal and was ferreted out and crushed by the state police, both secret and regular. The all-powerful Communist party was organized on an authoritarian basis. The Politburo, sixteen men meeting in secret and responsible only to the secretariat of the party, made all decisions, which were transmitted without question down through the chain of command to the local cells. The real center of power in the Soviet system was the secretariat of the Communist party, and the first (or general) secretary of the party was the most powerful figure in the Soviet Union. Obedience to superiors was demanded of all party members. Party members were carefully selected and trained. As set up by Lenin, the total number was kept relatively small.

Soviet Culture and Society

In 1917 more than 60 percent of the Russian people were illiterate. It was Lenin's belief that a Communist state required an educated populace in order to succeed. Nearly all the top Bolsheviks themselves were educated—in fact, they would be considered members of the intelligentsia in almost any time or place. Little could be done in the educational field in the first turbulent years of the Communist regime, but education received major attention in Stalin's five-year plans. In 1928 the Communists launched a vast program of free compulsory secular education. The program covered all levels—elementary, secondary, and higher—for both the young and adults. It included a comprehensive system of technical and on-the-job training. Science and engineering were particularly stressed. Of course, Soviet education was interlarded with Communist propaganda, but its standards were high, and it turned out the trained people who were needed. In 1941 Stalin announced that illiteracy had been banished from Russia.

Advanced scholarship and the arts were not neglected in the Soviet Union. An extensive program of scholarships, prizes, and institutes was inaugurated for the purpose of encouraging and subsidizing superior talent. Soviet musicians, architects, painters, and dancers more than held their own in international competition. Yet the arts were subject to official Communist ideology. All liberal, bourgeois, or capitalistic literature (which was most of it) was heavily censored. Such world-renowned composers as Prokofiev and Shostakovich occasionally fell into official disfavor because of their modern "bourgeois" music. When some powerful commissar decided that the Mendelian law of genetics, which is generally accepted in the world of science, ran counter to the party line, Soviet geneticists were forced to disclaim it.

FIGURE 54.4. **Women Workers and Architects Conferring** The Soviet government promoted social realism to make art relevant to the working masses and carry explicit messages. Here the sun streams in on women workers and architects conferring over plans for a new factory. On the left, a bust of Stalin looks on. (Tass from Sovfoto)

Soviet society was made more egalitarian. Although the party, governmental, military, and cultural elite enjoyed some advantages, most class distinctions were eliminated. Women particularly benefited, because all formal discrimination against them was eliminated (see Figure 54.4). Indeed, Soviet women probably gained unparalleled economic equality with men. They received equal pay and were offered equal educational and professional opportunities. However, stronger patterns of discrimination within the household left Soviet women with some of the realities of inequality that generally prevailed elsewhere in the West.

In many ways Soviet society displayed the marks of totalitarian control. Most social organi-

zations were saturated with official Communist ideology. The Communist party and the state took direct control when any social organization showed signs of gaining significant influence. Agents of the state, ranging from minor bureaucrats to members of the secret police, pervaded Soviet society. Terror, most evident during Stalin's Great Purges, was an ever-present weapon.

Religious Policy

The religious policy of the Bolsheviks, upon gaining power in Russia, was quite similar to that of the French revolutionists in 1789–1794. All church property was confiscated. The churches themselves were turned into museums or clubs of various kinds, although they were sometimes leased to religious congregations for purposes of worship. No religious instruction whatever was permitted in the schools, which were all public and secular. The churches were forbidden to give organized religious instruction and even to maintain seminaries for the training of their own clergy. At the same time, the schools were flooded with Communist propaganda.

The Communist leaders claimed that their harsh treatment of the churches was necessitated by the active opposition of the churches to the Communist government. They claimed that when they first came to power, they granted religious freedom for the first time in Russian history, but that the churches immediately used this freedom to advocate the overthrow of the very government that granted it. They further claimed that churches had always been the tools and agents of capitalistic governments and interests. Whatever truth there may be in these claims, it would appear that religion was perceived as a problem and danger to the Soviet regime.

6. THE SOVIET UNION AND THE WORLD

When the Bolsheviks first took over in 1917, they confidently expected some of the capitalistic governments in the war-weary world to collapse and follow Russia along the path to communism. To encourage them to do so and to avoid fulfillment of the harsh terms of the Treaty of Brest-Litovsk, the Communist leaders began an active campaign of revolutionary infiltration and subversion abroad, particularly in Germany. Although some headway was made in Germany, Bavaria falling under Communist control for a brief time, the only country to embrace communism was Hungary, where in 1919 Béla Kun set up a Communist dictatorship that lasted four months. To guide and aid the Communist parties in other countries in the common cause of world revolution, the Bolsheviks set up the Comintern (Communist International), with headquarters in Moscow.

The Western capitalistic powers were antagonistic to the Soviet Union. Thinking that the Bol-

shevik regime would soon collapse, France, Great Britain, Japan, and the United States landed troops on Russian soil in 1918 and aided the counterrevolutionary White forces. France helped the Poles to seize a large strip of Russian-speaking territory. Great Britain and France organized the anti-Soviet regimes in the countries of eastern Europe bordering the Soviet Union into a *cordon sanitaire* (health or quarantine belt). For several years, no Western power would recognize the Bolshevik regime. The Soviet Union was refused admission to the League of Nations until 1934, eight years after Germany had been admitted and one year after it had withdrawn under the guidance of Hitler. Even then the Western powers steadfastly refused to cooperate with the Soviet Union in any collective action against the rising Fascist menace.

Nonetheless, the failure of the Communist movements abroad and of the Bolsheviks' early efforts to communize Russia overnight caused the Soviet leaders to adopt a more conciliatory attitude toward the capitalistic powers. The NEP needed foreign commerce and foreign capital in order to function. The Soviet Union gained official recognition abroad. In 1922 Germany established official relations with the Soviet Union. Great Britain and France recognized the Soviet Union in 1924. The last capitalist state of the West to recognize the Soviet Union was the United States, which held off until 1933.

The five-year plans, which began in 1928, required much Western capital and technical assistance. Therefore, the next ten years represented the high tide of Soviet tractability toward the capitalistic Western democracies. Stalin, unlike Trotsky, was more interested in "socialism in one country" than in world revolution, which he believed would come later. The Comintern was allowed to languish. His foreign minister, Maxim Litvinov, became a respected and even popular figure in Geneva, Paris, London, and Washington. Of course, the Soviet Union's fear of the growing Nazi German menace after 1933 was a significant factor in its conciliatory attitude toward the capitalistic democracies. This honeymoon ended in 1938 with the Munich crisis (see p. 706). From that time, Stalin was apparently convinced that real cooperation with the Western democracies was impossible. The cooperation forced upon the Soviet Union and most of the capitalistic world by the menace of the Axis during World War II lasted only until victory was assured. Meanwhile, after Hitler came to power in 1933, the greatest threat to both the Soviet Union and the capitalistic democracies was Nazi Germany.

SUGGESTED READING

General

E. H. Carr, *A History of Soviet Russia*, 7 vols. (1951–1964). Scholarly and highly respected.

I. Deutscher, *Stalin: A Political Biography* (1967). Not only a scholarly biography of Stalin but also a good history of the whole Communist movement in Russia.

I. Deutscher, *Trotsky: 1879–1940*, 3 vols.: *The Prophet Armed* (1954); *The Prophet Unarmed* (1959); *The Prophet Outcast* (1963). A classic study of Trotsky.

The Russian Revolution and the Rise of the Bolsheviks

R. Daniels, *Red October* (1969). Well-written account of the Bolshevik revolution.

A. Ulam, *The Bolsheviks* (1968). A good introduction stressing Lenin's doctrines.

B. Wolfe, *Three Who Made a Revolution* (1955). Good study of Lenin, Trotsky, and Stalin; for the nonspecialist.

The Bolsheviks in Power, the Five-Year Plans, and the Purges

R. Conquest, *The Great Terror* (1968). Excellent study of Stalin's purges.

S. Fitzpatrick. *The Russian Revolution.* (1982). A brief, analytical treatment of the period.

G. Leggett, *The Cheka: Lenin's Secret Police* (1981). Good study of this topic.

J. P. Nettl, *The Soviet Achievement* (1967). Good analysis of economic development in the Soviet Union.

Totalitarian Control

S. Fitzpatrick, *Cultural Revolution in Russia, 1928–1931* (1978). A good analysis.

K. Geiger, *The Family in Soviet Russia* (1968). Well written.

R. Marshall, *Aspects of Religion in the Soviet Union, 1917–1967* (1971). A good book on this difficult subject.

R. Pipes, *The Formation of the Soviet Union* (1964). Stresses the problem of Soviet minorities.

The Soviet Union and the World

G. Kennan, *Russia and the West Under Lenin and Stalin.* By a former American ambassador to the Soviet Union; a harsh perspective.

A. Ulam, *Expansion and Coexistence: Soviet Foreign Policy* (1974). Scholarly, by a respected expert.

Historical Fiction

A. Koestler, *Darkness at Noon* (1956). Classic novel of bolshevism and the purges.

B. Pasternak, *Doctor Zhivago* (1974). Nobel Prize–winning novel depicting life in the Soviet Union by a man who experienced it.

A. Solzhenitsyn, *The Gulag Archipelago* (1974). Vivid account of terror.

CHAPTER 55

The Rise of Fascism and Authoritarianism

FIGURE 55.1. Mussolini Addresses the Masses This photo of Mussolini addressing a huge crowd in Rome after a victory of the Italian forces in Ethiopia shows some of the typical traits of fascism and authoritarianism during 1920s and 1930s: nationalism (the flag), militarism (the uniform), and mass politics (the cheering crowd). (UPI/Bettmann Newsphotos)

During World War I many hoped that victory against the Central Powers would be a blow to authoritarianism and a triumph for liberal democracy. By the time of the Paris Peace Conference in 1919, a shadow was already being cast on these hopes by the triumph of the Bolsheviks in Russia. Nevertheless, the arrangements made at Paris seemed to establish parliamentary democracy in the states of eastern Europe and affirm it in western Europe. But in only a few years these optimistic hopes were dashed by the rise of authoritarian governments in southern, eastern, and central Europe and by the growth of authoritarian political movements within several Western democracies.

1. TOTALITARIANISM, FASCISM, AND AUTHORITARIANISM

The 1920s and 1930s witnessed a great growth of totalitarianism, fascism, and right-wing authoritarianism. Of these political systems, totalitarianism was the most revolutionary and rigorous. In a totalitarian system, a single political party with a revolutionary ideology controls the government. It appeals for active support from the masses and is dominated by a dictatorial leader. No opposition is tolerated. Propaganda, force, and terror are openly used to ensure control and further the goals of the government. Modern communications, technology, and organization are used to control the economic, social, religious, and cultural life of the nation as much as possible. The liberal ideology of limited government and individual rights is formally rejected in a totalitarian system.

As we have already seen in Chapter 54, totalitarianism had its beginnings in the Soviet Union under Lenin and came to full flower under Stalin during the 1930s. Since this totalitarianism was based on Communist ideology, it is often called totalitarianism of the Left. Totalitarianism arose in a mild form in Italy during the 1920s and in a virulent form in Germany during the 1930s. Since this totalitarianism was based on Fascist ideology, it is often called totalitarianism of the Right.

Both fascism and communism were ideologies—sets of ideas and values—that were gaining strength in the West throughout the 1920s and 1930s, but fascism proved to be the greater immediate threat to liberal democracy. Generally fascism was antiliberal, antidemocratic, anti-individualistic, and anti-Communist. It was ultranationalistic and militaristic. It was tied to somewhat mystical ideas of the all-powerful expansive state, of race, and of will. Fascism was initiated by Mussolini during the 1920s. During the 1920s and 1930s Fascist parties spread throughout Europe. The greatest triumph of fascism came with the rise to power of Hitler and nazism in Germany during the 1930s. Some other governments in southern, central, and eastern Europe were influenced by fascism and had some of its trappings, but for the most part they were right-wing authoritarian regimes.

Right-wing authoritarian regimes were less ideologically based than Fascist regimes, and they controlled life in their nations to a much lesser degree than totalitarian systems. Usually they amounted to a dictatorship backed by the military and conservative forces of the nation. They tended to be most concerned with preserving order and protecting the established status quo against perceived threats from liberal democracy, socialism, or communism.

Together totalitarianism, fascism, and right-wing authoritarianism posed a serious threat to the advocates of liberal democracy in the West. Indeed, the hoped for triumph of liberal democracy after World War I seemed to be turning into a triumph for its enemies—a triumph that would lead to growing conflict and a renewal of war in 1939. The story of the rise of fascism and authoritarianism begins with Italy, where Mussolini set up the first Fascist dictatorship.

2. MUSSOLINI CREATES THE FIRST FASCIST STATE

Italy emerged from World War I battered and humiliated. Although it was one of the victorious Allies, Italy's armies had made a poor showing, and Italy had realized few of the grandiose ambitions for which it had entered the war. In the Paris peace settlements Italy had been awarded the adjacent Italian-speaking areas of Austria-

Hungary but had been denied further acquisitions east of the Adriatic and in Asia and Africa, some of which it ardently desired. These frustrations were severe blows to Italian national pride.

Italy's weak economy emerged from the war acutely maladjusted. The national debt was huge and the treasury empty. The inflated currency, together with a shortage of goods, raised prices ruinously. Hundreds of thousands of demobilized veterans could find no jobs. In the summer of 1919, there was widespread disorder. Veterans began seizing and squatting on idle, and sometimes on cultivated, lands. Sit-down strikes developed in the factories. During the winter of 1920–1921, several hundred factories were seized by the workers, and Marxism seemed to be gaining strength. The Italian government, torn by factions, seemed too weak to prevent the disorder and protect private property. Although the strife diminished and the Marxist threat waned before the end of 1921, the landlords and the factory owners were thoroughly frightened. Many of them, and indeed many small-business and professional people, longed for vigorous leadership and a strong government. The vigorous leader who stepped forward was Benito Mussolini. The strong government was his Fascist dictatorship.

Mussolini was a dynamic organizer and leader. The son of a blacksmith, he became first a teacher and later a radical journalist and agitator. Before World War I he was a pacifistic socialist, but during the war he became a violent nationalist. After the war he began organizing unemployed veterans into a political action group with a socialistic and extremely nationalistic program. During the labor disturbances of 1919–1921, Mussolini stood aside until it became apparent that the radical workers' cause would lose; then he threw his support to the capitalists and the landlords. Crying that he was saving Italy from communism and waving the flag of nationalism, Mussolini organized his veterans into terror squads of black-shirted "Fascisti," who beat up the leaderless radical workers and their liberal supporters. He thereby gained the support of the frightened capitalists and landed aristocracy. By 1922 Mussolini's Fascist party was strong enough to "march on Rome" and seize control of the faction-paralyzed government. Appointed premier by the weak and

distraught King Victor Emmanuel III, Mussolini acquired extraordinary powers. Between 1924 and 1926 Mussolini turned his premiership into a dictatorship. All opposition was silenced. Only the Fascist party could engage in organized political activity. The press and the schools were turned into propaganda agencies. The secret police were everywhere. Eventually, the Chamber of Deputies itself was replaced by Mussolini's handpicked Fascist political and economic councils.

Italy's economic life was strictly regimented but in such a way as to favor the capitalistic classes. Private property and profits were carefully protected. All labor unions were abolished except those controlled by the Fascist party. Strikes and lockouts were forbidden. Wages, working conditions, and labor-management disputes were settled by compulsory arbitration under party direction. An elaborate system of planned economy was set up to modernize, coordinate, and increase Italy's production of both industrial and agricultural goods. The very complicated economic and political machinery that Mussolini created for these purposes was called the corporate state. On the whole there was probably a small decline in per capita income under Italian fascism despite some superficial gains. The budget was balanced and the currency was stabilized. But Italy's taxes were the highest in the world, and labor's share of economic production was small.

Fascism, however, was primarily political in character, not economic. The essence of its ideology was nationalism run wild. Although Italy never became such a full-blown, viciously anti-Semitic police state as Germany, Mussolini understood the dynamic, energizing quality of militant nationalism. His writings and speeches rang with such words as *will, discipline, sacrifice, decision,* and *conquest.* "The goal," he cried, "is always—Empire! To build a city, to found a colony, to establish an empire, these are the prodigies of the human spirit. . . . We must resolutely abandon the whole liberal phraseology and way of thinking. . . . Discipline. Discipline at home in order that we may present the granite block of a single national will. . . . War alone brings up the highest tension, all human energy and puts the stamp of nobility upon the people who have the courage to meet it." This grandiose vision was reflected in Fascist

FIGURE 55.2. Max Beckmann, "The Night," 1918–1919 Beckmann, a German artist, reflects the sense of violence and disillusionment stemming from World War I in this scene of overwhelming, absurd torture. (Kunstsammlung Nordrhein-Westfalen, Dusseldorf)

trappings and symbols, which were adopted from ancient Rome.

Fascism clashed head-on with Christianity both in spirit and in deeds. Nevertheless, Mussolini realized the advantage of coming to terms with the powerful Catholic church and made a treaty with Pope Pius XI—the Lateran Treaty of 1929. The pope recognized Mussolini's regime. [Since the pope had been despoiled of his territories (1860–1870), he had refused to recognize the Italian government.] In return, Mussolini paid him nearly $100 million in cash and government bonds from a hard-pressed national treasury and allowed the teaching of religion by Catholic clergy in the public schools. This seeming accord, however, was uneasy and quarrelsome from the start.

The building of a powerful army and navy and the recovery of Italy's national prestige were always uppermost in Mussolini's thoughts. Fascist Italy's militarism, self-assertiveness, and expansive ambitions played an important part in the

breakdown of the peace settlement and the return to war. But before we examine these activities, we must examine the rise of fascism in Germany and authoritarianism elsewhere, all of which contributed to the outbreak of World War II.

3. THE WEIMAR REPUBLIC IN GERMANY

Germany emerged from World War I defeated, humiliated, and angry. As late as July 1918 the nation had seemed to be close to victory; four months later it had been forced to surrender, hopelessly beaten. Then Germany was compelled to sign a dictated peace treaty, the terms of which it considered unjust. The Weimar Republic (so-called from the city famous for Goethe and Schiller, where its constitution was drawn up), which the Germans set up in 1919, was structured to be a model liberal democracy. Politically divided and inexperienced, it inherited the taint of defeat from World War I and had to face tremendous postwar problems (see Figure 55.2).

Almost as soon as the Social Democrats, led by Friedrich Ebert, came to power, they were challenged, first by an uprising of radical Marxists (Spartacists), then by right-wing nationalists (under Wolfgang Kapp). Both of these challenges were met, but then economic problems threatened the new government. In the early 1920s inflation grew at an alarming rate. In January 1923, after the German government chose to default on its first payment of the huge reparations bill, French and Belgian troops occupied the Ruhr Valley, Germany's richest industrial area. The Germans fought back sullenly with passive resistance. The French countered by trying to stir up a secession movement from Germany in the Rhineland. Bloodshed between the occupying troops and the civilian population was frequent. Although the occupying forces were unable to collect any reparations, Germany's economy was paralyzed and a wild inflation swept the country. Thus more seeds of bitterness were sown.

In August 1923, Gustav Stresemann became head of the German government and offered conciliation. An international commission headed by Charles G. Dawes of the United States drew up a plan for the withdrawal of the occupying forces, for an international loan to Germany, and for the orderly payment of Germany's reparations installments. The German economy quickly recovered. From 1924 to 1929 Germany was the most prosperous nation in Europe and made its reparations payments as scheduled, mostly with loans from the United States. Under Stresemann's leadership Germany sought a *rapprochement* with its former enemies. In 1925 it signed the Treaty of Locarno with France, Great Britain, Italy, and Belgium, guaranteeing Germany's existing frontiers with France and Belgium. In 1926 Germany was admitted to the League of Nations, and Stresemann was elected president of the League. However, at home power was slipping from the moderate political parties toward the extremes, reflecting Germany's underlying economic and social maladjustments. One of the growing extremes was National Socialism, organized and led by Adolf Hitler.

4. THE RISE OF HITLER AND NATIONAL SOCIALISM

Adolf Hitler was the son of a middle-aged Austrian customs official and a young, sensitive, unhappily married mother. Of an artistic temperament, he went off to Vienna at an early age to seek an artist's career. Denied admission to the art academies for lack of training and too proud to work as a laborer, he lived for years in poverty and sometimes in squalor. He fed his ego with German master-race theories and filled his heart with hatred of the Jews. At the outbreak of World War I Hitler was in Munich, Germany, eking out a living at crude art work such as making posters. The ardent young German nationalist threw himself eagerly into the war, which he considered to be a righteous crusade for the beloved fatherland. Attaining the rank of corporal, he got his first taste for command. The experience of war—the sense of mission and unified struggle—would stay with Hitler and prove to be a source of appeal to many in future years. When the war ended, he was in a hospital, a victim of poison gas.

After the war Hitler frequented beer cellars, haranguing demobilized and unemployed troops and organizing them into violent political action groups. He soon discovered his magnetic powers of oratory and of leadership. The disgruntled and the disenchanted, particularly the frustrated university students and demobilized lesser army officers, began attaching themselves to Hitler in increasing numbers. He organized them into the National Socialist (Nazi) party. Among his most important early followers were Hermann Goering, who became second in command; Rudolph Hess, who became head of the political section of the party; and Paul Joseph Goebbels, who became the chief Nazi propagandist. As early as 1923 Hitler, in league with the popular war hero Field Marshal Ludendorff, made his first grab for power (the famous Beer Hall Putsch). It was premature, however, and Hitler was jailed for nearly a year. While in jail he wrote *Mein Kampf (My Struggle)*, which became the Nazi bible.

National Socialism, as outlined in *Mein Kampf*, was the German brand of fascism. In fact, the Nazis were heavily indebted to Mussolini for both ideology and methodology. At the center of its basic philosophy is the German master-race concept. The old Nordic myth of Gobineau and Chamberlain was revived. The terms *German, Nordic,* and *Aryan* were used interchangeably without regard to scientific fact. It was held that the Germans, the only pure representatives of the tall, blond Nordic "race," are superior to and destined to conquer and rule all other peoples. Militarism, indomitable will, pride, aggressiveness, and brute strength were held to be virtues; gentleness, peacefulness, tolerance, pity, and modesty, vices.

As a specific program of action, National Socialism was primarily concerned with foreign affairs. It called for repudiation of the Treaty of Versailles; all-out rearmament; the recovery of all territories, including colonies, lost at the end of World War I; and the annexation of all neighboring German-speaking territories such as Austria, the Netherlands, and most of Switzerland. Then the master race must have *Lebensraum* (living space), which was to be obtained by driving to the east (*Drang nach Osten*), particularly by conquering and enslaving the Soviet Union. There is little doubt that in the Nazi mind world domination was the ultimate goal.

The domestic program was vague and contradictory. Trusts and department stores were to be nationalized. Unearned income was to be abolished. Communism was to be destroyed and labor unions rigidly controlled. Finally, persecution of the Jews was part of the Nazi program. Over time, persecution escalated from legal discrimination, to economic exploitation, to violence, and finally, to literal extermination. The capitalistic classes never took the socialistic aspects of Hitler's program seriously. As in Italy, they looked to the Fascists to provide strong government, protect property, and control the working classes.

Hitler copied many of Mussolini's techniques. The rank and file of Nazi party members, wearing brown shirts, were organized along military lines as storm troopers. They marched, sang, and intimidated and beat up the opposition. An elite corps of black-shirted "SS" troops supervised and policed the brown shirts. Pagan symbolism, such as the swastika, was adopted. All party members swore unquestioning and undying allegiance to Hitler.

5. THE TRIUMPH OF HITLER

At first National Socialism grew slowly but steadily. National Socialism appealed particularly to youth, to displaced veterans, and to people from many classes who felt insecure and threatened by change. It promised much, seemed to provide membership in a movement with a clear cause and direction, and offered simple solutions to difficult problems. From 1925 to 1929, when Germany under Stresemann's leadership was the most prosperous nation in Europe and was being wooed by her former enemies, Nazi party membership grew from 27,000 to 178,000.

After the Great Depression of 1929, which struck Germany along with the rest of the capitalistic world, the Nazis gained rapidly. In the parliamentary elections of 1930 they obtained several million votes and increased their seats in the Reichstag from 12 to 107. They appealed to a broad spectrum of disaffected workers, members of the middle and lower middle classes, veterans, and particularly the young. They were now strong enough to disrupt the orderly functioning of parliamentary government, and President Hindenburg resorted to ruling by presidential decree. In the presidential election of 1932 Hitler ran as the Nazi candidate. The moderate and liberal parties, which in 1925 had feared and opposed Hindenburg, now persuaded him to run again as the only man who could stop Hitler (Hindenburg was now eighty-five years old). Hitler got enough votes to force a runoff election against the popular and venerable idol. In the runoff election Hindenburg was elected, but Hitler received more than 13 million votes. In parliamentary elections a few months later, the Nazis obtained 230 out of 608 seats in the Reichstag, the largest number ever held by any party under the Weimar Republic. Hindenburg now offered to make Hitler vice-chancellor, but Hitler, sensing complete dictatorship in the offing, refused.

Meanwhile, the Nazis, under Hitler's instructions, paralyzed Germany's political life with terror. When chaos threatened to play into the hands of the Communists, in January 1933, Hindenburg offered and Hitler accepted the chancellorship. Franz von Papen, head of the militaristic Nationalist party, was made vice-chancellor. It was the

FIGURE 55.3. Adolf Hitler at Buckeberg Walking between two lines of Nazi banners, Adolf Hitler makes a carefully staged, dramatic entrance to a mass meeting at Buckeberg, Germany, in 1934. (Heinrich Hoffman, *Life Magazine* © 1945 Time, Inc.)

great industrialists who finally gave the Nazis the necessary support to come to power. Hitler, determined to have nothing less than complete dictatorship, immediately called for parliamentary elections. Now in official control of the state police and the agencies of information in addition to their own highly disciplined party machinery, the Nazis skillfully used every device of propaganda to frighten and confuse the people. Like the Fascists in Italy, they exaggerated and exploited the Communist threat. Five days before the elections, they made use of the burning of the Reichstag building, blaming the Communists. The elections themselves, however, were by secret ballot and were relatively free. The Communists polled 4.8 million

votes, the Center (Roman Catholic) party 5.5 million, the Social Democrats (workers and small-business and professional people's party) 7.2 million, the Nazis 17 million, and von Papen's Nationalists 3 million. The Nazi and the Nationalist vote combined gave Hitler 52 percent of the seats in the Reichstag. A few days later, Hitler, wearing his Nazi party uniform, appeared before the newly elected Reichstag, from which the Communists were excluded, and demanded dictatorial powers for four years. They were granted with only 94 opposing (Social Democratic) votes. Long before the four years had expired, the moderate parties had been destroyed, and the Nazi dictatorship was complete (see Figure 55.3).

WHERE HISTORIANS DISAGREE

What Caused Nazism?

The rise of nazism in Germany was so dramatic and of such consequence that it demands explanation. Yet perhaps no other development has remained more difficult to explain.

Perhaps the simplest explanation for the rise of nazism focuses on the politics of Hitler's rise in the 1920s and 1930s—that the political parties of the Weimar Republic were disorganized, that political leaders were weak, that there was so much political struggle and intrigue going on that Hitler did not even need to seize power. This interpretation stresses the political failure of the Social Democrats and Communists to unify against the Nazi threat and the political blindness of those conservatives who offered him the chancellorship (even though they opposed him, believing that they could gain power themselves while controlling Hitler).

The economic interpretation, favored by many Marxists, holds that nazism was a logical consequence of the last, monopoly stage of capitalism—that large landowners and industrialists resorted to nazism in a period of economic crisis in order to prevent the collapse of capitalism and the spread of socialism. This interpretation stresses the growing strength of the Communist party and the restlessness of the working class. Thus Germany's real power holders tried to use Hitler and his nazism to control the threatening masses and maintain the endangered economic system that served the Junkers and industrialists.

A third interpretation holds that nazism was a logical continuation of German history itself. It stresses that the German people had long displayed tendencies favoring the authoritarianism, militarism, and racism that came to characterize nazism. This interpretation argues that in retrospect it is no surprise that Prussia had always been militaristic, that the liberal revolutions of 1848 failed in Germany, that Bismarck united the nation by blood and iron, that leading philosophers of racism were German, and that the democratic Weimar Republic was never very popular or effective.

More recently, psychosocial interpretations have been proposed to explain the rise of nazism in Germany. According to these interpretations, nazism both reflected and responded to the desires of certain large groups of Germans—people traumatized by the war such as the veterans and the young who suffered hunger and loss of their fathers, people disoriented by the political and economic upheavals immediately following the war, and people weakened and immobilized by the Great Depression. Nazism seemed to promise a sense of direction, action, purpose, power, and pride to these people.

An underlying controversy among historians is whether nazism should be viewed as an aberration of Western history. Many historians stress that nazism should be viewed as limited in time and place, that it was an unlikely product of circumstances. They stress the extraordinary character and role of Hitler, the peculiar circumstances of Germany after World War I, and the extreme qualities of nazism.

Others argue that there were many points of continuity between nazism and Western history. They stress the growth of fascism and totalitarianism in the West, the widespread nationalism and racism, and the general appeal of authoritarian practices in times of war or socioeconomic crises.

These and other interpretations are evolving as historians gain distance from the 1920s, 1930s, and 1940s. The topic remains controversial, and the debate over the causes of nazism are likely to continue for some time.

6. NAZI GERMANY

The Reichstag, having voted Hitler dictatorial powers, adjourned, to meet henceforth only on the call of the *Führer* (leader) for the purpose of voting approval of his acts. Hitler disbanded all political parties except the National Socialist party. Freedom of speech, press, and assembly was abolished. An elaborate and all-powerful secret police, the Gestapo, was established under the direction of Heinrich Himmler to spy out and destroy opposition. Hitler's most intense hatred was vented on the Jews, who were subjected to every conceivable humiliation. As fast as their services could be dispensed with, they were driven out of public and professional life. Eventually, the Nazis embarked on a program to exterminate all the Jews under their control. It is estimated that by the end of World War II the Nazis had murdered 6 million Jews out of a world total of 15 million.

The control and molding of thought always held high priority in Nazi activities. Indeed, this control appears to be an absolute necessity for any totalitarian dictatorship. Under the direction of Goebbels, minister of propaganda, the German press and radio spewed forth a constant stream of false or distorted information. To read or listen to foreign newspapers or broadcasts was made a crime. An incessant hate campaign was waged against the liberal democratic world. The schools were, of course, nazified. Only Nazi party members could be school administrators. Unsympathetic teachers were dismissed and punished. Members of Nazi youth organizations were set to spy on their teachers and parents. Textbooks were rewritten to conform to German master-race theories. The burning of liberal books, sometimes even those of Germany's greatest literary figures, such as Goethe and Schiller, became a national fad. The Nazi minister of education admitted that the sole function of education was the creation of Nazis. Hitler wrote in *Mein Kampf* that the German youth's "entire education and development has to be directed at giving him the conviction of being absolutely superior to the others . . . the belief in the invincibility of his entire nationality." The arts were nazified and only party members or sympathizers were permitted to publish, exhibit, or perform.

Since National Socialism was essentially an anti-Christian ideology, the Nazis realized the necessity of controlling the religious establishment. Much of the Lutheran church, which was the official state church and included more than half the German people in its membership, was brought under Nazi domination. Nazi officials attempted to turn it into a propaganda agency. The few Lutheran pastors, like Martin Niemöller, who resisted were thrown into concentration camps. The smaller Protestant denominations met the same fate. Hitler found it much more difficult to deal with the Catholic church, whose higher authority lay outside Germany. Although he soon signed a concordat with the pope, the terms proved to be unworkable. Catholic clergy, churches, and schools were subjected to constantly increasing pressures, indignities, and physical abuse.

The Nazis rejuvenated and regimented Germany's economic life. The property and the profits of the capitalistic classes were given special consideration. Labor unions were brought under Nazi control, and a system of enforced arbitration of disputes between labor and management was set up along the lines that Mussolini had established in Italy. Strikes and lockouts were forbidden. The entire German economy was forced into the overall pattern and policies of the Nazi government. The vast rearmament program gave employment to millions. Superhighways, airfields, hospitals, and apartment houses were built all over Germany. The most intricate financial trickery was resorted to, but the Nazis expected eventually to finance their huge undertakings out of the spoils of victorious war.

All other activities were subordinated to the prime purpose of making a military comeback. Shortly after assuming power, Hitler took Germany out of the League of Nations and out of the disarmament conference that was in progress in Geneva. Rearmament was pushed as rapidly as possible, and in 1935 Hitler openly repudiated the disarmament clauses of the Treaty of Versailles. In 1936 Hitler remilitarized the Rhineland and sent decisive aid to General Franco's Fascist rebels in Spain (see Chapter 56). The following year he made an alliance with Italy and Japan. This Berlin-Rome-Tokyo Axis was aimed specifically at the Soviet Union. More broadly, it was an aggressive antiliberal alliance for military expansion. Meanwhile, other events taking place elsewhere in Europe also threw liberal democracy into retreat.

7. AUTHORITARIAN REGIMES IN EASTERN AND SOUTHERN EUROPE

Beginning in the 1920s hopes for permanently establishing parliamentary regimes in eastern and southern Europe were dashed by the rise of right-wing authoritarian governments. Some of them had elements of Fascist ideology and policy, but most were dictatorships by royal or military figures and individuals backed by the military and conservative powers of the nation.

The rise of right-wing authoritarian regimes in eastern and southeastern Europe was initiated in Hungary under the regency of Admiral Miklós Horthy and the rule of Count Stephen Bethlen during the 1920s and General Julius Gömbös during the 1930s. In 1926 General Josef Pilsudaski set up a military dictatorship in Poland. In 1929 a royal dictatorship was established in Yugoslavia under King Alexander I; after his assassination in 1934 an authoritarian regime was set up under the regent Prince Paul. During the 1930s royal dictatorships were established in Rumania and Bulgaria. After 1934 Austria succumbed to authoritarian rule under Engelbert Dollfuss and then Kurt von Schuschnigg until its annexation by Hitler in 1938. In 1936 Greece's shaky parliamentary regime fell to the dictatorship of General Joannes Metaxas. Czechoslovakia was an exception. There parliamentary democracy survived until the nation fell to Hitler in 1938.

The Iberian peninsula, a scene of considerable turmoil, was an area where fascism became attractive to many. In Portugal authoritarianism and political instability was the rule rather than the exception during the 1920s and eventually led to the establishment of a strong dictatorship under Antonio de Oliveira Salazar in 1932. In Spain General Miguel Primo de Rivera ruled as de facto dictator between 1923 and 1930. After a democratic interlude between 1930 and 1936, the rise of the Fascist Falange and the revolt of Spanish generals led to a civil war and the triumph of General Francisco Franco as dictator in 1939.

Almost all these authoritarian regimes emphasized nationalism and militarism. They were bolstered by a fundamental fear of change, particularly the kind of change liberal democracy and socialism represented. Many regimes provided fertile grounds for the growth of Fascist organizations and the enactment of Fascist policies, but with the possible exception of Franco's Spain, these governments were not Fascist in the same sense as Italy under Mussolini and Germany under Hitler. This description of Europe's authoritarian regimes also describes Japan's government during the 1930s, which would become one of the Axis powers in 1937.

8. THE TRIUMPH OF AUTHORITARIANISM IN JAPAN

We have already observed (see p. 621) Japan's remarkable modernization and emergence as a great power between 1853 and 1914. Japan participated in World War I on the side of the Allies and received Germany's island possessions in the Pacific north of the equator as a reward. Japan in the early 1920s stood at the crossroads. It could use its great energies and skills either to develop Japanese institutions and raise the standard of living or to become a predatory military state.

Three divergent groups competed for the leadership of postwar Japan. The dominant group was made up of the great industrialists. Seventy-five percent of Japan's industry and capital was concentrated in the hands of five great families, called the *zaibatsu*. This handful of industrial giants had such a stranglehold on the Japanese economy that it was also able to control the highly restricted government. The *zaibatsu*, enjoying this economic and political monopoly, wished to see no fundamental change in Japan's undemocratic society; it advocated instead the peaceful economic penetration of Asia.

The liberals constituted the second group. This faction, with university professors and students providing much of the leadership, set out to broaden the suffrage, which was restricted to the well-to-do, to encourage the more effective unionization of labor, and to diminish the power of the military. Because of the political inexperience and

FIGURE 55.4. Japan Invades China Here Japanese soldiers are celebrating victory after a new assault on China in 1937. This photograph, showing armed Japanese troops on Chinese soil under the Japanese flag, symbolizes key elements of Japanese policy during the 1930s: nationalism, militarism, and expansionism. (Ullstein Bilderdienst, West Berlin)

the long tradition of passive submission to authority on the part of the Japanese masses, these were difficult undertakings. They were made more difficult by the activities of Marxists, who confused liberal reform movements and tainted them with the suspicion of treason. Nevertheless, Japan made encouraging progress toward liberal democracy. In 1925 the suffrage was broadened. Soon afterward, two liberal political parties appeared. The military budget was reduced. The prestige of the professional military declined to such an extent that many officers ceased wearing their uniforms in public.

The professional military, however, was determined to strengthen and exploit its own traditional power. In the late 1920s a group of restless and ambitious young army officers began to accuse their leaders of softness and plotted to seize control of both the armed forces and the government. When a coup planned for early 1931 was exposed and blocked, the conspirators decided on a bold move to throw the country into such hysteria and confusion that they could seize power. In October 1931 the Japanese army stationed in Manchuria made an unauthorized attack on the Chinese forces and began the conquest of all Manchuria. The next year Japanese forces attacked Shanghai, the chief port of China (see Figure 55.4). Once fighting with huge and potentially dangerous China began, war fever and patriotic hysteria swept Japan, just as the army plotters had foreseen. They now assassinated the premier and numerous other government officials and civilian leaders and cowed the rest into submission. Once in control, the military immediately turned to the destruction of the liberals. Liberal university professors were accused of disloyalty and silenced, dismissed, or imprisoned. The schools and the press and radio were made organs of propaganda. All democratic processes of government and civil

rights were destroyed. The military and state police were given unlimited authority. The *zaibatsu* were corrupted and won over with lush military contracts.

Meanwhile, Japanese overran all Manchuria, which was made into a puppet state of Manchukuo. When the League of Nations declared Japan an aggressor and ordered its withdrawal from Manchuria, Japan defied the League and instead withdrew from the organization. In 1937 Japan joined the Berlin-Rome Axis. In the same year Japan began an all-out assault on China proper. By 1937, therefore, the Axis powers were on the march.

SUGGESTED READING

Totalitarianism, Fascism, and Authoritarianism

H. Arendt, *The Origins of Totalitarianism* (1951). A brilliant but difficult analysis.

F. L. Carsten, *The Rise of Fascism* (1982). Good, scholarly analysis.

E. Nolte, *The Three Faces of Fascism* (1963). A respected but difficult intellectual history of fascism in Italy, Germany, and France.

H. Rogger and E. Weber, *The European Right: A Historical Profile* (1965). Compares the rise of right-wing politics in various countries.

H. A. Turner, Jr., ed., *Reappraisals of Fascism* (1975). A good collection of articles.

Mussolini and Italian Fascism

A. Lyttleton, *The Seizure of Power: Fascism in Italy, 1919–1929* (1973). Excellent analysis of the rise of fascism in Italy.

D. M. Smith, *Mussolini's Roman Empire* (1976). Solid, informative account of Mussolini's rule.

E. R. Tannenbaum, *The Fascist Experience: Italian Society and Culture, 1922–1945* (1972). Fine examination of life in Fascist Italy.

The Weimar Republic

E. Eyck, *A History of the Weimar Republic*, 2 vols. (1963). Comprehensive.

P. Gay, *Weimar Culture: The Outsider as Insider* (1968). Excellent examination of Weimar Germany.

Hitler and Nazi Germany

K. D. Bracher, *The German Dictatorship* (1970). Excellent study of the Nazi state.

A. Bullock, *Hitler: A Study in Tyranny* (1971). Classic biography of Hitler.

D. Schoenbaum, *Hitler's Social Revolution: Class and Status in Nazi Germany, 1933–1939* (1966). Good study of social policies and social life in Germany.

J. Stephenson, *The Nazi Organization of Women* (1980). Useful study of women in Nazi Germany.

Authoritarian Regimes in Eastern and Southern Europe

C. A. Macartney and A. W. Palmer, *Independent Eastern Europe: A History* (1967). Good survey.

J. Rothschild, *East Central Europe Between the Two World Wars* (1973). Useful general account.

The Triumph of Authoritarianism in Japan

R. Benedict, *The Chrysanthemum and the Sword* (1967). Examines the role of the professional military in Japan.

E. O. Reischauer, *The Japanese* (1977). A highly respected survey.

CHAPTER 56

Paralysis of the Democratic West

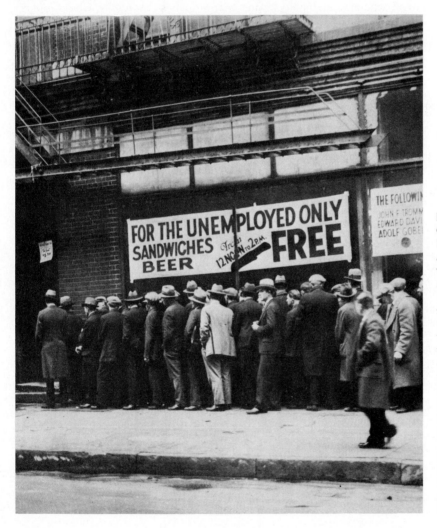

FIGURE 56.1. **The Great Depression in New York** Jobless and homeless men wait in line for a free meal in New York in 1930. These Depression breadlines are part of the reason for the seeming impotence of the democratic nations in the face of the growing Fascist menace. The Great Depression, which began in 1929, did not end unitl 1942, when World War II pumped billions of dollars into the American economy. (UPI/Bettmann Newsphotos)

The Western democracies emerged from World War I victorious. In many ways, each hoped to return to how things had been before the war, to quickly get back to "normal." But instead of the hoped-for smooth sailing, the Western democracies were faced with a series of challenges in the two decades following the war.

1. CHALLENGES OF THE 1920s AND 1930s

The first challenge was the immediate problem of postwar dislocation and recovery. The human, material, and economic losses were unprecedented and unequally borne—France and Belgium suffered most among the Western democracies. Soldiers had to be reintegrated into civilian life, economies had to be shifted from wartime production, and trade patterns had to be reestablished.

The second challenge was the roller-coaster ride of tension, optimism, and disillusionment that characterized international affairs in the 1920s and 1930s. The Treaty of Versailles left few happy and many resentful. The payment of reparations and wartime debts threatened the international order during the years immediately following the war. Then from 1925 to 1929, a period known as the Locarno Era, international tensions diminished and progress was made toward peace and disarmament. The Locarno Pact in 1925 (guaranteeing international boundaries in Europe), the admission of Germany to the League of Nations in 1926, the Kellogg-Briand Pact of 1928 (proclaiming a commitment to international friendship), and the earlier Washington Conference of 1921–1922 (limiting naval strength) seemed to establish a basis for optimism in international affairs. After 1930, however, this optimism gave way to disillusionment as discord, rearmament, and aggression marked international affairs.

The third challenge was the Great Depression. Economic depressions were not new to the West, but one of this magnitude and duration was unprecedented. In October 1929 the American stock market, bloated by speculation and borrowed money, crashed. Since the end of World War I, the international economic order had become dependent on the United States—particularly to keep up the flow of loans, debt payments, and trade. The financial crisis in America quickly spread to Europe. Stocks lost their value, banks failed, and confidence collapsed. This sudden financial crisis reflected the fragility of the postwar economic order, and between 1929 and 1933 economies almost everywhere were in a tailspin. World industrial production fell by more than 33 percent. Unemployment grew to massive proportions. Policies adopted to deal with the crisis probably made things worse—trade barriers rather than cooperation typified international economic policy, and cuts in spending instead of deficit spending marked domestic economic policy. Some countries started to recover after 1933, but in other cases the Great Depression extended until World War II.

The final challenge was the threat from the political extremes—communism on the left, fascism on the right. The most obvious threats were international, since communism was growing stronger in the Soviet Union and fascism was spreading in central and southern Europe. But the threats were internal as well, for both Communist and Fascist political organizations were growing within Western democracies—particularly during the 1930s.

The political and social development of each of the Western democracies greatly depended on how they met these four challenges. In retrospect it is easy to be harsh on the leaders of these societies, for in the end the world was immersed in another war even more destructive than World War I. However, these challenges were extraordinary and the leaders trying to deal with them often labored under overwhelming difficulties.

2. THE HARASSED BRITISH EMPIRE

At the end of World War I the British Empire still included one-fourth of all the land and people on the globe. Nevertheless, the British economy, empire, and world position were shaken beyond recovery. Britain's far-flung possessions in Asia and Africa were beginning to stir restlessly, as the spirit of nationalism, which long had provided the European world with so much of its expansive energy, spread eastward. Great Britain found it advisable to grant freedom to its already self-governing dominions, hoping to retain their loyalty. The Statute of Westminster in 1931 gave complete independence and equality with the mother country to Canada, Australia, New Zealand, the Union of South Africa, Newfoundland, and the Irish Free State (free since 1922). Great Britain could no longer count on their material support in world policies, nor could it count on its restless colonies. Furthermore, Britain was now clearly second to the United States as an industrial and financial power. (It would require many years, however, for the British to readjust their thinking to the reality of their country's reduced position.)

At home, postwar Britain was harassed with acute economic problems. National debt had quintupled during the war. Britain owed the United States a heavy war debt. German submarines had taken a toll of 9 million tons of British ships with their cargoes. British exports met sharply increased competition in the world markets, particularly from the United States. Rising protective tariffs all over the world hindered its commerce. Mines and industrial plants were antiquated and in disrepair. Returning servicemen found few jobs. Unemployment hovered around 3 million, a figure that came to be accepted as normal. Government support for the unemployed, sick, aged, and destitute increased Britain's financial problems.

These chronic economic ills were reflected in Great Britain's troubled postwar policies. In 1922 the Conservatives broke up Lloyd George's wartime coalition government of Liberals and Conservatives and won the ensuing parliamentary elections. They sought to restore classical nineteenth-century capitalism by means of rigid entrenchment of government spending, particularly for social services. This policy was so hard on the distressed masses that in 1924 a Labour-Liberal coalition headed by the Labour party leader, Ramsay MacDonald, ousted the Conservatives. The Labour party was now stronger than the Liberal party, and as times grew harder and feelings more bitter, the once great Liberal party was virtually crushed between the more extreme parties—Labour on the left and Conservative on the right.

But the majority of the British people were not yet ready to accept the mildly socialistic program that the Labour party advocated. MacDonald's ministry lasted less than a year. Dependent on the Liberals for his majority, he was forced to follow a moderate course. When he recognized the Soviet Union and made a commercial treaty with it, the Conservatives were able to capitalize on public suspicion and drive him from power. From 1925 to 1929 the Conservatives wrestled with rising discontent, strikes, and the steady growth of the Labour party. In 1929 a Labour victory, supported by the much dwindled Liberals, again brought Ramsay MacDonald to the head of the government. His moderation in the face of the deepening economic depression, however, caused the majority of his Labour followers to repudiate him two years later. But MacDonald was unwilling to give up the honors of office. In 1931 he therefore formed a national coalition of right-wing Labourites, Liberals, and Conservatives to deal with the mounting domestic and foreign crises. This national coalition was dominated by the Conservatives and MacDonald was really a captive of the Conservatives until he resigned in 1935. The Conservative-dominated coalition ruled Great Britain until the end of World War II. Although Great Britain was recovering from the Great Depression, the government was on the whole ineffective in dealing with social maladjustments at home and Fascist aggressions abroad. The Conservative prime ministers Stanley Baldwin and Neville Chamberlain, who followed Ramsay MacDonald as head of the national government, were unimaginative and unprepared for the challenges that would face them.

3. FRUSTRATED FRANCE

Although France enjoyed the advantage of being economically more self-sufficient than Great Britain, France had suffered greater wounds in World War I than had its island neighbor. Most of the· fighting had taken place on French soil. A tenth—the most productive tenth—of its land area had been devastated. The retreating Germans had lain waste much of what had not been destroyed in battle. Orchards were chopped down, and mines were wrecked, many beyond repair. Even more tragic was the loss of life. France, with the lowest birth rate of any major nation in the world, suffered by far the heaviest casualties per capita of any of the combatants. Out of a population of less than 40 million, it suffered almost 1.4 million battle deaths and 1.7 million wounded. The civilian death rate from direct and indirect causes had also been high. France had fewer people in 1918 than in 1914, even after the return of Alsace and Lorraine.

Postwar France was confronted with a staggering job of economic reconstruction and an equally staggering war debt. To meet these obligations and to finance the reconstruction, the French government counted on German reparations, but little was forthcoming. Inflation became a chronic headache. A more basic and long-range problem was French industry, which was rapidly falling behind its competitors. The highly individualistic French had not gone in for large-scale corporate industry to the same extent as the Americans, British, and Germans. The little French family industries had difficulty competing with mass production. A like situation prevailed in French agriculture, most of which occurred on thousands of little family farms too tiny to use machinery profitably. Industrial and agricultural production per worker was lower in France than in most other major Western nations.

Considering the serious plight of France's postwar economy and the habitual disorderliness with which its multiparty democracy traditionally functioned, one is impressed by the remarkable stability of the French government during the decade of the 1920s. From 1919 to 1924, a bloc of conservative parties was in power. It followed an antilabor, probusiness policy. It also favored the Roman Catholic church and pressed hard for collection of German reparations. Meanwhile, discontent among the laboring classes was mounting. In 1924, the year of MacDonald's first Labour ministry in Great Britain, the parties of the Left under the leadership of Edouard Herriot were victorious. Like MacDonald, Herriot pursued a prolabor policy, advocating an increase in social services, and soft money. He was also conciliatory toward Russia and Germany. But, also like MacDonald, he lasted less than a year.

From 1926 to 1929, a strong right-of-center national bloc under the leadership of Raymond Poincaré was in power. Poincaré checked the inflation by rigid retrenchment. Upon his retirement in 1929, however, the increasing pressure of discontent threw the country into political turmoil. No leader or political combination seemed to be capable of dealing with the economic crisis brought on by the world depression, the growing menace of fascism, or the unrest in the French colonies. Ministry followed ministry in rapid succession. Scandals and riots occurred, and Fascist groups appeared. In 1936 the Popular Front, consisting of left-wing parties under the leadership of the mild Socialist Léon Blum, came to power (see Figure 56.2). The Blum ministry obtained a forty-hour week and two weeks' annual vacation with pay for the workers. It also nationalized the Bank of France and the great munitions industries. This was too much for the powerful propertied interests, who drove Blum from office the following year. But the conservative parties who regained control were unable to agree upon firm policies, domestic or foreign.

Thus France, like Great Britain, in the face of resurgent Nazi Germany, swashbuckling Mussolini, and militaristic Japan, could summon little strength or unity. The propertied classes were unwilling to share their wealth or privileges or to change their nineteenth-century practices. They feared and hated Léon Blum. The Great Depression persisted and fueled political turmoil. The army was basking in past glory. Seeking to maintain the status quo, the French were defense-minded. They constructed the Maginot line fortifications along the German border and formed defensive alliances with Poland, Czechoslovakia, Yugoslavia, and Rumania. These alliances were no stronger than the faith those small countries had in France's ability to defend them, which by the late 1930s was very little.

4. ISOLATIONISM, BOOM, AND BUST IN THE UNITED STATES

The United States emerged from World War I the world's richest nation. Although its entry into the war at its most critical phase was probably decisive in determining the outcome, the United States suffered far less war damage than any of the other major participants. President Wilson assumed a

FIGURE 56.2.   The Popular Front   In 1935 Socialists, Communists, and others on the French Left united for the first time as the Popular Front. In 1936 the Popular Front came to power under the leadership of the Socialist premier, Léon Blum. This photo shows Blum (on the left) and Maurice Thorez, secretary of the French Communist party, at a 1937 Bastille Day rally in Paris. (Photo Trends)

leading role in the making of the peace settlements and in the creation of the League of Nations.

When President Wilson returned from Paris in the summer of 1919 and sought to persuade his country to join the League of Nations, he faced a strong challenge from his political enemies, led by Henry Cabot Lodge. Wilson's opponents refused to accept the treaty, and particularly the League of Nations, as proposed by Wilson. Wilson, seeing the treaty and the League as a matter of principle, refused to compromise. In his struggle to rally support, Wilson suffered a paralytic stroke. Since he was unable thereafter to lead the fight for the treaty and was unwilling to give the leadership to others, his opponents easily defeated ratification in the Senate.

The League was not an issue in the presidential election of 1920. However, the victor, Warren G. Harding, announced that the League was now a dead issue. And during the cynical and disillu-

sioned decade of the 1920s American public opinion became overwhelmingly isolationist. When during the international crises of the 1930s the League and the harassed British and French governments sought the support of the United States against the Fascist aggressors, they sought in vain.

The decade following World War I was a period of relative but uneven prosperity in the United States. The all-out war effort brought about a great expansion of American industry and unleashed huge quantities of money and credit. In 1914 the United States had been a debtor nation. It emerged from the war a creditor to most of Europe to the amount of $10 billion, a figure that doubled during the next ten years. Its chief economic competitors came out of the war battered and shaken. Production, profits, and purchasing power reached new heights. However, it was an uneven and unsound prosperity. Agriculture was depressed with surplus commodities and low prices, which meant low purchasing power for the farm population of the South and the Middle West. Nor did wages climb as rapidly as profits and prices in the industrial Northeast. These facts, plus increasing automation, meant growing unemployment and industrial surpluses. Labor unions declined in membership and bargaining power. Foreign markets were diminished by a policy of higher and higher tariffs designed to protect American industry from foreign competition. The government's philosophy of noninterference with free enterprise (except for tariffs) permitted unlimited speculation in the soaring stock market, often with other people's money and with unrestrained use of credit.

The stock market crashed in October 1929. Values tumbled. Thousands of banks and businesses failed. Millions were thrown out of work. The economic depression spread over the entire capitalistic world. For four years the Hoover administration, confident of the essential soundness of laissez-faire economy, refused to permit large-scale government relief measures, expecting and promising that the natural economic laws would soon bring back prosperity. But the depression only deepened.

In the presidential election of 1932 the Democratic candidate, Franklin D. Roosevelt, defeated Hoover, ending twelve years of Republican rule. The Roosevelt administration immediately launched a series of sweeping economic and social reforms that came to be called the New Deal. The New Deal was not a radical, new departure but, rather, a further advance along progressive lines established by Theodore Roosevelt and Woodrow Wilson and during World War I when the government engaged in economic planning and control. First, emergency measures were taken to relieve the suffering of the 12 million unemployed and their families. The chief of these was the setting up of the huge Works Progress Administration, which provided a large number of jobs. The Wagner Act strengthened the position of the labor unions by guaranteeing the right of collective bargaining. Old-age and unemployment insurance was inaugurated. For the desperate farmers, measures were passed that granted debt relief, commodity loans, price supports, and payments for acreage reduction. Deflation was checked by a de-

valuation of the dollar. Investments and deposits were protected by strict government supervision. Steps were taken to conserve the nation's natural resources against wasteful private exploitation. Gradually, some popular confidence was restored and the nation's economy began to recover. However, economic problems persisted and full recovery was not achieved until World War II, which forced the government to finance the war with greater deficit spending.

5. THE ROAD TO WAR

Early in the 1930s international affairs started slipping out of control. The League of Nations was challenged, rearmament spread, and aggression became the order of the day. Efforts to appease the aggressors and prevent the dreaded return to total war failed. By the end of the decade a new world war had broken out.

Breakdown of the League of Nations

The only international agency that existed for the maintenance of the peace was the League of Nations, which after the defection of the United States was largely dependent on Great Britain and France for support. For twelve years the League supervised the implementation of the peace treaties, administered relief to tens of thousands of war victims, promoted international good will, and settled numerous international disputes. None of these settlements, however, involved the disciplining of a major power, and thoughtful observers dreaded the time when the League would be called on to do so.

When in 1931 Japan began the conquest of Manchuria, China appealed to the League for protection. The League appointed a commission headed by Britain's Earl of Lytton to make an on-the-spot investigation. The Lytton Commission reported that Japan was guilty of aggression, having violated its solemn obligations both as a League member and as a signatory of the Kellogg-Briand Pact of Paris (1928), which outlawed war as an instrument of national policy. Forceful League action, however, would be largely dependent upon

Great Britain and France, who were unwilling to act without American support. President Hoover, reflecting the isolationist sentiment of American public opinion, would not consent to the use of force, the threat of force, or even economic pressure by the United States. The British and French governments, harassed by their own domestic economic and political problems and the rising menace of fascism in Europe, could not bring themselves to act alone. The League, without their backing, did nothing. It had failed its first major test and was on the way out as a potent force for peace. Japan's successful defiance of the League of Nations helped convince Mussolini and Hitler that they could safely launch aggressions of their own.

The deathblow was struck by Mussolini. Late in 1935 the Italian dictator invaded Ethiopia in East Africa. Ethiopia was a member of the League and appealed to it for protection. Great Britain, concerned for its numerous interests in the Near and Middle East and for its lifeline to the Far East, now became greatly agitated. Under the leadership of Great Britain and France, the League declared Mussolini to be the aggressor and invoked economic sanctions (Article XVI) against him. A list of commodities that League members were not to sell Mussolini was drawn up. However, the list did not include oil, and it soon became obvious that this was the commodity upon which the success of his aggression depended. But it quickly became apparent that, to be effective, an embargo on oil would require the cooperation of the United States. American exports of oil to Mussolini had trebled since the beginning of his campaign against Ethiopia. When the British and French governments requested the cooperation of the United States in withholding excess oil from Mussolini, Secretary of State Cordell Hull and President Roosevelt were sympathetic but were unable to get the oil companies to comply or to get Congress to force compliance. The press and public opinion were overwhelmingly isolationist, and Congress reflected that view. Mussolini got his oil. Britain and France, unwilling to resort to the only other means of stopping him, a shooting war, gave up the League struggle. Mussolini conquered Ethiopia. The League of Nations, for all practical purposes, was dead.

Appeasement

Since the triumph of the Nazis in 1933 Germany had been preparing for a military comeback. In March 1936 Hitler ordered his armed forces into the Rhineland, which, according to the Treaty of Versailles, was to be permanently demilitarized. France, recognizing this move as the gravest threat and challenge to itself, called for Great Britain's support. The British offered none. The French fretted and fumed but in the end did nothing. Hitler had won his gamble.

Fascism's next triumph was in Spain. Until 1931, it was dominated by the landed aristocracy, a few rich capitalists, aristocratic army officers, and the Catholic church. Most people were poor, landless peasants. Since the turn of the century and particularly since 1918, the pressure of discontent had been rising. In 1931 the king yielded, restored the constitution, and granted elections. The liberal and radical groups won such a sweeping victory that the king fled the country. The reformers then proceeded to make over the Spanish nation. They drew up a democratic constitution, granted local autonomy to Catalonia (the northeastern-most section of Spain, including Barcelona), began a sweeping program of public education, started to modernize the army by placing promotions on a merit basis, granted religious freedom, seized the lands and schools of the Catholic church, and planned to break up the great estates into peasant-owned farms.

There was much violence—riots and attacks on priests, nuns, and private property. After two years the conservative propertied interests, with the vigorous support of the pope, won the elections by a narrow margin and began to undo the reforms. Early in 1936, however, the liberal and radical parties won again and resumed their drastic reform program. The privileged classes were now desperate. In July 1936 a group of generals led by General Francisco Franco launched an armed rebellion against the government. Although the Rebels enjoyed the advantage of professional military leadership, the regular army, and most of the country's wealth, they were unable to make headway against the Loyalists, who enjoyed the support of the majority of the rank and file of the people.

FIGURE 56.3. **The Munich Conference** The chief participants at the Munich Conference pose for the photographer in September 1938. Left to right: Chamberlain, Daladier, Hitler, and Mussolini. The sellout of Czechoslovakia and the Soviet Union at Munich by Chamberlain and Daladier, in an attempt to appease Hitler, destroyed any hope of maintaining a unified front in Europe against Nazi Germany. (UPI/ Bettmann Newsphotos)

The Spanish Civil War soon became a battlefield in the world struggle of fascism, liberalism, and communism. Hitler and Mussolini, seeing in it an opportunity to advance the cause of fascism, gain a like-minded ally and a strategic military position, and test their new weapons, sent abundant arms and troops to aid Franco. The Loyalists appealed to the democracies for aid but received none, although a few volunteers from the democracies fought as individuals in the Loyalist cause. The only nation that supported the Loyalists was the Soviet Union, but the amount of aid it could send was quite small and tainted the Loyalist cause with the suspicion of communism. After three years of slaughter, Franco and his German and Italian allies beat down the last organized Loyalist resistance. A dictatorship was established over Spain. Liberalism was shattered. The world prestige of Fascist Germany and Italy rose while that of the democracies declined further.

The year 1937 was the year of decision—the point of no return on the road to war. In that year the three great Fascist powers formed the Berlin-Rome-Tokyo Axis, which was aimed specifically at the Soviet Union but was in reality an alliance of these aggressor nations for expansion. In that year the military strength of the Axis powers—their war plants running day and night—forged ahead of that of the rest of the world. In that year the Nazis blueprinted their timetable of conquests, and Japan began its all-out assault on China.

Early in 1938 the Nazis' timetable began to function. In March they overran Austria without opposition, annexing the 6.5 million Austrians to the German Reich (Empire). Great Britain and France denounced this open aggression and violation of the Treaty of Versailles but did nothing.

Almost immediately Hitler turned his big propaganda guns on his next victim, Czechoslovakia. In constructing this little country out of Austro-Hungarian territory at the end of World War I, the Allied peacemakers had left 3.5 million German-speaking people on the Czech side of the border. Although these Sudeten Germans had never been a part of Germany and were separated from Germany by the Sudeten Mountain Wall, Hitler now claimed them. The Czech republic was allied with France and Russia, and in the coming war that Hitler was planning against those two countries, Czechoslovakia could be a threat to the German flank.

As early as May 1938 Hitler threatened Czechoslovakia. The Czechs, however, surprised him by rushing to their defenses. Hitler spent the next four months arousing his people to readiness for war and softening up the democracies by keeping them in a constant state of tension and alarm. This psychological warfare culminated in a giant Nazi rally at Nuremberg in mid-September. There Hitler screamed to his frenzied followers that if the Sudeten areas were not surrendered to him by October 1, he would march. With France and the Soviet Union standing firm in their alliance with Czechoslovakia, the world anxiously awaited the beginning of a major conflict that was likely to become World War II.

At this juncture, the British Prime Minister Neville Chamberlain took it upon himself to fly to Hitler's retreat at Berchtesgaden and plead for a compromise. The upshot was a conference at Munich on September 29, 1938 (see Figure 56.3). The participants were Hitler, Mussolini, Chamberlain, and Premier Edouard Daladier of France.

Chamberlain persuaded Daladier to yield to Hitler's demands for the Sudeten areas of Czechoslovakia. Czechoslovakia and the Soviet Union, France's allies, were not consulted. This was one of Hitler's greatest triumphs. By enticing Great Britain and France to abandon France's allies, Czechoslovakia and the Soviet Union, Hitler had driven a wedge between the Soviet Union and the Western democracies. The Soviet leaders never trusted the Western democracies again. Neither did many of the other countries that were watching to see where their greatest safety lay.

The Outbreak of War

Although the four participating powers at Munich had agreed to become joint protectors of what remained of Czechoslovakia, in March 1939 Hitler overran without warning the remainder of the stricken little republic. This crass act of betrayal opened the eyes even of Neville Chamberlain to the fact that Hitler could not be appeased. When Hitler threatened Poland, Great Britain and France decided to draw a line. In April 1939 they made a guarantee to Poland that they would come to its aid if it were attacked and resisted the attack. Hitler, however, was not deterred. He was demanding, among other things, the return to Germany of the Polish Corridor, which separated East Prussia from the rest of Germany, and the city of Danzig, which was governed by the League of Nations. But by now it was apparent to almost everybody that specific Nazi demands were tied to unlimited aggression. Throughout the summer of 1939 the Germans made feverish preparations for war and kept up a drumfire of vilification of Poland and the democracies. Meanwhile, both sides were bidding for the support of the Soviet Union. But after Munich, Stalin had no confidence in the integrity of the capitalistic democracies. He decided to try to make his own peace with Hitler.

On August 23, 1939, the world was stunned by the signing of a ten-year peace pact by Hitler and Stalin. In return for the Soviet Union's neutrality while Germany conquered Poland, Hitler gave Stalin a free hand to reannex the territories in eastern Europe, including eastern Poland, that Russia had lost at the end of World War I.

With the Soviet Union safely neutralized, Hitler readied the attack on Poland as quickly as possible. At the last moment the British government instructed its ambassador in Berlin to ask Hitler what concessions by Poland he would accept to refrain from war. Hitler informed the ambassador that he was not interested in concessions, that his army and his people were ready and eager for war, and that he could not disappoint them now.

The wires between Warsaw and Berlin were cut, lest the Poles make a last-minute peaceable surrender to Hitler's demands. At dawn on September 1 the Germans launched an all-out attack on Poland by land, sea, and air. Two days later Great Britain and France declared war on Germany, Hitler having ignored their ultimatum to desist. World War II had begun.

SUGGESTED READING

General

C. Kindleberger, *The World in Depression, 1929–1939* (1973). Excellent examination of the Great Depression.

R. J. Sontag, *A Broken World, 1919–1939* (1971). An excellent survey of the period.

E. Wiskeman, *Europe of the Dictators, 1919–1945* (1966). A good general examination of the period.

R. Wohl, *The Generation of 1914* (1979). A creative interpretation of the impact of World War I in the postwar years.

The Harassed British Empire

N. Branson and M. Heinemann, *Britain in the Nineteen Thirties* (1971). A social and economic perspective.

R. Graves and A. Hodge, *The Long Weekend: A Social History of Great Britain, 1918–1939* (1963). A vivid and witty picture of the British ruling classes between the wars.

J. Stevenson, *British Society 1914–1945* (1984). An important new analysis.

D. Thomson, *England in the Twentieth Century, 1914–1963* (1965). A good survey.

Frustrated France

J. Colton, *Léon Blum, Humanist in Politics* (1966). Excellent biography of Blum.

N. Greene, *From Versailles to Vichy: The Third Republic, 1919–1940* (1970). A good survey of France during the period.

Isolationism, Boom, and Bust in the United States

R. Dallek, *Franklin D. Roosevelt and American Foreign Policy, 1932–1945* (1971). Thorough and highly respected.

J. K. Galbraith, *The Great Crash, Nineteen Twenty-Nine* (1955). By a distinguished economist and lively writer.

G. Perrett, *America in the Twenties* (1982). A good general account.

The Road to War

G. A. Craig and F. Gilbert, eds., *The Diplomats, 1919–1939* (1965). Good collection of essays on international relations.

W. Neuman, *The Balance of Power in the Interwar Years, 1919–1939* (1968). A good study of international relations.

A. Rowse, *Appeasement* (1961). By a bitter eyewitness of British appeasement efforts.

H. Thomas, *The Spanish Civil War* (1961). A highly respected account.

CHAPTER 57
World War II, 1939–1945

FIGURE 57.1. A German Concentration Camp   World War II was the most destructive war in history. Of particular brutality were the genocidal programs of Nazi Germany, which resulted in scenes like this one from the Landsberg concentration camp. (AP/Wide World Photos)

To much of the disillusioned and paralyzed democratic world, the outbreak of World War II seemed the beginning of the end of liberal Western civilization. For over two years these dire fears appeared to be justified. The seemingly invincible German and Japanese military machines swept on to victory after victory. Although liberal Western civilization would survive, World War II was by far the most destructive conflict in history. It served as a capstor.e to the period of unmatched death, loss, disruption, and terror begun by World War I.

1. TWO YEARS OF AXIS TRIUMPH

Striking without official warning at dawn, September 1, 1939, the German air force caught the Polish air force on its various airfields and destroyed it on the ground. Thereafter the German *Luftwaffe*, by ravaging Polish cities and communications centers and harassing troop movements, prevented the complete mobilization of the Polish army. Meanwhile, Nazi tanks and infantry poured into Poland from the north, west, and south. The Poles cried for help from France and Great Britain. The French and the British mobilized their armies along the German West Wall fortifications, and the British fleet blockaded Germany by sea. But that was all. The mechanized might of Nazi Germany overwhelmed Poland in a matter of days.

The Soviet Union, in accordance with its agreement with Hitler, proceeded to reannex territories in Poland and eastern Europe that it had lost at the end of World War I. Estonia, Latvia, and Lithuania were absorbed politically into the Soviet Union. In October 1939, the Soviet Union demanded three strategic little strips of Finnish territory. When the Finnish government refused, the Soviet Union attacked Finland and took these territories by force. In June 1940, while Hitler was busy in western Europe, the Soviet Union demanded and procured from Rumania the return of Bessarabia.

Early in April 1940 the Germans suddenly overran Denmark and Norway. The British fleet, attempting to intercept the invasion of Norway, was beaten off with heavy losses by the German air force. Denmark and Norway provided the Na-

zis with important food, timber, and mineral resources, sea and air bases, and a safe route for vital iron ore coming from Sweden.

On May 10, 1940, the German armies assaulted Luxembourg, the Netherlands, Belgium, and France. Luxembourg offered no resistance. The Netherlands fought heroically but was overwhelmed in six days. Trusting to the Maginot line to hold along the German border, the British army and a large part of the French army moved into Belgium to support the hard-pressed Belgian forces. In a surprise move through the Ardennes forest, powerful German mechanized forces on May 14 smashed through the French defenses at Sedan and drove quickly to the English Channel, cutting off the Belgian, British, and French armies in Belgium. Again the German "blitzkrieg"—a combir .ion of highly coordinated air strikes and rapid deployment of tanks and motorized columns—proved overwhelming. Although some 300,000 British and a few French troops escaped by sea from Dunkirk, all the Belgian troops, the bulk of the French troops together with their weapons and supplies, and the British weapons and supplies were captured.

Only five more days of fighting, June 5–10, were required for the Germans to crush the remaining organized French resistance and turn the French retreat into a disorderly rout. On June 10 Paris was declared an open city (see Figure 57.2). And on that day Mussolini, thinking it safe, declared war on France and Great Britain. On June 16 Marshal Philippe Pétain became premier of France and the following day dispatched a surrender team to Hitler. On June 25 the "fighting" ceased. The collapse of the French military machine after five days of fighting was a colossal military debacle. Hitler forced a harsh treaty on the helpless French. The northern half of France and all the Atlantic coastal area were placed under German occupation. The unoccupied portion was compelled to disarm and cooperate with Germany. Some 2 million French prisoners were held as hostages to ensure French good behavior. In unoccupied France, Marshal Pétain and Pierre Laval set up a semi-Fascist regime, with headquarters at Vichy, and undertook to cooperate with Hitler.

Not all of the French accepted defeat. Many resisted the German army of occupation coura-

FIGURE 57.2. Hitler at Eiffel Tower, Paris, June 1940   The first year of World War II was marked by a series of stunning German victories. In June 1940, Hitler was in Paris. The Eiffel Tower, a symbol of French independence and power, is behind him. (Brown Brothers)

geously throughout the war, suffering heavy casualties in so doing. General Charles de Gaulle, having unsuccessfully attempted to warn his superiors of the unreadiness of the French army, escaped to Great Britain and declared himself leader of the Free French. With energy and skill he strove to rally the French both inside and outside the homeland to resist the Germans and the Vichy collaborators and to restore the dignity and honor of France.

The collapse of France left Great Britain to face the German fury alone. Hitler now demanded that Britain surrender or suffer annihilation. The situation was desperate. Nearly all Britain's land ar-

maments had been lost at Dunkirk. Against the nearly one hundred fifty battle-tried Nazi divisions, Britain had only one fully equipped division. And although Great Britain did have the English Channel and the world's greatest navy, the fighting around Norway had demonstrated that navies could no longer control narrow waters dominated by a hostile air force. Britain's chief weapon of defense was its relatively small but efficient air force. Not the least of its assets was Winston Churchill, who on May 10, 1940, had at last replaced Neville Chamberlain as prime minister. The dynamic and eloquent Churchill defied Hitler. "We shall fight on the beaches; we shall fight on the landing grounds; we shall fight in the fields and in the streets; we shall fight in the hills; we shall never surrender.''

Throughout the month of July 1940 Nazi invasion forces gathered along the French coast opposite Britain, twenty-four miles away. To make the crossing, however, absolute control of the air over the Channel was required. Early in August, therefore, swarms of German bombers and fighter escorts flew over the Channel, seeking to destroy the British air force and its landing fields. In the ensuing air battles, the British pilots in their swift Spitfires and heavily armed and manueverable Hurricanes knocked down German planes at the ratio of two or three to one. Nevertheless, by the end of August the British air forces were facing annihilation by sheer weight of numbers. At this critical juncture the Nazis suddenly shifted to massive daylight attacks on London, the world's largest city. The destruction and the suffering were immense, but the British defenses were improving, thanks to the use of radar, the total mobilization of the economy, the breaking of the German secret code (project Ultra), and the high morale of the people. The loss of German planes was so great that early in October the Nazis once more shifted their tactics to night attacks, which were more terrifying but less effective. Although the destructive air raids on Great Britain's cities, together with the even more menacing submarine attacks on British shipping, continued until the end of the war, the immediate threat of invasion had now passed (a winter crossing of the Channel would be too risky); the Battle of Britain had been won.

While the Battle of Britain was at its height, Mussolini set in operation his grandiose schemes for conquering an empire. Upon entering the war in June 1940 he had closed the Mediterranean to British shipping. In September his armies moved on Egypt and the Suez Canal from Libya to the west and from Ethiopia to the south. In October his armies attacked Greece from Albania. To meet this threat, Churchill made a daring and farsighted military move. Believing Suez to be the most strategic spot in the world in a global war, he sent half of Britain's scarce supply of tanks and artillery around Africa to Egypt while the Nazis stood poised across the Channel for the invasion of Great Britain. Mussolini's forces met everywhere. The Greeks defeated them and them back into Albania. A squadron of B torpedo planes delivered a lethal blow to the ian fleet at its base in southern Italy. During th winter of 1940–1941, the Fascist armies moving on Egypt were completely destroyed by light, mobile British forces; Mussolini's bubble had burst with a feeble plop; henceforth he was hardly more than a prisoner of the German forces that were sent to save him.

When in October 1940 it became evident that Great Britain could not be invaded that year, Hitler ordered his planners to complete blueprints for the earliest possible invasion of the Soviet Union. The conquest of the Soviet Union had always been uppermost in Hitler's thoughts, but he had hoped first to dispose of the French and British threat to his rear. The plans called for an assault date not later than May 15, 1941. But first the Balkan flank was to be secured. Hungary and Rumania yielded to Hitler's threats and joined the Axis Alliance in November 1940, Bulgaria, in March 1941. Immediately, Nazi forces poured into those countries. Yugoslavia and Greece, however, refused to yield, and the Germans attacked them in April 1941. Yugoslavia was overrun in eleven days, Greece in three weeks. British forces that Churchill had dispatched to Greece were driven out of the peninsula and also off the island of Crete. Suez now appeared to be doomed. It was open to attack from the north; to the west Germany's Afrika Korps, which had been sent to replace the defeated Italians, had driven the British back to the border of Egypt; pro-Nazi movements had broken out in Iraq, Iran, and French Syria. At this point, however, Hitler hurled his main forces against the Soviet Union, giving the British a breathing spell to recoup their strength in the Near and Middle East.

On June 22, 1941, the Germans launched against the Soviet Union the most massive assault in history. They were joined by the Hungarians, the Rumanians, and the Finns. Although Stalin was able to throw an equal number of divisions against the invaders, his troops were not so well trained or equipped. Hitler expected to crush Soviet resistance in six weeks; the top British and American military leaders were of the same opinion. The Russians fought with unexpected skill

the Nazi war machine
...til by December 1 it was
... Leningrad was sur-
...teway to the Cauca-
...he richest and most
...et Union was in Ger-
...ans had suffered such stag-
... that Hitler announced that the
...n was destroyed and would never rise
... The Japanese, taking him at his word and
...unking the golden hour had struck, attacked the
United States on December 7, 1941. By that time,
however, the Arctic winter and the Soviet counterattacks had forced the Germans to halt and in
some places to retreat. The Soviet Union was still
alive, and the United States was now in the war.

2. THE NAZI EMPIRE

By 1942 Hitler ruled most of continental Europe
from the English Channel to Moscow. He had
initiated his "New Order"—basically a program
of racial imperialism—in the lands he controlled.
The conquered peoples were used according to
their ranking in Hitler's racial hierarchy. Those
more directly related to the Nazi conception of the
"Aryan race," such as the Scandinavians, the Anglo-Saxons, and the Dutch, were treated well and
would supposedly be absorbed into the Nazi Empire as partners with the Germans. The "Latin
races," such as the French, were considered clearly
inferior but tolerable as supportive cogs in the
New Order. Slavs were toward the bottom of Hitler's ranking; they were to be isolated, shoved
aside, and treated like slaves. Large numbers of
Russians, Poles, and others were removed from
their lands and turned into slave laborers, more
often than not perishing under the harsh conditions of their new existence.

Lowest on Hitler's scale were the Jews and
such other groups as socialists, gypsies, intellectuals, Jehovah's Witnesses, and the mentally ill.
These people were systematically hunted,
rounded up, transported to concentration camps,
and exterminated. This process was the "Final
Solution of the Jewish Problem," and the SS, under Heinrich Himmler, was given the special duty
of carrying it out. The quantity and quality of

programmed inhumanity, torture, and death was
so unprecedented that it could not be believed or
understood. In the end some 6 million Jews were
killed in that systematic, bureaucratized horror
along with perhaps another 6 million victims of
Nazi concentration camps.

This massive effort to racially reorganize Europe and perpetuate genocidal policies took priority over even the war effort—continuing until the
last days of the war and using up needed troops
and materials. Indeed, Nazi Germany itself was
only partially organized for the military effort in
the early years of the war, finally turning to full
mobilization after 1942. Under the leadership of
Albert Speer, German production multiplied in
1943 and 1944 despite Allied bombing.

The resources and treasures of conquered
lands were taken or put under the control of the
Nazis and used to further the Nazi war effort and
implement the New Order. The Nazis attempted
to gain the submission and cooperation of conquered peoples through the use of force and terror. While the Nazis always managed to find collaborators in occupied lands, they were never able
to stamp out persistent resistance. Such resistance
movements grew in France, Poland, Denmark,
Greece, Yugoslavia—indeed, in almost every occupied territory. They established underground
networks, provided intelligence for the Allied
forces, conducted guerrilla actions, aided escaping
prisoners or Jews, sabotaged military installations,
and generally tied down Nazi forces that might
have been used on the war fronts.

3. THE ENTRY OF THE UNITED STATES INTO THE WAR

The outbreak of the war in Europe caused hardly
a ripple in the isolationist sentiment of the American public and of Congress. Most isolationists
believed the French army and Maginot line and
the British navy were capable of containing the
Nazis.

But suddenly in May–June 1940, the picture
drastically changed. The French army and Maginot line ceased to exist, and the British navy was
in grave danger. Much of it would be used up in
the defense of Britain in case of invasion. Roose-

FIGURE 57.3. **Pearl Harbor**   On December 7, 1941, the Japanese attacked Pearl Harbor, Hawaii, and destroyed the Pacific fleet in the harbor and the air force on the ground. The attack brought the United States into the war. This photo shows the USS California as it went down. (UPI/Bettmann Newsphotos)

velt promptly came forward with a three-point program: (1) all-out rearmament, (2) bipartisanship in foreign affairs, (3) all aid short of war to those fighting the Axis (which at the moment meant Great Britain). There was little opposition to the first two points, and Roosevelt managed to overcome objections to aiding the British. American involvement grew from the supply of arms to the convoying of ships across the Atlantic by the American navy. Aid was extended to the Soviet Union, and in June 1941 Axis consulates were closed.

In August 1941 Roosevelt and Churchill had met at sea and drawn up the Atlantic Charter, a joint statement of ideals and war purposes. In it appeared such pregnant phrases as ". . . their

Sequence of German Expansion to 1942
1. Austria, Czechoslovakia, Poland, 1939
2. 1940, Denmark, Norway
3. 1940, Low Countries, France
4. 1940-1941, Balkans
5. 1942-1943, Russian Front
6. 1942, Vichy

Axis Powers, 1939   Axis Allies

Greater Germany, 1942

Areas of Axis Control, 1942

Neutral Countries

Areas Annexed by Russia, 1939-1940

Pre-1939 Political Boundaries

Map 57.1   EUROPE, 1942   This map shows the farthest extent of Axis power during World War II. By the end of the year German expansion had been stopped at Stalingrad in the East and Egypt in North Africa.

countries seek no aggrandizement, territorial or other; . . . they respect the right of all peoples to choose the form of government under which they will live; . . . after the final destruction of the Nazi tyranny, . . . the establishment of a wider and permanent system of general security. . . ." The Soviet Union subscribed to the Atlantic Charter shortly afterward. Thus, by October 1941 the United States was engaged in a shooting—but not yet official—war with Germany and was in a virtual alliance with Great Britain, one of the belligerents. The American people's eyes were on the Atlantic, where at any moment some new German act of aggression might make war official and total.

It was not in the Atlantic, however, but in the Pacific that the history-changing blow was struck; and not by Germany, but by Japan. Early in 1939 the Japanese, having conquered all the populous coastal areas of China and having driven Chiang Kai-shek's forces far into the Chinese interior, turned southward toward the territories of Southeast Asia and the Southwest Pacific. These territories, rich in rubber, tin, rice, copra, and oil, belonged (with the exception of independent Thailand) to France, the Netherlands, Great Britain, and the United States. Since the French, Dutch, and British had their hands full in Europe with the growing Nazi menace, President Roosevelt transferred the American fleet from the Atlantic to Pearl Harbor in Hawaii as a deterrent to further Japanese aggression. He also gave the Japanese the required six months' notice of the termination of the commercial treaty of 1911. These moves appear to have given the Japanese pause.

In 1940, however, after Hitler's conquest of France and the Netherlands and threatened conquest of Great Britain, the Japanese became much bolder. They took advantage of France's helplessness to occupy northern French Indochina and threatened the Dutch East Indies. But in the following year, 1941, when the Germans overran the Balkans and launched what promised to be a lethal attack on the Soviet Union, the Japanese leaders decided that the day of Axis world triumph was at hand.

Tensions rose between Japan and the United States. Finally on December 7, 1941, a large squadron of Japanese bombers and torpedo planes took off from carriers in a position north of Hawaii and caught by surprise the American fleet anchored in Pearl Harbor (see Figure 57.3). With little loss to themselves, the Japanese planes crippled the American navy in the Pacific and destroyed the air force in Hawaii on the ground. In rapid succession Japan and the United States declared war on each other and within four days the United States was at war with the other Axis powers.

4. CLIMAX AND TURNING POINT OF THE WAR, JUNE–AUGUST 1942

The entry of the United States, with its enormous resources and industrial potential, changed the whole complexion of the war. Together with the totally mobilized British economy and the massive economic and military resources of the Soviet Union, the long-term advantage was now clearly on the side of the Allies. However, many months would be required to mobilize America's resources, and the Axis was determined to win decisively before that mobilization could be achieved (see Map 57.1). To bring about Allied solidarity, Churchill hastened to Washington, where on January 1, 1942, he and Roosevelt launched the United Nations Alliance. Twenty-six nations, of which the United States, Great Britain, and the Soviet Union were the Big Three, promised to give their all to the common effort, to make no separate peace, and to abide by the principles of the Atlantic Charter. By the end of the war, the number of member nations had risen to forty-seven.

The now-global war was fought in three major theaters: (1) the Soviet Union, (2) the Mediterranean and western Europe, and (3) the Pacific. The Axis powers made their climactic bid for victory on all three fronts between June and August 1942. The biggest front in terms of numbers of troops, weapons, and casualties involved was that in the Soviet Union. Despite frightful losses, the Soviets had managed to keep their well-led army intact and to relocate or rebuild their wartime factories. The Soviet people were unified against the foreign aggressors in what they called the "Great Patriotic War of the Fatherland." The Germans, after having been stopped in December 1941 by the Russian winter and the counterattacks, resumed their forward thrust in June 1942, this time in the southern sector. Refreshed and reequipped, they seemed irresistible. By August they had reached the outskirts of Stalingrad on the Volga. Here Stalin ordered a stand: The battle of Stalingrad raged for six months. In February 1943, the Russians, having closed a pincer behind the Germans in Stalingrad, captured all who had not been killed of an army of almost three hundred thousand men. This action was the turning point; the Germans began a slow but general retreat.

The critical battle on the Mediterranean and western European front was fought in Egypt. General Rommel's tough Afrika Korps in its first drive on Suez in 1941 had been stopped and pushed back into Libya by the British. In June 1942 Rommel's forces, greatly strengthened, struck the British desert forces a shattering blow and chased them in near rout to El Alamein, only sixty-five miles from Alexandria. Suez seemed doomed, and the British fleet prepared to evacuate the Mediterranean before it could be bottled up. Churchill rushed to the scene and put in a team of winning commanders: Sir Harold Alexander in overall command and General Bernard Montgomery as field commander. In August Rommel's forces assaulted the British positions at El Alamein and were stopped. A race to build up men and supplies ensued; the British, with massive aid from the United States, won. Late in October 1942 Montgomery's superior Eighth Army attacked Rommel's forces and, after a desperate battle, drove them back across the desert in defeat. Suez and the Middle East were now saved from the Axis, and for the first time Great Britain and the United States were in a position to assume the offensive.

President Roosevelt had agreed with Churchill that first priority should be given to defeating Germany, which represented the gravest threat. Therefore the United States concentrated most of its efforts toward Europe, which made the war in the Pacific more difficult and predominantly naval in character.

Three days after Pearl Harbor, Japanese carrier-based torpedo planes struck the British Asiatic fleet a crippling blow in the Gulf of Siam. Now, with unchallenged mastery of the Pacific, the Japanese within the space of a few months were able to conquer with relative ease a vast area in the Southwest Pacific and Southeast Asia. The American islands of Wake, Guam, and the Philippines; British Hong Kong, Malaya, Singapore, and Burma; and the Dutch East Indies were overrun. In May 1942 Japanese naval forces were turned back by the Americans in the Battle of the Coral Sea, northeast of Australia. However, the main Japanese fleet was preparing a major thrust at Hawaii, which it could have taken easily immediately after Pearl Harbor. The United States navy, which had broken the Japanese code, massed for an all-out battle. Early in June 1942, just as the Stalingrad and El Alamein campaigns were beginning, the two powerful naval forces came within carrier plane range of each other off Midway Island, a thousand miles west of Hawaii. The climactic Battle of Midway was fought at long range entirely by aircraft and submarines. American planes sank all four of the Japanese carriers, while the Japanese were able to destroy only one of three American carriers. Pounded from the air and without air cover, the Japanese commander ordered a retreat, never to become so bold again. In August 1942 the Americans assumed the offensive by attacking Guadalcanal in the Solomon Islands northeast of Australia. By that time, it was evident that the tide was beginning to turn on all three fronts.

5. VICTORY

Although the greatest crises had passed by the end of 1942, two and a half more years of bloody fighting were required to subdue the Axis. In fact, the defeat of the Axis could not have been achieved at all without a high degree of cooperation among the Big Three allies. President Roosevelt, with his winsome personality, played an important part in maintaining mutual confidence and cooperation among the Allied powers, which were so divergent in their ideologies and specific interests. The chief planners of the coordinated global strategy were Churchill for Great Britain, Stalin for the Soviet Union, and Army Chief of Staff George Marshall for the United States.

Map 57.2 THE PACIFIC WAR This map shows the farthest extent of Japanese expansion, attained in June 1942, and the course of the American counterattack across the Pacific islands toward the Japanese mainland between 1942 and 1945.

FIGURE 57.4. Hiroshima After A-Bomb This photo of Hiroshima, taken shortly after the first atom bomb was dropped, shows the incredible destructive power of atomic weapons. (Sygma)

The Russian Front

The Battle of Russia was the greatest and most destructive battle in history. Some 9 million men (five hundred divisions) were engaged. For two and a half years after Stalingrad, the Germans were slowly beaten back, doggedly contesting every foot of ground. At last, in April of 1945, the Russians entered Berlin. Along the fifteen hundred miles between Stalingrad and Berlin lay the wreckage of the greater part of Hitler's war machine. But the richest and most productive part of the Soviet Union lay devastated. At least twenty million Russians had been killed—possibly many more.

The Mediterranean and Western European Front

In November 1942, just as the Germans were beginning to retreat from El Alamein, a combined Anglo-American force under the command of General Dwight D. Eisenhower landed in French North Africa. Early in 1943, the converging forces of Eisenhower and Montgomery cornered the Afrika Korps in Tunisia, where it surrendered in May.

Meanwhile most of the threats from German submarines and planes were being eliminated, as the British and Americans gained in the air and seas. Massive bombing raids pounded Germany.

The distinction between strategic military targets and civilian populations blurred as Germany's cities were leveled.

In July 1943 the Anglo-Americans conquered the island of Sicily, which they used as a base for the invasion of southern Italy. Mussolini was forced to resign (July 25), and Italy surrendered. However, the peninsula was held by strong German forces. By the end of 1943, the Allies had reached Cassino Pass, about 75 miles south of Rome. At this point, the major objectives in the Mediterranean area had been achieved, and Eisenhower, along with most of his forces, was transferred to Great Britain to command the main Anglo-American thrust across the Channel.

This thrust came on June 6, 1944. Thanks in large measure to complete Allied mastery of the skies, successful landings were made on the Normandy coast. After a rapid buildup, the Anglo-Americans broke out of the beachhead and before the end of the year cleared practically all of France. Germany, meanwhile, was being pulverized from the air. Early in 1945 the American and British forces, now joined by French units, broke through the German West Wall, crossed the Rhine, and joined forces with the Russians on the Elbe. Germany surrendered on May 8, ending the war in Europe. Near the end, Hitler and several other top Nazis committed suicide, and Mussolini was shot by Italian partisans.

The Pacific Front

Early in 1943 American forces under the command of General Douglas MacArthur began with a strong naval escort an island-hopping campaign northwestward from their base in Australia (see Map 57.2). At the same time the main American fleet, under the command of Admiral Chester Nimitz, now definitely superior to the Japanese fleet, thrust westward from Hawaii toward Japan, capturing the numerous Japanese-held islands in its path. Although the islands, many of them covered by jungles, were bloodily defended, the American forces moved steadily toward Japan itself. In October 1944 the American forces made a bold landing on Leyte Island in the Philippines, which brought the Japanese fleet out for a last desperate effort. In the Battle of Leyte Gulf, the Japanese fleet was annihilated. Cut off, uncovered, and subjected to ceaseless air and sea attacks, Japan was doomed. After Germany surrendered in May 1945, American, British, and Russian troops that had been engaged in the European theater were rapidly deployed to the Far East. In mid-July the atomic bomb, which American and British scientists had been developing for several years, was successfully completed and tested. The United States wanted to avoid the heavy casualties that a direct assault on the Japanese home islands would cause. The United States thus decided to use the bomb to shock Japan into surrender, a decision that has remained controversial ever since that time. On August 6, 1945, the first atomic bomb to be used in warfare destroyed the Japanese city of Hiroshima (see Figure 57.4) and some eighty thousand of its inhabitants. Two days later, the Soviet Union declared war on Japan and began to overrun Manchuria and northern Korea. The next day, August 9, the second and last atomic bomb then in existence demolished the industrial city of Nagasaki. The Japanese surrendered five days later, August 14, 1945.

World War II had ended. Estimates of soldiers and civilians killed range from 30 million to 50 million; even more had suffered injuries from the war. Western society now faced an overwhelming task of recovery and reorganization.

SUGGESTED READING

General

M. Baumont, *The Origins of the Second World War* (1978). A solid, brief treatment.

B. Liddell Hart, *History of the Second World War* (1980). A good military history.

G. Wright, *The Ordeal of Total War, 1939–1945* (1968). Thoughtful analysis; goes far beyond the military aspects.

Two Years of Axis Triumph

W. Churchill, *Their Finest Hour* (1949). The second and best of Churchill's great six-volume history of the war. Covers the defeat of France and the Battle of Britain.

A. Clark, *Barbarossa* (1964). Good history of the war on the Russian front.

The Nazi Empire

N. Cohn, *Warrant for Genocide* (1966). An in-depth analysis.

A. Dallin, *German Rule in Russia, 1941–1945* (1957). A good analysis.

L. Dawidowicz, *The War Against the Jews, 1933–1945* (1976). A thorough study.

T. Des Pres, *The Survivors* (1976). A good analysis of life in Hitler's concentration camps.

J. Haestrup, *Europe Ablaze* (1978). Thorough study of the resistance movements.

E. Kogon, *The Theory and Practice of Hell* (1958). A classic study of the concentration camps.

The Entry of the United States

A. R. Buchanan, *The United States and World War II*, 2 vols. (1964). A good survey.

R. Devine, *Reluctant Belligerent: American Entry into World War II* (1969). Good brief study.

H. Feis, *The Road to Pearl Harbor: The Coming of the War Between the United States and Japan* (1967). A scholarly work.

Allied Victory

M. Sherwin, *A World Destroyed: The Atomic Bomb and the Grand Alliance* (1975). Analyzes the final years and the role of the atomic bomb.

J. Toland, *The Last Hundred Days* (1966). A fine account of the end.

RETROSPECT

A long period of relative peace, growing prosperity, and sense of progress ended in August 1914. World War I initiated a three-decade period in which Europe would be shattered politically, economically, and socially by war, revolution, and depression.

European nations were plunged into World War I by an entangling alliance system that enhanced nationalistic rivalries and by persisting domestic tensions that encouraged national governments searching for unity to adopt belligerent policies. The hoped-for short war turned into a nightmarish struggle between the Central Powers and the Allies. The destruction went beyond the massive human and material toll to the political entities themselves. The German, Austro-Hungarian, Russian, and Ottoman empires did not survive the war. The British and French empires were both weakened, as indeed were Britain and France themselves. Efforts to make a durable peace and to set up an international organization, the League of Nations, to keep the peace foundered on the rocks of national self-interest. Instead, the peace settlements left a legacy of resentment that would haunt the West during the following two decades.

The victors in World War I were the liberal-democratic nations, and it was hoped that this victory would be turned into a permanent gain for liberal democracy. The trend toward totalitarianism, fascism, and authoritarianism during the 1920s and 1930s dashed these hopes. The first blow to liberalism and capitalism came during the final stages of World War I when revolution brought a Communist regime to power in Russia. Lenin led the revolutionary Bolsheviks to victory in November 1917 and over the next few years extracted the Soviet Union from World War I, defeated rivals in a bloody civil war, and established the foundations for a totalitarian state. By the end of the 1920s Lenin's successor, Stalin, had initiated the five-year plans that would collectivize Soviet agriculture and industrialize the nation. His Great Purges in the 1930s eliminated all possible resistance, completing the transformation of the Soviet Union into a totalitarian state.

The next blow to liberalism came with the rise of fascism in Italy under Mussolini during the early 1920s. Over the next few years Mussolini took steps to turn his Fascist regime into a totalitarian state, but these steps were always incomplete. Full-blown totalitarian fascism was established during the 1930s in Nazi Germany under Hitler. Much more than the Italian variety, German fascism was tinged with violence and racism. Both regimes denounced liberal democracy and, indeed, most of the developments since the French Revolution that Western liberals had pointed to with pride. With their emphasis on nationalism, militarism, and expansion, these Fascist regimes represented a direct threat to peace and the democratic West.

Two more blows to liberalism seriously undermined the position of the democratic West. The first was the rise of authoritarian regimes in southern Europe, eastern Europe, and Japan—almost all replacing governments that had more liberal leanings. The second was the Great Depression, which encouraged authoritarian movements everywhere and caused the Western democracies to turn inward. Thus, during the 1930s, when the threat from Fascist and authoritarian nations was growing, the Western democracies were increasingly paralyzed by their own domestic problems.

Neither the foundering League of Nations nor a policy of appeasement could restrain Germany, Italy, and Japan from pursuing their policies of expansion. In 1939 World War II broke out. For over two years the Axis powers seemed unstoppable, gaining victory after victory. By the end of 1942, however, overexpansion by the Axis forces, the stiff resistance by Soviet troops, the heroic struggle by the British, and the entrance of the United States into the war had started to turn the tide. Almost three years of struggle on a worldwide basis were necessary to end the war in 1945. By that time the Nazis had carried out a policy of genocide and enslavement as part of Hitler's racist "New Order," and war had claimed some 40 million lives.

In 1945 Europe lay in ruin. World War I, the interlude of turmoil and depression during the 1920s and 1930s, and World War II had changed Western civilization in irreversible ways. Indeed, many questioned whether Europe, the heart of Western civilization for so long, could recover from the devastation.

PART TWELVE

GLOBAL INTERDEPENDENCE IN THE CONTEMPORARY WORLD, 1945–PRESENT

The year 1945 was a watershed between two different eras in several ways. First, when the last shots were fired, an end came not only to World War II, which had raged since 1939, but also to three decades of devastating turmoil in Europe that had begun with the outbreak of World War I in 1914. In the decades following 1945 the West would face problems, but not on the scale of the destructive wars, political upheavals, and economic fluctuations that dominated the 1914–1945 period. Indeed, for most of the period after 1945 the basic trend would be toward recovery, growth, and relative stability. Second, 1945 marked the last time when the bulk of power and leadership in Western civilization would be located in Western Europe. After 1945 the two new competing superpowers, the United States and the Soviet Union, would be the dominating nations in the West and, to a considerable extent, the world. Third, 1945 marked the beginning of the end of Western colonialism. Over the next two decades the imperial powers would lose colonies they had controlled since the end of the nineteenth century or even longer. As these former colonies became independent nations, they, along with other nations of the non-Western world, would become assertive in a world that could no longer ignore them. Finally, 1945 marked the beginning of an age of rapidly growing global interdependence. The West was increasingly becoming tied to the non-Western world by expanding communications, economic dependence, international organizations, systems of alliances, ideological competition, and cultural exchange. Western ideals, values, institutions, and problems were spreading to and interacting with those of the rest of the world. As we approach the present, it becomes increasingly difficult to make a firm demarcation between the Western and non-Western worlds. More than ever before, Western civilization must be studied within a global context.

CHAPTER 58

The Recovery of Europe and the Superpowers, 1945–Present

FIGURE 58.1. The Division Between East and West The post–World War II division between East and West in Europe is symbolized by the Berlin Wall and the Brandenburg Gate in Berlin blocked by barbed wire and troops in 1961. (AP/Wide World Photos)

In 1945 much of Europe was in ashes. Disorganization was the rule, and effective governments often were virtually nonexistent. Economic destruction was so great that the immediate problem was not so much how to rebuild factories and initiate economic growth but how to minimize the starvation that faced millions and create shelter for the dislocated. European nations would revive with amazing speed and go on to establish new patterns of relative political stability and economic growth. However, before that could happen, Europeans had to deal with the immediate problems of the settlement of World War II and the beginnings of the Cold War.

1. THE SETTLEMENT AND THE COLD WAR

In 1945 the leaders of the victorious nations were confronted with the tasks of making a lasting peace and restoring a shattered world. From the beginning these tasks were hampered by hostility between the United States and the Soviet Union. This hostility, which came to be called the "Cold War," pervaded and poisoned every area of postwar international relations. To understand the nature of the peace settlement and the origins of the Cold War, one must go back to the conferences held by the Allies during the war and to the legacy of assumptions held by participants in those conferences.

Legacy of Assumptions

Although Great Britain, the United States, and the Soviet Union were cooperating allies during most of World War II, they approached each other with differing perceptions and a history of distrust. Since the Communists came to power in Russia in 1917, leaders of the Soviet Union and the capitalist democracies had viewed each other as opponents. As ideologies, communism and capitalism had always been in direct opposition. As practiced in the Soviet Union under Lenin and Stalin, communism took a totalitarian form, in sharp contrast to the democracies of Great Britain and the United States. Specific developments between the Rus-

sian Revolution of 1917 and World War II added to the hostility between the Soviet Union and the capitalist democracies. During the Russian civil war, the Western nations had supported anti-Bolshevik forces with materials and some troops. The United States had not recognized the Bolshevik government until 1933. The Soviet Union had not even been invited to the Munich Conference of 1938. In viewing the rise of Fascist and authoritarian governments during the 1920s and 1930s, many in the Western democracies found consolation in the opposition of these governments to communism. The Western democracies failed to ally with the Soviet Union in the 1930s against the growing threat of Nazi Germany. In 1939 Stalin entered into an astonishing pact with Hitler, enabling Nazi forces to concentrate on Western Europe during the first years of World War II.

Hitler's invasion of the Soviet Union and the entry of the United States into the war united Great Britain, the United States, and the Soviet Union as allies more in opposition to Nazi Germany than in agreement over principles or goals. When concrete negotiations for war aims and terms of a settlement took place, the history of hostility, distrust, and fear between capitalist and Communist powers caused problems. These problems would increase after the war when the threat of Nazi Germany no longer held the Allies together.

The Conferences and the Settlement

The decisions that led to the peace settlements, that helped shape Europe in the immediate postwar years, and that laid the groundwork for the Cold War were made in a series of conferences held by the leaders of Great Britain, the United States, and the Soviet Union. The first conference took place in December 1943 at Teheran. There Stalin agreed to enter the war against Japan after the defeat of Germany, and Great Britain and the United States agreed to open a second front in France. The most crucial decision was to reject Churchill's plan to open a front in Eastern Europe, which would have given Great Britain and the United States more influence over developments there. With British and American forces concentrated in Western Europe, Eastern Europe was

FIGURE 58.2.   Allied Leaders at Yalta   With victory over the Axis in sight, the terms of the settlement were negotiated at the Yalta Conference, February 1945. Churchill, Roosevelt, and Stalin, representing the Big Three Allied powers, made a series of agreements concerning the major postwar problems. (UPI/ Bettmann Newsphotos)

open to the advancing Russian troops.

The next meeting of the three heads of state was in February 1945 at Yalta (see Figure 58.2). The four main areas of discussion were (1) the United Nations charter, (2) Germany, (3) Eastern Europe, and (4) the Far East. All quickly reached agreement on questions concerning the United Nations charter. They also agreed on most matters concerning Germany: complete denazification with severe punishment for the top Nazis; demilitarization; the division of the country into four occupation zones; and a long period of occupation by the Allies. There was no agreement on the stiff reparations demanded by Stalin. In the discussion

over Eastern Europe a sharp cleavage soon developed. Stalin argued that Eastern Europe, already behind Soviet lines, was vital to the Soviet Union's security. Russia had been invaded through these countries in both world wars and many of them had been Hitler's allies. Therefore, he asserted, the Soviet Union should maintain a measure of control over these countries. Roosevelt and Churchill insisted that these countries must be given complete independence. These disagreements were not resolved; they were papered over with a general agreement that elections would be held as soon as possible in the liberated states of Eastern Europe but that these states were to be friendly to the Soviet Union. In regard to the Far East, Stalin agreed to enter the war within three months after Germany's surrender in return for islands and port facilities that Japan had earlier taken from Russia and for increased Soviet influence in Korea.

The last meeting of the heads of state of Great Britain, the United States, and the Soviet Union took place in July 1945 at Potsdam. At this conference Clement Attlee had replaced Winston Churchill as British prime minister and Truman had replaced Roosevelt as the American president. Matters that had already been agreed on were affirmed in greater detail, but there was still no fundamental agreement over Eastern Europe. Despite a general accord to work out peace treaties with the various nations as soon as possible, treaties with Germany's allies were not signed until February 10, 1947, and a final treaty with Germany was never signed.

While the war ended in 1945 with a complete victory for the Allies, the basis for postwar problems was already present. The legacy of distrust and hostility between Communist Russia and the capitalist West was not eradicated by the temporary period of cooperation during the war years. Decisions and disagreements at the wartime conferences resulted in resentments and accusations on both sides, particularly over Eastern Europe. Faced with the reality of Eastern Europe's being behind Soviet lines, Great Britain and the United States were at a disadvantage. Europe, though struggling to recover, was already politically divided. Political divisions would merge into Cold War divisions in the years following 1945.

The Cold War

The Cold War was the struggle between the United States and the Soviet Union, each supported by its respective non-Communist and Communist allies, that colored international relations during the four decades following World War II (see Map 58.1). On the one side the Soviet Union strove to secure itself from external threats and to spread its version of communism to the border states and elsewhere in the world. On the other side the United States strove to contain Soviet

influence and to counter Communist threats wherever they were perceived throughout the world. It was a war fought in almost all ways except open military conflict, and the threat of military force was always present. At times, the Cold War became violent, but the two superpowers never came together in direct armed combat.

The spirit of cooperation between the Western democracies and the Soviet Union was already being deflated by verbal salvos in 1945. Truman denounced the establishment of new governments through force, a clear attack on Soviet policies in Eastern Europe. In February 1946 Stalin described the Western democracies as enemies of communism. In March 1946 Churchill attacked Soviet actions in Eastern Europe and warned against Communist subversion. He described a Russian iron curtain "dividing a free and democratic West from an East under totalitarian rule."

These accusations focused mainly on developments in Eastern Europe. The United States and its allies felt that wartime agreements and a sense of justice should compel the Soviet Union to allow free elections in Eastern European states, all of which should be independent from Soviet control. The Soviet Union felt that these same wartime agreements and a higher sense of justice recognized the overriding need for the Soviet Union to make sure Eastern European states remained friendly and under Soviet influence. The United States became increasingly outraged when developments in Eastern Europe seemed to go Stalin's way. In 1945 the Soviets were already exerting control over the governments of Rumania and Poland, despite the protests of the British and Americans. By 1947 Soviet dominance in these two countries was solidified and spreading to other Eastern European countries. In 1948 Soviet threats forced non-Communist leaders out of the Czechoslovakian government, placing that country in Communist hands. By 1950 all the states of Eastern Europe were controlled by Communists and, with the exception of Yugoslavia under Tito, were dominated by the Soviet Union.

Struggles over Eastern Europe spread to Western Europe, where strong Communist parties in France and Italy pursued policies approved by Moscow. The United States and its allies feared these parties would subvert non-Communist gov-

Map 58.1 EUROPE DURING THE COLD WAR This map indicates the Cold War divisions in Europe during the 1950s. With some exceptions, nations in Western Europe joined NATO, a non-Communist military organization headed by the United States. Also with a few exceptions, nations in Eastern Europe joined the Warsaw Pact, a Communist military organization headed by the Soviet Union.

ernments and help spread Soviet control further south and west.

The verbal denunciations and discord over events in Europe were accompanied by a breakdown of cooperation between the United States and the Soviet Union. President Truman, who succeeded Roosevelt on April 12, 1945, was in favor of a tougher policy toward the Soviet Union. In May he cut off aid to the Soviet Union. When the possibility of international control of atomic weapons arose, the Americans and Russians could not agree. This led to the nuclear weapons race, which has flourished ever since.

The breakdown of cooperation was most striking in Germany. In accordance with the Potsdam agreements, most of Germany was divided into four occupation zones: American, Russian, British, and French. Berlin, which was in the Russian zone, was divided into four sectors and made the headquarters of a four-power coordinating commission. Sharp cleavages soon developed among the occupying powers, particularly between the United States and the Soviet Union. The Soviet Union, having suffered more at the hands of Germany during World Wars I and II than any other major nation, was determined to keep Germany permanently weak and as much as possible under Soviet domination. The United States, on the other hand, having little fear of Germany and seeing it as a valuable potential ally against the Soviet Union, soon set out to restore and rearm the nation. Matters came to a head in 1948–1949. In March 1948 the United States, having succeeded in merging the three Western zones and stepping up their economy to a level much higher than that agreed upon at Potsdam, announced plans for the creation of an independent West German state. To the Soviet leaders, this was the last straw. They attempted to dissuade the Western powers from going ahead with the project by blockading the three Western zones of Berlin in the hope of starving them out. For eleven months, from June 1948 to May 1949, the Soviets stopped all land traffic across their zone from the West to Berlin. The Western powers defeated the blockade through a giant airlift. The United States proceeded to set up the German Federal Republic, which began to function in September 1949. One month later the Soviet Union set up the German Democratic Republic in its zone.

Policies initiated in 1947 raised the Cold War to a higher level. The immediate occasion prompting the United States to inaugurate a new and harsher policy toward the Soviet Union was the situation in Greece and Turkey, both of which were under severe Soviet pressure. In February 1947 the British government, which had been supporting both Greece and Turkey with troops and money since the end of the war, announced that after March 31 it would be unable to continue to do so. On March 12, 1947, President Truman appeared before Congress and requested authorization to send American military and civilian personnel into Greece and Turkey. "I believe," he said, "that it must be the policy of the United States to support free peoples who are resisting attempted subjugation by armed minorities or by outside pressures." He asked for $400 million to implement the new program and warned that this was only a starter. Congress greeted this announcement with a standing ovation.

The new policy, which was soon called the Truman Doctrine, meant that the United States would draw a military ring around the Soviet Union and its satellites from Manchuria to Norway. It was the policy of military containment. All real diplomatic negotiations between the United States and the Soviet Union, of course, ceased immediately. The Soviet Union made no further pretense of withdrawing from the areas of Eastern Europe occupied by its troops; instead, the Soviet Union tightened the iron curtain that it had drawn around them.

In June 1947 Secretary of State General George Marshall supplemented the Truman Doctrine with the Marshall Plan. This plan was an offer of comprehensive economic aid to all European countries (except Fascist Spain) who would improve their economies, stabilize their currencies, and cooperate with each other in bringing about general economic recovery. All the countries of Europe except the Soviet Union and its satellites hastened to accept Marshall's terms and American aid. The Soviet Union regarded the Marshall Plan as an American scheme to shore up Europe's and its own tottering capitalism, to lure away the Soviet satellites, and to make the European countries economic dependencies of the United States. The Soviet Union therefore forbade the countries of Eastern Europe under its control or influence to participate. Congress voted $5.3 billion as the first of four installments totaling some $17 billion for Marshall Plan aid. In 1949 the United States took the initiative in organizing the North Atlantic Treaty Organization (NATO), which was a firm military alliance among the United States, Canada, and most of the nations of Western Europe against the Soviet Union (see p. 742 for details).

In the fall of 1947 the Soviet Union began a series of vigorous moves to counter the Truman Doctrine and the Marshall Plan. In September 1947 the Soviet Union set up the Communist Information Bureau, or Cominform, the better to coordinate policies of the Soviet Union, Poland, Hungary, Rumania, Bulgaria, Albania, Yugoslavia, and Czechoslovakia. This agency was in reality a restoration of the old Comintern, which was the Communist International working for world revolution. The following year the Cominform was supplemented by the Council for Economic Mutual Assistance, a Soviet Marshall Plan. At the same time the Soviet Union severely tightened its grip on its satellites. The local Communist parties were rigorously purged of moderates and national patriots. The Soviet Union strengthened military ties with its allies, eventually countering NATO with the establishment of the Warsaw Pact Organization in 1955.

By 1950 one stage of the Cold War was completed. Europe was clearly divided into a Communist camp in the East under the control of the Soviet Union and a non-Communist camp in the West under the leadership of the United States. The Cold War would continue in different ways and with varying intensity over the next four decades. Both sides were pitted against each other in a world-wide war of propaganda. Political struggles almost anywhere, whether purely internal matters or not, became potential fields for a victory or defeat in a Cold War competition. This competition expanded to the non-Western world and to a variety of fields not usually thought of as political, from the exploration of space to the Olympic games.

In 1950 the Korean War shifted the focus of the Cold War from Europe to the non-Western world. It also revealed how real the risk of military combat was in the struggle between Communist and non-Communist forces. In the mid-1950s there were some signs of a relaxation in the Cold War. Stalin died in 1953, and later that year an armistice was signed in Korea. The Soviet government made overtures to the United States to end the Cold War. In 1955 Soviet troops left Austria, which became an independent, neutral state. That same year a conference was held in Geneva between the leaders of Great Britain, France, the United States, and the Soviet Union. Little of substance was accomplished, but at least it symbolized an effort to solve problems peacefully. Talk of "peaceful coexistence" between the superpowers became popular and seemed confirmed when the two powers agreed to talks for a nuclear test ban treaty in 1958.

This apparent thaw in the Cold War was mitigated by some chilling developments. In the same year that Stalin died, John Foster Dulles became United States secretary of state in the new Eisenhower administration. It was his belief that all communism was a Moscow-directed conspiracy

bent upon world conquest. The time had come, he proclaimed, to pass over from containment to liberation. The United States tried to apply lessons learned in the struggles over Eastern Europe and Korea to Southeast Asia, where the French had lost to Communist-led insurgents in Vietnam. Efforts to hold a meeting between the American and Soviet heads of state in 1960 broke down amid Cold War accusations. In 1961 irritations over Germany were exacerbated by the construction of the Berlin Wall, sealing off democratic West Berlin from East Berlin and the rest of Communist East Germany. In 1962 the Cuban missile crisis, a Cold War confrontation over the placement of Russian missiles in Cuba, came close to erupting into a real war.

Nevertheless, the 1960s and most of the 1970s witnessed a general lessening of tensions in the Cold War. A nuclear test ban treaty between the two powers was signed in 1963, and strategic arms limitation talks were initiated in 1969. After 1969 relations between the United States and the Soviet Union were often described by the word *détente*, emphasizing cooperation rather than confrontation.

In the later 1970s and early 1980s events proved that the Cold War was not over. The increasing ties between Communist China and the United States were perceived as a threat by the Soviet Union. When Jimmy Carter became president in 1977, the Soviet leaders quickly took offense at his insistence on the granting of human rights throughout the world, including the Soviet Union, and they were uncomfortable with his more open style of diplomacy. A Soviet invasion of Afghanistan in 1979 led to the American boycott of the Olympic Games in 1980 and an embargo on grain shipments to the Soviet Union. The Reagan administration took a much tougher stand toward the Soviet Union and communism in general, reviving Cold War rhetoric and dramatically increasing arms production. In the 1980s the Polish crisis, American attempts to limit exportation of certain technology and materials by Western nations to the Soviet Union, the deployment of new American missiles in Europe, the American Strategic Defense Initiative, and the rejection of the 1979 Strategic Arms Limitation Treaty heightened tensions between the two powers. However, since 1985 the new arms limitations talks, the signing of an Intermediate-Range Nuclear Forces Treaty, a unilateral reduction of conventional forces in Eastern Europe, a more conciliatory foreign policy, a Soviet commitment in internal political and economic reforms, and the Soviet withdrawal from Afghanistan have contributed to improving relations between the United States and the Soviet Union.

2. REVIVAL OF A DIVIDED EUROPE AND THE WEST

Within the context of the Cold War struggle, Europe survived the difficult years immediately following World War II, recovered by the 1950s, and grew in new directions in the following decades. Yet there was a fundamental division between West and East in Europe, with Western Europe turning toward parliamentary democracy and support from the United States and Eastern Europe turning toward communism and support from the Soviet Union.

Western Europe

After World War II nations in Western Europe returned to liberal democratic forms of government. The political parties of the center generally came to power. On the Continent the Christian Democratic parties were particularly strong in France, West Germany, and Italy. They had ties to traditional prewar conservative parties but became more progressive after World War II. They stood for democracy, economic growth, moderate social reform, antifascism, and anticommunism. Their main competitors were a variety of moderate, democratic Socialist parties with ties to traditional prewar Socialist parties. With the exception of Great Britain, where the Labour party came to power in 1945, these Socialist parties usually found themselves in opposition rather than in power. Initially, Communist parties were also strong, but after 1947, when the Cold War heated up, these parties were systematically excluded from participation in national governments.

While the United States emerged from World War II economically strong, the postwar European governments were faced with the tremendous task of leading their countries to economic and social recovery. After the first few very difficult years, when hunger and dislocation were more a rule than an exception, Western Europe entered into a period of strong economic recovery lasting well into the 1960s. The economic recovery was fueled by money from the American Marshall Plan, pent-up demand since the beginning of the war for goods and services, cheap skilled labor, and a surprisingly strong birth rate. Different mixtures of national planning and free enterprise were used to direct the recovery. International cooperation, such as with the Organization of European Economic Cooperation (OEEC) and the European Coal and Steel Community, and the already high level of industrial and technological sophistication attained by Western Europeans, facilitated the recovery. Accompanying economic growth were government social policies providing for health care, unemployment relief, old-age benefits, and family support.

In the late 1960s and 1970s new problems appeared. The economic growth of the 1950s and early 1960s leveled off. Inflation became widespread, particularly after 1973, when oil prices started their dramatic rise. At the same time, growth rates started to decline and unemployment began to rise. This "stagflation"—economic stagnation coupled with sharp inflation—persisted into the 1980s. Partial recovery in the mid-1980s, led by the United States, was uneven and purchased at a high price. Governmental deficits and problems with trade balances became common in the West.

Social dissatisfaction was evidenced in a variety of movements, from the student protests of the late 1960s to the radical separatist movements of the 1970s and 1980s. While the period cannot be called one of political instability, voters often turned out incumbent parties in hopes that the opposition parties could solve problems. Socialist parties that came to power seemed to have as much trouble dealing with apparently intractable problems as their conservative counterparts.

These general trends and variations of them can best be understood by examining developments in some individual countries between 1945 and the present.

Great Britain

In Great Britain the Labour party swept to victory in elections held in July 1945, just as the war was coming to an end. Clement Attlee succeeded Churchill as prime minister. The problems confronting Britain and the Labour government were indeed formidable. More than half of Great Britain's merchant marine had been sunk; a third of its buildings had been destroyed or damaged; its foreign investments had been liquidated and used up; Great Britain owed the United States a huge debt; its empire was tottering. The Labour government strictly rationed the short supplies, raised taxes on the rich, and lowered taxes on the poor. It nationalized the Bank of England, the coal mines and the electrical and gas industries, inland transportation, and the steel industry. Altogether, some 20 percent of Britain's economy was socialized. A vast program of social security, public education, public housing, and national health insurance was launched. The dismantling of the British Empire was begun—India, the biggest of all of Britain's colonial prizes, was given its independence in 1947 (see Chapter 59). The six years of Labour rule were years of austerity for the middle and upper classes. However, the general morale of the people was high, and Britain recovered. By 1948 British production and exports were higher than before the war, and the masses of the people were enjoying more security, services, and material goods than ever before.

Unfortunately, Great Britain's economic condition was fundamentally unsound. The loss of its overseas investments and resources and of the income from most of its prewar shipping, together with the antiquated state of most of its mines and factories, left Britain far short of the funds needed for war repair, debt repayment, and social services. By 1949 the serious deficit in the balance of trade had become apparent, followed by a weakening of the pound and mounting inflation. Rising discontent enabled Churchill and the Conservatives to return to power in 1951. With the exception of denationalizing the steel and trucking industries, they tampered little with the Labour party's program, most of which the great majority of the British people now clearly favored.

But neither the Conservatives, who governed Britain from 1951 to 1964 and again from 1970 to 1974, nor the Labourites, who governed from 1964 to 1970 and again from 1974 to 1979, were able to strengthen Britain's deteriorating economy, which was not yet socialistic but was too restricted to allow free competitive capitalism to function as it had in the nineteenth century. Furthermore, it was difficult for many Britishers to adjust to their greatly diminished place in the world. Many could still remember the glamorous days when Britain ruled the seas and an empire over which the sun never set. But increasing numbers of the young and the poor knew and cared little about past glories. Lawlessness and violence escalated, reaching its peak of intensity in Ulster. There the Roman Catholic minority struggled fiercely to gain equality with the Protestant majority; many of the Roman Catholics demanded separation from Britain and union with Ireland. The Protestants fought equally fiercely to maintain their supremacy. Violence begat violence. Hundreds on both sides were killed and hopes for a harmonious society were destroyed for the foreseeable future.

Widespread dissatisfaction with the inability of the Labour party to discipline its own trade unions and to lessen the rate of inflation resulted in a sweeping victory for the Conservatives in 1979. Margaret Thatcher became Britain's first female prime minister. The coming into production of the North Sea oil discoveries of several years earlier promised to strengthen Britain's economy, which had been in decline since World War I. Nevertheless, during the early 1980s Britain's economy remained troubled. With unemployment at more than 12 percent year after year and economic growth modest, Britain was burdened with one of the poorest performing economies in Western Europe. Urban riots reflected growing dissatisfaction. Yet thanks to the nationalistic unity fostered by the brief Falklands War with Argentina in the spring of 1982, the divisions within the Labour party (which led to the creation of a new party, the Social Democrats), and a moderately improving economy, Thatcher's Conservatives managed to maintain control over the government in the elections of 1983 and 1987.

France

France emerged from the war not only ravaged but also, unlike Britain, defeated and demoralized. General Charles de Gaulle returned to France in 1944 with the American and British liberators, who gave official recognition to the government he set up in Paris. However, the first postwar elections, held in October 1945, resulted in a sweeping victory for the parties of the Left, with which the authoritarian de Gaulle could not cooperate. Early in 1946 he went into temporary retirement. The leftist coalition, suspicious of authority, drew up a constitution very similar to that of the Third Republic, with its weak executive. The one noteworthy advance made by the new constitution was the granting at long last of woman suffrage. The Fourth Republic, like the Third, was plagued by a multiplicity of parties and political instability.

Despite these difficulties the Fourth French Republic made some noteworthy changes in French economic and social life. Under the Monnet Plan, free enterprise was combined with economic planning. Major banking and insurance facilities, coal mines, and gas and electrical utilities were nationalized. Social services, somewhat less comprehensive than those of the British Labour government, were inaugurated. A strong if uneasy economic recovery was achieved. By 1958 the output of goods and services was far in excess of that before World War II. These accomplishments of the Fourth Republic, however, were offset by its unsuccessful effort to hold onto the French Empire. A costly attempt to put down a war for independence in Indochina, which had broken out in 1942, resulted in humiliating defeat for the French (see p. 752). In 1954 France was forced to grant independence to Indochina. An even costlier war to try to save Algeria, in 1954–1962, also ended in failure (see p. 757). Inability to solve the Algerian problem led to the mutiny of the French army in Algeria in May 1958, which brought down the government. Charles de Gaulle was recalled from his twelve-year retirement. The problems confronting him were formidable—a mutinous army, a disintegrating empire, a seemingly endless war in Algeria, a disgruntled working class, an inflated currency, governmental weakness amounting to anarchy, widespread cynicism.

De Gaulle was probably the only person in France who could have reestablished civilian control over the mutinous army, which he deftly proceeded to do. He drew up a new constitution that greatly strengthened the executive branch of the government, and in December 1958 he was elected by an overwhelming majority first president of this Fifth French Republic (see Figure 58.3). He immediately granted independence to all of France's colonies except Algeria with its large French population. Algerian independence was granted four years later. He undertook to strengthen France's capitalistic economy by means of an austerity program. In spite of widespread strikes and sabotage by the working classes, much of it Communist-inspired, France's economy was soon operating at its highest level in history, and the French masses were enjoying new prosperity.

In foreign affairs, de Gaulle set out to restore France's "greatness"—its prestige in world affairs and its hegemony in Western Europe. He also sought to make Western Europe a "third force" independent of both American and Soviet domination. To achieve these ends, he created at great cost an independent nuclear striking force, cultivated cordial relations with Germany, withdrew France's military forces from NATO because of its domination by the United States, and vetoed Great Britain's entry into the European Common Market because of its close ties to its Commonwealth associates and to the United States.

For eleven years these policies worked with remarkable success. France regained much of the stability and prestige it had lost in 1940. De Gaulle's strong role, of course, encountered much opposition, mostly from the extreme Right and the extreme Left. His position and that of France's economy were weakened by massive student and labor union strikes and riots in 1968. When, in early 1969, de Gaulle asked for a vote of confidence from the French people and lost by a narrow margin, he resigned.

During the early 1970s Gaullists remained in power under the more moderate leadership of Georges Pompidou. In 1974 the elegant, urbane Valéry Giscard d'Estaing, a moderate conservative, defeated his Communist- and Socialist-backed opponent by the narrowest of margins. Giscard d'Estaing represented France's techno-

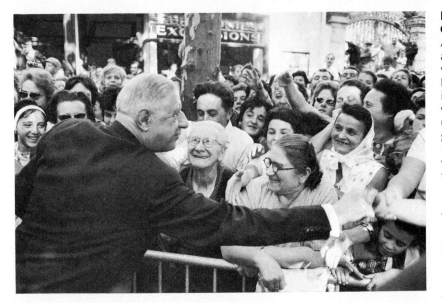

**FIGURE 58.3.
Charles de Gaulle**
After the French army in Algeria revolted against the French government in 1958, de Gaulle was recalled by popular acclaim and given an overwhelming mandate to rewrite the constitution. With dispatch he set up the Fifth French Republic and was elected its first president. This photo shows de Gaulle on tour of the French provinces. (Henri Cartier-Bresson/Magnum)

cratic Right and pursued a policy of slow modernization and social conservatism. Stunning change came in the elections of 1981, which brought the Socialists, under the leadership of François Mitterand, into power. Immediately, policies stressing nationalization of industries and banks, shorter hours and increased pay for workers, and progressive social programs were enacted. Yet several years of persistent economic problems, particularly inflation and high unemployment, dampened the reforming zeal of the Socialists. In 1986 the Socialists lost their majority to conservatives, but in 1988 the popular Mitterand was reelected president.

West Germany

The German Federal Republic was formally established in September 1949. It was a liberal democratic government similar to the Weimar Republic. The Christian Democratic party, a slightly right-of-center party with Roman Catholic leanings, won the first election, and its leader, the elderly and pro-Western Dr. Konrad Adenauer, became the first chancellor. The Western powers replaced their military governors with civilian commissioners and relaxed their control over Germany.

West Germany's industrial economy recovered rapidly, in part thanks to American assistance in replacing wrecked industrial plants with the most modern equipment and to American military protection, which relieved West Germany of the enormous military costs that burdened the economies of the United States, Great Britain, and France. By 1957 West Germany had regained its former industrial supremacy in Western Europe.

In 1963 Konrad Adenauer finally stepped down (at eighty-seven) as chancellor of West Germany. His Christian Democratic successors vigorously pursued his policies of strengthening West Germany's military ties with the United States, demanding the reunification of Germany and the recovery of lost territories in Eastern Europe, and establishing a place in the family of nuclear nations.

In 1969 Willy Brandt, a Social Democrat, became chancellor and launched Germany on a new course. His government quickly signed a nuclear nonproliferation treaty that had been long pending and entered into bilateral talks with East Germany and the Soviet Union. In August 1970 Chancellor Brandt and the Soviet premier Kosygin signed a treaty renouncing force or the threat of force in international relations and accepting the existing boundary lines of Eastern Europe including the Oder-Neisse line between East Germany and Poland. An official accompanying letter specified that the treaty left open the possibility of the future reunion of the two Germanies. This possibly momentous treaty was accompanied by trade agreements that promised a greatly stepped-up commerce between West Germany and the Soviet Union. The Social Democrats instituted and implemented many social programs, such as a comprehensive system of national health insurance and government ownership of public utilities. In economic policy, the German Social Democrats, unlike the French and British Socialists who advocated government ownership or control, followed a policy of codetermination between labor and management—*mitbestimmung*. West Germany's industrial economy had become the most prosperous of the Western world.

Economic problems plaguing other Western nations finally caught up with West Germany in the 1980s. By 1982 West Germany was experiencing negative economic growth, inflation of about 5 percent, and unemployment of almost 7 percent. In October 1982 Helmut Schmidt and his Social Democratic party fell from power and were replaced by the more conservative Christian Democratic party, led by the new chancellor Helmut Kohl. The rise to power of Kohl and the Christian Democrats was affirmed by elections in 1983, which also witnessed the first substantial entry into national politics of the environmentalist Green party, and again in 1987. While Germany's economy has recovered, unemployment remains a persistent problem.

Southern Europe

Italy   After the end of World War II, Italy abolished the monarchy and established itself as a republic. The Christian Democrats under the leadership of Alcide de Gasperi emerged as the dominant political party. The Italian Communist party also came out of World War II in a strong position, initially sharing power with the Christian Democrats in a coalition government. After 1947 the Communists, although continuing to command 25 to 35 percent of the vote and winning control of local elections throughout Italy, were excluded

from national governments. For the next three decades the Christian Democrats dominated Italian governments, although almost always in shaky alliances with other parties. Even though governments did not last long, the government bureaucracy was resistant to change and the same group of high governmental officials continued in office in succeeding governments.

Italy, and particularly northern Italy, enjoyed rapid economic growth and modernization in the 1950s and 1960s, for the first time becoming a leading industrial power in Europe. After the late 1960s Italy experienced greater economic, social, and political instability. Inflation became a perennial problem. Industrial growth slowed. The government, with its entrenched and sometimes corrupt bureaucracy, became less able to react to problems. In the mid-1970s voters turned increasingly to the Italian Communist party, which under Enrico Berlinguer was adopting more moderate policies. Radical groups, such as the Red Brigades, resorted to terrorism. By the 1980s the dominant Christian Democratic party was losing control of the government for the first time. In August 1983 Bentino Craxi was named the first Socialist premier in Italy and he managed to remain in power until 1987, but his coalition government was only moderately different from preceding governments. With inflation still a problem, unemployment averaging over 11 percent, and growth only moderate, prospects for governmental stability are dim.

Spain, Portugal, and Greece   The three southern European nations of Spain, Portugal, and Greece did not enter the mainstream of European developments until the 1970s. Both Spain, under Francisco Franco, and Portugal, under Antonio Salazar, remained out of World War II and retained their prewar authoritarian governments. Compared with the economies of other nations of Western Europe, their economies were less modernized and their people had a lower standard of living. Major political change came for both in the mid-1970s. In Portugal in 1974 General Antonio de Spinola headed a revolt that removed Marcelo Caetono, Salazar's authoritarian successor, from power. A year later Portugal held its first elections, and the Socialists, led by Mario Soares, gained control of the government. Again in 1986 the Socialist Soares was elected to power, this time as president. Spain underwent similar changes after the death of Franco in 1975. With the support of King Juan Carlos, a democratic constitution was approved in 1976. In 1982 the Socialists, under the popular Felipe Gonzáles, were elected to power for the first time. Since then Spain has enjoyed relative political stability and, recently, significant economic growth.

Greece, which suffered greatly during World War II, emerged in chaos and civil war. The Greek Royalists, with the help of first the British and then the Americans, were victorious. Greece became politically stable and remained so until the mid-1960s, when threats from the Left and Right led to the fall of the monarchy and, in 1967, a coup by conservative army officers. Their strong, authoritarian grip on Greek life was broken in 1974 when a confrontation with Turkey in Cyprus proved too difficult to handle. Since 1975 Greece has been governed by democratic rule, culminating in the election of the Socialists under Andreas Papandreou in 1981.

All three countries have followed a similar pattern: They broke from authoritarian rule in the mid-1970s, established a democratic form of government, and eventually elected a Socialist government. All three governments have had to deal with economies less modern than those in Western Europe and with societies that have had a lower standard of living. Yet recent events are pulling these southern European countries into the mainstream of Western European affairs; in the 1980s all three gained membership in the Common Market.

The United States

Of the Western powers, only the United States emerged from World War II virtually unscathed materially. The war had forced billions of dollars into circulation, ended the long depression, and destroyed much of the nation's foreign competition. The end of the war found big business and a high-spending military machine in close alliance and firmly entrenched. For most of the three decades following 1945, the United States enjoyed great economic prosperity. The pinnacle of prosperity came in the early and mid-sixties. Under presidents Kennedy and Johnson, the government pursued liberal policies of social reform, which included attacks on poverty, new educational programs, low-income housing projects, and governmental support of medical services. These policies put the United States more in line with other Western nations that had already established these social and "welfare state" institutions. However, the expansion of new social programs and unquestioned prosperity would come to an end in the 1970s and 1980s with new economic and political problems. Indeed, underlying the prosperity and confidence of the decades after World War II were a series of problems, which often resulted in anxiety, unrest, fear, and violence.

The first problem for Americans was the Soviet Union and communism. From the very beginning of the postwar era, Americans feared the Soviet Union and communism. Many journalists, military leaders, politicians, and business and professional people exploited this fear. During the early 1950s Senator Joseph McCarthy of Wisconsin fanned this fear into hysteria. In the eyes of McCarthy and his millions of followers, the American government, defense industries, armed forces, and educational system were honeycombed with Communists and fellow travelers.

In 1957, just as McCarthyism was subsiding, the American people were shocked by the news that the Soviet Union had orbited a satellite—Sputnik. The implication was that the lean and eager Russians had forged ahead in nuclear weapons and delivery systems while the soft and contented Americans had slept. The United States had, of course, for some time been working on a satellite of its own and in 1958 successfully orbited one. In 1961 the Soviet Union and the United States sent men into space and began to race each other to the moon. This race was won by the United States in 1969 at a cost of some $40 billion.

Americans were strongly concerned over repeated Communist successes in Asia (see Chapter 59), and closer to home a Communist takeover in Cuba in 1959 caused grave anxiety. The Cuban rebel leader, Fidel Castro, overthrew an American-supported rightist dictatorship. In 1961 the American government encouraged and aided an unsuccessful attempt by Cuban refugees to overthrow the Castro regime and the following year, by heavy threats, forced the Soviet Union to dismantle the missile bases it had constructed in Cuba. This was the most frightening of all the confrontations between the two nuclear powers, both of which had the nuclear capacity to destroy all the people on the earth.

America's next problem was the long-festering failure to integrate its large black population. By 1945 the blacks numbered some 20 million—about a tenth of the total population—and although considerable advancement in material well-being and social equality had been made, the gains fell far short of the promise. The curve of expectation was rising faster than the curve of achievement. Black veterans returning from World War II were particularly frustrated. In 1954 the Supreme Court outlawed segregation in the public schools and later specified forced busing as a means of implementing the decision. In the following years the civil rights movement was born, as blacks struggled for greater equality within American society. White resistance varied in close proportion to the number of blacks in the affected population—resistance flared up first in the Deep South and later in the large industrial cities of the North. Federal troops and marshals were used to overcome white resistance in the South. Millions of whites in the large northern industrial cities fled to the suburbs, leaving many cities primarily black. In 1964 Congress passed civil rights acts that guaranteed voting rights and broadly outlawed racial discrimination. Nevertheless, this legislation did not end the turmoil that had been unleashed. Riots occurred in major cities during the 1960s, reaching a climax in 1968 following the murder of Dr. Martin Luther King, Jr., the most prominent of the black leaders.

During the 1970s and 1980s, the position of blacks in American society has evolved, but the record is mixed. On the one hand, the elevation of many blacks to positions of political leadership and the growing numbers of blacks in middle-class jobs and residential areas indicate important change. On the other hand, blacks remain overrepresented in the growing core of inner-city unemployed who live below the poverty line.

Violence was by no means limited to the blacks nor to the United States. During the decade of the 1960s, youth all over the world was in revolt. However, violence and the crime rate were higher in the United States than in any other country and were constantly increasing. President Kennedy was assassinated in 1963 and his brother Robert, a major candidate for the Democratic presidential nomination, in 1968. College and university students staged protests, which often turned violent. Among the factors contributing to this unrest were continued racial inequality, widespread poverty alongside great wealth, inflation, wasteful destruction of natural resources, and growing dissatisfaction with American involvement in the war in Vietnam (see pp. 753–754).

While some of these problems became less immediate in the 1970s, new problems arose. In 1974, confidence in the American political system was shaken by the Watergate scandal, which revealed widespread misconduct and crimes within the highest levels of President Nixon's administration. Numerous high officials in the Nixon administration were forced to resign and were convicted and imprisoned. In August 1974, after it had become obvious that the president would be impeached by the full House and convicted by the Senate, Nixon resigned. He was succeeded by Gerald Ford, the conservative Republican leader who granted Nixon full pardon for all crimes he "may have committed while in office."

At almost the same time, economic problems stemming from the cost of the Vietnam War, from an unfavorable balance of trade, from growing inflation, and from the fourfold increase of oil prices between 1973 and 1974 started catching up with the United States. The country was entering a new period of declining growth rates, increasing unemployment, and rising prices. In the world marketplace, it was losing its dominance.

In 1976 Ford was narrowly defeated by Jimmy Carter. The Carter administration was confronted by spiraling inflation, a threatened fuel shortage, a high rate of unemployment (particularly among blacks and youths), a sense of disillusionment over the Vietnam War and its end, and widespread distrust of government at all levels—difficult problems that were not solved. The Carter administration was further burdened with trying to free American hostages from a hostile Iran and a new rise of oil prices.

In 1980 Ronald Reagan and the Republican party were elected to power and initiated a series of conservative policies in an attempt to undo several of the liberal reforms of the previous decades: Defense spending increased; a harsher line was taken toward communism; American arms and forces were sent to several areas throughout the world; programs to protect the environment, the worker, and the unemployed were attacked; and tax reforms that benefited mainly the corporations, the wealthy, and the middle class were enacted. The recession that began in the late 1970s deepened, with unemployment figures higher than in any years since the Great Depression of the 1930s. After 1983 the economy was in recovery, but the relative prosperity was purchased by a series of huge governmental deficits. In 1988 George Bush was elected president, promising to maintain the conservative policies of the Reagan administration.

Eastern Europe and the Soviet Union

The Soviet Union and Eastern Europe participated in the general European recovery from World War II, but their recovery was slower, not nearly as spectacular as in Western Europe. The Soviet Union initially set the pattern of economic and political development, but over time the various nations within the Soviet sphere of dominance moved in their own directions. In the decades following the 1960s, economic problems appeared and persisted. Agricultural production became an almost yearly disappointment. High administrative costs, inflexibility to market demand, and lethargy in productivity plagued industry. The gap between the economies of Western and Eastern Europe seemed to be widening rather than narrowing. In recent years these economic problems and the Soviet Union's own efforts at political and economic reform have led to considerable unrest and demands for economic decentralization in Eastern Europe. There are signs that the Soviet Union and Eastern Europe are embarking on a series of major long-term reforms.

The Soviet Union The Soviet Union emerged victorious from World War II, but the social and economic costs had been high. Few changes from prewar policies were evident. Stalin continued to assert totalitarian rule with a tightly planned economy stressing heavy industrialization. Political dissent was not allowed, and purges removed those perceived as potential threats. Prisons and forced-labor camps remained a feature of Stalin's rule. Despite the heavy expenditures required to maintain the Red Army, the Soviet Union recovered.

The death of Stalin in 1953 led to a liberalization of policies within the Soviet Union. Initially, Malenkov and Khrushchev struggled for power, but by 1955 Khrushchev had emerged as Stalin's successor. The most dramatic indication of changes from the Stalin era came in a 1956 speech in which Khrushchev denounced the crimes of Stalin before startled Communist leaders in Moscow. Khrushchev removed many of the conservative Stalinists within the party hierarchy but avoided the use of harsh Stalinist purges. Controls over cultural life were slightly loosened, as evidenced by the publication of novels by Boris Pasternak. Economically, there was a new stress on consumer goods and an attempt was made to reform agricultural policy. He embarked on an ambitious foreign policy. But Khrushchev may have tried to do too much at once, for domestic and international difficulties began to undermine his position. The gravest problems occurred in foreign affairs. The Soviet Union became involved in a growing ideological dispute with the Chinese Communists, who were younger and more evangelical in the Marxist faith than the Russians (see p. 749). The split between the Soviet Union and China was intensified by boundary disputes. Then in 1962 Khrushchev blundered into a showdown with the United States by trying to set up Soviet nuclear missiles in Cuba and was forced to make a humiliating retreat.

In October 1964 Khrushchev was suddenly ousted from power by his colleagues in the party's Central Committee. Leonid Brezhnev replaced him as party secretary, eventually emerging as the actual head of government by the late 1960s. Brezhnev reversed some of the liberalization of the Khrushchev years but did not fully return to Stalinist policies or practices. The Brezhnev era was marked by relative stability within the Soviet Union, a stability that seemed to persist under

Andropov, his successor. The Soviet economy has continued to expand but unevenly and not as rapidly as expected—in part thanks to the drain of military and administrative expenditures. By the 1980s the Soviet Union was a world leader in the production of steel, oil, coal, and cotton, and its industry was being computerized. Soviet agriculture was less successful. Although mechanization constantly increased, periodic droughts, poor management, and lack of incentive forced the government to make repeated and expensive grain purchases from the United States and Canada. The standard of living rose, but it still trailed that of the West and even that of some of the satellite countries in Eastern Europe. Soviet citizens enjoyed free education and medical services and relative job security. The Soviet Union continued to assert itself internationally as a world power, as indicated by its involvement and intervention in Czechoslovakia in 1968, Africa in the 1970s, Afghanistan in 1979, and Poland during the 1980s.

After Brezhnev died in 1982, Yuri Andropov (1982–1984) and then Konstantin Chernenko (1984–1985) came to power, but they did little to change the policies of the Brezhnev era. However, in 1985 the relatively young fifty-four-year-old Mikhail Gorbachev rose to power and initiated a series of important reforms (*glasnost*—"openness"; *perestroika*—"restructuring") in both foreign and domestic policy, including remodeling of the political system, attacks on corruption within the bureaucracy, decentralization of economic policy, relaxation of controls over political and cultural dissent, and new efforts to relax international tensions and stimulate disarmament agreements. These reforms seem to be producing both resistance and change within the Soviet Union.

Eastern Europe The governments and economies of Eastern Europe were brought under Stalin's control and set up in imitation of the Soviet model during the late 1940s. Initially, the Soviet Union drained off economic resources from these countries to strengthen its own economy. Soon single-party "people's democracies" were established in Poland, East Germany, Czechoslovakia, Hungary, Rumania, Yugoslavia, and Albania. Each of these governments was dominated by the head of its Communist party, who usually ruled in Stalinist

pattern. Each developed a planned economy stressing industrialization and collectivization of agriculture, and generally a high rate of economic growth was achieved. Each was required to cooperate politically, economically, and militarily with the Soviet Union. All major policies were tightly coordinated to the wishes of Moscow. Contact with the West was strictly limited. The one exception was Yugoslavia, where in 1948 Tito managed to break from the rest of the Communist bloc and take an independent course. Tito initiated a more decentralized form of communism stressing increased local control and worker participation in management.

Nevertheless, Eastern Europe should not be thought of as a mere appendage to the Soviet Union, even during the Stalinist period. Each state had its own sense of nationalism, each had its own particular ethnic mix, and each had its own history. The Soviet Union has not found it easy to gain or maintain control.

The first stirrings of revolt from Soviet control followed Stalin's death. In 1953 East Berliners rose but were quickly crushed by force. Following Khrushchev's 1956 speech denouncing Stalin and some of his policies, Poland rose in revolt. A compromise that left Poland within the Soviet sphere of control avoided the use of Soviet troops in Poland. Poland would enjoy a mild liberalization of its intellectual life and some economic independence. Shortly thereafter, a more violent armed revolt took place in Hungary. This more challenging demand for independence was met by an invasion of troops and the ouster of the new government. Nevertheless, under the Moscow-approved but moderate Janos Kádár, Hungarians were allowed increased individual freedom and greater national self-determination.

These revolts revealed some of the discontent and hopes for greater independence within East European nations, but the Soviet response also indicated the allowable limits to any deviance from the Soviet line. National differences between the various East European states and the Soviet Union were recognized. Contact with the West would be allowed. Cultural activities might be less restricted than in the Soviet Union. But fundamental political, economic, and military cooperation with Moscow was not to be violated.

FIGURE 58.4. Soviet Tanks in Prague Efforts by Czechoslovakia to reform its socialist system and gain greater independence from Moscow were brought to an end in August 1968 by a Soviet invasion. Here Soviet tanks overwhelm any potential resistance in the streets of Prague. (Josef Koudelka/Magnum)

Since the late 1950s the various Eastern European nations have pursued separate courses within the limits set by the Soviet Union. East Germany, Hungary, and Rumania remained relatively tranquil during the 1960s, 1970s, and 1980s. East Germany has closely followed the Soviet line while developing its industrial capacity. Hungary has successfully managed to orient its economy toward consumer goods, due to a loosening of state control and the introduction of limited capitalistic practices at the local level. In 1989 Hungary took new steps toward substantial democratic reform. Rumania has taken a more politically independent and conservative course under the leadership of president Nicolae Ceauşescu.

Albania, Czechoslovakia, and Poland have proven to be more of a problem to Moscow. In 1961 Albania, under Enver Hoxha, broke from Moscow and took the side of the Chinese in the Sino-Soviet split. Since Albania was surrounded by the already independent Yugoslavia and Greece, there was little the Soviet Union could do. In 1968 the Dubĉek government in Czechoslovakia went too far in allowing intellectual freedom and some democratization. The Soviet Union mobilized the troops of the Warsaw Pact nations and occupied Czechoslovakia (see Figure 58.4). Dubĉek and his supporters were removed from power along with their liberalizing policies. In 1980 the Polish government began to have difficulty maintaining its control over the nation. Mainly protesting the continuing economic mismanagement and corruption within the government, Polish workers struck and organized a union, Solidarity, under the leadership of Lech Walesa. Solidarity became increasingly powerful and was succeeding in forcing the government to grant concessions. When the union seemed to go too far, pressure from Moscow and resistance from conservative elements in the Polish government stiffened. In December 1981 martial law was declared by the new leader of the Polish Communist party, General Wojciech Jaruzelski. After a series of governmental crackdowns, Solidarity was outlawed in October 1982. In 1983 martial law was lifted and the government, pressured in part by the Catholic church, made some minor conciliatory gestures. Yet the fundamental political and economic problems that led to the unrest still keep Poland in a state of tension, as revealed by new strikes, a renewal of Solidarity's activities in 1988, new agreements between Solidarity and the government, and elections in 1989 giving Solidarity even greater power.

When compared with the economies of nations in Western Europe, the economies of Eastern Europe seem deficient. This deficiency is particularly apparent in recent years as the gap between Western and Eastern Europe seems to have widened. In the late 1980s Eastern Europe has been marked by growing discontent, greater political instability, and new demands for decentralization of economic decision making (as in Western capitalistic countries). On the other hand the economies of Eastern Europe started from a lower base and had to overcome greater difficulties. On the whole these economies have been modernizing, and Eastern Europeans have been enjoying a rising standard of living. Basic social services are extensive. With the exception of the elite of the Communist party and certain professionals, the gap between rich and poor classes has been narrowed. In a variety of fields, outstanding cultural productions have been created. The Eastern European nations, while still under the shadow of the Soviet Union, are distinct states with their own pasts and futures.

3. INTEGRATION AND INTERNATIONAL ORGANIZATIONS

In the years following World War II it became evident that there were advantages to dealing with problems cooperatively and through international organizations. European nations had long suffered from competitive nationalistic rivalries. The world in 1945 was no longer a place where a country such as Great Britain or France was strong enough to get its way. The developing Cold War was forcing countries to take sides whether or not they wanted to. After the destruction of World War II and particularly under the new threat of atomic weapons, the international pursuit of peace seemed even more pressing.

During the 1940s and 1950s a number of cooperative and international organizations were formed. Some were military, such as NATO (an alliance of the United States, Canada, and non-Communist nations of Europe) and its counterpart, the Warsaw Pact (an alliance of the Soviet Union and the Communist nations it dominated in Eastern Europe). Others were economic, such as the Organization for European Economic Cooperation (for coordination among recipients of Marshall Plan funds) and the Council for Economic Mutual Assistance (the Soviet response to the Marshall Plan). The most important of these organizations were the efforts toward integration in Western Europe and in the United Nations.

European Integration

In 1949 several nations in Western Europe took an initial step toward political integration by setting up the Council of Europe. Many hoped that this organization would develop into a parliament of Europe with real political power. However, the major European nations have been unwilling to give the council significant power, and it remains an organization of potential rather than concrete importance.

Western Europe has been more successful in taking steps toward economic integration. In 1950 France and Germany created the French-German Coal and Steel Authority. In 1952 it was expanded into the European Coal and Steel Community with the addition of Italy, Belgium, Luxembourg, and the Netherlands. In 1957 these same six nations signed the Treaty of Rome establishing the European Economic Community (the Common Market). Its purpose was to eliminate tariff barriers, cut restrictions on the flow of labor and capital, and generally integrate the economies of the member nations. The organization was a surprising success in the 1960s, eliminating tariff and immigration barriers ahead of schedule while its member nations enjoyed relative prosperity. During the 1970s and 1980s other nations joined the Common Market: Great Britain, Ireland, and Denmark in 1973; Greece in 1981; Portugal and Spain in 1986. Although at times further steps toward integration have been slow and difficult, in 1986 the Common Market agreed to eliminate almost all economic barriers among member states in 1992. This agreement would create a single market of some 320 million people.

The United Nations

In 1945 the world's leaders set up the United Nations to provide for international cooperation and act as a watchdog over peace. Since then, it has done an enormous amount of work in economic, cultural, and humanitarian fields, most of which has not made headlines. It has assisted in arranging cease-fires in several conflicts between Israel and the Arab states and has helped stop wars between India and Pakistan, and the Netherlands and Indonesia. Under the leadership of the United States, it fought in the Korean War, 1950–1953 (see pp. 750–751). In recent years the United Nations has won prestige for its effective role in areas of conflict such as the Middle East (particularly in facilitating the cease-fire between Iran and Iraq in 1988), southern Africa, and the western Sahara. Yet from the beginning the United Nations has been hampered by the unwillingness of the major powers to submit to its authority, embodied formally in the right of the permanent members of the Security Council to veto any action involving the use of force or the threat of force. Often it has proven unable to prevent wars or assert its will over defiant nations. The United Nations reflects more than it controls the domestic and international problems of its member nations over the past forty years.

SUGGESTED READING

General

W. Laqueur, *Europe Since Hitler* (1982). A scholarly, respected survey.

J. R. Wegs, *Europe Since 1945* (1983). A concise, up-to-date survey.

The Settlement and the Cold War

L. Halle, *The Cold War as History* (1967). A balanced account.

A. Ulam, *The Rivals: America and Russia Since World War II* (1972). Broad analysis of the significance of the Cold War.

D. Yergin, *The Shattered Peace* (1977). A balanced, well-written study of the Cold War.

Revival of a Divided Europe and the West

R. Aron, *The Imperial Republic: The United States and the World, 1945–1973* (1974). A sophisticated analysis of American dominance.

T. Ash, *The Polish Revolution: Solidarity* (1984). A full account.

L. T. Caldwell and W. Diebold, Jr., *Soviet American Relations in the 1980s* (1980). A good study of present problems.

W. Connor, *Socialism, Politics and Equality: Hierarchy and Change in Eastern Europe and the USSR* (1979). A good recent account.

R. Dahrendorf, *Society and Democracy in Germany* (1971). A respected but difficult analysis of Germany.

A. W. De Porte, *Europe Between the Superpowers: The Enduring Balance* (1979). A good recent analysis of Europe in the context of the superpowers.

D. L. Hanley et al., eds., *France: Politics and Society Since 1945* (1979). A good collection of essays.

J. Hough and M. Fainsod, *How the Soviet Union Is Governed* (1978). A useful general study.

F. Fejto, *A History of the People's Democracies: Eastern Europe Since Stalin* (1971). A solid study emphasizing differences among Eastern European nations.

A. H. Halsey, *Change in British Society* (1981). A solid recent study.

W. Leonhard, *Three Faces of Communism* (1974). Analyzes the ideological divisions of the Communist world.

A. Marwick, *British Society Since 1945* (1982). A good survey.

R. Mayne, *The Recovery of Europe, 1945–1973* (1973). Emphasizes Europe's economic progress and economic integration.

Integration and International Organizations

R. Mowat, *Creating the European Community* (1973). A study of European integration.

C. Tugenhat, *Making Sense of Europe* (1986). A recent evaluation of the Common Market.

CHAPTER 59

Decolonization and the Non-Western World, 1945–Present

FIGURE 59.1. Victory Parade in China, 1970 An imposing ninety-foot statue of Chairman Mao Tse-tung towers over marchers celebrating the twenty-first anniversary of the Communist victory in China. The rise of China as a world power in recent decades exemplifies the growing importance of connections between the Western and non-Western worlds. (Sipahioglu/Sipa/Special Features)

T he devastation of two world wars and the rising movements for independence with their
colonies was too much for the European imperial
powers to handle. Sometimes gracefully and
sometimes only after protracted violence, Europe
lost almost all her colonies in the two decades
following World War II. As the formerly colonized
peoples acquired their independence, they began
to assert their power in many areas of the non-
Western world. By the 1970s and 1980s it was
becoming clear that neither Europe nor the superpowers could act without taking into account the
concerns, power, and problems of the non-Western world.

1. JAPAN BETWEEN EAST AND WEST

Japan emerged from World War II defeated on sea
and land, the shocked victim of history's first two
atomic bombs used for military purposes. Since
the United States had played by far the major role
in the defeat of Japan, the United States refused
to share the occupation and governing of the Japanese islands with its former allies. President Truman appointed General Douglas MacArthur supreme commander of the Allied powers in Japan
and gave him absolute authority.

During the first year and a half of MacArthur's
command, a democratic constitution similar to
that of Great Britain was drawn up and put into
effect. In the first elections under the new constitution, which gave women the right to vote and
guaranteed civil liberties, the Social Democrats,
who were somewhat similar to the British Labourites, won the largest number of seats in the
national legislature. The activities of Japanese labor unions were encouraged, and they became
effective for the first time. The five great families
(the *zaibatsu*) who had monopolized Japan's industry and finance disbanded their great business
combinations under pressure from the occupation
authorities. Demilitarization was carried out and
a number of top Japanese war leaders were tried
and executed or imprisoned.

Of greatest significance was MacArthur's land-
reform program. The great mass of Japanese farmers were poverty-stricken, landless sharecroppers,

giving up from 50 to 70 percent of their yield to
absentee landlords. Laws sponsored by Mac-
Arthur forced the landlords to sell to the government all land in excess of seven and a half acres
(more in less fertile areas). The government, in
turn, sold the land in plots of seven and a half
acres to the tenant farmers, who were given thirty
years to pay for them. By the end of 1946 Japan
appeared to be on the way to becoming a liberal
democracy.

Early in 1947, when the Cold War was being
stepped up in intensity, General MacArthur suddenly reversed his liberal policy in Japan. He first
cracked down on the newly formed labor unions.
Industrial decentralization ceased, and land redistribution slowed down. Obviously, the United
States was now interested in making Japan, like
Germany, a link in the containment chain that it
was forging around the Soviet Union. By 1949 the
more conservative Liberal party, which later became the Liberal Democratic party, gained power
and would hold it in elections through the following four decades.

In 1951 the United States drew up a formal
treaty with Japan. The terms granted the United
States military bases in Japan and a protectorate
over the Ryukyu Islands (including Okinawa) and
Japan's former mandated islands in the Pacific.
(The United States gave up this protectorate in
1972.) Japan was to pay no indemnity and was to
be free to rearm and to make its own alliances.
Although forty-eight nations signed the treaty, India, Burma, the Soviet Union, and the Soviet satellites refused. China was not invited to sign.

During the 1950s and 1960s Japan made an
astounding economic recovery that surpassed
even that of West Germany. Like West Germany,
Japan received massive American aid. In rebuilding its ruined industries, Japan adopted the most
modern and scientific labor-saving devices (see
Figure 59.2). It benefited from the rapid expansion
of higher education and readily available, high-
quality labor. By the mid-1960s Japan was the third
greatest industrial power in the world, outranked
only by the United States and the Soviet Union,
and the Japanese people were enjoying a standard
of living and social peace such as they had never
known before. The Japanese, like the Germans,
benefited greatly from American military protec-

FIGURE 59.2. **Matsushita Electrical Industrial Company** By the 1970s, Japan was a leading industrial power, particularly in electronics. Plants such as this Matsushita Electrical Industrial Company (producing VCRs) used technology and disciplined labor to manufacture products for the home and foreign markets. (Courtesy Matsushita)

tion, which relieved them of the enormous cost of maintaining a big military establishment. They also sold large quantities of industrial products, particularly electronics and automobiles, to the United States and bought relatively few American goods in return. Furthermore, the Japanese labor unions, like the German, but unlike the American, British, and French unions, have followed a policy of cooperation—codetermination—with their corporate managers.

Political stability and economic prosperity continued through the 1970s. In 1978 Japan signed a treaty of friendship and commerce with the People's Republic of China. During the 1980s Japan has managed to maintain a striking degree of economic health with a comparatively high growth rate and lower rates of unemployment and inflation than any industrial power of the West. But the Japanese economy would appear to be fragile. Japan has few natural resources. In an area smaller than California, of which only 14 percent is arable, live more than 100 million people. Any prolonged interruption of foreign trade would probably be calamitous, and new competition from other Asian nations such as Taiwan, South Korea, and Singapore may prove costly.

2. THE RISE OF COMMUNIST CHINA

Across the Sea of Japan a very different and even more exciting drama was being enacted in China. Here, a massive upheaval involving one-fourth of the world's population took place. Sun Yat-sen, after launching his revolution against both China's foreign exploiters and its own reactionary and conniving government (see pp. 696–697), died in 1925, in the midst of the struggle. His place at the head of the revolutionary Chinese government was taken by his young and vigorous supporter, General Chiang Kai-shek, who soon gained control of all China. Chiang Kai-shek, a professional soldier, was much more interested in making China a powerful and independent nation than in liberalizing its government and society. Under him, the revolutionary Kuomintang party, then dominant in China, swung definitely to the right. When the Chinese Nationalist armies were defeated by the Japanese in 1937–1938 and driven deep into the interior, Chiang Kai-shek and the Kuomintang party were cut off from the chief bases of their liberal support, which were the great coastal cities. Heavily dependent then on the war-lords and landlords of the interior, they moved still further to the right.

Meanwhile, as China's Confucian civilization was crumbling faster than Sun Yat-sen's Western liberalism could replace it, another Western influence moved into the vacuum: Marxism. The hostility that the Western democracies showed to Sun Yat-sen's revolutionary liberal movement encouraged the Chinese Communists. In 1927 the Communists found an able leader in the scholarly and shrewd Mao Tse-tung (see Figure 59.3). This dedicated revolutionary from well-to-do peasant stock had risen to leadership by sheer force of intellect, personality, and energy. Chiang Kai-shek exerted every effort to crush the Chinese Communists—much more, in fact, than he spent to drive out the Japanese invaders. During the years 1939–1945, when the Kuomintang forces were inactive in Chungking and getting further and further out of touch with the Chinese masses, Mao Tse-tung's Communists were waging incessant guerrilla warfare against the Japanese and gaining a greater following among the Chinese people.

Following the surrender of Japan in August 1945, a bitter struggle for the control of China ensued between Chiang Kai-shek's Kuomintang forces, now known as the Chinese Nationalists, and the Chinese Communists. In this struggle the United States supported the Nationalists. However, the Communists won the support of ever-increasing numbers of the Chinese people. Morale in the long inactive and graft-ridden Nationalist armies was low, while that in the Communist armies, toughened by the continuous fighting against the Japanese, was high. Using Japanese weapons that had been left behind by the Russians, and American weapons and munitions that were surrendered by the Nationalists, the Communists began to gain the upper hand in 1947. During 1949 the victorious Communists swept over the entire Chinese mainland. Chiang Kai-shek, with a remnant of his Nationalist forces, mostly officers, fled to the island of Formosa (Taiwan), where after June 1950 they were protected by the United States navy. In 1949 Mao Tse-tung proclaimed the People's Republic of China and the following year formed an alliance with the Soviet Union. With Soviet aid, he began the enormous task of industrializing and communizing the world's most populous nation.

This formidable undertaking was interrupted shortly after it had begun by China's involvement in the Korean War, 1950–1953 (see the following section). When the United Nations forces, which were mostly American, defeated the North Korean Communists and approached the Manchurian border, the Chinese Communist armies crossed the Yalu River into Korea, drove the Americans back, and stalemated the war. This was a remarkable accomplishment for such an industrially backward country fighting against the world's greatest military power, and it cost the Chinese Communists nearly a million casualties.

In 1953 Mao Tse-tung launched his First Five-Year Plan, which was similar to Stalin's First Five-Year Plan twenty-five years earlier. The Chinese Communists, however, were starting from a much lower base than the Russians. Industry and agriculture were both collectivized. The emphasis was on building heavy industry. These were years of bleak austerity, but the Chinese masses had never known anything else. In 1957 the government announced that the First Five-Year Plan had been a great success. Most production quotas had been met or surpassed.

The following year it launched its Second Five-Year Plan. The vast new goals in industry and agriculture were to be achieved by communizing Chinese society more completely than had ever been attempted in the Soviet Union. The entire population was organized into strictly regimented communes; the ancient and sacred Chinese family structure was drastically altered. China's huge and rapidly growing population was set to building irrigation dams and ditches, steel mills, factories, railroads, schools, and hospitals, and in a frenzied hurry. This plan was called the "Great Leap Forward." But the plan was too ambitious. In 1959 a series of droughts and floods produced near-famine conditions in many areas. Overzealous local party officials provoked resentment and resistance among the harried populace. The realistic Red leaders slackened the pace and eased the regimentation.

The failure of the Great Leap Forward gave rise to ideological differences and set off a power struggle within the Communist party hierarchy. A

moderate group led by Liu Shaoqi, president of the republic and second in command to Party Chairman Mao Tse-tung, wished to slow down the pace of communization, produce more consumer goods, and encourage, at least temporarily, individual initiative. Mao took a different line. He believed many dangerous remnants of prerevolutionary capitalistic China and the newly bloated bureaucracy had to be destroyed. In 1966 he unleashed tens of thousands of Red Guards—fanatical Communist youths—upon the moderate element in what he called a "cultural revolution" and with the support of the regular army succeeded, after three years of turmoil, in crushing the moderates.

Of great concern to the Chinese Communists was their growing rift with the Soviet Union. In 1956 an ideological dispute had begun when Khrushchev denounced Stalin. Peking accused Moscow of becoming soft toward the capitalistic, imperialist West. In 1960 the Soviet Union began to withhold promised economic and technological aid from China. In 1964 Red China exploded its first nuclear device. This event, in addition to China's impressive military growth, appeared to give the Soviets grave concern. They moved many of their best mechanized divisions to the Far East, where in 1968 they clashed with Chinese units along the disputed border—the longest international border in the world. Both Red giants, fearful of each other, sought a détente with the United States.

In 1971 the United States government, shaken by its disastrous intervention in the Vietnam War (see pp. 753–754), began to face the changed realities in the Far East and to accept détente with both Red China and the Soviet Union. The United States ceased to block the admission of Red China to the United Nations, making it possible for the

FIGURE 59.3. Mao Tse-tung and Ho Chi Minh
These men were two of East Asia's most dynamic leaders since World War II. The North Vietnamese, though eager to get aid from China, were always suspicious and fearful of their big neighbor to the north. (Brian Brake/Rapho/Photo Researchers)

UN to admit the People's Republic of China (1971) and expel the Republic of China on Taiwan. Emissaries were exchanged between Peking and Washington. Only the continued American support of the Chinese Nationalist government on Taiwan (Chiang Kai-shek died in 1975) prevented the establishment of full diplomatic relations between the two great powers.

Mao Tse-tung died in 1976. The most influential and energetic leader in the new regime was Deputy Prime Minister Deng Xiaoping, who had been purged from the government by Mao. Late in 1978 Deng led a movement to diminish the image of Mao, reminiscent of Khrushchev's downgrading of Stalin in 1956. For the time being the fervor of permanent political revolution in Com-

Map 59.1 ASIA, 1989 Containing more than one-half of the world's population, Asia has been of growing concern to Western nations since 1945. Two wars (the Korean and the Vietnamese) have directly involved Western nations, while the economic might of Japan and the potential power of China are seen as threatening to many Western interests.

munist China had waned. Deng and his followers stressed rapid economic development, some economic decentralization, and opening more contacts with industrial powers. In the late 1970s and the 1980s these policies resulted in the treaty of friendship and commerce with Japan, improved relations with the United States, the quest for foreign loans, the opening of China to tourism and foreign investment, new economic growth, and greater economic freedom. However, in 1989 demands by students and workers for greater cultural and political freedom shook China, calling into question the stability of China's political system.

3. THE KOREAN WAR

The bitter Left-Right conflict among the Asiatic peoples and the global Cold War struggle between the United States and the Soviet Union merged in Korea to produce a shooting war of major proportions. In August 1945, in accordance with the Yalta Agreements, the forces of the Soviet Union overran Japanese-held Korea north of the thirty-eighth parallel, and the forces of the United States began to occupy Korea south of the thirty-eighth parallel. These moves were supposed to be for the purpose of setting up a free and united Korean nation. However, the Soviet Union immediately proceeded to set up a Communist dictatorship in North Korea under Kim Il-sung. The land was distributed to the peasants, and industry was nationalized. In South Korea the United States authorities sponsored a right-wing government under the leadership of the aged and reactionary Korean patriot Syngman Rhee. Late in 1948 the Soviet forces withdrew from North Korea, leaving behind an energetic Communist regime well armed with the latest Soviet weapons. Six months later the American forces withdrew from South Korea, leaving behind the Syngman Rhee landlord regime armed mostly with the weapons that had been captured from the Japanese. Both the North and South Korean governments talked loudly of conquering each other.

On June 25, 1950, North Korea suddenly attacked South Korea. The high-spirited and well-armed North Korean Communists easily defeated the South Koreans. The armies of Syngman Rhee, quer the world by military force and that there must not be another Munich. Secretary of State Dean Acheson persuaded the United Nations to take drastic action. Taking advantage of the absence of the Soviet Union's representative, the Security Council called upon the members of the United Nations to furnish military forces to repel the North Korean aggression and asked President Truman to name the commander of the United Nations forces. Truman named General MacArthur to command them. Truman also announced that he had already ordered American forces into the Korean War, that the American navy would protect Chiang Kai-shek's Chinese Nationalists on Taiwan against the Chinese Communists, and that American aid to the French fighting the native Communists in Indochina would be greatly increased.

The forces of the United Nations, mostly Americans, quickly defeated the North Koreans. By late November 1950, MacArthur's forces were approaching the Yalu River, which forms the Korean-Chinese border. At this point Red China entered the war and severely defeated MacArthur's forces, driving them in headlong retreat back down the peninsula. Eventually—January to March 1951—the battle line became stabilized roughly along the thirty-eighth parallel, where the war had started. Two years of negotiations brought an armistice in 1953. Total casualties—dead, wounded, and missing—are estimated to have been approximately a million and a half on each side, of which some 145,000 were Americans (including 54,000 dead) and 900,000 Chinese Communists. Most of the rest were Koreans. The war ended just about where it had started. However, Communist military aggression had been checked with severe punishment. The United Nations had functioned effectively and increased its prestige. Probably of equal significance is the fact that a revolutionary new Asiatic power, Red China, had fought the greatest Western power, the United States, to a standstill.

Since the end of the war, North and South Korea have gone their separate ways. North Korea has remained a tightly controlled Communist state under the long rule of Kim Il-sung. South Korea

FIGURE 59.4. Nehru and Gandhi Two great charismatic leaders of Asian independence, India's Jawaharlal Nehru and Mahatma Gandhi, are shown during a meeting of the All India Congress in Bombay in 1946. (UPI/Bettmann Newsphotos)

has remained under the control of right-wing authoritarian leaders, but its society is more open and more economically dynamic than that of the North. During the 1970s and 1980s it has become one of the most rapidly growing and industrializing economies in the world, and recently it has shown signs of broadening political participation.

4. THE REVOLT OF SOUTHERN ASIA

The end of World War II found the huge British, Dutch, and French empires in southern Asia aflame with the spirit of nationalism and revolt. Of the Western imperial powers, only the United States escaped direct embroilment in this revolt by granting independence to the Philippines in 1946.

In India, the world's second most populous country, the leader of the independence movement was Mohandas K. Gandhi (1869–1948), one of the most dynamic personalities of the twentieth century. This middle-class Hindu, educated in Great Britain, was a master of the psychology of the Indian masses. His chief tactics were passive resistance and civil disobedience. The British were unable to cope with him.

Indian nationalism reached its peak during World War II, but Churchill would not hear of Indian independence. "I did not become the king's first minister," said the doughty warrior, "in order to preside over the liquidation of the British Empire." The British Labour party, however, upon coming to power in 1945 immediately announced its determination to grant India independence. In 1947 independence was granted to India, containing some 350 million people, and Pakistan, with more than 70 million people.

Religious and national strife soon broke out between Hindu India and Moslem Pakistan. Gandhi tried to quell the strife, but he was assassinated in 1948 by a fanatical Hindu nationalist. Open war between the two states began in 1948 over possession of the disputed state of Kashmir. The United Nations was able to end the shooting but not the dispute.

One of Gandhi's most devoted followers, Jawaharlal Nehru, a charming, wealthy British-educated Hindu of the highest (Brahmin) caste, became the first prime minister of India (see Figure 59.4). The problems confronting him were staggering. Most of India's millions were poverty-stricken and illiterate. They spoke more than eight hundred languages and dialects (fewer than 50 percent spoke the official Hindi). Some 100 million Indians were of the untouchable class. Nehru inaugurated a liberal and mildly socialistic program somewhat similar to that of the British Labour government. For many observers, India would be watched as a test case. Could liberal democracy with a mixed capitalist-socialist economic policy do for the Indian people what Communism could do for the Chinese people in the way of modernization and material advancement? Not the least of Nehru's problems was avoiding embroilment in the Soviet-American Cold War. However, border clashes with Pakistan and with Red China frightened India into accepting military aid from both the United States and the Soviet Union.

Nehru's great charm and prestige kept India's restive millions fairly quiet. But when he died in 1964, his successors were confronted by rising discontent. In 1966 Nehru's daughter, Indira Gandhi, became prime minister. Many Indians felt that the economic and social reform program of the Nehrus was not drastic enough. In spite of sizable loans and much technical assistance from the United States, Great Britain, and the Soviet Union, India's standard of living was not keeping abreast of its ever-mounting population. In 1974, while millions of its people stood on the brink of starvation, India exploded its first nuclear device. In 1975 the opposition to Prime Minister Gandhi's administration became so disruptive that she invoked constitutional emergency decrees that amounted to dictatorship. Thousands of her most vocal opponents were imprisoned. But the opposition only increased. In 1977 Mrs. Gandhi granted national elections and was driven from power. However, her successors had little success in dealing with the overwhelming problems facing India. Indira Gandhi returned to power as prime minister in 1980, but she was assassinated by Sikh extremists in 1984 and has been succeeded by her son, Rajiv Gandhi. India still struggles with the problems of religious differences (particularly with the Sikhs of Punjab) and linguistic differences (as with the Tamils in the south) in a difficult environment of uneven economic development, overpopulation, and poverty.

Pakistan, divided into two states more than a thousand miles apart (see Map 59.1) and with a fragile constitutional government, soon became a military dictatorship closely aligned with the United States. In 1971 East Pakistan rebelled against the less populous but dominant West Pakistan and, with the help of India, gained its independence as the Republic of Bangladesh—but not before some 3 million of its helpless citizens had been slaughtered by the West Pakistani army. From 1977 to his death in 1988, Zia ul-Haq held power and remained an important if difficult ally of the United States.

The British Labour government also granted independence to Ceylon, Burma, and Malaya. This left only Hong Kong as a reminder of British imperialism in Asia.

The rich and populous Dutch East Indies declared independence at the end of World War II. The Dutch resisted fiercely for four years but yielded to pressure from the United Nations. In 1949 the Republic of Indonesia was recognized as an independent nation—a nation of approximately 125 million people, mostly Moslems, living on several thousand tropical islands rich in tin, rubber, oil, and many other valuable products.

Of all the European colonial regimes in Asia, that of the French in Indochina was probably the most predatory and the most hated. Immediately after the surrender of Japan in August 1945, the Indochinese nationalists, under the leadership of Ho Chi Minh, a Russian-trained Communist, proclaimed the independent "democratic" Republic of Vietnam. The returning French imperialists were fiercely resisted by the native Communist nationalists. Heavy fighting ensued, in which the French were aided by American Marshall Plan money. The majority of the Vietnamese people apparently preferred the Communists to the French, and the forces of Ho Chi Minh won victory after victory despite American aid to the French.

In 1954 the French government admitted defeat and ceded the northern half of Vietnam to the Communists. Although South Vietnam technically remained a part of the French Union, French influence quickly vanished. The United States, in accordance with its policy of military containment of communism—both Russian and Chinese—undertook to establish its power not only in South Vietnam but in Laos and Cambodia as well, which the French had also freed. Vigorous military and

FIGURE 59.5.   Vietnam, 1969   The intervention of the United States in Vietnam for the purpose of containing communism (Russian and Chinese, it was believed) resulted in greater bombing and destruction than in World War II. Millions of Vietnamese were killed, maimed, and made homeless. (Jones Griffiths/ Magnum)

financial aid was given to the conservative Ngo Dinh Diem regime in South Vietnam. Fearful of a Communist victory at the polls, American authorities refused to permit the holding of national elections, which had been promised by an international commission when the French withdrew. Diem became increasingly unpopular. Almost immediately, he was faced with a rebellion of his own people supported and soon led by the Communists in both South and North Vietnam. No amount of American aid seemed to be able to hold back the tide against the unpopular and faltering Diem regime. In 1963 Diem, having lost the confidence and support of his American protectors, was overthrown and assassinated by a group of his own officers, who set up a harsh military dictatorship of their own. Early in 1965 the Vietnam-

ese Communists, with significant material aid from both the Soviet Union and Red China, greatly stepped up their war against the American-supported but weakening South Vietnamese forces. The United States retaliated with heavy bombing of North Vietnam and increased its armed forces to over 500,000 troops. Vietnam was rapidly being devastated (see Figure 59.5).

Meanwhile, public opinion all over the world, including the United States, was becoming incensed at the wanton destruction. In 1968 a massive North Vietnamese surprise offensive convinced the American government that victory could not be won, and the United States began long, dreary peace talks with the North Vietnamese in Paris. In 1969 Ho Chi Minh died, but the war and new massive bombings (the United States dropped more explosives on Vietnam than were used by all combatants during World War II) dragged on until 1973, when peace agreements were finally signed and the United States withdrew its armed forces, leaving behind huge stores of war matériel for the South Vietnamese. The civil war in Vietnam, however, continued as both sides refused to abide by the terms of the peace agreements.

As in China and Korea, the graft-ridden armed forces of a corrupt government trying to maintain the old aristocratic society of a bygone era were no match for the high-spirited Communist forces. In 1975 the Communists swept to victory over all Vietnam and shortly thereafter over the rest of Indochina—Cambodia and Laos. Even then the violence did not end. In Cambodia the Communist Pol Pot regime devastated that society, resulting in the death of over a million people and ending in an invasion and occupation of Cambodia by Vietnam. Relations between Vietnam and China remain shaky, with violence having broken out along their border more than once during the past decade.

5. THE EMBATTLED MIDDLE EAST

One of the most explosive areas in the latter half of the twentieth-century world was the Middle East—that area between and including Egypt and Iran, where East meets West (see Map 59.2). In global terms it is probably the most strategic area in the world. It forms the bridge between the world's two greatest land masses, Eurasia and Africa; and through it pass the chief communication lines between the East and the West. The Middle East is the heart of the Moslem world, which stretches from Morocco to Indonesia and contains over 500 million followers of the Prophet. It is also the heart of the tumultuous Arab world. Moreover, the area contains more than half the world's known oil reserves.

During the early part of the century, while the great European powers competed for control of the Middle East, Arab nationalism was rising. This nationalism was vented first against the British, who were the dominant power in that area. As anti-British hostility mounted in the years between

the two world wars, Great Britain began to relax its control. By the end of World War II only Cyprus, Palestine, and the Suez Canal remained in Britain's possession, and the British were bidding strongly for Arab friendship. But continued British possession of the Suez Canal and the admission of tens of thousands of Jews into Palestine under the Balfour Declaration of 1917 proved to be effective barriers to Anglo-Arab accord.

Palestine was the ancient home of the Jews. However, in A.D. 70 they were dispersed by the government of the Roman Empire. In the seventh century the Moslem Arabs conquered Palestine and lived there until the twentieth century—thirteen hundred years. In the late nineteenth century, the Zionist movement began—a movement to restore Palestine as a national home for the Jews. During the anti-Semitic persecutions of the Hitler era, thousands of European Jewish refugees, many of them wealthy, poured into Palestine, buying up the land and dispossessing the Arabs. The whole Arab and Moslem world became incensed.

In 1948 the British Labour government turned Palestine over to the United Nations. The Jews immediately proclaimed the State of Israel and accepted the boundary lines that the United Nations had drawn to divide Palestine between the Jews and the Arabs. The Arab League refused to accept this arrangement and began hostilities with a view to eliminating the Jewish state. Tiny Israel, however, well armed and well financed, was more than a match for the Arabs. After a year of fighting, the United Nations succeeded in bringing about a truce. Israel had somewhat expanded its original borders, and it had expelled nearly half a million Arabs who had fought to destroy the State of Israel. Arab nationalism was thoroughly aroused, and border raids recurred as the Arabs armed for a renewal of the struggle. Israel, in the meantime, receiving financial aid from Jews abroad, prospered, built modern cities, introduced irrigation and scientific agriculture, and became a vigorous, democratic, cooperative Western society.

The Arabs found a vigorous leader when in 1952 a military coup in Egypt brought to power Gamel Abdul Nasser. Nasser set out to unite the Arab world and inflame it against the West. When

Map 59.2   **THE MIDDLE EAST, 1989**   Since 1945 the Middle East has been wracked by several outbreaks of war involving Israel and its neighbors. Cold war involvements, the growing strength of Arab nationalism, and OPEC control over oil production have made this part of the world of crucial concern to the West.

he threatened Israel, seized the Suez Canal, and aided France's rebellious subjects in North Africa, he was attacked by Israel, Great Britain, and France in 1956. He was saved only by the threatened intervention of the Soviet Union, which caused the United States to exert sufficient pressure on the three invading powers to force them to give up their assault. But nothing had been settled. Nasser continued to arouse Arab nationalism against Israel, and the Arab states received a swelling stream of arms from the Soviet Union.

In 1967 Nasser again brought on a showdown. He had prohibited the use of the Suez Canal by the Israelis since the 1956 war. When he blockaded Israel's only port on the Red Sea and Egyptian, Syrian, and Jordanian armies massed along the Israeli borders, the Israelis suddenly attacked them and crushed them in six days' time. The Israelis then occupied Egyptian territory east of the Suez Canal, Syria's Golan Heights, and Jordanian territory west of the Jordan—territories that the Israelis claimed were necessary for their security.

The six-day 1967 war humiliated not only the Arab world but also the Soviet Union, who rushed billions of dollars' worth of arms, including deadly surface-to-air missiles (SAMs), together with thousands of military "advisers," to Egypt and Syria. Nasser died in 1970 and was succeeded as president of Egypt by Anwar Sadat.

As the Israelis were celebrating their Yom Kippur holidays in October 1973, Egypt and Syria, supported by the rest of the Arab states (except Morocco), suddenly attacked them. This time the Arabs, much better armed and trained than before, inflicted serious casualties on the Israelis and pushed them back on all fronts. Several weeks were required for the heavily outnumbered Israelis to recover from their initial shock, receive massive fresh supplies from the United States, and mount offensives of their own. They then crossed the Suez Canal, surrounded an entire Egyptian army, and began advancing on Cairo to the west and Damascus, the Syrian capital, to the east. At this juncture the Soviet Union threatened to intervene. The United States alerted its armed forces and forced the Israelis to halt their advance. The United Nations helped to arrange a cease-fire.

Ever since the 1967 war most of the world—much of it undoubtedly influenced by its hunger for Arab oil—has supported the Arab states in their demand for the return of all occupied territories. The Israelis, claiming these territories as necessary buffer zones and bargaining pawns, have refused to give them up without adequate guarantees of security, which under the circumstances are hard to envision. Only the United States and the Netherlands supported Israel.

The Arabs now made full use of their oil weapon; they quadrupled the price of their oil, curtailed production, and placed a complete embargo on its shipment to the United States and the Netherlands. These measures added greatly to the strain of inflation that had long gripped the capitalistic world. The poorer nations of Asia and Africa were particularly distressed.

In November 1977 Egypt's President Sadat surprised the world by going to Jerusalem and beginning negotiations with Israel's Premier Begin for a peace settlement. Sadat was denounced by all his Arab neighbors for breaking the solid Arab front against Israel. Negotiations soon broke down, however, over the disposition of the Palestinian West Bank, which the Israelis had seized during the 1967 war, and over the claims of the Palestinian refugees. Again the world was surprised when President Carter in September 1978 succeeded in bringing Sadat and Begin to his retreat at Camp David, Maryland, and persuading

them to sign the first draft of a peace treaty. Since 1978 the only major step that has been taken to lessen tensions in this area of the world has been the Israeli withdrawal from the Sinai, completed in 1982.

The Palestinian refugees were one of the most tumultuous elements in the whole Middle Eastern complex. Fleeing Palestine after the 1948 war, they first attempted to overthrow the government of Jordan. Failing there, they took refuge in Lebanon, which was too weak to expel them. Their numbers grew constantly until by 1975 there were between 2 million and 3 million of them. In that year they joined the Moslem Lebanese majority in attempting to overthrow the Christian-dominated government. In the civil war that followed, Beirut, the capital city and one of the most prosperous banking and commercial centers in the Middle East, was wrecked. Syria took advantage of the turmoil to move in and gain military control over most of the country. In 1982 Israel invaded Lebanon and occupied the southern half of the country. In vain, troops from Western nations, including Italy, France, Great Britain, and the United States, were stationed in Beirut by 1983, only to be withdrawn in 1984. Lebanon continues to be wracked by civil war and international animosities, and the Palestinian's struggles with Israel seem far from over. Under the leadership of the Palestine Liberation Organization and other radical groups, Palestinians have continued to resist Israeli troops from within Israeli-occupied territories and resort to guerrilla and terrorist tactics almost everywhere. Israel has responded with intransigence. Recently, however, the Palestine Liberation Organization, under the leadership of Yasir Arafat, has gained increased international stature. By admitting Israel's right to exist and rejecting terrorism, the Palestine Liberation Organization has convinced the United States to open negotiations with it for the first time.

The enormous oil wealth pouring into the Middle East accelerated the demands for change. Countries such as Saudi Arabia and Kuwait became suddenly wealthy, commanding strategic oil reserves and great financial muscle. But in other countries, problems arose. In 1978 Iran, second only to Saudi Arabia in the production of oil and precariously situated between the Soviet Union and the Persian Gulf, was the scene of massive uprisings. The Shah's government was strongly supported by the United States as a military strong point on the border of the Soviet Union. Though modernizing the country, the Shah's government was a military dictatorship. Now it was beset on the one hand by young liberals who wanted to democratize and further modernize Iran and on the other by the masses led by Islamic fundamentalists who rejected the West and secularism in favor of old Islamic values. Early in 1979 the Shah was forced to flee, and the reins of government were seized by the seventy-nine-year-old popular Moslem mystic Ayatollah Khomeini, who set up an Islamic republic (see Figure 59.6). The nationalistic Khomeini was strongly anti-American, anti-Soviet, and anti-Israeli. The violence and instability continued and indeed was increased in 1980 by the outbreak of a costly war between Iran and Iraq that lasted until 1988. The Soviet invasions of Afghanistan in 1979 and the Islamic resistance that followed indicate that the turmoil that has marked the Middle East has few boundaries. The Soviet withdrawal from Afghanistan initiated in 1988 offers some hope for greater peace in that country.

6. THE EMANCIPATION OF AFRICA

Africa was the last of the continents to rise against European imperialism, and the history of Africa since the end of World War II has been largely the story of emancipation from European domination (see Map 59.3). France and Great Britain, who held the most territory in Africa, were the first to begin to dismantle their vast empires there.

The end of World War II found France's huge North African empire seething with unrest. Its population, largely Moslem, was agitated by the rampaging Arab nationalism in the Middle East. France, in 1956, granted independence to Morocco and Tunisia. The problem of independence or autonomy for Algeria was much more complex because of the presence there of more than a million French settlers who feared reprisals from the 8 million Moslem Algerians. Efforts to hold back independence resulted in open revolt by Algerians that France could not handle and that helped bring de Gaulle back to power in France. Bowing to the

FIGURE 59.6. Khomeini In 1979 the Shiites' leader, Ayatollah Khomeini, gained power in Iran. As spiritual head of an Islamic fundamentalist movement, Khomeini commanded the passionate allegiance of masses of followers. (UPI/Bettmann Newsphotos)

force of Arab nationalism, in 1962 he granted Algeria independence. Meanwhile, he had granted independence to all the other French colonies, most of which were in Africa, and invited them to form a voluntary union with France. All but one, French Guinea, did so.

Great Britain's experiences in Africa following World War II were quite similar to those of France. All the native populations caught the spirit of na-

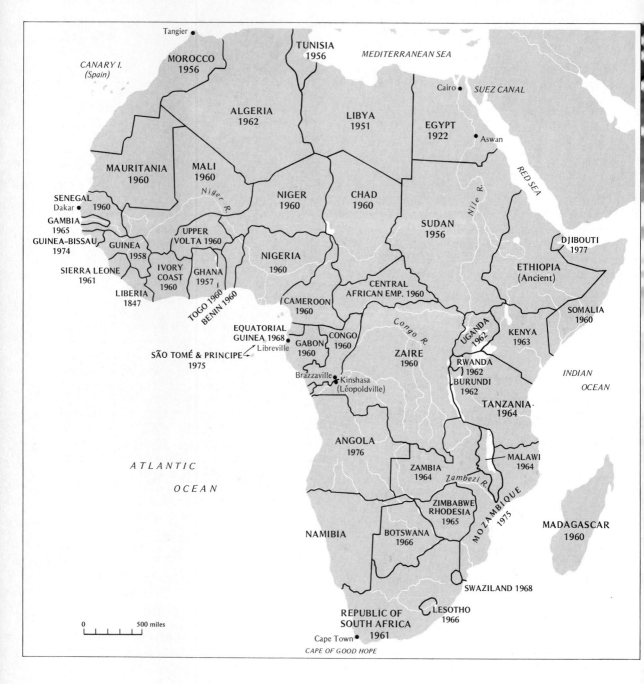

Tangier •

CANARY I.
(Spain)

MOROCCO
1956

TUNISIA
1956

MEDITERRANEAN SEA

Cairo • SUEZ CANAL

ALGERIA
1962

LIBYA
1951

EGYPT
1922

Aswan •

MAURITANIA
1960

MALI
1960

Niger R.

NIGER
1960

CHAD
1960

SUDAN
1956

RED SEA

Nile R.

SENEGAL
Dakar • 1960

GAMBIA
1965

GUINEA-BISSAU
1974

GUINEA
1958

UPPER
VOLTA 1960

SIERRA LEONE
1961

IVORY
COAST
1960

GHANA
1957

NIGERIA
1960

DJIBOUTI
1977

LIBERIA
1847

TOGO 1960
BENIN 1960

CAMEROON
1960

CENTRAL
AFRICAN EMP. 1960

ETHIOPIA
(Ancient)

SOMALIA
1960

EQUATORIAL
GUINEA 1968 •
Libreville

SÃO TOMÉ & PRINCIPE
1975

GABON
1960

CONGO
1960

Congo R.

ZAIRE
1960

UGANDA
1962

KENYA
1963

Brazzaville •

• Kinshasa
(Léopoldville)

RWANDA
1962
BURUNDI
1962

INDIAN

OCEAN

TANZANIA
1964

ATLANTIC

OCEAN

ANGOLA
1976

ZAMBIA
1964

MALAWI
1964

Zambezi R.

MOZAMBIQUE 1975

ZIMBABWE
RHODESIA
1965

MADAGASCAR
1960

NAMIBIA

BOTSWANA
1966

SWAZILAND 1968

REPUBLIC OF
SOUTH AFRICA
Cape Town • 1961

LESOTHO
1966

CAPE OF GOOD HOPE

0   500 miles

tionalism and turned in resentment against their white masters. Native terror bands, notably the Mau Mau in Kenya, made British life and property increasingly unsafe. In 1957 Great Britain granted independence to its Gold Coast colony, which became the Republic of Ghana. This proved to be the first step in the eventual freeing of Britain's remaining African colonies. During the next few years one after another of Britain's African territories was freed. By 1965 all of Britain's African empire had been dismantled.

In two of the former British African colonies sizable white minorities attempted to continue their domination over the black majorities and in so doing created tensions that became global in scope. In Rhodesia approximately a quarter million whites ruled 6 million blacks. When in 1965 the British government pressed the all-white government of Rhodesia to grant suffrage to blacks, that government declared its independence from Great Britain. Almost immediately the black majority demanded suffrage and civil equality; when it was refused, many of them resorted to guerrilla warfare, aided by neighboring black nations and by the Soviet Union. In 1979 the all-white government, under pressure from the United States, Great Britain, and the United Nations, formed a coalition with a group of moderate black leaders and granted universal suffrage. In the ensuing elections the coalition won a majority in parliament and named a black prime minister. However, the voting was so weighted and unfree that the black guerrillas continued their struggle for complete freedom and equality and an end to white privilege. In 1980 that freedom was gained. Zimbabwe acquired full independence from Great Britain, and Robert Mugabe, one of the principal black guerrilla leaders, was named prime minister.

South Africa was the scene of a bigger and potentially even more dangerous racial conflict.

Map 59.3 AFRICA, 1989 As this map indicates, the vast majority of African nations gained their independence during the 1950s and 1960s. Instability, often stemming from the legacy of Western colonialism, has plagued much of the continent.

The Dominion of South Africa had since 1931 (the Statute of Westminster) been completely free. There the prosperous white minority (4 million whites and 18 million blacks and other nonwhites) clung desperately to its superiority. In 1948 and thereafter, the white minority took severe measures to suppress the increasingly restless black majority and to enforce *apartheid* (racial segregation). When in 1961 several fellow members of the British Commonwealth censured South Africa because of its racial policies, South Africa withdrew from the Commonwealth, taking its large mandate, South-West Africa (Namibia), with it. Under pressure from the angry black majority and from the Organization of African Unity (set up in 1963 by the completely freed African nations), the United Nations, and world opinion, the all-white government of the Republic of South Africa from time to time made token concessions to *apartheid* but steadfastly refused to grant majority rule. During the 1970s and 1980s the situation became increasingly polarized and explosive. White South Africa now remains almost completely isolated in the world, censured because of its racism, a place where massive violence is expected to break out as peaceful alternatives for change are rejected.

The decision of the World War II allies to free oil-rich Moslem Libya from Italian control was consummated in 1951. In 1960 Italy granted independence to Somalia in East Africa, and Belgium gave up the Congo. Finally, Portugal freed her large African colonies in 1975, bringing to an end (with the exception of a few bits of territory here and there) the era of European domination of Africa that began in the fifteenth century.

The granting of independence, of course, did not bring peace and prosperity to the African people. The boundaries of the African states were drawn in many cases quite arbitrarily by nineteenth-century European imperialists sitting around plush green-topped tables in London or Brussels dividing up the spoils. In the Congo, for instance, tribal warfare flamed up immediately after independence. Russian and Chinese Communist agents moved in to exploit the chaos. UN Secretary-General Dag Hammarskjöld lost his life there in a plane accident while trying to mediate the differences. In Nigeria, the Ibos in the eastern region attempted to secede and set up the inde-

FIGURE 59.7. Ethiopian Refugee In recent decades, large areas of Africa have suffered from war, drought , and overpopulation. The results have been malnutrition, disease, starvation, and death. This photo of a starving child at a refugee camp in Ethiopia is all too common. (Michel Philippot/Sygma)

pendent Republic of Biafra. Thousands died in the futile struggle, and tens of thousands died by starvation. Since the newly freed African people were left without political experience and with few, if any, self-generated political institutions, instability, bloodshed, and rule by military strong men were often the result. Charismatic liberation leaders such as Kwame Nkrumah in Ghana and Jomo Kenyatta in Kenya (where a relatively stable parliamentary system was established) were more the exception than the rule.

Economically the European colonial powers did not leave African countries with a firm basis for balanced prosperity or self-sufficiency. In the early 1980s, Africa's economy was still primarily agricultural, despite a large development of oil and gas production in Libya, Algeria, and Nigeria and a beginning of industrialization (mostly foreign) in the Ivory Coast. Of course, gold and diamond mining in South Africa was still a source of

great wealth. Africa's rapidly growing population, dependent for the most part on agriculture, was faced with an increasing threat of hunger and starvation. An unprecedented drought in the huge sub-Sahara region of northern Africa during the late 1960s, the 1970s, and the 1980s brought death by starvation to tens of thousands (see Figure 59.7).

With the freeing of Africa, the expansion of the European world, which began in the fifteenth century, had after five hundred years been very definitely reversed. The non-Western world now challenged the West.

7. LATIN AMERICA

Finally, there remains to be examined a large and populous area of the world which is, in a sense, neither East nor West—Latin America (see Map 59.4). Just as Japan is a highly industrialized nation located in the East, Latin America is *in* but, in many respects, not *of* the West. Its religion and languages are, of course, Western. But the poverty and the illiteracy of the masses, the underdeveloped economy, and the unstable political institutions more closely resemble southern Asia and Africa than Western Europe and the United States.

At the end of World War II the governments of the twenty independent Latin American states were all republics in name. In reality, however, most of them were rightist dictatorships, representing the interests of the well-to-do bourgeoisie, the landowning classes, and the professional military. The Roman Catholic church, which during the nineteenth century had been one of the most powerful rightist forces, had during the twentieth century tended to become much more liberal. In some of the Latin American republics, notably

Map 59.4 LATIN AMERICA, 1989 With one of the world's highest population growth rates and seemingly unbridgeable gaps between the rich few and the poor masses, Latin America has become an area of great political, economic, and social instability. This instability has drawn Western powers, particularly the United States, into Latin American affairs.

UNITED STATES

Ciudad Juárez

Rio Grande

Monterrey *GULF OF MEXICO*

MEXICO

Guadalajara

Mexico City

Veracruz

YUCATÁN PEN.

Havana

CUBA

Santiago de Cuba

BELIZE
Belmopan
GUATEMALA HONDURAS Tegucigalpa
Guatemala
EL SALVADOR
San Salvador
Managua NICARAGUA
San José *PANAMA CANAL*
COSTA RICA
PANAMA Panamá

JAMAICA Kingston
GREATER ANTILLES

CARIBBEAN SEA

LESSER ANTILLES

Barranquilla Maracaibo
LAKE MARACAIBO Caracas
Barquisimeto
VENEZUELA

Medellín
Cali Bogotá
COLOMBIA

Quito
ECUADOR
Guayaquil

GALAPAGOS ISLANDS (ECUADOR)

Georgetown
GUYANA SURINAM Paramaribo
FRENCH GUIANA
Cayenne

Orinoco R.

Negro R. *Amazon R.*

Manaus

MARAJÓ ISLAND
Belém

Fortaleza

SELVAS

Ucayali R.
Madeira R.
Xingu R.
Tocantins R.

PERU

Lima

LAKE TITICACA

Arequipa

BOLIVIA
La Paz
Santa Cruz
LAKE POOPÓ

Antofagasta

PACIFIC OCEAN

CHILE

Valparaíso
Santiago

BRAZIL

Brasília

São Francisco R.
BRAZILIAN HIGHLANDS

Belo Horizonte

Paraguay R.

Paraná R.

São Paulo
Santos
Curitiba

Pôrto Alegre

Córdoba
Mendoza
Rosario URUGUAY
PAMPAS Montevideo
Buenos Aires *Río de la Plata*
ARGENTINA
Bahía Blanca

Recife

Salvador

Rio de Janeiro

ATLANTIC OCEAN

PARAGUAY
Asunción

PATAGONIA

FALKLAND ISLANDS (ISLAS MALVINAS) (U.K.)

Magellan Strait
Punta Arenas
TIERRA DEL FUEGO
Cape Horn

◎ **Capital Cities**

0   500   1000 MILES

HAITI
Port-au-Prince
DOMINICAN REPUBLIC
Santo Domingo
San Juan
PUERTO RICO (U.S.A.)
VIRGIN ISLANDS (U.S.A., U.K.)
ANGUILLA (U.K.)
ST. MARTIN (FR & NETH.)
BARBUDA (U.K.)
ANTIGUA
ST. KITTS, NEVIS (U.K.)
GUADELOUPE (FR.)
MONTSERRAT (U.K.)
DOMINICA
MARTINIQUE (FR.)
ST. LUCIA
BARBADOS
ST. VINCENT AND THE GRENADINES
GRENADA
TOBAGO
TRINIDAD & TOBAGO
Port-of-Spain
TRINIDAD

CARIBBEAN SEA

NETHERLANDS
ARUBA ANTILLES
CURAÇAO
BONAIRE

COLOMBIA

VENEZUELA

Chile, the Church was now actively engaged in liberal social and economic reform movements. Costa Rica was the most democratic of the republics. In Mexico a stable (though primarily a one-party) democratic regime had since 1934 been pursuing a liberal program of economic, social, and educational reforms.

Throughout most of Latin America the poor, illiterate, and ever more numerous masses became increasingly restive after World War II. Many of them turned to communism and were encouraged and supported by the Soviet Union. The United States, on the other hand, supported the rightist governments. In 1954 a military force armed by the United States invaded and overthrew the leftist government of Guatemala. Ten years later a rightist military takeover in Brazil was encouraged and applauded by the United States. In 1948 the twenty Latin American "republics" were persuaded to join the United States in an Organization of American States (OAS) for the purpose of resisting outside (Communist) interference. The Latin Americans were primarily interested in economic aid from the United States and were generally disappointed.

In Cuba the policy of the United States backfired. In 1959 the rightist dictator, Fulgencio Batista, long supported by the United States, was overthrown by the leftist revolutionary, Fidel Castro. Castro began a sweeping program of social and economic reforms including the seizure of property owned by citizens and corporations of the United States. Fumbling efforts of the United States to overthrow the Castro regime drove it into the arms of the Soviet Union. Cuba became a Communist beachhead in the Western Hemisphere.

In 1970 Chile became the first nation in the world to vote into power a Marxist regime. As a result of a split between the conservatives and the moderate liberals, Salvador Allende was elected president (with 36 percent of the vote) and immediately launched a Marxist program. All industrial properties, the biggest of which were owned by United States corporations, were nationalized. The government of the United States determined to destroy the Allende regime. In 1974 the American Central Intelligence Agency admitted that it had spent $11 million bribing Chilean legislators, stirring up labor strife, and supporting right-wing elements. In 1973 the Allende regime was overthrown by the professional military, which set up a rightist military dictatorship. Allende and thousands of his followers were executed.

In 1979 the Sandinistas, a leftist revolutionary force, overthrew the Somoza dictatorship in Nicaragua. During the 1980s, the new government pursued policies of radical social and economic reform, but it was weakened by pressure from the United States and the American-backed contra guerrillas. Although still fragile, this revolutionary regime—with support from Cuba and the Soviet Union—has managed to maintain control in Nicaragua.

In the 1980s Latin America, like much of the non-Western world, remains an area of sharp and dangerous contrasts. Rich natural resources are not being developed and used for the benefit of the rapidly increasing population, which for the most part is poor and illiterate. Increases in productivity seem more than matched by a rapid inflation of prices for goods and services. Great modern cities such as Mexico City and São Paulo, which rival New York and Chicago in size and modernity, stand surrounded by wretched hovels and an economically depressed countryside. Wealth is enjoyed by a small class of large landowners, industrialists, financiers, and governmental officials. The government of the United States supplies financial and technical assistance, but as in other parts of the world, it often supports rightist military regimes that are more interested in retaining their power than in aiding their people. Moreover a massive and mounting debt burden threatens relations with the United States and international financial stability. Even countries bolstered by income from oil production, such as Venezuela and Mexico, seem unable to keep their debts from growing to alarming proportions. Latin America thus remains an area of political instability and potential revolutionary activity, as revealed by the continuing guerrilla activity, coup d'états, mass demonstrations, and revolutions of recent years.

SUGGESTED READING

General

R. von Albertini, *Decolonization* (1971). A good survey.

G. Barraclough, *An Introduction to Contemporary History* (1975). An interpretive analysis of world history in an age of globalism.

C. E. Black, *The Dynamics of Modernization: A Study in Comparative History* (1966). Spans the Western and non-Western worlds.

A. Boyd, *An Atlas of World Affairs*, 7th ed. (1983). Useful, brief reference.

R. Critchfield, *Villages* (1980). Focuses on rural life in non-Western nations.

Asia and Africa

W. Brown, *The United States and India, Pakistan, and Bangladesh* (1972). An excellent brief survey.

F. Butterfield, *China, Alive in the Bitter Sea* (1982). Well-written observations by a journalist.

P. Caputo, *A Rumor of War* (1977). Fine book on the Vietnam War, by a Marine officer who served in Vietnam.

B. Davidson, *Let Freedom Come* (1978). Surveys modern Africa.

C. Fitzgerald, *The Birth of Communist China*. By a leading expert.

I. K. Y. Hsu, *China Without Mao: The Search for a New Order* (1982). A highly respected work.

E. Reischauer, *The Japanese* (1977). A brilliant and highly readable analysis.

The Middle East

W. Polk, *The Elusive Peace: The Middle East in the Twentieth Century* (1980). A fine survey.

J. Voll, *Islam: Continuity and Change in the Modern World* (1982). A brief survey.

Latin America

D. Collier, ed., *The New Authoritarianism in Latin America* (1979). Points to political problems in contemporary Latin America.

W. La Faber, *Inevitable Revolutions: The United States in Central America* (1984). A good background to this tension-filled area.

R. J. Shafer, *A History of Latin America* (1978). A useful survey.

CHAPTER 60

Culture and Society in the Twentieth Century

FIGURE 60.1 Don Eddy, "New Shoes for H," 1973–1974 This painting of a shoe store display in Manhattan reveals several trends of contemporary society and culture. The environment is one of urbanism and commercialism. The effect of the window panes is to show things from different perspectives and to distort. The style, photo-realism, combines technology and the newest painting techniques. (The Cleveland Museum of Art)

As we come closer to the present, it becomes more difficult to see and understand history. Current events—yesterday's headlines—may prove to be historically unimportant. Time must elapse before we can gain the perspective necessary to grasp their significance. This problem of perspective becomes magnified when the focus is not on dramatic political, military, or economic events but, rather, on the more subtle social and cultural developments of Western civilization. However, certain trends can be discerned.

Social, intellectual, and cultural trends have followed two broad patterns since World War I. Until 1945, there was a widespread sense of anxiety, disillusionment, and uncertainty in the West. In part, these feelings were an extension of a trend already developing in the two or three decades prior to World War I, but after World War I it was no longer confined to elite intellectual and cultural circles. It was also a reflection of the social turmoil and sense of decay that spread and deepened after 1914 in frightening ways. Much of the art, literature, philosophy, and even science of the 1920s and 1930s reflected this insecurity, this doubting of established values, this questioning of the future.

Since 1945, social, intellectual, and cultural trends have been marked by a complex mixture of continuity and change. There is still much of the disillusionment and anxiety that characterized the earlier decades of the twentieth century. At the same time, there has developed a new sense of experimentation and productivity, which reflects the lessening of social turmoil and a greater sense of stability compared with the difficult decades prior to World War II.

With these two broad patterns in mind, let us attempt to identify and explore some of the social, religious, intellectual, and cultural developments of Western civilization in the twentieth century.

1. WESTERN SOCIETY IN THE TWENTIETH CENTURY

Demographic and Social Changes

Population in the West has been growing since World War I but at varying rates. The broad pattern shows a slowing down of population growth as societies became more fully modernized, a pattern that has been evident in some countries since the end of the nineteenth century. During the 1940s and 1950s birth rates in most Western countries were relatively high (the "baby boom"), supporting an increase in the population. During the 1960s birth rates started to decline and reverse, to the point in the 1970s and 1980s where several countries have birth rates that are sufficient only to maintain the population or will result in a declining population. Some governments, such as France and East Germany, have begun to encourage larger families with financial aid. Changes in the makeup of the population are also evident. As a result of improved life expectancy, populations in the West have been growing older on the average, giving elderly groups more potential political power and making the social needs of the elderly more pressing.

Perhaps more important than population changes have been changes in where and how people live. Urbanization has increased in recent decades. Large cities have been swollen by migration from rural areas and immigration from southern areas. Northern European cities have absorbed large numbers of people from southern Italy, Greece, Turkey, and Africa, just as cities in North America have been expanded by people from Latin America and Asia. With the people came the traditional urban problems: congestion, overburdened transportation systems, insufficient social services, pollution, crime, and inadequate housing. At times the inner core of great cities has deteriorated and even suffered a decline in population, but this has usually been more than matched by the growth of surrounding suburbs. New shopping and industrial centers have grown up in the periphery of the older cities and even on the fringes of older suburbs. In reference to cities such as Paris, London, New York, and Moscow, it has become more accurate to include the metropolitan areas around them rather than merely the city itself.

In recent decades the most modern societies in the West have been termed "postindustrial," to emphasize the declining importance of traditional manufacturing industries and the growing importance of providing services—often through the use of high technology. The key figures in this postindustrial society are the financiers, technicians, managers, and professionals rather than the industrial entrepreneurs.

There have also been some broad shifts in the social classes that make up Western society. Generally, the shift has been away from rural classes to urban classes, away from traditional industrial jobs to service and white-collar jobs, and away from small firms toward corporate and governmental organizations. Class distinctions remain but are less clear than before. Society has become generally more mobile, both geographically and socially. While birth into wealth and position remains a great advantage, education or technical skill has increasingly become a relatively democratic avenue for social mobility.

In Western Europe and the United States the very wealthy have generally managed to retain their position at the top of society despite efforts in several countries to redistribute the wealth and lessen the gap between rich and poor. Most of the remnants of the traditional aristocracy have disappeared or merged with the wealthy upper middle class. While this elite class retains some protective barriers against intrusion from below and maintains itself through the aid of inheritance, it is increasingly being joined by a newer elite of corporate and governmental managers, successful professionals, and those with high scientific or technological expertise. These people tend to be highly educated, pragmatic, with a stake in the status quo, and yet always threatened by their younger, more recently educated competitors in the corporate or bureaucratic hierarchy.

Just below this upper middle class is the bulk of the middle class. Made up primarily of middle- and lower-level managers in corporate and governmental bureaucracies, those who hold salaried white-collar jobs in services, and professionals in a growing number of fields, this class has grown substantially. Entrance into this class is gained primarily through education, specialization, and technical expertise.

Since the end of World War II the industrial working class has generally seen an improvement in its standard of living and, at least until the 1960s, relative job security. Yet its ranks were thinning as the traditional industrial base eroded, forcing many to become service workers or enter the bottom level of white-collar employment. As economic problems became more acute in the 1970s and early 1980s, industrial workers faced unemployment matched only by pre–World War II statistics and declines in real income that had to be compensated for by more married women entering the paid work force. As they have grown more affluent, the distinction between them and the lower middle class has lessened: The incomes, diets, housing, leisure-time activities, and often even political affiliations of the two classes are becoming similar. Yet the working class has remained distinct in many ways; it has fewer opportunities for social mobility and greater frustrations at the workplace, as manifested by numerous strikes.

In many countries there remains a core of inner-city slum dwellers. They are usually without regular jobs, often marked by race or ethnic origin, and subject to the worst problems of urban life. In recent years there have been disturbing signs. This care of often homeless urban poor is growing.

The decline of rural populations has continued, with variations in each country. Generally agricultural productivity has been increasing, lessening the need for people on the farms. Many rural people have moved into the cities, leaving a small percentage of the population to grow food for the rest and for export. Those who adjusted to changing rural life—by mechanizing, enlarging their land holdings, joining cooperatives, and specializing—have enjoyed an uneven, but generally rising standard of living. But there remains a core of rural poor who have not adjusted to the agricultural changes since World War II or who have fallen victim to economic forces beyond their control. Rural life has also become less isolated with the spread of highways, cars, telephones, radio, and television.

In Eastern Europe social changes followed the model established in Russia since the revolution in 1917. The traditional landed aristocracy disappeared rapidly as their lands were taken away and redistributed or nationalized. Large collectivized farms arose. Eastern European states nationalized the factories, the banks, the commercial houses, and the large retail outlets of the middle class. The distinctions between urban classes were lessened as the state standardized basic housing, social ser-

FIGURE 60.2. Family Life
The changing roles of
women and men within
the family are reflected in
this photo of domestic
life. (Jim Harrison/Stock,
Boston)

vices, consumption, and even leisure activities. Nevertheless, a new privileged order arose. High-level party and governmental leaders, certain professionals, and the cultural elite have enjoyed more access to consumer goods, improved housing, better educational opportunities, and greater political influence than the rest of the population. This social inequality within these Eastern European socialist societies has been a source of discontent and turmoil in recent years.

The Family

Since World War I, and in particular over the past few decades, the family in the West has become smaller, more mobile, and less stable. Although people still tend to marry within their social, religious, and ethnic groups and with an eye toward economic considerations, emotional attraction continues to grow as the primary consideration in mate selection. In the past two decades sexual fulfillment has been added as an increasingly important condition for marriage and its continuation. The development of new methods of contra-

ception, particularly the contraceptive pill in the 1960s, and the accompanying acceptance of the idea of contraception (and, to a lesser extent, abortion) has given women and men greater sexual freedom and choice over marriage and childbearing. Since the baby boom of the immediate post–World War II years, married couples have fewer children on the average. The nuclear family—the couple and its children—has become more geographically mobile, and ties with extended family members such as grandparents, uncles, aunts, and cousins have become more distant. Other institutions, such as the school, the university, peer groups, family courts, family therapists, child psychologists, and day-care centers, have grown to take over functions that the family used to perform more exclusively.

The increase in premarital sex, cohabitation, gay life styles, divorce, and nontraditional family arrangements and a recent trend toward declining marriage rates and postponing marriage and childbearing have led many to question the viability of the modern family. The single-parent household and the childless household are gain-

FIGURE 60.3 French Women's Movement The women's movement since the 1960s has been international. Here French women demonstrate for equal pay with men for equal work. (Martine Franck/Magnum)

ing acceptance. The rate of divorce has risen sharply since World War II, particularly since the 1960s. Yet the family is not disappearing, as some critics have argued. Rather its form and its functions are evolving, as are the roles that its members are expected to play, particularly women.

Women

Some of the most important social changes have involved the role of women within the family and in society as a whole. In both World War I and World War II women assumed jobs and responsibilities previously thought beyond their "legitimate sphere," but with the return of the soldiers those women were pressured to return to their more traditional domestic roles. However, the long-run trend in the twentieth century, and particularly since the 1950s, has been for women to enter the paid working force in a greater variety of jobs. In particular, married women have been moving out of their middle-class roles as housekeepers, child rearers, and supporters of their income-producing husbands. The female wage-earning work force is no longer dominated by the young and single, as it was earlier in the twentieth century. With a growing life expectancy (now over seventy-five years in most Western countries), a

relatively early age of marriage and childbearing, and an infusion of appliances to aid in housekeeping chores, more women have been turning to "second careers" at middle age, often involving a return to school to acquire new skills. Over 50 percent of all married women now work outside the home in the United States, a dramatic increase from pre–World War II levels and a pattern that has generally prevailed in the West. Women, married and unmarried, are moving into jobs that were once the almost exclusive domain of men, from the legal and medical professions to all varieties of blue-collar work. However, discrimination based on gender is far from over. Women remain underrepresented in most higher-paying, higher-status occupations and still earn only between 60 and 80 percent of men's salaries.

The women's liberation movement, gaining force since the 1960s, has made many women more conscious of their common concerns (see Figure 60.3). Generally, this movement demands that women no longer be oppressed or considered second-class citizens, whether it be in their political rights, the wages they earn, the positions they hold, or the attitudes they or their society share. This movement has struggled not only to open political, economic, and social life to all, regardless of sex, but also to change stereotypical portrayals of femininity and common assumptions about differences between the sexes that contribute to barriers facing women. These changes are of great potential significance to women and by necessity, to men (see Figure 60.2). As with most fundamental historical changes, they will take a long time to have full effect. The changes women are initiating will require numerous subtle changes in the way we raise our children and the messages our culture transmits about gender and sex roles.

Youth and Education

One of the institutions most affected by social changes, and in particular changes in the family, has been education. Schools have been expected to adapt to social and economic change and take up functions that were once handled by parents as part of child rearing. Schools are expected to assist children who have emotional, social, and family problems as well as purely academic problems.

With the growing demands for democratization of educational opportunities, universities have had to open their doors to more than the traditional elite. The number of students attending college and going on for advanced degrees has increased dramatically since World War II. Universities have had to change their curriculums to fit the new demands of a mobile society and a modern economy. The strains on universities were particularly great in the 1960s, when students in many Western nations combined discontent with the university with attitudes critical of the values and behavior of their parents' generation. Students attacked the lack of humaneness, the restrictive behavior and values, the social inequities, and the competitive impersonality of the traditional adult world of their parents represented by the large, bureaucratized, impersonal university. They criticized governmental policies and rallied around issues such as opposition to the Vietnam War and support for national liberation movements in the non-Western world. The numerous demonstrations and disruptions of university life often spread into the surrounding communities, involving clashes with police and other public authorities. The most dramatic confrontations took place in France in 1968, where a student revolt threat-ened to overturn the government, particularly when students gained the sympathetic but temporary support of workers. The government eventually retained control, but numerous reforms of universities in France and elsewhere were instituted in the late 1960s and early 1970s. Since then student activism has diminished. Students have veered away from the traditional liberal arts curriculum and have become more concerned with preparing for careers in an increasingly competitive economic environment. Programs and majors in fields such as business administration, computer science, and the professions have proliferated.

Social Welfare

After World War I and particularly after World War II, trends toward increased governmental responsibility for social welfare accelerated. Most countries increased their traditional social security benefits for unemployment, retirement, sickness, and old age. Government expenditures for education expanded. In some countries, particularly Great Britain, steps were taken to ensure that medical services were available to all. New governmental programs were established to provide family allowances, maternity grants, and low-income housing.

In general, governments were being held responsible for providing a floor of social and economic well-being below which their citizens should not be allowed to fall. The expanded role of the state in providing a large array of social services within an economic system that still remained substantially capitalistic has been termed the creation of the "welfare state." The degree of involvement varied in each country. Governments of Communist nations in Eastern Europe assumed the most control over social and economic matters, but the services they could provide were limited by the economic well-being of the nation. Among the nations of Western Europe the Scandinavian countries have generally gone the furthest in providing social services for its citizens. The United States, with its own particular problems and aversion to programs that hint of socialism, lags behind in governmental provision of social services.

Of course, these services come at a price. Taxes

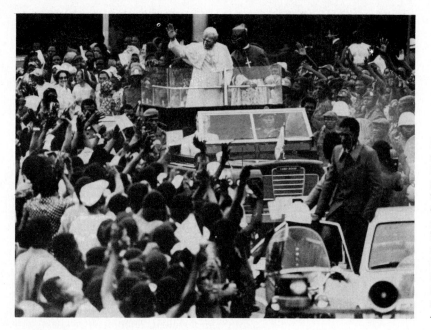

FIGURE 60.4. Areas such as Africa and Latin America have gained increasing attention within the Catholic Church in recent decades. Here, in one of his many trips outside of Europe, John Paul II rides in a motorcade in Zaire. (UPI/Bettmann Newsphotos)

have risen to pay for them. Governmental bureaucracies have grown to administer them. Moreover, critics question the quality of some of the services provided, particularly medical services. Yet once established, such social programs are rarely reversed—although the Reagan administration in the United States during the 1980s made efforts to do just that.

However efforts by governments to promote social welfare have not brought to an end persisting social problems. In addition to poverty, the high rate of crime and the proliferation of drug abuse in recent decades, particularly in the United States, attests to the sense of alienation and dissatisfaction in many Western societies. In the 1980s the spread of AIDS challenges the ability of government and science to solve difficult new problems.

2. RELIGION AND THEOLOGY IN THE TWENTIETH CENTURY

Christianity remains an important religious force in Western civilization despite the secularization that has taken place during the twentieth century. However, in the long run, Christian churches as institutions have continued to suffer a decline in influence in the West, particularly since World War II. Strenuous efforts were made to restore some of the lost unity of Christendom to enable the Christian church to face its problems with a united front. In 1948 leaders of hundreds of Protestant and Orthodox denominations met in Geneva and set up the World Council of Churches. The most spectacular step in this direction was taken by Pope John XXIII (1958–1963), who called the Second Vatican Council (1962–1965) in the spirit of Christian tolerance and unity. Although John XXIII died during the first year of the council and was succeeded by Paul VI (1963–1978), who was a less vigorous innovator, the Second Vatican Council introduced an ecumenical spirit into the Catholic church and showed a willingness to modernize the ritual and discipline that had been formalized by the Council of Trent in the sixteenth century. When Paul VI died in 1978, the College of Cardinals elected John Paul I, a man of great personal charm, who lived less than a month. The new pope, John Paul II, a Pole, was the first non-Italian pope since the early sixteenth century. Relatively young, forceful, and knowledgeable, John Paul II has traveled extensively, particularly to politically controversial areas such as Africa, Central America and Poland (see Figure 60.4). He has managed to convey an image of renewed dynamism and activism in the Catholic church. Nevertheless, he has been conservative in matters of faith and morals, refusing to liberalize Church policy toward theological doctrines, the priesthood, the family, and sex.

Theology in the Western world during the twentieth century for the most part reflected the materialism of the age and the influence of existentialist philosophy. Strong efforts were made to update Christian theology by making it a more secular philosophy. Paul Tillich (1886–1965), a German Protestant who spent his later years in the United States, conceived of God as "ultimate truth" and "inner reality." Such traditional terms as *original sin, salvation, forgiveness, immortality,* and *atonement* were useful symbols under his pen, actually referring to personal and social ethics. Harvey Cox (1929–) of Harvard University, in his widely read *The Secular City* (1965), defined Christianity as a continuing social revolution. During the decade of the 1960s the phrase "God is dead" enjoyed popularity among quite a number of divinity school teachers and students. The phrase apparently had a wide variety of meanings to its various users, including the belief that God is dead. Numerous religious cults sprang up, some of them quite wealthy and some violent, offering companionship and certainty to many of the lonely and the losers in this materialistic, competitive, and perplexing world.

On the other hand, a few powerful voices called for a return to an enlightened orthodox Christianity, notably the neo-Calvinists Karl Barth (1886–1968) in Switzerland and Reinhold Niebuhr (1892–1971) in the United States. God, they said, created the universe and runs it for his holy purpose, but selfish pride separates human beings from God. Only the Christian religion can remove that pride and bring men and women into God's purpose. Jacques Maritain (1882–1973) in France called for a return to the teachings of St. Thomas Aquinas. These learned theologians contributed dignity to the continuing claims of traditional Christianity.

3. TWENTIETH-CENTURY SCIENCE

After World War I, most scientific research was still carried out by individuals or small groups of scientists in a university setting. There was a sense of separation between theoretical and applied sciences, between research carried out by the best scientific minds and the later application of their discoveries by engineers or technicians. After World War II, that pattern would be modified by closer ties between science and technology and by a new infusion of funds for scientific research by government and big business (see Figure 60.5). Scientists tended to work in organized teams, in larger research laboratories with extremely expensive and sophisticated equipment, and with specific goals in mind. These trends are most clear in the physical sciences, particularly physics.

In the two decades after World War I, the main thrust in physics was to continue the probing of the atom, which was begun in the nineteenth century, to discover the truths concerning the nature of matter. The results tended to be disillusioning. Albert Einstein had undermined the Newtonian world of physical stability with his relativity theory (see p. 643). A more shattering blow was delivered by Max Planck (1858–1947). Although he published his quantum theory in 1900, its full impact was not realized until the decades following World War I. According to this theory, energy is not transmitted in a steady, measurable stream, as had long been supposed, but in little leaps or packets (quanta), and the behavior of subatomic particles is so irregular and complex that the ultimate secrets of nature can never be fathomed by objective observation. In 1919 Ernest Rutherford (1871–1937) opened the world of subatomic particles and the possibility of changing the structure of atoms by bombarding them with subatomic particles. The sense of relativity and uncertainty in physics was furthered by Werner Heisenberg (1901–1976), who in 1927 formulated the "principle of uncertainty." He argued that any model or measurement of atoms was inherently approximate and relative.

Since World War II, teams of physicists have used huge, powerful, expensive accelerators to explore the subatomic world to a far greater degree than was possible before the war. Astrophysicists

FIGURE 60.5 Moon Walk In July 1969, man walked on the moon. The United States' Apollo 11 moon mission is an example of the powerful combination of government and science. (NASA)

have combined new computer and radio telescope technology to expand our understanding of the universe. At the same time, many of these scientists have been employed by government and industry to create new, more destructive weapons of war or products, such as computer chips and superconductors, of economic importance to our consumer society.

The most exciting discoveries in the biological sciences were in the field of genetics. In 1953 the nature of the complicated DNA molecule, which controls the pattern of all living things, was discovered. It is assumed that by tampering with this molecule new forms of life may be created, and that given characteristics in all living things, including humans, can be controlled. Recent research with gene splitting and genetic engineering gives truth to this assumption.

The most beneficial discoveries in the field of biological science during the twentieth century

have been those that prevent and cure human ailments. Viruses were isolated and their role in the cause of many diseases, including infantile paralysis, influenza, and the common cold, was recognized. Vaccines were developed to combat successfully the infantile paralysis virus and a number of others—but the common cold still plagues most of humanity. During the late 1920s and the 1930s penicillin and sulfa drugs were discovered. These "miracle drugs" kill or control the bacteria causing many human infections. Since World War II, drugs have been found useful in treating mental illness, and artificial and transplanted kidneys and hearts have saved or lengthened many lives.

The chief drawback in the application of these wonderful discoveries has been their high and continually soaring cost and the shortage of trained personnel to administer them. Many nations, Great Britain and Sweden among the first, have recognized the enormous importance of public health by developing comprehensive programs of national health insurance. Communist regimes, of course, have always made the practice of medicine a public rather than a private matter.

The social sciences have continued to emphasize the application of the methods being used so successfully in the natural sciences—rigorous empirical research, inductive and deductive reasoning, conclusions couched in the value-free language of relativism and probabilities. In recent decades, three new approaches have been used in several of the social sciences. The first is an extension of previous methods—quantitative research aided by computers and newly developed statistical tools. Computers have enabled researchers to work with massive quantities of materials and factors. Statistical tools have sharpened the probability or predictability of their conclusions. The second is structuralism, which stresses the rules or the forms of behavior rather than the specific content. The third is relativism, which rejects universal values and assumes that societies and cultures should be viewed within their own time, place, and context.

Of all the social scientists, the sociologists and the anthropologists have been the most optimistic and energetic. Like all other social scientists, they attempted to apply the scientific method to the study of human behavior. Max Weber (1864–1920) of Germany set up ideal types or models as a method of scientifically analyzing various sociological problems—a method that has been widely used ever since. Emile Durkheim (1858–1917) established a sociological tradition emphasizing the use of statistics for analyzing social behavior. Karl Mannheim (1893–1947), a refugee from Nazi Germany to Great Britain, developed a sociology of knowledge. He argued that ideas are related to and influenced by social forces to a much greater degree than had been suspected. Anthropologists tended to move from their earlier measurements of skulls and other physical features to the concept that differing cultures are based essentially on differing ways of interpreting experience and adapting to the environment. Claude Lévi-Strauss, perhaps the most influential anthropologist in recent decades, used a structuralist perspective to analyze the forms and rules of culture.

Between World War I and the 1950s psychology continued to be strongly influenced by Freudian theory and practice, which emphasized the irrational, the unconscious, the sexual, and the aggressive elements in human thought and behavior. Behaviorism was also growing, and by the 1960s it overshadowed Freudianism. In the past two decades so many theories, approaches, therapies, and subdisciplines have proliferated within psychology that no single trend can be identified as dominant. Perhaps the most promising discoveries in recent years have been in physiological psychology. With so many people turning inward for answers and with secular explanations for human behavior deemed so important, psychology remains a field of growing influence.

Of all the social sciences, economics has taken most advantage of computer-aided quantitative research and sophisticated statistical tools. It is also the social science that most directly influences policy. Both governmental and private institutions rely on economists for the decisions they make. Underlying the quantitative research and statistical tools used by economists are more fundamental economic theories. Since the 1930s Keynesian economic thought has been most influential in countries with capitalistic or mixed economies. In 1936, in the midst of the Great Depression, John Maynard Keynes (1883–1946) published *The General Theory of Employment, Interest and Money,* advocating government regulation of the capitalistic system. He claimed that in times of recession the government should increase the supply of money in circulation by lowering interest rates and by deficit spending on public works. In times of inflationary boom it should restrict the money supply by raising interest rates and by other means. Liberals, not only in Keynes' native Britain but throughout the capitalistic world, accepted his theories, as indeed did many conservatives. But by the late 1970s and early 1980s it appeared that Keynesian theory could not account for many economic problems, particularly the combination of inflation and economic stagnation (with accompanying unemployment) that many termed "stagflation." Some theorists have called for greater governmental controls over wages and prices as well as general economic planning; others have attacked governmental involvement in the econ-

FIGURE 60.6. The development of tiny computer chips such as this has resulted in vast changes in science, business, and industry. (Charles Feil/Stock, Boston)

omy as doing more harm than good.

Probably the most important new tool for both the natural and social sciences is the computer (see Figure 60.6). The computer first became a tool of significance in the 1940s. By the 1950s and 1960s it was becoming linked with modern technology in a variety of ways, with strong impact on the sciences and in the economy. With developments in computer technology, particularly miniaturization, the use of computers proliferated in almost all fields of science during the 1970s and 1980s. Its ability to store and manipulate information has made the computer a necessity rather than a luxury for most scientists. Yet it is still no more than a tool: The scientist must feed the computer the right information, ask the useful questions, and interpret the answers.

4. TWENTIETH-CENTURY CULTURE

Philosophy

Philosophical thought in the twentieth century has been dominated by four trends, all of which can be traced back to the period just before World War I. The first was a wave of attacks on nineteenth-century optimism and rationalism that expanded the ideas set forth earlier by philosophers such as Friedrich Nietzsche in Germany and Henri Bergson in France (see p. 653). The most widely read of these post–World War I philosophers was Oswald Spengler. In his *Decline of the West* (1918), Spengler argued that the West was in decline, that World War I was the beginning of the end. This sense of decay and crisis appeared in many other works, most notably in José Ortega y Gasset's *Revolt of the Masses* (1930), which lamented the decline of liberal civilization and the rise of "mass man" in the West.

The second trend, which has clearly prevailed in Great Britain and the United States, is a combination of analytical philosophy and logical positivism. Analytical philosophy was first developed by Alfred North Whitehead (1861–1947) and Bertrand Russell (1872–1970) of Great Britain on the eve of World War I. The outstanding philosopher of logical positivism (or logical empiricism) was Ludwig Wittgenstein (1889–1951). Both analytical philosophy and logical positivism spurned any concept that could not be rationally and mathematically expressed. Under the influence of these doctrines, philosophy became highly technical, focusing on the exact meaning of words and logical relationships rather than the broad and ethical questions that traditionally concerned philosophers.

The third trend, which became more dominant on the European continent, is existentialism. Existentialism has its roots in the disenchantment of the late nineteenth century and the environment of anxiety resulting from the two world wars, the Great Depression, and the tensions of the Cold War. Existentialism drew heavily from Friedrich Nietzsche, who argued that there were no absolutes when he said "God is dead." Existential philosophy was also influenced by the mid-nineteenth-century Danish theologian, Søren Kierkegaard, who rejected systematized and institutionalized Christianity in favor of personal inspiration and individual commitment. In Germany during the 1920s Martin Heidegger and Carl Jaspers developed aspects of existentialist philosophy. Thereafter, the center of existentialist thought shifted to France. The most influential existentialist philosopher has been Jean-Paul Sartre (1905–1980). He argued that ultimately there is no meaning to existence and no final rights or wrongs. Individuals are born and simply exist. Individuals are free and responsible for the decisions and actions they take in life. Individuals must establish their own standards and their own rules, and each must take responsibility for living up to them. In the end, one simply dies.

The fourth trend, which has been a school of philosophy of varying strength, is Marxism (see pp. 565–566). Marxism has emphasized historical determinism, ethical relativism, and social meaning behind philosophical concepts. During the 1920s and 1930s, it grew in influence in several academic circles and disciplines. Since World War II its influence has waxed and waned, and its doctrines have been modified in several ways. But on the whole, it has remained influential as a philosophical and historical perspective in a variety of disciplines.

Literature

The literature of the twentieth century, like the philosophy, is essentially an outgrowth and continuation of the literature of the late nineteenth century. A number of the great realistic writers of the early twentieth century lived and wrote until the middle of the century. The realism that had shocked many Victorians was succeeded by the more starkly naked naturalism. The focus tended to shift to a more subjective point of view and to the feelings, uncertainties, and unconscious motives of individuals.

In English-speaking Europe, James Joyce (1882–1941), an Irish expatriate in Paris, Virginia Woolf (1882–1941), an English novelist and critic, and T. S. Eliot (1888–1965), an American expatriate in London, developed the stream-of-consciousness technique. They placed words and thoughts out of sequence, providing new insights into the psyche with dramatic effect. This method clearly reflected the introspection of Freudian psychology.

In Germany, Franz Kafka (1883–1924) depicted the alienation and frustrations of an intellectual in the World War I era. The haunting, ambiguous quality of his fiction symbolizes the uncertainties and fears of his age. Most of his work was published after his death, and he enjoyed wide popularity only after World War II. Hermann Hesse (1877–1962) also reflected the uncertainty and sense of alienation in Germany during the World War I era in his novels. His writings, particularly those stressing a youthful and psychologically insightful search for meaning in a life always threatened by despair, became particularly popular after World War II. Perhaps the towering figure of twentieth-century German literature was Thomas Mann (1875–1955). His style and content were more traditional than that of Kafka or Hesse, always stressing a reverence for human beings in the often distressing environment of Mann's lifetime.

In France, Marcel Proust (1871–1922) developed introspective writing to new depths in his influential *Remembrance of Things Past*. In seven volumes of exquisitely polished prose, he subjects to withering psychological analysis the remnants of French noble society and the vulgar social-

FIGURE 60.7 Picasso's "Guernica" This large mural in black and white by one of the greatest artists of the twentieth century captures some of the worst features of the century—war, terror, brutality, disjointedness, lack of direction, and despair. Guernica was a small Spanish town destroyed by the German air force during the Spanish Civil War. (Museo Nacional del Prado)

climbing *nouveau riche* bourgeoisie who were trying to imitate the nobility. During the 1940s and 1950s, Albert Camus (1913–1960) popularized existentialism in his novels and plays—stressing the plight of the individual seeking understanding and identity in an amoral and purposeless universe. During the 1960s writers such as Alain Robbe-Grillet and film directors such as François Truffaut and Jean-Luc Godard made France the center of the *nouvelle vague* (new wave) in literature and film, stressing experimentation and imaginative techniques.

In the Soviet Union, Boris Pasternak (1890–1960) wrote in the grand manner of Tolstoy and Dostoyevski. His most well-known novel is *Doctor Zhivago*, which traces life in Russia before, during, and after the Bolshevik Revolution in 1917. More recently, Alexander Solzhenitszen (1919–), living in the United States since his expulsion from the Soviet Union in 1974, has written novels critically depicting life in the Soviet Union during the Stalinist era.

In the United States Sinclair Lewis (1885–1951), much like Theodore Dreiser, ridiculed both the hypocritical and "puritanical" bourgeoisie and the stupid, vulgar masses. Babbitt, Elmer Gantry, and Arrowsmith, deflated heroes in Sinclair Lewis' novels by those titles, became stereotypes of typical Americans in the minds of thousands of untypical American readers of books. Eugene O'Neill (1888–1953) wrote plays in which the dramatic tension was maintained by psychological conflict (like those of Anton Chekhov—see p. 655) rather than development of plot and action. Ernest Hemingway (1898–1961) was an existentialist, entertaining his readers with his crisp and sophisticated prose. William Faulkner (1897–1962), with great depth and artistry, tore away the veil woven by civilization to conceal the violent and animallike nature of ordinary people. He extended the complex stream-of-consciousness technique.

The Fine Arts

The fine arts in the Western world in the twentieth century, like the philosophy and the literature, have proceeded generally along the guidelines laid down by the artists and writers of the late nineteenth century—disenchantment, rejection of tradition, search for new values, and experimentation. These characteristics have become intensified by the materialism and the uncertainties of the twentieth century.

Without a doubt, the most gifted and influential painter of the twentieth century was Pablo Picasso (1881–1973) (see Figure 60.7). A Spaniard, he emigrated to Paris as a young man. There he was influenced by the French postimpressionists (see pp. 656–657). In order to penetrate the surface and reveal the inner reality of things, Picasso would take his subjects apart—arms, heads, violin parts—and rearrange and distort them for maximum effect. Early in the century, at about the same time that young Whitehead and Russell were proclaiming their analytic philosophy based on mathematics, Picasso introduced cubism into the world of painting (see Figure 52.1). This technique was an effort, suggested by Cézanne, to demonstrate the solidity of the material universe by portraying the geometric composition of objects—spheres, cones, and cylinders. Cubism suggests the twentieth century's obsession with science.

Another prominent style of twentieth-century painting came to be called surrealism, whose chief proponents were Max Ernst (1891–1976) (see Color Plate 28), a German who later moved to the United States, and Salvador Dali (1904–1989) (see Color Plate 29), a Spaniard who lived many years in the United States. The surrealists, under the influence of Freud and his psychoanalytical techniques, attempted to express their imagination uncontrolled by reason and to suggest the activities of the subconscious mind, whether dreaming or awake. Picasso and Matisse (see p. 656), who were really laws unto themselves, painted many canvases in the surrealist style.

A third popular twentieth-century style of painting was expressionism, which had its origin in northern Europe, particularly Germany (see Figure 55.2). Its chief proponent was Vasili Kandinsky (1866–1944), a Russian who came to live in Germany. The expressionists, motivated by inner necessity, attempted to express freely their emotional reactions rather than the representation of the natural appearance of objects, resorting to abstraction and to violent distortion of color and form.

In recent decades, artistic styles such as pop art, op art, and photo-realism (see Figure 60.1) have continued to proliferate, often crossing boundaries between commercial and high art, between representational and abstract art (see Color Plate 30), and between traditional and nontraditional mediums (see Color Plate 31). All these styles reflect the artistic and the speculative mind of the Western world in the twentieth century—disenchantment, rejection of tradition, search for new values, and a turning inward for inspiration.

Twentieth-century architecture has been dominated by the functional style (see Figure 60.8), developed in Germany by Walter Gropius' Bauhaus school, in France by architects such as Le Corbusier, and in the United States by Louis Henry Sullivan (see p. 657). Sullivan's most illustrious student, and perhaps the most well-known architect of the twentieth century, was Frank Lloyd Wright (1869–1959). Like his teacher, Wright believed that function is the sole purpose of architecture. He further insisted that form should conform to the materials used and to the setting. He made brilliant use of the cantilever (a projecting member supported at only one end) to achieve striking horizontal lines and an unobstructed spaciousness. These effects were made possible by the tensile strength of steel. Wright combined artistic skill with a Shavian scorn for traditional values and institutions. The most spectacular monuments of functional architecture are, of course, the great bridges and skyscrapers, most of them in the United States.

Twentieth-century music, too, is for the most part a continuation and development of styles formulated during the period 1871–1914. Richard Strauss (1864–1949) and Igor Stravinsky (1882–1971), two of the originators of modern music, lived far into the twentieth century. During the course of the century, music in the Western world became increasingly dissonant, atonal, and experimental. These qualities probably found their ultimate composer in the Viennese Arnold Schoenberg (1874–1951), who abolished key, revolutionized the conception of melody, and replaced the seven-tone scale with one of twelve tones. Recent decades have witnessed the introduction of a universe of everyday and electronically produced sounds into music.

FIGURE 60.8 Pompidou Center of Art and Culture, Paris The controversial Pompidou Center of Art and Culture, built in the center of Paris during the 1970s, carries the idea of functionalism in architecture to an aesthetic extreme. Structural and functional elements of the building show prominently on the outside, creating a vast open space on the inside. (Bernard Annebicque/Sygma)

Popular Culture

The twentieth century has witnessed an explosion of popular culture. Several developments account for the huge variety and availability of popular literature, art, and music. There has been a tremendous expansion of communications—from cheap newspapers and paperback novels to radio, cinema, and television. Numerous and large public facilities—from museums and concert halls to stadiums—have been built. The rising level of education has stimulated greater interest in cultural activities. Increasing affluence and leisure time among the urban classes has enabled more people to take advantage of cultural offerings.

The products of popular culture are usually distinct from those of elite culture, but there has been some blurring of the lines between the two in recent decades. In cinema, an almost endless stream of what critics consider undistinguished but popular films are produced year after year. Yet cinema is perhaps the most original art form produced during the twentieth century (see Figure 60.9). The works of filmmakers such as Ingmar Bergman in Sweden and Federico Fellini in Italy reveal the potential of cinema as a sophisticated, creative, artistic medium. In music there is much that distinguishes the dissonant, atonal music of Arnold Schoenberg from rock and roll performed

FIGURE 60.9 Fritz Lang's "Metropolis" This eerie, futuristic scene from Fritz Lang's film "Metropolis" (1925) illustrates the overwhelming power of urban architecture and technology as well as the potential of the cinema as an artistic medium. (National Film Archive, London)

by groups such as the Beatles, but the distinction blurs with jazz, a development of America's black culture emphasizing sophisticated improvisation and rhythm. In art, most of the abstract or expressionistic paintings of the twentieth century remain outside popular tastes, but what was once elite art, such as the romantic or realistic paintings of the nineteenth century, or even avant-garde, such as impressionism, is now extremely popular.

5. PROBLEMS OF THE PRESENT AND FUTURE

Despite many real gains that have been made since the end of World War II, several persisting and growing problems in Western civilization contribute to a spreading sense of pessimism. Experience in the 1970s and 1980s shows us that eco-

FIGURE 60.10. Oil spills are one of the threats to the environment posed by modern industry. Here sea lions are trapped in oily waters off Alaska after a 1989 spill. (Reuters/Bettmann Newsphotos)

nomic growth can no longer be taken for granted; inflation, unemployment, and declining personal incomes for many have created social discontents that governments seem impotent to master. Moreover, the price we pay for economic growth and modernization seems to have been rising in recent years. Industrialization, urbanization, and affluence have strained our natural resources. Our air, our fresh water, and even our seas are becoming more polluted (see Figure 60.10). Depletion of the protective ozone layer and a heating up of the atmosphere threaten us. Our land is becoming blighted by concrete, tasteless commercial development, and poisonous wastes. The relentless march of technology with its accompanying urbanization has brought many creature comforts to the masses, but it has robbed millions of their manual skills and social contacts and lost people in the lonely crowd. At the higher levels of industry, corporate individuals have tended to lose their independence and individual identities. Government has expanded the social services it provides but that has not created a greater sense

of inclusion in modern society; rather, a sense of alienation seems to persist or even grow.

War, of course, has always brutalized those who are engaged in it, but the wars of the twentieth century have vastly exceeded those of the past in size and destructiveness. The threat of obliteration from nuclear war hangs over the post–World War II generations unabated as major powers refine their nuclear arsenals and other countries develop their own nuclear weapons. In other ways, violence seems to threaten us more than ever, whether it be from crime, terrorism, or potentially explosive smaller wars.

There is a growing awareness that the relatively affluent West can no longer ignore the non-Western areas of the world, with their pressing needs and growing demands. Clearly, the West must change its relationship to the non-Western world, but it is not clear how. There is a sense among many that the traditional values of the Western world are being eroded, but it is not clear what is replacing these values.

All these problems now weigh upon the West

and are not likely to go away in the foreseeable future. In some ways Western civilization and its institutions, which have been so long developing—the family, the governments, the courts of law, the churches, the traditions of social and moral behavior—are being severely tested. While problems of the present always seem more difficult than those of the past, the consequences of not dealing with today's problems are likely to be catastrophic. Whether and how Western civilization handles these challenges remains to be seen.

SUGGESTED READING

General

M. Crouzet, *The European Renaissance Since 1945* (1971). A balanced account emphasizing society and culture.

S. Hoffmann and P. Kitromilides, *Culture and Society in Contemporary Europe* (1981). Good collection of recent essays.

Western Society in the Twentieth Century

S. de Beauvoir, *The Second Sex* (1962). A classic, crucial analysis of women.

A. Cherlin, *Marriage, Divorce, Remarriage* (1981). Interpretive analysis of the American family.

E. Shorter, *The Making of the Modern Family* (1978). Well-written, controversial.

E. Wolf, *Europe and the People Without History* (1982). A provocative interdisciplinary analysis.

Religion and Theology in the Twentieth Century

S. P. Schilling, *Contemporary Continental Theologians* (1966). A good survey of modern theology.

Twentieth-Century Science

J. Ziman, *The Force of Knowledge: The Scientific Dimension of Society* (1976). Excellent analysis and bibliography.

J. Galbraith, *Age of Uncertainty* (1978). Writing lucidly for the nonspecialist, Galbraith argues for tight economic controls.

Twentieth-Century Culture

M. Biddiss, *Age of the Masses: Ideas and Society Since 1870* (1977). A fine intellectual history.

W. Barrett, *Irrational Man* (1958). A good treatment of existentialism.

M. Marrus, ed., *Emergence of Leisure* (1974). An important collection.

A. Neumeyer, *The Search for Meaning in Modern Art*. A useful guide for the nonspecialist.

J. Passmore, *A Hundred Years of Philosophy* (1968). A good, concise survey.

H. Read, *A Concise History of Modern Painting* (1974). Excellent brief survey.

E. Salzman, *Twentieth Century Music: An Introduction*. A good survey.

R. Stromberg, *After Everything: Western Intellectual History Since 1945* (1975). An interpretive, scholarly analysis.

R. Williams, *Communications* (1976). Analyzes the media.

Problems of the Present and Future

R. Heilbroner, *An Inquiry into the Human Prospect* (1980). Excellent analysis of our problems and our attitudes toward those problems.

C. Lasch, *Culture of Narcissism* (1978). A broad, controversial, insightful analysis of American life.

RETROSPECT

At the end of World War II devastation and disorganization were the rule rather than the exception. Most nations of Europe were so weakened that they had to rely on one of the two new superpowers that had emerged from World War II: the United States and the Soviet Union. Soon, even the unity of the victorious allies, which included the United States and the Soviet Union, proved too fragile to last. Deep-seated discord between these respective leaders of the non-Communist and Communist worlds broke out into the Cold War. Europe became divided into two camps—one of democratic capitalism (though often with elements of socialism mixed in) led by the United States, the other of communism modeled and led by the Soviet Union. This division of Europe and the broader Cold War struggle would dominate international policies for decades to come. Yet, despite the destruction of World War II, the emergence of the dominating superpowers, and the disunity brought about by the Cold War, European nations recovered, expanded their economies, and enjoyed relative political stability during the following decades. Problems in the 1970s and 1980s do not diminish from that record; rather, they indicate that Western civilization must face and deal with new and previously ignored difficulties. One way that nations have attempted to solve common problems has been through regional integration and internationalism, but the results have been mixed at best.

In the decades following World War II, France, England, Belgium, the Netherlands, and other Western nations lost most of their colonial empires. The new and old nations of the non-Western world struggled to get on their feet and assert themselves in an environment marked by Cold War rivalries, deep-rooted internal discord, and the disruption caused by the incomplete spread of Western values and institutions to their lands. In different ways, Japan and China emerged as leading economic and political powers in the Far East. The struggle between Hindu and Moslem in India, Pakistan, and Bangladesh and the wars in Southeast Asia made the British and French (and, later, American) withdrawals from southern Asia problematic. The Middle East has been marked by a series of wars and disruptions as well as the emergence of a new power bloc based on wealth from oil production. The long-lasting lack of peace between Israel and most of its neighbors, violence in divided Lebanon, and the war between Iran and Iraq suggest that this area of the world will remain explosive for the foreseeable future. Africans face tremendous difficulties in creating unity in nations artificially created by colonial powers and burdened by harsh economic conditions. The political instability of most African nations attests to these difficulties. Most Latin American nations have for decades been dominated by a wealthy elite and right-wing authoritarian governments (supported, and usually staffed, by the military). As the area's population grows, so does the contrast between the few haves and the mass of have-nots. Revolutions, guerrilla activities, and political upheavals indicate that stability is likely to be the exception rather than the rule in Latin America.

The most significant social, intellectual, and cultural changes in Western civilization during the twentieth century are more difficult to pinpoint than the concrete political and economic developments. For the most part, the social, intellectual, and cultural developments have been a continuation of trends already underway by the end of the nineteenth century. Western society became more urbanized as it adjusted to the demands of continuing economic modernization. Women changed their roles and the perception of themselves, a reflection of some of the changes occurring within the basic unit of Western society: the family. Christian churches continued to have difficulty adjusting to a changing, secularizing, scientific world. Intellectual and cultural trends reflected the richness of Western life as well as the often discouraging problems encountered by the West since the end of the nineteenth century. New problems have been added to the persisting problems, testing the spirit and ability of Western civilization in disturbing ways.

INDEX

Page references in *italic* refer to illustrations, maps, and their captions.